Basic Standard Deduction Amounts

Filing Status	2008 Deduction	2009 Deduction
Single	$ 5,450	$ 5,700
Qualifying widow or widower	$10,900	$11,400
Married filing jointly	$10,900	$11,400
Married filing separately	$ 5,450	$ 5,700
Head of household	$ 8,000	$ 8,350

Additional Standard Deduction Amounts

	2008 Deduction	2009 Deduction
Married taxpayers 65 or over or blind	$1,050	$1,100
Single taxpayer or head of household who is 65 or over or blind	$1,350	$1,400

Personal and Dependency Exemption Amounts

2008 Exemption	2009 Exemption
$3,500	$3,650

Corporate Income Tax Rates

Taxable Income	Tax
< $50,000	15% of taxable income
$50,000–$75,000	$7,500 + 25% of taxable income over $50,000
$75,000–$100,000	$13,750 + 34% of taxable income over $75,000
$100,000–$335,000	$22,250 + 39% of taxable income over $100,000
$335,000–$10,000,000	$113,900 + 34% of taxable income over $335,000
$10,000,000–$15,000,000	$3,400,000 + 35% of taxable income over $10,000,000
$15,000,000–$18,333,333	$5,150,000 + 38% of taxable income over $15,000,000
Over $18,333,333	35% of taxable income

McGraw-Hill's
TAXATION *of* INDIVIDUALS
2010 Edition

The McGraw·Hill Companies

McGraw-Hill
Irwin

MCGRAW-HILL'S TAXATION OF INDIVIDUALS: 2010 EDITION

Published by McGraw-Hill/Irwin, a business unit of The McGraw-Hill Companies, Inc., 1221 Avenue of the Americas, New York, NY, 10020. Copyright © 2010 by The McGraw-Hill Companies, Inc. All rights reserved. No part of this publication may be reproduced or distributed in any form or by any means, or stored in a database or retrieval system, without the prior written consent of The McGraw-Hill Companies, Inc., including, but not limited to, in any network or other electronic storage or transmission, or broadcast for distance learning.

Some ancillaries, including electronic and print components, may not be available to customers outside the United States.

This book is printed on acid-free paper.

1 2 3 4 5 6 7 8 9 0 QPD/QPD 0 9

ISBN 978-0-07-352695-9
MHID 0-07-352695-9
ISSN 1943-9318

Vice president and editor-in-chief: *Brent Gordon*
Editorial director: *Stewart Mattson*
Publisher: *Tim Vertovec*
Developmental editor II: *Daryl Horrocks*
Marketing manager: *Scott S. Bishop*
Lead project manager: *Pat Frederickson*
Senior production supervisor: *Debra R. Sylvester*
Lead designer: *Matthew Baldwin*
Senior photo research coordinator: *Lori Kramer*
Senior media project manager : *Susan Lombardi*
Cover design: *Matthew Baldwin*
Interior design: *Kay Lieberherr*
Cover image: *©Photolibrary*
Typeface: *10.5/12 Times New Roman*
Compositor: *Aptara®, Inc.*
Printer: *Quebecor World Dubuque Inc.*

www.mhhe.com

McGraw-Hill's
TAXATION *of* INDIVIDUALS
2010 Edition

Brian C. Spilker
Brigham Young University

Benjamin C. Ayers
The University of Georgia

John R. Robinson
The University of Texas – Austin

Edmund Outslay
Michigan State University

Ron G. Worsham
Brigham Young University

John A. Barrick
Brigham Young University

Connie D. Weaver
Texas A&M University

 **McGraw-Hill
Irwin**

Boston   Burr Ridge, IL   Dubuque, IA   New York   San Francisco   St. Louis
Bangkok   Bogotá   Caracas   Kuala Lumpur   Lisbon   London   Madrid   Mexico City
Milan   Montreal   New Delhi   Santiago   Seoul   Singapore   Sydney   Taipei   Toronto

Dedications

We dedicate this book to:

My children Braxton, Cameron, Ethan, and Lauren and to my parents Ray and Janet. Last but not least, to my wife Kim for allowing me to take up valuable kitchen space while I was working on the project. I love you all.

Brian Spilker

Wife Marilyn, daughters Margaret Lindley and Georgia, son Benjamin, and parents Bill and Linda.

Ben Ayers

JES, Tommy, Michelle, and Laura.

John Robinson

Family Jane, Mark, Sarah, and Jeff and to Professor James E. Wheeler, my mentor and friend.

Ed Outslay

Wife Anne, sons Matthew and Daniel, and daughters Whitney and Hayley.

Ron Worsham

Wife Jennifer and daughters Annika, Corinne, and Lina.

John Barrick

Husband Dan, son Travis, daughter Alix, and parents Charles and Helen.

Connie Weaver

ABOUT THE AUTHORS

Brian Spilker (Ph.D., University of Texas at Austin, 1993) is the tax group coordinator and the Georgia White Professor in the School of Accountancy at Brigham Young University. He teaches taxation in the graduate and undergraduate programs at Brigham Young University. He received both B.S. and M.Acc. (tax emphasis) degrees from Brigham University before working as a tax consultant for Arthur Young & Co. (now Ernst & Young). After his professional work experience, Brian earned his Ph.D. at the University of Texas at Austin. In 1996, he was selected as one of two nationwide recipients of the Price Waterhouse Fellowship in Tax award. In 1998, he was a winner of the American Taxation Association and Arthur Andersen Teaching Innovation award for his work in the classroom; he has also been honored for his use of technology in the classroom at Brigham Young University. Brian researches issues relating to tax information search and professional tax judgment. His research has been published in such journals as *The Accounting Review*, *Organizational Behavior and Human Decision Processes*, *Journal of the American Taxation Association*, *Behavioral Research in Accounting*, *Journal of Accounting Education*, *Journal of Corporate Taxation*, and *Journal of Accountancy*.

Ben Ayers (Ph.D., University of Texas at Austin, 1996) is the Director of the J.M. Tull School of Accounting at the University of Georgia. He holds a Ph.D. from the University of Texas at Austin and an M.T.A and B.S. from the University of Alabama. Prior to entering the Ph.D. program at the University of Texas, Professor Ayers was a tax manager at KPMG in Tampa, Florida, and a contract manager with Complete Health, Inc. in Birmingham, Alabama.

Professor Ayers teaches tax planning and research courses in the undergraduate and graduate programs at the University of Georgia. He is the recipient of eleven teaching awards at the School, College, and University levels, including the Richard B. Russell Undergraduate Teaching Award, the highest teaching honor for University of Georgia junior faculty members. Professor Ayers' current research interests include the effects of taxation on firm structure, mergers and acquisitions, and capital markets and the effects of accounting information on security returns. He has published articles in journals such as the *Accounting Review*, *Journal of Finance*, *Journal of Accounting and Economics*, *Contemporary Accounting Research*, *Review of Accounting Studies*, *Journal of Law and Economics*, *Journal of the American Taxation Association*, and *National Tax Journal*. Professor Ayers was the 1997 recipient of the American Accounting Association's Competitive Manuscript Award and the 2003 and 2008 recipient of the American Taxation Association's Outstanding Manuscript Award.

John Robinson (Ph.D., University of Michigan, 1981) is the C. Aubrey Smith Professor of Accounting in the McCombs School of Business at the University of Texas at Austin. Professor Robinson received his J.D. (*Cum Laude*) from The University of Michigan in 1979, and he was awarded his Ph.D. in accounting from The University of Michigan in 1981. Prior to joining the faculty at Texas in 1985, he taught at The University of Kansas where he was The Arthur Young Faculty Scholar from 1982–1984. John teaches introductory taxation, corporate tax, taxation of partnerships, and tax planning. He is the recipient of the Henry A. Bubb Award For Outstanding Teaching, the Texas Blazer's Faculty Excellence Award and the MPA Council Outstanding Professor Award. John conducts research in a broad variety of topics involving financial accounting, mergers and acquisitions, and the influence of taxes on financial structures and performance. His scholarly articles have appeared in *Accounting Review*, *Journal of Finance*, *National Tax Journal*, *Journal of Law and Economics*, *Journal of the American Taxation Association*, *The Journal of the American Bar Association*, and *The Journal of Taxation*. In addition, John was the editor of *The Journal of the American Taxation Association*, from 2002 through 2005, and he was a co-author of the articles honored with the 2003 and 2008 ATA Outstanding Manuscript Awards.

Ed Outslay (Ph.D., University of Michigan, 1981) is a Professor of Accounting and the Deloitte/Michael Licata Endowed Professor of Taxation in the Department of Accounting and Information Systems at Michigan State University, where he has taught since 1981. He received a B.A. from Furman University in 1974 and an MBA and Ph.D. from The University of Michigan in 1977 and 1981. Ed currently teaches graduate classes in corporate taxation, multiunit enterprises, accounting for income taxes, and international taxation. In February 2003, Ed testified before the Senate Finance Committee on the Joint Committee on Taxation's Report on Enron Corporation. MSU has honored Ed with the Presidential Award for Outstanding Community Service, Distinguished Faculty Award, John D. Withrow Teacher-Scholar Award, Roland H. Salmonson Outstanding Teaching Award, Senior Class Council Distinguished Faculty Award, MSU Teacher-Scholar Award, and MSU's 1st Annual Curricular Service-Learning and Civic Engagement Award in 2008. Ed received the Ray M. Sommerfeld Outstanding Tax Educator Award in 2004 from the American Taxation Association. He has also received the ATA Outstanding Manuscript Award twice, the ATA/Deloitte Teaching Innovations Award, and the 2004 Distinguished Achievement in Accounting Education Award from the Michigan Association of CPAs. Ed has been recognized for his community service by the Greater Lansing Chapter of the Association of Government Accountants, the City of East Lansing (Crystal Award), and the East Lansing Education Foundation. He received a National Assistant Coach of the Year Award in 2003 from AFLAC and was named an Assistant High School Baseball Coach of the Year in 2002 by the Michigan High School Baseball Coaches Association.

ABOUT THE AUTHORS

Ron Worsham (Ph.D., University of Florida, 1994) is an associate professor in the School of Accountancy at Brigham Young University. He teaches taxation in the graduate, undergraduate, MBA, and Executive MBA programs at Brigham Young University. He has also taught as a visiting professor at the University of Chicago. He received both B.S. and M.Acc. (tax emphasis) degrees from Brigham University before working as a tax consultant for Arthur Young & Co. (now Ernst & Young) in Dallas, Texas. While in Texas, he became licensed to practice as a CPA. After his professional work experience, Ron earned his Ph.D. at the University of Florida. He has been honored for outstanding innovation in the classroom at Brigham Young University. Ron has published academic research in the areas of taxpayer compliance and professional tax judgment. He has also published legal research in a variety of areas. His work has been published in such journals as *The Journal of the American Taxation Association*, *The Journal of International Taxation*, *The Tax Executive*, *The Journal of Accountancy*, and *Practical Tax Strategies*.

John Barrick (Ph.D., University of Nebraska at Lincoln, 1998) is currently an Accountant at the United States Congress Joint Committee on Taxation; he is also an associate professor in the Marriott School at Brigham Young University. He teaches taxation in the graduate and undergraduate programs at Brigham Young University. He received both B.S. and M.Acc. (tax emphasis) degrees from Brigham University before working as a tax consultant for Price Waterhouse (now PricewaterhouseCoopers). After his professional work experience, John earned his Ph.D. at the University of Nebraska at Lincoln. Professor Barrick was the 1998 recipient of the American Accounting Association, Accounting, Behavior, and Organization Section's Outstanding Dissertation Award. John researches issues relating to professional tax judgment and tax information search. His research has been published in such journals as *Organizational Behavior and Human Decision Processes*, *Contemporary Accounting Research*, and the *Journal of the American Taxation Association*.

Connie Weaver (Ph.D., Arizona State University, 1996) is an associate professor in the Mays Business School at Texas A&M University and a certified public accountant. She holds a Ph.D. from Arizona State University, a Masters of Professional Accounting from the University of Texas at Arlington, and a Bachelors of Science in Chemical Engineering from the University of Texas at Austin. Prior to obtaining her Ph.D., Professor Weaver was a tax manager at Ernst & Young in Dallas, TX.

Professor Weaver teaches introductory taxation in the undergraduate program at Texas A&M University. She has also taught undergraduates and graduate students at the University of Texas at Austin and the University of Wisconsin–Madison. She is the recipient of several teaching awards, including the 2006 American Taxation Association/Deloitte Teaching Innovations Award. Connie's current research interests include the effects of tax and financial incentives on corporate decisions and reporting. She has published articles in journals such as the *Accounting Review*, *Contemporary Accounting Research*, *Journal of the American Taxation Association*, and *Tax Notes*. She serves on the editorial board of *The Journal of the American Taxation Association* and was the 1997 recipient of the American Taxation Association/Price Waterhouse Outstanding Dissertation Award.

TEACHING THE CODE IN CONTEXT

  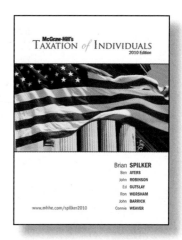

The basic approach to teaching taxation hasn't changed in decades. **Today's student deserves a new approach.** McGraw-Hill's Taxation of Individuals and Business Entities *is a bold and innovative new textbook that's already generating enthusiasm across the country.*

McGraw-Hill's Taxation is designed to provide a unique, innovative, and engaging learning experience for students studying taxation. The breadth of the topical coverage, **the storyline approach to presenting the material**, the emphasis on the tax and nontax consequences of multiple parties involved in transactions, and the integration of financial and tax accounting topics make this book ideal for the modern tax curriculum.

> **This text is one of the best written textbooks I have ever read.** It covers the material using real world examples. It is easy to understand but provides the student with everything they need for the course. This textbook would make teaching the class easy.
>
> – Hughlene Burton, University of North Carolina – Charlotte

> A lot of thought and planning went into the structure and content of the text, and a great product was achieved. **One of the most unique and helpful features is the common storyline** throughout each chapter.
>
> – Raymond J. Shaffer, Youngstown State University

Development on these chapters started in December of 2005, when the first of more than 140 instructors completed **180 manuscript reviews** and attended symposia or focus groups. Throughout this preface, their comments on the book's organization, pedagogy, and unique features are a testament to the **grass-roots nature of *Taxation*'s development**.

> This is a **very thorough tax textbook** covering many details about corporate tax. The authors include real life examples and several stories that make the **materials more understandable and "accessible" to students.**
>
> – Sonja Pippin, University of Nevada – Reno

A MODERN APPROACH FOR TODAY'S STUDENT

> *Very innovative organization of topics* with text that is very readable and some of the best quantitative examples I've seen.
> – Melanie James Earles,
> Tennessee Technological University

Key to this new tax series' remarkably positive reception are the five core precepts around which the text is built:

1 **Storyline Approach:** Each chapter begins with a storyline that introduces a set of characters or a business entity facing specific tax-related situations. Each chapter's examples are related to the storyline, giving students the opportunities to **learn the code in context**.

2 **Conversational Writing Style:** The authors took special care to write a textbook that fosters a friendly dialogue between the text and each individual student. The tone of the presentation is intentionally conversational—creating the impression of *speaking* **with the student**, as opposed to *teaching* to the student.

3 **Superior Organization of Related Topics:** *McGraw-Hill's Taxation* takes a fresh approach to taxation by grouping related topics together in **theme chapters**, including separate chapters on home ownership, compensation, investments, and retirement savings & deferred compensation.

> It's a **better alternative to the West text** than anything else I have seen.
> – Lyn Wheeler,
> Washington & Lee University

4 **Real World Focus:** Students learn best when they see how concepts are applied in the real world. For that reason, real-world examples and articles are included in "**Taxes in the Real World**" boxes throughout the book. These vignettes demonstrate current issues in taxation and show the relevance of tax issues in all areas of business.

5 **Integrated Examples:** The examples used throughout the chapter relate directly to the storyline presented at the beginning of each chapter, so students become familiar with one fact set and learn how to apply those facts to different scenarios. In addition to providing in-context examples, we provide "**What if**" scenarios within many examples to **illustrate how variations in the facts might or might not change the answers**.

> It is a breath of fresh air in its very original approach.
> – Alan Davis,
> Truman State University

A STORYLINE APPROACH THAT WILL RESONATE WITH STUDENTS

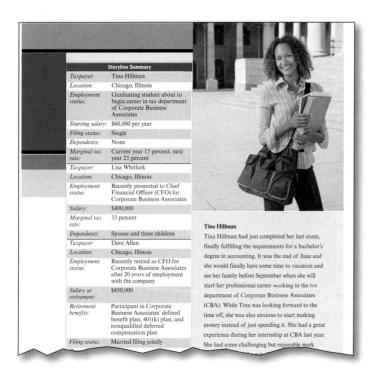

Storyline Summary	
Taxpayer:	Tina Hillman
Location:	Chicago, Illinois
Employment status:	Graduating student about to begin career in tax department of Corporate Business Associates
Starting salary:	$60,000 per year
Filing status:	Single
Dependents:	None
Marginal tax rate:	Current year 15 percent, next year 25 percent
Taxpayer:	Lisa Whitlark
Location:	Chicago, Illinois
Employment status:	Recently promoted to Chief Financial Officer (CFO) for Corporate Business Associates
Salary:	$400,000
Marginal tax rate:	33 percent
Dependents:	Spouse and three children
Taxpayer:	Dave Allan
Location:	Chicago, Illinois
Employment status:	Recently retired as CFO for Corporate Business Associates after 20 years of employment with the company
Salary at retirement:	$450,000
Retirement benefits:	Participant in Corporate Business Associates' defined benefit plan, 401(k) plan, and nonqualified deferred compensation plan
Filing status:	Married filing jointly

Tina Hillman

Tina Hillman had just completed her last exam, finally fulfilling the requirements for a bachelor's degree in accounting. It was the end of June and she would finally have some time to vacation and see her family before September when she will start her professional career working in the tax department of Corporate Business Associates (CBA). While Tina was looking forward to the time off, she was also anxious to start making money instead of just spending it. She had a great experience during her internship at CBA last year. She had some challenging but enjoyable work

Each chapter begins with a storyline that introduces a set of characters facing specific tax-related situations. This revolutionary approach to teaching tax emphasizes real people facing real tax dilemmas. Students learn to apply practical tax information to specific business and personal situations.

> I really like the use of the chapter storylines that tie together the different examples and exhibits. It definitely accomplishes the goal of providing a big picture background and allowing tax rules to be applied in real world settings.
> – Scott White,
> Lindenwood University

Examples

Examples are the cornerstone of any textbook covering taxation. For this reason, *McGraw-Hill's Taxation* took special care to create clear and helpful examples that relate to the storyline of the chapter. Students learn to refer to the facts presented in the storyline and apply them to other scenarios—in this way, they build a greater base of knowledge through application. Many examples also include "What if?" scenarios that add more complexity to the example or explore related tax concepts.

Example 8-4

Rick employs Joan, an arborist who specializes in trimming trees and treating local tree ailments. Joan generates a great deal of revenue for Rick's business, but is in her mid-60s and suffers from diabetes. In November, Rick purchased a "key-employee" term-life insurance policy on Joan's life. The policy cost Rick $720 and will pay him a $20,000 death benefit if Joan passes away during the next 12 months. What amount of life insurance policy premium can Rick deduct?

Answer: $0. Rick cannot deduct the $720 premium on the life insurance policy because the life insurance proceeds from the policy are tax-exempt.

What if: Suppose Rick purchased the life insurance policy on Joan's life and allowed Joan to name the beneficiary. The policy cost Rick $720 and will pay the beneficiary a $20,000 death benefit if Joan passes away during the next 12 months. What amount of life insurance policy premium can Rick deduct?

Answer: $720. In this scenario, Rick can deduct the entire premium of $720 as a *compensation* expense because the benefit of the policy inures to Joan and not to Rick's business.

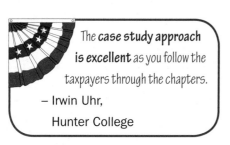

> The **case study approach** **is excellent** as you follow the taxpayers through the chapters.
> – Irwin Uhr,
> Hunter College

THE PEDAGOGY YOUR STUDENTS NEED TO PUT THE CODE IN CONTEXT

Taxes in the Real World

Taxes in the Real World are short boxes used throughout the book to demonstrate the real-world use of tax concepts. Current articles on tax issues, real-world application of chapter-specific tax rules, and short vignettes on popular news in tax are some of the issues covered in Taxes in the Real World boxes.

ment... These nontaxable awards are limited to $400 of tangible property *other than cash* per employee per year.[22] The award is not excluded from the employee's income if circumstances suggest it is disguised compensation.[23]

Taxes in the Real World   Oprah Car Winners Hit with Hefty Tax

Like any prize, the value is counted as income; winners must pay up to $7,000 or forfeit the car.

**September 22, 2004: 7:05 PM EDT
NEW YORK (CNN/Money)—Leave it to Uncle Sam to spoil the party.**

When Oprah Winfrey gave away 276 cars last week to the audience of her show, images of people laughing, jumping, crying—some hysterically—filled the airwaves and the give-away became stuff of legend. Late night talk show hosts and newspaper columnists are still talking about it. But now some of those eager prize-winners have a choice: Fork over $7,000 or give up the car.

According to a spokeswoman for Harpo Productions Inc., Oprah's company, the recipients must pay a tax on the winnings, just like any prize. For a brand new Pontiac G-Six, the model given away on the show, the sticker price is $28,500. The $28,500 would need to be claimed as income so, depending on the individual's tax bracket, the tax could be as high as $7,000. And that was after Pontiac agreed to pay most of the local charges, including state sales tax and licensing fees. The Harpo Spokeswomen said winners had three choices. They could keep the car and pay the tax, sell the car and pay the tax with the profits, or forfeit the car.

Source: http://money.cnn.com/2004/09/ 22/news/ newsmakers/oprah_car_tax/

Taxpayers must include the *gross* amount of their gambling winnings for the year in gross income. Taxpayers are allowed to deduct their gambling losses to the extent

> Best I've seen in giving real world explanations and examples that apply the complex IRS rules.
>
> — James E. Racic, Lakeland Community College

Key Facts

The Key Facts provide quick synopses of the critical pieces of information presented throughout each chapter.

THE KEY FACTS

Employee FICA Tax

- **Social Security Tax**
  · 6.2 percent rate on wage base.
  · 2009 wage base limit is $106,800.

- **Medicare Tax**
  · 1.45 percent rate on wage base.
  · Wage base unlimited.

Self-Employment Taxes

While employees equally share their FICA (Social Security and Medicare) tax burden with employers, self-employed taxpayers must pay the *entire* FICA tax burden on their self-employment earnings.[20] Just as it is with FICA taxes for employees, self-employment taxes consist of both Social Security and Medicare taxes. Because their FICA taxes are based on their self-employment earnings, FICA taxes for self-employed taxpayers are referred to as **self-employment taxes.** Just as it is with employees, the base for the Social Security component of the self-employment tax is limited to $106,800. The base for the Medicare portion of the self-employment tax is unlimited. The process for determining the taxpayer's self-employment taxes payable requires the following three steps:

Step 1: Compute the amount of the taxpayer's net income from self-employment activities (this is generally the taxpayer's net income from **Schedule C** of

Exhibits

Today's students are visual learners, and *McGraw-Hill's Taxation* delivers with a textbook that makes appropriate use of charts, diagrams, and tabular demonstrations of key material.

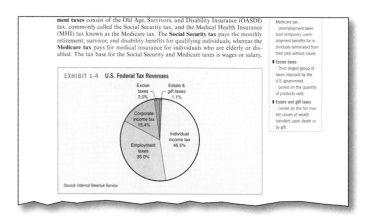

ment taxes consist of the Old Age, Survivors, and Disability Insurance (OASDI) tax, commonly called the Social Security tax, and the Medical Health Insurance (MHI) tax known as the Medicare tax. The **Social Security tax** pays the monthly retirement, survivor, and disability benefits for qualifying individuals, whereas the **Medicare tax** pays for medical insurance for individuals who are elderly or disabled. The tax base for the Social Security and Medicare taxes is wages or salary,

Medicare tax.
· Unemployment taxes fund temporary unemployment benefits for individuals terminated from their jobs without cause.

- **Excise taxes**
  · Third largest group of taxes imposed by the U.S. government.
  · Levied on the quantity of products sold.

- **Estate and gift taxes**
  · Levied on the fair market values of wealth transfers upon death or by gift.

EXHIBIT 1-4   U.S. Federal Tax Revenues

- Excise taxes 2.0%
- Estate & gift taxes 1.1%
- Corporate income tax 15.4%
- Individual income tax 46.5%
- Employment taxes 35.0%

Source: Internal Revenue Service

> Spilker's text adds **examples that flow through the chapter** with "Key Facts" boxes.
>
> — Deb Oden,
>   Missouri State
>   University

> Spilker's use of examples immediately following the concept is a **great way to reinforce the concepts.**
>
> — Karen Wisniewski, County College of Morris

PRACTICE MAKES PERFECT WITH A...

SUMMARY	
LO1	Describe the tax and nontax aspects of employer-provided defined benefit plans from both the employer's and employee's perspective.
	■ Benefits are determined based on years of service and salary. The maximum annual benefit is capped and adjusted upward annually for inflation.
	■ Benefits vest over time using either a five-year cliff or seven-year graded vesting schedule.
	■ Employers deduct cash contributions to fund the plan and employees treat cash distributions as ordinary income in the year received.
	■ Employers bear market risk with defined benefit plans.
	■ Premature distribution and minimum distribution penalties don't typically apply to defined benefit distributions.
	■ Because of the high cost of funding and maintaining defined benefit plans, they are waning in popularity.
LO2	Explain and determine the tax consequences associated with employer-provided defined contribution plans, including traditional 401(k) and Roth 401(k) plans.

Summary

A unique feature of *McGraw-Hill's Taxation* is the end of chapter summary organized around learning objectives. Each objective has a brief, bullet-point summary that covers the major topics and concepts for that chapter, including references to critical exhibits and examples.

All end of chapter material is tied to learning objectives:

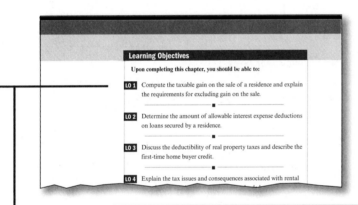

Learning Objectives

Upon completing this chapter, you should be able to:

LO 1 Compute the taxable gain on the sale of a residence and explain the requirements for excluding gain on the sale.

LO 2 Determine the amount of allowable interest expense deductions on loans secured by a residence.

LO 3 Discuss the deductibility of real property taxes and describe the first-time home buyer credit.

LO 4 Explain the tax issues and consequences associated with rental

> This promises to be the best tax and business strategy book around.
> – Dave Harris,
> Syracuse University

DISCUSSION QUESTIONS

1. **(LO1)** What is a tax bracket? What is the rel the width of the tax brackets in the tax rate s

2. **(LO1)** In 2009, for a taxpayer with $50,000 any actual computations, which filing status tax liability? Which filing status provides the

3. **(LO1)** What is the tax marriage penalty and circumstances would a couple experience a t

4. **(LO1)** Once they've computed their taxable mine their regular tax liability? What additic compute their tax liability when they have pi

Questions are provided for each of the major concepts in each chapter, providing students with an opportunity to review key parts of the chapter and answer evocative questions about what they have learned. Each question is linked to a learning objective.

> [The] end of chapter material relates to the text of each chapter; the chapter coverage emphasizes only the most important concepts for each topic. **Chapter summary eliminates need for study guide**.
> – David B. Bojarsky,
> California State University, Long Beach

...WIDE VARIETY OF ASSIGNMENT MATERIAL

Problems are designed to test the comprehension of more complex topics. Each problem at the end of the chapter is tied to that chapter's learning objective, with multiple problems for critical topics.

PROBLEMS

54. **(LO1)** Whitney received $75,000 of taxable income in 2009. All of the income was salary from her employer. What is her income tax liability in each of the following alternative situations?
   a. She files under the single filing status.
   b. She files a joint tax return with her spouse. Together their taxable income is $75,000.

> The author's approach is **very helpful for students like mine that often have very little actual business experience.** The storyline provides a context for understanding the tax laws and presenting a variety of tax issues. – Anne Christensen, Montana State University

Research Problems are special problems throughout the end of the chapter's assignment material. These require students to do both basic and

research 47. **(LO2)** Jennifer has been living in her current principal residence for three years. Six months ago Jennifer decided that she would like to purchase a second home near a beach so she can vacation there for part of the year. Despite her best efforts, Jennifer has been unable to find what she is looking for. Consequently, Jennifer recently decided to change plans. She purchased a parcel of land for $200,000 with the intention of building her second home on the property. To acquire the land, she borrowed $200,000 secured by the land. Jennifer would

more complex research on topics outside of the scope of the book. Each Research Problem includes an icon to differentiate it from regular problems.

> The questions and problems associated with the text are good and of varying levels. There are also **more questions and problems to choose from.**
> – Laurie Hagberg, Trident Technical College

Planning Problems are another unique set of problems, also located at the end of the chapter's assignment material. These require students to test their tax planning skills after covering the chapter's topics. Each Planning Problem includes an icon to differentiate it from regular problems.

home but doesn't plan to live in the home for 37 months?

planning 48. **(LO2)** Rajiv and Laurie Amin are recent college graduates looking to purchase a new home. They are purchasing a $200,000 home by paying $20,000 down and borrowing the other $180,000 with a 30-year loan secured by the home. The Amins have the option of (1) paying no discount points on the loan and paying interest at 8 percent or (2) paying one discount point on the loan and paying interest of 7.5 percent. Both loans require the Amins to make interest-only payments for the first five years. Unless otherwise stated, the

Comprehensive and Tax Return Problems address multiple concepts in a single problem. Comprehensive problems are ideal for cumulative topics; for this reason, they are located at the end of all chapters. In the end of book Appendix C, we include Tax Return Problems that cover multiple chapters.

COMPREHENSIVE PROBLEMS

40. Marc and Michelle are married and earned salaries this year (2009) of $64,000 and $12,000, respectively. In addition to their salaries, they received interest of $350 from municipal bonds and $500 from corporate bonds. Marc and Michelle also paid $2,500 of qualifying moving expenses, and Marc paid alimony to a prior spouse in the amount of $1,500. Marc and Michelle have a 10-year-old son, Matthew, who lived with them throughout the entire year. Thus, Marc and Michelle are allowed to claim a $1,000 child tax credit for Matthew. Marc and Michelle paid $6,000 of expenditures that qualify as itemized deductions and they had a total of $5,500 in federal income taxes withheld from their paychecks during the course of the year.

   a. What is Marc and Michelle's gross income?
   b. What is Marc and Michelle's adjusted gross income?
   c. What is the total amount of Marc and Michelle's deductions *from* AGI?

A Logical Organization

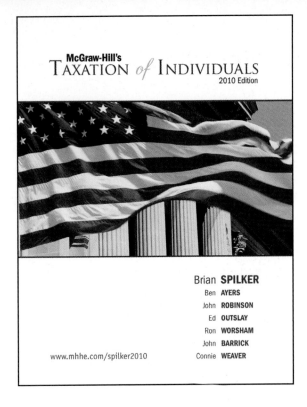

McGraw-Hill's Taxation of Individuals is organized to maximize topical efficiency and to emphasize topics that are most important to undergraduates taking their first tax course. The first three chapters provide an introduction to taxation and then carefully guide students through tax research and tax planning. Part II discusses the fundamental elements of individual income tax, starting with the tax formula in chapter 4 and then proceeding to more depth on individual topics in chapters 5–7. Part III then discusses tax issues associated with business and investment activities. On the business side, it addresses business income and deductions, accounting methods, and tax consequences associated with purchasing assets, property dispositions (sales, trades, or other dispositions). For investments it covers portfolio-type investments such as stocks and bonds and business investments including loss limitations associated with these investments. Part IV is unique among tax textbooks; this section combines related tax issues for compensation, retirement savings, and home ownership. The storylines in all of these chapters show how realistic individuals and business owners benefit from a clear understanding of the tax code.

Part I: Introduction to Taxation
1. An Introduction to Tax
2. Tax Compliance, the IRS, and Tax Authorities
3. Tax Planning Strategies and Related Limitations

Part II: Basic Individual Taxation
4. Individual Income Tax Overview
5. Gross Income and Exclusions
6. Individual Deductions
7. Individual Income Tax Computation and Tax Credits

Part III: Business and Investment–Related Transactions
8. Business Income, Deductions, and Accounting Methods
9. Property Acquisition and Cost Recovery
10. Property Dispositions
11. Investments

Part IV: Specialized Topics
12. Compensation
13. Retirement Savings and Deferred Compensation
14. Tax Consequences of Home Ownership

Makes Learning Efficient

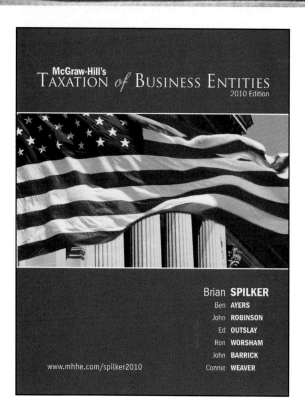

McGraw-Hill's Taxation of Business Entities begins with the process for determining gross income and deductions for businesses, and the tax consequences associated with purchasing assets, property dispositions (sales, trades, or other dispositions). Part II provides a comprehensive overview of entities, and the formation, reorganization and liquidation of corporations. Unique to this series is a complete chapter on FAS 109, which provides a primer on the basics of calculating the income tax provision. Included in the narrative is a discussion of temporary and permanent differences and their impact on a company's book "effective tax rate." Part III provides a detailed discussion of partnerships and S corporations. The last part of the book covers state and local taxation, multinational taxation and transfer taxes and wealth planning.

McGraw-Hill's Taxation of Individuals and Business Entities covers all chapters included in the two split volumes in one convenient volume.
See the next page!

AUTHOR-WRITTEN SUPPLEMENTS ENSURE QUALITY AND CONSISTENCY

The authors write all of the supplements for *McGraw-Hill's Taxation*, including the Testbank, Solutions Manual, PowerPoints® and Instructor's Manual. Each supplement has been reviewed by the author team to ensure consistency with the text material and accuracy. With the author's personal involvement in each supplement, you can be assured that *McGraw-Hill's Taxation's* supplements are the same high quality as the book.

Instructor's Resource Manual
This manual provides for each chapter: (a) a chapter overview; (b) a comprehensive lecture outline; (c) a variety of suggested class activities (real world, ethics, professional development activities including research, analysis, communication and judgment, and others); and (d) an assignment chart indicating topic, learning objective, and difficulty for every question and problem.

Solutions Manual
The Solutions Manual includes detailed solutions for every question, problem, and comprehensive problem in the text.

Testbank
Written by the authors, this comprehensive Testbank contains over 2,500 problems and true/false, multiple-choice, and problems.

PowerPoints®
The PowerPoint® slides are available on the Online Learning Center (OLC). Separate sets of PowerPoints® are available for instructors and students.

TaxACT®
McGraw-Hill's Taxation can be packaged with tax software from TaxACT, one of the leading tax preparation software companies in the market today.

ONLINE LEARNING OPPORTUNITIES THAT ACCOMMODATE A VARIETY OF LEARNING STYLES
www.mhhe.com/spilker2010

Today's students are every bit as comfortable using a web browser as they are reading a printed book. That's why we offer an Online Learning Center (OLC) that follows *McGraw-Hill's Taxation* chapter-by-chapter. It requires no building or maintenance on your part, and is ready to go the moment you and your students type in the URL. As your students study, they can access the OLC Website for such benefits as:

- Self-grading quizzes
- Kaplan Schweser CPA Simulations
- Tax forms
- Student PowerPoint® Presentations
- Text updates

A secured Instructor Resource Center stores your essential course materials to save you prep time before class. The Instructor Center includes:

- Instructor's Resource Manual
- Solutions Manual
- Instructor PowerPoint® Presentations
- EZ Test
- Sample syllabi

KAPLAN SIMULATIONS

> An all-inclusive textbook that clearly explains the tax code, and **uses extensive realistic examples that brings the code to life.** – Sarah C. Nash, DeKalb Technical College

Apply the knowledge you've gained through *McGraw-Hill's Taxation* with CPA simulations from Kaplan Schweser and McGraw-Hill Higher Education! Each CPA simulation demonstrates taxation concepts in a Web-based interface, identical to that used in the actual CPA Exam.

Kaplan Schweser's Online Review Courses for the CPA Exam provide the interactive benefits of a live classroom from the comfort and convenience of your home or office. Each course includes a variety of interconnected study materials to further reinforce the lessons taught. Kaplan Schweser is CPA Exam Review for today's candidate.

CPA simulations are found in the homework material after the very last case in selected chapters in your book.

A HEARTFELT THANKS TO THE MANY VOICES WHO SHAPED THIS BOOK

The version of the book you are reading would not be the same book without the valuable suggestions, keen insights, and constructive criticisms of the list of reviewers below. Each professor listed here contributed in substantive ways to the organization of chapters, coverage of topics, and the use of pedagogy. We are grateful to them for taking the time to read chapters or attend reviewer conferences, focus groups, and symposia in support of the development for the book:

Robert Adkins, *Clark State Community College*

Akinloye Akindayomi, *University of Massachusetts – Dartmouth*

Glenn Alan, *University of Arizona*

Susan M. Albring, *University of South Florida*

Raquel Alexander, *University of Kansas*

David L. Allen, *Harding University*

Mary Anderson, *University of Southern Mississippi*

Frank J. Aquilino, *Montclair State University*

A. David Austill, *Union University*

Jeff Austin, *Southern Methodist University*

Timothy Baker, *California State University – Fresno*

Anthony Basile, *Hofstra University*

Terry W. Bechtel, *Northwestern State University*

Katherine D. Black, *Utah Valley University*

Israel Blumenfrucht, *Queens College*

David B. Bojarsky, *California State University – Long Beach*

Patrick Borja, *Citrus College*

Darryl Brown, *Illinois State University*

Michael Brown, *University of Missouri*

Ronald Bruce, *Gwynedd-Mercy College*

Ann Burstein Cohen, *University at Buffalo (SUNY)*

Hughlene Burton, *University of North Carolina – Charlotte*

Sandra Callaghan, *Texas Christian University*

Julia M. Camp, *Providence College*

Lloyd Carroll, *Borough of Manhattan Community College*

Anne L. Christensen, *Montana State University*

Robert Cockrum, *University of South Florida*

Lisa Cole, *Johnson County Community College*

Caroline K. Craig, *Illinois State University*

Terry L. Crain, *University of Oklahoma*

Charles D'Alessandro, *Dowling College*

John Darcy, *University of Texas – Pan American*

Alan Davis, *Truman State University*

James DeSimpelare, *University of Michigan – Ann Arbor*

John Dexter, *Northwood University*

Melanie James Earles, *Tennessee Technological University*

Rafi Efrat, *California State University – Northridge*

Elizabeth Ekmekjian, *William Paterson University*

Charles Enis, *The Pennsylvania State University*

Philip R. Fink, *University of Toledo*

Ira Kaye Frashier, *Eastern New Mexico University*

Stephen Gara, *Drake University*

Greg Geisler, *University of Missouri*

Steve Gill, *San Diego State University*

Ruth Goran, *Northeastern Illinois University*

Diane Green, *Sam Houston State University*

Sanjay Gupta, *Michigan State University*

Roger W. Guyette, *University of West Florida*

Laurie Hagberg, *Trident Technical College*

Jerry W. Hanwell, *Robert Morris University*

Phil Harper, *Middle Tennessee State University*

David Harris, *Syracuse University*

Charles Hartman, *Cedarville University*

John W. Hatcher, *Purdue University*

Keith Hendrick, *DeKalb Technical College*

Daniel Holder, *University of Illinois*

William C. Hood, *Central Michigan University*

Bambi A. Hora, *University of Central Oklahoma*

Jana Hosmer, *Blue Ridge Community College*

Anne Jones, *University of Massachusetts*

Lynn C. Jones, *University of North Florida*

Elliot Kamlet, *Binghamton University*

John E. Karayan, *California State Polytechnic University – Pomona*

Jocelyn Kauffunger, *University of Pittsburgh*

Carl Keller, *Indiana University/Purdue University – Ft. Wayne*

Connie Kertz, *Emory University*

Kim Key, *Auburn University*

Dieter M. Kiefer, *American River College*

Paul Krazeise, *Bellarmine University*

Teresa Lang, *Columbus State University*

David Lanning, *Tompkins Cortland Community College*

Ernest R. Larkins, *Georgia State University*

Melissa P. Larson, *Brigham Young University*

Sharon Lassar, *Florida International University*

Leonard Lauricella, *Montclair State University*

Bruce Lindsey, *Genesee Community College*

Avi Liveson, *Hunter College*

Mariah Lynch, *University of South Carolina*

Richard Malamud, *California State University – Dominguez Hills*

Kate Mantzke, *Northern Illinois University*

Bobbie Martindale, *Dallas Baptist University*

Bruce W. McClain, *Cleveland State University*

Debra McGilsky, *Central Michigan University*

Gerard J. Mellnick, *Schoolcraft College*

Valerie C. Milliron, *California State University – Chico*

Lillian F. Mills, *University of Arizona*

Alfonsina Minchella, *Roxbury Community College*

Walter Montgomery, *Alabama State University*

Bill Moser, *University of Missouri*

Brigitte W. Muehlmann, *Suffolk University*

Cathryn Nash, *DeKalb Technical College*

Adolph A. Neidermeyer, *West Virginia University*

Richard Newmark, *University of Northern Colorado*

Nancy Nichols, *James Madison University*

Patricia Nodoushani, *University of Hartford*

Tracy Noga, *Bentley University*

Priscilla O'Clock, *Xavier University*

Debra Oden, *Missouri State University*

Thomas C. Omer, *Texas A&M University*

Simon R. Pearlman, *California State University – Long Beach*

Dennis Pelzek, *Waukesha County Technical College*

Sonja Pippin, *University of Nevada – Reno*

J. Kent Poff, *North Georgia College*

Thomas Purcell, *Creighton University*

James E. Racic, *Lakeland Community College*

David W. Randolph, *University of Dayton*

Ian Redpath, *Canisius College*

Tim Rupert, *Northeastern University*

Michael Schadewald, *University of Wisconsin – Milwaukee*

Ananth Seetharaman, *Saint Louis University*

Mark Sellner, *University of Minnesota – Minneapolis*

Ray Shaffer, *Youngstown State University*

James Shimko, *Sinclair Community College*

Harold Silverman, *Bridgewater State College*

Gene Smith, *Eastern New Mexico University*

Jim Smith, *University of San Diego*

Keith E. Smith, *George Washington University*

Will Snyder, *San Diego State University*

Andrew Somers, *University of California – San Diego*

Susan Sorensen, *University of Houston – Clear Lake*

W. Joey Styron, *Augusta State University*

Judyth A. Swingen, *University of Arkansas – Little Rock*

Bill Terando, *Iowa State University*

D. James Tiburzi, *University of Missouri*

James Trebby, *Marquette University*

Karen Trott, *University of North Carolina – Chapel Hill*

Ski VanderLaan, *Delta College*

Mark Washburn, *University of Texas – Tyler*

Wayne Wells, *St. Cloud State University*

Lyn F. Wheeler, *Washington & Lee University*

Scott White, *Lindenwood University*

Marvin Williams, *University of Houston – Downtown*

Karen Wisniewski, *County College of Morris*

Jennifer J.Wright, *Drexel University*

Timothy Yoder, *Mississippi State University*

Marilyn Young, *Belmont University*

Acknowledgments

Many talented people contributed to the creation of this first edition, and we would like to thank them for their valuable contributions. The keen editorial instincts of Elisa Adams and Laura Edwards helped shape the first draft of manuscript. William A. Padley of Madison Area Technical College and Ilene Persoff of CW Post Campus/Long Island University accuracy checked the pageproof and Solutions Manual; we greatly appreciate the hours they spent checking tax forms and double-checking our calculations throughout the book. Many thanks also to Jim Young for providing the tax numbers for 2009 well before the IRS made them available.

We also appreciate the expert attention given to this project by the staff at McGraw-Hill/ Irwin, especially Stewart Mattson, Editorial Director; Tim Vertovec, Publisher; Daryl Horrocks, Developmental Editor; Pat Frederickson, Lead Project Manager & K4 Liaison; Scott Bishop, Marketing Manager; Susan Lombardi, Media Product Manager; Matthew Baldwin, Lead Designer; and Debra Sylvester, Production Supervisor.

AS WE GO TO PRESS

We provide this page to inform you of any last-minute tax changes that occur as the book goes to the printer. This book is current through the Worker, Retiree, and Employer Recovery Act of 2008 signed by the President on December 23, 2008. It is possible and perhaps likely that economic stimulus tax legislation affecting the 2009 tax year will be passed after this book goes to press. You can go to our website (www.mhhe.com/spilker2010) for updates on these changes.

Table of Contents

Chapter 3

TAX PLANNING STRATEGIES AND RELATED LIMITATIONS

PART II
BASIC INDIVIDUAL TAXATION

Chapter 4

INDIVIDUAL INCOME TAX OVERVIEW

Chapter 5

GROSS INCOME AND EXCLUSIONS

Chapter 6

INDIVIDUAL DEDUCTIONS

Chapter 7

**INDIVIDUAL INCOME TAX COMPUTATION
AND TAX CREDITS**

PART III
BUSINESS AND INVESTMENT–RELATED
TRANSACTIONS

Chapter 8
BUSINESS INCOME, DEDUCTIONS, AND
ACCOUNTING METHODS

Chapter 9
PROPERTY ACQUISITION AND COST
RECOVERY

PART IV
SPECIALIZED TOPICS

Chapter 14
TAX CONSEQUENCES OF HOME OWNERSHIP

An Introduction to Tax

Learning Objectives

Upon completing this chapter, you should be able to:

LO 1 Demonstrate how taxes influence basic business, investment, personal, and political decisions.

■

LO 2 Discuss what constitutes a tax and the general objectives of taxes.

■

LO 3 Describe the different tax rate structures and calculate a tax.

■

LO 4 Identify the various federal, state, and local taxes.

■

LO 5 Apply appropriate criteria to evaluate alternate tax systems.

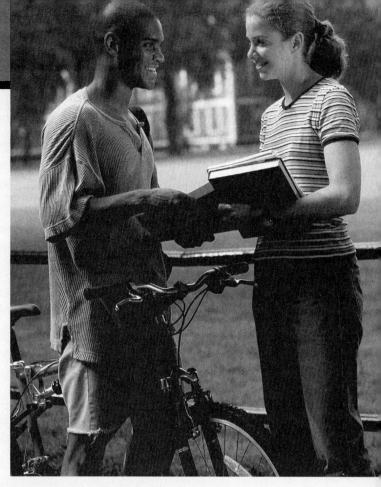

M argaret is a junior beginning her first tax course. She is excited about her career prospects as an accounting major but hasn't had much exposure to taxes. On her way to campus she runs into an old friend, Eddy, who is going to Washington, D.C., to protest recent proposed changes to the U.S. tax system. Eddy is convinced the IRS is evil and that the current tax system is blatantly unfair and corrupt. He advocates a simpler, fairer way of taxation. Margaret is intrigued by Eddy's passion but questions whether he has a complete understanding of the U.S. tax system. She decides to withhold all judgments about it (or about pursuing a career in taxation) until the end of her tax course. ∎

Storyline Summary	
Taxpayer:	Margaret
Employment status:	Margaret is a full-time student at the University of Georgia.
Current situation:	She is beginning her first tax class.

WHO CARES ABOUT TAXES AND WHY?

A clear understanding of the role of taxes in everyday decisions will help you make an informed decision about the value of studying taxation or pursuing a career in taxation. One view of taxation is that it represents an inconvenience every April 15th (the annual due date for filing federal individual tax returns without extensions). However, the role of taxation is much more pervasive than this view suggests. Your study of this subject will provide you a unique opportunity to develop an informed opinion about taxation. As a business student, you can overcome the mystery that pervades popular impressions of the tax system and perhaps, one day, share your expertise with friends or clients.

What are some common decisions you face that taxes may influence? In this course, we alert you to situations in which you can increase your return on investments by up to one third! Even the best lessons in finance courses can't approach the increase in risk-adjusted return that smart tax planning provides. Would you like to own your home someday? Tax deductions for home mortgage interest and real estate taxes can reduce the after-tax costs of owning a home relative to renting. Thus, when you face the decision to buy or rent, you can make an informed choice if you understand the relative tax advantages of home ownership. Would you like to retire someday? Understanding the tax-advantaged methods of saving for retirement can increase the after-tax value of your retirement nest egg—and thus increase the likelihood that you can afford to retire, and do so in style. Other common personal financial decisions that taxes influence include: choosing investments, evaluating alternative job offers, saving for education expenses, and doing gift or estate planning. Indeed, taxes are a part of everyday life and have a significant effect on many of the personal financial decisions all of us face.

The role of taxes is not limited to personal finance. Taxes play an equally important role in fundamental business decisions such as the following:

- What organizational form should a business use?
- Where should the business locate?
- How should business acquisitions be structured?
- How should the business compensate employees?
- What is the appropriate mix of debt and equity for the business?
- Should the business rent or own its equipment and property?
- How should the business distribute profits to its owners?

Savvy business decisions require owners and managers to consider all costs and benefits in order to evaluate the merits of a transaction. Although taxes don't necessarily dominate these decisions, they do represent large transaction costs that businesses should factor into the financial decision-making process.

Taxes also play a major part in the political process. U.S. presidential candidates often distinguish themselves from their opponents based upon their tax rhetoric. Indeed, the major political parties generally have very diverse views of the appropriate way to tax the public.[1] Determining who is taxed, what is taxed, and how much is taxed are tough questions with nontrivial answers. Voters must have a basic understanding of taxes to evaluate the merits of alternative tax proposals. Later in this chapter, we'll introduce criteria you can use to evaluate alternative tax proposals.

---

[1] The U.S. Department of the Treasury provides a "history of taxation" on its Web site (www.treas.gov/education/fact-sheets/taxes/ustax.shtml). You may find it interesting to read this history in light of the various political parties in office at the time.

Taxes in the Real World   *No New Taxes*

George H. W. Bush famously stated in his 1988 presidential election campaign, "Read my lips, no new taxes." In 1990, he signed legislation increasing individual income tax rates. Political observers cite this as one reason he lost the 1992 presidential election to Bill Clinton.

In summary, taxes affect many aspects of personal, business, and political decisions. Developing a solid understanding of taxation should allow you to make informed decisions in these areas. Thus, Margaret can take comfort that her semester will likely prove useful to her personally. Who knows? Depending on her interest in business, investment, retirement planning, and the like, she may ultimately decide to pursue a career in taxation.

WHAT QUALIFIES AS A TAX?

L02

Taxes have been described in many terms, some positive, some negative, some printable, some not. Let's go directly to a formal definition of a tax, which should prove useful in identifying alternative taxes and discussing alternative tax systems.

A **tax** *is a payment required by a government that is unrelated to any specific benefit or service received from the government.* The general purpose of a tax is to fund the operations of the government (to raise revenue). Taxes differ from fines and penalties in that taxes are not intended to punish or prevent illegal behavior. Nonetheless, by allowing deductions from income, our federal tax system does encourage certain behaviors like charitable contributions, retirement savings, and research and development, and we can view it as discouraging other legal behavior. For example, "**sin taxes**" impose relatively high surcharges on alcohol and tobacco products.[2]

Key components of the definition of a tax are that

- the payment is required (it is not voluntary),
- the payment is imposed by a government agency (federal, state, or local), and
- the payment is not tied directly to the benefit received by the taxpayer.

This last point is not to say that taxpayers receive no benefits from the taxes they pay. They benefit from national defense, a judicial system, law enforcement, government-sponsored social programs, an interstate highway system, public schools, and many other government-provided programs and services. The distinction is that taxes paid are not *directly* related to any specific benefit received by the taxpayer.

Can taxes be assessed for special purposes, such as a 1 percent sales tax for education? Yes. Why is an **earmarked tax,** a tax that *is* assessed for a specific purpose, still considered a tax? Because the payment made by the taxpayer does not directly relate to the specific benefit *received by the taxpayer.*

THE KEY FACTS

What Qualifies as a Tax?

- The general purpose of taxes is to fund government agencies.

- Unlike fines or penalties, taxes are not meant to punish or prevent illegal behavior; but "*sin taxes*" are meant to discourage some behaviors.

- The three criteria necessary to be a tax are that the payment is
  · required
  · imposed by a government
  · and not tied directly to the benefit received by the taxpayer.

Example 1-1

Margaret travels to Birmingham, Alabama, where she rents a hotel room and dines at several restaurants. The price she pays for her hotel room and meals includes an additional 2 percent city surcharge to fund roadway construction in Birmingham. Is this a tax?

Answer: Yes. The payment is required by a local government and does not directly relate to a specific benefit that Margaret receives.

---

[2]Sin taxes represent an interesting confluence of incentives. On the one hand, demand for such products as alcohol, tobacco, and gambling is often relatively inelastic because of their addictive quality. Thus, taxing such a product can raise substantial revenues. On the other hand, one of the arguments for sin taxes is frequently the social goal of *reducing* demand for such products.

Example 1-2

Margaret's parents, Bill and Mercedes, recently built a house and were assessed $1,000 by their county government to connect to the county sewer system. Is this a tax?

Answer: No. The assessment was mandatory and it was paid to a local government. However, the third criterion was not met since the payment directly relates to a specific benefit (sewer service) received by the payees. For the same reason, tolls, parking meter fees, and annual licensing fees are also not considered taxes.

L03

HOW TO CALCULATE A TAX

THE KEY FACTS

How to Calculate a Tax

■ Tax = Tax Base × Tax Rate

■ The tax base defines what is actually taxed and is usually expressed in monetary terms.

■ The tax rate determines the level of taxes imposed on the tax base and is usually expressed as a percentage.

■ Different portions of a tax base may be taxed at different rates.

In its simplest form, the amount of tax equals the tax base multiplied by the tax rate:

$$\text{Tax} = \text{Tax Base} \times \text{Tax Rate} \qquad \textbf{Eq. 1-1}$$

The **tax base** defines what is actually taxed and is usually expressed in monetary terms, whereas the **tax rate** determines the level of taxes imposed on the tax base and is usually expressed as a percentage. For example, a sales tax rate of 6 percent on a purchase of $30 yields a tax of $1.80 ($1.80 = $30 × .06).

Federal, state, and local jurisdictions use a large variety of tax bases to collect tax. Some common tax bases (and related taxes) include taxable income (federal and state income taxes), purchases (sales tax), real estate values (real estate tax), and personal property values (personal property tax).

Different portions of a tax base may be taxed at different rates. A single tax applied to an entire base constitutes a **flat tax.** In the case of **graduated taxes,** the base is divided into a series of monetary amounts, or **brackets,** and each successive bracket is taxed at a different (gradually higher or gradually lower) percentage rate.

Calculating some taxes—income taxes for individuals or corporations, for example—can be quite complex. Advocates of flat taxes argue that the process should be simpler. But as we'll see throughout the text, most of the difficulty in calculating a tax rests in determining the tax *base,* not the tax rate. Indeed, there are only three basic tax rate structures (proportional, progressive, and regressive), and each can be mastered without much difficulty.

DIFFERENT WAYS TO MEASURE TAX RATES

Before we discuss the alternative tax rate structures, let's first define three different tax rates that will be useful in contrasting the different tax rate structures: the marginal, average, and effective tax rates.

The **marginal tax rate** is the tax rate that applies to the *next additional increment* of a taxpayer's taxable income (or deductions). Specifically,

$$\text{Marginal Tax Rate} = \frac{\Delta \text{Tax}}{\Delta \text{Taxable Income}} = \frac{(\text{New Total Tax} - \text{Old Total Tax})}{(\text{New Taxable Income} - \text{Old Taxable Income})} {}_{3} \qquad \textbf{Eq. 1-2}$$

---

[3]Δ means *change in.*

where "old" refers to the current tax and "new" refers to the tax given the additional income (or deductions) in question. In graduated income tax systems, additional income (deductions) can push a taxpayer into a higher (lower) tax bracket, thus changing the marginal tax rate.

Example 1-3

Margaret's parents, Bill and Mercedes, file a joint tax return. They have $140,000 of taxable income this year (after all tax deductions). Assuming the following federal tax rate schedule applies, how much federal income tax will they owe this year?[4]

2009 Federal Married Filing Jointly Tax Rate Schedule

If taxable income is over-	But not over	The tax is:
$ 0	16,700	10% of the amount over $0
16,700	67,900	1,670 plus 15% of the amount over 16,700
67,900	137,050	9,350 plus 25% of the amount over 67,900
137,050	208,850	26,637.50 plus 28% of the amount over 137,050
208,850	372,950	46,741.50 plus 33% of the amount over 208,850
372,950	no limit	100,894.50 plus 35% of the amount over 372,950

Answer: Bill and Mercedes will owe $27,463.50 computed as follows:

$$\$27,463.50 = \$26,637.50 + 28\% (\$140,000 - \$137,050).$$

Note that in this graduated tax rate structure, the first $16,700 of taxable income is taxed at 10 percent, the next $51,200 of taxable income (between $16,700 and $67,900) is taxed at 15 percent, the next $69,150 of taxable income (between $67,900 and $137,050) is taxed at 25 percent. Bill and Mercedes' last $2,950 of taxable income (between $137,050 and $140,000) is taxed at 28 percent.

Many taxpayers incorrectly believe that all their income is taxed at their marginal rate. This mistake leads people to say, "I don't want to earn any additional money because it will put me in a higher tax bracket." Bill and Mercedes are currently in the 28 percent marginal tax rate bracket, but notice that *not* all their income is taxed at this rate. Their *marginal* tax rate is 28 percent. This means that small increases in income will be taxed at 28 percent, and small increases in tax deductions will generate tax *savings* of 28 percent. If Bill and Mercedes receive a large increase in income (or in deductions) such that they would change tax rate brackets, we cannot identify their marginal tax rate by simply identifying their current tax bracket.

Example 1-4

Bill, a well-known economics professor, signs a publishing contract with an $80,000 royalty advance. Using the rate schedule from Example 1-3, what would Bill and Mercedes' marginal tax rate be on this additional $80,000 of taxable income?

(*continued on page 1-6...*)

---

[4]The tax rate schedules for single, married filing jointly, married filing separately, and head of household are included inside the front cover of the text.

Answer: 28.70 percent, computed as follows:

Description	Amount	Explanation
(1) Taxable income with additional $80,000 of taxable income	$ 220,000	$80,000 plus $140,000 taxable income stated in Example 1-3
(2) Tax on $220,000 taxable income	$ 50,421	Using the rate schedule in Example 1-3. $50,421 = $46,741.50 + 33% (11,150)
(3) Taxable income before additional $80,000 of taxable income	$ 140,000	Example 1-3
(4) Tax on $140,000 taxable income	$27,463.50	Example 1-3
Marginal tax rate on additional $80,000 of taxable income	28.70%	$\frac{\Delta \text{Tax}}{\Delta \text{Taxable Income}} = [(2) - (4)]/[(1) - (3)]$

Note that Bill and Mercedes' marginal tax rate on the $80,000 increase in taxable income rests *between* the 28 percent and 33 percent bracket rates because a portion of the additional income ($208,850 − $140,000 = $68,850) is taxed at 28 percent with the remaining income ($220,000 − $208,850 = 11,150) taxed at 33 percent.

Example 1-5

Assume now that, instead of receiving a book advance, Bill and Mercedes start a new business that *loses* $80,000 this year (it results in $80,000 of additional tax deductions). What would be their marginal tax rate for these deductions?

Answer: 24.12 percent, computed as follows:

Description	Amount	Explanation
(1) Taxable income with additional $80,000 of tax deductions	$ 60,000	$140,000 taxable income stated in Example 1-3 less $80,000
(2) Tax on $60,000 taxable income	$ 8,165	Using the rate schedule in Example 1-3. $8,165 = $1,670 + 15% ($60,000 − $16,700)
(3) Taxable income before additional $80,000 of tax deductions	$ 140,000	Example 1-3
(4) Tax on $140,000 taxable income	$27,463.50	Example 1-3
Marginal tax rate on additional $80,000 of taxable income	24.12%	$\frac{\Delta \text{Tax}}{\Delta \text{Taxable Income}} = [(2) - (4)]/[(1) - (3)]$

Bill and Mercedes' marginal tax rate on $80,000 of additional deductions (24.12 percent) differs from their marginal tax rate on $80,000 of additional taxable income (28.70 percent) in these scenarios because of the relatively large increase in income and deductions. Taxpayers often will face the same marginal tax rates for small changes in income and deductions.

THE KEY FACTS

Different Ways to Measure Tax Rates

- **Marginal tax rate**
  - The tax that applies to next increment of income or deduction.
  - $= \dfrac{\Delta \text{Tax}}{\Delta \text{Taxable Income}}$
  - Useful in tax planning.

- **Average tax rate**
  - A taxpayer's average level of taxation on each dollar of *taxable* income.
  - $= \dfrac{\text{Total Tax}}{\text{Taxable Income}}$
  - Useful in budgeting tax expense.

  (continued)

The marginal tax rate is particularly useful in tax planning because it represents the rate of taxation or savings that would apply to additional taxable income (or tax deductions). In Chapter 3, we discuss basic tax planning strategies that use the marginal tax rate.

The **average tax rate** represents a taxpayer's average level of taxation on each dollar of taxable income. Specifically,

$$\text{Average Tax Rate} = \frac{\text{Total Tax}}{\text{Taxable Income}} \qquad \textbf{Eq. 1-3}$$

The average tax rate is often used in budgeting tax expense as a portion of income (what percent of taxable income earned is paid in tax) or to compare the relative tax burdens of taxpayers.

The **effective tax rate** represents the taxpayer's average rate of taxation on each dollar of total income, including taxable *and* nontaxable income. Specifically,

$$\text{Effective Tax Rate} = \frac{\text{Total Tax}}{\text{Total Income}} \qquad \textbf{Eq. 1-4}$$

Relative to the average tax rate, the effective tax rate provides a better depiction of a taxpayer's tax burden because it depicts the taxpayer's total tax paid as a ratio of the sum of both taxable and nontaxable income earned.

> (*concluded*)
> ▌ **Effective tax rate**
> · A taxpayer's average rate of taxation on each dollar of *total* income (taxable *and* nontaxable income).
> · $= \frac{\text{Total Tax}}{\text{Total Income}}$
> · Useful in comparing the relative tax burdens of taxpayers.

Example 1-6

Assuming Bill and Mercedes have $140,000 of taxable income and $10,000 of nontaxable income, what is their average tax rate?

Answer: 19.62 percent, computed as follows:

Description	Amount	Explanation
(1) Taxable income	$ 140,000	
(2) Tax on $140,000 taxable income	$27,463.50%	Example 1-3
Average tax rate	19.62%	$\frac{\text{Total Tax}}{\text{Taxable Income}} = (2)/(1)$

We should not be surprised that Bill and Mercedes' average tax rate is *lower* than their marginal tax rate because although they are currently in the 28 percent tax rate bracket, not all of their taxable income is subject to tax at 28 percent. The first $16,700 of their taxable incomeis taxed at 10 percent, their next $51,200 is taxed at 15 percent, their next $69,150 is taxed at 25 percent, and only their last $2,950 of taxable income is taxed at 28 percent. Thus, their average tax rate is considerably lower than their marginal tax rate.

Example 1-7

Again, given the same income figures as in Example 1-6 ($140,000 of taxable income and $10,000 of nontaxable income), what is Bill and Mercedes' effective tax rate?

Answer: 18.31 percent, computed as follows:

Description	Amount	Explanation
(1) Total income	$ 150,000	$140,000 taxable income plus $10,000 in nontaxable income (Example 1-6)
(2) Tax on $140,000 taxable income	$27,463.50	Example 1-3
Effective tax rate	18.31%	$\frac{\text{Total Tax}}{\text{Total Income}} = (2)/(1)$

Should we be surprised that the effective tax rate is lower than the *average* tax rate? No, because except when the taxpayer has more nondeductible expenses (such as fines or penalties) than nontaxable income (such as tax-exempt interest), the effective tax rate will be equal to or less than the average tax rate.

TAX RATE STRUCTURES

There are three basic tax rate structures used to determine a tax: proportional, progressive, and regressive.

Proportional Tax Rate Structure

A **proportional tax rate structure,** also known as a flat tax, imposes a constant tax rate throughout the tax base. As the tax base increases, the taxes paid increase proportionally. Because this rate stays the same throughout all levels of the tax base, the marginal tax rate remains constant and, in fact, equals the average tax rate (see Exhibit 1-1). The most common example of a proportional tax is a sales tax.

To calculate the tax owed for a proportional tax, simply use Equation 1-1 to multiply the tax base by the tax rate.

$$\text{Tax} = \text{Tax Base} \times \text{Tax Rate}$$

Example 1-8

Knowing her dad is a serious Bulldog fan, Margaret buys a $100 sweatshirt in downtown Athens. The city of Athens imposes a sales tax rate of 7 percent. How much tax does Margaret pay on the purchase?

Answer: $100 purchase (tax base) × 7% (tax rate) = $7

Progressive Tax Rate Structure

A **progressive tax rate structure** imposes an increasing marginal tax rate as the tax base increases. Thus as the tax base increases, both the marginal tax rate and the taxes paid increase. Common examples of progressive tax rate structures include

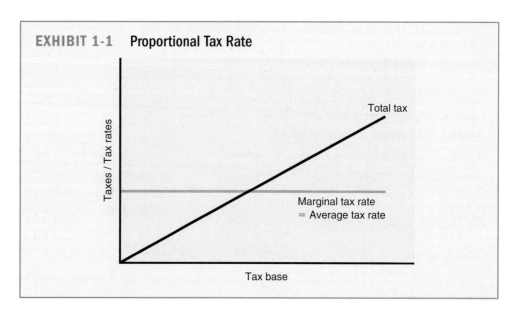

EXHIBIT 1-1   Proportional Tax Rate

Taxes / Tax rates

Total tax

Marginal tax rate
= Average tax rate

Tax base

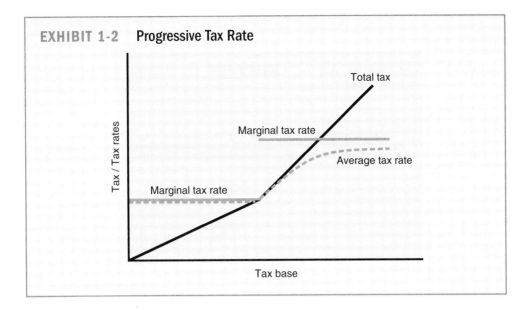

EXHIBIT 1-2   Progressive Tax Rate

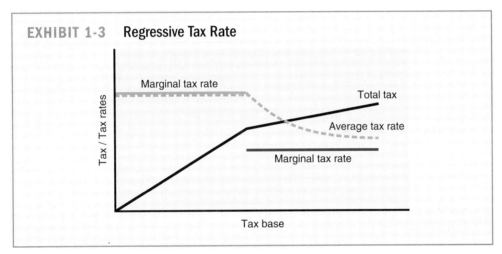

EXHIBIT 1-3   Regressive Tax Rate

federal and state income taxes. The tax rate schedule in Example 1-3 is a progressive tax rate structure. As illustrated in Exhibit 1-2, the average tax rate in a progressive tax rate structure will always be less than or equal to the marginal tax rate.

Regressive Tax Rate Structure

A **regressive tax rate structure** imposes a decreasing marginal tax rate as the tax base increases (see Exhibit 1-3). As the tax base increases, the taxes paid increases, but the marginal tax rate decreases. Regressive tax rate structures are not common. In the United States, only the Social Security tax employs a regressive tax rate structure.[5]

However, some taxes are regressive when viewed in terms of effective tax rates. For example, a sales tax is a proportional tax by definition, because as taxable purchases increase, the sales tax rate remains constant. Nonetheless, when you consider that the proportion of your total income spent on taxable purchases likely decreases as your total income increases, you can see the sales tax as a regressive tax.

[5]Wages subject to the Social Security tax (6.2 percent tax rate) are capped each year ($106,800 in 2009). Wages in excess of the cap are not subject to the tax. As might be expected, the maximum Social Security retirement benefit is capped as a function of the maximum wage base.

Example 1-9	

Bill and Mercedes have two single friends, Elizabeth and Marc, over for dinner. Elizabeth earns $300,000 as CFO of a company and spends $70,000 for purchases subject to the 7 percent sales tax. Marc, who earns $75,000 as a real estate agent, spends $30,000 of his income for taxable purchases. Let's compare their marginal, average, and effective tax rates for the sales tax with Bill and Mercedes, who spend $50,000 of their income for taxable purchases:

	Elizabeth	Bill and Mercedes	Marc
Total income (1)	$300,000	$150,000	$75,000
Total purchases subject to 7% sales tax (2)	$ 70,000	$ 50,000	$30,000
Sales tax paid (3)	$ 4,900	$ 3,500	$ 2,100
Marginal Tax Rate—Provided in Example	7%	7%	7%
Average Tax Rate (3)/(2)	7%	7%	7%
Effective Tax Rate (3)/(1)	1.6%	2.3%	2.8%

Is the sales tax regressive?

Answer: In terms of *effective* tax rates, the answer is yes.

When we consider the marginal and average tax rates in Example 1-9, the sales tax has a proportional tax rate structure. But when we look at the *effective* tax rates, the sales tax is a regressive tax. Indeed, Marc, who has the smallest total income, bears the highest effective tax rate, despite all three taxpayers being subject to the same marginal and average tax rates. Why do we see such a different picture when considering the effective tax rate? Because unlike the marginal and average tax rates, the effective tax rate captures the *incidence* of taxation, which relates to the ultimate economic burden of a tax. Thus, a comparison of effective tax rates is more informative about taxpayers' relative tax burdens.

TYPES OF TAXES

L04

"You can't live with 'em. You can't live without 'em." This statement has often been used in reference to bosses, parents, spouses, and significant others. To some degree, it applies equally well to taxes. Although we all benefit in multiple ways from tax revenues, and all civilized nations impose them, it would be hard to find someone who *enjoys* paying them. Most people don't object to the idea of paying taxes. Instead, it's the way they're levied that many people, like Margaret's friend Eddy, dislike. Hence, the search for the "perfect" tax. The following paragraphs describe the major types of taxes currently used by federal, state, and local governments. After this discussion, we describe the criteria for evaluating alternative tax systems.

Federal Taxes

The federal government imposes a variety of taxes to fund federal programs such as national defense, Social Security, an interstate highway system, educational programs, and Medicare. Major federal taxes include the individual and corporate income taxes, employment taxes, estate and gift taxes, and excise taxes (each discussed in detail in the following paragraphs). Noticeably absent from this list are a sales tax (a common tax for most state and local governments) and a **value-added tax** (a type of sales tax). Value-added taxes are imposed on the producers of goods and services based on the value added to the goods and services at each stage of production. They are quite common in Europe.

Income Tax   The most significant tax assessed by the U.S. government is the **income tax,** representing approximately 62 percent of all tax revenues collected in the United States in 2007. Despite the magnitude and importance of the federal income tax, its history is relatively short. Congress enacted the first U.S. personal income tax in 1861 to help fund the Civil War. This relatively minor tax (maximum tax rate of 5 percent) was allowed to expire in 1872. In 1892, Congress resurrected the income tax, but not without dissension among the states. In 1895, the income tax was challenged in *Pollock v. Farmers' Loan and Trust Company,* 157 U.S. 429 (1895). The U.S. Supreme Court ruled that the income tax was unconstitutional because direct taxes were prohibited by the Constitution unless the taxes were apportioned across states based upon their populations. This ruling, however, did not deter Congress. In July 1909, Congress sent a proposed constitutional amendment to the states to remove any doubt as to whether income taxes were allowed by the Constitution—and in February 1913, the 16th amendment was ratified.

Congress then enacted the Revenue Act of 1913, which included a graduated income tax structure with a maximum rate of 7 percent. The income tax has been an important source of tax revenues for the U.S. government ever since. Today, income taxes are levied on individuals (maximum rate of 35 percent), corporations (maximum rate of 39 percent), estates (maximum rate of 35 percent), and trusts (maximum rate of 35 percent). As Exhibit 1-4 illustrates, the individual income tax represents the largest source of federal tax revenues followed by employment taxes and the corporate income tax. We discuss each of these taxes in greater detail later in the text.

Employment and Unemployment Taxes   Employment and unemployment taxes are the second largest group of taxes imposed by the U.S. government. **Employment taxes** consist of the Old Age, Survivors, and Disability Insurance (OASDI) tax, commonly called the Social Security tax, and the Medical Health Insurance (MHI) tax known as the Medicare tax. The **Social Security tax** pays the monthly retirement, survivor, and disability benefits for qualifying individuals, whereas the **Medicare tax** pays for medical insurance for individuals who are elderly or disabled. The tax base for the Social Security and Medicare taxes is wages or salary,

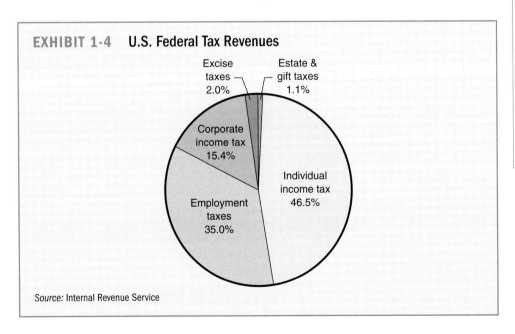

EXHIBIT 1-4   U.S. Federal Tax Revenues

Excise taxes 2.0%
Estate & gift taxes 1.1%
Corporate income tax 15.4%
Employment taxes 35.0%
Individual income tax 46.5%

Source: Internal Revenue Service

and the rates are 12.4 percent and 2.9 percent, respectively. In 2009, the tax base for the Social Security tax is capped at $106,800. The tax base for the Medicare tax is not capped. Employers *and* employees split these taxes equally. Self-employed individuals, however, must pay these taxes in their entirety. In this case, the tax is often referred to as the **self-employment tax.** We discuss these taxes in more depth later in the text.

In addition to the Social Security and Medicare taxes, employers are also required to pay federal and state **unemployment taxes,** which fund temporary unemployment benefits for individuals terminated from their jobs without cause. As you might expect, the tax base for the unemployment taxes is also wages or salary. Currently, the Federal Unemployment Tax rate is 6.2 percent on the first $7,000 of wages. The U.S. government allows a credit for state unemployment taxes paid up to 5.4 percent. Thus, the Federal Unemployment Tax rate may be as low as 0.8 percent (6.2% − 5.4% = 0.8%).

Excise Taxes   **Excise taxes** are taxes levied on the retail sale of particular products. They differ from other taxes in that the tax base for an excise tax typically depends on the *quantity* purchased, rather than a monetary amount. The federal government imposes a number of excise taxes on goods such as alcohol, diesel fuel, gasoline, and tobacco products and on services such as telephone use and air transportation. In addition, states often impose excise taxes on these same items.

Example 1-10

On the drive home from Athens, Georgia, Margaret stops at Gasup-n-Go. On each gallon of gasoline she buys, Margaret pays 18.4 cents of federal excise tax and 7.5 cents of state excise tax (plus 4 percent sales tax). Could Margaret have avoided paying excise tax had she stopped in Florida instead?

Answer: No. Had she stopped in Florida instead, Margaret would have paid the same federal excise tax. Additionally, Florida imposes 14.9 cents of state excise tax per gallon of gas.

Because the producer of the product pays the government the excise tax, many consumers are not even aware that businesses build these taxes into the prices consumers pay. Nonetheless, consumers bear the incidence of the taxes because of the higher price.

Transfer Taxes   Although they are a relatively minor tax compared to the income tax in terms of revenues collected, federal **transfer taxes**—estate and gift taxes—can be substantial for certain individual taxpayers and have been the subject of much debate in recent years. The **estate tax** (labeled the "death tax" by its opponents) and **gift taxes** are based on the fair market values of wealth transfers upon death or by gift, respectively. The estate and gift tax rates are high (maximum tax rate of 45 percent) compared to income tax rates and can be burdensome without proper planning. Most taxpayers, however, are not subject to estate and gift taxation because of the annual gift exclusion and gift and estate unified tax credits. The annual gift exclusion allows a taxpayer to transfer $13,000 of gifts per donee (gift recipient) each year without gift taxation. The unified tax credit exempts from taxation up to $1,000,000 in lifetime gifts and up to $3,500,000 in bequests (transfers upon death) and gifts.[6] Thus, only large transfers are subject to the gift and estate taxes.

---

[6]The gift tax credit is currently $345,000, which exempts $1,000,000 of lifetime gifts from taxation. The estate tax credit is currently $1,455,800, which exempts $3,500,000 of bequests and gifts from taxation.

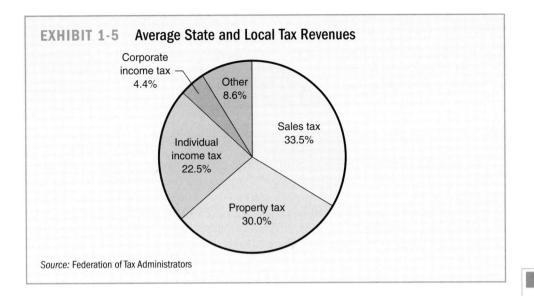

EXHIBIT 1-5   Average State and Local Tax Revenues

Source: Federation of Tax Administrators

State and Local Taxes

Like the federal government, state and local governments (such as counties, cities, and school districts) use a variety of taxes to generate revenues for their programs (such as education, highways, and police and fire departments). Some of the more common **state and local taxes** include income taxes, sales and use taxes, excise taxes, and property taxes. Typically, as shown in Exhibit 1-5, the largest state and local revenues are generated by state sales taxes and local property taxes.

Income Taxes   Currently, most states and the District of Columbia impose income taxes on individuals and corporations who either reside in or earn income within the state.[7] Calculations of individual and corporate taxable income vary with state law. Nonetheless, most state taxable income calculations largely conform to the federal taxable income calculations, with a limited number of modifications. The state of California is a notable exception. Certain local governments such as New York City also impose an income tax, and again, these generally follow the respective state taxable income calculation.

Sales and Use Taxes   Most states, the District of Columbia, and local governments impose sales and use taxes. The tax base for a **sales tax** is the retail sales of goods and some services, and retailers are responsible for collecting and remitting the tax; typically, sales tax is collected at the point of sale. The tax base for the **use tax** is the retail price of goods owned, possessed, or consumed within a state that were *not* purchased within the state. The purpose of a use tax is to discourage taxpayers from buying goods out of state in order to avoid or minimize the sales tax in their home state. At the same time, by eliminating the incentive to purchase goods out of state, a use tax removes any competitive disadvantage a retailer may incur from operating in a state with a high sales tax. States with a sales tax allow taxpayers to take a use tax credit on goods purchased out of state to mitigate the potential for double taxation on goods subject to sales tax in another state.

[7]Currently, Alaska, Florida, Nevada, South Dakota, Texas, Washington, and Wyoming have no personal income tax, and New Hampshire and Tennessee only tax individual dividend and interest income. Nevada, South Dakota, Washington, and Wyoming do not impose taxes on corporate income.

Example 1-11

Margaret buys three new Lands' End shirts for her dad for $100. Because Lands' End does not have a business presence in Florida, it does not collect Florida sales tax on the $100 purchase. Does Margaret's purchase escape Florida taxation?

Answer: No. Because Florida has a 6 percent use tax, Margaret is liable for $6 in use tax on the purchase ($6 = $100 × .06).

Despite the potential importance of the use tax as a source of state tax revenue, states have only recently begun to enforce it. Poor compliance is therefore not surprising; indeed, many individuals have never heard of the use tax. While it is relatively easy to enforce it on goods obtained out of state if they are subject to a registration requirement, such as automobiles, it is quite difficult for states to tax most other out-of-state purchases. The state of Florida is not likely to search your closet to look for tax-evaded Lands' End shirts. Note, however, that the majority of states have joined together (www.streamlinedsalestax.org) to try to subject all Internet sales to sales taxes.

Property Taxes   State and local governments commonly use two types of property taxes as sources of revenue: **real property taxes** and **personal property taxes.** Both are **ad valorem** taxes, meaning that the tax base for each is the fair market value of the property, and both are generally collected annually (if imposed at all).

Real property consists of land and structures permanently attached to land, whereas *personal property* includes all other types of property, both tangible and intangible. Common examples of tangible personal property potentially subject to state and local taxation include automobiles, boats, private planes, business inventory, equipment, and furniture. Intangible personal property potentially subject to state and local taxation includes stocks, bonds, and intellectual property. Relative to personal property tax, real property taxes are easier to administer because real property is not moveable and purchases often have to be registered with the state, thereby making it easy to identify the tax base and taxpayer. Furthermore, the taxing body can estimate market values for real property without much difficulty. In contrast, personal property is generally mobile (easier to hide) and may be more difficult to value, which make personal property taxes difficult to enforce. Accordingly, whereas all states and the District of Columbia provide for a real property tax, only a majority of states currently impose personal property taxes, most of which are assessed at the time of licensing or registration.

Excise Taxes   We've said that the tax base for excise taxes is typically based on the quantity of an item or service purchased. States typically impose excise taxes on items subject to federal excise tax. Transactions subject to state excise tax often include the sale of alcohol, diesel fuel, gasoline, tobacco products, and telephone services.

Implicit Taxes

All the taxes discussed above are **explicit taxes;** that is, they are taxes directly imposed by a government and are easily quantified. **Implicit taxes,** on the other hand, are indirect taxes—not paid directly to the government—that result from a tax advantage the government grants to certain transactions to satisfy social, economic, or other objectives. Implicit taxes are defined as the reduced before-tax return that a tax-favored asset produces because of its tax-advantaged status. Let's examine this concept more closely.

First of all, what does it mean to be *tax-favored?* An asset is said to be tax-favored when the income the asset produces is either excluded from the tax base or subject to a lower (preferential) tax rate, or if the asset generates some other tax benefit such as large tax deductions. These tax benefits, *all things equal,* result in higher after-tax profits (or lower after-tax costs) from investing in the tax-advantaged assets.

Why do tax-advantaged assets bear an implicit tax, or a reduced before-tax return as a result of the tax advantage? The answer is simple economics. The tax benefits associated with the tax-favored asset increase the demand for the asset. Increased demand drives up the price of the asset, which in turn, reduces its before-tax return, which is an implicit tax by definition. Consider Example 1-12.

Example 1-12

Consider two bonds, one issued by the Coca-Cola Co. and the other issued by the state of Georgia. Both bonds have similar nontax characteristics (risk, for example), the same face value of $10,000, and the same market interest rate of 10 percent. The only difference between the two bonds is that the interest income from the Coca-Cola Co. bond is subject to 20 percent income tax, whereas the interest income from the State of Georgia bond is tax-exempt with a 0 percent tax rate. Which of the two bonds is a better investment and should therefore have a higher demand?

	Price	Before-Tax[8] Return	Interest Income	Income[9] Tax	After-Tax Income	After-Tax[10] Return
Coca-Cola Bond	10,000	10%	1,000	200	800	8%
State of GA Bond	10,000	10%	1,000	0	1,000	10%

Answer: Compare the after-tax returns of the bonds. Given the difference between the return after taxes (10 percent vs. 8 percent), the better investment—again, all other investment features being equal—is the State of Georgia bond because it provides a higher *after*-tax return. Because all investors in this example should prefer to buy the State of Georgia bond, the demand for the bond will be high, and its price should increase. This increase in price leads to a lower before-tax return due to the bond's tax-favored status (this is an implicit tax).

Example 1-12 is a basic illustration of the need to consider the role of taxes in investment decisions. Without understanding the relative tax effects associated with each bond, we cannot correctly compare their after-tax returns.

At what point in Example 1-12 would you be indifferent between investing in the Coca-Cola Co. bond and the State of Georgia bond? Assuming each bond has the same nontax characteristics, you would be indifferent between them when they both provide the same after-tax rate of return. This could occur if the state of Georgia raised the price of its bond from $10,000 to $12,500 ($1,000 interest/$12,500 price = 8% return). Or the state of Georgia could lower its bond interest payment from $1,000 to $800 ($800 interest/$10,000 price = 8% return). Either way, the state of Georgia benefits from selling the tax-exempt bonds—either at a higher price or at a lower interest rate relative to other bonds. Let's look more closely at this latter option, because it is, in fact, what many tax-exempt bond issuers choose to do.

	Price	Before-Tax Return	Interest Income	Income Tax	After-Tax Income	After-Tax Return
Coca-Cola Bond	10,000	10%	1,000	200	800	8%
State of GA Bond	10,000	8%	800	0	800	8%

---

[8]Before-tax return is calculated as the before-tax income divided by the price of the bond. Likewise, after-tax return is calculated as the after-tax income divided by the price of the bond.

[9]Income tax equals the taxable interest income ($1,000) multiplied by the assumed income marginal tax rate (20 percent).

THE KEY FACTS

Implicit Taxes

■ Implicit taxes are indirect taxes that result from a tax advantage the government grants to certain transactions to satisfy social, economic, or other objectives.

■ Implicit taxes are defined as the reduced before-tax return that a tax-favored asset produces because of its tax-advantaged status.

■ Implicit taxes are difficult to quantify, but are important to understand in evaluating the relative tax burdens of tax-advantaged investments.

At this point, assuming each bond has the same nontax characteristics, an investor should be indifferent between the Coca-Cola Co. bond and the State of Georgia bond. What is the tax burden on investors choosing the Coca-Cola Co. bond? Coca-Cola Co. bond investors are paying $200 of income taxes (explicit taxes). What is the tax burden on investors choosing the State of Georgia bond? While it is true they are subject to zero income taxes (explicit taxes), they are subject to implicit taxes in the form of the $200 less in interest income they accept. This $200 reduced interest income (2 percent reduced before-tax rate of return) is an implicit tax. Although the investors in the State of Georgia bond are not paying this tax directly, they are paying it indirectly.

Does this happen in real life? Yes. Municipal bond interest income (interest income paid on bonds issued by state and local governments) generally is not subject to federal income taxation. Because of their tax-advantaged status, municipalities are able to pay a lower interest rate on their bond issuances and investors are willing to accept the lower rate. This type of indirect federal subsidy allows municipalities to raise money at a reduced cost without the need of direct federal subsidy or approval.

Although we were able to quantify the implicit taxes paid in the above example, in reality it is very difficult to estimate the amount of implicit taxes paid. For example, the federal government subsidizes housing by allowing taxpayers to deduct mortgage interest on their principal residence. Does this subsidy result in an implicit tax in the form of higher housing prices? Probably. Nonetheless, it would be difficult to quantify this implicit tax.

Despite the difficulty in quantifying implicit taxes, you should understand the concept of implicit taxes so you can make informed judgments about the attractiveness of alternative investments, and about the relative total tax burdens of tax-advantaged investments (considering both explicit and implicit taxes).

LO5   EVALUATING ALTERNATIVE TAX SYSTEMS

Although it may appear that tax systems are designed without much forethought, in truth lawmakers engage in continuous debate over the basic questions of whom to tax, what to tax, and how much to tax. Margaret's friend Eddy is obviously upset with what he views as an unfair tax system. But fairness, as we will discuss shortly, is often like beauty—it is in the eye of the beholder. What is fair to one may seem blatantly unfair to others. In the following paragraphs, we offer various criteria (sufficiency, equity, certainty, convenience, and economy) you can use to evaluate alternative tax systems.[10] Satisfying everyone at the same time is difficult. Hence, the spirited debate on tax reform.

Sufficiency

Judging the **sufficiency** of a tax system means assessing the size of the tax revenues it must generate and ensuring that it provides them. For a tax system to be successful, it must provide sufficient revenues to pay for governmental expenditures for a defense system, social services, and so on. This sounds easy enough: Estimate the amount of government expenditures that will be required, and then design the system to generate enough revenues to pay for these expenses. In reality, however, accurately estimating governmental expenditures and revenues is a rather daunting and imprecise process. Estimating governmental expenditures is difficult because it is impossible to predict the unknown. For example, in recent years governmental expenditures have increased due to the terrorist attacks of September 11, 2001, the Iraq

THE KEY FACTS

Evaluating Alternative Taxes—Sufficiency

■ Sufficiency involves assessing the aggregate size of the tax revenues that must be generated and ensuring that the tax system provides these revenues.

■ Static forecasting ignores how taxpayers may alter their activities in response to a proposed tax law change and bases projected tax revenues on the existing state of transactions.

■ Dynamic forecasting attempts to account for possible taxpayer responses to a proposed tax law change.

---

[10]Adam Smith identified and described the latter four criteria in *The Wealth of Nations*.

War, and natural disasters such as the hurricanes in the Gulf Coast area. Likewise, estimating governmental revenues is difficult because tax revenues are the result of transactions influenced by these same national events, the economy, and other factors. Thus, precisely estimating and matching governmental expenditures with tax revenues is nearly impossible.

The task of estimating tax revenues becomes even more daunting when the government attempts to make significant changes to the existing tax system or design a new one. Whenever Congress proposes changing who is taxed, what is taxed, or how much is taxed, its members must consider the taxpayer response to the change. That affects the amount of tax collected, and how forecasters predict what taxpayers will do affects how much revenue they estimate.

Static vs. Dynamic Forecasting   One option in forecasting revenue is to ignore how taxpayers may alter their activities in response to a tax law change and to base projected tax revenues on the existing state of transactions, a process referred to as **static forecasting.** However, this type of forecasting may result in a large discrepancy in projected versus actual tax revenues if taxpayers do change their behavior. The other choice is to attempt to account for possible taxpayer responses to the tax law change, a process referred to as **dynamic forecasting.** Dynamic forecasting is ultimately only as good as the assumptions underlying the forecasts and does not guarantee accurate results. Nonetheless, considering how taxpayers may alter their activities in response to a tax law change is a useful exercise to identify the potential ramifications of the change, even if the revenue projections ultimately miss the mark.

Example 1-13

The city of Heflin would like to increase tax revenues by $2,000,000 to pay for needed roadwork. A concerned taxpayer recently proposed increasing the cigarette excise tax from $1.00 per pack of cigarettes to $6.00 per pack to raise the additional needed revenue. Last year, 400,000 packs of cigarettes were sold in the city. Will the tax be successful in raising the $2,000,000 revenue?

Answer: Not likely. The proposed tax increase of $5, and the assumption that 400,000 packs will still be sold, is an example of static forecasting: it ignores that many taxpayers may respond to the tax change by quitting, cutting down, or buying cheaper cigarettes in the next town.

In some cases, static forecasting can lead to a tax consequence opposite the desired outcome. In Example 1-13, we might estimate that given Heflin's close proximity to other cities with a $1.00 cigarette tax, the number of packs of cigarettes sold within the city would drop significantly to, say, 50,000. In this case, the tax increase would actually *decrease* tax revenues by $100,000 ($400,000 existing tax − $300,000 new tax), not a good outcome if the goal was to increase tax revenues.

Income vs. Substitution Effects   The example above described proposed changes in an excise tax, which is a proportional tax. In terms of a progressive tax such as an *income* tax, a tax rate increase or an expansion of the tax base can result in one of two taxpayer responses, both of which are important for dynamic forecasting. The **income effect** predicts that when taxpayers are taxed more (when, say, a tax rate increases from 25 to 28 percent), they will work harder to generate the same after-tax dollars. The **substitution effect** predicts that when taxpayers are taxed more, rather than work more, they will substitute nontaxable activities like leisure pursuits for taxable ones because the marginal value of taxable activities has decreased. Which view is accurate? The answer depends on the taxpayer. Consider the following examples.

Example 1-14

Margaret's friend George, who earns $40,000 taxable income as a mechanic, is taxed at an average rate of 10 percent ($4,000 of tax). If Congress increases the income tax rate such that George's average tax rate increases from 10 percent to 25 percent, how much more income tax will he pay?

Answer: It depends on whether the income effect or the substitution effect is operating. Assuming George is single and cannot afford a net decrease in his after-tax income, he will likely work more (the income effect rules). Prior to the tax rate increase, George had $36,000 of after-tax income ($40,000 taxable income less $4,000 tax). With the increased tax rate, George will have to earn $48,000 of taxable income to keep $36,000 after taxes ($48,000 − [$48,000 × .25] = $36,000). Thus, if the income effect rules, the government will collect $12,000 of federal income tax from George, or $8,000 more than under the previous lower tax rate. In this scenario, the tax change increases government revenues because of the increased tax rate *and* the increased tax base.

Whether the substitution effect or the income effect will describe any individual taxpayer's reaction to a tax increase is something we can only guess. But some factors—such as having higher disposable income—are likely to correlate with the substitution effect.

Example 1-15

What if: Now let's assume that George is married and has two young children, both he and his wife work, and they file a tax return jointly with a 10 percent average tax rate. Either of their incomes is sufficient to meet necessities, even after the tax rate increase. But fixed child care costs make the marginal wage rate (the after-tax hourly wage less hourly child care cost) more sensitive to tax rate increases. In this case, the lower-earning spouse may choose to work less. Suppose George quits his full-time job and takes a part-time position that pays $20,000 to spend more time with his kids and to pursue his passion, writing sports novels. What are the taxes on George's income?

Answer: In this case, George will owe $5,000 tax ($20,000 × .25 = $5,000). Here, the substitution effect operates, and the government collects much less than it would have if George had maintained his full-time position, because the tax rate increase had a negative effect on the tax base.

As the previous examples illustrate, the response to a tax law change can vary by taxpayer and can greatly affect the magnitude of tax revenues generated by the change. Herein lies one of the challenges in significantly changing an existing tax system or designing a new one. If a tax system fails to generate sufficient revenues, the government must seek other sources to pay for governmental expenditures. The most common source of these additional funds for the federal government is the issuance of debt instruments such as Treasury bonds. This, however, is only a short-term solution to a budget deficit. Debt issuances require both interest and principal payments, which require the federal government to identify even more sources of revenue to service the debt issued, or to cut governmental spending (both of which may be unpopular choices with voters). A third option is for the government to default on its debt obligations. However, the costs of this option are potentially devastating. If the historical examples of Mexico, Brazil, and Argentina are any guide, a U.S. government default on its debt obligations would likely devalue the U.S. dollar severely and have extreme negative consequences for the U.S. capital markets.

The best option is for the government to match its revenues with its expenses—that is, not to spend more than it collects. State governments seem to be more successful in this endeavor than the U.S. federal government. Indeed, all states except Vermont require a balanced budget each year, whereas the federal government has had deficit spending for most of the last 40 years.

Equity

We've looked at the challenges of designing a tax system that provides sufficient revenues to pay for governmental expenditures. An equally challenging issue is how the tax burden should be distributed across taxpayers. At the heart of this issue is the concept of **equity** or fairness. Fairness is inherently subject to personal interpretation, and informed minds often disagree about what is fair. There is no "one-size-fits-all" definition of equity or fairness. Nonetheless, it is informative to consider in broad terms what makes a fair or equitable tax system.

In general terms, a tax system is considered fair or equitable if the tax is based on the taxpayer's ability to pay. Taxpayers with a greater ability to pay tax, pay more tax. In broad terms, each of the federal, state, and local taxes we've discussed satisfies this criterion. For example, those individuals with greater taxable income, purchases, property, and estates (upon death) generally pay higher dollar amounts in federal income tax, sales tax, property tax, and estate tax. If this is the case, why is there so much debate over the fairness of the U.S. income tax system? The answer is that equity is more complex than our first definition suggests. Let's take a closer look.

Horizontal vs. Vertical Equity   Two basic types of equity are relevant to tax systems. **Horizontal equity** means that two taxpayers in similar situations pay the same tax. In broad terms, each of the federal, state, and local taxes discussed satisfy this definition. Two individual taxpayers with the same taxable income, same purchases, same value of property, and same estate value pay the same federal income tax, sales tax, property tax, and estate tax. However, on closer inspection we might argue that each of these tax systems is *not* horizontally equitable. Here are some examples:

> **THE KEY FACTS**
>
> **Evaluating Alternative Taxes—Equity**
>
> ▪ Equity considers how the tax burden should be distributed across taxpayers.
>
> ▪ Horizontal equity means that two taxpayers in similar situations pay the same tax.
>
> ▪ Vertical equity is achieved when taxpayers with greater ability to pay tax, pay more tax relative to taxpayers with a lesser ability to pay tax.

- Two individual taxpayers with the same income will not pay the same federal income tax if one individual's income was earned as salary and the other individual's income was tax-exempt municipal bond interest income, dividend income, or capital gain income, which can be subject to a lower tax rate.
- Two individuals with the same dollar amount of purchases will not pay the same sales tax if one buys a higher proportion of goods that are subject to a lower sales tax rate, such as groceries.
- Two individuals with real estate of the same value will not pay the same property tax if one individual owns farmland, which is generally subject to a lower property tax rate.
- Finally, two individuals with estates of the same value will not pay the same estate tax if one individual bequeaths more of her property to charity or a spouse, because these transfers are not subject to estate tax.

These failures of horizontal equity are due to what we call *tax preferences.* Governments provide tax preferences for a variety of reasons, such as to encourage investment or further social objectives. Whether we view these tax preferences as appropriate greatly influences whether we consider a tax system to be fair in general and horizontally equitable in particular.

The second type of equity to consider in evaluating a tax system is **vertical equity.** Vertical equity is achieved when taxpayers with greater ability to pay tax, pay more tax than taxpayers with less ability to pay. We can think of vertical equity in terms of tax dollars paid or in terms of tax rates. Proponents of a flat income tax or of a sales tax—both of which are proportional tax rate structures—are more likely to argue that vertical equity is achieved when taxpayers with a greater ability to pay tax, simply pay more in tax *dollars*. Proponents of a progressive tax system are more likely to argue that taxpayers with a greater ability to pay should be subject to a higher tax *rate*. This view is based upon the argument that the *relative* burden of a flat tax rate decreases as a taxpayer's income increases. Which is the correct answer? There is no correct answer. Nonetheless, many feel very strongly regarding one view or the other.

Our discussion has focused on how we can view alternative tax rate structures in terms of vertical equity, ignoring the role that the tax base plays in determining vertical equity. Indeed, focusing on the tax rate structure in evaluating a tax system is appropriate only if the tax base chosen—whether it's taxable income, purchases, property owned, or something else—accurately portrays a taxpayer's ability to pay. This can be a rather strong assumption. Consider the sales tax in Example 1-9. Although taxable purchases in this example increase as the taxpayers' total incomes increase, total incomes increase at a much faster rate than taxable purchases. Thus, the gap between taxable purchases and total income widens as total income increases. The end result is that the effective tax rates for those with a greater ability to pay are *lower* than for those taxpayers with a lesser ability to pay, making this tax regressive. Regressive tax rate structures are generally considered not to satisfy vertical equity, unless you strongly believe that those with a greater ability to pay do so simply by paying more tax dollars, albeit at a lower tax rate. In sum, evaluating vertical equity in terms of effective tax rates may be much more informative than simply evaluating tax rate structures.

Certainty

Certainty means that taxpayers should be able to determine when to pay the tax, where to pay the tax, and how to determine the tax. Determining when and where to pay each of the taxes previously discussed is relatively easy. For example, individual federal income tax returns and the remaining balance of taxes owed must be filed with the Internal Revenue Service each year on or before April 15th. Likewise, sales taxes, property taxes, and excise taxes are each determined with relative ease: Sales taxes are based on the value of taxable purchases, property taxes are generally based on assessed property values, and excise taxes are based on the number of taxable units purchased. Indeed, these taxes are calculated for the taxpayer and often charged at regular intervals or at the point of purchase; they do not require a tax return.

In contrast, income taxes are often criticized as too complex. What are taxable vs. nontaxable forms of income? What are deductible/nondeductible expenses? When should income or expenses be reported? For wage earners with few investments, the answers to these questions are straightforward. For business owners and individuals with a lot of investments, the answers are nontrivial. Yearly tax law changes enacted by Congress can make it more difficult to determine a taxpayer's current tax liability, much less plan for the future.

Convenience

Convenience suggests that a tax system should be designed to facilitate the collection of tax revenues without undue hardship on the taxpayer or the government. Various tax systems meet this criterion by tying the collection of the tax as closely as possible to the transaction that generates it. For example, retailers collect sales taxes when buyers purchase goods. Thus, it is difficult for the buyer to avoid paying sales tax, assuming she is transacting with an ethical retailer. Likewise, employers withhold federal income and Social Security taxes directly from wage earners' paychecks, which speeds the government's collection of the taxes and makes it difficult for the taxpayer to evade the taxes. If tax withholdings are not sufficient relative to the taxpayer's anticipated income tax liability, the taxpayer is required to make quarterly estimated tax installments. Individual quarterly estimated payments are due on April 15, June 15, September 15, and January 15, whereas corporate estimated tax payments are due on the 15th day of the third, sixth, ninth, and twelfth months of the corporation's fiscal year.

Economy

Economy requires that a good tax system should minimize the compliance and administration costs associated with the tax system. We can view economy from both the taxpayers' and the government's perspectives. Believe it or not, most tax systems fare well in terms of economy, at least from the government's perspective. For example, the current IRS budget represents approximately 1/2 of a percent of every tax dollar collected. Compared to the typical costs of a collection agency, this is quite low.

How about from the taxpayer's perspective? Here the picture is a bit different. The sales tax imposes no administrative burden on the taxpayer and only small administrative costs on the local retailer. However, out-of-state sellers argue that collecting and remitting use taxes for thousands of state and city jurisdictions would be a substantial burden. Other taxes such as excise taxes and property taxes also impose minimal administrative costs on the taxpayer. In contrast, as we've seen, the income tax is often criticized for the compliance costs imposed on the taxpayer. Indeed, for certain taxpayers, record-keeping costs, accountant fees, attorney fees, and so on can be substantial. Advocates of alternative tax systems often challenge the income tax on this criterion.

Evaluating Tax Systems—The Trade-off

At the heart of any debate on tax reform are fundamental decisions and concessions based on the five criteria we've just discussed. Interestingly enough, much of the debate regarding alternative tax systems reduces to a choice between simplicity and fairness. Those taxes that generally are simpler and easier to administer, such as the sales tax, are typically viewed as less fair. Those taxes that may be viewed as more fair, such as the federal income tax, often are more complex to administer. Thus, Margaret's friend Eddy faces a difficult choice about which type of tax system to advocate, as do all taxpayers. An understanding of the evaluative criteria should be helpful to anyone trying to reconcile the trade-offs among alternative tax proposals.

CONCLUSION

In almost any society taxes are a part of life. They influence decisions about personal finance, investment, business, and politics. In this chapter, we introduced the basic concepts of why one should study tax, what is a tax, and how to calculate a tax. We also discussed various tax rates, tax rate structures, and different types of taxes imposed by federal, state, and local governments. Finally, we discussed the criteria that one might use to evaluate alternative tax rate systems. To make informed personal finance, investment, business, and political decisions, one must have a basic understanding of these items. In the following chapters we expand the discussion of how taxes influence these decisions while providing a basic understanding of our federal income tax system. Read on and learn more!

SUMMARY

LO1 Demonstrate how taxes influence basic business, investment, personal, and political decisions.

- Taxes are significant costs that influence many basic business, investment, and personal decisions.
  - *Business decisions:* what organization form to take; where to locate; how to compensate employees; appropriate debt mix; owning vs. renting equipment; how to distribute profits, and so forth.
  - *Investment decisions:* alternative methods for saving for education or retirement, and so forth.
  - *Personal finance decisions:* evaluating job offers; gift or estate planning; owning vs. renting home, and so forth.
- Taxes also play a major part in the political process. Major parties typically have very diverse views on whom, what, and how much to tax.

LO2 Discuss what constitutes a tax and the general objectives of taxes.

- The general purpose of taxes is to fund the government. Unlike fines or penalties, taxes are not meant to punish or prevent illegal behavior; but "*sin taxes*" (on alcohol, tobacco, etc.) are meant to discourage some behaviors.
- The three criteria necessary to be a tax are that the payment is (1) required (it is not voluntary), (2) imposed by a government (federal, state, or local), and (3) not tied directly to the benefit received by the taxpayer.

LO3 Describe the different tax rate structures and calculate a tax.

- Tax = tax rate × tax base, where the tax base is what is taxed and the tax rate is the level of taxes imposed on the base. Different portions of a tax base may be taxed at different rates.
- There are three different tax rates that are useful in contrasting the different tax rate structures, tax planning, and/or assessing the tax burden of a taxpayer: the marginal, average, and effective tax rates.
- The marginal tax rate is the tax that applies to the next increment of income or deduction. The average tax rate represents a taxpayer's average level of taxation on each dollar of taxable income. The effective tax rate represents the taxpayer's average rate of taxation on each dollar of total income (taxable *and* nontaxable income).
- The three basic tax rate structures are proportional, progressive, and regressive.
  - A *proportional tax rate* structure imposes a constant tax rate throughout the tax base. As a taxpayer's tax base increases, the taxpayer's taxes increase proportionally. The marginal tax rate remains constant and always equals the average tax rate. A common example is a sales tax.
  - A *progressive tax rate* imposes an increasing marginal tax rate as the tax base increases. As a taxpayer's tax base increases, both the marginal tax rate and the taxes paid increase. A common example is the U.S. federal income tax.
  - A *regressive tax rate* imposes a decreasing marginal tax rate as the tax base increases. As a taxpayer's tax base increases, the marginal tax rate decreases while the total taxes paid increases.

LO4 Identify the various federal, state, and local taxes.

- Federal taxes include the income tax, employment taxes (Social Security and Medicare taxes), unemployment taxes, excise taxes (levied on quantity purchased), and transfer taxes (estate and gift taxes).
- State and local taxes include the income tax (levied by most states), sales tax (levied on retail sales of goods and some services), use tax (levied on the retail price of goods owned or consumed within a state that were purchased out of state), property taxes (levied on fair market value of real and personal property), and excise taxes.

- Implicit taxes are indirect taxes that result from a tax advantage the government grants to certain transactions to satisfy social, economic, or other objectives. They are defined as the reduced before-tax return that a tax-favored asset produces because of its tax-advantaged status.

Apply appropriate criteria to evaluate alternate tax systems.   **LO5**

- Sufficiency involves assessing the aggregate size of the tax revenues that must be generated and ensuring that the tax system provides these revenues. Static forecasting ignores how taxpayers may alter their activities in response to a proposed tax law change and bases projected tax revenues on the existing state of transactions. Dynamic forecasting attempts to account for possible taxpayer responses to a proposed tax law change.

- Equity considers how the tax burden should be distributed across taxpayers. Generally, a tax system is considered fair or equitable if the tax is based on the taxpayer's ability to pay—that is, taxpayers with a greater ability to pay tax, pay more tax. Horizontal equity means that two taxpayers in similar situations pay the same tax. Vertical equity is achieved when taxpayers with greater ability to pay tax, pay more tax relative to taxpayers with a lesser ability to pay tax.

- Certainty means taxpayers should be able to determine when, where, and how much tax to pay.

- Convenience means a tax system should be designed to facilitate the collection of tax revenues without undue hardship on the taxpayer or the government.

- Economy means a tax system should minimize its compliance and administration costs.

KEY TERMS

ad valorem (1-14)

average tax rate (1-7)

bracket (1-4)

certainty (1-20)

convenience (1-20)

dynamic forecasting (1-17)

earmarked tax (1-3)

economy (1-21)

effective tax rate (1-7)

employment taxes (1-11)

equity (1-19)

estate tax (1-12)

excise taxes (1-12)

explicit tax (1-14)

flat tax (1-4)

gift tax (1-12)

graduated taxes (1-4)

horizontal equity (1-19)

implicit tax (1-14)

income effect (1-17)

income tax (1-11)

local tax (1-13)

marginal tax rate (1-4)

Medicare tax (1-11)

personal property tax (1-14)

progressive tax rate structure (1-8)

proportional tax rate structure (1-8)

real property tax (1-14)

regressive tax rate structure (1-9)

sales tax (1-13)

self-employment tax (1-12)

sin taxes (1-3)

Social Security tax (1-11)

state tax (1-13)

static forecasting (1-17)

substitution effect (1-17)

sufficiency (1-16)

tax (1-3)

tax base (1-4)

tax rate (1-4)

transfer taxes (1-12)

unemployment tax (1-12)

use tax (1-13)

value-added tax (1-10)

vertical equity (1-19)

DISCUSSION QUESTIONS

1. **(LO1)** Margaret's friend Eddy once stated that he couldn't understand why someone would take a tax course. Why is this a rather naïve view?

2. **(LO1)** What are some aspects of business that require knowledge of taxation? What are some aspects of personal finance that require knowledge of taxation?

3. **(LO1)** Describe some ways in which taxes affect the political process in the United States.

4. **(LO2)** Margaret recently received a speeding ticket on her way to the university. Her fine was $200. Is this considered a tax? Why or why not?

5. **(LO2)** Bill and Mercedes recently started building a house. They had to pay $300 to the county government for a building permit. Is the $300 payment a tax? Why or why not?

6. **(LO2)** The city of Birmingham recently enacted a 1 percent surcharge on hotel rooms that will help pay for the city's new stadium. Is this a tax? Why or why not?

7. **(LO2)** As noted in Example 1-2, tolls, parking meter fees, and annual licensing fees are not considered taxes. Can you identify other fees that are similar?

8. **(LO2)** If the general objective of our tax system is to raise revenue, why does the income tax allow deductions for charitable contributions and retirement plan contributions?

9. **(LO2)** One common argument for imposing so-called sin taxes is the social goal of *reducing* demand for such products. Using cigarettes as an example, is there a segment of the population that might be sensitive to price and for whom high taxes might discourage purchases?

10. **(LO3)** Eddy stated that he didn't want to earn any more money because it would "put him in a higher tax bracket." What is wrong with Eddy's reasoning?

11. **(LO3)** Describe the three different tax rates discussed in the chapter and how taxpayers might use them.

12. **(LO3)** Which is a more appropriate tax rate to use to compare taxpayers' tax burdens—the average or the effective tax rate? Why?

13. **(LO3)** Describe the differences between a proportional, progressive, and regressive tax rate structure.

14. **(LO3)** Margaret and Eddy have recently had a heated discussion about whether a sales tax is a proportional tax or a regressive tax. Margaret argues that a sales tax is regressive. Eddy counters that the sales tax is a flat tax. Who is correct?

15. **(LO4)** Which is the largest tax collected by the U.S. government? What types of taxpayers are subject to this tax?

16. **(LO4)** What is the tax base for the Social Security and Medicare taxes for an employee or employer? What is the tax base for Social Security and Medicare taxes for a self-employed individual? Is the self-employment tax in addition to or in lieu of federal income tax?

17. **(LO4)** What are unemployment taxes?

18. What is the distinguishing feature of an excise tax?

19. **(LO4)** What are some of the taxes that currently are unique to state and local governments? What are some of the taxes that the federal, state, and local governments each utilize?

20. **(LO4)** The state of Georgia recently increased its tax on a pack of cigarettes by $2.00. What type of tax is this? Why might Georgia choose this type of tax?

21. **(LO4)** What is the difference between a sales tax and a use tax?

22. **(LO4)** What is an ad valorem tax? Name an example of this type of tax.

23. **(LO4)** What are the differences between an explicit and an implicit tax?

24. **(LO4)** When we calculate average and effective tax rates, do we consider implicit taxes? What effect does this have on taxpayers' perception of equity?

25. **(LO4)** Eddy recently bought a truck in Alabama for his business in Georgia. What different types of federal and state taxes may affect this transaction?

26. **(LO5)** Eddy strongly dislikes SUVs and is appalled that so many are on the road. He proposes to eliminate the federal income tax and replace it with a $50,000 annual tax per SUV. Based on the number of SUVs currently owned in the United States, he estimates the tax will generate exactly the amount of tax revenue currently collected from the income tax. What is wrong with Eddy's proposal? What type of forecasting is Eddy likely using?

27. **(LO5)** What is the difference between the income and substitution effects? For which types of taxpayers is the income effect more likely descriptive? For which types of taxpayers is the substitution effect more likely descriptive?

28. **(LO5)** What is the difference between horizontal and vertical equity? How do tax preferences affect people's view of horizontal equity?

29. **(LO3, LO5)** Eddy argues that a flat income tax rate system is vertically equitable. Margaret argues that a progressive tax rate structure is vertically equitable. How do their arguments differ? Who is correct?

30. **(LO3, LO5)** Discuss why evaluating vertical equity simply based on tax rate structure may be less than optimal.

31. **(LO4, LO5)** Compare the federal income tax to sales taxes using the "certainty" criterion.

32. **(LO5)** Many years ago a famous member of Congress proposed eliminating federal income tax withholding. What criterion for evaluating tax systems did this proposal violate? What would likely have been the result of eliminating withholding?

33. **(LO5)** "The federal income tax scores very high on the economy criterion because the current IRS budget is relatively low compared to the costs of a typical collection agency." Explain why this statement may be considered wrong.

PROBLEMS

34. **(LO3)** Marc, a single taxpayer, earns $75,000 in taxable income and $10,000 in interest from an investment in City of Heflin bonds. Using the U.S. tax rate schedule, how much federal tax will he owe? What is his average tax rate? What is his effective tax rate? What is his current marginal tax rate?

35. **(LO3)** Using the facts in the previous problem, if Marc earns an additional $40,000 of taxable income, what is his marginal tax rate on this income? What is his marginal rate if, instead, he had $40,000 of additional deductions?

36. **(LO3)** In reviewing the tax rate schedule for a single taxpayer, Marc notes that the tax on $75,000 is $4,675 plus 25 percent of the taxable income over $33,950. What does the $4,675 represent?

37. **(LO3)** Elizabeth, a single taxpayer, earns $400,000 in taxable income and $2,000 in interest from an investment in State of New York bonds. Using the U.S. tax rate schedule, how much federal tax will she owe? What is her average tax rate? What is her effective tax rate? What is her current marginal tax rate?

38. **(LO3)** Using the facts in the previous problem, if Elizabeth earns an additional $15,000 of taxable income, what is her marginal tax rate on this income? What is her marginal rate if, instead, she had $15,000 of additional deductions?

39. **(LO3)** Jorge and Anita, married taxpayers, earn $150,000 in taxable income and $40,000 in interest from an investment in City of Heflin bonds. Using the U.S. tax rate schedule for married filing jointly, how much federal tax will they owe? What is their average tax rate? What is their effective tax rate? What is their current marginal tax rate?

40. **(LO3)** Using the facts in the previous problem, if Jorge and Anita earn an additional $100,000 of taxable income, what is their marginal tax rate on this income? What is their marginal rate if, instead, they reported an additional $100,000 in deductions?

41. **(LO3)** In reviewing the tax rate schedule for married filing jointly, Jorge and Anita note that the tax on $150,000 is $26,637.50 plus 28 percent of the taxable income over $137,050. What does the $26,637.50 represent?

42. **(LO3)** Scot and Vidia, married taxpayers, earn $240,000 in taxable income and $5,000 in interest from an investment in City of Tampa bonds. Using the U.S. tax rate schedule for married filing jointly, how much federal tax will they owe? What is their average tax rate? What is their effective tax rate? What is their current marginal tax rate?

43. **(LO3)** Using the facts in the previous problem, if Scot and Vidia earn an additional $70,000 of taxable income, what is their marginal tax rate on this income? How would your answer differ if they, instead, had $70,000 of additional deductions?

44. **(LO4)** Elizabeth invests $200,000 in a City of Heflin bond that pays 6 percent interest. Alternatively, Elizabeth could have invested the $200,000 in a bond recently issued by Surething, Inc., that pays 8 percent interest with similar risk and other nontax characteristics to the City of Heflin bond. Assume Elizabeth's marginal tax rate is 25 percent.

    a. What is her after-tax rate of return for the City of Heflin bond?
    b. How much explicit tax does Elizabeth pay on the City of Heflin bond?
    c. How much implicit tax does she pay on the City of Heflin bond?
    d. How much explicit tax would she have paid on the Surething, Inc., bond?
    e. What is her after-tax rate of return on the Surething, Inc. bond?

■ planning   45. **(LO4)** Marc has the choice between investing in a City of Heflin bond at 6 percent or a Surething bond at 9 percent. Assuming that both bonds have the same nontax characteristics and that Marc has a 40 percent marginal tax rate, in which bond should he invest?

■ planning   46. **(LO4)** Using the facts in the previous problem, what interest rate does Surething, Inc., need to offer to make Marc indifferent between investing in the two bonds?

■ planning   47. **(LO3, LO4)** Elizabeth has the choice between investing in a State of New York bond at 5 percent and a Surething bond at 8 percent. Assuming that both bonds have the same nontax characteristics and that Elizabeth has a 30 percent marginal tax rate, in which bond should she invest?

■ planning   48. **(LO4)** Using the facts in the previous problem, what interest rate does the state of New York need to offer to make Elizabeth indifferent between investing in the two bonds?

49. **(LO3)** Given the following tax structure, what minimum tax would need to be assessed on Shameika to make the tax progressive with respect to average tax rates?

Taxpayer	Salary	Muni-Bond Interest	Total Tax
Mihwah	10,000	10,000	600
Shameika	50,000	30,000	???

50. **(LO3)** Using the facts in the previous problem, what minimum tax would need to be assessed on Shameika to make the tax progressive with respect to effective tax rates?

51. **(LO5)** Song earns $100,000 taxable income as an interior designer and is taxed at an average rate of 20 percent (i.e., $20,000 of tax). If Congress increases the income tax rate such that Song's average tax rate increases from 20 percent to 25 percent, how much more income tax will she pay assuming that the income effect is descriptive? What effect will this tax rate change have on the tax base and tax collected?

52. **(LO5)** Using the facts from the previous problem, what will happen to the government's tax revenues if Song chooses to spend more time pursuing her other passions besides work in response to the tax rate change and earns only $75,000 in taxable income? What is the term that describes this type of reaction to a tax rate increase? What types of taxpayers are likely to respond in this manner?

53. **(LO5)** Given the following tax structure, what tax would need to be assessed on Venita to make the tax horizontally equitable?

Taxpayer	Salary	Total Tax
Mae	10,000	600
Pedro	20,000	1,500
Venita	10,000	???

54. **(LO5)** Using the facts in the previous problem, what is the minimum tax that Pedro should pay to make the tax structure vertically equitable based on the tax rate paid? This would result in what type of tax rate structure?

55. **(LO5)** Using the facts in the previous problem, what is the minimum tax that Pedro should pay to make the tax structure vertically equitable with respect to the amount of tax paid? This would result in what type of tax rate structure?

56. **(LO5)** Consider the following tax rate structure. Is it horizontally equitable? Why or why not? Is it vertically equitable? Why or why not?

Taxpayer	Salary	Total Tax
Rajiv	10,000	600
LaMarcus	20,000	600
Dory	10,000	600

57. **(LO5)** Consider the following tax rate structure. Is it horizontally equitable? Why or why not? Is it vertically equitable? Why or why not?

Taxpayer	Salary	Total Tax
Marilyn	10,000	600
Kobe	20,000	3,000
Alfonso	30,000	6,000

58. **(LO5)** Consider the following tax rate structure. Is it horizontally equitable? Why or why not? Is it vertically equitable? Why or why not?

Taxpayer	Salary	Total Tax
Rodney	10,000	600
Keisha	10,000	600

59. **(LO1, LO4)** Lorenzo is considering starting a trucking company either in Texas or Oklahoma. He will relocate his family, which includes his wife, children, and parents, to reside in the same state as his business. What types of taxes may influence his decision of where to locate his business?

■ **planning**

■ planning

60. **(LO5)** Congress would like to increase tax revenues by 10 percent. Assume that the average taxpayer in the United States earns $65,000 and pays an average tax rate of 15 percent. If the income effect is in effect for all taxpayers, what average tax rate will result in a 10 percent increase in tax revenues? This is an example of what type of forecasting?

■ research

61. **(LO5)** Locate the IRS Web site at www.irs.gov/index.html. For every $100 the IRS collected, how much was spent on the IRS collection efforts? What tax system criterion does this information help you to evaluate with respect to the current U.S. tax system?

■ research

62. **(LO4)** Using the Internet, find a comparison of income tax rates across states. What state currently has the highest income tax rate? In considering individual tax burdens across states, what other taxes should you consider?

2

Tax Compliance, the IRS, and Tax Authorities

Learning Objectives

Upon completing this chapter, you should be able to:

LO 1 Identify the filing requirements for income tax returns and the statute of limitations for assessment.

———————————————— ■ ————————————————

LO 2 Outline the IRS audit process, how returns are selected, the different types of audits, and what happens after the audit.

———————————————— ■ ————————————————

LO 3 Evaluate the relative weights of the various tax law sources.

———————————————— ■ ————————————————

LO 4 Describe the legislative process as it pertains to taxation.

———————————————— ■ ————————————————

LO 5 Perform the basic steps in tax research and evaluate various tax law sources when faced with ambiguous statutes.

———————————————— ■ ————————————————

LO 6 Describe tax professional responsibilities in providing tax advice.

———————————————— ■ ————————————————

LO 7 Identify taxpayer and tax professional penalties.

Bill and Mercedes received a notice from the Internal Revenue Service (IRS) that their return is under audit for certain interest deductions. As you might expect, they are quite concerned, especially because it has been several years since they claimed the deductions and they worry that all their supporting documentation may not be in place. Several questions run through their minds. How could the IRS audit a return that was filed so long ago? Why was their tax return selected, and what should they expect during the audit? The interest deductions they reported were based on advice from their CPA. What would cause the IRS and a CPA to interpret the law differently? What is their financial exposure if the deductions are ultimately disallowed?

Will they have to pay interest and penalties in addition to the tax they might owe? ■

Storyline Summary	
Taxpayers:	Bill and Mercedes
Family description:	Bill and Mercedes are married with one daughter, Margaret.
Employment status:	Bill is an economics professor; Mercedes is a small business owner.
Filing status:	Married, filing jointly
Current situation:	Bill and Mercedes face an IRS audit involving a previous year's interest deductions.

Even the most conservative taxpayer is likely to feel anxiety after receiving an IRS notice. This chapter will help answer Bill and Mercedes' questions and provide an overview of the audit process and tax research. While all taxpayers should understand these basics of our tax system, aspiring accountants should be especially familiar with them.

TAXPAYER FILING REQUIREMENTS

To file or not to file? Unlike Hamlet's "to be or not to be," this question has a pretty straightforward answer. Filing requirements are specified by law for each type of taxpayer. All corporations must file a tax return annually regardless of their taxable income. Estates and trusts are required to file annual income tax returns if their gross income exceeds $600.[1]

The filing requirements for individual taxpayers are a little more complex. Specifically, they depend on the taxpayer's filing status (single, married filing jointly, and so on, discussed in more detail in Chapter 4), age, and gross income (income before deductions). Exhibit 2-1 lists the 2009 gross income thresholds for taxpayers based on their filing status, gross income, and age.[2] These amounts are indexed for inflation and thus change each year. For certain taxpayers such as the self-employed and those claimed as dependents by another taxpayer, lower gross income thresholds apply.

EXHIBIT 2-1 **2009 Gross Income Thresholds by Filing Status**

Filing Status and Age (in 2009)	2009 Gross Income
Single	$ 9,350
Single, 65 or older,	$10,750
Married, filing a joint return	$18,700
Married, filing a joint return, one spouse 65 or older,	$19,800
Married, filing a joint return, both spouses 65 or older	$20,900
Married, filing a separate return	$ 3,650
Head of household	$12,000
Head of household, 65 or older	$13,400
Surviving spouse with a dependent child	$15,050
Surviving spouse, 65 or older, with a dependent child	$16,150

Whether a taxpayer is due a refund (which occurs when taxes paid exceed tax liability) does *not* determine whether a taxpayer must file a tax return. Gross income determines whether a tax return is required. Further, note that a taxpayer whose gross income falls below the respective threshold is not precluded from filing a tax return. Indeed, taxpayers due a refund *should* file a tax return to receive the refund (or claim a refundable tax credit), even if they are not required to file a tax return.

Tax Return Due Date and Extensions

Like the filing requirements, due dates for tax returns vary based on the type of taxpayer. Individual tax returns are due on the fifteenth day of the fourth month following year-end—that is, April 15 for calendar year individuals. (Due dates that fall on

---

[1]Estates file income tax returns during the administration period (i.e., before all of the estate assets are distributed).

[2]The gross income thresholds are calculated as the sum of the standard deduction and personal exemption(s) that apply to each respective filing status. We describe the standard deduction and personal exemptions in detail later in the text.

a Saturday, Sunday, or holidays are automatically extended to the next day that is not a Saturday, Sunday, or holiday.) Similarly, partnership returns are also due on the fifteenth day of the fourth month following the partnership's year-end. For corporations, tax returns must be filed by the fifteenth day of the third month following the corporation's year-end (March 15 for calendar-year corporations). Any individual or corporation unable to file a tax return by the original due date can, by that same deadline, request a six-month extension to file, which is granted automatically by the IRS. Similarly, partnerships may request an automatic five-month extension to file.

An extension allows the taxpayer to delay filing a tax return but does *not* extend the due date for tax payments. Thus, when a taxpayer files an extension, she must estimate how much tax will be owed. If a taxpayer fails to pay the entire balance of tax owed by the original due date of the tax return, the IRS charges the taxpayer interest on the underpayment from the due date of the return until the taxpayer pays the tax.[3] The interest rate charged depends on taxpayer type (individual or corporation) and varies quarterly with the federal short-term interest rate.[4] For example, the interest rate for tax underpayments for individuals equals the federal short-term rate plus three percentage points.[5]

What happens if the taxpayer does not file a tax return by the time required, whether April 15 or an extended deadline? As you might guess, the IRS imposes penalties on taxpayers failing to comply with the tax law. In many cases, the penalties can be quite substantial (see later discussion in this chapter). In the case of failure to file a tax return, the penalty equals 5 percent of the tax due for each month (or partial month) that the return is late. However, the maximum penalty is generally 25 percent of the tax owed, and the failure to file penalty does not apply if the taxpayer owes no tax.

Statute of Limitations

Despite the diligent efforts of taxpayers and tax professionals, it is quite common for tax returns to contain mistakes. Some may be to the taxpayer's advantage and others may be to the government's advantage. Regardless of the nature of the mistake, the taxpayer is obligated to file an amended return to correct the error (and request a refund or pay a deficiency) if the statute of limitations has not expired for the tax return. Likewise, the IRS can propose adjustments to the taxpayer's return if the statute of limitations for the return has not expired.

By law, the **statute of limitations** defines the period in which the taxpayer can file an amended tax return or the IRS can assess a tax deficiency for a specific tax year. For both amended tax returns filed by a taxpayer and proposed tax assessments by the IRS, the statute of limitations generally ends three years from the *later* of (1) the date the tax return was actually filed or (2) the tax return's original due date.

The statute of limitations for IRS assessment can be extended in certain circumstances. For example, a six-year statute of limitations applies to IRS assessments if the taxpayer omits items of gross income that exceed 25 percent of the gross income reported on the tax return. For fraudulent returns, or if the taxpayer fails to file a tax return, the news is understandably worse. The statute of limitations remains open indefinitely in these cases.

---

[3]The tax law also imposes a penalty for late payment in addition to the interest charged on the underpayment. We briefly discuss this penalty later in the chapter and in Chapter 7.

[4]The federal short-term rate is determined from a one-month average of the market yields from marketable obligations of the United States with maturities of three years or less.

[5]This same interest rate applies to individuals who overpay their taxes (i.e., receive a tax refund and interest payment as a result of an IRS audit or from filing an amended tax return).

Example 2-1

Bill and Mercedes file their 2005 federal tax return on September 6, 2006, after receiving an automatic extension to file their return by October 15, 2006. In 2009, the IRS selects their 2005 tax return for audit. When does the statute of limitations end for Bill and Mercedes' 2005 tax return?

Answer: Assuming the six-year and "unlimited" statute of limitation rules do not apply, the statute of limitations ends on September 6, 2009 (three years after the later of the actual filing date and the *original* due date).

What if: When would the statute of limitations end for Bill and Mercedes for their 2005 tax return if the couple filed the return on March 22, 2006 (before the original due date of April 15, 2006)?

Answer: In this scenario the statute of limitations would end on April 15, 2009, because the later of the actual filing date and the original due date is April 15, 2006.

Taxpayers should prepare for the possibility of an audit by retaining all supporting documents (receipts, cancelled checks, etc.) for a tax return until the statute of limitations expires. After the statute of limitations expires, taxpayers can discard much but should still keep a copy of the tax return itself, as well as any documents that may have on-going significance, such as those establishing the taxpayer's *basis* or original investment in existing assets like personal residences and long-term investments.

L02   IRS AUDIT SELECTION

Why me? This is a recurring question in life and definitely a common taxpayer question after receiving an IRS audit notice. The answer, in general, is that a taxpayer's return is selected for audit because the IRS has data suggesting the taxpayer's tax return has a high probability of a significant understated tax liability. Budget constraints limit the IRS's ability to audit a majority or even a large minority of tax returns. Currently, fewer than 2 percent of all tax returns are audited. Thus, the IRS must be strategic in selecting returns for audit in an effort to promote the highest level of voluntary taxpayer compliance and increase tax revenues.

Specifically, how does the IRS select tax returns for audit? The IRS uses a number of computer programs and outside data sources (newspapers, financial statement disclosures, informants, and other public and private sources) to identify tax returns that may have an understated tax liability. Common computer initiatives include the **DIF (Discriminant Function) system, document perfection program,** and **information matching program.** The most important of these initiatives is the DIF system. The DIF system assigns a score to each tax return that represents the probability the tax liability on the return has been underreported (a higher score = a higher likelihood of underreporting). The IRS derives the weights assigned to specific tax return attributes from historical IRS audit adjustment data from the National Research Program.[6] The DIF system then uses these (undisclosed) weights to score each tax return based on the tax return's characteristics. Returns with higher DIF scores are then reviewed to determine whether an audit is the best course of action.

---

[6]Similar to its predecessor, the Taxpayer Compliance Measurement Program, the National Research Program (NRP) analyzes a large sample of tax returns that are randomly selected for audit. From these randomly selected returns, the IRS identifies tax return characteristics (e.g., deductions for a home office, unusually high tax deductions relative to a taxpayer's income) associated with underreported liabilities, weights these characteristics, and then incorporates them into the DIF system. The NRP analyzes randomly selected returns to ensure that the DIF scorings are representative of the population of tax returns.

All returns are checked for mathematical and tax calculation errors, a process referred to as the document perfection program. Individual returns are also subject to the information matching program. This program compares the taxpayer's tax return to information submitted to the IRS from other taxpayers like banks, employers, mutual funds, brokerage companies, and mortgage companies. Information matched includes items such as wages (Form W-2 submitted by employers), interest income (Form 1099-INT submitted by banks), and dividend income (Form 1099-DIV submitted by brokerage companies). For tax returns identified as incorrect via the document perfection and information matching programs, the IRS recalculates the taxpayer's tax liability and sends a notice explaining the adjustment. If the taxpayer owes tax, the IRS will request payment of the tax due. If the taxpayer overpaid tax, the IRS will send the taxpayer a refund of the overpayment.

In addition to computer-based methods for identifying tax returns for audit, the IRS may use a number of other audit initiatives that target taxpayers in certain industries, engaged in certain transactions like the acquisition of other companies, or having specific attributes like home office deductions. Taxpayers of a given size and complexity, such as large publicly traded companies, may be audited every year.

> **THE KEY FACTS**
>
> **IRS Audit Selection**
>
> ■ The IRS uses a number of computer programs and outside data sources to identify tax returns that may have an understated tax liability.
>
> ■ Common computer initiatives include the DIF (Discriminant Function) system, document perfection program, and information matching program.
>
> ■ The DIF system assigns a score to each tax return that represents the probability the tax liability on the return has been underreported.
>
> ■ The document perfection program checks all returns for mathematical and tax calculation errors.
>
> ■ The information matching program compares the taxpayer's tax return to information submitted to the IRS from other taxpayers.

Taxes in the Real World   *Survivor Winner Can't Outwit and Outsmart the IRS*

The IRS appears to have stepped up its use of television as an audit source in recent years. In 2006, the original winner of the CBS reality show *Survivor*, Richard Hatch, was convicted of tax evasion for failing to report his $1,000,000 prize. Also in 2006, the IRS targeted the much-publicized Academy Awards gift baskets (aka Oscar Swag). Prior to the 2006 Academy Awards, IRS Commissioner Mark Everson issued a press release stating, "there's no special red-carpet tax loophole for the stars. The gift basket industry has exploded, and it's important that the groups running these events keep in mind the tax consequences." Although termed "gift baskets," the famous Oscar baskets do not meet the definition of nontaxable gifts for federal tax purposes (a transfer made solely out of detached and disinterested generosity, out of affection, respect, admiration, charity or like impulses). Later in 2006, the IRS and Academy settled the tax obligations for gift baskets awarded through 2005 and agreed that 2006 recipients of the gift baskets (estimated to be worth more than $100,000) would be fully responsible for taxes on the gift baskets. The Academy also decided to discontinue the practice of awarding gift baskets.

How was Bill and Mercedes' tax return selected for audit? Given the audit focus on certain deductions, the IRS likely selected their return for audit because the amount or type of the deductions resulted in a high DIF score. IRS personnel then determined that the deductions warranted further review and, thus, selected the tax return for audit.

Types of Audits

The three types of IRS audits are correspondence, office, and field examinations. **Correspondence examinations** are the most common. These audits, as the name suggests, are conducted by mail and generally are limited to one or two items on the taxpayer's return. Of the three types of audits, correspondence audits are generally the narrowest in scope and the least complex. The IRS typically requests supporting documentation for one or more items on the taxpayer's return, like charitable contributions deducted, for example. When appropriate documentation is promptly supplied, these audits typically can be concluded relatively quickly. Of course, they can also be expanded to address other issues that arise as a result of the IRS's inspection of taxpayer documents.

Office examinations are the second most common audit. As the name suggests, the IRS conducts them at its local office. These audits are typically broader in scope and more complex than correspondence examinations. Small businesses, taxpayers operating sole proprietorships, and middle- to high-income individual taxpayers are more likely, if audited, to have office examinations. In these examinations, the taxpayer receives a notice that identifies the items subject to audit; requests substantiation for these items as necessary; and notifies the taxpayer of the date, time, and location of the exam. Taxpayers may attend the examination alone or with representation, such as their tax adviser or attorney.

Field examinations are the least common audit. The IRS conducts these at the taxpayer's place of business or the location where the taxpayer's books, records, and source documents are maintained. Field examinations are generally the broadest in scope and the most complex of the three audit types. They can last months to years and generally are limited to business returns and the most complex individual returns.

What type of exam do you think Bill and Mercedes will have? Because their return is an individual tax return and the audit is restricted to a relatively narrow set of deductions, their return will likely be subject to a correspondence audit. If the audit were broader in scope, an office examination would be more likely.

THE KEY FACTS

IRS Audits

▮ The three types of IRS audits are correspondence, office, and field examinations.

▮ After the audit, the IRS will send the taxpayer a 30-day letter, which provides the taxpayer the opportunity to pay the proposed assessment or request an appeals conference.

▮ If an agreement is not reached at appeals or the taxpayer does not pay the proposed assessment, the IRS will send the taxpayer a 90-day letter.

▮ After receiving the 90-day letter, the taxpayer may pay the tax or petition the U.S. Tax Court to hear the case.

▮ If the taxpayer chooses to pay the tax, the taxpayer may then request a refund of the tax and eventually sue the IRS for refund in the U.S. District Court or the U.S. Court of Federal Claims.

After the Audit   After the examination, the IRS agent provides a list of proposed adjustments (if any) to the taxpayer for review. If he or she agrees to the proposed changes, the taxpayer signs an agreement form (Form 870) and pays the additional tax owed or receives the proposed refund. If the taxpayer disputes the proposed changes, the taxpayer will receive a **30-day letter** giving him or her 30 days to either (1) request a conference with an appeals officer, who is independent and resides in a separate IRS division from the examining agent, or (2) agree to the proposed adjustment. An appeals officer would consider the merits of the unresolved issues as well as the "hazards of litigation"—that is, the probability that the IRS will lose if the case is brought to court and the resulting costs of a taxpayer-favorable ruling. If the taxpayer chooses the appeals conference and reaches an agreement with the IRS there, the taxpayer can then sign the Form 870. If the taxpayer and IRS still do not agree on the proposed adjustment at the appeals conference, or the taxpayer chooses not to request an appeals conference, the IRS will send the taxpayer a 90-day letter. See Exhibit 2-2.

The **90-day letter** (also known as a *statutory notice of deficiency*) explains that the taxpayer has 90 days to either (1) pay the proposed deficiency or (2) file a petition in the U.S. Tax Court to hear the case. The **U.S. Tax Court** is a national court whose judges are tax experts and who hear only tax cases. If the taxpayer would like to litigate the case but prefers it to be heard in the local **U.S. District Court** or the **U.S. Court of Federal Claims,** the taxpayer must pay the tax deficiency first and then sue the IRS for refund in the court.

Why would a taxpayer prefer one trial court over others? To understand this, we must appreciate the basic distinguishing factors of each. First and foremost, it is relatively common for the U.S. Tax Court, local U.S. District Court, or the U.S. Court of Federal Claims to interpret and rule differently on the same basic tax issue. Given a choice of courts, the taxpayer should prefer the court most likely to rule favorably on his or her particular issues. The courts also differ in other ways. For example, the U.S. District Court is the only court that provides for a jury trial; the U.S. Tax Court is the only court that allows tax cases to be heard *before* the taxpayer pays the disputed liability and the only court with a small claims division

EXHIBIT 2-2 IRS Appeals/Litigation Process

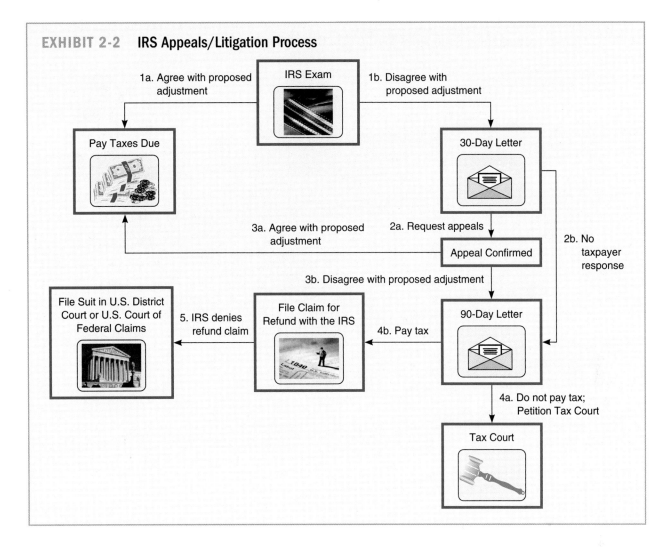

(hearing claims involving disputed liabilities of $50,000 or less); the U.S. Tax Court judges are tax experts, whereas the U.S. District Court and U.S. Court of Federal Claims judges are generalists. The taxpayer should consider each of these factors in choosing a trial court. For example, if the taxpayer feels very confident in her tax return position but does not have sufficient funds to pay the disputed liability, she will prefer the U.S. Tax Court. If, instead, the taxpayer is litigating a tax return position that is low on technical merit but high on emotional appeal, a jury trial in the local U.S. District Court may be the best option.

What happens after the taxpayer's case is decided in a trial court? The process may not be quite finished. After the trial court's verdict, the losing party has the right to request one of the 13 **U.S. Circuit Courts of Appeal** to hear the case. Both the U.S. Tax Court and local U.S. District Court cases are appealed to the specific U.S. Circuit Court of Appeals based on the taxpayer's residence. Cases litigated in Alabama, Florida, and Georgia, for example, appeal to the U.S. Circuit Court of Appeals for the 11th Circuit; whereas those tried in Louisiana, Mississippi, and Texas appeal to the 5th Circuit. In contrast, all U.S. Court of Federal Claims cases appeal to the U.S. Circuit Court of Appeals for the Federal Circuit (located in Washington, D.C.). Exhibit 2-3 depicts the geographic regions for each of the 11 U.S. Circuit Courts of Appeal defined by numerical region. Not depicted are the U.S. Circuit Court of Appeals for the District of Columbia and the U.S. Circuit Court of Appeals for the Federal Circuit.

EXHIBIT 2-3   Geographic Boundaries for the U.S. Circuit Courts of Appeal

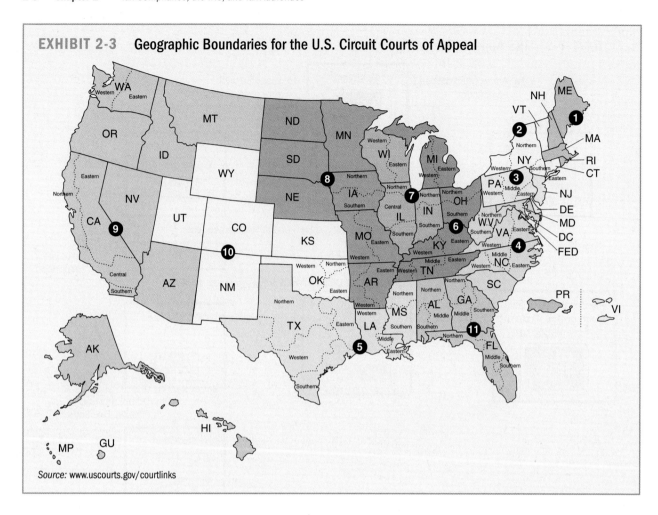

Source: www.uscourts.gov/courtlinks

Through the initial selection of a trial court—U.S. District Court, U.S. Tax Court, or U.S. Court of Federal Claims—the taxpayer has the ability to determine which circuit court would hear an appeal of the case (the U.S Circuit Court of Appeals based on residence or the U.S. Circuit Court of Appeals for the Federal Circuit). Because alternative circuit courts may interpret the law differently, the taxpayer should consider in choosing a trial-level court the relevant circuit courts' judicial histories to determine which circuit court (and thus, which trial court) would be more likely to rule in his or her favor.

After an appeals court hears a case, the losing party has one last option to receive a favorable ruling: a petition to the **U.S. Supreme Court** to hear the case. However, given the quantity of other cases appealed to the U.S. Supreme Court that are of national importance, the Supreme Court agrees to hear only a few tax cases a year with great significance to a broad cross-section of taxpayers, or cases litigating issues in which there has been disagreement among the circuit courts. For most tax cases, the Supreme Court refuses to hear the case (denies the ***writ of certiorari***) and litigation ends with the circuit court decision.

Although litigation of tax disputes is quite common, taxpayers should carefully consider the pros and cons. Litigation can be very costly financially and emotionally, and thus it is more appropriately used as an option of last resort, after all other appeal efforts have been exhausted.

What is the likely course of action for Bill and Mercedes' audit? It is too soon to tell. Before you can assess the likely outcome of their audit, you need a better understanding of both the audit issue and the relevant tax laws that apply to the issue. The next section explains alternative tax law sources. After we discuss the various sources of our tax laws, we'll describe how Bill and Mercedes (or their CPA) can research the sources to identify the best possible course of action.[7]

TAX LAW SOURCES

L03 L04

There are two broad categories of tax authorities: primary authorities and secondary authorities. **Primary authorities** are official sources of the tax law generated by the legislative branch (statutory authority issued by Congress), judicial branch (rulings by the U.S. District Court, U.S. Tax Court, U.S. Court of Federal Claims, U.S. Circuit Court of Appeals, or U.S. Supreme Court), and executive/administrative branch (Treasury and IRS pronouncements). Exhibit 2-4 displays the most common primary sources, and their relative authoritative weight (precedential

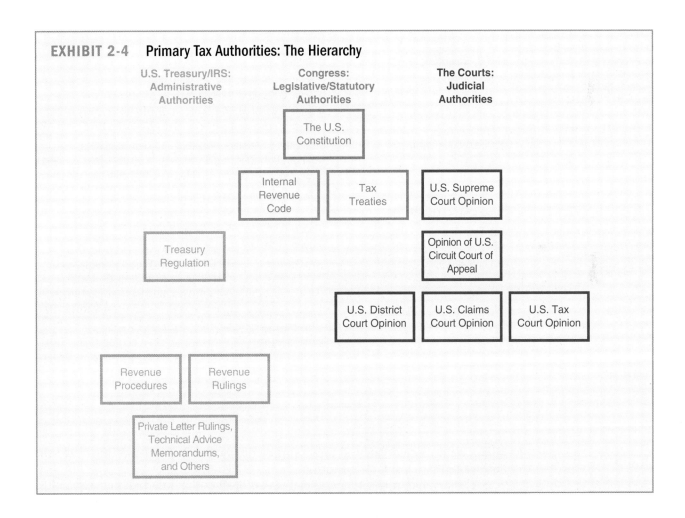

EXHIBIT 2-4   Primary Tax Authorities: The Hierarchy

U.S. Treasury/IRS: Administrative Authorities

Congress: Legislative/Statutory Authorities

The Courts: Judicial Authorities

The U.S. Constitution

Internal Revenue Code

Tax Treaties

U.S. Supreme Court Opinion

Treasury Regulation

Opinion of U.S. Circuit Court of Appeal

U.S. District Court Opinion

U.S. Claims Court Opinion

U.S. Tax Court Opinion

Revenue Procedures

Revenue Rulings

Private Letter Rulings, Technical Advice Memorandums, and Others

[7]Accountants should be mindful to not engage in the unauthorized practice of law. In years past, several court cases have addressed this issue without providing a clear understanding between practicing tax accounting and the unauthorized practice of law. At present, tax accountants are not likely to overstep their responsibilities if they limit their advice to tax issues and leave the general legal advice and drafting of legal documents to attorneys.

EXHIBIT 2-5   **Citations to Common Primary Authorities**

Statutory Authorities:	*Citation:*
Internal Revenue Code	IRC Sec. 162(e)(1)(A)
Committee Reports:	
Senate Finance Committee Report	S. Rep. No. 353, 82d Cong., 1st Sess. 14 (1951).
House Ways and Means Committee Report	H. Rep. No. 242, 82d Cong., 1st Sess. 40 (1951).

Administrative Authorities:	*Citation:*
Final Regulation	Reg. Sec. 1.217-2(c)(1)
Temporary Regulation	Temp. Reg. Sec. 1.217-2(c)(1)
Proposed Regulation	Prop. Reg. Sec. 1.217-2(c)(1)
Revenue Ruling	Rev. Rul. 77-262, 1977-2 C.B. 42
Revenue Procedure	Rev. Proc. 99-10, 1999-1 C.B. 272
Private Letter Ruling	PLR 200601001
Technical Advice Memorandum	TAM 200402004

Judicial Authorities:	*Citation:*
U.S. Supreme Court	*Comm. v. Kowalski*, 434 U.S. 77 (S. Ct., 1977)
	Comm. v. Kowalski, 98 S. Ct. 315 (S. Ct., 1977)
	Comm. v. Kowalski, 77-2 USTC par. 9,748 (S. Ct., 1977)
	Comm. v. Kowalski, 40 AFTR2d 77-6128 (S. Ct., 1977)
U.S. Circuit Court of Appeals	*Azar Nut Co. v. Comm.*, 931 F.2d 314 (5th Cir., 1991)
	Azar Nut Co. v. Comm., 91-1 USTC par. 50,257 (5th Cir., 1991)
	Azar Nut Co. v. Comm., 67 AFTR2d 91-987 (5th Cir., 1991)
U.S. Tax Court—Regular decision	*L.A. Beeghly*, 36 TC 154 (1962)
U.S. Tax Court—Memorandum decision	*Robert Rodriguez*, RIA TC Memo ¶2005-012
	Robert Rodriguez, 85 TCM 1162 (2005)
U.S. Court of Federal Claims	*J.R. Cohen v. U.S.*, 510 F. Supp. 297 (Fed. Cl., 1993)
	J.R. Cohen v. U.S., 72 AFTR 2d 93-5124 (Fed. Cl., 1993)
	J.R. Cohen v. U.S., 93-1 USTC par. 50,354 (Fed. Cl., 1993)
U.S. District Court	*Waxler Towing Co., Inc. v. U.S.*, 510 F. Supp. 297 (W.D, TN, 1981)
	Waxler Towing Co., Inc. v. U.S., 81-2 USTC par. 9,541 (W.D., TN, 1981)
	Waxler Towing Co., Inc. v. U.S., 48 AFTR2d 81-5274 (W.D., TN, 1981)

value). We'll discuss each of these authorities below. Exhibit 2-5 illustrates the citations to these primary authorities.

Secondary authorities are unofficial tax authorities that interpret and explain the primary authorities, such as tax research services (discussed below), tax articles from professional journals and law reviews, and newsletters. For quick questions, practitioners often use the *CCH Master Tax Guide* or *RIA Federal Tax Handbook*. Secondary authorities may be very helpful in understanding a tax issue, but they hold little weight in a tax dispute (hence their "unofficial" status). Thus, tax advisors should always be careful to verify their understanding of tax law by examining primary authorities directly. Exhibit 2-6 lists some of the common sources of secondary authority.

EXHIBIT 2-6   Common Secondary Tax Authorities

Tax Research Services:	***Professional Journals:***
BNA Tax Management Portfolios	*Journal of Accountancy*
CCH Standard Federal Tax Reporter	*Journal of Taxation*
CCH Tax Research Consultant	*Practical Tax Strategies*
RIA Federal Tax Coordinator	*Taxes*
RIA United States Tax Reporter	*Tax Adviser*
Newsletters:	***Quick Reference Sources:***
Daily Tax Report	*IRS Publications*
Federal Tax Weekly Alert	*CCH Master Tax Guide*
Tax Notes	*RIA Federal Tax Handbook*
Law Reviews:	
Tax Law Review (New York University School of Law)	
Virginia Tax Review (University of Virginia School of Law)	

Legislative Sources: Congress and the Constitution

The three legislative or statutory tax authorities are the U.S. Constitution, the Internal Revenue Code, and tax treaties. The **U.S. Constitution** is the highest authority in the United States, but it provides very little in the way of tax law since it contains no discussion of tax rates, taxable income, or other details. Instead, the 16th Amendment provides Congress the ability to tax income directly, from whatever source derived, without apportionment across the states.

Various attempts to amend the U.S. Constitution with regard to taxation—for example, one effort to repeal the 16th amendment entirely and one to require a two-thirds majority in both houses to raise taxes—have so far met with failure.

Internal Revenue Code   The second (and main) statutory authority is the **Internal Revenue Code of 1986,** as amended, known as the Code. As indicated in Exhibit 2-4, the Internal Revenue Code has the same authoritative weight as tax treaties and Supreme Court rulings. Thus, a taxpayer should feel very confident in a tax return position, such as taking a deduction that is specifically allowed by the Code. The Internal Revenue Code is unique in that every other authority—all administrative and judicial authorities except tax treaties and the Constitution—can be seen as an interpretation of it. Hence, understanding the relevant code section(s) is critical to being an efficient and effective tax professional.

Congress enacts tax legislation virtually every year that changes the Code; 1986 was simply the last major overhaul. Prior to 1986, tax law changes were incorporated into the Internal Revenue Code of 1954, the year a new numbering system and other significant changes were introduced. Before that, tax law changes were incorporated into the Internal Revenue Code of 1939, which was the year of the first Code.

The Legislative Process for Tax Laws   Exhibit 2-7 illustrates the legislative process for enacting tax laws. As required by the U.S. Constitution (Article 1, Section 7), "All bills for raising revenue shall originate in the House of Representatives." The Senate may propose tax legislation, but the first to formally consider a bill will be the House, typically within its Ways and Means Committee. After the committee debates

EXHIBIT 2-7 **Tax Legislation Process**

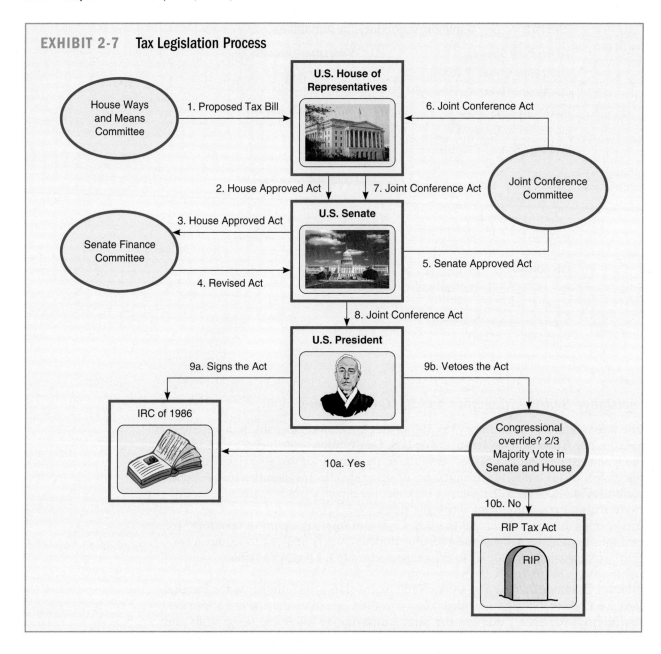

the proposed legislation and drafts a bill, the bill goes to the House of Representatives floor for debate and ultimately a vote (either yea or nay without modification). If the bill is approved, it becomes an *act* and is sent to the Senate, which typically refers the act to the Senate Finance Committee. Not to be outdone by the House, the Senate Finance Committee usually amends the act during its deliberations. After the revised act passes the Senate Finance Committee, it goes to the Senate for debate and vote. Unlike representatives, senators may modify the proposed legislation during their debate.

If the Senate passes the act, both the House and Senate versions of the legislation are sent to the Joint Conference Committee, which consists of members of the House Ways and Means Committee and the Senate Finance Committee. During the Joint Conference Committee deliberations, committee members debate the two versions of the proposed legislation. Possible outcomes for any specific provision in the proposed legislation include adoption of the Senate version, the House version, or some compromise version of the two acts. Likewise, the Joint

Conference Committee may simply choose to eliminate specific provisions from the proposed legislation or fail to reach a compromise, thereby terminating the legislation.

After the Joint Conference Committee approves the act, the revised legislation is sent to the House and Senate for vote. If both the House and Senate approve it, the act is sent to the president for his or her signature. If the president signs the act, it becomes law and is incorporated into the Internal Revenue Code of 1986 (Title 26 of the U.S. Code, which contains *all* codified laws of the United States). If the president vetoes the legislation, Congress may override the veto with a two-thirds positive vote in both the House and the Senate.

The House Ways and Means Committee, Senate Finance Committee, and Joint Conference Committee each produce a committee report that explains the current tax law, proposed change in the law, and reasons for the change. These committee reports are considered statutory sources of the tax law and may be very useful in interpreting tax law changes and understanding Congressional intent. This is especially important after new legislation has been enacted because, with the exception of the Code, there will be very little authority interpreting the new law (that is, no judicial or administrative authorities because of the time it takes for the new law to be litigated or for the IRS to issue interpretative guidance).

Basic Organization of the Code   The Internal Revenue Code is segregated into subtitles, chapters, subchapters, parts, subparts, and sections. All existing and any new tax laws are placed in the Code within a specific subtitle, chapter, subchapter, part, subpart, and section of the Code. When referencing a tax law, the researcher generally refers to the law simply by its code section. Code sections are numbered from 1 to 9833, with gaps in the section numbers to allow new code sections to be added to the appropriate parts of the Code as needed. Each code section is further segregated into subsections, paragraphs, subparagraphs, and clauses to allow more specific reference or citation.

Memorizing the various subtitles and chapters of the Code has limited value (except to impress your friends at cocktail parties). However, understanding the *organization* of the Code is important, especially for the aspiring tax accountant. First, you must understand the organization of a code section, its subsections, paragraphs, subparagraphs, and clauses to be able to cite the respective law correctly as, for example, IRC Sec. 162(b)(2). Second, note that many provisions in the Code apply only to specific parts of the Code. For example, it is quite common for a code section to include the phrase "for purposes of this chapter, ..." If you do not understand what laws are encompassed in the chapter, it would be very difficult for you to interpret the code section and determine its applicability to a research question.

Finally, remember that code sections addressing similar transactions, such as deductions, or topics, such as taxable corporations, are grouped together. Consider a researcher faced with the question of whether an item of income is taxable. If the researcher understands the organization of the Code, she can quickly focus her research on code sections 61–140, which provide a broad definition of gross income, list items specifically included in gross income, and identify items specifically excluded from gross income.

Tax Treaties   **Tax treaties** are negotiated agreements between countries that describe the tax treatment of entities subject to tax in both countries, such as U.S. citizens earning investment income in Spain. The U.S. president has the authority to enter into a tax treaty with another country after receiving the Senate's advice. If you are a U.S. citizen earning income abroad or an accountant with international clients, you

EXHIBIT 2-8   Example of Code Organization

Subtitle A—Income Taxes

  Chapter 1—Income Taxes

  Subchapter A—Determination of Tax Liability

    Part I—Definition of Gross Income, Adjusted Gross Income, Taxable Income, etc. (Sec. 61–68)

      Sec. 61—Gross Income Defined

      Sec. 62—Adjusted Gross Income Defined

      Sec. 63—Taxable Income Defined

        Subsection 63(c)—Standard Deduction

          Paragraph 63(c)(2)—Basic Standard Deduction

            Subparagraph 63(c)(2)(A) . . .

              Clause 63(c)(2)(A)(i) . . .

    Part II—Items Specifically Included in Gross Income (Sec. 71–90)

      Sec. 71—Alimony

      Sec. 72—Annuities

      Sec. 73—Services of Child

      Sec. 74—Prizes & Awards - . . .

    Part III—Items Specifically Excluded from Gross Income (Sec. 101–140)

      Sec. 101—Certain Death Benefits

      Sec. 102—Gifts and Inheritances

      Sec. 103—Interest on State & Local Bonds

need knowledge of U.S. tax laws, the foreign country's tax laws, and the respective tax treaty between the U.S. and the foreign country for efficient tax planning. Because the focus in this text is on U.S. tax laws, we only briefly mention the importance of tax treaties as a statutory authority.

Example 2-2

Bill recently spent a summer in Milan, Italy, teaching a graduate level economics course. While in Italy he earned a $20,000 stipend from Bocconi University and some interest in a temporary banking account that he established for the trip. What tax laws must Bill consider to determine the taxation of his $20,000 stipend?

Answer: U.S. tax laws, Italian tax laws, and the U.S.-Italy tax treaty will determine the tax consequences of the amounts Bill earned in Italy.

THE KEY FACTS

Judicial Authorities

■ Our judicial system is tasked with the ultimate authority to interpret the Internal Revenue Code and settle disputes between taxpayers and the IRS.

■ The Supreme Court is the highest judicial authority.

■ Beneath the Supreme Court, the decisions of the 13 Circuit Courts of Appeal represent the next highest judicial authority.

(continued)

Judicial Sources: The Courts

Our judicial system has the ultimate authority to interpret the Internal Revenue Code and settle disputes between the IRS and taxpayers. As Exhibit 2-4 illustrates, there are five basic sources of judicial authority (three trial-level courts, 13 U.S. Circuit Courts of Appeal, and the Supreme Court). We've noted that the Supreme Court, along with the Code, represents the highest tax-specific authority. An important distinction between the two, however, is that the Supreme Court does not establish law, but instead simply interprets and applies the Code (along with other authorities). Thus, the Code and the Supreme Court should never be in conflict.[8]

---

[8]The Supreme Court does have the authority to declare a Code provision unconstitutional.

Below the Supreme Court, the decisions of the 13 U.S. Circuit Courts of Appeal represent the next highest judicial authority. The lowest level of judicial authority consists of three different types of trial-level courts (U.S. District Courts, U.S. Court of Federal Claims, and the U.S. Tax Court). Given that the U.S. Tax Court hears only tax cases and that its judges are "tax experts," its decisions typically have more weight than those rendered by a district court or the U.S. Court of Federal Claims.[9] Likewise, because the U.S. Court of Federal Claims hears a much narrower set of issues than U.S. District Courts (only monetary claims against the U.S. government), its decisions have more weight than district court decisions.

In rendering court decisions, all courts apply the judicial doctrine of *stare decisis.* This doctrine means that a court will rule consistently with (a) its previous rulings (unless, due to evolving interpretations of the tax law over time, the court decides to overturn an earlier decision) and (b) the rulings of higher courts with appellate jurisdiction (the courts its cases are appealed to). The implication of *stare decisis* is that a circuit court will abide by Supreme Court rulings and its own rulings, whereas a trial-level court will abide by Supreme Court rulings, its respective circuit court's rulings, and its own rulings. For example, a district court in California would follow U.S. 9th Circuit and Supreme Court rulings as well as the court's own rulings.

The doctrine of *stare decisis* presents a special problem for the U.S. Tax Court because it appeals to different circuit courts based on the taxpayer's residence. To implement the doctrine of *stare decisis,* the tax court applies the **Golsen rule.** The Golsen rule simply states that the tax court will abide by rulings of the circuit court that has appellate jurisdiction for a case.

<table>
<tr><td>(concluded)</td></tr>
<tr><td>■ The lowest level of judicial authority consists of three different types of trial-level courts (U.S. District Courts, U.S. Court of Federal Claims, and the U.S. Tax Court).</td></tr>
<tr><td>■ U.S. Tax Court decisions typically are considered to have more authoritative weight than decisions rendered by a district court or the U.S. Court of Federal Claims.</td></tr>
<tr><td>■ All courts apply the judicial doctrine of *stare decisis,* which means that a court will rule consistently with its previous rulings and the rulings of higher courts with appellate jurisdiction.</td></tr>
</table>

Example 2-3

What if: If Bill and Mercedes opt to litigate their case in tax court, by which circuit court's rulings will the tax court abide?

Answer: Because Bill and Mercedes live in Florida, the U.S. Tax Court will abide the circuit court with appellate jurisdiction in Florida, which happens to be U.S. 11th Circuit Court.

Administrative Sources: The U.S. Treasury

Regulations, Revenue Rulings, and Revenue Procedures   The Treasury Department, of which the IRS is a bureau, is charged with administering and interpreting the tax laws of the United States, among other duties such as printing money and advising the president on economic issues. **Regulations** are the Treasury Department's official interpretation of the Internal Revenue Code, have the highest authoritative weight, and often contain examples of the application of the Code that may be particularly helpful to the tax researcher. Regulations are issued in three different forms: final, temporary, and proposed. The names are very descriptive. **Final regulations** are regulations that have been issued in final form, and thus, unless or until revoked, they represent the Treasury's interpretation of the Code. **Temporary regulations** have a limited life (three years for regulations issued after November 20, 1988). Nonetheless, during their life, they carry the same authoritative weight as final regulations.

<table>
<tr><td>**THE KEY FACTS**</td></tr>
<tr><td>Administrative Authorities</td></tr>
<tr><td>■ The Treasury Department is charged with administering and interpreting the tax laws.</td></tr>
<tr><td>■ Regulations
· Regulations are the Treasury Department's official interpretation of the Internal Revenue Code and have the highest authoritative weight.
· Regulations are issued in three different forms (proposed, temporary, and final) and serve three basic purposes (interpretative, procedural, and legislative).</td></tr>
<tr><td>(continued)</td></tr>
</table>

[9]The Tax Court renders both "regular" and "memorandum" decisions. Regular decisions involve new or unusual points of law, whereas memorandum decisions involve questions of fact or the application of existing law. Both decisions have similar authoritative weight. Decisions issued by the Tax Court's Small Claims division may not be cited as precedent.

(concluded)

■ **Revenue rulings and revenue procedures**
· Revenue rulings and revenue procedures are second in administrative authoritative weight after regulations.
· Revenue rulings address the application of the Code and regulations to a specific factual situation.
· Revenue procedures explain in greater detail IRS practice and procedures in administering the tax law.

■ **Letter rulings**
· Letter rulings are less authoritative but more specific than revenue rulings and regulations.
· Private letter rulings represent the IRS' application of the Code and other tax authorities to a specific transaction and taxpayer.

Finally, all regulations are issued in the form of **proposed regulations** first, to allow public comment on them. They do not carry the same authoritative weight as temporary or final regulations.

In addition to being issued in three different forms, regulations also serve three basic purposes: interpretative, procedural, and legislative. Most regulations are issued as interpretative or procedural regulations. As the names suggest, **interpretative regulations** represent the Treasury's interpretation of the Code. In Bill and Mercedes' case, these might be the regulations issued under IRC Sec. 163, which discuss interest deductions. **Procedural regulations** explain Treasury Department procedures as they relate to administering the Code. Again, for Bill and Mercedes' case, these might be the regulations issued under IRC Sec. 6501 regarding the statute of limitations for IRS assessment and collection. **Legislative regulations,** the rarest type, are issued when Congress specifically directs the Treasury Department to create regulations to address an issue in an area of law. In these instances, the Treasury is actually writing the law instead of interpreting the Code. Because legislative regulations represent tax law instead of interpretation of tax law, legislative regulations have more authoritative weight than interpretative and procedural regulations. Nonetheless, it is a very difficult process to challenge any regulation and thus, taxpayers are cautioned not to take tax return positions inconsistent with regulations.

As illustrated in Exhibit 2-4, revenue rulings and revenue procedures are second in administrative authoritative weight after regulations. But unlike regulations, revenue rulings address the application of the Code and regulations to a specific factual situation. Thus, while **revenue rulings** have less authoritative weight, they provide a much more detailed interpretation of the Code as it applies to a specific transaction and fact pattern. For example, Rev. Rul. 87-22 discusses the deductions of prepaid interest (points) a taxpayer may claim when refinancing the mortgage for a principal residence, whereas the Code and regulations do not specifically address this issue. **Revenue procedures** are also much more detailed than regulations. They explain in greater detail IRS practice and procedures in administering the tax law. For example, Rev. Proc. 87-56 provides the specific depreciation lives for depreciable assets (discussed in Chapter 9).

Letter Rulings   Below revenue rulings and revenue procedures in authoritative weight rest letter rulings. As you might guess, letter rulings are less authoritative but more specific than revenue rulings and regulations. Indeed, **private letter rulings** represent the IRS's application of the Code and other tax authorities to a specific transaction and taxpayer. Private letter rulings are issued in response to a taxpayer request and are common for proposed transactions with potentially large tax implications. For example, companies commonly request a private letter ruling to ensure that a proposed corporate acquisition meets the definition of a tax-free exchange. However, the IRS also maintains a list of certain issues on which it refuses to rule, such as the tax consequences of proposed federal tax legislation. Each year, the IRS publishes an updated list of these transactions in a revenue procedure.

Other types of letter rulings include determination letters and technical advice memorandums. **Determination letters,** issued by local IRS directors, are generally not controversial. An example of a determination letter is the request by an employer for the IRS to rule that the taxpayer's retirement plan is a "qualified plan." **Technical advice memorandums** differ from private letter rulings in that they are generated for completed transactions and usually are requested by an IRS agent during an IRS audit.

Is this a comprehensive list of IRS pronouncements? No. In addition to the pronouncements listed above, the IRS issues several less common types, which are beyond the scope of this text. A couple of other pronouncements, however, warrant some discussion. As we mentioned above, the IRS and taxpayers litigate tax cases in a number of courts and jurisdictions. Obviously, the IRS wins some and loses some of these cases. Except for Supreme Court cases, whenever the IRS loses, it may issue an **acquiescence** or **nonacquiescence** as guidance for how the IRS intends to respond to the loss. Although an acquiescence indicates that the IRS has decided to *follow* the court's adverse ruling in the future, it does not mean that the IRS *agrees* with it. Instead, it simply means that the IRS will no longer litigate this issue. A nonacquiescence has the exact opposite implications and alerts taxpayers that the IRS does plan to continue to litigate this issue. Finally, the IRS also issues **actions on decisions,** which explain the background reasoning behind an IRS acquiescence or nonacquiescence.

TAX RESEARCH

L05

Now that you have a basic understanding of the different types of tax authority, why do you think that the IRS and taxpayers disagree with respect to the tax treatment of a transaction? In other words, why would the IRS and Bill and Mercedes' CPA reach different conclusions regarding the deductibility of certain expenses? The answer is that, because the Code does not specifically address the tax consequences of each transaction type or every possible variation of a particular transaction, the application of the tax law is subject to debate and differing interpretations by the IRS, courts, tax professionals, taxpayers, and so on. Tax research, therefore, plays a vital role in allowing us to identify and understand the varying authorities that provide guidance on an issue, to assess the relative weights of differing authorities, to understand the risks associated with different tax return positions, and ultimately to draw an appropriate conclusion regarding the application of the tax law to the issue. The following paragraphs describe the basic process of tax research that tax professionals use to identify and analyze tax authorities to answer tax questions. We will then revisit Bill and Mercedes' issue and view the research memo prepared by their CPA.

Step 1: Understand Facts

To answer a tax question, you must understand the question. To understand the question, you must know the facts. There are two basic types of facts: open facts and closed facts. Open facts have not yet occurred, such as the facts associated with a proposed transaction. Closed facts have already occurred. The distinction between open and closed facts is important because unlike closed facts, open facts can be altered, and different facts may result in very different tax consequences. Open facts allow the taxpayer to arrange a transaction to achieve the most advantageous outcome. Thus, they are especially important in tax planning.

How do you determine the facts for a research question? Interview clients, speak with third parties such as attorneys and brokers, and review client documents such as contracts, prior tax returns, wills, trust documents, deeds, and corporate minutes. When interviewing clients, remember that not many are tax experts. Thus, it is up to the tax professional to ask the correct initial and follow-up questions to obtain all the relevant facts. Also consider nontax factors, such as a client's personal values or objectives, as these often put constraints on tax planning strategies.

Step 2: Identify Issues

A tax professional's ability to identify issues is largely a function of his or her type of tax expertise. A tax expert in a particular area will typically be able to identify quickly the specific tax issues that relate to transactions in that area. For example, an expert in corporate acquisitions would quickly identify the tax consequences and specific issues of alternative acquisition types. A novice, on the other hand, would likely

---

THE KEY FACTS

Tax Research

- The five steps in tax research are (1) understand the facts, (2) identify issues, (3) locate relevant authorities, (4) analyze the tax authorities, and (5) communicate research results.

- The two types of tax services that tax professionals use in tax research are annotated tax services, arranged by code section, and topical services, arranged by topic.

- Research questions often consist of questions of fact or questions of law.
  · The answer to a question of fact hinges upon the facts and circumstances of the taxpayer's transaction.
  · The answer to a question of law hinges upon the interpretation of the law, such as interpreting a particular phrase in a code section.

- When the researcher identifies that different authorities have conflicting views, she should evaluate the "hierarchy," jurisdiction, and age of the authorities.

(continued)

identify broader issues first and then more specific issues as he or she researched the relevant tax law.

What's the best method to identify tax issues? First of all, get a good understanding of the client's facts. Then, combine your understanding of the facts with your knowledge of the tax law. Let's consider the example of Bill and Mercedes' interest deduction. For an expert in this particular area, the issues will be immediately evident. For a novice, the initial response may take the form of a series of general questions: (1) Is this item of expense deductible? (2) Is that item of income taxable? (3) In what year should the expense be deducted? (4) In what year should the item of income be taxed? After you identify these types of general issues, your research will enable you to identify the more specific issues that ultimately determine the tax ramifications of the transaction.

Example 2-4	

(concluded)

■ Once the tax researcher has identified relevant authorities, she must make sure that the authorities are still valid and up to date

■ The most common end product of a research question is a research memo, which has five basic parts: (1) facts, (2) issues, (3) authority list, (4) conclusion, and (5) analysis.

Elizabeth, Bill and Mercedes' friend who is a shareholder and the CFO of a company, loaned money to her company to help prevent the company from declaring bankruptcy. Despite Elizabeth's loan, the company did file bankruptcy, and Elizabeth was not repaid the loan. What issues would a researcher consider?

Answer: The first questions to ask are whether Elizabeth can deduct the bad debt expense and if so, as what type of deduction? As the researcher delves more into the general issue, he would identify that the type of deduction depends on whether Elizabeth's debt is considered a business or nonbusiness bad debt. This more specific issue depends on whether Elizabeth loaned the money to the company to protect her job (business bad debt) or to protect her stock investment in the company (nonbusiness bad debt). Bad debt expenses incurred for nonbusiness debts (investment-related debts) are deducted as capital losses and thus subject to limitations (discussed in Chapter 11), whereas bad debt expenses for business debts (business-related debts) are ordinary deductions and not limited.

Why might this case be a good one to litigate in U.S. District Court?

Answer: Because a jury might be more likely to be convinced to assess Elizabeth's motives favorably.

Step 3: Locate Relevant Authorities

Step three in the research process is to locate the relevant authorities (code sections, regulations, court cases, revenue rulings) that address the tax issue. Luckily, tax services can aid the researcher in identifying relevant authorities. Most, if not all, of these services are available on the Internet (with a subscription), and thus offer the flexibility to conduct research almost anywhere.[10]

There are two basic types of tax services: annotated and topical. **Annotated tax services** are arranged by Internal Revenue Code Section. That is, for each code section, an annotated service includes the code section; a listing of the code section history; copies of congressional committee reports that explain changes to the code section; a copy of all the regulations issued for the specific code section; the service's unofficial explanation of the code section; and brief summaries (called annotations) of relevant court cases, revenue rulings, revenue procedures, and letter rulings that address issues specific to the code section. Two examples of annotated tax services are Commerce Clearing House's (CCH) Standard Federal Tax Reporter and Research Institute of America's (RIA) United States Tax Reporter.

---

[10]www.IRS.gov contains a lot of information (tax forms, IRS publications, etc.) that may be especially useful for answering basic tax questions. In addition, tax publishers, such as CCH and RIA, produce quick reference tax guides (e.g., the *CCH Master Tax Guide* or the *RIA Tax Handbook*) that may be used to answer basic tax questions.

Topical tax services are arranged by topic, such as taxable forms of income, tax-exempt income, and trade or business expenses. For each topic, the services identify tax issues that relate to each topic, and then explain and cite authorities relevant to the issue (code sections, regulations, court cases, revenue rulings, etc.). Beginning tax researchers often prefer topical services, because they generally are easier to read. Some examples of topical federal tax services include BNA's Tax Management Portfolios, CCH's Tax Research Consultant, and RIA's Federal Tax Coordinator.

How does a researcher use these services? An expert would probably go directly to the relevant portions of an annotated or topical service. A novice may conduct a keyword search in the service, use the tax service's topical index, or "browse" the tax service to identify the relevant portions. Some suggestions for identifying keywords: Try to describe the transaction in three to five words. An ideal keyword search typically includes (1) the relevant area of law and (2) a fact or two that describes the transaction. Try to avoid keywords that are too broad (income, deduction, taxable) or that may be too narrow.

Example 2-5

Bill and Mercedes refinanced the mortgage on their principal residence a couple of years ago when their original mortgage's four-year balloon payment came due. Their mortgage institution charged Bill and Mercedes $3,000 of points (prepaid interest) upon the refinancing in order to give them a reduced interest rate. On their CPA's advice, Bill and Mercedes deducted the $3,000 in the year they paid it, but upon audit, the IRS disallowed the deduction. What is the research issue?

Answer: The issue is, should Bill and Mercedes have deducted the $3,000 of points in the year they paid it?

What are some keywords that could identify relevant tax authority?

Answer: Points (area of law), interest (area of law), refinancing (fact that describes the transaction).

Keyword searching is more an art than an exact science. As you gain a better understanding of different areas of the tax law, you'll become much more efficient at using keywords. If keyword searching is not proving beneficial, check your spelling, make sure you're searching within the correct database, rethink your keywords, use another research method, use another tax service, or as a last resort, take a break.

While utilizing keyword searches or other research methods to identify potentially relevant areas of law and tax authorities, constantly ask yourself whether you are indeed in the correct area of law. Once the answer to this question is an authoritative yes, you can delve deeper into the area of law and related authorities to answer the question.

Step 4: Analyze Tax Authorities

Once a researcher identifies relevant authorities, she must read carefully to ensure she fully understands them, as well as their application to the research problem. Two basic types of issues researchers will encounter are questions of fact and questions of law.

The answer to a **question of fact** hinges upon the facts and circumstances of the taxpayer's transaction. For example, whether a trade or business expense is "ordinary," "necessary," "reasonable," and thus deductible, is a question of fact. If you're researching a question of fact, understand *which* facts determine the answer—in this case, which facts make an expense "ordinary," "necessary," and "reasonable" and which do not. In this type of question, the researcher will focus on understanding how various facts affect the research answer and identifying authorities with fact patterns similar to her client's.

The answer to a **question of law** hinges upon the interpretation of the law, such as interpreting a particular phrase in a code section. If a researcher is faced with this type of question, she will spend much of her time researching the various interpretations of the code section and take note of which authorities interpret the code differently and why.

For many tax questions, the answer is clear with no opposing interpretations or contrary authorities. For other questions, the researcher may identify that different authorities have conflicting views. In this situation, the tax researcher should evaluate the hierarchical level, jurisdiction, and age of the authorities, placing more weight on higher and newer authorities that have jurisdiction over the taxpayer. A tax researcher will become more adept at this process as she gains experience.

Once the tax researcher has identified relevant authorities, she must make sure the authorities are still valid and up to date. For court cases, a **citator,** which is a research tool that allows you to check the status of several types of tax authorities, will review the history of the case to find out, for example, whether it was subsequently appealed and overturned, and to identify subsequent cases that cite the case. Favorable citations strengthen a case, while unfavorable ones weaken it. Citators can also check the status of revenue rulings, revenue procedures, and other IRS pronouncements. Checking the status of the Code is fairly simple: just locate the current version. Checking the status of regulations is a little more complicated. Most tax services alert researchers if a regulation has not been updated for certain changes in the Code. If this is the case, the researcher should evaluate whether the changes in the Code make the regulation obsolete.

As you will see in the analysis section of the sample research memo drafted by Bill and Merccdes' CPA (see Exhibit 2-9, below), the question whether they should amortize or currently deduct the points paid to refinance the mortgage on their principal residence ultimately depends upon the interpretation of a particular phrase: "in connection with the purchase or improvement of" found in IRC Sec. 461(g)(2). Is there a correct answer to this question? No. There is no clear-cut answer. Rather, this is a situation where the tax professional must use professional judgment. Because there is substantial authority supporting the current deduction of the points (discussed in detail in the sample memo), Bill and Mercedes should be able to deduct the points currently without risk of penalty. However, Bill and Mercedes should be aware that the IRS has clearly stated in an action on decision that it will fight this issue outside the 8th Circuit—for example, in the 11th Circuit, where Bill and Mercedes live.

Step 5: Communicate the Results

After a researcher finishes her research, the final step of the process is to communicate the results. The most common end product of a research question is the internal research memo the researcher drafts for her supervisor's attention. The memo has five basic parts: (1) facts, (2) issues, (3) authority list, (4) conclusion, and (5) analysis. The purpose of the memo is to inform the reader of the answer to a research question, and thus, it should be written in an objective manner by discussing all relevant authorities to the research question, including those authorities that support, as well as those that conflict with, the answer. Below are some suggestions for each part of the memo. Compare these to the execution within the sample internal research memo presented in Exhibit 2-9.

Facts   Discuss facts relevant to the question presented—that is, facts that provide necessary background of the transaction and those facts that may influence the research answer. Keeping the fact discussion relatively brief will focus the reader's attention on the relevant characteristics of the transaction.

EXHIBIT 2-9   Sample Research Memo

Below is the memo that Bill and Mercedes' CPA drafted after researching their issue.

Facts:	Four years ago Bill and Mercedes' credit union provided them a $250,000 mortgage loan for their new home. The mortgage loan was a four-year interest-only note with a balloon payment at the end of four years. Bill and Mercedes (Floridians residing in the 11th Circuit) chose this type of loan to allow them to minimize their mortgage payment until their previous house was sold. After 18 months, Bill and Mercedes sold their previous house and refinanced their original short-term loan with a 15-year conventional mortgage. The credit union charged Bill and Mercedes $3,000 in points (prepaid interest) upon the refinancing.
Issue:	Can Bill and Mercedes deduct the points in the year they paid them?
Authorities:	IRC Sec. 461(g) Rev. Rul. 87-22, 1987-1 CB 146. *J.R. Huntsman v. Comm.* (8 Cir., 1990), 90-2 USTC par. 50,340, rev'g 91 TC 917 (1988). AOD 1991-002. *P.G. Cao v. Comm.* (9 Cir., 1996), 96-1 USTC par. 50,167, aff'g 67 TCM 2171 (1994)
Conclusion:	Because Bill and Mercedes' refinancing represents an integrated step in securing permanent financing for their home, substantial authority supports their deduction of the $3,000 points this year.
Analysis:	IRC Sec. 461(g)(1) provides that cash-method taxpayers (Bill and Mercedes) must amortize prepaid interest (points) over the life of the loan instead of receiving a current deduction. IRC Sec. 461(g)(2) provides an exception to the general rule of Sec. 461(g)(1). Specifically, IRC Sec. 461(g)(2) allows cash-method taxpayers to deduct points in the year paid if the related debt was incurred "in connection with the purchase or improvement of," and secured by, the taxpayer's principal residence. The question whether Bill and Mercedes should amortize or currently deduct the points paid to refinance the mortgage on the their principal residence depends upon the interpretation of "in connection with the purchase or improvement of" found in IRC Sec. 461(g)(2).
	There are two basic interpretations of "in connection with the purchase or improvement of." In Revenue Ruling 87-22, the IRS rules that points incurred in refinancing a mortgage on a taxpayer's residence are deductible in the year paid to the extent that the taxpayer uses the loan proceeds to improve the taxpayer's residence. Thus, points paid to simply refinance an existing mortgage without improving the residence must be amortized over the life of the loan. In contrast, in *J.R. Huntsman v. Comm.*, the 8th Circuit Court interpreted the phrase "in connection with the purchase or improvement of" much more broadly and held that points incurred to refinance a mortgage on the taxpayer's principal residence are currently deductible if the refinancing represents an *integrated step to secure permanent financing* for the taxpayer's residence. The facts in *J.R. Huntsman v. Comm.* are very similar to Bill and Mercedes' facts. Like Bill and Mercedes, the taxpayers in *J.R. Huntsman v. Comm.* also purchased their principal residence using a short-term loan with a "balloon" payment. When the balloon payment came due, the taxpayers obtained a permanent mortgage on their home (a 30-year conventional mortgage). The 8th Circuit Court held that in this case the permanent mortgage was acquired to extinguish the short-term financing and finalize the purchase of the home. "Thus, where taxpayers purchase a principal residence with a short-term three-year loan secured by a mortgage on the residence, and replace the loan with permanent financing . . . , the permanent mortgage obtained is sufficiently in connection with the purchase of the home to fall within the exception provided for by section 461(g)(2)." In Action on Decision 1991-002, the IRS has indicated that it will not follow the *J.R. Huntsman v. Comm.* decision outside the 8th Circuit (in the 11th Circuit where Bill and Mercedes live). Nonetheless, other courts (the 9th Circuit in *P.G. Cao v. Comm.*) have indicated a willingness to apply the 8th Circuit's interpretation of IRC Sec. 461(g)(2). That is, they have allowed deductibility of points incurred in refinancing if the refinancing occurred to secure permanent financing, instead of for some other reason such as to secure a lower interest rate.
	Given the similarity in facts between Bill and Mercedes' refinancing and those in *J.R. Huntsman v. Comm.* (refinancing of a short-term note to secure permanent financing), substantial authority supports a current deduction of the points paid.

Issues   State the specific issues that the memo addresses. This section confirms that you understand the research question, reminds the reader of the question being analyzed, and allows future researchers to determine whether the analysis in the memo is relevant. Issues should be written as specifically as possible and be limited to one or two sentences per issue.

Authorities   In this section, the researcher cites the relevant tax authorities that apply to the issue, such as the IRC, court cases, and revenue rulings. How many authorities should you cite? Enough to provide a clear understanding of the issue and interpretation of the law. Remember, in order to reach an accurate assessment of the strength of your conclusion, you should consider authorities that may support your desired conclusion, as well as those that may go against it.

Conclusion   There should be one conclusion per issue. Each conclusion should answer the question as briefly as possible, and preferably indicate why the answer is what it is.

Analysis   The goal of the analysis is for the researcher to provide the reader a clear understanding of the area of law and specific authorities that apply. Typically, an analysis will be organized to discuss the general area(s) of law first (the Code section) and then the specific authorities (court cases, revenue rulings) that apply to the research question. How many authorities should you discuss? As many as necessary to provide the reader an understanding of the issue and relevant authorities. After you discuss the relevant authorities, apply the authorities to your client's transaction and explain how the authorities result in your conclusion.

In the case of Bill and Mercedes' interest deduction, their CPA recommended a tax return position that the IRS disallowed upon audit. Did their CPA violate her professional responsibilities by recommending a position the IRS disallowed? Good question. Let's take a look at the rules governing tax professional responsibilities.

TAX PROFESSIONAL RESPONSIBILITIES

LO6

Tax practitioners are subject to a variety of statutes, rules, and codes of professional conduct. Some examples include the American Institute of CPAs (AICPA) Code of Professional Conduct, the AICPA Statements on Standards for Tax Services (SSTS), the IRS's Circular 230, and statutes enacted by a CPA's specific state board of accountancy. Tax practitioners should absolutely have a working knowledge of these statutes, rules, and guidelines because (1) they establish the professional standards for the practitioner and (2) failure to comply with the standards could result in adverse consequences for the tax professional, such as being admonished, suspended, or barred from practicing before the IRS; being admonished, suspended, or expelled from the AICPA; or suffering suspension or revocation of the CPA license. Given the voluminous nature of applicable statutes, rules, and codes, we will simply provide a brief overview of the major common sources of tax professional standards.

CPAs who are members of the AICPA are bound by the AICPA Code of Professional Conduct and Statements on Standards for Tax Services. Other tax professionals use these provisions as guidance of professional standards. The AICPA Code of Professional Conduct is not specific to tax practice and provides broader professional standards that are especially relevant for auditors—that is, for those independent CPAs charged with examining an entity's financial statements. Provisions included in the Code of Professional Conduct address the importance of a CPA maintaining independence from the client and using due professional care in carrying out responsibilities. Additional provisions limit the acceptance of contingent fees, preclude discreditable acts such as signing a false return, and prohibit false advertising and charging commissions. Most of these provisions rightly fall under the heading of common sense. Nonetheless, a regular review should prove useful to the practicing CPA.

The AICPA's **Statements on Standards for Tax Services (SSTS)** recommend appropriate standards of practice for tax professionals. One objective of these standards is to encourage increased understanding by the Treasury, IRS, and the public of a CPA's professional standards. Many state boards of accountancy have adopted similar standards, thus making the SSTS especially important. Currently, eight SSTS describe the tax professional standards when recommending a tax return position, answering questions on a tax return, preparing a tax return using data supplied by a client, using estimates on a tax return, taking a tax return position inconsistent with a previous year's tax return, discovering a tax return error, discovering a tax return error during an IRS audit, and giving tax advice to taxpayers. Exhibit 2-10 provides a brief summary of each SSTS. Most important from a research perspective, SSTS No. 1 provides that a tax professional may recommend any tax return position in which she has a good-faith belief that the position has a **realistic possibility** (defined elsewhere as a one-third probability, or greater) of being sustained administratively by the IRS or judicially by the courts on its merits if challenged. A tax professional may also recommend a tax return position if the position is *not frivolous*—not patently improper—and is *adequately disclosed* on the tax return.

Note, however, that Congress recently amended IRC Sec. 6694 to impose a penalty on a *tax practitioner* for any position that that is not supported by **substantial authority**.[11] A good tax professional evaluates whether supporting authority is substantial based upon the supporting and opposing authorities' weight and relevance. Substantial authority suggests the probability that the taxpayer's position is sustained upon audit or litigation is in the 40 plus percent range or above. The tax practitioner can also avoid penalty under IRC Sec. 6694 if the tax return position has at least a reasonable basis (i.e., supported by one or more tax authorities) and the position is disclosed on the taxpayer's return. The AICPA currently has not updated SSTS No. 1 to conform to the tax practitioner standards in IRC Sec. 6694, but we expect that it is only a matter of time before it does.

Example 2-6

Did Bill and Mercedes' CPA meet her professional standards as provided by SSTS No. 1?

Answer: Yes. Based on *J.R. Huntsman v. Comm.*, it is safe to conclude that there is a one-third or greater probability that the current points deduction will be sustained upon judicial review. Specifically, Bill and Mercedes' facts are very similar to those in *J.R. Huntsman v. Comm.*, and subsequent courts have interpreted the phrase "in connection with" consistently with *J.R. Huntsman v. Comm.*

Circular 230, issued by the IRS, provides regulations governing tax practice and applies to all persons practicing before the IRS. There are three parts of Circular 230: Subpart A describes who may practice before the IRS (CPAs, attorneys, enrolled agents) and what practicing before the IRS means (tax return preparation, representing clients before the IRS, and so on).[12] Subpart B describes the duties and restrictions that apply to individuals governed by Circular 230. Included in Subpart B are provisions discussing the submission of records to the IRS, guidelines when a practitioner

---

[11]The "more likely than not" standard, defined as a greater than 50 percent chance of a position being sustained on its merits, applies to tax shelters and other reportable transactions specified by the IRS.

[12]Similar to attorneys and CPAs, enrolled agents can represent taxpayers before the IRS. To become an enrolled agent, you must have either worked for the IRS for five years or pass a comprehensive examination.

EXHIBIT 2-10 **Summary of the AICPA Statements on Standards for Tax Services**

SSTS No 1: Tax Return Positions

A tax professional may recommend a tax return position when she has a good-faith belief that the position has a realistic possibility of being sustained if challenged. A tax professional may also recommend a tax return position if the position is *not frivolous*—not patently improper—and is *adequately disclosed* on the tax return.

SSTS No. 2: Answers to Questions on Returns

A tax professional should make a reasonable effort to obtain from the taxpayer the information necessary to answer all questions on a tax return.

SSTS No. 3: Certain Procedural Aspects of Preparing Returns

In preparing or signing a tax return, a tax professional may rely without verification on information that a taxpayer or a third party has provided, unless the information appears to be incorrect, incomplete, or inconsistent.

SSTS No. 4: Use of Estimates

Unless prohibited by statute or rule, a tax professional may use taxpayer estimates in preparing a tax return if it is impractical to obtain exact data and if the estimated amounts appear reasonable based on the facts and circumstances known by the professional.

SSTS No. 5: Departure from a Position Previously Concluded in an Administrative Proceeding or Court Decision

A tax professional may sign a tax return that contains a departure from a position previously concluded in an administrative or court proceeding if the tax professional adheres to the standards of SSTS No. 1. This rule does not apply if the taxpayer is bound to a specific tax treatment in the later year, such as by a formal closing agreement with the IRS.

SSTS No. 6: Knowledge of Error: Return Preparation

A tax professional must advise the taxpayer promptly when she learns of an error in a previously filed tax return or the taxpayer's failure to file a required return. The tax professional should include a recommendation for appropriate measures the taxpayer should take. The professional is not obligated to inform the IRS of the error, nor may she do so without the taxpayer's permission, except when required by law.

SSTS No. 7: Knowledge of Error: Administrative Proceedings

When a tax professional represents a taxpayer in an administrative proceeding, such as an audit, and the professional is aware of an error on the tax return involved in the proceeding, the tax professional should notify the taxpayer promptly, advise the taxpayer on corrective action, and request the taxpayer's agreement to disclose the error to the IRS. If the taxpayer refuses to disclose the error to the IRS, the professional may consider terminating the professional relationship with the taxpayer. The professional is not obligated to inform the IRS of the error, nor may she do so without the taxpayer's permission, except when required by law.

SSTS No. 8: Form and Content of Advice to Taxpayers

In providing advice to taxpayers, tax professionals must use judgment that reflects professional competence and serves the taxpayer's needs. The professional should ensure that the standards under SSTS No. 1 are satisfied for all advice rendered. The professional is not obligated to communicate with a taxpayer when subsequent events affect advice previously provided except when implementing plans associated with the advice provided or when the professional is obligated to do so by specific agreement.

> **THE KEY FACTS**
>
> **Tax Professional Responsibilities**
>
> - Tax practitioners are subject to a variety of statutes, rules, and codes of professional conduct.
>
> - The AICPA's eight Statements on Standards for Tax Services (SSTS) recommend appropriate standards of practice for tax professionals.
>   · Many state boards of accountancy have adopted similar standards to the SSTS standards.
>
> - Circular 230 provides regulations governing tax practice and applies to all persons practicing before the IRS.
>   · There is a good bit of overlap between Circular 230 and the AICPA SSTS.

discovers a tax return error, restrictions on charging contingency fees, prohibition of sharing employment with someone suspended from practicing before the IRS, stringent rules relating to providing advice for tax shelters, and standards for when a practitioner can recommend a tax return position. Subpart C explains disciplinary proceedings for practitioners violating the Circular 230 provisions. There is a good bit of overlap between Circular 230 and the AICPA SSTS. Indeed, Circular 230's current standard for when a practitioner can recommend a tax return position is virtually identical to the current AICPA SSTS No. 1. We anticipate, however, that the

EXHIBIT 2-11 Civil Penalties Imposed for Tax Violations

Taxpayers		Tax Practitioners	
Failure to file a tax return.	5% of tax due per month.	Failure to provide a copy of the tax return to a taxpayer.	$50 per violation.
Failure to pay tax owed.	5% of tax due per month. Reduces the failure to file a tax return penalty, if applicable. Maximum failure to file and failure to pay tax penalty is 5% of tax due per month.	Failure to sign a tax return.	$50 per violation.
Failure to make estimated payments.	Penalty varies with federal short-term interest rate and underpayment.	Failure to include the tax practitioner's ID number on the tax return.	$50 per violation.
Substantial understatement of tax.	20% of understatement.	Failure to keep a listing of taxpayers or tax returns.	$50 per violation.
Providing false withholding information.	$500.	Failure to keep a listing of employees.	$50 per violation.
Fraud.	75% of liability attributable to fraud.	Understatement due to unreasonable position.	Greater of $1,000 or 50% of income derived from preparing the taxpayer's tax return.
		Willful understatement of tax.	Greater of $5,000 or 50% of income derived from preparing the taxpayer's tax return.
		Organizing, promoting, etc. an abusive tax shelter.	Lesser of $1,000 or 100% of gross income derived from tax shelter. If activity is based on fraudulent statements, the penalty equals 50% of gross income derived from tax shelter.
		Aiding and abetting the understatement of a tax liability.	$1,000.

IRS will revise the tax return position standards in Circular 230 to conform to the new standards in IRC Sec. 6694.

TAXPAYER AND TAX PRACTITIONER PENALTIES

L07

In addition to motivating good behavior via tax professional standards, the IRS can impose both criminal and civil penalties to encourage tax compliance by both tax professionals and taxpayers. **Civil penalties** are much more common, generally come in the form of monetary penalties, and may be imposed when tax practitioners or taxpayers violate tax statutes without reasonable cause—say, as the result of negligence, intentional disregard of pertinent rules, willful disobedience, or outright fraud. Some common examples of civil penalties are listed in Exhibit 2-11.

Criminal penalties are much less common than civil penalties, although they have been used to incarcerate some of the most notorious criminals. (Notorious mobster Al Capone was convicted and put in prison for tax evasion.) They are commonly

THE KEY FACTS

Taxpayer and Tax Practitioner Penalties

■ The IRS can impose both criminal and civil penalties to encourage tax compliance by both tax professionals and taxpayers.

(continued)

charged in tax evasion cases, which include willful intent to defraud the government, but are imposed only after normal due process, including a trial. Compared to civil cases, the standard of conviction is higher in a criminal trial; guilt must be proven beyond a reasonable doubt (versus a "clear and convincing evidence" standard for civil tax fraud). However, the penalties are also much higher, such as fines up to $100,000 for individuals plus a prison sentence.

Assuming the IRS assesses additional tax upon audit, will the taxpayer always be subject to penalty? No. While the taxpayer will have to pay interest on the underpayment, he or she will *not* be subject to an underpayment penalty *if there is* substantial authority *that supports the tax return position*.[13] As previously discussed, substantial authority suggests the probability that the taxpayer's position is sustained upon audit or litigation is in the 40 plus percent range or above.

Example 2-7	
(concluded)	What is Bill and Mercedes' exposure to penalties in their IRS audit?
▪ The standard of conviction is higher in a criminal trial, but the penalties are also much higher.	**Answer:** None. Why? Because "substantial tax authority" supports their tax return position and the disputed tax liability is relatively small (the tax savings on a $3,000 tax deduction), Bill and Mercedes have no penalty exposure. Nonetheless, Bill and Mercedes will owe interest on the disputed tax liability unless the IRS recants its position in the audit or appeals process (or if the case is litigated and Bill and Mercedes win).
▪ A taxpayer will not be subject to an underpayment penalty if there is substantial authority that supports the tax return position.	
▪ A tax practitioner will also not be subject to penalty for recommending a tax return position if there is substantial authority that supports the position.	

As we explained in Example 2-6, Bill and Mercedes' CPA met her professional standards (as defined currently in SSTS No. 1) by recommending a tax return position that has a realistic possibility (one-third or greater probability) of being sustained upon judicial review. Likewise, because "substantial tax authority" supports the tax return position, Bill and Mercedes' CPA should also not have penalty exposure under IRC Sec. 6694.

Taxes in the Real World   *Even the Largest Tax Return Preparers Can't Escape Scrutiny*

In spring of 2007, the federal government investigated Jackson Hewitt, the nation's second largest tax return preparer, on charges that certain franchisees helped their customers file fraudulent tax returns to get bigger refunds. The government alleges a wide range of fraudulent actions, such as filing returns claiming re- funds based on phony wage forms and using fabricated businesses and business expenses on returns to claim bogus deductions. The IRS estimates that the fraud resulted in more than $70 million in combined losses to the Treasury. Upon news of the charges, Jackson Hewitt's stock price fell 18 percent.

CONCLUSION

Now that we have a full understanding of the issue under audit for Bill and Mercedes, what is their likely outcome? Another good question. The IRS has stated that it will continue to disallow a current deduction for points incurred for refinanced mortgages. Nonetheless, the courts appear to follow *J.R. Huntsman v. Comm.,* and

---

[13]The taxpayer can also avoid penalty if the tax return position has at least a reasonable basis (i.e., supported by one or more tax authorities) and the position is disclosed on the taxpayer's return.

therefore, the IRS stands a strong possibility of losing this case if litigated. In an IRS appeals conference, the appeals officer may consider the hazards of litigation. Accordingly, Bill and Mercedes have a good likelihood of a favorable resolution at the appeals conference.

In this chapter we discussed several of the fundamentals of tax practice and procedure: taxpayer filing requirements, the statute of limitations, the IRS audit process, the primary tax authorities, tax research, tax professional standards, and taxpayer and tax practitioner penalties. For the tax accountant, these fundamentals form the basis for much of her work. Likewise, tax research forms the basis of much of a tax professional's compliance and planning services. Even for the accountant who doesn't specialize in tax accounting, gaining a basic understanding of tax practice and procedure is important, as assisting clients with the IRS audit process is a valued service that accountants provide, and clients expect all accountants to understand basic tax procedure issues and how to research basic tax issues.

SUMMARY

Identify the filing requirements for income tax returns and the statute of limitations for assessment.   **LO1**

- All corporations must file a tax return annually regardless of their taxable income. Estates and trusts are required to file annual income tax returns if their gross income exceeds $600. The filing requirements for individual taxpayers depend on the taxpayer's filing status, age, and gross income.

- Individual and partnership tax returns are due on the fifteenth day of the fourth month following year-end. For corporations, tax returns must be filed by the fifteenth day of the third month following the corporation's fiscal year end. Any taxpayer unable to file a tax return by the original due date can request an extension to file.

- For both amended tax returns filed by a taxpayer and proposed tax assessments by the IRS, the statute of limitations generally ends three years from the *later* of (1) the date the tax return was actually filed or (2) the tax return's original due date.

Outline the IRS audit process, how returns are selected, the different types of audits, and what happens after the audit.   **LO2**

- The IRS uses a number of computer programs and outside data sources to identify tax returns that may have an understated tax liability. Common computer initiatives include the DIF (Discriminant Function) system, document perfection program, and information matching program.

- The three types of IRS audits consist of correspondence, office, and field examinations.

- After the audit, the IRS will send the taxpayer a 30-day letter, which provides the taxpayer the opportunity to pay the proposed assessment or request an appeals conference. If an agreement is not reached at appeals or the taxpayer does not pay the proposed assessment, the IRS will send the taxpayer a 90-day letter. At this time, the taxpayer may pay the tax or petition the U.S. Tax Court to hear the case. If the taxpayer chooses to pay the tax, the taxpayer may then request a refund of the tax and eventually sue the IRS for a refund in the U.S. District Court or the U.S. Court of Federal Claims.

Evaluate the relative weights of the various tax law sources.   **LO3**

- Primary authorities are official sources of the tax law generated by the legislative branch (statutory authority issued by Congress), judicial branch (rulings by the U.S. District Court, U.S. Tax Court, U.S. Court of Federal Claims, U.S. Circuit Court of Appeals, or U.S. Supreme Court), or executive/administrative branch (Treasury and IRS pronouncements).

Exhibit 2-4 in the chapter displays the most common primary sources and their relative authoritative weight. Secondary authorities are unofficial tax authorities that interpret and explain the primary authorities.

LO4   Describe the legislative process as it pertains to taxation.

- Exhibit 2-7 illustrates the legislative process for enacting tax law changes. Bills proceed from the House Ways and Means Committee to the House of Representatives. If approved, the act is sent to the Senate Finance Committee with a revised version then sent to the U.S. Senate. If approved, the Joint Conference Committee considers the acts passed by the House of Representative and Senate. If a compromise is reached, the revised act is sent to the House of Representatives, if approved then to the Senate, and if approved then to the president. If signed by the president, the act is incorporated into the IRC of 1986. If the president vetoes the legislation, Congress may override the veto with a two-thirds positive vote in both the House of Representatives and Senate.

LO5   Perform the basic steps in tax research and evaluate various tax law sources when faced with ambiguous statutes.

- The five basic steps in tax research are (1) understand the facts, (2) identify issues, (3) locate relevant authorities, (4) analyze the tax authorities, and (5) communicate research results.
- When the researcher identifies that different authorities have conflicting views, she should evaluate the "hierarchy," jurisdiction, and age of the authorities, placing more weight on higher and newer authorities that have jurisdiction over the taxpayer.

LO6   Describe tax professional responsibilities in providing tax advice.

- Tax practitioners are subject to a variety of statutes, rules, and codes of professional conduct. Some examples include the American Institute of CPAs (AICPA) Code of Professional Conduct, the AICPA Statements on Standards for Tax Services (SSTS), the IRS's Circular 230, and statutes enacted by a CPA's specific state board of accountancy.
- The AICPA's Statements on Standards for Tax Services (SSTS) recommend appropriate standards of practice for tax professionals. Many state boards of accountancy have adopted similar standards, thus making the SSTS especially important. Currently, there are eight SSTS summarized in Exhibit 2-10 that describe the tax professional standards.
- Circular 230 provides regulations governing tax practice and applies to all persons practicing before the IRS. There is a good bit of overlap between Circular 230 and the AICPA SSTS.

LO7   Identify taxpayer and tax professional penalties.

- The IRS can impose both criminal and civil penalties to encourage tax compliance by both tax professionals and taxpayers. Civil penalties are much more common, generally come in the form of monetary penalties, and may be imposed when tax practitioners or taxpayers violate tax statutes without reasonable cause. Some common examples of civil penalties are listed in Exhibit 2-11.
- Criminal penalties are much less common than civil penalties and are commonly charged in tax evasion cases. Compared to civil cases, the standard of conviction is higher in a criminal trial, but the penalties are also much higher.
- A taxpayer will not be subject to an underpayment penalty if there is substantial authority that supports the tax return position.
- A tax practitioner will also not be subject to penalty for recommending a tax return position if there is substantial authority that supports the position.

KEY TERMS

30-day letter (2-6)
90-day letter (2-6)
acquiescence (2-17)
action on decision (2-17)
annotated tax service (2-18)
Circular 230 (2-23)
citator (2-20)
civil penalties (2-25)
correspondence examination (2-5)
criminal penalties (2-25)
determination letters (2-16)
DIF (Discriminant Function) system (2-4)
document perfection program (2-4)
field examination (2-6)
final regulations (2-15)
Golsen rule (2-15)

information matching program (2-4)
Internal Revenue Code of 1986 (2-11)
interpretative regulations (2-16)
legislative regulations (2-15)
nonacquiescence (2-17)
office examination (2-6)
primary authority (2-9)
private letter rulings (2-16)
procedural regulations (2-16)
proposed regulations (2-16)
question of fact (2-19)
question of law (2-20)
realistic possibility (2-23)
regulations (2-15)
revenue procedures (2-16)
revenue rulings (2-16)
secondary authority (2-10)

stare decisis (2-15)
Statements on Standards for Tax Services (SSTS) (2-23)
statute of limitations (2-3)
substantial authority (2-23)
tax treaties (2-13)
technical advice memorandum (2-16)
temporary regulations (2-15)
topical tax service (2-19)
U.S. Circuit Courts of Appeal (2-7)
U.S. Constitution (2-11)
U.S. Court of Federal Claims (2-6)
U.S. District Court (2-6)
U.S. Supreme Court (2-8)
U.S. Tax Court (2-6)
writ of certiorari (2-8)

DISCUSSION QUESTIONS

1. **(LO1)** Name three factors that determine whether a taxpayer is required to file a tax return.

2. **(LO1)** Benita is concerned that she will not be able to complete her tax return by April 15. Can she request an extension to file her return? By what date must she do so? Assuming she requests an extension, what is the latest date that she could file her return this year without penalty?

3. **(LO1)** Agua Linda, Inc., is a calendar-year corporation. What is the original due date for the corporate tax return? What happens if the original due date falls on a Saturday?

4. **(LO2)** Approximately what percentage of tax returns does the IRS audit? What are the implications of this number for the IRS's strategy in selecting returns for audit?

5. **(LO2)** Explain the difference between the DIF system and the National Research Program? How do they relate to each other?

6. **(LO2)** Describe the differences between the three types of audits in terms of their scope and taxpayer type.

7. **(LO2)** Simon just received a 30-day letter from the IRS indicating a proposed assessment. Does he have to pay the additional tax? What are his options?

8. **(LO2)** Compare and contrast the three trial-level courts.

9. **(LO3)** Compare and contrast the three types of tax law sources and give examples of each.

10. **(LO3)** The U.S. Constitution is the highest tax authority but provides very little in the way of tax laws. What are the next highest tax authorities beneath the U.S. Constitution?

11. **(LO3)** Jackie has just opened her copy of the Code for the first time. She looks at the table of contents and wonders why it is organized the way it is. She questions whether it makes sense to try and understand the Code's organization.

What are some reasons why understanding the organization of the Internal Revenue Code may prove useful?

12. **(LO3)** Laura Li, a U.S. resident, works for three months this summer in Hong Kong. What type of tax authority may be especially useful in determining the tax consequences of her foreign income?

13. **(LO3)** What are the basic differences between regulations, revenue rulings, and private letter rulings?

14. **(LO3)** Under what circumstance would the IRS issue an acquiescence? a non-acquiescence? An action on decision?

15. **(LO3)** Carlos has located a regulation that appears to answer his tax research question. He is concerned because the regulation is a temporary regulation. Evaluate the authoritative weight of this type of regulation. Should he feel more or less confident in his answer if the regulation was a proposed regulation?

16. **(LO3)** Tyrone recently read a regulation that Congress specifically requested the IRS to issue. What type of regulation is this? How does this regulation's authoritative weight compare to other regulations?

17. **(LO3)** In researching a tax question, you find only one authority (a trial-level court opinion) that is directly on point. Which court would you least prefer to have heard this case and why?

18. **(LO3)** What is *stare decisis* and how does it relate to the Golsen rule?

19. **(LO3)** Mason was shocked to learn that the current Code is the Internal Revenue Code of 1986. He thought that U.S. tax laws change more frequently. What is wrong with Mason's perception?

20. **(LO4)** Describe in general the process by which new tax legislation is enacted.

21. **(LO4)** What are the three committees that debate proposed tax legislation? What documents do these committees generate, and how might they be used?

22. **(LO4)** The president recently vetoed a tax act passed by the House and Senate. Is the tax act dead? If not, what will it take for the act to be passed?

23. **(LO5)** What are the five basic parts of an internal research memo?

24. **(LO5)** What is the difference between primary and secondary authorities? Explain the role of each authority type in conducting tax research.

25. **(LO5)** Jorge is puzzled that the IRS and his CPA could legitimately reach different conclusions on a tax issue. Why does this happen?

26. **(LO5)** What is the difference between open and closed facts? How is this distinction important in conducting tax research?

27. **(LO5)** In writing a research memo, what types of facts should be included in the memo?

28. **(LO5)** Amber is a tax expert, whereas Rob is a tax novice. Explain how their process in identifying tax issues may differ.

29. **(LO5)** Discuss the basic differences between annotated and topical tax services. How are these services used in tax research?

30. **(LO5)** In constructing a keyword search, what should the keyword search include?

31. **(LO5)** Lindley has become very frustrated in researching a tax issue using keyword searches. What suggestions can you give her?

32. **(LO5)** Nola, a tax novice, has a fairly simple tax question. Besides tax services, what are some sources that she can use to answer her question?

33. **(LO5)** Armando identifies a tax research question as being a question of fact. What types of authorities should he attempt to locate in his research?

34. **(LO5)** How are citators used in tax research?

35. **(LO5)** What is the general rule for how many authorities a research memo should discuss?

36. **(LO6)** Identify some of the sources for tax professional standards. What are the potential ramifications of failing to comply with these standards?

37. **(LO6)** Levi is recommending a tax return position to his client. What standard must he meet to satisfy his professional standards? What is the source of this professional standard?

38. **(LO6)** What is Circular 230?

39. **(LO7)** What are the basic differences between civil and criminal tax penalties?

40. **(LO7)** What are some of the most common civil penalties imposed on taxpayers?

41. **(LO7)** What are the taxpayer's standards to avoid the substantial understatement of tax penalty?

42. **(LO7)** What are the tax practitioner's standards to avoid a penalty for recommending a tax return position?

PROBLEMS

43. **(LO1)** Ahmed does not have enough cash on hand to pay his taxes. He was excited to hear that he can request an extension to file his tax return. Does this solve his problem? What are the ramifications if he doesn't pay his tax liability by April 15?

44. **(LO1)** Molto Stancha Corporation had zero earnings this fiscal year; in fact, they lost money. Must they file a tax return?

45. **(LO1)** The estate of Monique Chablis earned $450 of income this year. Is the estate required to file an income tax return?

46. **(LO1)** Jamarcus, a full-time student, earned $2,500 this year from a summer job. He had no other income this year and will have zero federal income tax liability this year. His employer withheld $300 of federal income tax from his summer pay. Is Jamarcus required to file a tax return? Should Jamarcus file a tax return?

47. **(LO1)** Shane has never filed a tax return despite earning excessive sums of money as a gambler. When does the statute of limitations expire for the years in which Shane has not filed a tax return?

48. **(LO1)** Latoya filed her tax return on February 10 this year. When will the statute of limitations expire for this tax return?

49. **(LO1)** Using the facts from the previous problem, how would your answer change if Latoya understated her income by 40 percent? How would your answer change if Latoya intentionally failed to report as taxable income any cash payments she received from her clients?

50. **(LO2)** Paula could not reach an agreement with the IRS at her appeals conference and has just received a 90-day letter. If she wants to litigate the issue but does not have sufficient cash to pay the proposed deficiency, what is her best court choice?

51. **(LO2)** In choosing a trial-level court, how should a court's previous rulings influence the choice? How should circuit court rulings influence the taxpayer's choice of a trial-level court?

52. **(LO2)** Sophia recently won a tax case litigated in the 7th Circuit. She recently heard that the Supreme Court denied the *writ of certiorari*. Should she be happy or not, and why?

53. **(LO2)** Campbell's tax return was audited because she failed to report interest she earned on her tax return. What IRS audit selection method identified her tax return?

54. **(LO2)** Yong's tax return was audited because he calculated his tax liability incorrectly. What IRS audit procedure identified his tax return for audit?

55. **(LO2)** Randy deducted a high level of itemized deductions two years ago relative to his income level. He recently received an IRS notice requesting documentation for his itemized deductions. What audit procedure likely identified his tax return for audit?

planning   56. **(LO2)** Jackie has a corporate client that has recently received a 30 day notice from the IRS with a $100,000 tax assessment. Her client is considering requesting an appeals conference to contest the assessment. What factors should Jackie advise her client to consider before requesting an appeals conference?

planning   57. **(LO2)** The IRS recently completed an audit of Shea's tax return and assessed $15,000 additional tax. Shea requested an appeals conference but was unable to settle the case at the conference. She is contemplating which trial court to choose to hear her case. Provide her a recommendation based on the following alternative facts:

a. Shea resides in the 2nd Circuit, and the 2nd Circuit has recently ruled against the position Shea is litigating.

b. The Federal Circuit Court of Appeals has recently ruled in favor of Shea's position.

c. The issue being litigated involves a question of fact. Shea has a very appealing story to tell but little favorable case law to support her position.

d. The issue being litigated is highly technical, and Shea believes strongly in her interpretation of the law.

e. Shea is a local elected official and would prefer to minimize any local publicity regarding the case.

58. **(LO3)** Juanita, a Texas resident (5th Circuit), is researching a tax question and finds a 5th Circuit case ruling that is favorable and a 9th Circuit case that is unfavorable. Which circuit case has more "authoritative weight" and why? How would your answer change if Juanita were a Kentucky resident (6th Circuit)?

59. **(LO3)** Faith, a resident of Florida (11th Circuit) recently found a circuit court case that is favorable to her research question. Which two circuits would she prefer to have issued the opinion?

60. **(LO3)** Robert has found a "favorable" authority directly on point for his tax question. If the authority is a court case, which court would he prefer to have issued the opinion? Which court would he least prefer to have issued the opinion?

61. **(LO3)** Jamareo has found a "favorable" authority directly on point for his tax question. If the authority is an administrative authority, which specific type of authority would he prefer to answer his question? Which administrative authority would he least prefer to answer his question?

62. **(LO4)** Justine would like to clarify her understanding of a code section recently enacted by Congress. What tax law sources are available to assist Justine?

63. **(LO5)** Aldina has identified conflicting authorities that address her research question. How should she evaluate these authorities to make a conclusion?

64. **(LO5)** Georgette has identified a 1983 court case that appears to answer her research question. What must she do to determine if the case still represents "current" law?

65. **(LO5)** Sandy has determined that her research question depends upon the interpretation of the phrase "not compensated by insurance." What type of research question is this?

research   66. **(LO5)** J. C. has been a professional gambler for many years. He loves this line of work and believes the income is tax-free. Use an available tax research service to determine whether J. C.'s thinking is correct. Is the answer to this question found in the Internal Revenue Code? If not, what type of authority answers this question?

67. **(LO5)** Katie recently won a ceramic dalmatian valued at $800 on a television game show. She questions whether this prize is taxable since it was a "gift" she won on the show. Use an available tax research service to answer Katie's question.

68. **(LO5)** Pierre recently received a tax penalty for failing to file a tax return. He was upset to receive the penalty, but he was comforted by the thought that he will get a tax deduction for paying the penalty. Use an available tax research service to determine if Pierre is correct.

69. **(LO5)** Paris was happy to provide a contribution to her friend Nicole's campaign for mayor, especially after she learned that charitable contributions are tax deductible. Use an available tax service to determine whether Paris can deduct this contribution.

70. **(LO5)** Matt and Lori recently were divorced. Although grief stricken, Matt was at least partially comforted by his monthly receipt of $10,000 alimony. He was particularly excited to learn from his friend, Denzel, that the alimony was not taxable. Use an available tax service to determine if Denzel is correct. Would your answer change if Matt and Lori continued to live together?

71. **(LO5)** Shaun is a huge college football fan. In the past, he has always bought football tickets on the street from ticket scalpers. This year, he decided to join the university's ticket program, which requires a $2,000 contribution to the university for the "right" to purchase tickets. Shaun will then pay $400 per season ticket. Shaun understands that the price paid for the season tickets is not tax deductible as a charitable contribution. However, contributions to a university are typically tax deductible. Use an available tax service to determine how much, if any, of Shaun's $2,000 contribution for the right to purchase tickets is tax deductible.

72. **(LO5)** Latrell recently used his Delta Skymiles to purchase a free roundtrip ticket to Milan, Italy (value $1,200). The frequent flyer miles used to purchase the ticket were generated from Latrell's business travel as a CPA. Latrell's employer paid for his business trips, and he was not taxed on the travel reimbursement. Use an available tax research service to determine how much income, if any, does Latrell have to recognize as a result of purchasing an airline ticket with Skymiles earned from business travel.

73. **(LO6)** Randy has found conflicting authorities that address a research question for one of his clients. The majority of the authorities provide an unfavorable answer for his client. Randy estimates that if the client takes the more favorable position on its tax return that there is approximately a 48 percent chance that the position will be sustained upon audit or judicial proceeding. If the client takes this position on its tax return, will Randy be subject to penalty? Will the client potentially be subject to penalty?

74. **(LO6)** Using the same facts from the previous problem, how would your answer change if Randy estimates that there is only a 20 percent chance that the position will be sustained upon audit or judicial proceeding?

75. **(LO7)** Sasha owes additional tax imposed in a recent audit. In addition to the tax, will she be assessed other amounts? If so, how will these amounts be determined?

76. **(LO7)** Maurice has a client that recently asked him about the odds of the IRS detecting cash transactions not reported on a tax return. What are some of the issues that Maurice should discuss with his client?

chapter

3

Tax Planning Strategies and Related Limitations

Learning Objectives

Upon completing this chapter, you should be able to:

LO 1 Identify the objectives of basic tax planning strategies.

———————————— ■ ————————————

LO 2 Apply the timing strategy and describe its applications and limitations.

———————————— ■ ————————————

LO 3 Apply the concept of present value to tax planning.

———————————— ■ ————————————

LO 4 Apply the strategy of income shifting, provide examples, and describe its limitations.

———————————— ■ ————————————

LO 5 Apply the conversion strategy, provide examples, and describe its limitations.

———————————— ■ ————————————

LO 6 Describe basic judicial doctrines that limit tax planning strategies.

———————————— ■ ————————————

LO 7 Contrast tax avoidance and tax evasion.

While working with their CPA during their audit, Bill and Mercedes decide to inquire about less risky tax planning opportunities. Specifically, they would like to gain a better understanding of how to maximize their after-tax returns without increasing their potential for another audit. (Although it was fun and educational, one audit is enough!) Mercedes is convinced that, as a small-business owner (Lavish Interior Designs, Inc.), she feels she pays more than her fair share of taxes. Likewise, Bill, an avid investor, wonders whether he is missing the mark by not considering taxes in his investment decisions. ∎

Storyline Summary	
Taxpayers:	Bill and Mercedes
Family description:	Bill and Mercedes are married with one daughter, Margaret.
Employment status:	Bill is an economics professor; Mercedes is a small-business owner.
Filing status:	Married, filing jointly
Current situation:	Bill and Mercedes want to engage in less risky tax planning strategies.

Bill and Mercedes have come to the right place. This chapter describes the basic tax planning concepts that form the basis of the simplest to most complex tax planning transactions. In the process we also discuss the judicial doctrines that serve as basic limits on tax planning.

BASIC TAX PLANNING OVERVIEW

LO1

Effective tax planning requires a basic understanding of the roles that taxes and nontax factors play in structuring business, investment, and personal decisions. Although taxes may not be the sole or even the primary determinant of a transaction or its structure, taxes can significantly affect the costs or benefits associated with business, investment, and personal transactions. Thus, the tax implications of competing transactions warrant careful consideration. Likewise, nontax factors, such as the taxpayer's financial goals or legal constraints, are an integral part of every transaction.

In general terms, effective tax planning maximizes the taxpayer's after-tax wealth while achieving the taxpayer's nontax goals. Maximizing after-tax wealth is not necessarily the same as minimizing taxes. Specifically, maximizing after-tax wealth requires us to consider both the tax and nontax costs and benefits of alternative transactions, whereas tax minimization focuses solely on a single cost—taxes. Indeed, if the goal of tax planning were simply to minimize taxes, the simplest way to achieve it would be to earn no income at all. Obviously, this strategy has potential limitations—most notably, the unattractive nontax consequence of poverty. Thus, it is necessary to consider the nontax ramifications of any planning strategy.

Virtually every transaction includes three parties: the taxpayer, the other transacting party, and the uninvited silent party that specifies the tax consequences of the transaction—the government. Astute tax planning requires an understanding of the tax and nontax costs from the taxpayer's *and* the other party's perspective. For example, as discussed in Chapter 12, it would be impossible for an employer to develop an effective compensation plan without considering the tax and nontax costs associated with different compensation arrangements from both the employer's and the employees' perspectives. With sound tax planning, the employer can design a compensation package that generates value for employees while reducing costs for the employer. (One way to achieve this goal is through the use of nontaxable fringe benefits, such as health insurance, which are deductible by the employer but not taxable income to employees.) Throughout the text, we highlight situations where this multilateral approach to tax planning is especially important.

In this chapter we discuss three basic tax planning strategies that represent the building blocks of tax planning:

1. *Timing* (deferring or accelerating taxable income and tax deductions**)**.
2. *Income shifting* (shifting income from high to low tax rate taxpayers).
3. *Conversion* (converting income from high to low tax rate activities).

> ### THE KEY FACTS
> **The Basics of Tax Planning**
>
> ■ Effective tax planning maximizes the taxpayer's after-tax wealth while achieving the taxpayer's nontax goals.
>
> ■ Virtually every transaction includes three parties: the taxpayer, the other transacting party, and the uninvited silent party that specifies the tax consequences of the transaction—the government.
>
> ■ Astute tax planning requires an understanding of the tax and nontax costs from the taxpayer's *and* the other party's perspectives.

TIMING STRATEGIES

LO2 **LO3** **LO6**

One of the cornerstones of basic tax planning is the idea of *timing. When* income is taxed or an expense is deducted affects the associated "real" tax costs or savings. This is true for two reasons. First, the time that income is taxed or an expense is deducted affects the *present value* of the taxes paid on income or the tax savings on deductions. Second, the tax costs of income and tax savings income vary as *tax rates* change. The tax costs on income are higher when tax rates are higher and lower when tax rates are lower. Likewise, the tax savings on deductions are higher when tax rates are higher and lower when tax rates are lower. Let's look at the effects of present value and tax rates on the timing strategy.

Present Value of Money

The concept of **present value**—also known as the time value of money—basically states that $1 today is worth *more* than $1 in the future. Is this true or is this some type of new math?

It's true. Assuming an investor can earn a positive after-tax rate of return such as 5 percent, $1 invested today should be worth $1.05 in one year.[1] Specifically

$$\text{Future Value} = \text{Present Value} \times (1 + r)^n$$
$$= \$1 \times (1 + .05)^1 = \$1.05$$

Eq. 3-1

where $1 is the present value, r is the after-tax rate of return (5 percent), and n is the investment period (1 year). Hence, $1 today is equivalent to $1.05 in one year. The implication of the time value of money for tax planning is that the timing of a cash inflow or a cash outflow affects the present value of the income or expense.

Example 3-1

Bill is given the choice of receiving a $1,000 nontaxable gift today or a $1,000 nontaxable gift in one year. Which would Bill prefer? Assume Bill could invest $1,000 today and earn an 8 percent return after taxes in one year. If he receives the gift today, how much would the $1,000 be worth in one year?

Answer: The $1,000 gift today would be worth $1,080 in one year and thus, Bill should prefer to receive the gift today. Specifically,

$$\text{Future Value} = \text{Present Value} \times (1 + r)^n$$
$$= \$1,000 \times (1 + .08)^1 = \$1,080$$

In terms of *future value,* the choice in the above example of receiving either $1,000 today or $1,000 in one year simplifies to a choice of $1,080 or $1,000. For even the least materialistic individual, choosing $1,080—that is, $1,000 *today*— should be straightforward.

Often tax planners find it useful to consider sums not in terms of future value, but rather in terms of present value. How would we restate the choice in Example 3-1 in terms of present value? Obviously, the present value of receiving $1,000 today is $1,000, but what is the *present value* of $1,000 received in one year? The answer depends on the **discount rate,** which we derive from the taxpayer's expected after-tax rate of return. The discount rate is a very useful factor for calculating the present value of future inflows or outflows of cash. We can derive the discount rate for a given rate of return simply by rearranging the future value equation (Eq. 3-1) from above:

$$\text{Present Value} = \text{Future Value}/(1 + r)^n$$
$$= \$1/(1 + .08)^1 = \$0.926$$

Eq. 3-2

$$\text{Therefore, the discount rate} = 0.926$$

THE KEY FACTS

Present Value of Money

■ The concept of present value—also known as the time value of money—states that $1 today is worth *more* than $1 in the future.

■ The implication of the time value of money for tax planning is that the timing of a cash inflow or a cash outflow affects the present value of the income or expense.

■ When considering cash inflows, higher present values are preferred; when considering cash outflows, lower present values are preferred.

■ Present Value = Future Value/$(1 + r)^n$.

---

[1]Assuming a constant marginal tax rate (tr), after-tax rate of return (r) may be calculated as follows. $r = R \times (1 - tr)$, where R is the taxpayer's before-tax rate of return.

EXHIBIT 3-1   Present Value of a Single Payment at Various Annual Rates of Return

Year	4%	5%	6%	7%	8%	9%	10%	11%	12%
1	.962	.952	.943	.935	.926	.917	.909	.901	.893
2	.925	.907	.890	.873	.857	.842	.826	.812	.797
3	.889	.864	.840	.816	.794	.772	.751	.731	.712
4	.855	.823	.792	.763	.735	.708	.683	.659	.636
5	.822	.784	.747	.713	.681	.650	.621	.593	.564
6	.790	.746	.705	.666	.630	.596	.564	.535	.507
7	.760	.711	.665	.623	.583	.547	.513	.482	.452
8	.731	.677	.627	.582	.540	.502	.467	.434	.404
9	.703	.645	.592	.544	.500	.460	.424	.391	.361
10	.676	.614	.558	.508	.463	.422	.386	.352	.322
11	.650	.585	.527	.475	.429	.388	.350	.317	.287
12	.625	.557	.497	.444	.397	.356	.319	.286	.257
13	.601	.530	.469	.415	.368	.326	.290	.258	.229
14	.577	.505	.442	.388	.340	.299	.263	.232	.205
15	.555	.481	.417	.362	.315	.275	.239	.209	.183

Applying the discount rate, we can see that $1,000 received in one year is worth $926 in today's dollars. Thus, in terms of present value, Bill's choice in Example 3-1 simplifies to a choice between a cash inflow of $1,000 today and a cash inflow worth $926 today. Again, choosing $1,000 is pretty straight-forward.

Exhibit 3-1 provides the discount rates for a lump sum (single payment) received in *n* periods using various rates of return. Tax planners frequently utilize such tables for quick reference in calculating present value for sums under consideration.

Example 3-2

At a recent holiday sale, Bill and Mercedes purchased $1,000 worth of furniture with "no money down and no payments for one year!" How much money is this deal really worth? (Assume their after-tax rate of return on investments is 10 percent.)

Answer: The discount rate of .909 (Exhibit 3-1, 10% Rate of Return column, Year 1 row) means the present value of $1,000 is $909 ($1,000 × .909 = $909)—so Bill and Mercedes save $91 ($1,000 − $909 = $91).

While Example 3-1 considers a $1,000 cash inflow, Example 3-2 addresses a $1,000 cash *outflow.* In terms of present value, a choice between $1,000 paid today and $1,000 paid in a year simplifies to incurring a cash outflow of either $1,000 (by paying today) or $909 (by paying in one year). Most people would prefer to pay $909. Indeed, financial planners always keep the following general rule of thumb in mind: When considering *cash inflows, prefer higher present values;* when considering *cash outflows, prefer lower present values.*

The Timing Strategy When Tax Rates Are Constant

In terms of tax planning, remember that *taxes paid* represent cash *outflows,* while *tax savings* generated from tax deductions are cash *inflows*. This perspective leads us to two basic tax-related timing strategies when tax rates are constant (not changing):

1. Accelerate tax deductions (deduct in an earlier period).
2. Defer recognizing taxable income (recognize in a later period).

Accelerating tax deductions to an earlier period increases the present value of the tax savings from the deduction. That is, tax savings received now have a higher present value than the same amount received a year from now.

Deferring income to a later period decreases the present value of the tax cost of the income. That is, taxes paid a year from now have a lower present value than taxes paid today. These two strategies are summarized in Exhibit 3-2.

EXHIBIT 3-2   The Timing Tax Strategy When Tax Rates Are Constant

Item	Recommendation	Why?
Tax deductions	Accelerate tax deductions into earlier years.	Maximizes the present value of tax savings from deductions.
Taxable income	Defer taxable income into later tax years.	Minimizes the present value of taxes paid.

Example 3-3

Mercedes, a calendar-year taxpayer, uses the cash method of accounting for her small business.[2] On December 28, she receives a $10,000 bill from her accountant for consulting services related to her small business. She can avoid late payment charges by paying the $10,000 bill before January 10 of next year. Let's assume that Mercedes' marginal tax rate is 30 percent *this year and next* and that she can earn an after-tax rate of return of 10 percent on her investments. When should she pay the $10,000 bill—this year or next?

Answer: If Mercedes pays the bill this year, she will receive a tax deduction on this year's tax return.[3] If she pays the bill in January, she will receive a tax deduction on next year's tax return (one year later). She needs to compare the after-tax cost of the accounting service using the present value of the tax savings for each scenario:

Description	Option 1: Pay $10,000 bill *this year*	Option 2: Pay $10,000 bill *next year*
Present Value Comparison		
Tax deduction	$10,000	$10,000
Marginal tax rate	× 30%	× 30%
Tax savings	$ 3,000	$ 3,000
Present value factor	× 1	× .909
Present value tax savings	$ 3,000	$ 2,727
After-tax cost of accounting services:		
Before tax cost	$10,000	$10,000
Less: Present value tax savings	−$ 3,000	−$ 2,727
After-tax cost of accounting services	$ 7,000	$ 7,273

Since Mercedes would surely rather spend $7,000 than $7,273 for accounting services, paying the bill in December is the clear winner.

---

[2]In Chapter 8, we discuss the basic accounting methods (e.g., cash vs. the accrual method), which influence the timing of when income and deductions are recognized for tax purposes.

[3]Accelerating her payment from January 10 to December 31 will increase the present value of the $10,000 cash outflow by 10 days. Thus, there is a minor present value cost associated with accelerating her payment.

In terms of accelerating deductions, the intent of the timing strategy is to accelerate the tax deduction significantly *without* accelerating the actual cash outflow that generates the expense. Indeed, if we assume a marginal rate of 30 percent and an after-tax return of 8 percent, accelerating a $1,000 cash outflow by one year to realize $300 in tax savings actually *increases* the after-tax *cost* of the expense from $648.20 to $700.

	Present Value Comparison	
Description	**Present value of net cash outflow *today***	**Present value of net cash outflow in *one year***
Cash outflow	$1,000	$ 1,000
Less: Tax savings (outflow × 30% tax rate)	– $ 300	– $ 300
Net cash outflow	$ 700	$ 700
Present value factor	× 1	× .926
Present value of net cash outflow today	$ 700	$648.20

Generally speaking, whenever a taxpayer can accelerate a deduction without also accelerating the cash outflow, the timing strategy will be more beneficial.

Is the accelerating deductions strategy utilized in the real world? Yes. While the strategy is particularly effective for cash-method taxpayers who can often control the year in which they pay their expenses, all taxpayers have *some* latitude in timing deductions. Common examples of the timing strategy include accelerating depreciation deductions for depreciable assets, using LIFO instead of FIFO for inventory, and accelerating the deduction of certain prepaid expenses.[4] For large corporations, the benefits associated with this timing strategy can be quite substantial. Thus, tax planners spend considerable time evaluating the proper period in which to recognize expenses and identifying opportunities to accelerate deductions.

Are there certain taxpayer or transaction attributes that enhance the advantages of accelerating deductions? Absolutely. Higher tax rates, higher rates of return, larger transaction amounts, and the ability to accelerate deductions by two or more years all increase the benefits of accelerating deductions. To demonstrate this for yourself, simply rework Example 3-3 and substitute any of the following: 50 percent tax rate, 12 percent after-tax rate of return, $100,000 expense, or a five-year period difference in the timing of the expense deduction. The benefits of accelerating deductions become much more prominent with these changes.

Deferring income recognition is an equally beneficial timing strategy, especially when the taxpayer can defer the recognition of income significantly without deferring the actual receipt of income very much. Consider the following example.

Example 3-4

In early December, Bill decides he would like to sell $100,000 of his Dell Inc. stock, which cost $20,000 10 years ago. Assume Bill's tax rate on the $80,000 gain will be 15 percent and his typical after-tax rate of return on investments is 7 percent. What effect would deferring the sale to January have on Bill's after-tax income on the sale?

(*continued on page 3-7...*)

---

[4]See the discussion of accounting methods in Chapter 8.

Answer:

Description	Option 1: Sell the $100,000 stock in *December*[5]	Option 2: Sell the $100,000 stock in *January*[6]
Sales price	$100,000	$100,000
Less: Cost of stock	− $ 20,000	− $ 20,000
Gain on sale	$ 80,000	$ 80,000
Marginal tax rate	× 15%	× 15%
Tax on gain	$ 12,000	$ 12,000
Present value factor	× 1	× .935
Present value tax cost	$ 12,000	$ 11,220
After-tax income from sale:		
Before tax income	$100,000	$100,000
Less: Present value tax cost	− $ 12,000	− $ 11,220
After-tax income from sale	$ 88,000	$ 88,780

Present Value Comparison

Bill would doubtlessly prefer to earn $88,780 to $88,000, so from a tax perspective, selling the Dell Inc. stock in January is preferable.

Income deferral represents an important aspect of investment planning (Chapter 11), retirement planning (Chapter 13), and certain property transactions (Chapter 10). Income-related timing considerations also affect tax planning for everyday business operations, such as determining the appropriate period in which to recognize sales income (upon product shipment, on delivery, or on customer acceptance).

Taxes in the Real World   *The Timing Strategy and the Daimler-Chrysler Merger*

Although the two firms have since broken apart again, the 1998 Daimler–Chrysler merger provides a good example of the importance of the timing strategy for major business transactions. By structuring the acquisition as a stock-for-stock tax-free exchange, Chrysler allowed investors to defer paying tax on their gains from the acquisition, thereby reducing the present value of the tax to them. To ensure the acquisition qualified as a tax-free exchange, Chrysler requested a private letter ruling from the IRS regarding the tax ramifications of the proposed acquisition. The following excerpts from the Daimler–Chrysler Merger Prospectus (Form F-4, filed August 6, 1998, pages 47–48) describe the role of taxes in the merger discussions.

> During the course of these discussions and thereafter [referring to discussions between Daimler and Chrysler representatives the week of February 17, 1998, and thereafter], representatives of Chrysler stated that it was important to Chrysler that any potential transaction maximize value for its shareholders, that it be tax-free to Chrysler's U.S. stockholders and tax efficient for DaimlerChrysler AG, . . .

(continued on page 3-8...)

---

[5]This will require Bill to pay the tax on the gain no later than April 15 of the following year (i.e., three months after the sale). If Bill and Mercedes' current-year withholding and estimated payments do not equal or exceed 110 percent of their previous year's tax liability, they will have to make an estimated payment by January 15 to avoid the failure to make estimated tax payment penalty discussed later in Chapter 7. This example assumes that Bill and Mercedes can avoid the underpayment of estimated tax penalty discussed in Chapter 7 by paying 110 percent of their previous year's tax liability in both options 1 and 2. Thus, they can defer paying the tax on the gain until April 15 of the year following the sale.

[6]This will require Bill to pay the tax on the gain no later than April 15 of the following year (i.e., 15 months after the sale).

> Representatives of Daimler-Benz indicated that it was important to Daimler-Benz that any potential transaction maximize value for its stockholders, that it be tax-free to Daimler-Benz' German stockholders and tax efficient for DaimlerChrysler AG and . . .
>
> The prospectus later describes discussions on April 7 and 9 and states: "Major points of discussion during that period and thereafter involved: . . . (c) finding a structure that would (i) result in a tax-free transaction in the United States and Germany for both companies' stockholders and result in ongoing tax efficiency . . ."

Do certain taxpayer or transaction attributes enhance the advantages of deferring income? Yes. The list is very similar to that for accelerating deductions: Higher tax rates, higher rates of return, larger transaction amounts, and the ability to defer revenue recognition for longer periods of time increase the benefits of deferral. To demonstrate this for yourself, simply rework Example 3-4 using any of the following: 50 percent tax rate, 12 percent after-tax rate of return on investments, or $200,000 gain.[7]

The Timing Strategy When Tax Rates Change

When tax rates change, the timing strategy requires a little more consideration because the tax costs of income and the tax savings from deductions will now vary. The higher the tax rate, the higher the tax savings for a tax deduction. The lower the tax rate, the lower the tax costs for taxable income. *All things being equal, taxpayers should prefer to recognize deductions during high-tax-rate years and income during low-tax-rate years.* The implication is that before a taxpayer implements the timing strategies suggested above (accelerate deductions, defer income), she should consider whether her tax rates are likely to change. In fact, as we discuss below, increasing tax rates may even suggest the taxpayer should *accelerate* income and *defer* deductions.

What would cause a taxpayer's marginal tax rate to change? The taxpayer's taxable income can change, perhaps due to changing jobs, retiring, or starting a new business. Indeed, in Chapter 1, we demonstrated how a taxpayer's marginal tax rate changes as income or deductions change. Marginal tax rates can also change because of tax legislation. We discussed the tax legislative process in Chapter 2 and noted that Congress frequently enacts tax legislation, because lawmakers use taxes to raise revenue, stimulate the economy, and so on. In the last 25 years, Congress has changed the maximum statutory tax rates that apply to ordinary income, such as wages and business income, or capital gains, such as gains from the sale of stock, for individual taxpayers no fewer than nine times (see Exhibit 3-3).

Let's take a look at how changing tax rates affect the timing strategy recommendations. Exhibit 3-4 presents recommendations when tax rates are increasing. The taxpayer must actually calculate the optimal tax strategies for deductions and income when tax rates are increasing. Specifically, because accelerating deductions causes them to be recognized in a *lower*-tax-rate year, the taxpayer must calculate whether the benefit of accelerating the deduction outweighs the disadvantage. Likewise, because deferring income causes income to be recognized in a *higher*-tax-rate year, the taxpayer must calculate whether the benefit of deferring it outweighs the disadvantage.

---

[7]In Example 3-4, increasing the deferral period (e.g., from one to five years) also increases the benefits of tax deferral but requires additional assumptions regarding the expected five-year return of the Dell Inc. stock (assuming he does not sell the stock for five years) and his new investment (assuming he sells the Dell Inc. stock and immediately reinvests the after-tax proceeds).

THE KEY FACTS

The Timing Strategy

- The timing of when income is taxed or an expense is deducted affects the *present value* of the taxes paid on income or tax savings on deductions.

- The tax costs of income and tax savings of deductions vary as *tax rates* change.

- When tax rates are constant, tax planners prefer to defer income and accelerate deductions.

- When tax rates are increasing, the taxpayer must calculate the optimal tax strategies for deductions and income.

- When tax rates are decreasing, taxpayers should accelerate tax deductions into earlier years and defer taxable income to later years.

EXHIBIT 3-3   **Historical Maximum Ordinary and Capital Gains Tax Rates for Individuals Since 1982**

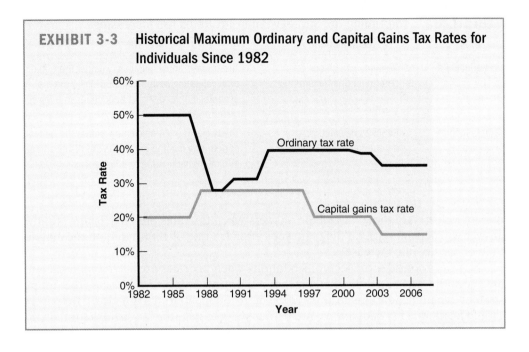

Example 3-5

Having decided she needs new equipment for her business, Mercedes is now considering whether to make the purchase and claim a corresponding $10,000 deduction at year-end or next year. Mercedes anticipates that, with the new machinery, her business income will rise such that her marginal rate will increase from 20 percent this year to 28 percent next year. Assuming her after-tax rate of return is 8 percent, what should Mercedes do?

Answer: Given rising tax rates, Mercedes must calculate the after-tax cost of the equipment for *both* options and compare present values.

	Present Value Comparison	
Description	**Option 1: Pay $10,000 bill *this year***	**Option 2: Pay $10,000 bill *next year***
Tax deduction	$10,000	$10,000
Marginal tax rate	× 20%	× 28%
Tax savings	$ 2,000	$ 2,800
Present value factor	× 1	× .926
Present value tax savings	$ 2,000	$ 2,593
After-tax cost of equipment:		
Before tax cost	$10,000	$10,000
Less: Present value tax savings	–$ 2,000	–$ 2,593
After-tax cost of equipment	$ 8,000	$ 7,407

Paying the $10,000 in January is the clear winner.

In the above example, if the choice were either to recognize $10,000 of *income* this year or next, the *amounts* would be exactly the same but the conclusion would be different, and Mercedes would prefer to receive $8,000 of after-tax income this year instead of $7,407. (Remember, when considering cash *inflows,* we prefer the *higher*

EXHIBIT 3-4 **The Timing Tax Strategy When Tax Rates Are *Increasing***

Item	Recommendation	Why?
Tax deductions	Requires calculation to determine optimal strategy.	The taxpayer must calculate whether the benefit of accelerating deductions outweighs the disadvantage of recognizing deductions in a *lower*-tax-rate year.
Taxable income	Requires calculation to determine optimal strategy.	The taxpayer must calculate whether the benefit of deferring income outweighs the disadvantage of recognizing income in a *higher*-tax-rate year.

present value.) Are these always the answers when tax rates are increasing? No, the answer will depend both on the taxpayer's after-tax rate of return and on the magnitude of the tax rate increase.

Now let's consider the recommendations when tax rates are *decreasing*—a common scenario when an individual reaches retirement. Exhibit 3-5 presents the timing strategy recommendations in this case. The recommendations are clear. Taxpayers should accelerate tax deductions into earlier years to reap the tax savings from *accelerating* deductions to *higher*-tax-rate years. Likewise, taxpayers should defer taxable income to later years to enjoy the tax benefits of *deferring* taxable income to *lower*-tax-rate years.

EXHIBIT 3-5 **The Timing Tax Strategy When Tax Rates Are *Decreasing***

Item	Recommendation	Why?
Tax deductions	Accelerate tax deductions into earlier years.	Maximizes the present value of tax savings from deductions due to the acceleration of the deductions into *earlier* years with a *higher*-tax-rate year.
Taxable income	Defer taxable income into later tax years.	Minimizes the present value of taxes paid due to the deferral of the income to later years with a *lower* tax rate.

THE KEY FACTS

Limitation on the Timing Strategy

■ Timing strategies contain several inherent limitations.

■ Whenever a taxpayer is unable to accelerate a deduction without also accelerating the cash outflow, the timing strategy will be less beneficial.

■ Tax law generally requires taxpayers to continue their investment in an asset in order to defer income recognition for tax purposes.

■ A deferral strategy may not be optimal if the taxpayer has severe cash flow needs, if continuing the investment would generate a low rate of return compared to other investments, if the current investment would subject the taxpayer to unnecessary risk, and so on.

■ The constructive receipt doctrine, which provides that a taxpayer must recognize income when it is actually *or* constructively received, also restricts income deferral for cash-basis taxpayers.

Limitations to Timing Strategies   Timing strategies contain certain inherent limitations. First, tax laws generally require taxpayers to continue their investment in an asset in order to defer income recognition for tax purposes. In other words, deferral is generally not an option if a taxpayer has "cashed out" of an investment.[8] For example, Bill could not sell his Dell stock in December and then choose not to recognize the income until January. A deferral strategy may not be optimal (1) if the taxpayer has severe cash flow needs, (2) if continuing the investment would generate a low rate of return compared to other investments, or (3) if the current investment would subject the taxpayer to unnecessary risk. For example, the risk that the value of Bill's investment in Dell Inc. will decline from December to January in Example 3-4 may lead Bill to forego deferring his stock sale until January. Again, the astute taxpayer considers both the tax *and* nontax ramifications of deferring income.

A second limitation results from the **constructive receipt doctrine,** which also restricts income deferral for cash-basis taxpayers.[9] Unlike accrual-method taxpayers,

[8]See the discussions of like-kind exchanges in Chapter 10, investment planning in Chapter 11, and retirement planning in Chapter 13.

[9]Later in this chapter we discuss other judicial doctrines that apply to all planning strategies.

cash-method taxpayers report income for tax purposes when the income is *received,* whether it is in the form of cash, property, or services.[10] The cash method affords taxpayers some leeway in determining when to recognize income because such taxpayers can control when they bill their clients. However, the constructive receipt doctrine provides that a taxpayer must recognize income when it is actually *or* constructively received. Constructive receipt is deemed to have occurred if the income has been credited to the taxpayer's account or if the income is unconditionally available to the taxpayer, the taxpayer is aware of the income's availability, and there are no restrictions on the taxpayer's control over the income.

Example 3-6

Mercedes' brother-in-law, Carlos, works for King Acura, which recently instituted a bonus plan that pays year-end bonuses each December to employees rated above average for their customer service. Carlos is expecting a $10,000 bonus this year that will be paid on December 31. Thinking he'd prefer to defer this income until next year, Carlos plans to take a vacation on December 30 so that he will not receive his bonus check until January. Will Carlos's strategy work?

Answer: No, the constructive receipt doctrine applies here. Because Carlos's check was unconditionally available to him on December 31, he was aware of its availability, and there were no restrictions on his control over the income on that date, Carlos must report the income in the current year.

What could taxpayers do to avoid Carlos's problem in the future? They could request that their employer institute a company policy of paying bonuses on January 1, which would allow all employees to report the bonus income in that year. However, if the employer is a cash-method taxpayer, this creates a potential conflict with its employees.[11] Such an employer would most likely prefer to deduct the bonus in the current year, which requires the bonuses to be paid in December. This conflict would not exist if the employer were an accrual-method taxpayer, because paying the bonuses in January would not affect its ability to deduct the bonuses in the previous year.[12]

INCOME-SHIFTING STRATEGIES

LO4 LO6

We've seen that the value of a tax deduction, or the tax cost of income, varies with the marginal tax rate. We've also seen that tax rates can vary across time, which leads to basic tax planning strategies regarding when to recognize deductions and income. Tax rates can also vary across *taxpayers* or *jurisdictions* (states, countries), which leads to still other tax planning strategies—for example, shifting income from high-tax-rate taxpayers to low-tax-rate taxpayers or shifting deductions from low-tax-rate taxpayers to high-tax-rate taxpayers.

---

[10]As we discuss in depth in Chapter 8, accrual-basis taxpayers report income when it is earned. In general, income is deemed earned when all events have occurred that fix the taxpayer's right to the income and the income can be estimated with reasonable accuracy. Thus, income recognition for accrual-basis taxpayers generally is not tied to payment. Receipt of prepaid income by accrual-basis taxpayers may trigger income recognition in certain circumstances. The constructive receipt doctrine may apply in these situations.

[11]Because King Acura carries inventory, the cash method is not allowed for transactions related to its inventory (e.g., cost of goods sold, sales, etc.). However, King Acura is permitted to use the cash method for other transactions. This mixed method is referred to the "hybrid" method of accounting.

[12]When an employee/shareholder and an employer/corporation are related (i.e., the employee/shareholder owns more than 50 percent of the value of the employer corporation), the corporation is not allowed to deduct the compensation expense until the employee/shareholder includes the payment in income. §267(a)(2).

The type of taxpayers who benefit most from this strategy are (1) related parties, such as family members or businesses and their owners, who have varying marginal tax rates and are willing to shift income for the benefit of the group; and (2) taxpayers operating in multiple jurisdictions with different marginal tax rates. In any case, tax planners should seek only legitimate methods of shifting income that will withstand IRS scrutiny. In the following section we discuss transactions between family members, followed by a discussion of transactions between owners and their businesses, and finally a discussion of income shifting across jurisdictions.

Transactions between Family Members and Limitations

One of the most common examples of income shifting is high-tax-rate parents shifting income to low-tax-rate children. For example, Bill and Mercedes have a 30 percent marginal tax rate, whereas their daughter, Margaret, has a 10 percent marginal tax rate. Assuming their marginal tax rates remain constant with relatively modest changes in income, every $1 of income that Bill and Mercedes shift to Margaret reduces the family's tax liability by 20 cents [$1 × (30% − 10%)]. Thus, if Bill and Mercedes shift $10,000 of taxable income to Margaret, the family's after-tax income will increase by $2,000. Can taxpayers legally do this? Yes and no. As you might expect, there are limitations on this type of income shifting.

The **assignment of income doctrine** requires income to be taxed to the taxpayer who actually earns it.[13] Merely attributing your paycheck or dividend to another taxpayer does not transfer the tax liability associated with the income. The assignment of income doctrine implies that, in order to shift income to a taxpayer, that taxpayer must actually earn the income. For example, if Mercedes would like to shift some of her business income to Margaret, Margaret must actually earn it. One way to accomplish this would be for Mercedes to employ Margaret in her business and pay her a $10,000 salary. The effects of this transaction are to decrease Mercedes' taxable income by $10,000 because of tax-deductible salary expense, and increase Margaret's income by the $10,000 taxable salary. What if Margaret is paid $10,000 to answer Mercedes' business phone one Saturday afternoon every month? Does this seem reasonable? Not likely. The IRS frowns upon this type of aggressive strategy.

Indeed, the IRS closely scrutinizes such **related-party transactions**—that is, financial activities among family members (also among owners and their businesses, or among businesses owned by the same owners). Unlike **arm's-length transactions**, where each transacting party negotiates for his or her own benefit, related-party transactions involve taxpayers who are much more willing to negotiate for their own common good to the detriment of the IRS. For example, would Mercedes pay an unrelated party $10,000 to answer the phone once a month? Doubtful.[14]

Are there other ways to shift income to children? For example, could Bill shift some of his investment income to Margaret? Yes, but there's a catch. The assignment of income applies what is referred to as the "fruit and the tree" analogy (*Lucas v. Earl* (S. Ct., 1930), 8 AFTR 10287). For the owner to avoid being taxed on the fruit from the tree (the income), the owner must transfer the tree. Thus, to shift investment income, Bill would also have to transfer ownership in the underlying investment assets to Margaret.[15] Is there a problem with this requirement? Not for Margaret. However, Bill would likely prefer to maintain his wealth. The nontax disadvantages

---

[13]Later in this chapter we discuss other judicial doctrines that apply to all planning strategies.

[14]The Internal Revenue Code also contains specific provisions to curtail benefits from related-party transactions. For example, as we discuss in Chapter 10, §267 disallows a tax deduction for losses on sales to related parties (even if the sale was consummated at the asset's fair market value).

[15]Further, as we discuss in Chapter 7, the "kiddie tax" may apply when parents shift too much investment income to children. The kiddie tax restricts the amount of a child's investment income that can be taxed at the child's (lower) tax rate instead of the parents' (higher) tax rate.

of transferring wealth to implement the income-shifting strategy often outweigh the tax benefits of the transfer. For example, most parents either could not afford to or would have serious reservations about transferring significant wealth to their children—a prime example of how nontax costs may override tax considerations.

Transactions between Owners and Their Businesses and Limitations

Income shifting is not limited to transactions within a family unit. One of the most common examples occurs between owners and their businesses. Let's consider Mercedes' interior design business. Currently, Mercedes operates her business as a sole proprietorship. A sole proprietorship (unlike a taxable corporation) is not a separate reporting entity, and thus, Mercedes reports her business income and deductions on her individual tax return. Shifting income to or from her sole proprietorship offers little benefit, because all of her sole proprietorship income is reported on her tax return regardless of whether it is attributed to her personally or to her business. On the other hand, if Mercedes operated her interior design business as a taxable corporation, shifting income to or from the taxable corporation may make good financial sense because the corporation would be a separate entity with tax rates distinct from Mercedes' individual tax rate. Shifting income to herself may allow Mercedes to decrease the tax on her business profits, thereby increasing her after-tax income. Example 3-7 illustrates the savings obtainable from this strategy.

In order to shift income from the corporation to the owner, the corporation must create a tax deduction for itself in the process. Compensation paid to employee–owners is the most common method of shifting income from corporations to their owners. Compensation expense is deductible by the corporation and is generally taxable to the employee. (See Chapter 12 for a broader discussion of nontaxable compensation benefits.) Having the business owner rent property to the corporation or loan money to the corporation are also effective income-shifting methods, because both transactions generate tax deductions for the corporation and income for the shareholder. Because corporations don't get a tax deduction for dividends paid, paying dividends is *not* an effective way to shift income. Having a business pay dividends actually results in "double taxation"—the profits generating the dividends are taxed first at the corporate level, and then at the shareholder level. Recommending this tax planning strategy may not be a good way to keep your job as a tax consultant.

Example 3-7

Mercedes is considering incorporating her interior design business. She projects $200,000 of business profit next year. Excluding this profit, Bill and Mercedes expect $140,000 of taxable income next year. If Mercedes would like to minimize her current-year tax liability, should she incorporate her business? [Use the married filing jointly and corporate tax rates inside the front cover of the book to answer this question.]

Answer: If Mercedes does not incorporate her business, the first $68,850 of her business profits will be taxed at 28 percent (from $140,000 to $208,850 of taxable income, the marginal tax rate is 28 percent). The remaining $131,150 (from $208,850 to $340,000 of taxable income) would be taxed at 33 percent. Upon reviewing the above corporate tax rate schedule, you should note that the first two corporate tax rates (15 percent and 25 percent) are lower than Bill and Mercedes' current marginal tax rate of 33 percent. Thus, there appears to be some opportunity for Mercedes to reduce her current year tax exposure by incorporating her business.[16]

---

[16]Note that this is a simplified discussion of one of many tax issues associated with incorporating a business.

After a taxpayer identifies the opportunity and appropriate method to shift income (compensation paid to a related party), he or she can easily determine the optimal amount to shift depending on the taxpayers' marginal tax rates.

Example 3-8	

Assuming Mercedes' goal is to minimize her current year federal income tax liability, how much of the $200,000 business income should her corporation report?

Answer: It should report $75,000. Comparing the two tax rate schedules reveals how to calculate this number.

Step 1: Would Mercedes rather have income taxed at 15 percent (the corporation's marginal tax rate from zero to $50,000 taxable income) or 28 percent (Bill and Mercedes' marginal tax rate before recognizing any profit from Mercedes' business)? 15 percent is the obvious answer. To take advantage of the 15 percent corporate tax bracket, Mercedes should retain $50,000 of the expected $200,000 in profits in the corporation, because $50,000 is the width of the 15 percent corporate tax bracket.

Step 2: Assuming the corporation reports $50,000 of income, its marginal tax rate will now be 25 percent, and thus Mercedes' choice is to have income taxed at 25 percent (the corporation's marginal tax rate) or at 28 percent (Bill and Mercedes' marginal tax rate before recognizing any profit from Mercedes' business). Twenty-five percent is the clear answer. To take advantage of the 25 percent corporate tax bracket, the corporation should retain another $25,000 of the expected $200,000 in profits. ($25,000 is the width of the 25 percent corporate tax bracket.) The corporation's marginal tax rate will now be 34 percent.

Step 3: Continuing this same decision process, Mercedes should shift the remaining $125,000 of profits ($68,850 taxed at 28 percent and $56,150 taxed at 33 percent) to herself and Bill—via a salary paid to Mercedes—because their marginal tax rates (28 percent and 33 percent) will be lower than the corporation's marginal tax rate (34 percent).

How much current federal income tax does this strategy save Bill and Mercedes? The corporation's and Bill and Mercedes' combined federal income tax liability will be $79,021 ($13,750 for the corporation plus $65,271 for Bill and Mercedes) compared to $90,021 for Bill and Mercedes if the business is operated as a sole proprietorship. Thus, they will save $11,000.[17]

Are there nontax disadvantages of the income-shifting-via-incorporating strategy? Yes. For example, one nontax disadvantage for Mercedes is that her new corporation now has $61,250 of her after-tax profits ($75,000 profits less $13,750 of corporate tax). If Mercedes has personal cash flow needs that require use of the $61,250, this is not a viable strategy. Indeed, it's advantageous only if the business owner intends to reinvest the business profits into the business. Furthermore, any subsequent transactions between Mercedes and the corporation would clearly be related-party transactions. Thus, Mercedes should be prepared for IRS scrutiny.[18] If the salary, rent, and other costs are deemed to be unreasonable, the IRS may reclassify any excess payments above the value of services and property provided as nondeductible corporate dividends. In this scenario, the corporation and Mercedes would both pay income tax on each dollar of deemed dividend payment. This is not a good outcome for Mercedes or any business owner.

[17]This strategy will result in the eventual double taxation of the income retained in Mercedes' corporation. Specifically, Mercedes will eventually have to pay tax on the income retained by the corporation, either in the form of taxable dividends from the corporation or a taxable gain when she sells or liquidates the corporation. The present value of this additional layer of tax reduces the tax savings from this strategy. The longer that the second layer of tax is deferred, the more advantageous this strategy will be. This calculation is beyond the scope of this chapter.

[18]The taxpayer should maintain documentation for related-party transactions (e.g., notes for related-party loans and contemporaneous documentation of reasonable compensation paid to related parties).

Example 3-9

Upon reviewing Bill and Mercedes' tax return, the IRS reclassifies $65,000 of Mercedes's $125,000 salary in Example 3-8 as a dividend. What are the tax consequences of this reclassification?

Answer: (1) The corporation's taxable income will increase from $75,000 to $140,000 because dividends are not deductible, thereby increasing the corporation's tax liability from $13,750 to $37,850; and (2) Bill and Mercedes' taxable income will remain the same, except $65,000 of their $265,000 of taxable income will be dividends taxed at a preferential 15 percent tax rate. Thus, Bill and Mercedes will have $200,000 of taxable income taxed at their ordinary tax rates ($44,263.50 of tax) and $65,000 of dividend income taxed at 15 percent ($9,750 of tax), resulting in a tax liability of $54,013,50.

Under this scenario, the combined tax liabilities of the corporation and Bill and Mercedes will be $91,863.50, which is $1,842.50 *higher* than Bill and Mercedes' $90,021 tax liability had they not incorporated Mercedes' business.[19]

As the above examples illustrate, tax-avoiding strategies can be quite beneficial, but they also entail some financial risks if the structure fails to pass muster with the IRS.

Income Shifting across Jurisdictions and Limitations

Taxpayers that operate in multiple jurisdictions (states, countries) also apply the income-shifting strategy. Specifically, income earned in different jurisdictions—whether in the United States or abroad, and for state income tax purposes, income earned in different states—is often taxed very differently. With a proper understanding of the differences in tax laws across jurisdictions, taxpayers can use these differences to maximize their after-tax wealth.

Example 3-10

Carlos's employer, King Acura, has two locations. Its main location is in South Dakota (a state with no corporate tax), with a secondary location in North Dakota (maximum corporate state tax rate of 7 percent). What tax planning strategy may save money for King Acura?

Answer: The most obvious strategy is to shift income from the North Dakota location to the South Dakota location, thereby reducing King Acura's state income tax liability by seven cents for every dollar of income shifted.[20]

A number of possibilities exist to execute a strategy such as King Acura's in Example 3-10. Assuming that the North Dakota and South Dakota locations exchange cars, the firm could shift income via *transfer pricing* (using the price the South Dakota location charges the North Dakota location for cars transferred to North Dakota). Likewise, if the South Dakota location (the corporate headquarters) provides a legitimate support function for the North Dakota location, the firm should allocate a portion of the overhead and administrative expenses from the South Dakota location to the North Dakota location.

---

[19]Chapter 12 discusses the consequences of unreasonable compensation to employee–owners.

[20]Because state taxes are deductible for federal tax purposes, every dollar of state taxes reduced with this strategy will increase King Acura's federal income tax liability by its federal marginal tax rate (e.g., 35 percent). Thus, the net tax savings for every dollar of income shifted from North Dakota to South Dakota will be 4.55 percent, which equals the state tax savings (7 percent) less the federal tax increase resulting from the lost state tax deduction (7 percent × 35 percent).

What are some of the limitations of income shifting across jurisdictions? First, taxing authorities are fully aware of the tax benefits of strategically structuring transactions across tax borders (across countries or states). Thus, the IRS closely examines transfer pricing on international transactions. Similarly, state tax authorities scrutinize interstate transactions between related taxpayers. Second, when taxpayers locate in low-tax-rate jurisdictions to, in effect, shift income to a tax-advantaged jurisdiction, they may bear *implicit* taxes (that is, additional costs attributable to the jurisdiction's tax advantage). For example, the demand for workers, services, or property in low-tax-rate jurisdictions, whether a foreign country or a low-tax state, may increase the nontax costs associated with operating a business there enough to offset the tax advantages. Finally, negative publicity from moving operations (and jobs) from the United States to a lower-tax jurisdiction may more than offset any tax benefits associated with these strategies.

Taxes in the Real World   *Corporate Inversions and Income Shifting*

In the ultimate income-shifting strategy, several high-profile U.S. companies—including Cooper Industries, Fruit of the Loom, Helen of Troy, and Ingersoll-Rand—executed corporate "inversions" in the 1990s and early 2000s to escape U.S. taxation of foreign income. In a corporate inversion, a U.S. company becomes a subsidiary of a foreign company organized in a tax haven (a low-tax jurisdiction). The end result is that the former U.S. company avoids U.S. taxation on its foreign income.

Cooper Industries estimated that its corporate inversion saved the company (and cost the U.S. government) approximately $55 million in U.S. taxes per year. Not surprisingly, corporate inversions were not well received by Congress and the IRS. Congress acted swiftly to eliminate the tax benefits of these transactions.

The public also reacted very negatively to corporate inversions, which may have deterred other companies from utilizing this strategy. Indeed, Stanley Works abandoned its planned corporate inversion (expected to generate annual tax savings of $30 million) after heavy public and political pressure.

CONVERSION STRATEGIES

We've now seen how tax rates can vary across time and taxpayers. They can also vary across different *activities*. For example, ordinary income such as salary, interest income, and business income received by individual taxpayers is taxed at their ordinary marginal tax rates, whereas long-term capital gains, which are gains from the sale of investment assets held longer than one year, and dividends are taxed at lower tax rates (currently a maximum of 15 percent), and still other forms of income like nontaxable compensation benefits and municipal bond interest are tax-exempt. Expenses from different types of activities may also be treated very differently for tax purposes. Business expenses are generally fully tax deductible, whereas tax deductions for investment expenses may be limited, and tax deductions for personal expenses may be completely disallowed. In sum, the tax law does not treat all types of income or deductions the same. This understanding forms the basis for the conversion strategy—recasting income and expenses to receive the most favorable tax treatment.

To implement the conversion strategy, the taxpayer must be aware of the underlying differences in tax treatment across various types of income, expenses, and activities and have some ability to alter the nature of the income or expense to receive the more advantageous tax treatment. What are some common examples of the conversion strategy? In Chapter 11, we consider investment planning and the advantages of investing in assets that generate preferentially taxed income. In Chapter 8, we explain the basic differences between business and investment activities and what characteristics result in the more favorable "business" designation for expense deductions.

In Chapters 12 and 13, we discuss compensation planning and the benefits of restructuring employee compensation from currently taxable compensation to nontaxable or tax-deferred forms of compensation, such as employer-provided health insurance and retirement contributions.

To analyze the benefits of the conversion strategy, you often compare the after-tax returns of alternative investments. Given a stationary marginal tax rate, you can calculate an investment's after-tax rate of return as follows:

$$\text{After-Tax Return} = \text{Before-Tax Return} - (\text{Before-Tax Return} \times \text{Marginal Tax Rate}) \qquad \textbf{Eq. 3-3}$$

which simplifies to:

$$\text{After-Tax Return} = \text{Before-Tax Return} \times (1 - \text{Marginal Tax Rate}) \qquad \textbf{Eq. 3-4}$$

> (concluded)
> ■ The Internal Revenue Code contains specific provisions that prevent the taxpayer from changing the nature of expenses, income, or activities to a more tax-advantaged status.
> ■ Implicit taxes may also reduce or eliminate the advantages of conversion strategies.

Example 3-11

Bill is contemplating three different investments, each with the same amount of risk:

1. A high-dividend stock that pays 8 percent dividends annually but has no appreciation potential.
2. Taxable corporate bonds that pay 9 percent interest annually.
3. Tax-exempt municipal bonds that pay 6 percent interest annually.

Assuming that dividends are taxed at 15 percent and that Bill's marginal tax rate on ordinary income is 30 percent, which investment should Bill choose?

Answer: To answer this question, we must compute Bill's after-tax rate of return for each investment. The after-tax returns for the 3 investments are:

Investment Choice	Computation	After-Tax Return
High-dividend stock	8% × (1 − 15%) =	6.8%
Corporate bond	9% × (1 − 30%) =	6.3%
Municipal bond	6% × (1 − 0%) =	6.0%

Accordingly, Bill should choose the dividend-yielding stock.

What marginal tax rate on ordinary income would make Bill indifferent between the dividend-yielding stock and the corporate bond?

Answer: The dividend-yielding stock has an after-tax rate return of 6.8 percent. For Bill to be indifferent between this stock and the corporate bond, the corporate bond would need a 6.8 percent after-tax rate of return. We can use Eq. 3-4 above to solve for the marginal tax rate.

$$\text{After-Tax Return} = \text{Pre-Tax Return} \times (1 - \text{Marginal Tax Rate})$$
$$6.8\% = 9\% \times (1 - \text{Marginal Tax Rate})$$
$$\text{Marginal Tax Rate} = 24.44\%$$

Let's check this answer: After-Tax Return = 9% × (1 − 24.44%) = 6.8%

Limitations of Conversion Strategies

Like other tax planning strategies, conversion strategies face potential limitations. The Code itself also contains several specific provisions that prevent the taxpayer from changing the nature of expenses, income, or activities to a more

LO6

tax-advantaged status, including (among many others) the depreciation recapture rules discussed in Chapter 10 and the luxury auto depreciation rules discussed in Chapter 9. In addition, as discussed in Chapter 1, implicit taxes may reduce or eliminate the advantages of tax-preferred investments (such as municipal bonds or any investment taxed at preferential tax rates) by decreasing their before-tax rate of returns. Thus, implicit taxes may reduce the advantages of the conversion strategy.

ADDITIONAL LIMITATIONS TO TAX PLANNING STRATEGIES: JUDICIAL DOCTRINES

The IRS also has several other doctrines at its disposal for situations where it expects taxpayer abuse. These doctrines apply across a wide variety of transactions and planning strategies (timing, income shifting, and conversion). The **business purpose doctrine,** for instance, allows the IRS to challenge and disallow business expenses for transactions with no underlying business motivation, such as the travel cost of a spouse accompanying a taxpayer on a business trip. The **step-transaction doctrine** allows the IRS to collapse a series of related transactions into one transaction to determine the tax consequences of the transaction. Finally, the **substance-over-form doctrine** allows the IRS to consider the transaction's substance regardless of its form, and where appropriate, to reclassify the transaction according to its substance. In Chapter 2, we noted that the Internal Revenue Code is the ultimate tax authority. The business purpose, step-transaction, and substance-over-form doctrines allow the IRS to determine the tax consequences of transactions that follow only the form of the Internal Revenue Code and not the spirit.

You can often assess whether the business purpose, step-transaction, or substance-over-form doctrines apply by using the "smell test": If the transaction "smells bad," one of these doctrines likely applies. (Transactions usually smell bad when the primary purpose is to avoid taxes and not to accomplish an independent business objective.) For example, using the substance-over-form doctrine, the IRS would likely reclassify most of the $10,000 paid to Margaret for answering the phone one Saturday afternoon a month as a gift from Mercedes to Margaret (see the earlier discussion of income shifting and transactions between family members), even though the transaction was structured as compensation and Margaret did do some work for her mother. This recharacterization would unwind the income-shifting benefits for the amount considered to be a gift, as gifts to family members are not tax deductible. In sum, the *substance* of the transaction must be justifiable, not just the form.

LO7

TAX AVOIDANCE VERSUS TAX EVASION

Each of the tax planning strategies discussed in this book falls within the confines of legal **tax avoidance.** Tax avoidance has long been endorsed by the courts and even Congress. For example, remember that Congress specifically encouraged tax avoidance by excluding municipal bond income from taxation, preferentially taxing dividend and capital gain income, and other strategies. Likewise, the courts have often made it quite clear that taxpayers are under no moral obligation to pay more taxes than required by law. As an example, in *Commissioner v. Newman,* 159 F.2d 848 (2 Cir., 1947), which considered a taxpayer's ability to shift income to his children using trusts, Judge Learned Hand included the following statement in his dissenting opinion:

> Over and over again courts have said that there is nothing sinister in so arranging one's affairs as to keep taxes as low as possible. Everybody does so, rich or poor; and all do right, for nobody owes any public duty to pay more than the law demands: taxes are enforced exactions, not voluntary contributions. To demand more in the name of morals is mere cant.

In contrast to tax avoidance, **tax evasion**—that is, the willful attempt to defraud the government—falls outside the confines of legal tax avoidance and thus may land the perpetrator within the confines of a federal prison. (Recall from Chapter 2 that the rewards of tax evasion include stiff monetary penalties and imprisonment.) When does tax avoidance become tax evasion? Very good question. In many cases a clear distinction exists between avoidance (such as not paying tax on municipal bond interest) and evasion (not paying tax on a $1,000,000 game show prize). In other cases, the line is less clear. In these situations, professional judgment, the use of a smell test, and consideration of the business purpose, step-transaction, and substance-over-form doctrines may prove useful.

As you might expect, tax evasion is a major area of concern and focus for the IRS. While the IRS vigorously prosecutes suspected tax evaders, its actions alone have not been able to solve this problem. Is tax evasion a victimless crime? No. Because the federal government must replace lost tax revenues by imposing higher taxes on others, honest taxpayers are the true victims of tax evasion. Currently, the federal government estimates that tax evasion costs the federal government annually more than $200 billion in lost tax revenues. As citizens and residents of the United States, each of us must recognize our obligation to support our country. As future accountants and business professionals, we also must recognize the inherent value of high ethical standards, which call for us to do the right thing in *all* situations. As business professionals have learned over and over, the costs of doing otherwise far exceed any short-term gains.

> **THE KEY FACTS**
>
> Tax Evasion versus Tax Avoidance
>
> ■ Tax avoidance is the legal act of arranging one's transactions to minimize taxes paid.
>
> ■ Tax evasion is the willful attempt to defraud the government by not paying taxes legally owed.
>
> ■ Tax evasion falls outside the confines of legal tax avoidance.

CONCLUSION

In this chapter we discussed three basic tax planning strategies—timing, income shifting, and conversion—and their related limitations. Each of these strategies exploits the variation in taxation across different dimensions. The timing strategy exploits the variation in taxation across time: The "real" tax costs of income decrease as taxation is deferred; the "real" tax savings associated with tax deductions increase as tax deductions are accelerated. However, because tax rates may change over time and the tax costs of income and tax savings of deductions vary with tax rates, tax planning should consider the effects of such changes on the timing strategy. The income-shifting strategy exploits the variation in taxation across taxpayers or jurisdictions. The assignment of income doctrine limits aggressive attempts to shift income across taxpayers. In addition, related-party transactions receive close IRS attention given the increased likelihood of taxpayer abuses in these transactions. Finally, the conversion strategy exploits the variation in taxation rates across activities although implicit taxes may reduce the advantages of this strategy. In addition to limitations specific to each planning strategy, the judicial doctrines of business purpose, step-transaction, and substance-over-form broadly apply to a wide range of transactions and planning strategies.

The timing, income-shifting, and conversion strategies represent the building blocks for the more sophisticated tax strategies that tax professionals employ on a daily basis. Combining an understanding of these basic tax planning strategies with knowledge of our tax law will provide you with the tools necessary to identify, evaluate, and implement tax planning strategies. Throughout the remainder of the text, we will discuss how these strategies can be applied to different transactions.

SUMMARY

LO1 Identify the objectives of basic tax planning strategies.

- Effective tax planning maximizes the taxpayer's after-tax wealth while achieving the taxpayer's nontax goals. Maximizing after-tax wealth is not necessarily the same as tax minimization. Maximizing after-tax wealth requires one to consider both the tax and nontax costs and benefits of alternative transactions, whereas tax minimization focuses solely on a single cost (i.e., taxes).

- Virtually every transaction involves three parties: the taxpayer, the other transacting party, and the uninvited silent party that specifies the tax consequences of the transaction (i.e., the government). Astute tax planning requires an understanding of the tax and nontax costs from the taxpayer's *and* the other party's perspectives.

LO2 Apply the timing strategy and describe its applications and limitations.

- One of the cornerstones of basic tax planning involves the idea of *timing*—that is, *when* income is taxed or an expense is deducted affects the associated "real" tax costs or savings. This is true for two reasons. First, the timing of when income is taxed or an expense is deducted affects the *present value* of the taxes paid on income or tax savings on deductions. Second, the tax costs of income and tax savings income vary as *tax rates* change.

- When tax rates are constant, tax planners prefer to defer income (i.e., to reduce the present value of taxes paid) and accelerate deductions (i.e., to increase the present value of tax savings). Higher tax rates, higher rates of return, larger transaction amounts, and the ability to accelerate deductions or defer income by two or more years increase the benefits of the timing strategy.

- When tax rates change, the timing strategy requires a little more consideration because the tax costs of income and the tax savings from deductions vary as *tax rates* change. When tax rates are increasing, the taxpayer must calculate the optimal tax strategies for deductions and income. When tax rates are decreasing, the recommendations are clear. Taxpayers should accelerate tax deductions into earlier years and defer taxable income to later years.

- Timing strategies contain several inherent limitations. Generally speaking, whenever a taxpayer must accelerate a cash outflow to accelerate a deduction, the timing strategy will be less beneficial. Tax law generally requires taxpayers to continue their investment in an asset in order to defer income recognition for tax purposes. A deferral strategy may not be optimal if the taxpayer has severe cash flow needs, if continuing the investment would generate a low rate of return compared to other investments, if the current investment would subject the taxpayer to unnecessary risk, and so on. The constructive receipt doctrine, which provides that a taxpayer must recognize income when it is actually or constructively received, also restricts income deferral for cash-basis taxpayers.

LO3 Apply the concept of present value to tax planning.

- The concept of present value—also known as the time value of money—basically states that $1 today is worth *more* than $1 in the future. For example, assuming an investor can earn a positive return (e.g., 5 percent after taxes), $1 invested today should be worth $1.05 in one year. Hence, $1 today is equivalent to $1.05 in one year.

- The implication of the time value of money for tax planning is that the timing of a cash inflow or a cash outflow affects the present value of the income or expense.

LO4 Apply the strategy of income shifting, provide examples, and describe its limitations.

- The income-shifting strategy exploits the differences in tax rates across taxpayers or jurisdictions. Three of the most common examples of income shifting are high-tax-rate parents shifting income to low-tax-rate children, businesses shifting income to their owners, and taxpayers shifting income from high-tax jurisdictions to low-tax jurisdictions.

■ The assignment of income doctrine requires income to be taxed to the taxpayer who actually earns the income. In addition, the IRS closely monitors such related-party transactions—that is, financial activities among family members, among owners and their businesses, or among businesses owned by the same owners. Implicit taxes may also limit the benefits of income shifting via locating in tax-advantaged jurisdictions.

Apply the conversion strategy, provide examples, and describe its limitations.   **L05**

■ Tax law does not treat all types of income or deductions the same. This understanding forms the basis for the conversion strategy—recasting income and expenses to receive the most favorable tax treatment. To implement the conversion strategy, one must be aware of the underlying differences in tax treatment across various types of income, expenses, and activities, and have some ability to alter the nature of the income or expense to receive the more advantageous tax treatment.

■ Common examples of the conversion strategy include investment planning to invest in assets that generate preferentially taxed income, compensation planning to restructure employee compensation from currently taxable compensation to nontaxable or tax-deferred forms of compensation, and corporate distribution planning to structure corporate distributions to receive the most advantageous tax treatment.

■ The Internal Revenue Code contains specific provisions that prevent the taxpayer from changing the nature of expenses, income, or activities to a more tax-advantaged status. Implicit taxes may also reduce or eliminate the advantages of conversion strategies.

Describe basic judicial doctrines that limit tax planning strategies.   **L06**

■ The constructive receipt doctrine, which may limit the timing strategy, provides that a tax-payer must recognize income when it is actually *or* constructively received. Constructive receipt is deemed to have occurred if the income has been credited to the taxpayer's account or if the income is unconditionally available to the taxpayer, the taxpayer is aware of the income's availability, and there are no restrictions on the taxpayer's control over the income.

■ The assignment of income doctrine requires income to be taxed to the taxpayer who actually earns the income. The assignment of income doctrine implies that, in order to shift income to a taxpayer, that taxpayer must actually earn the income.

■ The business purpose, step-transaction, and substance-over-form doctrines apply across a wide variety of transactions and planning strategies (timing, income shifting, and conversion).

■ The business purpose doctrine allows the IRS to challenge and disallow business expenses for transactions with no underlying business motivation, such as a travel cost of a spouse accompanying a taxpayer on a business trip.

■ The step-transaction doctrine allows the IRS to collapse a series of related transactions into one transaction to determine the tax consequences of the transaction.

■ The substance-over-form doctrine allows the IRS to consider the transaction's substance regardless of its form, and where appropriate, reclassify the transaction according to its substance.

Contrast tax avoidance and tax evasion.   **L07**

■ Tax avoidance is the legal act of arranging one's transactions, and so on, to minimize taxes paid. Tax evasion is the willful attempt to defraud the government (i.e., by not paying taxes legally owed). Tax evasion falls outside the confines of legal tax avoidance.

■ In many cases a clear distinction exists between avoidance (e.g., not paying tax on municipal bond interest) and evasion (e.g., not paying tax on a $1,000,000 game show prize). In other cases, the line between tax avoidance and evasion is less clear. In these situations, professional judgment, the use of a "smell test," and consideration of the business purpose, step-transaction, and substance-over-form doctrines may prove useful.

KEY TERMS

arm's-length transaction (3-12)	discount rate (3-3)	substance-over-form doctrine (3-18)
assignment of income doctrine (3-12)	present value (3-3)	tax avoidance (3-18)
business purpose doctrine (3-18)	related-party transaction (3-12)	tax evasion (3-19)
constructive receipt doctrine (3-10)	step-transaction doctrine (3-18)	

DISCUSSION QUESTIONS

1. **(LO1)** "The goal of tax planning is to minimize taxes." Explain why this statement is not true.

2. **(LO1)** Describe the three parties engaged in every business transaction and how understanding taxes may aid in structuring transactions.

3. **(LO1)** In this chapter we discuss three basic tax-planning strategies. What different features of taxation does each of these strategies exploit?

4. **(LO2)** What are the two basic timing strategies? What is the intent of each?

5. **(LO2)** Why is the timing strategy particularly effective for cash-basis taxpayers?

6. **(LO2)** What are some common examples of the timing strategy?

7. **(LO2)** What factors increase the benefits of accelerating deductions or deferring income?

8. **(LO2, LO3)** How do changing tax rates affect the timing strategy? What information do you need to determine the appropriate timing strategy when tax rates change?

9. **(LO2, LO6)** Describe the ways in which the timing strategy has limitations.

10. **(LO3)** The concept of the time value of money suggests that $1 today is not equal to $1 in the future. Explain why this is true.

11. **(LO3)** Why is understanding the time value of money important for tax planning?

12. **(LO3)** What two factors increase the difference between present and future values?

13. **(LO4)** What factors have to be present for income shifting to be a viable strategy?

14. **(LO4)** Name three common types of income shifting.

15. **(LO4)** What are some ways that a parent could effectively shift income to a child? What are some of the disadvantages of these methods?

16. **(LO4)** What is the key factor in shifting income from a business to its owners? What are some methods of shifting income in this context?

17. **(LO4)** Explain why paying dividends is not an effective way to shift income from a corporation to its owners.

18. **(LO5)** What are some of the common examples of the conversion strategy?

19. **(LO5)** What is needed to implement the conversion strategy?

20. **(LO5)** Explain how implicit taxes may limit the benefits of the conversion strategy.

21. **(LO6)** Several judicial doctrines limit basic tax planning strategies. What are they? Which planning strategies do they limit?

22. **(LO6)** What is the constructive receipt doctrine? What types of taxpayers does this doctrine generally affect? For what tax planning strategy is the constructive receipt doctrine a potential limitation?

23. **(LO6)** Explain the assignment of income doctrine. In what situations would this doctrine potentially apply?
24. **(LO6)** Relative to arm's-length transactions, why do related-party transactions receive more IRS scrutiny?
25. **(LO6)** Describe the business purpose, step-transaction, and substance-over-form doctrines. What types of tax planning strategies may these doctrines inhibit?
26. **(LO7)** What is the difference between tax avoidance and tax evasion?
27. **(LO7)** What are the rewards of tax avoidance? What are the rewards of tax evasion?
28. **(LO7)** "Tax avoidance is discouraged by the courts and Congress." Is this statement true or false? Please explain.

PROBLEMS

29. **(LO2)** Yong recently paid his accountant $10,000 for elaborate tax planning strategies that exploit the timing strategy. Assuming this is an election year and there could be a power shift in the White House and Congress, what is a potential risk associated with Yong's strategies? *planning*
30. **(LO2, LO3)** Billups, a physician and cash-method taxpayer, is new to the concept of tax planning and recently learned of the timing strategy. To implement the timing strategy, Billups plans to establish a new policy that allows all his clients to wait two years to pay their co-pays. Assume that Billups does not expect his marginal tax rates to change. What is wrong with his strategy? *planning*
31. **(LO2, LO3)** Tesha works for a company that pays a year-end bonus in January of each year (instead of December of the preceding year) to allow employees to defer the bonus income. Assume Congress recently passed tax legislation that decreases individual tax rates as of next year. Does this increase or decrease the benefits of the bonus deferral this year? What if Congress passed legislation that increased tax rates next year? Should Tesha ask the company to change its policy this year? What additional information do you need to answer this question? *planning*
32. **(LO2, LO3)** Isabel, a calendar-year taxpayer, uses the cash-basis method of accounting for her sole proprietorship. In late December she received a $20,000 bill from her accountant for consulting services related to her small business. Isabel can pay the $20,000 bill anytime before January 30 of next year without penalty. Assume her marginal tax rate is 40 percent this year and next year, and that she can earn an after-tax rate of return of 12 percent on her investments. When should she pay the $20,000 bill—this year or next? *planning*
33. **(LO2, LO3)** Using the facts from the previous problem, how would your answer change if Isabel's after-tax rate of return were 8 percent? *planning*
34. **(LO2, LO3)** Manny, a calendar-year taxpayer, uses the cash-basis method of accounting for his sole proprietorship. In late December he performed $20,000 of legal services for a client. Manny typically requires his clients to pay his bills immediately upon receipt. Assume Manny's marginal tax rate is 40 percent this year and next year, and that he can earn an after-tax rate of return of 12 percent on his investments. Should Manny send his client the bill in December or January? *planning*
35. **(LO2, LO3)** Using the facts from the previous problem, how would your answer change if Manny's after-tax rate of return were 8 percent? *planning*
36. **(LO2, LO3)** Reese, a calendar-year taxpayer, uses the cash-basis method of accounting for her sole proprietorship. In late December, she received a $20,000 *planning*

bill from her accountant for consulting services related to her small business. Reese can pay the $20,000 bill anytime before January 30 of next year without penalty. Assume Reese's marginal tax rate is 30 percent this year and will be 40 percent next year, and that she can earn an after-tax rate of return of 12 percent on her investments. When should she pay the $20,000 bill—this year or next?

planning   37. **(LO2, LO3)** Using the facts from the previous problem, when should Reese pay the bill if she expects her marginal tax rate to be 33 percent next year? 25 percent next year?

planning   38. **(LO2, LO3)** Hank, a calendar-year taxpayer, uses the cash-basis method of accounting for his sole proprietorship. In late December, he performed $20,000 of legal services for a client. Hank typically requires his clients to pay his bills immediately upon receipt. Assume his marginal tax rate is 30 percent this year and will be 40 percent next year, and that he can earn an after-tax rate of return of 12 percent on his investments. Should Hank send his client the bill in December or January?

planning   39. **(LO2, LO3)** Using the facts from the previous problem, when should Hank send the bill if he expects his marginal tax rate to be 33 percent next year? 25 percent next year?

40. **(LO3)** Geraldo recently won a lottery and chose to receive $100,000 today instead of an equivalent amount in 10 years, computed using an 8 percent rate of return. Today, he learned that interest rates are expected to increase in the future. Is this good news for Geraldo given his decision?

planning   41. **(LO3)** Assume Rafael can earn an 8 percent after-tax rate of return. Would he prefer $1,000 today or $1,500 in five years?

planning   42. **(LO3)** Assume Ellina earns a 10 percent after-tax rate of return, and that she owes a friend $1,200. Would she prefer to pay the friend $1,200 today or $1,750 in four years?

planning   43. **(LO3)** Jonah has the choice of paying Rita $10,000 today or $40,000 in 10 years. Assume Jonah can earn a 12 percent after-tax rate of return. Which should he choose?

planning   44. **(LO3)** Bob's Lottery, Inc., has decided to offer winners a choice of $100,000 in 10 years or some amount currently. Assume that Bob's Lottery, Inc., earns a 10 percent after-tax rate of return. What amount should Bob offer lottery winners currently, in order for him to be indifferent between the two choices?

planning   45. **(LO4)** Tawana owns and operates a sole proprietorship and has a 40 percent marginal tax rate. She provides her son, Jonathon, $8,000 a year for college expenses. Jonathon works as a pizza delivery person every fall, and has a marginal tax rate of 15 percent. What could Tawana do to reduce her family tax burden? How much pretax income does it currently take Tawana to generate the $8,000 after taxes given to Jonathon? If Jonathon worked for his mother's sole proprietorship, what salary would she have to pay him to generate $8,000 after taxes (ignoring any Social Security, Medicare, or self-employment tax issues)? How much money would this strategy save?

planning   46. **(LO4)** Moana is a single taxpayer who operates a sole proprietorship. She expects her taxable income next year to be $250,000, of which $200,000 is attributed to her sole proprietorship. Moana is contemplating incorporating her sole proprietorship. Using the single individual tax brackets and the corporate tax brackets inside the book's front cover, find out how much current tax this strategy could save Moana (ignore any Social Security, Medicare, or self-employment tax issues). How much income should be left in the corporation?

planning   47. **(LO4)** Orie and Jane, husband and wife, operate a sole proprietorship. They expect their taxable income next year to be $275,000, of which $125,000 is attributed to the sole proprietorship. Orie and Jane are contemplating incorporating their sole proprietorship. Using the married-joint tax brackets and the corporate tax brackets inside the book's front cover, find out how much current tax this strategy could save Orie and Jane. How much income should be left in the corporation?

48. **(LO4)** Hyundai is considering opening a plant in two neighboring states. One state has a corporate tax rate of 10 percent. If operated in this state, the plant is expected to generate $1,000,000 pretax profit. The other state has a corporate tax rate of 2 percent. If operated in this state, the plant is expected to generate $930,000 of pretax profit. Which state should Hyundai choose? Why do you think the plant in the state with a lower tax rate would produce a lower before-tax income?

■ **planning**

49. **(LO4, LO6)** Bendetta, a high-tax-rate taxpayer, owns several rental properties and would like to shift some income to her daughter, Jenine. Bendetta instructs her tenants to send their rent checks to Jenine so Jenine can report the rental income. Will this shift the income from Bendetta to Jenine? Why, or why not?

■ **planning**

50. **(LO4, LO6)** Using the facts in the previous problem, what are some ways that Bendetta could shift some of the rental income to Jenine? What are the disadvantages associated with these income-shifting strategies?

■ **planning**

51. **(LO5)** Dennis is currently considering investing in municipal bonds that earn 6 percent interest, or in taxable bonds issued by the Coca-Cola Company that pay 8 percent. If Dennis's tax rate is 20 percent, which bond should he choose? Which bond should he choose if his tax rate is 30 percent? At what tax rate would he be indifferent between the bonds? What strategy is this decision based upon?

■ **planning**

52. **(LO7)** Duff is really interested in decreasing his tax liability, and by his very nature he is somewhat aggressive. A friend of a friend told him that cash transactions are more difficult for the IRS to identify and, thus, tax. Duff is contemplating using this "strategy" of not reporting cash collected in his business to minimize his tax liability. Is this tax planning? What are the risks with this strategy?

53. **(LO7)** Using the facts from the previous problem, how would your answer change if instead, Duff adopted the cash method of accounting to allow him to better control the timing of his cash receipts and disbursements?

54. **(LO2, LO4, LO5)** Using an available tax service or the Internet, identify three basic tax planning ideas or tax tips suggested for year-end tax planning. Which basic tax strategy from this chapter does each planning idea employ?

■ **planning**

■ **research**

55. **(LO7)** Jayanna, an advertising consultant, is contemplating instructing some of her clients to pay her in cash so that she does not have to report the income on her tax return. Use an available tax service to identify the three basic elements of tax evasion and penalties associated with tax evasion. Write a memo to Jayanna explaining tax evasion and the risks associated with her actions.

■ **research**

56. **(LO7)** Using the IRS Web site (www.irs.gov/index.html), how large is the current estimated "tax gap" (i.e., the amount of tax underpaid by taxpayers annually)? What group of taxpayers represents the largest "contributors" to the tax gap?

■ **research**

4

Individual Income Tax Overview

Learning Objectives

Upon completing this chapter, you should be able to:

LO 1 Describe the formula for calculating an individual taxpayer's taxes payable or refund and generally explain each formula component.

■

LO 2 Explain the requirements for determining a taxpayer's personal and dependency exemptions.

■

LO 3 Determine a taxpayer's filing status.

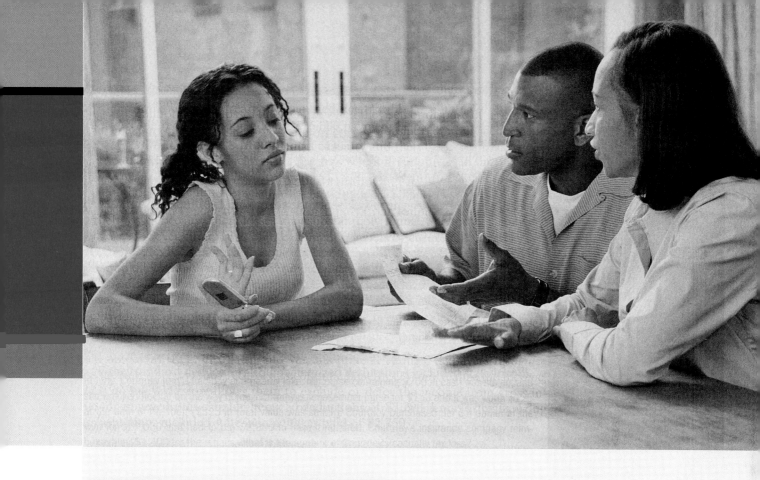

Storyline Summary	
Taxpayer:	Rodney and Anita Hall
Other household members:	Tara, their 21-year-old daughter, and Braxton, their 12-year-old son. Shawn, Rodney's brother, also lives with the Halls.
Location:	Brookings, South Dakota
Employment status:	Rodney is a manager for a regional grocery chain. His salary is $64,000. Anita works part-time as a purchasing-card auditor at South Dakota State University. Her salary is $46,000.
Current situation:	Determining their tax liability

Tara Hall just completed a unit on individual taxation in her undergraduate tax class at South Dakota State University. She was excited to share her knowledge with her parents, Rodney and Anita Hall, as they prepared their tax return. Rodney and Anita have been married for over 25 years, and they have filed a joint tax return each year. The Halls's 12-year-old son Braxton lives at home but Tara, who is 21, lives nearby in the university dorms. Further, in January of this year, Rodney's younger brother Shawn moved in with the Halls. They expect Shawn to live with them for at least one year and maybe two. Every year Rodney and Anita use tax-preparation software to complete their tax return, but they are not always sure they understand the final result. This year, with Tara's help, they hope that will change. ∎

This and the next three chapters discuss the fundamental elements of the individual income tax formula. This is the overview chapter; the other chapters provide more depth on individual income tax topics. Here we introduce the individual income tax formula, summarize its components, describe requirements for dependency exemptions, and explain how to determine a taxpayer's filing status. Chapter 5 explains gross income, and Chapter 6 describes deductible expenses to determine adjusted gross income and taxable income. Finally, Chapter 7 addresses issues associated with calculating a taxpayer's tax liability and discusses tax return filing concerns.

LO1 THE INDIVIDUAL INCOME TAX FORMULA

Each year, individuals file tax returns to report their **taxable income,** the tax base for the individual income tax, to the Internal Revenue Service. Exhibit 4-1 presents a simplified formula for calculating taxable income.

EXHIBIT 4-1   Individual Tax Formula

	Realized income from whatever source derived
Minus:	Excluded or deferred income
Equals:	Gross income
Minus:	*For* AGI deductions
Equals:	Adjusted gross income (AGI)
Minus:	*From* AGI deductions:
	(1) *Greater* of
	(a) Standard deduction or
	(b) Itemized deductions and
	(2) Personal and dependency exemptions
Equals:	Taxable income
Times:	Tax rates
Equals:	Income tax liability
Plus:	Other taxes
Equals:	Total tax
Minus:	Credits
Minus:	Prepayments
Equals:	Taxes due or (refund)

Beginning with gross income, this formula is imbedded in the first two pages of the individual income tax Form 1040, the form individuals generally use to report their taxable income. Exhibit 4-2 presents the first two pages from the form. Note that income excluded from taxation is usually not reported on the tax return (though line 8b asks for tax-exempt interest). However, deferred income is generally reported on the tax return, but it is usually provided on supporting schedules rather than on the first two pages of the tax return. Also, note that the last line on page 1 of Form 1040 is adjusted gross income (AGI), an important reference point in the income tax formula.

Let's look at the components of the individual tax formula and provide a brief description of each of the key elements.

Realized Income, Exclusions, Deferrals, and Gross Income

The U.S. tax laws are based on the **all-inclusive income concept.** Under this concept, taxpayers generally must include in taxable income *all* **realized income** *from whatever source derived.*[1] Realized income is income generated in a transaction with a second party in which there is a measurable change in property rights between parties.

[1]§61(a).

EXHIBIT 4-2   Form 1040, pages 1 and 2

Form **1040**   Department of the Treasury—Internal Revenue Service

U.S. Individual Income Tax Return 2008   (99) IRS Use Only—Do not write or staple in this space.

		OMB No. 1545-0074

For the year Jan. 1–Dec. 31, 2008, or other tax year beginning   , 2008, ending   , 20

Label
(See instructions on page 14.)
Use the IRS label. Otherwise, please print or type.

L A B E L   H E R E

Your first name and initial   Last name   **Your social security number**

If a joint return, spouse's first name and initial   Last name   **Spouse's social security number**

Home address (number and street). If you have a P.O. box, see page 14.   Apt. no.   ▲ You **must** enter your SSN(s) above. ▲

City, town or post office, state, and ZIP code. If you have a foreign address, see page 14.   Checking a box below will not change your tax or refund.

Presidential Election Campaign ▶ Check here if you, or your spouse if filing jointly, want $3 to go to this fund (see page 14) ▶ ☐ You ☐ Spouse

Filing Status

Check only one box.

1 ☐ Single
2 ☐ Married filing jointly (even if only one had income)
3 ☐ Married filing separately. Enter spouse's SSN above and full name here. ▶
4 ☐ Head of household (with qualifying person). (See page 15.) If the qualifying person is a child but not your dependent, enter this child's name here. ▶
5 ☐ Qualifying widow(er) with dependent child (see page 16)

Exemptions

6a ☐ **Yourself.** If someone can claim you as a dependent, **do not** check box 6a
b ☐ **Spouse**
c Dependents:

(1) First name Last name	(2) Dependent's social security number	(3) Dependent's relationship to you	(4) ✓ if qualifying child for child tax credit (see page 17)
			☐
			☐
			☐
			☐

If more than four dependents, see page 17.

Boxes checked on 6a and 6b ____
No. of children on 6c who:
• lived with you ____
• did not live with you due to divorce or separation (see page 18) ____
Dependents on 6c not entered above ____
Add numbers on lines above ▶ ☐

d Total number of exemptions claimed

Income

Attach Form(s) W-2 here. Also attach Forms W-2G and 1099-R if tax was withheld.

If you did not get a W-2, see page 21.

Enclose, but do not attach, any payment. Also, please use Form 1040-V.

7	Wages, salaries, tips, etc. Attach Form(s) W-2	7	
8a	**Taxable** interest. Attach Schedule B if required	8a	
b	**Tax-exempt** interest. **Do not** include on line 8a 8b		
9a	Ordinary dividends. Attach Schedule B if required	9a	
b	Qualified dividends (see page 21) 9b		
10	Taxable refunds, credits, or offsets of state and local income taxes (see page 22)	10	
11	Alimony received	11	
12	Business income or (loss). Attach Schedule C or C-EZ	12	
13	Capital gain or (loss). Attach Schedule D if required. If not required, check here ▶ ☐	13	
14	Other gains or (losses). Attach Form 4797	14	
15a	IRA distributions 15a b Taxable amount (see page 23)	15b	
16a	Pensions and annuities 16a b Taxable amount (see page 24)	16b	
17	Rental real estate, royalties, partnerships, S corporations, trusts, etc. Attach Schedule E	17	
18	Farm income or (loss). Attach Schedule F	18	
19	Unemployment compensation	19	
20a	Social security benefits 20a b Taxable amount (see page 26)	20b	
21	Other income. List type and amount (see page 28)	21	
22	Add the amounts in the far right column for lines 7 through 21. This is your **total income** ▶	22	

Adjusted Gross Income

23	Educator expenses (see page 28)	23	
24	Certain business expenses of reservists, performing artists, and fee-basis government officials. Attach Form 2106 or 2106-EZ	24	
25	Health savings account deduction. Attach Form 8889	25	
26	Moving expenses. Attach Form 3903	26	
27	One-half of self-employment tax. Attach Schedule SE	27	
28	Self-employed SEP, SIMPLE, and qualified plans	28	
29	Self-employed health insurance deduction (see page 29)	29	
30	Penalty on early withdrawal of savings	30	
31a	Alimony paid b Recipient's SSN ▶	31a	
32	IRA deduction (see page 30)	32	
33	Student loan interest deduction (see page 33)	33	
34	Tuition and fees deduction. Attach Form 8917	34	
35	Domestic production activities deduction. Attach Form 8903	35	
36	Add lines 23 through 31a and 32 through 35	36	
37	Subtract line 36 from line 22. This is your **adjusted gross income** ▶	37	

For Disclosure, Privacy Act, and Paperwork Reduction Act Notice, see page 88.   Cat. No. 11320B   Form **1040** (2008)

(continued)

EXHIBIT 4-2   Form 1040, pages 1 and 2 (*continued*)

Form 1040 (2008)   Page **2**

Tax and Credits	38	Amount from line 37 (adjusted gross income)	38

39a	Check if: { **You** were born before January 2, 1944, ☐ ☐ Blind. } { **Spouse** was born before January 2, 1944, ☐ ☐ Blind. } **Total boxes** checked ▶ 39a	
b	If your spouse itemizes on a separate return or you were a dual-status alien, see page 34 and check here ▶ 39b ☐	
c	Check if standard deduction includes real estate taxes or disaster loss (see page 34) ▶ 39c ☐	

Standard Deduction for—

- People who checked any box on line 39a, 39b, or 39c **or** who can be claimed as a dependent, see page 34.
- All others:

Single or Married filing separately, $5,450

Married filing jointly or Qualifying widow(er), $10,900

Head of household, $8,000

Line	Description	Amount
40	**Itemized deductions** (from Schedule A) **or** your **standard deduction** (see left margin) .	40
41	Subtract line 40 from line 38	41
42	If line 38 is over $119,975, or you provided housing to a Midwestern displaced individual, see page 36. Otherwise, multiply $3,500 by the total number of exemptions claimed on line 6d .	42
43	**Taxable income.** Subtract line 42 from line 41. If line 42 is more than line 41, enter -0- .	43
44	**Tax** (see page 36). Check if any tax is from: **a** ☐ Form(s) 8814 **b** ☐ Form 4972 .	44
45	**Alternative minimum tax** (see page 39). Attach Form 6251	45
46	Add lines 44 and 45 . . . . ▶	46
47	Foreign tax credit. Attach Form 1116 if required	47	
48	Credit for child and dependent care expenses. Attach Form 2441	48	
49	Credit for the elderly or the disabled. Attach Schedule R . .	49	
50	Education credits. Attach Form 8863	50	
51	Retirement savings contributions credit. Attach Form 8880 .	51	
52	Child tax credit (see page 42). Attach Form 8901 if required .	52	
53	Credits from Form: **a** ☐ 8396 **b** ☐ 8839 **c** ☐ 5695	53	
54	Other credits from Form: **a** ☐ 3800 **b** ☐ 8801 **c** ☐ ____	54	
55	Add lines 47 through 54. These are your **total credits**	55
56	Subtract line 55 from line 46. If line 55 is more than line 46, enter -0- . . . . . ▶	56

Other Taxes	57	Self-employment tax. Attach Schedule SE	57
	58	Unreported social security and Medicare tax from Form: **a** ☐ 4137 **b** ☐ 8919 . .	58
	59	Additional tax on IRAs, other qualified retirement plans, etc. Attach Form 5329 if required .	59
	60	Additional taxes: **a** ☐ AEIC payments **b** ☐ Household employment taxes. Attach Schedule H	60
	61	Add lines 56 through 60. This is your **total tax** . . . . ▶	61

Payments	62	Federal income tax withheld from Forms W-2 and 1099 . .	62	
	63	2008 estimated tax payments and amount applied from 2007 return	63	
If you have a qualifying child, attach Schedule EIC.	64a	**Earned income credit (EIC)**	64a	
	b	Nontaxable combat pay election 64b	
	65	Excess social security and tier 1 RRTA tax withheld (see page 61)	65	
	66	Additional child tax credit. Attach Form 8812	66	
	67	Amount paid with request for extension to file (see page 61) .	67	
	68	Credits from Form: **a** ☐ 2439 **b** ☐ 4136 **c** ☐ 8801 **d** ☐ 8885	68	
	69	First-time homebuyer credit. Attach Form 5405	69	
	70	Recovery rebate credit (see worksheet on pages 62 and 63) .	70	
	71	Add lines 62 through 70. These are your **total payments** . . . . ▶	71

Refund	72	If line 71 is more than line 61, subtract line 61 from line 71. This is the amount you **overpaid**	72
Direct deposit? See page 63 and fill in 73b, 73c, and 73d, or Form 8888.	73a	Amount of line 72 you want **refunded to you.** If Form 8888 is attached, check here ▶ ☐	73a
	▶ b	Routing number	▶ c Type: ☐ Checking ☐ Savings
	▶ d	Account number	
	74	Amount of line 72 you want **applied to your 2009 estimated tax** ▶	74

Amount You Owe	75	**Amount you owe.** Subtract line 71 from line 61. For details on how to pay, see page 65 ▶	75
	76	Estimated tax penalty (see page 65)	76	

Third Party Designee

Do you want to allow another person to discuss this return with the IRS (see page 66)? ☐ **Yes.** Complete the following. ☐ **No**

Designee's name ▶	Phone no. ▶ ( )	Personal identification number (PIN) ▶	

Sign Here

Under penalties of perjury, I declare that I have examined this return and accompanying schedules and statements, and to the best of my knowledge and belief, they are true, correct, and complete. Declaration of preparer (other than taxpayer) is based on all information of which preparer has any knowledge.

Joint return? See page 15.

Keep a copy for your records.

Your signature	Date	Your occupation	Daytime phone number ( )
Spouse's signature. If a joint return, **both** must sign.	Date	Spouse's occupation	

Paid Preparer's Use Only

Preparer's signature ▶	Date	Check if self-employed ☐	Preparer's SSN or PTIN
Firm's name (or yours if self-employed), address, and ZIP code ▶		EIN	
		Phone no. ( )	

Form **1040** (2008)

Exhibit 4-3 provides a listing of common income items that meet the realization threshold and indicates where in the text we provide more detail on each income item.

EXHIBIT 4-3   **Common Income Items**

Income Item	Discussed in More Detail in
Compensation for services including fringe benefits	Chapter 12
Business income	Chapter 8
Gains from selling property	Chapters 10 and 11
Interest and dividends	Chapters 5 and 11
Rents and royalties	Chapters 5, 11, and 14
Alimony received and annuities	Chapter 5
Retirement income	Chapter 13
Income from the discharge of indebtedness	Chapter 5

Taxpayers are allowed to permanently exclude certain types of realized income from taxation or defer paying taxes to a later year on certain types of realized income if, and only if, *a specific tax provision allows them to do so.* Income items that taxpayers permanently exclude from taxation are referred to as **excluded income** or **exclusions.** Income items that taxpayers realize in one year, but are allowed to defer paying taxes on until a later year, are called **deferral items, deferred income,** or simply **deferrals.** Exhibit 4-4 provides a listing of common exclusions and deferrals and indicates where in the text we discuss each in more detail. **Gross income** is realized income minus exclusions and deferrals. That is, gross income is the income that taxpayers actually report on their tax returns.

EXHIBIT 4-4   **Common Exclusions and Deferrals**

Exclusion or Deferral Item	Exclusion or Deferral	Discussed in
Interest income from municipal bonds	Exclusion	Chapters 5 and 11
Gifts and inheritances	Exclusion	Chapter 5
Gain on sale of personal residence	Exclusion	Chapter 14
Life insurance proceeds	Exclusion	Chapters 5 and 11
Installment sale	Deferral	Chapter 10
Like-kind exchange	Deferral	Chapter 10

Example 4-1

In 2009, Rodney earned a salary of $64,000, and Anita earned a salary of $46,000 working part-time. The Halls also received $600 of interest income from investments in corporate bonds and $300 of interest income from investments in municipal bonds. This was their only income during the year. What is the Halls's 2009 gross income?

Answer: $110,600, computed as follows:

Description	Amount	Explanation
(1) Rodney's salary	$ 64,000	
(2) Anita's salary	46,000	
(3) Interest from corporate bonds	600	
(4) Interest from municipal bonds	300	
(5) Realized income	$110,900	(1) + (2) + (3) + (4).
(6) Exclusions and deferrals	(300)	(4) Exclusion for municipal bond interest.
Gross income	**$110,600**	(5) + (6).

Deductions

Taxpayers reduce their gross income by subtracting their **deductions** to determine their taxable income. In stark contrast to the all-inclusive treatment of income, taxpayers are *not allowed to deduct anything unless a specific tax provision allows them to do so*. Thus, deductions are a matter of **legislative grace.** The tax laws provide for two distinct types of deductions in the individual tax formula: **deductions *for* AGI** and **deductions *from* AGI.** Deductions *from* AGI are also referred to as **deductions below the line,** while deductions *for* AGI are referred to as **deductions above the line.** In both cases, the "line" is adjusted gross income (AGI), which is the last line on the front page of the individual tax return Form 1040 (see Exhibit 4-2). When it enacts new legislation that grants deductions, Congress typically identifies whether the deductions are for or from AGI. In general, deductions *for* AGI tend to be related to business activities and certain investing activities, whereas deductions *from* AGI tend to be more personal in nature.

Deductions for AGI   Taxpayers first reduce their gross income by deductions *for* AGI, so we discuss these first. They are called for AGI deductions because they are used *for* calculating AGI, or come *before* AGI in the tax formula. In contrast to *from* AGI deductions, which may be limited or may generate no tax benefit, *for* AGI deductions *always* reduce gross income and therefore reduce taxable income dollar for dollar. For these reasons, deductions *for* AGI are typically considered more valuable than deductions *from* AGI. Exhibit 4-5 provides a listing of common for AGI deductions and indicates where in the text we discuss them.

EXHIBIT 4-5   **Common *for* AGI Deductions**

For AGI Deduction	Discussed in
Alimony paid	Chapter 6
Health insurance deduction for self-employed taxpayers	Chapter 6
Moving expenses	Chapter 6
Rental and royalty expenses	Chapter 6
One-half of self-employment taxes paid	Chapter 7
Business expenses	Chapter 8
Losses on dispositions of assets used in a trade or business	Chapter 10
Losses from flow-through entities	Chapter 11
Losses on dispositions of investment assets (*net* losses limited to $3,000 for the year).	Chapter 11
Contributions to qualified retirement accounts	Chapter 13

Gross income reduced by *for* AGI deductions is termed **adjusted gross income (AGI).**

Example 4-2

In 2009, the Halls paid $5,000 of deductible moving expenses when the family relocated due to an employment transfer for Rodney. What is the Halls's 2009 adjusted gross income?

Answer: $105,600, computed as follows:

Description	Amount	Explanation
(1) Gross income	$110,600	Example 4-1.
(2) Moving expenses	(5,000)	*For* AGI deduction (see Exhibit 4-5).
Adjusted gross income	**$105,600**	(1) + (2).

AGI is an important reference point in the tax formula because it is often used in other tax-related calculations. Specifically, limits on certain *from* AGI expenses depend on AGI (certain from AGI deductions are reduced for taxpayers with high AGI). Because *for* AGI deductions reduce AGI, they *increase* the deductibility of the *from* AGI deductions subject to AGI limitations.

Deductions from AGI   Taxpayers reduce their AGI by deductions *from* AGI to determine their taxable income. Deductions from AGI include **itemized deductions,** the **standard deduction,** and **exemptions.** Individuals have the choice of deducting their itemized deductions *or* deducting a fixed amount called the standard deduction amount. Exhibit 4-6 identifies the primary categories of itemized deductions.

EXHIBIT 4-6   Primary Categories of Itemized Deductions

- *Medical and dental expenses:* Deductible to the extent these expenses exceed 7.5 percent of AGI.
- *Taxes:* State and local income taxes, real estate taxes, personal property taxes, and other taxes.
- *Interest expense:* Mortgage, home equity, and investment interest expense.
- *Gifts to charity (charitable contributions)*
- *Casualty and theft losses:* Deductible to the extent they exceed 10 percent of AGI.
- *Job expenses and certain miscellaneous deductions:* Deductible to the extent the sum of these expenses exceeds 2 percent of AGI.
- *Other miscellaneous deductions:* Gambling losses (to the extent of gambling winnings) and certain other deductions not subject to AGI limitation.

Note: Itemized deductions are discussed in more detail in Chapter 6.

The amount of the standard deduction varies by taxpayer filing status; the government indexes this deduction for inflation. Exhibit 4-7 presents the standard deduction amounts by filing status for 2008 and 2009. (We use 2008 forms because the 2009 forms were not available at the time this book went to press.)

Exemptions are the final amount taxpayers deduct *from* AGI in determining their taxable income. An exemption is a flat deduction allowed for the taxpayer, the taxpayer's spouse, and each person who qualifies as a dependent of the taxpayer. The exemptions for the taxpayer(s) filing the tax return are called **personal exemptions,** while the others are referred to as **dependency exemptions.** In 2009 the amount of the exemption deduction is $3,650 for both exemption types. We discuss the dependency qualification requirements later in this chapter.

EXHIBIT 4-7   Standard Deduction Amounts by Filing Status*

	2008	2009
Married filing jointly	$10,900	$11,400
Qualifying widow or widower	$10,900	$11,400
Married filing separately	$ 5,450	$ 5,700
Head of household	$ 8,000	$ 8,350
Single	$ 5,450	$ 5,700

*Taxpayers 65 years of age and/or blind taxpayers are entitled to additional standard deduction amounts (see discussion in Chapter 6). Also, the standard deduction amount for an individual claimed as a dependent on another return may be limited (see discussion in Chapter 7).

Example 4-3

Tara's parents, Rodney and Anita, annually file a joint tax return. Tara determined that during 2009 her parents paid a total of $14,000 for expenditures that qualify as itemized deductions. Assuming Tara and her younger brother Braxton qualify as Rodney and Anita's dependents, what

(*continued on page 4-8...*)

is the total amount of *from* AGI deductions Rodney and Anita are allowed to deduct on their 2009 tax return?

Answer: $28,600, computed as follows:

Description	Amount	Explanation
(1) Standard deduction	$11,400	Married filing joint filing status (see Exhibit 4-7).
(2) Itemized deductions	$14,000	
(3) Greater of (1) or (2)	$14,000	Itemized deductions exceed the standard deduction.
(4) Personal and dependency exemptions	$14,600	($3,650 × 4) One exemption each for Rodney, Anita, Tara, and Braxton.
Total deductions from AGI	**$28,600**	(3) + (4). (Also referred to as deductions "below the line.")

What if: What would be the amount of the Halls's from AGI deductions for 2009 if, instead of the original facts, Rodney and Anita had paid a total of $8,000 in expenditures that qualified as itemized deductions, such as interest expense and gifts to charity?

Answer: $26,000, computed as follows:

Description	Amount	Explanation
(1) Standard deduction	$11,400	Married filing joint filing status (see Exhibit 4-7).
(2) Itemized deductions	$ 8,000	
(3) Greater of (1) or (2)	$11,400	The standard deduction exceeds itemized deductions.
(4) Personal and dependency exemptions	$14,600	($3,650 × 4) One personal exemption each for Rodney, Anita, Tara, and Braxton.
Total deductions from AGI	**$26,000**	(3) + (4).

Income Tax Calculation

After determining taxable income, taxpayers can generally calculate their regular income tax liability using either a **tax table** or a **tax rate schedule,** depending on their filing status and income level (see inside front cover for the regular tax rate schedule and see Appendix A to this chapter for an excerpt from a tax table). Taxpayers with taxable income under $100,000 generally must use the tax tables.[2] However, as we discuss in other chapters, certain types of income that are included in taxable income are taxed at rates different from the rates embedded in the tables or published in the tax rate schedules. Exhibit 4-8 identifies these income items and indicates where in the text we discuss the income items in more detail.

EXHIBIT 4-8 Income Taxed at Rate Other Than Rate from Tax Rate Schedule for That Taxpayer*

Income Item	Applicable Tax Rate	Discussed in
Long-term capital gains	Generally 15%. Can be as low as 0% and as high as 28%.[3]	Chapters 10 and 11
Qualifying dividends	Generally 15%. Can be as low as 0%.	Chapter 11

*As we discuss in Chapter 7, certain income of children may be taxed at the parents' marginal tax rate.

[2]For administrative convenience and to prevent low- and middle-income taxpayers from making mathematical errors using a rate schedule, the IRS provides tax tables that present the gross tax for various amounts of taxable income. For simplicity, we use the tax rate schedule to determine tax liabilities in the examples presented in this text.

[3]§1(h).

Example 4-4

With Tara's help, the Halls determined their taxable income to be $77,000 as follows:

Description	Amount	Explanation
(1) Adjusted gross income	$105,600	Example 4-2.
(2) From AGI deductions	(28,600)	Example 4-3.
Taxable income	$ 77,000	(1) + (2).

They have also determined that all of their income is taxed at the rates provided in the tax rate schedule. What is their tax liability for the year (use the tax rate schedule rather than the tax tables to answer the question)?

Answer: $11,625. See the married filing jointly tax rate schedule inside front cover. [$9,350 + $2,275 {25% × (77,000 − 67,900)}]

What if: Suppose the Halls reported $77,000 of taxable income in 2008, what would be their 2008 tax liability using the tax tables (see Appendix A at the end of this chapter)?

Answer: $11,944.

What if: What would the Halls's tax liability be if their taxable income was $12,000 (all taxed at the ordinary rates in the tax rate schedule)?

Answer: $1,200 ($12,000 × 10%).

What if: Assume that in addition to the $77,000 of income taxed at the normal rates described in the original facts, the Halls also reported $5,000 of qualified dividends subject to a 15 percent tax rate. How much tax would they pay on the additional $5,000 dividend?

Answer: $750 ($5,000 × 15%). Qualifying dividends are generally taxed at a 15 percent rate. Note that the Halls's taxable income is $82,000. $77,000 of the income is taxed at the normal rates and $5,000 is taxed at the preferential 15 percent rate.

Other Taxes

In addition to the individual income tax, individuals may also be required to pay other taxes such as the **alternative minimum tax (AMT)** or **self-employment taxes.** These taxes are imposed tax bases other than the individual's regular taxable income. We discuss both taxes in more detail in Chapter 7.

Tax Credits

Individual taxpayers may reduce their tax liabilities by **tax credits** to determine their total taxes payable. Like deductions, tax credits are specifically granted by Congress and are narrowly defined. Unlike deductions, which reduce *taxable income,* tax credits *directly reduce taxes payable*. That is, a $1 credit reduces taxes payable by $1. Common credits include the child tax credit ($1,000 per child that qualifies for the credit), the child and dependent care credit, the earned income credit, Hope scholarship credit, and the lifetime learning credit. We discuss credits in more detail in Chapter 7.

Tax Prepayments

After calculating the total tax and subtracting their available credits, taxpayers determine their taxes due (or tax refund) by subtracting tax prepayments from the total tax remaining after credits. Tax prepayments include (1) **withholdings,** or income taxes withheld from the taxpayer's salary or wages by her employer; (2) **estimated tax payments** the taxpayer makes for the year; and (3) taxes the taxpayer overpaid in the previous year that the taxpayer elects to apply as an estimated payment for the current year.

If tax prepayments exceed the total tax after subtracting credits, the taxpayer receives a tax refund for the difference. If tax prepayments are less than the total tax after credits, the taxpayer owes additional tax and potentially a penalty for the underpayment.

Example 4-5

Based on their calculation in Example 4-4, Rodney and Anita Hall's tax liability for 2009 is $11,625. The Halls had $10,552 of federal income taxes withheld by their employers from their 2009 paychecks and are able to claim a $1,000 child tax credit for their 12-year old son Braxton (Tara is too old to qualify). What is the Halls's tax due or tax refund for 2009?

Answer: $73 taxes due, computed as follows:

Description	Amount	Explanation
(1) Tax liability	$11,625	Example 4-4.
(2) Tax credits	(1,000)	$1,000 child tax credit for 12-year old son Braxton.
(3) Tax prepayments	(10,552)	
Tax due	**$ 73**	(1) + (2) + (3).

Although not explicitly stated in the individual tax formula, a taxpayer's filing status affects many parts of the tax formula, including the standard deduction amount and the applicable income tax rate schedule among others. Below, we describe the rules for determining a taxpayer's filing status. However, because a taxpayer's filing status may depend on whether the taxpayer has dependents for tax purposes, we discuss how to determine who qualifies as a taxpayer's dependent before we address filing status.

L02 PERSONAL AND DEPENDENCY EXEMPTIONS

In 2009, taxpayers are allowed to deduct $3,650 for each personal and dependency exemption they are entitled to claim.[4] Individual taxpayers generally may deduct a personal exemption for themselves. Married couples filing jointly may claim two personal exemptions (one for each spouse).[5] Further, to provide some tax relief for taxpayers supporting others, individuals may claim additional exemptions for each person who qualifies as the taxpayer's dependent.[6] Individuals who qualify as a dependent of another taxpayer may *not* claim a personal exemption for themselves on their own individual tax returns.

Example 4-6

Assume that Tara (the Halls's 21-year-old daughter who is a full-time college student) qualifies as Rodney and Anita's dependent. Tara earned $9,000 at a summer job this year, and she files her own tax return. Is Tara allowed to claim a personal exemption for herself on her own tax return?

Answer: No. Because Tara qualifies as the Halls's dependent, the Halls may deduct a dependency exemption for Tara, but Tara may *not* deduct a personal exemption for herself.

---

[4]The amount of the exemption is indexed for inflation.
[5]§151(b).
[6]§151(c).

Dependency Requirements

Taxpayers may claim exemptions only for persons qualifying as their **dependents.** To qualify as a dependent of another, an individual (1) must be a resident of the United States, Canada, or Mexico; (2) must *not* file a joint return with the individual's spouse unless there is no tax liability on the couple's joint return and there would not have been any tax liability on either spouse's tax return if they had filed separately[7]; and (3) must be considered either a **qualifying child** of the taxpayer *or* a **qualifying relative** of the taxpayer.[8]

Qualifying Child   To be considered a qualifying child of a taxpayer, an individual must satisfy the following four tests: (1) relationship, (2) age, (3) residence, and (4) support.[9]

Relationship test.   A qualifying child must be a relative of the taxpayer. Eligible relatives include the taxpayer's son, daughter, stepchild, an eligible foster child, brother, sister, half-brother, half-sister, stepbrother, stepsister or a descendant of any of these relatives. This definition does not include cousins.

Age test.   A qualifying child must be younger than the taxpayer claiming such individual as a qualifying child and *either* (1) under age 19 at the end of the year, (2) under age 24 at the end of the year *and* a full-time student.[10] A person is a full-time student if she was in school full-time during any part of each of five calendar months during the calendar year.[11] An individual who is permanently and totally disabled is deemed to have met the age test.[12]

Residence test.   A qualifying child must have the same principal residence as the taxpayer for *more* than half the year. Time that a child (or the taxpayer) is temporarily away from the taxpayer's home because the child (or taxpayer) is ill, is pursuing an education, or has other special circumstances is counted as though the child (or taxpayer) were living in the taxpayer's home.[13]

Support test.   A qualifying child must *not* have provided more than half his or her *own* support (living expenses) for the year. When determining who provided the support for a *child* of the taxpayer who is a full-time student, scholarships are excluded from the computation.[14] Otherwise, support generally includes:

- Food, school lunches, toilet articles, and haircuts.
- Clothing.
- Recreation—including toys, summer camp, horseback riding, entertainment, and vacation expenses.
- Medical and dental care.
- Child care expenses.
- Allowances and gifts.
- Wedding costs.
- Lodging.
- Education—including board, uniforms at military schools, and tuition.

[7]Rev. Rul. 54-567, 1954-2 C.B. 108.

[8]§152.

[9]Technically, an individual is not eligible to be a qualifying child of another if she filed a joint return with her spouse (other than to claim a refund) [see §151(c)(2)(e)]. However, because this is also a requirement to be claimed as a dependent we do not discuss the requirement separately here.

[10]§152(c)(3)(A).

[11]§152(f)(2).

[12]§151(c)(3)(B).

[13]Reg. §1.152-1(b).

[14]§151(f)(5) and §151(f)(1). This provision requires that the student be a son, daughter, stepson, stepdaughter, or an eligible foster child of the taxpayer.

Example 4-7

Rodney and Anita have two children: Braxton, age 12, who lives at home and Tara, age 21, who is a full-time student and does not live at home. While Tara earned $9,000 in a summer job (see previous example), she did *not* provide more than half of her own support during the year. Are Braxton and Tara qualifying children to Rodney and Anita?

Answer: Yes, see analysis of factors below:

Test	Braxton	Tara
Relationship	Yes, son.	Yes, daughter.
Age	Yes, under age 19 at end of year (and younger than his parents).	Yes, under age 24 at year-end *and* full-time student (and younger than her parents).
Residence	Yes, lived at home entire year.	Yes, time away at college is considered as time at home.
Support	Yes, does not provide more than half of own support.	Yes, does not provide more than half of own support (note that her scholarship does not count as support she provides for herself).

Because they both meet all the requirements, Braxton and Tara are qualifying children to the Halls. So, the Halls may claim one dependency exemption for Braxton and one for Tara.

Tiebreaking rules.   The requirements for determining who is a qualifying child leave open the possibility that one person could be a qualifying child to more than one taxpayer. In these circumstances, the taxpayer who has priority for claiming the dependency exemption is based on the following tiebreaking rules:

1. If the person is a qualifying child of a parent, the parent is entitled to the dependency exemption for the child. This situation could arise, for example, when a child lives with her mother *and* her grandparents. In this case, the mother has priority for claiming the dependency exemption over the grandparents.
2. If the individual is a qualifying child to both parents, the parent with whom the child has resided for the longest period of time during the year has priority for claiming the dependency exemption. This situation may arise in a year when the child lives with both parents for more than half of the year but the parents divorce in the latter part of the year.[15]
3. Finally, if the child resides with both parents for the same amount of time or the qualifying child resides with taxpayers who are not the parents, the taxpayer with the *highest AGI* has priority for claiming the dependency exemption for the child.[16]

Example 4-8

In the previous example, we determined that Braxton (Rodney and Anita's son) is Rodney and Anita's qualifying child. Braxton's Uncle Shawn (Rodney's brother) lived in the Halls's home (the same home Braxton lived in) for more than 11 months during 2009. Does Braxton meet the requirements to be considered Shawn's qualifying child?

(*continued on page 4-13...*)

[15]The dependency exemption for a child of divorced parents can be specifically allocated in the divorce decree or separation agreement to the noncustodial parent.

[16]However, if the parents may claim the child as a qualifying child but no parent does so, another taxpayer may claim the individual as a qualifying child but only if the other individual's AGI is higher than the AGI of any parent of the child [§152(c)(4)(C)].

Answer: Yes, see analysis of factors below.

Test	Braxton
Relationship	Yes, son of Shawn's brother.
Age	Yes, under age 19 at end of year (and younger than Shawn).
Residence	Yes, lived in same residence as Shawn for more than half the year.
Support	Yes, does not provide more than half of own support.

Thus, Braxton is considered to be Rodney and Anita's qualifying child *and* he is considered to be Shawn's qualifying child. Under the tiebreaker rules, who is allowed to claim Braxton as a dependent for the year?

Answer: Rodney and Anita. Under the first tiebreaking rule, Rodney and Anita are allowed to claim the dependency exemption for Braxton because they are Braxton's parents.

Qualifying Relative   A qualifying relative is a person who is *not* a qualifying child *and* satisfies (1) a relationship test, (2) a support test, and (3) a gross income test.

Relationship test.   As you might expect, the relationship test for a qualifying relative is more inclusive than the relationship test for a qualifying child. In fact, it even includes people who are *unrelated* to the taxpayer if the unrelated person lived as a member of the taxpayer's household for the *entire* year.[17] A person is "related" to the taxpayer if the person is a descendant or ancestor of the taxpayer (child, grandchild, parent, or grandparent), a sibling of the taxpayer, or a stepmother, stepfather, stepbrother, stepsister, nephew, niece, aunt, uncle, or in-law (mother-in law, father-in-law, sister-in-law, and brother-in-law) of the taxpayer.[18] Cousins are *not* considered related to the taxpayer for purposes of this test.

Support test.   The support test requires that the taxpayer pay *more than half* the qualifying relative's living expenses.[19] As we discussed above, living expenses include rent, food, medicine, and clothes, among other things. Just as with the qualifying child support test, scholarships of children of a taxpayer who are full-time students are excluded from the support test.[20]

Gross income test.   The gross income test requires that a qualifying relative's gross income for the year be *less* than the personal exemption amount. As we noted above, the personal exemption amount for 2009 is $3,650.

---

[17]A person is considered to live with the taxpayer for the entire year if he or she was either born during the year or died during the year and resided with the taxpayer for the remaining part of the year. For example, a person who dies in March is deemed to live with the taxpayer for the entire year if the person resided with the taxpayer from the beginning of the year.

[18]Persons who are adopted qualify as if they are blood relatives.

[19]A multiple support agreement may be used to allocate a dependency exemption when multiple taxpayers provide support for an individual, but no single taxpayer provides a majority of support. The agreement can allocate the exemption to any taxpayer who provides at least 10 percent of the total support and would otherwise qualify to claim the individual as a dependent as a qualifying relative.

[20]§151(f)(5) and §151(f)(1). Just as with a qualifying child, this provision requires that the student be a son, daughter, stepson, stepdaughter, or an eligible foster child of the taxpayer.

Example 4-9

In determining their dependency exemptions for the year, Rodney and Anita evaluated whether Shawn is their *qualifying relative*. Assuming Shawn's gross income for the year is $42,000, the Halls provided food and lodging for Shawn valued at $8,000, and Shawn paid for his other living expenses valued at $14,000, is Shawn a qualifying relative of the Halls?

Answer: No, as analyzed below.

Test	Explanation
Relationship	Yes, Rodney's brother.
Support	No, the Halls provided $8,000 of support to Shawn, but Shawn provided $14,000 of his own support. Because the Halls provided less than half of Shawn's support, Shawn does not pass the support test.
Gross income	No, Shawn's gross income for the year is $42,000, which exceeds the exemption amount, so Shawn fails the gross income test.

Because Shawn fails the support test and the gross income test, he is not a qualifying relative of the Halls. Consequently, they cannot claim a dependency exemption for him. Thus, Shawn can claim a personal exemption for himself on his own tax return.

What if: Assume that Shawn received $5,000 of tax-exempt interest during the year and that is his only source of income. Does he fail the gross income test?

Answer: No. Because tax-exempt interest is excluded from gross income Shawn's gross income is $0, so he passes the gross income test.

What if: Assume the original facts in the example except that Shawn paid for his $14,000 of living expenses with interest he had received from tax-exempt bonds. Would Shawn pass the support test?

Answer: No. The Halls would not have provided more than half of Shawn's support. The fact that Shawn received the money he spent on his support from tax-exempt income does not matter. All that matters is that he provided more than half of his own support with his own funds.

What if: Assume that in 2009 Anita's 92-year-old grandfather Juan lives in an apartment by himself near the Halls's residence. His gross income for the year is $3,000. Assuming the Halls provide more than half of Juan's living expenses for the year, would Juan be a qualifying relative of the Halls?

Answer: Yes, as analyzed below.

Test	Explanation
Relationship	Yes, Anita's father.
Support	Yes, as assumed in the facts, the Halls provide more than half of Juan's support.
Gross income	Yes, Juan's gross income for the year is $3,000, which is below the $3,650 exemption amount, so Juan passes the gross income test.

What if: Assume Juan was a friend of the family but was not related to either Rodney or Anita, that his gross income is $3,000, and that the Halls provided over half of his support. Is Juan a qualifying relative of the Halls?

Answer: No, as analyzed below.

Test	Explanation
Relationship	No, not related to Halls and did not live as a member of the Halls's household for the *entire* year. If he had lived with the Halls, he would meet the relationship test even though he's not actually related to anyone in the Hall family.
Support	Yes, as assumed in the facts, the Halls provide more than half of Juan's support.
Gross income	Yes, Juan's gross income for the year is $3,000, which is below the $3,650 exemption amount, so Juan passes the gross income test.

The Halls would not be able to claim an exemption for Juan as a qualifying relative because he fails the relationship test under this set of facts.

The rules for determining who qualifies as a dependent as a qualifying child and who qualifies as a dependent as a qualifying relative overlap to some extent. The primary differences between the two are (1) the relationship requirement is more broadly defined for qualifying relatives than qualifying children, (2) qualifying children are subject to age restrictions while qualifying relatives are not, (3) qualifying relatives are subject to a gross income restriction while qualifying children are not, and (4) taxpayers need not provide more than half a qualifying child's support (though the child cannot provide more than half of her own support) but they must provide more than half the support of a qualifying relative. Exhibit 4-9 summarizes the dependency requirements.

EXHIBIT 4-9 Summary of Dependency Requirements

Test	Qualifying Child	Qualifying Relative
Relationship	Taxpayer's child, stepchild, foster child, sibling, half-brother or sister, stepbrother or sister, or a descendant of any of these relatives.	Taxpayer's descendant or ancestor, sibling, stepmother, stepfather, stepbrother or sister, nephews, nieces, aunts, uncles, in-laws, and anyone else who lives with the taxpayer for the entire year.
Age	Younger than the taxpayer claiming the individual as a qualifying child and under age 19 or a full-time student under age 24. Also anyone totally and permanently disabled.	Not applicable.
Residence	Lives with taxpayer for more than half of the year (includes temporary absences for things such as illness and education).	Not applicable.
Support	The qualifying child must not provide more than half of his or her own support.	Taxpayer must have provided more than half of the support for the qualifying relative.
Gross income	Not applicable.	Gross income less than exemption amount ($3,650 in 2009).
Other	Not applicable.	Not a qualifying child.

L03

FILING STATUS

THE KEY FACTS

Filing Status for Married Taxpayers

■ **Married filing jointly**
· Taxpayers are legally married as of the last day of the year.
· When one spouse dies during the year the surviving spouse is still considered to be married for tax purposes during the year of the spouse's death.
· Both spouses are ultimately responsible for paying the joint tax.

■ **Married filing separately**
· Taxpayers are legally married as of the last day of the year.
· Generally no tax advantage to filing separately (usually a disadvantage).
· Each spouse is ultimately responsible for paying own tax.
· Couples may choose to file separately (generally for nontax reasons).

■ **Qualifying widow or widower**
· When a taxpayer's spouse dies, the surviving spouse can file as qualifying widow or widower for two years after the year of the spouse's death if the surviving spouse remains unmarried and maintains a household for a dependent child.

Each year taxpayers determine their **filing status** according to their marital status at year-end and whether they have any dependents. A taxpayer's filing status is important because, as we discussed above, it determines:

1. The applicable tax rate schedule for determining the taxpayer's tax liability.
2. The taxpayer's standard deduction amount.
3. The AGI threshold for reductions in certain tax benefits such as itemized deductions, personal and dependency exemption deductions, and certain tax credits, among others.

Each year, all taxpayers filing tax returns file under one of the following five filing statuses:

- Married filing jointly
- Married filing separately
- Qualifying widow or widower (surviving spouse)
- Head of household
- Single

Married Filing Jointly and Married Filing Separately

Married couples may file tax returns jointly **(married filing jointly)** or separately **(married filing separately).** To be married for filing status purposes, taxpayers must be married on the last day of the year. When one spouse dies during the year, the surviving spouse is considered to be *married* to the decedent spouse at the end of the year unless the surviving spouse remarries during the year. Married couples filing joint returns combine their income and deductions and agree to share joint and several liability for the resulting tax. That is, they are both ultimately responsible to see that the tax is paid.

When married couples file separately, each spouse reports the income he or she received during the year and the deductions he or she paid on a tax return separate from that of the other spouse.[21] So that married taxpayers can't file separately to gain more combined tax benefits than they are entitled to if they filed jointly, tax-related items for married filing separate (MFS) taxpayers—such as tax rate schedules and standard deduction amounts, among others—are generally *one-half* what they are for married filing joint (MFJ) taxpayers. Also, if one spouse deducts itemized deductions, the other spouse is required to deduct itemized deductions even if his or her itemized deductions are less than the standard deduction. Thus, only in unusual circumstances does it make sense for *tax* purposes for married couples to file separately.

However, it may be wise for married couples to file separately for *nontax* reasons. For example, a spouse who does not want to be liable for the other spouse's income tax liability, or a spouse who is not in contact with the other spouse, may want to file separately (see abandoned spouse discussion below).

Example 4-10

Rodney and Anita Hall are married at the end of the year. What is their filing status?

Answer: Married filing jointly, unless they choose to file separately.

(*continued on page 4-17...*)

---

[21]As we discuss in the next chapter, under community property laws of certain states, one spouse may be treated as receiving income earned by the other spouse.

What if: Assume that this year (year 2009), the Halls file a joint return. In year 2010, Rodney and Anita divorce and the IRS audits their year 2009 tax return and determines that due to overstating their deductions, the Halls underpaid their taxes by $2,000. Who must pay the tax?

Answer: Both Rodney and Anita are responsible for paying. If the IRS can't locate Rodney, it can require Anita to pay the full $2,000 even though Anita earned $40,000 and Rodney earned $59,000.

What if: Assume that this year (year 2009), the Halls file separate tax returns. In year 2010, Rodney and Anita divorce and the IRS audits the Halls's separate tax returns. It determines that by overstating deductions, Rodney understated his tax liability by $1,500 and Anita understated her tax liability by $500. Further, the IRS cannot locate Rodney. What is the maximum amount of taxes Anita is liable for?

Answer: $500. Because she filed a separate return, she is responsible for the tax liability associated with her separate tax return and she is not responsible for the taxes associated with Rodney's tax return.

Qualifying Widow or Widower

When a taxpayer's spouse dies during the year, the taxpayer is no longer legally married. However, to provide tax relief for widows and widowers *with dependents,* taxpayers who qualify for the **qualifying widow or widower** filing status may file as though they are married filing jointly for up to two years *after* the end of the year in which the other spouse died (recall that for tax purposes, they are still considered to be married for the year of the spouse's death).[22] Taxpayers qualify for this exception as long as they (1) remain unmarried and (2) maintain a household for a dependent child during the two years after the year in which their spouses die.[23]

Example 4-11

What if: Assume that last year Rodney passed away, and during the current year Anita did not remarry but maintained a household for Braxton and Tara, her dependent children. Under these circumstances, what would Anita's filing status be?

Answer: Qualifying widow. Last year, the year of Rodney's death, Anita qualified to file a joint return with Rodney. This year, Anita qualifies as a qualifying widow (also referred to as a surviving spouse) because she has not remarried and she maintains a household for her dependent children. She will qualify as a surviving spouse next year (two years after Rodney's death) if she does not remarry and she continues to maintain a household for Braxton and/or Tara.

Head of Household

A taxpayer who is unmarried at the end of the year and who is not a qualifying widow or widower may be able to file as a **head of household.** To qualify as head of household, the taxpayer must either (1) pay more than half the costs of maintaining a household that is, for *more* than half the taxable year, the principal place of abode for a dependent who is either (A) a qualifying child or (B) a qualifying relative who meets the relationship test (that is, the dependent must still be considered to be related to the taxpayer even if the dependent did not live with the taxpayer for the entire year); or (2) pay more than half the costs of maintaining a separate household that is the principal place of abode for the taxpayer's mother or father if the mother or father also qualifies as a dependent of the taxpayer.[24]

[22]The qualifying widow or widower is not allowed to claim a dependency exemption for the deceased spouse for the two years after the spouse's death.
[23]§2(a).
[24]§2(b)(1)(B).

Example 4-12

What if: Assume Rodney and Anita divorced last year. During the current year, Braxton lives with Anita and Anita pays all the costs of maintaining the household for herself and Braxton. Under these circumstances, what is Anita's filing status for the current year?

Answer: Head of household. Anita is unmarried at the end of the year, and she provides more than half the costs of maintaining a household that is the principal place of abode for more than half the year for Braxton who is her qualifying child.

What if: Assume Shawn (Rodney's brother) lived with the Halls, but Shawn paid more than half the costs of maintaining a separate apartment that is the principal residence of his mother, Sharon, whose gross income is $1,500. Because Shawn provided more than half of Sharon's support during the year, and because Sharon's gross income was only $1,500, she qualifies as Shawn's dependent (as a qualifying relative). In these circumstances, what is Shawn's filing status?

Answer: Head of household. Shawn paid more than half the costs of maintaining a separate household that is the principal place of abode for his mother, and his mother qualifies as his dependent.

If Sharon's gross income exceeded $3,650 she would fail the dependency gross income test and would not qualify as Shawn's dependent. If she did not qualify as his dependent, Shawn would not qualify for the head of household filing status. Also, if Sharon were Shawn's grandmother rather than his mother, Shawn would not qualify for head of household status—Sharon must be Shawn's parent for him to qualify as a head of household.

In certain situations a couple may be legally married at the end of the year, but living apart. Although the couple could technically file a joint tax return, this is often not desirable from a nontax perspective, because each spouse would be assuming responsibility for paying tax on income earned by either spouse whether it was reported or not. However, because both spouses are married at the end of the year, their only other option is to file under the unfavorable status of married filing separately.

To provide tax relief in these situations, the tax laws treat married taxpayers who qualify as **abandoned spouses** *as though they were unmarried* at the end of the year. This allows them to qualify for the more favorable head of household filing status. An abandoned spouse is a taxpayer who meets all of the following requirements:

1. Is married at the end of the year (or is not *legally* separated from the other spouse).
2. Files a tax return for the year separate from the other spouse's.
3. Pays *more than half* the costs of maintaining his or her home for the entire year, and this home is the principal residence for a dependent qualifying child for *more than* half the year.
4. Whose spouse does not live in the taxpayer's home for the last six months of the year.

Example 4-13

What if: Assume that last year, Rodney and Anita informally separated (they did not legally separate). Rodney moved out of the home and into his own apartment. Anita stayed in the Halls's home with Braxton. During the current year, Anita paid more than half the cost of maintaining the home for herself and Braxton. Even though Rodney and Anita were legally married at the end of the year, they filed separate tax returns. Under these circumstances, what is Anita's filing status for the current year?

Answer: Head of household, determined as follows (see numbered requirements above):

1. Anita is married to Rodney at the end of the year.
2. Anita filed a tax return separate from Rodney's.

3. Anita paid more than half the costs of maintaining her home, and her home was the principal residence for Braxton who is her dependent qualifying child.

4. Rodney did not live in Anita's home for the last six months of the year (in fact, he didn't live there at any time during the entire year).

Without the abandoned spouse rule, Anita would have been required to file as married filing separately. Rodney's filing status, however, is married filing separately.

Single

Unmarried taxpayers who do not qualify for head of household status file as **single** taxpayers.

Example 4-14

Shawn Hall, Rodney's brother, was divorced in January and is unmarried at the end of the year. What is his filing status?

Answer: Single. Because Shawn is unmarried at the end of the year, and he did not maintain a household for any other person, his filing status is single.

SUMMARY OF INCOME TAX FORMULA

Tara crunched some numbers and put together a summary of her parents' taxable income calculation. She determined that her parents will be required to pay $73 of tax when they file their 2009 tax return. Tara's summary is provided in Exhibit 4-10.

EXHIBIT 4-10   **2009 Taxable Income and Tax Calculation Summary for Rodney and Anita Hall**

Description	Amount	Explanation
(1) Realized income from all sources	$ 110,900	Example 4-1, line (5).
(2) Excluded or deferred income:	(300)	Example 4-1, line (6).
(3) Gross income	110,600	(1) + (2)
(4) For AGI deductions	(5,000)	Example 4-2, line (2).
(5) Adjusted gross income	$ 105,600	(3) + (4)
(6) Itemized deductions	(14,000)	Example 4-3, line (2).
(7) Personal and dependency exemptions	(14,600)	Example 4-3, line (4).
(8) Taxable income	$ 77,000	(5) + (6) + (7).
(9) Income tax liability	$ 11,625	Example 4-4.
(10) Other taxes	0	
(11) Total tax	$ 11,625	(9) + (10).
(12) Credits	(1,000)	Example 4-5, line (2).
(13) Prepayments	(10,552)	Example 4-5, line (3).
Tax due with return	$ 73	(11) + (12) + (13).

CONCLUSION

This chapter presents an overview of the individual income tax formula and provides rules for determining a taxpayer's filing status and who qualifies as a taxpayer's dependents. In Chapter 5, we turn our attention to determining gross income. In Chapter 6, we describe deductions available to taxpayers when computing their taxable income. In Chapter 7, we conclude our review of the individual income tax formula by determining how to compute a taxpayer's tax liability and her taxes due or tax refund.

APPENDIX A   EXCERPT FROM 2008 TAX TABLE

2008 Tax Table–Continued

If line 43 (taxable income) is— At least	But less than	Single	Married filing jointly*	Married filing separately	Head of a household
77,000					
77,000	77,050	15,600	11,944	15,939	14,319
77,050	77,100	15,613	11,956	15,953	14,331
77,100	77,150	15,625	11,969	15,967	14,344
77,150	77,200	15,638	11,981	15,981	14,356
77,200	77,250	15,650	11,994	15,995	14,369
77,250	77,300	15,663	12,006	16,009	14,381
77,300	77,350	15,675	12,019	16,023	14,394
77,350	77,400	15,688	12,031	16,037	14,406
77,400	77,450	15,700	12,044	16,051	14,419
77,450	77,500	15,713	12,056	16,065	14,431
77,500	77,550	15,725	12,069	16,079	14,444
77,550	77,600	15,738	12,081	16,093	14,456
77,600	77,650	15,750	12,094	16,107	14,469
77,650	77,700	15,763	12,106	16,121	14,481
77,700	77,750	15,775	12,119	16,135	14,494
77,750	77,800	15,788	12,131	16,149	14,506
77,800	77,850	15,800	12,144	16,163	14,519
77,850	77,900	15,813	12,156	16,177	14,531
77,900	77,950	15,825	12,169	16,191	14,544
77,950	78,000	15,838	12,181	16,205	14,556
78,000					
78,000	78,050	15,850	12,194	16,219	14,569
78,050	78,100	15,863	12,206	16,233	14,581
78,100	78,150	15,875	12,219	16,247	14,594
78,150	78,200	15,888	12,231	16,261	14,606
78,200	78,250	15,900	12,244	16,275	14,619
78,250	78,300	15,913	12,256	16,289	14,631
78,300	78,350	15,925	12,269	16,303	14,644
78,350	78,400	15,938	12,281	16,317	14,656
78,400	78,450	15,950	12,294	16,331	14,669
78,450	78,500	15,963	12,306	16,345	14,681
78,500	78,550	15,975	12,319	16,359	14,694
78,550	78,600	15,988	12,331	16,373	14,706
78,600	78,650	16,000	12,344	16,387	14,719
78,650	78,700	16,013	12,356	16,401	14,731
78,700	78,750	16,025	12,369	16,415	14,744
78,750	78,800	16,038	12,381	16,429	14,756
78,800	78,850	16,050	12,394	16,443	14,769
78,850	78,900	16,063	12,406	16,457	14,781
78,900	78,950	16,077	12,419	16,471	14,794
78,950	79,000	16,091	12,431	16,485	14,806
79,000					
79,000	79,050	16,105	12,444	16,499	14,819
79,050	79,100	16,119	12,456	16,513	14,831
79,100	79,150	16,133	12,469	16,527	14,844
79,150	79,200	16,147	12,481	16,541	14,856
79,200	79,250	16,161	12,494	16,555	14,869
79,250	79,300	16,175	12,506	16,569	14,881
79,300	79,350	16,189	12,519	16,583	14,894
79,350	79,400	16,203	12,531	16,597	14,906
79,400	79,450	16,217	12,544	16,611	14,919
79,450	79,500	16,231	12,556	16,625	14,931
79,500	79,550	16,245	12,569	16,639	14,944
79,550	79,600	16,259	12,581	16,653	14,956
79,600	79,650	16,273	12,594	16,667	14,969
79,650	79,700	16,287	12,606	16,681	14,981
79,700	79,750	16,301	12,619	16,695	14,994
79,750	79,800	16,315	12,631	16,709	15,006
79,800	79,850	16,329	12,644	16,723	15,019
79,850	79,900	16,343	12,656	16,737	15,031
79,900	79,950	16,357	12,669	16,751	15,044
79,950	80,000	16,371	12,681	16,765	15,056

If line 43 (taxable income) is— At least	But less than	Single	Married filing jointly*	Married filing separately	Head of a household
80,000					
80,000	80,050	16,385	12,694	16,779	15,069
80,050	80,100	16,399	12,706	16,793	15,081
80,100	80,150	16,413	12,719	16,807	15,094
80,150	80,200	16,427	12,731	16,821	15,106
80,200	80,250	16,441	12,744	16,835	15,119
80,250	80,300	16,455	12,756	16,849	15,131
80,300	80,350	16,469	12,769	16,863	15,144
80,350	80,400	16,483	12,781	16,877	15,156
80,400	80,450	16,497	12,794	16,891	15,169
80,450	80,500	16,511	12,806	16,905	15,181
80,500	80,550	16,525	12,819	16,919	15,194
80,550	80,600	16,539	12,831	16,933	15,206
80,600	80,650	16,553	12,844	16,947	15,219
80,650	80,700	16,567	12,856	16,961	15,231
80,700	80,750	16,581	12,869	16,975	15,244
80,750	80,800	16,595	12,881	16,989	15,256
80,800	80,850	16,609	12,894	17,003	15,269
80,850	80,900	16,623	12,906	17,017	15,281
80,900	80,950	16,637	12,919	17,031	15,294
80,950	81,000	16,651	12,931	17,045	15,306
81,000					
81,000	81,050	16,665	12,944	17,059	15,319
81,050	81,100	16,679	12,956	17,073	15,331
81,100	81,150	16,693	12,969	17,087	15,344
81,150	81,200	16,707	12,981	17,101	15,356
81,200	81,250	16,721	12,994	17,115	15,369
81,250	81,300	16,735	13,006	17,129	15,381
81,300	81,350	16,749	13,019	17,143	15,394
81,350	81,400	16,763	13,031	17,157	15,406
81,400	81,450	16,777	13,044	17,171	15,419
81,450	81,500	16,791	13,056	17,185	15,431
81,500	81,550	16,805	13,069	17,199	15,444
81,550	81,600	16,819	13,081	17,213	15,456
81,600	81,650	16,833	13,094	17,227	15,469
81,650	81,700	16,847	13,106	17,241	15,481
81,700	81,750	16,861	13,119	17,255	15,494
81,750	81,800	16,875	13,131	17,269	15,506
81,800	81,850	16,889	13,144	17,283	15,519
81,850	81,900	16,903	13,156	17,297	15,531
81,900	81,950	16,917	13,169	17,311	15,544
81,950	82,000	16,931	13,181	17,325	15,556
82,000					
82,000	82,050	16,945	13,194	17,339	15,569
82,050	82,100	16,959	13,206	17,353	15,581
82,100	82,150	16,973	13,219	17,367	15,594
82,150	82,200	16,987	13,231	17,381	15,606
82,200	82,250	17,001	13,244	17,395	15,619
82,250	82,300	17,015	13,256	17,409	15,631
82,300	82,350	17,029	13,269	17,423	15,644
82,350	82,400	17,043	13,281	17,437	15,656
82,400	82,450	17,057	13,294	17,451	15,669
82,450	82,500	17,071	13,306	17,465	15,681
82,500	82,550	17,085	13,319	17,479	15,694
82,550	82,600	17,099	13,331	17,493	15,706
82,600	82,650	17,113	13,344	17,507	15,719
82,650	82,700	17,127	13,356	17,521	15,731
82,700	82,750	17,141	13,369	17,535	15,744
82,750	82,800	17,155	13,381	17,549	15,756
82,800	82,850	17,169	13,394	17,563	15,769
82,850	82,900	17,183	13,406	17,577	15,781
82,900	82,950	17,197	13,419	17,591	15,794
82,950	83,000	17,211	13,431	17,605	15,806

If line 43 (taxable income) is— At least	But less than	Single	Married filing jointly*	Married filing separately	Head of a household
83,000					
83,000	83,050	17,225	13,444	17,619	15,819
83,050	83,100	17,239	13,456	17,633	15,831
83,100	83,150	17,253	13,469	17,647	15,844
83,150	83,200	17,267	13,481	17,661	15,856
83,200	83,250	17,281	13,494	17,675	15,869
83,250	83,300	17,295	13,506	17,689	15,881
83,300	83,350	17,309	13,519	17,703	15,894
83,350	83,400	17,323	13,531	17,717	15,906
83,400	83,450	17,337	13,544	17,731	15,919
83,450	83,500	17,351	13,556	17,745	15,931
83,500	83,550	17,365	13,569	17,759	15,944
83,550	83,600	17,379	13,581	17,773	15,956
83,600	83,650	17,393	13,594	17,787	15,969
83,650	83,700	17,407	13,606	17,801	15,981
83,700	83,750	17,421	13,619	17,815	15,994
83,750	83,800	17,435	13,631	17,829	16,006
83,800	83,850	17,449	13,644	17,843	16,019
83,850	83,900	17,463	13,656	17,857	16,031
83,900	83,950	17,477	13,669	17,871	16,044
83,950	84,000	17,491	13,681	17,885	16,056
84,000					
84,000	84,050	17,505	13,694	17,899	16,069
84,050	84,100	17,519	13,706	17,913	16,081
84,100	84,150	17,533	13,719	17,927	16,094
84,150	84,200	17,547	13,731	17,941	16,106
84,200	84,250	17,561	13,744	17,955	16,119
84,250	84,300	17,575	13,756	17,969	16,131
84,300	84,350	17,589	13,769	17,983	16,144
84,350	84,400	17,603	13,781	17,997	16,156
84,400	84,450	17,617	13,794	18,011	16,169
84,450	84,500	17,631	13,806	18,025	16,181
84,500	84,550	17,645	13,819	18,039	16,194
84,550	84,600	17,659	13,831	18,053	16,206
84,600	84,650	17,673	13,844	18,067	16,219
84,650	84,700	17,687	13,856	18,081	16,231
84,700	84,750	17,701	13,869	18,095	16,244
84,750	84,800	17,715	13,881	18,109	16,256
84,800	84,850	17,729	13,894	18,123	16,269
84,850	84,900	17,743	13,906	18,137	16,281
84,900	84,950	17,757	13,919	18,151	16,294
84,950	85,000	17,771	13,931	18,165	16,306
85,000					
85,000	85,050	17,785	13,944	18,179	16,319
85,050	85,100	17,799	13,956	18,193	16,331
85,100	85,150	17,813	13,969	18,207	16,344
85,150	85,200	17,827	13,981	18,221	16,356
85,200	85,250	17,841	13,994	18,235	16,369
85,250	85,300	17,855	14,006	18,249	16,381
85,300	85,350	17,869	14,019	18,263	16,394
85,350	85,400	17,883	14,031	18,277	16,406
85,400	85,450	17,897	14,044	18,291	16,419
85,450	85,500	17,911	14,056	18,305	16,431
85,500	85,550	17,925	14,069	18,319	16,444
85,550	85,600	17,939	14,081	18,333	16,456
85,600	85,650	17,953	14,094	18,347	16,469
85,650	85,700	17,967	14,106	18,361	16,481
85,700	85,750	17,981	14,119	18,375	16,494
85,750	85,800	17,995	14,131	18,389	16,506
85,800	85,850	18,009	14,144	18,403	16,519
85,850	85,900	18,023	14,156	18,417	16,531
85,900	85,950	18,037	14,169	18,431	16,544
85,950	86,000	18,051	14,181	18,445	16,556

* This column must also be used by a qualifying widow(er).

SUMMARY

Describe the formula for calculating an individual taxpayer's taxes payable or refund and generally explain each formula component.

- Generally, taxpayers are taxed on all income they realize during the year, no matter the source. However, the tax laws allow taxpayers to permanently exclude or defer to a later year certain types of income they realize during the year.

- Income items that taxpayers are allowed to permanently exclude from income are called exclusions. Realized income items that taxpayers are not taxed on until a future period are called deferrals.

- Taxpayers include gross income on their tax returns. Gross income is realized income minus exclusions and deferrals.

- Taxpayers subtract deductions from their gross income to determine their taxable income. Taxpayers are not allowed to reduce income for any deductions unless a specific provision in the tax laws provides for the deduction.

- For AGI deductions tend to relate to business activities and certain investment activities. These deductions always reduce taxable income, dollar for dollar. For AGI deductions are deductions "above the line," the line being the last line on the front page of the individual tax Form 1040.

- Gross income minus for AGI deductions equals adjusted gross income (AGI).

- AGI is an important reference point in the individual tax formula because it is often used in other tax-related calculations, including determining limitations on from AGI deductions.

- From AGI deductions are subtracted from AGI to determine taxable income. From AGI deductions include itemized deductions, the standard deduction, and exemptions. From AGI deductions are referred to as "deductions below the line."

- Taxpayers generally deduct itemized deductions when the amount of the itemized deductions exceeds the standard deduction. The standard deduction varies by filing status and is indexed for inflation.

- Taxpayers are allowed to deduct personal exemptions for themselves and their spouses (if any) and dependency exemptions for those who qualify as their dependents.

- Taxpayers generally calculate the tax on their taxable income by referring to tax tables or tax rate schedules. However, certain types of income such as long-term capital gains and qualifying dividends may be taxed at rates other than the rates provided in the tax rate schedule.

- Taxpayers may be required to pay the alternative minimum tax (AMT) or self-employment taxes in addition to their regular income tax.

- Tax credits reduce taxpayers' tax liability dollar for dollar.

- Taxpayers prepay taxes during the year through withholdings by employers, estimated tax payments, or a prior year overpayment applied toward the current year tax liability.

- If tax prepayments exceed the taxpayer's total tax after credits, the taxpayer receives a refund. If tax prepayments are less than the total tax after credits, the taxpayer owes additional tax with his or her tax return.

Explain the requirements for determining a taxpayer's personal and dependency exemptions.

- In 2009, taxpayers are allowed to deduct $3,650 for each personal and dependency exemption they are entitled to claim.

- Individuals may claim an exemption for themselves and their spouses if they are married and file jointly. They may also claim dependency exemptions for each person who qualifies as their dependent.

- If an individual qualifies as a dependent of another taxpayer, the dependent may not deduct a personal exemption for him- or herself on his or her individual return.

- Taxpayers may claim dependency exemptions for those qualifying as their qualifying child or qualifying relative.

- A child must meet a relationship test, an age test, a residence test, and a support test to qualify as a qualifying child.
- A person may be considered a qualifying relative by meeting a relationship test, a support test, and a gross income test.

L03   Determine a taxpayer's filing status

- Taxpayers may file their tax returns as married filing jointly, married filing separately, qualifying widow or widower (or surviving spouse), head of household, or single.
- Married taxpayers may file a joint return or they may choose to file separately. It is generally more advantageous for tax purposes to file jointly if married. However, for nontax reasons, it may be advantageous to file separately.
- Each spouse is ultimately responsible for paying the tax on a joint return.
- For two years after the year in which one spouse dies, qualifying widows or widowers may file as if they were married filing jointly as long as they (1) remain unmarried and (2) maintain a household for a dependent child. However, they are not allowed to claim a dependency exemption for the deceased spouse beyond the year of the spouse's death.
- An unmarried taxpayer who is not a qualifying widow or widower may file as head of household if the person either (1) pays more than half the costs of maintaining a household that is, for *more* than half the taxable year, the principal place of abode for a dependent who is either a qualifying child or a qualifying relative who meets the exemption relationship test; or (2) pays more than half the costs of maintaining a separate household that is the principal place of abode for the taxpayer's mother or father if the mother or father also qualifies as a dependent of the taxpayer.
- Unmarried taxpayers who do not qualify for head of household status file as single taxpayers.

KEY TERMS

abandoned spouse (4-18)

adjusted gross income (AGI) (4-6)

all-inclusive income concept (4-2)

alternative minimum tax (AMT) (4-9)

deductions (4-6)

deductions above the line (4-6)

deductions below the line (4-6)

deductions *for* AGI (4-6)

deductions *from* AGI (4-6)

deferral items, deferred income, or deferrals (4-5)

dependency exemptions (4-7)

dependent (4-11)

estimated tax payments (4-9)

excluded income or exclusions (4-5)

exemptions (4-7)

filing status (4-16)

gross income (4-5)

head of household (4-17)

itemized deductions (4-7)

legislative grace (4-6)

married filing jointly (4-16)

married filing separately (4-16)

personal exemptions (4-7)

qualifying child (4-11)

qualifying relative (4-11)

qualifying widow or widower (4-17)

realized income (4-2)

single (4-19)

self-employment taxes (4-9)

standard deduction (4-7)

taxable income (4-2)

tax credits (4-9)

tax rate schedule (4-8)

tax tables (4-8)

withholdings (4-9)

DISCUSSION QUESTIONS

1. **(LO1)** How are realized income, gross income, and taxable income similar, and how are they different?
2. **(LO1)** Are taxpayers required to include all realized income in gross income? Explain.
3. **(LO1)** All else equal, should taxpayers prefer to exclude income or to defer it? Why?
4. **(LO1)** Compare and contrast *for* and *from* AGI deductions. Why are *for* AGI deductions likely more valuable to taxpayers than *from* AGI deductions?

5. **(LO1)** What is the difference between gross income and adjusted gross income, and what is the difference between adjusted gross income and taxable income?

6. **(LO1)** How do taxpayers determine whether they should deduct their itemized deductions or utilize the standard deduction?

7. **(LO1)** Why are some deductions called "above the line" deductions and others are called "below the line" deductions? What is the "line"?

8. **(LO1)** What is the difference between a tax deduction and a tax credit? Is one more beneficial than the other?

9. **(LO1)** What types of income are taxed at rates different than the rates provided in tax rate schedules and tax tables?

10. **(LO1)** What types of federal income-based taxes, other than the regular income tax, might taxpayers be required to pay? In general terms, what is the tax base for each of these other taxes on income?

11. **(LO1)** Identify three ways taxpayers can pay their income taxes to the government.

12. **(LO2)** Emily and Tony are recently married college students. Can Emily qualify as her parents' dependent? Explain.

13. **(LO2)** In general terms, what are the differences in the rules for determining who is a qualifying child and who qualifies as a dependent as a qualifying relative? Is it possible for someone to be a qualifying child and a qualifying relative of the same taxpayer? Why or why not?

14. **(LO2)** How do two taxpayers determine who has priority to claim the dependency exemption for a qualifying child of both taxpayers when neither taxpayer is a parent of the child (assume the child does not qualify as a qualifying child of either parent)? How do parents determine who gets to deduct the dependency exemption for a qualifying child of both parents when the parents are divorced or file separate returns?

15. **(LO3)** What requirements do the abandoned spouse and qualifying widow or widower have in common?

16. **(LO3)** For tax purposes, why is the married filing jointly tax status generally preferable to the married filing separately filing status? Why might a married taxpayer prefer *not* to file a joint return with the taxpayer's spouse?

17. **(LO3)** What does it mean to say that a married couple filing a joint tax return has joint and several liability for the taxes associated with the return?

PROBLEMS

18. **(LO1)** Jeremy earned $100,000 in salary and $6,000 in interest income during the year. Jeremy has two qualifying dependent children who live with him. He qualifies to file as head of household and has $17,000 in itemized deductions. Neither of his dependents qualifies for the child tax credit.

    a. Use the 2009 tax rate schedules to determine Jeremy's taxes due.

    b. Assume that in addition to the original facts, Jeremy has qualifying dividends of $4,000. What is Jeremy's tax liability including the tax on the dividends (use the tax rate schedules rather than the tax tables)?

    c. Assume the original facts except that Jeremy had only $7,000 in itemized deductions. What is Jeremy's total income tax liability (use the tax rate schedules rather than the tax tables)?

19. **(LO1)** David and Lilly Fernandez have determined their tax liability on their joint tax return to be $1,700. They have made prepayments of $1,500 and also have a child tax credit of $1,000. What is the amount of their tax refund or taxes due?

■ planning

20. **(LO1)** In 2009, Rick, who is single, has been offered a position as a city land-scape consultant. The position pays $125,000 in cash wages. Assume Rick files single and is entitled to one personal exemption. Rick deducts the standard deduction instead of itemized deductions.

a. What is the amount of Rick's after-tax compensation (ignore payroll taxes)?

b. Suppose Rick receives a competing job offer of $120,000 in cash compensation and nontaxable (excluded) benefits worth $4,000. What is the amount of Rick's after-tax compensation for the competing offer? Which job should he take if taxes were the only concern?

21. **(LO1)** Through November 2009, Tex has received gross income of $120,000. For December, Tex is considering whether to accept one more work engagement for the year. Engagement 1 will generate $7,000 of revenue at a cost of $4,000 which is deductible for AGI. In contrast, engagement 2 will generate $7,000 of revenue at a cost of $3,000, which is deductible as an itemized deduction. Tex files a single tax return.

a. Calculate Tex's taxable income assuming he chooses engagement 1 and assuming he chooses engagement 2. Assume he has no itemized deductions other than those generated by engagement 2.

b. Calculate Tex's taxable income assuming he chooses engagement 1 and assuming he chooses engagement 2. Assume he has $4,500 of itemized deductions other than those generated by engagement 2.

c. Calculate Tex's taxable income assuming he chooses engagement 1 and assuming he chooses engagement 2. Assume he has $7,000 of itemized deductions other than those generated by engagement 2.

■ planning

22. **(LO1)** Matteo, who is single and has no dependents, was planning on spending the weekend repairing his car. On Friday, Matteo's employer called and offered him $500 in overtime pay if he would agree to work over the weekend. Matteo could get his car repaired over the weekend at Autofix for $400. If Matteo works over the weekend, he will have to pay the $400 to have his car repaired but he will earn $500. Assume Matteo pays a tax at a flat rate of 15 percent rate.

a. Strictly considering tax factors, should Matteo work or repair his car if the $400 he must pay to have his car fixed is not deductible?

b. Strictly considering tax factors, should Matteo work or repair his car if the $400 he must pay to have his car fixed is deductible for AGI?

23. **(LO1, LO2)** Rank the following three single taxpayers in order of the magnitude of taxable income for 2009 (from lowest to highest) and explain your results.

	Ahmed	Baker	Chin
Gross income	$80,000	$80,000	$80,000
Deductions *for* AGI	8,000	4,000	0
Itemized deductions	0	4,000	8,000

24. **(LO2)** The Samsons are trying to determine whether they can claim their 22-year-old adopted son, Jason, as a dependent. Jason is currently a full-time student at an out-of-state university. Jason lived in his parents' home for three months of the year and he was away at school for the rest of the year. He received $9,500 in scholarships this year for his outstanding academic performance and earned $3,900 of income working a part-time job during the year. The Samsons paid a total of $4,000 to support Jason while he was away at college. Jason used the

scholarship, the earnings from the part-time job, and the money from the Samsons as his only sources of support.

a. Can the Samsons claim Jason as their dependent?

b. Assume the original facts except that Jason's grandparents, not the Samsons, provided him with the $4,000 worth of support. Can the Samsons (Jason's parents) claim Jason as their dependent? Why or why not?

c. Assume the original facts except substitute Jason's grandparents for his parents. Determine whether Jason's grandparents can claim Jason as a dependent.

d. Assume the original facts except that Jason earned $4,500 while working part-time and used this amount for his support. Can the Samsons claim Jason as their dependent? Why or why not?

25. **(LO2)** John and Tara Smith are married and have lived in the same home for over 20 years. John's uncle Tim, who is 64 years old, has lived with the Smiths since March of this year. Tim is searching for employment but has been unable to find any—his gross income for the year is $2,000. Tim used all $2,000 toward his own support. The Smiths provided the rest of Tim's support by providing him with lodging valued at $5,000 and food valued at $2,200.

a. Are the Smiths able to claim a dependency exemption for Tim?

b. Assume the original facts except that Tim earned $10,000 and used all the funds for his own support. Are the Smiths able to claim Tim as a dependent?

c. Assume the original facts except that Tim is a friend of the family and not John's uncle.

d. Assume the original facts except that Tim is a friend of the family and not John's uncle and Tim lived with the Smiths for the entire year.

26. **(LO2)** Francine's mother Donna and her father Darren separated and divorced in September of this year. Francine lived with both parents until the separation. Francine does *not* provide more than half of her own support. Francine is 15 years old at the end of the year.

a. Is Francine a qualifying child to Donna?

b. Is Francine a qualifying child to Darren?

c. Assume Francine spends more time living with Darren than Donna after the separation. Who may claim Francine as a dependency exemption for tax purposes?

d. Assume Francine spends an equal number of days with her mother and her father and that Donna has AGI of $52,000 and Darren has AGI of $50,000. Who may claim a dependency exemption for Francine?

27. **(LO2)** By the end of 2009, Jamel and Jennifer have been married 30 years and have filed a joint return every year of their marriage. Their three daughters, Jade, Lindsay, and Abbi, are ages 12, 17, and 22 respectively and all live at home. None of the daughters provides more than half of her own support. Abbi is a full-time student at a local university and does not have any gross income.

a. How many personal and dependency exemptions are the Harrisons allowed to claim?

b. Assume the original facts except that Abbi is married. She and her husband live with Jamel and Jennifer while attending school and they file a joint return. Abbi and her husband reported a $1,000 tax liability on their 2009 tax return. If all parties are willing, can Jamel and Jennifer claim Abbi as a dependent on their 2009 tax return? Why or why not?

c. Assume the same facts as part b., except that Abbi and her husband report a $0 tax liability on their 2009 joint tax return. Also, if the couple had filed separately, Abbi would have not had a tax liability on her return but her husband would owe $250 of tax on his separate return. Can Jamel and Jennifer claim Abbi as a dependent on their 2009 tax return? Why or why not?

d. Assume the original facts except that Abbi is married. Abbi files a separate tax return for 2009. Abbi's husband files a separate tax return and owes $250 in taxes. Can Jamel and Jennifer claim Abbi as a dependent in 2009?

research

28. **(LO2)** Mel and Cindy Gibson's 12-year-old daughter Rachel was abducted on her way home from school on March 15, 2009. Police reports indicated that a stranger had physically dragged Rachel into a waiting car and sped away. Everyone hoped that the kidnapper and Rachel would be located quickly. However, as of the end of the year, Rachel was still missing. The police were still pursuing several promising leads and had every reason to believe that Rachel was still alive. In 2010, Rachel was returned safely to her parents.

a. Are the Gibsons allowed to claim an exemption deduction for Rachel in 2009 even though she only lived in the Gibson's home for two-and-one-half months? Explain and cite your authority.

b. Assume the original facts except that Rachel is unrelated to the Gibsons but she has been living with them since January 2004. The Gibsons have claimed a dependency exemption for Rachel for the years 2004 through 2008. Are the Gibsons allowed to claim a dependency exemption for Rachel in 2009? Explain and cite your authority.

research

29. **(LO2)** Bob Ryan filed his 2009 tax return and claimed a dependency exemption for his 16-year-old son Dylan. Both Bob and Dylan are citizens and residents of the United States. Dylan meets all the necessary requirements to be considered a qualifying child; however, when Bob filed the tax return he didn't know Dylan's Social Security number and, therefore, didn't include an identifying number for his son on the tax return. Instead, Bob submitted an affidavit with his tax return stating he had requested Dylan's Social Security number from Dylan's birth state. Is Bob allowed to claim a dependency exemption for Dylan without including Dylan's identifying number on the return?

30. **(LO2, LO3)** Kimberly is divorced and the custodial parent of 5-year-old twins, Bailey and Cameron. All three live with Kimberly's parents, who pay all the costs of maintaining the household (such as mortgage, property taxes, and food). Kimberly pays for her own and the children's clothing, entertainment, and health insurance costs. These costs comprised only a small part of the total costs of maintaining the household.

a. Determine the appropriate filing status for Kimberly.

b. What if Kimberly lived in her own home and provided all the costs of maintaining the household?

31. **(LO3)** Juan and Bonita are married and have two dependent children living at home. This year, Juan is killed in an avalanche while skiing.

a. What is Bonita's filing status this year?

b. Assuming Bonita doesn't remarry and still has two dependent children living at home, what will her filing status be next year?

c. Assuming Bonita doesn't remarry and doesn't have any dependents next year, what will her filing status be next year?

32. **(LO3)** Gary and Lakesha were married on December 31 last year. They are now preparing their taxes for the April 15 deadline and are unsure of their filing status.

a. What filing status options do Gary and Lakesha have for last year?

b. Assume instead that Gary and Lakesha were married on January 1 of this year. What is their filing status for last year (neither has been married before and neither had any dependents last year)?

33. **(LO3)** Elroy, who is single, has taken over the care of his mother Irene in her old age. Elroy pays the bills relating to Irene's home. He also buys all her groceries and provides the rest of her support. Irene has no gross income.

    a. What is Elroy's filing status?
    b. Assume the original facts except that Elroy has taken over the care of his grandmother, Renae, instead of his mother. What is Elroy's filing status?
    c. Assume the original facts except that Elroy's mother, Irene, lives with him and that she receives an annual $4,000 taxable distribution from her retirement account. Elroy still pays all the costs to maintain the household. What is his filing status?

34. **(LO3)** Kano and his wife, Hoshi, have been married for 10 years and have two children under the age of 12. The couple has been living apart for the last two years and both children live with Kano. Kano has provided all the means necessary to support himself and his children. Kano and Hoshi do not file a joint return.

    a. What is Kano's filing status?
    b. Assume the original facts except that Kano and Hoshi separated in May of the current year. What is Kano's filing status?
    c. Assume the original facts except that Kano and Hoshi separated in November of this year. What is Kano's filing status?
    d. Assume the original facts except that Kano's parents, not Kano, paid more than half of the cost of maintaining the home in which Kano and his children live. What is Kano's filing status?

35. **(LO2, LO3)** In each of the following *independent* cases, determine the taxpayer's filing status and the number of personal and dependency exemptions the taxpayer is allowed to claim.

    a. Frank is single and supports his 17-year-old brother, Bill. Bill earned $3,000 and did not live with Frank.
    b. Geneva and her spouse reside with their son, Steve, who is a 20-year-old undergraduate student at State University. Steve earned $13,100 at a part-time summer job, but he deposited this money in a savings account for graduate school. Geneva paid all of the $12,000 cost of supporting Steve.
    c. Hamish's spouse died last year and Hamish has not remarried. Hamish supports his father, Reggie, age 78, who lives in a nursing home and had interest income this year of $2,500.
    d. Irene is married but has not seen her spouse since February. She supports her spouse's 18-year-old child, Dolores, who lives with Irene. Dolores earned $4,500 this year.

36. **(LO2, LO3)** In each of the following *independent* cases, determine the taxpayer's filing status and the number of personal and dependency exemptions the taxpayer is allowed to claim.

    a. Alexandra is a blind widow who provides a home for her 18-year-old nephew, Newt. Newt's parents are dead and so Newt supports himself. Newt's gross income is $5,000.
    b. Bharati supports and maintains a home for her daughter, Daru, and son-in-law, Sam. Sam earned $15,000 and filed a joint return with Daru, who had no income.
    c. Charlie intended to file a joint return with his spouse, Sally. However, Sally died in December. Charlie has not remarried.
    d. Deshi cannot convince his spouse to consent to signing a joint return. The couple has not separated.
    e. Edith and her spouse support their 35-year-old son, Slim. Slim is a full-time college student who earned $5,500 over the summer in part-time work.

37. **(LO3)** Jasper and Crewella Dahvill were married in year 0. They filed joint tax returns in years 1 and 2. In year 3, their relationship was strained and Jasper insisted on filing a separate tax return. In year 4, the couple divorced. Both Jasper and Crewella filed single tax returns in year 4. In year 5, the IRS audited the couple's joint year 2 tax return and each spouse's separate year 3 tax returns. The IRS determined that the year 2 joint return and Crewella's separate year 3 tax return understated Crewella's self-employment income causing the joint return year 2 tax liability to be understated by $4,000 and Crewella's year 3 separate return tax liability to be understated by $6,000. The IRS also assessed penalties and interest on both of these tax returns. Try as it might, the IRS has not been able to locate Crewella, but they have been able to find Jasper.

    a. What amount of tax can the IRS require Jasper to pay for the Dahvill's year 2 joint return? Explain.

    b. What amount of tax can the IRS require Jasper to pay for Crewella's year 3 separate tax return? Explain.

38. **(LO3)** Janice Traylor is single. She has an 18-year-old son named Marty. Marty is Janice's only child. Marty has lived with Janice his entire life. However, Marty recently joined the Marines and was sent on a special assignment to Australia. During 2009, Marty spent nine months in Australia. Marty was extremely homesick while in Australia, since he had never lived away from home. However, Marty knew this assignment was only temporary, and he couldn't wait to come home and find his room just the way he left it. Janice has always filed as head of household, and Marty has always been considered a qualifying child (and he continues to meet all the tests with the possible exception of the residence test due to his stay in Australia). However, this year Janice is unsure whether she qualifies as head of household due to Marty's nine-month absence during the year. Janice has come to you for advice on whether she qualifies for head of household filing status in 2009. What do you tell her?

39. **(LO3)** Doug Jones timely submitted his 2009 tax return and elected married filing jointly status with his wife, Darlene. Doug and Darlene did not request an extension for their 2009 tax return. Doug and Darlene owed and paid the IRS $124,000 for their 2009 tax year. Two years later, Doug amended his return and claimed married filing separate status. By changing his filing status, Doug sought a refund for an overpayment for the tax year 2009 (he paid more tax in the original joint return than he owed on a separate return). Is Doug allowed to change his filing status for the 2009 tax year and receive a tax refund with his amended return?

COMPREHENSIVE PROBLEMS

40. Marc and Michelle are married and earned salaries this year (2009) of $64,000 and $12,000, respectively. In addition to their salaries, they received interest of $350 from municipal bonds and $500 from corporate bonds. Marc and Michelle also paid $2,500 of qualifying moving expenses, and Marc paid alimony to a prior spouse in the amount of $1,500. Marc and Michelle have a 10-year-old son, Matthew, who lived with them throughout the entire year. Thus, Marc and Michelle are allowed to claim a $1,000 child tax credit for Matthew. Marc and Michelle paid $6,000 of expenditures that qualify as itemized deductions and they had a total of $5,500 in federal income taxes withheld from their paychecks during the course of the year.

    a. What is Marc and Michelle's gross income?

    b. What is Marc and Michelle's adjusted gross income?

    c. What is the total amount of Marc and Michelle's deductions *from* AGI?

d. What is Marc and Michelle's taxable income?

e. What is Marc and Michelle's taxes payable or refund due for the year? (Use the tax rate schedules.)

41. Demarco and Janine Jackson have been married for 20 years and have four children who qualify as their dependents. Their income from all sources this year (2009) totaled $200,000 and included a gain from the sale of their home, which they purchased a few years ago for $200,000 and sold this year for $250,000. The gain on the sale qualified for the exclusion from the sale of a principal residence. The Jacksons incurred $16,500 of itemized deductions.

a. What is the Jackson's taxable income?

b. What would their taxable income be if their itemized deductions totaled $6,000 instead of $16,500?

c. What would their taxable income be if they had $0 itemized deductions and $6,000 of for AGI deductions?

d. Assume the original facts except that they also incurred a loss of $5,000 on the sale of some of their investment assets. What effect does the $5,000 loss have on their *taxable income*?

e. Assume the original facts except that the Jacksons owned investments that appreciated by $10,000 during the year. The Jacksons believe the investments will continue to appreciate, so they did not sell the investments during this year. What is the Jackson's taxable income?

42. Camille Sikorski was divorced last year. She currently owns and provides a home for her 15-year-old daughter, Kaly, and 18-year-old son, Parker. Both children lived in Camille's home for the entire year, and Camille paid for all the costs of maintaining the home. She received a salary of $105,000 and contributed $6,000 of it to a qualified retirement account. She also received $10,000 of alimony from her former husband. Finally, Camille paid $5,000 of expenditures that qualified as itemized deductions. (The current year is 2009.)

a. What is Camille's taxable income?

b. What would Camille's taxable income be if she incurred $14,000 of itemized deductions instead of $5,000?

c. Assume the original facts except that Camille's daughter, Kaly, is 25 years old and a full-time student. Kaly's gross income for the year was $5,000. Kaly provided $3,000 of her own support, and Camille provided $5,000 of support. What is Camille's taxable income?

43. In 2009, Tiffany is unmarried and has a 15-year-old qualifying child. Tiffany has determined her tax liability to be $3,525, and her employer has withheld $1,500 of federal taxes from her paycheck. Tiffany is allowed to claim a $1,000 child credit for her qualifying child. What amount of taxes will Tiffany owe (or what amount will she receive as a refund) when she files her tax return?

5

Gross Income and Exclusions

Learning Objectives

Upon completing this chapter, you should be able to:

LO 1 Apply the concept of realization and explain when taxpayers recognize gross income.

---■---

LO 2 Understand the distinctions between the various sources of income, including income from services and property.

---■---

LO 3 Apply basic income exclusion provisions to compute gross income.

T he past year has kept Courtney Wilson very busy. Last October Courtney divorced her husband, Al Wilson. Courtney has sole custody of their 10-year-old son, Deron, and their 20-year-old daughter, Ellen. Looking for a fresh start after the divorce, in January, Courtney quit her job as an architect in Cincinnati, Ohio, and moved to Kansas City, Missouri. Courtney wanted to pursue several promising job opportunities in Kansas City and be close to Ellen while she attends the University of Missouri-Kansas City. Courtney's 70-year-old mother "Gram" also lives in Kansas City and is in relatively good health. However, Courtney's father, "Gramps," passed away last December from cancer. At Courtney's insistence, Gram moved in with Courtney and Deron in April.

In late April, Courtney broke her wrist in a mountain biking accident and was unable to work for two weeks. Thankfully, Courtney's disability insurance paid her for lost wages during her time away from work.

While her personal life has been in disarray, Courtney's financial prospects have been improving. Shortly after arriving in Kansas City, Courtney was fortunate to land a job as an architect with Earth Wise Design (EWD). EWD provided Courtney the following compensation and benefits this year:

- Salary $98,000.

- Medical and life insurance premiums.

- Contribution of 10 percent of her base salary to her qualified retirement account.

- No-interest loan with a promise to forgive the loan principal over time if she continues her employment with EWD.

- Performance bonus for her first year on the job.

Storyline Summary	
Taxpayers:	Courtney Wilson, age 40 Courtney's mother, Dorothy "Gram" Weiss, age 70
Family description:	Courtney is divorced with a son, Deron, age 10, and a daughter, Ellen, age 20. Gram is currently residing with Courtney.
Location:	Kansas City, Missouri
Employment status:	Courtney works as an architect for EWD. Her salary is $98,000. Gram is unemployed.
Current situation:	Determining what income is taxable

Courtney also received other payments unrelated to her employment with EWD as follows:

- Alimony from her ex-husband Al.
- Child support from her ex-husband Al.
- Consulting income.
- Dividend, interest, and rental income.
- Refund of state taxes she paid last year.

Before Gram moved in with Courtney, she lived alone in an apartment in Kansas City. After Gramps died, Gram was dependent on her Social Security benefits. In March, Gram's landlord agreed to allow Gram to babysit his infant son in lieu of paying rent. In early April, Gram received the proceeds from Gramp's life insurance policy. She invested part of the proceeds in an annuity contract that will pay Gram a fixed amount per year. Gram also invested some of the proceeds in the stock of a local corporation. She used the rest of the life insurance proceeds to purchase a certificate of deposit and start a savings account. Gram also spent some of her spare time completing sweepstakes entries. Her hard work paid off when she won a WaveRunner in a sweepstakes contest.

Until last year, Courtney's husband always prepared their income tax return. Since EWD hired her, Courtney has become anxious about her income tax and whether her withholding will be sufficient to cover her tax bill. Courtney is also worried about Gram's tax situation, because Gram did not make any tax payments this year. ■

In the previous chapter, we presented an overview of individual taxation. In this chapter, we begin to dig deeper into the tax formula to determine a taxpayer's gross income. We focus on whether income is included or excluded from a taxpayer's gross income rather than the rate at which the income is taxed. In the next two chapters, we continue to work through the individual tax formula to determine the tax liabilities for Courtney and Gram. Chapter 6 describes deductible expenses to determine adjusted gross income and taxable income, and Chapter 7 addresses issues associated with calculating the tax liability, tax credits, and tax return filing concerns.

LO1   REALIZATION AND RECOGNITION OF INCOME

As we learned in the previous chapter, **gross income** is income that taxpayers realize and recognize and report on their tax returns for the year. In the individual tax formula, gross income is computed as income *realized* during the year, minus realized income that is either **excluded** from taxation or **deferred** until a subsequent year. In the previous chapter, we discussed gross income in general terms. In this chapter we explain the requirements for taxpayers to recognize gross income, and we discuss the most common sources of gross income.

What Is Included in Gross Income?

The definition of gross income for tax purposes is provided in §61(a) as follows:

> GENERAL DEFINITION.—Except as otherwise provided in this subtitle, gross income means all income *from whatever source derived* (emphasis added).

In addition to providing this **all-inclusive definition of income,** §61 includes a list of examples of gross income such as compensation for services, business income, rents, royalties, interest, and dividends. However, it is clear that unless a tax provision says otherwise, gross income includes *all* income. Thus, gross income is *broadly* defined. Reg. §1.61-(a) provides further insight into the definition of gross income as follows:

> Gross income means all income from whatever source derived, unless excluded by law. Gross income includes income realized in any form, whether in money, property, or services.

Based on §61(a), Reg. §1.61-(a), and various judicial rulings, taxpayers *recognize* gross income when (1) they receive an economic benefit, (2) they realize the income, *and* (3) no tax provision allows them to exclude or defer the income from gross income for that year.[1] Let's address each of these three requirements for recognizing gross income.

Economic Benefit   Taxpayers must receive an economic benefit to have gross income. Thus, when a taxpayer borrows money, the borrowed funds do *not* represent gross income because the increase in the taxpayer's assets from receiving the borrowed funds is completely offset by the liability the taxpayer is required to pay from borrowing the funds.

Realization Principle   As indicated in Reg. §1.61-(a), the tax definition of income adopts the **realization principle.** Under this principle, income is realized when (1) a taxpayer engages in a transaction with another party, and (2) the transaction results in a measurable change in property rights.

The concept of realization for tax purposes closely parallels the concept of realization for financial accounting purposes. A transaction has the benefit of reducing the uncertainty associated with determining the *amount* of income because a change in rights can typically be traced to a specific moment in time and is generally accompanied by legal documentation.

Example 5-1

In April, Gram used part of the life insurance proceeds she received from Gramps's death to purchase 50 shares in Acme Corporation for $30 per share. From April to the end of December, the value of the shares fluctuated between $40 and $25, but on December 31, the shares were worth $35. If Gram does *not* sell the shares, how much income from her stockholdings in Acme Corporation does she *realize* for the year?

Answer: $0 is realized. Unless Gram sells the stock, she does not enter into a transaction resulting in a measurable change of property rights with a second party. Thus, she does not realize income even though she experienced an economic benefit from the appreciation of the stock from $30 per share to $35 per share.

---

[1]For tax purposes it matters not whether income is obtained through legal or illegal activities.

Adopting the realization principle for defining gross income provides two major advantages. First, because parties to the transaction must agree to the value of the exchanged property rights, the transaction allows the income to be measured objectively. Second, the transaction generally provides the taxpayer with the **wherewithal to pay** taxes. That is, the transaction itself provides the taxpayer with the funds to pay taxes on income generated by the transaction. Thus, it reduces the possibility that the taxpayer will be required to sell other assets to pay the taxes on the income from the transaction.

Recognition   Taxpayers who realize an economic benefit must include it in gross income unless a specific provision of the tax code says otherwise. That is, taxpayers are generally required to *recognize* all realized income by reporting it as gross income on their tax returns. However, as we describe later in this chapter, through exclusions Congress allows taxpayers to permanently exclude certain types of income from gross income and through deferrals they allow taxpayers to defer certain types of income from gross income until a subsequent year. Thus, it is important to distinguish between realized and recognized income.

Other Income Concepts

The tax laws, administrative authority, and judicial rulings have established several other concepts important for determining an individual's gross income.

Form of Receipt   A common misperception is that taxpayers must receive cash to realize and recognize gross income. However, Reg. §1.61-(a) indicates that taxpayers realize income whether they receive money, property, *or* services in a transaction. For example, **barter clubs** facilitate the exchange of rights to goods and services between members, many of whom have the mistaken belief that they need not recognize income on the exchanges. However, when members exchange property, they realize and recognize income at the market price, the amount that outsiders are willing to pay for the goods or services. Also, other taxpayers who exchange or trade goods or services with each other must recognize the value of the goods or services as income, even when they do not receive any cash. Indeed, taxpayers have the legal and ethical responsibility to report realized income no matter the form of its receipt or whether the IRS knows the taxpayer received the income.

Example 5-2

During March, Gram paid no rent to her neighbor (also her landlord). Although the neighbor typically charges $500 per month for rent, he allowed Gram to live rent free in exchange for babysitting his infant son. What income must Gram and Gram's neighbor realize and recognize on this exchange?

Answer: $500. Gram and the neighbor each must recognize $500 of income for March. The neighbor recognizes $500 of rental receipts, because this is the value of the babysitting services the neighbor received in lieu of a cash payment for rent from Gram (an economic benefit the neighbor realized through the exchange). Gram recognizes $500 of babysitting income, because this is the value of the services provided to her neighbor (an economic benefit was realized because Gram was not required to pay rent).

Return of Capital Principle   When taxpayers sell assets, they must determine the extent to which they include the sale proceeds in gross income. Initially, the IRS was convinced that Congress's all-inclusive definition of income required taxpayers to include *all* sale proceeds in gross income. Taxpayers, on the other hand, argued that a portion of proceeds from a sale represented a return of the cost or capital investment in the underlying property (called **tax basis**). The courts determined that when receiving a payment for property, taxpayers are allowed to recover the cost of the property tax free. Consequently, when taxpayers sell property, they are allowed to reduce the sale proceeds by their unrecovered investment in the property to determine the realized gain from the sale.[2] When the tax basis exceeds the sale proceeds, the **return of capital** principle generally applies to the extent of the sale proceeds. The excess of basis over sale proceeds is generally not considered to be a return of capital, but rather a loss that is deductible only if specifically authorized by a specific provision of the tax code. Below, we revisit the return of capital principle when we discuss asset dispositions.

The return of capital principle gets complicated when taxpayers sell assets and collect the sale proceeds over several periods. In these cases, the principle is usually modified by law to provide that the return of capital occurs evenly (pro rata) over the collection period. We discuss this issue in more detail later in this chapter when we discuss the taxation of annuities.

Recovery of Amounts Previously Deducted Taxpayers sometimes deduct a current expenditure and then later receive a refund of the expenditure they previously deducted. For example, taxpayers may pay and deduct medical expenses in one year but have these expenditures reimbursed or refunded by their insurance company in a subsequent year. The question then arises whether the reimbursement or refund should be included in gross income. In these situations, taxpayers generally deduct the expenditure in the year it was paid and include the refund in gross income in the year it is received. However, the **tax benefit rule** limits the amount of the refund that the taxpayer is required to include in gross income. According to the tax benefit rule, taxpayers receiving a refund of an expenditure that they deducted in a prior year are only required to include the amount in gross income *to the extent that the amount refunded actually reduced the taxpayer's taxable income and tax liability in the year of the deduction.*[3] If the expenditure and corresponding deduction didn't reduce the taxpayer's taxable income and ultimately the taxpayer's taxes payable in the prior year, then it did not provide any tax benefit. Hence, the taxpayer is not required to include the refund in gross income.

Example 5-3

In March 2009 (the current year), Courtney received a $420 refund of the $3,500 in state income taxes her employer withheld from her pay in 2008 (the withholdings were taxes paid by Courtney in 2008). Including the $3,500 of state income taxes, Courtney reported $15,500 in itemized deductions last year. Courtney filed as a head of household in 2008. The standard deduction for head of household filing status in 2008 was $8,000. How much of the $420 refund, if any, is Courtney required to include in her gross income in 2009?

Answer: All $420. Courtney is required to include the entire refund in her 2009 gross income because her itemized deduction for the $420 of state income taxes that she overpaid last year reduced her taxable income by $420. Accordingly, because she received a tax benefit (deduction) for the entire $420 overpayment, she must include it all in gross income in 2009. See the following for the calculation of the amount of tax benefit Courtney received from the $420 overpayment of taxes in 2008.

(*continued on page 5-6...*)

---

[2]§1001(a).
[3]§111.

Deduction	Amount	Explanation
(1) Itemized deductions with $420 overpayment	$15,500	
(2) 2008 standard deduction	8,000	Head of household filing status.
(3) Reduction in taxable income with $420 overpayment	15,500	Greater of (1) and (2).
(4) Itemized deductions *without* the $420 overpayment that was refunded	15,080	(1) – $420.
(5) Reduction in taxable income *without* the $420 overpayment that was refunded	15,080	Greater of (2) and (4).
Tax benefit from prior year $420 overpayment of state taxes	$ 420	(3) – (5).

What if: Let's consider *alternative* fact patterns provided in Scenarios A and B to further illustrate the application of the tax benefit rule.

Scenario A: In 2008 Courtney's itemized deductions, including $3,500 in state taxes, were $5,500.

Scenario B: In 2008 Courtney's itemized deductions, including $3,500 in state taxes, were $8,250.

How much of the $420 refund would Courtney include in her 2009 gross income in Scenarios A and B?

Answer Scenario A: $0. As computed below, Courtney received $0 tax benefit from the $420 tax overpayment in 2008, so she need not include any of the refund in her gross income.

Answer Scenario B: $250. As computed below, Courtney received a $250 tax benefit (reduction in taxable income) from the $420 state tax overpayment in 2008, so she must include $250 of the refund in her 2009 gross income.

Deduction	Scenario A Amount	Scenario B Amount	Explanation
(1) Itemized deductions with $420 overpayment	$5,500	$8,250	
(2) 2008 standard deduction	8,000	8,000	Head of household filing status.
(3) Reduction in taxable income with $420 overpayment	8,000	8,250	Greater of (1) and (2).
(4) Itemized deductions *without* the $420 overpayment that was refunded	5,080	7,830	(1) – $420.
(5) Reduction in taxable income *without* the $420 overpayment that was refunded	8,000	8,000	Greater of (2) and (4).
Tax benefit from prior year $420 overpayment of state taxes	$ 0	$ 250	(3) – (5).

When Do Taxpayers Recognize Income?

Individual taxpayers generally file tax returns reporting their taxable income for a calendar-year period, whereas corporations often use a fiscal year end. In either case, the taxpayer's method of accounting generally determines the calendar year in which realized income is recognized and included in gross income.

Accounting Methods   Most large corporations use the accrual method of accounting. Under the **accrual method,** income is generally recognized when earned, and expenses are generally deducted in the period when liabilities are incurred. In contrast, most individuals use the **cash method** as their overall method of accounting.[4] Under the cash method, taxpayers recognize income in the period they receive it (in the form of cash, property, or services), rather than when they actually earn it. Likewise, cash-method taxpayers claim deductions when they make expenditures, rather than when they incur liabilities. The cash method greatly simplifies the computation of income for the overwhelming majority of individuals, many of whom have neither the time nor the training to apply the accrual method. Another advantage of the cash method is that taxpayers may have some control over when income is received and expenses are paid. Because of this control, taxpayers can more easily use the timing tax planning strategy (described in Chapter 3) to lower the present value of their tax bill.

Constructive Receipt   Taxpayers using the cash method of accounting may try to shift income from the current year to the next year when they receive payments near year-end. For instance, taxpayers may merely delay cashing a check or avoid picking up a compensation payment until after year-end. The courts responded to this ploy by devising the **constructive receipt doctrine**.[5] The constructive receipt doctrine states that a taxpayer must realize and recognize income when it is actually or *constructively* received. Constructive receipt is deemed to occur when the income has been credited to the taxpayer's account or when the income is unconditionally available to the taxpayer, the taxpayer is aware of the income's availability, and there are no restrictions on the taxpayer's control over the income.

> **THE KEY FACTS**
>
> *Income Recognition*
>
> - Cash-method taxpayers recognize income when it is received.
>
> - Income is realized regardless of whether payments are received in money, property, *or* services.
>
> - Income is taxed in the period in which a cash-basis taxpayer has a right to receive payment without substantial restrictions.

Example 5-4

Courtney is a cash-method taxpayer. Based on her outstanding performance, Courtney earned a $4,800 year-end bonus. On December 28, Courtney's supervisor told her that her bonus was issued as a separate check and that Courtney could pick up the check in the accounting office anytime. Courtney did not pick up the check until January 2 of next year, and she did not cash it until late January. When does Courtney realize and recognize the $4,800 income?

Answer: On December 28 of the current year. Courtney *constructively* received the check this year because it was unconditionally available to her on December 28, she was aware of the check's availability, and there were no restrictions on her control over the check. Courtney must include the $4,800 bonus in gross income this year, even though she did not actually receive the funds until late January of next year.[6]

Who Recognizes the Income?

In addition to determining when taxpayers realize and recognize income, it is important to consider *who* (which taxpayer) recognizes the income. This question often arises when taxpayers attempt to shift income to other related taxpayers through the income-shifting strategy. For example, a father (with a high marginal income tax rate) might wish to assign his paycheck to his baby daughter (with a low marginal income tax rate) to minimize their collective tax burden.

---

[4]Taxpayers involved in a business may use the accrual or hybrid overall method of accounting. We discuss these methods in Chapter 8.

[5]Justice Holmes summarized this doctrine as follows: "The income that is subject to a man's unfettered command and that he is free to enjoy at his own option may be taxed to him as his income, whether he sees fit to enjoy it or not." *Corliss v. Bowers,* 281 US 378 (1930).

[6]Note also that Courtney's employer would include her bonus on Courtney's W-2 for the year in which it issued the check.

Assignment of Income   The courts developed the **assignment of income doctrine** to prevent this strategy. In essence, the assignment of income doctrine holds that the taxpayer who earns income from services must recognize the income. Likewise, income from property such as dividends and interest is taxable to the person who actually owns the income-producing property.[7] For example, interest income from a bond is taxable to the person who owns the bond during the time the interest income accrues. Thus, to shift income from property to another person, a taxpayer must also transfer the *ownership* in the property to the other person.

Example 5-5

Courtney would like to begin saving for Deron's college tuition. If Courtney were to direct EWD to deposit part of her salary in Deron's bank account, who would pay tax on the salary income?

Answer: Courtney would be taxed on her entire salary as income because she earned the income.[8] The payment to Deron would be treated as a gift and would not be taxable to him (gifts are excluded from the recipient's income as discussed later in the chapter).

What if: Suppose that Courtney wanted to shift her rental income to Deron. What would Courtney need to do to ensure that her rental income is taxed to Deron?

Answer: Courtney would have to transfer her ownership in the rental property to Deron in order for Deron to be taxed on the rental income.[9]

Community Property Systems   The state laws of nine states (Arizona, California, Idaho, Louisiana, Nevada, New Mexico, Texas, Washington, and Wisconsin) implement **community property systems.** Under community property systems, the income earned from services by one spouse is treated as though it was earned equally by both spouses. Also, property acquired by either spouse during the marriage is usually community property and is treated as though it is owned equally by each spouse. Property that a spouse brings into a marriage is treated as that spouse's separate property. For federal income tax purposes, the community property system has the following consequences:

- Half of the income earned from the services of one spouse is included in the gross income of the other spouse. In contrast, in common law states, all of the income earned by one spouse is included in the gross income of the spouse who earned it.
- Half of the income from property held as community property by the married couple is included in the gross income of each spouse.
- In all common law states and in five community property states (Arizona, California, Nevada, New Mexico, and Washington), all of the income from property owned separately by one spouse is included in that spouse's gross income.
- In Texas, Louisiana, Wisconsin, and Idaho, half of the income from property owned separately by one spouse is included in the gross income of each spouse.

---

[7]This rule of thumb is also referred to as the "fruit and the tree" doctrine because of the analogy to fruit belonging the tree upon which it was grown. See *Lucas v. Earl* (1930) 281 US 111 and *Helvering v. Horst* (1940) 311 US 112.

[8]Note also, that EWD has the responsibility of issuing a W-2 to the taxpayer who provided the services—Courtney in this case.

[9]As explained in Chapter 7, the tax savings from such a transfer would be mitigated in the calculation of Deron's tax by the so-called "kiddie" tax.

Example 5-6

Last year (2008), Courtney and Al Wilson divorced on October 1. Through September 30, 2008, Al had earned $90,000 of salary, and Courtney had earned $60,000. Al and Courtney lived in Cincinnati, Ohio. Ohio is a common law state. How much of the income earned by Al and by Courtney was Al required to include on his 2008 tax return, and how much of the income earned by Al and by Courtney was Courtney required to report on her 2008 individual tax return?

Answer: Because they resided in a common law state, Al reports the $90,000 that he earned through September (and the income he earned through the end of the year) on his own return, and Courtney reports the entire $60,000 she earned through September (and the income she earned through the rest of the year) on her own tax return.

What if: How much of this income would Al have been required to include on his 2008 tax return and how much of this income would Courtney have been required to report on her 2008 individual tax return if they lived in California, a community property state?

Answer: If they resided in a community property state, both Al and Courtney would have included $75,000 of the $150,000 the couple had jointly earned through September [(Al's $90,000 + Courtney's $60,000)/2] on their 2008 individual tax returns. Whether they resided in a community property state or not, Al and Courtney also would have included on their 2008 tax returns the income they individually earned and received from October through December of 2008.

The treatment of income from property is relatively simple when the property is jointly owned in a common law state. In this instance, each co-owner is taxed on the income attributable to his share of the property. For example, suppose that a parcel of property is jointly owned by three individuals in equal shares. One-third of the income from this property will be included in the gross income of each co-owner.

Of course, if a couple files a joint tax return, all the income from both spouses is included on the return, so the community property rules do not affect the aggregate taxes payable by the couple. However, when couples file separate tax returns, their combined tax liability may depend on whether they live in a common law state, a community property state that shares income from separate property equally between spouses, or a community property state that does not split income from separate property between spouses.[10]

TYPES OF INCOME

LO2

Now that we have a basic understanding of the general definition of gross income and related concepts, let's turn our attention to specific *types* of income subject to taxation. Our discussion is organized around income from services, income from property, and other sources of income.

Income from Services

Income from labor is one of the most common sources of gross income, and it is rarely exempt from taxation. Payments for services including salary, wages, and fees that a taxpayer earns through services in a nonemployee capacity are all considered income from services.[11] Income from services is also referred to as **earned income**

---

[10]§66 provides rules that allow spouses living apart but living in community property states to be taxed on his or her own income from services as long as (1) the taxpayers live apart for the entire year, (2) they do not file a joint tax return with each other, and (3) they do not transfer any of the income from services between each other.

[11]Under Reg. §1.165-10 unemployment compensation (amounts received from state unemployment compensation systems) is included in the recipient's gross income because it represents replacement "wages."

because it is generated by the efforts of the taxpayer (this also includes business income earned by a taxpayer even if the taxpayer's business is selling inventory).

Example 5-7

EWD pays Courtney a salary of $98,000. In addition, Courtney earned and received $19,500 of fees from consulting work she did on weekends outside of her employment with EWD. She incurred $1,500 of miscellaneous expenses for supplies and transportation while doing the consulting work. What is Courtney's *gross income* from services (earned income) from her employment and her self-employment activities?

Answer: $117,500, consisting of her $98,000 of salary and $19,500 of her business income from her consulting activities. Note that Courtney's $1,500 of expenses will be used to calculate her net income from the business but do not reduce her gross income from the business (these expenses are deductions *for* AGI and are not a reduction in Courtney's gross income).

Income from Property

Income from property, often referred to as **unearned income,** may take different forms, such as gain or losses from the sale of property, **dividends, interest,** rents, **royalties,** and **annuities.**[12] The tax treatment of unearned income depends upon the type of income and, in some circumstances, the type of the transaction generating the income. For example, while gains or losses are typically recognized in the current period, certain gains or losses are postponed indefinitely. We discuss annuity income and property dispositions briefly in the following paragraphs. We discuss income from property in more detail in subsequent chapters.

Example 5-8

Dividends: Courtney owns 1,000 shares of GE stock that she registered in a dividend reinvestment plan. Under this plan, all dividends are automatically used to purchase more shares of the stock. This year, GE declared and paid $700 in dividends on Courtney's stock. Must Courtney include the dividend in her gross income for the year?

Answer: Yes. Courtney includes the $700 dividend (unearned income) in her gross income.

Example 5-9

Interest income: Gram purchased a $100,000, three-year certificate of deposit (CD) with a portion of the life insurance proceeds she received on Gramps's death. At year-end, her CD account is credited with $4,100 of interest, and her savings account is credited with $300 of interest. Courtney had a total of $550 of interest credited to her savings account and $50 credited to her checking account during the year. How much interest must Gram and Courtney include in their gross income for the year?

Answer: Gram must include the $4,100 of interest credited to her CD account and the $300 of interest credited to her savings account this year regardless of whether she withdraws the interest or not. Courtney must include the $600 of interest credited to her savings account ($550) and her checking account ($50) regardless of whether she withdraws it or not.

---

[12]The tax definition of unearned income is different from the financial accounting definition. Unearned income for financial accounting purposes is a liability that represents advance payments for goods or services.

Example 5-10

Rental income: Courtney owns a condo in town that she rents to tenants. This year, the condo generated $14,000 of rental revenue. Courtney incurred $4,000 in real estate taxes, $2,500 in utility expenses, $500 in advertising expenses, and $2,000 of depreciation and other expenses associated with the rental. What effect does the rental have on Courtney's *gross income*? What effect does the rental have on Courtney's *taxable income*?

Answer: The rent increases Courtney's *gross income* by $14,000. However, after considering her allowable deductions for the rental, Courtney will only report $5,000 of *taxable income* from rental activities computed as follows:

Description	Amount	
Rental revenue		$14,000
Less:		
Real estate taxes	(4,000)	
Utilities	(2,500)	
Advertising	(500)	
Depreciation and other expenses	(2,000)	
Total rental expenses		(9,000)
Net rental income		$ 5,000

Annuities   An annuity is an investment that pays a stream of equal payments over time. Individuals often purchase annuities as a means of generating a set income stream during retirement. There are two basic types of annuities: (1) annuities paid over a fixed period and (2) annuities paid over a person's life (for as long as the person lives). The challenge from a tax perspective is to determine how much of each annuity payment represents gross income (income taxed at ordinary tax rates) and how much represents a nontaxable *return of capital* (return of the original investment). For both types of annuities, the tax law deems a *portion* of each annuity payment as a nontaxable return of capital and the remainder as gross income. Taxpayers use the annuity *exclusion* ratio to determine the return of capital (nontaxable) portion of each payment.

$$\text{Annuity Exclusion Ratio} = \frac{\textit{Original Investment}}{\textit{Number of Payments}} = \text{Return of capital } \textit{per payment}$$

The number of payments are uncertain for annuities paid over a person's life. For these annuities, taxpayers must use IRS tables to determine the *expected* number of payments based upon the taxpayer's life expectancy at the start of the annuity.[13] Taxpayers with an annuity paid over the life of one person (a single-life annuity) use the table presented in Exhibit 5-1.

EXHIBIT 5-1   **Table for Expected Monthly Annuity Payments for Single-Life Annuity**

Age at Annuity Starting Date	Expected Monthly Payments
55 or under	360
56–60	310
61–65	260
66–70	210
71 or older	160

[13]See Reg. §1.72-9.

Some annuities provide payments over the lives of two people. For example, a taxpayer may purchase an annuity that provides an annual payment each year until both the taxpayer *and* the taxpayer's spouse pass away. This type of annuity is called a joint-life annuity. The IRS provides a separate table for determining the expected number of payments from joint-life annuities.

A taxpayer who lives longer than his or her estimated life expectancy will ultimately receive more than the expected number of payments. The full amount of these "extra" payments is included in the taxpayer's gross income because the taxpayer would have completely recovered her investment in the annuity by the time she receives them. If the taxpayer dies *before* receiving the expected number of payments, the amount of the unrecovered investment (the initial investment less the amounts received that is treated as a nontaxable return of capital) is deducted on the taxpayer's final income tax return.[14]

Example 5-11

In January of this year, Gram purchased an annuity from UBET Insurance Co. that will pay her $10,000 per year for the next 15 years. Gram received the first $10,000 payment in December. Gram paid $99,000 for the annuity and will receive $150,000 over the life of the annuity (15 years × $10,000 per year). How much of the $10,000 payment Gram receives in December should she include in her gross income?

Answer: $3,400. Because Gram purchased a fixed-payment annuity, the portion of the annuity payment included in gross income is calculated as follows:

Description	Amount	Explanation
(1) Investment in annuity contract	$99,000	
(2) Number of payments	15	
(3) Return of capital per payment	6,600	(1)/(2).
(4) Amount of each payment:	10,000	
Gross income per payment	**$ 3,400**	(4) − (3).

What if: Assume the annuity Gram purchased pays her $1,000 per month over the remainder of her life. Gram paid $99,000 for the annuity, and she received her first $1,000 payment in December of this year. How much income would she recognize on the $1,000 payment?

Answer: $528, computed as follows:

Description	Amount	Explanation
(1) Investment in annuity contract	$99,000.00	
(2) Number of expected payments	210	Exhibit 5-1, 70 years old.
(3) Return of capital per payment	471.43	(1)/(2).
(4) Amount of each payment:	1,000.00	
(5) Taxable income per payment	528.57	(4) − (5).

After Gram receives 210 monthly annuity payments, each subsequent $1,000 annuity payment would be fully taxable.

What if: Assume that instead of receiving all 210 expected annuity payments, Gram dies after only receiving 100 payments. What amount would be deducted on her final tax return for the unrecovered investment in the annuity?

(continued on page 5-13...)

---

[14]The unrecovered cost of the annuity is deducted as a miscellaneous itemized deduction not subject to the 2 percent of AGI floor. See §72(a)(3) and §67(b)(10).

Answer: $51,857, computed as follows:

Description	Amount	Explanation
(1) Investment in annuity contract	$99,000.00	
(2) Number of expected payments	210	Exhibit 5-1, 70 years old.
(3) Return of capital per payment	471.43	(1)/(2).
(4) Number of payments received	100	
(5) Total amount of payments considered nontaxable recovery of investment	47,143	(3) × (4).
Tax deduction for unrecovered investment in annuity	$ 51,857	(1) − (5).

Property Dispositions Taxpayers can realize a gain or loss when disposing of an asset. Consistent with the return of capital principle we discussed above, taxpayers are allowed to recover their investment in property (tax basis) before they realize any gain. A loss is realized when the proceeds are less than the tax basis in the property. Because the return of capital principle generally applies only to the extent of the sale proceeds, a loss does not necessarily reduce the taxpayer's gross income. A loss will only reduce the taxpayer's taxable income if the loss is deductible. Exhibit 5-2 presents a general formula for computing the gain or loss from a sale of an asset.

> **THE KEY FACTS**
>
> **Return of Capital**
>
> ▪ Taxpayers are allowed to recover the capital invested in property tax free.
>
> ▪ Payments from purchased annuities are part income and part return of capital.
>
> ▪ When property is sold or disposed, the realized gain or loss equals the sale proceeds reduced by the tax basis of the property.

EXHIBIT 5-2 Formula for Calculating Gain (Loss) from Sale of an Asset

Sales proceeds
Less: Selling expenses
= Amount realized
Less: Basis (investment) in property sold
Gain (Loss) on sale

The rate at which taxpayers are taxed on *gains* from property dispositions and the extent to which they can deduct *losses* from property dispositions depends on whether the taxpayer used the asset for business purposes, investment purposes, or personal purposes. We discuss specific rules associated with property dispositions in Chapters 10 and 11.

Example 5-12

On December 31, Gram sold her 50 shares of Acme Corporation stock for $40 per share. Gram also paid $150 of selling expenses to enter into the transaction. Gram originally purchased the shares in April of this year for $30 per share. How much gross income does Gram recognize from the stock sale?

Answer: Gram recognizes $350 gross income on the sale, computed as follows:

Sales proceeds ($40 × 50 shares)	$2,000
Less: Selling expenses	−150
= Amount realized	$1,850
Less: Tax basis (investment) in property sold ($30 × 50 shares)	−1,500
Gain (Loss) on sale	$ 350

Other Sources of Gross Income

Taxpayers may receive income from sources other than their efforts (earned income from wages or business) and their property (unearned income such as dividends and interest). In this section we briefly summarize other common types of gross income. If by chance you encounter other types of income that are not specifically discussed here, remember that the tax law is based upon the all-inclusive income concept. That is, unless a specific provision grants exclusion or deferral, economic benefits that are realized generate gross income. This basic understanding of the structure of our tax law (and research skills to investigate the taxability of specific income types) will serve you well as you evaluate whether realized income should be included in gross income.

Income from Flow-through Entities   Individuals may invest in various business entities. The legal form of the business affects how the income generated by the business is taxed. If the entity is a **flow-through entity** such as a partnership or S corporation, the income and deductions of the entity "flow through" to the owners of the entity (partners or shareholders). That is, the owners report income as though they operated a portion of the business personally. Specifically, each partner or S corporation shareholder reports his or her share of the entity's income and deductions, generally in proportion to his or her ownership percentage, on his or her individual tax return.[15]

Because different types of income and deductions may be treated differently for tax purposes (dividends may be eligible for a special low tax rate), each item the partners or shareholders report on their tax returns retains its underlying tax characteristics. That is, the partners are treated as if they personally received their share of each item of the flow-through entity's income. For example, corporate dividend income paid to a partnership is reported and taxed as dividend income on the partners' individual tax returns.[16] Also, it is important to note that owners of flow-through entities are taxed on their share of the entity's income whether or not cash is distributed to them. When owners receive cash distributions from the entity, the distributions are generally treated as a return of capital and, therefore, not included in the owner's gross income.

Example 5-13

What if: Suppose that Courtney is a 40 percent partner in KJZ partnership. KJZ reported $20,000 of business income and $3,000 of interest income for the year. KJZ also distributed $1,000 of cash to Courtney. What amount of gross income from her ownership in KJZ partnership would Courtney report for the current year?

Answer: $9,200, consisting of $8,000 of business income ($20,000 × 40%) and $1,200 of interest income ($2,000 × 40%). Courtney would not include the $1,000 distribution in her gross income because it was a return of her investment.

Alimony   When couples legally separate or divorce, one spouse may be required to provide financial support to the other in the form of **alimony.** The tax law defines

---

[15]Losses from partnerships and S corporations are subject to several limitations that we discuss in Chapter 11.

[16]Partnerships and S corporations report to each partner or shareholder, that partner's or shareholder's share of partnership and S corporation income (or loss) on Schedule K-1 filed with the partnership and S corporation's annual information returns (Form 1065 and 1120S, respectively). See the Forms 1065 and 1120S on the IRS Web site, www.IRS.gov.

alimony as (1) a transfer of *cash* made under a written separation agreement or divorce decree, (2) the separation or divorce decree does not designate the payment as something other than alimony, and (3) the payments cannot continue after the death of the recipient.[17]

For tax purposes, a transfer between former spouses represents alimony only if it meets this definition. If the payment is alimony, then the amount of the payment is included in the gross income of the person receiving it and is deductible *for* AGI by the person paying it. Thus, alimony shifts income from one spouse to the other.

Example 5-14

Last year, Courtney divorced Al Wilson. In addition to paying child support, under the divorce decree Al is required to pay Courtney $20,000 cash each year until she dies. The agreement does not designate the payment as a payment for something other than alimony. Does this payment qualify as alimony?

Answer: Yes. Courtney is taxed on the $20,000 as income for alimony. These payments qualify as alimony for tax purposes because they are cash payments (1) made under a divorce decree, (2) the payments are not designated as something other than alimony, and (3) the payments cease on Courtney's death. In the current year, Al made a $20,000 alimony payment to Courtney. Courtney includes all $20,000 in her gross income. To ensure that the income is taxed only once, Al is allowed to deduct the entire payment as a deduction *for* AGI.

There may be other types of payments that *do not qualify as alimony*. These include (1) property divisions (for example, who gets the car, house, or china?) and (2) child support payments fixed by the divorce or separation agreement.[18] In any event, if a transfer of property between spouses does *not* meet the definition of alimony, the *recipient* of the transfer *excludes* the value of the transfer from income, and the person transferring the property is not allowed to deduct the value of the property transferred.

Example 5-15

As required by the divorce decree, Al made $10,000 in child support payments during the year to Courtney to help her support Deron. Al is required to make child support payments until Deron is 18 years old. Is the current-year payment considered alimony?

Answer: No. The $10,000 of child support payments are not income to Courtney. The payments are not alimony because the divorce decree specifies that the payments are for child support. Consequently, Courtney does not include these payments in gross income, and Al does not deduct them.

The objective definition of alimony eliminates uncertainty regarding which transfers are treated as alimony. However, it creates a second problem. Since the purpose of the transfer is irrelevant to the tax consequences, it is possible to use alimony transfers to assign income from the (higher tax rate) payer of the alimony to the (lower tax rate) recipient. For example, instead of transferring ownership of an asset to the recipient as a nondeductible/nontaxable property settlement, the payer could

---

[17]§71(b). Another requirement for alimony is that spouses who are legally separated (but not divorced) may not live in the same household. In addition, certain payments to third parties on behalf of the spouse, such as mortgage payments, can also qualify as payments in cash.

[18]A payment that is not specifically designated as child support may nonetheless be treated as child support if the payment is reduced on the happening of a specific contingency related to the child. For example, a payment that ceases once a child reaches the age of 18 would be treated as child support.

claim an alimony deduction by making a transfer that meets the alimony requirements. The spouses can share the tax savings from this transaction if they can agree on structuring the payments to qualify as alimony (this may be a little difficult for a couple going through a divorce). To address this tax-avoidance opportunity, Congress enacted a complex set of restrictions called *front loading* that make it difficult for taxpayers to disguise property payments as alimony payments. In general terms, when taxpayers attempt to disguise property payments as alimony payments (large alimony payments shortly after the divorce, followed by smaller alimony payments in subsequent years), the tax laws may require the taxpayers to recharacterize (or "recapture") part of the alimony payments as nondeductible property transfers.[19]

Example 5-16

As part of the divorce agreement, Al transferred his interest in their joint residence to Courtney. The couple did not have any outstanding debt on the home. At the time of the divorce, the home was valued at $500,000 and Al's share was valued at $250,000. What are the tax consequences of the home ownership transfer to Courtney?

Answer: Because the transfer is not a cash transfer, it does not qualify as alimony. Consequently, Courtney does not recognize the $250,000 as income, and Al is not allowed to deduct the $250,000 transfer.

What if: Assume that Al's marginal tax rate is 35 percent and Courtney's marginal tax rate is 15 percent. To generate tax savings, in lieu of transferring his share of the ownership in the home, Al and Courtney agreed that Al would make a $250,000 cash transfer to Courtney. The divorce agreement stipulated that this payment was alimony. What are Al and Courtney trying to accomplish under this arrangement? Will they be successful?

Answer: They are trying to convert a property payment into alimony that is deductible by Al (at a high tax rate) and includible in Courtney's income (at a lower tax rate). As we discussed above, under a complex set of alimony recapture rules, it is likely that a portion of this payment will be treated as a nonalimony property settlement.

Prizes, Awards, and Gambling Winnings Prizes, awards, and gambling winnings, such as raffle or sweepstake prizes or lottery winnings, are included in gross income.

Example 5-17

After devoting much of her free time during the year to filling out sweepstakes entries, Gram hit the jackpot. She won a WaveRunner worth $7,500 in a sweepstakes sponsored by *Reader's Digest*. How much of the prize, if any, must Gram include in her gross income?

Answer: Gram must include the full $7,500 value of the WaveRunner in her gross income. Note that because she must pay taxes on the winnings, she's not really getting the WaveRunner for "free."

There are two specific, narrowly defined exceptions to this rule. First, awards for scientific, literary, or charitable achievement such as the Nobel prize are excluded from gross income, *but only if* the taxpayer *immediately* transfers the award to a federal, state, or local governmental unit or qualified charity such as a church, school, or charitable organization.[20] The obvious downside of this exception is that the award recipient does not actually get to keep the award. However, for tax purposes it is more

---

[19]See §71(f) for details. The specifics of these provisions are beyond the scope of this text.
[20]§74(b).

beneficial for the recipient to exclude the award from income entirely by immediately transferring it to a charitable organization than it is to receive the award, recognize the income, and then contribute funds to a charity for a charitable deduction. Transferring the award has the same effect as claiming the transfer as a deduction *for* AGI. However, by receiving the award, recognizing the income, and then contributing funds to a charity, the taxpayer is deducting the donation as a deduction *from* AGI. As we discussed in Chapter 4, deductions *for* AGI are likely more advantageous than deductions *from* AGI.

The second exception is for employee *awards for length of service or safety achievement.*[21] These nontaxable awards are limited to $400 of tangible property *other than cash* per employee per year.[22] The award is not excluded from the employee's income if circumstances suggest it is disguised compensation.[23]

Taxes in the Real World   *Oprah Car Winners Hit with Hefty Tax*

Like any prize, the value is counted as income; winners must pay up to $7,000 or forfeit the car.

September 22, 2004: 7:05 PM EDT
NEW YORK (CNN/Money)—Leave it to Uncle Sam to spoil the party.
When Oprah Winfrey gave away 276 cars last week to the audience of her show, images of people laughing, jumping, crying—some hysterically—filled the airwaves and the give-away became stuff of legend. Late night talk show hosts and newspaper columnists are still talking about it. But now some of those eager prize-winners have a choice: Fork over $7,000 or give up the car.

According to a spokeswoman for Harpo Productions Inc., Oprah's company, the recipients must pay a tax on the winnings, just like any prize. For a brand new Pontiac G-Six, the model given away on the show, the sticker price is $28,500. The $28,500 would need to be claimed as income so, depending on the individual's tax bracket, the tax could be as high as $7,000. And that was after Pontiac agreed to pay most of the local charges, including state sales tax and licensing fees. The Harpo Spokeswomen said winners had three choices. They could keep the car and pay the tax, sell the car and pay the tax with the profits, or forfeit the car.

Source: http://money.cnn.com/2004/09/ 22/news/ newsmakers/oprah_car_tax/

Taxpayers must include the *gross* amount of their gambling winnings for the year in gross income. Taxpayers are allowed to deduct their gambling losses to the extent of their gambling winnings, but the losses are usually deductible as **miscellaneous itemized deductions.**[24] For professional gamblers, however, the losses are deductible (to the extent of gambling winnings) *for* AGI.

Social Security Benefits   Over the last 30 years, the taxation of Social Security benefits has changed considerably. Thirty years ago, Social Security benefits were completely excluded from income. Today, taxpayers may be required to include *up to* 85 percent of the benefits in gross income *depending* on the amount of the taxpayer's Social Security benefits and the taxpayer's *modified* AGI.[25] Modified AGI is regular

---

[21]Prizes or awards from an employer-sponsored contest are fully taxable.

[22]§74(c).

[23]The $400 limit is increased to $1,600 for qualified award plans (plans in writing that do not discriminate in favor of highly compensated employees). However, the *average* cost of all qualified plan awards from an employer is limited to $400.

[24]See Rev. Rul. 83-130, 1983-2 CB 148.

[25]§86(d) applies to monthly benefits under title II of the Social Security Act and tier 1 railroad retirement benefits.

AGI (before including Social Security benefits) plus tax-exempt interest income and certain other deductions *for* AGI.[26] The calculation of the amount of Social Security benefits to be included in income is depicted on the IRS worksheet in Appendix A at the end of this chapter.[27] The calculation is complex, to say the least. However, the taxability of Social Security benefits can be summarized as follows:

1. Low income individuals exclude all Social Security benefits from gross income. Low income is defined to include single taxpayers whose modified AGI plus one-half of their Social Security benefits are below $25,000 and married taxpayers whose modified AGI plus one-half of their Social Security benefits is below $32,000.

2. High-income individuals include a portion of their benefits up to a maximum of 85 percent of the total Social Security benefits. High income is defined to include single taxpayers whose modified AGI plus one-half of their Social Security benefits is above $34,000 and married taxpayers whose modified AGI plus one-half of their Social Security benefits is above $44,000.

3. Taxpayers not in groups (1) and (2) above include a portion of their benefits up to 50 percent of the total Social Security benefits.

Example 5-18

Gram received $7,200 of Social Security benefits this year. Suppose that Gram's modified AGI is $16,150. What amount of the Social Security benefits must Gram include in her gross income?

Answer: $0. Gram's modified AGI plus one-half of her Social Security benefits is $19,750, which is below $25,000. Hence, Gram may *exclude* the entire $7,200 of Social Security income from gross income.

What if: Assume that Gram received $7,200 of Social Security benefits this year and that her modified AGI is $50,000. What amount of benefits must Gram include in her gross income?

Answer: $6,120 ($7,200 × 85%).

Imputed Income   Besides realizing *direct* economic benefits like wages and interest, taxpayers sometimes realize *indirect* economic benefits that they must include in gross income. For example, taxpayers realize an economic benefit when (1) they are allowed to purchase products or services from an employer at less than the market price or (2) they are allowed to borrow money at less than the market rate of interest. Even though these types of transactions provide an indirect economic benefit, taxpayers receiving such benefits may be required to include a certain amount of **imputed income** from these transactions in their gross income. For example, employees must recognize income to the extent they receive a greater than 20 percent discount from their employer for the employer's services or purchase goods from their employer at a price below the employer's cost.

Example 5-19

As part of her compensation package, EWD agreed to provide Courtney with EWD architectural design services (to create more space for Gram) at an 80 percent discount. EWD provided Courtney with services valued at $10,000 but charged her only $2,000 for the services. How much of the discount must Courtney include in gross income?

(continued on page 5-19...)

---

[26]See §86(b)(2)(A).

[27]Because the 2009 worksheet was not available at the time the book went to press, we include the 2008 worksheet in the Appendix A. The 2008 worksheet can be used to determine the taxable portion of social security benefits received in 2009.

Answer: $6,000, computed as follows:

Description	Amount	Explanation
(1) Value of services EWD provided to Courtney	$10,000	
(2) Courtney's cost of the services	2,000	
(3) Discount on services	8,000	(1) − (2).
(4) Excludable discount	2,000	(1) × 20%.
Discount in excess of 20% is included in gross income	$ 6,000	(3) − (4).

Employees may also recognize imputed income when they borrow money from an employer at a below-market interest rate. The amount of imputed income is the difference between the amount of the loan multiplied by an applicable federal interest rate and the amount of interest the taxpayer actually pays. Fortunately the imputed interest rules do not apply to loans of $10,000 or less.

Example 5-20

At the beginning of January, EWD provides Courtney with a $50,000 zero-interest loan. Assume that the applicable federal interest rate is 8 percent. Courtney used the loan proceeds to acquire several personal-use assets (an automobile and other items). What amount is Courtney required to include in gross income in the current year?

Answer: $4,000, computed as follows:

Description	Amount	Explanation
(1) Loan principal	$50,000	
(2) Applicable federal interest rate	8%	
(3) Interest on loan principal at federal rate	4,000	(1) × (2).
(4) Interest paid by Courtney	0	
(5) Imputed interest included in Courtney's gross income[28]	$ 4,000	(3) − (4).

What if: Assume the same facts except that EWD had loaned Courtney $10,000 at a zero-interest rate, how much imputed interest income would Courtney be required to include in her gross income for the year?

Answer: $0. The imputed interest rules don't apply because the loan did not exceed $10,000.

Discharge of Indebtedness   In general, when a taxpayer's debt is forgiven by a lender (the debt is discharged), the taxpayer must include the amount of debt relief in gross income.[29]

THE KEY FACTS
Other Sources of Income
▌ Alimony is taxed to recipient when paid in cash, pursuant to written agreement or decree and contingent on life of the recipient.
▌ Awards are included in gross income unless made for scientific, literary, or charitable achievement and transferred to a qualified charity.
▌ A maximum of 85% of Social Security benefits are included in gross income depending on level of AGI.
▌ Discharge of debt is included in gross income unless taxpayer is insolvent before and after forgiveness.

Example 5-21

In the previous example, Courtney borrowed $50,000 from EWD. Because EWD wants to keep Courtney as an employee, it agreed to forgive $10,000 of loan principal at the end of each year that Courtney stays on board. On December 31 of this year, EWD formally cancels $10,000 of Courtney's indebtedness. How much of this debt relief is Courtney required to include in gross income?

Answer: All $10,000 is included in Courtney's gross income.

---

[28]Courtney will also incur an imputed interest expense of $4,000 for the year and EWD will also deduct $4,000 of compensation expense. As we learn in the next chapter, business interest expense is a deduction *for* AGI, investment interest expense is an itemized deduction subject to limitations, and personal interest is generally not deductible. In this example, we assume Courtney used the proceeds for personal purposes so she is not allowed to deduct the interest expense.

[29]§61(a)(12).

To provide tax relief for insolvent taxpayers—taxpayers with liabilities, including tax liabilities, exceeding their assets—a **discharge of indebtedness** is *not* taxable if the taxpayer is insolvent before *and* after the debt forgiveness.[30] If the discharge of indebtedness makes the taxpayer solvent, the taxpayer recognizes taxable income to the extent of his solvency.[31] For example if a taxpayer is discharged of $30,000 of debt and this causes him to be solvent by $10,000 (after the debt relief, the taxpayer's assets exceed his liabilities by $10,000), the taxpayer must include $10,000 in gross income.[32]

L02 EXCLUSION PROVISIONS

So far in this chapter, we've discussed various types of income taxpayers must realize and recognize by reporting it on their tax returns in the current year. However, there are specific types of income that taxpayers realize but are allowed to permanently *exclude* from gross income or temporarily defer from gross income until a subsequent period. As we discussed in the previous chapter, *exclusions* and *deferrals* are the result of *specific Congressional action* and are *narrowly defined*. Because taxpayers are not required to recognize income that is excluded or deferred, we refer to tax laws allowing exclusions or deferrals as **nonrecognition provisions.** Nonrecognition provisions result from various policy objectives. In very general terms, Congress allows most exclusions and deferrals for two primary reasons: (1) to subsidize or encourage particular activities or (2) to be fair to taxpayers (such as mitigating the inequity of double taxation). Our discussion in this chapter focuses on exclusions.

Common Exclusions

Because exclusion provisions allow taxpayers to permanently remove certain income items from their tax base, they are particularly taxpayer friendly. We begin by introducing two common exclusion provisions, the exclusion of municipal interest and fringe benefits. We continue with a survey of other exclusion provisions based on their underlying purpose: education, double taxation, and sickness and injury.[33]

Municipal Interest   The most common example of an exclusion provision is the exclusion of interest on **municipal bonds.** Municipal bonds include bonds issued by state and local governments located in the United States, and this exclusion is generally recognized as a subsidy to state and local governments.

Example 5-22

Courtney holds a $10,000 City of Cincinnati municipal bond. The bond pays 5 percent interest annually. Courtney acquired the bond a few years ago. The city used the proceeds from the bond issuance to help pay for renovations on a major league baseball stadium. In late December, Courtney received $500 of interest income from the bond for the year. How much of the $500 interest from the municipal bond may Courtney *exclude* from her gross income?

Answer: All $500 because the interest is from a municipal bond.

---

[30]§108(a)(1)(B).

[31]§108(a)(3).

[32]Other circumstances in which taxpayers may exclude a discharge of indebtedness are beyond the scope of this chapter.

[33]Two other common exclusions we discuss in detail in subsequent chapters include the exclusion of gain on the sale of a personal residence (Chapter 14) and the exclusion of earnings on "Roth" retirement savings accounts (Chapter 13).

Fringe Benefits In addition to paying salary and wages, many employers provide employees with **fringe benefits.** For example, an employer may provide an employee with an automobile to use for personal purposes, pay for an employee to join a health club, or pay for an employee's home security. In general, the value of these benefits is *included* in the employee's gross income as compensation for services. However, certain fringe benefits, called "qualifying" fringe benefits, are excluded from gross income.[34] Exhibit 5-3 lists some of the most common fringe benefits that are excluded from an employee's gross income. We discuss fringe benefits in more depth in Chapter 12.

EXHIBIT 5-3 **Common Qualifying Fringe Benefits**
(excluded from employee's gross income)

Item	Description
Medical and dental health insurance coverage	An employee may exclude from income the cost of medical and dental health insurance premiums the employer pays on an employee's behalf.
Life insurance coverage	Employees may exclude from income the value of life insurance premiums the employer pays on an employee's behalf for up to $50,000 of **group-term life insurance.**
De minimis (small) benefits	As a matter of administrative convenience, Congress allows employees to exclude from income relatively small and infrequent benefits employees receive at work (such as limited use of a business copy machine).

Example 5-23

EWD paid $6,000 this year for Courtney's health insurance premiums and $150 in premiums for her $40,000 group-term life insurance policy. How much of the $6,150 in benefits can Courtney exclude from her gross income?

Answer: Courtney can exclude all $6,150 in benefits from her gross income. All health insurance premiums paid by an employer on an employee's behalf are excluded from the employee's income. In addition, premiums employers pay on an employee's behalf for group-term life insurance (up to $50,000 of coverage) are also excluded from the employee's gross income.

Example 5-24

In December, Courtney mailed a newsletter to several dozen friends and relatives with a recent picture of her son, daughter, and grandmother. Courtney printed both the newsletter and the photos on printers at work (with permission of EWD). Courtney would have paid $55 for the duplicate newsletters and photos at a nearby copy center. How much of this $55 benefit that Courtney received from EWD may Courtney *exclude* from her gross income?

Answer: All $55 is excluded. The $55 benefit is considered a nontaxable de minimis fringe benefit because it is small in amount and infrequent.

---

[34]Most nontaxable fringe benefits are listed with "items specifically excluded from gross income" in §§101-140 of the Internal Revenue Code. Employers are generally prohibited from discriminating among employees with respect to nontaxable fringe benefits (that is, they cannot offer them only to executives).

Education-Related Exclusions

As an incentive for taxpayers to participate in higher education (education beyond high school), Congress excludes certain types of income if the funds are used for higher education. In the following paragraphs, we discuss exclusions for scholarships and exclusions for certain types of investment plans used to save for college.[35]

Scholarships   College students seeking a degree can exclude from gross income scholarships that pay for tuition, fees, books, supplies, and other equipment *required* for the student's courses.[36] Any excess scholarship amounts (such as for room or meals) are fully taxable. The scholarship exclusion applies only if the recipient is *not* required to perform services in exchange for receiving the scholarship. "Scholarships" that represent compensation for past, current, or future services are fully taxable. Consequently, students working at school for compensation must include these payments in gross income.

Example 5-25

Ellen, Courtney's daughter, received a scholarship from the University of Missouri–Kansas City that pays for her tuition and provides $300 cash for books. Ellen spent $400 on books. How much of the scholarship may she exclude from gross income?

Answer: All $700 is excluded. Ellen may exclude all of the scholarship for tuition and she may exclude the $300 cash she received for books because she spent all $300 purchasing her books for school.

What if: How much is Ellen allowed to exclude if she spent only $250 on books?

Answer: $650 is excluded. Ellen excludes all of the scholarship for her tuition and $250 of the $300 in cash payments because she spent $250 on books. She must include the excess cash payment of $50 ($300 − $250) in her gross income.

Other Educational Subsidies   Taxpayers are allowed to exclude from gross income earnings on investments in qualified education plans such as 529 plans and Coverdell education savings accounts as long as they use the earnings to pay for qualifying educational expenditures. We discuss these plans in more detail in Chapter 11.

The federal government issues bonds that allow taxpayers to acquire the bonds at a discount and redeem the bonds for a fixed amount over stated time intervals. These bonds don't generate any cash in the form of interest until the taxpayer redeems the bond. At redemption, the amount of the redemption price in excess of the acquisition price is interest included in gross income.[37] U.S. Series EE bonds fall into this category. However, an exclusion is available for interest from Series EE bonds. This exclusion requires that the redemption proceeds be used to pay for higher education expenses of the taxpayer, the taxpayer's spouse, or a dependent of the taxpayer. Qualified higher education expenses include the tuition and fees required for enrollment or attendance at an eligible educational institution. Taxpayers may also exclude the interest income if they contribute the proceeds to a qualified tuition program.

The exclusion is partially reduced or eliminated for taxpayers exceeding a fixed level of modified adjusted gross income (adjusted gross income before the

THE KEY FACTS

Education Exclusions

- Students seeking a college degree can exclude scholarships that pay for required tuition, fees, books, and supplies.

- Taxpayers can elect to exclude interest earned on Series EE savings bonds when the redemption proceeds are used to pay qualified higher education expenses.

- The exclusion of interest on Series EE savings bonds is restricted to taxpayers with modified AGI below specific limits.

---

[35]A detailed explanation is available in IRS Publication 970 *Tax Benefits for Education* available on the Web at www.IRS.gov.

[36]§177(b)(2).

[37]Alternatively, taxpayers can elect to include the annual increase in the redemption value in gross income rather than waiting to recognize all the income on redemption. See §454(a).

educational savings bond exclusion, the foreign earned income exclusion, and certain other deductions).[38] If the taxpayer's modified AGI exceeds the thresholds in the redemption year, the exclusion is phased out (gradually reduced) until all of the interest from the bonds is taxed.[39]

Exclusions to Mitigate Double Taxation

Congress provides certain exclusions to eliminate the potential double tax that may arise for gifts, inheritances, and life insurance proceeds.

Gifts and Inheritances Individuals may transfer property to other taxpayers without receiving or expecting to receive value in return. If the *transferor* is alive at the time of the transfer, the property transfer is called a **gift.** If the property is transferred from the decedent's estate (*transferor* is deceased), it is called an **inheritance.** These transfers are generally subject to a federal transfer tax, *not* the income tax. Gifts are typically subject to the federal gift tax and inheritances are typically subject to a federal estate tax.[40] Thus, gift and estate taxes are imposed on *transfer* of the property and not included in income by the recipient. Congress excludes property transferred as gifts and inheritances from income taxation to avoid the potential double taxation (transfer and income taxation) on these transfers.

Example 5-26

Ellen graduated from high school last year. As a graduation present, Gram purchased a $1,500 travel package for Ellen, so that Ellen could go on a Caribbean cruise. Last year, Ellen also received an inheritance of $2,000 from Gramps's estate. How much gross income does Ellen recognize on the $1,500 gift she received from Gram and the $2,000 inheritance she received from Gramps's estate?

Answer: $0. Ellen is allowed to exclude the entire gift and the entire amount of the inheritance from her gross income. Consequently, she does not recognize any gross income from these transactions.

Life Insurance Proceeds In some ways, life insurance proceeds are similar to inheritances. When the owner of the life insurance policy dies, the beneficiary receives the death benefit proceeds. The decedent (or the decedent's estate) is generally subject to estate taxation on the amount of the insurance proceeds. In order to avoid potential double taxation on the life insurance proceeds, the tax laws allow taxpayers receiving life insurance proceeds to exclude the proceeds from taxable income.[41] However, when the insurance proceeds are paid over a period of time rather than in a lump sum, a portion of the payments represents interest and must be included in gross income.

Foreign-Earned Income U.S. citizens are subject to tax on all income whether it is generated in the United States or in foreign countries. Because most foreign countries also impose tax on income earned within their borders, U.S. citizens could be subject to both U.S. and foreign taxation on income earned abroad. To

---

[38]§135(c)(4).

[39]In 2009, the phase-out range begins at $104,900 of modified adjusted gross income for married taxpayers filing joint returns. For all other taxpayers, the phase-out range begins at $69,950.

[40]As a general rule, the federal gift tax does not apply to relatively small gifts (under $13,000), and the federal estate tax does not apply to transfers from relatively small estates (under $3.5 million).

[41]§101. The exclusion is lost if the insurance policy is sold by the owner.

THE KEY FACTS

Exclusions to Mitigate
Double Taxation

▌ Gifts and inheritances are
subject to Federal trans-
fer taxes and are, there-
fore, excluded from the
income of the recipient.

▌ A maximum of $91,400
(2009) of foreign
earned income can be
excluded from gross
income for qualifying
individuals.

▌ To be eligible for the foreign earned income ex-
clusion, the taxpayer must
live in the foreign country
for 330 days in a consec-
utive 12-month period.

provide relief from this potential double taxation, Congress allows taxpayers to exclude foreign earned income up to an annual maximum amount. The maximum exclusion is indexed for inflation, and in 2009 the maximum is $91,400. Rather than claim this exclusion, taxpayers may deduct foreign taxes paid as itemized deductions or they may claim the foreign tax credit for foreign taxes paid on their foreign earned income.[42] Thus, each year taxpayers must choose to (1) exclude the income from U.S. taxation, (2) deduct the taxes, *or* (3) claim the foreign tax credit to offset their U.S. income tax liability. To determine whether claiming the annual exclusion, the deduction, or the foreign tax credit is most advantageous, taxpayers should compare the tax effects of each option on an annual basis.

As you might expect, individuals must meet certain requirements to qualify for the foreign earned income exclusion. To be eligible for the annual exclusion, a taxpayer must (1) be considered a resident of the foreign country or (2) live in the foreign country for 330 days in a consecutive 12-month period. However, because the exclusion is computed on a *daily* basis, the *maximum* exclusion is reduced pro rata for each day during the calendar year the taxpayer is not considered to be a resident of the foreign country or does not actually live in the foreign country.

Example 5-27

What if: Assume that Courtney is considering a one-year rotation in one of EWD's overseas offices in 2009. If Courtney agrees to do the rotation, she anticipates she will earn approximately $120,000 in salary. How much of her expected $120,000 salary will Courtney be allowed to exclude from her gross income assuming she meets the residency requirements?

Answer: She is eligible to exclude $91,400 of her $120,000 of compensation from U.S. taxation. However, her entire $120,000 salary may be subject to the foreign country's income tax.

What if: Assume that Courtney agrees to the rotation but she expects to live in the foreign country for only 340 days. How much of her expected $120,000 salary will she be allowed to exclude from gross income?

Answer: $85,140 [$91,400 full exclusion × 340/365 (days in foreign country/days in year)].

What if: Assume that Courtney expects to live in the foreign country for 340 days and that she expects her salary to be $60,000. How much of her expected $60,000 salary will she be allowed to exclude from gross income?

Answer: All $60,000. She can exclude up to $85,140 of salary from income (see above computation).

Sickness and Injury-Related Exclusions

The tax laws provide several exclusion provisions for taxpayers who are sick or injured. One explanation for these exclusions is that payments for sickness or injury should not be taxable to reflect an inability to pay the tax and facilitate recovery.

Workers' Compensation The provision for workers' compensation is relatively straightforward. Taxpayers receive workers' compensation benefits when they are unable to work because of a work-related injury. Any payments a taxpayer receives from a state-sponsored workers' compensation plan are excluded from the taxpayer's income.[43] Note that this treatment is *opposite* that of *unemployment* compensation, which is fully taxable.

---

[42]See §911(b)(2) and Chapters 6 and 7.
[43]§104.

Payments Associated with Personal Injury Historically, the question of which payments associated with a personal injury were excludible was a matter of controversy. In 1996 Congress settled the matter by deciding that all payments associated with compensating a taxpayer for a *physical* injury are excluded from gross income. That is, the tax laws specify that any payments on account of a *physical injury* or *physical sickness* are nontaxable. Thus, damages taxpayers receive for emotional distress associated with a physical injury are excluded. In contrast, punitive damages are *fully taxable*, because they are intended to punish the harm-doer rather than to compensate the taxpayer for injuries. Likewise, taxpayers receiving damages for emotional distress that are not associated with a physical injury must include those payments in income and only exclude payments for medical expenses attributable to the emotional distress. In general, all other awards (those that do not relate to physical injury or sickness or are payments for the medical costs of treating emotional distress) are included in gross income.

Example 5-28

In February, Courtney's cousin, Kelsey, was struck and injured by a bus as she was attempting to cross a street in a crosswalk. Because the bus driver was negligent, the bus company settled Kelsey's claim by paying her $1,500 for medical expenses and $500 for emotional distress associated with the accident. How much of the $2,000 Kelsey received from the bus company may she *exclude* from her gross income?

Answer: All $2,000. Kelsey may exclude the $1,500 she received for medical expenses and the $500 payment she received for emotional distress because these damages were associated with Kelsey's physical injury.

What if: Assume Kelsey sued the bus company and was awarded $5,000 in punitive damages by the court. How much of the $5,000 would Kelsey be able to exclude from her gross income?

Answer: $0. Payments for punitive damages are not excludable. Kelsey would be required to include the entire $5,000 in her gross income.

Health Care Reimbursement Any reimbursement a taxpayer receives from a health and accident insurance policy for medical expenses paid by the taxpayer during the current year is excluded from gross income. This exclusion applies regardless of whether the taxpayer or the taxpayer's employer purchased the insurance policy.

Disability Insurance The exclusion provisions for **disability insurance** are more restrictive than those for workers' compensation payments or reimbursements from a health and accident insurance plan. Disability insurance, sometimes called wage replacement insurance, pays the insured individual for wages lost when the individual misses work due to injury or disability. If an individual purchases disability insurance directly, the cost of the policy is not deductible, but any disability benefits are excluded from gross income.

Disability insurance may also be purchased on an individual's behalf by an employer. When an employer pays disability insurance premiums, the employer may allow employees to choose whether the payments on their behalf are to be considered taxable compensation or a nontaxable fringe benefit. If the premiums paid on the employee's behalf are taxable compensation to the employee, the policy is considered to have been purchased by the employee. If the premium paid for by the employer is a nontaxable fringe benefit to the employee, the policy is considered to have been purchased by the employer. This distinction is important because only payments taxpayers receive from an *employee-purchased* policy are excluded from an employee's gross income. If the employer pays the premiums for an employee as a nontaxable fringe benefit, the employee must include all disability benefits in gross income.

THE KEY FACTS

Exclusions Related to Sickness and Injury

▪ Payments from workers' compensation plans are excluded from gross income.

▪ Payments received as compensation for a *physical* injury are excluded from gross income, but punitive damages are included in gross income.

▪ Reimbursements by health and accident insurance policies for medical expenses paid by the taxpayer are excluded from gross income.

▪ Disability payments received from an *employee-purchased* policy are excluded from gross income.

Example 5-29	

Courtney purchased disability insurance last year. In late April of this year, she broke her wrist in a mountain biking accident and could not work for two weeks. Courtney's doctor bills totaled $2,000, of which $1,600 were reimbursed by her health insurance purchased by EWD. How much of the $1,600 health insurance reimbursement for medical expenses is Courtney allowed to *exclude* from her gross income?

Answer: All $1,600 is excluded. All medical expense reimbursements from health insurance are excluded from a taxpayer's gross income.

Courtney also received $600 for lost wages due to the accident from her disability insurance policy. How much of the $600 is Courtney allowed to exclude from her gross income?

Answer: All $600 is excluded. Courtney can exclude the entire amount because she paid the premiums on the policy.

What if: How much of the $600 payment for lost wages from the disability insurance policy would Courtney exclude if EWD paid the disability insurance premium on her behalf as a nontaxable fringe benefit?

Answer: $0 is excluded. In this circumstance the policy would be considered to be purchased by the employer, so Courtney would not be allowed to exclude any of the payment from gross income. She would include the payment in gross income and be taxed on the entire $600.

What if: How much of the $600 payment for lost wages from the disability insurance policy would Courtney be allowed to exclude if she paid half the cost of the policy with after-tax dollars and EWD paid the other half as a nontaxable fringe benefit?

Answer: $300 is excluded. Because Courtney paid for half the cost of the policy with after-tax dollars, she is allowed to exclude half of the disability insurance benefit.

Deferral Provisions

We've described exclusion provisions that allow taxpayers to permanently eliminate certain types of income from their tax base. Other code sections, called *deferral provisions,* allow taxpayers to defer (but not permanently exclude) the recognition of certain types of realized income. Transactions generating deferred income include **installment sales,** like-kind exchanges, involuntary conversions, and contributions to non-Roth **qualified retirement accounts.** We "defer" our detailed discussion of these transactions to subsequent chapters.

GROSS INCOME SUMMARY

At the end of the year, Courtney calculated her gross income and Gram's gross income. Exhibit 5-4 presents Courtney's gross income calculation and Exhibit 5-5 displays how this income would be reported on the front page of Courtney's tax return. Note that line 22 of the first page of the Form 1040 sums to "total income" not gross income. The difference between these two numbers is that "total income" is gross income minus certain deductions *for* AGI such as business expenses and deductible capital losses. Exhibit 5-4 reconciles from Courtney's gross income to her total income as displayed on her tax return.

Exhibit 5-6 presents Gram's gross income calculation. Because Gram doesn't have any business, rental, or royalty deductions, her gross income is equal to her total income on line 22 of page 1 of her tax return.

EXHIBIT 5-4   Courtney's Gross Income

Description	Amount	Reference
(1) State tax refund (line 10, 1040 page 1)	$ 420	Example 5-3.
(2) Employment bonus award (line 7, 1040 page 1)	4,800	Example 5-4.
(3) Salary (line 7, 1040 page 1)	98,000	Example 5-7.
(4) Gross business income (line 12, 1040 page 1)	19,500	Example 5-7.
(5) Dividends (lines 9a and 9b, 1040, page 1)	700	Example 5-8.
(6) Interest income (line 8a, 1040 page 1)	600	Example 5-9.
(7) Gross rental income (line 17, 1040 page 1)	14,000	Example 5-10.
(8) Alimony (line 11, 1040 page 1)	20,000	Example 5-14.
(9) Discount architectural design services (line 7, 1040 page 1)	6,000	Example 5-19.
(10) Compensation on below market loan from EWD (line 7, 1040 page 1)	4,000	Example 5-20.
(11) Discharge of indebtedness (line 7, 1040 page 1)	10,000	Example 5-21.
(12) Gross income for current year	**$178,020**	Sum of (1) through (11).
(13) Business expenses associated with consulting activities (line 12, 1040 page 1)	(1,500)	Example 5-7.
(14) Rental expenses (line 17, 1040 page 1)	(9,000)	Example 5-10.
Total income as presented on line 22 of front page of 1040 (see Exhibit 5-5)	**$167,520**	(12) + (13) + (14)

EXHIBIT 5-5   Courtney's Tax Return

(total income as reported on 1040 page 1, lines 7–22)

Income	7	Wages, salaries, tips, etc. Attach Form(s) W-2		7	122,800
	8a	**Taxable** interest. Attach Schedule B if required		8a	600
Attach Form(s) W-2 here. Also attach Forms W-2G and 1099-R if tax was withheld.	b	**Tax-exempt** interest. **Do not** include on line 8a . . .	8b 500		
	9a	Ordinary dividends. Attach Schedule B if required		9a	700
	b	Qualified dividends (see page 21)	9b		
	10	Taxable refunds, credits, or offsets of state and local income taxes (see page 22) . .		10	420
	11	Alimony received		11	20,000
	12	Business income or (loss). Attach Schedule C or C-EZ		12	18,000
If you did not get a W-2, see page 21.	13	Capital gain or (loss). Attach Schedule D if required. If not required, check here ▶ ☐		13	
	14	Other gains or (losses). Attach Form 4797		14	
	15a	IRA distributions . .	15a	b Taxable amount (see page 23)	15b	
	16a	Pensions and annuities	16a	b Taxable amount (see page 24)	16b	
Enclose, but do not attach, any payment. Also, please use Form 1040-V.	17	Rental real estate, royalties, partnerships, S corporations, trusts, etc. Attach Schedule E		17	5,000
	18	Farm income or (loss). Attach Schedule F		18	
	19	Unemployment compensation		19	
	20a	Social security benefits . 20a		b Taxable amount (see page 26)	20b	
	21	Other income. List type and amount (see page 28) - - - - - - - - - - - - -		21	
	22	Add the amounts in the far right column for lines 7 through 21. This is your **total income** ▶		22	167,520

EXHIBIT 5-6   Gram's Gross Income and Total Income

Description	Amount	Reference
Babysitting services	$ 500	Example 5-2.
Interest income	4,400	Example 5-9.
Annuity income	3,400	Example 5-11.
Gain on stock sale	350	Example 5-12.
Sweepstakes winnings (WaveRunner)	7,500	Example 5-17.
Gross income for current year	**$16,150**	

CONCLUSION

In this chapter we explained the basic concepts of income realization and recognition, identified and discussed the major types of income, and described the most common income exclusions. We discovered that many exclusions are related to specific Congressional objectives, but that absent an specific exclusion, realized income should be included in gross income. In the next two chapters, we turn our attention to the deductions available to taxpayers when computing their taxable income, and we conclude our review of the individual income tax formula by determining how to compute taxpayers' tax liability and their taxes due or tax refund. We will continue to follow Courtney and Gram in their quest to determine their taxable income and corresponding tax liability.

PUBLICATION 915 (2008)

Worksheet 1. **Figuring Your Taxable Benefits**

Before you begin:

- If you are married filing separately and you lived apart from your spouse for all of 2008, enter "D" to the right of the word "benefits" on Form 1040, line 20a, or Form 1040A, line 14a.
- Do not use this worksheet if you repaid benefits in 2008 and your total repayments (box 4 of Forms SSA-1099 and RRB-1099) were more than your gross benefits for 2008 (box 3 of Forms SSA-1099 and RRB-1099). None of your benefits are taxable for 2008. For more information, see *Repayments More Than Gross Benefits.*

---

1. Enter the total amount from box 5 of ALL your Forms SSA-1099 and RRB-1099. Also enter this amount on Form 1040, line 20a, or Form 1040A, line 14a . . . . **1.** _____

2. Enter one-half of line 1 . . . . **2.** _____

3. Enter the total of the amounts from:
   Form 1040: Lines 7, 8a, 9a, 10 through 14, 15b, 16b, 17 through 19, and 21
   Form 1040A: Lines 7, 8a, 9a, 10, 11b, 12b, and 13 . . . . **3.** _____

4. Enter the amount, if any, from Form 1040 or 1040A, line 8b . . . . **4.** _____

5. *Form 1040 filers:* Enter the total of any exclusions/adjustments for:
   - Qualified U.S. savings bond interest (Form 8815, line 14)
   - Adoption benefits (Form 8839, line 30)
   - Foreign earned income or housing (Form 2555, lines 45 and 50, or Form 2555-EZ, line 18), and
   - Certain income of bona fide residents of American Samoa (Form 4563, line 15) or Puerto Rico
   Form 1040A filers: Enter the total of any exclusions for:
   - Qualified U.S. savings bond interest (Form 8815, line 14)
   - Adoption benefits (Form 8839, line 30) . . . . **5.** _____

6. Add lines 2, 3, 4, and 5 . . . . **6.** _____

7. *Form 1040 filers:* Enter the amounts from Form 1040, lines 23 through 32, 34, and any write-in adjustments you entered on the dotted line next to line 36. *Form 1040A filers:* Enter the amounts from Form 1040A, lines 16, 17, and 19 . . . . **7.** _____

8. Is the amount on line 7 less than the amount on line 6?
   No. (STOP) None of your social security benefits are taxable. Enter -0- on Form 1040, line 20b, or Form 1040A, line 14b.
   Yes. Subtract line 7 from line 6 . . . . **8.** _____

9. If you are:
   - Married filing jointly, enter $32,000
   - Single, head of household, qualifying widow(er), or married filing separately and you **lived apart** from your spouse for all of 2008, enter $25,000 . . . . **9.** _____
   Note. If you are married filing separately and you lived with your spouse at any time in 2008, skip lines 9 through 16; multiply line 8 by 85% (.85) and enter the result on line 17. Then go to line 18.

10. Is the amount on line 9 less than the amount on line 8?
    No. (STOP) None of your benefits are taxable. Enter -0- on Form 1040, line 20b, or on Form 1040A, line 14b. If you are married filing separately and you **lived apart** from your spouse for all of 2008, be sure you entered "D" to the right of the word "benefits" on Form 1040, line 20a, or on Form 1040A, line 14a.
    Yes. Subtract line 9 from line 8 . . . . **10.** _____

11. Enter $12,000 if married filing jointly; $9,000 if single, head of household, qualifying widow(er), or married filing separately and you **lived apart** from your spouse for all of 2008 . . . . **11.** _____

12. Subtract line 11 from line 10. If zero or less, enter -0- . . . . **12.** _____

13. Enter the **smaller** of line 10 or line 11 . . . . **13.** _____

14. Enter one-half of line 13 . . . . **14.** _____

15. Enter the **smaller** of line 2 or line 14 . . . . **15.** _____

16. Multiply line 12 by 85% (.85). If line 12 is zero, enter -0- . . . . **16.** _____

17. Add lines 15 and 16 . . . . **17.** _____

18. Multiply line 1 by 85% (.85) . . . . **18.** _____

19. **Taxable benefits.** Enter the **smaller** of line 17 or line 18. Also enter this amount on Form 1040, line 20b, or Form 1040A, line 14b . . . . **19.** _____

 If you received a lump-sum payment in 2008 that was for an earlier year, also complete Worksheet 2 or 3 and Worksheet 4 to see if you can report a lower taxable benefit.

SUMMARY

LO1 Apply the concept of realization and explain when taxpayers recognize gross income.

- Income is typically realized with a transaction that allows economic benefit to be identified and measured.
- Unless income is deferred or excluded, it is included in gross income in the period dictated by the taxpayer's accounting method.
- The accrual method of accounting recognizes income in the period it is earned, and this method is typically used by large corporations.
- The cash method of accounting recognizes income in the period received, and this method offers a simple and flexible method of accounting typically used by individuals.
- The return of capital principle, constructive receipt doctrine, and assignment of income doctrine affect how much income is recognized, when income is recognized, and who recognizes income, respectively.

LO2 Understand the distinctions between the various sources of income, including income from services and property.

- Income from services is called earned income, whereas income from property is called unearned income.
- A portion of annuity payments and proceeds from sales of property is a nontaxable return of capital.
- Earned and unearned income generated by flow-through business entities is reported by partners and Subchapter S shareholders.
- Other sources of income include alimony payments, unemployment compensation, Social Security benefits, prizes and awards, bargain purchases, imputed interest on below-market loans, and discharge of indebtedness.

LO3 Apply basic income exclusion provisions to compute gross income.

- Interest received from holding state and local indebtedness (municipal interest) is excluded from gross income.
- Employment-related nonrecognition provisions include a variety of excludable fringe benefits.
- Gifts, inheritances, life insurance proceeds, and foreign earned income are excluded from gross income in order to mitigate the effects of double taxation.
- Common injury-related nonrecognition provisions include the exclusions for worker's compensation, personal injury payments and reimbursements from health insurance policies, and certain payments from disability policies.

KEY TERMS

accrual method (5-6)
alimony (5-14)
all-inclusive definition of income (5-3)
annuity (5-10)
assignment of income doctrine (5-8)
barter clubs (5-4)
cash method (5-7)
community property systems (5-8)
constructive receipt doctrine (5-7)
deferred income (5-2)
disability insurance (5-25)
discharge of indebtedness (5-20)
dividends (5-10)

earned income (5-9)
excluded income (5-2)
flow-through entity (5-14)
fringe benefits (5-21)
gift (5-23)
gross income (5-2)
group-term life insurance (5-21)
imputed income (5-18)
inheritance (5-23)
installment sale (5-26)
interest (5-10)
miscellaneous itemized deductions (deductions *from* AGI) (5-17)

municipal bond (5-20)
nonrecognition provisions (5-20)
qualified retirement accounts (5-26)
realization principle (5-3)
return of capital (5-5)
royalties (5-10)
tax basis (5-5)
tax benefit rule (5-5)
unearned income (5-10)
wherewithal to pay (5-4)

DISCUSSION QUESTIONS

1. **(LO1)** Explain why Congress adopted the definition of gross income in §61.

2. **(LO1)** Discuss why it might be difficult to determine taxable income using an economist's definition of income.

3. **(LO1)** Describe the co1ncept of realization for tax purposes.

4. **(LO1)** Explain why the definition of gross income for tax purposes might vary from the definition of income for financial accounting income.

5. **(LO1)** Compare and contrast realization of income with recognition of income.

6. **(LO1)** Tim is a plumber who joined a barter club. This year Tim exchanges plumbing services for a new roof. The roof is properly valued at $2,500, but Tim would have only billed $2,200 for the plumbing services. What amount of income should Tim recognize on the exchange of his services for a roof? Would your answer change if Tim would have normally billed $3,000 for his services?

7. **(LO1)** Andre constructs and installs cabinets in residential homes. Blair sells and installs carpet in residential homes. Andre and Blair worked out an arrangement whereby Andre installed cabinets in Blair's home and Blair installed carpet in Andre's home. Neither Andre nor Blair believes they are required to recognize any gross income on this exchange because neither received cash. Do you agree with them? Explain.

8. **(LO1)** What issue precipitated the return of capital principle? Explain.

9. **(LO1)** Compare how the return of capital principle applies when (1) a taxpayer sells an asset and collects the sale proceeds all at once and (2) a taxpayer sells an asset and collects the sale proceeds over several periods (an installment sale). If Congress wanted to maximize revenue from installment sales, how would they have applied the return of capital principle for installment sales?

■
■**research**
■■

10. **(LO1)** This year, Jorge received a refund of property taxes that he deducted on his tax return last year. Jorge is not sure whether he should include the refund in his gross income. What would you tell him?

11. **(LO1)** Describe in general how the cash method of accounting differs from the accrual method of accounting.

12. **(LO1)** Janet is a cash-method calendar-year taxpayer. She received a check for services provided in the mail during the last week of December. However, rather than cash the check, Janet decided to wait until the following January because she believes that her delay will cause the income to be realized and recognized next year. What would you tell her? Would it matter if she didn't open the envelope? Would it matter if she refused to check her mail during the last week of December? Explain.

13. **(LO1)** The cash method of accounting means that taxpayers don't recognize income unless they receive cash or cash equivalents. True or false? Explain.

14. **(LO1)** Dewey is a lawyer who uses the cash method of accounting. Last year Dewey provided a client with legal services worth $55,000, but the client could not pay the fee. This year Dewey requested that in lieu of paying Dewey $55,000 for the services, the client could make a $45,000 gift to Dewey's daughter. Dewey's daughter received the check for $45,000 and deposited it in her bank account. How much of this income is taxed, if any, to Dewey? Explain.

15. **(LO1)** Clyde and Bonnie were married this year. Clyde has a steady job that will pay him about $37,000, while Bonnie does odd jobs that will produce about $28,000 of income. They also have a joint savings account that will pay about $400 of interest. If Clyde and Bonnie reside in a community property state and

file married-separate tax returns, how much gross income will Clyde and Bonnie each report? Any difference if they reside in a common law state? Explain.

16. **(LO2)** Distinguish earned income from unearned income, and provide an example of each.

research

17. **(LO2)** Jim purchased 100 shares of stock this year and elected to participate in a dividend reinvestment program. This program automatically uses dividends to purchase additional shares of stock. This year Jim's shares paid $350 of dividends and he used these funds to purchase additional shares of stock. These additional shares are worth $375 at year-end. What amount of dividends, if any, should Jim declare as income this year? Explain.

18. **(LO2)** Jerry has a certificate of deposit at the local bank. The interest on this certificate was credited to his account on December 31 of last year, but he didn't withdraw the interest until January of this year. Explain to Jerry when the interest income is taxed to him.

19. **(LO2)** Conceptually, when taxpayers receive annuity payments, how do they determine the amount of the payment they must include in gross income?

20. **(LO2)** George purchased a life annuity to provide him monthly payments for as long as he lives. Based on IRS tables, George's life expectancy is 100 months. Is George able to recover his cost of the annuity if he dies before he receives 100 monthly payments? Explain. What happens for tax purposes if George receives more than 100 payments?

21. **(LO2)** Brad purchased land for $45,000 this year. At year end Brad sold the land for $51,700 and paid a sales commission of $450. What effect does this transaction have on Brad's gross income? Explain.

22. **(LO2)** Tomiko is a 50 percent owner (partner) in the Tanaka partnership. During the year, the partnership reported $1,000 of interest income and $2,000 of dividends. How much of this income must Tomiko include in her gross income?

23. **(LO2)** Clem and Ida have been married for several years, but this year they decided to get divorced. In the divorce decree, Clem agreed to deed his car to Ida and pay Ida $10,000 per year for four years. Will either of these transfers qualify as alimony for tax purposes? Explain.

planning

24. **(LO2)** Otto and Fiona are negotiating the terms of their divorce. Otto has agreed to transfer property to Fiona over the next two years, but he has reserved the right to make cash payments in lieu of property transfers. Will tax considerations play a role in Otto's decision to transfer property or pay cash? How will Otto's choice affect the combined gross income and income taxes paid by Otto and Fiona? Explain.

25. **(LO2)** Larry Bounds has won the gold bat award for hitting the longest home run in major league baseball this year. The bat is worth almost $35,000. Under what conditions can Larry exclude the award from his gross income? Explain.

26. **(LO2)** Both Rory and Nicholi each annually receive Social Security benefits of $15,000. Rory's taxable income from sources other than Social Security exceeds $200,000. In contrast, the Social Security benefits are Nicholi's only source of income. What percentage of the Social Security benefits must Rory include in his gross income? What percentage of Social Security benefits is Nicholi required to include in his gross income?

27. **(LO2)** Explain why taxpayers are required to include indirect benefits, such as imputed interest, in gross income. Provide an example of how imputed interest can increase a taxpayer's gross income.

28. **(LO2)** Explain why an insolvent taxpayer is allowed to exclude income from the discharge of indebtedness if the taxpayer remains insolvent after receiving the debt relief.

29. **(LO3)** Cassie works in an office and has access to several professional color printers. Her employer allows Cassie and her fellow employees to use the printers to print color postcards for the holidays. This year Cassie printed out two dozen postcards worth almost $76. Must Cassie include this amount in her gross income this year? Explain your answer.

30. **(LO3)** Why does Congress allow taxpayers to exclude certain fringe benefits from gross income?

31. **(LO3)** Explain how state and local governments benefit from the provisions that allow taxpayers to exclude interest on state and local bonds from their gross income.

32. **(LO3)** Explain why taxpayers are allowed to exclude gifts and inheritances from gross income even though these payments are realized and clearly provide taxpayers with wherewithal to pay.

33. **(LO3)** Describe the kinds of insurance premiums an employer can pay on behalf of an employee without triggering includible compensation to the employee.

34. **(LO3)** Jim was injured in an accident and his surgeon botched the medical procedure. Jim recovered $5,000 from the doctors for pain and suffering and $2,000 for emotional distress. Determine the taxability of these payments and briefly explain to Jim the apparent rationale for including or excluding these payments from gross income.

35. **(LO3)** Tom was just hired by Acme Corporation and has decided to purchase disability insurance. This insurance promises to pay him weekly benefits to replace his salary should he be unable to work because of disability. Disability insurance is also available through Acme as part of its compensation plan. Acme pays these premiums as a nontaxable fringe benefit, but the plan promises to pay about 10 percent less in benefits. If he elects to have Acme pay the premiums it will reduce his taxable compensation by an equivalent amount. Should tax considerations play a role in Tom's choice to buy disability insurance through Acme or on his own? Explain.

36. **(LO3)** Why does Congress allow taxpayers to defer recognizing certain types of realized income?

PROBLEMS

37. **(LO1)** For the following independent cases, determine whether economic income is present and, if so, whether it must be included in gross income (that is, is it realized and recognized for tax purposes?).

    a. Asia owns stock that is listed on the New York Stock Exchange, and this year the stock increased in value by $20,000.

    b. Ben sold stock for $10,000 and paid a sales commission of $250. Ben purchased the stock several years ago for $4,000.

    c. Devon owns 1,000 shares of stock worth $10,000. This year he received 200 additional shares of this stock from a stock dividend. His 1,200 shares are now worth $12,500.

    d. Bessie is a partner in SULU Enterprises LLC. This year SULU reported that Bessie's share of rental income was $2,700 and her share of municipal interest was $750.

38. **(LO1)** XYZ declared a $1 per share dividend on August 15. The dividend was paid to shareholders of record on September 1 (the stock began selling *ex-dividend* on September 2). Ellis is a cash-method taxpayer. Determine if

■ **research**
■■

he must include the dividends in gross income under the following independent circumstances.

   a. Ellis bought 100 shares of XYZ stock on August 1 for $21 per share. Ellis received $100 on September 10. Ellis still owns the shares at year-end.

   b. Ellis bought 100 shares of XYZ stock on August 1 for $21 per share. Ellis sold his XYZ shares on September 5 for $23 per share. Ellis received the $100 dividend on September 10 (note that even though Ellis didn't own the stock on September 10, he still received the dividend because he was the shareholder on the record date).

   c. Ellis bought 100 shares of XYZ stock for $22 per share on August 20. Ellis received the $100 dividend on September 10. Ellis still owns the shares at year-end.

■ research
■■

39. **(LO1)** For the following independent cases, determine whether economic income is present and, if so, whether it must be included in gross income. Identify the tax authority that supports your analysis.

   a. Hermione discovered a gold nugget (valued at $10,000) on her land.

   b. Jay embezzled $20,000 from his employer and has not yet been apprehended.

   c. Keisha found $1,000 inside an old dresser. She purchased the dresser at a discount furniture store at the end of last year and found the money after the beginning of the new year. No one has claimed the money.

40. **(LO1)** Although Hank is retired, he is an excellent handyman and often works part-time on small projects for neighbors and friends. Last week his neighbor, Mike, offered to pay Hank $500 for minor repairs to his house. Hank completed the repairs in December of this year. Hank uses the cash method of accounting and is a calendar-year taxpayer. Compute Hank's gross income for this year from each of the following alternative transactions:

   a. Mike paid Hank $200 in cash in December of this year and promised to pay the remaining $300 with interest in three months.

   b. Mike paid Hank $100 in cash in December of this year and gave him a negotiable promissory note for $400 due in three months with interest. Hank sold the note in January for $350.

   c. Mike gave Hank tickets to the big game in January. The tickets have a face value of $50 but Hank could sell them for $400. Hank went to the game with his son.

   d. Mike bought Hank a new set of snow tires. The tires typically sell for $500, but Mike bought them on sale for $450.

41. **(LO1)** Jim recently joined the Austin Barter Club, an organization that facilitates the exchange of services between its members. This year Jim provided lawn-mowing services to other club members. Jim received the following from the barter club. Determine the amount, if any, Jim should include in his gross income in each of the following situations:

   a. Jim received $275 of car repair services from another member of the club.

   b. Jim received a $150 credit that gave him the option of receiving a season pass at a local ski resort from another member of the club. However, he forgot to request the pass by the end of the ski season and his credit expired.

   c. Jim received a $450 credit that can only be applied for goods or services from club members next year.

■ research
■■

42. **(LO1)** Last year Acme paid Ralph $15,000 to install a new air-conditioning unit at its headquarters building. The air conditioner did not function properly, and this year Acme requested that Ralph return the payment. Because Ralph could

not repair one critical part in the unit, he refunded the cost of the repair, $5,000, to Acme.

   a. Is Ralph required to include the $15,000 payment he received last year in his gross income from last year?

   b. What are the tax implications of the repayment if Ralph was in the 35 percent tax bracket when he received the $15,000 payment from Acme, but was in the 28 percent tax bracket when he refunded $5,000 to Acme?

   c. How would you answer the question in part (b) if Ralph refunded $2,500 to Acme and not $5,000?

43. **(LO1)** Louis files as a single taxpayer. In April of this year he received a $900 refund of state income taxes that he paid last year. How much of the refund, if any, must Louis include in gross income under the following independent scenarios? Assume the standard deduction last year was $5,450.

   a. Last year Louis claimed itemized deductions of $5,800. Louis's itemized deductions included state income taxes paid of $1,750.

   b. Last year Louis had itemized deductions of $4,550 and he chose to claim the standard deduction. Louis's itemized deductions included state income taxes paid of $1,750.

   c. Last year Louis claimed itemized deductions of $7,290. Louis's itemized deductions included state income taxes paid of $2,750.

44. **(LO1)** Clyde is a cash-method taxpayer who reports on a calendar-year basis. This year Paylate Corporation has decided to pay Clyde a year-end bonus of $1,000. Determine the amount Clyde should include in his gross income this year under the following circumstances:

   a. Paylate Corporation wrote the check and put it in his office mail slot on December 30 of this year, but Clyde did not bother to stop by the office to pick it up until after year-end.

   b. Paylate Corporation mistakenly wrote the check for $100. Clyde received the remaining $900 after year-end.

   c. Paylate Corporation mailed the check to Clyde before the end of the year, but although he expected the bonus payment, he decided not to collect his mail until after year-end.

   d. Clyde picked up the check in December, but the check could not be cashed immediately because it was postdated January 10.

45. **(LO1)** Identify the amount, if any, that these individuals must include in gross income in the following independent cases. Assume that the individuals are on the cash method of accounting and report income on a calendar-year basis.

   a. Elmer was an extremely diligent employee this year and his employer gave him three additional days off with pay (Elmer's gross pay for the three days totaled $1,200, but his net pay was only $948).

   b. Amax purchased new office furniture and allowed each employee to take home $250 of old office furniture.

   c. In January each Ajax employee was given a $300 gift card as a bonus. However, half of Ajax employees allowed the gift card to expire without using the credits.

46. **(LO2)** Ralph owns a building that he is trying to lease. Ralph is a calendar-year, cash-method taxpayer and is trying to evaluate the tax consequences of three different lease arrangements. Under lease 1 the building rents for $500 per month, payable on the first of the next month, and the tenant must make a $500 security deposit that is refunded at the end of the lease. Under lease 2 the

research

building rents for $5,500 per year, payable at the time the lease is signed, but no security deposit is required. Under lease 3 the building rents for $500 per month, payable at the beginning of each month, and the tenant must pay a security deposit of $1,000 that is to be applied toward the rent for the last two months of the lease.

   a. What amounts are included in Ralph's gross income this year if a tenant signs lease 1 on December 1 and makes timely payments under that lease?

   b. What amounts are included in Ralph's gross income this year if the tenant signs lease 2 on December 31 and makes timely payments under that lease?

   c. What amounts are included in Ralph's gross income this year if the tenant signs lease 3 on November 30 and makes timely payments under that lease?

47. **(LO2)** Anne purchased an annuity from an insurance company that promised to pay her $20,000 per year for the next ten years. Anne paid $145,000 for the annuity, and in exchange she will receive $200,000 over the life of the annuity.

   a. How much of the first $20,000 payment should Anne include in gross income?

   b. How much income will Anne recognize over the term of the annuity?

48. **(LO2)** Larry purchased an annuity from an insurance company that promises to pay him $1,000 per month for the rest of his life. Larry paid $159,900 for the annuity. Larry is in good health and he is 62 years old. Larry received the first annuity payment of $1,000 this month.

   a. How much of the first payment should Larry include in gross income?

   b. If Larry lives that long, how much of the 270th payment should Larry include in gross income?

   c. What are the tax consequences if Larry dies just after he receives the 100th payment?

research

49. **(LO2)** Gramps purchased a joint survivor annuity that pays $500 monthly over his remaining life and that of his wife, Gram. Gramps is 70 years old and Gram is 65 years old. Gramps paid $97,020 for the contract. How much income will Gramps recognize on the first payment?

50. **(LO2)** Lanny and Shirley are recently divorced. Shirley has custody of their child, Art, and Lanny pays Shirley $22,000 per year. All property was divided equally.

   a. How much should Shirley include in income if Lanny's payments are made in cash but will cease if Shirley dies or remarries?

   b. How much should Shirley include in income if only $12,000 of Lanny's payments is designated as "nonalimony" in the divorce decree?

   c. How much should Shirley include in income if Lanny's payments drop to $15,000 once Art reaches the age of 18?

planning

51. **(LO2)** Todd and Margo are seeking a divorce. Margo has offered to pay Todd $42,000 per year for five years if Margo receives sole title to the art collection. This collection cost them $100,000, but is now worth $360,000. All other property is to be divided equally.

   a. If Margo's payments cease in the event of Todd's death, how are the payments treated for tax purposes?

   b. How much of the gain would be taxed to Todd if Margo sells the art at the end of five years?

   c. Compute the tax cost (benefit) to Todd (Margo) if the payments qualify as alimony. Assume that Todd (Margo) has a marginal tax rate of 15 percent (35 percent), and ignore the time value of money.

   d. How much more should Todd demand in order to agree to allow the payments to cease in the event of his death?

52. **(LO2)** For each of the following independent situations, indicate the amount the taxpayer must include in gross income and explain your answer:

    a. Phil won $500 in the scratch-off state lottery. There is no state income tax.

    b. Ted won a compact car worth $17,000 in a TV game show. Ted plans to sell the car next year.

    c. Al Bore won the Nobel Peace Prize of $500,000 this year. Rather than take the prize, Al designated that the entire award should go to Weatherhead Charity, a tax-exempt organization.

    d. Jerry was awarded $2,500 from his employer, Acme Toons, when he was selected most handsome employee for Valentine's Day this year.

    e. Ellen won a $1,000 cash prize in a school essay contest. The school is a tax-exempt entity, and Ellen plans to use the funds to pay her college education.

    f. Gene won $400 in the office March Madness pool. He paid $40 to join the pool.

53. **(LO2)** Grady received $8,205 of Social Security benefits this year. Grady also reported salary and interest income this year. What amount of the benefits must Grady include in his gross income under the following two independent situations?

    a. Grady files single and reports salary of $12,100 and interest income of $245.

    b. Grady files married joint and reports salary of $75,000 and interest income of $500.

54. **(LO2)** Wally is employed as an executive with Pay More Incorporated. To entice Wally to work for Pay More, the corporation loaned him $20,000 at the beginning of the year at an interest rate of 1 percent. Wally would have paid interest of $2,400 this year if the interest rate on the loan had been set at the prevailing federal interest rate.

    a. Wally used the funds as a down payment on a vacation home and repaid the $20,000 loan (including $200 of interest) at year-end. Does this loan result in any income to either party, and if so, how much?

    b. Assume that in addition to the facts described in part (a), Pay More forgave the loan and interest on December 31. What amount of gross income does Wally recognize this year? Explain.

55. **(LO3)** Jimmy has fallen on hard times recently. Last year he borrowed $250,000 and added an additional $50,000 of his own funds to purchase $300,000 of undeveloped real estate. This year the value of the real estate dropped dramatically, and Jimmy's lender agreed to reduce the loan amount to $230,000. For each of the following independent situations, indicate the amount Jimmy must include in gross income and explain your answer:

    a. The real estate is worth $175,000 and Jimmy has no other assets or liabilities.

    b. The real estate is worth $235,000 and Jimmy has no other assets or liabilities.

    c. The real estate is worth $200,000 and Jimmy has $45,000 in other assets but no other liabilities.

56. **(LO3)** Grady is a 45-year-old employee with AMUCK Garbage Corporation. AMUCK pays group-term life insurance premiums for employees, and Grady chose the maximum face amount of $120,000. What amount, if any, of the premium AMUK paid on his behalf, must Grady include in his gross income for the year? Provide a tax authority to support your answer.

    research

57. **(LO3)** Fred currently earns $9,000 per month. Fred has been offered the chance to work overseas on a temporary assignment next year. His employer is willing to pay Fred $10,000 per month if he accepts the assignment. Assume that the maximum foreign earned income exclusion for next year is $91,400.

    a. How much U.S. gross income will Fred report if he accepts the assignment abroad on January 1 of next year and works overseas for the entire year?

b. Suppose that Fred's employer has offered Fred only a six-month overseas assignment beginning on January 1 of next year. How much U.S. gross income will Fred report next year if he accepts the six-month assignment abroad and returns home on July 1 of next year?

c. Suppose that Fred's employer offers Fred a permanent overseas assignment beginning on March 1 of next year. How much U.S. gross income will Fred report next year if he accepts the permanent assignment abroad? Assume that Fred will be abroad for 305 days next year.

58. **(LO3)** For each of the following situations, indicate how much the taxpayer is required to include in gross income and explain your answer:

a. Steve was awarded a $5,000 scholarship to attend State Law School. The scholarship pays Steve's tuition and fees.

b. Hal was awarded a $15,000 scholarship to attend State Hotel School. All scholarship students must work 20 hours per week at the school residency during the term.

c. Bill was the recipient of an athletic scholarship that pays his $12,000 tuition to State University and provides him with a $500 per month stipend to pay for food and housing. The scholarship requires Bill to participate in athletic competition each term.

59. **(LO3)** Cecil cashed in a Series EE savings bond with a redemption value of $14,000 and an original cost of $9,800. For each of the following independent scenarios, calculate the amount of interest Cecil will include in his gross income assuming he files as a single taxpayer:

a. Cecil plans to spend all of the proceeds to pay his tuition at State University and estimates his modified adjusted gross income at $63,100.

b. Cecil plans to spend $4,200 of the proceeds to pay his tuition at State University and estimates his modified adjusted gross income at $60,600.

60. **(LO3)** Grady is a member of a large family and received the following payments this year. For each payment, determine whether the payment constitutes realized income and determine the amount of each payment Grady must include in his gross income.

a. A gift of $20,000 from Grady's grandfather.

b. 1,000 shares of GM stock worth $120 per share inherited from Grady's uncle. The uncle purchased the shares for $25 each, and the shares are worth $125 at year-end.

c. A gift of $50,000 of Ford Motor Bonds. Grady received the bonds on October 31, and he received $1,500 of semiannual interest from the bonds on December 31.

d. A loan of $5,000 for school expenses from Grady's aunt.

61. **(LO3)** Bart is the favorite nephew of his aunt Thelma. Thelma transferred several items of value to Bart. For each of the following transactions, determine the effect on Bart's gross income.

a. Thelma gave Bart an auto worth $22,000. Thelma purchased the auto three years ago for $17,000.

b. Bart eventually sold the automobile he received in part (a) for $15,000 (assume his basis in the auto was $17,000).

c. Thelma elects to cancel her life insurance policy, and she gives the cash surrender value of $15,000 to Bart.

d. Bart is the beneficiary of a $100,000 whole life insurance policy on the life of Thelma. Thelma died this year, and Bart received $100,000 in cash.

e. Bart inherited 500 shares of stock from Thelma's estate. Thelma purchased the shares many years ago for $1,200, and the shares are worth $45,000 at her death.

62. **(LO3)** Terry was ill for three months and missed work during this period. During his illness, Terry received $4,500 in sick pay from a disability insurance policy. What amounts are included in Terry's gross income under the following independent circumstances?

a. Terry has disability insurance provided by his employer as a nontaxable fringe benefit. Terry's employer paid $2,800 in disability premiums for Terry this year.

b. Terry paid $2,800 in premiums for his disability insurance this year.

c. Terry's employer paid the $2,800 in premiums for Terry, but Terry elected to have his employer include the $2,800 as compensation on Terry's W-2.

d. Terry has disability insurance whose cost is shared with his employer. Terry's employer paid $1,800 in disability premiums for Terry this year as a nontaxable fringe benefit, and Terry paid the remaining $1,000 of premiums from his after-tax salary.

63. **(LO3)** Tim's parents plan to provide him with $50,000 to support him while he establishes a new landscaping business. In exchange for the support, Tim will maintain the landscape at his father's business. Under what conditions will the transfer of $50,000 be included in Tim's gross income? Explain. Do you have a recommendation for Tim and his parents?

■ planning

64. **(LO3)** What amounts are included in gross income for the following taxpayers? Explain your answers.

a. Janus sued Tiny Toys for personal injuries from swallowing a toy. Janus was paid $30,000 for medical costs and $250,000 for punitive damages.

b. Carl was injured in a car accident. Carl's insurance paid him $500 to reimburse his medical expenses and an additional $250 for the emotional distress Carl suffered as a result of the accident.

c. Ajax published a story about Pete and as a result Pete sued Ajax for damage to his reputation. Ajax lost in court and paid Pete an award of $20,000.

d. Bevis was laid off from his job last month. This month he drew $800 in unemployment benefits.

COMPREHENSIVE PROBLEMS

65. Charlie was hired by Ajax this year as a corporate executive and a member of the board of directors. During the current year, Charlie received the following payments or benefits paid on his behalf.

Salary payments	$92,000
Contributions to qualified pension plan	10,200
Qualified health insurance premiums	8,400
Year-end bonus	15,000
Annual director's fee	10,000
Group-term life insurance premiums (face = $40,000)	750
Whole life insurance premiums (face = $100,000)	1,420
Disability insurance premiums (no special elections)	4,350

a. Charlie uses the cash method and calendar year for tax purposes. Calculate Charlie's gross income for the current year.

b. Suppose that Ajax agrees to pay Charlie an additional $100,000 once Charlie completes five years of employment. Will this agreement alter Charlie's gross income this year relative to your part (a) answer? Explain.

c. Suppose that in exchange for his promise to remain with the firm for the next four years, Ajax paid Charlie four years of director's fees in advance. Will this arrangement alter Charlie's gross income this year relative to your part (a) answer? Explain.

d. Assume that in lieu of a year-end bonus Ajax transferred 500 shares of Bell stock to Charlie as compensation. Further assume that the stock was listed at $35 per share and Charlie would sell the shares by year-end, at which time he expected the price to be $37 per share. Will this arrangement alter Charlie's gross income this year relative to your part (a) answer? Explain.

e. Suppose that in lieu of a year-end bonus Ajax made Charlie's house payments (a total of $23,000). Will this arrangement alter Charlie's gross income this year relative to your part (a) answer? Explain.

66. Irene is retired and receives payments from a number of sources. The interest payments are from bonds that Irene purchased over past years and a disability insurance policy that Irene purchased after her retirement. Calculate Irene's gross income.

Interest, bonds issued by City of Austin, Texas	$2,000
Social Security benefits	8,200
Interest, U.S. Treasury bills	1,300
Interest, bonds issued by Ford Motor Company	1,500
Interest, bonds issued by City of Quebec, Canada	750
Disability insurance benefits	9,500
Distributions from qualified pension plan	5,400

67. Ken is 63 years old and unmarried. He retired at age 55 when he sold his business, Understock.com. Though Ken is retired, he is still very active. Ken reported the following financial information this year. *Assume* Ken's modified adjusted gross income for purposes of the bond interest exclusion and for determining the taxability of his Social Security benefits is $70,000 and that Ken files as a single taxpayer. Determine Ken's 2009 gross income.

a. Ken won $1,200 in an illegal game of poker (the game was played in Utah, where gambling is illegal).

b. Ken sold 1,000 shares of stock for $32 a share. He inherited the stock two years ago. His tax basis (or investment) in the stock was $31 per share.

c. Ken received $25,000 from an annuity he purchased eight years ago. He purchased the annuity, to be paid annually for 20 years, for $210,000.

d. Ken received $13,000 in Social Security benefits for the year.

e. Ken resided in Ireland from July 1, 2008, through June 30, 2009, visiting relatives. While he was there he earned $35,000 working in his cousin's pub. He was paid $17,000 for his services in 2008 and $18,000 for his services in 2009. Assume Ken elects to use the foreign-earned income exclusion to the extent he is eligible.

f. Ken decided to go back to school to learn about European history. He received a $500 cash scholarship to attend. He used $300 to pay for his books and he applied the rest toward his new car payment.

g. Ken's son, Mike, instructed his employer to make half of his final paycheck of the year payable to Ken. Ken received the check on December 30 in the amount of $1,100.

h. Ken received a $610 refund of the $3,600 in state income taxes his employer withheld from his pay last year. Ken claimed $5,500 in itemized deductions last year (the standard deduction for a single filer was $5,450).

i. Ken received $30,000 of interest from corporate bonds and money market accounts.

68. Consider the following letter and answer Shady's question.

December 31, 2009

To my friendly student tax preparer:

Hello, my name is Shady Slim. I understand you are going to help me figure out my gross income for the year . . . whatever that means. It's been a busy year and I'm a busy man, so let me give you the lowdown on my life and you can do your thing.

I was unemployed at the beginning of the year and got $2,000 in unemployment compensation. I later got a job as a manager for Roca Cola. I earned $55,000 in base salary this year. My boss gave me a $5,000 Christmas bonus check on December 22. I decided to hold on to that check and not cash it until next year, so I won't have to pay taxes on it this year. Pretty smart, huh? My job's pretty cool. I get a lot of fringe benefits like a membership to the gym that costs $400 a year and all the Roca Cola I can drink, although I can't really drink a whole lot. I also got an award for having the department with the least number of accidents. My boss gave me a gold watch worth $300!

As part of my manager duties, I get to decide on certain things like contracts for the company. My good buddy, Eddie, runs a bottling company. I made sure that he won the bottling contract for Roca Cola for this year (even though his contract wasn't quite the best). Eddie bought me a Corvette this year for being such a good friend. The Corvette cost $50,000 and he bought it for me out of the goodness of his own heart. What a great guy!

Here's a bit of good luck for the year. Upon leaving my office one day, I found $10,000 lying in the street! Well, one person's bad luck is my good luck, right?

I like to gamble a lot. I won a $22,000 poker tournament in Las Vegas this year. I also won about $5,000 over the year playing the guys at our Friday night poker game. Can you believe that I didn't lose anything this year?

Speaking of the guys, one of them hit me with his car as we were leaving the game one night. He must have been pretty ticked that he lost! I broke my right leg and my left arm. I sued the guy and got $11,000 for my medical expenses, $3,000 to pay my psychotherapist for the emotional problems I had relating to the injuries (I got really depressed!), and I won $10,000 in punitive damages. That'll teach him that he's not so tough without his car!

Another bit of bad luck. My uncle Monty died this year. I really liked the guy, but the $200,000 inheritance I received from him made me feel a little better about the loss. I did the smart thing with the money and invested it in stocks and bonds and socked a little into my savings account. As a result, I received $600 in dividends from the stock, $400 in interest from the municipal bonds, and $300 in interest from my savings account.

My ex-wife, Alice, is still paying me alimony. She's a lawyer who divorced me a few years ago because I was "unethical" or something like that. Since she was making so much money and I was unemployed at the time, the judge ruled that she had to pay ME alimony. Isn't that something? She sent me $3,000 in alimony payments this year. She still kind of likes me, though. She sent me a check for $500 as a Christmas gift this year. I didn't get her anything, though.

So there you go. That's 2009 in a nutshell. Can you figure out my gross income for me? And since you're a student, this is free, right? Thanks, I owe you one! Let me know if I can get you a six-pack of Roca Cola or something.

69. Diana and Ryan Workman were married on January 1 of last year. Diana has an eight-year-old son, Jorge, from her previous marriage. Ryan works as a computer programmer at Datafile Inc. (DI) earning a salary of $96,000. Diana is self-employed and runs a day care center. The Workmans reported the following financial information pertaining to their activities during the current year.

a. Ryan earned a $96,000 salary for the year.

b. Ryan borrowed $12,000 from DI to purchase a car. DI charged him 2 percent interest on the loan, which Ryan paid on December 31, but the applicable federal interest rate is 6 percent.

c. Diana received $2,000 in alimony and $4,500 in child support payments from her former husband.

d. Diana won a $900 cash prize at her church-sponsored Bingo game.

e. The Workmans received $500 of interest from corporate bonds and $250 of interest from a municipal bond. Diana owned these bonds before she married Ryan.

f. The couple bought 50 shares of ABC Inc. stock for $40 per share on July 2. The stock was worth $47 a share on December 31. The stock paid a dividend of $1.00 per share on December 1.

g. Diana's father passed away on April 14. She inherited cash of $50,000 and his baseball card collection, valued at $2,000. As the beneficiary of her father's life insurance policy, Diana also received $150,000.

h. The couple spent a weekend in Atlantic City in November and came home with gambling winnings of $1,200.

i. Ryan received $400 cash for reaching 10 years of continuous service at DI.

j. Ryan was hit and injured by a drunk driver while crossing a street at a crosswalk. He was unable to work for a month. He received $6,000 from his disability insurance. DI paid the premiums for Ryan, but they reported the amount of the premiums as compensation to Ryan on his year-end W-2.

k. The drunk driver who hit Ryan in part (j) was required to pay his $2,000 medical costs, $1,500 for the emotional trauma he suffered from the accident, and $5,000 for punitive damages.

l. For meeting his performance goals this year, Ryan was informed on December 27 that he would receive a $5,000 year-end bonus. DI mailed the check to Ryan on December 30 but Ryan didn't receive the check at his home until January 2.

m. Diana is a 10 percent owner of MNO Inc., a Subchapter S corporation. The company reported ordinary business income for the year of $92,000. Diana acquired the MNO stock last year.

n. Diana's day care business received $35,000 in revenues. In addition, customers owed her $3,000 at year-end. During the year, Diana spent $5,500 for supplies, $1,500 for utilities, $15,000 for rent, and $500 for miscellaneous expenses. One customer gave her free advertising (worth $2,500) on a local radio station he owned in exchange for Diana allowing his child to attend the day care center free of charge. Diana accounts for her business activities using the cash method of accounting.

o. Ryan's employer pays the couple's annual health insurance premiums of $5,500.

Required:

A. Assuming the Workmans file a joint tax return, determine their 2009 gross income.

B. Assuming the Workmans live in California, a community property state, and that Diana and Ryan file separately, what is Ryan's gross income?

Individual Deductions

Learning Objectives

Upon completing this chapter, you should be able to:

LO 1 Identify the common deductions necessary for calculating adjusted gross income (AGI).

—————————— ■ ——————————

LO 2 Describe the different types of itemized deductions available to individuals and compute itemized deductions.

—————————— ■ ——————————

LO 3 Explain the operation of the standard deduction, determine the deduction for personal and dependency exemptions, and compute taxable income.

N ow that Courtney has determined her gross income, she still must determine her deductions to compute taxable income. Fortunately, Courtney keeps detailed records of all the expenditures she believes to be deductible. Besides expenses associated with her weekend consulting work and rental property, Courtney incurred some significant costs moving from Cincinnati to Kansas City. She also paid self-employment taxes on her consulting income and paid tuition for Ellen to attend summer school. Courtney is confident most of these items are deductible, but she isn't quite sure about the tuition.

Based on her review of prior-year tax returns (prepared by a professional), Courtney has a pretty good handle on her itemized deductions. She incurred some extra medical expenses to treat a broken wrist from a mountain biking accident and had additional state income taxes withheld from her paycheck. Courtney paid real estate taxes for her personal residence and investment property and interest expense on loans secured by her new home. She also donated (cash and property) to her favorite charities. Courtney experienced losses when her purse was stolen and when she damaged her car in an accident. She isn't sure if these losses are deductible.

In a push to improve her job performance, Courtney incurred costs to attend motivational seminars and travel to

Storyline Summary	
Taxpayers:	Courtney Wilson, age 40 Courtney's mother Dorothy "Gram" Weiss, age 70
Family description:	Courtney is divorced with a son, Deron, age 10, and a daughter, Ellen, age 20. Gram is currently residing with Courtney. Ellen is currently a full-time student.
Location:	Kansas City, Missouri
Employment status:	Courtney works as an architect for EWD. Gram is retired.
Filing status:	Courtney files as head-of-household. Gram files as a single taxpayer.
Current situation:	Determining allowable deductions and computing taxable income

other parts of the country to study different architectural designs. Despite the fact that she was trying to improve her job performance, EWD did not reimburse her for these costs.

Gram wasn't as busy as Courtney this year. Gram paid a penalty for cashing in her certificate of deposit early. She also paid some medical expenses and donated money to her local church. Gram is a little frustrated because she doesn't incur enough itemized deductions to exceed the standard deduction amount. Gram recently learned that that she might be able to save taxes by "bunching" her itemized deductions into one year. She's hoping to learn a little bit more about this technique. In any event, Gram didn't pay any taxes during the year and she wants to learn how much she's going to owe. ∎

In the previous chapter, we determined *gross income* for both Courtney and Gram. To compute their taxable income, however, we need to identify their deductions. As emphasized previously, taxpayers are not allowed to deduct expenditures unless there is a specific tax law authorizing the deductions. And as we learn in this chapter, Congress grants many deductions for taxpayers for a variety of reasons.

As we discussed in Chapter 4, deductions appear in one of two places in the individual income tax formula. Deductions "for AGI" (also called deductions "above the line") are subtracted directly from gross income.[1] Next, deductions "from AGI" (also called deductions "below the line" or "itemized" deductions) are subtracted directly from AGI, resulting in taxable income. Deductions for AGI are generally preferred over deductions from AGI because deductions above the line reduce taxable income dollar for dollar. In contrast, deductions from AGI sometimes have no effect on taxable income. Further, because many of the limitations on tax benefits for higher income taxpayers are based upon AGI, deductions for AGI often reduce these limitations thereby increasing potential tax benefits. Thus, it's important to determine both the amount of the deduction and whether it's a deduction *for* AGI or *from* AGI. We begin our discussion of deductions by describing deductions for AGI, and we conclude by tackling itemized deductions, the standard deduction, and exemptions.

L01 DEDUCTIONS FOR AGI

Congress allows taxpayers to claim a variety of deductions for AGI.[2] To provide an overview, we select a cross section of deductions for AGI and classify them into three categories:

1. Deductions *directly* related to **business activities.**
2. Deductions *indirectly* related to business activities.
3. Deductions subsidizing specific activities.

[1]Most, but not all, deductions for AGI appear on lines 23 through 35 on page 1 of Form 1040. The term "above the line" refers to the placement of deductions for AGI before the last line of the first page of Form 1040. This last line is the taxpayer's AGI.

[2]§62 identifies deductions for AGI.

We've organized our discussion around these categories to illustrate the variety of deductions for AGI and explain why Congress provides preferential treatment for certain deductions.

Deductions Directly Related to Business Activities

As a matter of equity, Congress allows taxpayers involved in business activities to deduct expenses incurred to generate business income. That is, because taxpayers include the revenue they receive from doing business in gross income, they should be allowed to deduct against gross income the expenses they incur to generate those revenues.

To begin, we must define "business activities" and, for reasons we discuss below, we must distinguish business activities from **investment activities.** In general, for tax purposes activities are either *profit-motivated* or motivated by personal objectives. Profit-motivated activities are, in turn, classified as either (1) business activities or (2) investment activities. Business activities are sometimes referred to as a **trade or business**, and these activities require a relatively high level of involvement or effort from the taxpayer. For example, if an individual is a full-time employee, the individual is in the business of being an employee. Self-employed individuals are also engaged in business activities. Unlike business activities, investment activities are profit-motivated activities that *don't* require a high degree of taxpayer involvement or effort.[3] Instead, investment activities involve investing in property for appreciation or for income payments. An individual who occasionally buys land or stock in anticipation of appreciation or dividend payments would be engaged in an investment activity.

Example 6-1

Suppose that Courtney purchased a parcel of land for its appreciation potential. Would her ownership in the land be considered a business or investment activity?

Answer: Courtney's activity would most likely be considered an investment activity, because she acquired the land for its appreciation potential and she does not plan to exercise any special effort to develop the property or to become actively involved in other real estate speculation.

What if: Suppose that Courtney frequently buys and sells land or develops land to sell in small parcels to those wanting to build homes. Would Courtney's activity be considered a business or investment activity?

Answer: Courtney's activity would most likely be considered a business activity because she is actively involved in generating profits from the land by developing it rather than simply holding the land for appreciation.

The distinction between business and investment activities is critical for determining whether a deduction associated with the activity is above the line or below. With one exception, business expenses are deducted for AGI. The lone exception is unreimbursed employee business expenses, which are deductible as itemized (from AGI) deductions.[4] In contrast, investment expenses are deductible as itemized deductions, with one exception. Expenses associated with rental and royalty activities are deductible for AGI regardless of whether the activity qualifies as an investment or a business. Exhibit 6-1 summarizes the rules for classifying business and investment expenses as for and from AGI deductions.

---

[3]§162 authorizes trade or business expense deductions, while §212 authorizes deductions for investment activities. The distinction between these activities is discussed in Chapter 8.

[4]For example, an employee may use her own automobile to make a business delivery for her employer. The expenses she incurs to make the delivery (cost of operating the automobile and parking) are business expenses that are deducted from AGI as miscellaneous itemized deductions that are deducted from AGI as miscellaneous itemized deductions.

EXHIBIT 6-1   Individual Business and Investment Expense Deductions for AGI and from AGI

	Deduction Type	
Activity Type	**Deduction for AGI**	**Deduction from AGI** (itemized deduction)
Business activities	Self-employed business expenses	Employee business expenses
Investment activities	Rental and royalty expenses	Other investment expenses

Trade or Business Expenses   Congress limits business deductions to expenses directly related to the business activity and those that are **ordinary and necessary** for the activity.[5] This means that deductible expenses must be appropriate and helpful for generating a profit. Although business deductions are one of the most common deductions for AGI, they are not readily visible on the front page of Form 1040. Instead, these deductions are reported with business revenues on Schedule C of Form 1040. Schedule C, presented in Exhibit 6-2, is essentially an income statement for the business that identifies typical ordinary and necessary business expenses.

EXHIBIT 6-2   Parts I and II from Schedule C Profit or Loss from Business

Part I   Income

1. Gross receipts or sales. **Caution.** See page C-4 and check the box if:
   - This income was reported to you on Form W-2 and the "Statutory employee" box on that form was checked, or
   - You are a member of a qualified joint venture reporting only rental real estate income not subject to self-employment tax. Also see page C-4 for limit on losses.   ▶ ☐
2. Returns and allowances
3. Subtract line 2 from line 1
4. Cost of goods sold (from line 42 on page 2)
5. **Gross profit.** Subtract line 4 from line 3.
6. Other income, including federal and state gasoline or fuel tax credit or refund (see page C-4).
7. **Gross income.** Add lines 5 and 6   ▶

Part II   Expenses. Enter expenses for business use of your home **only** on line 30.

8. Advertising
9. Car and truck expenses (see page C-5).
10. Commissions and fees
11. Contract labor (see page C-5)
12. Depletion
13. Depreciation and section 179 expense deduction (not included in Part III) (see page C-5).
14. Employee benefit programs (other than on line 19).
15. Insurance (other than health)
16. Interest:
   a. Mortgage (paid to banks, etc.)
   b. Other
17. Legal and professional services
18. Office expense
19. Pension and profit-sharing plans
20. Rent or lease (see page C-6):
   a. Vehicles, machinery, and equipment
   b. Other business property
21. Repairs and maintenance
22. Supplies (not included in Part III)
23. Taxes and licenses
24. Travel, meals, and entertainment:
   a. Travel
   b. Deductible meals and entertainment (see page C-7)
25. Utilities
26. Wages (less employment credits)
27. Other expenses (from line 48 on page 2)

28. **Total expenses** before expenses for business use of home. Add lines 8 through 27   ▶
29. Tentative profit or (loss). Subtract line 28 from line 7.
30. Expenses for business use of your home. Attach **Form 8829**
31. **Net profit or (loss).** Subtract line 30 from line 29.
   - If a profit, enter on both **Form 1040, line 12,** and **Schedule SE, line 2,** or on **Form 1040NR, line 13** (if you checked the box on line 1 as a statutory employee, see page C-7). Estates and trusts, enter on **Form 1041, line 3.**
   - If a loss, you **must** go to line 32.
32. If you have a loss, check the box that describes your investment in this activity (see page C-8).
   - If you checked 32a, enter the loss on both **Form 1040, line 12,** and **Schedule SE, line 2,** or on **Form 1040NR, line 13** (if you checked the box on line 1 as a statutory employee, see the line 31 instructions on page C-7). Estates and trusts, enter on **Form 1041, line 3.**
   - If you checked 32b, you **must** attach **Form 6198.** Your loss may be limited.

   32a ☐ All investment is at risk.
   32b ☐ Some investment is not at risk.

For Paperwork Reduction Act Notice, see page C-9 of the instructions.   Cat. No. 11334P   Schedule C (Form 1040) 2008

Taxpayers transfer the *net* income or loss from Schedule C to Form 1040 (page 1), line 12. Business deductions are not listed on the front of Form 1040, because these expenses reduce the net income on Schedule C that is reported on page 1 of Form 1040.

[5]§162. In Chapter 8, we address the requirements for deductible business expenses in detail.

Example 6-2

Besides being employed by EWD, Courtney is also a self-employed consultant (a business activity). This year her consulting activity generated $19,500 of revenue and incurred $1,500 in expenses (primarily travel and transportation expenses). How does she report the revenue and deductions from the activity?

Answer: Courtney reports the $19,500 of revenue and deducts the $1,500 of business expenses for AGI on her Schedule C. Her net income of $18,000 from her consulting activities is included on the front page (line 12) of her individual tax return.

Rental and Royalty Expenses   Taxpayers are allowed to deduct their expenses associated with generating rental or royalty income for AGI.[6] Similar to business expenses, rental and royalty expenses do not appear directly on the front page of Form 1040. Instead, rental and royalty deductions are reported with rental and royalty revenues on Schedule E of Form 1040. Schedule E, presented in Exhibit 6-3, is

EXHIBIT 6-3   Page 1 of Schedule E Rental or Royalty Income

Income:		Properties		
		A	B	C
3 Rents received	3			
4 Royalties received	4			
Expenses:				
5 Advertising	5			
6 Auto and travel (see page E-4)	6			
7 Cleaning and maintenance	7			
8 Commissions	8			
9 Insurance	9			
10 Legal and other professional fees	10			
11 Management fees	11			
12 Mortgage interest paid to banks, etc. (see page E-5)	12			
13 Other interest	13			
14 Repairs	14			
15 Supplies	15			
16 Taxes	16			
17 Utilities	17			
18 Other (list) ▶	18			
19 Add lines 5 through 18	19			
20 Depreciation expense or depletion (see page E-5)	20			
21 Total expenses. Add lines 19 and 20	21			
22 Income or (loss) from rental real estate or royalty properties. Subtract line 21 from line 3 (rents) or line 4 (royalties). If the result is a (loss), see page E-5 to find out if you must file **Form 6198**	22			
23 Deductible rental real estate loss. **Caution.** Your rental real estate loss on line 22 may be limited. See page E-5 to find out if you must file **Form 8582.** Real estate professionals **must** complete line 43 on page 2	23	( ) (	) (	)

24 Income. Add positive amounts shown on line 22. **Do not** include any losses . . . .
25 Losses. Add royalty losses from line 22 and rental real estate losses from line 23. Enter total losses here.
26 **Total rental real estate and royalty income or (loss).** Combine lines 24 and 25. Enter the result here. If Parts II, III, IV, and line 40 on page 2 do not apply to you, also enter this amount on Form 1040, line 17, or Form 1040NR, line 18. Otherwise, include this amount in the total on line 41 on page 2 . .

For Paperwork Reduction Act Notice, see page E-8 of the instructions.   Cat. No. 11344L

[6]§212(a)(4).

essentially an income statement for the taxpayer's rental or royalty activities. Taxpayers transfer the *net* income or loss from Schedule E to Form 1040 (page 1), line 17.

Rental and royalty endeavors are most commonly considered to be investment activities, but like trade or business expenses, rental and royalty deductions are claimed above the line.[7] Perhaps rental and royalty expenses are deductible for AGI because Congress believed that these activities usually require more taxpayer involvement than other types of investment activities.

Example 6-3

Courtney owns a condominium that she rents to tenants. This year she received $14,000 in rental revenue and incurred $9,000 of expenses associated with the rental, including management fees, maintenance, and depreciation. How does she report the revenue and expenses for tax purposes?

Answer: Courtney reports the $14,000 of rental receipts and deducts the $9,000 of rental expenses for AGI on Schedule E. The net rental income of $5,000 is reported on the front page (line 17) of her individual tax return.

Losses   As we discuss in more detail in Chapter 10, taxpayers disposing of business assets at a loss are allowed to deduct the loss as an AGI deduction. Also, individual taxpayers selling investment (capital) assets at a loss are allowed to deduct the "capital" losses against other capital gains. If the capital losses exceed the capital gains, they can deduct up to $3,000 as a net capital loss in a particular year. Losses in excess of the $3,000 limit are carried forward indefinitely to subsequent years when they are deductible subject to the same limitations.

Flow-Through Entities   Income from flow-through entities such as partnerships, LLCs, and S corporations passes through to the owners of those entities and is reported on the tax returns of the owners. Similarly, any expenses and losses incurred by the entity pass through to the entity owners, who typically treat them as deductions for AGI, subject to certain restrictions that we discuss in Chapter 11.

Deductions Indirectly Related to Business Activities

Taxpayers can incur expenses in activities that are not directly related to making money but that they would not have incurred if they were not involved in a business activity. Taxpayers are allowed to deduct several of these expenses that are indirectly related to business activities as deductions for AGI. We describe several of these deductions below.

Moving Expenses   The cost of moving personal possessions is not a direct cost of doing business or being employed. Nonetheless, individuals qualify for a moving expense deduction if they move *and* change their principal place of work. Specifically, individuals can deduct moving expenses as deductions for AGI if they meet two tests: (1) a distance test and (2) a business test associated with the move.[8]

---

[7]Royalties are received for allowing others to use property or rights to property. For example, royalties are paid for allowing others to use or sell copyrighted material such as books or plays, or extract natural resources from property. The amount of the royalty is often a percentage of total revenues derived from the property or rights to property.

[8]§217.

To satisfy the distance test, the distance from the taxpayer's old residence to the new place of work must be at least 50 miles more than the distance from the old residence to the old place of work. In other words, if the taxpayer were staying in her old home, the new place of work must increase her commute by at least 50 miles, thereby justifying a move to a new residence. To satisfy the business test, the taxpayer must either be employed full-time for 39 of the first 52 weeks after the move or be self-employed for 78 of the first 104 weeks after the move.

Taxpayers can qualify for a moving expense deduction by beginning their first job or by beginning a job after a prolonged absence from the workforce. However, individuals need not change employers if they meet both tests. Indeed, a taxpayer's reasons for moving may be entirely personal, such as wanting to move to a milder climate; business-related, such as wanting to change jobs or start a new business; or some of both.

Example 6-4

Before moving to Kansas City, Courtney lived in Cincinnati, Ohio, where she commuted 10 miles to her place of work. The distance from Courtney's home in Cincinnati to EWD in Kansas City, her new place of work, is 580 miles. Can Courtney deduct the expenses of moving her residence to Kansas City?

Answer: Yes. Courtney meets both the distance and the business tests because 580 miles is more than 60 miles (her original 10-mile commute from her former residence to her former place of work, plus 50 miles), and because she worked for EWD for the requisite 39 weeks during her first 52 weeks after her move (she worked from mid-January through December 31).

What if: Suppose that Courtney started a new job at an office just outside of Cincinnati and she moved into a new residence. The distance from Courtney's former residence to her former place of work was 12 miles. The distance from Courtney's former residence to her new place of work is 55 miles. Does Courtney meet the distance test for moving expenses?

Answer: No, because if she had stayed in her former residence her commute would have increased by only 43 miles. To qualify, the commute from her former residence to her new work must be at least 50 miles longer than her commute from her former residence to her former place of work. Note that the location of her new residence is irrelevant to the distance test.

What if: Suppose that Courtney started a new job at an office just outside of Cincinnati and she moved into a new residence. If the distance from Courtney's former residence to her former place of work was 12 miles, and the distance from her former residence to her new work place was 80 miles, would Courtney meet the distance test for moving expenses?

Answer: Yes, the commute from her former residence to her new job is 68 miles longer than the commute from her former residence to her old job.

Deductible moving expenses are limited to reasonable expenses associated with moving personal possessions and traveling to the new residence, including transportation and lodging. Taxpayers are allowed to deduct a mileage rate in lieu of the actual costs of driving their personal automobiles during the move. In 2009, taxpayers are allowed to deduct 24 cents a mile for driving their personal automobiles during a move. Taxpayers may also deduct the cost of moving their personal belongings and the belongings of members of their households. Taxpayers are *not* allowed to deduct costs such as meals during the move or costs associated with house-hunting trips. Taxpayers who are reimbursed by their employers for actual moving expenses exclude the reimbursement from income but do not deduct the reimbursed expenses. However, taxpayers who receive a flat amount as a moving allowance from their employers are required to include the allowance in gross income, and can deduct their actual moving expenses for AGI.

THE KEY FACTS

Moving Expenses

- Deductible for AGI for individuals who pass a mileage test and a business test.
- Mileage test: New job site must extend existing commute by 50 miles.
- Business test: Taxpayer must be employed at least 39 of 52 weeks or be self-employed for 78 of the 104 weeks following the move.

Example 6-5

Courtney drove 650 miles in her move from Cincinnati to Kansas City and incurred the following expenses related to the move:

Description	Amount
Moving company (personal belongings)	$5,000
Lodging (one night en route)	123
Meals en route	75
House-hunting trip	520

What amount can Courtney deduct as moving expenses?

Answer: Courtney can deduct $5,279 computed as follows:

Description	Deduction
Transportation (24¢ per mile times 650 miles)	$ 156
Moving company (personal belongings)	5,000
Lodging (one night en route)	123
Total deduction	**$5,279**

The meals and house-hunting are not deductible.

What if: Suppose that EWD agreed to reimburse Courtney for $2,000 of actual moving expenses. What amount would Courtney deduct for moving expenses?

Answer: $3,279. Courtney would deduct $3,279 in moving expenses ($5,279 minus $2,000 reimbursement). She would not include the reimbursement in income and she would not deduct the $2,000 of expenses for which she was reimbursed.

Health Insurance Deduction by Self-Employed Taxpayers   The cost of health insurance is essentially a personal expense. However, *employers* often pay a portion of health insurance premiums for employees as a qualified fringe benefit. Employers are allowed to deduct health insurance premiums as compensation expense while employees are allowed to *exclude* these premiums from gross income. In contrast to employees, the health insurance fringe benefit does not apply to self-employed taxpayers because they are not an "employee." To provide equitable treatment, Congress allows self-employed taxpayers to deduct personal health insurance premiums as deductions for AGI.[9]

This deduction is intended to help self-employed taxpayers who must pay their own insurance premiums. Consequently, self-employed taxpayers are *not* allowed to deduct health care insurance premiums if the taxpayer is *eligible* to participate in an employer-provided health plan. This restriction applies regardless of whether the health plan is sponsored by either an employer of the taxpayer or an employer of the taxpayer's spouse, and it is irrelevant whether the taxpayer actually participates in the plan.[10]

Self-Employment Tax Deduction   Employees and employers each pay one-half of employees' Social Security tax liability. Employers deduct the Social Security taxes on the half they pay for employees. In contrast, because self-employed individuals do not have an employer, these individuals are required to pay self-employment

---

[9]§162(l). As we'll explain shortly, health insurance premiums also qualify as itemized deductions as medical expenses, but itemizing these deductions may not produce any tax benefits.

[10]§162(l)(2)(B).

tax. This tax is double that paid by employees because it represents both the employee's *and* the employer's share of the Social Security tax. Unfortunately, the self-employment tax is *not* considered a business expense. To put self-employed individuals on somewhat equal footing with other employers who are allowed to deduct the *employer's* share of the Social Security tax, self-employed taxpayers are allowed to deduct one-half of the self-employment tax they pay.

Example 6-6

As we indicated in Example 6-2, Courtney reported $18,000 of net income from her self-employed consulting activities. She paid $482 in self-employment taxes on this income.[11] What amount of self-employment tax can she deduct this year?

Answer: $241. ($482 × 50% = $241).

Penalty for Early Withdrawal of Savings   This provision allows a deduction for AGI for any interest income an individual forfeits to a bank as a penalty for prematurely withdrawing a certificate of deposit or similar deposit. This deduction reduces the taxpayer's net interest income to the amount she actually received. Otherwise, taxpayers would be required to report the full amount of interest income as taxable income and could deduct only the forfeited interest as an investment-expense itemized deduction. As we discuss below, investment expenses deducted as itemized deductions are subject to limitations that substantially reduce their tax benefits.

Example 6-7

Gram invested $100,000 in a three-year certificate of deposit (CD). On December 31, she decided to cash out the certificate of deposit after holding it for less than a year. She receives the $4,100 of interest income the CD had generated up to the withdrawal date, less a $410 early withdrawal penalty. How will Gram report the interest and early withdrawal for tax purposes?

Answer: Gram reports $4,100 as interest income this year and deducts the $410 early withdrawal penalty as a deduction for AGI.

Deductions Subsidizing Specific Activities

To address specific policy objectives, Congress provides that certain expenditures are deductible for AGI. For example, alimony payments are deductible for AGI to maintain equity and contributions to retirement savings are deductible for AGI to encourage savings.[12] Further, Congress created two important deductions for AGI to encourage and subsidize higher education. Taxpayers are allowed to deduct for AGI, subject to certain limitations, (1) interest expense on **qualified educational loans** and (2) **qualified educational expenses.**[13] As we discuss throughout the text, Congress has also created a number of related provisions, including education tax credits, to encourage and subsidize higher education.

---

[11]In this case, Courtney uses the following equation to determine her self-employment tax $18,000 × .9235 × .029 (Courtney's business income is subject to the Medicare tax but not the Social Security tax due to the level of her salary). We discuss how to compute the self-employment tax in detail in Chapter 7.

[12]See Chapter 5 for detailed discussion of alimony and Chapter 13 for detailed discussion of the tax consequences of retirement savings.

[13]See §221 and §222. At press time, the deduction for qualified education is scheduled to expire at the end of 2009.

Deduction for Interest on Qualified Education Loans   Qualified education loans are loans whose proceeds are used to pay qualified education expenses.[14] Qualified education expenses encompass expenses paid for the education of the taxpayer, the taxpayer's spouse, or a taxpayer's dependent to attend a postsecondary institution of higher education.[15] These expenses include tuition and fees, books and expenses required for enrollment, room and board, and other necessary supplies and expenses including travel.

The maximum deduction for interest expense on qualified education loans is $2,500. However, the maximum deduction is reduced (phased-out) for taxpayers depending on the taxpayer's filing status and **modified AGI.** Modified AGI for this purpose is AGI *before* deducting interest expense on the qualified education loans and *before* deducting qualified education expenses (discussed below). Married individuals who file separately are not allowed to deduct this expense under any circumstance. The deduction limitations for other taxpayers are summarized in Exhibit 6-4 as follows:

EXHIBIT 6-4   Summary of Limitations on Deduction of Interest on Education Loans

Panel A: AGI limitations	
Modified AGI Level	**Maximum Deduction**
Equal to or above $75,000 ($150,000 for married filing jointly)	Zero
Not over $60,000 ($120,000 for married filing jointly)	Amount paid up to $2,500
Above $60,000 ($120,000 for married filing jointly) but below $75,000 ($150,000 for married filing jointly)	Lesser of (1) amount paid or (2) $2,500 times phase-out percentage (see Panel B for the details of the phase-out computation).

Panel B: Phase-out Percentage*	
Filing Status	**Phase-out Percentage**
Single or Head of Household	(Modified AGI − $60,000)/$15,000
Married filing jointly	(Modified AGI − $120,000)/$30,000

*Married taxpayers filing separately are ineligible for the deduction.

Example 6-8

What if: Assume that Courtney's brother Jason paid interest on a qualified education loan he used to pay the tuition and fees for his three daughters to attend State University. In 2009, Jason was married and filed a joint return, paid $3,000 of interest expense on the loan, and reported modified AGI of $132,000. What amount of interest expense on the education loan is Jason allowed to deduct as a for AGI deduction?

(*continued on page 6-11...*)

[14]Home equity loans cannot qualify as education loans regardless of how the loan proceeds are spent.

[15]Postsecondary education includes courses at a university, college, or vocational school including internship programs leading to a degree or certificate. Qualifying costs claimed as deductions for AGI cannot be reimbursed by scholarships or Coverdell education savings accounts and are also ineligible for Hope and Lifetime Learning Credit purposes.

Answer: $1,500, computed as follows:

Description	Amount	Explanation
(1) Modified AGI	$132,000	AGI before higher education deductions.
(2) Actual interest expense on loan	3,000	Amount paid.
(3) Maximum interest expense deduction before phase-out	2,500	
(4) Phase-out (reduction) percentage	40%	[(1) − 120,000]/30,000.
(5) Phase-out amount (reduction in maximum)	1,000	(3) × (4).
(6) Maximum deduction after phase-out	1,500	(3) − (5).
(7) Deductible interest expense	$ 1,500	Lesser of (2) and (6).

Deduction for Qualified Education Expenses   For purposes of this deduction, qualified education expenses are limited to the tuition and fees required for enrollment at a postsecondary institution of higher education. Thus, the definition of qualifying expenses is more restrictive for the qualified education expense deduction than it is for the education loan interest expense deduction. However, similar to the education interest expense deduction, the amount of the maximum education expense deduction depends on filing status and level of modified AGI. For purposes of the qualified education expense deduction, modified AGI is AGI *after* deducting the education loan interest expense but *before* deducting qualified education expenses.[16] Just as with the qualified education loan interest deduction, married individuals filing separately are ineligible for the qualified education expense deduction. The rules for determining the allowable education expense deduction for taxpayers who qualify for the deduction are summarized in Exhibit 6-5.

EXHIBIT 6-5   **Summary of 2009 Limitations on Qualified Education Expenses**

Modified AGI Level	Deduction
Equal to or above 80,000 ($160,000 for married filing jointly)	Zero
Not over $65,000 ($130,000 for married filing jointly)	Amount paid up to $4,000
Above $65,000 ($130,000 for married filing jointly) but below $80,000 ($160,000)	Lesser of amount paid or $2,000

There are two important differences between the AGI limits on the interest on education loans deduction (summarized in Exhibit 6-4) and the AGI limits on the educational expense deduction (summarized in Exhibit 6-5). First, the definition of modified AGI for qualified education expenses in Exhibit 6-5 includes the deduction for interest on education loans. Second, there is no gradual phase-out of the deduction for education expenses as there is for the deduction for interest on education loans.

Example 6-9

Courtney paid $2,100 of tuition for Ellen to attend the University of Missouri–Kansas City during the summer. How much of this payment can Courtney deduct as a qualifying education expense?

Answer: None. The cost of the tuition is a qualified education expense but Courtney's modified AGI exceeds $80,000 (Courtney files as a head of household). Hence, Courtney is not allowed to deduct any of the cost of the tuition she paid for Ellen.

(continued on page 6-12...)

---

[16]At press time, the deduction for qualified education expenses is scheduled to expire after 2009.

THE KEY FACTS

Education Expenses

■ Up to $4,000 of qualified education expenses can be deducted for AGI.

■ Qualified education expenses include tuition and related costs for postsecondary or higher education.

■ The deduction is reduced for taxpayers with modified AGI over $65,000 ($130,000 married filing jointly) and eliminated for taxpayers with modified AGI of $80,000 ($160,000 married filing jointly) or more.

What if: Assume the same facts except that Courtney is married filing jointly and her modified AGI is $57,000. What amount can Courtney deduct as a qualifying education expense in this situation?

Answer: $2,100. She can deduct the full amount of the expenditure (limited to $4,000) because she is married filing jointly and her modified AGI is less than $65,000.

What if: Assume the original facts except that Courtney's modified AGi is $77,000. How much of the $2,100 tuition for Ellen would Courtney be allowed to deduct as a for AGI qualified education expense?

Answer: $2,000. Because Courtney's AGI is greater than $65,000 but not greater than $130,000 (she files as head of household) her deduction is the lesser of (1) her actual qualified education expenditures and (2) $2,000. Since Courtney's actual education expenditures were $2,100, her deduction is $2,000.

Because there are several education-related tax incentives, individuals can sometimes select among different tax benefits. For example, certain education expenses that qualify as deductions for AGI may also qualify for an education tax credit. Typically, a single expenditure *cannot* generate multiple tax benefits. Consequently, individuals should select the tax provision to apply to the expenses that generates the most benefit.

Summary: Deductions for AGI

Business expenses and rental and royalty expenses are two of the most important deductions for AGI. There are a variety of other important deductions for AGI that are indirectly related to business or provided to subsidize certain activities. After we have determined the deductions for AGI, we can compute AGI. Exhibits 6-6 and 6-7 summarize the computation of AGI for Courtney and for Gram, respectively. Exhibit 6-8 shows Courtney's AGI calculation as presented on the front page of her Form 1040.

EXHIBIT 6-6　Courtney's Adjusted Gross Income

Description	Amount	Reference
Gross income for current year	$178,020	Exhibit 5-4
Deductions for AGI:		
Business expenses	(1,500)	Example 6-2
Rental expenses	(9,000)	Example 6-3
Moving expenses	(5,279)	Example 6-5
One-half of self-employment taxes	(241)	Example 6-6
Adjusted gross income	**$162,000**	

EXHIBIT 6-7　Gram's Adjusted Gross Income

Description	Amount	Reference
Gross income for current year	$16,150	Exhibit 5-6
Deduction for AGI:		
Penalty for early withdrawal of savings	(410)	Example 6-7
Adjusted gross income	**$15,740**	

EXHIBIT 6-8   Courtney's AGI Computation on Form 1040, Page 1

Income	7	Wages, salaries, tips, etc. Attach Form(s) W-2	**7**	122,800
	8a	**Taxable** interest. Attach Schedule B if required	**8a**	600
Attach Form(s) W-2 here. Also attach Forms W-2G and 1099-R if tax was withheld.	b	**Tax-exempt** interest. **Do not** include on line 8a . . . **8b** 500		
	9a	Ordinary dividends. Attach Schedule B if required	**9a**	700
	b	Qualified dividends (see page 21) **9b**		
	10	Taxable refunds, credits, or offsets of state and local income taxes (see page 22) . .	**10**	420
	11	Alimony received	**11**	20,000
	12	Business income or (loss). Attach Schedule C or C-EZ	**12**	18,000
	13	Capital gain or (loss). Attach Schedule D if required. If not required, check here ▶ ☐	**13**	
If you did not get a W-2, see page 21.	14	Other gains or (losses). Attach Form 4797	**14**	
	15a	IRA distributions . . **15a**	b Taxable amount (see page 23)	**15b**	
	16a	Pensions and annuities **16a**	b Taxable amount (see page 24)	**16b**	
Enclose, but do not attach, any payment. Also, please use Form 1040-V.	17	Rental real estate, royalties, partnerships, S corporations, trusts, etc. Attach Schedule E	**17**	5,000
	18	Farm income or (loss). Attach Schedule F	**18**	
	19	Unemployment compensation	**19**	
	20a	Social security benefits . **20a**	b Taxable amount (see page 26)	**20b**	
	21	Other income. List type and amount (see page 28)	**21**	
	22	Add the amounts in the far right column for lines 7 through 21. This is your **total income** ▶	**22**	167,520
Adjusted Gross Income	23	Educator expenses (see page 28) **23**		
	24	Certain business expenses of reservists, performing artists, and fee-basis government officials. Attach Form 2106 or 2106-EZ **24**		
	25	Health savings account deduction. Attach Form 8889 . . **25**		
	26	Moving expenses. Attach Form 3903 . . . . . . **26** 5,279		
	27	One-half of self-employment tax. Attach Schedule SE . . **27** 241		
	28	Self-employed SEP, SIMPLE, and qualified plans . . . **28**		
	29	Self-employed health insurance deduction (see page 29) **29**		
	30	Penalty on early withdrawal of savings **30**		
	31a	Alimony paid b Recipient's SSN ▶ _____ **31a**		
	32	IRA deduction (see page 30) **32**		
	33	Student loan interest deduction (see page 33) **33**		
	34	Tuition and fees deduction. Attach Form 8917 . . . . **34**		
	35	Domestic production activities deduction. Attach Form 8903 **35**		
	36	Add lines 23 through 31a and 32 through 35	**36**	5,520
	37	Subtract line 36 from line 22. This is your **adjusted gross income** . . . . . ▶	**37**	162,000

Once we have determined AGI, we calculate taxable income by identifying deductions *from* AGI. These deductions consist of (1) the greater of itemized deductions or the standard deduction and (2) personal and dependency exemption deductions. We address itemized deductions next.

DEDUCTIONS FROM AGI: ITEMIZED DEDUCTIONS

LO2

There is a variety of itemized deductions, a few of which relate to profit-motivated activities (employee business expenses and investment expenses that are unrelated to rental or royalty activities). Many itemized deductions are personal in nature but are allowed in order either to subsidize desirable activities such as home ownership and charitable giving. Other itemized deductions, such as medical expenses and casualty losses, provide relief for taxpayers whose ability to pay taxes has been involuntarily reduced. We discuss itemized deductions in the order they appear on the individual tax return, Form 1040, Schedule A.

Medical Expenses

The medical expense deduction is designed to provide relief for taxpayers whose ability to pay taxes is seriously hindered by health-related circumstances. Qualifying medical expenses include any payments for the care, prevention, diagnosis, or cure of injury, disease, or bodily function that are not reimbursed by health insurance or are not paid for through a "flexible spending account."[17] Taxpayers may also deduct

---

[17]Taxpayers participating in flexible spending accounts are allowed to direct that a fixed amount of their salary be placed in an account to pay for medical expenses. The salary paid into these accounts is excluded from gross income and used to pay for medical expenses. See Chapter 12.

medical expenses incurred to treat their spouses and their dependents.[18] Common medical expenses include:

- Prescription medication and medical aids such as eyeglasses, contact lenses, and wheel chairs.
- Payments to medical care *providers* such as doctors, dentists, and nurses and medical care *facilities* such as hospitals.
- Transportation for medical purposes.
- Hospitals and long-term care facilities.
- Health insurance premiums (if not deducted for AGI by self-employed taxpayers) and insurance for long-term care services.[19]

Example 6-10

In April, Courtney broke her wrist in a mountain biking accident. She paid $2,000 for a visit to the hospital emergency room and follow-up visits with her doctor. While she recuperated, Courtney paid $300 for prescription medicine and $700 to a therapist for rehabilitation. Courtney's insurance reimbursed her $1,840 for these expenses. What is the amount of Courtney's qualifying deductible medical expenses?

Answer: $1,160, computed as follows:

Description	Deduction
Emergency room and doctor visits	$2,000
Prescription medication	300
Physical therapy	700
Total qualifying medical expenses	$3,000
Less insurance reimbursement	−1,840
Qualifying medical expenses from the accident	**$1,160**

Medical expenses for cosmetic surgery or other similar procedures are not deductible unless the surgery or procedure is necessary to ameliorate a deformity arising from, or directly related to, a congenital abnormality, a personal injury resulting from an accident or trauma, or disfiguring disease.[20]

Transportation and Travel for Medical Purposes   Taxpayers traveling for the primary purpose of receiving essential and deductible medical care may deduct the cost of the travel (including meals and lodging, with certain restrictions) and transportation.[21] Taxpayers using personal automobiles for medical transportation purposes may deduct a standard mileage allowance in lieu of actual costs. For 2009, the mileage rate is 24 cents a mile.

---

[18]For the purpose of deducting medical expenses a dependent need not meet the gross income test (§213(a)) and a child of divorced parents is considered a dependent of both parents (§213(d)(5)). We discuss the general requirements for dependency in Chapter 4.

[19]This includes the annual cost of Medicare and prescription insurance withheld from Social Security recipient's benefits checks.

[20]§213(d)(9)(A).

[21]The cost of travel for and essential to medical care, including meals and lodging (with certain limitations) is also deductible if the expense is not extravagant and the travel has no significant element of personal pleasure. However, under §213(d)(2) the deduction for the cost of lodging is limited to $50 per night per individual.

Example 6-11

Gram drove Courtney, *in Courtney's car,* 75 miles back and forth from the doctor's office and the physical therapist's facility during the period Courtney was being treated for her broken wrist. What is the amount of Courtney's qualifying medical expense for her trips to the doctor's office?

Answer: $18 (75 miles × $0.24)

Hospitals and Long-Term Care Facilities   Taxpayers may deduct the cost of meals and lodging at hospitals. However, the costs of meals and lodging at other types of facilities such as nursing homes are deductible only when the principal purpose for the stay is medical care rather than convenience. Of course, taxpayers may deduct the costs of actual medical care whether the care is provided at hospitals or other long-term care facilities.

Example 6-12

Gram considered moving into a long-term care facility before she eventually decided she would move in with Courtney. The facility was not primarily for medical care and would have cost Gram $36,000 a year. During discussions with facility administrators, Gram learned that typically 20 percent of the total cost for the facility is allocable to medical care. If Gram were to stay in the facility for an entire year, what amount of the long-term care costs would qualify as a deductible medical expense for Gram?

Answer: $7,200 ($36,000 × 20% allocable to medical care)

Medical Expense Deduction Limitation   The deduction for medical expenses is limited to the amount of unreimbursed qualifying medical expenses paid during the year (no matter when the services were provided) *reduced* by 7.5 percent of the taxpayer's AGI. This restriction is called a **floor limitation** because it eliminates any deduction for amounts below the floor. The purpose of a floor limitation is to restrict a deduction to taxpayers with substantial qualifying expenses. Because this floor limitation is set at a high percentage of AGI, unreimbursed medical expenses rarely produce tax benefits, especially for high income taxpayers.

Example 6-13

This year Courtney incurred $2,400 in unreimbursed qualifying medical expenses (including the $1,160 of qualifying medical expenses associated with the accident and the $18 transportation deduction for mileage). Given that Courtney's AGI is $162,000, what is the amount of Courtney's itemized medical expense deduction?

Answer: $0 computed as follows:

Description	Expense
Total unreimbursed qualifying medical expenses	$ 2,400
Minus: 7.5% of AGI ($162,000 × 7.5%)	(12,150)
Medical expense itemized deduction	$ 0

What if: What amount of medical expenses would Courtney be allowed to deduct if her AGI was $30,000?

(*continued on page 6-16...*)

Answer: $150, computed as follows:

Description	Expense
Total unreimbursed qualifying medical expenses	$ 2,400
Minus: 7.5% of AGI ($30,000 × 7.5%)	(2,250)
Medical expense itemized deduction	**$ 150**

Taxes

Individuals may deduct as itemized deductions payments made during the year for the following taxes:

- State, local, and foreign *income* taxes, including state and local taxes paid during the year through employer withholding, estimated tax payments, and overpayments on the prior year return that the taxpayer applies to the current year (the taxpayer asks the state to keep the overpayment rather than refund it).
- Real estate taxes on property held for personal or investment purposes.
- Personal property taxes that are assessed on the *value* of the specific property.[22]

Taxpayers may elect to deduct state and local sales taxes *instead of* deducting state and local income taxes.[23] This is particularly good news for taxpayers working in states that don't have an individual state income tax. Many common taxes are *not* deductible because there is no specific tax law allowing taxpayers to deduct these taxes. For example, gasoline taxes, excise taxes, Social Security taxes, federal estate and gift taxes, and the federal income tax are not deductible taxes for federal income tax purposes.

Another nonitemizer deduction exists for state and local property taxes. Typically, only individuals who itemize deductions may deduct real property taxes imposed by state and local governments. However, nonitemizers are allowed to increase their standard deduction for the state and local real property taxes paid.[24] This addition is limited to the lesser of:

1. The amount of real property taxes paid during the year, or
2. $500 ($1,000 for a married couple filing jointly).

Example 6-14

During the year, Courtney paid $6,700 of state income taxes through withholding from her paycheck. She also paid $2,700 of real estate taxes on her personal residence and $850 of real estate taxes on an investment property she owns in Oklahoma. Finally, Courtney paid $180 as a registration fee for her automobile (the fee is based on the year the automobile was manufactured, not its value). What amount of these payments can Courtney deduct as itemized deductions?

(*continued on page 6-17...*)

---

[22]§164.

[23]The deduction can be based upon either the amount paid or the amount published in the IRS tables (IRS Publication 600) based upon the state of residence, income, and number of exemptions. The states with no income tax are Alaska, Florida, Nevada, South Dakota, Texas, Washington, and Wyoming. Tennessee and New Hampshire have no state income tax on wages, but do impose a tax on unearned income.

[24]§62(c)(1)(C). At press time, this deduction is scheduled to expire after 2009.

Answer: $10,250 ($6,700 state taxes + $2,700 real estate taxes on residence + $850 real estate taxes on investment property). Courtney is not allowed to deduct the registration fee for her car because the fee is not based on the value of the automobile.

What if: Suppose that on April 15, 2009, Courtney filed her 2008 state tax return and was due a refund from the state in the amount of $420. However, Courtney elected to have the state keep the overpayment and apply it to her 2009 tax payments. What amount of state income taxes is Courtney allowed to deduct as an itemized deduction in 2009?

Answer: $7,120 ($6,700 withholding + $420 overpayment applied to 2009). The treatment of the overpayment is the same as if Courtney had received the refund in 2009 and then remitted it to the state as payment of 2009 taxes. Because she paid the tax in 2009, she is allowed to deduct the tax in 2009. Recall that under the tax benefit rule (see Chapter 5), Courtney will be required to include the $420 in gross income in 2009 if she itemized deductions in 2008.

What if: Suppose that Gram paid $755 in property taxes but did not itemize her deductions. What amount of property taxes is Gram allowed to deduct as a nonitemized deduction?

Answer: Gram cannot deduct the property taxes because she does not itemize her deductions. However, she can choose to increase her standard deduction by $500 (the lesser of the property taxes paid or $500).

Interest

There are two itemized deductions for interest expense.[25] Subject to limitations to be discussed in Chapter 14, individuals can deduct interest paid on loans secured by a personal residence. Individuals can also deduct interest paid on loans used to purchase investment assets such as stocks, bonds, or land (investment interest expense). The deduction of investment interest is limited to a taxpayer's net investment income (investment income minus investment expenses). Any investment interest in excess of the net investment income limitation carries forward to the subsequent year. Taxpayers are not allowed to deduct interest on personal credit card debt or on loans to acquire (and secured by) personal-use automobiles.

Example 6-15

Courtney acquired her home in Kansas City in January of this year for $300,000 (also its value throughout the year). She purchased it by paying $40,000 as a down payment and borrowing $260,000 from a credit union. Her home is the collateral for the loan. During the year, Courtney paid $15,800 in interest on the loan. How much of this interest may Courtney deduct?

Answer: $15,800. Because Courtney's home mortgage is secured by her home, she is allowed to deduct the interest expense on the home as an itemized deduction.

What if: Suppose that Courtney borrowed $26,000 to purchase a new car (the loan was secured by the car). Would she be allowed to deduct the interest on the loan?

Answer: No, the loan was not used to purchase a personal residence or investment assets.

Example 6-16

In March, Courtney borrowed $2,000 from her bank to purchase stock in Delta, Inc. During the year, she paid $130 of interest expense on the loan and realized $200 of investment income. What amount of the $130 in interest expense can Courtney deduct as an itemized deduction this year?

(*continued on page 6-18...*)

---

[25]Interest paid on loans where the proceeds are used in a trade or business is fully deductible as a business expense deduction for AGI.

Answer: $130. Courtney can deduct investment interest expense as an itemized deduction to the extent of her net investment income. Courtney recognized $200 of investment income, but she had no deductible investment expenses (investment interest expense is not an investment expense). Hence, Courtney's net investment income is $200. Because net investment income exceeds the amount of Courtney's investment interest expense, she can deduct the entire $130 of investment interest expense on her return.[26]

What if: Suppose that Courtney received net investment income of only $100 this year. How much of the $130 investment interest expense would she be allowed to deduct?

Answer: $100. Her deduction is limited to the net investment income of $100. Courtney would be allowed to carry over the $30 of interest expense that was not deductible to deduct in a future year when she has net investment income.

Charitable Contributions

Congress encourages donations to charities by allowing taxpayers to deduct contributions of money and other property to *qualified* charitable organizations. Qualifying charitable organizations include organizations that engage in educational, religious, scientific, governmental, and other public activities.[27]

Example 6-17

This year Courtney donated $1,700 to the Red Cross. She also gave $200 in cash to various homeless people she met on the streets during the year. What amount of these donations is Courtney allowed to deduct as a charitable contribution?

Answer: $1,700. Because the Red Cross is a public charity recognized by the IRS, Courtney may deduct her $1,700 charitable contribution to it as an itemized deduction. However, despite Courtney's charitable intent, her donations to the homeless are not deductible as charitable contributions because individuals do not qualify as charitable organizations.

What if: Suppose that instead of transferring cash to homeless people on the streets, Courtney donated $200 cash to a local food bank that is listed in IRS Publication 78 as a qualified charity. The food bank provides meals to those in need. Would Courtney be allowed to deduct this contribution?

Answer: Yes, because the food bank is a qualified charity.

The *amount* of the charitable contribution deduction depends on whether the taxpayer contributes money or other property to the charity. Note that in virtually all circumstances, donations are only deductible if the contribution is substantiated by written records.[28]

Contributions of Money   Cash contributions are deductible in the year paid, including donations of cash or by check, electronic funds transfers, credit card charges, and payroll deductions.[29] Taxpayers are also considered as making monetary contributions for the cost of transportation and travel for charitable purposes if there is no significant element of pleasure or entertainment in the travel. When taxpayers use

---

[26]Courtney also had $700 of investment income in the form of dividends on her 1,000 shares of GE stock. However, this income is subject to a preferential tax rate, and absent a special election, it would not qualify as net investment income. We describe this election in Chapter 11.

[27]§170(c). IRS Publication 78 lists the organizations that the IRS has determined to be qualified charities.

[28]For example, to deduct monetary donations, taxpayers must keep a bank record or a written communication from the charity showing the name of the charity and the date and amount of the contribution. See Publication 526 for more information.

[29]When individual taxpayers mail a contribution, they are allowed to deduct the contribution when they place the payment in the mail. When they pay via credit card, they are allowed to deduct the contribution on the day of the charge. Rev. Rul. 78-38, 1978-1 CB 67.

their personal vehicles for charitable transportation purposes, they may deduct, as a cash contribution, a standard mileage allowance for each mile driven (14 cents a mile). While taxpayers are allowed to deduct their transportation costs and other out-of-pocket costs of providing services for charities, they are not allowed to deduct the value of the services they provide for charities.

Example 6-18

Once a month, Courtney does volunteer work at a Goodwill Industries outlet about 20 miles from her home. Altogether, Courtney traveled 500 miles during the year driving to and from the Goodwill outlet. Courtney has determined that the services she provided during the year are reasonably valued at $1,500. What amount is Courtney allowed to deduct for her volunteer work with Goodwill Industries?

Answer: $70. Courtney is *not* allowed to deduct the value of the services she provides to Goodwill. However, in 2009 she is allowed to deduct the $70 cost of her transportation to and from the Goodwill outlet (500 miles × 14 cents per mile).

Taxpayers receiving goods or services from a charity in exchange for a contribution may only deduct the amount of the contribution *in excess of the fair market value of the goods or services they receive* in exchange for their contribution.[30]

Contributions of Property Other Than Money   When a taxpayer donates *property* to charity, the *amount* the taxpayer is allowed to deduct depends on whether the property is **capital gain property** or **ordinary income property.**

Capital gain property.   In general, taxpayers are allowed to deduct the *fair market value* of capital gain property on the date of the donation. Capital gain property is any appreciated asset that would have generated a *long-term* capital gain if the taxpayer had sold the property for its fair market value instead of contributing the asset to charity. To qualify as long-term, the taxpayer must have held the asset for more than a year. Capital assets include the following assets:

- Investment assets (stocks, bonds, land held for investment, paintings, etc.).
- Business assets (to the extent that gain on the sale of the business asset would *not* have been considered ordinary income).[31]
- Personal-use assets.

Contributing capital gain property is a particularly tax efficient way to make charitable contributions, because taxpayers are allowed to deduct the fair market value of the property, and they are *not* required to include the appreciation on the asset in gross income.

Example 6-19

In December of the current year, Courtney donated 100 shares of stock in JBD Corp. to her church, a qualified charity. Courtney purchased the stock several years ago for $2,600, but the shares were worth $10,600 at the time of the donation. What is the amount of Courtney's charitable deduction for donating the stock?

Answer: $10,600. Because the stock is an appreciated investment asset held for more than a year, it qualifies as capital gain property. Hence, Courtney is allowed to deduct the $10,600 fair market value of the stock, and she is *not* required to recognize any of the $8,000 realized gain ($10,600 − $2,600).

---

[30]Reg. §1.170A-1(h). To help with this determination, a charity that provides goods or services in return for a contribution of more than $75 must provide contributors with a written statement estimating the value of goods and services that the charity has provided to the donor.

[31]These assets are considered to be §1231(b) assets. We discuss the tax treatment of dispositions of business assets in Chapter 10.

Certain contributions of capital gain property do not qualify for a fair market value deduction. The deduction for capital gain property that is *tangible personal property* is limited to the *adjusted basis* of the property if the charity uses the property for a purpose that is *unrelated* to its charitable purpose.[32] That is, this restriction applies to capital gains property that is (1) tangible, (2) personal property (not realty), and (3) unrelated to the charity's operations. The third requirement does not apply if, at the time of the donation, the taxpayer reasonably anticipates that the charity will put the property to a related use.

Example 6-20

What if: Suppose that Courtney donated a religious-themed painting to her church. Courtney purchased the painting several years ago for $2,600, but the painting was worth $10,600 at the time of the donation. When Courtney contributed the painting, she reasonably expected the church to hang the painting in the church chapel. What would be the amount of Courtney's charitable contribution deduction?

Answer: $10,600. Because Courtney reasonably expected the church to use the painting in a manner related to its tax-exempt purpose, Courtney is allowed to deduct the full fair market value of the painting without recognizing the $8,000 realized gain.

What if: Suppose that Courtney was told at the time she donated the painting that the church intended to sell it and use the cash to help fund expansion of the church building. What would be Courtney's charitable contribution deduction?

Answer: $2,600, the adjusted basis of the property. Because the church is selling the painting, it is using it for a purpose unrelated to its charitable purposes. Thus, Courtney may deduct only the tax basis of the painting.

What if: Suppose that Courtney donated stock to her church and the church informed her that it intended to immediately sell the stock. What would be the amount of Courtney's charitable contribution deduction?

Answer: $10,600. Stock is intangible property, not tangible personal property. Hence, Courtney would deduct the fair market value of the stock.

Ordinary income property.   Taxpayers contributing ordinary income property can only deduct the *lesser* of (1) the property's fair market value or (2) the property's adjusted basis. Ordinary income property consists of all assets other than capital gain property. That is, ordinary income property is property that if sold would generate income taxed at ordinary rates. This includes the following types of assets:

- Assets the taxpayer has held for a year or less.
- Inventory the taxpayer sells in a trade or business.
- Business assets held for more than a year to the extent the taxpayer would recognize ordinary income under the depreciation recapture rules if the taxpayer had sold the property.[33]
- Assets, including investment assets and personal-use assets, with a value *less than* the taxpayer's basis in the assets (they have declined in value).

---

[32]Reg. §1.170A-4(b)(2). The taxpayer's deduction for donating capital gain property is also limited to basis if the taxpayer contributes capital gain property other than stock to a private nonoperating foundation. There are also other exceptions in which capital gain property might not otherwise qualify for deduction at value such as the subsequent sales of donated property by the charity. These exceptions are beyond the scope of this text.

[33]We discuss depreciation recapture in Chapter 9.

Example 6-21

Before her move from Cincinnati, Courtney decided to donate her excess possessions to Goodwill Industries. Courtney estimated that she paid over $900 for these items, including clothing, a table, and a couch. However, although the items were in excellent condition, they were worth only $160. What amount can Courtney deduct for her donation of these items?

Answer: $160. Because Courtney's possessions have declined in value, they are considered to be ordinary income property. Consequently, Courtney may deduct the lesser of (1) the fair market value of $160 or (2) her tax basis in the property of $900.

Charitable Contribution Deduction Limitations   The amount of a taxpayer's charitable contribution deduction for the year is limited to a **ceiling** or maximum deduction. The ceiling depends upon the type of property the taxpayer donates and the nature of the charity receiving the donation; donations to public charities (charities that are publicly supported such as churches and schools) and **private operating foundations** (privately sponsored foundations that actually fund and conduct charitable activities) are subject to less stringent restrictions than other charities. In general, cash and property donations to public charities and private operating foundations are limited to 50 percent of the taxpayer's AGI. Deductions for contributions of capital gain property to public charities and private operating foundations are generally limited to 30 percent of the taxpayer's AGI. Deductions for cash and property contributions to **private nonoperating foundations** (privately sponsored foundations that disburse funds to other charities) are limited to 30 percent of the taxpayer's AGI. Finally, deductions for contributions of capital gain property to private nonoperating foundations are limited to 20 percent of the taxpayer's AGI. Exhibit 6-9 summarizes the charitable contribution limitations for individual taxpayers.

EXHIBIT 6-9   Summary of Charitable Contribution Limitation Rules

Contribution Type	Public Charity and Private Operating Foundation	Private Nonoperating Foundation
Cash:		
Amount	Cash amount	Cash amount
AGI limit	50%	30%
Capital gain property:		
Amount	FMV	Basis
AGI limit	30%	20%
Ordinary income property:		
Amount	Lesser of Basis or FMV	Lesser of Basis or FMV
AGI limit	50%	30%

When taxpayers make contributions that are subject to different percentage limitations, they apply the AGI limitations in the following sequence:

Step 1: Determine the limitation for the 50 percent contributions.

Step 2: Apply the limitations to the 30 percent contributions. The 30 percent contribution limit is the *lesser* of (a) AGI × 30% or (b) AGI × 50% minus the amount of contributions deducted in Step 1.

Step 3: Apply the limitations to the 20 percent contributions. The 20 percent contribution limit is the *lesser* of (a) AGI × 20% or (b) AGI × 30% minus the amount of contributions from Step 2.

When a taxpayer's contributions exceed the AGI ceiling limitation for the year, the excess contribution is treated as though it were made in the subsequent tax year and is subject to the same AGI limitations in the next year. The excess contribution can be carried forward for five years before it expires. However, because the ceiling limitations are fairly generous, taxpayers exceed the ceiling limitations only in unusual circumstances.

Example 6-22

This year Courtney made the following contributions to qualified charities:

Organization	Amount	Type	AGI Limitation	Reference
Red Cross	$ 1,700	Cash	50%	Example 6-17.
Goodwill Industries	70	Cash-mileage	50%	Example 6-18.
Goodwill	160	Ordinary income property	50%	Example 6-21.
Church	10,600	Capital gain property	30%	Example 6-19.
Total contributions	$12,530			

After applying the AGI limitations, how much of the $12,530 in contributions is Courtney allowed to deduct?

Answer: $12,530, computed as follows:

Description	Amount	Explanation
(1) AGI	$162,000	Exhibit 6-6.
(2) 50% contributions	1,930	($1,700 + 70 + 160).
(3) 50% AGI contribution limit	81,000	(1) × 50%.
(4) Allowable 50% deductions	**1,930**	Lesser of (2) or (3).
(5) 30% contributions	10,600	
(6) 30% AGI contribution limit	48,600	(1) × 30%.
(7) Remaining 50% AGI limitation	79,070	(3) − (4).
(8) Allowable 30% deductions	**10,600**	Lesser of (5), (6), or (7).
Deductible charitable contributions	**$ 12,530**	(4) + (8).

What if: Suppose that Courtney's AGI was $30,000. After applying the AGI limitations, how much of the $12,530 in contributions would Courtney be allowed to deduct?

Answer: $10,930, computed as follows:

Description	Amount	Explanation
(1) AGI	$ 30,000	
(2) 50% contributions	1,930	
(3) 50% AGI contribution limit	15,000	(1) × 50%.
(4) Allowable 50% deductions	**1,930**	Lesser of (2) and (3).
(5) 30% contributions	10,600	
(6) 30% AGI contribution limit	9,000	(1) × 30%.
(7) Remaining 50% AGI limitation	13,070	(3) − (4).
(8) Allowable 30% deductions	**9,000**	Lesser of (5), (6), or (7).
Deductible charitable contributions	**$ 10,930**	(4) + (8).

Courtney would not be allowed to deduct this year $1,600 of her $10,600 capital gain property contribution to her church. However, she will carry forward the $1,600 to next year (and the four years after that, if necessary) and treat it as though she made a $1,600 contribution next year subject to the 30 percent of AGI limitation.

Casualty and Theft Losses on Personal-Use Assets

Individuals cannot deduct losses they realize when they sell or dispose of assets used for personal purposes (personal-use assets as opposed to business or investment assets). However, individuals *are* allowed to deduct casualty and theft losses realized on personal-use assets.[34] A **casualty** loss is defined as a loss arising from a *sudden, unexpected,* or *unusual* event such as a "fire, storm, or shipwreck" or loss from theft.[35]

Tax Loss from Casualties   Congress allows deductions for unreimbursed casualty and theft losses because these losses may substantially reduce a taxpayer's ability to pay taxes. However, limitations on the deduction generally ensure that taxpayers receive a tax benefit from such losses only when the losses are relatively large. The *amount* of the tax loss from any *specific casualty event* (including theft) is the *lesser* of (1) the decline in value of the property caused by the casualty or (2) the taxpayer's tax basis in the damaged or stolen asset. The loss is reduced by any reimbursements the individual is eligible to receive, such as insurance reimbursements.

Example 6-23

In June, Courtney had a bad day at a nearby lake. Her purse containing $200 in cash was stolen, and she wrecked her car on the way home. Courtney purchased her purse for $150 and it was worth $125 at the time of the theft ($325 in total value was stolen). Courtney purchased her car earlier in the year for $22,000 and had to pay $2,000 to have it repaired. Courtney's insurance company reimbursed her $1,400 for the repairs. What is the amount of Courtney's casualty tax loss?

Answer: $925 ($325 theft + $600 accident). The theft and the automobile accident are considered to be two separate casualty events generating two different casualty losses. The amount of each casualty loss, before considering limitations, is computed as follows:

	Theft	Accident
Fair market value (FMV) before casualty	$325	
FMV after the casualty	–0	
(1) Decline in FMV (cost to repair)	$325	$ 2,000
(2) Tax basis in property before casualty	$400	$22,000
Loss before reimbursement [lesser of (1) or (2)]	$325	$ 2,000
Insurance reimbursement	–0	–1,400
Unreimbursed casualty losses	$325	$ 600

Casualty Loss Deduction Floor Limitations   Casualty losses must exceed two separate floor limitations to qualify as itemized deductions. The first floor is $500 for *each* casualty event during the year.[36] This floor eliminates deductions for small losses. The second floor limitation is 10 percent of AGI and it applies to the sum of all casualty losses for the year (after applying the $500 floor). In other words, the itemized deduction is the aggregate amount of casualty losses that exceeds 10 percent of AGI.

Example 6-24

Courtney's total casualty loss before applying the deduction limitations is $925. What amount of the $925 loss is Courtney allowed to deduct after applying the two floor limitations?

(*continued on page 6-24...*)

---

[34]§165. As we discuss in more detail in Chapter 8, businesses may deduct casualty and theft losses of business property as a deduction for AGI. Further, casualty or theft losses on investment assets are deductible as a miscellaneous itemized deduction not subject to the 2 percent of AGI floor.

[35]§165(c)(3). See also IRS Publication No. 547 (Casualties, Disasters, and Thefts), 2006, p. 2.

[36]At press time, the $500 limit is scheduled to drop to $100 after 2009.

Answer: $0 Computed as follows:

	Theft	Accident	Total
Losses before limitations	$325	$600	
Less $500 per casualty floor	−500	−500	
Casualty loss before AGI limit	$ 0	$100	$ 100
Less 10% of $162,000			−16,200
Casualty loss deduction after AGI limit			$ 0

What if: Suppose that Courtney's automobile was worth $20,000, and that it was completely destroyed in the accident. What would be Courtney's casualty loss deduction if she received only $3,100 of insurance reimbursement for her loss?

Answer: $625, computed as follows:

	Theft	Accident	Total
Fair market value (FMV) before casualty	$325	$20,000	
FMV after the casualty	0	0	
(1) Decline in FMV (cost to repair)	$325	$20,000	
(2) Tax basis in property before casualty	$400	$22,000	
Loss before reimbursement [lesser of (1) or (2)]	$325	$20,000	
Less Insurance reimbursement	−0	−3,100	
Less $500 per casualty floor	−500	−500	
Unreimbursed casualty losses	$ 0	$16,400	$16,400
Less 10% of $162,000			−16,200
Casualty loss deduction after AGI limit			$ 200

Taxes in the Real World

In order to qualify for a casualty loss deduction, a taxpayer's personal loss must be sudden or unexpected. Taxpayers and the IRS sometimes disagree about what is a casualty. Consider the following three case summaries (sometimes called the "trilogy of the rings") and, for each case, see whether you can determine whether the taxpayer or the IRS was victorious.

Case 1

Nancy Carpenter cleaned her wedding ring by placing it in some ammonia near the kitchen sink. Nancy's husband, William, later emptied the ammonia into the drain along with the ring while doing the dishes. He then turned on the garbage disposal, destroying the ring [*William H. Carpenter,* decided by the Tax Court in 1966, 25 TCM 1186].

Case 2

John lovingly helped his wife Agnes from the car and started to shut the door. Agnes, upon realizing she had left something on the seat, reached her hand back toward the car only to have the door shut directly on her engagement ring. The setting of the ring broke on impact and the diamond was flung into the leaf-covered driveway as she retracted her hand. Despite all their efforts, John and Agnes never found the stone [*John P. White,* decided by the Tax Court in 1967, 48 TC 430].

Case 3

Mr. and Mrs. Keenan spent the night at a hotel. Mr. Keenan, who was suffering from a stuffy nose, used tissues he had placed near his bed throughout the night. During the night Mrs. Keenan removed her rings and placed them within a tissue at the bedside. Mr. Keenan awoke before his wife the following morning, and he gathered the tissues, including the ring, and flushed them down the toilet [*Keenan v. Bowers,* decided in 1950 by the South Carolina District Court, 50-2 USTC ¶9444].

So, what do you think?

The taxpayers won Case 1 and Case 2 because the losses were deemed to be "sudden and unexpected" in nature. However, the taxpayer lost Case 3 because the loss was due to a "chain of events on the parts of Mrs. Keenan and Mr. Keenan." Thus, the loss was not considered to be sudden in nature.

Miscellaneous Itemized Deductions Subject to AGI Floor

There are a variety of deductions that address specific objectives but do not fit easily into any category. Congress called these deductions **miscellaneous itemized deductions** and subjected most of these deductions to an AGI floor (only amounts over the floor are deductible). Miscellaneous itemized deductions subject to the floor limitation include employee business expenses, investment expenses, and certain other expenses. These miscellaneous deductions are lumped together at the end of the year and are deductible only to the extent that their sum *exceeds* 2 percent of the taxpayer's AGI.

Employee Business Expenses   While business expenses are typically deductible as deductions for AGI, employee business expenses are deductible as miscellaneous itemized deductions. Expenses that qualify include those that are appropriate and helpful for the employee's work such as the cost of professional dues, uniforms (unless suitable as normal attire), and subscriptions to publications related to employment.

Example 6-25

Courtney subscribes to several architectural publications at an annual cost of $410. She finds these publications helpful, and it is certainly appropriate that an architect read current publications to keep up with new trends. Her employer does not reimburse Courtney for the cost of the subscriptions. What amount, if any, qualifies as a deductible employee business expense?

Answer: All $410 qualifies as a deductible employee business expense because the expense is appropriate and helpful to Courtney's employment.

Several types of employee expenses are restricted. For example, the costs of job hunting qualify if the job is in the employee's current trade or business, but not for the individual's first job. In addition, the cost of education qualifies if it serves to maintain or improve the employee's skill in the business, but not if the education is *required* to qualify for a new business or profession. Thus, a high school teacher would not be able to deduct the cost of attending law school because a law degree would qualify him for a different profession.

Example 6-26

During the year, Courtney paid $1,550 to attend motivational seminars sponsored by a continuing education provider. Courtney has found these seminars helpful, and her employer has encouraged Courtney to attend. How much of the cost of the seminars qualifies as a deductible employee business expense?

Answer: All $1,550. The cost qualifies an an employee business expense because the courses are appropriate and helpful and do not qualify Courtney for a new business.

Travel and transportation.   The cost of travel and transportation associated with the employee's work responsibilities may also qualify as miscellaneous itemized deductions. The cost of travel is deductible if the primary purpose of the trip is business. However, the cost of **commuting**—traveling from a residence to the place of business—is personal and never deductible.[37] When employees drive their personal automobiles for business purposes, they may deduct a standard mileage rate in lieu of deducting actual costs. In 2009, the standard business mileage rate is 55 cents per mile. When employees travel on business trips long enough to be away from home overnight, meals and lodging also qualify as employee business expenses. Although meals and lodging are deductible employee business expenses, employees are allowed to deduct only half the cost of the meals.

Example 6-27

Because Courtney is extremely motivated to reach her potential as an architect (the seminars are doing wonders), she spent a week in September, at her own expense, driving her personal car to several large cities to study different architectural designs. During the trip, she drove a total of 1,940 miles, spent $796 on lodging, and paid $500 for meals. What amount can Courtney deduct as unreimbursed employee business expenses before considering the 2 percent of AGI floor?

Answer: $2,113, computed for 2009 as follows:

Description	Expense	Calculation
Transportation	$1,067	1,940 miles × 55 cents
Lodging	796	
Meals	250	$500 × 50%
Total employee business expense from trip	$2,113	

Employee expense reimbursements.   Many employees are reimbursed for their business expenses by their employers. As a general rule, employees *include* reimbursements in gross income and deduct employee business expenses as miscellaneous itemized deductions. However, if an employee is required to submit documentation supporting expenses to receive reimbursement and the employer reimburses only legitimate business expenses, then the employer's reimbursement plan qualifies as an **accountable plan**, Under an accountable plan employees *exclude* expense reimbursements from gross income and do *not* deduct the reimbursed expenses. If the expenses exceed the reimbursements, the excess (unreimbursed) portion is deductible as an employee business expense. Thus, miscellaneous itemized deductions for employee business expenses are commonly referred to as deductions for *unreimbursed* employee business expenses.

Example 6-28

In November, Courtney went on a business trip to Los Angeles to meet with a prospective client and spent $1,700 on business travel including meals and lodging. EWD reimbursed Courtney for the entire $1,700 cost of the trip under an accountable plan. What amount can Courtney deduct?

Answer: $0. Because EWD's reimbursement is made under an accountable plan, Courtney ignores the reimbursement and the expenses for tax purposes; the reimbursement and expenses completely offset each other.

What if: Suppose that EWD provided Courtney with a flat amount of $2,000 to cover her expenses for the trip and did not require her to account for expenditures. How would Courtney treat the reimbursement and the expenses for tax purposes?

(continued on page 6-27...)

[37]See a discussion of the deduction limitation on meals in Chapter 8. Costs of commuting to and from a temporary place of work are deductible and costs of commuting from a first job to a second job are deductible. Employees may take *temporary* business trips that last for months. For these trips, the costs of the travel, including meals and lodging, are deductible for the duration of the trip. However, because trips in excess of one year are deemed to be *permanent,* the cost of travel on indefinite trips is *not* deductible.

Answer: Courtney would include the $2,000 in gross income and claim the $1,700 from the trip from AGI as an employee business expense, miscellaneous itemized deduction subject to the 2 percent of AGI floor. The reimbursement was not made under an accountable plan because Courtney was not required to substantiate her expenses.

Investment Expenses   As previously explained, investment expenses are itemized deductions. These expenses are classified as miscellaneous itemized deductions and include expenditures necessary for the production or collection of income, or for the management, conservation, or maintenance of property held for the production of income.[38] Common investment expenses include:

- Expenses associated with investment income or property.
- Investment advisory fees.
- Safe-deposit box fees.
- Subscriptions to investment-related publications.

Tax Preparation Fees   Ordinary and necessary expenses incurred in connection with determining their tax obligations imposed by federal, state, municipal, or foreign authorities are also deductible as miscellaneous itemized deductions subject to the 2 percent AGI floor.[39] While the most common of tax preparation fees are the costs of preparing taxpayers' tax returns, taxpayers may also deduct other related expenses such as the cost of property appraisals for tax purposes and the costs of contesting tax liabilities.

Example 6-29

In 2009, Courtney paid Quick Taxes, Inc., $250 to prepare her 2008 income tax return. What amount of this expenditure can Courtney deduct before considering the 2 percent of AGI floor?

Answer: $250. The entire amount qualifies as a miscellaneous itemized deduction for 2009.

Hobby Losses   As stated previously, individuals engaged in *business* activities are allowed to deduct their business expenses as deductions for AGI. However, taxpayers may engage in certain activities for primarily personal enjoyment but these activities may also generate revenue. For tax purposes, this type of activity is considered a **hobby** rather than a business. Hobby expenses are deductible only to the extent of the revenue generated by the hobby. Sometimes referred to as the *hobby loss limitation,* this limit is less taxpayer-friendly for a hobby than the limits on business expenses. Thus, it's important to determine whether an activity should be considered a business or a hobby for tax purposes. This determination hinges upon whether the taxpayer is engaged in the activity *primarily* to make a profit or *primarily* for personal enjoyment.

To help make this subjective determination, the regulations provide a list of following factors to consider.[40]

- The manner in which the taxpayer carries on the activity.
- The expertise of the taxpayer or his advisors.
- The time and effort expended by the taxpayer in carrying on the activity.
- The expectation that assets used in the activity may appreciate in value.
- The success of the taxpayer in carrying on other, similar activities.
- The taxpayer's history of income or losses with respect to the activity.

[38]§212. As we discussed earlier in the chapter, rental and royalty expenses are the only investment expenses that qualify as a deduction for AGI.
[39]§212.
[40]See Reg. §1.183-2.

- The amount of occasional profits, if any.
- The financial status of the taxpayer.
- The elements of personal pleasure or recreation.

One of the most important factors is the taxpayer's history of income or loss in the activity. In fact, the tax law explicitly presumes that an activity is a business if it generates a profit in three of five consecutive years.[41] This presumption is difficult for the IRS to overcome in disputes with taxpayers.

If an activity is determined to be a hobby, the taxpayer must *include* the revenue from the activity in gross income and may deduct the expenses, to the extent of the gross income from the activity, *as miscellaneous itemized deductions* (see discussion below).[42] Thus, the revenue from the activity increases the taxpayer's AGI (and taxable income) dollar for dollar. However, the deductions may or may not decrease taxable income depending on whether and the extent to which they exceed the 2 percent of AGI floor.

Example 6-30

Courtney's cousin, Phil T. Thrill, played golf at Arizona State University. He turned pro and tried to qualify for the PGA tour when he graduated from college. Unfortunately, he couldn't support his family playing golf and is currently employed as a high school physical education instructor. Every summer, Phil plays in several local and a few regional professional golf tournaments. His only source of revenue from golf is the prize money he wins in these tournaments. Phil has managed to earn prize money in excess of his expenses in only one of the previous five years. This year Phil received golf revenues of $3,200 and incurred golf-related expenses of $8,800 consisting of tournament entry fees, equipment, food, transportation, clothing, and lodging. For tax purposes, are Phil's golf activities considered to be a business or a hobby? If Phil's golfing activities are determined to be a *hobby*, how does Phil account for his revenues and expenses for tax purposes?

Answer: Most likely a hobby. Because Phil has only generated golf revenue in excess of expenses in one of the past five years, the activity is not presumed to be a business activity. To qualify as a business, Phil would have to convince the IRS that he is primarily engaging in golf activities to make a profit rather than for personal enjoyment. If the activity is determined to be a hobby, Phil includes the $3,200 of revenue in gross income as miscellaneous income. He is allowed to deduct $3,200 of his expenses as miscellaneous itemized deductions subject to the 2 percent floor (the deduction is limited to gross income from the activity).

What if: Suppose that Phil's golfing activities are determined to be a hobby and (1) his AGI is $70,000 before considering the effects of his golfing activity and (2) he has no miscellaneous itemized deductions other than his golfing expenses. What is the effect of his golfing activities on his AGI and taxable income this year?

Answer: The golfing activities will increase Phil's AGI by $3,200 and his taxable income by $1,464 because the full amount of the revenue is included in gross income but his expense deductions are limited. Phil's AGI and taxable income are computed as follows:

Description	Amount	Explanation
(1) AGI before activity	$70,000	
(2) Golf revenue (increase in AGI)	3,200	
(3) AGI after activity	73,200	(1) + (2).
(4) Golf expenses	3,800	
(5) Golf expenses after revenue limit	3,200	Lesser of (2) or (4).
(6) 2% of AGI floor	1,464	(3) × 2%.
(7) Deductible golf expenses (as itemized deduction)	1,736	(5) − (6).
Increase in taxable income	**$ 1,464**	(2) − (7).

---

[41]For activities involving breeding, training, or racing horses, the taxpayer need show a profit in only two of seven years for the activity to be presumed to be a business.

[42]When expenses of a hobby exceed revenue, the expenses must be deducted in a particular sequence. Taxpayers first deduct expenses that are deductible anyway, such as mortgage interest or property taxes. Second, taxpayers deduct all other expenses except depreciation expense. Finally, they deduct depreciation expense.

Limitation on Miscellaneous Itemized Deductions (2 percent of AGI Floor)   To apply the 2 percent floor limit and determine the miscellaneous itemized deduction, the sum of all deductions subject to the 2 percent floor limitation is reduced by 2 percent of AGI. If the 2 percent floor equals or exceeds the sum of miscellaneous itemized deductions, the deductions do not increase the taxpayer's itemized deductions (they don't provide any tax benefit). The 2 percent floor limitation makes it likely that most taxpayers will receive limited, if any, tax benefit from the deductions subject to the floor.

Example 6-31

What amount is Courtney's deduction for miscellaneous itemized deductions that are subject to the 2 percent floor?

Answer: $1,083, computed as follows:

Description	Amount	Reference
Subscriptions to publications	$ 410	Example 6-25.
Educational costs	1,550	Example 6-26.
Business trip to observe architecture	2,113	Example 6-27.
Tax preparation fees	250	Example 6-29.
Total deductions subject to 2% floor	$4,323	
2% of AGI floor (162,000 × 2%)	−3,240	
Total miscellaneous itemized deductions	$1,083	

Courtney incurred a total of $4,323 of miscellaneous itemized deductions, but she can deduct only $1,083 of them due to the 2 percent of AGI restriction.

THE KEY FACTS

Miscellaneous Itemized Deductions

■ Employee business expenses not reimbursed by an accountable plan.

■ Investment expenses if not in a rental or royalty activity.

■ Tax preparation fees and allowable hobby expenses

■ Total miscellaneous itemized deductions are subject to a 2 percent of AGI floor limit.

Taxes in the Real World

Mrs. Tschetschot was a database project engineer residing in Cedar Rapids, Iowa, but she was also a professional tournament poker player. In 2000, Mrs. Tschetschot participated in nine poker tournament series, winning in excess of $11,000. In contrast, Mr. Tschetschot occasionally played slot machines and blackjack while accompanying his wife on her poker tournament trips. In 2000, Mr. and Mrs. Tschetschot claimed a net loss of $29,933 on Schedule C from "professional" (business) gambling activities. The IRS assessed a deficiency of $10,071 based on the view that the deductions were not appropriately Schedule C deductions, but rather should be claimed as miscellaneous itemized deductions on Schedule A and limited to the extent of gambling winnings.

Mr. and Mrs. Tschetschot petitioned the Tax Court, and at trial the IRS conceded Mrs. Tschetschot's status as a professional and allowed her deductions. The IRS, however, disputed Mr. Tschetschot's deductions.

In deciding the case, the Tax Court noted that "a player's tournament success depends on a combination of both luck and skill. A player might have a decent hand, but as Kenny Rogers tells us in 'The Gambler,' he or she would still have to 'know when to hold 'em, know when to fold 'em, know when to walk away and know when to run' to actually be a success." Despite that, the Tax Court decided that Congress made a policy decision to treat businesses based on wagering activities differently than other businesses, and that the court was not free to rewrite the Internal Revenue Code. Accordingly, the court held that tournament poker is a "wagering" activity and that deductions are limited by gambling winnings. Given this decision, do you think the IRS regrets conceding Mrs. Tschetschot's deductions?

Source: George E. Tschetschot, TC Memo 2007-38

Miscellaneous Itemized Deductions Not Subject to AGI Floor

Several deductions are considered to be miscellaneous itemized deductions but are not subject to the 2 percent of AGI floor. Perhaps because gambling includes a significant element of personal enjoyment (losers may think otherwise), individuals include all gambling winnings for the year in gross income but may also deduct gambling losses *to the extent of gambling winnings* for the year. The deductible gambling losses are miscellaneous itemized deductions; therefore, *losses don't directly offset winnings*. However, unlike other miscellaneous itemized deductions, gambling losses are *not* subject to the 2 percent of AGI floor. Casualty and theft losses on property held for investment and the unrecovered cost of a life annuity (the taxpayer died before recovering the full cost of the annuity) also qualify as miscellaneous itemized deductions not subject to the AGI floor.

Phase-out of Itemized Deductions

In addition to limits on specific deductions, the amount of a taxpayer's *total* itemized deductions *other than* medical expenses, casualty losses, investment *interest* expense, and gambling losses is subject to **phase-out**.[43] That is, when AGI exceeds a certain threshold, itemized deductions are reduced. In 2009, the threshold begins at $166,800 of AGI for all taxpayers except married taxpayers filing separately. For these taxpayers, the amount is $83,400 (one-half the standard amount). The computational details of the phase-out are provided in Appendix A to this chapter.

Summary of Itemized Deductions

This part of the chapter examined the various itemized deductions (deductions from AGI). We found that both medical expense and casualty loss deductions are designed to reduce the tax burden on individuals whose ability to pay has been involuntarily impaired, but because of large floor limitations these itemized deductions are unlikely to produce tax benefits. Most miscellaneous itemized deductions, including unreimbursed employee business expense and investment expenses (excluding rental and royalty expenses), are likewise hampered by a relatively large floor limitation.

Example 6-32

Given Courtney's current year AGI of $162,000, what is the amount of her total itemized deductions she may claim on her tax return after computing the itemized deduction phase-out?

Answer: Courtney's itemized deductions for the year are $39,793 calculated as follows:

Description	Amount	Reference
Taxes	$10,250	Example 6-14.
Interest on loans secured by residence	15,800	Example 6-15.
Charitable contributions	12,530	Example 6-22.
Miscellaneous itemized deductions	+1,083	Example 6-31.
Total itemized deductions subject to phase-out	$39,663	
Less phase-out of itemized deductions*	-0	
Plus investment interest expense	+130	Example 6-16.
Total itemized deductions	$39,793	

*Because Courtney's AGI of $162,000 is below the beginning of the phase-out threshold of $166,800 for taxpayers filing as a head of household, none of her itemized deductions is phased out.

[43]§68. Certain charitable contributions made for hurricane relief are also exempt from the phase-out.

Exhibit 6-10 presents Courtney's itemized deductions on Form 1040, Schedule A.

EXHIBIT 6-10   Courtney's Form 1040, Schedule A

SCHEDULES A&B	Schedule A—Itemized Deductions	OMB No. 1545-0074
(Form 1040)	(Schedule B is on back)	20**08**
Department of the Treasury Internal Revenue Service (99)	▶ Attach to Form 1040. ▶ See Instructions for Schedules A&B (Form 1040).	Attachment Sequence No. **07**

Name(s) shown on Form 1040 — **COURTNEY WILSON**   Your social security number

Medical and Dental Expenses		**Caution.** Do not include expenses reimbursed or paid by others.			
	1	Medical and dental expenses (see page A-1).	1	2,400	
	2	Enter amount from Form 1040, line 38 ⌊ 2 ⌋			
	3	Multiply line 2 by 7.5% (.075)	3	12,150	
	4	Subtract line 3 from line 1. If line 3 is more than line 1, enter -0-.	**4**		0
Taxes You Paid	5	State and local (**check only one box**):			
		a ☑ Income taxes, **or**	5	6,700	
(See page A-2.)		b ☐ General sales taxes			
	6	Real estate taxes (see page A-5)	6	3,550	
	7	Personal property taxes	7		
	8	Other taxes. List type and amount ▶ _____	8		
	9	Add lines 5 through 8	**9**		10,250
Interest You Paid	10	Home mortgage interest and points reported to you on Form 1098	10	15,800	
	11	Home mortgage interest not reported to you on Form 1098. If paid to the person from whom you bought the home, see page A-6 and show that person's name, identifying no., and address ▶			
(See page A-5.)		_____	11		
Note. Personal interest is not deductible.	12	Points not reported to you on Form 1098. See page A-6 for special rules.	12		
	13	Qualified mortgage insurance premiums (see page A-6)	13		
	14	Investment interest. Attach Form 4952 if required. (See page A-6.)	14	130	
	15	Add lines 10 through 14	**15**		15,930
Gifts to Charity	16	Gifts by cash or check. If you made any gift of $250 or more, see page A-7	16	1,770	
If you made a gift and got a benefit for it, see page A-7.	17	Other than by cash or check. If any gift of $250 or more, see page A-8. You **must** attach Form 8283 if over $500	17	10,760	
	18	Carryover from prior year	18		
	19	Add lines 16 through 18	**19**		12,530
Casualty and Theft Losses	20	Casualty or theft loss(es). Attach Form 4684. (See page A-8.)	**20**		
Job Expenses and Certain Miscellaneous Deductions	21	Unreimbursed employee expenses—job travel, union dues, job education, etc. Attach Form 2106 or 2106-EZ if required. (See page A-9.) ▶ _____	21	3,663	
	22	Tax preparation fees	22	250	
(See page A-9.)	23	Other expenses—investment, safe deposit box, etc. List type and amount ▶ _____ **SUBSCRIPTIONS TO BUSINESS PUBLICATIONS**	23	410	
	24	Add lines 21 through 23	24	4,323	
	25	Enter amount from Form 1040, line 38 ⌊ 25 ⌋			
	26	Multiply line 25 by 2% (.02)	26	3,240	
	27	Subtract line 26 from line 24. If line 26 is more than line 24, enter -0-	**27**		1,083
Other Miscellaneous Deductions	28	Other—from list on page A-10. List type and amount ▶ _____	**28**		
Total Itemized Deductions	29	Is Form 1040, line 38, over $159,950 (over $79,975 if married filing separately)?			
		☐ **No.** Your deduction is not limited. Add the amounts in the far right column for lines 4 through 28. Also, enter this amount on Form 1040, line 40.	**29**		39,793
		☑ **Yes.** Your deduction may be limited. See page A-10 for the amount to enter.			
	30	If you elect to itemize deductions even though they are less than your standard deduction, check here . . . . ▶ ☐			

For Paperwork Reduction Act Notice, see Form 1040 instructions.   Cat. No. 11330X   **Schedule A (Form 1040) 2008**

L03

THE STANDARD DEDUCTION AND EXEMPTIONS

Standard Deduction

The **standard deduction** is a flat amount that most individuals can elect to deduct *instead* of deducting their itemized deductions (if any). That is, taxpayers generally *deduct the greater of their standard deduction or their itemized deductions.*

The amount of the standard deduction varies according to the taxpayer's filing status, age, and eyesight. The basic standard deduction is greater for married taxpayers filing jointly and those supporting a family (head of household) than it is for married taxpayers filing separately and unmarried taxpayers not supporting a family. Taxpayers who are at least 65 years of age on the last day of the year or blind are entitled to additional standard deduction amounts above and beyond their basic standard deduction.[44] Exhibit 6-11 summarizes the standard deduction amounts.[45]

EXHIBIT 6-11   Standard Deduction Amounts*

	2008 Amounts	
Filing Status	**Basic Standard Deduction**	**Additional Standard Deduction for Age and/or Blindness at End of Year**
Married filing jointly	$10,900	$1,050
Head of household	8,000	1,350
Single	5,450	1,350
Married filing separately	5,450	1,050
	2009 Amounts	
Filing Status	**Basic Standard Deduction**	**Additional Standard Deduction for Age and/or Blindness at End of Year**
Married filing jointly	$11,400	$1,100
Head of household	8,350	1,400
Single	5,700	1,400
Married filing separately	5,700	1,100

*For individuals claimed as a dependent on another return, the 2009 standard deduction is the greater of (1) $950 or (2) $300 plus earned income not to exceed the basic standard deduction plus any additional standard deduction amounts. See Chapter 7 for more discussion.

For 2009, the additional standard deduction for either age and/or blindness is $1,100 for married taxpayers and $1,400 for taxpayers who are not married. Thus, a blind individual who is 65 years old and single is entitled to a standard deduction of $8,500 (5,700 + 1,400 + 1,400). A married couple filing a joint return with one spouse over age 65 and one spouse considered legally blind is entitled to a standard deduction of $13,600 (11,400 + 1,100 + 1,100). Finally, for an individual who is claimed as a dependent on another's return, the standard deduction is the greater of (1) $950 or (2) $300 plus the individual's earned income limited to the regular standard deduction (including the additional standard deduction amounts, if any).

[44]Taxpayers are considered to be blind if they have a certified statement from their eye doctor or registered optometrist that their corrected vision of their better eye is no better than 20/200 or their field of vision is 20 degrees or less.

[45]The standard deduction amount is indexed for inflation.

Example 6-33

What is Courtney's standard deduction for the year?

Answer: $8,350. Because Courtney is unmarried at the end of the year and she maintains a household for more than six months for Deron and Ellen who both qualify as her dependents (as qualifying children), Courtney's filing status is head of household, which allows her to claim a $8,350 standard deduction.

Given that Courtney's itemized deductions are $39,793, will Courtney deduct her itemized deductions or her standard deduction?

Answer: She will deduct her itemized deductions because they exceed her standard deduction.

From the government's standpoint, the standard deduction serves two purposes. First, to help taxpayers with lower income, it automatically provides a minimum amount of income that is not subject to taxation. Second, it eliminates the need for the IRS to verify and audit itemized deductions for those taxpayers who chose to deduct the standard deduction. From the taxpayers' perspective, the standard deduction allows them to avoid taxation on a portion of their income, and for those not planning to itemize deductions, it eliminates the need to substantiate and collect information about them. The standard deduction, however, is a double-edged sword. While it reduces taxes by offsetting income with an automatic deduction, it eliminates the tax benefits of itemized deductions up to the amount of the standard deduction. This is a very important point to consider when evaluating the tax benefits of itemized deductions.

Example 6-34

In Example 6-32, we determined that Courtney is entitled to deduct $39,793 of itemized deductions this year. How much do Courtney's itemized deductions reduce her taxable income relative to a situation in which she had $0 itemized deductions?

Answer: $31,443. Because Courtney files as a head of household, she would have been able to deduct $8,350 as a standard deduction even if she had not incurred *any* itemized deductions. Consequently, her itemized deductions reduce her taxable income by only $31,443 ($39,793 − $8,350) beyond what her taxable income would have been if she did not itemize deductions.

Bunching Itemized Deductions   Some taxpayers may deduct the standard deduction every year because their itemized deductions always fall just short of the standard deduction amount and thus never produce any tax benefit. They may gain some tax benefit from their itemized deductions by implementing a simple timing tax planning strategy called **bunching itemized deductions.** The basic strategy consists of shifting itemized deductions into one year such that the amount of itemized deductions exceeds the standard deduction for the year, and then deducting the standard deduction in the next year (or vice versa).

Because individuals are cash-method taxpayers, they may shift certain itemized deductions by accelerating payment into the current year. For example, a taxpayer could make charitable contributions at the end of December rather than at the beginning of January in the following year. Taxpayers' ability to shift itemized deductions is limited because the timing of these payments is not completely discretionary. For example, real estate taxes have due dates, state taxes are generally paid throughout the year via withholding, and employees may incur and be required to pay business expenses throughout the year. However, taxpayers who annually make a certain amount of charitable contributions, for example, may consider lumping contributions for two years into one year and not contributing in the next year.[46]

Example 6-35

What if: Gram is 70 years old and files as a single taxpayer. Last year Gram paid deductible medical expenses (after the 7.5 percent AGI floor) of $4,000. She also contributed $2,000 to her local church. Last year her total itemized deductions were $6,000 ($4,000 medical + 2,000 charitable). Assuming Gram has similar expenditures this year, what amount of additional deductions would Gram have been able to deduct last year if she had bunched her deductions by making her 2008 and 2009 charitable contributions in 2008?

Answer: $900, computed as follows:

	No Bunching		Bunching	
	2008	**2009**	**2008**	**2009**
(1) Standard deduction*	$6,650	$7,100	$6,650	$7,100
(2) itemized deductions	6,000	6,000	4,000	8,000
Greater of (1) and (2)	$6,650	$7,100	$6,650	$8,000
Total deductions (combined years)	$13,750 ($6,650 + 7,100)		$14,650 ($6,650 + 8,000)	
Deductions gained through bunching	$900 ($14,650 bunching deductions − $13,750 nonbunching deductions)			

*Her 2008 standard deduction is the $5,350 standard deduction for single taxpayers plus an additional $1,300 standard deduction amount for age. Her 2009 standard deduction is the $5,700 standard deduction for single taxpayers plus an additional $1,400 standard deduction amount for age.

Deduction for Personal and Dependency Exemptions

As we learned in Chapter 4, taxpayers are generally allowed to deduct $3,650 in 2009 for each **personal** and **dependency exemption.** In general, then, a taxpayer's from AGI deduction for personal and dependency exemptions is $3,650 multiplied by the number of the taxpayer's **exemptions.** However, just as with itemized deductions, a taxpayer's total exemption deduction is phased out based on AGI for relatively high income taxpayers. The AGI threshold for the beginning of the phase-out and the AGI for the maximum phase-out depends on the taxpayer's filing status. The amounts for 2009 are presented in Exhibit 6-12. We discuss the computational details of the phase-out in Appendix B to this chapter.

EXHIBIT 6-12   Maximum Phase-out Range for Personal and Dependency Exemptions for 2009

Filing Status	Threshold	AGI Maximum Phase-out
Married filing jointly	250,200	372,701
Head of household	208,500	331,001
Single	166,800	291,801
Married filing separately	125,100	186,351

[46]Of course, as we discussed in Chapter 3, taxpayers adopting this strategy must also consider the time value of money for the contributions amounts they pay in advance to determine whether a tax planning strategy designed to save taxes makes economic sense.

Example 6-36

This year, Courtney is allowed to claim a personal exemption for herself and dependency exemptions for her daughter Ellen and her son Deron. Courtney's filing status for her 2009 tax return is head of household. What amount is Courtney allowed to deduct for her personal and dependency exemptions?

Answer: $10,950 ($3,650 × 3). Because Courtney's AGI is $162,000 and she files as a head of household, her AGI is below the $208,500 threshold for the exemption phase-out, so she is allowed to deduct her full exemption amounts without phase-out.

Taxable Income Summary

We now have enough information to calculate Courtney's and Gram's taxable income. Exhibit 6-13 shows Courtney's taxable income calculation and Exhibit 6-14 illustrates how this information would be displayed on page 2 of Courtney's Form 1040. Exhibit 6-15 provides Gram's taxable income calculation.

EXHIBIT 6-13   Courtney's Taxable Income

Description	Amount	Reference
AGI	$162,000	
Less: Greater of (1) itemized deductions ($39,681) or (2) standard deduction ($8,350)	(39,793)	Example 6-32.
Less: Personal and dependency exemptions	(10,950)	Example 6-36.
Taxable income	$111,257	

EXHIBIT 6-14   Courtney's Taxable Income Computation as Presented on Form 1040, Page 2

Form 1040 (2008)   Page **2**

Tax and Credits	**38**	Amount from line 37 (adjusted gross income)	**38**	162,000	
	39a	Check { ☐ **You** were born before January 2, 1944, ☐ Blind. } **Total boxes** if: { ☐ **Spouse** was born before January 2, 1944, ☐ Blind. } checked ▶ **39a**	0		
	b	If your spouse itemizes on a separate return or you were a dual-status alien, see page 34 and check here ▶ **39b** ☐			
Standard Deduction for—	**c**	Check if standard deduction includes real estate taxes or disaster loss (see page 34) ▶ **39c** ☐			
	40	**Itemized deductions** (from Schedule A) **or** your **standard deduction** (see left margin) .	**40**	39,793	
● People who checked any box on line 39a, 39b, or 39c **or** who	**41**	Subtract line 40 from line 38	**41**	122,207	
	42	If line 38 is over $119,975, or you provided housing to a Midwestern displaced individual, see page 36. Otherwise, multiply $3,500 by the total number of exemptions claimed on line 6d .	**42**	10,950	
	43	**Taxable income.** Subtract line 42 from line 41. If line 42 is more than line 41, enter -0- .	**43**	111,257	

EXHIBIT 6-15   Gram's Taxable Income

Description	Amount	Explanation
(1) AGI	$15,740	
(2) Greater of (a) itemized deductions ($6,000) or (b) standard deduction ($6,400)	(7,100)	Example 6-35.
(3) Personal and dependency exemptions	(3,650)	One exemption.
Taxable income	$ 4,990	(1) + (2) + (3).

Note that because Gram's gross income of $16,150 (Exhibit 5-6) is more than the sum of her basic standard deduction amount plus her personal and dependency exemption ($10,750), therefore, she is required to file a tax return.

CONCLUSION

We started this chapter with Courtney's and Gram's gross incomes. In this chapter, we first identified the duo's separate *deductions for AGI* and we computed their AGI. We then determined their *from* AGI deductions. Courtney deducted her itemized deductions because they exceeded her standard deduction. Gram, on the other hand, deducted her standard deduction. Finally, Courtney deducted three exemptions: a personal exemption for herself and dependency exemptions for each of her two children, Deron and Ellen. Gram deducted one personal exemption for herself. By subtracting their *from* AGI deductions from their AGI, we determined taxable income for both Courtney and Gram. With this knowledge, we proceed to the next chapter and address issues relating to determining the amount of tax Courtney and Gram are required to pay on their taxable income. As we'll discover, it's not always as simple as applying taxable income to a tax rate schedule to determine the tax liability.

APPENDIX A — CALCULATION OF ITEMIZED DEDUCTION PHASE-OUT FOR 2009

The amount of the itemized deduction phase-out for 2009 is determined using the following two-step process.

Step 1: Determine the lesser of (1) 3 percent × [AGI minus $166,800 (or $83,400 if married filing separately)] or (2) 80 percent of the total itemized deductions subject to phase-out.

Step 2: Multiply the amount determined in Step 1 by one-third. The product is the amount of the itemized deduction phase-out (the amount of the *reduction* to the taxpayer's itemized deductions).

The reason for Step 2 is that for 2009 the tax laws limit the phase-out to one-third of the full amount (Step 1 determines the full amount of the phase-out under the original tax law). Consequently, for 2009, no matter how high a taxpayer's AGI, the taxpayer will always be allowed to deduct at *least* 73.33 percent of her itemized deductions that are subject to phase-out computed as follows:

$$[100\% - (80\% \times 1/3 \text{ max phase-out})]$$

Because itemized deductions can be reduced but not completely eliminated, the phase-out provision is sometimes referred to as a **cutback** or **haircut.** In 2010, the phase-out (and thus Step 1 and Step 2) is completely eliminated.

Example 6-1A

What if: Suppose Courtney's AGI was $260,000. What would be the amount of her total itemized deductions she may claim on her tax return after computing the itemized deduction phase-out?

Answer: Courtney's itemized deductions for the year are $39,793, calculated as follows:

Description	Amount	Reference
Taxes	$10,250	Example 6-14.
Interest on loans secured by residence	15,800	Example 6-15.
Charitable contributions	12,530	Example 6-22.
Miscellaneous itemized deduction	+1,083	Example 6-31.
Total itemized deductions subject to phase-out	$39,663	
Less phase-out of itemized deductions	−932	See calculation below.
Plus investment interest expense (not subject to phase-out)	+130	Example 6-16.
Total itemized deductions	$38,861	

Calculation of the phase out: Step 1: the phase-out is the lesser of (1) 3 percent × (AGI minus $166,800) or (2) 80 percent of the deductions subject to the phase-out ($39,663). Step 2: for 2009, the amount of the phase-out is reduced by one-third as follows:

Step 1: Phase-out amount is $2,796. This is the lesser of:

3% × ($260,000 − $166,800)	$2,796
80% × 39,663	$31,730

Step 2: Multiply Step 1 amount

by one-third	$932	($2,796 × 1/3)

PERSONAL EXEMPTION
PHASE-OUT COMPUTATION FOR 2009

APPENDIX B

Before 2006, taxpayers could have had their personal and dependency exemption deductions *completely* phased out. In 2009 taxpayers may have up to one-third of their exemptions phased-out. In 2010 and subsequent years, the phase-out no longer applies.

The process of determining the amount of the phase-out involves several steps. First, in general terms, the phase-out requires the taxpayer to reduce her *total* amount of personal and dependency deductions by a percentage that depends on the extent to which the taxpayer's AGI exceeds the threshold (see Exhibit 6-12). Specifically, the process to determine the taxpayer's allowable personal and dependency exemptions after the phase-out involves the following six steps.

Step 1: Subtract the taxpayer's AGI from the AGI threshold based on the taxpayer's filing status. If the threshold equals or exceeds the taxpayer's AGI, the taxpayer deducts her full personal and dependency exemptions.

Step 2: Divide the excess AGI (the amount from Step 1) by 2,500. If the result is not a whole number (i.e., the excess AGI is not evenly divisible by 2,500), round *up* to the next whole number.[47]

Step 3: Multiply the outcome of Step 3 by 2 percent, but limit the product to 100 percent. This is the *full* phase-out percentage.

Step 4: Multiply the full phase-out percentage from Step 3 by one-third.

Step 5: Multiply the percentage determined in Step 4 by the taxpayer's total personal and dependency exemptions (i.e., number of personal and dependent exemptions times $3,650 in 2009). The product is the amount of personal and dependency exemption deductions that is phased-out (i.e., the taxpayer is *not* allowed to deduct this amount).

[47]For married filing separate taxpayers, replace the $2,500 amount with $1,250.

Step 6: Subtract the Step 5 result from the taxpayer's total personal and dependency exemptions that would be deductible without any phase-out (i.e., number of personal and dependent exemptions times $3,650 in 2009).[48]

Example 6-1B

What if: Assume Courtney files as a head of household, has three personal and dependency exemptions, and has AGI of $260,000. Before the phase-out, her deductible personal and dependency exemption total is $10,950 ($3,650 × 3). What amount of this exemption amount would she be allowed to deduct with the phase-out?

Answer: $9,792, computed as follows:

	Amount	Explanation
Step 1:	$51,500	$260,000 − 208,500 (Excess AGI).
Step 2:	17	Divide $51,500 by 2,500 and round up to nearest whole number $51,500/2,500 = 20.6 → 21.
Step 3:	42%	Multiply the amount in Step 2 by 2% (i.e., 21 × 2%). This is the full phase-out percentage.
Step 4:	14%	Multiply the Step 3 result by one-third (i.e., 42% × 1/3).
Step 5:	$ 1,533	Multiply the Step 4 result by total exemption amount (i.e., $10,950 × 14%). This is the amount of the phase-out.
Step 6:	$ 9,417	Subtract the Step 5 result from total exemption amounts (i.e., $10,950 − $408). This is the deductible exemption amount.

SUMMARY

LO1   Identify the common deductions necessary for calculating adjusted gross income (AGI).

- Deductions for AGI may be categorized into those that are directly or indirectly business-related and those that address specific policy issues.
- The business-related deductions for AGI include business expenses, rent and royalty expenses, self-employment taxes, moving expenses, medical and health insurance by self-employed taxpayers, and forfeited interest.
- Other common deductions for AGI include the deductions for alimony, interest on student loans, for qualified education expenses and early withdrawal penalties.

LO2   Describe the different types of itemized deductions available to individuals and compute itemized deductions.

- The medical expense and casualty loss deductions are designed to provide tax benefits to needy individuals but both are subject to significant floor limitations.
- The itemized deduction for interest is limited to interest related to a personal residence and investment interest, and the latter is limited by net investment income.
- The deduction for charitable contributions extends to contributions of money and property to qualifying charities. The charitable deduction is subject to ceiling limitations, which are more restrictive for donations of property.

---

[48]From a compliance standpoint, taxpayers calculate both the phase-out of itemized deductions and the phase-out of exemptions on worksheets rather than on the Form 1040. Taxpayers report itemized deductions on Schedule A, and the total deduction net of the cutback is transferred from line 28 of Schedule A to Form 1040, line 40. Taxpayers report personal and dependency exemptions (net of the phase-out) on Form 1040, line 42.

- The deduction for taxes includes state income and property taxes. Sales taxes can be deducted in lieu of deducting state and local income taxes.
- Employee business expenses and investment expenses (except rental and royalty expenses) are miscellaneous itemized deductions subject to a 2 percent of AGI floor limitation.

Explain the operation of the standard deduction, determine the deduction for personal and dependency exemptions, and compute taxable income.

LO3

- Itemized deductions do not produce any tax benefit unless the total itemized deductions exceed the standard deduction.
- Certain itemized deductions are subject to a phase-out limitation for high income individuals.
- Personal exemptions are allowed for the taxpayer and spouse but are subject to a phase-out for higher income individuals.

KEY TERMS

accountable plan (6-26)
bunching itemized deductions (6-33)
business activities (6-2)
capital gain property (6-19)
casualty (6-23)
ceiling (6-21)
commuting (6-25)
cutback (6-36)
dependency exemption (6-34)

exemption (6-34)
floor limitation (6-15)
haircut (6-36)
hobby (6-27)
investment activities (6-3)
miscellaneous itemized deductions (6-25)
modified AGI (6-10)
ordinary and necessary (6-4)

ordinary income property (6-19)
personal exemption (6-34)
phase-outs (6-30)
private nonoperating foundations (6-21)
private operating foundations (6-21)
qualified educational expenses (6-9)
qualified educational loans (6-9)
standard deduction (6-32)
trade or business (6-3)

DISCUSSION QUESTIONS

1. **(LO1)** It has been suggested that tax policy favors deductions for AGI compared to itemized deductions. Describe two ways in which deductions for AGI are treated more favorably than itemized deductions.

2. **(LO1)** How is a business activity distinguished from an investment activity? Why is this distinction important for the purpose of calculating federal income taxes?

3. **(LO1)** Describe how a business element is reflected in the requirements to deduct moving expenses and how Congress limited this deduction to substantial moves.

4. **(LO1)** Explain why Congress allows self-employed taxpayers to deduct the cost of health insurance above the line (for AGI) when employees can only itemize this cost as a medical expense. Would a self-employed taxpayer ever prefer to claim health insurance premiums as an itemized deductions rather than a deduction for AGI? Explain.

5. **(LO1)** Explain why Congress allows self-employed taxpayers to deduct half of their self-employment tax.

6. **(LO1)** Using the Internal Revenue Code, describe two deductions for AGI that are not described in this chapter.

 research

7. **(LO1)** Explain why Congress allows taxpayers to deduct interest forfeited as a penalty on the premature withdrawal from a certificate of deposit.

8. **(LO1)** Describe the mechanical limitation on the deduction of qualified educational expenses and explain how it differs from the limitation on the deduction for interest on qualified educational loans.

9. **(LO1)** Congress has tried to subsidize the cost of higher education through the federal income tax system. Compare and contrast the operation of the deduction for qualified educational costs and the operation of the deduction for interest on qualified educational loans.

10. **(LO2)** Explain why the medical expense and casualty loss provisions are sometimes referred to as "wherewithal" deductions and how this rationale is reflected in the limits on these deductions.

11. **(LO2)** Describe the type of medical expenditures that qualify for the medical expense deduction. Will the cost of meals consumed while hospitalized qualify for the deduction? Will over-the-counter drugs and medicines qualify for the deduction? Why or why not?

12. **(LO2)** Under what circumstances can a taxpayer deduct medical expenses paid for a member of his family? Does it matter if the family member reports significant amounts of gross income and cannot be claimed as a dependent?

13. **(LO2)** What types of taxes qualify to be deducted as itemized deductions? What sort of taxes don't qualify for the deduction? Would a vehicle registration fee qualify as a deductible tax? Why or why not?

research 14. **(LO2)** Compare and contrast the limits on the deduction of interest on home acquisition indebtedness versus home equity loans. Are these limits consistent with horizontal equity? Explain.

15. **(LO2)** Explain the argument that the deductions for charitable contributions, home mortgage interest, and state and local taxes all represent indirect subsidies for these activities.

research 16. **(LO2)** Cash donations to charity are subject to a number of very specific substantiation requirements. Describe these requirements and how charitable gifts can be substantiated. Describe the substantiation requirements for property donations.

17. **(LO2)** Describe the conditions in which a donation of property to a charity will result in a charitable contribution deduction of fair market value and when it will result in a deduction of the tax basis of the property.

18. **(LO2)** Describe the type of event that qualifies as a casualty for tax purposes.

19. **(LO2)** A casualty loss from the complete destruction of a personal asset is limited to the lesser of fair market value or the property's adjusted basis. Explain the rationale for this rule as opposed to just allowing a deduction for the basis of the asset.

research 20. **(LO2)** This week Jim's residence was heavily damaged by a storm system that spread destruction throughout the region. While Jim's property insurance covers some of the damage, there is a significant amount of uninsured loss. The governor of Jim's state has requested that the president declare the region a federal disaster area and provide federal disaster assistance. Explain to Jim the income tax implications of such a declaration and any associated tax planning possibilities.

21. **(LO2)** Describe the types of expenses that constitute miscellaneous itemized deductions and explain why these expenses rarely produce any tax benefits.

22. **(LO2)** Explain why the cost of commuting from home to work is not deductible as a business expense.

23. **(LO2)** When is the cost of education deductible as an employee business expense?

24. **(LO2)** How might the reimbursement of a portion of an employee expense influence the deductibility of the expense for the employee?

25. **(LO2)** Explain why an employee should be concerned about whether his employer reimburses business expenses using an "accountable" plan?

26. **(LO2)** Jake is a retired jockey who takes monthly trips to Las Vegas to gamble on horse races. Jake also trains race horses part time at his Louisville ranch. So far this year, Jake has won almost $47,500 during his trips to Las Vegas while spending $27,250 on travel expenses and incurring $62,400 of gambling losses. Jake also received $60,000 in revenue from his training activities and he incurred $72,000 of associated costs. Explain how Jake's gambling winnings and related costs will be treated for tax purposes. Describe the factors that will influence how Jake's ranch expenses are treated for tax purposes.

27. **(LO2)** Frank paid $3,700 in fees for an accountant to tabulate business information (Frank operates as a self-employed contractor and files a Schedule C). The accountant also spent time tabulating Frank's income from his investments and determining Frank's personal itemized deductions. Explain to Frank whether or not he can deduct the $3,700 as a business expense or as an itemized deduction, and provide a citation to an authority that supports your conclusion.

    ■ research

28. **(LO2)** Contrast ceiling and floor limitations, and give an example of each.

29. **(LO2)** Identify which itemized deductions are subject to floor limitations, ceiling limitations, phase-out limitations, or some combination of these limits.

30. **(LO3)** Describe the tax benefits from "bunching" itemized deductions in one year. Describe the characteristics of the taxpayers who are most likely to benefit from using bunching and explain why this is so.

31. **(LO3)** Explain how the standard deduction is rationalized and why the standard deduction might be viewed as a floor limit on itemized deductions.

32. **(LO3)** Explain why the overall phase-out of itemized deductions has been described as both a "stealth" tax and a "haircut" of itemized deductions. Explain whether it is possible for a taxpayer to lose all itemized deductions under the phase-out rules.

33. **(LO3)** Describe the mechanism for phasing out exemptions. Can a taxpayer lose the benefit of all of her personal and dependency exemptions?

34. **(LO3)** Determine if a taxpayer can change his election to itemize deductions once a return is filed. (*Hint:* Read about itemization under Reg. §1.63-1.)

    ■ research

35. **(LO3)** Determine whether a taxpayer who is claimed as a dependent on another return is entitled to an addition to the standard deduction for age or blindness. (*Hint:* Read the calculation of the standard deduction under IRC §63.)

    ■ research

PROBLEMS

36. **(LO1)** Clem is married and is a skilled carpenter. Clem's wife, Wanda, works part-time as a substitute grade school teacher. Determine the amount of Clem's expenses that are deductible *for AGI* this year (if any) under the following circumstances:

    a. Clem is self-employed and this year he incurred $525 for tools and supplies related to his job. Wanda paid health insurance premiums of $3,600 to provide coverage for herself and Clem.

b. Clem and Wanda own a garage downtown that they rent to a local business for storage. This year they incurred $1,250 in utilities and depreciation of $780.

c. Clem paid self-employment tax of $14,200 and Wanda had $3,000 of Social Security taxes withheld from her pay.

d. Clem paid $45 to rent a safe deposit box to store his coin collection. Clem has collected coins intermittently since he was a boy, and he expects to sell his collection when he retires.

37. **(LO1)** Clyde currently commutes 55 miles to work in the city. He is considering a new assignment in the suburbs on the other side of the city that would increase his commute considerably. He would like to accept the assignment, but he thinks it might require that he move to the other side of the city. Determine if Clyde's move qualifies for a moving expense deduction and calculate the amount (if any) under the following circumstances:

a. Clyde estimates that unless he moves across town, his new commute would be almost 70 miles. He also estimates the costs of a move as follows:

Lodging while searching for an apartment	$ 125
Transportation—auto	75
Mover's fee (furniture and possessions)	1,500
Lodging while waiting for movers	210
Meals while en route	35

b. Same as (a) above, except Clyde estimates that unless he moves across town, his new commute would be almost 115 miles.

c. Same as (a) above, except Clyde's new commute would be almost 150 miles, and in addition to the above expenses, Clyde estimates that he would also need to spend $225 to break his current lease.

38. **(LO1)** Smithers is a self-employed individual who earns $30,000 per year in self-employment income. Smithers pays $2,200 in annual health insurance premiums. In each of the following situations, determine the amount of his health insurance premium Smithers may deduct and indicate where on his tax return he will deduct it.

a. Smithers is single and the self-employment income is his only source of income.

b. Smithers is single, but besides being self-employed, Smithers is also employed part-time by SF Power Corporation. This year Smithers elected not to participate in SF's health plan.

c. Smithers is self-employed and he is also married. Smithers's spouse, Samantha, is employed full-time by Burns Corporation and is covered by SF's health plan. Smithers is not eligible to participate in SF's health plan and the insurance premiums cover his medical care.

d. Smithers is self-employed and he is also married. Smithers' spouse, Samantha, is employed full-time by SF Power Corporation and is covered by SF's health plan. Smithers elected not to participate in SF's health plan and the insurance premiums cover his medical care.

39. **(LO1)** Hardaway earned $100,000 of compensation this year. He also paid (or had paid for him) $3,000 of health insurance. What is Hardaway's AGI in each of the following situations (ignore the effects of Social Security and self-employment taxes)?

a. Hardaway is an employee and his employer paid Hardaway's $3,000 of health insurance for him as a nontaxable fringe benefit. Consequently, Hardaway received $97,000 of taxable compensation and $3,000 of nontaxable compensation.

b. Hardaway is a self-employed taxpayer, and he paid $3,000 of health insurance himself. He is not eligible to participate in an employer-sponsored plan.

40. **(LO1)** Betty operates a beauty salon as a sole proprietorship. Betty also owns other property including a half interest in a partnership that operates a delivery service, a half interest in a partnership that operates a movie theatre, and an apartment building. This year Betty paid or reported the following expenses related to her salon and other property. Determine Betty's AGI.

Interest income	$11,255
Salon sales and revenue	86,360
Salaries paid to beauticians	45,250
Beauty salon supplies	23,400
Revenues from delivery service partnership	18,200
Expenses from delivery service partnership	5,200
Operating income for theatre partnership	17,250
Rental revenue from apartment building	31,220
Depreciation on apartment building	12,900
Real estate taxes paid on apartment building	11,100
Real estate taxes paid on personal residence	6,241
Contributions to charity	4,237

41. **(LO1)** Lionel is an unmarried law student at State University Law School, a qualified educational institution. This year Lionel borrowed $24,000 from Counti Bank and paid interest of $1,440. Lionel used the loan proceeds to pay his law school tuition. Calculate the amounts Lionel can deduct for higher education expenses and interest on higher education loans under the following circumstances:

a. Lionel's AGI before deducting either the deduction for higher education expenses or interest on higher education loans is $50,000.

b. Lionel's AGI before deducting either the deduction for higher education expenses or interest on higher education loans is $69,000.

c. Lionel's AGI before deducting either the deduction for higher education expenses or interest on higher education loans is $90,000.

d. Lionel's AGI is $50,000 before deducting either the deduction for higher education expenses or interest on higher education loans. Lionel used $16,000 of the loan to pay law school tuition and $8,000 of the loan to purchase a car.

42. **(LO1)** Ned is a head of household with a dependent son, Todd, who is a full-time student. Todd is studying auto mechanics at Mechanics Tech, a qualified educational institution. This year Ned made the following expenditures related to Todd's education:

Tuition (required for enrollment)	$1,700
Room and board	2,200
Books (required for enrollment)	700
Travel (to and from school)	350

a. Ned reports that his AGI is $45,000. What is the maximum amount of Ned's deduction for qualified educational expenses?

b. Ned reports that his AGI is $115,000. What is the maximum amount of Ned's deduction for qualified educational expenses?

43. **(LO1)** This fall Jacob decided to return to school and entered State University during the fall semester. In September, he paid tuition of $2,800. The same amount of tuition for spring term is due by January 15 of next year. However,

■ **planning**

Jacob is considering whether tax considerations dictate that he should pay his spring tuition before December 31. Advise Jacob whether he should pay his tuition in December of this year or in January of next year for each of the following independent circumstances:

a. Jacob expects to file single with a modified AGI of $55,000 this year and he expects to have about the same AGI next year.

b. Jacob expects to file single with a modified AGI of $67,700 this year and he expects to have about the same AGI next year.

c. Jacob expects to file single with a modified AGI of $83,000 this year and he expects to have about the same AGI next year.

research

44. **(LO1)** This year Jack intends to file a married-joint return with two dependents. Jack received $157,500 of salary. and paid $5,000 of qualified tuition costs for his dependent daughter, Deb. This year Jack has also paid qualified moving expenses of $4,300 and $24,000 of alimony.

a. What is Jack's adjusted gross income? Assume that Jack will opt to treat tax items in a manner to minimize his AGI.

b. Suppose that Jack also reported income of $8,800 from a half share of profits from a partnership and paid $3,000 of interest expense on a loan made to pay qualified educational expenses. What AGI would Jack report under these circumstances? Again, assume that Jack will opt to treat tax items in a manner to minimize his AGI.

45. **(LO1, LO2)** In each of the following independent cases, indicate whether the amount involved is (1) deductible *for* AGI, (2) deductible *from* AGI, or (3) not deductible at all.

a. Ted paid $8 rent on a safety deposit box at the bank. In this box he kept the few shares of stock that he owned.

b. Tyler paid $85 for minor repairs to the fence at a rental house he owned.

c. Timmy paid $545 for health insurance premiums this year. Timmy is employed full-time and his employer paid the remaining premiums as a qualified fringe benefit.

d. Tess paid $850 for self-employment taxes and $1,150 of state income taxes on her consulting income.

46. **(LO1, LO2)** In each of the following independent cases, indicate whether the amount involved is (1) deductible *for* AGI, (2) deductible *from* AGI, or (3) not deductible at all.

a. Fran spent $90 for uniforms for use on her job. Her employer reimbursed her for $75 of this amount under an accountable plan.

b. Timothy, a plumber employed by ACE Plumbing, spent $65 for small tools to be used on his job, but he was not reimbursed by ACE.

c. Jake is a perfume salesperson. Because of his high pay, he receives no allowance or reimbursement from his employer for advertising expenses even though his position requires him to advertise frequently. During the year, he spent $2,200 on legitimate business advertisements.

d. Trey is a self-employed special-duty nurse. He spent $120 for uniforms.

e. Mary, a public school teacher, spent $340 for magazine subscriptions. The magazines were used in her classroom activities.

f. Wayne lost $325 on the bets he made at the race track, but he won $57 playing online poker.

47. **(LO2)** Ted is a successful attorney, but when he turned 50 years old he decided to retire from his law practice and become a professional golfer. Ted has been a

very successful amateur golfer, so beginning this year Ted began competing in professional golf tournaments. At year-end, Ted reported the following expenses associated with competing in 15 professional events:

Transportation from his home to various tournaments	$25,000
Lodging for the 15 weeks on the road	18,200
Meals while traveling and during golf tournaments	5,200
Entry fees	7,500
Lessons from various golf teachers	12,500
Golf supplies (balls, tees, etc.)	783
Total expenses	$69,183

a. Suppose that Ted reports $275,000 in gross income from his pension and various investments. Describe the various considerations that will dictate the extent to which Ted can deduct the expenses associated with professional golf.

b. Calculate the maximum amount of his golf expenses that Ted could deduct if the IRS and the courts are convinced that Ted engages in competitive golf primarily for enjoyment rather than the expectation of making a profit. Assume Ted's AGI is $275,000.

48. **(LO2)** Simpson is a single individual who is employed full-time by Duff Corporation. This year Simpson reports AGI of $50,000 and has incurred the following medical expenses:

Dentist charges	$ 900
Physician's charges	1,800
Optical charges	500
Cost of eyeglasses	300
Hospital charges	2,100
Prescription drugs	250
Over-the-counter drugs	450
Medical insurance premiums	775

a. Calculate the amount of medical expenses that will be included with Simpson's itemized deductions.

b. Suppose that Simpson was reimbursed for $650 of the physician's charges and $1,200 for the hospital costs. Calculate the amount of medical expenses that will be included with Simpson's itemized deductions.

49. **(LO2)** This year Tim is age 45 and is considering enrolling in an insurance program that provides for long-term care insurance. He is curious about whether the insurance premiums are deductible as a medical expense and, if so, what is the maximum amount that can be deducted in any year.

research

50. **(LO2)** Doctor Bones prescribed physical therapy in a pool to treat Jack's broken back. In response to this advice (and for no other reason), Jack built a swimming pool in his backyard and strictly limited use of the pool to physical therapy. Jack paid $25,000 to build the pool, but he wondered if this amount could be deducted as a medical expenses? Determine if a capital expenditure such as the cost of a swimming pool qualifies for the medical expense deduction.

research

51. **(LO1, LO2)** Charles has AGI of $50,000 and has made the following payments related to (1) land he inherited from his deceased aunt and (2) a personal vacation taken last year. Calculate the amount of taxes Charles

may include in his itemized deductions for the year under the following circumstances:

State inheritance tax on the land	$1,200
County real estate tax on the land	1,500
School district tax on the land	690
City special assessment on the land (replacing curbs and gutters)	700
State tax on airline tickets (paid on vacation)	125
Local hotel tax (paid during vacation)	195

a. Suppose that Charles holds the land for appreciation.

b. Suppose that Charles holds the land for rent.

c. Suppose that the vacation was actually a business trip.

52. **(LO2)** Dan has AGI of $50,000 and paid the following taxes during this tax year. Calculate the amount of taxes Dan may include in his itemized deductions for the year.

State income tax withholding	$1,400
State income tax estimated payments	750
Federal income tax withholding	3,000
Social security tax withheld from wages	2,100
State excise tax on liquor	400
Automobile license (based on the car's weight)	300
State sales tax paid	475

53. **(LO1, LO2)** Tim is a single, cash-basis taxpayer with one personal exemption. In April of this year Tim paid $1,020 with his state income tax return for the previous year. During the year, Tim had $5,400 of state income tax and $18,250 of federal income tax withheld from his salary. In addition, Tim made estimated payments of $1,360 and $1,900 of state and federal income taxes, respectively. Finally, Tim expects to receive a refund of $500 for state income taxes when he files his state tax return for this year in April next year. What is the amount of taxes that Tim can deduct as an itemized deduction?

54. **(LO2)** This year Randy paid $28,000 of interest (Randy borrowed $450,000 to buy his residence and it is currently worth $500,000). Randy also paid $2,500 of interest on his car loan and $4,200 of margin interest to his stockbroker. How much of this interest can Randy deduct as an itemized deduction under the following circumstances?

a. Randy received $2,200 of interest this year and no other investment income or expenses.

b. Randy had no investment income this year.

55. **(LO2)** Calvin reviewed his cancelled checks and receipts this year for charitable contributions. Calculate Calvin's charitable contribution deduction and carryover (if any) under the following circumstances:

Donee	Item	Cost	FMV
Hobbs Medical Center	IBM stock	$5,000	$22,000
State Museum	painting	5,000	3,000
A needy family	food and clothes	400	250
United Way	cash	8,000	8,000

a. Calvin's AGI is $100,000.

b. Calvin's AGI is $100,000 but the State Museum told Calvin that it plans to sell the painting.

c. Calvin's AGI is $50,000.

d. Calvin's AGI is $100,000 and Hobbs is a nonoperating private foundation.

e. Calvin's AGI is $100,000 but the painting is worth $10,000.

56. **(LO2)** In addition to cash contributions to charity, Dean decided to donate shares of stock and a portrait painted during the earlier part of the last century. Dean purchased the stock and portrait many years ago as investments. Dean reported the following recipients:

Charity	Property	Cost	FMV
State University	cash	$15,000	
Red Cross	cash	14,500	
State History Museum	antique auto	5,000	$82,000
City Medical Center	Dell stock	28,000	17,000

a. Determine the maximum amount of charitable deduction for each of these contributions *ignoring* the AGI ceiling on charitable contributions.

b. Assume that Dean's AGI this year is $150,000. Determine Dean's itemized deduction for his charitable contributions this year and any carryover.

c. Assume that Dean's AGI this year is $240,000. Determine Dean's itemized deduction for his charitable contributions this year and any carryover.

d. Suppose Dean is a dealer in antique autos and he held the auto for sale before the contribution. Determine Dean's itemized deduction for his charitable contributions this year and any carryover.

e. Suppose that Dean's objective with the donation to the museum was to finance expansion of the historical collection. Hence, Dean was not surprised when the museum announced the sale of the portrait because of its limited historical value. What is Dean's charitable contribution for the auto in this situation (ignoring AGI limitations)?

57. **(LO2)** Tim suffered greatly this year. In January a freak storm damaged his sailboat and in July Tim's motorcycle was stolen from his vacation home. Tim originally paid $27,000 for the boat, but he was able to repair the damage for $6,200. Tim paid $15,500 for the motorcycle, but it was worth $17,000 before it was stolen. Insurance reimbursed $1,000 for the boat repairs and the cycle was uninsured.

a. Calculate Tim's deductible casualty loss if his AGI is $50,000.

b. Calculate Tim's deductible casualty loss if his AGI is $150,000.

c. How would you answer (a) if Tim received an additional $65,000 in interest from municipal bonds this year?

58. **(LO2)** Trevor is a single individual who is a cash-method calendar-year taxpayer. For each of the next two years (year 1 and year 2), Trevor expects to report AGI of $80,000, contribute $3,000 to charity, and pay $2,200 in state income taxes and $400 in real estate taxes.

■ **planning**

a. Estimate Trevor's taxable income for year 1 and year 2 using the current amounts for the standard deduction and personal exemption for both years.

b. Now assume that Trevor combines his anticipated charitable contributions for the next two years and makes the combined contribution in December of year 1. Estimate Trevor's taxable income for each of the next two years using the current amounts for the standard deduction and personal exemption. Reconcile the total taxable income to your solution to (a) above.

c. Trevor plans to purchase a residence next year, and he estimates that additional property taxes and residential interest will each cost $4,000 annually

($8,000 in total). Estimate Trevor's taxable income for each of the next two years (year 1 and year 2) using the current amounts for the standard deduction and personal exemption.

d. Assume that Trevor makes the charitable contribution for year 2 and pays the real estate taxes for year 2 in December of year 1. Estimate Trevor's taxable income for year 1 and year 2 using the current amounts for the standard deduction and personal exemption. Reconcile the total taxable income to your solution to (c) above.

e. Explain the conditions in which the bunching strategy in part (d) will generate tax savings for Trevor.

59. **(LO2)** Baker paid $775 for the preparation of his tax return and incurred $375 of employee business expenses, of which $60 was reimbursed by his employer through an accountable plan. Baker also paid a $100 fee for investment advice. Calculate the amount of these expenses that Baker is able to deduct assuming he itemizes his deductions in each of the following situations:

a. Baker's AGI is $50,000.

b. Baker's AGI is $100,000.

60. **(LO2)** Zack is employed as a full-time airport security guard. This year Zack's employer transferred him from Dallas to Houston. At year-end, Zack discovered a number of unreimbursed expenses related to his employment in Dallas prior to his move to Houston. Identify which expenses are deductible and whether the deductions are *for* or *from* AGI.

Cost of bus transportation from his home to the airport	$ 150
Subscription to *Journal of Security Guards*	52
Lunch with colleagues	195
Cost of self-defense course at local college	500
Lunch with supervisor during evaluations	383
Total	$1,280

61. **(LO3)** This year Jeff, who is single, is entitled to the following deductions before phase-outs:

State income taxes	$7,850
Real estate taxes	1,900
Home mortgage interest	8,200
Charitable contributions	1,700

a. Assuming Jeff's AGI is $196,800, calculate Jeff's itemized deductions after considering the overall phase-out of itemized deductions.

b. Suppose that Jeff's AGI is $1,996,800. Calculate Jeff's itemized deductions after considering the overall phase-out of itemized deductions.

62. **(LO3)** Jim who is single is considering expending $30,000 that will be deductible. He is eligible to claim the standard deduction and one personal exemption. Assuming Jim has no other deductions and his taxable income is subject to a tax rate of 25 percent, calculate the amount of tax savings Jim will gain from the deduction under the following independent conditions:

a. Jim has AGI of $150,000 (without the deduction) and the deduction is *for AGI*.

b. Jim has AGI of $150,000 and the deduction is *from AGI*. Assume that the deduction is a charitable contribution and Jim has no other itemized deductions.

c. Jim has AGI of $250,000 (without the deduction) and the deduction is *for AGI*.

63. **(LO1, LO2, LO3)** Tammy teaches elementary school history for the Metro School District. This year she has incurred the following expenses associated with her job:

Noncredit correspondence course on history	$ 900
Teaching publications	1,800
Tuition for university graduate course in physics	1,200
Transportation between school and home	750
Photocopying class materials	100
Transportation from school to extracurricular activities	110
Cost of lunches eaten during study halls	540

Tammy's base salary is $45,000 and she receives a $200 salary supplement to help her cover expenses associated with her school extracurricular activities.

a. Identify the amount and type (*for* AGI or *from* AGI) of deductible expenses.

b. Calculate Tammy's AGI and taxable income for this year assuming she files single with one personal exemption.

COMPREHENSIVE PROBLEMS

64. Evan graduated from college, and took a job as a deliveryman in the city. Evan was paid a salary of $64,500 and he received $700 in hourly pay for part-time work over the weekends. Evan summarized his expenses below.

Cost of moving his possessions to the city	$1,200
Interest paid on accumulated student loans	2,800
Cost of purchasing a delivery uniform	1,100
Contribution to State University deliveryman program	1,300

Calculate Evan's AGI and taxable income if he files single with one personal exemption.

65. Read the following letter and help Shady Slim with his tax situation.

December 31, 2009

To the friendly student tax preparer:

Hi, it's Shady Slim again. I'm told that you need some more information from me in order to complete my tax return. I'm an open book! I'll tell you whatever I think you need to know. Please remember that you figured out that my gross income is $172,900.

Let me tell you a few more things about my life. As you may recall, I am divorced from my wife, Alice. I know that it's unusual, but I have custody of my son, Shady, Jr. The judge owed me a few favors and I really love the kid. He lives with me full-time and my wife gets him every other weekend. I pay the vast majority of my son's expenses. I think Alice should have to pay some child support, but she doesn't have to pay a dime. The judge didn't owe me that much, I guess.

I had to move this year after getting my job at Roca Cola. We moved on February 3 of this year, and I worked my job at Roca Cola all year. I still live in the same state, but I moved 500 miles away from my old house. I left a little bit early to go on a house-hunting trip that cost me a total of $450. I hired a moving company to move our stuff at a cost of $2,300. Junior and I got a hotel room along the way that cost us $40 (I love Super 8!). We spent $35 on meals on the way to our new home. Oh yeah, I took Junior to a movie on the way and that cost $20.

Can you believe I'm still paying off my student loans, even after 15 years! I paid a total of $900 in interest on my old student loans this year.

Remember when I told you about that guy that hit me with his car? I had a bunch of medical expenses that were not reimbursed to me by the lawsuit or by my insurance. I incurred a total of $20,000 in medical expenses, and I was only reimbursed for $11,000. Good thing I can write off medical expenses, right?

I contributed a lot of money to charity this year. I'm such a nice guy! I gave $1,000 in cash to the March of Dimes. I contributed some of my old furniture to the church. It was some good stuff! I gave a red velvet couch and my old recliner. The furniture is considered vintage and is worth $5,000 today (the appraiser surprised me!), even though I only paid $1,000 for it back in the day. I'm told that the pastor didn't appreciate the fabric, though, and he's selling the furniture to pay for some more pews in the church. Some people just have no taste, right? Roca Cola had a charity drive this year and I contributed $90. Turns out, I don't even miss it, because Roca Cola takes it right off my paycheck every month . . . $15 a month starting in July. Oh, one other bit of charity from me this year. An old buddy of mine was down on his luck. He lost his job and his house. I gave him $500 to help him out.

I paid a lot of money in interest this year. I paid a total of $950 in personal credit card interest. I also paid $12,000 in interest on my home mortgage. When I bought the new house, the bank made me pay something called "points" to the tune of $1,000. I paid the points to get a lower interest rate. I also paid $2,000 in real estate taxes for my new house.

A few other things I want to tell you about last year. Someone broke into my house and stole my kid's brand new bicycle and my set of golf clubs. The total loss from theft was $900. I paid $100 in union dues this year. I had to pay $1,000 for new suits for my job. Roca Cola requires its managers to wear suits every day on the job. I spent a total of $1,300 to pay for gas to commute to my job this year.

Oh, this is pretty cool. I've always wanted to be a firefighter. I spent $1,000 in tuition to go to the local firefighter's school. I did this because someone told me that I can deduct the tuition as an itemized deduction, so the money would be coming back to me.

That should be all the information you need right now. Please calculate my taxable income. You're still doing this for free, right?

66. Jeremy and Alyssa Johnson have been married for five years and do not have any children. Jeremy was married previously and has one child from the prior marriage. He is self-employed and operates his own computer parts store. For the first two months of the year, Alyssa worked for Staples, Inc., as an employee. In March, Alyssa accepted a new job with Super Toys, Inc. (ST), where she worked for the remainder of the year. This year, the the Johnsons received $255,000 of gross income. Determine the Johnson's AGI given the following information:

   a. Expenses associated with Jeremy's store include $40,000 in salary (and employment taxes) to employees, $45,000 of cost of goods sold, and $18,000 in rent and other administrative expenses.

   b. As a salesperson, Alyssa incurred $2,000 in travel expenses related to her employment that were not reimbursed by her employer.

   c. The Johnsons own a piece of investment real estate. They paid $500 of real property taxes on the property and they incurred $200 of expenses in travel costs to see the property and to evaluate other similar potential investment properties.

   d. The Johnsons own a rental home. They incurred $8,500 of expenses associated with the property.

   e. The Johnson's home was only five miles from the Staples store where Alyssa worked in January and February. The ST store was 60 miles from their home, so the Johnsons decided to move to make the commute easier for Alyssa. The Johnson's new home was only ten miles from the ST store. However, it was 50 miles from their former residence. The Johnsons paid a moving company $2,000 to move their possessions to the new location. They also drove the 50 miles to their new residence. They stopped along the way for lunch and spent $60 eating at Denny's. None of the moving expenses were reimbursed by ST.

   f. Jeremy paid $4,500 for health insurance coverage for himself. Alyssa was covered by health plans provided by her employer, but Jeremy is not eligible for the plan until next year.

g. Jeremy paid $2,500 in self-employment taxes.

h. Alyssa contributed $4,000 to ST's employer-provided traditional 401k plan.

i. Jeremy paid $5,000 in alimony and $3,000 in child support from his prior marriage.

j. Alyssa paid $3,100 of tuition and fees to attend night classes at a local university. The Johnsons would like to deduct as much of this expenditure as possible rather than claim a credit.

k. The Johnsons donated $2,000 to their favorite charity.

67. Shauna Coleman is single. She works as an architectural designer for Streamline Design (SD). Shauna wanted to determine her taxable income for this year. She correctly calculated her AGI. However, she wasn't sure how to compute the rest of her taxable income. She provided the following information with hopes that you could use it to determine her taxable income.

a. Shauna paid $2,000 for medical expenses and Blake, Shauna's boyfriend, drove Shauna (in her car) a total of 115 miles so that she could receive care for a broken ankle she sustained in a biking accident.

b. Shauna paid a total of $3,400 in health insurance premiums during the year. SD did not reimburse any of this expense. Besides the health insurance premiums and the medical expenses for her broken ankle, Shauna had Lasik eye surgery last year and she paid $3,000 for the surgery (she received no insurance reimbursement). She also incurred $450 of other medical expenses for the year.

c. SD withheld $1,800 of state income tax, $7,495 of Social Security tax, and $14,500 of federal income tax from Shauna's paychecks throughout the year.

d. In 2009, Shauna was due a refund of $250 for overpaying her 2008 state taxes. On her 2008 state tax return that she filed in April 2009, she applied the overpayment toward her 2009 state tax liability. She estimated that her state tax liability for 2009 will be $2,300.

e. Shauna paid $3,200 of property taxes on her personal residence. She also paid $500 to the developer of her subdivision, because he had to replace the sidewalk in certain areas of the subdivision.

f. Shauna paid a $200 property tax based on the state's estimate of the value of her car.

g. Shauna has a home mortgage loan in the amount of $220,000. The home is worth about $400,000. Shauna paid interest of $12,300 on the loan this year. She also paid $1,000 of interest on a home equity loan. She used the proceeds of the loan to buy a car and to go on a vacation. Both loans are secured by her residence.

h. Shauna made several charitable contributions throughout the year. She contributed stock in ZYX Corp. to the Red Cross. On the date of the contribution, the fair market value of the donated shares was $1,000 and her basis in the shares was $400. Shauna also contributed $300 cash to State University and religious artifacts she has held for several years to her church. The artifacts were valued at $500 and Shauna's basis in the items was $300. Shauna had every reason to believe the church would keep them on display indefinitely. Shauna also drove 200 miles doing church-related errands for her minister. Finally, Shauna contributed $1,200 of services to her church last year.

i. Shauna's car was totaled in a wreck in January. The car was worth $14,000 and her cost basis in the car was $16,000. The car was a complete loss. Shauna received $2,000 in insurance reimbursements for the loss.

j. Shauna paid $300 for architectural design publications, $100 for continuing education courses to keep her up to date on the latest design technology, and

$200 for professional dues to maintain her status in a professional designer's organization.

k. Shauna paid $250 in investment advisory fees and another $150 to have her tax return prepared last year (that is, she paid $150 in 2009 to have her 2008 tax return prepared).

l. Shauna is involved in horse racing as a hobby. During the year, she won $2,500 in prize money and incurred $10,000 in expenses. She has never had a profitable year with her horse racing activities, so she acknowledges that this is a hobby for federal income tax purposes.

m. Shauna sustained $2,000 in gambling losses over the year (mostly horse-racing bets) and only had $200 in winnings.

Required

A. Determine Shauna's taxable income assuming her AGI is $107,000.

B. Determine Shauna's taxable income assuming her AGI is $207,000.

68. Joe and Jessie are married and have one dependent child, Lizzie. Lizzie is currently in college at State University. Joe works as a design engineer for a manufacturing firm while Jessie runs a craft business from their home. Jessie's craft business consists of making craft items for sale at craft shows that are held periodically at various locations. Jessie spends considerable time and effort on her craft business and it has been consistently profitable over the years. Joe and Jessie own a home and pay interest on their home loan (balance of $220,000) and a personal loan to pay for Lizzie's college expenses (balance of $35,000). Neither Joe nor Jessie is blind or over age 65, and they plan to file as married-joint. Based on their estimate, determine Joe and Jessie's AGI and taxable income for the year. They have summarized the income and expenses they expect to report this year as follows:

Income:

Joe's salary	$109,100
Jessie's craft sales	18,400
Interest from certificate of deposit	1,650
Interest from Treasury bond funds	730
Interest from municipal bond funds	920

Expenditures:

Federal income tax withheld from Joe's wages	$13,700
State income tax withheld from Joe's wages	6,400
Social Security tax withheld from Joe's wages	7,482
Real estate taxes on residence	6,200
Automobile licenses (based on weight)	310
State sales tax paid	1,150
Home mortgage interest	14,000
Interest on Masterdebt credit card	2,300
Medical expenses (unreimbursed)	1,690
Joe's employee expenses (unreimbursed)	2,400
Cost of Jessie's craft supplies	4,260
Postage for mailing crafts	145
Travel and lodging for craft shows	2,230
Meals during craft shows	770
Self-employment tax on Jessie's craft income	1,620
College tuition paid for Lizzie	5,780
Interest on loans to pay Lizzie's tuition	3,200
Lizzie's room and board at college	12,620
Cash contributions to the Red Cross	525

Individual Income Tax Computation and Tax Credits

Learning Objectives

Upon completing this chapter, you should be able to:

LO 1 Determine a taxpayer's regular tax liability and identify tax issues associated with the process.

LO 2 Compute a taxpayer's alternative minimum tax liability and describe the tax characteristics of taxpayers most likely to owe the alternative minimum tax.

LO 3 Calculate a taxpayer's employment and self-employment taxes payable and explain tax considerations relating to whether a taxpayer is considered to be an employee or a self-employed independent contractor.

LO 4 Describe the different general types of tax credits, identify specific tax credits, and compute a taxpayer's allowable child tax credit, child and dependent care credit, earned income credit, Hope scholarship credit, and lifetime learning credit.

LO 5 Explain taxpayer filing and tax payment requirements and describe in general terms how to compute a taxpayer's underpayment, late filing, and late payment penalties.

Courtney has already determined her taxable income. Now she's working on computing her tax liability. She knows she owes a significant amount of regular income tax on her employment and business activities. However, she's not sure how to compute the tax on the qualifying dividends she received from General Electric. Courtney is worried that she may be subject to the alternative minimum tax this year because she's heard that an increasing number of taxpayers in her income range must pay the tax. Finally, Courtney knows she owes some self-employment taxes on her business income. Courtney would like to determine whether she is eligible to claim any tax credits such as the child tax credit for her two children and education credits because she paid for a portion of her daughter Ellen's tuition at the University of Missouri–Kansas City this year. Courtney is hoping that she has paid enough in taxes during the year to avoid underpayment penalties. She's planning on filing her tax return and paying her taxes on time.

Gram's tax situation is much more straightforward. Gram needs to determine the regular income tax on her taxable income. Gram's income is so low she knows she need not worry about the alternative minimum tax, and she doesn't have any self-employment income so she need not pay any self-employment taxes. Gram didn't prepay any taxes this year, so she is concerned that she might be required to pay an underpayment penalty. She also expects to file her tax return and pay her taxes by the looming due date.

to be continued . . .

Storyline Summary	
Taxpayers:	Courtney Wilson, age 40 Courtney's mother Dorothy "Gram" Weiss, age 70.
Family description:	Courtney is divorced with a son, Deron, age 10, and a daughter, Ellen, age 20. Gram is currently residing with Courtney.
Location:	Kansas City, Missouri.
Employment status:	Courtney works as an architect for EWD. Gram is unemployed.
Filing status:	Courtney is head of household. Gram is single.
Current situation:	Courtney and Gram have computed their taxable income. Now they are trying to determine their tax liability, tax refund or additional taxes due, and whether they owe any payment-related penalties.

In prior chapters we've learned how to compute taxable income for taxpayers such as Courtney and Gram. This chapter describes how to determine a taxpayer's tax liability for the year. We discover that the process is not as easy as simply applying taxable income to the applicable tax rate schedule or tax table. Taxpayers may generate taxable income that is taxed at rates not provided in the tax rate schedules or tax tables. We will learn that they may also be required to pay taxes in addition to the regular income tax. We also describe tax credits taxpayers may use to reduce their gross taxes payable. We conclude the chapter by describing taxpayer filing requirements and identifying certain penalties taxpayers may be required to pay when they underpay or are late paying their taxes. We start our coverage by explaining how to compute one's regular tax liability.

LO1 REGULAR FEDERAL INCOME TAX COMPUTATION

When taxpayers have determined their taxable income, they are ready to compute their gross tax from a series of progressive tax rates called a **tax rate schedule.**

Tax Rate Schedules

Congress has constructed four different tax rate schedules for individuals. The applicable tax rate schedule is determined by the taxpayer's filing status, which we discussed in depth in Chapter 4. Recall that a taxpayer's filing status is one of the following:

1. Married filing jointly.
2. Qualifying widow or widower, also referred to as surviving spouse.
3. Married filing separately.
4. Head of household.
5. Single.

As we describe in Chapter 1, a tax rate schedule is composed of several ranges of income taxed at different (increasing) rates. Each separate range of income subject to a different tax rate is referred to as a **tax bracket.** While each filing status has its own tax rate schedule (married filing jointly and qualifying widow or widower use the same rate schedule), all tax rate schedules consist of tax brackets taxed at 10 percent, 15 percent, 25 percent, 28 percent, 33 percent, and 35 percent. However, the width or range of income within each bracket varies by filing status. In general, the tax brackets are widest and higher levels of income are taxed at the lowest rates for the married filing jointly filing status, followed by the head of household filing status, single filing status, and finally the married filing separately filing status.

The tax rate schedule for each filing status is provided inside the front cover of this book. Notice that the married filing separately schedule is the same as the married filing jointly schedule except that the taxable income levels listed in the schedule are exactly one-half the taxable income levels for married filing jointly.

Example 7-1

As we determined in Chapter 6, Courtney files under the head of household filing status and her 2009 taxable income is $111,257 (see Exhibit 6-12).

What if: For now, let's *assume* that all of Courtney's income is taxed as ordinary income. That is, assume that none of her income is taxed at a preferential rate (some is, but we'll address this in a bit). What is the tax on her taxable income?

(Continued on page 7-3...)

Answer: $22,667 Using the head of household tax rate schedule, her taxable income falls in the 25 percent marginal tax rate bracket, in between $45,500 and $117,450, so her tax is computed as follows:

Description	Amount	Explanation
(1) Base tax	$ 6,228	From head of household tax rate schedule for tax-payer with taxable income in 25 percent bracket.
(2) Income taxed at marginal tax rate	65,757	($111,257 − 45,500) from head of household tax rate schedule.
(3) Marginal tax rate	25%	From head of household tax rate schedule.
(4) Tax on income at marginal tax rate	16,439	(2) × (3).
Tax on taxable income	**$22,667**	(1) + (4).

For administrative convenience and to prevent low and middle income taxpayers from making mathematical errors using a tax rate schedule, the IRS provides **tax tables** that present the gross tax for various amounts of taxable income under $100,000 and filing status (it's impractical to provide a table for essentially unlimited amounts of income).

Example 7-2

As we determined in Chapter 6, Gram files under the single filing status. In Chapter 6 we calculated her 2009 taxable income to be $5,690 (see Exhibit 6-15). None of her income is taxed at a preferential rate. What is the tax on her taxable income using the tax rate schedules?

Answer: $569. ($5,690 × 10%).

What if: Suppose that Gram's 2008 taxable income was $5,690. What would be her tax liability using the 2008 tax table for single taxpayers (see the excerpt of the 2008 tax table for single taxpayers in the Appendix A to this chapter)?

Answer: $568.

Because the tax tables generate nearly the same tax as calculated from the tax rate schedule, we use the tax rate schedules throughout this chapter.[1]

Marriage Penalty or Benefit

An interesting artifact of the tax rate schedules is that they can impose what some refer to as a **marriage penalty,** but they may actually produce a **marriage benefit.** A marriage penalty (benefit) occurs when, for a given level of income, a married couple has a greater (lesser) tax liability when they use the married filing jointly tax rate schedule to determine the tax on their joint income than they would have owed (in total) if each spouse would have used the single tax rate schedule to compute the tax on each spouse's individual income. Exhibit 7-1 explores the marriage penalty in a scenario in which both spouses earn income and another in which only one spouse earns income. As the exhibit illustrates, the marriage penalty applies to couples with two wage earners, but a marriage benefit applies to couples with single breadwinners.

Exceptions to the Basic Tax Computation

In certain circumstances, taxpayers cannot completely determine their final tax liability from their tax rate schedule or tax table. Taxpayers must perform additional

---

[1]Further, the tax rate tables for 2009 were unavailable at the time this book went to press.

EXHIBIT 7-1 2009 Marriage Penalty (Benefit) Two Income vs. Single Income Married Couple*

Married Couple	Taxable Income	Tax if File Jointly (1)	Tax if File Single (2)	Marriage Penalty (Benefit) (1) − (2)
Scenario 1: *Two wage-earners*				
Wife	$100,000		$21,720	
Husband	100,000		21,720	
Combined	$200,000	$44,264	$43,440	$824
Scenario 2: *One wage-earner*				
Wife	$200,000		$51,143	
Husband	0		0	
Combined	$200,000	$44,264	$51,143	($6,879)

*This analysis assumes the taxpayers do not owe any alternative minimum tax (discussed below).

computations to determine their tax liability (1) when they recognize long-term capital gains or receive dividends that are taxed at preferential (lower) rates and/ or (2) when the taxpayer is a child and the child's unearned taxable income is taxed at her parent's **marginal tax rate.** We describe these additional computations in detail below.

Preferential Tax Rates for Capital Gains and Dividends As we describe in detail in Chapter 11, certain capital gains and certain dividends are taxed at a lower or **preferential tax rate** relative to other types of income. In general, the preferential tax rate is 15 percent.[2] While we discuss this in more depth in that chapter, let's briefly introduce the capital gains and dividends that are taxed at preferential rates. A capital gain is the gain recognized on the disposition of a capital asset. In general terms, a capital asset is any asset *other than*

- Accounts receivable from the sale of goods or services.
- Inventory and other assets held for sale in the ordinary course of business.
- Assets used in a trade or business, including supplies.

Thus, assets held for investment, such as stocks or bonds, are capital assets. When a taxpayer sells a capital asset at a gain or loss, the gain or loss is considered to be a long-term capital gain or loss if the taxpayer owned the asset for *more than* a year before selling it. Otherwise, the capital gain or loss is considered to be a short-term capital gain or loss. Only net long-term capital gains in excess of net short-term capital losses are taxed at preferential rates.

Qualified dividends (distributions from corporations to shareholders) are also taxed at preferential tax rates. Qualified dividends generally include dividends paid by a U.S. corporation (including mutual funds)[3] and dividends on stock that the taxpayer has held for a certain amount of time.[4] In Chapter 11, we describe in more depth how to determine the amount of capital gains and dividends that qualify for

---

[2]As we discover in Chapter 11, some types of income may be taxed at a preferential rate of 28 percent or 25 percent. Further, as we discuss below, income that would otherwise be taxed at the 15 percent preferential rate is taxed at 0 percent if it would have been taxed at a 15 percent or lower rate if it were ordinary income taxed at the rates in the tax rate schedule.

[3]Dividends from "qualified foreign corporations" may also qualify [see §1(h)(11)(B)].

[4]We discuss the holding period in Chapter 11. See §1(h)(11)(B)(iii).

the preferential tax rate. Here, we focus on how to determine a taxpayer's tax liability when the taxpayer recognizes income taxed at a preferential tax rate.

The tax rate tables and tax rate schedules allow taxpayers to compute their tax on ordinary but not **preferentially taxed income.** This is true even though preferentially taxed income is included in adjusted gross income (AGI) and in taxable income. Taxpayers with income subject to the preferential rate (long-term capital gains and qualifying dividends) can use the following three-step process to determine their tax liability.

Step 1: Split taxable income into the portion that is subject to the preferential rate and the portion taxed at the ordinary rates.

Step 2: Compute the tax separately on each type of income. Note that the income that is not taxed at the preferential rate is taxed at the ordinary tax rates using the tax rate schedule for the taxpayer's filing status.

Step 3: Add the tax on the income subject to the preferential tax rates and the tax on the income subject to the ordinary rates. This is the taxpayer's regular tax liability.

Example 7-3

Courtney's taxable income of $111,257 includes $700 of qualifying dividends from GE (Exhibit 5-4). What is her tax liability on her taxable income?

Answer: $23,174, computed at head of household rates as follows:

Description	Amount	Explanation
(1) Taxable income	$111,257	Exhibit 6-13.
(2) Preferentially taxed income	700	Exhibit 5-4.
(3) Income taxed at ordinary rates	110,557	(1) − (2).
(4) Tax on income taxed at ordinary rates	22,492	[$6,228 + (110,557 − 45,500) × 25%].
(5) Tax on preferentially taxed income	105	(2) × 15% [Note that if (2) were ordinary income it would have been taxed at 25 percent].
Tax on taxable income	**$22,597**	(4) + (5).

In this example, what is Courtney's tax savings from having the dividends taxed at the preferential rate rather than the ordinary rate?

Answer: $70. $700 × (25% − 15%). This is the amount of the dividend times the difference in the ordinary and preferential tax rate.

To ensure that taxpayers receive some tax benefit from preferentially taxed income, *to the extent* that this income would have been taxed at 15 percent or 10 percent if it were ordinary income, it is taxed at a 0 percent preferential rate.

Example 7-4

What if: Gram's taxable income is $5,690. We computed her tax on this income in Example 7-2. Suppose that Gram's taxable income included $350 of long-term capital gains taxable at the preferential rate (the $350 capital gain she *actually* recognized was a short-term gain not subject to the preferential rate). What is Gram's tax liability under these circumstances?

(continued on page 7-6...)

Answer: $534, calculated as follows:

Description	Amount	Explanation
(1) Taxable income	$5,690	Exhibit 6-15.
(2) Preferentially taxed income	350	
(3) Income taxed at ordinary rates	5,340	(1) − (2).
(4) Tax on income taxed at ordinary rates	534	(3) × 10% (see tax rate schedule for single taxpayers).
(5) Tax on preferentially taxed income	0	(2) × 0% [Note that if (2) were ordinary income it would have been taxed at 10 percent; since this is equal to or less than 15 percent the income is taxed at 0 percent].
Tax	**$ 534**	(4) + (5).

Example 7-5

What if: Assume that Gram's taxable income is $35,000 including $4,000 of qualifying dividends taxed at the preferential rate. What would be Gram's tax liability on her income under these circumstances?

Answer: $4,732, computed using the single tax rate schedule as follows:

Description	Amount	Explanation
(1) Taxable income	$35,000	
(2) Preferentially taxed income	4,000	
(3) Income taxed at ordinary rates	31,000	(1) − (2).
(4) Tax on income taxed at ordinary rates	4,233	$835 + [(31,000 − 8,350) × 15%] (see tax rate schedule for single taxpayers).
(5) Tax on preferentially taxed income	158	[($2,950 × 0%) + (1,050 × 15%)].**
Tax	**$ 4,391**	(4) + (5).

**Gram had $4,000 of preferentially taxed income. If this income was ordinary income, $2,950 of the income would have been taxed at 15 percent [$33,950 (end of 15 percent bracket) − $31,000 (ordinary taxable income)] and the remaining $1,050 would have been taxed at 25 percent [$35,000 (total taxable income) − $33,950 (end of 15 percent bracket)]. Consequently, $2,950 of the preferential income is taxed at 0 percent and the remaining $1,050 is taxed at 15 percent.

Kiddie Tax   Parents can reduce their family's income tax bill by shifting income that would otherwise be taxed at their higher tax rates to their children whose income is taxed at lower rates. However, as we described in Chapter 5, under the assignment of income doctrine, taxpayers cannot simply assign or transfer income to other parties. Earned income, or income from services or labor, is taxed to the person who earns it. Thus, it's difficult for a parent to shift *earned* income to a child. However, unearned income or income from property such as dividends from stocks or interest from bonds is taxed to the *owner* of the property. Thus, a parent can shift unearned income to a child by transferring actual ownership of the income-producing property to the child. By transferring ownership, the parent runs the risk that the child will sell the asset or use it in a way unintended by the parent. However, this risk is relatively small for parents transferring property ownership to younger children.

The tax laws reduce parents' ability to shift unearned income to children in two ways. First, they limit the standard deductions for taxpayers who are claimed as dependents on another's tax return to the *greater* of (1) $950 or (2) $300 *plus* the dependent's earned income.[5] However, the standard deduction cannot exceed the basic standard deduction amount.[6] In 2009, the basic standard deduction is $5,700 for single taxpayers.

Example 7-6

At the beginning of the year Al (Courtney's ex-husband) gave a $20,000 IBM bond to Deron. The bond pays 5 percent interest annually. In December of the current year, Deron received $1,000 of interest from the bond. This is Deron's only source of income for the year. What is Deron's taxable income for the year?

Answer: $50, determined as follows:

Description	Amount	Explanation
(1) Gross income	$1,000	
(2) Minimum standard deduction	950	Minimum for taxpayer claimed as dependent on another return.
(3) Earned income + $300	300	$0 + $300.
(4) Standard deduction for dependent on another tax return	950	Greater of (2) or (3).
(5) Personal exemption	0	Deron is claimed as a dependent on Courtney's return (see Example 6-36) so he is *not* allowed to claim a *personal* exemption.
Taxable income	**$ 50**	(1) − (4) − (5).

What if: Would Deron's taxable income change if an unrelated taxpayer rather than Al gave the bond to Deron?

Answer: No, Deron would still report $50 of taxable income. Because Deron qualifies as a dependent of another taxpayer (no matter who that taxpayer is), his standard deduction is limited to $950 in this scenario.

What if: Suppose that Deron's income for the year consists of $1,000 of wages (earned income) rather than interest (unearned income). What would Deron's taxable income be under these circumstances?

Answer: $0. In this case, Deron would be entitled to a standard deduction of $1,300 [greater of (1) $950 or (2) $300 + $1,000 earned income]. Thus, he would not have any taxable income ($1,000 − 1,300).

What if: Assume that Deron received $8,000 of earned income and $500 of unearned income during the year. What is the amount of his standard deduction?

Answer: $5,700. Because he is claimed as a dependent on another's tax return, his standard deduction is the greater of (1) $950 or (2) $300 + earned income of $8,000. It appears as though he may claim a standard deduction of $8,300; however, his standard deduction is limited to the $5,700 basic standard deduction available for single taxpayers.

The second way the tax laws limit parents' ability to shift (or at least to benefit from shifting) unearned income to children is through the so-called **kiddie tax.** The kiddie tax provisions apply (or potentially apply) to a child if (1) the child is under 18 years old at year end, (2) the child is 18 at year end but her earned income does *not* exceed half of her support, or (3) the child is over age 18 but under age 24 at year end, is a full-time student during the year, and her earned income does not exceed half of her support (excluding scholarships).[7]

In general terms, if the kiddie tax applies, children must pay tax on a certain amount of their unearned income (their **net unearned income,** discussed below) at

---

[5]§63(c)(5).

[6]The taxpayer who is a dependent of another taxpayer may add any additional standard deduction amounts for age or blindness to her standard deduction amount whether she is able to claim the full basic standard deduction or whether it is limited due to a lack of earned income (Rev. Proc. 2006-53).

[7]§1(g)(2)(A).

their parents' marginal tax rate rather than at their own marginal tax rate, unless the parents' marginal tax rate on the income (the preferential tax rate if the income is long-term capital gain or qualifying dividends) would be lower than the child's marginal tax rate.[8] (When the parents of the child are not married, this provision applies to the custodial parent.[9]) That is, the kiddie tax will never allow children to pay less tax than they would have been required to pay without the kiddie tax provision.

The kiddie tax base is the child's net unearned income. Net unearned income is the *lesser* of (1) the child's gross *unearned income* minus $1,900[10] or (2) the child's taxable income (the child is not taxed on more than her taxable income).[11] Consequently, the kiddie tax does not apply unless the child has *unearned* income in *excess* of $1,900.[12] Thus the kiddie tax significantly limits, but does not eliminate, the tax benefit gained by a family unit when parents transfer income-producing assets to children.

Example 7-7

What if: Suppose that during 2009, Deron received $1,000 in interest from the IBM bond, and he received another $2,100 in interest income from a money market account that his parents have been contributing to over the years. Is Deron potentially subject to the kiddie tax?

Answer: Yes, Deron is younger than 18 years old at the end of the year and his net unearned income exceeds $1,900.

What is Deron's taxable income and corresponding tax liability?

Answer: $2,150 taxable income and $395 tax liability, calculated as follows under the single filing status:

Description	Amount	Explanation
(1) Gross income/AGI	$3,100	$1,000 dividends + $2,100 interest. All unearned income.
(2) Standard deduction	950	Minimum for taxpayer claimed as a dependent on another return (no earned income, so must use minimum).
(3) Personal exemption	0	Claimed as a dependent on Courtney's return.
(4) Taxable income	**$2,150**	(1) − (2) − (3).
(5) Gross unearned income minus $1,900	1,200	(1) − $1,900.
(6) Net unearned income	$1,200	Lesser of (4) or (5).
(7) Courtney's ordinary marginal rate	25%	See Example 7-3 (use Courtney's rate because she is the custodial parent).
(8) Kiddie tax	$ 300	(6) × (7) (Deron's income taxed at Courtney's marginal rate).
(9) Taxable income taxed at Deron's rate	950	(4) − (6).
(10) Tax on taxable income using Deron's tax rates	$ 95	(9) × 10% (See single filing status, $950 taxable income).
Deron's total tax liability	**$ 395**	(8) + (10).

(continued on page 7-9...)

[8]§1(g).

[9]§1(g)(5).

[10]The $1,900 consists of $950 of the child's standard deduction (even if the child is entitled to a larger standard deduction) plus an *extra* $950. If the child itemizes deductions, then the calculation becomes more complex and is beyond the scope of this text.

[11]§1(g)(4).

[12]Under §1(g)(7), subject to certain requirements, parents may elect to include on their own tax return. (on Form 8814) their child's unearned income.

What if: Assume Deron's only source of income is qualifying dividends of $2,100 (unearned income). What is his taxable income and tax liability?

Answer: Taxable income is $1,250; tax liability is $60, computed as follows:

Description	Amount	Explanation
(1) Gross income/(AGI)	$2,100	Qualifying dividends, all unearned income
(2) Minimum standard deduction	950	Minimum for taxpayer claimed as a dependent on another return (all unearned income, so must use minimum).
(3) Personal exemption	0	Claimed as a dependent on Courtney's return.
(4) Taxable income	**$1,150**	(1) − (2) − (3).
(5) Gross unearned income minus $1,900	200	(2) − $1,900.
(6) Net unearned income	$ 200	Lesser of (4) or (5).
(7) Courtney's marginal tax rate on qualifying dividend income	15%	See Example 7-3 (her marginal rate on ordinary income is 25 percent, so her marginal rate on preferentially taxed income is 15 percent).
(8) Kiddie tax	$ 30	(6) × (7) (Deron's income taxed at Courtney's marginal rate on the dividend income).
(9) Taxable income taxed at Deron's rate	950	(4) − (6).
(10) Tax on taxable income using Deron's tax rates	$ 0	(9) × 0% (Deron's marginal rate on the dividend would be 10 percent if it were ordinary income so he qualifies for 0 percent rate on dividend).
Deron's total tax liability	**$ 30**	(8) + (10).

As we've just described, all individual taxpayers must pay federal income taxes on their federal taxable income. However, taxpayers may be liable for other federal taxes in addition to the regular tax liability. Many taxpayers are also required to pay the alternative minimum tax, and some working taxpayers are required to pay employment or self-employment taxes. We delve into these additional taxes below.

ALTERNATIVE MINIMUM TAX

L02

Each year, an increasing number of taxpayers are required to pay the **alternative minimum tax (AMT)** in *addition to* their *regular* tax liability. The **alternative minimum tax system** was implemented in 1986 (earlier variations date back to the late 1960s) to ensure that taxpayers generating income pay some *minimum* amount of income tax each year. The tax was originally targeted at higher-income taxpayers who were benefiting from (or were perceived by the public to be benefiting from) the *excessive* use (more than Congress intended) of tax preference items such as exclusions, deferrals, and deductions to reduce or even eliminate their tax liabilities. However, for reasons we discuss below, the tax is forcing many taxpayers who don't fit this description to pay the tax. In fact, the alternative minimum tax is referred to by some as the "ticking time bomb" of the tax code.[13] While in 2002, only about 2 million taxpayers paid

---

[13]Amy Feldman, "The Tax of Unintended Consequences," *Money,* September 2003, pp. 86–92.

AMT, estimates indicate that nearly 46% of taxpayers with incomes between $75,000 and $100,000 will pay the the AMT in 2010.[14]

In general terms, the alternative minimum tax is a tax on an *alternative* tax base meant to more closely reflect economic income than the regular income tax base. Thus the **AMT base** is more inclusive (or more broadly defined) than is the regular income tax base. To compute their AMT, taxpayers first compute their regular income tax liability. Then, they compute the AMT base and multiply the base by the applicable alternative tax rate.[15] They must pay the AMT only when the tax on the AMT base exceeds their regular tax liability.

Alternative Minimum Tax Formula

Regular taxable income is the starting point for determining the alternative minimum tax. As the AMT formula in Exhibit 7-2 illustrates, taxpayers make several "plus" and "minus" adjustments to regular taxable income to compute alternative minimum taxable income (AMTI). They then arrive at the AMT base by subtracting an AMT exemption from AMTI. Taxpayers multiply the AMT base by the AMT rate to determine their **tentative minimum tax.** Finally, to determine their alternative minimum tax, taxpayers subtract their regular tax liability from the tentative minimum tax. The alternative minimum tax is the *excess* of the tentative minimum tax over the regular tax. If the regular tax liability equals or exceeds the tentative minimum tax, taxpayers need not pay any AMT. Individual taxpayers compute their AMT on Form 6251.

Alternative Minimum Taxable Income (AMTI)   In order to compute alternative minimum taxable income (AMTI), taxpayers make several **alternative minimum tax adjustments** to regular taxable income. Many of these are plus adjustments that are added to regular taxable income to reach AMTI and some are minus adjustments

EXHIBIT 7-2   **Formula for Computing the Alternative Minimum Tax**

Regular Taxable Income

Plus: Personal exemptions and standard deduction if taxpayer deducted the standard deduction in computing regular taxable income

Minus: Phase-out of itemized deductions for regular tax purposes (if applicable)

Plus or minus other adjustments*
Alternative minimum taxable income

Minus: AMT exemption amount (if any)
Equals: **Tax base for AMT**

Times AMT rate
Equals: **Tentative minimum tax**

Minus: **Regular tax**
Equals: **Alternative minimum tax**

*Technically, some of these adjustments are referred to as preference items and some are referred to as adjustments. We refer to all of these items as adjustments for simplicity's sake.

[14]See Burman, L., J. Koch, G. Leiserson, and J. Rohaly (2008). "The Individual Alternative Minimum Tax: 12 Facts and Projections." Urbans-Brookings Tax Policy Center: June 30, 2008 (http://www.taxpolicycenter.org).

[15]The rate of the alternative minimum tax (AMT) was set below that of the income tax with the objective of avoiding the perception that the AMT was an additional assessment.

that are subtracted from regular taxable income to determine AMTI. Consequently, these adjustments tend to expand the regular income tax base to more closely reflect economic income.

Exemptions, standard deduction, and itemized deduction phase-out.   Taxpayers first add back to regular taxable income the amount of personal and dependency exemptions they actually deducted, after considering phase-outs, in determining their regular taxable income. The exemption deduction is added back because it does not represent an actual economic outflow. Next, taxpayers add back the standard deduction amount, but only *if they deducted it* in determining taxable income. Again, just like exemptions, taxpayers add back the standard deduction because it is a deduction that does not reflect an actual economic outflow from the taxpayer. Finally, taxpayers *subtract* the amount of itemized deductions they incurred but did not deduct because the deductions were phased-out or reduced for regular tax purposes (see discussion in Chapter 6). The phase-out is subtracted because it represents an economic outflow that did not reduce taxable income.

Example 7-8

Courtney started the process of determining whether she owed any AMT by adjusting her regular taxable income for her exemptions. What is Courtney's AMTI before other adjustments?

Answer: $122,207, computed as follows:

Description	Amount	Explanation
(1) Taxable income	$111,257	Exhibit 6-13.
(2) Exemptions	10,950	Exhibit 6-13.
AMTI before other adjustments	$122,207	(1) + (2).

Other adjustments.   Taxpayers are required to make several other adjustments to compute AMTI. Exhibit 7-3 describes the most common of these adjustments.

As Exhibit 7-3 indicates, several itemized deductions are not deductible for AMT purposes. The major itemized deductions that are deductible for both regular tax and AMT purposes using the *same limitations* are

- Casualty and theft losses.
- Charitable contributions.
- Home mortgage interest expenses.
- Gambling losses.

Deductions that are deductible for regular tax and AMT purposes but have *different limitations* are

- Medical expenses.
- Home-equity interest.
- Investment interest expense.

Example 7-9

Courtney continued to work on her AMT computation by determining the other adjustments she needs to make to determine her alternative minimum taxable income (AMTI). What is Courtney's AMTI?

(continued on page 7-12...)

EXHIBIT 7-3   Common AMT Adjustments

Adjustment	Description
Plus adjustments:	
Tax-exempt interest from private activity bonds	Taxpayers must add back interest income that was excluded for regular tax purposes if the bonds were used to fund private activities (privately owned baseball stadium or private business subsidies) and not for the public good (build or repair public roads).
Real property and personal property taxes deducted as itemized deductions	Deductible for regular tax purposes, but not for AMT purposes.
State income or sales taxes	Deductible for regular tax purposes, but not for AMT purposes.
Home-equity interest expense	This is *not deductible* for AMT purposes if the proceeds from the loan are used for *purposes other than to acquire or substantially improve the home.*
Miscellaneous itemized deductions (subject to the 2 percent floor) in excess of the 2 percent floor	Deductible for regular tax purposes but not for AMT purposes.
Plus or Minus adjustment:	
Depreciation	Taxpayers must compute their depreciation expense for AMT purposes. For certain types of assets, the regular tax method is more accelerated than the AMT method. In any event, if the regular tax depreciation exceeds the AMT depreciation, this is a plus adjustment. If the AMT depreciation exceeds the regular tax depreciation, this is a minus adjustment.
Minus adjustments:	
State income tax refunds included in regular taxable income	Because state income taxes paid are not deductible for AMT purposes, refunds are not taxable (they do not increase the AMT base).
Gain or loss on sale of depreciable assets	Due to differences in regular tax and AMT depreciation methods, taxpayers may have a different adjusted basis (cost minus accumulated depreciation) for regular tax and for AMT purposes. Thus, they may have a different gain or loss for regular tax purposes than they do for AMT purposes. If regular tax gain exceeds AMT gain, this is a minus adjustment. Because AMT accumulated depreciation will never exceed regular tax accumulated depreciation, this would never be a plus adjustment.

(continued from page 7-11...)
Answer: $133,620, computed as follows:

Description	Amount	Explanation
(1) AMTI before other adjustments	$122,207	Example 7-8.
Plus adjustments:		
(2) Tax-exempt interest on Cincinnati bond used to pay for renovations to major league baseball stadium (private activity bond)	500	Example 5-22.
(3) Real estate property taxes	3,550	Example 6-14.
(4) State income taxes	6,700	Example 6-14.
(5) Miscellaneous itemized deductions in excess of 2 percent floor	1,083	Example 6-31.
Minus adjustments:		
(6) State income tax refund	(420)	Example 5-3.
Alternative minimum taxable income	$133,620	Sum of (1) through (6).

AMT Exemption   To help ensure that low-income taxpayers aren't required to pay the alternative minimum tax, Congress allows taxpayers to deduct an **AMT exemption** amount to determine their alternative minimum tax base.[16] The amount of the exemption depends on the taxpayer's filing status. The exemption is phased-out (reduced) by 25 cents for every dollar the AMTI exceeds the threshold amount. Exhibit 7-4 identifies, by filing status, the base exemption amount, the phase-out threshold, and the range of AMTI over which the exemption is phased-out for 2008. Because the 2009 AMT exemption amounts were unavailable when this book went to press, we use the 2008 exemption amounts in all examples and problems.

EXHIBIT 7-4   2008 AMT Exemptions

Filing Status	Exemption	Phase-out Begins at This Level of AMTI	Phase-out Complete for This Level of AMTI
Married filing jointly	$69,950	$150,000	$415,000
Married filing separately	34,975	75,000	207,500
Head of household and Single	46,200	112,500	289,900

Example 7-10

What is Courtney's AMT base?

Answer: $96,300 computed by subtracting her allowable exemption amount from her AMTI as follows:

Description	Amount	Explanation
(1) AMTI	$133,620	Example 7-9.
(2) Full AMT Exemption (Head of Household):	46,200	Exhibit 7-4.
(3) Exemption phase-out threshold	112,500	
(4) AMTI in excess of exemption phase-out threshold	21,120	(1) − (3).
(5) Exemption phase-out percentage	25%	
(6) Exemption phase-out amount	5,280	(4) × (5).
(7) Deductible exemption amount	40,920	(2) − (6).
AMT base	**$ 92,700**	(1) − (7).

Tentative Minimum Tax and AMT Computation   Taxpayers compute the tentative minimum tax by multiplying the AMT base by the applicable AMT rates. The AMT rate schedule consists of just two regular brackets as follows:

- 26 percent on the first $175,000 of AMT base ($87,500 for married taxpayers filing separately).
- 28 percent on AMT base in excess of $175,000.

However, for AMT purposes long-term capital gains and dividends are taxed at the same preferential rate as they were taxed for regular tax purposes (generally 15 percent).

Example 7-11

Courtney's AMT base is $92,700 However, Courtney also received $700 in dividends that are included in the base but are subject to a maximum tax rate of 15 percent even under the AMT system. The remaining $92,000 ($92,700 − 700) is taxed at the normal AMT rates. What is Courtney's tentative minimum tax?

(continued on page 7-14...)

---

[16]Unlike exemption and standard deduction amounts, the AMT exemption is not indexed for inflation. However, Congress usually increases the exemption amount for that particular year.

Answer: $24,025, computed as follows:

Description	Amount	Reference
(1) AMT base	$92,700	Example 7-10.
(2) Dividends taxed at preferential rate	700	Example 7-3.
(3) Tax rate applicable to dividends	15%	
(4) Tax on dividends	105	(2) × (3).
(5) AMT base taxed at regular AMT rates	92,000	(1) − (2).
(6) Regular AMT tax rate	26%	For AMT base below $175,000.
(7) Tax on AMT base taxed at regular AMT rates	23,920	(5) × (6).
Tentative minimum tax	**$24,025**	(4) + (7).

Taxpayers subtract their regular tax liability from their tentative minimum tax to determine their AMT. If the taxpayer's regular tax liability is equal to or exceeds the tentative minimum tax liability, the taxpayer does not owe any AMT.

Example 7-12

What is Courtney's alternative minimum tax liability?

Answer: $1,787, computed as follows:

Description	Amount	Reference
(1) Tentative minimum tax	$ 24,025	Example 7-11.
(2) Regular tax liability	(22,597)	Example 7-3.
Alternative minimum tax	$ 1,428	(1) − (2).

Courtney owes $1,428 of alternative minimum tax in addition to her regular tax liability.

In some situations, taxpayers who pay the AMT are entitled to a **minimum tax credit** to use when the regular tax exceeds the tentative minimum tax. They can use the credit to offset regular tax but not below the tentative minimum tax for that year.[17]

Other AMT Considerations

Above we mentioned that the number of taxpayers subject to the AMT is increasing over time and is projected to continue to increase until 2010. Why is this happening? The two primary contributing factors are

1. The AMT exemption amount is not indexed for inflation. Consequently, as taxpayers' incomes increase over time through inflation, the exemption amount does not. Increasing income combined with a stable exemption exposes more income to the AMT (income over exemption amount). Congress has been applying a temporary fix to this problem each year by increasing the exemption amount for that particular year. However, there are no guarantees that Congress will continue this trend.

---

[17]The credit only applies when the taxpayer has positive adjustments that will reverse and become negative adjustments in the future. For example, depreciation, gain or loss on asset sales, and incentive stock option bargain element adjustments (see Chapter 12) fall into this category. Due to the nature of her adjustments, Courtney does not qualify for the minimum tax credit.

2. Individual tax rates have been decreasing while AMT rates have remained constant. For example, the top tax rate from 1993 through 2000 was 39.6 percent, in 2001 it was 39.1 percent, in 2002 it was 38.6 percent, and from 2003 to today it is 35 percent. Further, the lowest tax bracket was reduced from 15 percent to 10 percent with no corresponding reduction in the AMT rates. Because taxpayers pay the AMT only when the tax on the AMT base exceeds the regular tax liability, taxpayers may owe the AMT because their regular tax is decreasing (due to lower rates) and not necessarily because their tentative minimum tax is increasing.

Based on the nature of the adjustments we've explained, it's clear that the taxpayers who tend to get hit the hardest by AMT are taxpayers who (1) have many dependents, (2) live in a high-income-tax state (they deduct state taxes for regular tax purposes but not AMT purposes), (3) pay high real estate or other property taxes, and/or (4) have relatively high capital gains (the capital gains increase AMTI, which reduces the exemption amount and thus exposes more income to the AMT).

General AMT Planning Strategies   In certain circumstances, taxpayers can implement tax planning strategies to mitigate the impact of the AMT. For example, consistent with the tax rate timing strategy we discussed in Chapter 3, taxpayers who pay AMT at 26 percent (or 28 percent) one year and expect to pay regular tax at 35 percent in the next year may want to consider accelerating income into the AMT year to ensure that it is taxed at a lower rate than it would be in a regular tax year. In any event, taxpayers who either pay or may pay the AMT should consider their tax situation to determine whether and how to use timing tax planning strategies to reduce their combined tax burden (regular tax and AMT) given their circumstances.

THE KEY FACTS

Alternative Minimum Tax (AMT)

- Implemented to ensure taxpayers pay some minimum level of income tax.

- Alternative minimum tax base.
  · More broad than regular income tax base.
  · No deductions for exemptions, standard deduction, state income taxes, property taxes, and others.

- AMT exemption amounts for 2008.
  · $69,950 married filing jointly.
  · $34,975 married filing separately.
  · $46,200 other.
  · Phased-out by 25 cents for each dollar of AMTI over threshold.

- AMT rates.
  · 26 percent on first $175,000 of AMT base.
  · 28 percent on AMT base in excess of $175,000.
  · Net long-term capital gains and qualifying dividends taxed at same preferential rates used for regular tax purposes.

- AMT is the excess of tentative minimum tax (tax on AMT base) over regular tax liability.

Taxes in the Real World   *Alternative Minimum Taxes*

Excerpts from: The ABCs of Dealing With the AMT; As Dreaded Tax Ensnares More People, Advisers Suggest Ways to Avoid It Next Year

Ouch.

As of this week's filing deadline, some four million people wound up owing more in taxes—sometimes several thousand dollars more—for 2006 than they would have otherwise, thanks to the federal alternative minimum tax.

Despite the AMT's rapid expansion, it still hasn't completely eliminated the problem that led to its birth. For 2003, of the 2.5 million income-tax returns with adjusted gross income of $200,000 or more, 2,416 reported a worldwide income-tax liability of zero, according to the IRS.

Neither President Bush nor Vice President Dick Cheney, whose tax returns were released recently, had to worry about the AMT for 2006. That's because they owed more under the regular system, where the top federal rate is 35 percent. President and Mrs. Bush filed jointly and reported adjusted gross income of $765,801. Their taxable income totaled $642,905, and they paid $186,378 in federal tax.

Among those most likely to be affected by the AMT this tax season were people with income between $200,000 and $500,000 and who live in high-tax areas, such as New York City; Washington, D.C.; California; Connecticut; and New Jersey, says Mr. Burman of the Tax Policy Center. Mr. Hopwood, the American Express executive who works in Manhattan but lives in Fair Lawn, New Jersey, took a big hit when he realized he could no longer deduct his state and local taxes. "I'm kind of being punished for working in a high-tax state," he says.

People with large families also may be affected because they lose personal exemptions.

Source: Tom Herman, The Wall Street Journal, April 18, 2007, p. D-1.

L03 EMPLOYMENT AND SELF-EMPLOYMENT TAXES

As we discussed in Chapter 1, employees and self-employed taxpayers must pay employment (or self-employment) taxes known as FICA taxes.[18] The FICA tax consists of a Social Security and a Medicare component that are payable by both employees and employers. The **Social Security tax** is intended to provide basic pension coverage for the retired and disabled. The **Medicare tax** helps pay medical costs for qualifying individuals. Because Social Security and Medicare taxes are paid by working taxpayers but received by retired taxpayers, Social Security and Medicare taxes represent intergenerational transfers. The Social Security tax rate is 12.4 percent on the tax base (limited to $106,800 in 2009), and the Medicare tax rate is 2.9 percent on the tax base. The party responsible for paying the tax and the tax base depends on whether the taxpayer is an employee or whether the taxpayer is self-employed.

Employee FICA Taxes Payable

Employees must pay **FICA taxes** on their salary, wages, and other compensation provided to them by their employer. However, employers are responsible for paying one-half of employees' FICA tax liabilities. Consequently, the Social Security tax rate for employees is 6.2 percent (12.4% × 1/2) of their salary or wages and the Medicare tax rate for employees is 1.45 percent (2.9% × 1/2) of their salary or wages. Employers withhold the employees' FICA tax liabilities from the employees' paychecks.

Example 7-13

While she was attending school full-time, Ellen received $15,000 in wages working part-time for an off-campus employer during 2009. How much in FICA taxes should Ellen's employer have withheld from her paychecks during the year?

Answer: $1,148, computed as follows:

Description	Amount	Reference
(1) Wages	$15,000	
(2) Social Security tax rate	6.2%	
(3) Social Security tax	930	(1) × (2).
(4) Medicare tax rate	1.45%	
(5) Medicare tax	218	(1) × (4).
FICA taxes withheld	$ 1,148	(3) + (5).

The wage base on which employees pay Social Security taxes is limited to an annually determined amount, reflecting the fact that the benefits the employee may ultimately receive are also capped. The limits apply to *each* taxpayer's wages regardless of marital or tax filing status. That is, the earnings of each spouse are subject to a *separate* limit. The 2009 limit is $106,800, which is a $4,800 increase over the $102,000 limit in 2008. There is no wage base limit for the Medicare component of the FICA tax (all wages are subject to the 1.45 percent Medicare tax).

Example 7-14

During 2009, Courtney received a total of $122,800 in employee compensation from EWD. Recall that the compensation consisted of $98,000 in wages, $4,800 performance bonus, $6,000 discount

(continued on page 7-17...)

---

[18]FICA stands for Federal Insurance Contributions Act.

for architectural design services, $4,000 compensation for a below-market loan, and $10,000 forgiveness of debt (see Exhibit 5-4). What is her FICA tax liability on this income?

Answer: $8,403, computed as follows:

Description	Amount	Reference
(1) Compensation subject to FICA tax	$122,800	
(2) Social Security tax base limit for 2009	106,800	
(3) Compensation subject to Social Security tax	106,800	Lesser of (1) or (2).
(4) Social Security tax rate	6.2%	
(5) Social Security tax	6,622	(3) × (4).
(6) Medicare tax rate	1.45%	
(7) Medicare tax*	1,781	(1) × (6).
FICA taxes	$ 8,403	(5) + (7).

*Note that Courtney's compensation subject to the Social Security tax wage base is capped at $106,800, but her Medicare tax wage base is not.

What amount of FICA taxes for the year must EWD pay on Courtney's behalf?

Answer: $8,403. Courtney paid one-half of her FICA tax liability and EWD is required to pay the other half. Consequently, EWD would calculate its liability exactly as Courtney calculated hers.

Employees who work for multiple employers within a calendar year may receive aggregate compensation that exceeds the Social Security wage base. Because each employer is required to withhold Social Security taxes on the employee's wages until the employee has reached the wage base limit *with that employer,* the employee may end up paying Social Security tax in *excess* of the required maximum. In such cases, the IRS treats the excess Social Security tax paid through withholding as an additional federal income tax payment (or credit) on Page 2 of Form 1040. The government refunds the excess withholding to the employee through either lower taxes payable with the tax return or a greater tax refund.[19] Employers, on the other hand, are *not* able to recover excess Social Security taxes paid on behalf of their employees.

Example 7-15

What if: Suppose that Courtney worked for her former employer LA, Inc. (Landmark Architects), in Cincinnati for two weeks in January 2009 before moving to Kansas City. During those two weeks, Courtney would have earned $4,000 in salary. LA, Inc., would have withheld $306 in FICA taxes from her final paycheck consisting of $248 of Social Security taxes ($4,000 × 6.2%) and $58 of Medicare taxes ($4,000 × 1.45%). How much excess Social Security tax would have been withheld from Courtney's combined salaries from LA, Inc., and EWD during 2009?

Answer: $248 ($4,000 wages earned with LA, Inc., × 6.2 percent Social Security rate). Due to the $106,800 Social Security tax wage base for the year, Courtney's Social Security tax liability is limited to $6,622 ($106,800 × 6.2%). However, through employer withholding, she would have paid a total of $6,870 in Social Security taxes, consisting of $248 withheld by LA, Inc., ($4,000 × 6.2%) and $6,622 withheld by EWD ($106,800 × 6.2%). Thus, given these facts, Courtney's *excess* Social Security tax withheld was $248 ($6,870 − 6,622). Courtney would get this amount back from the government through either lower taxes payable with her tax return or a greater tax refund. Because there is no limit on Medicare taxes, Courtney's entire 2009 compensation from both employers would be subject to the 1.45 percent Medicare tax.

[19]Because employees meet their FICA tax payment obligations through withholding, no FICA taxes are due with their returns.

Self-Employment Taxes

While employees equally share their FICA (Social Security and Medicare) tax burden with employers, self-employed taxpayers must pay the *entire* FICA tax burden on their self-employment earnings.[20] Just as it is with FICA taxes for employees, self-employment taxes consist of both Social Security and Medicare taxes. Because their FICA taxes are based on their self-employment earnings, FICA taxes for self-employed taxpayers are referred to as **self-employment taxes.** Just as it is with employees, the base for the Social Security component of the self-employment tax is limited to $106,800. The base for the Medicare portion of the self-employment tax is unlimited. The process for determining the taxpayer's self-employment taxes payable requires the following three steps:

Step 1: Compute the amount of the taxpayer's net income from self-employment activities (this is generally the taxpayer's net income from **Schedule C** of Form 1040—Schedule C reports the taxpayers self-employment-related income and expenses) that is subject to self-employment taxes.

Step 2: Multiply the amount from Step (1) by 92.35 percent. The product is called **net earnings from self-employment.**[21] Net earnings from self-employment is the base for the self-employment tax.

Step 3: The computation of the self-employment tax depends on the amount of the taxpayer's net earnings from self-employment as follows:

- If the taxpayer's net earnings from self-employment are less than $400, the taxpayer is not required to pay *any* self-employment tax.
- If the taxpayer's net earnings from self-employment are $106,800 or less (in 2009) multiply the amount from Step (2) by 15.3 percent.
- If the taxpayer's net earnings from self-employment exceeds $106,800, multiply the amount from Step (2) by 2.9 percent and add $13,243 ($106,800 × 12.4%). This reflects the fact that the Medicare tax base is unlimited but the Social Security tax base is limited to $106,800.

Note that as we discussed in Chapter 6, taxpayers are allowed to deduct one-half of their self-employment taxes as a *for* AGI deduction.

Example 7-16

What if: Assume that Courtney's only income for the year is her $18,000 in net self-employment income from her weekend consulting business. What amount of self-employment taxes would Courtney be required to pay on this income?

Answer: $2,543, computed as follows:

Step 1: $18,000 of net self-employment income subject to self-employment taxes.

Step 2: $18,000 × .9235 = $16,623. This is net earnings from self-employment.

Step 3: $16,623 × 15.3% = $2,543. This is the Courtney's self-employment taxes payable.

Under these circumstances, Courtney would be able to deduct $1,272 as a *for* AGI deduction for one-half of the self-employment taxes she paid ($2,543 × 50%).

---

[20]As we discussed in Chapters 5 and 6, self-employed taxpayers report their self-employment earnings on Schedule C of Form 1040. Individuals who are partners in partnerships and who are actively involved in the partnerships' business activities may be required to pay self-employment taxes on the income they are allocated from the partnerships. They would report these earnings on Schedule E of Form 1040.

[21]Because self-employed taxpayers are responsible for paying the *entire* amount of their FICA taxes, they are allowed an implicit deduction for the 7.65 percent "employer's portion" of the taxes, leaving 92.35 percent (100% − 7.65%) of the full amount subject to self-employment taxes. Note that the 7.65 percent consists of the 6.2 percent Social Security tax and 1.45 percent Medicare tax.

When a taxpayer receives *both* employee compensation and self-employment earnings in the same year, the taxpayer's *total earnings* subject to the Social Security tax is capped at $106,800 and the earnings subject to Medicare tax is unlimited. In these situations, the taxpayer's FICA tax liability on the employee compensation is determined as if the employee had no self-employment income. The taxpayer then computes her self-employment tax liability. This ordering is favorable for taxpayers because it allows them to use up all or a portion of the Social Security wage base limit with their employee income (taxed at 6.2 percent) before they determine the Social Security tax on their net earnings from self-employment (taxed at 12.4 percent). Consequently, if an employee's wages exceed the Social Security tax wage base limitation, she would not be required to pay any Social Security tax on her self-employment earnings. After calculating the FICA taxes on the taxpayer's employee wages, the taxpayer's self-employment taxes payable are determined as follows:

Step 1: Determine the limit on the Social Security portion of the self-employment tax base by subtracting the employee compensation from the Social Security wage base ($106,800 in 2009) (not below $0).

Step 2: Determine the net earnings from self-employment (self-employment earnings times 92.35 percent).

Step 3: Multiply the *lesser* of Step (1) and Step (2) by 12.4 percent. This is the amount of Social Security taxes due on the self-employment income.

Step 4: Multiply Step (2) by 2.9 percent. This is the amount of Medicare taxes due on the self-employment income.

Step 5: Add the amounts from Steps (3) and (4).

Example 7-17

In 2009, Courtney received $122,800 in taxable compensation from EWD (see Example 7-14) and $18,000 in self-employment income from her weekend consulting activities (see Example 6-2). What are Courtney's *self-employment taxes* payable on her $18,000 of income from self-employment?

Answer: $482, computed as follows:

Description	Amount	Explanation
(1) Limit on Social Security wage base	$106,800	
(2) Employee compensation	122,800	
(3) Limit on Social Security base for self-employment tax purposes	0	Step 1: (1) − (2), limited to $0.
(4) Self-employment income	18,000	
(5) Net earnings from self-employment percentage	92.35%	
(6) Net earnings from self-employment	16,623	Step 2: (4) × (5).
(7) Social Security portion of self-employment tax	0	Step 3: [Lesser of (3) or (6)] × 12.4%.
(8) Medicare portion of self-employment tax	482	Step 4: (6) × 2.9%.
Total self-employment taxes	**$ 482**	Step 5: (7) + (8).

As we reported in Chapter 6, Courtney is entitled to a $241 *for* AGI deduction for one half of her $482 self-employment taxes she incurred during the year ($482 × 50%).

Example 7-18

What if: Let's change the facts and assume that Courtney received $100,000 of taxable compensation from EWD in 2009, and she received $18,000 in self-employment income from her weekend consulting activities. What amount of self-employment taxes is Courtney required to pay on her $18,000 of business income?

Answer: $1,412 computed as follows:

Description	Amount	Explanation
(1) Limit on Social Security wage base	$106,800	
(2) Employee compensation	100,000	
(3) Limit on Social Security base for self-employment tax purposes	6,800	Step 1: (1) − (2).
(4) Self-employment income	18,000	
(5) Net earnings from self employment percentage	92.35%	
(6) Net earnings from self employment	16,623	Step 2: (4) × (5).
(7) Social Security portion of self-employment tax	843	Step 3: [Lesser of (3) or (6)] × 12.4%.
(8) Medicare portion of self-employment tax	482	Step 4: (6) × 2.9%.
Total self-employment taxes	**$ 1,325**	Step 5: (7) + (8).

Because the extra FICA taxes paid by the self-employed represent an incremental cost of doing business for them, as we discussed in Chapter 6, self-employed taxpayers are allowed to deduct half of the self-employment taxes they pay as a *for* AGI deduction.

Unlike employees, whose employers withhold tax throughout the year on their behalf, self-employed taxpayers must satisfy their self-employment tax obligations through periodic, usually quarterly, estimated tax payments. Taxpayers who are employed and self-employed (an employee with a business on the side, like Courtney) may have their employers withhold enough taxes to cover both their income and self-employment tax obligations.[22] Any self-employment taxes not paid through these mechanisms must be paid with the self-employed taxpayer's individual tax return.

continued from page 7-1...

Courtney was enjoying her work with EWD but she also really liked her weekend consulting work. A couple of months ago, after Courtney had played an integral part in completing a successful project, Courtney's boss jokingly mentioned that if Courtney ever decided to leave EWD to work for herself as a full-time consultant that EWD would love to hire her back for contract work. This caused Courtney to start thinking about the possibilities of starting her own consulting business. She's always had some interest in working for herself, but she is not at a point in her life where she can take significant financial risks even if it might mean a more satisfying career. Courtney knew that before making such a move she would need to seriously consider the non-tax issues associated with self-employment and she would need to learn more about the tax consequences of working as an independent contractor. She was particularly interested in the tax consequences of working for EWD as an independent contractor (contract worker) relative to working for EWD as an employee. ∎

[22]As we describe in Chapter 12, employees can manage their employer withholdings with Form W-4.

Employee vs. Self-Employed (Independent Contractor)

Determining whether an individual is taxed as an **employee** or as an **independent contractor** can be straightforward or quite complex, depending on the specific arrangement between the parties. In its published guidance, the IRS stipulates that an employer/employee relationship exists when the party for whom services are performed has the right to direct or control the individual performing services.[23] To assist taxpayers in deciding whether the party receiving services has the requisite amount of control over the individual providing services, the IRS has published a list of 20 factors to consider.[24] A few of the factors suggesting independent contractor rather than employee status include the contractor's ability to

1. Set her own working hours.
2. Work part-time.
3. Work for more than one firm.
4. Realize either a profit or a loss from the activities.
5. Perform work somewhere other than on an employer's premises.
6. Work without frequent oversight.

When these factors are absent, individuals are more likely to be classified as employees. Rather than simply summing the number of factors in favor of independent contractor status and those in favor of employee status, however, taxpayers and their advisors should use the factors as guides in determining the overall substance of the contractual relationship.

Whether a taxpayer is classified as an employee or as an independent contractor (self-employed) has both tax and nontax consequences to the employer and the taxpayer. The best classification for the taxpayer is situation specific.

Employee vs. Independent Contractor Comparison The two primary *tax* differences between independent contractors and employees relate to (1) the amount of their FICA taxes payable and (2) the deductibility of their business expenses.[25] However, there are several nontax factors to consider as well. In the previous section, we detailed how to determine the FICA taxes payable for employees and independent contractors (self-employed taxpayers). In terms of the deductibility of business expenses, as we discussed in Chapter 6, *employees* who incur unreimbursed business expenses relating to their employment can deduct these expenses as miscellaneous itemized deductions subject to a 2 percent of AGI floor. This floor means, in many cases, that employees receive little or no tax benefit for their employee business expenses. In contrast, as we also described in Chapter 6, self-employed independent contractors are able to deduct expenses relating to their business activities as *for* AGI deductions, which they can deduct without restriction. While these factors appear to favor independent contractor status over employee status, note that employees generally don't incur many unreimbursed expenses relating to their employment. Thus, even though independent contractors may be able to deduct more expenses than employees, they typically incur more costs in doing business.

When taxpayers are classified as independent contractors rather than employees, they are not eligible for nontaxable fringe benefits available to employees, such as health care insurance, retirement plan benefits, and other fringe benefits provided to employees. Further, independent contractors are responsible for paying their

[23]IRS Publication 1779. Independent Contractor or Employee brochure (Rev. 1 – 2005).

[24]Rev. Rul. 87-41, 1987-1 CB 296.

[25]Also, independent contractors generally receive a Form 1099 from each client reporting the gross income they received from the client during the year. Employees receive Form W-2 reporting the compensation the employee received from the employer during the year.

estimated tax liability throughout the year through estimated tax payments because the employer does not withhold taxes from an independent contractor's pay. However, as we mentioned above, taxpayers are allowed to deduct one-half of the self-employment taxes they pay.

From the employer's perspective, it is generally less costly to hire an independent contractor than an employee because the employer need not provide these benefits and the employer need not withhold or pay any FICA taxes on behalf of an independent contractor. As a result, an employer may be willing to offer an apparently higher level of taxable compensation to an independent contractor than a similarly situated employee. However, after considering all relevant factors, the taxpayer may do better receiving less compensation as an employee than slightly higher compensation as an independent contractor.

Example 7-19	

What if: Let's compare Courtney's compensation as an employee with EWD to her compensation if she were to work for EWD as an independent contractor. *Assume* that Courtney works an average of 40 hours per week for 50 weeks per year to earn a salary of $100,000; in addition she receives fringe benefits including a 10 percent contribution to her retirement plan, life insurance coverage, and health insurance coverage. Would Courtney be "made whole" in terms of her hourly rate if EWD agreed to pay her $55 an hour for her contract work (10 percent more than her hourly rate as an employee)?

Answer: Not very likely. As an independent contractor, Courtney would receive the same gross income, but she must pay more costly self-employment taxes (at nearly twice the rate of employment taxes) under the new arrangement. In addition, she will be ineligible for nontaxable the fringe benefits (retirement plan contributions, life insurance, and health coverage) she was receiving as an employee and will not receive as a contractor.

THE KEY FACTS

Employee vs. Independent Contractor

■ **Employees**
· Less control over how, when, and where to perform duties.
· Pay 6.2 percent Social Security tax subject to limit.
· Pay 1.45 percent Medicare tax.

■ **Independent contractors**
· More control over how, when, and where to perform duties.
· Report income and expenses on Form 1040, Schedule C.
· Pay 12.4 percent self-employment (Social Security) tax subject to limit.
· Pay 2.9 percent self-employment (Medicare tax) tax (no limit).
· Self-employment tax base is 92.35 percent of net self-employment income.
· Deduct half of self-employment taxes paid.

We've described how to calculate a taxpayer's regular tax liability, alternative minimum tax liability, and self-employment tax liability. These tax liabilities sum to a taxpayer's gross tax liability. While Gram's gross tax is simply her regular income tax liability of $569 (see Example 7-2), Courtney's gross tax includes other taxes. Courtney's gross tax liability is calculated in Exhibit 7-5.

EXHIBIT 7-5 Courtney's Gross Tax

Description	Amount	Explanation
(1) Regular federal income tax	$22,597	Example 7-3.
(2) Alternative minimum tax	1,428	Example 7-12.
(3) Self-employment tax	482	Example 7-17.
Gross tax	$24,507	(1) + (2) + (3).

Taxpayers reduce their gross tax by tax credits and tax prepayments (withholding and estimated tax payments) for the year. As indicated in Exhibit 7-6, if the gross

EXHIBIT 7-6 Formula for Computing Net Tax Due or Refund

Gross tax
Minus: Tax credits
Minus: Prepayments
Net tax due (refund)

tax exceeds the tax credits and prepayments, the taxpayer owes additional taxes when she files her tax return. In contrast, if the prepayments exceed the gross tax after applying tax credits, the taxpayer is entitled to a tax refund. We next explore available tax credits and conclude the chapter by dealing with taxpayer prepayments.

TAX CREDITS

L04

Congress provides a considerable number of credits for taxpayers. **Tax credits** reduce a taxpayer's *tax liability* dollar for dollar. In contrast, deductions reduce *taxable income* dollar for dollar, but the tax savings deductions generate depend on the taxpayer's marginal tax rate. Because tax credits generate tax savings *independent of* a taxpayer's marginal tax rate, they are a popular tax policy tool for avoiding the perception that tax benefits for certain tax policies are distributed disproportionately to taxpayers with higher incomes and corresponding higher marginal tax rates. Further, tax credits are powerful tax policy tools because they directly affect taxes due. By using tax credits, policy makers can adjust the magnitude of the tax effects of tax policy without changing tax rates.

Tax credits may be either nonrefundable or refundable. A nonrefundable credit may reduce a taxpayer's gross tax liability to zero, but if the amount of the credit exceeds the amount of the taxpayer's gross tax liability, the credit in excess of the gross tax liability is not refunded to the taxpayer and expires without ever providing tax benefits (unless the unused credit can be carried over to a different year). Refundable credits in excess of a taxpayer's gross tax liability are refunded to the taxpayer.

Tax credits are generally classified into one of three categories: nonrefundable personal, refundable personal, or business credits, depending on the nature of the credit. The primary exception to this general rule is the foreign tax credit. The foreign tax credit is a hybrid between personal and business credits because, like nonrefundable personal credits, it reduces the taxpayer's liability before business credits but, like business credits, unused foreign tax credits can be carried over to use in other years.

Nonrefundable Personal Credits

Congress provides many **nonrefundable personal tax credits** to generate tax relief for certain groups of individuals. For example, the child tax credit provides tax relief for taxpayers who provide a home for dependent children and the child and-dependent care credit provides tax relief for taxpayers who incur expenses to care for their children and other dependents in order to work. The adoption expense credit helps parents pay the cost of adopting children. The Hope scholarship credit and the lifetime learning credit help taxpayers pay for the cost of higher education. Because the child tax credit, the dependent care credit, and the Hope scholarship and lifetime learning credits are some of the most common nonrefundable personal credits, we discuss them in detail.

Child Tax Credit   Taxpayers may claim a $1,000 **child tax credit** for *each qualifying child* (same definition for dependency exemption purposes—see §152(c) and Chapter 4) who is under age 17 at the end of the year and who is claimed as their dependent.[26] The credit is subject to phase-out based on the taxpayer's AGI. The phase-out threshold depends on the taxpayer's filing status and is provided in Exhibit 7-7.

> **THE KEY FACTS**
>
> **Child Tax Credit**
>
> ▪ $1,000 credit for each qualifying child under age 17.
>
> ▪ Credit is nonrefundable credit.
>
> ▪ Credit is phased out for taxpayers with AGI above $110,000.
>   · Lose $50 for every $1,000 or portion thereof that AGI exceeds $110,000.

[26]§24(a).

EXHIBIT 7-7   **Child Tax Credit Phase-out Threshold**

Filing Status	Phase-out Threshold
Married filing jointly	$110,000
Married filing separately	55,000
Head of household and single	75,000

The total amount of the credit ($1,000 × number of qualifying children) is phased-out, but not below zero, by $50 for each $1,000 *or portion thereof* by which the taxpayer's AGI exceeds the applicable threshold. Taxpayers can determine their allowable child tax credit after the phase-out by using the following four steps:

Step 1: Determine the excess AGI by subtracting the threshold amount (see Exhibit 7-7) from the taxpayer's AGI.

Step 2: Divide the excess AGI from step (1) by 1,000 and round up to the next whole number.

Step 3: Multiply the amount from step (2) by $50. This is the amount of the total credit that is phased-out or disallowed.

Step 4: Subtract the amount from step (3) from the total credit before phase-out (limited to $0) to determine the allowable child tax credit.

Because the phase-out is based upon a fixed amount ($50) rather than a percentage, the phase-out range varies according to the amount of credits claimed.[27]

Example 7-20

Both Ellen and Deron are Courtney's qualifying children. Courtney may claim a child tax credit for Deron but she may *not* claim a child tax credit for Ellen because Ellen is not under age 17 at the end of the year. What amount of child tax credit is Courtney allowed to claim for Deron after accounting for the credit phase-out?

Answer: $0. Because Courtney's AGI of $162,000 exceeds the $75,000 AGI phase-out threshold, she must determine her credit after the phase-out. Her phase-out is computed as follows:

1. $162,000 AGI (Exhibit 6-6) − $75,000 head of household threshold (Exhibit 7-7) = $87,000.
2. $87,000 excess AGI divided by 1,000 = 87 (if her AGI was $87,001, this would be 88)
3. 87 × $50 = $4,350. This is the amount of the phase-out.
4. $1,000 allowable credit minus $4,350 = $0 (limited to $0).

Courtney is *not able to claim any child tax credit* because the entire amount is phased out.

What if: How much child tax credit would Courtney be able to claim after the phase-out if she had claimed five qualifying children under the age of 17 as dependents?

Answer: $650. Her total child tax credit before phase-outs would be $5,000 ($1,000 × 5). Assuming the same AGI of $162,000, she would be required to phase-out $4,350 of the credit. Consequently, she would still be able to reduce her taxes by the $650 portion of the credit that was not phased-out ($5,000 − $4,350).

---

[27]The child tax credit is partially refundable for lower-income taxpayers and is considered an additional child tax credit. For 2009, the refundable portion of the credit is the lesser of (1) the taxpayer's earned income in excess of $12,550 times 15 percent, and (2) the amount of the unclaimed portion of the nonrefundable credit (the computation is modified for taxpayers with three or more qualifying children). Thus, if a taxpayer has enough tax liability to absorb the nonrefundable portion of the credit, the refundable portion is reduced to zero. See IRS Publication 972 for more information relating to the child tax credit.

Child and Dependent Care Credit   The child and dependent care credit (dependent care credit) is a tax subsidy to help taxpayers pay the cost of providing care for their dependents to allow taxpayers to work or look for work. The amount of the credit is based on the amount of the taxpayer's expenditures to provide care for one or more qualifying persons. A qualifying person includes (1) a dependent under the age of 13, and (2) a dependent or spouse who is physically or mentally incapable of caring for herself or himself and who lives in the taxpayer's home for more than half the year.

The amount of expenditures eligible for the credit is the *least* of the following three amounts:

1. The total amount of dependent care expenditures for the year.
2. $3,000 for one qualifying person or $6,000 for two or more qualifying persons.
3. The taxpayer's earned income including wage, salary, or other taxable employee compensation, or net earnings from self-employment. Married taxpayers must file a joint tax return and the amount of earned income for purposes of the dependent care credit limitation is the earned income of the lesser-earning spouse.[28]

Expenditures for care qualify whether the care is provided outside or within the home. But, expenditures for care do *not* qualify if the caregiver is a dependent relative or child of the taxpayer.[29] The amount of the credit is calculated by multiplying qualifying expenditures by the appropriate credit percentage. The credit percentage is based upon the taxpayer's AGI level and begins at 35 percent for taxpayers with AGI of $15,000 or less. The minimum dependent care credit is 20 percent for taxpayers with AGI over $43,000. Exhibit 7-8 provides the dependent care credit percentage for different levels of AGI.

THE KEY FACTS
Dependent Care Credit
▪ Credit to help taxpayers who work or seek work when they must provide care for dependents.
▪ Credit is a nonrefundable credit.
▪ Credit is based on maximum qualifying expenditures multiplied by the rate based on AGI.
· Maximum expenditures are $3,000 for one qualifying person or $6,000 for two or more qualifying persons.
· Highest rate (for low AGI taxpayers) is 35 percent for the lowest AGI taxpayers and 20 percent for the highest.

EXHIBIT 7-8   Child and Dependent Care Credit Percentage

If AGI is over	But not over	Then the percentage is:
$ 0	15,000	35%
15,000	17,000	34%
17,000	19,000	33%
19,000	21,000	32%
21,000	23,000	31%
23,000	25,000	30%
25,000	27,000	29%
27,000	29,000	28%
29,000	31,000	27%
31,000	33,000	26%
33,000	35,000	25%
35,000	37,000	24%
37,000	39,000	23%
39,000	41,000	22%
41,000	43,000	21%
43,000	No limit	20%

[28]If the lesser-earning spouse cannot work due to a disability or is a full-time student, the lesser-earning spouse is *deemed* to have earned $250 a month if the couple is computing the credit for one qualifying person or $500 a month if the couple is computing the credit for more than one qualifying person.

[29]§21(e)(6). Also, the regulations indicate that the costs of summer school and tutoring programs are indistinguishable from general education and, therefore, do not qualify for the credit [See Reg. §1.21-1(b)].

Example 7-21	

What if: Suppose that this year, Courtney paid a neighbor $3,200 to care for her 10-year-old son, Deron, so Courtney could work. Would Courtney be allowed to claim the dependent care credit for the expenditures she made for Deron's care?

Answer: Yes. (1) Courtney paid for Deron's care to allow her to work, and (2) Deron is a qualifying person for purposes of the credit because (a) he is Courtney's dependent and (b) he is under 13 years of age at the end of the year.

What amount of dependent care credit, if any, would Courtney be allowed to claim for the $3,200 she spent to provide Deron's care given her AGI is $162,000?

Answer: $600, computed as follows:

Description	Amount	Explanation
(1) Dependent care expenditures	$ 3,200	
(2) Limit on qualifying expenditures for one dependent	3,000	
(3) Courtney's earned income	140,800	$122,800 compensation from EWD + $18,000 business income (see Example 7-17).
(4) Expenditures eligible for credit	3,000	Lesser of (1), (2), and (3).
(5) Credit percentage rate	20%	AGI over $43,000. See Exhibit 7-8.
Dependent care credit	**$ 600**	(4) × (5).

What if: If Courtney's AGI (and her earned income) was only $31,500, what would be her dependent care credit?

Answer: $780, computed as follows:

Description	Amount	Explanation
(1) Dependent care expenditures	$ 3,200	
(2) Limit on qualifying expenditures for one dependent	3,000	
(3) Courtney's earned income	31,500	
(4) Expenditures eligible for credit	3,000	Lesser of (1), (2), and (3).
(5) Credit percentage rate	26%	See table for AGI between $31,000 and $33,000.
Dependent care credit	**$ 780**	(4) × (5).

THE KEY FACTS

Education Credits

■ Hope Scholarship Credits
· Qualifying expenses include tuition for a qualifying student incurred during the first two years at a qualifying institution of higher education.
· In 2009, maximum credit of $1,800 per student calculated as percentage of maximum of $2,400 qualifying expenses.

■ Lifetime Learning Credit
· Qualifying expenses include costs at a qualifying institution associated with acquiring or improving job skills.
· Maximum credit of $2,000 per taxpayer calculated as percentage of maximum of $10,000 in annual expenses.

■ Education credits are subject to a phase-out for taxpayers who exceed an AGI threshold.
· AGI threshold is $100,000 for married filing jointly taxpayers and $50,000 for all others.

Education Credits   Congress provides the Hope scholarship credit and the lifetime learning credit to encourage taxpayers and their dependents to obtain higher education by reducing the costs of the education. Both of these credits are based on tuition and fees the taxpayer pays for herself or pays on behalf of her spouse or dependents.[30] Amounts paid by dependents of the taxpayer and amounts paid by third parties on behalf of the taxpayer's dependents are treated as though they are paid by the taxpayer.[31] The payments must be made to a qualified postsecondary

---

[30]See Reg. §1.25A-2(d). The definition of qualifying educational expenses is the same as it is for the *for* AGI education deduction we discussed in Chapter 6.

[31]§25A(g)(3).

(post high school) educational institution.[32] The Hope scholarship credit is only available for students who are enrolled at least half time in either their first or second year of postsecondary education. In 2009 the amount of the credit is 100 percent of the first $1,200 of eligible expenses paid by the taxpayer plus 50 percent of the next $1,200 of eligible expenses paid by the taxpayer. Thus, the maximum Hope credit in 2009 for any one person is $1,800 [$1,200 + (50% × $1,200)]. The Hope credit is applied on a *per student* basis. Consequently, a taxpayer with three eligible dependents can claim a maximum Hope credit of $1,800 for *each* dependent. However, as we describe below, the credit is phased-out for taxpayers with moderately high AGI.

Example 7-22

Courtney paid $2,000 of tuition for Ellen to attend the University of Missouri–Kansas City during the summer at the end of her freshman year. What is the maximum Hope credit (before phase-out) Courtney may claim for these expenses?

Answer: $1,600. Because the $2,000 tuition is an eligible expense Courtney may claim a maximum Hope credit before phase-out of $1,600 [($1,200 × 100%) + ($2,000 − $1,200) x 50%].

The lifetime learning credit applies to the cost of any course of instruction to acquire or improve a taxpayer's job skills. This credit can be used for tuition costs beyond the first two years of postsecondary education, including professional or graduate school tuition. The credit is equal to 20 percent of eligible expenses up to an annual maximum of $10,000 of eligible expenses (maximum of $2,000). In contrast to the Hope credit, the lifetime learning credit limit applies to the taxpayer (a married couple filing a joint return may claim only $2,000 of lifetime learning credit). Thus, a taxpayer with multiple eligible dependents can claim a maximum lifetime learning credit of only $2,000 in 2009.

Example 7-23

Courtney paid $1,550 to attend motivation seminars to help her improve her job skills (see Example 6-26). Courtney could elect to claim the lifetime learning credit for these expenses instead of deducting them as miscellaneous itemized deductions. If Courtney decided to claim a credit for these expenditures, what would be her maximum lifetime learning credit (before phase-out)?

Answer: $310 ($1,550 × 20%)

The sum of a taxpayer's Hope scholarship credit and lifetime learning credit for the year is subject to phase-out based on the taxpayer's AGI. For 2009, these credits are phased-out prorata for taxpayers with modified AGI between $50,000 to $60,000 ($100,000 – 120,000 for married taxpayers filing jointly).[33]

---

[32]§25A. Generally, eligible institutions participate in the federal student loan program. While tuition and fees qualify for these credits, the cost of books generally does not. Qualified tuition and fees must be reduced by scholarships received to pay for these expenses or other amounts received as reimbursements for the expenses (employer-sponsored reimbursement plans, Educational IRAs, 529 plans, and the like). The credit does not apply to the cost of room and board or other personal expenses.

[33]Modified AGI is AGI without certain foreign income exclusions.

Example 7-24

In Example 7-22 we determined that Courtney was eligible for a maximum Hope credit of $1,600 and in Example 7-23 we learned that Courtney was eligible for a maximum lifetime learning credit of $310 (before phase-out). How much Hope scholarship credit and lifetime learning credit is Courtney allowed to report on her 2009 tax return (how much may she claim after phase-out)?

Answer: $0. Because Courtney's AGI of $162,000 exceeds the head of household limit of $60,000, her entire credit is phased-out. That is, *she is not allowed to claim any* Hope scholarship credit or life-time learning credit. The same AGI limitation applies to both credits.

What if: How much Hope scholarship credit and lifetime learning credit would Courtney have been allowed to claim after the phase-out if her AGI were only $53,000?

Answer: $1,085, computed as follows:

Description	Amount	Explanation
(1) Hope scholarship and lifetime learning credit before phase-out	$ 1,910	Examples 7-22, and 7-23 ($1,600 Hope credit + 310 lifetime learning).
(2) AGI	53,000	
(3) Phase-out threshold	50,000	
(4) Excess AGI	3,000	(2) − (3).
(5) Phase-out range for taxpayer filing as Head of Household	10,000	$60,000 − 50,000.
(6) Phase-out percentage	30%	(4)/(5).
(7) Phase-out amount	573	(1) × (6).
Hope scholarship credit and lifetime learning credit after phase-out	**$ 1,337**	(1) − (7).

For expenses that qualify for both the Hope and lifetime learning credits (freshman or sophomore tuition and fees), taxpayers may choose which credit to use, but they may not claim both credits for the same expenditure or for the same student. In addition, taxpayers may choose to *either* (1) deduct qualifying education expenses of an individual as *for* AGI deductions (see discussion of this *for* AGI deduction in Chapter 6) or claim educational credits for the individual's expenses. However, if a taxpayer claims *any* educational credits for an individual's educational expenditures, the taxpayer may not claim *any for* AGI deduction for that individual's qualifying expenditures (and vice versa).[34]

Example 7-25

What if: Assume Courtney paid $3,000 of tuition for Ellen to attend the University of Missouri–Kansas City during the summer at the end of her freshman year. Further assume that Courtney's AGI is $45,000, so her education credits are not subject to phase-out. Courtney would be allowed to claim the maximum Hope credit of $1,800 on the first $2,400 of the educational expenditures. Assuming Courtney used $2,400 of the educational expenses to claim the maximum Hope credit, would she be allowed to deduct the remaining $600 of tuition costs ($3,000 total expenses − $2,400 maximum Hope credit expenses) as a *for* AGI deduction?

Answer: No. If Courtney claims any Hope credit for Ellen's expenditures, she is not allowed to deduct any *for* AGI deduction for Ellen's expenditures (even the expenses not used in computing the Hope credit).

(*continued on page 7-29...*)

[34]§222(c)(2)(A).

What if: Assume that both Ellen and Deron were in their first year of college, and that Courtney paid tuition for both Ellen and Deron. Further assume that Courtney's AGI is below the phase-out threshold. Is Courtney allowed to claim a Hope credit for Ellen's expenses and claim a *for* AGI educational expense deduction for Deron's expenses?

Answer: Yes. Courtney may claim a Hope credit or a deduction for Ellen's expenses, and she may claim a Hope credit or a deduction for Deron's expenses.

Refundable Personal Credits

Several personal credits are refundable, the most common of which is the **earned income credit.**

Earned Income Credit The earned income credit is a **refundable credit** that is designed to help offset the effect of employment taxes on compensation paid to low-income taxpayers and to encourage lower-income taxpayers to seek employment. Because it is refundable (if the credit exceeds the tax after considering nonrefundable credits the taxpayer receives a refund for the excess), it is sometimes referred to as a *negative income tax.* The credit is available for qualified individuals who have earned income for the year.[35] Qualified individuals generally include (1) any individual who has at least one qualifying child (same definition of qualifying child for dependent purposes—see Chapter 4) or (2) any individual who does not have a qualifying child for the taxable year, but who lives in the United States for more than half the year, is at least 25 years old but younger than 65 years old at the end of the year, and is not a dependent of another taxpayer. Earned income includes wages, salaries, tips, and other employee compensation included in gross income and net earnings from self-employment.

The amount of the credit depends on the taxpayer's filing status, the number of the taxpayer's qualifying children who live in the home for more than half of the year, and the amount of the taxpayer's earned income. To be eligible for the credit, married taxpayers must file a joint tax return. The credit is computed by multiplying the appropriate credit percentage times the taxpayer's earned income up to a maximum amount. The credit percentage depends upon the number of qualifying children in the home and is subject to a phase-out based upon AGI (or earned income if greater). The earned income credit begins to phase-out for taxpayers with earned income (or AGI if greater) over a certain amount, and for higher levels of earned income or AGI it is completely phased-out. As summarized in Exhibit 7-9, the earned income credit increases as taxpayers receive earned income up to the maximum amount of earned income eligible for the credit. Finally, as taxpayers earn more income, the credit begins to phase-out and is completely eliminated once taxpayers' earned income reaches established levels.

Example 7-26

Courtney's earned income for the year is $140,800 and her AGI is $162,000. Deron and Ellen both qualify as Courtney's qualifying children. What amount of earned income credit is Courtney entitled to claim on her 2009 tax return?

Answer: $0. Courtney's AGI (which is greater than her earned income) exceeds the $40,295 limit for unmarried taxpayers with two or more qualifying children. Consequently, Courtney is not allowed to claim any earned income credit.

What if: Assume that Courtney's only source of income for the year was $30,000 in salary. Also assume Courtney's AGI for the year was also $30,000. What would be Courtney's earned income credit in these circumstances?

(continued on page 7-30...)

[35]§32.

EXHIBIT 7-9 **2009 Earned Income Credit Table**

Qualifying children	(1) Maximum earned income eligible for credit	(2) Credit %	(3) Maximum credit (1) × (2)	(4) Credit phase-out for AGI (or earned income if greater) over this amount	(5) Phase-out percentage	No credit when AGI (or earned income if greater) equals or exceeds this amount (4) + [(3)/(5)]
			Married taxpayers filing joint returns			
0	$ 5,970	7.65%	$ 457	$ 10,600	7.65%	$16,570
1	8,950	34%	3,043	19,550	15.98%	38,593
2+	12,570	40%	5,028	19,550	21.06%	43,425
			All taxpayers *except* married taxpayers filing joint returns			
0	$ 5,970	7.65%	$ 457	$ 7,470	7.65%	$13,440
1	8,950	34%	3,043	16,420	15.98%	35,463
2+	12,570	40%	5,028	16,420	21.06%	40,295

(*continued from page 7-29...*)
Answer: $1,639, computed as follows

Description	Amount	Explanation
(1) Earned income	$30,000	
(2) Maximum earned income eligible for earned income credit for taxpayers filing as head of household with two qualifying children	12,570	Exhibit 7-9.
(3) Earned income eligible for credit	12,570	Lesser of (1) and (2).
(4) Earned income credit percentage for taxpayer with two qualifying children	40%	
(5) Earned income credit before phase-out	$ 5,028	(3) × (4).
(6) Phase-out threshold begins at this level of AGI (or earned income if greater)	$16,420	See Exhibit 7-9 for head of household filing status and two qualifying children.
(7) AGI in excess of phase-out threshold	13,580	(1) − (6).
(8) Phase-out percentage	21.06%	See Exhibit 7-9.
(9) Credit phase-out amount	2,860	(7) × (8).
Earned income credit after phase-out	**$ 2,168**	(5) − (9).

Other Refundable Personal Credits   Other refundable personal tax credits include a portion of the child tax credit (discussed above), excess FICA withholdings (see discussion above under FICA taxes), and taxes withheld on wages and estimated tax payments. We address withholdings and estimated taxes below when we discuss tax prepayments.

Business Tax Credits

Business tax credits are designed to provide incentives for taxpayers to hire certain types of individuals or to participate in certain business activities. For example, Congress provides the employment tax credit to encourage business to hire certain unemployed individuals, and it provides the research and development credit to encourage businesses to expend funds to develop new technology. Business tax credits are *nonrefundable* credits. However, when business credits other than the foreign tax credit (discussed below), exceed the taxpayer's gross tax for the year, the credits are carried *back* one year and forward 20 years to use in years when the taxpayer has sufficient gross tax liability to use the credits.

Why discuss business credits in an individual tax chapter? We discuss business credits here because self-employed individuals may qualify for these credits. Also, individuals may be allocated business credits from flow-through entities (partnerships, LLCs, and S corporations). Finally, individuals working as employees overseas or receiving dividends from investments in foreign securities may qualify for the foreign tax credit.

Foreign Tax Credit   U.S. citizens must pay U.S. tax on their worldwide income. However, when they generate some or all of their income in other countries, they generally are required to pay income taxes to the foreign country where they earned their income. Without some form of tax relief, taxpayers earning income overseas would be double-taxed on this income. When taxpayers pay income taxes to foreign countries, for U.S. tax purposes, they may treat the payment in one of three ways: (1) as we discussed in Chapter 5 when we introduced the foreign earned income exclusion, taxpayers may exclude the foreign earned income from U.S. taxation (in which case they would *not* deduct or receive a credit for any foreign taxes paid); (2) taxpayers may include the foreign income in their gross income and deduct the foreign taxes paid as itemized deductions; or (3) taxpayers may include foreign income in gross income and claim a foreign tax credit for the foreign taxes paid. Here, we discuss the foreign tax credit.

The foreign tax credit helps reduce the double tax taxpayers may pay when they pay income taxes on foreign earned income to the United States and to foreign countries. Taxpayers are allowed to claim a foreign tax credit, against their U.S. tax liability, for the income taxes they pay to foreign countries.[36] In certain situations, taxpayers may not be able to claim the full amount of foreign tax paid as a credit. This restriction may apply when the taxpayer's effective foreign tax rate is higher than the effective U.S. tax rate on the foreign earnings. Taxpayers generally benefit from claiming credits rather than deductions for foreign taxes paid because credits reduce their liabilities dollar for dollar. However, in circumstances when the foreign tax credit is restricted (see above), taxpayers may benefit by claiming deductions for the taxes paid instead of credits.

As we discussed above, the foreign tax credit may be limited in circumstances where a taxpayer's effective foreign tax rate exceeds her U.S. tax rate. Further, the foreign tax credit offsets an individual's tax liability *after* all nonrefundable credits *except* for the adoption credit and the child tax credit.[37] As a nonrefundable credit, it may only reduce the taxpayer's tax liability to zero. When the use of a foreign tax credit is limited, taxpayers may carry back their unused credits one year and carry forward the credits up to 10 years.

Tax Credit Summary

Exhibit 7-10 identifies several tax credits and for each credit identifies the credit type, notes the IRC section allowing the credit, and describes the credit.

Credit Application Sequence

As we've discussed, credits are applied against a taxpayer's gross tax. However, we still must describe what happens when the taxpayer's allowable credits exceed the

[36]§904.

[37]The foreign tax credit also offsets an individual's liability after the saver's credit. We discuss the saver's credit in Chapter 13.

EXHIBIT 7-10   **Summary of Selected Tax Credits**

Credit	Type of Credit	IRC	Description
Dependent care credit	Nonrefundable personal	§21	Credit for taxpayers who pay dependent care expenses due to their employment activities.
Credit for elderly and disabled	Nonrefundable personal	§22	Credit for elderly low-income taxpayers who retired because of a disability.
Adoption expense credit	Nonrefundable personal	§23	Credit for qualified adoption-related expenses.
Child tax credit	Nonrefundable and refundable personal	§24	Credit for providing home for dependent children under the age of 17.
Hope scholarship credit	Nonrefundable personal	§25A	Credit for higher education expenses.
Lifetime learning credit	Nonrefundable personal	§25A	Credit for higher education expenses for the first two years of postsecondary education only.
Saver's credit	Nonrefundable personal	§25B	Credit for contributing to qualified retirement plans. See Chapter 13 for details.
Earned income credit	Refundable personal	§32	Credit to encourage low-income taxpayers to work.
Credit for increasing research activities	Business	§41	Credit to encourage research and development.
Employer-provided child care credit	Business	§45F	Credit for providing child care for employees.
Rehabilitation credit	Business	§47	Credit for expenditures to renovate or restore older business buildings.
Energy credit	Business	§48	Credit for businesses that invest in energy conservation measures.
Work opportunity credit	Business	§51	Credit for hiring certain economically disadvantaged individuals.
Welfare to work credit	Business	§51A	Credit for hiring those on welfare.
Foreign tax credit	Hybrid business and personal	§904	Credit to reduce effects of double taxation of foreign income.

taxpayer's gross tax. To set up this discussion, it is important to understand that non-refundable personal credits and business credits may be used to reduce a taxpayer's gross tax to zero, but not below zero.[38] In contrast, by definition, a refundable credit may reduce a taxpayer's gross tax below zero. This excess refundable credit generates a tax refund for the taxpayer.

When a nonrefundable personal credit exceeds the taxpayer's gross tax, it reduces the gross tax to zero, but the excess credit (credit in excess of the taxpayer's gross tax) disappears. That is, the taxpayer may *not* carry over any excess nonrefundable personal credits to use in other years. However, when a business credit or foreign tax credit exceeds the gross tax, it reduces the taxpayer's gross tax to zero, but the excess credit may be carried forward or back to be used in other years when the taxpayer has sufficient gross tax to use the credit (subject to certain time restrictions discussed above).

---

[38]In general, nonrefundable personal credits can offset a taxpayer's regular tax and AMT (§26). The limitation on business credits is more complex. We limit our discussion here to basic concepts. See §38(c) for the detailed limitations.

EXHIBIT 7-11   **Credit Application**

Credit Type	Order Applied	Excess Credit
Nonrefundable personal	First	Lost
Business	Second	Carryover
Refundable personal	Last	Refunded

Because the tax treatment of excess credits depends on the type of credit, it is important to identify the sequence in which taxpayers apply the credits when they have more than one type of credit for the year. When taxpayers have multiple credit types in the same year, they apply the credits against their gross tax in the following order: (1) nonrefundable personal credits, (2) business credits, and (3) refundable credits. This sequence maximizes the chances that taxpayers will receive full benefit for their tax credits.

Because, as we discuss above, the foreign tax credit is a hybrid credit subject to a unique set of application rules, we exclude it from our general discussion on applying credits. Exhibit 7-11 summarizes the order in which the credits are applied against gross tax and indicates the tax treatment of any excess credits.

Example 7-27

What if: As we describe in Example 7-2, Gram's gross tax liability is $569. For illustrative purposes, let's *assume* that Gram is entitled to an $800 nonrefundable personal tax credit, a $700 business tax credit, and a $600 refundable personal tax credit. What is the amount of Gram's refund or taxes due?

Answer: $600 refund. Gram would apply these credits as follows:

Description	Amount	Treatment of excess credit
Gross tax liability	$ 569	Example 7-2.
(1) Nonrefundable personal credits	(569)	$231 ($800 − 569) excess credit expires unused.
(2) Business credits	0	$700 carried back one year or forward 20 years (10 years for foreign tax credit).
Refundable personal credits	(600)	**Generates $600 tax refund to Gram.**

TAXPAYER PREPAYMENTS AND FILING REQUIREMENTS

L05

Even after determining their tax liabilities, taxpayers must still file a tax return and pay any additional tax due or receive a refund. When taxpayers don't pay enough taxes during the year or when they are late filing their tax return or late paying their taxes due, they may be subject to certain penalties.

Prepayments

The income tax must be paid on a *pay-as-you-go* basis. This means that the tax must be prepaid via **withholding** from salary or through periodic **estimated tax payments** during the tax year. Employees pay tax through withholding, and self-employed taxpayers generally pay taxes through estimated tax payments. Employers are required to withhold taxes from an employee's wages based upon the employee's marital status, exemptions, and estimated annual pay. Wages include both cash and noncash remuneration for services, and employers remit withholdings to the government on behalf of employees. At the end of the year employers report the amounts withheld to each employee via Form W-2. Estimated tax payments are required only if withholdings are insufficient to meet the taxpayer's tax liability. For calendar-year taxpayers, estimated tax payments are due on April 15, June 15, and September 15 of the current year and January 15 of the following year.

Example 7-28	

Courtney's gross tax liability for the year including federal income tax, alternative minimum tax, and self-employment taxes is $24,507 (see Exhibit 7-5). However, because she had only $21,569 withheld from her paycheck by EWD, she underpaid $2,938 for the year ($24,507 − $21,569). If she had been aware that her withholding would be insufficient, she could have increased her withholding at any time during the year (even in her December paycheck) or made estimated tax payments of $735 on April 15, June 15, and September 15 of 2009 and January 15, 2010 ($2,938/4).

What if: If Courtney was self-employed (instead of employed by EWD) and thus had no tax withholdings by an employer, she would be *required* to pay quarterly estimated tax payments. In this scenario, she would need to pay $6,127 ($24,507/4 = $6,127) by April 15, June 15, and September 15 of 2009 and $6,126 by January 15 of 2010 to cover her gross tax liability of $24,507.

Underpayment Penalties   When taxpayers like Courtney fall behind on their tax prepayments, they may be subject to an **underpayment penalty.**[39] Taxpayers with unpredictable income streams may be particularly susceptible to this penalty because it is difficult for them to accurately estimate their tax liability for the year. To help taxpayers who may not be able to predict their earnings for the year and to provide some margin of error for those who can, the tax laws provide some **safe-harbor provisions.** Under these provisions taxpayers can avoid underpayment penalties if their withholdings and estimated tax payments equal or exceed one of the following two safe harbors: (1) 90 percent of their *current tax liability* or (2) 100 percent of their *previous year tax liability* (110 percent for individuals with AGI greater than $150,000).

These two safe harbors determine on a quarterly basis the minimum tax prepayments that a taxpayer must have made to avoid the underpayment penalty. The first safe harbor requires that a taxpayer must have paid at least 22.5 percent (90 percent/4 = 22.5 percent) of the *current* year liability via withholdings or estimated tax payments by April 15 to avoid the underpayment penalty for the first quarter. Similarly by June 15, September 15, and January 15, the taxpayer must have paid 45 percent (22.5 percent × 2), 67.5 percent (22.5 percent × 3), and 90 percent (22.5 percent × 4), respectively, of the current year liability via withholding or estimated tax payments to avoid the underpayment penalty in the second, third, and fourth quarters.[40] In determining taxpayers' prepayments for a quarter, tax withholdings are generally treated as though they are withheld evenly through the year. In contrast, estimated tax payments are credited to the taxpayer's account when they are remitted.

Example 7-29	

Because all of Courtney's prepayments were made through withholding by EWD, the payments are treated as though they were made evenly throughout the year. What are Courtney's actual and required withholdings under the 90 percent safe-harbor provision throughout the year?

(continued on page 7-35...)

---

[39]§6654

[40]As an alternative method of estimating safe harbor, (1) taxpayers can compute 90 percent of the current liability using the seasonal method. This method allows the taxpayer to estimate 90 percent of their current tax liability by annualizing their taxable income earned through the month prior to the payment date (e.g., through March for April 15, May for June 15, and August for September 15). Taxpayers with uneven taxable income throughout the year with smaller taxable income earlier in the year benefit from this method.

Answer: See the following table:

Dates	(1) Actual Withholding	(2) Required Withholding	(1) − (2) Over (Under) Withheld
April 15, 2009	$5,392 ($21,569 × .25)	$5,514 ($24,507 × .9 × .25)	($122)
June 15, 2009	10,785 ($21,569 × .50)	11,028 ($24,507 × .9 × .50)	(243)
September 15, 2009	16,177 ($21,569 × .75)	16,542 ($24,507 × .9 × .75)	(365)
January 15, 2010	$21,569	22,056 ($24,507 × .9 × 1)	(487)

It looks like Courtney is underwithheld in each quarter.

The second safe harbor requires that by April 15, June 15, September 15, and January 15, the taxpayer must have paid 25 percent, 50 percent (25 percent × 2), 75 percent (25 percent × 3), and 100 percent (25 percent × 4), respectively, of the *previous* year tax liability via withholding or estimated tax payments to avoid the underpayment penalty in the first, second, third, and fourth quarters.

If the taxpayer does not satisfy either of the safe harbor provisions, the taxpayer can compute the underpayment penalty owed using Form 2210. The underpayment penalty is determined by multiplying the **federal short-term interest rate** plus 3 percentage points by the amount of tax underpayment per quarter. For purposes of this computation, the quarterly tax underpayment is the difference between the taxpayer's quarterly withholding and estimated tax payments and the required minimum tax payment under the first or second safe harbor (whichever is less). If the taxpayer does not complete the Form 2210 and remit the underpayment penalty with the taxpayer's tax return, the IRS will compute and assess the penalty for the taxpayer.

Example 7-30

In the previous example, we discovered that Courtney was underwithheld in each quarter based on the first (90 percent of current year) safe-harbor provision. Assuming Courtney was underwithheld by even more under the second (100 percent of prior year) safe-harbor provision, she is required to pay an underpayment penalty based on the underpayments determined using the first safe harbor. Assuming the federal short-term rate is 5 percent, what is Courtney's underpayment penalty for 2009?

Answer: $25, computed as follows:

Description	First Quarter	Second Quarter	Third Quarter	Fourth Quarter
Underpayment	$ 122	$243	$365	$ 487
Times: federal rate + 3% (5% + 3%)	× 8%	× 8%	× 8%	× 8%
	$ 10	$ 19	$ 29	$ 39
Times one quarter of a year[41]	× 25%	× 25%	× 25%	× 25%
Underpayment penalty per quarter	$ 3	$ 5	$ 7	$ 10

That's a lot of work to figure out a $25 penalty ($3 + $5 + $7 + $10 = $25).

---

[41]Form 2210 actually computes the penalty per quarter based on the number of days in the quarter divided by the number of days in the year. For simplicity, we assume this ratio is 1/4 per quarter.

As a matter of administrative convenience, taxpayers who either (1) had no tax liability in the previous year or (2) whose tax payable after subtracting their withholding amounts (but not estimated payments) is less than $1,000 are not subject to underpayment penalties.

Example 7-31

Gram's gross tax liability for the year is $569 (Example 7-2), but she did not have any taxes withheld during the year, and she did not make any estimated tax payments. What is Gram's underpayment penalty?

Answer: $0. Because Gram's $569 tax payable after subtracting her withholding amounts ($569 tax − $0 withholding) is less than $1,000, she is not subject to an underpayment penalty.

THE KEY FACTS

Taxpayer Prepayments and Underpayment Penalties

▪ Taxpayers prepay their tax via withholding from salary or through periodic estimated tax payments during the tax year.

▪ Estimated tax payments are required only if withholdings are insufficient to meet the taxpayer's tax liability.

▪ For calendar-year taxpayers, estimated tax payments are due on April 15, June 15, and September 15 of the current year and January 15 of the following year.

▪ Taxpayers can avoid an underpayment penalty if their withholdings and estimated tax payments equal or exceed one of two safe harbors.

▪ The underpayment penalty is determined by multiplying the federal short-term interest rate plus 3 percentage points by the amount of tax underpayment per quarter.

Filing Requirements

Individual taxpayers are required to file a tax return only if their *gross income* exceeds certain thresholds, which vary based on the taxpayer's filing status and age. However, a taxpayer may prefer to file a tax return even when she is not required to do so. For example, a taxpayer with gross income less than the threshold may want to file a tax return to receive a refund of income taxes withheld. In general, the thresholds are simply the standard deduction amount plus personal and dependency exemption amounts for different filing statuses. Individual tax returns are due on April 15 for calendar-year individuals (the fifteenth day of the fourth month following year-end). If the due date falls on a Saturday, Sunday, or holiday, it is automatically extended to the next day that is not a Saturday, Sunday, or holiday. Taxpayers unable to file a tax return by the original due date can request (by that same deadline) a six-month extension to file, which is granted automatically by the IRS. The extension gives the taxpayer additional time to file the tax return, but does *not* extend the due date for paying the tax.

Late Filing Penalty   The tax law imposes a penalty on taxpayers that do not file a tax return by the required date (the original due date plus extension).[42] The penalty equals 5 percent of the amount of tax owed for each month (or fraction thereof) that the tax return is late, with a maximum penalty of 25 percent. For fraudulent failure to file, the penalty is 15 percent of the amount of tax owed per month with a maximum penalty of 75 percent. If the taxpayer owes no tax as of the due date of the tax return (plus extension), the tax law does not impose a **late filing penalty.**

Late Payment Penalty   An extension allows the taxpayer to delay filing a tax return but does *not* extend the due date for tax payments. If a taxpayer fails to pay the entire balance of tax owed by the original due date of the tax return, the tax law imposes a **late payment penalty** from the due date of the return until the taxpayer pays the tax.[43] The late payment penalty equals .5 percent of the amount of tax owed for each month (or fraction thereof) that the tax is not paid. The *combined* maximum penalty that may be imposed for late payment and late filing

---

[42]§6651

[43]§6651. As we discussed in Chapter 2, the tax law also assesses interest on any tax underpayments until the tax is paid (§6601).

(nonfradulent) is 5 percent per month (25 percent in total). For late payment and filing due to fraud, the combined maximum penalty for late payment and late filing is 15 percent per month (75 percent in total).

Example 7-32

Courtney filed her tax return on April 10 and included a check with the return for $2,963 made payable to the United States Treasury. The $2,963 consisted of her underpaid tax liability of $2,938 (Example 7-28) and her $25 underpayment penalty (Example 7-30).

What if: If Courtney had waited until May 1 to file her return and pay her taxes, what late filing and late payment penalties would she owe?

Answer: Her combined *late filing penalty* and *late payment penalty* would be $147 ($2,938 late payment × 5 percent × 1 month or portion thereof—the combined penalty is limited to 5 percent per month).

TAX SUMMARY

Courtney's and Gram's net taxes due (sorry, no refunds this year) including an underpayment penalty for Courtney are provided in Exhibits 7-12 and 7-14, respectively. Exhibit 7-13 illustrates how this information would be presented on Courtney's tax return by providing Courtney's Form 1040, page 2.

EXHIBIT 7-12 **Courtney's Net Tax Payable**

Description	Amount	Reference
(1) Regular federal income tax	$22,597	Example 7-3.
(2) Alternative minimum tax	1,428	Example 7-12.
(3) Self-employment tax	482	Example 7-17.
(4) Gross tax	$24,507	(1) + (2) + (3).
(5) Tax credits	0	Examples 7-20, 7-24, and 7-26.
(6) Prepayments	(21,569)	Example 7-28.
(7) Underpayment penalties	25	Example 7-30.
Tax and penalties due with tax return	$ 2,963	

Taxes in the Real World *Late Payments and Filing Penalties*

Late payment and late filing penalties seem to be all the rage with the rich and famous. In Chapter 2, we mentioned the escapades of *Survivor*'s Richard Hatch. However, Mr. Hatch is not the only person of fame (big screen, little screen, or musical) that has had to pay significant tax penalties. One of the most famous cases involved country legend Willie Nelson.

In 1990, the IRS sent Nelson a bill for over $16 million in back taxes and penalties for his involvement in an "aggressive" tax shelter. To raise money to pay the taxes and interest, Nelson released the album entitled, "The IRS Tapes—Who'll Buy My Memories?" More recently, he has turned his tax "lemons" into lemonade by appearing in a commercial for H&R Block.

EXHIBIT 7-13   Courtney's Net Tax Payable (as presented on her Form 1040, page 2)

Form 1040 (2008)   Page **2**

Tax and Credits	38	Amount from line 37 (adjusted gross income)	38	162,000
	39a	Check if: { ☐ **You** were born before January 2, 1944, ☐ Blind. / ☐ **Spouse** was born before January 2, 1944, ☐ Blind. } **Total boxes** checked ► 39a		
	b	If your spouse itemizes on a separate return or you were a dual-status alien, see page 34 and check here ► 39b ☐		
	c	Check if standard deduction includes real estate taxes or disaster loss (see page 34) ► 39c ☐		
Standard Deduction for—	40	**Itemized deductions** (from Schedule A) or your **standard deduction** (see left margin) .	40	39,793
• People who checked any box on line 39a, 39b, or 39c **or** who can be claimed as a dependent, see page 34.	41	Subtract line 40 from line 38	41	122,207
	42	If line 38 is over $119,975, or you provided housing to a Midwestern displaced individual, see page 36. Otherwise, multiply $3,500 by the total number of exemptions claimed on line 6d .	42	10,950
	43	**Taxable income.** Subtract line 42 from line 41. If line 42 is more than line 41, enter -0-	43	111,257
	44	**Tax** (see page 36). Check if any tax is from: **a** ☐ Form(s) 8814 **b** ☐ Form 4972 .	44	22,597
• All others:	45	**Alternative minimum tax** (see page 39). Attach Form 6251	45	1,428
Single or Married filing separately, $5,450	46	Add lines 44 and 45 . . . . ►	46	24,025
	47	Foreign tax credit. Attach Form 1116 if required	47	
Married filing jointly or Qualifying widow(er), $10,900	48	Credit for child and dependent care expenses. Attach Form 2441	48	
	49	Credit for the elderly or the disabled. Attach Schedule R . .	49	
	50	Education credits. Attach Form 8863	50	
	51	Retirement savings contributions credit. Attach Form 8880 .	51	
	52	Child tax credit (see page 42). Attach Form 8901 if required .	52	
Head of household, $8,000	53	Credits from Form: **a** ☐ 8396 **b** ☐ 8839 **c** ☐ 5695	53	
	54	Other credits from Form: **a** ☐ 3800 **b** ☐ 8801 **c** ☐ ___	54	
	55	Add lines 47 through 54. These are your **total credits**	55	
	56	Subtract line 55 from line 46. If line 55 is more than line 46, enter -0- . . . . ►	56	24,025
Other Taxes	57	Self-employment tax. Attach Schedule SE	57	482
	58	Unreported social security and Medicare tax from Form: **a** ☐ 4137 **b** ☐ 8919	58	
	59	Additional tax on IRAs, other qualified retirement plans, etc. Attach Form 5329 if required . .	59	
	60	Additional taxes: **a** ☐ AEIC payments **b** ☐ Household employment taxes. Attach Schedule H	60	
	61	Add lines 56 through 60. This is your **total tax** . . . . ►	61	24,507
Payments	62	Federal income tax withheld from Forms W-2 and 1099 . .	62	21,569
	63	2008 estimated tax payments and amount applied from 2007 return	63	
If you have a qualifying child, attach Schedule EIC.	64a	**Earned income credit (EIC)**	64a	
	b	Nontaxable combat pay election 64b		
	65	Excess social security and tier 1 RRTA tax withheld (see page 61)	65	
	66	Additional child tax credit. Attach Form 8812	66	
	67	Amount paid with request for extension to file (see page 61)	67	
	68	Credits from Form: **a** ☐ 2439 **b** ☐ 4136 **c** ☐ 8801 **d** ☐ 8885	68	
	69	First-time homebuyer credit. Attach Form 5405	69	
	70	Recovery rebate credit (see worksheet on pages 62 and 63) .	70	
	71	Add lines 62 through 70. These are your **total payments** . . . . ►	71	21,569
Refund	72	If line 71 is more than line 61, subtract line 61 from line 71. This is the amount you **overpaid**	72	
Direct deposit? See page 63 and fill in 73b, 73c, and 73d, or Form 8888.	73a	Amount of line 72 you want **refunded to you.** If Form 8888 is attached, check here ► ☐	73a	
	► b	Routing number		► **c** Type: ☐ Checking ☐ Savings
	► d	Account number		
	74	Amount of line 72 you want **applied to your 2009 estimated tax** ► 74		
Amount You Owe	75	**Amount you owe.** Subtract line 71 from line 61. For details on how to pay, see page 65 ►	75	2,963
	76	Estimated tax penalty (see page 65) 76	25	

Third Party Designee	Do you want to allow another person to discuss this return with the IRS (see page 66)? ☐ **Yes.** Complete the following. ☐ **No**
	Designee's name ►	Phone no. ► ( )	Personal identification number (PIN) ►

Sign Here
Joint return? See page 15.
Keep a copy for your records.

Under penalties of perjury, I declare that I have examined this return and accompanying schedules and statements, and to the best of my knowledge and belief, they are true, correct, and complete. Declaration of preparer (other than taxpayer) is based on all information of which preparer has any knowledge.

Your signature	Date	Your occupation	Daytime phone number ( )
Spouse's signature. If a joint return, **both** must sign.	Date	Spouse's occupation	

Paid Preparer's Use Only

Preparer's signature ►		Date	Check if self-employed ☐	Preparer's SSN or PTIN
Firm's name (or yours if self-employed), address, and ZIP code ►			EIN	
			Phone no. ( )	

Form **1040** (2008)

✪ **Printed on recycled paper**

EXHIBIT 7-14   Gram's Tax Payable

Description	Amount	Reference
(1) Gross tax	$569	Example 7-2.
(2) Alternative minimum tax	0	
(3) Self-employment tax	0	
(4) Gross tax	$569	(1) + (2) + (3).
(5) Tax Credits	0	
(6) Prepayments	0	
(7) Penalties	0	
Tax due with return	$569	(4) − (5) − (6) − (7).

CONCLUSION

This chapter reviewed the process for determining an individual's gross and net tax liability. We discovered that taxpayers may be required to pay regular federal income tax, alternative minimum tax, and employment-related tax. Taxpayers are able to offset their gross tax liability dollar for dollar with various types of tax credits and by the amount of tax they prepay during the year. Taxpayers must pay additional taxes with their tax return or they may receive a refund when they file their tax return depending on their gross tax liability and their available tax credits and tax prepayments. The prior three chapters have covered the basic individual tax formula. The next three chapters (8–10) address issues relevant for taxpayers involved in business activities. In Chapters 11–14, we dig a little deeper into certain individual income taxation issues.

APPENDIX A — EXCERPT FROM SINGLE TAX TABLE

5,000

At least	But less than	Single	Married filing jointly *	Married filing separately	Head of a household
5,000	5,050	503	503	503	503
5,050	5,100	508	508	508	508
5,100	5,150	513	513	513	513
5,150	5,200	518	518	518	518
5,200	5,250	523	523	523	523
5,250	5,300	528	528	528	528
5,300	5,350	533	533	533	533
5,350	5,400	538	538	538	538
5,400	5,450	543	543	543	543
5,450	5,500	548	548	548	548
5,500	5,550	553	553	553	553
5,550	5,600	558	558	558	558
5,600	5,650	563	563	563	563
5,650	5,700	568	568	568	568
5,700	5,750	573	573	573	573
5,750	5,800	578	578	578	578
5,800	5,850	583	583	583	583
5,850	5,900	588	588	588	588
5,900	5,950	593	593	593	593
5,950	6,000	598	598	598	598

6,000

At least	But less than	Single	Married filing jointly *	Married filing separately	Head of a household
6,000	6,050	603	603	603	603
6,050	6,100	608	608	608	608
6,100	6,150	613	613	613	613
6,150	6,200	618	618	618	618
6,200	6,250	623	623	623	623
6,250	6,300	628	628	628	628
6,300	6,350	633	633	633	633
6,350	6,400	638	638	638	638
6,400	6,450	643	643	643	643
6,450	6,500	648	648	648	648
6,500	6,550	653	653	653	653
6,550	6,600	658	658	658	658
6,600	6,650	663	663	663	663
6,650	6,700	668	668	668	668
6,700	6,750	673	673	673	673
6,750	6,800	678	678	678	678
6,800	6,850	683	683	683	683
6,850	6,900	688	688	688	688
6,900	6,950	693	693	693	693
6,950	7,000	698	698	698	698

7,000

At least	But less than	Single	Married filing jointly *	Married filing separately	Head of a household
7,000	7,050	703	703	703	703
7,050	7,100	708	708	708	708
7,100	7,150	713	713	713	713
7,150	7,200	718	718	718	718
7,200	7,250	723	723	723	723
7,250	7,300	728	728	728	728
7,300	7,350	733	733	733	733
7,350	7,400	738	738	738	738
7,400	7,450	743	743	743	743
7,450	7,500	748	748	748	748
7,500	7,550	753	753	753	753
7,550	7,600	758	758	758	758
7,600	7,650	763	763	763	763
7,650	7,700	768	768	768	768
7,700	7,750	773	773	773	773
7,750	7,800	778	778	778	778
7,800	7,850	783	783	783	783
7,850	7,900	788	788	788	788
7,900	7,950	793	793	793	793
7,950	8,000	798	798	798	798

8,000

At least	But less than	Single	Married filing jointly *	Married filing separately	Head of a household
8,000	8,050	803	803	803	803
8,050	8,100	810	808	810	808
8,100	8,150	818	813	818	813
8,150	8,200	825	818	825	818
8,200	8,250	833	823	833	823
8,250	8,300	840	828	840	828
8,300	8,350	848	833	848	833
8,350	8,400	855	838	855	838
8,400	8,450	863	843	863	843
8,450	8,500	870	848	870	848
8,500	8,550	878	853	878	853
8,550	8,600	885	858	885	858
8,600	8,650	893	863	893	863
8,650	8,700	900	868	900	868
8,700	8,750	908	873	908	873
8,750	8,800	915	878	915	878
8,800	8,850	923	883	923	883
8,850	8,900	930	888	930	888
8,900	8,950	938	893	938	893
8,950	9,000	945	898	945	898

9,000

At least	But less than	Single	Married filing jointly *	Married filing separately	Head of a household
9,000	9,050	953	903	953	903
9,050	9,100	960	908	960	908
9,100	9,150	968	913	968	913
9,150	9,200	975	918	975	918
9,200	9,250	983	923	983	923
9,250	9,300	990	928	990	928
9,300	9,350	998	933	998	933
9,350	9,400	1,005	938	1,005	938
9,400	9,450	1,013	943	1,013	943
9,450	9,500	1,020	948	1,020	948
9,500	9,550	1,028	953	1,028	953
9,550	9,600	1,035	958	1,035	958
9,600	9,650	1,043	963	1,043	963
9,650	9,700	1,050	968	1,050	968
9,700	9,750	1,058	973	1,058	973
9,750	9,800	1,065	978	1,065	978
9,800	9,850	1,073	983	1,073	983
9,850	9,900	1,080	988	1,080	988
9,900	9,950	1,088	993	1,088	993
9,950	10,000	1,095	998	1,095	998

10,000

At least	But less than	Single	Married filing jointly *	Married filing separately	Head of a household
10,000	10,050	1,103	1,003	1,103	1,003
10,050	10,100	1,110	1,008	1,110	1,008
10,100	10,150	1,118	1,013	1,118	1,013
10,150	10,200	1,125	1,018	1,125	1,018
10,200	10,250	1,133	1,023	1,133	1,023
10,250	10,300	1,140	1,028	1,140	1,028
10,300	10,350	1,148	1,033	1,148	1,033
10,350	10,400	1,155	1,038	1,155	1,038
10,400	10,450	1,163	1,043	1,163	1,043
10,450	10,500	1,170	1,048	1,170	1,048
10,500	10,550	1,178	1,053	1,178	1,053
10,550	10,600	1,185	1,058	1,185	1,058
10,600	10,650	1,193	1,063	1,193	1,063
10,650	10,700	1,200	1,068	1,200	1,068
10,700	10,750	1,208	1,073	1,208	1,073
10,750	10,800	1,215	1,078	1,215	1,078
10,800	10,850	1,223	1,083	1,223	1,083
10,850	10,900	1,230	1,088	1,230	1,088
10,900	10,950	1,238	1,093	1,238	1,093
10,950	11,000	1,245	1,098	1,245	1,098

11,000

At least	But less than	Single	Married filing jointly *	Married filing separately	Head of a household
11,000	11,050	1,253	1,103	1,253	1,103
11,050	11,100	1,260	1,108	1,260	1,108
11,100	11,150	1,268	1,113	1,268	1,113
11,150	11,200	1,275	1,118	1,275	1,118
11,200	11,250	1,283	1,123	1,283	1,123
11,250	11,300	1,290	1,128	1,290	1,128
11,300	11,350	1,298	1,133	1,298	1,133
11,350	11,400	1,305	1,138	1,305	1,138
11,400	11,450	1,313	1,143	1,313	1,143
11,450	11,500	1,320	1,148	1,320	1,149
11,500	11,550	1,328	1,153	1,328	1,156
11,550	11,600	1,335	1,158	1,335	1,164
11,600	11,650	1,343	1,163	1,343	1,171
11,650	11,700	1,350	1,168	1,350	1,179
11,700	11,750	1,358	1,173	1,358	1,186
11,750	11,800	1,365	1,178	1,365	1,194
11,800	11,850	1,373	1,183	1,373	1,201
11,850	11,900	1,380	1,188	1,380	1,209
11,900	11,950	1,388	1,193	1,388	1,216
11,950	12,000	1,395	1,198	1,395	1,224

12,000

At least	But less than	Single	Married filing jointly *	Married filing separately	Head of a household
12,000	12,050	1,403	1,203	1,403	1,231
12,050	12,100	1,410	1,208	1,410	1,239
12,100	12,150	1,418	1,213	1,418	1,246
12,150	12,200	1,425	1,218	1,425	1,254
12,200	12,250	1,433	1,223	1,433	1,261
12,250	12,300	1,440	1,228	1,440	1,269
12,300	12,350	1,448	1,233	1,448	1,276
12,350	12,400	1,455	1,238	1,455	1,284
12,400	12,450	1,463	1,243	1,463	1,291
12,450	12,500	1,470	1,248	1,470	1,299
12,500	12,550	1,478	1,253	1,478	1,306
12,550	12,600	1,485	1,258	1,485	1,314
12,600	12,650	1,493	1,263	1,493	1,321
12,650	12,700	1,500	1,268	1,500	1,329
12,700	12,750	1,508	1,273	1,508	1,336
12,750	12,800	1,515	1,278	1,515	1,344
12,800	12,850	1,523	1,283	1,523	1,351
12,850	12,900	1,530	1,288	1,530	1,359
12,900	12,950	1,538	1,293	1,538	1,366
12,950	13,000	1,545	1,298	1,545	1,374

13,000

At least	But less than	Single	Married filing jointly *	Married filing separately	Head of a household
13,000	13,050	1,553	1,303	1,553	1,381
13,050	13,100	1,560	1,308	1,560	1,389
13,100	13,150	1,568	1,313	1,568	1,396
13,150	13,200	1,575	1,318	1,575	1,404
13,200	13,250	1,583	1,323	1,583	1,411
13,250	13,300	1,590	1,328	1,590	1,419
13,300	13,350	1,598	1,333	1,598	1,426
13,350	13,400	1,605	1,338	1,605	1,434
13,400	13,450	1,613	1,343	1,613	1,441
13,450	13,500	1,620	1,348	1,620	1,449
13,500	13,550	1,628	1,353	1,628	1,456
13,550	13,600	1,635	1,358	1,635	1,464
13,600	13,650	1,643	1,363	1,643	1,471
13,650	13,700	1,650	1,368	1,650	1,479
13,700	13,750	1,658	1,373	1,658	1,486
13,750	13,800	1,665	1,378	1,665	1,494
13,800	13,850	1,673	1,383	1,673	1,501
13,850	13,900	1,680	1,388	1,680	1,509
13,900	13,950	1,688	1,393	1,688	1,516
13,950	14,000	1,695	1,398	1,695	1,524

If line 43 (taxable income) is— And you are— Single / Married filing jointly * / Married filing separately / Head of a household — Your tax is—

* This column must also be used by a qualifying widow(er).

SUMMARY

Determine a taxpayer's regular tax liability and identify tax issues associated with the process.

- Individual income is taxed using progressive tax rate schedules with rates ranging from 10 percent to 35 percent.

- Marginal tax rates depend on filing status and amount of taxable income.

- Progressive tax rate schedules may lead to either a marriage penalty or a marriage benefit for married taxpayers.

- Long-term capital gains and qualifying dividends are taxed at either a 0 percent or 15 percent rate, depending on the amount of taxable income.

- Strategies to shift investment income from parents to children are limited by reducing the standard deduction for children and taxing investment income at the parents' marginal tax rate (the so-called kiddie-tax).

Compute a taxpayer's alternative minimum tax liability and describe the tax characteristics of taxpayers most likely to owe the alternative minimum tax.

- The AMT was designed to ensure that higher-income taxpayers pay some minimum level of income tax.

- The AMT base is broader than the regular income tax base. The AMT base is designed to more closely reflect economic income than is regular taxable income.

- The starting point for calculating AMT is regular taxable income. To compute AMTI, taxpayers add back items not deductible for AMT purposes such as personal exemptions, state income taxes, property taxes, and interest on home-equity loans not used to acquire or substantially improve the home. In some cases, taxpayers may subtract items not includible in AMTI and items deductible for AMT but not for regular tax purposes. Taxpayers then subtract the allowable AMT exemption to generate the AMT base. They then apply the AMT rates and compare the product (the tentative minimum tax) to their regular tax liability. They owe AMT if the tentative minimum tax exceeds the regular tax liability.

- The AMT exemption depends on the taxpayer's filing status and is subject to phase-out of 25 cents for each dollar of AMTI over the specific thresholds based on filing status.

- The AMT tax rates are 26 percent (up to $175,000 of AMT base) and 28 percent thereafter. However, long-term capital gains and qualifying dividends are subject to the same preferential rate they are taxed at for regular tax purposes.

- The amount of the AMT is the excess of the tentative minimum tax over the taxpayer's regular tax liability.

Calculate a taxpayer's employment and self-employment taxes payable and explain tax considerations relating to whether a taxpayer is considered to be an employee or a self-employed independent contractor.

- Employees' wages are subject to FICA tax. The Social Security component is 6.2 percent and the Medicare component is 1.45 percent. The Social Security tax applies to the first $106,800 of income in 2009. The wage base on the Medicare tax is unlimited.

- Self-employed taxpayers pay self-employment tax on their net self-employment income (92.65 percent of their net Schedule C income). They pay Social Security tax of 12.4 percent and Medicare tax of 2.9 percent on their net self-employment income. The Social Security tax applies to the first $106,800 of net Schedule C income in 2009. The base for the Medicare tax is unlimited.

- The decision of whether a worker should be treated as an independent contractor or as an employee for tax purposes is a subjective test based in large part on the extent of control the worker has over things such as the nature, timing, and location of work performed.

- Independent contractors are able to deduct ordinary and necessary business expenses as *for* AGI deductions. Employees incurring unreimbursed business expenses must deduct the items as miscellaneous itemized deductions subject to the 2 percent of AGI floor.

- Independent contractors may deduct one-half of their self-employment taxes paid during the year. Employees may not deduct their FICA taxes.

- Independent contractors are not eligible to receive benefits employers pay to employees such as health and life insurance and retirement savings.

- Independent contractors are required to pay self-employment tax, which is nearly double the amount they must pay in FICA taxes as employees. Further, independent contractors must pay estimated taxes on their income because the employer does not withhold taxes from the independent contractor's paychecks.

- Hiring independent contractors is generally less costly for employers than is hiring employees. Employers do not pay FICA taxes, withhold taxes, or provide fringe benefits for independent contractors.

LO4 Describe the different general types of tax credits, identify specific tax credits, and compute a taxpayer's allowable child tax credit, child and dependent care credit, earned income credit, Hope scholarship credit, and lifetime learning credit.

- Tax credits are generally classified into one of three categories, business, nonrefundable personal, or refundable personal credits.

- Personal tax credits are nonrefundable and provide tax relief to specified groups of individuals.

- The child tax credit is a $1,000 credit for low-income taxpayers who provide a home for dependent children under the age of 17.

- The child and dependent care credit is provided to help taxpayers pay the cost of providing care for their dependents to allow taxpayers to work or to look for work.

- The Hope scholarship credit provides a credit for a percentage of the costs of the first two years of a student's college education.

- The lifetime learning credit provides a credit for a percentage of the costs for instruction to acquire or improve a taxpayer's job skills.

- The two education credits are subject to a phase-out limitation for high-income taxpayers.

- Nonrefundable credits are first used to reduce a taxpayer's gross tax but cannot reduce the gross tax below zero. Any excess credit is lost unless it is allowed to be carried to a different tax year.

- The earned income credit is refundable but subject to a very complex calculation.

- Business credits reduce the tax after applying nonrefundable credits. Any credit in excess of the remaining tax is generally allowed to be carried over or back to be used in other years.

- Refundable credits are the last credit applied to the tax after applying nonrefundable and business credits. Any refundable credit in excess of the remaining tax is treated as an overpayment and refunded to the taxpayer.

LO5 Explain taxpayer filing and tax payment requirements and describe in general terms how to compute a taxpayer's underpayment, late filing, and late payment penalties.

- The income tax must be prepaid via withholding from salary or through periodic estimated tax payments during the tax year. Estimated tax payments are required only if withholdings are insufficient to meet the taxpayer's tax liability. For calendar-year taxpayers, estimated tax payments are due on April 15, June 15, and September 15 of the current year and January 15 of the following year.

- Taxpayers can avoid an underpayment penalty if their withholdings and estimated tax payments equal or exceed one of two safe harbors (90 percent of current year tax, 100 percent of previous year tax, or 110% if AGI exceeds $150,000). If the taxpayer does not satisfy either of the safe-harbor provisions, the underpayment penalty is determined by multiplying the federal short-term interest rate plus 3 percentage points by the amount of tax underpayment per quarter.

- Individual taxpayers are required to file a tax return only if their *gross income* exceeds certain thresholds, which vary based on the taxpayer's filing status, age, and gross income.
- Individual tax returns are due on April 15 for calendar-year individuals. Taxpayers unable to file a tax return by the original due date can request a six-month extension to file.
- The tax law imposes penalties on taxpayers that do not file a tax return (by the original due date plus extension) or pay the tax owed (by the original due date). The failure to file penalty equals 5 percent of the amount of tax owed for each month (or fraction thereof) that the tax return is late with a maximum penalty of 25 percent. The late payment penalty equals .5 percent of the amount of tax owed for each month (or fraction thereof) that the tax is not paid. The combined maximum penalty that may be imposed for late filing and late payment is 5 percent per month (25 percent in total). The late filing and late payment penalties are higher if fraud is involved.

KEY TERMS

alternative minimum tax (7-9)

alternative minimum tax adjustments (7-10)

alternative minimum tax base (AMT base) (7-10)

alternative minimum tax exemption (7-13)

alternative minimum tax system (7-9)

business tax credits (7-30)

child tax credits (7-23)

earned income credit (7-29)

employee (7-21)

estimated tax payments (7-33)

federal short-term interest rate (7-35)

FICA taxes (7-16)

independent contractor (7-21)

kiddie tax (7-7)

late filing penalty (7-36)

late payment penalty (7-36)

marginal tax rate (7-4)

marriage benefit (7-3)

marriage penalty (7-3)

Medicare tax (7-16)

minimum tax credit (7-14)

net earnings from self-employment (7-18)

net unearned income (7-7)

nonrefundable personal tax credits (7-23)

preferential tax rate (7-4)

preferentially taxed income (7-5)

refundable credits (7-29)

safe-harbor provisions (7-34)

Schedule C (7-18)

self-employment taxes (7-18)

Social Security tax (7-16)

tax bracket (7-2)

tax credits (7-23)

tax rate schedule (7-2)

tax tables (7-3)

tentative minimum tax (7-10)

underpayment penalty (7-34)

withholding (7-33)

DISCUSSION QUESTIONS

1. **(LO1)** What is a tax bracket? What is the relationship between filing status and the width of the tax brackets in the tax rate schedule?

2. **(LO1)** In 2009, for a taxpayer with $50,000 of taxable income, without doing any actual computations, which filing status do you expect to provide the lowest tax liability? Which filing status provides the highest tax liability?

3. **(LO1)** What is the tax marriage penalty and when does it apply? Under what circumstances would a couple experience a tax marriage benefit?

4. **(LO1)** Once they've computed their taxable income, how do taxpayers determine their regular tax liability? What additional steps must taxpayers take to compute their tax liability when they have preferentially taxed income?

5. **(LO1)** Are there circumstances in which preferentially taxed income (long-term capital gains and qualifying dividends) is taxed at the same rate as ordinary income? Explain.

 research

6. **(LO1)** Augustana received $10,000 of qualifying dividends this year. Under what circumstances would all $10,000 be taxed at the same rate? Under what circumstances might the entire $10,000 of income not be taxed at the same rate?

7. **(LO1)** What is the difference between earned and unearned income?

8. **(LO1)** How do the tax laws use the standard deduction to limit a parent's ability to shift unearned income to a child?

9. **(LO1)** Does the kiddie tax eliminate the tax benefits gained by a family when parents transfer income-producing assets to children? Explain.

10. **(LO1)** Does the kiddie tax apply to all children no matter their age? Explain.

11. **(LO1)** What is the kiddie tax and on whose tax return is the kiddie tax liability reported? Explain.

12. **(LO1)** Lauren is 17 years old. She reports earned income of $3,000 and unearned income of $2,000. Is it likely that she is subject to the kiddie tax? Explain.

13. **(LO2)** In very general terms, how is the alternative minimum tax system different from the regular income tax system? How is it similar?

14. **(LO2)** Describe, in general terms, why Congress implemented the AMT.

15. **(LO2)** In computing alternative minimum taxable income, why are taxpayers allowed to deduct the amount of their itemized deductions that were phased-out for regular tax purposes?

16. **(LO2)** Do taxpayers always add back the standard deduction when computing alternative minimum taxable income? Explain.

17. **(LO2)** The starting point for computing alternative minimum taxable income is regular taxable income. What are some of the plus adjustments, plus or minus adjustments, and minus adjustments to regular taxable income to compute alternative minimum taxable income?

18. **(LO2)** Describe what the AMT exemption is and who is and isn't allowed to deduct the exemption. How is it similar to the standard deduction and how is it dissimilar?

19. **(LO1, LO2)** How do the AMT tax rates compare to the regular income tax rates?

20. **(LO2)** Is it possible for a taxpayer who pays AMT to have a marginal tax rate higher than the stated AMT rate? Explain.

21. **(LO2)** What is the difference between the tentative minimum tax (TMT) and the AMT?

22. **(LO2)** Why is it that an increasing number of taxpayers are forced to pay the AMT?

■ planning

23. **(LO2)** Lee is single and he runs his own business. He uses the cash method of accounting to determine his business income. Near the end of the year, Lee performed work that he needs to bill a client for. The value of his services is $5,000. Lee figures that if he immediately takes the time to put the bill together and send it out, the client will pay him before year-end. However, if he doesn't send out the bill for one week, he won't receive the client's payment until the beginning of next year. Lee expects that he will owe AMT this year and that his AMT base will be around $200,000 before counting any of the additional business income. Further, Lee anticipates that he will not owe AMT next year. He anticipates his regular taxable income next year will be in the $200,000 range. Would you advise Lee to immediately bill his client or to wait? What factors would you consider in making your recommendation?

24. **(LO3)** Are an employee's entire wages subject to the FICA tax? Explain.

25. **(LO3)** Bobbie works as an employee for Altron Corp. for the first half of the year and for Betel Inc. for rest of the year. She is relatively well paid. What FICA tax issues is she likely to encounter? What FICA tax issues do Altron Corp. and Betel Inc. need to consider?

26. **(LO3)** Compare and contrast an employee's FICA tax payment responsibilities with those of a self-employed taxpayer.

27. **(LO3)** When a taxpayer works as an employee and as a self-employed independent contractor during the year, how does the taxpayer determine her employment and self-employment taxes payable?

28. **(LO3)** What are the primary factors to consider when deciding whether a worker should be considered an employee or a self-employed taxpayer for tax purposes?

29. **(LO3)** How do the tax consequences of being an employee differ from those of being self-employed?

30. **(LO3)** Mike wanted to work for a CPA firm but he also wanted to work on his father's farm in Montana. Because the CPA firm wanted Mike to be happy, they offered to let him work for them as an independent contractor during the fall and winter and let him return to Montana to work for his father during the spring and summer. He was very excited to hear that they were also going to give him a 5 percent higher "salary" for the six months he would be working for the firm over what he would have made over the same six-month period if he worked full-time as an employee. Should Mike be excited about his 5 percent raise? Why or why not? What counter offer could Mike reasonably suggest?   ■ **planning**

31. **(LO4)** How are tax credits and tax deductions similar? How are they dissimilar?

32. **(LO4)** What are the three types of tax credits, and explain why it is important to distinguish between the different types of tax credits.

33. **(LO4)** Explain why there is such a large number and variety of tax credits.

34. **(LO4)** What is the difference between a refundable and nonrefundable tax credit?

35. **(LO4)** Is the child tax credit a refundable or nonrefundable credit? Explain.

36. **(LO4)** How is the phase-out for the child tax credit similar to the phase-out of the overall amount of itemized deductions? How is it dissimilar?

37. **(LO4)** Diane has a job working three-quarter time. She hired her mother to take care of her two small children so Diane could work. Do Diane's child care payments to her mother qualify for the child and dependent care credit? Explain.

38. **(LO4)** The amount of the child and dependent care credit is based on the amount of the taxpayer's expenditures to provide care for one or more qualifying persons. Who is considered to be a qualifying person for this purpose?

39. **(LO4)** Compare and contrast the lifetime learning credit with the Hope scholarship credit.

40. **(LO4)** Jennie's grandfather paid her tuition this fall to State University (an eligible educational institution). Jennie is claimed as a dependent by her parents, but she also files her own tax return. Can Jennie claim an education credit for the tuition paid by her grandfather? What difference would it make, if any, if Jennie did not qualify as a dependent of her parents (or anyone else)?   ■ **research**

41. **(LO4)** Why is the earned income credit referred to as a negative income tax?

42. **(LO4)** Under what circumstances can a college student qualify for the earned income credit?

43. **(LO4)** What factors determine the amount of a taxpayer's earned income credit?

44. **(LO4)** How are business credits similar to personal credits? How are they dissimilar?

45. **(LO4)** Is the foreign tax credit a personal credit or a business credit? Explain.
46. **(LO4)** When a U.S. taxpayer pays income taxes to a foreign government, what options does the taxpayer have when determining how to treat the expenditure on her U.S. individual income tax return?
47. **(LO4)** Describe the order in which different types of tax credits are applied to reduce a taxpayer's tax liability.
48. **(LO5)** Describe the two methods that taxpayers use to prepay their taxes.
49. **(LO5)** What are the consequences of a taxpayer underpaying his or her tax liability throughout the year? Explain the safe-harbor provisions that may apply in this situation.
50. **(LO5)** Describe how the underpayment penalty is calculated.
51. **(LO5)** What determines if a taxpayer is required to file a tax return? If a taxpayer is not required to file a tax return, does this mean that the taxpayer should not file a tax return?
52. **(LO5)** What is the due date for individual tax returns? What extensions are available?
53. **(LO5)** Describe the consequences for failing to file a tax return and for paying tax owed late.

PROBLEMS

54. **(LO1)** Whitney received $75,000 of taxable income in 2009. All of the income was salary from her employer. What is her income tax liability in each of the following alternative situations?
    a. She files under the single filing status.
    b. She files a joint tax return with her spouse. Together their taxable income is $75,000.
    c. She is married but files a separate tax return. Her taxable income is $75,000.
    d. She files as a head of household.

55. **(LO1)** In 2009, Lisa and Fred, a married couple, have taxable income of $300,000. If they were to file separate tax returns, Lisa would have reported taxable income of $125,000 and Fred would have reported taxable income of $175,000. What is the couple's marriage penalty or benefit?

56. **(LO1)** In 2009, Jasmine and Thomas, a married couple, have taxable income of $150,000. If they were to file separate tax returns, Jasmine would have reported taxable income of $140,000 and Thomas would have reported taxable income of $10,000. What is the couple's marriage penalty or benefit?

57. **(LO1)** Lacy is a single taxpayer. In 2009, her taxable income is $37,000. What is her tax liability in each of the following alternative situations?
    a. All of her income is salary from her employer.
    b. Her $37,000 of taxable income includes $2,000 of qualifying dividends.
    c. Her $37,000 of taxable income includes $5,000 of qualifying dividends.

58. **(LO1)** Henrich is a single taxpayer. In 2009, his taxable income is $85,000. What is his tax liability in each of the following alternative scenarios?
    a. All of his income is salary from his employer.
    b. His $85,000 of taxable income includes $2,000 of long-term capital gain that is taxed at preferential rates.
    c. His $85,000 of taxable income includes $5,000 of long-term capital gain that is taxed at preferential rates.

59. **(LO1)** In 2009, Stephen is single and is claimed as a dependent on his parent's tax return. Stephen has two sources of income. He mows lawns during the summer and he receives interest income on his money market account. What is Stephen's standard deduction in each of the following alternative situations?

   a. Stephen is 14 years old and earned $400 mowing lawns and he received $1,000 of interest income?

   b. Stephen is 20 years old and earned $400 mowing lawns and he received $1,000 of interest income.

   c. Stephen is 14 years old and earned $1,000 mowing lawns and he received $1,000 of interest income.

   d. Stephen is 14 years old and earned $6,000 mowing lawns and he received $1,000 of interest income.

60. **(LO1)** In 2009, Sheryl is claimed as a dependent on her parents' tax return. Her parents' ordinary income marginal tax rate is 35 percent. Sheryl did not provide more than half her own support. What is Sheryl's tax liability for the year in each of the following alternative circumstances?

   a. She received $7,000 from a part-time job. This was her only source of income. She is 16 years old at year-end.

   b. She received $7,000 of interest income from corporate bonds she received several years ago. This is her only source of income. She is 16 years old at year-end.

   c. She received $7,000 of interest income from corporate bonds she received several years ago. This is her only source of income. She is 20 years old at year-end and is *not* a full-time student.

   d. She received $7,000 of interest income from corporate bonds she received several years ago. This is her only source of income. She is 20 years old at year-end and is a full-time student.

   e. She received $7,000 of qualifying dividend income. This is her only source of income. She is 16 years old at year-end.

61. **(LO2)** Brooklyn files as a head of household for 2009 and claims a total of three personal exemptions (3 × $3,650 = $10,950). She claimed the standard deduction of $8,350 for regular tax purposes . Her regular taxable income was $80,000. What is Brooklyn's AMTI?

62. **(LO2)** Sylvester files as a single taxpayer during 2009 and claims one personal exemption. He itemizes deductions for regular tax purposes. He paid charitable contributions of $7,000, real estate taxes of $1,000, state income taxes of $4,000, and interest on a home-equity loan of $2,000. Sylvester's regular taxable income is $100,000.

   a. What is Sylvester's AMTI if he used the home-equity proceeds to purchase a car?

   b. What is Sylvester's AMTI if he used the home-equity loan proceeds to build a new garage next to his home?

63. **(LO2)** In 2009, Nadia has $100,000 of regular taxable income. She itemizes her deductions as follows: real property taxes of $1,500, state income taxes of $2,000, and mortgage interest expense of $10,000 (not a home-equity loan). In addition, she receives tax-exempt interest of $1,000 from a municipal bond that was used to fund a new business building for a (formerly) out-of-state employer. Finally, she received a state tax refund of $300 from the prior year.

   a. What is Nadia's AMTI this year if she deducted $15,000 of itemized deductions last year (she did not owe any AMT last year)?

b. What is Nadia's AMTI this year if she deducted the standard deduction last year (she did not owe any AMT last year)?

64. **(LO2)** In 2009, Sven is single and has $120,000 of regular taxable income. He itemizes his deductions as follows: real property tax of $2,000, state income tax of $4,000, mortgage interest expense of $15,000 (not a home-equity loan). He also paid $2,000 in tax preparation fees. Assume that Sven was required to reduce his itemized deductions by $100 because his AGI was so high. In addition, he has a positive AMT depreciation adjustment of $500. What is Sven's alternative minimum taxable income (AMTI)?

65. **(LO2)** Olga is married and files a joint tax return with her husband. What amount of AMT exemption may she deduct under each of the following alternative circumstances (use the 2008 AMT exemption amount)?

   a. Her AMTI is $90,000.
   b. Her AMTI is $180,000.
   c. Her AMTI is $450,000.

66. **(LO2)** Corbett's AMTI is $130,000. What is his 2008 AMT exemption under the following alternative circumstances?

   a. He is married and files a joint return.
   b. He is married and files a separate return.
   c. His filing status is single.
   d. His filing status is head of household.

67. **(LO2)** In 2009, Juanita is married and files a joint tax return with her husband. What is her tentative minimum tax in each of the following alternative circumstances?

   a. Her AMT base is $100,000, all ordinary income.
   b. Her AMT base is $250,000, all ordinary income.
   c. Her AMT base is $100,000, which includes $10,000 of qualifying dividends.
   d. Her AMT base is $250,000, which includes $10,000 of qualifying dividends.

68. **(LO2)** Steve's tentative minimum tax (TMT) for 2009 is $15,000. What is his AMT if

   a. His regular tax is $10,000?
   b. His regular tax is $20,000?

69. **(LO2)** In 2009, Janet and Ray are married filing jointly. They have five dependent children under 18 years of age. The couple's AGI is $180,000 and their taxable income is $140,000. They itemize their deductions as follows: real property taxes of $5,000, state income taxes of $9,000, and mortgage interest expense of $15,000 (not a home-equity loan). They also had $132 of itemized deductions phased-out. What is Janet and Ray's AMT for 2009 (use the 2008 AMT exemption amount)?

70. **(LO3)** Brooke works for Company A for all of 2009, earning a salary of $50,000.

   a. What is her FICA tax obligation for the year?
   b. Assume Brooke works for Company A for half of 2009, earning $50,000 in salary, and she works for Company B for the second half of 2009, earning $70,000 in salary. What is Brooke's FICA tax obligation for the year?

71. **(LO3)** Rasheed works for Company A, earning $350,000 in salary during 2009. Assuming he has no other sources of income, what amount of FICA tax will Rasheed pay for the year?

72. **(LO3)** Alice is self-employed in 2009. Her net business profit on her Schedule C for the year is $140,000. What is her self-employment tax liability for 2009?

73. **(LO3)** Kyle worked as a free-lance software engineer for the first three months of 2009. During that time, he earned $44,000 of self-employment income. On April 1, 2009, Kyle took a job as a full-time software engineer with one of his former clients, Hoogle Inc. From April through the end of the year, Kyle earned $78,000 in salary. What amount of self-employment/FICA tax does Kyle owe for the year?

74. **(LO3)** Eva received $60,000 in compensation payments from JAZZ Corp. during 2009. Eva incurred $5,000 in business expenses relating to her work for JAZZ Corp. JAZZ did not reimburse Eva for any of these expenses. Eva is single and she deducts a standard deduction of $5,700 and a personal exemption of $3,650. Based on these facts answer the following questions:

   a. Assume that Eva is considered to be an *employee*. What amount of FICA taxes is she required to pay for the year?

   b. Assume that Eva is considered to be an *employee*. What is her regular income tax liability for the year?

   c. Assume that Eva is considered to be a *self-employed contractor*. What is her self-employment tax liability for the year?

   d. Assume that Eva is considered to be a *self-employed contractor*. What is her regular tax liability for the year?

75. **(LO3)** Terry Hutchison worked as a self-employed lawyer until two years ago when he retired. He used the cash method of accounting in his business for tax purposes. Five years ago, Terry represented his client ABC corporation in an antitrust lawsuit against XYZ corporation. During that year, Terry paid self-employment taxes on all of his income. ABC won the lawsuit but Terry and ABC could not agree on the amount of his earnings. Finally, this year, the issue got resolved and ABC paid Terry $90,000 for the services he provided five years ago. Terry plans to include the payment in his gross income, but because he spends most of his time playing golf and absolutely no time working on legal matters, he does not intend to pay self-employment taxes on the income. Is Terry subject to self-employment taxes on this income?

research

76. **(LO4)** In 2009, Trey claims a dependency exemption for both of his two daughters, ages 14 and 17, at year-end. Trey files a joint return with his wife. What amount of child credit will Trey be able to claim for his daughters under each of the following alternative situations?

   a. His AGI is $100,000.

   b. His AGI is $120,000.

   c. His AGI is $122,100, and his daughters are ages 10 and 12.

77. **(LO4)** In 2009, Julie paid a day care center to watch her two-year-old son while she worked as a computer programmer for a local start-up company. What amount of child and dependent care credit can Julie claim in each of the following alternative scenarios?

   a. Julie paid $2,000 to the day care center and her AGI is $50,000 (all salary).

   b. Julie paid $5,000 to the day care center and her AGI is $50,000 (all salary).

   c. Julie paid $4,000 to the day care center and her AGI is $25,000 (all salary).

   d. Julie paid $2,000 to the day care center and her AGI is $14,000 (all salary).

   e. Julie paid $4,000 to the day care center and her AGI is $14,000 ($2,000 salary and $12,000 unearned income).

78. **(LO4)** In 2009, Elaine paid $1,800 of tuition for her dependent son to attend State University this past fall as a freshman. Elaine files a joint return with her husband. What is the maximum amount of education credit that Elaine can claim for the tuition payment in each of the following alternative situations?

   a. Elaine's AGI is $80,000.

   b. Elaine's AGI is $108,000.

   c. Elaine's AGI is $124,000.

research

79. **(LO4)** In 2009, Amy paid $3,200 of qualified tuition and related expenses for her son Bryan to attend State University as a freshman. Can Amy claim a Hope credit for part of the tuition costs and a lifetime learning credit for the remaining tuition costs?

planning

80. **(LO4)** In 2009, Laureen is currently single. She paid $2,800 of qualified tuition and related expenses for each of her twin daughters Sheri and Meri to attend State University as freshmen ($2,800 each for a total of $5,600). Sheri and Meri qualify as Laureen's dependents. Laureen also paid $2,400 for her son Ryan (also Laureen's dependent) to attend his junior year at State University. Finally, Laureen paid $1,200 for herself to attend seminars at a community college to help her improve her job skills. What is the maximum amount of education credits Laureen can claim for these expenditures in each of the following alternative scenarios?

   a. Laureen's AGI is $45,000. If Laureen claims education credits is she allowed to deduct as *for* AGI expenses tuition costs for her daughters that do not generate credits? Explain.

   b. Laureen's AGI is $65,000. What options does Laureen have for deducting her continuing education costs to the extent the costs don't generate a credit?

   c. Laureen's AGI is $45,000 and Laureen paid $12,000 for Ryan to attend graduate school instead of $2,400.

81. **(LO4)** In 2009, Amanda and Jaxon Stuart have a daughter who is one year old. The Stuarts are full-time students and they are both 23 years old. Their only sources of income are gains from stock they held for three years before selling and wages from part-time jobs. What is their earned income credit in the following alternative scenarios?

   a. Their AGI is $15,000, consisting of $5,000 of capital gains and $10,000 of wages.

   b. Their AGI is $15,000, consisting of $10,000 of capital gains and $5,000 of wages.

   c. Their AGI is $25,000, consisting of $20,000 of wages and $5,000 of capital gains.

   d. Their AGI is $25,000, consisting of $5,000 of wages and $20,000 of capital gains.

   e. Their AGI is $10,000, consisting of $10,000 of capital gains (they had no wages).

82. **(LO4)** In 2009, Zach is single with no dependents. He is not claimed as a dependent on another's return. All of his income is from salary and he does not have any *for* AGI deductions. What is his earned income credit in the following alternative scenarios?

   a. Zach is 29 years old and his AGI is $5,000.

   b. Zach is 29 years old and his AGI is $14,000.

   c. Zach is 29 years old and his AGI is $19,000.

   d. Zach is 24 years old and his AGI is $5,000.

83. **(LO4)** This year Luke has calculated his gross tax liability at $1,800. Luke is entitled to a $2,400 nonrefundable personal tax credit, a $1,500 business tax credit,

and a $600 refundable personal tax credit. In addition, Luke has had $2,300 of income taxes withheld from his salary. What is Luke's net tax due or refund?

84. **(LO5)** This year Lloyd, a single taxpayer, estimates that his tax liability will be $10,000. Last year, his total tax liability was $15,000. He estimates that his tax withholding from his employer will be $7,800.

    a. Is Lloyd required to increase his withholding or make estimated tax payments this year to avoid the underpayment penalty? If so, how much?

    b. Assuming Lloyd does not make any additional payments, what is the amount of his underpayment penalty? Assume the federal short-term rate is 5 percent.

■ planning

85. **(LO5)** This year, Paula and Simon (married filing jointly) estimate that their tax liability will be $200,000. Last year, their total tax liability was $170,000. They estimate that their tax withholding from their employers will be $175,000. Are Paula and Simon required to increase their withholdings or make estimated tax payments this year to avoid the underpayment penalty? If so, how much?

■ planning

86. **(LO5)** This year, Santhosh, a single taxpayer, estimates that his tax liability will be $100,000. Last year, his total tax liability was $15,000. He estimates that his tax withholding from his employer will be $35,000. Is Santhosh required to increase his withholding or make estimated tax payments this year to avoid the underpayment penalty? If so, how much?

■ planning

87. **(LO5)** For the following taxpayers, determine if they are required to file a tax return in 2009.

    a. Ricko, single taxpayer, with gross income of $12,000.

    b. Fantasia, head of household, with gross income of $17,500.

    c. Ken and Barbie, married taxpayers with no dependents, with gross income of $12,000.

    d. Dorothy and Rudolf, married taxpayers, both age 68, with gross income of $19,000.

    e. Janyce, single taxpayer, age 73, with gross income of $12,500.

88. **(LO5)** For the following taxpayers, determine the due date of their tax returns.

    a. Jerome, a single taxpayer, is not requesting an extension this year. Assume the due date falls on a Tuesday.

    b. Lashaunda, a single taxpayer, requests an extension this year. Assume the extended due date falls on a Wednesday.

    c. Barney and Betty, married taxpayers, do not request an extension this year. Assume the due date falls on a Sunday.

    d. Fred and Wilma, married taxpayers, request an extension this year. Assume the extended date falls on a Saturday.

89. **(LO5)** Determine the amount of the late filing and late payment penalties that apply for the following taxpayers.

    a. Jolene filed her tax return by its original due date but did not pay the $2,000 in taxes she owed with the return until one and a half months later.

    b. Oscar filed his tax return and paid his $3,000 tax liability seven months late.

    c. Wilfred, attempting to evade his taxes, did not file a tax return or pay his $10,000 in taxes for several years.

COMPREHENSIVE PROBLEMS

■ planning

90. In 2009, Jack and Diane Heart are married with two children, ages 10 and 12. Jack works full-time and earns an annual salary of $75,000, while Diane works

as a substitute teacher and earns approximately $25,000 per year. Jack and Diane expect to file jointly and do not itemize their deductions. In the fall of this year, Diane was offered a full-time teaching position that would pay her an additional $20,000.

a. Calculate the marginal tax rate on the additional income, *excluding employment taxes,* to help Jack and Diane evaluate the offer.

b. Calculate the marginal tax rate on the additional income, *including employment taxes,* to help Jack and Diane evaluate the offer.

c. Calculate the marginal tax rate on the additional income, *including self-employment taxes,* if Diane would be working as a self-employed individual contractor.

■ planning   91. Matt and Carrie are married, have two children, and file a joint return. Their daughter Katie is 19 years old and was a full-time student at State University. During 2009, she completed her freshman year and one semester as a sophomore. Katie's expenses while she was away at school during the year were as follows:

Tuition	$5,000
Class fees	300
Books	500
Room and board	4,500

Katie received a half-tuition scholarship that paid for $2,500 of her tuition costs. Katie's parents paid the rest of these expenses. Matt and Carrie are able to claim Carrie as a dependent on their tax return.

Matt and Carrie's 23-year-old son Todd also attended school full time at a nearby college. Todd is a senior and his expenses while away at school during the year were as follows:

Tuition	$3,000
Class fees	0
Books	250
Room and board	4,000

Todd paid for his own tuition and books, but Matt and Carrie paid for his room and board.

Since Matt and Carrie still benefit from claiming Todd as a dependent on their tax return, they decided to provide Todd with additional financial assistance by making the payments on Todd's outstanding loans. Todd used the proceeds from these loans to pay his tuition costs. Besides paying off some of the loan principal, Matt and Carrie paid a total of $900 of interest on the loan.

This year Carrie decided to take some classes at the local community college to help improve her skills as a schoolteacher. The community college is considered to be a qualifying postsecondary institution of higher education. Carrie spent a total of $1,300 on tuition for the classes, and she was not reimbursed by her employer. Matt and Carrie's AGI for 2009 before any education-related tax deductions is $112,000 and their taxable income before considering any education-related tax benefits is $90,000. Matt and Carrie incurred $2,300 of miscellaneous itemized deductions subject to the 2 percent floor not counting any education-related expenses.

Required:

Determine the mix of tax benefits that maximize tax savings for Matt and Carrie. Their options for credits for each student are as follows:

a. They may claim either a credit or a qualified education deduction for Katie's expenses.

b. They may claim either a credit or a qualified education deduction for Todd.

c. They may claim (1) a credit or (2) a qualified education deduction for Carrie. They may deduct any amount not included in (1) or (2) as a miscellaneous itemized deduction subject to the 2 percent of AGI floor.

Remember to apply any applicable limits or phase-outs in your computations. Also, be sure to include the interest deduction for qualified educational loans in your computations.

92. Reba Dixon is a fifth grade school teacher who earned a salary of $38,000 in 2009. She is 45 years old and has been divorced for four years. She received $1,200 of alimony payments each month from her former husband. Reba also rents out a small apartment building. This year Reba received $30,000 of rental payments from tenants and she incurred $19,500 of expenses associated with the rental.

Reba and her daughter Heather (20 years old at the end of the year) moved to Florida in January of this year. They had been living in Texas for the past 15 years, but ever since her divorce, Reba has been wanting to move back to Florida to be closer to her family. Luckily, last December, a teaching position opened up and Reba and Heather decided to make the move. Reba paid a moving company $2,000 to move their personal belongings, and she and Heather spent two days driving the 1,000 miles to Florida. During the trip, Reba paid $150 for lodging and $85 for meals. Reba's mother was so excited to have her daughter and granddaughter move back to Florida that she gave Reba $3,000 to help out with the moving costs.

Reba rented a home in Florida. Heather decided to continue living at home with her mom, but she started attending school full-time at a nearby university. She was awarded a $3,000 partial tuition scholarship this year, and Reba helped out by paying the remaining $500 tuition cost. Reba thought it would be best to claim the education credit for these expenses.

Since Florida has no state income tax, Reba wasn't sure if she would have enough items to help her benefit from itemizing on her tax return. However, she kept track of several expenses this year that she thought might qualify if she was able to itemize. Reba paid $6,500 in charitable contributions during the year. She also paid the following medical-related expenses for her and Heather:

Insurance premiums	$3,200
Medical care expenses	1,100
Prescription medicine	350
Nonprescription medicine	100
New contact lenses for Heather	200

After living in Florida for a few months, Reba decided it was time to buy a new car. She paid $20,000 for the car and an additional $1,600 in sales tax on the automobile. Reba also kept records indicating she spent an additional $800 of sales taxes during the year. About a week after she purchased the car, Reba got distracted while driving and she ran into a street sign. The accident caused $900 in damage to the car and gave her whiplash. Because the repairs were less than her insurance deductible, she paid the entire cost of the repairs. Reba wasn't able to work for two months after the accident. Fortunately, she received $2,000 from her disability insurance. Her employer, the Central Florida School District, paid 60 percent of the premiums on the policy as a nontaxable fringe benefit and Reba paid the remaining 40 percent portion.

A few years ago, Reba acquired several investments with her portion of the divorce settlement. This year she reported the following income from her investments: $2,200 of interest income from corporate bonds and $1,500 interest income from City of Dallas municipal bonds. Overall, Reba's stock portfolio appreciated by $12,000 but she did not sell any of her stocks.

Heather reported $3,200 of interest income from corporate bonds she received as gifts from her father over the last several years. This was Heather's only source of income for the year.

Reba had $10,000 of federal income taxes withheld by her employer. Heather made $500 of estimated tax payments during the year. Reba did not make any estimated payments.

Required:

a. Determine Reba's federal income taxes due or taxes payable for the current year.

b. Is Reba allowed to file as a head of household or single?

c. Determine the amount of FICA taxes Reba was required to pay on her salary.

d. Determine Heather's federal income taxes due or payable.

93. John and Sandy Ferguson got married eight years ago and have a seven-year-old daughter Samantha. In 2009, John worked as a computer technician at a local university earning a salary of $52,000, and Sandy worked part-time as a receptionist for a law firm earning a salary of $29,000. John also does some Web design work on the side and reported revenues of $4,000 and associated expenses of $750. The Fergusons received $800 in qualified dividends and a $200 refund of their state income taxes. The Fergusons always itemize their deductions and their itemized deductions were well over the standard deduction amount last year.

The Fergusons reported making the following payments during the year:

- State income taxes of $4,400.
- Alimony payments to John's former wife of $10,000.
- Child support payments for John's child with his former wife of $4,100.
- $3,200 of real property taxes.
- Sandy was reimbursed $600 for employee business expenses she incurred. She was required to provide documentation for her expenses to her employer.
- In addition to the $750 of Web design expenses, John attended a conference to improve his skills associated with his Web design work. His trip was for three days and he incurred the following expenses: airfare $370, total taxi fares for trip $180, meals $80, and conference fee of $200.
- $3,600 to Kid Care day care center for Samantha's care while John and Sandy worked.
- $14,000 interest on their home mortgage.
- $3,000 interest on a home-equity loan. They used the loan to pay for family vacation and new car.
- $6,000 cash charitable contributions to qualified charities.
- Donation of used furniture to Goodwill. The furniture had a fair market value of $400 and cost $2,000.

Required:

What is the Ferguson's 2009 federal income taxes payable or refund, including any self-employment tax and AMT, if applicable (use the 2008 AMT exemption amount)?

94. Ellis has been a widower for a little over three years now. He is 63 years old and is legally blind. This year (2009) he received $12,000 of Social Security benefits; he also won $2,500 playing the slots during July. Unfortunately, his luck wasn't

so good for the rest of the year when he lost $4,000. Ellis earned $11,000 at a part-time job and he received $24,000 ($2,000 per month) from an annuity he purchased three years ago for $180,000 with the life insurance proceeds from his deceased spouse Wendrina. The annuity he purchased was a single life annuity. Ellis never has enough itemized deductions, so he always deducts the standard deduction.

Required:

a. Compute Ellis's taxable income and tax liability.

b. Assume that Ellis's only source of income is his $11,000 of wages and that he had $100 withheld from his paycheck. What taxes will he owe with his return or what refund will he receive?

KAPLAN SCHWESER CPA SIMULATIONS

Please visit the Online Learning Center   (www.mhhe.com/spilker2010) to access the following Kaplan Schweser CPA Simulation:

The simulation for **Lisa Harrison** covers individual income tax issues, including filing status and exemptions over two years; calculation of AGI; and tax treatment of numerous items.

Please visit the Online Learning Center   (www.mhhe.com/spilker2010) to access the following Kaplan Schweser CPA Simulation:

The simulation for **Steve and Raelene Sutton** covers individual income tax issues, including filing status and exemptions; job expenses and other miscellaneous deductions; casualty/theft; dependents and exemptions; capital gains and losses; and earned income.

Please visit the Online Learning Center   (www.mhhe.com/spilker2010) to access the following Kaplan Schweser CPA Simulation:

The simulation for **Michael and Marshall Morgan** covers individual income tax issues, including itemized deductions; rental income and expenses; deductions for AGI; filing requirements; AMT; and dependents with summer job income.

chapter
8

Business Income, Deductions, and Accounting Methods

Learning Objectives

Upon completing this chapter, you should be able to:

LO 1 Describe the general requirements for deducting business expenses and identify common business deductions.

■

LO 2 Apply the limitations on business deductions to distinguish between deductible and nondeductible business expenses.

■

LO 3 Identify and explain special business deductions specifically permitted under the tax laws.

■

LO 4 Explain the concept of an accounting period and describe accounting periods available to businesses.

■

LO 5 Identify and describe accounting methods available to businesses and apply cash and accrual methods to determine business income and expense deductions.

Storyline Summary	
Taxpayer:	Rick Grime, age 27
Location:	San Antonio, Texas
Family description:	Unmarried
Employment status:	Rick quit his landscaping job in Dallas and moved to San Antonio to start a business as a self-employed landscaper.

Rick Grime graduated from Texas State University with a degree in agronomy, and for the past few years he has been employed by a landscape architect in Dallas. Nearly every day that Rick went to work, he shared ideas with his employer about improving the business. In April, Rick finally decided he should take his ideas and start his own landscaping business in his hometown of San Antonio, Texas. In mid-April, Rick left his job and moved his belongings to San Antonio. Once in town, Rick discovered he had to do a lot of things to start his business. First, he registered his new business name (Green Acres Landscaping) and established a bank account for the business. Next, he rented a used sport utility vehicle (SUV) and a shop for his place of business. Rick didn't know much about accounting for business activities, so he hired a CPA, Jane Bronson, to help him. Jane and Rick decided that Rick should initially operate Green Acres as a sole proprietorship, but Jane suggested that as the business grew, he might want to consider organizing it as a different type of legal entity. Operating as a corporation, for instance, would allow him to invite new investors or business partners to help fund future expansion. Rick formally started his business on May 1. He spent a lot of time attracting new customers, and he figured he would hire employees as he needed them.

to be continued . . .

In previous chapters, we've emphasized the process of determining gross income and deductions for *individuals*. This chapter describes the process for determining gross income and deductions for *businesses*. Keep in mind that the concepts we discuss in this chapter generally apply to all types of business entities including sole proprietorships (such as Rick's company, Green Acres), partnerships, S corporations, and C corporations.[1] Because Rick is a sole proprietor, our examples emphasize business income and deductions from a proprietor's perspective. Proprietors report business income and deductions on Schedule C of their individual income tax returns. Schedule C income is subject to both individual income and self-employment taxes. Entities other than sole proprietorships report income on tax forms separate from the owners' tax returns. For example, partnerships report taxable income on Form 1065, S corporations report taxable income on Form 1120S, and C corporations report income on Form 1120. Of all these entity types, generally only C corporations pay taxes on their income.

BUSINESS GROSS INCOME

In most respects, the rules for determining business gross income are the same as for determining gross income for individuals. Gross income includes "all income from whatever source derived."[2] Further, the tax laws specifically indicate that this definition includes gross income from "business." Generally speaking, income from business includes gross profit from inventory sales (sales minus cost of goods sold), income from services provided to customers, and income from renting property to customers. Just like individuals, businesses are allowed to exclude certain types of realized income from gross income, such as municipal bond interest.

L01

BUSINESS DEDUCTIONS

Because Congress intended for taxable income to reflect the *net* increase in wealth from a business, it is only fair that businesses be allowed to deduct expenses incurred to generate business income. Typically, Congress provides *specific* statutory rules authorizing deductions. However, as you can see from the following excerpt from IRC §162, the provision authorizing business deductions is relatively broad and ambiguous:

> There shall be allowed as a deduction all the ordinary and necessary expenses paid or incurred during the taxable year in carrying on any trade or business . . .

This provision authorizes taxpayers to deduct expenses for "trade or business" activities.[3] The tax code does not define the phrase "trade or business," but it's clear that the objective of business activities is to make a profit. Thus, the tax law requires that a business expense be made in the pursuit of profits rather than the pursuit of other, presumably personal, motives.

When a taxpayer's activity does not meet the "for profit" requirement, it is treated as a **hobby** (an activity motivated by personal objectives). As we discussed in Chapter 6, a taxpayer engaged in a hobby that generates revenues includes all revenues from the activity in gross income and deducts associated expenses to the extent of gross income

---

THE KEY FACTS

Business Expenses

■ Business expenses must be incurred in pursuit of profits, not personal goals.

■ Only reasonable amounts are allowed as deductions.

■ A deduction must be ordinary and necessary (i.e., appropriate and helpful).

---

[1]Both S corporations and C corporations are incorporated for state law purposes. However, S corporations are taxed as flow-through entities (S corporation income is taxed to its owners) while C corporations (or taxable corporations) are taxed as separate taxable entities.

[2]IRC §61(a). See Chapter 5 for a detailed description of inclusions and exclusions of income.

[3]§212 contains a sister provision to §162 allowing deductions for ordinary and necessary expenses incurred for the production of income ("investment expenses") and for the management and maintenance of property (including expenses incurred in renting property in situations when the rental activity is not considered to be a trade or business).

from the activity as *miscellaneous itemized deductions* (subject to the 2 percent of AGI floor).

Ordinary and Necessary

Business expenditures must be both **ordinary and necessary** to be deductible. An *ordinary* expense is an expense that is normal or appropriate for the business under the circumstances.[4] An expense is *not* necessarily required to be typical or repetitive in nature to be considered ordinary. For example, a business could deduct the legal fees it expends to defend itself in an antitrust suit. Although an antitrust suit would be atypical and unusual for most businesses, defending the suit would probably be deemed ordinary, because it would be expected under the circumstances. A *necessary* expense is an expense that is helpful or conducive to the business activity, but the expenditure need not be essential or indispensable. For example, a deduction for metric tools would qualify as ordinary and necessary even if there was only a small chance that a repairman might need these tools. The "ordinary and necessary" requirements are applied on a case-by-case basis, and while the deduction depends on individual circumstances, the IRS is often reluctant to second-guess business decisions. Exhibit 8-1 presents examples of expenditures that are ordinary and necessary for typical businesses.

EXHIBIT 8-1 **Examples of Typical Ordinary and Necessary Expense**

• Advertising	• Office expenses
• Car and truck expenses	• Rent
• Depreciation	• Repairs
• Employee compensation and benefits	• Supplies
• Insurance	• Travel
• Interest	• Utilities
• Legal fees	• Wages

Example 8-1

Rick paid $50 to attend a two-week, nighttime meditation course ("Meditation for Dummies") to learn how to meditate. He is considering whether this expenditure qualifies as an ordinary and necessary business expense. Rick believes that meditation will improve his ability to produce innovative landscape designs and thus increase the demand for his business services. Further, he plans to meditate only for business purposes. Rick decides that the cost of the course is a deductible business expense, so he deducts the $50 cost as an ordinary and necessary business expense. Is he correct?

Answer: Under the regulations, educational expenses are deductible if they help the taxpayer maintain or improve skills in an existing trade or business. It is difficult, however, to know whether the IRS or a court would agree that meditation is ordinary and necessary. What do you think?

Reasonable in Amount

Ordinary and necessary business expenses are deductible only *to the extent* they are also **reasonable in amount.** The courts have interpreted this requirement to mean that an expenditure is not reasonable when it is extravagant or exorbitant.[5] If the expenditure is extravagant in amount, the courts presume the excess amount was spent for personal rather than business reasons, and thus not deductible.

---

[4] *Welch v. Helvering* (1933), 290 US 111.
[5] §162(a) and *Comm. v. Lincoln Electric Co.* (CA-6, 1949), 176 F.2d 815.

Determining whether an expenditure is reasonable is not an exact science and, not surprisingly, taxpayers and the IRS may have different opinions. Generally, the courts and the IRS test for extravagance by comparing the amount of the expense to a market price or an **arm's length amount.** If the amount of the expense is the amount typically charged in the market by unrelated parties, the amount is considered to be reasonable. Because the underlying issue is *why* a profit-motivated taxpayer would pay an extravagant amount, reasonableness is most likely to be an issue when a payment is made to an individual related to the taxpayer, or the taxpayer enjoys some incidental benefit from the expenditure, such as entertainment value.

Example 8-2

During the busy part of the year, Rick could not keep up with all the work. Therefore, he hired four part-time employees and paid them $10 an hour to mow lawns and pull weeds for an average of 20 hours a week. When things finally slowed down in late fall, Rick released his four part-time employees. In total, Rick paid a total of $22,000 in compensation to the four employees. He still needed some extra help now and then, so he hired his brother, Tom, on a part-time basis. Tom performed the same duties as the prior part-time employees (his quality of work was about the same). However, Rick paid Tom $25 per hour because Tom is a college student and Rick wanted to provide some additional support for Tom's education. At year end, Tom had worked a total of 100 hours and received $2,500 from Rick. What amount can Rick deduct for the compensation he paid to his employees?

Answer: $23,000. Rick can deduct the $22,000 paid to part-time employees. However, he can only deduct $10 an hour for Tom's compensation because the extra $15 per hour Rick paid Tom is unreasonable in amount.[6] The remaining $15 per hour is considered a personal (nondeductible) gift from Rick to Tom. Hence, Rick can deduct a total of $23,000 for compensation expense this year [$22,000 + ($10 × 100)].

LO2   LIMITATIONS ON BUSINESS DEDUCTIONS

THE KEY FACTS

Limitations on Business Expense Deductions

▌ No business deductions for expenditures against public policy (bribes) or political contributions.

▌ Expenditures that benefit a period longer than 12 months generally must be capitalized.

▌ No deductions for expenditures associated with the production of tax-exempt income.

▌ Personal expenditures are not deductible.

For a variety of reasons, Congress specifically prohibits or limits a business's ability to deduct certain expenditures that appear to otherwise meet the general business expense deductibility requirements.

Expenditures against Public Policy

Even though they incur the expenses as part of their business activities, businesses are not allowed to deduct fines, penalties, illegal bribes, or illegal kickbacks.[7] Congress disallows these expenditures under the rationale that allowing them would subsidize illegal activities and frustrate public policy. Interestingly enough, businesses conducting illegal activities (selling stolen goods or conducting illegal gambling activities) are allowed to deduct their cost of goods sold and their ordinary and necessary business expenses in conducting the business activities (note, however, that they are not allowed to deduct fines, penalties, illegal bribes, or illegal kickbacks).[8] Of course, the IRS is probably more concerned that many illegal businesses fail to report *any* income than about illegal businesses overstating deductions.[9]

[6]In practice, this distinction is rarely cut and dried. Rick may be able to argue for various reasons that Tom's work is worth more than $10 an hour but perhaps not as much as $25 per hour. We use this example to illustrate the issue of reasonable expenses and not to discuss the merits of what actually is reasonable compensation to Tom.

[7]§162(c) and Reg. §1.162-21.

[8]*Comm. v. Sullivan* (1958), 356 US 27.

[9]§280E explicitly prohibits drug dealers from deducting any business expenses associated with this "business" activity. However, drug dealers are able to deduct cost of goods sold because cost of goods sold is technically a reduction in gross income and not a business expense. See Reg. §1.61-3(a).

Taxes in the Real World   *Al Capone Put Away—By the IRS*

Al Capone, the notorious Chicago crime boss, wasn't put behind bars for murder, extortion, drug dealing, or even bootlegging. He went to prison because he didn't pay taxes on his illegal income. In the summer of 1929, Capone was alleged to owe more than $250,000 in taxes and over $150,000 in penalties and he was charged with 24 counts of income tax evasion and failure to file tax returns. Capone was ultimately convicted on three charges of tax evasion in 1925, 1926, and 1927 and two charges of failing to file a tax return in 1928 and 1929. He was sentenced to 11 years in prison and assessed fines totaling $80,000. Capone was brought to justice by the work of IRS agent Frank J. Wilson, who was able to follow Capone's money trail and establish that Capone's income required him to file tax returns and pay taxes.

Source: IN DEPTH: Crime: Al Capone. Last Updated March 20, 2007 by Robin Rowland, CBC News, http://www.cbc.ca/news/background/crime/capone.html.

Political Contributions and Lobbying Costs

Perhaps to avoid the perception that the federal government subsidizes taxpayer efforts to influence politics, the tax laws disallow deductions for political contributions and most lobbying expenses.[10]

Example 8-3

In July, the city fined Rick $200 for violating the city's watering ban when he watered a newly installed landscape. Later, Rick donated $250 to the mayor's campaign for reelection. Can Rick deduct these expenditures?

Answer: No. Rick cannot deduct either the fine or the political contribution as business expenses because the tax laws specifically prohibit deductions for these expenditures.

Capital Expenditures

Whether a business uses the cash or the accrual method of accounting, it generally must capitalize expenditures for *tangible* assets such as buildings, machinery and equipment, furniture and fixtures, and similar property that has a useful life of more than one year (12 months).[11] For tax purposes, businesses generally recover the cost of capitalized tangible assets (other than land) through depreciation.

Businesses also generally must capitalize the cost to create or acquire *intangible* assets such as patents, goodwill, **start-up costs,** and organizational expenditures.[12] They recover the costs of capitalized intangible assets either through amortization (when the tax laws allow them to do so) or upon disposition of the assets.[13]

Expenses Associated with the Production of Tax-Exempt Income

Expenses that do not help businesses generate *taxable* income are not allowed to offset taxable income. For example, this restriction disallows interest expense deductions for businesses that borrow money and invest the loan proceeds in municipal

---

[10]§162(e).

[11]Reg. §1.263(a)-2(d)(4). The act of recording the asset is sometimes referred to as *capitalizing* the expenditure.

[12]Reg. §1.263(a)-4(b). The extent to which expenditures for intangible assets must be capitalized is explored in *Indopco v. Comm.* (1992), 503 US 79.

[13]See §195, §197, and §248 for provisions that allow taxpayers to amortize the cost of certain intangible assets.

(tax-exempt) bonds. It also disallows deductions for life insurance premiums businesses pay on policies that cover the lives of officers or other key employees and compensate the business for the disruption and lost income they may experience due to a key employee's death. Because the death benefit from the life insurance policy is not taxable, the business is not allowed to deduct the insurance premium expense associated with this nontaxable income.

Example 8-4

Rick employs Joan, an arborist who specializes in trimming trees and treating local tree ailments. Joan generates a great deal of revenue for Rick's business, but is in her mid-60s and suffers from diabetes. In November, Rick purchased a "key-employee" term-life insurance policy on Joan's life. The policy cost Rick $720 and will pay him a $20,000 death benefit if Joan passes away during the next 12 months. What amount of life insurance policy premium can Rick deduct?

Answer: $0. Rick cannot deduct the $720 premium on the life insurance policy because the life insurance proceeds from the policy are tax-exempt.

What if: Suppose Rick purchased the life insurance policy on Joan's life and allowed Joan to name the beneficiary. The policy cost Rick $720 and will pay the beneficiary a $20,000 death benefit if Joan passes away during the next 12 months. What amount of life insurance policy premium can Rick deduct?

Answer: $720. In this scenario, Rick can deduct the entire premium of $720 as a *compensation* expense because the benefit of the policy inures to Joan and not to Rick's business.

Personal Expenditures

Taxpayers are not allowed to deduct **personal expenses** unless the expenses are "expressly" authorized by a provision in the law.[14] While the tax laws do not define personal expenses, they imply the scope of personal expenses by stating that "personal, living, or family expenses" are not deductible. Therefore, at a minimum, the costs of food, clothing, and shelter are assumed to be personal and nondeductible. Of course, there are the inevitable exceptions when otherwise personal items are specially adapted to business use. For example, taxpayers may deduct the cost of uniforms or special clothing they purchase for use in their business, if the clothing is not appropriate to wear as ordinary clothing outside the place of business. When the clothing is adaptable as ordinary clothing, the cost of the clothing is a nondeductible personal expenditure.[15]

Example 8-5

Rick spent $500 to purchase special coveralls that identify his landscaping service and provide a professional appearance. How much of the cost for the clothing can Rick deduct as a business expense?

Answer: All $500. While the cost of clothing is inherently personal, Rick can deduct the $500 cost of the coveralls because, due to the design and labeling on the coveralls, they are not suitable for ordinary use.

Many business owners, particularly small business owners such as sole proprietors, may be in a position to use business funds to pay for items that are entirely personal in nature. For example, a sole proprietor could use the business checking account to pay for family groceries. These expenditures, even though funded by the business, are not deductible.

---

[14]§262(a).

[15]An employee who purchases clothing for work would go through a similar analysis to determine if the cost of the clothing qualifies as an employee business expense.

Mixed-Motive Expenditures

Business owners in general, and owners of small or closely held businesses in particular, often make expenditures that are motivated by *both* business and personal concerns. These **mixed-motive expenditures** are of particular concern to lawmakers and the IRS because of the tax incentive to disguise nondeductible personal expenses as deductible business expenses. Thus, deductions for business expenditures with potential personal motives are closely monitored and restricted. The rules for determining the amount of *deductible* mixed-motive expenditures depend on the type of the expenditure. Here we review the rules for determining the deductible portion of mixed-motive expenditures for meals and entertainment, travel and transportation, and the use of property for both business and personal purposes. In Chapter 14, we discuss rules for determining deductible expenses for taxpayers with business offices in their homes.

Meals and Entertainment   Because everyone needs to eat, even business meals contain a significant personal element. To allow for this personal element, taxpayers may only deduct 50 percent of actual business meals. In addition, to deduct any portion of the cost of a meal as a business expense, (1) the amount must be reasonable under the circumstances, (2) the taxpayer (or an employee) must be present when the meal is furnished, and (3) the meal must be directly associated with the active conduct of the taxpayer's business.

Similar to business meals, entertainment associated with business activities contains a significant element of enjoyment. Hence, only 50 percent of allowable business entertainment may be deducted as a business expense.[16] Further, entertainment deductions are allowable only if (1) "business associates" are entertained, (2) the amounts paid are reasonable in amount, and (3) the entertainment is either "directly related" or "associated with" the active conduct of business.

Business associates are individuals with whom the taxpayer reasonably expects to do business, such as customers, suppliers, employees, or advisors. Entertainment is directly related to business if there is an active discussion aimed at generating revenue or fees or the discussion occurs in a clear business setting (such as a hospitality room). The cost of entertainment that occurs in a setting with little possibility of conducting a business discussion, such as a theatre or sports venue, will only be deductible if the entertainment directly precedes or follows a substantial business discussion, thereby satisfying the "associated with" test. In addition, to deduct the cost of meals and entertainment, taxpayers generally must meet strict record-keeping requirements we discuss below.[17]

> **THE KEY FACTS**
>
> Mixed-Motive Expenditures
>
> ■ Only 50 percent of business meals and entertainment are deductible.
>
> ■ Special limits are imposed on expenditures that have both personal and business benefits.
>
> ■ Contemporaneous written records of business purpose are required.

Example 8-6

Rick went out to dinner with a prospective client to discuss Rick's ideas for landscaping the homeowner's yard. After dinner, Rick and the prospective client attended the theatre. Rick paid $190 for the meal and $350 for the tickets, amounts that were reasonable under the circumstances. What amount of these expenditures can Rick deduct as a business expense?

Answer: Rick can deduct $270 [($190 + $350) × 50%], representing half the cost of the meal and entertainment, as a business expense, as long as Rick can substantiate the business purpose and substantial nature of the dinner discussion.

(*continued on page 8-8...*)

---

[16]§274 also provides some exceptions to the 50 percent reduction for meals and entertainment, such as meals and entertainment provided for special events or as employee compensation. Taxpayers can also use a *per diem* rate (an automatic, flat amount per meal) in lieu of actual expenditures to determine the amount of the deduction. There are special limits placed on entertainment expenses associated with spouses.

[17]Under §274, there are special limits placed on certain entertainment expenditures, such as those related to spouses, club dues and entertainment facilities, skyboxes, and entertainment associated with corporate officers, directors, and large shareholders.

What if: Suppose that Rick did not discuss business with the client either before, during, or after the meal. What amount of the expenditures can Rick deduct as a business expense?

Answer: $0. In this scenario, Rick cannot deduct the costs of the meal or entertainment because the activity was not directly related to or associated with a substantial business discussion.

Travel and Transportation   Under certain conditions, sole proprietors and self-employed taxpayers may deduct the cost of travel and transportation for business purposes. Transportation expenses include the direct cost of transporting the taxpayer to and from business sites. However, the cost of commuting between the taxpayer's home and regular place of business is personal and, therefore, not deductible. If the taxpayer uses a vehicle for business, the taxpayer can deduct the costs of operating the vehicle plus depreciation on the vehicle's tax basis. Alternatively, in lieu of deducting these costs, the taxpayer may simply deduct a standard amount for each business mile she drives. The standard mileage rate represents the per-mile cost of operating an automobile (including depreciation or lease payments).[18] For 2009 the standard mileage rate has been set at 55 cents per mile. Once a taxpayer uses the mileage rate to claim deductions for automobile expenses, she must continue to do so in subsequent years. To be deductible, the transportation must be for business reasons. If the transportation is primarily for personal purposes, the cost is not deductible.

Example 8-7

Rick leases an SUV to drive between his shop and various work sites. Rick carefully documents the business use of the SUV (8,100 miles in 2009) and his $5,335 of operating expenses ($3,935 for gas, oil, and repairs and $1,400 for lease payments). At no time does Rick use the SUV for personal purposes. What amount of these expenses may Rick deduct as business expenses?

Answer: $5,335. Since Rick uses the SUV in his business activities, he can deduct (1) the $5,335 cost of operating and leasing the SUV or (2) $4,445 for the 8,100 business miles he drove (55 cents per mile × 8,100 miles). Assuming Rick chooses to deduct operating expenses and lease payments in lieu of using the mileage rate, he can deduct $5,335. Note that if Rick chose the mileage rate this year, he would be required to continue to use the mileage rate for the SUV's business use in future years.

In contrast to transportation expenses, travel expenses are only deductible if the taxpayer is away from home overnight while traveling. This distinction is important because besides the cost of transportation, the deduction for **travel expenses** includes meals (50 percent), lodging, and incidental expenses. A taxpayer is considered to be away from home overnight if she has left her primary place of business on a trip of sufficient duration to require sleep or rest. When a taxpayer travels solely for business purposes, *all* of the costs of travel are deductible (only 50 percent of meals). When the travel has both business and personal aspects, the deductibility of the transportation costs depends upon whether business is the *primary* purpose for the trip. If the primary purpose of a trip is business, the transportation costs are fully deductible, but meals (50 percent), lodging, and incidental expenditures are limited to those incurred during the business portion of the travel.[19] If the taxpayer's primary purpose for the trip is personal, the

---

[18]This mileage rate is updated periodically (sometimes two or three times within a year) to reflect changes in the cost of operating a vehicle. For example, the mileage rate was 50.5¢ per mile for the first half of 2008 and 58.5¢ per mile from July 1, 2008 until year-end. The mileage option is only available for vehicles not previously depreciated, vehicles previously depreciated on the straight-line method, or for leased vehicles where this method has been used throughout the term of the lease.

[19]Special limitations apply to a number of travel expenses that are potentially abusive, such as luxury water travel, foreign conventions, conventions on cruise ships, and travel expenses associated with taking a companion.

taxpayer may not deduct *any* transportation costs to arrive at the location but may deduct meals (50 percent), lodging, transportation, and incidental expenditures for the *business* portion of the trip.

The rule for business travel is modified somewhat if a trip abroad includes both business and personal activities. Like the rule for domestic travel, if foreign travel is primarily for personal purposes, then only those expenses directly associated with business activities are deductible. However, unlike the rule for domestic travel, when foreign travel is primarily for business purposes, a portion of the transportation costs to arrive abroad is not deductible. The nondeductible portion is typically computed based on a time ratio such as the proportion of personal days to total days (travel days count as business days).[20]

Example 8-8

Rick paid a $300 registration fee for a three-day course in landscape design. The course was held in New York (Rick paid $700 for airfare to attend) and he spent four days in New York. He spent the last day sightseeing. During the trip, Rick paid $150 a night for three nights' lodging, $50 a day for meals, and $70 a day for a rental car. What amount of these travel-related expenditures may Rick deduct as business expenses?

Answer: $1,435 for travel and $300 for business education. The primary purpose for the trip appears to be business because Rick spent three days on business activities versus one personal day. He can deduct travel costs, computed as follows:

Deductible Travel Costs

Description	Amount	Explanation
Airfare to New York	$ 700	Primary purposes is business
Lodging in New York	450	3 business days × $150 a day
Meals	75	3 business days × $50 a day × 50% limit
Rental car	210	3 business days × $70 a day
Total business travel expenses	$1,435	

What if: Assume Rick stayed in New York for ten days, spending three days at the seminar and seven days sightseeing. What amount could he deduct?

Answer: In this scenario Rick can deduct $735 for travel and $300 for business education. Rick would not be able to deduct the $700 cost of airfare because the trip is primarily personal, as evidenced by the seven days of personal activities compared to only three days of business activities.

Deductible Travel Costs

Description	Amount	Explanation
Airfare to New York	$ 0	Primary purposes is personal
Lodging in New York	450	3 business days × $150 a day
Meals	75	3 business days × $50 a day × 50% limit
Rental car	210	3 business days × $70 a day
Total business travel expenses	$735	

(*continued on page 8-10...*)

---

[20]Foreign transportation expense is deductible without prorating under special circumstances authorized in §274(c). For example, the cost of getting abroad is fully deductible if the travel is for one week or less or if the personal activity constitutes less than one-fourth of the travel time.

What if: Assume the original facts in the example except Rick traveled to London (rather than New York) for five days spending three days at the seminar and two days sightseeing. What amount could he deduct?

Answer: In this scenario Rick can deduct $1,155 for travel (computed below) and $300 for business education.

Deductible Travel Costs

Description	Amount	Explanation
Airfare to London	$ 420	3 business days/5 total days × $700
Lodging in London	450	3 business days × $150 a day
Meals	75	3 business days × $50 a day × 50% limit
Rental car	210	3 business days × $70 a day
Total business travel expenses	$1,155	

Rick is allowed to deduct $420 of the $700 airfare (60 percent) because he spent three of the five days on the trip conducting business activities.

Property Use   Several types of property may be used for both business and personal purposes. For example, business owners often use automobiles, computers, or cell phones for both business and personal purposes.[21] However, because expenses relating to these assets are deductible only to the extent the assets are used for business purposes, taxpayers must allocate the expenses between the business and personal use portions.

Example 8-9

Rick occasionally uses his personal auto (a BMW) to drive to interviews with prospective clients and to drive back and forth between his shop and various work sites. This year Rick carefully recorded that the BMW was driven 375 miles for business activities and 10,500 miles in total. What expenses associated with the BMW may Rick deduct?

Answer: $206. Based on the 2009 standard mileage rate of 55¢ per mile, Rick can deduct $206 (375 × 55¢) for business use of his BMW. Alternatively, Rick can track the operating expenses of the BMW (including depreciation) and deduct the business portion [based upon the percentage of business miles driven to total miles driven in 2009 (375 business miles/10,500 total miles)].

When taxpayers use other business assets for both business and personal purposes, the deductible business expense is determined by prorating the expenses based upon the percentage of the time the asset is used for business purposes. For example, if a full year's expense for a business asset is $1,000, but the asset is only used for business purposes 90 percent of the time, then only $900 of expense can be deducted ($1,000 × 90%). Special rules apply when the business usage for an asset drops below 50 percent. We discuss these issues in the next chapter.

---

[21]These types of assets are referred to as "listed property."

Record Keeping and Other Requirements   Because distinguishing business purposes from personal purposes is a difficult and subjective task, the tax laws include provisions designed to help the courts and the IRS determine the business element of mixed-motive transactions. Under these provisions, taxpayers must maintain specific, written, contemporaneous records (of time, amount, and business purpose) for mixed-motive expenses. For example, as we discussed above, the tax laws prohibit any deductions for business meals and entertainment unless substantial business discussions accompany the entertainment activity. Consequently, when taxpayers incur meals and entertainment expenses, they must document the business purpose and the extent of the discussion to deduct any of the expenditures.[22]

SPECIFIC BUSINESS DEDUCTIONS

L03

As we discuss above, the tax code provides general guidelines for determining whether business expenditures are deductible. We learned that to be deductible, business expenditures must be must be ordinary, necessary, and reasonable in amount. In some cases, however, the tax laws identify *specific* items businesses are allowed to deduct. We discuss several of these deductions below.

Start-Up Costs and Organizational Expenditures

Businesses may make expenditures to create, establish, or organize new trades or businesses. These expenditures are typically immediately expensed for financial accounting purposes. The tax rules associated with these expenditures are summarized in Exhibit 8-2. We summarize the rules in the exhibit because we discuss the tax treatment of these expenditures in depth in the next chapter.

Bad Debt Expense

Businesses are allowed to deduct bad debt expense when a debt owed to the business becomes worthless or uncollectible.[23] While this business deduction is specifically allowed by the tax laws, it is available only to businesses using the accrual method of accounting for tax purposes. Thus, we defer a detailed discussion of bad debt expense until we discuss accrual method deductions.

Domestic Manufacturing Deduction

Businesses that manufacture goods are allowed to deduct an *artificial* business deduction for tax purposes called the U.S. domestic production activities deduction. This deduction, also known as the **domestic manufacturing deduction (DMD),** is designed to reduce the tax burden on domestic manufacturers to make investments in domestic manufacturing facilities more attractive. The DMD provides a special tax deduction for businesses, large and small, that "manufacture, produce, grow or extract" tangible products entirely or in significant part within the United States.[24]

> **THE KEY FACTS**
>
> Domestic Manufacturing Deduction
>
> ■ A subsidy for the cost of producing goods or certain construction services within the United States.
>
> ■ The deduction for 2009 is 6 percent of qualified production activity income.
>
> ■ The deduction is limited to overall income (AGI for individuals) and 50 percent of wages associated with the production.

[22]§274 requires substantiation of all elements of travel and entertainment including sufficient corroborating evidence. Although there are a few exceptions to this rule, approximations and estimates are generally not sufficient. Also, taxpayers must maintain records to deduct the business portion of mixed-use assets such as cars used for both business and personal purposes.

[23]§166(a).

[24]§199 also allows this deduction for qualifying taxpayers in the domestic film and sound recording industries, those engaged in a construction business in the United States, and engineering and architectural firms providing services for U.S. construction projects. Because the domestic manufacturing deduction does not represent a real expenditure, the deduction is not an expense for financial accounting purposes.

EXHIBIT 8-2   Start-Up Costs and Organizational Expenditures

Item	Description	Discussed in
Start-up costs	• Costs associated with investigating and creating or acquiring a business. • Normal business expenditures before business actually begins. • Capitalized unless formally *elect* to deduct on first tax return. • Immediately expense up to $5,000. • If start-up costs exceed $50,000, immediate expense is reduced dollar for dollar. Once start-up costs reach $55,000, no immediate expense. • Amount not immediately expensed is amortized over 180 months on straight-line basis beginning in the month the business begins. • Applies to any business regardless of form.	Chapter 9
Organizational expenditures	• Expenditures to organize business, including: cost of organizational meetings, state fees, accounting service costs, and legal service expenditures incident to the organization. • Capitalized unless formally *elect* to deduct on first tax return. • Costs of selling or marketing stock or ownership interests are not deductible. • Same rules for immediate expensing and amortizing as start-up costs. • Applies to corporations (§248) and to partnerships (§709).	Chapter 9

This deduction is artificial because it does not represent an expenditure per se, but merely serves to reduce the income taxes the business must pay and thereby increase the after-tax profitability of domestic manufacturing.

The formula for computing the DMD is 6 percent times the *lesser* of (1) the business's taxable income before the deduction (or modified AGI for individuals) or **(2) qualified production activities income (QPAI).**[25] Generally speaking, QPAI is the *net* income from selling or leasing property that was manufactured in the United States. Thus, to compute QPAI, businesses need to determine the amount of revenues, cost of goods sold, and expenses attributable to U.S. production activities. Obviously, the calculation of the income allocable to domestic production can be exceedingly complex, especially in the case of large multinational businesses. The final deduction cannot exceed 50 percent of the wages the business paid to employees for working in qualifying production activities during the year.[26]

Example 8-10

This fall Rick constructed a greenhouse that qualified for the domestic manufacturing deduction. Rick received $5,000 for the construction project from his client and allocated $3,500 in expenses to the project. These expenses included $2,000 of qualified wages. Thus, the greenhouse project generated $1,500 of qualified production activity income (QPAI) for Rick ($5,000 minus $3,500). What is Rick's domestic manufacturing deduction for this project?

(*continued on page 8-13...*)

---

[25]See §199(d)(2). Modified AGI is AGI before the DMD and certain other specified deductions. The percentage increases to 9 percent in 2010 and later years.

[26]Taxpayers show the deduction computations on Form 8903.

Answer: $90. Assuming Rick's QPAI of $1,500 is less than his modified AGI, the DMD is $90, calculated by multiplying 6 percent times $1,500 of QPAI. The entire computation is summarized as follows:

DMD Calculation

Description	Amount	Explanation
Qualified domestic gross receipts	$5,000	Must be a qualified activity
Allocable costs and expenses	−3,500	Allocate to qualified activity
Qualified production activity income	$1,500	Limited to modified AGI
Statutory percentage for 2009	× 6%	Increases to 9% in 2010
Domestic manufacturing deduction	$ 90	Limited to 50% of wages

The 50 percent wage limitation is $1,000 (50% × $2,000 in wages Rick paid to employees working on the project). Thus, Rick is allowed to deduct the entire $90 domestic manufacturing deduction even though the $90 deduction doesn't represent a specific liability or payment to anyone.

Taxes in the Real World   *Starbucks the Manufacturer?*

When you think of Starbucks, do you think of a manufacturing company? Apparently Congress does. The tax law describing business activities that qualify for the domestic manufacturing deduction explicitly states that "the sale of food and beverages prepared by the taxpayer at a retail establishment" is *not* a qualifying activity. However, a footnote in the House-Senate Conference Committee report of the tax act creating the deduction explicitly indicates that *roasting* coffee beans is a qualifying activity but *brewing* coffee is not. Since the retail price of brewed coffee includes the cost of roasted beans, businesses that roast and brew coffee are able to claim a domestic manufacturing deduction for the profit they make from directly selling roasted beans to walk-up customers (and other retailers), and for a portion of the profit they make from selling brewed coffee to customers attributable to the value of the coffee beans. The footnote describing the proper classification of roasted coffee beans for purposes of determining the domestic manufacturing deduction is frequently referred to as the "Starbucks footnote" due to the influence Starbucks had in helping lawmakers see things its way.

Sources: Janet Novack, "Business in the Beltway: Domestic Help," Forbes, May 10, 2006. www.forbes.com/taxes/ 2006/05/10/intel-aol-ge-; §199(c)(4)(B)(i).

Losses on Dispositions of Business Property

Besides operating expenses, businesses are generally allowed to deduct losses incurred when selling or disposing of business assets.[27] The calculation of losses from business property dispositions can be complex, but the main idea is that businesses realize and recognize a loss when the asset's tax basis exceeds the sale proceeds. We discuss the rules governing the tax treatment of gains and losses on asset disposition in more detail in Chapter 10.

Example 8-11

What if: Assume that in late October, Rick purchased a used trailer to transport equipment to work sites. Rick bought the trailer for what he thought was a bargain price of $1,000. However, shortly after Rick acquired it and before he has an opportunity to use the trailer, the axle snapped and was not

(continued on page 8-14...)

---

[27]In most circumstances businesses may *not* deduct losses on assets sold to related parties.

repairable. Rick was forced to sell the trailer to a parts shop for $325. What amount can Rick deduct as a loss from the trailer sale?

Answer: $675, because the trailer was a business asset (amount realized of $325 minus adjusted basis of $1,000). (Note, as we discuss later in Chapter 9, Rick is not allowed to deduct depreciation on the trailer because he did not place it in service this year).

Business Casualty Losses

Besides selling assets, businesses can incur losses when their assets are stolen, damaged, or completely destroyed by a force outside the control of the business.[28] These events are called **casualty losses.** Businesses may deduct casualty losses in the year the casualty occurs or in the year the theft of an asset is discovered. The amount of the loss deduction depends on whether the asset is (1) completely destroyed or stolen or (2) only partially destroyed. When its asset is *completely* destroyed or stolen, the business calculates the amount of the loss as though it sold the asset for the insurance proceeds, if any. That is, the loss is the amount of insurance proceeds minus the adjusted tax basis of the asset. If the asset is damaged but not completely destroyed, the amount of the loss is the amount of the insurance proceeds minus the *lesser* of (1) the asset's tax basis or (2) the decline in the value of the asset due to the casualty. While individuals deduct business casualty losses and casualty losses associated with rentals and royalties as deductions *for* AGI, casualty and theft losses of assets used for the production of income (investments) and personal-use assets are generally deductible as itemized deductions.[29] We summarize the casualty and theft loss rules for business, production of income, and personal-use assets in Exhibit 8-3, which appears on the following page.

Example 8-12

What if: Suppose Rick acquired a personal-use asset several years ago for $9,000. Suppose further that a casualty event destroyed the asset, and at that time the asset was worth $1,000 and insured for $250. What is the amount of Rick's casualty loss (before applying the $500 per casualty floor and the 10 percent of AGI restriction)?

Answer: $750, computed as follows:

Insurance proceeds		$250
Minus the *lesser* of:		
(1) adjusted tax basis or	$9,000	
(2) value at time of casualty	$1,000	−1,000
Casualty loss deduction (before limitations)		($750)

Suppose instead that Rick's asset was a business-use asset and Rick had deducted $4,000 of depreciation expense against the asset. Hence, the asset's tax basis was $5,000 ($9,000 − $4,000), what would be the amount of his business casualty loss?

Answer: $4,750, computed as follows:

Insurance proceeds	$ 250
Minus adjusted tax basis	−5,000
Casualty loss deduction	($4,750)

---

[28]Casualties can be described as unexpected events driven by forces outside the control of the taxpayer that damage or destroy a taxpayer's property. For example, §165 lists "fire, storm, and shipwreck" as examples of casualties.

[29]For example, a taxpayer with a coin collection that is stolen or valuable antique collection that burns is potentially eligible for a casualty loss deduction on assets used for the production of income.

EXHIBIT 8-3   Comparison of Casualty and Theft Loss Rules for Property Used in Business, for Production of Income, and Personal Purposes

	Property Used in Business (including losses from rental and royalty property)	Property Used for the Production of Income	Personal-Use Property
Amount of loss if property completely destroyed or stolen	Insurance proceeds minus adjusted basis	Same as business	Insurance proceeds minus lesser of (1) adjusted basis or (2) decline in asset's value due to casualty or theft
Amount of loss if property is not completely destroyed	Insurance proceeds minus lesser of (1) adjusted basis or (2) decline in asset's value	Same as business	Same as business
Loss limitation	None	None	$500 floor per casualty and 10 percent of AGI floor for total casualty losses for year
Type of deduction	For AGI	Miscellaneous itemized deduction (not subject to 2 percent floor)	Itemized deduction

ACCOUNTING PERIODS

So far we've discussed how to determine a business's income and how to determine its deductible business expenses. In this section, we discuss accounting periods, which affect when taxpayers determine their income and deductions. Businesses must report their income and deductions over a fixed **accounting period** or **tax year.** A full tax year consists of 12 full months. A tax year can consist of a period less than 12 months (a short tax year) in certain circumstances. For instance, a business may report income for such a short year in its first year of existence (for example, it reports income on a calendar year-end and starts business after January 1) or in its final year of existence (for example, a calendar-year business ends its business before December 31). Short tax years in a business's initial or final year are treated the same as full years. A business may also have a short year when it changes its tax year. In these situations, special rules may apply for computing the tax liability of the business.[30]

There are three types of tax years, each with different year-ends:

- A calendar year ends on December 31.
- A **fiscal year** ends on the last day of a month other than December.
- A 52/53 week year ends on the same day of the week every year. In other words, a 52/53 week year could end on the same day of the week that is the last such day in the month or on the same day of the week nearest the end of the month. For example, a business could adopt a 52/53 week fiscal year that (1) ends on the last Saturday in July each year or (2) ends on the Saturday closest to the end of July (although this Saturday might be in August rather than July).[31]

> **THE KEY FACTS**
>
> **Accounting Periods**
>
> ■ Individuals and proprietorships account for income on a calendar year.
>
> ■ Corporations are allowed to choose a fiscal year.
>
> ■ Partnerships and other flow-through entities generally use a required year.

---

[30]§443. Discussion of tax consequences associated with these short years is beyond the scope of this text.

[31]Businesses with inventories may benefit from 52/53 year-ends to facilitate an inventory count when the store is closed (e.g., over a weekend).

Not all types of tax years are available to all types of businesses. The rules for determining the tax years available to the business depends on whether the business is a sole proprietorship, a **flow-through entity,** or a C corporation. These rules are summarized as follows:

- *Sole proprietorships:* Because individual proprietors must report their business income on their individual returns, proprietorships use a calendar year-end to report their business income.[32]
- *Flow-through entities:* Because partnerships and S corporations are flow-through entities (partners and S corporation owners report the entity's income directly on their own tax returns), these entities generally must adopt tax years consistent with the owners' tax years.[33] Because owners are allocated income from flow-through entities on the last day of the entity's taxable year, the tax laws impose the tax year consistency requirement to minimize income tax deferral opportunities for the owners.
- *C corporations:* C corporations are generally allowed to select a calendar, fiscal, or 52/53 week year-end.

A business adopts a calendar year-end or fiscal year-end by filing its initial tax return. In contrast, a business adopts a 52/53 week year-end by filing a special election with the IRS. Once a business establishes its tax year, it generally must receive permission from the IRS to change.

Example 8-13

Rick is a calendar-year taxpayer. What tax year should Rick use to report income from his business Green Acres?

Answer: Calendar year. This is true even though Rick began his business in May of this year. He will calculate income and expense for his landscaping business over the calendar year and include the net business income from May through December of this year on Schedule C of his individual tax return.

What if: Suppose that Rick incorporated Green Acres at the time he began his business. What tax year could Green Acres adopt?

Answer: If Green Acres was operated as a C corporation, it could elect a calendar year-end, a fiscal year-end, or a 52/53 week year-end. If it were an S corporation, it likely would have a calendar year-end.

L05

ACCOUNTING METHODS

Once a business adopts a tax year, it must determine which items of income and deductions to recognize during a *particular* year. Generally speaking, the taxpayer's **accounting methods** determine the tax year in which a business recognizes a particular item of income or deduction. Because accounting methods affect the *timing* of when a taxpayer reports income and deductions, accounting methods are very important for taxpayers using a timing tax strategy to defer income or accelerate deductions.[34]

---

[32]Virtually all individual taxpayers use a calendar year tax year.

[33]See §706 for the specific restrictions on year-ends for partnerships and §1378 for restrictions on S corporations. If they can show a business purpose (not easy to do), both partnerships and S corporations may adopt year-ends other than those used by their owners.

[34]Accounting methods do not determine *whether* an item of income is taxable or an expense is deductible. Accordingly, accounting methods generally do not affect the total income or deductions recognized over the taxpayer's lifetime.

Financial and Tax Accounting Methods

Many businesses are required to generate financial statements for nontax reasons. For example, publicly traded corporations must file financial statements with the Securities and Exchange Commission (SEC) based on generally accepted accounting principles (GAAP). Also, privately owned businesses borrowing money from banks are often required to generate financial statements under GAAP, so that the lender can evaluate the business's creditworthiness. In reporting financial statement income, businesses have incentives to select accounting methods permissible under GAAP that accelerate income and defer deductions. In contrast, for tax planning purposes, businesses have incentives to choose accounting methods that *defer income* and *accelerate deductions*. This natural tension between financial reporting incentives and tax reporting incentives may be the reason the tax laws sometimes require businesses to use the same accounting methods for tax purposes that they use for financial accounting purposes. In other words, in many circumstances, if businesses want to defer taxable income, they must also defer book income.[35]

However, sometimes the tax laws require businesses to use different, presumably more appropriate, accounting methods for tax purposes. Consequently, for policy and administrative reasons, the tax laws also identify several circumstances when businesses must use specific tax accounting methods to determine taxable income no matter what accounting method they use for financial reporting purposes. We now turn our attention to accounting methods prescribed by the tax laws. With certain restrictions, businesses are able to select their *overall* accounting methods and accounting methods for *specific* items or transactions. We cover each of these in turn.

Overall Accounting Method

Businesses must choose an overall method of accounting to track and report their business activities for tax purposes. The overriding requirement for any tax accounting method is that the method must "clearly reflect income" and be applied consistently.[36] The two primary overall methods are the cash method and the accrual method. Businesses may also choose a hybrid method (some accounts on the cash method and others on the accrual method).

Cash Method   A taxpayer (or business) using the cash method of accounting recognizes revenue when property or services are actually or constructively received. This is generally true no matter when the business sells the good or performs the service that generates the revenue. Likewise, a business adopting the cash method generally recognizes deductions when the expense is paid. Thus, the timing of the liability giving rise to the expense is usually irrelevant.

Keep in mind that a cash-method business receiving payments in *noncash* form (as property or services) must recognize the noncash payments as gross income. Also, in certain circumstances, a business expending cash on ordinary and necessary business expenses may not be allowed to *currently* deduct the expense at the time of the payment. For example, cash-method taxpayers (and accrual-method taxpayers) are not allowed to deduct prepaid interest expense and cannot usually deduct prepaid expenses or payments that create a tangible or intangible asset.[37] However, the regulations provide a **12-month rule** for prepaid business expenses to simplify the process of determining whether to capitalize or immediately expense payments that create benefits for a relatively brief period of time, such as insurance, security, rent, and

---

[35]§446(a).
[36]§446(b).
[37]§461(g).

warranty service contracts. When a business prepays business expenses, it may *immediately* deduct the prepayment if (1) the contract period does not last more than a year *and* (2) the contract period does not extend beyond the end of the taxable year following the tax year in which the taxpayer makes the payment.[38] If the prepaid expense does not meet both of these criteria, the business must capitalize the prepaid amount and amortize it over the length of the contract whether the business uses the cash or accrual method of accounting.[39]

Example 8-14

On July 1, 2009, Rick paid $1,200 for a 12-month insurance policy that covers his business property from accidents and casualties from July 1, 2009, through June 30, 2010. How much of the $1,200 expenditure may Rick deduct in 2009 if he uses the cash method of accounting for his business activities?

Answer: $1,200. Because the insurance coverage does not exceed 12 months and does not extend beyond the end of 2010, Rick is allowed to deduct the entire premium payment under the 12-month rule.

What if: Suppose the insurance policy was for 12 months but the policy ran from February 1, 2010, through January 31, 2011. How much of the expenditure may Rick deduct in 2009 if he uses the cash method of accounting for his business activities?

Answer: $0. Even though the contract period is 12 months or less, Rick is required to capitalize the cost of the prepayment for the insurance policy because the contract period extends beyond the end of 2010.

What if: Suppose Rick had paid $1,200 for an *18-month* policy beginning July 1, 2009 and ending December 31, 2010. How much may he deduct in 2009 if he uses the cash method of accounting for his business activities?

Answer: $400. In this scenario, because the policy exceeds 12 months, Rick is allowed to deduct the portion of the premium pertaining to 2009. In 2009, he would deduct $400 (6 months/ 18 months × $1,200). He would deduct the remaining $800 in 2010.

Accrual Method   Businesses using the accrual method to determine taxable income follow rules similar to GAAP with two basic differences. First, as we discuss below, requirements for recognizing taxable income tend to be structured to recognize more income than the recognition rules for financial accounting. Second, requirements for accruing tax deductions tend to be structured to recognize less accrued expenses than the recognition rules for financial reporting purposes. These differences reflect the underlying objectives of financial accounting income and taxable income. The objective of financial accounting is to provide useful information to stakeholders such as creditors, prospective investors, and shareholders. Because financial accounting methods are designed to guard against businesses overstating their profitability to these users, financial accounting tends to bias *against overstating* income. In contrast, the government's main objective for writing tax laws is to collect revenues. Thus, tax accounting rules for accrual-method businesses tend to bias *against understating* income. These differences should be apparent as we describe tax accounting rules for businesses.

---

[38]This 12-month rule applies to both cash-method and accrual-method taxpayers. However, for accrual-method taxpayers to deduct prepaid expenses they must meet the 12-month rule requirements and they must meet an economic performance requirement that we discuss in the next section.

[39]Reg. §1.263(a)-4(f).

continued from page 8-1...

Rick's CPA, Jane, informed him that he needs to select an overall method of accounting for Green Acres to compute its taxable income. Jane advised Rick to use the cash method. However, Rick wanted to prepare GAAP financial statements and use the accrual method of accounting. He decided that if Green Acres was going to become a big business, it needed to act like a big business. Finally, after much discussion, Rick and Jane reached a compromise. For the first year, they would track Green Acres' business activities using both the cash *and* the accrual method. In addition, they would also keep GAAP-based books for financial purposes. When filing time comes, Rick would decide which method to use in reporting taxable income. Jane told Rick that he could wait until he filed his tax return to select the accounting method for tax purposes. ∎

Accrual Income

Businesses using the accrual method of accounting generally recognize income when they meet the "all-events test."

All-Events Test for Income   The all-events test requires that businesses recognize income when (1) all events have occurred that determine or fix their right to receive the income and (2) the amount of the income can be determined with reasonable accuracy.[40] Assuming the amount of income can be determined with reasonable accuracy, businesses meet the all-events requirement on the *earliest* of the following three dates:

1. When they complete the task required to earn the income. Businesses earn income for services as they provide the services, and they generally earn income from selling property when the title of the property passes to the buyer.
2. When the payment for the task is due from the customer.
3. When the business receives payment for the task.

Example 8-15

In early fall, Rick contracted with a dozen homeowners to relandscape their yards. Rick agreed to do the work for an aggregate of $11,000. Rick and his crew started in the fall and completed the jobs in December 2009. However, he didn't mail the bills until after the holidays and didn't receive any payments until January 2010. When must Rick recognize the income from this work?

Answer: Under the accrual method, Rick must recognize the entire $11,000 as income in 2009 because his right to the income is fixed when Rick and his crew complete the work. Under the cash method, however, Rick would not recognize the $11,000 as income until 2010 when he received it.

Taxation of Advance Payments of Income (Prepaid Income)

In some cases, businesses receive income payments *before* they actually earn the income (they receive a prepayment). *When* the business must recognize a prepayment as income depends on the type of income. The rule for interest and rental income is

---

[40]Reg. §1.451-1(a).

relatively strict. Businesses must recognize prepaid rental and prepaid interest income *immediately* upon receipt (the income is recognized before it is earned). However, businesses are not required to recognize security deposits received from rental customers because they incur a liability to return security deposits when they receive the payments.[41] The income recognition rules are less strict when businesses receive advance payments for services or goods.

Advance Payment for Services   For financial reporting purposes, a business does not immediately recognize income on advance payments it receives for services to be provided in the future. For financial reporting purposes, an advance payment for services is recorded as a debit for cash received and a credit to a liability account (unearned financial accounting income). The business then recognizes the *financial* income from the services as it performs the services. In contrast, for tax purposes, the all-events test generally requires businesses receiving *advance* payments for services to recognize the income when they receive the payment, rather than when they perform the services.

The IRS provides an exception to this immediate recognition general rule. Specifically, businesses receiving advance payments for services may *defer* recognizing the *prepayment* as income until the tax year *following* the year they receive the payment.[42] This one-year deferral does *not* apply (1) if (or the extent to which) the income is actually earned by the end of the year of receipt, (2) if the prepayment was included in financial reporting income, or (3) if the prepayment was for interest or rent (taxpayers must recognize prepaid interest and rental income on receipt).

Advance Payment for Goods

When an accrual-basis business receives an advance payment for *goods* it will provide to customers in the future, the business may account for the prepayment for tax purposes under the **full-inclusion method** or the **deferral method.**[43] Businesses electing the full-inclusion method *immediately* recognize the advance payment as income. Businesses using the deferral method recognize advance payments for goods by the earlier of (1) when the business would recognize the income for tax purposes if it had not received the *advance* payment or (2) when it recognizes the income for financial reporting purposes. Thus, the deferral method is comparable to the deferral allowed for advance payments received for future services. However, unlike the treatment of advance payments for services, advance payments for goods could be deferred for more than a year, if the business defers the income for financial reporting purposes for more than a year.

Example 8-16

In late November 2009, Rick received a $7,200 payment from a client for monthly landscaping services from December 1, 2009, through November 30, 2011 ($300 a month for 24 months). When must Rick recognize the income from the advance payment for services?

Answer: Under the accrual method, Rick would initially recognize the $300 income he earned in December 2009. However, in 2010, he would recognize the remaining $6,900 (rather than only the

(*continued on page 8-21...*)

[41]*Comm. v. Indianapolis Power & Light Co.* (1990), 493 US 203.
[42]Rev Proc. 2004-34, 2004-1 CB 991.
[43]Reg. §1.141-5

$3,600 related to 2010) because he is not allowed to defer the prepayments for services for more than a year. However, under the cash method, Rick must recognize the entire prepayment, $7,200, as income upon receipt in 2009.

What if: Suppose the $7,200 prepayment was for the delivery of 15 pallets of sod at a cost to Rick of $1,800. Suppose further that five pallets were to be delivered in 2010 and the remainder was to be delivered in 2011. When would Rick recognize the income from the advance payment of goods under the accrual method?

Answer: If Rick elected the full-inclusion method, then he would recognize the entire prepayment of $7,200 as income (minus his cost of goods sold of $1,800) in 2009. However, if Rick elected the deferral method, then he would recognize the income as the sod is delivered, $2,400 in 2010 (minus $600 cost of goods sold) and $4,800 in 2011 (minus $1,200 cost of goods sold).

Inventories

Many businesses generate income by selling products they acquire for resale or products they manufacture. Businesses for which selling inventory is a material income-producing factor generally must account for gross profit (sales minus cost of goods sold) using the accrual method, even when they are otherwise cash-method taxpayers.[44]

However, the business is not allowed to deduct the cost of the inventory to the extent it has the product at the end of the year. How does this exception benefit a cash-method business if the business is not allowed to fully deduct the cost of inventory until it sells the inventory? It may benefit the business because it allows it to use the cash method to account for sales revenue. Without the exception, cash-method service businesses would be required to account for sales revenue from inventory sales on the accrual method, which means they may be required to recognize revenue before they actually receive it. With the exception, they are allowed to defer the revenue recognition until they receive the payments from customers.

Businesses selling inventory must determine their inventory costs to accurately compute taxable income. This requires businesses to maintain records of balances for finished goods inventory and, if applicable, for partially finished goods and raw materials. Inventory costs include the purchase price of raw materials (minus any discounts), shipping costs, and any indirect costs it allocates to the inventory under the **uniform cost capitalization rules (UNICAP rules).**[45]

Uniform Capitalization The tax laws require businesses to capitalize in the cost of inventory certain direct and indirect costs associated with inventories.[46] Congress enacted these rules primarily for two reasons. First, the rules accelerate tax revenues for the government by deferring deductions for the capitalized costs until the business sells the associated inventory. Thus, there is generally a one-year lag between when businesses initially capitalize the costs and when they deduct them. Second, Congress designed the "uniform" rules to reduce variation in the costs businesses include in

> **THE KEY FACTS**
>
> **Inventories**
>
> ∎ Businesses must use the accrual method to account for substantial inventories.
>
> ∎ The UNICAP rules require capitalization of most indirect costs of production.
>
> ∎ The LIFO method is allowed if also used for financial reporting purposes.

---

[44]As an exception to this general rule, cash-method businesses are allowed to use the cash method to account for their gross profit under a "small business" exception if the business's average annual gross receipts for the three-year period prior to the current year do not exceed $10,000,000 *and* the business's primary business activity is to provide services to customers but the business also provides a product incident to (as a secondary or small part of) the services.

[45]Inventory valuation allowances are generally not allowed, but taxpayers can adopt the lower of cost or market method of inventory valuation. In addition, specific goods not salable at normal prices can be valued at bona fide selling prices less direct cost of disposition.

[46]§263A(a).

inventory. Congress intended the UNICAP provisions to apply to large businesses. Consequently, businesses with average annual gross receipts of $10 million or less over the three-year period ending with the taxable year prior to the current year are not *required* to use the UNICAP rules.

Under these uniform cost capitalization rules, large businesses are generally required to capitalize more costs to inventory for tax purposes than they capitalize under financial accounting rules. Under GAAP, businesses generally include in inventory only those costs incurred within their production facility. In contrast, the UNICAP rules require businesses to allocate to inventory the costs they incur inside the production facility and the costs they incur outside the facility to support production (or inventory acquisition) activities. For example, under the UNICAP provisions, a business must capitalize at least a portion of the compensation paid to employees in its purchasing department, general and administrative department, and even its information technology department, to the extent these groups provide support for the production process. In contrast, businesses immediately expense these costs as period costs for financial accounting purposes. The regulations provide guidance on the costs that must be allocated to inventory. Selling, advertising, and research costs are specifically identified as costs that do not have to be allocated to inventory under the UNICAP provisions.[47]

Example 8-17

Green Acres sells trees but Rick anticipates selling flowers, shrubs, and other plants in future years. Ken is Rick's employee in charge of purchasing inventory. Ken's compensation this year is $30,000, and Rick estimates that Ken spends about 5 percent of his time acquiring inventory and the remaining time working on landscaping projects. How would Rick allocate Ken's compensation under the UNICAP rules?

Answer: If the UNICAP rules applied to Green Acres, Rick would allocate $1,500 ($30,000 × 5%) of Ken's compensation to the cost of the inventory Green Acres acquired this year. (Note, however, because Green Acres gross receipts for the year are under $10,000,000, it is not *required* to and it does not apply the UNICAP rules.) In contrast, Ken's entire salary would be expensed as a period cost for financial accounting purposes.

Inventory Cost-Flow Methods   Once a business determines the cost of its inventory, it must use an inventory cost-flow method to determine its cost of goods sold. Three primary cost-flow methods are (1) first-in, first-out (**FIFO**), (2) last-in, first-out (**LIFO**), and (3) **specific identification.** Businesses might be inclined to use FIFO or LIFO methods when they sell similar, relatively low-cost, high-volume products such as cans of soup or barrels of oil. These methods simplify inventory accounting because the business need not track the individual cost of each item it sells. In contrast, businesses that sell distinct, relatively high-cost, low-volume products might be more likely to adopt the specific identification method. For example, jewelry and used-car businesses would likely use the specific identification method to account for their cost of sales. In general terms, when costs are increasing, a business using the FIFO method will report a higher gross margin than if it used the LIFO method. The opposite is true if costs are decreasing.

---

[47]Reg. §1.263A–1(e)(3)(iii).

Example 8-18

In late August, Rick purchased 10 oak saplings (immature trees) for a total purchase price of $3,000. In September, he purchased 12 more for a total price of $3,900, and in late October, he purchased 15 more for $5,000. The total cost of each lot of trees was determined as follows:

Purchase Date	Trees	Direct Cost	Other Costs	Total Cost
August 20	10	$ 3,000	$200	$ 3,200
September 15	12	3,900	300	4,200
October 22	15	5,000	400	5,400
Totals	37	$11,900	$900	$12,800

Before the end of the year, Green Acres sold 20 of the oak saplings (5 from the August lot, 5 from the September lot, and 10 from the October lot) for cash. What is Green Acres' gross profit from sales of oak saplings if the sales revenue totaled $14,000 (all collected by year-end), and what is its ending oak sapling inventory under the accrual and the cash method of accounting?

Answer: Under the accrual method, Green Acres' gross profit from sapling sales and its ending inventory balance for the remaining oak saplings under the FIFO, LIFO, and specific identification cost-flow methods is as follows:

	FIFO	LIFO	Specific ID
Sales	$14,000	$14,000	$14,000
Cost of goods sold	−6,700	−7,150	−6,950
Gross profit	$ 7,300	$ 6,850	$ 7,050
Ending inventory:			
August 20 trees	$ 0	$ 3,200	$ 1,600
September 15 trees	700	2,450	2,450
October 22 trees	5,400	0	1,800
Total ending inventory	$ 6,100	$ 5,650	$ 5,850

Using the cash method, the answer is the same as it is under the accrual method. Green Acres is not allowed to deduct the cost of its ending inventory even if it qualifies to use the cash method to account for gross profit under the small business ($10M) exception.

What if: Assume the same original facts except that Green Acres received $10,000 sales revenue from customers this year and the remaining $4,000 early next year. Assuming Green Acres qualifies to use the cash method to account for gross profit under the small business ($10M) exception, what is the amount of Green Acres' gross profit this year if it uses the specific identification method of accounting for its ending inventory?

Answer: $3,050 ($10,000 revenue minus $6,950 cost of goods sold). In this situation Green Acres would be allowed to defer $4,000 of the sales revenue until it collected it next year.

When costs are subject to inflation over time, a business would get the best of both worlds if it adopted the FIFO method for financial reporting purposes and the LIFO method for tax purposes. Not surprisingly, the tax laws require that a business can use LIFO for tax purposes only if it also uses LIFO for financial reporting purposes.[48] While this "consistency" requirement may not matter to entities not required to generate financial reports, it can be very restrictive to publicly traded corporations.

[48]§472(c).

Accrual Deductions

Generally, when accrual-method businesses incur a liability relating to a business expense, they account for it by crediting a liability account (or cash if they pay the liability at the time they incur it) and debiting an expense account. However, to record an expense and the corresponding deduction for tax purposes, the business must meet (1) an all-events test for the liability *and* (2) an **economic performance test** with respect to the liability.[49] While the all-events test for recognizing deductions is similar to the all-events test for recognizing income, the additional economic performance requirement makes the deduction recognition rules more stringent than the income recognition rules. The deduction rules generally preclude businesses from deducting estimated expenses or reserves.

All-Events Test for Deductions   For a business to recognize a deduction, all events that establish its liability giving rise to the deduction must have occurred and it must be able to determine the amount of the liability with reasonable accuracy.[50]

Example 8-19	

On November of this year, Rick agreed to a one-year $6,000 contract with Ace Advertising to produce a radio ad campaign. Ace agreed that Rick would owe nothing under the contract unless his sales increase a minimum of 25 percent over the next six months. What amount, if any, may Rick deduct this year for this contract under the accrual and cash methods?

Answer: Under the accrual method, Green Acres is not allowed to recognize *any* deduction this year for the liability. Even though Ace will have completed two months of advertising for Green Acres by the end of the year, its guarantee means that Rick's liability is not fixed until and unless his sales increase by 25 percent.

Under the cash method, Rick would not deduct any of the cost of the campaign this year because he has not paid anything to Ace.

Economic Performance   Even when businesses meet the all-events test, they still must clear the economic performance hurdle to recognize the tax deduction. This requirement specifies that businesses may not recognize a deduction for an expense until the underlying activity generating the associated liability (called *economic performance*) has occurred. Thus, an accrual-method business would not be allowed to deduct a prepaid business expense even if it qualified to do so under the 12-month rule (discussed above) unless it also met the economic performance test with respect to the liability associated with the expense.

The specific requirements for the economic performance test differ based on whether the liability arose from:

- Receiving goods or services *from* another party.
- Renting or leasing property *from* another party.
- Providing goods or services *to* another party.
- Certain activities creating **payment liabilities.**

Receiving goods and (or) services from another party.   When a business agrees to pay another party for goods or services the other party will provide, the business deducts the expense associated with the liability as the other party provides the goods or

---

THE KEY FACTS

Accrual of Business-Expense Deductions

- Both all-events and economic performance are required for deducting accrued business expenses.

- The all-events test requires that the business be liable for the payment.

- Economic performance generally requires that underlying activity generating liability has occurred in order for the associated expense to be deductible.

---

[49] §461(h)
[50] §461.

services (assuming the all-events test is met for the liability). As an exception to this general rule, when a business hires another party to provide goods or services, and in this situation the business actually *pays* the liability before the other party provides the goods or services, the business may treat the *actual payment as economic performance* as long as it *reasonably expects* the other party to provide the goods or all of the services within three and one-half months after it makes the payment.[51]

Example 8-20

On December 15, 2009, Rick hires Your New Fence, LLC (YNF), to install a concrete wall for one of his clients by paying $1,000 of the cost as a down payment and agreeing to pay the remaining $7,000 when YNF finishes the wall. YNF was not going to start building the wall until early 2010, so as of the end of the year Rick has not billed his client for the wall. Rick expects YNF to finish the wall by the end of April. What amount associated with his liability to YNF is Rick allowed to deduct in 2009 and 2010?

Answer: Under the accrual method, Rick will deduct his full $8,000 cost of the wall in 2010 when YNF builds the wall, because economic performance occurs as YNF provides the services, even though Rick paid for part of the goods and services in 2009. Under the cash method, Rick would deduct $1,000 (his down payment) in 2009 and the remainder in 2010 when he pays the remainder on the contract.

What if: Assume that Rick expected YNF to finish building the wall by the end of January 2010. What amount associated with this liability to YNF is Rick allowed to deduct in 2009 and 2010?

Answer: Under the accrual method, Rick is allowed to deduct $1,000 in 2009 because Rick actually paid this amount in 2009 and he reasonably expected YNF to finish its work on the wall within three and one-half months after he made the payment to them on December 15. Rick would deduct the remaining $7,000 cost of the wall in 2010 when YNF builds the wall.

Under the cash method, Rick deducts the $1,000 down payment in 2009 and the remaining $7,000 when he makes the payment in 2010.

Renting or leasing property from another party.   When a business enters into an agreement to rent or lease property from another party, economic performance occurs over the rental period. Thus, the business is allowed to deduct the rental expense over the rental period.

Example 8-21

On May 1, 2009, Rick paid $7,200 in advance to rent his shop for 12 months ($600 per month). What amount may Rick deduct for rent in 2009 if he accounts for his business activities using the accrual method?

Answer: $4,800 ($600 × 8 months use in 2009). Even though the rent is a prepaid business expense and Rick may deduct the expense under the 12-month rule (the contract period is for 12 months and the contract period does not extend beyond 2010), he must deduct the rent expense over the term of the lease because that is when economic performance occurs.

What if: Assuming the original facts, what amount of the $7,200 rental payment may Rick deduct in 2009 if he is using the cash method of accounting for his business?

Answer: $7,200. In this case, Rick may deduct the expense under the 12-month rule. He does not have to meet the economic performance requirement to deduct the expense because the economic performance requirements apply to accrual—not cash-method taxpayers.

---

[51]Reg. §1.461-4(d)(6).

Example 8-22

On November 1, 2009, Rick paid $2,400 to rent a trailer for 24 months. What amount of this payment may Rick deduct and when may he deduct it?

Answer: Under the accrual method, even though Rick paid the entire rental fee in advance, economic performance occurs over the 24-month rental period. Thus, Green Acres deducts $200 for the trailer rental in 2009, $1,200 in 2010, and $1,000 in 2011. Because the rental period exceeds 12 months, the amount and timing of the deductions is the same under the cash method.

Providing goods and services to another party. Businesses liable for providing goods and services to other parties meet the economic performance test for these liabilities as they incur costs in satisfying the liabilities.

Example 8-23

In the summer, Rick landscaped a city park. As part of this service, Rick agreed to remove a fountain from the park at the option of the city parks committee. In December 2009, the committee decided to have Rick remove the fountain. Rick began the removal in December and completed the removal in the spring of 2010. Rick paid a part-time employee $850 for the removal work in December and an additional $685 to complete the removal the following spring. What is the amount and timing of Rick's deductions for the removal project?

Answer: Under the accrual method, Rick is allowed to deduct his payments for services to others as he incurs costs to satisfy his liability for removing the fountain. Consequently, Rick can deduct the $850 payment to meet this obligation in 2009 and the remaining $685 in 2010. Under the cash method, the amount and timing of his deductions would be the same as it is under the accrual method.

What if: Suppose that in December 2009, Rick paid $1,000 to a subcontractor to remove the fountain and the subcontractor removed the fountain in 2010. What is the amount and timing of Rick's deductions for the removal project in this situation?

Answer: Under the accrual method, because Rick is hiring another person to provide the service that he is liable to perform, economic performance occurs once the service is provided (rather than as costs are incurred). Hence, Rick can only deduct the $1,000 payment once the fountain has been removed in 2010.[52] Under the cash method, however, Rick can deduct $1,000 in 2009 when he makes the payment to the subcontractor.

Payment liabilities. Economic performance occurs for certain liabilities only when the business actually *pays* the liability. Thus, accrual-method businesses incurring payment liabilities are essentially on the *cash method* for deducting the associated expenses. Exhibit 8-4 describes different categories of these payment liabilities.

EXHIBIT 8-4   Categories of Payment Liabilities

Economic performance occurs when taxpayer pays liability associated with:

- Worker's compensation, tort, breach of contract, or violation of law.
- Rebates and refunds.
- Awards, prizes, and jackpots.
- Insurance, warranties, and service contracts provided *to* the business. (Note: This is insurance, warranties, and product service contracts that cover the taxpayer and *not* a warranty like the one in Example 8-24 that the taxpayer provides to others.)
- Taxes.[53]
- Other liabilities not provided for elsewhere.

---

[52]Reg. §1.461-4(d)(4) and Reg. §1.461-4(d)(7), example 1.

[53]While taxes are generally not deducted until they are paid, §461(c) allows businesses to elect to accrue the deduction for real property taxes as time passes instead of deducting them when they actually pay them.

Example 8-24

If clients are not completely satisfied with Green Acres' landscaping work, Rick offers a $200 refund with no questions asked. Near the end of the year, Rick had four clients request refunds. Rick incurred the liability for the refunds this year, but he was busy during the holiday season, so he didn't pay the refunds until January 2010. When should Rick deduct the customer refunds?

Answer: Because refunds are payment liabilities, economic performance does not occur until Rick actually pays the refunds. Consequently, Rick deducts the $800 of refunds in 2010 even though the liability for the refunds met the all-events test in 2009. Under the cash method, Rick would not deduct the refunds until he paid them in 2010.

Accrual-method taxpayers that prepay business expenses for *payment liabilities* (insurance contracts, warranties, and product service contracts provided to the taxpayer) are allowed to immediately deduct the prepayments subject to the 12-month rule for prepaid expenses. Thus, the deductible amounts for Rick's prepaid insurance contracts in Example 8-14 are the same for both the cash method and accrual method of accounting. Exhibit 8-5 describes the requirements for economic performance for the different types of liabilities.[54]

EXHIBIT 8-5   Economic Performance

Taxpayer incurs liability from	Economic performance occurs
Receiving goods and services *from* another party	When the goods or services are provided to the taxpayer or with payment if the taxpayer reasonably expects actual performance within 3½ months.
Renting or leasing property *from* another party	Ratably over the time period during which the taxpayer is entitled to use the property or money.
Providing goods and services *to* another party	When the taxpayer incurs costs to satisfy the liability or provide the goods and services.
Activities creating "payment" liabilities	When the business actually makes payment.
Interest expense	As accrued. This technically does not fall within the economic performance rules but it is a similar concept.

Bad Debt Expense   When accrual method businesses sell a product or a service on credit, they debit accounts receivable and credit sales revenue for both financial and tax purposes. However, because businesses usually are unable to collect the full amount of their accounts receivable, they incur bad debt expense (a customer owes them a debt that the customer will not pay). For financial reporting purposes, the business estimates the amount of the bad debt, debits bad debt expense, and credits an allowance for doubtful accounts. However, for tax purposes, businesses are allowed to deduct bad debt expense only when the debt actually becomes worthless within the taxable year.[55] Consequently, for tax purposes, businesses determine which debts are

---

[54]Reg. §1.461-5 provides a "recurring items" exception to the economic performance rules. If the taxpayer elects to use this exception, businesses generally may deduct recurring expenses as if economic performance occurred in a year as long as economic performance actually occurs by 8½ months after the year ends. In the case of services, all of the services must be provided within 8½ months to qualify for this exception. This exception only applies if deducting the item in the earlier year results in better matching of expenses with income or the item is immaterial.

[55]§166(a).

uncollectible and write them off by debiting bad debt expense and *directly* crediting the actual account receivable account that is uncollectible. This required method of determining bad debt expense for tax purposes is called the **direct write-off method.** In contrast, the method used for financial reporting purposes is called the **allowance method.** Businesses reporting taxable income on the cash method of accounting are *not* allowed to deduct bad debt expenses, because they do not include receivables in taxable income (they do not credit revenue until they actually receive payment).

Example 8-25

At year-end, Rick estimates that about $900 of the receivables from his landscaping services will be uncollectible, but he has identified only one client, Jared, who will definitely not pay his bill. Jared, who has skipped town, owes Rick $280 for landscaping this fall. What amount of bad debt expense may Rick deduct for the year?

Answer: For financial reporting purposes, Rick recognizes a $900 bad debt expense. However, for tax purposes, under the accrual method, Rick can only deduct $280—the amount associated with specifically writing off Jared's receivable. Under the cash method, Rick would not be able to claim any deduction, because he did not receive a payment from Jared and thus did not recognize income on the amount Jared owed him.

Limitations on Accruals to Related Parties   To prevent businesses and related parties from working together to defer taxes, the tax laws prevent an accrual-method business from accruing (and deducting) an expense for a liability owed to a related party using the cash method until the related party recognizes the income associated with the payment.[56] For this purpose, related parties include:

- Family members including parents, siblings, and spouses.
- Shareholders and C corporations when the shareholder owns more than 50 percent of the corporation's stock.[57]
- Owners of partnerships and S corporations no matter the ownership percentage.[58]

This issue frequently arises in situations in which a business employs the owner or a relative of an owner. The business is not allowed to deduct compensation expense owed to the related party until the year in which the related party includes the compensation in income. However, this related-party limit extends beyond compensation to *any* accrued expense the business owes to a related cash-basis taxpayer.

Example 8-26

In December, Rick asked his retired father, Henry, to help him finish a landscaping job. By the end of the year, Rick owed Henry $2,000 of (reasonable) compensation for his efforts, which he paid in January 2010. What amount of this compensation may Rick deduct and when may he deduct it?

Answer: If Rick uses the accrual method and Henry the cash method, Rick will not be able to deduct the $2,000 compensation expense until 2010. Rick is Henry's son, so Rick and Henry are "related" parties for tax purposes. Consequently, Rick can deduct the compensation only when Henry includes the payment in his taxable income in 2010. If Rick uses the cash method, he will deduct the expense when he pays it in January 2010.

---

[56]§267(a).

[57]Certain constructive ownership rules apply in determining ownership percentages for this purpose. See §267(c).

[58]See §267(b) for related-party definitions.

Comparison of Accrual and Cash Methods

From a business perspective, the two primary advantages of adopting the cash method over the accrual method are that (1) the cash method provides the business with more flexibility to time income and deductions by accelerating or deferring payments (timing tax planning strategy) and (2) bookkeeping for the cash method is easier. For example, a cash-method taxpayer could defer revenue by waiting to bill clients for goods or services until after year-end, thereby increasing the likelihood that customers would send payment after year-end. There are some concerns with this tax strategy. For example, delaying the bills might increase the likelihood that the customers will not pay their bills at all.

The primary advantage of the accrual method over the cash method is that it better matches revenues and expenses. For that reason, external financial statement users who want to evaluate a business's financial performance prefer the accrual method. Consistent with this idea, the cash method is not allowed for financial reporting under GAAP.

Although the cash method is by far the predominate accounting method among sole proprietors, it is less common in other types of businesses. In fact, tax laws generally prohibit C corporations and partnerships with corporate partners from using the cash method of accounting.[59] Exhibit 8-6 details the basic differences in accounting for income and deductions under the accrual and the cash method of accounting.

EXHIBIT 8-6   Comparison of Cash and Accrual Methods

Income or Expense Item	Cash Method	Accrual Method
Income recognition	Actually or constructively received.	Earned under the all-events test.
Prepaid rental and interest income	Taxable on receipt.	Taxable on receipt.
Prepaid income for services	Taxable on receipt.	Taxed when earned or in the following year of receipt if not earned by end of year of receipt.
Prepaid income for goods	Taxable on receipt.	Full-inclusion is taxed on receipt but deferral election allows taxation when earned.
Deduction recognition	Deduct when paid; economic performance does not apply.	Deduct under all-events test and economic performance test.
Expenditures for tangible assets with a useful life more than one year	Capitalize and apply cost recovery.	Same as cash method.
Expenditures for intangible assets other than prepaid business expenses	Capitalize and amortize if provision in code allows it.	Same as the cash method.
Prepaid business expenses	Immediately deductible unless contract period exceeds 12 months or extends beyond the end of the next taxable year.	Same as cash method if payment liability, otherwise, capitalize and apply 12-month rule and economic performance rules to determine timing of deduction.
Prepaid interest expense	Not deductible until interest accrues.	Same as the cash method.
Bad debt expense	Not deductible because sales on account not included in income.	Deduct under direct write-off method.

[59]These entities are able to adopt the cash method if their average annual gross receipts for the three tax years ending with the prior tax year do not exceed $5 million (see §448).

Example 8-27

At year-end, Rick determined that Green Acres had collected a total of $71,000 of service revenue (not described elsewhere in examples). Rick is debating whether to adopt the cash or accrual method. To help him resolve his dilemma, Jane includes these revenues in a calculation of Green Acres' taxable income under the cash and accrual methods (Exhibit 8-7). What are the differences between the two calculations?

Answer: Jane provided the following summary of the differences between taxable income under the cash method and taxable income under the accrual method:

Description	Cash (less)	Accrual (equals)	Difference	Example
Revenue:				
Credit sales	0	11,000	−11,000	8-15
Prepaid revenue	7,200	300	+6,900	8-16
Expenses:				
Prepaid services	−1,000	0	−1,000	8-20
Prepaid rent expense	−7,200	−4,800	−2,400	8-21
Bad debts	−	−280	+280	8-25
Total difference (accrual income > cash income)			**−7,220**	

Jane explains that by comparing the revenue and expenses recognized under the two accounting methods, the selection of the accrual method for Green Acres means that Rick will be taxed on an additional $7,220 of income this year than if Green Acres adopts the cash method.

The business income for Green Acres under the accrual and cash methods is summarized in Exhibit 8-7. After reflecting on these numbers and realizing that he would recognize $7,220 more taxable income (and self-employment income subject to self-employment tax) this year under the accrual method than under the cash method, Rick decided it made sense to adopt the cash method of accounting for Green Acres' first tax return. He figured Green Acres could always act like a big business next year. Meanwhile, he knew he had to include Green Acres' business income on Schedule C of his individual tax return. Exhibit 8-8 presents Rick's Schedule C for Green Acres using the cash method of accounting.

Adopting an Accounting Method

We've seen that businesses use overall accounting methods (cash, accrual, or hybrid) and many specific accounting methods (inventory cost-flow assumption, methods of accounting for prepaid income for goods, and methods for accounting for prepaid expenses, among other methods) to account for their business activities. For tax purposes, it's important to understand how and when a business technically *adopts* an accounting method because once it does so, it must get the IRS's permission to change the method.

Businesses generally elect their accounting methods by using the methods on their tax returns. However, *when* the business technically adopts a method depends on whether the method it uses on its tax return is a **permissible accounting method** or an **impermissible accounting method.** So far, our discussion has emphasized accounting methods permissible under the tax laws. However, businesses may unwittingly (or

EXHIBIT 8-7 Green Acres' Net Business Income for 2009

Description	Cash	Accrual	Example
Income			
Service revenue:			
Greenhouse construction	$ 5,000	$ 5,000	8-10
December landscape service	0	11,000	8-15
Prepaid landscape services	7,200	300	8-16
Landscaping revenue	71,000	71,000	8-27
Sales of inventory:			
Trees sales	14,000	14,000	8-18
Cost of goods sold (LIFO method)	−7,150	−7,150	8-18
Gross Profit	**$90,050**	**$94,150**	
Car and truck expense:			
SUV operating expense	5,335	5,335	8-7
BMW operating expense	206	206	8-9
Insurance	1,200	1,200	8-14
Rent			
Shop	7,200	4,800	8-21
Trailer	200	200	8-22
Travel, meals, and entertainment:			
Travel to NY seminar	1,435	1,435	8-8
Dinner and Theatre with client	270	270	8-6
Wages and subcontractor fees:			
Part-time employees	23,000	23,000	8-2
Full time employee (Ken)	30,000	30,000	8-17
Fountain removal	850	850	8-23
Fence installation (prepaid subcontractor)	1,000	0	8-20
Other deductions:			
Education—meditation class	50	50	8-1
Education—seminar	300	300	8-8
Domestic manufacturing deduction	90	90	8-10
Uniforms	500	500	8-5
Bad debts	0	280	8-25
Other expenses not in examples:			
Advertising	1,200	1,200	
Depreciation	4,000	4,000	
Interest	300	300	
Legal and professional services	1,100	1,100	
Office expense	1,500	1,500	
Repairs and maintenance	1,975	1,975	
Taxes and licenses	400	400	
Utilities	2,200	2,200	
Total Deductions	**$84,311**	**$81,191**	
Taxable Income	$ 5,739	$12,959	

intentionally) use an impermissible accounting method. For example, a business using the allowance method for determining bad debt expense for tax purposes is using an impermissible accounting method because the tax laws prescribe the use of the direct write-off method for determining bad debt expense. A business *adopts* a *permissible* accounting method by using and reporting the tax results of the method for at least *one year*. A business *adopts* an *impermissible* method by using and reporting the results of the method for *two consecutive years*.

EXHIBIT 8-8   Green Acres 2008 Schedule C

SCHEDULE C **(Form 1040)**	**Profit or Loss From Business**
	(Sole Proprietorship)

OMB No. 1545-0074

2008

Department of the Treasury
Internal Revenue Service (99)

► Partnerships, joint ventures, etc., generally must file Form 1065 or 1065-B.
► Attach to Form 1040, 1040NR, or 1041.   ► See Instructions for Schedule C (Form 1040).

Attachment Sequence No. **09**

Name of proprietor   **RICK GRIME**

Social security number (SSN)

A Principal business or profession, including product or service (see page C-3 of the instructions)
LANDSCAPER

B Enter code from pages C-9, 10, & 11   ► 5 7 1 6 3 0

C Business name. If no separate business name, leave blank.
GREEN ACRES LANDSCAPING

D Employer ID number (EIN), if any

E Business address (including suite or room no.) ► **SAN ANTONIO TEXAS**
City, town or post office, state, and ZIP code

F Accounting method: (1) ☑ Cash (2) ☐ Accrual (3) ☐ Other (specify) ► ....
G Did you "materially participate" in the operation of this business during 2008? If "No," see page C-4 for limit on losses ☑ Yes ☐ No
H If you started or acquired this business during 2008, check here . . . . ► ☑

Part I   Income

1	Gross receipts or sales. **Caution.** See page C-4 and check the box if: • This income was reported to you on Form W-2 and the "Statutory employee" box on that form was checked, or • You are a member of a qualified joint venture reporting only rental real estate income not subject to self-employment tax. Also see page C-4 for limit on losses. ► ☐	1	97,200
2	Returns and allowances	2	
3	Subtract line 2 from line 1	3	97,200
4	Cost of goods sold (from line 42 on page 2)	4	7,150
5	**Gross profit.** Subtract line 4 from line 3.	5	90,050
6	Other income, including federal and state gasoline or fuel tax credit or refund (see page C-4). . . .	6	
7	**Gross income.** Add lines 5 and 6 . . . . ►	7	90,050

Part II   Expenses. Enter expenses for business use of your home **only** on line 30.

8	Advertising	8	1,200	18	Office expense	18	1,500
9	Car and truck expenses (see page C-5)	9	5,541	19	Pension and profit-sharing plans	19	
10	Commissions and fees . .	10		20	Rent or lease (see page C-6):		
11	Contract labor (see page C-5)	11	1,000		a Vehicles, machinery, and equipment .	20a	7,400
12	Depletion	12			b Other business property . .	20b	
13	Depreciation and section 179 expense deduction (not included in Part III) (see page C-5)	13	4,000	21	Repairs and maintenance . .	21	1,975
				22	Supplies (not included in Part III) .	22	
				23	Taxes and licenses	23	400
				24	Travel, meals, and entertainment:		
14	Employee benefit programs (other than on line 19) .	14			a Travel	24a	1,435
15	Insurance (other than health) .	15	1,200		b Deductible meals and entertainment (see page C-7)	24b	270
16	Interest:			25	Utilities	25	2,200
a	Mortgage (paid to banks, etc.) .	16a		26	Wages (less employment credits) .	26	53,850
b	Other	16b	300	27	Other expenses (from line 48 on page 2)	27	940
17	Legal and professional services	17	1,100				

28	**Total expenses** before expenses for business use of home. Add lines 8 through 27 . . . . ►	28	84,311
29	Tentative profit or (loss). Subtract line 28 from line 7	29	5,739
30	Expenses for business use of your home. Attach **Form 8829**	30	
31	**Net profit or (loss).** Subtract line 30 from line 29. • If a profit, enter on both **Form 1040, line 12,** and **Schedule SE, line 2,** or on **Form 1040NR, line 13** (if you checked the box on line 1, see page C-7). Estates and trusts, enter on **Form 1041, line 3.** • If a loss, you **must** go to line 32.	31	5,739
32	If you have a loss, check the box that describes your investment in this activity (see page C-8). • If you checked 32a, enter the loss on both **Form 1040, line 12,** and **Schedule SE, line 2,** or on **Form 1040NR, line 13** (if you checked the box on line 1, see the line 31 instructions on page C-7). Estates and trusts, enter on **Form 1041, line 3.** • If you checked 32b, you **must** attach **Form 6198.** Your loss may be limited.	32a ☑ All investment is at risk. 32b ☐ Some investment is not at risk.	

For Paperwork Reduction Act Notice, see page C-9 of the instructions.   Cat. No. 11334P   Schedule C (Form 1040) 2008

Changing Accounting Methods

Once a business has adopted an accounting method, it must receive permission to change the method, regardless of whether the existing method is a permissible method or an impermissible method. A taxpayer requests permission to change accounting methods by filing Form 3115 with the IRS. The IRS automatically approves certain types of accounting method changes, but for others the business must provide a good business purpose for the change and pay a fee. The IRS also requires permission when a business must change from using an impermissible method; this requirement helps the IRS to certify that the business properly makes the transition to a permissible method. In essence, the IRS requires the business to report its own noncompliance. Why would a business do so? Besides complying with the tax laws, a business might report its own noncompliance to receive leniency from the IRS. Without getting into the details, the IRS is likely to assess fewer penalties and less interest expense for noncompliance when the business reports the noncompliance before the IRS discovers it on its own.

Tax Consequences of Changing Accounting Method   When a business changes from one accounting method to another, the business determines its taxable income for the year of change using the new method. Further, the business must make an adjustment to taxable income that effectively represents the *cumulative difference,* as of the beginning of the tax year, between the amount of income (or deductions) recognized under the old accounting method and the amount that would have been recognized for all prior years if the new method had been applied. This adjustment is called a **Section 481 adjustment.** The §481 adjustment prevents the duplication or omission of items of income or deduction due to a change in accounting method. If the §481 adjustment *increases* taxable income, the taxpayer recognizes it over *four years* beginning with the year of the change (25 percent of the full adjustment each year). If the adjustment *decreases* taxable income, the taxpayer recognizes it *entirely in the year of change*.

Example 8-28

What if: Suppose that at the end of 2009, Green Acres has $24,000 of accounts receivable. Assuming Green Acres uses the cash method of accounting in 2009, it would not include the $24,000 of receivables in income in determining its 2009 taxable income. Suppose further that Rick decides to switch Green Acres to the accrual method of accounting in 2010 by filing a Form 3115 and receiving permission from the IRS. What is Rick's §481 adjustment for his change in accounting method from the cash to the accrual method?

Answer: $24,000 increase to income ($6,000 in 2010 and each of the subsequent three years). Since Rick would use the accrual method in 2010, he would *not* include payments he receives for the $24,000 receivables as income because he earned this income in 2009 (not 2010). Instead, Rick would be required to make a §481 adjustment to ensure that he does not *omit* these items from taxable income. His total §481 adjustment is to increase net income by $24,000. Because this is an income-increasing adjustment, Rick includes $6,000 of the adjustment (25 percent) in Green Acres taxable income in 2010. He would likewise include a $6,000 §481 adjustment in each of the subsequent three years.

What if: Suppose that at the end of 2009, Green Acres has $4,000 of accounts payable instead of $24,000 of accounts receivable. What is Rick's §481 adjustment for his change in accounting method from the cash to the accrual method?

Answer: In this instance Green Acres would have a negative (income-decreasing) §481 adjustment of $4,000 because the $4,000 of expenses would have accrued in 2009 but would not have been deducted. Hence, Green Acres would be entitled to deduct the full $4,000 as a negative §481 adjustment amount in 2010.

CONCLUSION

This chapter discussed issues relating to business income and deductions. We learned that the income rules for businesses are very similar to those for individuals, and that businesses may deduct only ordinary and necessary business expenses and other business expenses specifically authorized by law. We also described several business expense limitations. Finally, we discussed the accounting periods and methods businesses may use in reporting taxable income to the IRS. The issues described in this chapter are widely applicable to all types of business entities including sole proprietorships, partnerships, S corporations, and C corporations. In the next chapter, we determine how businesses recover the costs of assets they use in their business activities.

SUMMARY

LO1 Describe the general requirements for deducting business expenses and identify common business deductions.

- Ordinary and necessary business expenses are allowed as deductions to calculate net income from activities entered into with a profit motive.
- Only reasonable amounts are allowed as business expense deductions. Extravagant or excessive amounts are likely to be characterized by personal motives and are disallowed.

LO2 Apply the limitations on business deductions to distinguish between deductible and nondeductible business expenses.

- The law specifically prohibits deducting expenses against public policy (such as fines or bribes) and expenses that produce tax-exempt income.
- Expenses benefiting multiple periods must be capitalized and special limits and record-keeping requirements are applied to business expenses that may have personal benefits, such as entertainment and meals.

LO3 Identify and explain special business deductions specifically permitted under the tax laws.

- Special calculations are necessary for deductions such as bad debt expenses, the domestic manufacturing deduction, and casualty losses.

LO4 Explain the concept of an accounting period and describe accounting periods available to businesses.

- Accounting periods and methods are chosen at the time of filing the first tax return.
- There are three types of tax years, calendar year, fiscal year, and 52/53 week year, and each tax year is distinguished by year-end.

LO5 Identify and describe accounting methods available to businesses and apply cash and accrual methods to determine business income and expense deductions.

- Under the cash method, taxpayers recognize revenue when they actually or constructively receive property or services and recognize deductions when they actually pay the expense.
- Under the accrual method, the all-events test requires that income be recognized when all the events have occurred that are necessary to fix the right to receive payments and the amount of the payments can be determined with reasonable accuracy.
- The accrual method must be used to account for sales and purchases for businesses where inventories are an income-producing factor.
- Under the accrual method, accrued expenses can only be deducted once both the all-events test and the economic performance tests are met. The application of the economic performance test depends, in part, on the type of business expense.
- Changes in accounting method or accounting period typically require the consent of the IRS and a §481 adjustment to taxable income.

KEY TERMS

12-month rule (8-17)
accounting method (8-16)
accounting period (8-15)
allowance method (8-28)
arm's length amount (8-4)
casualty losses (8-14)
deferral method (8-20)
direct write-off method
(business only) (8-28)
domestic manufacturing deduction
(DMD) (8-11)
economic performance test (8-24)
FIFO (8-22)

fiscal year (8-15)
flow-through entities (8-16)
full-inclusion method (8-20)
hobby (8-2)
impermissible accounting
method (8-30)
LIFO (8-22)
mixed-motive expenditures (8-7)
ordinary and necessary (8-3)
payment liability (8-24)
permissible accounting method (8-30)
personal expenses (8-6)

qualified production activities income
(QPAI) (8-12)
reasonable in amount (8-3)
Section 481 adjustment (8-33)
specific identification (8-22)
start-up costs (8-5)
tax year (8-15)
travel expenses (8-8)
uniform cost capitalization rules
(UNICAP rules) (8-21)

DISCUSSION QUESTIONS

1. **(LO1)** What is an "ordinary and necessary" business expenditure?

2. **(LO1)** Is cost of goods sold deductible as a business expense for a business selling inventory? Explain.

3. **(LO1)** Tom is an attorney who often represents individuals injured while working (worker liability claims). This year Tom spent $50 on a book entitled *Plumbing for Dummies* and paid $500 to take a course on plumbing residences and rental housing. Can you imagine circumstances in which these expenditures would be deductible as "ordinary and necessary" for an attorney. Explain.

4. **(LO1)** Jake is a professional dog trainer who purchases and trains dogs for use by law enforcement agencies. Last year Jake purchased 500 bags of dog food from a large pet food company at an average cost of $30 per bag. This year, however, Jake purchased 500 bags of dog food from a local pet food company at an average cost of $45 per bag. Under what circumstances would the IRS likely challenge the cost of Jake's dog food as unreasonable?

5. **(LO2)** What kinds of deductions are prohibited as a matter of public policy? Why might Congress deem it important to disallow deductions for expenditures against public policy?

6. **(LO2)** Provide an example of an expense associated with the production of tax-exempt income and explain what might happen if Congress repealed the prohibition against deducting expenses incurred to produce tax exempt income.

7. **(LO2)** Jerry is a self-employed rock star and this year he expended $1,000 on special "flashy" clothes and outfits. Jerry would like to deduct the cost of these clothes as work-related because the clothes are not adaptable for normal wear. Under what circumstances can Jerry deduct the cost of these work clothes?

8. **(LO2)** Jimmy is a sole proprietor of a small dry cleaner. This month Jimmy paid for his groceries by writing checks from the checking account dedicated to the dry cleaning business. Why do you suppose Jimmy is using his business checking account rather than his personal checking account to pay for personal expenditures?

9. **(LO2)** Tim employs three sales representatives who often take clients to dinner and provide entertainment in order to increase sales. This year Tim reimbursed the representatives $2,500 for the cost of meals and $8,250 for the cost of

entertaining clients. Describe the conditions under which Tim can claim deductions for meals and entertainment.

10. **(LO2)** Jenny uses her car for both business and personal purposes. She purchased the auto this year and drove 11,000 miles on business trips and 9,000 miles for personal transportation. Describe how Jenny will determine the amount of deductible expenses associated with the auto.

11. **(LO1, LO2)** What expenses are deductible when a taxpayer combines both business and personal activities on a trip? How do the rules for international travel differ from the rules for domestic travel?

12. **(LO2)** Clyde lives and operates a sole proprietorship in Dallas, Texas. This year Clyde found it necessary to travel to Fort Worth (about 25 miles away) for legitimate business reasons. Is Clyde's trip likely to qualify as "away from home," and why would this designation matter?

13. **(LO2)** Describe the record-keeping requirements for business deductions expenses including mixed-motive expenditures.

14. **(LO3)** Explain why the domestic manufacturing deduction is sometimes described as an "artificial" expense and the apparent rationale for this deduction. How might a business begin to determine the domestic portion of revenues and expenses for products that are assembled in the United States from parts made overseas?

15. **(LO3)** Describe the two limitations placed on the calculation of the domestic manufacturing deduction and explain the apparent reason for each limitation.

16. **(LO3)** Compare and contrast start-up costs and organizational expenditures. Describe how the tax treatment of these expenditures differs from the treatment for financial accounting purposes.

17. **(LO3)** Explain the difference between calculating a loss deduction for a business asset that was partially damaged in an accident and a loss deduction for a business asset that was stolen or completely destroyed in an accident.

18. **(LO3)** How do casualty loss deductions differ when a business asset is completely destroyed as opposed to the destruction of a personal-use asset?

19. **(LO4)** What is the difference between a full tax year and a short tax year? Describe circumstances in which a business may have a short tax year.

20. **(LO4)** Compare and contrast the different tax year-ends available to businesses and why a taxpayer might choose one tax year end over another if given a choice.

21. **(LO4)** Compare and contrast the different year-ends available to sole proprietorships, flow-through entities, and C corporations.

22. **(LO4)** Why does the law generally require partnerships to adopt a tax year consistent with the year used by the partners?

23. **(LO4)** How does an entity choose its tax year? Is it the same process no matter the type of tax year-end the taxpayer adopts?

24. **(LO5)** Explain when an expenditure should be "capitalized" rather than expensed based upon accounting principles. From time to time, it is suggested that all business expenditures should be expensed for tax purposes. Do you agree with this proposition, and if so, why?

25. **(LO5)** Describe the 12-month rule for determining whether and to what extent businesses should capitalize or immediately deduct prepaid expenses such as insurance or security contracts. Explain the apparent rationale for this rule.

26. **(LO5)** Explain why Congress sometimes mandates that businesses use particular accounting methods while other times Congress is content to require businesses to use the same accounting methods for tax purposes that they use for financial accounting purposes.

27. **(LO5)** Why is it not surprising that specific rules differ between tax accounting and financial accounting?

28. **(LO5)** Fred is considering using the accrual method for his next business venture. Explain to Fred the conditions for recognizing income for tax purposes under the accrual method.

29. **(LO5)** Describe the all-events test for determining income and describe how to determine the date in which the all-events test has been met.

30. **(LO5)** Compare and contrast the tax treatment for rental income received in advance and advance payments for services.

31. **(LO5)** Compare and contrast the rules for determining the tax treatment of advance payments for services versus advance payments for goods.

32. **(LO5)** Jack operates a plumbing business as a sole proprietorship on the cash basis. Besides providing plumbing services, Jack also sells plumbing supplies to homeowners and other plumbers. The sales of plumbing supplies constitute less than $20,000 per year, and this is such a small portion of Jack's income that he does not keep physical inventories for the supplies. Describe the conditions in which Jack must account for sales and purchases of plumbing supplies on the accrual method.

33. **(LO5)** Explain why Congress enacted the UNICAP rules and describe the burdens these rules place on taxpayers.

34. **(LO5)** Compare and contrast financial accounting rules with the tax rules under UNICAP (§263A). Explain whether the UNICAP rules tend to accelerate or defer income relative to the financial accounting rules.

35. **(LO5)** Compare and contrast the tests for accruing income and those for accruing deductions for tax purposes.

36. **(LO5)** Compare and contrast when taxpayers are allowed to deduct amounts for warranties provided by others to the taxpayer and when taxpayers are allowed to deduct expenses associated with warranties they provide to others.

37. **(LO5)** Describe when economic performance occurs for the following expenses:
    Worker's compensation
    Rebates and refunds
    Insurance, warranties, and service contracts provided *to* the business
    Taxes

38. **(LO5)** On December 31 of the current year, a taxpayer prepays an advertising company to provide advertising services for the next 10 months. Using the 12-month rule and the economic performance rules, contrast when the taxpayer would be able to deduct the expenditure if the taxpayer uses the cash method of accounting versus if the taxpayer uses the accrual method of accounting.

39. **(LO5)** Compare and contrast how bad debt expense is determined for financial accounting purposes and how the deduction for bad debts is determined for accrual-method taxpayers. How do cash-method taxpayers determine their bad debt expense for accounts receivable?

40. **(LO5)** Describe the related-party limitation on accrued deductions. What tax savings strategy is this limitation designed to thwart?

41. **(LO5)** What are the relative advantages of the cash and accrual methods of accounting?

42. **(LO5)** Describe how a business adopts a permissible accounting method. Explain whether a taxpayer can adopt an impermissible accounting method.

43. **(LO5)** Describe why the IRS might be skeptical of permitting requests for changes in accounting method without a good business purpose?

44. **(LO5)** What is a §481 adjustment and what is its purpose?

PROBLEMS

45. **(LO1)** Michael hired his brother's firm to provide accounting services to his business. During the current year, Michael paid his brother's firm $82,000 for services even though other firms were willing to provide the same services for $40,000. How much of this expenditure, if any, is deductible as an ordinary and necessary business expenditure?

46. **(LO1, LO2)** Indicate the amount (if any) that Michael can deduct as ordinary and necessary business deductions in each of the following situations and explain your solution.

    a. From time to time, Michael rents a dump truck for his business. While hauling gravel to a job site, Michael was stopped for speeding. He paid a fine of $125 for speeding and a fine of $80 for carrying an overweight load.

    b. Michael paid a part-time employee $750 to drive his rented dump truck. Michael reimbursed the employee $35 for gasoline for the truck.

    c. Michael gave a member of the city council a new watch, which cost $200. He hopes that the city councilman will "throw" some contracts to his business.

47. **(LO1, LO2)** Indicate the amount (if any) that Josh can deduct as ordinary and necessary business deductions in each of the following situations and explain your solution.

    a. Josh borrowed $50,000 from the First State Bank using his business assets as collateral. He used the money to buy City of Blanksville bonds. Over the course of a year, Josh paid interest of $4,200 on the borrowed funds, but he received $3,500 of interest on the bonds.

    b. Josh purchased a piece of land for $45,000 in order to get a location to expand his business. He also paid $3,200 to construct a new driveway for access to the property.

    c. This year Josh paid $15,000 to employ the mayor's son in the business. Josh would typically pay an employee with these responsibilities about $10,000 but the mayor assured Josh that after his son was hired, some city business would be coming his way.

    d. Josh paid his brother, a mechanic, $3,000 to install a robotic machine for Josh's business. The amount he paid to his brother is comparable to what he would have paid to an unrelated party to do the same work. Once the installation was completed by his brother, Josh began calibrating the machine for operation. However, by the end of the year, he had not started using the machine in his business.

48. **(LO2)** Ralph invited a potential client to dinner and the theatre. Ralph paid $250 for the dinner and $220 for the theatre tickets in advance. They first went to dinner and then they went to the theatre.

    a. What amount can Ralph deduct if, prior to the dinner, he met with the potential client to discuss future business prospects?

    b. What amount can Ralph deduct if he and the client only discussed business during the course of the dinner?

    c. What amount can Ralph deduct if he and the potential client tried to discuss business during the course of the theatre performance but did not discuss business at any other time?

    d. What amount can Ralph deduct if the potential client declined Ralph's invitation, so Ralph took his accountant to dinner and the theatre to reward his accountant for a hard day at work? At dinner, they discussed the accountant's workload and upcoming assignments.

49. **(LO2)** Melissa recently paid $400 for round-trip airfare to San Francisco to attend a business conference for three days. Melissa also paid the following expenses: $250 fee to register for the conference, $300 per night for three night's lodging, $200 for meals, and $150 for cab fare.

   a. What amount of the travel costs can Melissa deduct as business expenses?

   b. Suppose that while Melissa was on the coast, she also spent two days sight-seeing the national parks in the area. To do the sightseeing, she paid $1,000 for transportation, $800 for lodging, and $450 for meals during this part of her trip, which she considers personal in nature. What amount of the travel costs can Melissa deduct as business expenses?

   c. Suppose that Melissa made the trip to San Francisco primarily to visit the national parks and only attended the business conference as an incidental benefit of being present on the coast at that time. What amount of the travel costs (airfare) can Melissa deduct as business expenses?

   d. Suppose that Melissa's permanent residence and business was located in San Francisco. She attended the conference in San Francisco. She drove 100 miles over the course of three days and paid $90 for parking at the conference hotel. In addition, she spent $150 for breakfast and dinner over the three days of the conference. She bought breakfast on the way to the conference hotel and she bought dinner on her way home each night from the conference. What amount of the travel costs can Melissa deduct as business expenses?

50. **(LO2)** Kimberly is a self-employed taxpayer. She recently spent $1,000 for airfare to travel to Italy. What amount of the airfare is she allowed to deduct in each of the following alternative scenarios?

   a. Her trip was entirely for personal purposes.

   b. On the trip, she spent eight days on personal activities and two days on business activities.

   c. On the trip, she spent eight days on business activities and two days on personal activities.

   d. Her trip was entirely for business purposes.

51. **(LO2)** Ryan is self-employed. This year Ryan used his personal auto for several long business trips. Ryan paid $1,500 for gasoline on these trips. His depreciation on the car if he was using it fully for business purposes would be $3,000. During the year, he drove his car a total of 12,000 miles (a combination of buisness and personal travel).

   a. Ryan can provide written documentation of the business purpose for trips totaling 3,000 miles. What business expense amount can Ryan deduct (if any) for these trips?

   b. Ryan estimates that he drove approximately 1,300 miles on business trips, but he can only provide written documentation of the business purpose for trips totaling 820 miles. What business expense amount can Ryan deduct (if any) for these trips?

52. **(LO1, LO2)** Christopher is a cash-method, calendar-year taxpayer, and he made the following cash payments related to his business this year. Calculate the after-tax cost of each payment assuming he has a 30 percent marginal tax rate.   ■ **planning**

   a. $500 fine for speeding while traveling to a client meeting.

   b. $240 of interest on a short-term loan incurred in September and repaid in November. Half of the loan proceeds were used immediately to pay salaries and the other half was invested in municipal bonds until November.

c. $600 for office supplies in May of this year. He used half of the supplies this year and he will use the remaining half by February of next year.

d. $450 for several pair of work boots. Christopher expects to use the boots about 80 percent of the time in his business and the remainder of the time for hiking. Consider the boots to be a form of clothing.

research

53. **(LO2)** Heather paid $15,000 to join a country club in order to meet potential clients. This year she paid $4,300 in greens fees when golfing with clients. Under what circumstances, if any, can Heather deduct the $15,000 cost of country club dues and the costs of the golf played with clients?

planning

54. **(LO1, LO2)** Assume Sarah is a cash-method, calendar-year taxpayer, and she is considering making the following cash payments related to her business. Calculate the after-tax cost of each payment assuming she has a 25 percent marginal tax rate.

a. $2,000 payment for next year's property taxes on her place of business.

b. $800 to reimburse the cost of meals incurred by employees while traveling for the business.

c. $1,200 for football tickets to entertain out-of-town clients during contract negotiations.

d. $500 contribution to the mayor's re-election campaign.

55. **(LO3)** Renee manufactured and sold a "gadget," a specialized asset used by auto manufacturers that qualifies for the domestic manufacturing deduction. Renee incurred $15,000 in direct expenses in the project, which includes $2,000 of wages Renee paid to employees in the manufacturing of the gadget. What is Renee's domestic manufacturing deduction for the gadget in each of the following alternative scenarios?

a. Renee sold the gadget for $25,000 and she reported AGI of $75,000 before considering the manufacturing deduction.

b. Renee sold the gadget for $25,000 and she reported AGI of $5,000 before considering the manufacturing deduction.

c. Renee sold the gadget for $40,000 and she reported AGI of $50,000 before considering the manufacturing deduction.

planning

56. **(LO3)** Andrew is considering starting a business of constructing and selling prefabricated greenhouses. There are three very different methods to constructing these greenhouses, and each method results in different revenue and cost projections. Below, Andrew has projected the qualifying revenue and costs for each method. The selling price includes qualifying receipts. The allocable expenses include wages and allocable expenses are included in total costs.

Method	Selling Price	Qualifying Receipts	Total Cost	Allocable Expenses	Allocable Wages
#1	$13,000	$ 9,000	$6,500	$2,500	$2,000
#2	14,000	9,000	7,400	5,500	1,500
#3	15,000	14,000	8,600	2,000	1,000

a. Estimate the tax benefit from domestic manufacturing deduction for each construction technique. You may assume that Andrew has sufficient AGI to utilize the deduction.

b. Which construction technique should Andrew use if his marginal tax rate is 30 percent?

57. **(LO3)** This year Amy purchased $2,000 of equipment for use in her business. However, the machine was damaged in a traffic accident while Amy was transporting the equipment to her business. Note that because Amy did not place the equipment into service during the year, she does not claim any depreciation expense for the equipment.

    a. After the accident, Amy had the choice of repairing the equipment for $1,800 or selling the equipment to a junk shop for $300. Amy sold the equipment. What amount can Amy deduct for the loss of the equipment?

    b. After the accident, Amy repaired the equipment for $800. What amount can Amy deduct for the loss of the equipment?

    c. After the accident, Amy could not replace the equipment so she had the equipment repaired for $2,300. What amount can Amy deduct for the loss of the equipment?

58. **(LO3)** Stephen operates a small hardware store on the cash basis. On July 1 of this year, Stephen purchased a "key-employee" term-life policy that insures the life of his best store clerk. The policy cost Stephen $1,220 and will pay him a $40,000 death benefit if his clerk passes away any time during the next 12 months.

    a. What amount of the $1,220 life insurance policy premium can Stephen deduct this year?

    b. Suppose that Stephen purchased the life insurance policy on the clerk's life but allowed the clerk to name the clerk's wife as the beneficiary. What amount of the life insurance policy can Stephen deduct this year?

59. **(LO5)** Nicole is a calendar-year taxpayer who accounts for her business using the cash method. On average, Nicole sends out bills for about $12,000 of her services at the first of each month. The bills are due by the end of the month, and typically 70 percent of the bills are paid on time and 98 percent are paid within 60 days.   ■ **planning**

    a. Suppose that Nicole is expecting a 2 percent reduction in her marginal tax rate next year. Ignoring the time value of money, estimate the tax savings for Nicole if she postpones mailing of bills for December until January 1 of next year.

    b. Describe how the time value of money affects your calculations.

    c. Would this tax savings strategy create any additional business risks? Explain.

60. **(LO5)** Jeremy is a calendar-year taxpayer who sometimes leases his business equipment to local organizations. He recorded the following receipts this year. Indicate the extent to which these payments are taxable income to Jeremy this year if Jeremy is (1) a cash-method taxpayer and (2) he is an accrual-method taxpayer.

    a. $1,000 deposit from the Ladies' Club, which wants to lease a trailer. The club will receive the entire deposit back when the trailer is returned undamaged.

    b. $800 from the Ladies' Club for leasing the trailer from December of this year through March of next year ($200 per month).

    c. $300 lease payment received from the Men's Club this year for renting Jeremy's trailer last year. Jeremy billed the club last year but by year-end of last year he determined that the Men's Club would never pay him, so he was surprised when he received the check.

61. **(LO5)** Brown Thumb Landscaping is a calendar-year, accrual-method taxpayer. In September, Brown Thumb negotiated a $14,000 contract for services it would provide to the city in November of the current year. The contract specifies that Brown Thumb will receive $4,000 in October as a down payment

for these services and it will receive the remaining $10,000 in January of next year when the city budget is reviewed.

a. How much income from this $14,000 contract will Brown Thumb recognize in the current year? Explain.

b. How much income from this $14,000 contract will Brown Thumb recognize in the current year if it uses the cash method of accounting?

c. Suppose that the total amount to be paid under the contract with the city is estimated at $14,000 but may be adjusted to $12,000 next year during the review of the city budget. What amount from the contract, if any, should Brown Thumb recognize as income this year? Explain.

d. Suppose that in addition to the basic contract, Brown Thumb will be paid an additional $3,000 if their city landscape design wins the annual designer's competition next year. Should Brown Thumb accrue a $3,000 revenue this year? Why or why not?

62. **(LO5)** In January of year 0, Justin paid $4,800 for an insurance policy that covers his business property for accidents and casualties. Justin is a calendar-year taxpayer who uses the cash method of accounting. What amount of the insurance premium may Justin deduct in year 0 in each of the following alternative scenarios?

a. The policy covers the business property from April 1 of year 0 through March 31 of year 1.

b. The policy begins on February 1 of year 1 and extends through January 31 of year 2.

c. Assume Justin paid $6,000 for a 24-month policy that covers from April 1, year 0 through March 31, year 2.

d. Assume that instead of paying an insurance premium, Justin paid $4,800 to rent his business property from April 1 of year 0 through March 31 of year 1.

research

63. **(LO5)** Tiffany decided to promise her full-time employees a two-week paid vacation. When, if ever, may Tiffany deduct the expense for the vacation pay? {*Hint: See Reg. §1.404b.-1T, Q&A-2(b)(1).*}

a. Assume Tiffany's business uses the cash method of accounting.

b. Assume Tiffany's business uses the accrual method of accounting.

64. **(LO5)** On April 1 of year 0 Stephanie received a $9,000 payment for full payment on a three-year service contract (under the contract Stephanie is obligated to provide advisory services for the next three years).

a. What amount of income should Stephanie recognize in year 0 if she uses the accrual method of accounting (she recognized $2,250 for financial accounting purposes)?

b. What amount of income will Stephanie recognize in year 1 if she uses the accrual method of accounting?

c. What amount of income will Stephanie recognize in year 2 if she uses the accrual method of accounting?

d. What amount of income will Stephanie recognize in year 0 if she recognizes $5,000 of income from the contract for financial statement purposes?

65. **(LO5)** In October of year 0, Janine received a $6,000 payment from a client for 25 months of security services she will provide starting on November 1 of year 0. This amounts to $240 per month.

a. When must Janine recognize the income from the $6,000 advance payment for services if she uses the cash method of accounting?

b. When must Janine recognize the income from the $6,000 advance payment for services if she uses the accrual method of accounting?

c. Suppose that instead of services, Janine received the payment for a security system (inventory) that she will deliver and install in year 2. When would Janine recognize the income from the advance payment for inventory sale if she uses the accrual method of accounting and she uses the deferral method for reporting income from advance payments? For financial accounting purposes, she reports the income when the inventory is delivered.

d. Suppose that instead of services, Janine received the payment for the delivery of inventory to be delivered next year. When would Janine recognize the income from the advance payment for sale of goods if she uses the accrual method of accounting and she uses the full-inclusion method for advance payments?

66. **(LO5)** Nicole's business uses the accrual method of accounting and accounts for inventory with specific identification. In year 0, Nicole received a $4,500 payment with an order for inventory to be delivered to the client early next year. Nicole has the inventory ready for delivery at the end of year 0 (she purchased the inventory in year 0 for $2,300).

a. When does Nicole recognize the $2,200 of gross profit ($4,500 revenue minus $2,300 cost of the inventory) if she uses the full-inclusion method?

b. When does Nicole recognize the $2,200 of gross profit from the inventory sale if she if she uses the deferral method?

c. How would Nicole account for the inventory-related transactions if she uses the cash method of accounting and her annual sales are usually less than $100,000?

d. How would Nicole account for the inventory-related transactions if she uses the cash method of accounting and her annual sales are usually over $2,000,000 per year?

67. **(LO5)** This year Amber opened a factory to process and package landscape mulch. At the end of the year, Amber's accountant prepared the following schedule for allocating manufacturing costs to the mulch inventory, but her accountant is unsure of what costs need to be allocated to the inventory under UNICAP. Approximately 20 percent of management time, space, and expenses are spent on this manufacturing process.

		Costs	Tax Inventory
Material:	Mulch and packaging	$ 5,000	?
	Administrative supplies	250	?
Salaries:	Factory labor	12,000	?
	Sales & advertising	3,500	?
	Administration	5,200	?
Property taxes:	Factory	4,600	?
	Offices	2,700	?
Depreciation:	Factory	8,000	?
	Offices	1,500	?

a. At the end of the year, Amber's accountant indicated that the business had processed 10,000 bags of mulch but only 1,000 bags remained in the ending inventory. What is Amber's tax basis in her ending inventory after applying the UNICAP rules to allocate indirect costs to inventory? (Assume direct costs are allocated to inventory according to the level of ending inventory. In contrast, indirect costs are first allocated by time spent and then according to level of ending inventory.)

b. Under what conditions could Amber's business avoid having to apply UNICAP to allocate indirect costs to inventory for tax purposes?

68. **(LO5)** Suppose that David adopted the last-in, first-out (LIFO) inventory-flow method for his business inventory of widgets (purchase prices below).

Widget	Purchase Date	Direct Cost	Other Costs	Total Cost
#1	August 15	$2,100	$100	$2,200
#2	October 30	$2,200	$150	$2,350
#3	November 10	$2,300	$100	$2,400

In late December, David sold widget #2 and next year David expects to purchase three more widgets at the following estimated prices:

Widget	Purchase Date	Estimated Cost
#4	Early spring	$2,600
#5	Summer	$2,260
#6	Fall	$2,400

a. What cost of goods sold and ending inventory would David record if he elects to use the LIFO method this year?

b. If David sells two widgets next year, what will be his cost of goods sold and ending inventory next year under the LIFO method?

c. How would your answers to (a) and (b) change if David had initially selected the first-in, first-out (FIFO) method instead of LIFO?

d. Suppose that David initially adopted the LIFO method, but wants to apply for a change to FIFO next year. What would be his Section 481 adjustment for this change, and in what year(s) would he make the adjustment?

69. **(LO5)** On November 1 of year 0, Jaxon borrowed $50,000 from Bucksnort Savings and Loan for use in his business. In December, Jaxon paid interest of $4,500 relating to the 12-month period from November of year 0 through October of year 1.

a. How much interest, if any, can Jaxon deduct in year 0 if his business uses the cash method of accounting for tax purposes?

b. How much interest, if any, can Jaxon deduct in year 0 if his business uses the accrual method of accounting for tax purposes?

70. **(LO5)** Matt has contracted with Apex Services to provide routine repair and maintenance services for several pieces of his business equipment. On November 1of year 0, Matt paid $2,000 for the repairs that he expects will begin in early March of year 1.

a. What amount of the cost of the repairs can Matt deduct in year 0 if he uses the cash method of accounting for his business?

b. What amount of the cost of the repairs can Matt deduct in year 0 if he uses the accrual method of accounting for his business?

c. What amount of the cost of the repairs can Matt deduct in year 0 if he uses the accrual method and he expects the repairs to be done by early February?

d. What amount of the cost of the repairs can Matt deduct in year 0 if he uses the cash method of accounting and he expects the repairs to be done by early February?

71. **(LO5)** Circuit Corporation (CC) is a calendar-year, accrual-method taxpayer. CC manufactures and sells electronic circuitry. On November 15, year 0, CC enters into a contract with Equip Corp (EC) that provides CC with exclusive use of EC's specialized manufacturing equipment for the five-year period

beginning on January 1 of year 1. Pursuant to the contract, CC pays EC $1,000,000 on December 30, year 0. How much of this $1,000,000 expenditure is CC allowed to deduct in year 0 and in year 1?

72. **(LO5)** This year (year 0) Elizabeth agreed to a three-year service contract with an engineering consulting firm to improve efficiency in her factory. The contract pays the consulting firm $1,500 for each instance that Elizabeth requests their assistance. The contract also provides that Elizabeth only pays the consultants if their advice increases efficiency as measured 12 months from the date of service. This year Elizabeth requested advice on three occasions and she has not yet made any payments to the consultants.

    a. How much should Elizabeth deduct in year 0 under this service contract if she uses the accrual method of accounting?

    b. How much should Elizabeth deduct in year 0 under this service contract if she uses the cash method of accounting?

73. **(LO5)** Travis is a professional landscaper. He provides his clients with a one-year (12-month) warranty for retaining walls he installs. In June of year 1, Travis installed a wall for an important client, Sheila. In early November, Sheila informed Travis that the retaining wall had failed. To repair the wall, Travis paid $700 cash for additional stone that he delivered to Sheila's location. Travis also offered to pay a mason $800 to repair the wall. Due to some bad weather and the mason's work backlog, the mason agreed to finish the work by the end of January of year 2. Even though Travis expected the mason to finish the project as agreed (end of January), Travis informed the mason that he would pay the mason the $800 when he completed the job.

    a. Assuming Travis is an accrual-method taxpayer, how much can he deduct in year 1 from these activities?

    b. Assuming Travis is a cash-method taxpayer, how much can he deduct in year 1 from these activities?

74. **(LO5)** Adam elects the accrual method of accounting for his business. What amount of deductions does Adam recognize in year 0 for the following transactions?

    a. Adam guarantees that he will refund the cost of any goods sold to a client that fails within a year of delivery. In December of year 0, Adam agreed to refund $2,400 to clients, and he expects to make payment in January of year 1.

    b. On December 1 of year 0, Adam paid $480 for a one-year contract with CleanUP Services to clean his store. The agreement calls for services to be provided on a weekly basis.

    c. Adam was billed $240 for annual personal property taxes on his delivery van. Because this was the first time Adam was billed for these taxes, he did not make payment until January. However, he considers the amounts immaterial.

75. **(LO5)** Rebecca is a calendar-year taxpayer who operates a business. She made the following business-related expenditures in December of year 0. Indicate the amount of these payments that she may deduct in year 0 under both the cash method of accounting and the accrual method of accounting.

    a. $2,000 for an accountant to evaluate the accounting system of Rebecca's business. The accountant spent three weeks in January of year 1 working on the evaluation.

    b. $2,500 for new office furniture. The furniture was delivered on January 15.

    c. $3,000 for property taxes payable on her factory.

    d. $1,500 for interest on a short-term bank loan relating to the period from November 1 through March 31.

76. **(LO5)** BCS Corporation is a calendar-year, accrual-method taxpayer. BCS was formed and started its business activities on January 1, year 0. It reported the following information for year 0. Indicate BCS's deductible amount for year 0 in each of the following alternative scenarios.

    a. BCS provides two-year warranties on products it sells to customers. For its year 0 sales, BCS estimated and accrued $200,000 in warranty expense for financial accounting purposes. During year 0, BCS actually spent $30,000 repairing its product under the warranty.

    b. BCS accrued an expense for $50,000 for amounts it anticipated it would be required to pay *under* the worker compensation act. During year 0, BCS actually paid $10,000 for workers' compensation–related liabilities.

    c. In June of year 0, a display of BCS's product located in its showroom fell on and injured a customer. The customer sued BCS for $500,000. The case is scheduled to go to trial next year. BCS anticipates that it will lose the case and accrued a $500,000 expense on its financial statements.

    d. Assume the same facts as in (c) except that BCS was required to pay $500,000 to a court-appointed escrow fund in year 0. If BCS loses the case in year 1, the money from the escrow fund will be transferred to the customer suing BCS.

    e. In December of year 0, BCS acquired equipment from Equip Company. As part of the purchase, BCS signed a warranty agreement with Equip so that Equip would warranty the equipment for two years. The cost of the warranty was $10,000. BCS paid Equip for the warranty in January of year 1.

77. **(LO5)** This year William provided $4,200 of services to a large client on credit. Unfortunately, this client has recently encountered financial difficulties and has been unable to pay William for the services. Moreover, William does not expect to collect for his services for at least a year. William has "written off" the account and would like to claim a deduction for tax purposes.

    a. What amount of deduction for bad debt expense can William claim this year if he uses the accrual method?

    b. What amount of deduction for bad debt expense can William claim this year if he uses the cash method?

78. **(LO5)** Dustin has a contract to provide services to Dado Enterprises. In November of year 0, Dustin billed Dado $10,000 for the services he rendered during the year. Dado is an accrual-method proprietorship that is owned and operated by Dustin's father.

    a. What amount of revenue must Dustin recognize in year 0 if Dustin uses the cash method and Dado remits payment for the services in December of year 0? What amount can Dado deduct in year 0?

    b. What amount of revenue must Dustin recognize in year 0 if Dustin uses the accrual method and Dado remits payment for the services in December of year 0? What amount can Dado deduct in year 0?

    c. What amount of revenue must Dustin recognize in year 0 if Dustin uses the cash method and Dado remits payment for the services in January of year 1? What amount can Dado deduct in year 0?

    d. What amount of revenue must Dustin recognize in year 0 if Dustin uses the accrual method and Dado remits payment for the services in January of year 1? What amount can Dado deduct in year 0?

79. **(LO5)** Nancy operates a business that uses the accrual method of accounting. In December, Nancy asked her brother, Hank, to provide her business with consulting advice. Hank billed Nancy for $5,000 of consulting services in year 0

(a reasonable amount), but Nancy was only able to pay $3,000 of the bill by the end of year 0. However, Nancy paid the remainder of the bill in year 1.

a. How much of the $5,000 consulting services will Hank include in his income in year 0 if he uses the cash method of accounting? What amount can Nancy deduct in year 0 for the consulting services?

b. How much of the $5,000 consulting services will Hank include in his income in year 0 if he uses the accrual method of accounting? What amount can Nancy deduct in year 0 for the consulting services?

80. **(LO5)** Erin is considering switching her business from the cash method to the accrual method at the beginning of next year (year 1). Determine the amount and timing of her §481 adjustment assuming the IRS grants Erin's request in the following alternative scenarios.

a. At the end of end of year 0/beginning of year 1, Erin's business has $15,000 of accounts receivables and $18,000 of accounts payables that have not been recorded for tax purposes.

b. At the end of year 0/beginning of year 1, Erin's business reports $25,000 of accounts receivables and $9,000 of accounts payables that have not been recorded for tax purposes.

COMPREHENSIVE PROBLEMS

81. Joe operates a business that locates and purchases specialized assets for clients, among other activities. Joe uses the accrual method of accounting but he doesn't keep any significant inventories of the specialized assets that he sells. Joe reported the following financial information for his business activities during year 0. Determine the effect of each of the following transactions on the taxable business income.

a. Joe has signed a contract to sell gadgets to the city. The contract provides that sales of gadgets are dependent upon a test sample of gadgets operating successfully. In December, Joe delivers $12,000 worth of gadgets to the city that will be tested in March. Joe purchased the gadgets especially for this contract and paid $8,500.

b. Joe paid $180 for entertaining a visiting out-of-town client. The client didn't discuss business with Joe during this visit, but Joe wants to maintain good relations to encourage additional business next year.

c. On November 1, Joe paid $600 for premiums providing for $40,000 of "key man" insurance on the life of Joe's accountant over the next 12 months.

d. At the end of the year (year 1), Joe's business reports $9,000 of accounts receivable. Based upon past experience, Joe believes that at least $2,000 of his new receivables will be uncollectible.

e. In December of year 0, Joe rented equipment for a large job. The rental agency required a minimum rental of three months ($1,000 per month), but Joe completed the job before year-end.

f. Joe hired a new sales representative as an employee and sent her to Dallas for a week to contact prospective out-of-state clients. Joe ended up reimbursing his employee $300 for airfare, $350 for lodging, $250 for meals, and $150 for entertainment. Joe requires the employee to account for all expenditures in order to be reimbursed.

g. Joe uses his BMW (a personal auto) to travel to and from his residence to his factory. However, he switches to a business vehicle if he needs to travel after he reaches the factory. Last month, the business vehicle broke down and he was forced to use the BMW both to travel to and from the factory and to visit work sites. He drove 120 miles visiting work sites and 46 miles driving to and from the factory from his home.

h. Joe paid a visit to his parents in Dallas over the Christmas holidays. While he was in the city, Joe spent $50 to attend a half-day business symposium. Joe paid $200 for airfare, $50 for meals during the symposium, and $20 on cab fare to the symposium.

82. Jack, a geologist, had been debating for years whether or not to venture out on his own and operate his own business. He had developed a lot of solid relationships with clients and he believed that many of them would follow him if he were to leave his current employer. As part of a New Year's resolution, Jack decided he would finally do it. In January, Jack put his business plan together and in February, opened his doors for business as a C corporation called Geo-Jack (GJ). Jack contributed $50,000 of cash to get the business started and Jack is the sole shareholder. Jack reported the following financial information for the year (assume Geo-Jack reports on a calendar year).

a. Geo-Jack incurred $3,000 of organizational expenditures in January.

b. GJ earned and collected $290,000 performing geological-related services and selling its specialized digging tool [see part (i)].

c. GJ received $50 interest from municipal bonds and $2,100 interest from other investments.

d. GJ purchased some new equipment in February for $42,500. It claimed depreciation on these assets during the year in the amount of $6,540.

e. GJ paid $7,000 to buy luxury season tickets for Jack's parents for State U football games.

f. GJ paid Jack's father $10,000 for services that would have cost no more than $6,000 if Jack had hired any other local business to perform the services. While Jack's dad was competent, he does not command such a premium from his other clients.

g. In an attempt to get his name and new business recognized, GJ paid $7,000 for a one-page ad in the *Geologic Survey.* It also paid $15,000 in radio ads to be run through the end of December.

h. GJ leased office space in a building downtown. GJ paid rent of $27,000 for the year.

i. In August, GJ began manufacturing a special geological digging tool that it sells to wholesalers. GJ's QPAI from the activity for the year is $100,000 [included in revenues reported in part (b)]. GJ paid $10,000 of wages to the employees working on the project during the year and its cost of goods sold on the sales is $15,000. (Assume that taxable income does not limit the amount of the DMD.)

j. In November, Jack's office was broken into and equipment valued at $5,000 was stolen. The tax basis of the equipment was $5,500. Jack received $2,000 of insurance proceeds from the theft.

k. GJ incurred a $4,000 fine from the state government for digging in an unauthorized digging zone.

l. GJ contributed $3,000 to lobbyists for their help in persuading the state government to authorize certain unauthorized digging zones.

m. On July 1, GJ paid $1,800 for an 18-month insurance policy for its business equipment.

n. GJ borrowed $20,000 to help with the company's initial funding needs. GJ used $2,000 of funds to invest in municipal bonds. At the end of the year, GJ paid the $1,200 of interest expense that accrued on the loan during the year.

o. Jack lives 12 miles from the office. He carefully tracked his mileage and drove his truck 6,280 miles between the office and his home. He also drove an additional 7,200 miles between the office and traveling to client sites. Jack did not use the truck for any other purposes. He did not keep track of the specific expenses associated with the truck. However, while traveling to a client site, Jack received a $150 speeding ticket. GJ reimbursed Jack for business mileage and for the speeding ticket.

p. Geo-Jack purchased two season tickets (20 games) to attend State U baseball games for a total of $1,100. Jack took existing and prospective clients to the games to maintain contact and find further work. This was very successful for Jack as GJ gained many new projects through substantial discussions with the clients following the games.

q. Geo-Jack reimbursed employee-salespersons $3,500 for meals involving substantial business discussion.

r. GJ had a client who needed Jack to perform work in Florida. Because Jack had never been to Florida before, he booked an extra day and night for sightseeing. Jack spent $400 for airfare and booked a hotel for 3 nights ($120/night). He also rented a car for $45 per day. The client arranged for Jack's meals while Jack was doing business. GJ reimbursed Jack for all expenses.

Required:

A. What is Geo-Jack's taxable income for the year?

B. As a C corporation, does GJ have a required tax year? If so, what would it be?

C. If GJ were a sole proprietorship, would it have a required tax year-end? If so, what would it be?

D. If GJ were an S corporation, would it have a required tax year-end? If so, what would it be?

83. Rex loves to work with his hands and is very good at making small figurines. In 2005, Rex opened Bronze Age Miniatures (BAM) for business as a sole proprietorship. BAM produces miniature characters ranging from sci-fi characters (his favorite) to historical characters like George Washington (the most popular). Business has been going very well for him—so well, in fact, that he has decided to hire you to determine his business (Schedule C) income for this year. Rex provided the following information relating to his business.

a. Rex received approval from the IRS to switch from the cash method of accounting to the accrual method of accounting effective January 1 of this year. At year-end of last year, BAM reported accounts receivable that had not been included in income under the accrual method of $14,000 and accounts payable that had not been deducted under the accrual method of $5,000.

b. In March, BAM sold 5,000 miniature historical figures to History R Us, Inc. (HRU), a retailer of historical artifacts and figurines, for $75,000.

c. HRU was so impressed with the figurines that they purchased in March that they wanted to contract with BAM to continue to produce the figurines for them for the next three years. HRU paid BAM $216,000 ($12 per figurine) on October 30 of this year, to produce 500 figurines per month for 36 months beginning on November 1 of this year. BAM delivered 500 figurines on November 30 and again on December 30. Rex elects to use the deferral method to account for the transaction.

d. Though the sci-fi figurines were not quite as popular, BAM sold 400 figurines at a sci-fi convention in April. He accepted cash only and received $11,000 for these sales.

e. In January, BAM determined that it would not be able to collect on $2,000 of its beginning-of-the-year receivables, so it wrote off $2,000 of specific receivables. BAM sold 100,000 other figurines on credit for $120,000. BAM estimates that it will be unable to collect 5 percent of the sales revenue from these sales but it has not been able to specifically identify any accounts to write off.

f. Assume that BAM correctly determined that its cost of goods sold this year is $54,000.

g. The sci-fi convention in April was held in Chicago, Illinois. Rex attended the convention because he felt it was a good opportunity to gain new customers and to get new ideas for figurines. He paid $350 round-trip airfare, $100 for entrance to the convention, $210 for lodging, $65 for cab fare, and $110 for meals during the trip. He was busy with business activities the entire trip.

h. On August 1, BAM purchased a 12-month insurance policy that covers its business property for accidents and casualties through July 31 of next year. The policy cost BAM $3,600.

i. BAM reported depreciation expense of $8,200 for this year.

j. Rex had previously operated his business out of his garage, but in January he decided to rent a larger space. He entered into a lease agreement on February 1 and paid $14,400 ($1,200 per month) to possess the space for the next 12 months (February of this year through January of next year).

k. Before he opened his doors for business in 2005, Rex spent $30,000 investigating and otherwise getting ready to do business. He expensed $5,000 immediately and is amortizing the remainder using the straight-line method over 180 months.

l. In December, BAM agreed to a 12-month $8,000 contract with Advertise-With-Us (AWU) to produce a radio ad campaign. BAM paid $3,000 up front (in December of this year) and AWU agreed that BAM would owe the remaining $5,000 only if BAM's sales increased by 15 percent over the nine-month period after the contract was signed.

m. In November of this year, BAM paid $2,500 in business property taxes (based on asset values) covering the period December 1 of this year through November 30 of next year. In November of last year, BAM paid $1,500 for business property taxes (based on asset values) covering the period December 1 of last year through November 30 of this year.

Required:

A. Compute BAM's business income.

B. Complete a Schedule C for BAM (page 1 only).

84. Bryan followed in his father's footsteps and entered into the carpet business. He owns and operates I Do Carpet (IDC). Bryan prefers to install carpet only, but in order to earn additional revenue, he also cleans carpets and sells carpet cleaning supplies. Compute his taxable income considering the following items:

a. IDC contracted with a homebuilder in December of last year to install carpet in 10 new homes being built. The contract price of $80,000 includes $50,000 for materials (carpet). The remaining $30,000 is for IDC's service of installing the carpet. The contract also stated that all money was to be paid upfront. The homebuilder paid IDC in full on December 28 of last year. The contract required IDC to complete the work by January 31 of this year. Bryan purchased the necessary carpet on January 2 and began working on the first home January 4. He completed the last home on January 27 of this year.

b. IDC entered into several other contracts this year and completed the work before year-end. The work cost $130,000 in materials. Bryan billed out $240,000 but only collected $220,000 by year-end. Of the $20,000 still owed to him, Bryan wrote off $3,000 he didn't expect to collect as a bad debt from a customer experiencing extreme financial difficulties.

c. IDC entered into a three-year contract to clean the carpets of an office building. The contract specified that IDC would clean the carpets monthly from July 1 of this year through June 30 three years hence. IDC received payment in full of $8,640 ($240 a month for 36 months) on June 30 of this year.

d. IDC sold 100 bottles of carpet stain remover this year for $5 per bottle (he collected $500). He sold 40 bottles on June 1 and 60 bottles on November 2. IDC had the following carpet cleaning supplies on hand for this year and it uses the LIFO method of accounting for inventory:

Purchase Date	Bottles	Total Cost
November last year	40	$120
February this year	35	$112
July this year	25	$ 85
August this year	40	$140
Totals	140	$457

e. On August 1 of this year, IDC needed more room for storage and paid $900 to rent a garage for 12 months.

f. On November 30 of this year, Bryan decided it was time to get his logo on the sides of his work van. IDC hired We Paint Anything, Inc. (WPA), to do the job. It paid $500 down and agreed to pay the remaining $1,500 upon completion of the job. WPA indicated they wouldn't be able to begin the job until January 15 of next year, but the job would only take one week to complete. Due to circumstances beyond their control, WPA wasn't able to complete the job until April 1 of next year, at which time IDC paid the remaining $1,500.

g. In December, Bryan's son, Aiden, helped him finish some carpeting jobs. IDC owed Aiden $600 (reasonable) compensation for his work. However, Aiden did not receive the payment until January of next year.

h. IDC also paid $1,000 for interest on a short-term bank loan relating to the period from November 1 of this year through March 31 of next year.

85. Hank started a new business in June of last year, Hank's Donut World (HW for short). He has requested your advice on the following specific tax matters associated with HW's first year of operations. Hank has estimated HW's income for the first year as follows:

Revenue:		
Donut sales	$252,000	
Catering revenues	71,550	$323,550
Expenditures:		
Donut supplies	$124,240	
Catering expense	27,910	
Salaries to shop employees	52,500	
Rent expense	40,050	
Accident insurance premiums	8,400	
Other business expenditures	6,850	−259,950
Net Income		$ 63,600

HW operates as a sole proprietorship and Hank reports on the calendar-year basis. Hank uses the cash method of accounting and plans to do the same with HW (HW has no inventory of donuts because unsold donuts are not salable). HW does not purchase donut supplies on credit nor does it generally make sales on credit. Hank has provided the following details for specific first-year transactions.

- A small minority of HW clients complained about the catering service. To mitigate these complaints, Hank's policy is to refund dissatisfied clients 50 percent of the catering fee. By the end of the first year, only two HW clients had complained but had not yet been paid refunds. The expected refunds amount to $1,700, and Hank reduced the reported catering fees for the first year to reflect the expected refund.

- In the first year, HW received a $6,750 payment from a client for catering a monthly breakfast for 30 consecutive months beginning in December. Because the payment didn't relate to last year, Hank excluded the entire amount when he calculated catering revenues.

- In July, HW paid $1,500 to ADMAN Co. for an advertising campaign to distribute fliers advertising HW's catering service. Unfortunately, this campaign violated a city code restricting advertising by fliers, and the city fined HW $250 for the violation. HW paid the fine, and Hank included the fine and the cost of the campaign in "other business" expenditures.

- In July, HW also paid $8,400 for a 24-month insurance policy that covers HW for accidents and casualties beginning on August 1 of the first year.

- On May of the first year, Hank signed a contract to lease the HW donut shop for 10 months. In conjunction with the contract, Hank paid $2,000 as a damage deposit and $8,050 for rent ($805 per month). Hank explained that the damage deposit was refundable at the end of the lease. At this time, Hank also paid $30,000 to lease kitchen equipment for 24 months ($1,250 per month). Both leases began on June 1 of the first year.

- Hank signed a contract hiring WEGO Catering to help cater breakfasts. At year-end, WEGO asked Hank to hold the last catering payment for the year, $9,250, until after January 1 (apparently because WEGO didn't want to report the income on their tax return). The last check was delivered to WEGO in January after the end of the first year. However, because the payment related to the first year of operations, Hank included the $9,250 in last year's catering expense.

- Hank believes that the key to the success of HW has been hiring Jimbo Jones to supervise the donut production and manage the shop. Because Jimbo is such an important employee, HW purchased a "key-employee" term-life insurance policy on his life. HW paid a $5,100 premium for this policy and it will pay HW a $40,000 death benefit if Jimbo passes away any time during the next 12 months. The term of the policy began on September 1 of last year and this payment was included in "other business" expenditures.

- In the first year, HW catered a large breakfast event to celebrate the city's anniversary. The city agreed to pay $7,100 for the event, but Hank forgot to notify the city of the outstanding bill until January of this year. When he mailed the bill in January, Hank decided to discount the charge to $5,500. On the bill, Hank thanked the mayor and the city council for their patronage and asked them to "send a little more business our way." This bill is not reflected in Hank's estimate of HW's income for the first year of operations.

Required:

A. Hank files his personal tax return on a calendar year, but he has not yet filed last year's personal tax return nor has he filed a tax return reporting HW's results for the first year of operations. Explain when Hank should file the tax return for HW and calculate the amount of taxable income generated by HW last year.

B. Determine the taxable income that HW will generate if Hank chooses to account for the business under the accrual method.

C. Describe how your solution might change if Hank incorporated HW before he commenced business last year.

86. R.E.M., a calendar-year corporation and Athens, Georgia, band, recently sold tickets ($20,000,000) for concerts scheduled in the United States for next year and the following year. For financial statement purposes, R.E.M. will recognize the income from the ticket sales when they perform the concerts. For tax purposes, they use the accrual method and would prefer to defer the income from the ticket sales until they perform the concerts. This is the first time that they have sold tickets one or two years in advance. Michael Stipe has asked your advice. Write a memo to Michael explaining your findings.

KAPLAN SCHWESER CPA SIMULATIONS

KAPLAN SCHWESER

Please visit the Online Learning Center (www.mhhe.com/spilker2010) to access the following Kaplan Schweser CPA Simulation:

The simulation for **Colt and Cara West** covers individual income tax issues, including business income/expense; home office deduction; NOL; charitable donations; and capital expenditures.

chapter

9

Property Acquisition and Cost Recovery

Learning Objectives

Upon completing this chapter, you should be able to:

LO 1 Explain the concept of basis and adjusted basis and describe the cost recovery methods used under the tax law to recover the cost of personal property, real property, intangible assets, and natural resources.

◼

LO 2 Determine the applicable cost recovery (depreciation) life, method, and convention for tangible personal and real property and calculate the deduction allowable under MACRS.

◼

LO 3 Explain the rationale behind amortization, describe the four categories of amortizable intangible assets, and calculate amortization expense.

◼

LO 4 Explain cost recovery of natural resources and the allowable depletion methods.

Storyline Summary	
Taxpayer:	Teton Mountaineering Technology, LLC (Teton)—a calendar-year single-member LLC (treated as a sole proprietorship for tax purposes)
Location:	Cody, Wyoming
President/ Founder:	Steve Dallimore
Current situation:	Teton must acquire property to start manufacturing operations and wants to understand the tax consequences of property acquisitions.

T wo years ago while climbing the Black Ice Couloir (pronounced "coo-lore") in Grand Teton National Park, Steve Dallimore and his buddy got into a desperate situation. The climbers planned to move fast and light and to be home before an approaching storm reached the Teton. But just shy of the summit, climbing conditions forced them to turn back. Huddled in a wet sleeping bag in a dark snow cave waiting for the tempest to pass, Steve had an epiphany—a design for a better ice-climbing tool. Since that moment, Steve has been quietly consumed with making his dream— designing and selling his own line of climbing equipment—a reality. Although his current sales career is challenging and financially rewarding, Steve has too often found himself watching the clock and dreaming of a more fulfilling and adventurous career based upon his early training as a mechanical engineer. Steve decided to exercise his stock options, leave his current position, and start Teton. The only problem is that Steve has no employees, no business location, and no manufacturing equipment. ■

Steve obviously has many issues to resolve and decisions to make. In this chapter, we focus on issues dealing with the assets Steve will acquire for use in his new business. In particular, we explain how Teton will determine its cost recovery (depreciation, amortization, and depletion) deductions for the assets in the year the business begins and in subsequent years. These deductions can generate significant tax savings for companies in capital-intensive industries.

This chapter explores the tax consequences of acquiring new or used property, depreciation methods businesses may use to recover the cost of their assets, and special cost recovery incentives for small businesses such as Teton. Along the way, we compare and contrast the process of computing depreciation for tax purposes and for financial accounting purposes. We also address the tax consequences of using intangible assets and natural resources in business activities.

L01 | COST RECOVERY

Most businesses make a significant investment in property, plant, and equipment that is expected to provide benefits over a number of years. For both financial accounting and tax accounting purposes, businesses must capitalize the cost of assets with a useful life of more than one year on the balance sheet rather than expense the cost immediately. Businesses are allowed to use various methods to recover the cost of these assets over time because the assets are subject to wear, tear, and obsolescence.

The method of **cost recovery** is referred to as **depreciation, amortization,** or **depletion**—depending on the nature of the underlying asset. Depreciation is the method of deducting the cost of *tangible* personal and real property (other than land) over a specific time period. Amortization is the method of deducting the cost of **intangible assets** over a specific time period. Finally, depletion is the method of deducting the cost of natural resources over time. Exhibit 9-1 summarizes these concepts.

Generally, a significant portion of a firm's assets is comprised of property, plant, equipment, intangibles, or even natural resources. In most cases, this holds true for small businesses like Teton and also for large publicly traded companies. For example, Exhibit 9-2 describes the assets held by Weyerhaeuser, a publicly traded timber company. As indicated in Exhibit 9-2, Weyerhaeuser has almost $7 billion in property and equipment (net of depreciation), $3.7 billion in timber (net of depletion), and $2.2 billion in goodwill.

Businesses must choose accounting methods for the assets acquired during the year from among the allowable cost recovery alternatives we describe in this chapter.

EXHIBIT 9-1   Assets and Cost Recovery

Asset Type	Cost Recovery Method
Personal property is comprised of tangible assets such as automobiles, equipment, and machinery.	Depreciation
Real property is comprised of buildings and land (although land is nondepreciable).	Depreciation
Intangible assets are nonphysical assets such as goodwill and patents.	Amortization
Natural resources are commodities that are considered valuable in their natural form such as oil, coal, timber, and gold.	Depletion

EXHIBIT 9-2   **Weyerhaeuser Assets**

Assets (in millions) per 10-K Statement	12/31/2007	12/25/2006
Total current assets	$ 3,014	$ 4,121
Property and equipment, net (Note 6)	6,817	7,061
Construction in progress	442	395
Timber and timberlands at cost, less depletion charged to disposals	3,769	3,681
Investments in and advances to equity affiliates (Note 7)	356	499
Goodwill (Note 8)	2,207	2,185
Deferred pension and other assets (Note 9)	2,505	1,368
Restricted assets held by special purpose entities (Note 10)	916	917
Noncurrent assets of discontinued operations (Note 3)	–	3,011
	$20,026	$23,238

Attention to detail is important because the basis of an asset must be reduced by the cost recovery deductions allowed or *allowable*.[1]

Basis for Cost Recovery

Businesses may begin recouping the cost of purchased business assets once they begin using the asset in their business (they place it in service).[2] Once the business establishes its cost basis in an asset, the basis is reduced as the business recovers the cost of the asset through cost recovery deductions such as depreciation, amortization, or depletion. The amount of an asset's cost that has yet to be recovered through cost recovery deductions is called the asset's **adjusted basis** or **tax basis.** An asset's adjusted basis can be computed by subtracting the accumulated depreciation (or amortization or depletion) from the asset's initial cost or historical basis.[3]

An asset's cost basis includes all of the expenses to purchase, prepare it for use, and begin using the asset. These costs may include sales tax, shipping, and installation. The financial accounting and tax rules for computing an asset's basis are very similar. Thus, a purchased asset's initial basis for both tax and book purposes is generally the same.[4]

When a business incurs additional costs associated with an asset after the asset has been placed in service, how are the additional costs treated for tax purposes? The answer depends on whether the expense constitutes routine maintenance on the asset or whether it significantly extends the useful life of the asset. Routine maintenance costs are immediately deductible as ordinary business expenses. For example, if Teton spent $35 to have a delivery truck's oil changed, it would immediately deduct the cost as routine maintenance. Alternatively, if an additional cost significantly extends an

---

> **THE KEY FACTS**
>
> *Cost Basis*
>
> ■ An asset's cost basis includes all expenses needed to purchase the asset, prepare it for use, and begin using it.
>
> ■ Cost basis is usually the same for book and tax purposes.
>
> ■ Special basis rules apply when personal assets are converted to business use and when assets are acquired through nontaxable transactions, gifts, or inheritances.

---

[1]This means that if a business fails to deduct the allowable amount of depreciation expense for the year, the business must still reduce the asset's basis by the depreciation expense the taxpayer could have deducted under the method the business is using to depreciate the asset (this reduces the future depreciation deductions for the asset). If a business discovers that it failed to claim allowable depreciation in a previous year, it cannot currently deduct the depreciation attributable to prior years. Rather, the business must file amended returns—assuming the statute of limitations is still open—to claim the depreciation expense.

[2]Cost basis is defined under §1012. The mere purchase of an asset does not trigger cost recovery deductions. A business must begin using the asset for business purposes (place it in service) in order to depreciate the asset. However, because businesses generally acquire and place assets in service at the same time, we refer to these terms interchangeably throughout the chapter.

[3]§1011.

[4]However, special basis rules apply when an asset is acquired through a nontaxable transaction. See discussion below.

asset's useful life, the expenditure generates a new asset (for cost recovery purposes) separate from the original asset.[5] For example, if Teton spends $3,000 on a rebuilt engine for a delivery truck in an attempt to add 50,000 miles to the truck's useful life, the cost of the engine would be accounted for as a separate, new asset.

When a business acquires multiple assets for one purchase price, the tax laws require the business to determine a cost basis for each separate asset. For example, if Teton were to acquire land and a building on the land, Teton must treat the building and land as separate assets. In these types of acquisitions, businesses determine the cost basis of each asset by allocating a portion of the purchase price to each asset based on that asset's value relative to the total value of all the assets the business acquired in the same purchase. The asset values are generally determined by an appraisal.[6]

<table>
<tr><td colspan="6">**Example 9-1**</td></tr>
</table>

Steve determined that he needed machinery and office furniture for a manufacturing facility and a design studio (located in Cody, Wyoming). During the year, Steve purchased the following assets and incurred the following costs to prepare the assets for business use. His cost basis in each asset is determined as follows:

Asset	Date Acquired	(1) Purchase Price	(2) Business Preparation Costs	(1) + (2) Cost Basis
Machinery	7/22/09	$250,000	$10,000 (delivery and setup)	$260,000
Office furniture	2/3/09	$ 10,000		$ 10,000
Delivery truck (used)	8/17/09	$ 15,000		$ 15,000
Warehouse	5/1/09	$270,000*	$5,000 (minor modifications)	$275,000
Land (10 acres)	5/1/09	$ 75,000*		$ 75,000

*Note that the warehouse and the land were purchased together for $345,000. Steve and the seller determined that the value (and cost) of the warehouse was $270,000 and the value (and cost) of the land was $75,000.

Special rules apply when determining the tax basis of assets converted from personal to business use or assets acquired through a nontaxable exchange, gift, or inheritance. If an asset is used for personal purposes and is later converted to business (or rental) use, the basis is the *lesser* of (1) the cost basis of the asset or (2) the fair market value of the asset on the date of conversion to business use.[7] This rule prevents taxpayers from converting a nondeductible personal loss into a deductible business loss. For example, if Steve had purchased a truck for $20,000 several years ago and decided to use it as a delivery truck when its value had declined to $15,000, his cost basis (or tax basis) in the truck for tax purposes would be $15,000. The $5,000 decline in the truck's value from $20,000 to $15,000 would be a nondeductible personal loss to Steve, and the reduction in basis ensures that he will not ever be allowed to deduct the loss. Assets acquired through a nontaxable exchange such as a like-kind exchange retain a carryover basis—the basis they had before the transaction. Assets acquired by gift have a carryover basis, which means that the taxpayer's basis in property received through a gift is generally the same basis the transferor had in the property.[8] For example, if Steve's parents gave him stock worth $45,000 to help him start his business and his parents had purchased the stock 10 years earlier for $25,000, Steve's basis in the stock

[5] §168(i)(6).
[6] Reg. §1.167(a)-5.
[7] Reg. §§1.168-2(j)(6) and 1.168(i)-4(b).
[8] §1015. The basis may be increased if the transferor is required to pay gift tax on the transfer [see §1015(d)].

would be $25,000 (the same basis his parents had in the stock). Assets acquired through inheritance generally receive a basis equal to the fair market value on the transferor's date of death.[9] For example, if Steve inherited a 1957 Porsche Speedster worth $90,000 from his grandfather who originally paid $3,500 for it, Steve's basis would be $90,000 (its fair market value) because Steve acquired it through an inheritance.

DEPRECIATION

Before 1981, tax depreciation methods closely resembled financial accounting methods. For both financial accounting and tax purposes, businesses were allowed to choose from among a wide range of depreciation methods and **recovery periods.** Computing both tax and financial accounting depreciation required businesses to determine the assets' useful lives and "salvage values." In 1981, tax and financial accounting depreciation methods parted ways when Congress introduced the **Accelerated Cost Recovery System (ACRS)** for computing depreciation expense. Under ACRS, businesses used accelerated depreciation methods to depreciate assets over predetermined, fixed recovery periods.

> **THE KEY FACTS**
> *Tax Depreciation*
> ■ To depreciate an asset, a business must determine:
> · Original basis
> · Depreciation method
> · Recovery period
> · Depreciation convention

Today, businesses calculate their tax depreciation using the **Modified Accelerated Cost Recovery System (MACRS)**—which is pronounced "makers" by tax accountants.[10] Compared to financial (book) depreciation, MACRS tax depreciation is quite simple. To compute MACRS depreciation for an asset, the business need only know the asset's *original cost,* the applicable *depreciation method,* the asset's *recovery period* (or depreciable "life"), and the applicable depreciation *convention* (the amount of depreciation deductible in the year of acquisition and the year of disposition). The method, recovery, period, and convention vary based on whether the asset is **personal property** or **real property.** We first turn our attention to determining depreciation expense for personal property.

Personal Property Depreciation

Personal property includes all tangible property, such as computers, automobiles, furniture, machinery, and equipment, other than real property. Note that personal property and *personal-use* property are *not* the same thing. Personal property denotes any property that is not real property (e.g., building and land) while personal-*use* property is any property used for personal purposes (for example, a personal residence is personal-use property even though it is real property). Personal property is relatively short-lived and subject to obsolescence when compared to real property.

Depreciation Method   MACRS provides three acceptable methods for depreciating personal property: 200 percent (double) declining balance, 150 percent declining balance, and straight-line.[11] The 200 percent declining balance method is the default method. This method takes twice the straight-line amount of depreciation in the first year, and continues to take twice the straight-line percentage on the asset's declining basis until switching to the straight-line method in the year that the straight-line method over the remaining life provides a greater depreciation expense. Fortunately, as we describe below, the IRS provides depreciation tables to simplify the calculations.

Profitable businesses with relatively high marginal tax rates generally choose to use the 200 percent declining balance method because it generates the largest depreciation expense in the early years of the assets' lives and, thus, the highest current

[9]§1014. The date for determining the fair market value is later if the alternate valuation date is elected by the estate.

[10]IRS Publication 946 provides a useful summary of MACRS depreciation.

[11]For personal property, the 200 DB is often referred to as the General Depreciation System (GDS) while the 150 percent DB or straight-line methods are referred to as the Alternative Depreciation System (ADS).

year after-tax cash flows. For tax planning purposes, companies that currently have lower marginal tax rates but expect their marginal tax rates to increase in the near future may elect the straight-line method because that method generates less depreciation expense in the early years of the asset's life and more depreciation expense in the later years when their marginal tax rates may increase.

Example 9-2

If Teton wants to accelerate its current depreciation deductions to the extent possible, what method should it use to depreciate its office furniture, machinery, and delivery truck?

Answer: The 200 percent declining balance method (switching to straight-line). Teton could have elected to use either the 150 percent declining balance or the straight-line method, if it wanted a less accelerated method for determining its depreciation deductions.

Each year, businesses elect the depreciation method for the assets placed in service during *that year*. Specifically, businesses elect one depreciation method for all similar assets they acquired that year.[12] Thus, if a business acquires several different machines during the year, it must use the same method to depreciate all of the machines.

Depreciation Recovery Period For financial accounting purposes, an asset's recovery period (depreciable life) is based on its taxpayer-determined estimated useful life. In contrast, for tax purposes an asset's recovery period is predetermined by the IRS in Rev. Proc. 87-56. Rev. Proc. 87-56 helps taxpayers categorize each of their assets based upon the property's description. Once the business has determined the appropriate categories for its assets, it can use the Revenue Procedure to identify the recovery period for all assets in a particular category. For example, Teton placed office furniture in service during the year. By examining the excerpt from Rev. Proc. 87-56 provided in Exhibit 9-3, you can see that Category or Asset Class 00.11 includes office furniture and that assets in this category, including Teton's office furniture, have a recovery period of seven years (emphasis in excerpt added through bold and italic text).[13]

EXHIBIT 9-3 **Excerpt from Revenue Procedure 87-56**

Description of Assets Included		Years	
Specific depreciable assets used in all business activities, except as noted:	**Class Life**	**General Recovery Period**	**Alternative Recovery Period**
00.11 **Office Furniture**, Fixtures, and Equipment: Includes furniture and fixtures that are not a structural component of a building. Includes such assets as desks, files, safes, and communications equipment. Does not include communications equipment that is included in other classes.	10	7	10
00.241 Light General Purpose Trucks: Includes trucks for use over the road (actual unloaded weight less than 13,000 pounds) . . .	4	5	5
34.0 Manufacture of Fabricated Metal Products Special Tools: Includes assets used in the production of metal cans, tinware . . .	12	7	12

[12]Technically, similar assets are assets in the same asset class. We discuss asset classes below.

[13]The "alternative" recovery period in Rev. Proc. 87-56 refers to an asset's life under the alternative depreciation system (which was discussed earlier under depreciation methods). The Class Life referred to in Rev. Proc. 87-56 refers to the midpoint of asset depreciation range (ADR) applicable under pre-ACRS and has little or no meaning under MACRS.

EXHIBIT 9-4 Recovery Period for Most Common Business Assets

Asset Description (summary of Rev. Proc. 87-57)	Recovery Period*
Cars, light general-purpose trucks, and computers and peripheral equipment.	5-year
Office furniture, fixtures, machinery, and equipment.	7-year

*Using 200 percent declining balance, switching to straight-line.

While even this excerpt from Rev. Proc. 87-56 may seem a bit intimidating, you can classify the vast majority of business assets acquired by knowing a few common recovery periods. You should know the recovery period for the commonly purchased assets described in Exhibit 9-4.

To this point, our discussion has emphasized computing depreciation for new assets. Does the process change when businesses acquire used assets? No, it is exactly the same. For example, Teton purchased a *used* delivery truck. The fact that the truck is used does not change its MACRS recovery period. No matter how long the previous owner used the truck, Teton will depreciate it over the five-year recovery period for light general purpose trucks (see Exhibit 9-4).

Compare this to the process of determining the life of each *individual* asset as required by financial accounting rules. Exhibit 9-5 provides an excerpt from

EXHIBIT 9-5 Weyerhaeuser Asset Depreciable Lives for Financial Accounting Purposes

	Weyerhaeuser		
	NOTE 6: PROPERTY AND EQUIPMENT		
(Dollar amounts in millions)	**Range of Lives (in years)**	**12/30/2007**	**12/31/2006**
Property and equipment, at cost:			
Land	N/A	$ 282	$ 303
Buildings and improvements	10–40	2,449	3,172
Machinery and equipment	2–25	12,640	17,900
Rail and truck roads	10–20	584	575
Other	3–10	391	457
		16,346	22,407
Less discontinued operations		–	(6,445)
		16,346	15,962
Allowance for depreciation and amortization		(9,529)	(12,398)
Less discontinued operations		–	3,497
		(9,529)	(8,901)
Property and Equipment, net		$ 6,817	$ 7,061

Weyerhaeuser, a portion of
NOTE 1. SUMMARY OF SIGNIFICANT ACCOUNTING POLICIES

Property and Equipment
We maintain property accounts on an individual asset basis.
Here's how we handle major items:

- Improvements to and replacements of major units of property are capitalized.
- Maintenance, repairs and minor replacements are expensed.
- Depreciation is calculated using a straight-line method at rates based on estimated service lives.
- Logging railroads and truck roads are generally amortized as timber is harvested at rates based on the volume of timber estimated to be removed.
- For property sold or retired, cost and accumulated depreciation are removed from the accounts and the gain or loss is included in earnings.

EXHIBIT 9-6   Teton Personal Property Summary (Base Scenario)

Asset	Date Acquired	Quarter Acquired	Cost Basis	Recovery Period	Reference
Machinery	7/22/09	3rd	$260,000	7	Example 9-1; Exhibit 9-3.
Office furniture	2/3/09	1st	10,000	7	Example-9-1; Exhibit 9-3.
Delivery truck	8/17/09	3rd	15,000	5	Example 9-1; Exhibit 9-3.
Total personal property			**$285,000**		

Weyerhaeuser's financial statements illustrating the complexities of financial accounting depreciation.

Notice that, for financial statement purposes, Weyerhaeuser has determined that the life of its machinery and equipment ranges from 2 to 25 years. Determining the tax recovery periods for these assets is very simple. Under MACRS, the tax recovery period for machinery and equipment is seven years. Using Rev. Proc. 87-57, Teton has determined the cost recovery periods for the personal property it purchased and placed in service during the year. Exhibit 9-6 summarizes this information.

Depreciation Conventions   Once a business has determined the depreciation methods and recovery periods for the assets it placed in service during the year, it must also determine the applicable depreciation conventions. The depreciation convention specifies the portion of a full year's depreciation the business can deduct for an asset in the year the asset is first placed in service *and* in the year the asset is sold. For *personal property,* taxpayers must use either the **half-year convention** or the **mid-quarter convention**. But, as we discuss below, taxpayers are *not* free to choose the convention of their choice.

Half-year convention.   The half-year convention allows one-half of a full year's depreciation in the year the asset is placed in service, regardless of when it was actually placed in service. For example, when the half-year convention applies to a calendar-year business, an asset placed in service on either February 3 or August 17 is treated as though it was placed in service on July 1, which is the middle of the calendar year. Thus, under this convention, Teton would deduct one-half of a year's worth of depreciation for the machinery, office furniture, and delivery truck even though it acquired the machinery, delivery truck, and office furniture at various times during the year (see Exhibit 9-6). The half-year convention is built into the depreciation tables provided by the IRS, which simplifies the depreciation calculation for the year the asset is placed into service.

The original ACRS system required the use of the half-year convention for all personal property placed in service during the year. However, Congress believed that many businesses took unfair advantage of the half-year convention by purposely acquiring assets at the end of the year that they otherwise would have acquired at the beginning of the next taxable year. Thus, businesses received one-half of a year's worth of depreciation for assets that they only used for a small portion of the year. Even though the half-year convention is the default convention, policy makers introduced the *mid-quarter convention* under MACRS to limit or prevent this type of opportunistic behavior.

Mid-quarter convention.   Under the mid-quarter convention, businesses treat assets *as though* they were placed in service during the middle of the *quarter* in which the business actually placed the assets into service. For example, when the

---

THE KEY FACTS

Half-Year Convention

■ One-half of a year's depreciation is allowed in the first and the last year of an asset's life.

■ The IRS depreciation tables automatically account for the half-year convention.

■ If an asset is disposed of before it is fully depreciated, only one-half of the table's applicable depreciation percentage is allowed in the year of disposition.

mid-quarter convention applies, if a business places an asset in service on December 1 (in the fourth quarter) it must treat the asset as though it was placed in service on November 15, which is the middle of the fourth quarter. Consequently, the business would only be able to deduct one-half of a quarter's worth of depreciation in the year the asset was placed in service (depreciation for the second half of November and the entire month of December).

Businesses must use the mid-quarter convention when *more* than 40 percent of their total *tangible personal property* that they place in service during the year is placed in service during the *fourth* quarter.[14] Thus, the steps to determine whether the mid-quarter convention applies are the following:

Step 1: Sum the total basis of the tangible personal property that was placed in service during the year.

Step 2: Sum the total basis of the tangible personal property that was place in service in the fourth quarter.

Step 3: Divide the outcome of Step 2 by the outcome of Step 1. If the quotient is greater than 40 percent, the business must use the mid-quarter convention to determine the depreciation for all personal property the business places in service during the year. Otherwise, the business uses the half-year convention for depreciating this property.

Example 9-3

The following excerpt from the base scenario in Exhibit 9-6 provides the information we need to determine if Teton must use the mid-quarter convention to compute depreciation:

Asset	Date Acquired	Quarter Acquired	Cost Basis
Machinery	7/22/09	Third	$260,000
Office furniture	2/3/09	First	10,000
Delivery truck	8/17/09	Third	15,000
Total personal property			$285,000

Is Teton required to use the mid-quarter convention to depreciate its personal property?

Answer: No. See computation below.

Description	Amount	Explanation
(1) Total basis of tangible personal property placed in service during year	$285,000	
(2) Total basis of tangible personal property placed in service in fourth quarter	$ 0	
(3) Percentage of basis of total tangible personal property placed in service during fourth quarter	0%	(2)/(1).

Teton is not required to use the mid-quarter convention because it did not place more than 40 percent of its assets in service during the fourth quarter. (In fact, Teton did not place any assets in service in the fourth quarter.) Consequently, Teton will use the half-year convention to calculate its depreciation expense.

THE KEY FACTS

Mid-Quarter Convention

▪ The mid-quarter convention is required when more than 40 percent of a taxpayer's personal property placed in service during the year was placed during the fourth quarter.

▪ Each quarter has its own depreciation table. Once you begin using a table, you must use the table over the asset's whole life.

▪ If an asset is disposed of before it is fully depreciated, use the formula given to determine the allowable depreciation in the year of disposition.

[14]Reg. §1.168-1(b)(4) indicates that property expensed under §179 (discussed later in the chapter) is not included in the numerator or denominator of the mid-quarter test.

Example 9-4

What if: Let's replace the facts from the base scenario presented in Exhibit 9-6 with the following alternative scenario 1 facts. In this alternative set of facts, we assume the machinery was acquired during the fourth quarter on October 25 as follows:

Asset	Date Acquired	Quarter Acquired	Cost Basis
Machinery	10/25/09	Fourth	$260,000
Office furniture	2/3/09	First	10,000
Delivery truck	8/17/09	Third	15,000
Total personal property			**$285,000**

Under alternative scenario 1, is Teton required to use the mid-quarter convention?

Answer: Yes. Of the personal property it placed in service during the year, it placed 91.2 percent in service in the last quarter (this is greater than 40 percent). See the calculations below:

Description	Amount	Explanation
(1) Cost of all personal property placed in service during current year.	$285,000	
(2) Cost of personal property placed in service in the fourth quarter during current year.	260,000	
(3) Percentage of all personal property placed in service during current year that was placed in service in the fourth quarter.	91.2%	(1)/(2).

What if: Assume that Teton also placed in service on July 1 a building costing $500,000. Is Teton subject to the mid-quarter convention?

Answer: Yes. Because the building is real property (not personal property), it is not included in the mid-quarter calculation. The calculation is exactly the same as the calculation in alternative scenario 1 above.

Calculating Depreciation for Personal Property   Once a business has identified the applicable method, recovery period, and convention for personal property, tax depreciation is relatively easy to calculate because the Internal Revenue Service provides depreciation percentage tables in Rev. Proc. 87-57. The percentages in the depreciation tables for tangible personal property incorporate the method and convention [accordingly there are separate tables for each combination of depreciation method (200 percent declining balance, 150 percent declining balance, and straight-line) and convention (half-year and mid-quarter; each quarter has its own table)]. To determine the depreciation for an asset for the year, use the following three steps:

Step 1: Locate the applicable table provided in Rev. Proc. 87-57.
Step 2: Select the column that corresponds with the asset's recovery period.
Step 3: Find the row identifying the year of the asset's recovery period.

The tables are constructed so that the intersection of the row and column provides the percentage of the asset's *original basis* that is deductible as depreciation expense for the particular year. Thus, depreciation expense for a particular asset is the product of the percentage from the table and the asset's *original basis*.

EXHIBIT 9-7   MACRS-200 percent Declining Balance Using the Half-Year Convention

Depreciation Rate for Recovery Period

Year	5-Year Property	7-Year Property
1	20.00%	14.29%
2	32.00	24.49
3	19.20	17.49
4	11.52	12.49
5	11.52	8.93
6	5.76	8.92
7	N/A	8.93
8	N/A	4.46

Applying the Half-Year Convention   Consider the excerpt from Rev. Proc. 87-57 provided in Exhibit 9-7 that shows the depreciation percentages for MACRS 200 percent declining balance using the half-year convention.[15] If a seven-year asset is placed into service during the current year, the depreciation percentage is 14.29 percent (the intersection of row 1 (year 1) and the seven-year property column).

Notice that the depreciation percentages for five-year property extend for six years and the percentages for seven-year property extend for eight years. Why does it take six years to fully depreciate an asset with a five-year recovery period and eight years for a seven-year asset? Because the business does not deduct a full year's depreciation in the first year (businesses must use either the half-year or mid-quarter convention), an entire year of depreciation is effectively split between the first and last year. For example, when the half-year convention applies to a five-year asset, the taxpayer deducts one-half of a year's depreciation in year 1 and one-half of a year's depreciation in year 6.

Example 9-5

Teton is using the 200 percent declining balance method and half-year convention to compute depreciation expense on its current year personal property additions. What is Teton's depreciation expense for these assets?

Answer: $41,583, computed as follows:

Asset	Date Placed in Service	(1) Original Basis	(2) Rate	(1) × (2) Depreciation
Machinery	July 22	$260,000	14.29%	$37,154
Office furniture	February 3	$ 10,000	14.29%	$ 1,429
Used delivery truck	August 17	$ 15,000	20.00%	$ 3,000
Total				$41,583

Because the machinery has a seven-year recovery period and it is the first year for depreciation, the depreciation rate is 14.29 percent (see Exhibit 9-7). The depreciation rate for the office furniture and the used delivery truck (five-year property) are determined in a similar manner.

---

[15]MACRS tables for the half-year and mid-quarter convention are also provided in the chapter Appendix A.

Calculating depreciation for assets in years after the year of acquisition is also relatively simple. Again, using the MACRS Half-Year Convention Table (see Exhibit 9-7) to compute depreciation for the second year, the taxpayer would multiply the asset's original basis times the rate factor in the *year 2* row and the *year 3* row in the following year and so on.

Example 9-6

What if: Assume that Teton holds the tangible personal property it acquired and placed in service this year until the assets are fully depreciated. Using the IRS provided tables (see Exhibit 9-7) how would Teton determine its depreciation expense for years 1 through 8?

Answer: See the following table:

Depreciation Over Asset Recovery Period

Year	Seven-Year Machinery	7-Year Office Furniture	5-Year Delivery Truck	Yearly Total
1	$ 37,154	$ 1,429	$ 3,000	$ 41,583
2	$ 63,674	$ 2,449	$ 4,800	$ 70,923
3	$ 45,474	$ 1,749	$ 2,880	$ 50,103
4	$ 32,474	$ 1,249	$ 1,728	$ 35,451
5	$ 23,218	$ 893	$ 1,728	$ 25,839
6	$ 23,192	$ 892	$ 864	$ 24,948
7	$ 23,218	$ 893	N/A	$ 24,111
8	$ 11,596	$ 446	N/A	$ 12,042
Accumulated Depreciation	$260,000	$10,000	$15,000	$285,000

Half-year convention for year of disposition. Businesses often sell or dispose of assets before they fully depreciate them. Recall that the half-year convention applies in both the year of acquisition and the year of disposition. Note, however, that the tables can't anticipate when a business may dispose of an asset. Accordingly, the tables only provide depreciation percentages for assets assuming the asset won't be disposed of before it is fully depreciated. That is, for each year in the asset's recovery period, the tables provide a percentage for an entire year's worth of depreciation. So, to calculate the depreciation for the year of disposition, the business first calculates depreciation for the *entire year* as if the property had not been disposed of. Then the business applies the half-year convention by multiplying the full year's depreciation by 50 percent (one-half of a year's depreciation). Note, however, that if a business acquires and disposes of an asset in the same year, it is not allowed to claim any depreciation on the asset.[16]

Example 9-7

What if: Assume that Teton sells all of its office furniture in year 2 (the year after it buys it). What is Teton's depreciation for the office furniture in the year of disposition (year 2)?

(*continued on page 9-13...*)

---

[16]Reg. §1.168(d)-1(b)(3).

Answer: $1,225, calculated using the MACRS Half-Year Convention Table as follows:

Asset	Amount	Explanation
(1) Office furniture	$10,000	Original basis.
(2) Depreciation percentage	24.49%	Seven-year property, year 2.
(3) Full year of depreciation	$ 2,449	(1) × (2).
(4) Half-year convention percentage	50%	Depreciation limit in year of disposal.
Depreciation in year of disposal	$ 1,225	(3) × (4).

What if: Assume that Teton sold all of its office furniture in year 1 (the year it bought it and placed it in service). How much deprecation expense can Teton deduct for the office furniture in year 1?

Answer: $0. A business is not allowed to claim any depreciation expense for assets it acquires and disposes of in the same year.

Applying the Mid-Quarter Convention   When the mid-quarter convention applies, the process for computing depreciation is the same as it is when the half-year convention applies, except that businesses use a different set of depreciation tables (a separate table for each quarter). After categorizing the assets by recovery period and grouping them into quarters, businesses consult the Mid-Quarter Convention Tables (which have been consolidated into Exhibit 9-8) to determine the depreciation rate for each asset group.

EXHIBIT 9-8   Mid-Quarter Depreciation Table for Personal Property by Quarter Placed in Service and Recovery Period (Excerpts from Rev. Proc. 87-57)

	First Quarter		Second Quarter		Third Quarter		Fourth Quarter	
Year	5-year	7-year	5-year	7-year	5-year	7-year	5-year	7-year
1	35.00%	25.00%	25.00%	17.85%	15.00%	10.71%	5.00%	3.57%
2	26.00	21.43	30.00	23.47	34.00	25.51	38.00	27.55
3	15.60	15.31	18.00	16.76	20.40	18.22	22.80	19.68
4	11.01	10.93	11.37	11.97	12.24	13.02	13.68	14.06
5	11.01	8.75	11.37	8.87	11.30	9.30	10.94	10.04
6	1.38	8.74	4.26	8.87	7.06	8.85	9.58	8.73
7		8.75		8.87		8.86		8.73
8		1.09		3.33		5.53		7.64

The depreciation expense for an asset is the product of the asset's original basis and the percentage from the table.

Example 9-8

What if: For this example, we assume the facts from alternative scenario 1 presented in Example 9-4 (see table below). What is Teton's year 1 depreciation expense for its personal property additions under the alternative scenario 1 presented in Example 9-4?

(*continued on page 9-14...*)

Answer: $14,032, computed as follows:

Asset	Purchase Date	Quarter	Original Basis	Rate	Depreciation
Machinery (7-year)	October 25	Fourth	$260,000	3.57%	$ 9,282
Office furniture (7-year)	February 3	First	$ 10,000	25.00%	$ 2,500
Delivery truck (5-year)	August 17	Third	$ 15,000	15.00%	$ 2,250
					$14,032

The machinery factor of 3.57 percent is located in Exhibit 9-8. See the columns for property placed into service during the fourth quarter (last two columns), select the 7-year recovery period column (last column), and the year 1 row. The process for determining the rate factor for the office furniture and used delivery truck follows the same methodology using the first and third quarter columns, respectively.

Teton's $41,583 depreciation expense under the half-year convention (see Example 9-5) is significantly higher than its $14,032 depreciation expense under the mid-quarter convention (see Example 9-8). Why the big disparity? Because the (high cost) machinery was placed into service during the fourth quarter and thus generated significantly less current depreciation expense (one-half of one quarter's depreciation) than it would have under the half-year convention. It is important to note, however, that when using the mid-quarter convention, assets placed in service in the first or second quarter will generate more depreciation than they would have under the half-year convention (10.5/12ths and 7.5/12ths of a full year, respectively). However, because the mid-quarter convention only applies when a large percentage of the cost of the assets was placed in service in the fourth quarter, the mid-quarter convention tends to generate less overall depreciation expense for new additions than the half-year convention.

The process for calculating depreciation for assets in years after the year of acquisition under the mid-quarter convention is nearly identical to the process we described for making this computation under the half-year convention. The only difference is that the business looks to the MACRS Mid-Quarter Convention Table (Exhibit 9-8) for the appropriate quarter rather than the MACRS Half-Year Convention Table (Exhibit 9-7).

Example 9-9

What if: Assume that Teton held and fully depreciated the tangible personal property it placed in service this year under the mid-quarter convention (alternative scenario 1). What would be Teton's depreciation expense for its personal property additions for years 1 through 8 using the mid-quarter tables provided in Exhibit 9-8?

Answer: See table below*:

Year	7-year Machinery 4th Quarter	7-year Office Furniture 1st Quarter	5-year Delivery Truck 3rd Quarter	Yearly Total
1	$ 9,282	$ 2,500	$ 2,250	$ 14,032
2	$ 71,630	$ 2,143	$ 5,100	$ 78,873
3	$ 51,168	$ 1,531	$ 3,060	$ 55,759
4	$ 36,556	$ 1,093	$ 1,836	$ 39,485
5	$ 26,104	$ 875	$ 1,695	$ 28,674
6	$ 22,698	$ 874	$ 1,059	$ 24,631
7	$ 22,698	$ 875	N/A	$ 23,573
8	$ 19,864	$ 109	N/A	$ 19,973
	$260,000	$10,000	$15,000	$285,000

*See Exhibit 9-8; the depreciation is calculated by multiplying the applicable rate by the cost basis.

Mid-quarter convention for year of disposition.   Calculating depreciation expense in the year of sale or disposition for mid-quarter convention assets is a bit more involved than it is when the half-year convention applies. When the mid-quarter convention applies, the asset is treated as though it is sold in the middle of the quarter of which it was actually sold. The process for calculating mid-quarter convention depreciation for the year of sale is exactly the same as the process for using the half-year convention, except that *instead of* multiplying the full year's depreciation by 50 percent, the business multiplies the amount of depreciation it would have been able to claim on the asset if it had not sold the asset (a full year's depreciation) by the applicable percentage in Exhibit 9-9 below.

EXHIBIT 9-9   **Mid-Quarter Convention Percentage of Full Year's Depreciation in Year of Disposition**

Quarter of Disposition	Percentage	Calculation*
First	12.5%	1.5/12
Second	37.5%	4.5/12
Third	62.5%	7.5/12
Fourth	87.5%	10.5/12

*The calculation is the number of months the taxpayer held or is deemed to have held the asset in the year of disposition divided by 12 months in the year.

Example 9-10

What if: Assume that Teton depreciates its personal property under the mid-quarter convention (alternative scenario 1, see Example 9-4) and that it sells its office furniture in the third quarter of year 2. The office furniture ($10,000 original basis) was placed into service during the first quarter of year 1 and has a seven-year recovery period. What depreciation expense can Teton deduct for the office furniture in year 2, the year of sale?

Answer: $1,339. Computed as follows:

Description	Amount	Explanation
(1) Original basis	$10,000	Example 9-4.
(2) Year 2 depreciation percentage	21.43%	Exhibit 9-8; Mid-quarter, first quarter table, 7-year property, year 2.
(3) Full year 2 depreciation	2,143	(1) × (2).
(4) Percentage of full year's depreciation in year of disposition if mid-quarter convention applies	62.5%	From Exhibit 9-9; asset disposed of in third quarter.
Depreciation in year of disposition	$1,339	(3) × (4).

What if: Assume Teton disposed of the office furniture on January 2 of year 2. How much depreciation expense would it be able to claim on the furniture in year 2?

Answer: $268 ($2,143 full year's depreciation × 12.5% from Exhibit 9-9).

Immediate Expensing   Policy makers created an important tax incentive designed to help small businesses purchasing new or used tangible personal property.[17] This incentive is commonly referred to as the **§179 expense** or *immediate expensing* election.

[17]Real property, intangibles, and tangible personal property used less than 50 percent for business are not eligible for immediate expensing.

As discussed earlier in the chapter, businesses must generally depreciate assets over the assets' recovery periods. However, under §179, businesses may elect to immediately expense up to $133,000 of tangible personal property placed in service during 2009 ($250,000 in 2008).[18] They may also elect to deduct less than the maximum. When businesses elect to deduct a certain amount of §179 expense, they immediately expense all or a portion of an asset's basis or several assets' bases. To reflect this immediate depreciation expense, they must reduce the basis of the asset or assets to which they applied the expense *before* they compute the MACRS depreciation expense on the remaining bases of these assets.

Example 9-11

What if: Assume Teton is eligible for and elects to immediately deduct $80,000 of §179 expense against the basis of the machinery. (Note that Teton could have elected to deduct up to $133,000.) What is the amount of Teton's current year depreciation expense, including regular MACRS depreciation and the §179 expense on its machinery (assuming half-year convention applies)?

Answer: $105,722, computed as follows:

Description	Amount	Explanation
(1) Machinery	$260,000	Example 9-1.
(2) §179 expense	$ 80,000	
(3) Remaining basis in machinery	$180,000	(1) − (2).
(4) MACRS depreciation rate for 7-year machinery	14.29%	Rate from Exhibit 9-7.
(5) MACRS deprecation expense on machinery	$ 25,722	(3) × (4).
Total depreciation on machinery	$105,722	(2) + (5).

What if: Assume that Teton was eligible for and elected to claim the maximum amount of §179 expense. What would be its total current-year depreciation expense, including MACRS depreciation and §179 expense (assuming half-year convention applies)?

Answer: $151,148, computed as follows:

Description	Amount	Explanation
(1) Machinery	$260,000	Example 9-1.
(2) §179 expense	$133,000	Maximum expense in 2009.
(3) Remaining basis in machinery	$127,000	(1) − (2).
(4) MACRS depreciation rate for 7-year machinery	14.29%	Rate from Exhibit 9-7.
(5) MACRS deprecation expense on machinery	$ 18,148	(3) × (4).
Total depreciation on machinery	$151,148	(2) + (5).

Limits on immediate expensing. The maximum amount of §179 expense a business may elect to claim for the year is subject to a phase-out limitation. Under the phase-out limitation, businesses must reduce the maximum available expense dollar for

[18]The maximum allowable expense under §179 is indexed for inflation and changes annually. Generally, the annual amount is released in a Revenue Procedure at the beginning of the taxable year. The 2009 amounts are based on the law as of the date this book went to press; however, there is legislative discussion regarding extending the larger amounts from the Economic Stimulus Act of 2008.

dollar for the amount of *tangible personal property* purchased and placed in service during 2009 *over* a $530,000 threshold ($800,000 in 2008, according to the Economic Stimulus Act of 2008 unless extended by Congress).[19] Thus, if a business places more than $663,000 ($530,000 threshold plus $133,000 expense) of tangible personal property into service during 2009, its maximum available §179 expense for the year is $0. The phased-out portion of the maximum expense disappears and does *not* carry over to another year.

Example 9-12

What if: Let's assume that during 2009, Teton placed into service $543,000 of machinery (up from the base scenario amount of $260,000), $10,000 of office furniture, and a $10,000 truck for a total of $543,000 of tangible *personal* property placed in service for the year. What is Teton's maximum §179 expense after applying the phase-out limitation?

Answer: $120,000 computed as follows:

Description	Amount	Explanation
(1) Property placed in service in 2009	$543,000	
(2) Threshold for §179 phase-out	(530,000)	2009 amount [§179(b)(1)].
(3) Phase-out of maximum §179 expense	$ 13,000	(1) − (2) (permanently disallowed).
(4) Maximum §179 expense before phase-out	$133,000	Assumed 2009 amount [§179(b)(2)].
(5) Phase-out of maximum §179 expense	13,000	From (3).
Maximum §179 expense after phase-out*	$120,000	(4) − (5).

*Note that this is the maximum expense after phase-out but *before* the taxable income limitation we discuss next.

What if: Assume further that Teton acquired and placed in service a warehouse costing $275,000. Taking the warehouse into account, what it Teton's maximum §179 expense after the phase-out?

Answer: $120,000. The same answer as above. The phase-out is based on the amount of tangible personal property placed in service during the year. Because the warehouse is *real property*, its acquisition has no effect on Teton's maximum §179 expense.

Businesses may elect to claim the §179 expense for the year up to the maximum amount available (after computing the phase-out—see the previous example). When a business elects to claim a certain amount of §179 expense, it must reduce the basis of the asset(s) to which the expense is applied. It then computes regular depreciation on the basis of the assets that remains after reducing the basis of the asset(s) for the §179 expense.

The business's *deductible* §179 expense is limited to the business's net income after deducting all expenses (including regular depreciation expense) except the §179 expense. Consequently, the §179 expense cannot create or extend a business's net operating loss. If a business claims more §179 expense than it is allowed to deduct due to the taxable income limitation, it carries the excess forward and deducts it in a subsequent year, subject to the taxable income limitation (but not the phase-out limitation) in the subsequent year.[20]

---

[19]The threshold under §179 is indexed for inflation and changes annually. Generally, the annual amount is released in a Revenue Procedure at the beginning of the taxable year. The 2009 amounts are based on the law as of the date this book went to press; however, there is legislative discussion regarding extending the larger amounts from the Economic Stimulus Act of 2008.

[20]Businesses typically elect only to expense the currently deductible amount since the taxable income limitation may also limit their §179 expense in future years just as it does for the current year.

Example 9-13

What if: Let's assume the facts of the previous example, where Teton's maximum §179 expense after applying the phase-out limitation is $120,000. Also assume that Teton elects to claim the entire $120,000 expense and it chooses to apply it against the machinery. Further assume that Teton reports $50,000 of taxable income before deducting any §179 expense [note that this is after deducting all regular (non-§179) depreciation (including the amount on line (5) in the table below]. What amount of total depreciation (including §179 expense) is Teton able to deduct on the machinery for the year?

Answer: $107,589 computed as follows:

Description	Amount	Explanation
(1) Machinery	$543,000	Example 9-12.
(2) Elected §179 expense	120,000	
(3) Remaining basis	423,000	(1) − (2).
(4) MACRS depreciation rate for seven-year machinery, year 1	14.29%	See Exhibit 9-7.
(5) MACRS deprecation expense on machinery	$ 60,447	(3) × (4).
(6) Deductible §179 expense	$ 50,000	Taxable income limitation.
(7) Total depreciation expense on machinery for the year	$110,447	(5) + (6).
(8) Excess §179 expense	$ 70,000	(2) − (6).

What is the amount of Teton's excess §179 expense (elected expense in excess of the deductible amount due to the taxable income limitation) and what does it do with it for tax purposes?

Answer: $70,000. See the above table for the computation (line 8). Teton carries this $70,000 excess §179 expense forward to future years and may deduct it subject to the same overall maximum limitation after the phase-out and the taxable income limitation.

THE KEY FACTS

§179 Expenses

- $133,000 of tangible personal property is expected to be immediately expensed in 2009 ($250,000 in 2008).

- Businesses are eligible for the full amount of this expense when tangible personal property placed in service is less than $530,000 ($800,000 in 2008). Beginning at $530,000, the §179 expense is phased out, dollar-for-dollar. When assets placed in service exceed $663,000, no §179 expense can be taken.

- §179 expenses are also limited to a business's taxable income before the §179 expense. §179 expenses cannot create losses.

Choosing the assets to immediately expense.   Businesses qualifying for immediate expensing are allowed to choose the asset or assets (from tangible personal property placed in service during the year) they immediately expense under §179. If a business's objective is to maximize its current depreciation expense and the half-year convention applies, it should immediately expense the property with the *longest* recovery period. For example, it should immediately expense a seven-year asset before a five-year asset, if given the choice. However, if the mid-quarter convention applies, the business should apply the §179 expense on the asset or assets with the *lowest* first year depreciation percentage, which might mean applying it against the shorter-lived asset if it was placed in service in a later quarter than the longer-lived asset. For example, looking at Exhibit 9-8, if a business had to choose between immediately expensing seven-year property placed in service in the first quarter or five-year property placed in service in the third quarter, which asset should it elect to expense under §179? The five-year asset because its first year depreciation percentage is 15 percent, while the seven-year asset's first year depreciation percentage is 25 percent. Finally, it is important to note that businesses reduce the basis of the assets for the §179 expense before computing whether the mid-quarter convention applies. Thus, applying the §179 expense against assets placed in service in the fourth quarter reduces the chances that the mid-quarter convention will apply.[21]

[21]§168(d)(3)(B)(ii).

Example 9-14

What if: Let's assume that Teton placed into service on June 1, five-year property costing $150,000 and seven-year property costing $150,000. Further assume that Teton is not subject to the taxable income limitation for the §179 expense. What is Teton's depreciation expense (including §179 expense) if it elects to apply the full §179 expense against the five-year property (Scenario A)? What is its depreciation expense if it applies it against its seven-year property (Scenario B)?

Answer: $157,835 if it applies the §179 to the five-year property (Scenario A) and $165,429 if it applies it to the seven-year property (Scenario B). See the computations below:

Description	(Scenario A) Amount 5-year Property	(Scenario B) Amount 7-year Property	Explanation
(1) Original basis	$150,000	$150,000	
(2) Elected §179 expense	133,000	133,000	Maximum expense.
(3) Remaining basis	17,000	17,000	(1) − (2).
(4) MACRS depreciation rate	20%	14.29%	See Exhibit 9-7.
(5) MACRS deprecation expense	$ 3,400	$ 2,429	(3) × (4).
(6) Deductible §179 expense	$133,000	$133,000	Example 9-12.
(7) MACRS depreciation on other property	$ 21,435	$ 30,000	This is the depreciation on the $150,000 seven-year property in the five-year column and on the $150,000 five-year property in the seven-year column.
Total 2009 depreciation expense	$157,835	$165,429	(5) + (6) + (7).

Note that Teton deducts $7,594 more in depreciation expense if it applies the §179 expense to the seven-year property.

What if: Assume the same facts, except that Teton placed the five-year property in service on December 1. Absent any §179 expense, Teton would be subject to the mid-quarter convention because 50 percent of its tangible personal property was placed in service in the fourth quarter. Assuming Teton wanted to avoid the mid-quarter convention, how should it apply its §179 expense?

Answer: It should apply the §179 expense against the five-year property. By doing so, the basis of the assets placed in service in the fourth quarter is $17,000 ($150,000 minus $133,000 §179 expense) and the basis of the assets placed in service in total is $167,000 ($150,000 7-year property + $17,000 5-year property). Thus, the percentage of tangible personal property placed in service in the fourth quarter is 10.18 percent ($17,000/$167,000), and the mid-quarter convention does not apply. If, however, it applies the §179 expense against the seven-year property, the mid-quarter convention would apply because the percentage of tangible personal property placed in service in the fourth quarter increases to 89.82 percent ($150,000/$167,000). Because this exceeds 40 percent, the mid-quarter convention applies.

Bonus Depreciation. To stimulate the economy, policy makers occasionally implement **bonus depreciation.**[22] In 2008, taxpayers could elect to immediately expense 50 percent of qualified property. Qualified property must have a recovery period of 20 years or less (no real property), the original use of the property must commence with the taxpayer (the property must be new rather than used), and the property

---

[22]§168(k)(1). Bonus depreciation is also allowable for purposes of the AMT.

must be placed in service during 2008 (with the exception of extension property).[23] The bonus depreciation is calculated after the §179 expense but before MACRS depreciation.[24]

Example 9-15

What if: Assume that the tangible personal property acquired in Exhibit 9-6 was purchased by Teton in 2008 rather than 2009.

Asset	Date Acquired	Quarter Acquired	Cost Basis	Recovery Period
Machinery	7/22/08	3rd	$260,000	7
Office furniture	2/3/08	1st	10,000	7
Delivery truck	8/17/08	3rd	15,000	5
Total			$285,000	

Assuming Teton elects no §179 expensing, what is Teton's bonus depreciation for 2008?

Answer: $142,500 computed as follows:

Description	Amount	Explanation
(1) Qualified property	$285,000	
(2) Bonus depreciation rate	50%	§168(k)(1).
Bonus depreciation	$142,500	(1) × (2).

What if: Also assume that Teton placed an order during 2008 for $100,000 of tangible property with a 15-year recovery period that is placed in service during 2009. Assume that the property qualifies as extension property eligible for bonus depreciation. If the property has a basis of $60,000 on December 31, 2008 what is the amount of Teton's bonus depreciation with respect to the extension property in 2009?

Answer: $30,000 ($60,000 × 50 percent). Teton is allowed bonus depreciation of 50 percent of the adjusted basis of the property as of December 31, 2008 [§168(k)(2)(B)(ii)].

Listed Property   Most business-owned assets are used for business rather than personal purposes. For example, Weyerhaeuser employees probably have little or no personal interest in using Weyerhaeuser's timber-harvesting equipment during their free time. In contrast, business owners and employees may find some business assets, such as company automobiles or laptop computers, conducive for personal use.

Business assets that tend to be used for both business and personal purposes are referred to as **listed property.** For example, automobiles, other means of transportation (planes, boats, and recreation vehicles), computer equipment, and even cell phones are considered to be listed property. The tax law limits the allowable depreciation on listed property to the portion of the asset used for business purposes.

How do taxpayers compute depreciation for listed property? First, they must determine the percentage of business vs. personal use of the asset for the year. If the business-use percentage for the year *exceeds* 50 percent, the deductible depreciation is limited to the full annual depreciation multiplied by the *business-use* percentage for the year.

[23]§168(k)(2). Property subject to a binding contract prior to 2008 is ineligible. A one-year extension of the placed-in service date (through 2009) is provided for property with a recovery period of 10 years or longer and certain transportation property (including aircraft).

[24]Reg. §1.168(k)-1(a)(2)(iii).

Example 9-16

What if: Assume that, in addition to the assets Teton purchased in the base scenario presented in Exhibit 9-6, it also purchased a new computer projector for $2,000 that its employees use for business presentations on weekdays. On weekends, Steve uses the projector as an integral part of his high-definition home theater system. Since the computer projector is listed property, Teton must assess the business-use percentage to properly calculate its deductible depreciation for the projector. Assuming that Teton determines the business-use percentage to be 75 percent, what is Teton's depreciation deduction on the projector for the year?

Answer: $300, computed as follows:

Description	Amount	Explanation
(1) Original basis of projector	$2,000	
(2) MACRS depreciation rate	20%	5-year property, year 1, half-year convention.
(3) Full MACRS depreciation expense	400	(1) × (2).
(4) Business-use percentage	75%	
Depreciation deduction for year	$300	(3) × (4).

When the business-use percentage of an asset is 50 percent or less, the business must compute depreciation for the asset using the MACRS *straight-line* method over the MACRS ADS (alternative depreciation system) recovery period.[25] For five-year assets such as automobiles and computers, the assets on which the personal use limitation is most common, the MACRS ADS recovery period is also five years. However, for seven-year assets, the ADS recovery period is generally 10 years.[26]

If a business initially uses an asset more than 50 percent of the time for business (and appropriately adopts the 200 percent declining balance method) but subsequently its business use drops to 50 percent or below, the *depreciation expense for all prior years must be recomputed* as if it had been using the straight-line depreciation over the ADS recovery period the entire time. It must then make up for any excess of accelerated depreciation it did deduct over the straight-line depreciation it should have deducted by adjusting the current year depreciation. In practical terms, the business can use the following five steps to determine its current depreciation expense for the asset:

Step 1: Compute depreciation for the year it drops to 50 percent or below using the straight-line method (this method also applies to all subsequent years).

Step 2: Compute the amount of depreciation the taxpayer would have deducted if the taxpayer had used the straight-line method over the ADS recovery period for all prior years (recall that depreciation is limited to the business-use percentage in those years).

Step 3: Compute the amount of depreciation the taxpayer had actually deducted on the asset for all prior years.

[25]This is the alternative recovery period listed in Rev. Proc. 87-56. See §168(g)(3)(C) and Temporary Reg. §1.280F-3T(d)(1).

[26]However, there are exceptions to this general rule. For example, the ADS recovery period for certain machinery for food and beverages is 12 years and the ADS recovery period for machinery for tobacco products is 15 years. Thus, it is important to check Rev. Proc. 87-56 to verify the ADS recovery period in these situations.

Step 4: Subtract the amount from Step 2 from the amount in Step 3. The difference is the prior year accelerated depreciation in excess of straight-line depreciation.

Step 5: Subtract the excess accelerated depreciation from Step 4 from the current year straight-line depreciation in Step 1. This is the business's allowable depreciation expense on the asset for the year. If the prior year excess depreciation from Step 4 exceeds the current year straight-line depreciation in Step 1, the business is not allowed to deduct any depreciation on the asset for the year and must actually recognize additional ordinary income for the amount of the excess.

This five-step process is designed to place the business in the same position it would have been in if it had used straight-line depreciation during all years of the asset's life.

Example 9-17

What if: Assume that, consistent with the previous example, in year 1 Teton used the projector for 75 percent of the time for business purposes and deducted $300 depreciation expense on the projector. However, in year 2, Teton's business-use percentage falls to 40 percent. What is Teton's depreciation deduction for the projector in year 2?

Answer: $10, computed using the five-step process described above as follows:

Description	Amount	Explanation*
(1) Straight-line depreciation in current year	$160	$2,000/5 years × 40 percent business use percentage (Step 1).
(2) Prior year straight-line depreciation	150	$2,000/5 × 50 percent (half-year convention) × 75 percent business-use percentage (Step 2).
(3) Prior year accelerated depreciation	300	Example 9-16 (prior example) (Step 3).
(4) Excess accelerated depreciation	150	(3) − (2) (Step 4).
Allowable current year depreciation	**$ 10**	(1) − (4) (Step 5).

*Note that the MACRS ADS recovery period (five years) for computers and peripherals (qualified technological equipment) is the same as the standard MACRS recovery period (five years).

What if: Now assume that, in year 1 Teton used the projector for 85 percent of the time for business purposes and deducted $340 depreciation expense on the projector. However, in year 2, Teton's business-use percentage falls to 40 percent. What is Teton's depreciation deduction for the projector in year 2?

Answer: $10 of ordinary income, computed as follows:

Description	Amount	Explanation
(1) Straight-line depreciation in current year	$160	$2,000/5 years × 40 percent business use.
(2) Prior year straight-line depreciation	170	$2,000/5 × 50 percent (half-year convention) × 85 percent business-use percentage.
(3) Prior year accelerated depreciation	340	Example 9-16 (prior example, if 85%).
(4) Excess accelerated depreciation	170	(3) − (2).
Allowable current year depreciation (income)	**($10)**	(1) − (4).

Luxury Automobiles   For good reason, policy makers believe that an element of personal pleasure or benefit is derived from passenger automobiles.[27] As we discussed in Chapter 8, §162 limits business deductions to those considered to be "ordinary, necessary, and reasonable" to prevent subsidizing (giving a tax deduction for) unwarranted business expenses. Although these terms are subject to interpretation, most taxpayers probably agree that for purposes of simply transporting passengers for business-related purposes, the cost of acquiring and using a Ford Focus is more likely to be ordinary, necessary, and reasonable than the cost of acquiring and using a Ferrari California—although not as exhilarating. Since either vehicle should be able to transport an employee or business owner from the office to a business meeting, the Ford Focus should be just as effective at accomplishing the business purpose as the Ferrari. If this is true, why should the government help taxpayers pay for expensive cars with tax savings from large depreciation deductions associated with automobiles? Congress decided it shouldn't. Therefore, with certain exceptions we discuss below, the tax laws generally limit the annual depreciation expense for automobiles.[28] Each year, the IRS provides a maximum depreciation schedule for automobiles placed in service during that particular year.[29] Exhibit 9-10 summarizes these schedules for automobiles placed in service for each year from 2009 back to 2006.

THE KEY FACTS
Luxury Vehicles
▪ Depreciation on automobiles weighing less than 6,000 lbs. is subject to luxury auto provisions.
▪ Luxury automobiles have a maximum depreciation limit for each year.
▪ Listed property rules are also applicable to luxury automobiles.

EXHIBIT 9-10   Automobile Depreciation Limits[30]

Recovery Year	Year Placed in Service			
	2009	**2008**	**2007**	**2006**
1	$2,960	$2,960	$3,060	$2,960
2	4,800	4,800	4,900	4,800
3	2,850	2,850	2,850	2,850
4 and after	1,775	1,775	1,775	1,775

*Rev. Proc. 2008-22 reports the luxury auto limits for 2008. This is for automobiles for which the 50 percent bonus depreciation is not taken.

Businesses placing automobiles into service during the year determine depreciation expense for the automobiles by first computing the regular MACRS depreciation expense (using the appropriate convention). They then compare it to the maximum depreciation amount for the first year of the recovery period based on the IRS-provided tables. Businesses are allowed to deduct the lesser of the two. If the automobile depreciation limits apply in the first year, the taxpayer must use the IRS maximum automobile depreciation table to compute depreciation for the asset(s) in all subsequent years. In 2009, if the half-year convention applies, the table limits the depreciation on automobiles placed in service during the year costing more than $14,800.[31] Automobiles to which the depreciation limits apply are commonly referred

---

[27]The passenger automobile definition excludes vehicles that charge for transportation such as taxi cabs, limousines, and hearses. It also excludes delivery trucks and vans.

[28]The tax law also limits the deduction for leased autos, which closed the leasing loophole that circumvented the luxury auto depreciation rules.

[29]The luxury automobile limitations are indexed for inflation and change annually. Generally, the annual amount is released in a Revenue Procedure at the beginning of the taxable year. The annual Rev. Proc. also provides slightly higher limits for hybrids, trucks, and SUVs.

[30]Rev. Proc. 2008-22 reports the luxury auto limits for 2008 and provides slightly higher limits for trucks and SUVs.

[31]In 2009, the full first-year depreciation on an automobile costing $14,800 is $2,960 ($14,800 × 20%). This is the amount of the first year limit for automobiles placed in service in 2009.

to as **luxury automobiles.**[32] For any two such luxury cars—say, a 2008 Honda Civic and a 2008 Porsche 911—the annual depreciation limit is the same, regardless of the cost of the vehicles. The only difference is the length of time it will take to fully depreciate the vehicle.

Example 9-18

What is the maximum annual depreciation expense available for 2008 (year 1) on a 2008 Honda Civic costing $15,460 and a 2008 Porsche Carrera costing $97,100 (ignoring bonus depreciation)?

Answer: $2,960 for both. See the following depreciation schedules for each automobile.

Luxury Auto Depreciation

Year/Make	2008 Honda Civic	2008 Porsche 911
Model	DX 2dr Coupe	Carrera 4S
Price	$15,460	$97,100
Depreciation		
Year 1	($2,960)	($2,960)
Year 2	($4,800)	($4,800)
Year 3	($2,850)	($2,850)
Year 4	($1,775)	($1,775)
Year 5	($1,775)	($1,775)
Year 6	($1,400)	($1,775)
Years 7–51		($1,775)
Year 52		($1,290)

Given the maximum deduction limitations, the depreciation of the Honda and Porsche are identical in years 1–5. However, beginning in year 6 the Porsche is depreciated at a maximum of $1,775 per year until fully depreciated in year 52—however, it is unlikely the business will actually hold the Porsche through year 51 and $1,290.

The luxury automobile limitations don't apply to vehicles weighing more than 6,000 pounds. Thus, businesses owning these vehicles are allowed to compute regular MACRS depreciation expense for these vehicles.[33]

Just like businesses using other types of listed property, businesses using luxury automobiles for business and personal purposes may only deduct depreciation on the asset to the extent of business use determined by miles driven for business purposes relative to total miles driven for the year.[34] Consequently, if a business places a luxury automobile into service in 2008 and uses the automobile 90 percent of the time for business purposes during the year (9,000 miles for business and 1,000 miles of personal use), the owner's depreciation on the auto for the year is limited to $2,664 (year 1 full depreciation of $2,960 × 90 percent business use—see Exhibit 9-10).[35] Further, if the business use falls below 50 percent in any subsequent year, just as with other listed property, the taxpayer must use the straight-line method of depreciation and reduce depreciation

---

[32]Correspondingly, the depreciation limits on automobiles are commonly referred to as the *luxury auto depreciation limits.*

[33]§280F(d)(5)(A). Congress regularly considers closing this loophole; however, it has not followed through (most recently it was considered as part of the 2007 Energy Bill).

[34]As an alternative to deducting depreciation expense and other costs of operating an automobile, taxpayers using automobiles for both personal and business purposes may deduct a standard mileage rate for each mile of business use. In 2008, the rate is 58.5 cents per mile after July 1, 2008 the rate is 55 cents per mile in 2009.

[35]Even if the business-use percentage multiplied by the MACRS depreciation is greater than the $2,960 maximum, the depreciation amount is limited to the maximum depreciation amount times the business-use percentage.

expense by the amount of excess accelerated depreciation (see Example 9-16). However, because straight-line depreciation is also limited by the luxury auto depreciation limits, it may turn out that the business doesn't have any excess accelerated depreciation.

Are businesses allowed to deduct §179 expensing on luxury automobiles? Yes, but the maximum depreciation *including* §179 expense is subject to the luxury auto limits ($2,960 for 2008). Thus, using the §179 expense on a luxury auto is unlikely to provide any tax benefit beyond the regular depreciation for most automobiles. However, businesses may deduct $25,000 of §179 expense for trucks and SUVs weighing over 6,000 pounds.[36] This $25,000 is part of the overall $250,000 maximum amount in 2008. Some companies use the §179 benefits to sell customers on purchasing automobiles that qualify for these tax benefits.

Taxes in the Real World   *Marketing Tax Advantages*

Small-Business Tax Advantage

When used for business purposes, Range Rover, Range Rover Sport, and LR3 models offer significant tax advantages in comparison to similarly priced luxury cars. Because the Range Rover, Range Rover Sport, and LR3 each have a Gross Vehicle Weight (GVW)[37] of more than 6,000 pounds, when used for business, they may be able to be depreciated much more rapidly than luxury cars.[38]

Source: www.landroverusa.com/us/en/Dealers/ Special_offers_finance/Small_Business_Owners.htm

---

Real Property

For depreciation purposes, real property is classified as land, *residential rental* property, or *nonresidential property*. Land is nondepreciable. Residential rental property consists of dwelling units such as houses, condominiums, and apartment complexes. Residential property has a 27.5-year recovery period. Nonresidential property consists of all other buildings (office buildings, manufacturing facilities, shopping malls, and the like). Nonresidential property placed in service on or after May 13, 1993, has a 39-year recovery period and nonresidential property placed in service after December 31, 1986, and before May 13, 1993, has a 31.5-year recovery period. Exhibit 9-11 summarizes the recovery periods for real property.

If a building is substantially improved (not a minor repair) at some point after the initial purchase, the building addition is treated as a new asset with the same recovery period of the original building. For example, if Teton expanded its warehouse 10 years after the building was placed in service, the expansion or building addition would be depreciated over 39 years because it is nonresidential property.

> **THE KEY FACTS**
>
> **Real Property Depreciation**
>
> ■ Real property is depreciated using the straight-line method.
>
> ■ Real property uses the mid-month convention.
>
> ■ Residential property has a recovery period of 27.5 years.
>
> ■ Nonresidential property placed in service after 1993 has a life of 39 years.

EXHIBIT 9-11   Recovery Period for Real Property

Asset Description (Summary of Rev. Proc. 87-57)	Recovery Period
Residential	27.5 years
Nonresidential property placed in service on or after May 13, 1993	39 years
Nonresidential property placed in service before May 13, 1993	31.5 years

---

[36]§179(b)(6).

[37]Individual tax situations may vary. The information on this page was accurate at the time of publishing. Federal rules and tax guidelines are subject to change. Consult your tax advisor for complete details on rules applicable to your transaction.

[38]Gross Vehicle Weight Rating (GVWR) is the manufacturer's rating of the vehicle's maximum weight when fully loaded. Under current law, owners of vehicles with GVW ratings of more than 6,000 pounds are eligible to expense up to $25,000 in Year One under Section 179 of the Internal Revenue Code. The Year One Benefit indicated on this page includes the $25,000 to be expensed under Section 179 of the I.R.C., plus the current year's depreciation allowance on the vehicle's remaining cost basis.

An important area of tax practice related to real property is cost segregation. This practice attempts to partition or divide the costs of a building into two or more categories. The first category is the building itself, which has a recovery period as noted in Exhibit 9-11. The second category is building components (tangible personal property associated with the building such as electrical and plumbing fixtures that have a shorter recovery period and accelerated depreciation method). Cost segregation utilizes engineers and construction experts who divide the costs between real and tangible personal property. This can generate significant tax savings due to the difference in the present value of the tax savings from the accelerated depreciation deductions associated with personal property.

Applicable Method   All depreciable real property is depreciated for tax purposes using the straight-line method. This is generally consistent with depreciation methods used for financial accounting purposes.

Applicable Convention   All real property is depreciated using the mid-month convention. The **mid-month convention** allows the owner of real property to expense one-half of a month's depreciation for the month in which the property was placed in service (and in the month of the year it is sold as well). This is true regardless of whether the asset was placed in service at the beginning or at the end of the month. For example, if Teton placed its warehouse into service on May 1 (or on *any* other day in May), it would deduct *one-half* a month's depreciation for May and then full depreciation for the months June through December.

Depreciation Tables   Just as it does for personal property, the IRS provides depreciation tables for real property. The depreciation tables for 27.5 year, 31.5 year, and 39 year real property are reproduced in this chapter's Appendix A. The percentage of the asset's original basis that is depreciated in a particular year is located at the intersection of the month the asset was placed in service (column) and the year of depreciation (row—first, second, etc.).

Example 9-19

As indicated in Example 9-1, Teton's basis in the warehouse it purchased on May 1 of year 1 is $275,000. What is Teton's year 1 depreciation on its warehouse?

Answer: $4,414, computed as follows:

Asset	Method	Recovery Period	Date Placed in Service	(1) Basis	(2) Rate*	(1) × (2) Depreciation
Warehouse	SL	39	May 1	$275,000	1.605%	$4,414

What if: What would be Teton's year 1 depreciation expense if the building was not a warehouse but was an apartment building that it rented to Teton's employees?

Answer: $6,251, computed as follows:

Asset	Method	Recovery Period	Date Placed in Service	(1) Basis	(2) Rate**	(1) × (2) Depreciation
Apt. Bldg.	SL	27.5	May 1	$275,000	2.273%	$6,251

* The 1.605 percent tax rate factor for the year is found in the 39-year table (see Appendix A to this chapter) in the fifth column (fifth month) and first row (first year).

** The 2.273 percent tax rate factor for the year is found in the 27.5-year table (see Appendix A to this chapter) in the fifth column (fifth month) and first row (first year).

When using depreciation tables for real property it is important to stay in the month column corresponding with the month the property was originally placed in service.[39] Thus, to calculate depreciation for a piece of real property placed in service in May (the fifth month), businesses will *always* (for each year of depreciation) find the current year rate factor in the fifth column for that asset. This is true even if the asset is sold in a subsequent year in July (it's easy to make the mistake of using the seventh column to calculate the depreciation for the year of disposition in this situation).

Mid-month convention for year of disposition.   Businesses deduct one-half of a month's depreciation in the month they sell or otherwise dispose of real property. For example, if Teton sold its warehouse on March 5 of year 2, it would deduct two and one-half months of depreciation in that year for the warehouse (depreciation for January, February, and one-half of March). Calculating depreciation expense in the year of sale or disposition for mid-month convention assets is similar to the calculation under the mid-quarter convention. When the mid-month convention applies, the asset is treated as though it is sold in the *middle of the month* of which it was actually sold. The simplest process for calculating mid-month convention depreciation for the year of sale consists of the following four steps:

Step 1: Determine the amount of depreciation expense for the asset as if the asset was held for the entire year,

Step 2: Subtract one-half of a month from the month in which the asset was sold (if sold in third month, subtract .5 from 3 to get 2.5). (Subtract half of a month because the business is treated as though the asset was disposed of in the middle of the third month—not the end),

Step 3: Divide the amount determined in Step 2 by 12 months (2.5/12). This is the fraction of the full year's depreciation the business is eligible to deduct.

Step 4: Multiply the Step 3 outcome by the full depreciation determined in Step 1.

These steps are summarized in the following formula:

Mid-month depreciation for year of disposition

$$= \text{Full year's depreciation} \times \frac{(\text{month in which asset was disposed of } -.5)}{12}$$

Example 9-20

What if: Assume that Teton sells its warehouse on March 5 in year 2 (the year after Teton buys it). What is Teton's depreciation for the warehouse in the year of disposition (year 2)?

Answer: $1,469, computed using the four-step procedure outlined above as follows.

   Step 1: Determine full year's depreciation [$275,000 × 2.564%*] = $7,051
   Step 2: 3 (month sold) − .5 = 2.5
   Step 3: 2.5/12
   Step 4: $7,051 × 2.5/12 = $1,469 (see formula above).

*The 2.564 percent rate factor (full year percentage) in Step 1 is obtained from the MACRS Mid-Month Table for 39-year property placed in service during the fifth month (year 2 row).

---

[39]Failure to do so will result in the wrong depreciation expense and is technically a change in accounting method (which requires filing of a Form 3115 with the IRS).

EXHIBIT 9-12 **MACRS Recovery Periods for Regular Tax and AMT Purposes**

	Regular Tax	AMT
Software	3-Year	3-Year
Cars, light general purpose trucks, and computers and peripheral equipment	5-Year	5-Year
Office furniture, fixtures, machinery, and equipment	7-Year	7-Year
Residential real property	27.5-Year	27.5-Year
Nonresidential real property	39-Year	39-Year

Depreciation for the Alternative Minimum Tax

Both individuals and corporations are subject to tax under the Alternative Minimum Tax (AMT) system. In determining their alternative minimum taxable income, individuals and corporations may be required to recalculate their depreciation expense. For AMT purposes, the allowable recovery period and conventions are the same for all depreciable assets as they are for regular tax purposes.[40] However, for AMT purposes, businesses are not allowed to use the 200 percent declining balance method to depreciate tangible personal property. Rather, they must choose from the 150 percent declining balance method or the straight-line method to depreciate the property for AMT purposes. The difference between regular tax depreciation and AMT depreciation is an adjustment that is either added to or subtracted from regular taxable income in computing the alternative minimum tax base.[41] In contrast, the §179 expense is equally deductible for both regular tax and AMT purposes. Depreciation of real property is the same for both regular tax and AMT purposes. Exhibit 9-12 summarizes the recovery periods for assets for regular tax purposes and AMT purposes.

Depreciation Summary

Teton's depreciation for the year is summarized in Exhibit 9-13 and Exhibit 9-14 presents Teton's depreciation expense as it would be reported on its tax return on Form 4562.

EXHIBIT 9-13 **Tax Depreciation Expense Summary**

Asset	Original Basis	§179 Expense	Remaining Basis*	Depreciation Expense	Reference
Machinery	$260,000	$80,000	$180,000	$ 25,722	Example 9-11 (What-if scenario).
Office furniture	$ 10,000		$ 10,000	$ 1,429	Example 9-5.
Delivery truck	$ 15,000	$ 0	$ 15,000	$ 3,000	Example 9-5.
Warehouse	$275,000	N/A	$275,000	$ 4,414	Example 9-19.
Land	$ 75,000	N/A	$ 75,000	$ 0	N/A.
§179 Expense				$ 80,000	Example 9-11.
Total Depreciation Expense				$114,565	

*Note that Teton's remaining basis is the original cost less the §179 expense.

[40]This is true for assets placed in service after 1998.

[41]If the taxpayer elected either the 150 percent declining nalance or the straight-line method for regular tax depreciation of tangible personal property, then there is no AMT adjustment with respect to that property.

EXHIBIT 9-14   Teton's Form 4562 Parts I – IV for Depreciation

(Assumes $100,000 of taxable income before the §179 expense)

Form **4562**	**Depreciation and Amortization**	OMB No. 1545-0172
Department of the Treasury Internal Revenue Service (99)	**(Including Information on Listed Property)** ► **See separate instructions.** ► **Attach to your tax return.**	**2008** Attachment Sequence No. **67**

Name(s) shown on return	Business or activity to which this form relates	Identifying number
Teton Mountaineering Technologies, LLC		

Part I   Election To Expense Certain Property Under Section 179
Note: *If you have any listed property, complete Part V before you complete Part I.*

1	Maximum amount. See the instructions for a higher limit for certain businesses	**1**	$250,000
2	Total cost of section 179 property placed in service (see instructions)	**2**	285,000
3	Threshold cost of section 179 property before reduction in limitation (see instructions) . . .	**3**	$800,000
4	Reduction in limitation. Subtract line 3 from line 2. If zero or less, enter -0-	**4**	0
5	Dollar limitation for tax year. Subtract line 4 from line 1. If zero or less, enter -0-. If married filing separately, see instructions	**5**	133,000

(a) Description of property	**(b)** Cost (business use only)	**(c)** Elected cost	
6 Machinery	260,000	80,000	

7	Listed property. Enter the amount from line 29	**7**	
8	Total elected cost of section 179 property. Add amounts in column (c), lines 6 and 7	**8**	80,000
9	Tentative deduction. Enter the **smaller** of line 5 or line 8.	**9**	80,000
10	Carryover of disallowed deduction from line 13 of your 2007 Form 4562	**10**	0
11	Business income limitation. Enter the smaller of business income (not less than zero) or line 5 (see instructions)	**11**	100,000
12	Section 179 expense deduction. Add lines 9 and 10, but do not enter more than line 11 . . .	**12**	80,000
13	Carryover of disallowed deduction to 2009. Add lines 9 and 10, less line 12 ► **13**		

Note: *Do not use Part II or Part III below for listed property. Instead, use Part V.*

Part II   Special Depreciation Allowance and Other Depreciation (Do not include listed property.) (See instructions.)

14	Special depreciation allowance for qualified property (other than listed property) placed in service during the tax year (see instructions)	**14**	0
15	Property subject to section 168(f)(1) election	**15**	0
16	Other depreciation (including ACRS)	**16**	0

Part III   MACRS Depreciation (Do not include listed property.) (See instructions.)

Section A

17	MACRS deductions for assets placed in service in tax years beginning before 2008	**17**	0
18	If you are electing to group any assets placed in service during the tax year into one or more general asset accounts, check here . . . . ► ☐		

Section B—Assets Placed in Service During 2008 Tax Year Using the General Depreciation System

(a) Classification of property	**(b)** Month and year placed in service	**(c)** Basis for depreciation (business/investment use only—see instructions)	**(d)** Recovery period	**(e)** Convention	**(f)** Method	**(g)** Depreciation deduction
19a 3-year property						
b 5-year property		15,000	5 year	HY	DDB	3,000
c 7-year property		190,000	7 year	HY	DDB	27,151
d 10-year property						
e 15-year property						
f 20-year property						
g 25-year property			25 yrs.		S/L	
h Residential rental property			27.5 yrs.	MM	S/L	
			27.5 yrs.	MM	S/L	
i Nonresidential real property	May 2009	275,000	39 yrs.	MM	S/L	4,414
				MM	S/L	

Section C—Assets Placed in Service During 2008 Tax Year Using the Alternative Depreciation System

20a Class life					S/L	
b 12-year			12 yrs.		S/L	
c 40-year			40 yrs.	MM	S/L	

Part IV   Summary (See instructions.)

21	Listed property. Enter amount from line 28	**21**	
22	**Total.** Add amounts from line 12, lines 14 through 17, lines 19 and 20 in column (g), and line 21. Enter here and on the appropriate lines of your return. Partnerships and S corporations—see instr.	**22**	114,565
23	For assets shown above and placed in service during the current year, enter the portion of the basis attributable to section 263A costs . . **23**		

For Paperwork Reduction Act Notice, see separate instructions.   Cat. No. 12906N   Form **4562** (2008)

L03

AMORTIZATION

Businesses recover the cost of intangible assets through amortization rather than depreciation expense. Intangible assets in the form of capitalized expenditures, such as capitalized **research and experimentation (R&E) costs** or **covenants not to compete,** do not have physical characteristics. Nonetheless, they may have determinable lives. While research and experimentation costs may have an indeterminate life, a covenant not to compete, for example, would have a life equal to the stated term of the contractual agreement. When the life of intangible assets cannot be determined, taxpayers recover the cost of the assets when they dispose of them—unless they are assigned a specific tax recovery period.

For tax purposes, an intangible asset can be placed into one of the following four general categories:

1. §197 purchased intangibles.
2. Start-up expenditures and organizational costs.
3. Research and experimentation costs.
4. Patents and copyrights.

Businesses amortize all intangible assets in these categories using the straight-line method for both book and tax purposes.

Section 197 Intangibles

> **THE KEY FACTS**
>
> **§197 Intangible Assets**
>
> ■ Purchased intangibles are amortized over a period of 180 months, regardless of their explicitly stated lifetimes.
>
> ■ The full-month convention applies to amortizable assets.

When a business purchases the *assets* of another business for a single purchase price, the business must determine the basis of each of the assets it acquired in the transaction. To determine basis, the business must allocate a portion of the purchase price to each of the individual assets acquired in the transaction. Generally, under this approach, each asset acquired in the purchase (cash, machinery, and real property, for example) takes a basis equal to its fair market value. However, some of the assets acquired in the transaction may not appear on the seller's balance sheet. In fact, a substantial portion of a business's value may exist in the form of intangible assets such as customer lists, patents, trademarks, trade names, goodwill, going-concern value, covenants not to compete, and so forth. Nearly all of these assets are amortized according to §197 of the Internal Revenue Code—hence, they are often referred to as **§197 purchased intangibles.** According to §197, these assets have a recovery period of 180 months (15 years), *regardless of their actual life.*[42] For example, when a business buys an existing business, the owner selling the business often signs a covenant not to compete for a specified period such as five years.[43] Even though a five-year covenant not to compete clearly has a fixed and determinable life, it must be amortized over 180 months (15 years). The **full-month convention** applies to the amortization of purchased intangibles. This convention allows taxpayers to deduct an entire month's worth of amortization for the month of purchase and all subsequent months in the year. The full-month convention also applies in the month of sale or disposition.

Special rules apply when a taxpayer sells a §197 intangible or the intangible becomes worthless and the taxpayer's basis in the asset exceeds the sale proceeds (if any). If, at the time of sale or disposal, the business does not hold any other §197 assets that the business acquired in the *same initial transaction* as the asset being sold or disposed of, the business may recognize a loss on the sale or disposition. Otherwise, the taxpayer may not deduct the loss on the sale or disposition until the business sells or disposes of *all* of the other §197 intangibles that it purchased in the

---

[42]§197 was Congress's response to taxpayers manipulating the valuation and recovery periods assigned to these purchased intangibles.

[43]A covenant not to compete is a contract between the seller of a business and its buyer that the seller will not operate a similar business that would compete with the previous business for a specified period of time.

same initial transaction.[44] The same loss disallowance rule applies if a §197 intangible expires before it is fully amortized. For example, a business would not be allowed to deduct a loss on a five-year covenant not to compete when it expires even though the covenant is worthless and still would have two-thirds of its original cost remaining (10 years left to amortize over a 15-year recovery period). In either case, the excess basis (basis in excess of sale proceeds or basis in excess of worthless intangible asset) is allocated to the remaining §197 intangibles that were initially acquired in the same transaction pro rata, based on the relative adjusted bases of the remaining §197 intangibles. The new basis allocated to each remaining §197 intangible is amortized over the remaining years of the initial 15-year recovery period.

	Example 9-21

What if: Assume that at the beginning of year 1, Teton acquires a competitor's assets for $350,000.[45] Of the $350,000 purchase price, $125,000 is allocated to tangible assets and $225,000 is allocated to §197 intangible assets (patent, goodwill, and a customer list with a three-year life).[46] For each of the first three years, Teton would deduct one-fifteenth of the basis of each asset as amortization expense. What is Teton's accumulated amortization and remaining basis in each of these §197 intangibles after three years?

Answer: See the table below:

Description	Patent	Goodwill	Customer List
Basis	$25,000	$150,000	$50,000
Accumulated amortization (3/15ths of original basis)	($5,000)	($30,000)	($10,000)
Remaining basis	$20,000	$120,000	$40,000

At the end of year 3, Teton's customer list is worthless (it has expired), but it still has a remaining basis of $40,000. Rather than deducting the $40,000 loss on the customer list, Teton must allocate it to the other §197 intangible assets that were initially purchased in the same transaction. After this allocation what is Teton's new basis in the patent and the goodwill?

Answer: Teton's new basis in the patent is $25,716 and its new basis in the goodwill is $154,284, computed as follows:

Description	(A) Remaining basis	(B) Percentage of remaining basis	(C) Allocated portion of remaining basis in customer list [(B) × $40,000]	(A) + (C) New basis
(1) Patent	$ 20,000	14.29% [(1)/(3)]	$ 5,716	$ 25,716
(2) Goodwill	120,000	85.71% [(2)/(3)]	34,284	154,284
(3) Total basis	$140,000	100%	$40,000	$180,000

The new basis of the patent and goodwill are amortized over the remaining 12-year (144-month) recovery period.

---

[44]Chapter 10 deals with asset dispositions; however, it is necessary to discuss the disposition of §197 intangibles in this chapter because it may affect future amortization expense.

[45]If a business acquires another business's stock (rather than assets) there is no goodwill assigned for tax purposes, and the purchase price simply becomes the basis of the stock purchased.

[46]A customer base is the value assigned to current customers (i.e. the lists that will allow the new owner to capture future benefits from the current customers).

When a taxpayer sells a §197 intangible for more than its basis, the taxpayer recognizes gain. We describe how to characterize this type of gain in the next chapter.

Organizational Expenditures and Start-Up Costs

Organizational expenditures include expenditures to form and organize a business in the form of a corporation or a partnership.[47] Organizational expenditures typically include costs of organizational meetings, state fees, accounting service costs incident to organization, and legal service expenditures such as document drafting, taking minutes of organizational meetings, and creating terms of the original stock certificates. These costs are generally incurred prior to the starting of business (or shortly thereafter) but relate to creating the business entity. The costs of selling or marketing stock do *not* qualify as organizational expenditures and cannot be amortized.[48]

Example 9-22

THE KEY FACTS
Organizational Expenditures and Start-up Costs
▮ Taxpayers may immediately expense up to $5,000 of organizational expenditures and $5,000 of start-up costs.
▮ The $5,000 immediate expense rule has a dollar-for-dollar phase-out that begins at $50,000, so that when expenses exceed $55,000, there is no immediate expensing.

What if: Suppose Teton was organized as a corporation rather than a sole proprietorship (recall that sole proprietorships cannot expense organizational expenditures). Steve paid $35,000 of legal costs to Scott, Tang, and Malan to draft the corporate charter and articles of incorporation; $10,000 to Harvey and Stratford for accounting fees related to the organization; and $7,000 for organizational meetings, $5,000 for stock issuance costs, and $1,000 for state fees related to the incorporation. What amounts of these expenditures qualify as organizational costs?

Answer: $53,000 computed as follows (with the exception of the stock issuance costs, each of Teton's expenses qualify as amortizable organizational expenditures):

Description	Qualifying Organizational Expenditures
Legal drafting of corporate charter and articles of incorporation	$35,000
Accounting fees related to organization	10,000
Organizational meetings	7,000
Stock issuance costs	0
State incorporation fees	1,000
Totals	$53,000

Businesses may *immediately expense* up to $5,000 of organizational expenditures.[49] However, businesses incurring more than $50,000 in organizational expenditures must phase-out (reduce) the $5,000 immediate expense amount dollar for dollar for expenditures exceeding $50,000. Thus, businesses incurring at least $55,000 of organizational expenditures are not allowed to immediately expense any of the expenditures.

Example 9-23

What if: Suppose Teton is a corporation and it wants to maximize its current year organizational expenditure deduction. As described in Example 9-22, Teton incurred $53,000 of organizational expenditures in year 1. How much of the organizational expenditures can Teton immediately expense in year 1?

(*continued on page 9-33...*)

---

[47]§248 for corporations and §709 for partnerships. Sole-proprietorships cannot deduct organizational expenditures.

[48]These costs are capitalized and deducted on the final tax return a business files.

[49]§248(a)(1) for corporations or §709 for partnerships.

Answer: $2,000, computed as follows:

Description	Amount	Explanation
(1) Maximum immediate expense	$ 5,000	§248(a)(1).
(2) Total organizational expenditures	53,000	Example 9-22.
(3) Phase-out threshold	50,000	§248(a)(1)(B).
(4) Immediate expense phase-out	3,000	(2) − (3).
(5) Allowable immediate expense	**2,000**	(1) − (4).
Remaining organizational expenditures	$51,000*	(2) − (5).

What if: Assuming that Teton is a corporation and that it incurred $41,000 of organizational expenditures in year 1. How much of the organizational expenditures could Teton immediately expense in year 1?

Answer: $5,000, computed as follows:

Description	Amount	Explanation
(1) Maximum immediate expense	$ 5,000	§248(a)(1).
(2) Total organizational expenditures	41,000	
(3) Phase-out threshold	50,000	§248(a)(1)(B).
(4) Immediate expense phase-out	$ 0	(2) − (3).
(5) Allowable immediate expense	**5,000**	(1) − (4).
Remaining organizational expenditures	$36,000*	(2) − (5).

What if: Assuming that Teton is a corporation and it incurred $60,000 of organizational expenditures in year 1, how much of the organizational expenditures could Teton immediately expense in year 1?

Answer: $0, computed as follows:

Description	Amount	Explanation
(1) Maximum immediate expense	$ 5,000	§248(a)(1).
(2) Total organizational expenditures	60,000	
(3) Phase-out threshold	50,000	§248(a)(1)(B).
(4) Immediate expense phase-out	10,000	(2) − (3).
(5) Allowable immediate expense	**$ 0**	(1) − (4).
Remaining organizational expenditures	$60,000*	(2) − (5).

*As we discuss below, Teton may elect to amortize the remaining organizational costs.

Businesses amortize organizational expenditures that they do not immediately expense using the straight-line method over a recovery period of 15 years (180 months).[50]

Example 9-24

What if: Assume Teton is a corporation and it amortizes the $51,000 of organizational expenditures remaining after it immediately expenses $2,000 of the costs (see Example 9-23). If Teton began business on February 1 of year 1, how much total cost recovery expense for the organizational expenditures is Teton able to deduct in year 1?

(*continued on page 9-34...*)

[50]§248(a)(2). Businesses incurring organizational expenditures before October 22, 2004 are allowed to amortize the expenditures on a straight-line basis over five years (60 months).

Answer: $5,117, computed as follows:

Description	Amount	Explanation
(1) Total organizational expenditures	$53,000	Example 9-21.
(2) Amount immediately expensed	2,000	Example 9-22.
(3) Expenditures subject to straight-line amortization	$51,000	(1) − (2).
(4) Recovery period in months	180	15 years §248(a)(2).
(5) Monthly straight-line amortization	283.33	(3)/(4).
(6) Teton business months during year 1	× 11	February through December.
(7) Year 1 straight-line amortization	3,117	(5) × (6).
Total year 1 cost recovery expense for organizational expenditures.	$ 5,117	(2) + (7).

Start-up costs are costs businesses incur to, not surprisingly, start up a business.[51] Start-up costs apply to all types of business forms.[52] These costs include costs associated with investigating the possibilities of and actually creating or acquiring a trade or business. For example, costs Teton incurs in deciding whether to locate the business in Cody, Wyoming, or Bozeman, Montana, are start-up costs. Start-up costs also include costs that would normally be deductible as ordinary business expenses except that they don't qualify as business expenses because they are incurred before the trade or business activity actually begins. For example, costs Teton incurs to train its employees before the business begins are start-up costs. The rules for immediately expensing and amortizing start-up costs are identical to those for immediately expensing and amortizing organizational expenditures (see discussion above). While the rules are the same, the limitations are computed separately for organizational expenditures and for start-up costs. Consequently, a business could immediately expense $5,000 of organizational expenditures and $5,000 of start-up costs in its first year of business.

Example 9-25

What if: Assume that in January of year 1 (before it began business on February 1) Teton spent $4,500 investigating the climbing hardware market, creating company logos, and determining the locations for both the office and manufacturing facility. The $4,500 of expenditures qualifies as start-up costs. Teton makes the proper election on its initial tax return. How much of the $4,500 of start-up costs is Teton allowed to immediately expense?

Answer: All $4,500. Teton is allowed to immediately expense the entire $4,500 because its total start-up costs do not exceed $50,000. Teton could have immediately expensed up to $5,000 of start-up costs as long as its total start-up costs did not exceed $50,000.

Exhibit 9-15 illustrates the timing of organizational expenditures, start-up costs, and normal trade or business expenses.

Research and Experimentation Expenditures

To stay competitive, businesses often invest in activities they believe will generate innovative products or significantly improve their current products or processes. These research and experimentation costs include expenditures for research laboratories including salaries, materials, and other related expenses. Businesses may immediately expense these costs or they may *elect* to capitalize these costs and amortize them

[51]§195.

[52]Recall that rules for amortizing organizational expenditures apply only to corporations and partnerships.

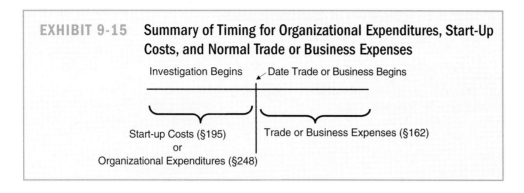

EXHIBIT 9-15   **Summary of Timing for Organizational Expenditures, Start-Up Costs, and Normal Trade or Business Expenses**

using the straight-line method over a period of not less than 60 months, beginning in the month benefits are first derived from the research.[53] However, if a business elects to capitalize and amortize the costs, it must stop amortizing the costs if and when the business receives a patent relating to the expenditures. When the business obtains a patent, it adds any remaining basis in the costs to the basis of the patent and it amortizes the basis of the patent over the patent's life (see discussion below).

Patents and Copyrights

The manner in which a business amortizes a patent or copyright depends on whether the business directly purchases the patent or copyright or whether it self-creates the intangibles. Businesses directly purchasing patents or copyrights (not in an asset acquisition to which §197 applies) amortize the cost over the remaining life of the patents or copyrights.[54] Businesses receiving "self-created" patents or copyrights amortize the cost or basis of the self-created intangible assets over their legal lives—up to a maximum of 17 years for patents and 28 years for copyrights. The costs included in the basis of a self-created patent or copyright include legal costs, fees, and, as we discussed above, unamortized research and experimentation expenditures associated with the creation of the patent or copyright. However, because the patent approval process is slow, the unamortized research and experimentation costs included in the patent's basis are likely to be relatively small because, with a five-year recovery period, the research and experimentation costs would likely be mostly or even fully amortized by the time the patent is approved.

Example 9-26

In September of year 1, Teton purchased a patent with a remaining life of 10 years from Chouinard Equipment for $60,000. What amount of amortization expense is Teton allowed to deduct for the patent in year 1?

Answer: $2,000, computed as follows:

Description	Amount	Explanation
(1) Cost of patent	$60,000	
(2) Remaining life of patent in months	120	10 years.
(3) Monthly amortization	$ 500	(1)/(2).
(4) Months in year 1 Teton held patent	× 4	September through December.
(5) Monthly straight-line amortization	**$ 2,000**	(3) × (4).
Unamortized cost of patent at end of year 1	$58,000	(1) − (5).

[53]See §174. High tax rate taxpayers may choose to deduct these costs while low tax rate taxpayers may prefer to capitalize and amortize them so that they will have more future deductions when they are hopefully generating more income. There is also the research and experimentation credit which is available to some businesses.

[54]§167(f).

EXHIBIT 9-16 **Summary of Amortizable Assets**

Asset Description	Recovery Period (months)	Applicable Method	Applicable Convention	Financial Accounting Treatment
§197 purchased intangibles including goodwill, trademarks, patents, and covenants not to compete.[55]	180	Straight-line	Full-month beginning with month of purchase.	FAS 142 tests for annual impairment.
Organizational expenditures and start-up costs are required to be capitalized.	180	Straight-line	Full-month in month business begins.	AICPA SOP 98-5.
Research and experimentation costs that are capitalized.	60 (not less than); ceases when patent is issued.	Straight-line	Full-month in first month that benefits from research are obtained.	Expensed.
Self-created patents (17 years maximum) and copyrights (28 years maximum).	Actual life.	Straight-line	Full-month month intangible is obtained.	Expensed.

Amortizable Intangible Asset Summary

Exhibit 9-16 summarizes the different types of amortizable intangible assets, identifies the recovery period of these assets, and describes the applicable amortization method for each asset. Exhibit 9-16 also identifies the applicable convention for each type of amortizable intangible asset and identifies the financial accounting treatment for recovering the cost of the intangible assets under GAAP.

Exhibit 9-17 presents Teton's amortization expense as it would be reported on its tax return on Form 4562.

EXHIBIT 9-17 **Teton Form 4562, Part VI Amortization Amortization of Organizational Expenditures and Patent**

Part VI Amortization					
(a) Description of costs	(b) Date amortization begins	(c) Amortizable amount	(d) Code section	(e) Amortization period or percentage	(f) Amortization for this year
42 Amortization of costs that begins during your 2008 tax year (see instructions):					
Organizational expenditures	2/1/2008	53,000	248	15 yrs	5,117
Patent	9/1/2008	60,000	167	10 yrs	2,000
43 Amortization of costs that began before your 2008 tax year. **43**					
44 **Total.** Add amounts in column (f). See the instructions for where to report. **44**					7,117

Form **4562** (2008)

[55]A patent or copyright that is part of a basket purchase (several assets together) is treated as a §197 intangible. A patent or copyright that is purchased separately is simply amortized over its remaining life (§167(f)).

continued from page 9-1 . . .

Teton was developing some additional employee parking on a lot adjacent to the warehouse when the excavation crew discovered a small gold deposit. Steve called his friend Ken, who had some experience in mining precious metals, to see what Ken thought of the find. Ken was impressed and offered Steve $150,000 for the rights to the gold. Steve accepted the offer on Teton's behalf. ■

DEPLETION

LO4

Depletion is the method taxpayers use to recover their capital investment in natural resources. Depletion is a particularly significant deduction for businesses in the mining, oil and gas, and forestry industries. These businesses generally incur depletion expense as they use up the natural resource. Specifically, businesses compute annual depletion expense under both the cost and percentage depletion methods and they deduct the larger of the two.[56]

Under **cost depletion,** taxpayers must estimate or determine the number of units or reserves (tons of coal, barrels of oil, board feet of timber, for example) that remain at the beginning of the year and allocate a pro rata share of that basis to each unit that is extracted during the year.[57]

Example 9-27

Ken's cost basis in the gold is the $150,000 he paid for it. Based on a mining engineer's estimate that the gold deposit probably holds 1,000 ounces of gold, Ken can determine his cost depletion. What is Ken's cost depletion for year 1 and year 2, assuming he extracts 300 and 700 ounces of gold in year 1 and year 2, respectively?

Answer: $45,000 in year 1 and $105,000 in year 2, computed as follows:

Description	Amount	Explanation
(1) Cost basis in gold	$150,000	Storyline.
(2) Estimated ounces of gold	1,000	
(3) Per ounce cost depletion rate	150	(1)/(3).
(4) Year 1 ounces extracted	300	
(5) Year 1 cost depletion	**$ 45,000**	(3) × (4).
(6) Basis remaining after year 1 depletion	105,000	(1) − (5).
(7) Year 2 ounces extracted	700	
(8) Year 2 cost depletion	**105,000**	(7) × (3).
Basis remaining after year 2 depletion	$ 0	(6) − (8).

Ken is not eligible for cost depletion after year 2 because as of the end of year 2, his cost basis has been reduced to $0.

Because the cost depletion method of depletion requires businesses to estimate the number of units of the resource they will actually extract, it is possible that their estimate will prove to be inaccurate. If they underestimate the number of units, they will fully deplete the cost basis of the resource before they have fully extracted the resource. Once they have recovered the entire cost basis of the resource, businesses are

---

[56]Depletion of timber and major integrated oil companies must be calculated using only the cost depletion method (no percentage depletion is available).

[57]§612.

> **THE KEY FACTS**
>
> Depletion
>
> ■ Cost depletion involves estimating resource reserves and allocating a pro-rata share of basis based on the number of units extracted.
>
> ■ Percentage depletion is determined by a statutory percentage of gross income that is permitted to be expensed each year. Different resources have different statutory percentages (i.e., gold, tin, coal).
>
> ■ Taxpayers may expense the larger of cost or percentage depletion.

EXHIBIT 9-18 **Applicable Percentage Depletion Rates**

Statutory Percentage	Natural Resources (Partial list)
5 percent [§613(b)(6)]	Gravel, pumice, and stone.
14 percent [§613(b)(3)]	Asphalt rock, clay, and other metals.
15 percent [§613(b)(2)]	Gold, copper, oil shale, and silver.
22 percent [§613(b)(1)]	Platinum, sulfur, uranium, and titanium.

not allowed to use cost depletion to determine depletion expense. Businesses, however, may continue to use percentage depletion (see discussion below). If a business overestimates the number of units to be extracted, it will still have basis remaining after the resource has been fully extracted. In these situations, the business would deduct the unrecovered basis once it had sold all the remaining units.

The amount of **percentage depletion** for a natural resource business activity is determined by multiplying the *gross income* from the resource extraction activity by a fixed percentage based on the type of natural resource as indicated in Exhibit 9-18.[58]

In many cases, percentage depletion may generate *larger* depletion deductions than does cost depletion. Recall that taxpayers are allowed to deduct the greater of cost and percentage depletion. Businesses reduce their cost basis in the resource when they deduct percentage depletion. However, once the cost basis is exhausted, they are allowed to continue to deduct percentage (but not cost) depletion. This provides a potentially significant governmental subsidy to extraction businesses that have completely recovered their costs in a natural resource.[59]

It is important to note that businesses deduct percentage depletion when they *sell* the natural resource and they deduct cost depletion in the year they *produce* or extract the natural resource. Also, percentage depletion cannot exceed 50 percent of the *net income* from the natural resource business activity before considering the depletion expense, while cost depletion has no such limitation.

Example 9-28

In Example 9-27, Ken determined his cost depletion expense for the gold. However, because he is allowed to deduct the greater of cost or percentage depletion each year, he set out to determine his percentage depletion for year 2. Assuming that Ken has gross (net) income from the gold mining activity before depletion expense of $200,000 ($50,000), $600,000 ($450,000), and $600,000 ($500,000) in year 1, year 2, and year 3, respectively, what is his percentage depletion expense for each of these three years?

Answer: $25,000, $90,000, and $90,000 for years 1, 2, and 3, respectively, computed as follows:

	Year 1	Year 2	Year 3	Explanation
(1) Net income from activity (before depletion expense)	$ 50,000	$450,000	$500,000	
(2) Gross income	$200,000	$600,000	$600,000	
(3) Percentage	× 15%	× 15%	× 15%	Exhibit 9-18.
(4) Percentage depletion expense before limit	$ 30,000	$ 90,000	$ 90,000	(2) × (3).
(5) 50 percent of net income limitation	$ 25,000	$225,000	$250,000	(1) × 50%.
Allowable percentage depletion	**$ 25,000**	**$ 90,000**	**$ 90,000**	Lesser of (4) or (5).

Finally, as we discussed above, a business's depletion expense deduction is the greater of either the annual cost or percentage depletion.

---

[58]§613.

[59]Percentage depletion in excess of basis is an AMT preference item.

Example 9-29

Based on his computations of cost depletion and percentage depletion, Ken was able to determine his deductible depletion expense. Using the cost and percentage depletion computations from Examples 9-27 and 9-28, what is Ken's deductible depletion expense for years 1, 2, and 3?

Answer: $45,000 for year 1, $105,000 for year 2, and $90,000 for year 3, computed as follows:

Tax Depletion Expense	Year 1	Year 2	Year 3	Explanation
(1) Cost depletion	$45,000	$105,000	$ 0	Example 9-27.
(2) Percentage depletion	$30,000	$ 90,000	$90,000	Example 9-28.
Allowable expense	$45,000	$105,000	$90,000	Greater of (1) or (2).

CONCLUSION

This chapter describes and discusses how businesses recover the costs of their tangible and intangible assets. Cost recovery expenses are important because they represent a significant tax deduction for many businesses. Businesses must routinely make choices that affect the amount and timing of these deductions. Further understanding cost recovery basics helps businesses determine how to compute and characterize gain and loss they recognize when they sell or otherwise dispose of business assets. We address the interaction between cost recovery expenses and gain and loss on property dispositions in the next chapter.

MACRS TABLES

MACRS Half-Year Convention

Year	Depreciation Rate for Recovery Period	
	5-year	7-year
1	20.00%	14.29%
2	32.00	24.49
3	19.20	17.49
4	11.52	12.49
5	11.52	8.93
6	5.76	8.92
7		8.93
8		4.46

MACRS Mid-Quarter Convention: *For property placed in service during the first quarter*

Year	Depreciation Rate for Recovery Period	
	5-year	7-year
1	35.00%	25.00%
2	26.00	21.43
3	15.60	15.31
4	11.01	10.93
5	11.01	8.75
6	1.38	8.74
7		8.75
8		1.09

MACRS Mid-Quarter Convention: *For property placed in service during the second quarter*

	Depreciation Rate for Recovery Period	
Year	5-year	7-year
1	25.00%	17.85%
2	30.00	23.47
3	18.00	16.76
4	11.37	11.97
5	11.37	8.87
6	4.26	8.87
7		8.87
8		3.33

MACRS Mid-Quarter Convention: *For property placed in service during the third quarter*

	Depreciation Rate for Recovery Period	
Year	5-year	7-year
1	15.00%	10.71%
2	34.00	25.51
3	20.40	18.22
4	12.24	13.02
5	11.30	9.30
6	7.06	8.85
7		8.86
8		5.53

MACRS-Mid Quarter Convention: *For property placed in service during the fourth quarter*

	Depreciation Rate for Recovery Period	
Year	5-year	7-year
1	5.00%	3.57%
2	38.00	27.55
3	22.80	19.68
4	13.68	14.06
5	10.94	10.04
6	9.58	8.73
7		8.73
8		7.64

Residential Rental Property Mid-Month Convention Straight Line—27.5 Years

Month Property Placed in Service

Year	1	2	3	4	5	6	7	8	9	10	11	12
1	3.485%	3.182%	2.879%	2.576%	2.273%	1.970%	1.667%	1.364%	1.061%	0.758%	0.455%	0.152%
2–9	3.636	3.636	3.636	3.636	3.636	3.636	3.636	3.636	3.636	3.636	3.636	3.636
10	3.637	3.637	3.637	3.637	3.637	3.637	3.636	3.636	3.636	3.636	3.636	3.636
11	3.636	3.636	3.636	3.636	3.636	3.636	3.637	3.637	3.637	3.637	3.637	3.637
12	3.637	3.637	3.637	3.637	3.637	3.637	3.636	3.636	3.636	3.636	3.636	3.636
13	3.636	3.636	3.636	3.636	3.636	3.636	3.637	3.637	3.637	3.637	3.637	3.637
14	3.637	3.637	3.637	3.637	3.637	3.637	3.636	3.636	3.636	3.636	3.636	3.636
15	3.636	3.636	3.636	3.636	3.636	3.636	3.637	3.637	3.637	3.637	3.637	3.637
16	3.637	3.637	3.637	3.637	3.637	3.637	3.636	3.636	3.636	3.636	3.636	3.636
17	3.636	3.636	3.636	3.636	3.636	3.636	3.637	3.637	3.637	3.637	3.637	3.637
18	3.637	3.637	3.637	3.637	3.637	3.637	3.636	3.636	3.636	3.636	3.636	3.636
19	3.636	3.636	3.636	3.636	3.636	3.636	3.637	3.637	3.637	3.637	3.637	3.637
20	3.637	3.637	3.637	3.637	3.637	3.637	3.636	3.636	3.636	3.636	3.636	3.636
21	3.636	3.636	3.636	3.636	3.636	3.636	3.637	3.637	3.637	3.637	3.637	3.637
22	3.637	3.637	3.637	3.637	3.637	3.637	3.636	3.636	3.636	3.636	3.636	3.636
23	3.636	3.636	3.636	3.636	3.636	3.636	3.637	3.637	3.637	3.637	3.637	3.637
24	3.637	3.637	3.637	3.637	3.637	3.637	3.636	3.636	3.636	3.636	3.636	3.636
25	3.636	3.636	3.636	3.636	3.636	3.636	3.637	3.637	3.637	3.637	3.637	3.637
26	3.637	3.637	3.637	3.637	3.637	3.637	3.636	3.636	3.636	3.636	3.636	3.636
27	3.636	3.636	3.636	3.636	3.636	3.636	3.637	3.637	3.637	3.637	3.637	3.637
28	1.97	2.273	2.576	2.879	3.182	3.485	3.636	3.636	3.636	3.636	3.636	3.636
29							0.152	0.455	0.758	1.061	1.364	1.667

Nonresidential Real Property Mid-Month Convention Straight Line—31.5 Years

Year	Month Property Placed in Service											
	1	2	3	4	5	6	7	8	9	10	11	12
1	3.042%	2.778%	2.513%	2.249%	1.984%	1.720%	1.455%	1.190%	0.926%	0.661%	0.397%	0.132%
2–7	3.175	3.175	3.175	3.175	3.175	3.175	3.175	3.175	3.175	3.175	3.175	3.175
8	3.175	3.174	3.175	3.174	3.175	3.175	3.175	3.175	3.175	3.175	3.175	3.175
9	3.174	3.175	3.174	3.175	3.174	3.175	3.174	3.175	3.175	3.175	3.174	3.175
10	3.175	3.174	3.175	3.174	3.175	3.174	3.175	3.174	3.175	3.174	3.175	3.174
11	3.174	3.175	3.174	3.175	3.174	3.175	3.174	3.175	3.174	3.175	3.174	3.175
12	3.175	3.174	3.175	3.174	3.175	3.174	3.175	3.174	3.175	3.174	3.175	3.174
13	3.174	3.175	3.174	3.175	3.174	3.175	3.174	3.175	3.174	3.175	3.174	3.175
14	3.175	3.174	3.175	3.174	3.175	3.174	3.175	3.174	3.175	3.174	3.175	3.174
15	3.174	3.175	3.174	3.175	3.174	3.175	3.174	3.175	3.174	3.175	3.174	3.175
16	3.175	3.174	3.175	3.174	3.175	3.174	3.175	3.174	3.175	3.174	3.175	3.174
17	3.174	3.175	3.174	3.175	3.174	3.175	3.174	3.175	3.174	3.175	3.174	3.175
18	3.175	3.174	3.175	3.174	3.175	3.174	3.175	3.174	3.175	3.174	3.175	3.174
19	3.174	3.175	3.174	3.175	3.174	3.175	3.174	3.175	3.174	3.175	3.174	3.175
20	3.175	3.174	3.175	3.174	3.175	3.174	3.175	3.174	3.175	3.174	3.175	3.174
21	3.175	3.175	3.174	3.175	3.174	3.175	3.174	3.175	3.174	3.175	3.174	3.175
22	3.174	3.174	3.175	3.174	3.175	3.174	3.175	3.174	3.175	3.174	3.175	3.174
23	3.175	3.175	3.174	3.175	3.174	3.175	3.174	3.175	3.174	3.175	3.174	3.175
24	3.174	3.174	3.175	3.174	3.175	3.174	3.175	3.174	3.175	3.174	3.175	3.174
25	3.174	3.175	3.174	3.175	3.174	3.175	3.174	3.175	3.174	3.175	3.174	3.175
26	3.175	3.174	3.175	3.174	3.175	3.174	3.175	3.174	3.175	3.174	3.175	3.174
27	3.174	3.175	3.174	3.175	3.174	3.175	3.174	3.175	3.174	3.175	3.174	3.175
28	3.175	3.174	3.175	3.174	3.175	3.174	3.175	3.174	3.175	3.174	3.175	3.174
29	3.174	3.175	3.174	3.175	3.174	3.175	3.174	3.175	3.174	3.175	3.174	3.175
30	3.175	3.174	3.175	3.174	3.175	3.174	3.175	3.174	3.175	3.174	3.175	3.174
31	3.174	3.175	3.174	3.175	3.174	3.175	3.174	3.175	3.174	3.175	3.174	3.175
32	1.720	1.984	2.249	2.513	2.778	3.042	3.175	3.174	3.175	3.174	3.175	3.174
33							0.132	0.397	0.661	0.926	1.190	1.455

Nonresidential Real Property Mid-Month Convention Straight Line—39 Years

Year	Month Property Placed in Service											
	1	2	3	4	5	6	7	8	9	10	11	12
1	2.461%	2.247%	2.033%	1.819%	1.605%	1.391%	1.177%	0.963%	0.749%	0.535%	0.321%	0.107%
2–39	2.564	2.564	2.564	2.564	2.564	2.564	2.564	2.564	2.564	2.564	2.564	2.564
40	0.107	0.321	0.535	0.749	0.963	1.177	1.391	1.605	1.819	2.033	2.247	2.461

SUMMARY

Explain the concept of basis and adjusted basis and describe the cost recovery methods used under the tax law to recover the cost of personal property, real property, intangible assets, and natural resources.

LO1

- Tangible personal and real property (depreciation), intangibles (amortization), and natural resources (depletion) are all subject to cost recovery.

- An asset's basis is the amount that is subject to cost recovery. Generally, an asset's initial basis is its purchase price, plus the cost of any other expenses incurred to get the asset in working condition.

- The basis of assets acquired in a nontaxable exchange is the transferor's adjusted basis—simply a carryover basis.

- Expenditures on an asset are either expensed currently or capitalized as a new asset. Expenditures for routine or general maintenance of the asset are expensed currently. Expenditures that extend the useful life of the asset are capitalized.

- When acquiring a business and purchasing a bundle of property, the basis of each asset is determined as the fair market value of the asset.

Determine the applicable cost recovery (depreciation) life, method, and convention for tangible personal and real property and calculate the deduction allowable under MACRS.

LO2

- Tax depreciation is currently calculated under the Modified Accelerated Cost Recovery System (MACRS).

- MACRS for tangible personal property is based upon recovery period (Rev. Proc. 87-56), method (200 percent declining balance, 150 percent declining balance, and straight-line), and convention (half-year or mid-quarter).

- §179 allows taxpayers to expense tangible personal property. The expense is limited by the amount of property placed in service and taxable income.

- Listed property includes automobiles, other means of transportation, computer equipment, and cell phones. Depreciation is limited to the expense multiplied by business-use percentage. Special rules apply if business use is less than 50 percent.

- Additional limitations apply to luxury automobiles.

- Real property is divided into two groups for tax purposes: residential rental and nonresidential. The recovery period is 27.5 years for residential property and 31.5 years or 39 years for nonresidential property, depending on when the property was placed in service. The depreciation method is straight-line and the convention is mid-month.

Explain the rationale behind amortization, describe the four categories of amortizable intangible assets, and calculate amortization expense.

LO3

- Intangible assets (such as patents, goodwill, and trademarks) have their costs recovered through amortization.

- Intangible assets are amortized (straight-line method) using the full-month convention.

- Intangibles are divided into four types (§197 purchased intangibles, start-up costs and organizational expenditures, research and experimentation, and self-created intangibles).

Explain cost recovery of natural resources and the allowable depletion methods.

LO4

- Depletion allows a taxpayer to recover his or her capital investment in natural resources.

- Two methods of depletion are available, and the taxpayer must calculate both and take the one that results in the larger depletion deduction each year.

- Cost depletion allows taxpayers to estimate number of units and then allocate a pro rata share of the basis to each unit extracted during the year.

- Percentage depletion allows the taxpayer to take a statutory determined percentage of gross income as an expense. Deductions are not limited to basis.

KEY TERMS

Accelerated Cost Recovery System (ACRS) (9-5)

adjusted basis (9-3)

amortization (9-2)

bonus depreciation (9-19)

cost depletion (9-37)

cost recovery (9-2)

covenant not to compete (9-30)

depletion (9-2)

depreciation (9-2)

full-month convention (9-30)

half-year convention (9-8)

intangible assets (9-2)

listed property (9-20)

luxury automobile (9-24)

mid-month convention (9-26)

mid-quarter convention (9-8)

Modified Cost Recovery System (MACRS) (9-5)

organizational expenditures (9-32)

percentage depletion (9-38)

personal property (9-5)

real property (9-5)

recovery period (9-5)

research and experimentation (R&E) costs (9-30)

§179 election (9-15)

§197 purchased intangibles (9-30)

start-up costs (9-34)

tax basis (9-3)

DISCUSSION QUESTIONS

1. **(LO1)** Explain the reasoning why the tax laws require the cost of certain assets to be capitalized and recovered over time rather than immediately expensed.

2. **(LO1)** Explain the differences and similarities between personal property, real property, intangible property, and natural resources. Also, provide an example of each type of asset.

3. **(LO1)** Explain the similarities and dissimilarities between depreciation, amortization, and depletion. Describe the cost recovery method used for each of the four asset types (personal property, real property, intangible property, and natural resources).

4. **(LO1)** Is an asset's initial or cost basis simply its purchase price? Explain.

5. **(LO1)** Compare and contrast the basis of property acquired via purchase, conversion from personal use to business or rental use, a nontaxable exchange, gift, and inheritance.

6. **(LO1)** Explain why the expenses incurred to get an asset in place and operable should be included in the asset's basis.

7. **(LO1)** Graber Corporation runs a long-haul trucking business. Graber incurs the following expenses: replacement tires, oil changes, and a transmission overhaul. Which of these expenditures may be deducted currently and which must be capitalized? Explain.

8. **(LO2)** MACRS depreciation requires the use of a recovery period, method, and convention to depreciate tangible personal property assets. Briefly explain why each is important to the calculation.

9. **(LO2)** Can a taxpayer with very little current year income choose to not claim any depreciation expense for the current year and thus save depreciation deductions for the future when the taxpayer expects to be more profitable?

■ planning 10. **(LO2)** What depreciation methods are available for tangible personal property? Explain the characteristics of a business likely to adopt each method.

11. **(LO2)** If a business places several different assets in service during the year, must it use the same depreciation method for all assets? If not, what restrictions apply to the business's choices of depreciation methods?

12. **(LO2)** Describe how you would determine the MACRS recovery period for an asset if you did not already know it.

 research 13. **(LO2)** Compare and contrast the recovery periods used by MACRS and those used under generally accepted accounting principles (GAAP).

14. **(LO2)** Fast and Furious Corporation (F&F) decided that it should cash in on the current popularity of stock car racing. F&F designed and built a track and related facilities including grandstands, garages, concession stands, landscaping, and a hotel on the property.

   a. What does Rev. Proc. 87-56 list for the recovery period of the land improvements such as landscaping?

   b. Now, conduct research (*hint:* use a tax service and the term "motorsports entertainment complex") to determine the recovery period for the various assets if the entire project was completed in July 2007 and the first race was held on October 10, 2007.

   c. Would your answers change if there were a one-year delay in construction? If so, how would it change and why?

15. **(LO2)** What are the two depreciation conventions that apply to tangible personal property under MACRS? Explain why Congress provides two methods.

16. **(LO2)** A business buys two identical tangible personal property assets for the same identical price. It buys one at the beginning of the year and one at the end of year. Under what conditions would the taxpayer's depreciation on each asset be exactly the same? Under what conditions would it be different?

17. **(LO2)** AAA, Inc., acquired a machine in year 1. In May of year 3, it sold the asset. Can AAA find its year 3 depreciation percentage for the machine on the MACRS table? If not, what adjustment must AAA make?

18. **(LO2)** Discuss why a small business might be able to deduct a greater percentage of the assets it places in service during the year than a larger business.

19. **(LO2)** Explain the two limitations placed on the §179 expense deduction. How are they similar? How are they different?

20. **(LO2)** Compare and contrast the types of businesses that would benefit from and those that would not benefit from the §179 expense.

21. **(LO2)** What strategies will help a business maximize its current depreciation deductions (including §179)? Why might a taxpayer choose not to maximize its current depreciation deductions?

22. **(LO2)** Why might a business elect only the §179 expense it can deduct in the current year rather than claiming the full amount available?

23. **(LO2)** Describe assets that are considered to be listed property. Why do you think Congress requires them to be "listed"?

24. **(LO2)** Are taxpayers allowed to claim deprecation expense on assets they use for both business and personal purposes? What are the tax consequences if the business use drops from above 50 percent in one year to below 50 percent in the next?

25. **(LO2)** Discuss why Congress limits the amount of depreciation expense businesses may claim on certain automobiles.

26. **(LO2)** Compare and contrast how a Land Rover SUV and a Mercedes Benz sedan are treated under the luxury auto rules. Also include a discussion of the similarities and differences in available §179 expense.

27. **(LO2)** There are two recovery period classifications for real property. What reasons might Congress have to allow residential real estate a shorter recovery period than nonresidential real property?

28. **(LO2)** Discuss why Congress has instructed taxpayers that real property be depreciated using the mid-month convention as opposed to the half-year or mid-quarter conventions used for tangible personal property.

research

29. **(LO2)** If a taxpayer has owned a building for 10 years and decides that it should make significant improvements to the building, what is the recovery period for the improvements?

30. **(LO2)** Compare and contrast the differences between computing depreciation expense for tangible personal property and depreciation expense for real property under both the regular tax and alternative tax systems.

31. **(LO3)** What is a §197 intangible? How do taxpayers recover the costs of these intangibles? How do taxpayers recover the cost of a §197 intangible that expires (such as a covenant not to compete)?

32. **(LO3)** Compare and contrast the tax and financial accounting treatment of goodwill. Are taxpayers allowed to deduct amounts associated with self-created goodwill?

33. **(LO3)** Compare and contrast the similarities and differences between organizational expenditures and start-up costs for tax purposes.

34. **(LO3)** Discuss the methodology used to determine the amount of organizational expenditures or start-up costs that may be immediately expensed in the year a taxpayer begins business.

35. **(LO3)** Explain the amortization convention applicable to intangible assets.

36. **(LO3)** Compare and contrast the recovery periods of §197 intangibles, organizational expenditures, start-up costs, and research and experimentation expenses.

37. **(LO4)** Compare and contrast the cost and percentage depletion methods for recovering the costs of intangible assets. What are the similarities and differences between the two methods?

38. **(LO4)** Explain why percentage depletion has been referred to as a government subsidy.

PROBLEMS

39. **(LO1)** Jose purchased a delivery van for his business through an online auction. His winning bid for the van was $24,500. In addition, Jose incurred the following expenses before using the van: shipping costs of $650; paint to match the other fleet vehicles at a cost of $1,000; registration costs of $3,200 which included $3,000 of sales tax and a registration fee of $200; wash and detailing for $50; and an engine tune-up for $250. What is Jose's cost basis for the delivery van?

40. **(LO1)** Emily purchased a building to store inventory for her business. The purchase price was $760,000. Beyond this, Emily incurred the following necessary expenses to get the building ready for use: $10,000 to repair the roof, $5,000 to make the interior suitable for her finished goods, and $300 in legal fees. What is Emily's cost basis in the new building?

41. **(LO1)** Dennis contributed business assets to a new business in exchange for stock in the company. The exchange did not qualify as a nontaxable exchange. The fair market value of these assets was $287,000 on the contribution date. Dennis's original basis in the assets he contributed was $143,000, and the accumulated depreciation on the assets was $78,000.

   a. What is the business's basis in the assets it received from Dennis?

   b. What would be the business's basis if the transaction qualified as a nontaxable exchange?

42. **(LO1)** Brittany started a law practice as a sole proprietor. She owned a computer, printer, desk, and file cabinet she purchased during law school (several years ago)

that she is planning to use in her business. What is the depreciable basis that Brittany should use in her business for each asset, given the following information?

Asset	Purchase Price	FMV at Time Converted to Business Use
Computer	$2,500	$ 800
Printer	$ 300	$ 150
Desk	$1,200	$1,000
File cabinet	$ 200	$ 225

43. **(LO1)** Meg O'Brien received a gift of some small-scale jewelry manufacturing equipment that her father had used for personal purposes for many years. Her father originally purchased the equipment for $1,500. Because the equipment is out of production and no longer available, the property is currently worth $4,000. Meg has decided to begin a new jewelry manufacturing trade or business. What is her depreciable basis for depreciating the equipment?

44. **(LO1)** Gary inherited a Maine summer cabin on 10 acres from his grandmother. His grandparents originally purchased the property for $500 in 1950 and built the cabin at a cost of $10,000 in 1965. His grandfather died in 1980 and when his grandmother recently passed away, the property was appraised at $500,000 for the land and $700,000 for the cabin. Since Gary doesn't currently live in New England, he decided that it would be best to put the property to use as a rental. What is Gary's basis in the land and in the cabin?

45. **(LO1)** Wanting to finalize a sale before year-end, on December 29, WR Outfitters discounted and sold to Bob a warehouse and the land it was built on for $125,000. The appraised fair market value of the warehouse was $75,000, and the appraised value of the land was $100,000.

a. What is Bob's basis in the warehouse and in the land?

b. What would be Bob's basis in the warehouse and in the land if the appraised value of the warehouse is $50,000, and the appraised value of the land is $125,000?

c. Which appraisal would Bob likely prefer?

46. **(LO2)** At the beginning of the year, Poplock began a calendar-year dog boarding business called Griff's Palace. Poplock bought and placed in service the following assets during the year:

Asset	Placed in Service Date	Cost Basis
Computer equipment	3/23	$ 5,000
Dog grooming furniture	5/12	$ 7,000
Pickup truck	9/17	$ 10,000
Commercial building	10/11	$270,000
Land (one acre)	10/11	$ 80,000

Assuming Poplock does not elect §179 expensing, answer the following questions:

a. What is Poplock's year 1 depreciation expense for each asset?

b. What is Poplock's year 2 depreciation expense for each asset?

c. What is Poplock's year 1 depreciation expense for each asset if the pickup truck was purchased and placed in service on 11/15 instead of 9/17?

d. Assuming the pickup truck was purchased and placed in service on 11/15, what is Poplock's year 2 depreciation expense for each asset?

47. **(LO2)** Evergreen Corporation acquired the following assets during the current year (ignore §179 expense for these problems and assume that the delivery truck is not subject to the luxury auto limitations):

Asset	Placed in Service Date	Original Basis
Machinery	October 25	$ 70,000
Computer equipment	February 3	$ 10,000
Used delivery truck*	August 17	$ 23,000
Furniture	April 22	$150,000

*The delivery truck is not a luxury automobile.

a. What is the allowable MACRS depreciation on Evergreen's property in the current year?

b. What is the allowable MACRS depreciation on Evergreen's property in the current year if the machinery had a basis of $170,000 rather than $70,000?

c. What is the allowable MACRS depreciation on Evergreen's property in the current year if the machinery had a basis of $270,000 rather than $170,000?

■ **planning**   48. **(LO2)** Parley needs a new truck to help him expand Parley's Plumbing Palace. Business has been booming and Parley would like to accelerate his tax deductions as much as possible. On April 1, Parley purchased a new delivery van for $25,000. It is now September 26 and Parley, already in need of another vehicle, has found a deal on buying a truck for $22,000 (all fees included). The dealer tells him if he doesn't buy the truck (Option 1), it will be gone tomorrow. There is an auction (Option 2) scheduled for October 5 where Parley believes he can get a similar truck for $21,500, but there is also a $500 auction fee.

a. Which option allows Parley to generate more depreciation expense deductions this year (the vehicles are not considered to be luxury autos)?

b. Assume the original facts, except that the delivery van was placed in service one day earlier on March 31 rather than April 1. Which option generates more depreciation expense?

49. **(LO2)** Way Corporation disposed of the following tangible personal property assets in the current year. Calculate Way Corporation's 2009 depreciation expense. Assume that the delivery truck is not a luxury auto.

Asset	Date Acquired	Date Sold	Convention	Original Basis
Furniture (7-year)	5/12/05	7/15/09	HY	$ 55,000
Machinery (7-year)	3/23/06	3/15/09	MQ	$ 72,000
Delivery truck* (5-year)	9/17/07	3/13/09	HY	$ 20,000
Machinery (7-year)	10/11/08	8/11/09	MQ	$270,000
Computer (5-year)	10/11/09	12/15/09	HY	$ 80,000

*Used 100 percent for business.

■ **planning**   50. **(LO2)** Assume that Green Corporation has 2009 taxable income of $250,000 before the §179 expense and acquired the following assets during 2009:

Asset	Placed in Service	Basis
Machinery	October 12	$170,000
Computer equipment	February 10	$ 70,000
Delivery truck	August 21	$ 93,000
Furniture	April 2	$180,000
Total		$513,000

a. What is the maximum amount of §179 expense Green may deduct for 2009?

b. What is the maximum total depreciation expense, including §179 expense, that Green may deduct in 2009 on the assets it placed in service in 2009?

c. What is the maximum total depreciation expense, including §179 expense, Green may deduct in 2009 on the assets it placed in service in 2009 if the delivery truck was purchased and placed in service on October 21 instead of August 21?

51. **(LO2)** Assume that Timberline Corporation has 2009 taxable income of $25,000 before the §179 expense.

Asset	Purchase Date	Basis
Furniture (7-year)	December 1	$150,000
Computer equipment (5-year)	February 28	$ 90,000
Copier (5-year)	July 15	$ 30,000
Machinery (7-year)	May 22	$280,000
Total		$550,000

a. What is the maximum amount of §179 expense Timberline may deduct for 2009?

b. What would Timberline's maximum depreciation expense be for 2009?

c. What would Timberline's maximum depreciation expense be for 2009 if the furniture cost $350,000 instead of $150,000?

52. **(LO2)** Dain's Diamond Bit Drilling purchased the following assets during 2009. Assume its taxable income for the year was $53,000 before deducting any §179 expense.

■ **planning**

Asset	Purchase Date	Original Basis
Drill bits (5-year)	January 25	$ 90,000
Drill bits (5-year)	July 25	$ 95,000
Commercial building	April 22	$220,000

a. What is Dain's maximum §179 expense for the year 2009?

b. What is Dain's maximum depreciation expense for the year 2009 (including §179 expense)?

c. If the January drill bits' original basis was $500,000, what is Dain's maximum §179 expense for the year 2009?

d. If the January drill bits' basis was $650,000, what is Dain's maximum §179 expense for the year 2009?

53. **(LO2)** Phil owns a ranch business and uses four-wheelers to do much of his work. Occasionally, though, he and his boys will go for a ride together as a family activity. Last year, Phil put 765 miles on the four-wheeler that he bought on January 15 for $6,500. Of the miles driven, only 175 miles were for personal use. Assume four-wheelers qualify to be depreciated according to the five-year MACRS schedule and the four-wheeler was the only asset Phil purchased this year.

a. Calculate the allowable depreciation for the current year (year 1) (ignore the §179 expense).

b. Calculate the allowable depreciation for year 2 if total miles were 930 and personal-use miles were 400.

54. **(LO2)** Assume that Ernesto purchased a laptop computer on July 10 of year 1 for $3,000. In year 1, 80 percent of his computer usage was for his business and 20 percent was for computer gaming with his friends. This was the only asset he placed in service during year 1. Ignoring any potential §179 expense, answer the questions for each of the following alternative scenarios:

a. What is Ernesto's depreciation deduction for the computer in year 1?

b. What would be Ernesto's depreciation deduction for the computer in year 2 if his year 2 usage was 75 percent business and 25 percent for computer gaming?

   c. What would be Ernesto's depreciation deduction for the computer in year 2 if his year 2 usage was 45 percent business and 55 percent for computer gaming?

   d. What would be Ernesto's depreciation deduction for the computer in year 2 if his year 2 usage was 30 percent business and 70 percent for computer gaming?

55. **(LO2)** Lina purchased a new car for use in her business during 2008. The auto was the only business asset she purchased during the year and her business was extremely profitable. Calculate her maximum depreciation deductions (including §179 expense unless stated otherwise) for the automobile in 2008 (Lina didn't elect bonus depreciation for 2008) and 2009 in the following alternative scenarios (assuming half-year convention for all):

   a. The vehicle cost $15,000 and business use is 100 percent (ignore §179 expense).

   b. The vehicle cost $40,000, and business use is 100 percent.

   c. The vehicle cost $40,000, and she used it 80 percent for business.

   d. The vehicle cost $40,000, and she used it 80 percent for business. She sold it on March 1 of year 2.

   e. The vehicle cost $40,000, and she used it 20 percent for business.

   f. The vehicle cost $40,000 is an SUV that weighed 6,500 pounds. Business use was 100 percent.

56. **(LO2)** On November 10 of year 1 Javier purchased a building, including the land it was on, to assemble his new equipment. The total cost of the purchase was $1,200,000; $300,000 was allocated to the basis of the land and the remaining $900,000 was allocated to the basis of the building.

   a. Using MACRS, what is Javier's depreciation expense on the building for the first three years?

   b. What would be the year 3 depreciation expense if the building was sold on August 1 of year 3?

   c. Answer the question in part (a), except assume the building was purchased and placed in service on March 3 instead of November 10.

   d. Answer the question in part (a), except assume that the building is residential property.

   e. What would be the depreciation for 2009, 2010, and 2011 if the property were nonresidential property purchased and placed in service November 10, 1992 (assume the same original basis)?

57. **(LO2)** Carl purchased an apartment complex for $1.1 million on March 17 of year 1. $300,000 of the purchase price was attributable to the land the complex sits on. When he purchased the complex, he made $25,000 in landscaping improvements. He also installed new furniture into half of the units at a cost of $60,000.

   a. What is Carl's allowable depreciation expense for his real property for years 1 and 2?

   b. What is Carl's allowable depreciation expense for year 3 if the property is sold on January 2 of year 3?

research

58. **(LO2)** Paul Vote purchased the following business assets this year (ignore §179 expensing when answering the questions below):

Asset	Purchase Date	Basis
Machinery	May 12	$ 23,500
Computers	August 13	$ 20,000
Warehouse	December 13	$180,000

   a. What is Paul's allowable MACRS depreciation expense for the property?

   b. What is Paul's allowable alternative minimum tax (AMT) depreciation expense for the property? You will need to find the AMT depreciation tables to compute the depreciation.

59. **(LO3)** After several profitable years running her business, Ingrid decided to acquire a small competing business. On May 1 of year 1, Ingrid acquired the competing business for $300,000. Ingrid allocated $50,000 of the purchase price to goodwill. Ingrid's business reports its taxable income on the calendar-year basis.

    a. How much amortization expense on the goodwill can Ingrid deduct in year 1, year 2, and year 3?

    b. In lieu of the original facts, assume that $40,000 of the purchase price was allocated to goodwill and $10,000 of the purchase price was allocated to a customer phone list that has an expected life of two years. How much amortization expense on the goodwill and the phone list can Ingrid deduct in year 1, year 2, and year 3?

    c. Assume that the only intangible asset Ingrid acquired was the customer phone list with a useful life of two years and that $10,000 of the purchase price was allocated to the customer list. How much amortization expense for the customer phone list can Ingrid deduct in year 1, year 2, and year 3, and how will she account for the fact that the phone list is no longer useful after April of year 3?

60. **(LO3)** Juliette formed a new business to sell sporting goods this year. The business opened its doors to customers on June 1. Determine the amount of start-up costs Juliette can immediately expense (not including amortization) this year in the following alternative scenarios.

    a. She incurred start-up costs of $2,000.

    b. She incurred start-up costs of $45,000.

    c. She incurred start-up costs of $53,500.

    d. She incurred start-up costs of $60,000.

    e. How would you answer parts (a–d) if she formed a partnership or a corporation and she incurred the same amount of organizational expenditures rather than start-up costs (how much of the organizational expenditures would be immediately deductible)?

61. **(LO3)** Nicole organized a new corporation. The corporation began business on April 1 of year 1. She made the following expenditures associated with getting the corporation started:

Expense	Date	Amount
Attorney fees for articles of incorporation	February 10	$32,000
March 1–March 30 wages	March 30	$ 4,500
March 1–March 30 rent	March 30	$ 2,000
Stock issuance costs	April 1	$20,000
April 1–May 30 wages	May 30	$12,000

    a. What is the total amount of the start-up costs and organizational expenditures for Nicole's corporation?

    b. What amount of the start-up costs and organizational expenditures may the corporation immediately expense in year 1?

    c. What amount could the corporation deduct as amortization expense for the organizational expenditures and for the start-up costs for year 1 (not including the amount it immediately expensed)?

    d. What would be the allowable organizational expenditures, including immediate expensing and amortization, if Ingrid started a sole proprietorship instead?

62. **(LO3)** Bethany incurred $20,000 in research and experimental costs for developing a specialized product during July of year 1. Bethany went through a lot of trouble and spent $10,000 in legal fees to receive a patent for the product in August of year 3.

    a. What amount of research and experimental expenses for year 1 through year 3 may Bethany deduct if she elects to amortize them over 60 months?

    b. How much *patent* amortization expense would Bethany deduct in year 3 assuming she elected to amortize the research and experimental costs over 60 months?

    c. If Bethany chose to capitalize but *not* amortize the research and experimental expenses she incurred in year 1, how much patent amortization expense would Bethany deduct in year 3?

63. **(LO4)** Last Chance Mine (LC) purchased a coal deposit for $750,000. It estimated it would extract 12,000 tons of coal from the deposit. LC mined the coal and sold it, reporting gross receipts of $1 million, $3 million, and $2 million for years 1 through 3, respectively. During years 1–3, LC reported net income (loss) from the coal deposit activity in the amount of ($20,000), $500,000, and $450,000, respectively. In years 1–3, LC actually extracted 13,000 tons of coal as follows:

(1)	(2)	Depletion (2)/(1)	Tons Extracted per Year		
Tons of Coal	Basis	Rate	Year 1	Year 2	Year 3
12,000	$750,000	$62.50	2,000	7,200	3,800

    a. What is Last Chance's cost depletion for years 1, 2, and 3?

    b. What is Last Chance's percentage depletion for each year (the applicable percentage for coal is 10 percent)?

    c. Using the cost and percentage depletion computations from the previous parts, what is Last Chance's actual depletion expense for each year?

COMPREHENSIVE PROBLEMS

64. Back in Boston, Steve has been busy creating and managing his new company, Teton Mountaineering (TM), which is based out of a small town in Wyoming. In the process of doing so, TM has acquired various types of assets. Below is a list of assets acquired during 2008:

Asset	Cost	Date Place in Service
Office equipment	$ 10,000	02/03/2008
Machinery	$260,000	07/22/2008
Used delivery truck*	$ 15,000	08/17/2008

*Not considered a luxury automobile, thus not subject to the luxury automobile limitations

During 2008, TM had huge success and Steve acquired more assets the next year to increase their production capacity. These are the assets that were acquired during 2009:

Asset	Cost	Date Place in Service
Computers & info. system	$ 40,000	03/31/2009
Luxury auto**	$ 80,000	05/26/2009
Assembly equipment	$175,000	08/15/2009
Storage building	$400,000	11/13/2009

**Used 100 percent for business purposes. Assume the year 2009 auto depreciation limits to be the same as in 2008.

TM did surprisingly well during 2009 by generating net income of $432,500. Although Steve is a good manager, he needs a little help with filing his tax return. He has hired you to minimize his tax liability for 2009, given the information he has provided.

Required

a. Determine the appropriate recovery period and convention for all of TM's assets using the MACRS method for cost recovery. After doing so, compute the allowable cost recovery deductions that minimize Steve's tax liability in 2009. Remember to consider any §179 expense. Steve is a calendar-year taxpayer.

b. In addition to the information in part (a), now assume that Steve acquired a new machine on September 1 that will greatly increase his efficiencies. The cost of the new machine was $300,000 plus $20,000 for delivery and setup costs. The machine was placed into service on October 2. Compute the allowable cost recovery deductions (including §179 expense) that minimize Steve's tax liability in 2009.

c. Ignoring part (b), now assume that during 2009, Steve decides to buy a competitor's assets for a purchase price of $350,000. Steve purchased the following assets for the lump-sum purchase price.

Asset	Cost	Date Placed in Service
Inventory	$ 20,000	09/15/2009
Office furniture	$ 30,000	09/15/2009
Machinery	$ 50,000	09/15/2009
Patent	$ 98,000	09/15/2009
Goodwill	$ 2,000	09/15/2009
Building	$130,000	09/15/2009
Land	$ 20,000	09/15/2009

Compute Steve's maximum 2009 cost recovery deductions for the assets Steve acquired in the purchase.

d. Complete Part I of Form 4562 for part (a). (Use 2008 form if 2009 form is unavailable.)

65. While completing undergraduate work in information systems, Dallin Bourne and Michael Banks decided to start a business called ISys Answers, which was a technology support company. They bought the following assets and incurred the following fees at start up:

Year 1 Assets	Purchase Date	Basis
Computers (5-year)	October 30, Y1	$15,000
Office equipment (7-year)	October 30, Y1	$10,000
Furniture (7-year)	October 30, Y1	$ 3,000
Start-up costs	October 30, Y1	$ 7,000

In April of the following year, they decided to purchase a customer list from a company started by fellow information systems students preparing to graduate that provided virtually the same services. The customer list cost $10,000, and the sale was completed on April 30. During their summer break, Dallin and Michael passed on internship opportunities in an attempt to really grow their business into something they could do full-time after graduation. In the summer, they purchased a small van (for transportation, not considered a luxury auto) and a pinball machine (to help attract new employees). They bought the van on June 15 of year 2 for $15,000, and spent $3,000 getting it ready to put into service. The pinball machine cost $4,000, and was placed in service on July 1 of year 2.

Year 2 Assets	Purchase Date	Basis
Van	June 15, Y2	$18,000
Pinball machine (7-year)	July 1, Y2	$ 4,000
Customer list	April 30, Y2	$10,000

Assume that ISys Answers does not elect any §179 expense. Also assume that year 2 is 2009.

a. What are the maximum cost recovery deductions for ISys Answers (excluding §179 expensing) for year 1 and year 2?

b. What is ISys Answers' basis in each of its assets at the end of year 1 and year 2?

66. Diamond Mountain was originally thought to be one of the few places in North America to contain diamonds, so Diamond Mountain Inc. (DM) purchased the land for $1,000,000. Later, DM discovered that the only diamonds on the mountain had been planted there and the land was worthless for mining. DM engineers discovered a new survey technology and discovered a silver deposit estimated at 5,000 pounds on Diamond Mountain. DM bought new drilling equipment and immediately began mining the silver.

In years 1–3 following the opening of the mine, DM had net (gross) income of $200,000 ($700,000), $400,000 ($1,100,000), and $600,000 ($1,450,000), respectively. Mining amounts for each year were as follows: 750 pounds (year 1), 1,450 pounds (year 2), and 1,800 pounds (year 3). At the end of year 2, engineers used the new technology (which had been improving over time) and estimated there was still an estimated 6,000 pounds of silver deposits.

DM also began a research and experimentation project with the hopes of gaining a patent for its new survey technology. Diamond Mountain Inc. chooses to capitalize research and experimentation expenditures and amortize the costs over 60 months or until it obtains a patent on its technology. In March of year 1, DM spent $95,000 on research and experimentation. DM spent another $75,000 in February of year 2 for research and experimentation. In September of year 2, DM paid $20,000 of legal fees and was granted the patent in October of year 2 (the entire process of obtaining a patent was unusually fast).

Answer the following questions regarding DM's activities (assume that DM tries to maximize its deductions if given a choice).

a. What is DM's depletion expense for years 1–3?

b. What is DM's research and experimentation amortization for years 1 and 2?

c. What is DM's basis in its patent and what is its amortization for the patent in year 2?

chapter
10
Property Dispositions

Learning Objectives

Upon completing this chapter you should be able to:

LO 1 Calculate the amount of gain or loss recognized on the disposition of assets used in a trade or business.

LO 2 Describe the general character types of gain or loss recognized on property dispositions.

LO 3 Explain the rationale for and calculate depreciation recapture.

LO 4 Describe the tax treatment of unrecaptured §1250 gains and determine the character of gains on property sold to related parties.

LO 5 Describe the tax treatment of §1231 gains or losses, including the §1231 netting process.

LO 6 Explain common exceptions to the general rule that realized gains and losses are recognized currently.

Storyline Summary
Taxpayer: Teton Mountaineering Technologies, LLC (Teton)—a calendar-year, single-member LLC (treated as a sole proprietorship for tax purposes)
President: Steve Dallimore
Location: Cody, Wyoming

By most measures, Teton Mountaineering Technologies, LLC (Teton) has become a success with sponsored climbers summiting the world's highest peaks, satisfied customers creating brand loyalty, and profitability improving steadily. However, after several years of operation, some of Teton's machinery is wearing out and must be replaced. Further, because Teton has outgrown its manufacturing capacity, Steve is considering whether to expand the company's current facility or sell it and build a new one in a different location. Steve would like to know how any asset dispositions will affect Teton's tax bill.

Steve has found a willing buyer for Teton's machinery, and he has options for trading the equipment. For tax purposes, does it matter whether he sells or trades the equipment? Steve also has questions about how to best manage Teton's acquisitions and dispositions of real property. It all seems a bit overwhelming. . . . He picks up the phone and dials his tax accountant's number. ■

You can imagine why Steve might be eager to reach his accountant. Tax accounting widely impacts business decisions: What are the tax consequences of selling, trading, or even abandoning business assets? Are the tax consequences the same whether taxpayers sell machinery, inventory, or investment assets? Does it matter for tax purposes whether Teton is structured as a sole proprietorship or a corporation when its sells its warehouse? If Steve sells his personal sailboat, car, or furniture, what are the tax consequences?

In the previous chapter we explained the tax consequences associated with purchasing assets and recovering the cost of the assets through depreciation, amortization, or depletion. This chapter explores fundamental tax issues associated with property dispositions (sales, trades, or other dispositions). We focus on the disposition of depreciable assets, but the same principles apply to the sale of intangible assets and natural resources.

LO1   DISPOSITIONS

Taxpayers can dispose of assets in many ways. For example, a taxpayer could sell an asset, donate it to charity, trade it for a similar asset, take it to the landfill, or have it destroyed in a natural disaster. No matter how it is accomplished, every asset disposition triggers a realization event for tax purposes. To calculate the amount of gain or loss taxpayers realize when they sell assets, they must determine the amount realized on the sale and their **adjusted basis** in each asset they are selling.

Amount Realized

Simply put, the **amount realized** by a taxpayer from the sale or other disposition of an asset is everything of *value* received from the buyer *less* any selling costs.[1] While taxpayers typically receive cash when they sell property, they may also accept marketable securities, notes receivable, similar assets, or any combination of these items as payment. Additionally, taxpayers selling assets such as real property subject to loans or mortgages must increase their amount realized by the amount of debt relief (the buyer's assumption of the seller's liability increases the seller's amount realized). The amount realized computation is captured in the following formula:

$$\text{Amount realized} = \text{Cash received} + \text{Fair market value of other property} \\ + \text{Buyer's assumption of liabilities} - \text{Seller's expenses}$$

Example 10-1

Teton wants to upgrade its old manufacturing machinery that is wearing out. On November 1 of the current year, Teton sells the old machinery for $30,000 cash and marketable securities valued at $70,500. Teton paid a broker $500 to find a buyer. What is Teton's amount realized on the sale of the machinery?

Answer: $100,000, computed as follows:

Description	Amount	Explanation
(1) Cash received	$ 30,000	
(2) Marketable securities received	70,500	
(3) Broker commission paid	(500)	
Amount realized	$100,000	(1) + (2) + (3).

---

[1]*S.C. Chapin,* CA-8, 50-1 USTC ¶9171.

Adjusted Basis

Recall from the previous chapter that an asset's *cost basis* is the amount *subject to* cost recovery. The *adjusted basis* however, is the original basis reduced by depreciation or other types of cost recovery deductions taken against the property. The adjusted basis of an asset can be determined using the following formula:

$$\text{Adjusted basis} = \text{Cost basis} - \text{Cost recovery deductions}$$

Example 10-2

To determine its realized gain or loss on the sale, Teton must calculate the adjusted basis of the machinery it sold in Example 10-1 for $100,000. Teton originally purchased the machinery for $260,000 three years ago. For tax purposes, Teton depreciated the machine using MACRS (seven-year recovery period, 200 percent declining balance method, and half-year convention). The machine's adjusted basis at the time of the sale is as follows:

Description	Tax	Explanation
(1) Original basis	$260,000	Example 9-1.
(2) Year 1	(37,154)	Example 9-6.
(3) Year 2	(63,674)	Example 9-6.
(4) Year 3	(45,474)	Example 9-6.
(5) Year 4	(16,237)	$32,474 (Example 9-6) × 50% (half-year convention).
(6) Accumulated depreciation	($162,539)	(2) + (3) + (4) + (5).
Adjusted basis	$ 97,461	(1) + (6).

Because businesses generally use more highly accelerated depreciation methods for tax purposes than they do for book purposes, the tax-adjusted basis of a particular asset is likely to differ from the book-adjusted basis.

Realized Gain or Loss on Disposition

The amount of gain or loss taxpayers realize on a sale or other disposition of assets is simply the amount they realize minus their adjusted basis in the disposed assets.[2] The formula for computing **realized gain or loss** is as follows:

$$\text{Gain or (loss) realized} = \text{Amount realized} - \text{Adjusted basis}$$

Example 10-3

In Example 10-1, we learned that Teton sold machinery for a total amount realized of $100,000, and in Example 10-2 we learned that its basis in the machinery was $97,461. What is Teton's realized gain or loss on the sale of the machinery?

Answer: $2,539, computed as follows:

Description	Amount	Explanation
(1) Amount realized	$100,000	Example 10-1.
(2) Adjusted basis	(97,461)	Example 10-2.
Gain realized	$ 2,539	(1) + (2).

[2]§1001(a).

EXHIBIT 10-1   Summary of Formulas for Computing Gain or Loss Realized on an Asset Disposition

- Gain (loss) realized = Amount realized − Adjusted basis
- Amount realized = Cash received + Fair market value of other property + Buyer's assumption of seller's liabilities − Seller's expenses
- Adjusted basis = Cost basis − Cost recovery deductions

Exhibit 10-1 details the important formulas necessary to determine realized tax gains and losses.

So far, our examples have used one of Teton's asset sales to demonstrate how to compute gain or loss realized when property is sold. However, as we describe in Exhibit 10-2, Teton disposed of several assets during the year. We refer to this exhibit throughout the chapter as a reference point for discussing the tax issues associated with property dispositions.

EXHIBIT 10-2   Teton's Asset Dispositions* Realized Gain (Loss) for Tax Purposes

Asset	(1) Amount Realized	(2) Cost	(3) Accumulated Depreciation	(4) [(2) − (3)] Adjusted Basis	(5) [(1) − (4)] Gain (Loss) Realized
Machinery	$100,000	$260,000	$162,539	$ 97,461	$ 2,539
Office furniture	$ 12,000	$ 10,000	$ 7,000	$ 3,000	$ 9,000
Delivery truck	$ 2,000	$ 15,000	$ 10,500	$ 4,500	($2,500)
Warehouse	$350,000	$275,000	$ 15,000	$260,000	$ 90,000
Land	$175,000	$ 75,000	$ 0	$ 75,000	$100,000
Total gain realized					$199,039

*These are the assets initially purchased by Teton in Example 9-1. Chapter 10 generally assumes that Teton has been in business for four years. However, for simplicity, this chapter assumes Teton did not previously elect any §179 immediate expensing.

Recognized Gain or Loss on Disposition

As a general rule, taxpayers realizing gains and losses during a year must recognize the gains or losses. **Recognized gains or losses** are gains (losses) that increase (decrease) taxpayers' gross income.[3] Thus, taxpayers must report recognized gains and losses on their tax returns. Although taxpayers must immediately recognize the vast majority of realized gains and losses, in certain circumstances they may be allowed to defer recognizing gains to subsequent periods, or they may be allowed to permanently exclude the gains from taxable income. However, taxpayers may also be required to defer losses to later periods and, in more extreme cases, they may have their realized losses permanently disallowed. We address certain nonrecognition provisions later in the chapter.

LO2   CHARACTER OF GAIN OR LOSS

In order to determine how a recognized gain or loss affects a taxpayer's income tax liability, the taxpayer must determine the *character* or type of gain or loss recognized. Ultimately, every gain or loss is characterized as either ordinary or capital

[3]Recall under the return of capital principle we discussed in Chapter 5, when a taxpayer sells an asset, the taxpayer's adjusted basis is a return of capital and not a deductible expense.

EXHIBIT 10-3 **Character of Assets Depending on Property Use and Holding Period**

	Property Use		
Holding Period	Trade or Business	Investment or Personal-Use Assets	Inventory and Accounts Receivable
Short-term (One year or less)	Ordinary	Short-term Capital	Ordinary
Long-term (More than one year)	§1231**	Long-term Capital	Ordinary

*Gains on the sale of personal-use assets are taxable capital gains but losses on the sale of personal-use assets are not deductible.

**Gain or loss is eventually characterized as ordinary or capital (long-term).

> **THE KEY FACTS**
>
> *Character of Assets*
>
> ▌ Ordinary Assets
> · Assets created or used in a taxpayer's trade or business.
> · Business assets held for less than a year.
>
> ▌ Capital Assets
> · Assets held for investment purposes.
> · Assets held for personal-use purposes.
>
> ▌ §1231 Assets
> · Depreciable assets and land used in a trade or business held for *more* than one year.

(long-term or short-term). As described below, businesses may recognize §1231 gains or losses on property dispositions but even the §1231 gains or losses are eventually characterized as ordinary or capital (long-term). The character of a gain or loss is important because gains and losses of different characters are treated differently for tax purposes. For example, ordinary income (loss) is generally taxed at ordinary rates (fully deductible against ordinary income). However, capital gains may be taxed at preferential (lower) rates while deductions for capital losses are subject to certain restrictions. The character of the gains or losses taxpayers recognize when they sell assets depends on the character of the assets they are selling. The character of an asset depends on how the taxpayer used the asset and how long the taxpayer owned the asset (the holding period) before selling it.

In general terms, property may be used in a trade or business, held for investment, used for personal purposes, sold as inventory, or held as accounts receivable. The holding period may be short-term (one year or less) or long-term (more than a year). Exhibit 10-3 provides a matrix of the character of assets (ordinary, capital, or §1231) depending on how taxpayers used the assets and the length of time they held the property before selling it.

Ordinary Assets

Ordinary assets are generally assets created or used in a taxpayer's trade or business. For example, inventory is an **ordinary asset** because it is held for sale to customers in the ordinary course of business. Accounts receivable are ordinary assets because receivables are generated from the sale of inventory or business services. Other assets used in a trade or business such as machinery and equipment are also considered to be ordinary assets if they have been used in a business for *one year or less*. For example, if Teton purchased a forklift for the warehouse but sold it six months later, the gain or loss would be ordinary. When taxpayers sell ordinary assets at a gain, they recognize an ordinary gain that is taxed at ordinary rates. When taxpayers sell ordinary assets at a loss, they deduct the loss against other ordinary income.

Capital Assets

A **capital asset** is generally something held for investment (stocks and bonds), for the **production of income** (a for-profit activity that doesn't rise to the level of a trade or business), or for personal use (your car, house, or personal computer).[4] Whether an asset qualifies as a capital asset depends on the purpose for which the taxpayer uses the asset. Thus, the same asset may be considered a capital asset to one taxpayer and

[4]§1221 defines what is not a capital asset. Broadly speaking, a *capital asset* is any property *other than* property used in a trade or business (e.g., inventory, manufacturing equipment) or accounts (or notes) receivable acquired in a business from the sale of services or property.

EXHIBIT 10-4   Review of Capital Gains and Losses

Taxpayer Type	Preferential Rates	Loss Limitations
Individuals	• Most capital gains taxed at 15 percent (0 percent to the extent the gain would have been taxed at a 15 percent or lower rate if it were ordinary income). • Unrecaptured §1250 gains taxed at a maximum rate of 25 percent. • Gains on collectibles held for more than a year taxed at a maximum rate of 28 percent.	• Individuals may annually deduct up to $3,000 of net capital losses against ordinary income. • Losses carried forward indefinitely but not carried back.
Corporations	• No preferential rates, taxed at ordinary rates.	• No offset against ordinary income. • Net capital losses can generally be carried back three years and forward five years to offset gains in those years.

an ordinary asset to another taxpayer. For example, a piece of land held as an investment because it is expected to appreciate in value over time is a capital asset to that taxpayer. However, the same piece of land held as inventory by a real estate developer would be an ordinary asset. Finally, the same piece of land would be a §1231 asset if the taxpayer held it for more than one year and used it in a trade or business (e.g., as a parking lot).

Individual taxpayers generally prefer capital gains to ordinary income because certain capital gains are taxed at lower rates and capital gains may offset capital losses that cannot be deducted against ordinary income. Individuals also prefer ordinary losses to capital losses, because ordinary losses are deductible without limit while individuals may deduct only $3,000 of net capital losses against ordinary income each year. Corporate taxpayers may prefer capital gains to ordinary income because capital gains may allow them to deduct capital losses that they would not be allowed to deduct otherwise. Corporations are not allowed to deduct any net capital losses, but they are allowed to carry capital losses back three years and forward five years. Exhibit 10-4 reviews the treatment of capital gains and losses for individuals and corporations.

§1231 Assets

Section 1231 assets are depreciable assets and land used in a trade or business (including rental property) held by taxpayers for *more* than one year.[5] At a general level, when a taxpayer sells a §1231 asset, the taxpayer recognizes a §1231 gain or loss. As discussed above, however, ultimately §1231 gains or losses are characterized as ordinary or capital on a taxpayer's return. When taxpayers sell multiple §1231 assets during the year, they combine or "net" their §1231 gains and §1231 losses together. If the taxpayer recognizes a net §1231 gain, the net gain is treated as a long-term capital gain. If the taxpayer recognizes a net §1231 loss, the net loss is treated as an ordinary loss. Because net §1231 gains are treated as capital gains and §1231 losses are treated as ordinary losses, §1231 assets are tax favored relative to other types of assets.

As we discuss below, §1231 gains on individual depreciable assets may be recharacterized as ordinary income under the depreciation recapture rules. However,

[5]As noted above, property used in a trade or business and held for *one year or less* is ordinary income property.

because land is not depreciable, when taxpayers sell or otherwise dispose of land that qualifies as §1231 property, the gain or loss from the sale is always characterized as §1231 gain or loss. Thus, we refer to land as a pure §1231 asset.

Example 10-4

So that it can acquire another parcel of land to expand its manufacturing capabilities, Teton sold five acres of land that it has been using in its trade or business for $175,000. Teton purchased the land several years ago for $75,000. What is the amount and character of Teton's gain recognized on the land?

Answer: $100,000 §1231 gain, calculated as follows:

Description	Amount	Explanation
(1) Amount realized	$175,000	Exhibit 10-2.
(2) Original basis and current adjusted basis	75,000	Example 9-1.
Gain (Loss) realized and recognized	**$100,000**	(1) − (2) §1231 gain.

What if: Assume that Teton sold the land for $50,000. What would be the character of the ($25,000) loss it would recognize?

Answer: §1231 loss.

What if: Assume that the land was the only asset Teton sold during the year. How would the §1231 gain or §1231 loss on the sale ultimately be characterized on its tax return?

Answer: If Teton recognized a §1231 gain on the sale, it would be characterized as a long-term capital gain on its return. If Teton recognized a §1231 loss on the sale, it would be characterized as an ordinary loss.

DEPRECIATION RECAPTURE

L03

Because all §1231 assets except land are subject to cost recovery, it is possible that a §1231 asset other than land could be sold at a gain in situations when the asset has not appreciated in value and even in situations when the asset has *declined* in value since it was placed in service. How does this happen? It happens because depreciation deductions relating to the asset could reduce the adjusted basis of the asset by more than the actual economic decline in the asset's value. In this situation, absent tax rules to the contrary, taxpayers selling these assets would recognize §1231 gains (likely treated as long-term capital gains) even though the gain was created by depreciation deductions (against ordinary income) that reduced the basis of the asset being sold.

While Congress intended for businesses to receive favorable treatment on economic gains from the *appreciation* of §1231 assets, it did not intend for this favorable treatment to apply to gains that were created artificially through depreciation deductions that offset ordinary income.[6] In response to this concern, Congress introduced the concept of **depreciation recapture.** Depreciation recapture potentially applies to gains (but not losses) on the sale of depreciable or amortizable business property. When depreciation recapture applies, it recharacterizes the gain on the sale of a §1231 asset (all or a portion of the gain) from §1231 gain into ordinary income. Note, however, that depreciation recapture does not affect §1231 losses.

The method for computing the amount of depreciation recapture depends on the type of §1231 assets the taxpayer is selling (personal property or real property). As

---

[6]Due to accelerated methods for determining depreciation expense, many assets are depreciated faster for tax purposes than their true economic decline in value.

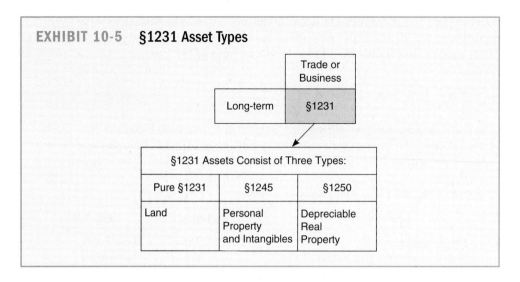

EXHIBIT 10-5   §1231 Asset Types

presented in Exhibit 10-5, §1231 assets can be categorized as pure §1231 assets (land), §1245 assets (personal property), or §1250 assets (real property). Whether taxpayers are selling personal property or real property, though, it is important to understand that depreciation recapture changes only the *character* but not the *amount* of gain taxpayers recognize when they sell a depreciable asset.

§1245 Property

Tangible personal property (machinery, equipment, and automobiles) and amortizable intangible property (patents, copyrights, and purchased goodwill) are a subset of §1231 property known as **§1245 property.**[7] The gain from the sale of §1245 property is characterized as ordinary income to the extent the gain was created by depreciation or amortization deductions. The amount of *ordinary income* (§1245 depreciation recapture) taxpayers recognize when they sell §1245 property is the lesser of (1) recognized gain on the sale *or* (2) total accumulated depreciation (or amortization) on the asset.[8] The remainder of any recognized gain is characterized as §1231 gain.[9] The sum of the ordinary income (due to depreciation recapture) and the §1231 gain on the sale equals the *total* gain recognized because depreciation recapture changes only the character (not the amount) of the gain.

When taxpayers sell or dispose of §1245 property, they encounter one of the following three scenarios involving gain or loss:

Scenario 1: They recognize a gain created solely through depreciation deductions.

Scenario 2: They recognize a gain created through both depreciation deductions and actual asset appreciation

Scenario 3: They recognize a loss.

[7]An exception in the law is that §1245 property also includes nonresidential real property placed in service between 1981 and 1986 (ACRS) for which the taxpayer elected accelerated depreciation.

[8]§1245 recapture is commonly referred to as "full" depreciation recapture because it may cause a taxpayer to recapture the entire accumulated depreciation amount as ordinary income. §1245 recapture applies notwithstanding any other provision of the IRS Code (depreciation recapture trumps all other tax rules).

[9]As a practical matter, taxpayers are unlikely to recognize any §1231 gain on the disposition of personal property because the real economic value of most tangible personal property does not increase over time as the property is used.

The following discussion considers each of these scenarios.

Scenario 1: Gain Created Solely Through Cost Recovery Deductions   Most
§1231 assets that experience wear and tear or obsolescence generally do not appreciate in value. Thus, when a taxpayer sells these types of assets at a gain, the gain is usually created because the taxpayer's depreciation deductions associated with the asset reduced the asset's adjusted basis faster than the real decline in the asset's economic value. In other words, the entire gain is artificially generated through depreciation the taxpayer claims before disposing of the asset. That is, absent depreciation deductions, the taxpayer would recognize a loss on the sale of the asset. Therefore, the entire gain on the disposition is recaptured (or characterized) as ordinary income under §1245 (recall that without depreciation recapture the gain would be §1231 gain, which can generate long-term capital gain and could create a double benefit for the taxpayer: ordinary depreciation deductions and capital gain upon disposition).

Example 10-5

As indicated in Exhibit 10-2, Teton sold machinery for $100,000. What is the amount and character of the gain Teton recognizes on the sale?

Answer: $2,539 of ordinary income under the §1245 depreciation recapture rules and $0 of §1231 gain, computed as follows:

Machinery Sale: Scenario 1
(Original scenario sales price = $100,000)

Description	Amount	Explanation
(1) Amount realized	$100,000	Exhibit 10-2.
(2) Original basis	260,000	Exhibit 10-2.
(3) Accumulated depreciation	162,539	Exhibit 10-2.
(4) Adjusted basis	$ 97,461	(2) − (3).
(5) Gain (Loss) recognized	$ 2,539	(1) − (4).
(6) Ordinary income (§1245 depreciation recapture)	$ 2,539	Lesser of (3) or (5).
§1231 gain	$ 0	(5) − (6).

Note that in this situation, because Teton's entire gain is created through depreciation deductions, the entire gain is treated as ordinary income under §1245.

What if: What would be the amount and character of Teton's gain without the depreciation recapture rules?

Answer: $2,539 of §1231 gain. Note that the recapture rules change the character of the gain but not the amount of the gain.

Scenario 2: Gain Due to Both Cost Recovery Deductions and Asset Appreciation
Assets subject to cost recovery deductions may actually *appreciate* in value over time. When these assets are sold, the recognized gain must be divided into ordinary gain from depreciation recapture and §1231 gain. The portion of the gain created through cost recovery deductions is **recaptured** as ordinary income. The remaining gain (the gain due to economic appreciation) is §1231 gain.

Example 10-6

What if: Let's assume the same facts as in the previous example and in Exhibit 10-2, except that Teton sells the machinery for $270,000. What is the amount and character of the gain Teton would recognize on this sale?

Answer: $162,539 of ordinary income under the §1245 depreciation recapture rules and $10,000 of §1231 gain due to the asset's economic appreciation, computed as follows:

Machinery Sale: Scenario 2
(Assumed sales price = $270,000)

Description	Amount	Explanation
(1) Amount realized	$270,000	
(2) Original basis	260,000	Exhibit 10-2.
(3) Accumulated depreciation	162,539	Exhibit 10-2.
(4) Adjusted basis	$ 97,461	(2) − (3).
(5) Gain (Loss) recognized	$172,539	(1) − (4).
(6) Ordinary income (§1245 depreciation recapture)	$162,539	Lesser of (3) or (5).
§1231 gain	$ 10,000	(5) − (6).

Note that taxpayers can quickly determine their §1231 gain (if any) when they sell §1245 property by subtracting the asset's *original* basis from the amount realized. In Scenario 2, presented above (Example 10-6), the §1231 gain is $10,000 ($270,000 amount realized less the $260,000 original basis).

Scenario 3: Asset Sold at a Loss Many §1231 assets, such as computer equipment or automobiles, tend to decline in value faster than the corresponding depreciation deductions reduce the asset's adjusted basis. When taxpayers sell or dispose of these assets before the assets are fully depreciated, they recognize a loss on the disposition. Because the depreciation recapture rules don't apply to losses, taxpayers selling §1245 property at a loss recognize §1231 loss.

Example 10-7

What if: Let's assume the same facts as in Example 10-5 and in Exhibit 10-2, except that Teton sells the machinery for $90,000. What is the amount and character of the gain or loss Teton would recognize on this sale?

Answer: A $7,461 §1231 loss, computed as follows:

Machinery Sale: Scenario 3
(Assumed sales price = $90,000)

Description	Amount	Explanation
(1) Amount realized	$ 90,000	
(2) Original basis	260,000	Exhibit 10-2.
(3) Accumulated depreciation	162,539	Exhibit 10-2.
(4) Adjusted basis	$ 97,461	(2) − (3).
(5) Gain (Loss) recognized	($7,461)	(1) − (4).
(6) Ordinary income (§1245 depreciation recapture)	$ 0	Lesser of (3) or (5) (limited to $0).
§1231 (loss)	($7,461)	(5) − (6).

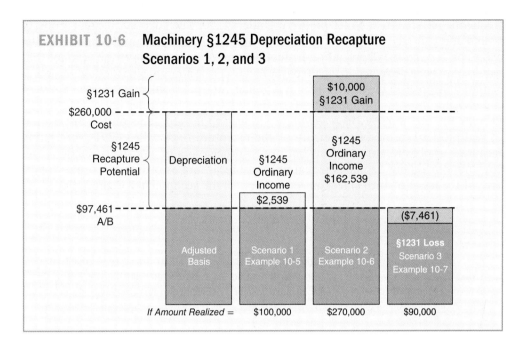

EXHIBIT 10-6   Machinery §1245 Depreciation Recapture Scenarios 1, 2, and 3

Exhibit 10-6 graphically illustrates the §1245 depreciation recapture computations for the machinery sold in Scenarios 1, 2, and 3, presented in Examples 10-5, 10-6, and 10-7, respectively.[10]

In Example 10-5 (Scenario 1), we characterized the gain Teton recognized when it sold its machinery. For completeness, let's characterize the gain or loss Teton recognized on the other two §1245 assets it sold during the year (see Exhibit 10-2). Teton sold its office furniture for $12,000 and its delivery truck for $2,000. What is the amount and character of gain or loss Teton recognizes on the sales of the office furniture and delivery truck?

Answer: Office furniture: $7,000 ordinary income and $2,000 §1231 gain. Delivery truck: ($2,500) §1231 loss.

The computations supporting the answers are as follows:

Description	Office Furniture	Delivery Truck	Explanation
(1) Amount realized	$12,000	$ 2,000	Exhibit 10-2.
(2) Original basis	10,000	15,000	Exhibit 10-2.
(3) Accumulated depreciation	7,000	10,500	Exhibit 10-2.
(4) Adjusted basis	$ 3,000	$ 4,500	(2) − (3).
(5) Gain (Loss) recognized	$ 9,000	($2,500)	(1) − (4).
(6) Ordinary income (§1245 depreciation recapture)	$ 7,000	$ 0	Lesser of (3) or (5), limited to $0.
§1231 gain (loss)	$ 2,000	($2,500)	(5) − (6).

§1250 Depreciation Recapture for Real Property

Depreciable real property, such as an office building or a warehouse, sold at a gain is *not* subject to §1245 depreciation recapture. Rather, it is subject to a different type of recapture called §1250 depreciation recapture. Thus, depreciable real property is

[10]The authors thank PriceWaterhouseCoopers for allowing us to use these figures.

frequently referred to as **§1250 property.** Under §1250, when depreciable real property is sold at a gain, the amount of gain recaptured as ordinary income is limited to the excess of *accelerated* depreciation deductions on the property over the amount that would have been deducted if the taxpayer had used the straight-line method of depreciation to depreciate the asset.[11] However, under current law, all real property is depreciated using the straight-line method so the §1250 recapture rules no longer apply.[12] Despite the fact that *§1250 recapture* no longer applies to gains on the disposition of real property, a modified version of the recapture rules called **§291 depreciation recapture** applies to corporations but not to other types of taxpayers. Under §291, corporations selling depreciable real property recapture as ordinary income 20 percent of the lesser of the (1) recognized gain or (2) the accumulated depreciation.

Example 10-9

What if: Suppose that Teton was organized as a corporation and that, as described in Exhibit 10-2, it sold its existing warehouse. Let's assume the same facts: that Teton sold the warehouse for $350,000, that it initially purchased the warehouse for $275,000, and has deducted $15,000 of straight-line depreciation deductions as of the date of the sale. What is Teton's recognized gain on the sale and what is the character of its gain on the sale?

Answer: $90,000 gain recognized; $3,000 ordinary income and $87,000 §1231 gain. Teton's recognized gain is $90,000 ($350,000 − $260,000 adjusted basis). Under §291, if Teton is a corporation, it must recapture $3,000 as ordinary income (20% × $15,000) [20 percent of the lesser of (1) recognized gain of $90,000 or (2) accumulated depreciation of $15,000].

L04

OTHER PROVISIONS AFFECTING THE RATE AT WHICH GAINS ARE TAXED

Other provisions, other than depreciation recapture, may affect the rate at which taxpayer gains are taxed. The first potentially applies when individuals sell §1250 property at a gain and the second potentially applies when taxpayers sell property to related parties at a gain.

Unrecaptured §1250 Gain for Individuals

When individual taxpayers sell §1250 property at a gain, they are not required to recapture any of the gain as ordinary income under the depreciation recapture rules. Consequently, a gain resulting from the disposition of §1250 property is a §1231 gain and is netted with other §1231 gains and losses to determine whether the taxpayer has a net §1231 gain for the year or a net §1231 loss for the year.

If, after the §1231 netting process (described below), the gain on the sale of the §1250 property is ultimately determined to be a long-term capital gain, the taxpayer must determine the rate at which the gain will be taxed. Tax policy makers determined that the portion of the gain caused by depreciation deductions reducing the basis (called **unrecaptured §1250 gain**) should be taxed at a maximum rate of 25 percent (taxed at the ordinary rate if the ordinary rate is lower than 25 percent) and not the 15 percent rate generally applicable to other types of long-term capital gains.

THE KEY FACTS

Unrecaptured §1250 Gains

- Depreciable real property sold at a gain is §1250 property, but is no longer subject to §1250 recapture.

- The gain that would be §1245 recapture if the asset were §1245 property is called *unrecaptured §1250 gain.*

- Unrecaptured §1250 gain is §1231 gain that, if ultimately characterized as a long-term capital gain, is taxed at a maximum rate of 25 percent.

---

[11]§1250 recapture is commonly referred to as *partial depreciation recapture.*

[12]Accelerated depreciation was allowed for real property placed in service before 1987. Such property had a maximum recovery period of 19 years, which means that as of 2005 all of this property is now fully depreciated under both the accelerated and straight-line depreciation methods—so §1250 recapture does not apply.

Consequently, when an individual sells §1250 property at a gain, the amount of the gain taxed at a maximum rate of 25 percent is the *lesser* of the (1) recognized gain or (2) the accumulated depreciation on the asset.[13] The remainder of the gain is taxed at a maximum rate of 15 percent.

Example 10-10

Teton bought its warehouse for $275,000, depreciated it $15,000, and sold it for $350,000. What is the amount and character of the gain Teton (and thus Steve) reports on the sale (recall that income of sole proprietorships is taxed directly to the owner of the business)?

Answer: $90,000 of §1231 gain, which includes $15,000 of unrecaptured §1250 gain, computed as follows:

Description	Amount	Explanation
(1) Amount realized	$350,000	
(2) Original basis	$275,000	
(3) Accumulated depreciation	($15,000)	
(4) Adjusted basis	$260,000	(2) + (3).
(5) Gain (Loss) recognized	$ 90,000	(1) − (4).
(6) Unrecaptured §1250 gain	$ 15,000	Lesser of (3) or (5).
(7) Remaining §1231 gain	$ 75,000	(5) − (6).
Total §1231 gain	**$ 90,000**	(6) + (7).

What if: Suppose Steve's marginal ordinary tax rate is 35 percent. What amount of tax will he pay on the gain (assuming no other asset dispositions)?

Answer: $15,000, computed as follows:

Description	(1) Gain	(2) Rate	(1) × (2) Tax	Explanation
Long-term capital gain (unrecaptured §1250 gain portion)	$15,000	25%	$ 3,750	This is the gain due to depreciation deductions.
Long-term capital gain (15 percent portion)	$75,000	15%	$11,250	
Totals	$90,000		$15,000	

Because Steve did not sell any other §1231 assets during the year, the entire §1231 gain is treated as a long-term capital gain that is split into a portion taxed at 25 percent and a portion taxed at 15 percent.

Characterizing Gains on the Sale of Depreciable Property to Related Parties

Under §1239, when a taxpayer sells property to a *related party* and the property is depreciable property to the *buyer,* the entire gain on the sale is characterized as ordinary income to the *seller.*[14] In these situations, the tax laws essentially treat the related parties (the buyer and the seller) as the same person. Because the buyer will be offsetting ordinary income with future depreciation deductions associated with the property, the tax laws require the seller to currently recognize ordinary income. Without

[13]The amount taxed at a maximum rate of 25 percent cannot exceed the amount of the taxpayer's net §1231 gain.

[14]§707(b)(2) contains a similar provision for partnerships.

THE KEY FACTS

Related-Party Transactions

▌ All gain recognized from selling property that is a depreciable asset to a related-party buyer is ordinary income (regardless of the character of the asset to the seller).

▌ Related parties include an individual and

· Siblings, spouses, ancestors, lineal descendants, and

· Corporations in which the individual owns more than 50 percent of the stock.

· See §267(b) for others.

this provision, related parties could create tax savings by currently generating capital or §1231 gains through selling appreciated assets to related parties and receiving future ordinary deductions through depreciation expense on the basis of the property (stepped up to fair market value through the sale) in exchange.

The §1239 recapture provision is different from depreciation recapture in the sense that the seller is required to recognize ordinary income *for depreciation deductions the buyer will receive in the future,* while depreciation recapture requires taxpayers to recognize ordinary income *for depreciation deductions they have received in the past.* In both cases, however, the tax laws are designed to provide symmetry between the character of deductions an asset generates and the character of income the asset generates when it is sold. When depreciation recapture and the §1239 recapture provision apply to the same gain, the depreciation recapture rule applies first.

For purposes of §1239, §267 provides the definition of related parties. The definition includes family relationships including siblings, spouses, ancestors, and lineal descendants. It also includes an individual and a corporation if the individual owns more than 50 percent of the stock of the corporation, a partnership and any of its partners, and an S corporation and any of its shareholders.[15]

Example 10-11	

What if: Suppose that Teton is organized as a corporation and Steve is the sole shareholder. Steve sells equipment that he was using for personal purposes to Teton for $90,000 (he originally purchased the equipment for $80,000). The equipment was a capital asset to Steve because he had been using it for personal purposes (he did not depreciate it). What is the amount and character of the gain Steve would recognize on the sale?

Answer: $10,000 of ordinary income (amount realized $90,000 − $80,000 adjusted basis). Even though Steve is selling what is a capital asset to him, because it is a depreciable asset to Teton and because Steve and Teton are considered to be related parties, Steve is required to characterize the entire amount of gain as ordinary under §1239. Without the §1239 provision, Steve would have recognized a capital gain.

L05

CALCULATING NET §1231 GAINS OR LOSSES

Once taxpayers determine the amount and character of gain or loss they recognize on *each* §1231 asset they sell during the year, they still have work to do to determine whether the gains or losses will be treated as ordinary or capital. After recharacterizing §1231 gain as ordinary income under the §1245 and §291 (if applicable) depreciation recapture rules and the §1239 related-party rules, the remaining §1231 gains and losses are netted together. If the gains exceed the losses, the net gain becomes a long-term capital gain (a portion of which may be taxed at maximum rate of 25 percent). If the losses exceed the gains, the net loss is treated as an ordinary loss.

A taxpayer could gain significant tax benefits by discovering a way to have all §1231 gains treated as long-term capital gains and all §1231 losses treated as ordinary losses. The *annual* netting process makes this task impossible for a *particular* year. However, a taxpayer who owns multiple §1231 assets could sell the §1231 loss assets at the end of year 1 and the §1231 gain assets at the beginning of year 2. The taxpayer could benefit from this strategy in three ways: (1) accelerating losses into

---

[15]See §267(b) for more related-party relationships. This section also details the constructive ownership rules where the taxpayer is deemed to own what another related taxpayer owns (for example a married taxpayer is considered to own what her spouse owns).

year 1, (2) deferring gains until year 2, and (3) characterizing the gains and losses due to the §1231 netting process. The **§1231 look-back rule** prevents this strategy.

§1231 Look-Back Rule

The §1231 look-back rule is a *nondepreciation* recapture rule that applies in situations like the one we just described to turn what would otherwise be §1231 gain into ordinary income. That is, the rule affects the character but not the amount of gains on which a taxpayer is taxed. In general terms, the §1231 look-back rule is designed to require taxpayers who recognize net §1231 gains in the current year to recapture (characterize) those gains as ordinary gains to the extent they recognized §1231 losses that were treated as ordinary losses in prior years. Without the look-back rule, taxpayers could carefully time the year in which the §1231 assets are sold to maximize the tax benefits.

In specific terms, the §1231 look-back rule indicates that anytime a taxpayer recognizes a net §1231 gain for a year, the taxpayer must "look-back" to the *five-year* period preceding the current tax year to determine if, during that period, the taxpayer recognized any **unrecaptured §1231 losses** (losses that were deducted as ordinary losses that have not caused subsequent §1231 gains to be recharacterized as ordinary income). The taxpayer starts the process by looking back to the year five years prior to the beginning of the current year. If the taxpayer recognized a net §1231 loss in that period, and had not previously recaptured the loss (by causing a subsequent §1231 gain to be recharacterized as ordinary) in a subsequent year (but prior to the current year), the taxpayer must recharacterize the *current year* net §1231 gain as ordinary income to the extent of that prior year unrecaptured §1231 loss. The prior year loss is then "recaptured," to the extent it caused the current year gain to be treated as ordinary income. If the current year net §1231 gain exceeds the unrecaptured §1231 loss from the year five-years prior, the taxpayer repeats the process for the year four-years prior, and then three-years prior, and so on. It is important to note that a prior year's unrecaptured losses are not netted against the current year's gains (they don't offset the current year gains); rather, they cause the taxpayer to recharacterize a net §1231 gain or a portion of that gain (that would otherwise be characterized as a long-term capital gain) as ordinary income.[16]

Example 10-12

What if: Suppose that Teton began business in year 1 and that it recognized a $7,000 net §1231 loss in year 1. Assume that the current year is year 6 and that Teton reports a *net* §1231 gain of $25,000 for the year. Teton did not recognize any §1231 gains or losses in years 2–5. For year 6, what would be the ultimate character of the $25,000 net §1231 gain?

Answer: $7,000 ordinary income and $18,000 as long-term capital gain. Because it recognized a net §1231 loss in year 1, it must characterize $7,000 of its net §1231 gain in year 6 as ordinary income. The remaining $18,000 §1231 gain is taxed as §1231 gain.

What if: Assume the same facts as above, except that Teton also recognized a $2,000 net §1231 loss in year 5. For year 6, what would be the ultimate character of the $25,000 net §1231 gain?

Answer: $9,000 ordinary income and $16,000 long-term capital gain. Note that the overall gain is still $25,000, but a portion of it is recharacterized as ordinary income under the §1231 look-back rule.

---

[16]If the taxpayer's net §1231 gains include unrecaptured §1250 gains and other 15 percent long-term capital gains, the unrecaptured §1231 losses first recharacterize the unrecaptured §1250 gains as ordinary income.

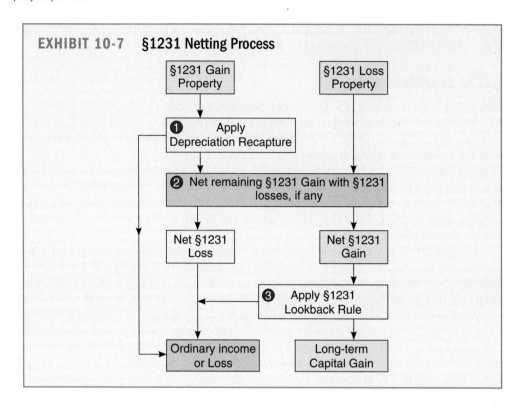

EXHIBIT 10-7   §1231 Netting Process

As we've mentioned several times, ultimately, all of a taxpayer's §1231 gains and losses must be characterized as ordinary or capital for purposes of determining a taxpayer's tax liability. Exhibit 10-7 summarizes the process of characterizing §1231 gains and losses as ordinary or capital.

The following provides details on Steps 1–3 from Exhibit 10-7:

Step 1: Apply the *depreciation* recapture rules (and the §1239 recapture rules) to §1231 assets sold at a gain (any recaptured amounts become ordinary).

Step 2: Net the remaining §1231 gains with the §1231 losses. If the netting process yields a §1231 loss, the net §1231 loss becomes an ordinary loss.

Step 3: If the netting process produces a net §1231 gain, the taxpayer applies the §1231 look-back rule to determine if any of the remaining §1231 gain should be characterized as ordinary gain. Any gain remaining after applying the look-back rule is treated as long-term capital gain (including unrecaptured §1250 gain). This gain is included in the capital gains netting process, which is discussed in Chapter 11.

GAIN OR LOSS SUMMARY

As indicated in Exhibit 10-2, Teton sold several assets during the year. Exhibit 10-8 summarizes the character of the gain or loss Teton (and thus Steve) recognized on each asset sale.

So, how would this information be reported on Steve's tax return? Exhibit 10-9 provides Steve's Form 4797, which summarizes Teton's property transactions and divides the gain and losses between the ordinary gain of $19,539 and the §1231 gain of $179,500. Because the net §1231 gain is treated as a long-term capital gain, it flows to Steve's Schedule D (the form for reporting capital gains and losses). Steve's Schedule D is presented in Exhibit 10-10.

EXHIBIT 10-8   Summary of Teton Gains and Losses on Property Dispositions

Asset	(1) §1245 Ordinary Gain	(2) Total Ordinary Gain	(3) §1231 Gain (Loss)	(2) + (3) Total Gain
Machinery	$2,539	$ 2,539	$ 0	$ 2,539
Office furniture	$7,000	$ 7,000	$ 2,000	$ 9,000
Delivery truck	$ 0	$ 0	($2,500)	($2,500)
Warehouse	$ 0	$ 0	$ 90,000*	$ 90,000
Land	$ 0	$ 0	$100,000	$100,000
§1231 look-back		$10,000	($10,000)**	$ 0
Totals	$9,539	$19,539	$179,500*	$199,039

*Because the warehouse is §1231 property, the $90,000 gain is included in the §1231 gain (loss) column. Further, $15,000 of the $90,000 gain is considered unrecaptured §1250 gain (see Example 10-10).

**This exhibit assumes that Teton had $10,000 of net §1231 losses in the prior five years.

NONRECOGNITION TRANSACTIONS

Taxpayers realizing gains and losses when they sell or exchange property must immediately recognize the gain for tax purposes unless a specific provision in the tax code says otherwise. Under certain tax provisions, taxpayers defer or delay recognizing a gain or loss until a subsequent period. We first explore tax provisions that allow taxpayers to defer recognizing realized gains. Congress allows taxpayers to defer recognizing gains in certain types of exchanges because the exchange itself does not provide the taxpayers with the wherewithal (cash) to pay taxes on the realized gain if the taxpayers were required to immediately recognize the gain. In particular, we discuss common **nonrecognition transactions** such as **like-kind exchanges, involuntary conversions, installment sales,** and other business-related transactions such as business formations and reorganizations.

Like-Kind Exchanges

Taxpayers involved in a business may have valid reasons to trade business assets to others for similar business assets. For example, to increase productivity a taxpayer may want to trade machinery used in the business for the latest model. As we discussed earlier in this chapter, taxpayers exchanging property *realize* gains (or losses) on exchanges just as taxpayers do by selling property for cash. However, taxpayers exchanging property for property are in a different situation than taxpayers selling the same property for cash. Taxpayers exchanging one piece of business property for another haven't changed their relative economic position in the sense that both before and after the exchange they hold an asset for use in their business. Further, exchanges of property do not generate the wherewithal (cash) for the taxpayers to pay taxes on the gain they realize on the exchanges. While taxpayers selling property for cash must immediately recognize gain on the sale, taxpayers exchanging property for assets other than cash must defer recognizing gain (or loss) realized on the exchange if they meet certain requirements. This type of deferred gain (or loss) transaction is commonly referred to as a like-kind (or §1031) exchange.[17]

LO6

[17]Like-kind exchanges are defined in §1031 of the Internal Revenue Code.

EXHIBIT 10-9   Teton's (On Steve's return) Form 4797

Form **4797**	**Sales of Business Property** (Also Involuntary Conversions and Recapture Amounts Under Sections 179 and 280F(b)(2)) ▶ Attach to your tax return. ▶ See separate instructions.	OMB No. 1545-0184 **2008** Attachment Sequence No. **27**

Department of the Treasury Internal Revenue Service

Name(s) shown on return: **Steve Dallimore (Teton Mountaineering Technologies, LLC)**   Identifying number

1 Enter the gross proceeds from sales or exchanges reported to you for 2008 on Form(s) 1099-B or 1099-S (or substitute statement) that you are including on line 2, 10, or 20 (see instructions) ... **1**

Part I   Sales or Exchanges of Property Used in a Trade or Business and Involuntary Conversions From Other Than Casualty or Theft—Most Property Held More Than 1 Year (see instructions)

2	(a) Description of property	(b) Date acquired (mo., day, yr.)	(c) Date sold (mo., day, yr.)	(d) Gross sales price	(e) Depreciation allowed or allowable since acquisition	(f) Cost or other basis, plus improvements and expense of sale	(g) Gain or (loss) Subtract (f) from the sum of (d) and (e)
	Delivery Truck	Yr 0	Yr 4	2,000	10,500	15,000	(2,500)
	Land	Yr 0	Yr 4	175,000	0	75,000	100,000

3 Gain, if any, from Form 4684, line 45	**3**	
4 Section 1231 gain from installment sales from Form 6252, line 26 or 37	**4**	
5 Section 1231 gain or (loss) from like-kind exchanges from Form 8824	**5**	
6 Gain, if any, from line 32, from other than casualty or theft	**6**	92,000
7 Combine lines 2 through 6. Enter the gain or (loss) here and on the appropriate line as follows:	**7**	189,500

Partnerships (except electing large partnerships) and S corporations. Report the gain or (loss) following the instructions for Form 1065, Schedule K, line 10, or Form 1120S, Schedule K, line 9. Skip lines 8, 9, 11, and 12 below.

Individuals, partners, S corporation shareholders, and all others. If line 7 is zero or a loss, enter the amount from line 7 on line 11 below and skip lines 8 and 9. If line 7 is a gain and you did not have any prior year section 1231 losses, or they were recaptured in an earlier year, enter the gain from line 7 as a long-term capital gain on the Schedule D filed with your return and skip lines 8, 9, 11, and 12 below.

8 Nonrecaptured net section 1231 losses from prior years (see instructions)	**8**	10,000
9 Subtract line 8 from line 7. If zero or less, enter -0-. If line 9 is zero, enter the gain from line 7 on line 12 below. If line 9 is more than zero, enter the amount from line 8 on line 12 below and enter the gain from line 9 as a long-term capital gain on the Schedule D filed with your return (see instructions)	**9**	179,500

Part II   Ordinary Gains and Losses (see instructions)

10 Ordinary gains and losses not included on lines 11 through 16 (include property held 1 year or less):

11 Loss, if any, from line 7	**11**	( )
12 Gain, if any, from line 7 or amount from line 8, if applicable	**12**	10,000
13 Gain, if any, from line 31	**13**	9,539
14 Net gain or (loss) from Form 4684, lines 37 and 44a	**14**	
15 Ordinary gain from installment sales from Form 6252, line 25 or 36	**15**	
16 Ordinary gain or (loss) from like-kind exchanges from Form 8824	**16**	
17 Combine lines 10 through 16	**17**	19,539

18 For all except individual returns, enter the amount from line 17 on the appropriate line of your return and skip lines a and b below. For individual returns, complete lines a and b below:

a If the loss on line 11 includes a loss from Form 4684, line 41, column (b)(ii), enter that part of the loss here. Enter the part of the loss from income-producing property on Schedule A (Form 1040), line 28, and the part of the loss from property used as an employee on Schedule A (Form 1040), line 23. Identify as from "Form 4797, line 18a." See **18a**

b Redetermine the gain or (loss) on line 17 excluding the loss, if any, on line 18a. Enter here and on Form 1040, line 14 **18b** 19,539

For Paperwork Reduction Act Notice, see separate instructions.   Cat. No. 13086I   Form **4797** (2008)

EXHIBIT 10-9   Teton's (On Steve's return) Form 4797 (*continued*)

Form 4797 (2008)   Page **2**

Part III	**Gain From Disposition of Property Under Sections 1245, 1250, 1252, 1254, and 1255** (see instructions)

19	(a) Description of section 1245, 1250, 1252, 1254, or 1255 property:				(b) Date acquired (mo., day, yr.)	(c) Date sold (mo., day, yr.)
	A	Machinery			Yr 0	11/1/Yr 4
	B	Office Furniture			Yr 0	Yr 4
	C	Warehouse			Yr 0	Yr 4
	D					

	These columns relate to the properties on lines 19A through		**Property A**	**Property B**	**Property C**	**Property D**
20	Gross sales price (**Note:** *See line 1 before completing.*)	20	100,000	12,000	350,000	
21	Cost or other basis plus expense of sale	21	260,000	10,000	275,000	
22	Depreciation (or depletion) allowed or allowable	22	162,539	7,000	15,000	
23	Adjusted basis. Subtract line 22 from line 21	23	97,461	3,000	260,000	
24	Total gain. Subtract line 23 from line 20	24	2,539	9,000	90,000	
25	**If section 1245 property:**					
a	Depreciation allowed or allowable from line 22	25a	162,539	7,000		
b	Enter the **smaller** of line 24 or 25a	25b	2,539	7,000		
26	**If section 1250 property:** If straight line depreciation was used, enter -0- on line 26g, except for a corporation					
a	Additional depreciation after 1975 (see instructions)	26a				
b	Applicable percentage multiplied by the **smaller** of line 24 or line 26a (see instructions)	26b				
c	Subtract line 26a from line 24. If residential rental property **or** line 24 is not more than line 26a, skip lines	26c				
d	Additional depreciation after 1969 and before 1976	26d				
e	Enter the **smaller** of line 26c or 26d	26e				
f	Section 291 amount (corporations only)	26f				
g	Add lines 26b, 26e, and 26f	26g				
27	**If section 1252 property:** Skip this section if you did not dispose of farmland or if this form is being completed for a partnership (other than an electing large					
a	Soil, water, and land clearing expenses	27a				
b	Line 27a multiplied by applicable percentage (see instructions)	27b				
c	Enter the **smaller** of line 24 or 27b	27c				
28	**If section 1254 property:**					
a	Intangible drilling and development costs, expenditures for development of mines and other natural deposits, and mining exploration costs (see instructions)	28a				
b	Enter the **smaller** of line 24 or 28a	28b				
29	**If section 1255 property:**					
a	Applicable percentage of payments excluded from income under section 126 (see instructions)	29a				
b	Enter the **smaller** of line 24 or 29a (see instructions)	29b				

Summary of Part III Gains. Complete property columns A through D through line 29b before going to line 30.

30	Total gains for all properties. Add property columns A through D, line 24	30	101,539
31	Add property columns A through D, lines 25b, 26g, 27c, 28b, and 29b. Enter here and on line 13	31	9,539
32	Subtract line 31 from line 30. Enter the portion from casualty or theft on Form 4684, line 39. Enter the portion from other than casualty or theft on Form 4797, line 6	32	92,000

Part IV	**Recapture Amounts Under Sections 179 and 280F(b)(2) When Business Use Drops to 50% or Less** (see instructions)

			(a) Section 179	(b) Section 280F(b)(2)
33	Section 179 expense deduction or depreciation allowable in prior years	33		
34	Recomputed depreciation (see instructions)	34		
35	Recapture amount. Subtract line 34 from line 33. See the instructions for where to report	35		

Form **4797** (2008)

EXHIBIT 10-10   Steve's Schedule D (Assumes Steve had no other capital gains and losses other than those incurred by Teton)

SCHEDULE D (Form 1040)	Capital Gains and Losses	OMB No. 1545-0074
Department of the Treasury Internal Revenue Service (99)	▶ Attach to Form 1040 or Form 1040NR. ▶ See Instructions for Schedule D (Form 1040). ▶ Use Schedule D-1 to list additional transactions for lines 1 and 8.	20**08** Attachment Sequence No. **12**

Name(s) shown on return
Steve Dallimore

Your social security number

Part I   Short-Term Capital Gains and Losses—Assets Held One Year or Less

	(a) Description of property (Example: 100 sh. XYZ Co.)	(b) Date acquired (Mo., day, yr.)	(c) Date sold (Mo., day, yr.)	(d) Sales price (see page D-7 of the instructions)	(e) Cost or other basis (see page D-7 of the instructions)	(f) Gain or (loss) Subtract (e) from (d)
1						

2	Enter your short-term totals, if any, from Schedule D-1, line 2 . .	**2**	
3	**Total short-term sales price amounts.** Add lines 1 and 2 in column (d)	**3**	
4	Short-term gain from Form 6252 and short-term gain or (loss) from Forms 4684, 6781, and 8824	**4**	
5	Net short-term gain or (loss) from partnerships, S corporations, estates, and trusts from Schedule(s) K-1	**5**	
6	Short-term capital loss carryover. Enter the amount, if any, from line 8 of your **Capital Loss Carryover Worksheet** on page D-7 of the instructions	**6**	( )
7	**Net short-term capital gain or (loss).** Combine lines 1 through 6 in column (f)	**7**	

Part II   Long-Term Capital Gains and Losses—Assets Held More Than One Year

	(a) Description of property (Example: 100 sh. XYZ Co.)	(b) Date acquired (Mo., day, yr.)	(c) Date sold (Mo., day, yr.)	(d) Sales price (see page D-7 of the instructions)	(e) Cost or other basis (see page D-7 of the instructions)	(f) Gain or (loss) Subtract (e) from (d)
8						

9	Enter your long-term totals, if any, from Schedule D-1, line 9	**9**	
10	**Total long-term sales price amounts.** Add lines 8 and 9 in column (d)	**10**	
11	Gain from Form 4797, Part I; long-term gain from Forms 2439 and 6252; and long-term gain or (loss) from Forms 4684, 6781, and 8824	**11**	179,500
12	Net long-term gain or (loss) from partnerships, S corporations, estates, and trusts from Schedule(s) K-1	**12**	
13	Capital gain distributions. See page D-2 of the instructions	**13**	
14	Long-term capital loss carryover. Enter the amount, if any, from line 13 of your **Capital Loss Carryover Worksheet** on page D-7 of the instructions	**14**	( )
15	**Net long-term capital gain or (loss).** Combine lines 8 through 14 in column (f). Then go to Part III on the back	**15**	179,500

For Paperwork Reduction Act Notice, see Form 1040 or Form 1040NR instructions.   Cat. No. 11338H   Schedule D (Form 1040) 2008

Like-kind exchange treatment can provide taxpayers with significant tax advantages by allowing them to defer gain (and current taxes payable) that would otherwise be recognized immediately.[18] For an exchange to qualify as a like-kind exchange for tax purposes, the transaction must meet the following three criteria:

1. The property is exchanged "solely for like-kind" property.
2. Both the property given up and the property received in the exchange by the taxpayer are either "used in a trade or business" or are "held for investment," by the taxpayer.
3. The "exchange" must meet certain time restrictions.

Below, we discuss each of these requirements in detail.

Definition of Like-Kind Property

The definition of like-kind property depends on whether the property exchanged is real property or tangible personal property. Generally, the definition of like-kind *real* property is much less restrictive than it is for like-kind *personal* property.

Real Property   All real property is considered to be "like-kind" with any other type of real property as long as the real property is used in a trade or business or held for investment. For example, from Teton's perspective, its warehouse on 10 acres would be considered to be like-kind with a nearby condominium complex, a 20-acre parcel of raw land for sale across town, or even a Manhattan skyscraper.

Personal Property   Determining what qualifies as like-kind property for tangible personal property is a little more involved. The Treasury regulations explain that tangible personal property qualifies as "like-kind" if the property transferred and the property received in the exchange is in the same general asset class in Rev. Proc. 87-56 (this is the concept we use in the previous chapter to determine the recovery period for MACRS depreciation).[19] In simpler terms, for personal property to qualify as like-kind property the property given in the exchange and the property received in the exchange must have the same general use to the taxpayer. For example, if Teton were to trade some machinery used in its manufacturing operations for some new machinery to be used in its manufacturing process, the transaction would qualify as a like-kind exchange. However, if Teton were to trade some machinery used in its manufacturing operations for a new delivery truck, the exchange would not qualify as a like-kind exchange.

Property Ineligible for Like-Kind Treatment   Certain types of property are, by definition, excluded from the definition of like-kind property and thus, are not eligible for like-kind treatment.[20] This property includes inventory held for resale (including land held by a developer), most financial instruments (such as stocks, bonds, or notes), domestic property exchanged for foreign property, and partnership interests.[21]

> **THE KEY FACTS**
>
> **Like-Kind Property**
>
> ▪ **Real Property**
>   · All real property used in a trade or business or held for investment is considered "like-kind" with other real property used in a trade or business or held for investment.
>
> ▪ **Personal Property**
>   · Personal property is considered "like-kind" if it has the same general use and is used in a business or held for investment.
>
> ▪ **Ineligible Property**
>   · Inventory.
>   · Most financial instruments.
>   · Partnerships interests.
>   · Domestic property exchanged for property used in a foreign country and all property used in a foreign country.

---

[18]In contrast, financial accounting rules require businesses to recognize (for financial accounting purposes) any gain they realize in a like-kind exchange transaction.

[19]Like-kind is defined in Reg. §1.1031(a)-2(b).

[20]§1031(a)(2).

[21]Property used more than 50 percent of the time in a foreign country is not like-kind with domestic or with other foreign property.

Taxes in the Real World   *A Super Like-Kind Exchange*

Long before the Indianapolis Colts won the 2007 NFL Super Bowl, they were called the Baltimore Colts. Back in 1972, Carrol Rosenbloom, the owner of the Baltimore Colts, wanted to move the Colts franchise to another city. When the NFL blocked the move, Mr. Rosenbloom wanted to sell the Colts franchise and buy another NFL franchise in a different city. However, if he sold the Colts, he would be required to pay a significant amount of tax on the capital gain he would recognize on the sale because the value of the franchise had appreciated significantly from the time he initially acquired the Colts. So, with the help of attorney Hugh Culverhouse, Mr. Rosenbloom engaged in an unprecedented NFL franchise swap. Mr. Culverhouse found Bob Irsay who was willing to buy and then trade the Los Angeles Rams to Mr. Rosenbloom for the Baltimore Colts in a qualifying like-kind exchange. When the dust had settled, Mr. Rosenbloom had acquired a different NFL franchise without having to currently pay tax on the exchange. How's that for a super tax planning strategy?

Property Use

Even when property meets the definition of like-kind property, taxpayers can only exchange the property in a qualifying like-kind exchange if the taxpayer used the transferred property in a trade or business or for investment *and* the taxpayer will use the property received in the exchange in a trade or business or for investment. For example, Teton could exchange its warehouse on 10 acres for a 200-acre parcel of land it intends to hold as an investment in a qualifying like-kind exchange because Teton was using the warehouse in its business and it would hold the land as an investment. However, if Steve exchanged his personal-use cabin in Maine for a personal residence in Wyoming, the exchange would not qualify because Steve used the residence for personal purposes, and he would be using the Wyoming property for personal rather than business or investment purposes. In fact, even if Steve was renting his Maine cabin (it qualifies as investment property) when he exchanged it for his principal residence in Wyoming, the exchange would not qualify for like-kind exchange treatment because *both* properties (the property the taxpayer is giving up and the property the taxpayer is receiving in the exchange) must meet the use test (the personal residence does not qualify as business or investment property). Likewise, if Teton exchanged a business computer for Steve's personal computer, which he uses for playing Halo and Warcraft with his friends, Teton would qualify for like-kind exchange treatment because Teton was using its computer equipment in its business and it will use Steve's computer in its business. However, the exchange would not qualify as a like-kind exchange for Steve because Steve used the computer for personal (not business or investment) purposes. A key takeaway here is that due to the use and other requirements, one party to an exchange may qualify for like-kind treatment and the other party may not. Each party to the exchange must individually determine whether or not the exchange qualifies as a like-kind exchange to her.

Timing Requirements for a Like-Kind Exchange

Many like-kind exchanges involve a simultaneous exchange of like-kind assets. For example, Teton could take its used machinery to a dealer and pick up its new machinery at the same time. However, a simultaneous exchange may not be practical or possible. For example, taxpayers may not always be able to immediately (or even eventually) find another party who is willing to exchange properties with the taxpayer. In these situations taxpayers often use **third-party intermediaries** to facilitate like-kind exchanges. When a third party is involved, the taxpayer transfers the like-kind property to the intermediary and the intermediary sells the property and uses the

---

THE KEY FACTS

Timing Requirements

- Like-kind property exchanges may involve intermediaries.

- Taxpayers must identify replacement "like-kind" property within 45 days of giving up their property.

- "Like-kind" property must be received within 180 days of when the taxpayer transfers property in a "like-kind" exchange.

EXHIBIT 10-11   Diagram of Deferred or Starker Exchange

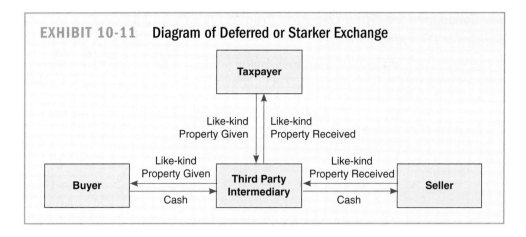

proceeds to acquire the new property for the taxpayer.[22] Because the third party must sell the taxpayer's old property and locate and purchase suitable replacement property, this process is subject to delay. In these types of situations, does a delay in the completion of the exchange disqualify an otherwise allowable like-kind exchange? Not necessarily. The tax laws do not require a simultaneous exchange of assets, but they do impose some timing requirements to ensure that a transaction is completed within a reasonable time in order to qualify as a **deferred** (not simultaneous) **like-kind exchange**—often referred to as a *Starker exchange*.[23]

The two timing rules applicable to like-kind exchanges are (1) the taxpayer must *identify* the like-kind replacement property within 45 days after transferring the property given up in the exchange, and (2) the taxpayer must receive the replacement like-kind property within 180 days (or the due date of the tax return including extensions) after the taxpayer initially transfers property in the exchange.[24] The time limits force the taxpayer to close the transaction within a specified time period, so that the taxpayers can report the tax consequences of the transaction. Exhibit 10-11 provides a diagram of a like-kind exchange involving a third-party intermediary.

When a taxpayer fails to meet the timing requirements, the exchange fails to qualify for like-kind treatment and it thus fully taxable.

Example 10-13

What if: Suppose that on July 1 of year 1 Steve transferred a parcel of real property that he was holding as an investment to a third-party intermediary with the intention of exchanging the property for another suitable investment property. By what date does Steve need to identify the replacement property?

Answer: August 16 of year 1, which is 45 days after Steve transferred the property to the intermediary.

Assuming Steve identifies the replacement property within the 45-day time period, by what date does he need to receive the replacement property in order to qualify for like-kind exchange treatment?

Answer: December 21 of year 1, which is 180 days from July 1, the date he transferred the property to the intermediary.

---

[22]Exchanges involving third-party intermediaries are very common with real estate exchanges. For real estate, taxpayers must use a "qualified exchange intermediary," such as a title company, and cannot use a personal attorney (because attorneys are considered to be the taxpayer's agent).

[23]The term *Starker exchange* refers to a landmark court case that first allowed deferred exchanges (*T.J. Starker, Appellant v. United States of America,* 79-2 USTC ¶9541). The rules for deferred exchanges are found in §1031(a)(3). The tax laws also allow for reverse like-kind exchanges where replacement property is acquired before the taxpayer transfers the like-kind property.

[24]The taxpayer must identify at least one like-kind asset; however, since failure to obtain the asset disqualifies the transaction from having deferred like-kind exchange status, the taxpayer may identify up to three alternatives to hedge against the inability to obtain the first identified asset. Generally, a taxpayer must obtain only one to facilitate the exchange [see Reg. §1.1031(k)-1(c)(4)].

Tax Consequences When Like-Kind Property Is Exchanged Solely for Like-Kind Property

As we've discussed, when taxpayers exchanging property meet the like-kind exchange requirements, they do not recognize gain or loss on the exchange. They also establish or receive an **exchanged basis** in the like-kind property they receive. That is, they exchange the basis they had in the property they gave up and transfer it to the basis of the property they receive.[25]

Example 10-14

Teton would like to trade machinery worth $29,500 (adjusted basis of $18,742), for new machinery worth $29,500. How much gain does Teton recognize on this exchange?

Answer: $0. Teton's exchange qualifies as a like-kind exchange and the $10,758 realized gain ($29,500 amount realized minus $18,742 adjusted basis) is deferred.

What is Teton's basis in the new machinery?

Answer: $18,742, the basis it had in the old machinery it traded in.

THE KEY FACTS

Like-Kind Exchanges Involving Boot

■ Non-like-kind property is known as boot.

■ When boot is given as part of a like-kind transaction:
· The asset received is recorded in two parts: property received in exchange for like-kind property and property received in a sale (bought by the boot).

■ When boot is received:
· Boot received usually creates recognized gain.
· Gain recognized is lesser of gain realized or boot received.

Tax Consequences of Transfers Involving Like-Kind and Non-Like-Kind Property (Boot)

A practical problem with like-kind exchanges is that the value of the like-kind property the taxpayer transfers may differ from the value of the like-kind property the taxpayer receives in the exchange. In these situations the party transferring the lesser-valued asset must also transfer additional property to the other party to equate the values. When this additional property or **"boot"** (non-like-kind property) is transferred, the party receiving it apparently fails the first like-kind exchange requirement that like-kind property be exchanged solely for like-kind property. Nevertheless, if a taxpayer receives boot in addition to like-kind property, the transaction can still qualify for like-kind exchange treatment, but the taxpayer is required to recognize realized gain *to the extent of the boot received.*[26] As a practical matter, this means the taxpayer's recognized gain is the *lesser of* (1) gain realized or (2) boot received.

The reason a taxpayer must recognize gain is that the taxpayer is essentially selling a portion of the like-kind property for the boot in a taxable exchange. The receipt of boot triggers taxable gain (but not a taxable loss) in an otherwise qualifying like-kind exchange. If the taxpayer transfers loss property (adjusted basis is greater than fair market value) in a qualifying like-kind exchange, the taxpayer defers recognition of the loss until the taxpayer sells or disposes of the loss property in a taxable transaction—so it may be important for tax planning purposes to avoid the like-kind exchange rules if the taxpayer wishes to currently recognize the loss.[27] When a taxpayer recognizes gain in a like-kind exchange, the character of the gain depends on the character of the asset transferred by the taxpayer (the depreciation recapture rules apply when characterizing gains).

---

[25]If the asset is a depreciable asset, the taxpayer continues to depreciate the new asset as if it were the old asset.

[26]§1031(b).

[27]§1031(a) states that no gain or loss is recognized in a qualifying like-kind exchange.

Example 10-15

What if: Suppose that Teton trades its used machinery with a value of $29,500 and an adjusted basis of $18,742 ($30,615 historical cost less $11,873 of accumulated depreciation) to the dealer for new machinery valued at $27,500. To equate the value of the property exchanged, the dealer also pays Teton $2,000. What gain or loss does Teton realize on the exchange and what gain or loss does Teton recognize on the exchange?

Answer: $10,758 realized gain and $2,000 recognized gain, calculated as follows:

Description	Amount	Explanation
(1) Amount realized from machine	$27,500	
(2) Amount realized from boot (cash)	2,000	
(3) Total amount realized	$29,500	(1) + (2).
(4) Adjusted basis	18,742	
(5) Gain realized	$10,758	(3) − (4).
Gain recognized	$ 2,000	Lesser of (2) and (5).

What is the character of Teton's $2,000 gain?

Answer: Ordinary income. Because Teton's accumulated depreciation on the asset exceeds its $2,000 gain, Teton must treat the gain as ordinary gain under the §1245 depreciation recapture rules discussed earlier.

What if: Suppose the same facts as above, except that Teton's adjusted basis in the machinery was $29,000. What amount of gain would Teton recognize on the exchange?

Answer: $500. Teton recognizes the lesser of (1) $500 gain realized ($29,500 minus 29,000) or (2) $2,000 boot received.

When taxpayers receive like-kind property and boot in a like-kind exchange, their basis in the like-kind property is computed using the following formula:

$$\text{Basis in like-kind property} = \text{Fair market value of like-kind property received} - \text{deferred gain} + \text{deferred loss}$$

The basis of boot received in the exchange is always the boot's fair market value. This formula for computing basis ensures that the taxpayer's deferred gain or loss on the exchange (the gain or loss realized that is not recognized) is captured in the difference between the value and the basis of the new property received. Consequently, taxpayers defer realized gain or loss on qualifying like-kind exchanges; they do not exclude them. Taxpayers will ultimately recognize the gain or loss when they dispose of the new asset in a taxable transaction.[28]

Example 10-16

What if: Assume the facts in the previous example where Teton traded its used machinery with a value of $29,500 and an adjusted basis of $18,742 to the dealer for new machinery valued at $27,500 and $2,000. Teton recognized $2,000 on the exchange. What is Teton's basis in the new machinery it received from the dealer?

(continued on page 10-26...)

---

[28]Additionally, the deferred gain is subject to depreciation recapture when the asset is eventually disposed of in a taxable disposition.

Answer: $18,742, computed as follows:

Description	Amount	Explanation
(1) Amount realized from machine	$27,500	Fair market value of new machine.
(2) Amount realized from boot (cash)	2,000	
(3) Total amount realized	$29,500	(1) + (2).
(4) Adjusted basis of used machinery	18,742	
(5) Gain realized	$10,758	(3) − (4).
(6) Gain recognized	$ 2,000	Lesser of (2) and (5).
(7) Deferred gain	$ 8,758	(5) − (6).
Adjusted basis in new property	$18,742	(1) − (7).

It is important to note that anything a taxpayer receives in an exchange other than like-kind property is considered boot. This includes cash, other property, or even the amount of a taxpayer's liability transferred to (assumed by) the other party in the exchange. For example, let's return to the previous example. If instead of paying Teton $2,000 of cash, the dealer assumed Teton's $2,000 liability secured by Teton's old machinery, the tax consequences would have been identical. The dealer relieved Teton of $2,000 of debt and the debt relief is treated the same as if the dealer had paid Teton cash and Teton had paid off its $2,000 liability. Finally, when a taxpayer transfers both like-kind property and boot and receives both like-kind property and boot, the amount of realized gain the taxpayer must recognize on the exchange, if any, depends on the form of the boot. When a taxpayer both transfers and receives boot in an otherwise qualifying like-kind exchange, the taxpayer must recognize any realized gain to the extent of the boot received. That is, as a general rule, the taxpayer is not allowed to offset boot received with boot paid.[29] However, when the taxpayer gives and receives boot in the form of liabilities, the taxpayer is allowed to net the boot received and the boot paid.[30]

Reporting Like-Kind Exchanges

Like-kind exchange transactions are reported on Form 8824. Exhibit 10-12 presents the computations from Form 8824 reflecting the like-kind exchange of the machinery in Example 10-14.

Involuntary Conversions

Usually, when taxpayers sell, exchange, or abandon property they intend to do so. However, in certain situations taxpayers may involuntarily dispose of property due to circumstances beyond their control. Thus, the tax law refers to these types of property dispositions as involuntary conversions.[31] Involuntary conversions occur when property is partially or wholly destroyed by a natural disaster or accident, stolen, condemned, or seized via eminent domain by a governmental agency. Tragic examples of this include the results of the September 11, 2001, terrorist attacks and the Hurricane Katrina-related events in 2005. Even in situations when taxpayers

---

[29]Reg. §1.1031(d)-2. However, Reg. §1.1031(j)-1 provides an exception where multiple like-kind exchanges are made in a single exchange.

[30]Further details of this important exception are beyond the scope of our discussion. See the examples provided in Reg. §1.1031(d)-2 for further guidance.

[31]§1033.

EXHIBIT 10-12   Form 8824, Part III (From machine exchange in Example 10-14)

Form 8824 (2008)   Page **2**

Name(s) shown on tax return. Do not enter name and social security number if shown on other side. Steve Dallimore (Teton Mountaineering Technologies, LLC)	Your social security number

| **Part III** | **Realized Gain or (Loss), Recognized Gain, and Basis of Like-Kind Property Received** |

Caution: If you transferred **and** received **(a)** more than one group of like-kind properties or **(b)** cash or other (not like-kind) property, see **Reporting of multi-asset exchanges** in the instructions.

Note: Complete lines 12 through 14 **only** if you gave up property that was not like-kind. Otherwise, go to line 15.

12	Fair market value (FMV) of other property given up	**12**	0	
13	Adjusted basis of other property given up	**13**	0	
14	Gain or (loss) recognized on other property given up. Subtract line 13 from line 12. Report the gain or (loss) in the same manner as if the exchange had been a sale	**14**	0
	Caution: If the property given up was used previously or partly as a home, see **Property used as home** in the instructions.		
15	Cash received, FMV of other property received, plus net liabilities assumed by other party, reduced (but not below zero) by any exchange expenses you incurred (see instructions)	**15**	0
16	FMV of like-kind property you received	**16**	29,500
17	Add lines 15 and 16	**17**	29,500
18	Adjusted basis of like-kind property you gave up, net amounts paid to other party, plus any exchange expenses **not** used on line 15 (see instructions)	**18**	18,742
19	**Realized gain or (loss).** Subtract line 18 from line 17	**19**	10,758
20	Enter the smaller of line 15 or line 19, but not less than zero	**20**	
21	Ordinary income under recapture rules. Enter here and on Form 4797, line 16 (see instructions) . . .	**21**	
22	Subtract line 21 from line 20. If zero or less, enter -0-. If more than zero, enter here and on Schedule D or Form 4797, unless the installment method applies (see instructions)	**22**	
23	**Recognized gain.** Add lines 21 and 22	**23**	
24	Deferred gain or (loss). Subtract line 23 from line 19. If a related party exchange, see instructions . .	**24**	10,758
25	**Basis of like-kind property received.** Subtract line 15 from the sum of lines 18 and 23 . . .	**25**	18,742

experience a loss of property due to theft, disaster, or other circumstances, they might realize a gain for tax purposes if they receive replacement property or insurance proceeds in excess of their basis in the property that was stolen or destroyed.

Taxpayers may experience a tremendous financial hardship if they were required to recognize the realized gain in these circumstances. For example, let's consider a business that acquired a building for $100,000. The building appreciates in value and when the building is worth $150,000 it is destroyed by fire. The building is fully insured at its replacement cost, so the business receives a check from the insurance company for $150,000. The problem for the business is that it realizes a $50,000 gain on this involuntary conversion ($150,000 insurance proceeds minus $100,000 basis in property without considering depreciation). Assuming the business's income is taxed at a 30 percent marginal rate, it must pay $15,000 of tax on the insurance money it receives. This leaves the business with only $135,000 to replace property worth $150,000. This hardly seems equitable. Congress provides special tax laws to allow taxpayers to defer the gains on such *involuntary* conversions.

Taxpayers may defer realized gains on both direct and indirect involuntary conversions. **Direct conversions** involve taxpayers receiving a direct property replacement for the involuntarily converted property. For example, a municipality that is widening its streets may seize land from a taxpayer through its eminent domain and compensate the taxpayer with another parcel of similar value. In this case, the taxpayer would not recognize gain on the exchange of property and would take an adjusted basis in the new parcel of land equal to the taxpayer's basis in the land that was claimed by the municipality. Just as with like-kind exchanges, an exchanged basis

(basis of old property exchanged for basis of new property) ensures that the gain built into the new property (fair market value minus adjusted basis) includes the same gain that was built into the old property.

Indirect conversions involve taxpayers receiving money for the involuntarily converted property through insurance reimbursement or some other type of settlement. Taxpayers meeting the involuntary conversion requirements may *elect* to either recognize or defer realized gain on the conversions. Indirect conversions are more common than direct conversions. Taxpayers can defer realized gains on indirect conversions *if* they acquire **qualified replacement property** within a prescribed time limit, which is generally two years (three years in case of condemnation) after the close of the tax year in which they receive the proceeds.[32]

For both personal and real property, qualified replacement property for an involuntary conversion is defined more narrowly than is like-kind property in a like-kind exchange. The property must be similar *and* related in service or use to qualify.[33] For example, a bowling alley is not qualified replacement property for a pool hall, even though both are real properties used for entertainment purposes. This is stricter than the like-kind exchange rules that would allow the bowling alley to be exchanged for any other real property including a pool hall. Taxpayers recognize realized gain to the extent that they do not reinvest the reimbursement proceeds in qualified property. However, just like in like-kind exchanges, taxpayers do not recognize more gain than they realize on involuntary conversions. That is, a taxpayer's recognized gain on an involuntary conversion can be determined by the following formula: Recognized gain on involuntary conversion = the *lesser of* (1) the gain realized on the conversion or (2) the amount of reimbursement the taxpayer does *not reinvest* in qualified property.

The character of any gain recognized in an involuntary conversion depends on the nature of the asset that was converted—including depreciation recapture if applicable. The basis of the replacement property in an involuntary conversion is calculated in the same way it is for like-kind exchange property. That is, the basis of the replacement property is the fair market value of the new property minus the deferred gain on the conversion.

Example 10-17

What if: Assume that one of Teton's employees was involved in a traffic accident while driving a delivery van. The employee survived without serious injury but the van was totally destroyed. Before the accident, Teton's delivery van had a fair market value of $15,000 and an adjusted basis of $11,000 (the cost basis was $15,000 and accumulated depreciation on the van was $4,000). Teton received $15,000 of insurance proceeds to cover the loss. Teton was considering two alternatives for replacing the van: Alternative 1 was to purchase a new delivery van for $20,000 and Alternative 2 was to purchase a used delivery van for $14,000. What gain or loss does Teton recognize under Alternative 1 and Alternative 2?

Answer: $0 gain recognized under Alternative 1 and $1,000 gain recognized under Alternative 2 (see computations below). Teton qualifies for a deferral because the new property (delivery van) has a similar and related use to the old property (delivery van). But it must recognize gain under Alternative 2 because it did not reinvest all of the insurance proceeds in a replacement van.

(continued on page 10-29...)

---

[32]§1033(a)(2)(B). The time period varies depending on the type of property converted. Additionally, the IRS may consent to an extension of the time period for replacement.

[33]The similar and related-use test has been developed through a variety of administrative pronouncements and judicial law.

What is Teton's basis in the replacement property it acquired under Alternative 1 and Alternative 2?

Answer: $16,000 in Alternative 1 and $11,000 in Alternative 2, computed as follows:

Description	Alternative 1 Amount	Alternative 2 Amount	Explanation
(1) Amount realized	$15,000	$15,000	
(2) Adjusted basis	11,000	11,000	
(3) Gain realized	$ 4,000	$ 4,000	(1) − (2).
(4) Insurance proceeds	$15,000	$15,000	
(5) Proceeds reinvested	$15,000	$14,000	
(6) Amount not reinvested	$ 0	$ 1,000	(4) − (6).
(7) **Gain recognized**	$ 0	$ 1,000	Lesser of (1) and (3).*
(8) Deferred gain	$ 4,000	$ 3,000	(3) − (7).
(9) Value of replacement property	$20,000	$14,000	
Basis of replacement property	**$16,000**	**$11,000**	(9) − (8).

*The character of the $1,000 recognized gain is ordinary income under §1245 (lesser of gain recognized or accumulated depreciation).

Involuntary conversions share several similar concepts with like-kind exchanges such as the concept of qualified property, time period restrictions, the method of computing gain recognized (lesser of realized gain or cash received in addition to qualifying property), and basis calculation (gain or loss from old property remains built into new property). However, one important difference between the two is that taxpayers experiencing a loss from involuntary conversion may immediately deduct the loss as a casualty loss (either personal or business depending on the nature of the loss—as described in Chapter 6).

Installment Sales

In general, when taxpayers sell property for cash and collect the entire sale proceeds in one lump-sum payment, they immediately recognize gain or loss for tax purposes. However, taxpayers selling property don't always collect the sale proceeds in one lump sum from the buyer. For example, the buyer may make a down payment in the year of sale and then agree to pay the remainder of the sale proceeds over a period of time. This type of arrangement is termed an *installment sale.* Technically, an installment sale is any sale of property where the seller receives at least one payment in a taxable year subsequent to the year of disposition of the property.[34] Taxpayers selling property via an installment sale realize gains to the extent the selling price (the amount realized) exceeds their adjusted basis in the property sold. The installment sale rules stay true to the wherewithal-to-pay concept and allow taxpayers selling property in this manner to use the installment method of recognizing *gain* on the sale over time.[35] The installment method does not apply to property sold at a loss. Under the installment method taxpayers determine the amount of realized gain on the transaction, and they recognize the gain pro rata as they receive the installment payments. So, by the time they have received all of the installment payments, they will have recognized all of the initial realized gain.[36] For financial accounting purposes,

[34]§453(b)(1).

[35]Technically, a taxpayer selling property on an installment basis at a gain is required to use the installment method of reporting the recognized gain from the transaction. However, taxpayers are allowed to *elect* out of using the installment method §453(d).

[36]Because the seller in an installment sale is essentially lending money to the buyer, the buyer makes the required installment payments to the seller and the buyer pays interest to the seller for the money the buyer is borrowing. Any interest income received by the seller is immediately taxable as ordinary income. Special rules apply regarding interest for installment sales of more than $150,000 (see §453A).

THE KEY FACTS

Installment Sales

■ Sale of property where the seller receives the sale proceeds in more than one period.

■ Must recognize a portion of gain on each installment payment received.

■ Gains from installments sales are calculated as follows:
 · Gross profit percentage = Gain realized / Amount realized.

■ Inventory, marketable securities, and depreciation recapture cannot be accounted for under installment sale rules.

■ Does not apply to losses.

businesses selling property on an installment basis generally immediately recognize the realized gain on their financial statements.[37]

To determine the amount of gain the taxpayer (seller) must recognize on each installment payment received, the seller must compute the gross profit percentage on the transaction. The gross profit percentage is calculated as follows:

$$\text{Gross profit percentage} = \frac{\text{Gain realized}}{\text{Amount realized}}$$

The gross profit percentage indicates the percentage of the total sales proceeds (or amount realized) that will ultimately be recognized as gain. To determine the portion of a particular payment that is currently recognized as gain, the seller multiplies the amount of the payments received during the year (including the year of sale) by the gross profit percentage (note that once established, the gross profit percentage does not change). Similar to fully taxable transactions, the character of gain taxpayers recognize using the installment method is determined by the character of the asset they sell.

Example 10-18

What if: Suppose Teton decides to sell 5 acres of land adjacent to the warehouse for $100,000. The cost basis for the land is $37,500. Teton agrees to sell the property for four equal payments of $25,000—one now (in year 1) and the other three on January 1 of the next three years—plus interest. What amount of gain does Teton realize on the sale and what amount of gain does it recognize in year 1?

Answer: The realized gain on the transaction is $62,500 ($100,000 amount realized less $37,500 adjusted basis), and the year 1 recognized gain is $15,625, computed as follows:

Description	Amount	Explanation
(1) Amount realized	$100,000	
(2) Adjusted basis	$ 37,500	
(3) Gain realized	$ 62,500	(1) − (2).
(4) Gross profit percentage	62.5%	(3)/(1).
(5) Payment received in year 1	$ 25,000	
Gain recognized in year 1	$ 15,625	(5) × (4).

Because Teton used the land in its trade or business and it held the land for more than a year, the character of the gain is §1231 gain.

The formula for determining the basis of an installment note receivable is (1 − gross profit percentage) × remaining payments on note. Because the gross profit percentage reflects the percentage of the installment payments that will be recognized as gain, (1 − gross profit percentage) is the percentage that is not recognized as gain because it reflects a return of capital (basis).

Gains Ineligible for Installment Reporting

Not all gains are eligible for installment sale reporting. Taxpayers selling marketable securities or inventory on an installment basis may not use the installment method to report gain on the sales. Similarly, any §1245 depreciation recapture is

---

[37]One exception is that the installment sale method similar to the tax installment method is used for financial accounting purposes when there is doubt that the business will collect the receivable.

not eligible for installment reporting and must be recognized in the year of sale.[38] However, the §1231 gain remaining after the §1245 depreciation recapture can be recognized using the installment method. To ensure that any §1245 depreciation recapture is not taxed twice (once immediately and then a second time as payments are received), immediately taxable recapture-related gains are *added to* the adjusted basis of the property sold to determine the gross profit percentage. The increase in basis reduces the gain realized, which also reduces the gross profit percentage and the amount of future gain that will ultimately be recognized as the taxpayer receives the installment payments.

Example 10-19

What if: Assume that Teton agrees to sell some of its machinery for $90,000 for two equal payments of $45,000 plus interest. Teton's original basis was $80,000 and depreciation of $30,000 was taken. Teton will receive one payment in year 1 (the current year) and the other payment in year 2. What is the amount and character of the gain Teton recognizes on the sale in year 1?

Answer: $30,000 ordinary income and $5,000 of §1231 gain, computed as follows:

Description	Amount	Explanation
(1) Amount realized	$90,000	
(2) Original basis	$80,000	
(3) Accumulated depreciation	($30,000)	
(4) Adjusted basis	$50,000	(2) + (3).
(5) Realized gain(loss)	$40,000	(1) − (4).
(6) Ordinary income from depreciation recapture (not eligible for installment reporting)	**$30,000**	Ordinary income. Lesser of (3) and (5).
(7) Gain eligible for installment reporting	$10,000	(5) − (6).
(8) Gross profit percentage	11.11%	(7)/(1).
(9) Payment received in year 1	$45,000	
Installment gain recognized in year 1	**$ 5,000**	(9) × (8) §1231 gain.

What is the amount and character of the gain Teton recognized upon receipt of the payment in year 2?

Answer: $5,000 of §1231 gain ($45,000 payment received times the gross profit percentage of 11.11 percent).

Other Nonrecognition Provisions

There are several tax law provisions that allow businesses to change the form or organization of their business while deferring the realized gains for tax purposes. For example, a sole proprietor can form his business as a corporation or contribute assets to an existing corporation and defer the gain realized on the exchange of assets for an ownership interest in the business entity.[39] Without the nonrecognition provision, the tax cost of forming a corporation may be large enough to deter taxpayers from doing so. Nonrecognition rules also apply to taxpayers forming partnerships or contributing assets to partnerships.[40] In still other transactions involving corporations, such as when corporations merge, a corporation divides (a spin-off or split-up), or corporations otherwise reorganize, they can often do so in

[38]§453(i).
[39]§351.
[40]§721.

THE KEY FACTS

Related-Party Losses

▌ The tax laws essentially treat related parties as though they are the same taxpayer.

▌ Related parties are defined in §267 and include certain family members, related corporations, and other entities (partnerships).

▌ Losses on sales to related parties are not deductible by the seller.

▌ The related party may deduct the previously disallowed loss *to the extent of the gain* on the sale to the unrelated third party.

a tax-free or deferred transaction.[41] While these transactions generally result in deferred gain or loss for the involved parties, the specific details of these topics can easily fill chapters worth of material, and will be not be considered further in this chapter.

Related-Party Loss Disallowance Rules

For equity reasons, the tax laws limit or disallow deductions for losses taxpayers realize when they sell property to related parties. Taxpayers selling business or investment property at a loss to unrelated parties are generally able to deduct the loss.[42] This makes sense in most situations because taxpayers are selling the property for less than their remaining investment (adjusted basis) in the property and after the sale, the taxpayer's investment in the property is completely terminated. In contrast, when a taxpayer sells property at a loss to a related party, she effectively retains some element of control over the property through the related party. Consistent with this idea, the tax laws essentially treat related parties as though they are the same taxpayer and, accordingly, disallow recognition of losses on sales to related parties. Related taxpayers include individuals with family relationships including siblings, spouses, ancestors, and lineal descendants. Related parties also include an individual and a corporation if the individual owns more than 50 percent of the stock of the corporation and a partner and the partnership no matter the partner's ownership percentage.[43]

Example 10-20

What if: Suppose Teton is formed as a corporation and Steve is its sole shareholder. Teton is looking to make some long-term investments to fund its anticipated purchase of a new manufacturing facility. Steve currently owns 1,000 shares of stock in his previous company Northeastern Corp., which he intends to sell in the near future. Steve initially paid $40 a share for the stock but the stock is currently valued at $30 a share. While Steve believes the stock has good long-term potential, he needs cash now to purchase a personal residence in Cody, Wyoming. Steve believes selling the shares to Teton makes good sense because he can deduct the loss and save taxes now and Teton can benefit from the expected long-term appreciation of the stock. If Steve sells 1,000 shares of Northeastern Corp. stock to Teton for $30 per share, what amount of loss will he realize and what amount of loss will he recognize for tax purposes?

Answer: $10,000 loss realized and $0 loss recognized, determined as follows:

Description	Amount	Explanation
(1) Amount realized on sale	$30,000	(1,000 × $30).
(2) Adjusted basis in stock	40,000	(1,000 × $40).
(3) **Loss realized on sale**	**($10,000)**	(1) − (2).
Loss recognized on sale	**$ 0**	Losses on sales to related parties are disallowed.

Because Steve owns more than 50 percent of Teton (he owns 100 percent), Steve and Teton are considered to be related parties. Consequently, Steve is not allowed to recognize any loss on the sale.

---

[41]§368 contains the numerous variations and requirements of these tax-deferred reorganizations.

[42]Capital losses are subject to certain limitations for individuals and corporate taxpayers (§1211).

[43]§267(a). The related-party rules include both direct ownership as well as indirect ownership (ownership attributed to the taxpayer from related parties). See §267(c) for a description of the indirect ownership rules

As we discussed above, the tax laws essentially treat related sellers and buyers as a single entity. Thus, while taxpayers are not allowed to immediately deduct losses when they sell property to related parties, the related party *buyer* may be able to deduct the related party *seller*'s disallowed loss if the related buyer subsequently sells the property to an *unrelated* third party at a gain. The rules follow:

- If the related buyer sells the property at a gain (the related-party buyer sells it for more than she purchased it for) greater than the disallowed loss, the entire loss that was disallowed for the related-party seller is deductible by the buyer.
- If the related-party buyer subsequently sells the property and the related-party seller's disallowed loss exceeds the related party's gain on the subsequent sale, the related-party buyer may only deduct or offset the previously disallowed loss *to the extent of the gain* on the sale to the unrelated third party—the remaining disallowed loss expires unused.
- If the related-party buyer sells the property for less than her purchase price from the related seller, the disallowed loss expires unused.

Example 10-21

What if: Let's return to the previous example where Steve sold 1,000 shares of Northeastern Corp. stock to Teton (a corporation) for $30,000. As we discovered in that example, Steve realized a $10,000 loss on the sale, but he was not allowed to deduct it because Steve and Teton are related parties. Let's assume that a few years after Teton purchased the stock from Steve, Teton sells the Northeastern Corp. stock to an unrelated third party. What gain or loss does *Teton* recognize when it sells the stock in each of three scenarios, assuming it sells the stock for $37,000 in Scenario 1, $55,000 in Scenario 2, and $25,000 in Scenario 3?

Answer: $0 gain or loss in Scenario 1, $15,000 gain in Scenario 2, and $5,000 loss in Scenario 3, computed as follows:

Description	Scenario 1	Scenario 2	Scenario 3	Explanation
(1) Amount realized	$37,000	$55,000	$25,000	
(2) Adjusted basis	$30,000	$30,000	$30,000	Example 10-20 (Teton's purchase price).
(3) Realized gain (loss)	$ 7,000	$25,000	($5,000)	(1) − (2).
(4) Benefit of Steve's ($10,000) disallowed loss	($7,000)	($10,000)	$ 0	Loss benefit limited to realized gain.
Recognized gain (loss)	$ 0	$15,000	($5,000)	(3) + (4).

In Scenario 1 $3,000 of Steve's $10,000 remaining disallowed loss expires unused. In Scenario 3, Steve's entire $10,000 disallowed loss expires unused.

CONCLUSION

This chapter describes and discusses the tax consequences associated with sales and other types of property dispositions. We've learned how to determine the amount of gain or loss taxpayers recognize when they sell or otherwise dispose of property, and we've learned how to determine the character of these gains and losses. Tax accountants who understand the rules and concepts of property dispositions are able to comply with the tax law and advise clients of potential tax-planning opportunities and avoid pitfalls associated with various nonrecognition provisions.

SUMMARY

LO1 Calculate the amount of gain or loss recognized on the disposition of assets used in a trade or business.

- Dispositions occur in the form of sales, trades, or other realization events.
- Gain realized is the amount realized less the adjusted basis of an asset.
- Amount realized is everything of value received in the transaction less any selling costs.
- Adjusted basis is the historical cost or basis of an asset less any cost recovery deductions applied against the asset.
- Gain is realized on every disposition; however, not all realized gains are recognized currently.

LO2 Describe the general character types of gain or loss recognized on property dispositions.

- Recognized gains must be characterized as ordinary, capital, or §1231. An asset's character is a function of the asset's use and holding period.
- Ordinary assets are derived from normal transactions of the business (revenues and accounts receivable), sale of short-term trade or business assets, and depreciation recapture.
- Capital assets are assets that are held either for investment or for personal use (a taxpayer's principal residence).
- §1231 assets consist of property used in a taxpayer's trade or business that has been held for more than one year.
- Net §1231 assets receive the best of both worlds—net §1231 gains become capital and net §1231 losses become ordinary.

LO3 Explain the rationale for and calculate depreciation recapture.

- §1231 assets, other than land, are subject to cost recovery deductions (depreciation), which generate ordinary deductions.
- Gains that are created through depreciation deductions are subject to depreciation recapture. Any remaining gain is §1231 gain.
- Depreciation recapture does not change the amount of the gain but simply converts or recharacterizes the gain from §1231 to ordinary.
- Different recapture rules apply to tangible personal property (§1245) and real property (§291).

LO4 Describe the tax treatment of unrecaptured §1250 gains and determine the character of gains on property sold to related parties.

- When individuals sell §1250 property at a gain, the portion of the gain generated by depreciation deductions is called unrecaptured §1250 gain.
- This gain is a §1231 gain that, if treated as a capital gain after the netting process, is taxed at a maximum rate of 25 percent.
- If a taxpayer sells an asset at a gain to a related party and the asset is a depreciable asset to the related party, the seller must characterize the entire gain as ordinary income.

LO5 Describe the tax treatment of §1231 gains or losses, including the §1231 netting process.

- After applying the depreciation recapture rules, taxpayers calculate the net §1231 gain or loss.
- If a net §1231 loss results, the loss will become ordinary and offset ordinary income.
- If a net §1231 gain results, the §1231 look-back rule must be applied.
- After applying the look-back rule, any remaining net §1231 gain is a long-term capital gain.

LO6 Explain common exceptions to the general rule that realized gains and losses are recognized currently.

- Like-kind exchanges involve trading or exchanging business assets for similar business assets. The gain is deferred unless boot or non-like-kind property is received.

■ Involuntary conversions are the losses on property through circumstances beyond tax-payers' control. Reasons include natural disasters, accidents, theft, or condemnation.

■ Installment sales occur when any portion of the amount realized is received in a year subsequent to the disposition.

■ §267 related-party losses are disallowed but the related-party buyer may be able to deduct the disallowed loss if she subsequently sells the property at a gain.

KEY TERMS

adjusted basis (10-2)	installment sale (10-17)	recognized gain or loss (10-4)
amount realized (10-2)	involuntary conversion (10-17)	§291 depreciation recapture (10-12)
boot (10-24)	like-kind exchange (10-17)	§1231 assets (10-6)
capital asset (10-5)	nonrecognition transaction (10-17)	§1231 look-back rule (10-15)
deferred like-kind exchange (10-23)	ordinary asset (10-5)	§1245 property (10-8)
depreciation recapture (10-7)	production of income (10-5)	§1250 property (10-12)
direct conversion (10-27)	qualified replacement property (10-28)	third-party intermediaries (10-22)
exchanged basis (10-24)	realized gain or loss (10-3)	unrecaptured §1231 losses (10-15)
indirect conversion (10-28)	recapture (10-9)	unrecaptured §1250 gain (10-12)

DISCUSSION QUESTIONS

1. **(LO1)** Compare and contrast different ways in which a taxpayer triggers a realization event by disposing of an asset.

2. **(LO1)** Potomac Corporation wants to sell a warehouse that it has used in its business for 10 years. Potomac is asking $450,000 for the property. The warehouse is subject to a mortgage of $125,000. If Potomac accepts Wyden Inc.'s offer to give Potomac $325,000 in cash and assume full responsibility for the mortgage on the property, what amount does Potomac realize on the sale?

3. **(LO1)** Montana Max sells a 2,500-acre ranch for $1,000,000 in cash, a note receivable of $1,000,000, and debt relief of $2,400,000. He also pays selling commissions of $60,000. In addition, Max agrees to build a new barn on the property (cost $250,000) and spend $100,000 upgrading the fence on the property before the sale. What is Max's amount realized on the sale?

4. **(LO1)** Hawkeye sold farming equipment for $55,000. It bought the equipment four years ago for $75,000, and it has since claimed a total of $42,000 in depreciation deductions against the asset. Explain how to calculate Hawkeye's adjusted basis in the farming equipment.

5. **(LO1)** When a taxpayer sells an asset, what is the difference between realized and recognized gain or loss on the sale?

6. **(LO2)** What does it mean to characterize a gain or loss? Why is characterizing a gain or loss important?

7. **(LO2)** Explain the difference between ordinary, capital, and §1231 assets.

8. **(LO2)** Discuss the reasons why individuals generally prefer capital gains over ordinary gains. Explain why corporate taxpayers might prefer capital gains over ordinary gains.

9. **(LO2)** Dakota Conrad owns a parcel of land he would like to sell. Describe the circumstances in which the sale of the land would generate §1231 gain or loss, ordinary gain or loss, or capital gain or loss. Also, describe the circumstances where Dakota would not be allowed to deduct a loss on the sale.

10. **(LO2)** Lincoln has used a piece of land in her business for the past five years. The land qualifies as §1231 property. It is unclear whether Lincoln will have to recognize a gain or loss when she eventually sells the asset. She asks her accountant how the gain or loss would be characterized if she decides to sell. Her accountant said that selling §1231 assets gives sellers "the best of both worlds." Explain what her accountant means by "the best of both worlds."

11. **(LO3)** Explain Congress's rationale for depreciation recapture.

12. **(LO3)** Compare and contrast §1245 recapture and §1250 recapture.

13. **(LO3)** Why is depreciation recapture not required when assets are sold at a loss?

14. **(LO3)** What are the similarities and differences between the tax benefit rule we discussed in Chapter 5 and depreciation recapture?

15. **(LO3, LO4)** Are both corporations and individuals subject to depreciation recapture when they sell depreciable real property at a gain? Explain.

16. **(LO4)** How is unrecaptured §1250 gain for individuals similar to depreciation recapture? How is it different?

17. **(LO4)** Explain why gains from depreciable property sold to a related taxpayer are treated as ordinary income under §1239.

18. **(LO5)** Bingaman Resources, a Taos-based corporation, sold two depreciable §1231 assets during the year. One asset resulted in a large gain (the asset was sold for more than it was purchased for) and the other resulted in a small loss. Describe the §1231 netting process for Bingaman.

19. **(LO5)** Jeraldine believes that when the §1231 look-back rule applies, the taxpayer deducts a §1231 loss in a previous year against §1231 gains in the current year. Explain whether Jeraldine's description is correct.

20. **(LO5)** Explain the purpose behind the §1231 look-back rule.

21. **(LO5)** Does a taxpayer apply the §1231 look-back rule in a year when the taxpayer recognizes a net §1231 loss? Explain.

22. **(LO5)** How would you describe the application of the §1231 look-back rule to a friend who knows little about taxation?

23. **(LO4, LO5)** Describe the circumstances in which an individual taxpayer with a net §1231 gain will have different portions of the gain taxed at different rates.

24. **(LO6)** Rocky and Bullwinkle Partnership sold a parcel of land during the current year and realized a gain of $250,000. Rocky and Bullwinkle did not recognize gain related to the sale of the land on its tax return. Is this possible? Explain how a taxpayer could realize a gain but not recognize it.

25. **(LO6)** Why does Congress allow taxpayers to defer gains on like-kind exchanges? How do the tax laws ensure that the gains (or losses) are deferred and not permanently excluded from a taxpayer's income?

26. **(LO6)** Compare and contrast the like-kind property requirements for real property and for personal property for purposes of qualifying for a like-kind exchange. Explain whether a car held by a corporation for delivering documents will qualify as like-kind property with a car held by an individual for personal use.

27. **(LO6)** Salazar Inc., a Colorado company, is relocating to a nearby town. It would like to trade its real property for some real property in the new location. While Salazar has found several prospective buyers for its real property and has also located several properties that are acceptable in the new location, it cannot find anyone that is willing to trade Salazar Inc. for its property in a like-kind exchange. Explain how a third-party intermediary could facilitate Salazar's like-kind exchange.

28. **(LO6)** Minuteman wants to enter into a like-kind exchange by exchanging its old New England manufacturing facility for a ranch in Wyoming. Minuteman is using a third-party intermediary to facilitate the exchange. The purchaser of

the manufacturing facility wants to complete the transaction immediately but, for various reasons, the ranch transaction will not be completed for three to four months. Will this delay cause a problem for Minuteman's desire to accomplish this through a like-kind exchange? Explain.

29. **(LO6)** Olympia Corporation, of Kittery, Maine, wants to exchange its manufacturing machinery for Bangor Company's machinery. Both parties agree that that Olympia's machinery is worth $100,000 and that Bangor's machinery is worth $95,000. Olympia would like the transaction to qualify as a like-kind exchange. What could the parties do to equalize the value exchanged but still allow the exchange to qualify as a like-kind exchange? How would the necessary change affect the tax consequences of the transaction?

30. **(LO6)** Compare and contrast the similarities and differences between like-kind exchanges and involuntary conversions for tax purposes?

31. **(LO6)** What is an installment sale? How do the tax laws ensure that taxpayers recognize all the gain they realize on an installment sale? How is depreciation recapture treated in an installment sale? Explain the gross profit ratio and how it relates to gains recognized under installment method sales.

32. **(LO6)** Mr. Kyle owns stock in a local publicly traded company. Although the stock price has declined since he purchased it two years ago, he likes the long-term prospects for the company. If Kyle sells the stock to his sister because he needs some cash for a down payment on a new home, is the loss deductible? If Kyle is right and the stock price increases in the future, how is his sister's gain computed if she sells the stock?

PROBLEMS

33. **(LO1)** Rafael sold an asset to Jamal. What is Rafael's amount realized on the sale in each of the following alternative scenarios?

    a. Rafael received $80,000 of cash and a vehicle worth $10,000. Rafael also pays $5,000 in selling expenses.
    b. Rafael received $80,000 of cash and was relieved of a $30,000 mortgage on the asset he sold to Jamal. Rafael also paid a commission of $5,000 on the transaction.
    c. Rafael received $20,000 of cash, a parcel of land worth $50,000, and marketable securities of $10,000. Rafael also paid a commission of $8,000 on the transaction.

34. **(LO1)** Shasta Corporation sold a piece of land to Bill for $45,000. Shasta bought the land two years ago for $30,600. What gain or loss does Shasta realize on the transaction?

35. **(LO1)** Lassen Corporation sold a machine to a machine dealer for $25,000. Lassen bought the machine for $55,000 and has claimed $15,000 of depreciation expense on the machine. What gain or loss does Lassen realize on the transaction?

36. **(LO2)** Identify each of White Corporation's following assets as an ordinary, capital, or §1231 asset.

    a. Two years ago, White used its excess cash to purchase a piece of land as an investment.
    b. Two years ago, White purchased land and a warehouse. It uses these assets in its business.
    c. Manufacturing machinery White purchased earlier this year.
    d. Inventory White purchased 13 months ago, but is ready to be shipped to a customer.

   e. Office equipment White has used in its business for the past three years.

   f. 1,000 shares of stock in Black corporation that White purchased two years ago because it was a good investment.

   g. Account receivable from a customer with terms 2/10 net 30.

   h. Machinery White held for three years and then sold at a loss of $10,000.

37. **(LO3, LO4)** In year 0, Canon purchased a machine to use in its business for $56,000. In year 3, Canon sold the machine for $42,000. Between the date of the purchase and the date of the sale, Canon depreciated the machine by $32,000.

   a. What is the amount and character of the gain Canon will recognize on the sale, assuming that it is a partnership?

   b. What is the amount and character of the gain Canon will recognize on the sale, assuming that it is a corporation?

   c. What is the amount and character of the gain Canon will recognize on the sale, assuming that it is a corporation and the sale proceeds were increased to $60,000?

   d. What is the amount and character of the gain Canon will recognize on the sale, assuming that it is a corporation and the sale proceeds were decreased to $20,000?

38. **(LO3, LO4)** In year 0, Longworth Partnership purchased a machine for $40,000 to use in its business. In year 3, Longworth sold the machine for $35,000. Between the date of the purchase and the date of the sale, Longworth depreciated the machine by $22,000.

   a. What is the amount and character of the gain Longworth will recognize on the sale?

   b. What is the amount and character of the gain Longworth will recognize on the sale if the sale proceeds were increased to $45,000?

   c. What is the amount and character of the gain Longworth will recognize on the sale if the sale proceeds were decreased to $15,000?

39. **(LO3, LO4)** On August 1 of year 0, Dirksen purchased a machine for $20,000 to use in its business. On December 4 of year 0, Dirksen sold the machine for $18,000.

   a. What is the amount and character of the gain Dirksen will recognize on the sale?

   b. What is the amount and character of the gain Dirksen will recognize on the sale if the machine was sold on January 15 of year 1 instead?

40. **(LO3, LO4)** Rayburn Corporation has a building that it bought during year 0 for $850,000. It sold the building in year 5. During the time it held the building Rayburn depreciated it by $100,000. What is the amount and character of the gain or loss Rayburn will recognize on the sale in each of the following alternative situations?

   a. Rayburn receives $840,000.

   b. Rayburn receives $900,000.

   c. Rayburn receives $700,000.

41. **(LO3, LO4)** Moran owns a building he bought during year 0 for $150,000. He sold the building in year 6. During the time he held the building he depreciated it by $32,000. What is the amount and character of the gain or loss Moran will recognize on the sale in each of the following alternative situations?

   a. Moran received $145,000.

   b. Moran received $170,000.

   c. Moran received $110,000.

42. **(LO3, LO4, LO5)** Hart, an individual, bought an asset for $500,000 and has   ■ **planning**
    claimed $100,000 of depreciation deductions against the asset. Hart has a
    marginal tax rate of 30 percent. Answer the questions presented in the follow-
    ing alternative scenarios (assume Hart had no property transactions other than
    those described in the problem):

    a. What is the amount and character of Hart's recognized gain if the asset is
       tangible personal property sold for $450,000? What effect does the sale have
       on Hart's tax liability for the year?

    b. What is the amount and character of Hart's recognized gain if the asset is
       tangible personal property sold for $550,000? What effect does the sale have
       on Hart's tax liability for the year?

    c. What is the amount and character of Hart's recognized gain if the asset is
       tangible personal property sold for $350,000? What effect does the sale have
       on Hart's tax liability for the year?

    d. What is the amount and character of Hart's recognized gain if the asset is a
       nonresidential building sold for $450,000? What effect does the sale have on
       Hart's tax liability for the year?

    e. Now assume that Hart is a corporation. What is the amount and character
       of its recognized gain if the asset is a nonresidential building sold for
       $450,000? What effect does the sale have on Hart's tax liability for the year
       (assume the same 30 percent marginal tax rate)?

    f. Now assuming that the asset is real property, which entity type should be
       used to minimize the taxes paid on real estate gains?

43. **(LO4)** Luke sold a building and the parcel of land the building is built on to
    his brother at fair market value. The fair market value of the building was
    determined to be $325,000; Luke built the building several years ago at a cost
    of $200,000. Luke had claimed $45,000 of depreciation expense on the build-
    ing. The fair market value of the land was determined to be $210,000; Luke
    purchased the land many years ago for $130,000. Luke's brother will use the
    building in his business.

    a. What is the amount and character of Luke's recognized gain or loss on the
       building?

    b. What is the amount and character of Luke's recognized gain or loss on the
       land?

44. **(LO5)** Buckley, an individual, began business two years ago and has never sold
    a §1231 asset. Buckley owned each of the assets for several years. In the current
    year, Buckley sold the following business assets:

Asset	Original Cost	Accumulated Depreciation	§1231 Gain/Loss
Computers	$ 6,000	$ 2,000	($3,000)
Machinery	$ 10,000	$ 4,000	($2,000)
Furniture	$ 20,000	$12,000	$7,000
Building	$100,000	$10,000	($1,000)

Assuming Buckley's marginal ordinary income tax rate is 35 percent, answer
the questions for the following alternative scenarios:

    a. What are Buckley's gains or losses for the current year? What effect do the
       gains and losses have on Buckley's tax liability?

    b. Assume that the building was sold at a $6,000 gain instead. What are
       Buckley's gains or losses for the current year? What effect do the gains and
       losses have on Buckley's tax liability?

    c. Assume that the building was sold at a $15,000 gain instead. What are Buckley's gains or losses for the current year? What effect do the gains and losses have on Buckley's tax liability?

■ planning 45. **(LO5)** Aruna, a sole proprietor, wants to sell two assets that she no longer needs for her business. Both assets qualify as §1231 assets. The first is machinery and will generate a $10,000 §1231 loss on the sale. The second is land that will generate a $7,000 §1231 gain on the sale. Aruna's ordinary marginal tax rate is 30 percent.

    a. Assuming she sells both assets in December of year 1 (the current year), what effect will the sales have on Aruna's tax liability?

    b. Assuming that Aruna sells the land in December of year 1 and the machinery in January of year 2, what effect will the sales have on Aruna's tax liability for each year?

    c. Explain why selling the assets in separate years will result in tax savings for Aruna.

46. **(LO5)** Bourne Guitars, a corporation, reported a $157,000 net §1231 gain for year 6.

    a. Assuming Bourne reported $50,000 of unrecaptured §1231 losses during years 1–5, what amount of Bourne's net §1231 gain for year 6, if any, is treated as ordinary income?

    b. Assuming Bourne's unrecaptured §1231 losses from years 1–5 were $200,000, what amount of Bourne's net §1231 gain for year 6, if any, is treated as ordinary income?

■ planning 47. **(LO5)** Tonya Jefferson, a sole proprietor, runs a successful lobbying business in Washington, DC. She doesn't sell many business assets, but she is planning on retiring and selling her historic townhouse, which she runs her business from, in order to buy a place somewhere sunny and warm. Tonya's townhouse is worth $1,000,000 and the land is worth another $1,000,000. The original basis in the townhouse was $600,000, and she has claimed $250,000 of depreciation deductions against the asset over the years. The original basis in the land was $500,000. Tonya has located a buyer that would like to finalize the transaction in December of the current year. Tonya's marginal ordinary income tax rate is 35 percent.

    a. What amount of gains or losses does Tonya recognize on the sale? What is the character of the gains or losses? What effect do the gains and losses have on her tax liability?

    b. In additional to the original facts, assume that Tonya reports the following unrecaptured 1231 loss:

Year	Net §1231 Gains/(Losses)
Year 1	($200,000)
Year 2	$0
Year 3	$0
Year 4	$0
Year 5	$0
Year 6 (current year)	?

    What amount of gains or losses does Tonya recognize on the sale? What is the character of the gains or losses? What effect do the gains or losses have on her year 6 (the current year) tax liability?

    c. Assuming the unrecaptured 1231 loss in part (b), as Tonya's tax advisor could you make a suggestion as to when Tonya should sell the townhouse in order to reduce her taxes? What would Tonya's tax liability be if she adopts your recommendation?

48. **(LO5)** Morgan's Water World (MWW), an LLC, opened several years ago and reports the following net §1231 gains and losses since it began business.

Year	Net §1231 Gains/(Losses)
Year 1	($11,000)
Year 2	$ 5,000
Year 3	($21,000)
Year 4	($4,000)
Year 5	$ 17,000
Year 6	($43,000)
Year 7 (current year)	$113,000

What amount, if any, of the year 7 $113,000 net §1231 gain is treated as ordinary income?

49. **(LO5)** Han runs a sole proprietorship. Hans reported the following net §1231 gains and losses since he began business:

Year	Net §1231 Gains/(Losses)
Year 1	($110,000)
Year 2	$15,000
Year 3	$ 0
Year 4	$ 0
Year 5	$10,000
Year 6	$ 0
Year 7 (current year)	$50,000

a. What amount, if any, of the year 7 (current year) $50,000 net §1231 gain is treated as ordinary income?

b. Assume that the $50,000 net §1231 gain occurs in year 6 instead of year 7. What amount of the gain would be treated as ordinary income in year 6?

50. **(LO6)** Independence Corporation needs to replace some of the assets used in its trade or business and is contemplating the following exchanges:

Exchange	Asset Given Up by Independence	Asset Received by Independence
a	Band saw	Band saw
b	Machinery used in textiles	Machinery used for wood working
c	Passenger automobile used for deliveries	Heavy duty van that seats two and has a large cargo box
d	Large warehouse on two acres	Small warehouse on twenty-two acres
e	Office building in Green Bay, WI, used in the business	Apartment complex in Newport Beach, CA, that will be held as an investment

Determine whether each exchange qualifies as a like-kind exchange? Also, explain the rationale for why each qualifies or does not qualify as a like-kind exchange.

51. **(LO6)** Kase, an individual, purchased some property in Potomac, Maryland, for $150,000 approximately 10 years ago. Kase is approached by a real estate agent representing a client who would like to exchange a parcel of

land in North Carolina for Kase's Maryland property. Kase agrees to the exchange. What are Kase's realized gain or loss, recognized gain or loss, and basis in the North Carolina property in each of the following alternative scenarios?

a. The transaction qualifies as a like-kind exchange and the fair market value of each property is $675,000.

b. The transaction qualifies as a like-kind exchange and the fair market value of each property is $100,000.

research

52. **(LO6)** Longhaul Trucking traded two smaller trucks (each had a 10,000-pound gross weight) for one larger truck (18,000-pound gross weight). Do the trucks qualify as like-kind property (*Hint:* because the trucks are tangible personal property they must be the same asset class to be like-kind assets). You should use Rev. Proc. 87-56 to determine the asset classes for the trucks.

research

53. **(LO6)** Twinbrook Corporation needed to upgrade to a larger manufacturing facility. Twinbrook first acquired a new manufacturing facility for $2,100,000 cash, and then transferred the facility it was using (building and land) to White Flint Corporation for $2,000,000 three months later. Does the exchange qualify for like-kind exchange treatment (*Hint:* examine Revenue Procedures 2000-37 and 2004-51)? If not, can you propose a change in the transaction that will allow it to qualify?

research

54. **(LO6)** Woodley Park Corporation currently owns two parcels of land (parcel 1 and parcel 2). It owns a warehouse facility on parcel 1. Woodley needs to acquire a new and larger manufacturing facility. Woodley was approached by Blazing Fast Construction (who specializes in prefabricated warehouses) about acquiring Woodley's existing warehouse on parcel 1. Woodley indicated that it prefers to exchange its existing facility for a new and larger facility in a qualifying like-kind exchange. Blazing Fast indicated that it could construct a new manufacturing facility on parcel 2 to Woodley's specification within four months. Woodley and Blazing Fast agreed to the following arrangement. First, Blazing Fast would construct the new warehouse on parcel 2 and then relinquish the property to Woodley within four months. Woodley would then transfer the warehouse facility and land parcel 1 to Blazing Fast. All of the property exchanged in the deal was identified immediately and the construction was completed within 180 days. Does the exchange of the new building for the old building and parcel 1 qualify as a like-kind exchange (see *DeCleene v. Commissioner,* 115 TC 457)?

55. **(LO6)** Metro Corp. traded machine A for machine B. Metro originally purchased machine A for $50,000 and machine A's adjusted basis was $25,000 at the time of the exchange. What is Metro's realized gain or loss, recognized gain or loss, and adjusted basis in machine B in each of the following alternative scenarios?

a. The fair market value of machine A and of machine B is $40,000 at the time of the exchange. The exchange does not qualify as a like-kind exchange.

b. The fair market value of machine A and of machine B is $40,000. The exchange qualifies as a like-kind exchange

c. The fair market value of machine A is $35,000 and machine B is valued at $40,000. Metro exchanges machine A and $5,000 cash for machine B. Machine A and machine B are like-kind property.

d. The fair market value of machine A is $45,000 and Metro trades machine A for machine B valued at $40,000 and $5,000 cash. Machine A and machine B are like-kind property.

56. **(LO6)** Prater Inc. enters into an exchange in which it gives up its warehouse on 10 acres of land and receives a tract of land. A summary of the exchange is as follows:

Transferred	FMV	Original Basis	Accumulated Depreciation
Warehouse	$300,000	$225,000	$45,000
Land	$ 50,000	$ 50,000	
Mortgage on warehouse	$ 30,000		
Cash	$ 20,000	$ 20,000	
Assets Received	FMV		
Land	$340,000		

a. What is Prater's realized and recognized gain on the exchange and its basis in the assets it received in the exchange?

b. What is Prater's realized and recognized gain on the exchange and its basis in the new property if, instead of paying $20,000 cash, Prater assumed a $20,000 mortgage on the new property?

57. **(LO6)** Baker Corporation owned a building located in Kansas. Baker used the building for its business operations. Last year a tornado hit the property and completely destroyed it. This year, Baker received an insurance settlement. Baker had originally purchased the building for $350,000 and had claimed a total of $100,000 of depreciation deductions against the property. What is Baker's realized and recognized gain or (loss) on this transaction and what is its basis in the new building in the following alternative scenarios?

a. Baker received $450,000 in insurance proceeds and spent $450,000 rebuilding the building during the current year.

b. Baker received $450,000 in insurance proceeds and spent $500,000 rebuilding the building during the current year.

c. Baker received $450,000 in insurance proceeds and spent $400,000 rebuilding the building during the current year.

d. Baker received $450,000 in insurance proceeds and spent $450,000 rebuilding the building during the next three years.

58. **(LO6)** Russell Corporation sold a parcel of land valued at $400,000. Its basis in the land was $275,000. For the land, Russell received $50,000 in cash in year 0 and a note providing that Russell will receive $175,000 in year 1 and $175,000 in year 2 from the buyer.

a. What is Russell's realized gain on the transaction?

b. What is Russell's recognized gain in year 0, year 1, and year 2?

59. **(LO6)** In year 0, Javens Inc. sold machinery with a fair market value of $400,000 to Chris. The machinery's original basis was $317,000 and Javens's accumulated depreciation on the machinery was $50,000, so its adjusted basis to Javens was $267,000. Chris paid Javens $40,000 immediately (in year 0) and provided a note to Javens indicating that Chris would pay Javens $60,000 a year for six years beginning in year 1. What is the amount and character of the gain that Javens will recognize in year 0? What amount and character of the gain will Javens recognize in years 1 through 6?

60. **(LO6)** Ken sold a rental property for $500,000. $400,000 of the sales price was allocated to the building and the remaining $100,000 was allocated to the land. Ken purchased the property several years ago for $300,000. $225,000 of

research

the purchase price was allocated to the building and $75,000 was allocated to the land. Ken has claimed $25,000 of depreciation deductions over the years against the building. If Ken had no other sales of §1231 or capital assets in the current year, determine what Ken's recognized gain or loss is, the character of Ken's gain, and calculate Ken's tax due because of the sale (assuming his marginal tax rate is 35 percent). (*Hint:* see the examples in Reg. §1.453-12.)

■ planning

61. **(LO6)** Hillary is in the leasing business and faces a marginal tax rate of 35 percent. She has leased equipment to Whitewater Corporation for several years. Hillary bought the equipment for $50,000 and claimed $20,000 of depreciation deductions against the asset. The lease term is about to expire and Whitewater would like to acquire the equipment. Hillary has been offered two options to choose from:

Option	Details
Like-kind exchange	Whitewater would provide Hillary with like-kind equipment. The like-kind equipment has a fair market value of $35,000.
Installment sale	Whitewater would provide Hillary with two payments of $19,000. She would use the proceeds to purchase equipment that she could also lease.

Ignoring time value of money, which option provides the greatest after-tax value for Hillary, assuming she is indifferent between the proposals based on nontax factors?

62. **(LO6)** Deirdre sold 100 shares of stock to her brother, James, for $2,400. Deirdre purchased the stock several years ago for $3,000.

a. What gain or loss does Deirdre recognize on the sale?

b. What amount of gain or loss does James recognize if he sells the stock for $3,200?

c. What amount of gain or loss does James recognize if he sells the stock for $2,600?

d. What amount of gain or loss does James recognize if he sells the stock for $2,000?

COMPREHENSIVE PROBLEMS

63. Two years ago, Bethesda Corporation bought a delivery truck for $30,000 (not subject to the luxury auto depreciation limits). Bethesda used MACRS 200 percent declining balance and the half-year convention to recover the cost of the truck, but it did not elect §179 expensing. Answer the questions for the following alternative scenarios.

a. Assuming Bethesda used the truck until March of year 3, what depreciation expense can it claim on the truck for years 1 through 3?

b. Assume that Bethesda claimed $18,500 of depreciation expense on the truck before it sold it in year 3. What is the amount and character of the gain or loss if Bethesda sold the truck in year 3 for $17,000, and incurred $2,000 of selling expenses on the sale?

c. Assume that Bethesda claimed $18,500 of depreciation expense on the truck before it sold it in year 3. What is the amount and character of the gain or loss if Bethesda sold the truck in year 3 for $35,000, and incurred $3,000 of selling expenses on the sale?

64. Hauswirth Corporation sold (or exchanged) some manufacturing equipment in year 0. Hauswirth bought the machinery several years ago for $65,000 and it has claimed $23,000 of depreciation expense against the equipment.

    a. Assuming that Hauswirth receives $50,000 in cash for the equipment, compute the amount and character of Hauswirth's recognized gain or loss on the sale.

    b. Assuming that Hauswirth receives like-kind equipment with a fair market value of $50,000 in exchange for its equipment, compute Hauswirth's gain realized, gain recognized, deferred gain, and basis in the new equipment.

    c. Assuming that Hauswirth receives $20,000 in cash in year 0 and a $50,000 note receivable that is payable in year 1, compute the amount and character of Hauswirth's gain in year 0 and in year 1.

65. Fontenot Corporation sold some machinery to its majority owner Gray (an individual who owns 60 percent of Fontenot). Fontenot purchased the machinery for $100,000 and has claimed a total of $40,000 of depreciation expense deductions against the property. Gray will provide Fontenot with $10,000 of cash today and provide a $100,000 note that will pay Fontenot $50,000 one year from now and $50,000 two years from now.

    research

    a. What gain does Fontenot's realize on the sale?

    b. What is the amount and character of the gain that Fontenot must recognize in the year of sale (if any) and each of the two subsequent years? (*Hint:* use the Internal Revenue Code and start with §453; please give appropriate citations.)

66. Moab Inc. manufactures and distributes high-tech biking gadgets. It has decided to streamline some of its operations so that it will be able to be more productive and efficient. Because of this decision it has entered into several transactions during the year.

    Part (1) Determine the gain/loss realized and recognized in the current year for each of these events. Also determine whether the gain/loss recognized will be §1231, capital, or ordinary.

    a. Moab Inc. sold a machine that it used to make computerized gadgets for $27,300 cash. It originally bought the machine for $19,200 three years ago and has taken $8,000 depreciation.

    b. Moab Inc. held stock in ABC Corp., which had a value of $12,000 at the beginning of the year. That same stock had a value of $15,230 at the end of the year.

    c. Moab Inc. sold some of its inventory for $7,000 cash. This inventory had a basis of $5,000.

    d. Moab Inc. disposed of an office building with a fair market value of $75,000 for another office building with a fair market value of $55,000 and $20,000 in cash. It originally bought the office building seven years ago for $62,000 and has taken $15,000 in depreciation.

    e. Moab Inc. sold some land held for investment for $28,000. It originally bought the land for $32,000.

    f. Moab Inc. sold another machine for a note payable in four annual installments of $12,000. The first payment was received in the current year. It originally bought the machine two years ago for $32,000 and has claimed $9,000 in depreciation expense against the machine.

    g. Moab Inc. sold stock it held for eight years for $2,750. It originally purchased the stock for $2,100.

    h. Moab Inc. sold another machine for $7,300. It originally purchased this machine six months ago for $9,000 and has claimed $830 in depreciation expense against the asset.

Part (2) From the recognized gains/losses determined in part 1, determine the net §1231 gain/loss and the net ordinary gain/loss Moab will recognize on its tax return. Moab Inc. also has $2,000 of unrecaptured §1231 losses from previous years

research

67. Vertovec Inc., a large local consulting firm in Utah, hired several new consultants from out of state last year to help service their expanding list of clients. To aide in relocating the consultants, Vertovec Inc. purchased the consultants' homes in their prior location if the consultants were unable to sell their homes within 30 days of listing them for sale. Vertovec Inc. bought the homes from the consultants for 5 percent less than the list price and then continued to list the homes for sale. Each home Vertovec Inc. purchased was sold at a loss. By the end of last year, Vertovec had suffered a loss totaling $250,000 from the homes. How should Vertovec treat the loss for tax purposes? Write a memo to Vertovec Inc. explaining your findings and any planning suggestions that you may have if Vertovec Inc. continues to offer this type of relocation benefit to newly hired consultants.

Investments

Learning Objectives

Upon completing this chapter, you should be able to:

LO 1 Explain how interest income and dividend income are taxed.

---■---

LO 2 Compute the tax consequences associated with the disposition of capital assets, including the netting process for calculating gains and losses.

---■---

LO 3 Describe common sources of tax-exempt investment income and explain the rationale for exempting some investments from taxation.

---■---

LO 4 Calculate the deduction for portfolio investment-related expenses, including investment expenses and investment interest expense.

---■---

LO 5 Understand the distinction between portfolio investments and passive investments and apply tax basis, at-risk, and passive activity loss limits to losses from passive investments.

Storyline Summary	
Taxpayers:	Nick and Rachel Sutton
Home:	Scottsdale, Arizona
Employment status:	Rachel—Software developer for national software company; current salary $120,000 Nick—High School science teacher; current salary $50,000
Filing status:	Married filing jointly
Dependents:	None currently, but they are expecting a baby girl
Marginal tax rate for ordinary income:	30 percent
Current situation:	Nick recently received an inheritance, and the Suttons are deciding how to invest it.

N ick and Rachel Sutton live in Scottsdale, Arizona. The couple has been married for 10 years and is expecting a first child, a girl, next month. Nick is a high school science teacher, earning an annual salary of $50,000, and Rachel is a software developer, earning an annual salary of $120,000. With their above-average family income, the Suttons invest in retirement accounts through their employers but have no other investments.

When Nick's grandmother recently passed away, he learned that she had left him an inheritance of $100,000 with the stipulation that he "invest it to financially benefit his family."

After considerable discussion, Nick and Rachel decide to invest the inheritance to help the family accomplish two financial goals. First, they want to save for their daughter's college education. They figure that if they immediately invest $50,000 of the inheritance for her college education, they should have a significant sum accumulated when Lea (yes, they've decided on the baby's name) starts college in 18 years. Second, they decided they will immediately invest the remaining $50,000 for five years and use the accumulation to make a significant down payment on a vacation home in Park City, Utah, a town they fell in love with while attending the 2002 Winter Olympics. The Suttons have a marginal income tax rate of 30 percent, and they have investment opportunities that earn an 8 percent **before-tax rate of return.**[1] Their objective is to devise an investment strategy that will maximize the **after-tax rate of return** on their investments while accomplishing their nontax objectives. ■

[1] Unless otherwise noted, all the investments discussed in the chapter are assumed to yield an 8 percent before-tax return. Although this rate may be somewhat unrealistic, this assumption is made to facilitate a comparison of investments based on their tax characteristics alone.

INVESTMENTS OVERVIEW

Investors are attracted to certain investments according to their investment philosophy and their appetite for risk, among other things. Some prefer investments that provide a consistent income stream. Others prefer investments that have significant appreciation potential but provide no current cash flows. These investment attributes affect the before-tax returns on investments. However, taxes are levied on **investment income,** and thus, it would be unwise to make an investment without considering the tax cost. For example, it is possible that two investments with identical before-tax rates of return will generate different after-tax rates of return because the investments are taxed differently. Indeed, it is possible that an investment with a lower before-tax rate of return compared to an alternative investment will have a higher after-tax rate of return because income from the investment is taxed at a later date or taxed at a lower rate than the alternative investment.

Two key tax characteristics that affect after-tax returns from investments are (1) the timing of tax payments or tax benefits (when investment income is taxed or when investment losses are deducted) and (2) the tax rate applied to investment income or losses (the rate at which investment income is taxed or deductible losses generate tax savings). Not surprisingly, these variables are directly related to the timing and conversion tax planning strategies introduced in Chapter 3.

Income from **portfolio investments** (investments producing **dividends,** interest, royalties, annuities, or capital gains) may be taxed at ordinary rates, preferential rates, or it may be exempt from taxation. Further, depending on the type of investment, tax on income from a portfolio investment may be imposed annually or may be deferred until the taxpayer sells the investment. Losses from portfolio investments are deferred until the investment is sold and are typically subject to limitations.

In contrast to portfolio investments, **passive investments** generate **operating income** and **operating losses.** Operating income is always taxed annually at ordinary rates while operating losses are either deducted annually at ordinary rates or deferred and deducted later at ordinary rates depending on the investor's circumstances. Losses from passive investments are also subject to limitations.

This chapter explores several common portfolio and passive investments, discusses important tax and nontax considerations relevant for those investments, and compares investment returns on an after-tax basis.

L01   PORTFOLIO INCOME: INTEREST AND DIVIDENDS

Taxpayers who desire current cash flows from their investments may choose investments that generate income in the form of interest or regular dividends. Investments generating interest income include **certificates of deposit** (CDs), savings accounts, corporate **bonds,** and governmental bonds. Investments generating dividend income include direct equity investments in corporate stocks or investments in **mutual funds** that invest in corporate stock.[2] Although all of these investments generate current cash flows, they differ significantly in terms of their economic and tax consequences.

By lending money to banks, governmental entities, or corporations, investors essentially become debt holders. As such, they are legally entitled to receive periodic interest payments *and* to recover the amount of principal loaned (in the case of bonds, principal is the **maturity value** or **face value** of the bonds). Interest payments

---

[2]Mutual funds are portfolios of investment assets managed by professional money managers. Generally, the income earned by mutual funds flows through to the owners of mutual fund shares who pay the resulting taxes due. The nature of the assets held by the mutual fund determines the character of the income.

EXHIBIT 11-1   Formulas for After-Tax Rate of Return and the After-Tax Future Value of Investment with *Constant Rate of Return*

After-tax rate of return = before-tax rate of return × (1 − marginal tax rate)

After-tax future value = $I \times (1 + r)^n$ where

I = the amount of the original investment,

r = the annual *after-tax rate* of return, and

n = the number of years the investment is maintained.

and the time and manner of repayment of the loan principal are defined either contractually for CDs and savings accounts or by bond covenants for loans made either to governments or corporations. In contrast, investors who purchase stocks become stockholders (also called equity holders) of a corporation. As stockholders, they are entitled to receive dividends if the company declares dividends and to *indirectly* share in either the future appreciation or depreciation in the value of a corporation through stock ownership. Unlike debt holders, stockholders are not legally entitled to receive dividend payments or to recover their initial investment. Thus, from an investor's perspective, debt tends to be less risky than equity.

For tax purposes, individual investors typically are taxed on both interest and dividend income when they receive it. However, interest income is taxed at ordinary rates while dividend income is generally taxed at lower capital gains rates.

Interest

In general, taxpayers recognize interest income from investments when they receive the interest payments.[3] Taxpayers investing in savings accounts, money market accounts, CDs, and most bonds receive interest payments based on a stated annual rate of return at yearly or more frequent intervals. When interest is paid annually at a stated rate of return, it is relatively straightforward to modify the rate of return and time value of money formulas you have seen in finance-type courses to account for taxes on interest income. Indeed, assuming constant tax rates, the after-tax rate of return and the future value of an investment *paying* interest annually at a *constant before-tax rate of return* can be determined after any number of years using the formulas provided in Exhibit 11-1. For bonds, the formulas assume the bonds are purchased at face value.

Example 11-1

Assume on January 1 of year 1 the Suttons invest the $50,000 earmarked for the Park City vacation home in General Electric (GE) bonds that mature in exactly five years and the $50,000 designated for Lea's education in General Electric bonds that mature in exactly 18 years. They will purchase both bonds at face value, and both bonds will pay 8 percent interest annually. How much interest income will Nick and Rachel report from this investment at the end of the first year?

Answer: $4,000 of interest income ($50,000 × .08) from each bond in the first year of the investment.

Assuming they reinvest their annual after-tax interest payments in the GE bonds, what after-tax rate of return will they earn on the bonds over the 5- and 18-year investment periods and what amount will the Suttons receive 5 and 18 years from now when the bonds mature?

(*continued on page 11-4...*)

---

[3]Interest income is reported on Part I of Schedule B filed with taxpayers' Form 1040.

Answer: See (1) and (2) in the table below.

Time to Maturity	5 Years	18 Years
(1) After-Tax Rates of Return = 8% × (1 − .3) (recall the Suttons' marginal tax rate = 30%)	5.6%	5.6%
(2) Nick and Rachel will receive after-tax: $50,000 (1 + .056)^n, where n is 5 and 18 years, respectively.	$65,658	$133,328

Why are the after-tax returns the same for both bonds? Because the investments are taxed annually, the investment horizon does not affect after-tax rates of return.

Special rules apply for determining the timing and amount of interest from bonds when there is a **bond discount** (bonds are issued at an amount below the maturity value) or a **bond premium** (bonds are issued at an amount above the maturity value). Below we discuss these rules as they apply to corporate, U.S. Treasury bonds, and **U.S. savings bonds.**

Corporate and U.S. Treasury Bonds   Both corporations and the U.S. Treasury raise money from debt markets by issuing bonds.[4] Corporate bonds, **Treasury bonds,** and **Treasury notes** are issued at maturity value, at a discount, or at a premium, depending on prevailing interest rates.[5] Treasury bonds and Treasury notes pay a stated rate of interest semiannually.[6] However, corporate bonds may pay interest at a stated "coupon" rate or they may not provide any periodic interest payments. Corporate bonds that do not pay periodic interest are called **zero-coupon bonds.** Overall, the tax consequences of corporate and Treasury bonds are very similar. The two primary differences are that (1) interest from Treasury bonds is exempt from *state* taxation while interest from corporate bonds is not and (2) Treasury bonds always pay interest periodically while corporate bonds may or may not. The rules for determining the timing and amount of interest income from corporate and U.S. Treasury bonds are as follows:

- Taxpayers include the actual interest payments they receive in gross income.
- If the bond was issued at a discount, special **original issue discount** (OID) rules apply. Taxpayers are required to amortize the discount and include the amount of the current year **amortization** in gross income in addition to any interest payments the taxpayer actually receives.[7] In the case of corporate zero-coupon bonds, this means taxpayers must report and pay taxes on income related to the bonds even though they did not receive *any* payments from the bonds. Bond issuers or brokers are responsible for calculating the yearly amortization of original issue discount and providing this information to investors using Form 1099-OID.

---

[4]Investors in corporate bonds assume more risk than investors in Treasury securities because they are relying on the creditworthiness of the corporation issuing the bonds. To compensate bondholders for this additional risk, corporate bonds usually yield higher before-tax rates of return than Treasury securities.

[5]The bonds are issued at a discount (premium) if the market interest rate is higher (lower) than the stated rate on the bonds.

[6]Treasury notes and bonds differ in terms of their maturities. Treasury notes are issued with two, five, and ten year maturities. In contrast, Treasury bonds are issued with maturities greater than ten years. From this point forward, we use the term Treasury bonds to refer to both Treasury notes and Treasury bonds.

[7]§1272. Original issue discount is amortized semiannually under the constant yield method, which is consistent with the approach used to amortize bond discount under GAAP.

- If the bond was issued at a premium, taxpayers may *elect* to amortize the premium.[8] Taxpayers or their advisors are responsible for determining the yearly amortization of bond premium if the election to amortize the premium has been made. The amount of the current year amortization offsets a portion of the actual interest payments that taxpayers must include in gross income. The original tax basis of the bond includes the premium and is reduced by any amortization of bond premium over the life of the bond.

- If the bond is purchased in the secondary bond market at a discount, the taxpayer treats some of or all of the **market discount** as interest income *when she sells the bond or the bond matures.*[9] If the bond is sold prior to **maturity,** a ratable amount of the market discount (based on the number of days the bond is held over the number of days until maturity when the bond is purchased), called the *accrued market discount,* is treated as interest income on the date of sale.[10] If the bond is held to maturity, the entire bond discount is treated as interest income at maturity.

- If the bond is purchased in the secondary bond market at a premium, the premium is treated exactly like original issue bond premiums. As a result, the taxpayer may elect to amortize the **market premium** to reduce the annual interest income received from the bond. Otherwise, the premium remains as part of the tax basis of the bond and affects the capital gain or loss the taxpayer recognizes when the taxpayer sells or redeems the bond.

U.S. Savings Bonds   U.S. savings bonds such as Series EE or Series I bonds are issued at either face value or at a discount. These bonds do not pay periodic interest; rather, interest accumulates over the term of the bonds and is paid when investors redeem them at maturity or earlier.[11] That is, the amount of interest income taxpayers recognize *when they redeem* the bonds is the excess of the bond proceeds over the taxpayer's **basis** (purchase price) in the bonds. Taxpayers may elect to include the increase in the bond redemption value in income each year, but this is generally not advisable because it accelerates the income from the bond without providing any cash to pay the taxes.[12] Finally, as we discuss in Chapter 5, interest from Series EE and Series I bonds may be excluded from gross income to the extent the bond proceeds are used to pay qualifying educational expenses. However, this exclusion benefit is subject to phase-out based on the taxpayer's AGI.

Example 11-2

What if: Assume that instead of buying GE bonds, Nick and Rachel were deciding whether to invest the $50,000 earmarked for the Park City vacation home in (1) Series EE savings bonds that mature in exactly five years, (2) original issue AMD Corporation *zero-coupon* bonds that mature in exactly five years, or (3) U.S. Treasury bonds that pay $46,250 at maturity in five years trading in the secondary bond market with a stated annual interest rate of 10 percent. Further, assume that all bonds yield 8

(continued on page 11-6...)

---

[8]§171. Like original issue discount, bond premium is amortized semiannually under the constant yield method—the same method used to amortize bond premiums under GAAP. Unlike premiums on taxable bonds, premiums on tax exempt bonds must always be amortized.

[9]§1276(a). Under §1278(b)(1), taxpayers may elect to include the amortization of market discount in their income annually. However, this election accelerates the recognition of income from the market discount and is therefore usually not advisable.

[10]§1276(b)

[11]Series EE savings bonds are issued at a discount and Series I savings bonds are issued at maturity value. EE bonds provide a constant rate of return while Series I bonds provides a return that is indexed for inflation and thus increases over time.

[12]§454(a). Investors that make this election report the annual increase in the redemption value of their savings bonds using savings bond redemption tables published by the Treasury Department.

percent annual before-tax returns compounded semiannually. At the end of the first year, the redemption value of the EE savings bond would be $54,080, or the Suttons would receive a Form 1099-OID from AMD reporting $4,080 of OID amortization for the year, or they would receive two semiannual interest payments of $2,312.50 from the Treasury bonds. Under the general rules, how much interest income from each bond would Nick and Rachel report at the end of the first year?

Answer: $0 from the Series EE savings bonds, $4,080 from the AMD bonds, and $4,625 (two semiannual payments of $2,312.50) from the Treasury bonds. Note, however, that the Suttons could *elect* to include the $4,080 redemption value of the Series EE bond in interest income even though they did not receive any interest payments on the bond (probably not optimal). They also could *elect* to amortize $637.50 of the $3,750 premium ($50,000 purchase price less the $46,250 maturity value) on the Treasury bond to offset the $4,625 in actual interest payments they received on the bond (probably a good idea). The calculations required to amortize the premium on the Treasury bond for the first year are reflected in the following table:

Semiannual Period	(A) Adjusted Basis of Bond at Beginning of Semiannual Period	(B) Interest Received ($46,250 × 10% × .5)	(C) Reported Interest (A) × 8% × .5	Premium Amortization (B) − (C)
1	$50,000.00	$2,312.50	$2,000.00	$312.50
2	$49,687.50	$2,312.50	$1,987.50	$325.00
Yearly Total		$4,625.00	$3,987.50	$637.50

Intuitively, would the Suttons be better or worse off purchasing the Series EE savings bonds rather than the GE bonds (see Example 11-1) to save for the Park City home?

Answer: They would better off in two respects. First, they wouldn't have to pay state income taxes on the interest earned from the savings bonds. Second, they would be able to defer paying taxes on the accumulated interest from the savings bonds until the savings bonds are cashed in at maturity. This will increase the after-tax returns from the savings bonds relative to the GE bonds.

Intuitively, would the Suttons be better or worse off purchasing the AMD zero-coupon bonds rather than the GE bonds to save for the Park City home?

Answer: They will be worse off because they will have to pay taxes currently from the OID amortization on the AMD bonds without receiving any cash flow from the bonds to pay the taxes due. This will reduce the after-tax returns from the AMD bonds relative to the GE bonds.

Example 11-3

What if: Assume that on January 1, Nick and Rachel use the $50,000 earmarked for the Park City vacation home to purchase AMD zero-coupon bonds in the *secondary bond market* almost immediately after it was originally issued. If the bonds mature in exactly five years and have a maturity value of $74,000, how much interest income will Nick and Rachel report at the end of the first year and in the year the bonds mature?

Answer: $0 in the first year and $24,000 in the year the bonds mature. Because the AMD zero-coupon bonds were not purchased at original issue, the entire $24,000 market discount on the bonds will be reported as interest income when the bonds mature. Thus, the Suttons will not report any income related to the AMD bonds until the year the bonds mature.

What if: Assume the same facts as above, except the Suttons purchased a U.S. Series EE bond instead of an AMD zero-coupon bond to fund the Park City vacation home in five years. How much interest income will the Suttons report at the end of the first year and in the year the bonds mature?

Answer: $0 in the first year and $24,000 in the year the EE savings bonds mature; exactly the same outcome as the investment in the AMD zero-coupon bonds.

EXHIBIT 11-2   Timing of Interest Payments and Taxes

General Rule	Exception	Exception
Interest Received Annually and Taxed Annually	**Interest Received at Sale or Maturity and Taxed at Sale or Maturity**	**Interest Received at Sale or Maturity but Taxed Annually**
• Savings accounts. • CDs. • Money market accounts. • Bond interest payments actually received in the year.	• Accrued market discount on bonds. • Interest earned on U.S. savings bonds.	• Original issue discount (OID) on corporate and Treasury bonds.

As our discussion suggests, for certain types of investments such as savings accounts, money market accounts, and CDs, computing the annual taxable interest income is relatively straightforward. However, for investments in bonds, the process is much more involved. Exhibit 11-2 summarizes the general rule and exceptions for the timing of interest payments and related tax payments.

Dividends

Historically, dividends received by investors have been taxed at the same rate as interest income. However, in 2003, Congress changed the law for dividends to mitigate the so-called "double tax" on dividend income.[13] Consistent with the general rule for taxing interest income, dividend payments (including reinvested dividends) are taxed annually.[14] However, **qualified dividends** generally are taxed at a 15 percent preferential rate (in some circumstances, qualified dividends may be taxed at rate as low as 0 percent depending on the taxpayer's ordinary income tax rate).[15] Qualified dividends are those paid by domestic or certain qualified foreign corporations provided investors hold the dividend-paying stock for *more than* 60 days during the 121-day period that begins 60 days before the **ex-dividend date** (the first day on which the purchaser of the stock would not be entitled to receive a declared dividend on the stock).[16] Nonqualifying dividends are not eligible for the reduced rate and are therefore taxed at ordinary rates. Corporations normally indicate whether their dividends are potentially eligible for the preferential rate when they send Form 1099-DIV to stockholders after year-end. However, stockholders ultimately must determine if they qualify for the preferential rate by confirming they held the stock for the required number of days around the ex-dividend date.

Example 11-4

What if: Assume that Nick and Rachel decide to purchase dividend-paying stocks to achieve their short- and long-term financial objectives. They invest $50,000 in Xerox stock, intend to hold the stock for five years, and then sell it to fund the Park City home down payment. They invest another $50,000

(*continued on page 11-8...*)

---

[13]Because corporations pay income taxes, dividends are taxed once at the corporate level when the income used to pay dividends is earned by the corporation, and a second time when dividends are received by investors.

[14]Dividends are reported on Part II of Schedule B filed with taxpayers' Form 1040.

[15]Certain dividends paid in the form of additional stock shares (stock dividends) are not taxable (see §305).

[16]Qualifying foreign corporations are those incorporated in a U.S. possession (e.g., Puerto Rico, U.S. Virgin Islands), those eligible for the benefits of a comprehensive income tax treaty with the United States, or those whose shares are readily traded on an established U.S. securities market.

in Xerox stock, intend to hold it for 18 years, and then sell it to fund their daughter's education. How much dividend income will Nick and Rachel report at the end of the first year if the dividend payments provide an 8 percent return on their investments?[17]

Answer: Nick and Rachel will report $4,000 ($50,000 × .08) of dividend income from each block of the Xerox stock for the first year of their investment.

What if: Assume that Xerox dividends continue to provide an 8 percent return for 5 and 18 years, respectively, that Nick and Rachel reinvest their after-tax dividends each year, and that the share price of Xerox remains constant. Given these assumptions, what will be their after-tax rate of return over the 5- and 18-year investment periods, and what will be the value of their investment in the Xerox 5-year block and the Xerox 18-year block of stock 5 and 18 years from now?

Answer: See (1) and (2) in the table below.

Time to Maturity	5 years	18 years
(1) After-tax rates of return: 8% × (1 − .15) Note that qualified dividends are taxed at 15%	6.80%	6.80%
(2) Nick and Rachel will receive after-tax: $50,000 (1 + .068)^n$, where n is 5 and 18 years, respectively.	$69,475	$163,400

Note that the formula for determining the after-tax rate of return and the after-tax accumulation is identical to the formula used in Example 11-2 to determine the rate of return and accumulation on the bond investments. The only difference is that the dividends are taxed at a 15 percent rate, which is *half the rate* at which the interest on the bonds was taxed to the Suttons.

Because dividend income is taxed generally at lower rates than interest income, it appears that taxpayers seeking current cash flows from their investments should favor dividend-paying investments over interest-paying investments. This raises the question of why anyone would ever prefer investments paying interest over those paying dividends. Remember, though, that savvy investors also should consider nontax factors such as before-tax rates of return, risk, and liquidity needs when choosing among alternative investments. These fundamental differences explain why investors may continue to seek out interest income in spite of the associated tax disadvantages.

LO2   PORTFOLIO INCOME: CAPITAL GAINS AND LOSSES

Investors who don't need annual cash flows from their investments may prefer to invest in assets with the expectation that the investments will appreciate in value over time, providing cash at some point in the future when they sell the assets. Investors also may be willing to assume greater risk in exchange for greater returns than those provided by interest or dividend-paying investments. For example, they might purchase raw land, fine art, rare coins, precious gems or metals, growth stocks (stock in corporations that reinvest their earnings to grow the company as opposed to distributing earnings to shareholders in the form of dividends), mutual fund shares, or even vintage automobiles.[18] Purchasing any such asset is

---

[17]Annual returns from dividend-paying stocks are typically lower than the return from taxable bonds. However, it is assumed here that the returns are equal for the sake of comparability.

[18]Mutual funds are portfolios of investment assets managed by professional money managers. Generally, the income earned and distributed by mutual funds flows through to the owners of mutual fund shares and the nature of the assets held by the mutual fund determines the character of the income. Mutual fund distributions are taxable even when investors choose to reinvest distributions in the same mutual fund.

not without risk. Indeed, investments held solely for appreciation potential *may* actually decline in value.

When taxpayers buy and hold assets with appreciation potential, they typically are investing in **capital assets.** As we discussed in the previous chapter, capital assets are typically investment-type assets and personal-use assets.[19] Thus, artwork, corporate stock, bonds, your personal residence, and even your iPod are capital assets.

While it may be enjoyable to view collectible fine art in your home or watch a stock portfolio grow in value on quarterly brokerage statements, from a tax perspective, the real advantages of investing in capital assets are (1) gains are deferred for tax purposes until the taxpayer sells or otherwise disposes of the assets[20] and (2) gains generally are taxed at preferential rates relative to ordinary income.[21] Why the favorable treatment? One reason is that taxpayers may not have the wherewithal (cash) to pay the tax on their gains until they sell the investment. A second reason is that the preferential rates compensate for the fact that the tax basis of a capital asset held for investment is not indexed for inflation. Another is that the preferential tax rate provides an incentive for taxpayers to invest in assets that may stimulate the economy. Investors can capture these tax benefits when they sell capital assets at a gain. However, when they sell capital assets at a loss, their ability to deduct the loss may be limited.

When a taxpayer sells a capital asset for more than its **tax basis,** the taxpayer recognizes a capital gain; if a taxpayer sells a capital asset for less than its tax basis, the taxpayer recognizes a capital loss (to the extent the loss is deductible).[22] The amount realized or selling price of a capital asset includes the cash and fair market value of other property received, less broker's fees and other selling costs. The adjusted basis of any asset, including a capital asset, is generally the taxpayer's "cost" of acquiring the asset, including the initial purchase price and other costs incurred to purchase or improve the asset. Thus, the tax basis of corporate stock purchased from a stockbroker includes the cost of the stock and any additional brokerage fees paid by the taxpayer to acquire the stock. Also, the tax basis in a personal residence includes the initial purchase price plus the cost of subsequent improvements to the home.

Because a taxpayer cannot accurately compute the gain or loss on the sale of a capital asset without knowing its basis, it is important for taxpayers to maintain accurate records to track their basis in capital assets. This process is relatively straightforward for unique assets such as a taxpayer's personal residence or individual jewels in a taxpayer's jewelry collection. However, capital assets such as shares of stock are much more homogeneous and difficult to track. For example, a taxpayer may purchase blocks of stock in a given corporation at different times over a period of several years, paying a different price per share for each block of stock acquired. When the taxpayer sells shares of this stock in subsequent years, what basis does she use to compute gain or loss? Taxpayers who haven't adequately

---

[19]§1221 defines capital assets in the negative. This section excludes inventory, depreciable property or real property used in a trade or business, certain self-created intangibles, accounts or notes receivable, U.S. government publications, certain commodities derivative financial instruments, certain hedging transactions, and supplies from the definition of a capital asset.

[20]Similarly, interest related to market discount on bonds and the original issue discount on U.S. EE savings bonds accumulates free of tax until the bonds mature or are sold. However, ordinary rather than capital gains rates apply when the tax must finally be paid.

[21]Mutual funds that generate current income by regularly selling capital assets or by holding income-producing securities are an exception to this general rule. Mutual fund investors are taxed on mutual fund income as it is recognized by mutual funds for tax purposes. However, tax-efficient mutual funds that only buy and hold growth stocks are treated like other capital assets for tax purposes (capital gains are deferred until mutual fund shares are sold).

[22]As discussed below, losses on personal assets are not deductible for tax purposes.

tracked the basis in their stock are required to use the **first-in first-out (FIFO) method** of determining the basis of the shares they sell.[23] However, if they maintain good records, they can use the **specific identification method** to determine the basis of the shares they sell. Taxpayers using the specific identification method can choose to sell their high-basis stock first, minimizing their gains or increasing their losses on stock dispositions.

Example 11-5

After Rachel's car broke down, Nick and Rachel decided to buy a new one. To fund the down payment, they sold 200 shares of Cisco stock at the current market price of $40 per share for a total amount realized of $8,000. The Suttons held the following blocks of Cisco stock at the time of the sale:

Cisco Corporation Stock Ownership

Acquisition Date	(1) Cost per share	(2) Shares	(1) × (2) Basis	Basis of 200 shares sold	Explanation
4/1/2002	$25	250	$6,250	$5,000	FIFO basis ($25 × 200)
11/5/2005	$32	250	$8,000	$6,400	Specific ID basis ($32 × 200)

How much capital gain will the Suttons recognize if they use the FIFO method of computing the basis in the Cisco shares sold?

Answer: $3,000. $8,000 amount realized ($40 × 200) minus $5,000 FIFO basis ($25 × 200). As indicated in the table above, under the FIFO (oldest first) method, they are treated as though they sold the stock purchased on 4/1/2002.

What if: How much capital gain will the Suttons recognize if they use the specific identification method of computing the basis in the shares sold to minimize the taxable gain on the sale?

Answer: $1,600. $8,000 amount realized ($40 × 200) minus $6,400 ($32 × 200). To minimize their gain on the sale under the specific identification method, the Suttons would choose to sell the 200 shares with the highest basis. As indicated in the table above, the shares with the higher basis are those acquired on 11/5/2005 for $32 per share.

Note in the above example that the Suttons receive $8,000 from the stock sale ($40 per share × 200 shares sold) regardless of the method they use to compute the basis of the shares they sell. The difference between the FIFO and specific identification methods lies in the amount of taxable gain on the *current* sale. Over time, as taxpayers sell all of their stock, both methods will ultimately allow taxpayers to fully recover their cost in the investments. However, applying the specific identification method will result in lower capital gains taxes currently and thereby minimize the present value of the taxes paid on stock sales.

---

[23]Reg. §1.1012-1(c)(1)

Types of Capital Gains and Losses

Taxpayers selling capital assets that they hold for a year or less recognize **short-term capital gains or losses.**[24] Alternatively, taxpayers selling capital assets they hold for more than a year recognize **long-term capital gains or losses.** Short-term capital gains are taxed at ordinary rather than preferential rates. In contrast, long-term capital gains are taxed at preferential rates. However, not all long-term capital gains are created equal. Although most long-term capital gains are taxed at a maximum 15 percent rate, certain long-term capital gains are taxed at a maximum rate of 25 percent and others are taxed at a maximum 28 percent rate for tax policy reasons.

Unrecaptured §1250 Gain   When individuals sell depreciable real property at a gain, some or all of the gain is subject to a maximum tax rate of 25 percent. As we discussed in Chapter 10, the amount of this **unrecaptured §1250 gain** is generally the *lesser* of (1) the recognized gain or (2) the accumulated depreciation on the property. Gains in excess of this unrecaptured § 1250 gain amount are subject to a maximum tax rate of 15 percent. Thus, even though unrecaptured §1250 gains are treated as long-term capital gains, they are taxed at a rate higher than most other long-term capital gains.[25] Unrecaptured §1250 gains are taxed at higher capital gains rates because the depreciation deductions responsible for these gains previously reduced ordinary income taxable at higher ordinary rates.

Example 11-6

What if: Assume Jeb Landers, Rachel's father, recently sold a rental home for $160,000. He originally acquired the home many years ago for $100,000, and he has fully depreciated it for tax purposes. Assuming Jeb's marginal ordinary tax rate is 35 percent, what tax does he owe on the gain if he did not sell any other property during the year?

Answer: $34,000. Because Jeb's tax basis in the home is $0 (he has fully depreciated it), his gain on the sale is $160,000. As we pointed out in Chapter 10, all of the gain qualifies as §1231 gain because Jeb held the rental home for more than one year. This gain will ultimately be treated as long-term capital gain because Jeb does not have any §1231 losses during the year. The unrecaptured §1250 gain is $100,000, which is the lesser of (1) the $160,000 gain recognized on the sale or (2) the $100,000 accumulated depreciation. Thus, Jeb must pay $25,000 in tax on this portion of the gain ($100,000 × 25%). The remaining $60,000 of gain is taxed at 15 percent, so he owes $9,000 of tax on this portion ($60,000 × 15%). In total, he owes $34,000 of tax on the sale ($25,000 + $9,000).

Collectibles and §1202 Gain   Gains from two types of capital assets are taxable at a maximum 28 percent rate. The first type, **collectibles,** consists of works of art, any rug or antique, any metal or gem, any stamp or coin, any alcoholic beverage, or other similar items held for more than one year.[26] The second type is **qualified small business stock**

---

[24]**Nonbusiness bad debt** is treated as a short-term capital loss no matter how long the debt was outstanding before it became worthless. Whether a bad debt is considered to be a business bad debt for individuals depends on the facts and circumstances. In general, if the taxpayer experiencing the loss is in the business of loaning money, the bad debt should be considered to be business bad debt; otherwise, the bad debt will likely be considered nonbusiness bad debt.

[25]As we discussed in Chapter 10, unrecaptured §1250 gain is technically a §1231 gain.

[26]§408(m)

held for *more than five years*.[27] In general, §1202 defines qualified small business stock as stock received at *original issue* from a C corporation with a gross tax basis in its assets both before and after the issuance of no more than $50,000,000 and with at least 80 percent of the value of its assets used in the active conduct of certain qualified trades or businesses. Under this definition, many investors and employees who hold stock in closely held corporations are likely to hold qualified small business stock. When taxpayers sell qualified small business stock after holding it for more then five years, they may exclude half of the gain on the sale from regular taxable income.[28] However, the capital gain not excluded from income is taxed at 28 percent. Thus, the effective maximum capital gains rate on the total gain from the sale is 14 percent—slightly less than the usual long-term capital gains rate of 15 percent. The 28 percent rate imposed on qualified small business stock was motivated by a desire in Congress to recapture a portion of the benefit from the 50 percent exclusion available when such stock is sold after five years.

Example 11-7

What if: Assume that Jeb sold his stock in Gangbusters, Inc., a qualified small business stock, for $200,000 after holding it for six years. His basis in the stock is $50,000. How much tax will he owe on the sale if his ordinary marginal rate is 35 percent if he is not subject to the alternative minimum tax?

Answer: $21,000. Because Jeb held the qualified small business stock for more than five years, he will exclude $75,000 of the gain from income (one-half), and he will be taxed on the other $75,000 at 28 percent.

What if: Assume instead that Jeb sold his Gangbusters stock after holding it for only two years, how much tax will he owe on the sale?

Answer: $22,500. Because Jeb didn't hold the stock for more than five years, he must recognize all $150,000 of long-term capital gain. This gain is taxed at 15 percent, yielding a total tax due of $22,500.

Exhibit 11-3 presents the maximum tax rates applicable to capital gains.

EXHIBIT 11-3   Classification of Capital Gains by Applicable Tax Rates

Short-Term or Long-Term	Type	Maximum Rate
Short-Term	All	35%
Long-Term	Collectibles	28%*
Held > 5 years	Qualified Small Business Stock	28%*
Long-Term	Unrecaptured §1250 Gain from Depreciable Realty	25%*
Long-Term	All Remaining Capital (and §1231 Gains) Gain Not Included Elsewhere	15%**

*Lower rates will apply when the taxpayer's ordinary rates are less than the rates reflected in this exhibit.
**This gain is taxed at 0 percent to the extent it would have been taxed at a rate of 15 percent or less if it were ordinary income.

---

[27]§1(h)(7)

[28]The maximum exclusion is the lesser of $10,000,000 ($5,000,000 for married taxpayers filing separately) or 10 times the adjusted basis of the stock [see §1202(b)(1)]. The amount of gain excluded from the sale of qualified small business stock is an AMT preference item. Consequently, the gain otherwise excludable for regular tax purposes may be taxed under the AMT system.

Netting Process for Gains and Losses   To this point, our discussion of applicable tax rates for capital gains hasn't considered situations in which taxpayers recognize both capital gains and capital losses in the same year. To determine the appropriate tax treatment for the capital gains and losses recognized during the year, the taxpayer must engage in a netting process. This netting process can be complex when taxpayers recognize capital losses and long-term capital gains subject to different maximum tax rates. We first describe the netting steps for taxpayers who do not recognize any 25 percent or 28 percent rate long-term capital gain.

Step 1: Net all short-term gains and short-term losses, including any short-term capital loss carried forward from a prior year. If the net amount is positive, it is termed a **net short-term capital gain** (NSTCG). If the net amount is negative, it is called a **net short-term capital loss** (NSTCL).

Step 2: Net long-term gains and losses, including any long-term capital loss carried forward from a prior year. If the net amount is positive, the amount is called a **net long-term capital gain** (NLTCG). If negative, the amount is termed a **net long-term capital loss** (NLTCL).

Step 3: If Step 1 and Step 2 both yield gains—*or* if they both yield losses—the netting process ends. Otherwise, net the short- and long-term outcomes against each other to yield a final net gain or net loss, which may be either classified as short-term (if the NSTCG exceeds the NLTCL or if the NSTCL exceeds the NLTCG) or long-term (if the NLTCG exceeds the NSTCL or if the NLTCL exceeds the NSTCG). When net long-term capital gains exceed net short-term capital losses, if any, the taxpayer is said to have a **net capital gain.**

Example 11-8

Jeb Landers has recently retired and now wants to pursue his life-long dream of owning a sailboat. To come up with the necessary cash, he sells the following investments:

Stock	Market Value	Basis	Capital Gain/Loss	Scenario 1 Type	Scenario 2 Type
A	$40,000	$ 5,000	$35,000	Long	Short
B	$20,000	$30,000	($10,000)	Long	Short
C	$20,000	$12,000	$ 8,000	Short	Long
D	$17,000	$28,000	($11,000)	Short	Long

What is the amount and nature of Jeb's capital gains and losses (Scenario 1)?

Answer: $22,000 net capital gain (treated as long-term capital gain), computed as follows:

Step 1: Net short-term gains and short-term losses. The $8,000 short-term gain on stock C is netted against the $11,000 short-term loss on stock D, yielding a NSTCL of $3,000.

Step 2: Net long-term gains and long-term losses. The $35,000 long-term gain on stock A is netted against the $10,000 long-term loss on stock B, producing a NLTCG of $25,000.

Step 3: Net the results of Step 1 and Step 2. The NSTCL from Step 1 is netted with the NLTCG from Step 2 yielding a $22,000 net capital gain [($3,000) + $25,000] taxable at long-term capital gains rates.

What if: Consider the original facts, except that Scenario 2 dictates the long- and short-term capital gains. What is the amount and character of Jeb's net gain (or loss) on the sale of the shares in this situation?

(continued on page 11-14...)

> **Answer:** $22,000 net short-term capital gain computed as follows:
>
> **Step 1:** The gain from stock A would first be netted with the loss from stock B to produce a $25,000 NSTCG [$35,000 + ($10,000)]
>
> **Step 2:** The loss from stock D and the gain from stock C are combined to provide a $3,000 NLTCL [($11,000) + $8,000].
>
> **Step 3:** The results from Step 1 and Step 2 are netted to reach a $22,000 net short-term capital gain [$25,000 NSTCG + ($3,000) NLTCL].
>
> **What if:** Assume the original facts (Scenario 1), except that stocks B and C were the only investments Jeb sold during the year. Walk through the outlined steps and see if you determine that Jeb would recognize a ($2,000) net long-term capital loss.

After completing the netting process, taxpayers must calculate the tax consequences of the resulting outcomes. Net short-term capital gains are taxed as ordinary income. As we discussed and illustrated in Chapter 7, net long-term capital gains generally are taxed at 15 percent to the extent the gains would have been taxed at a rate higher if they were ordinary income, and they are taxed at 0 percent to the extent they would have been taxed at a rate of 15 percent or lower if they were ordinary income. Taxpayers can deduct up to $3,000 ($1,500 if married filing separately) of net capital losses against ordinary income. Net capital losses in excess of $3,000 ($1,500 if married filing separately) retain their short- or long-term character and are carried forward and treated as though they were incurred in the subsequent year.[29] Short-term losses are applied first to reduce ordinary income when the taxpayer recognizes both short- and long-term net capital losses. Capital loss carryovers for individuals never expire.

Reporting Capital Gains.   When taxpayers sell capital assets, they report their sales on Schedule D of Form 1040 (dates of sale and purchase are additional items provided on Schedule D). After listing their sales, taxpayers then use Schedule D to apply the basic capital gains netting process. Exhibit 11-4 illustrates how Jeb would report his stock sales in Example 11-8, Scenario 1.

Netting Gains and Losses from 15 Percent, 25 Percent, and 28 Percent Capital Assets
When taxpayers sell long-term capital assets and recognize gains subject to the 25 percent or 28 percent capital gains rates, we must expand the basic netting process we've just described.[30] In these situations, apply the following steps to determine the amount of gain taxable at the different tax rates:

Step 1: Net all short-term gains and short-term losses, including any short-term capital loss carried forward from a prior year. If the net amount is positive, it is a net short-term capital gain. If the net amount is negative, it is a net short-term capital loss.

Step 2: Net all long-term capital gains and losses, including any long-term capital loss carried forward from a prior year. If the outcome is a net loss, proceed to Step 3; otherwise, ignore Step 3 and proceed to Step 4.

Step 3: If Step 1 generated a gain, net the gain against the loss from Step 2. If the outcome is a gain, the gain is a net short-term gain and you can ignore Steps 4–9. If the outcome is a loss, it is a net long-term capital

---

[29]When a taxpayer incurs both short- and long-term net capital losses that exceed the $3,000 annual deduction limit, the net short-term capital losses are first applied to the $3,000 deduction limit.
[30]§1(h)

EXHIBIT 11-4 Jeb's Schedule D

SCHEDULE D (Form 1040)	Capital Gains and Losses	OMB No. 1545-0074

Department of the Treasury
Internal Revenue Service   (99)

► Attach to Form 1040 or Form 1040NR.   ► See Instructions for Schedule D (Form 1040).
► Use Schedule D-1 to list additional transactions for lines 1 and 8.

2008

Attachment
Sequence No. **12**

Name(s) shown on return	Your social security number
Jeb Landers	450 : 28 : 2934

Part I Short-Term Capital Gains and Losses—Assets Held One Year or Less

(a) Description of property (Example: 100 sh. XYZ Co.)	(b) Date acquired (Mo., day, yr.)	(c) Date sold (Mo., day, yr.)	(d) Sales price (see page D-7 of the instructions)	(e) Cost or other basis (see page D-7 of the instructions)	(f) Gain or (loss) Subtract (e) from (d)
1 Stock C	3/01/08	11/05/08	20,000	12,000	8,000
Stock D	2/07/08	6/09/08	17,000	28,000	(11,000)
2 Enter your short-term totals, if any, from Schedule D-1, line 2 .	**2**				
3 Total short-term sales price amounts. Add lines 1 and 2 in column (d) .	**3**	37,000			

4 Short-term gain from Form 6252 and short-term gain or (loss) from Forms 4684, 6781, and 8824 | **4**

5 Net short-term gain or (loss) from partnerships, S corporations, estates, and trusts from Schedule(s) K-1 | **5**

6 Short-term capital loss carryover. Enter the amount, if any, from line 8 of your **Capital Loss Carryover Worksheet** on page D-7 of the instructions . | **6** ( )

7 **Net short-term capital gain or (loss).** Combine lines 1 through 6 in column (f) . | **7** (3,000)

Part II Long-Term Capital Gains and Losses—Assets Held More Than One Year

(a) Description of property (Example: 100 sh. XYZ Co.)	(b) Date acquired (Mo., day, yr.)	(c) Date sold (Mo., day, yr.)	(d) Sales price (see page D-7 of the instructions)	(e) Cost or other basis (see page D-7 of the instructions)	(f) Gain or (loss) Subtract (e) from (d)
8 Stock A	11/04/08	3/06/08	40,000	5,000	35,000
Stock B	7/09/05	9/01/08	20,000	30,000	(10,000)
9 Enter your long-term totals, if any, from Schedule D-1, line 9 .	**9**				
10 Total long-term sales price amounts. Add lines 8 and 9 in column (d) .	**10**	60,000			

11 Gain from Form 4797, Part I; long-term gain from Forms 2439 and 6252; and long-term gain or (loss) from Forms 4684, 6781, and 8824 . | **11**

12 Net long-term gain or (loss) from partnerships, S corporations, estates, and trusts from Schedule(s) K-1 . | **12**

13 Capital gain distributions. See page D-2 of the instructions . | **13**

14 Long-term capital loss carryover. Enter the amount, if any, from line 13 of your **Capital Loss Carryover Worksheet** on page D-7 of the instructions . | **14** ( )

15 **Net long-term capital gain or (loss).** Combine lines 8 through 14 in column (f). Then go to Part III on the back . | **15** 25,000

For Paperwork Reduction Act Notice, see Form 1040 or Form 1040NR instructions.   Cat. No. 11338H   **Schedule D (Form 1040) 2008** loss and you can ignore steps 4-9. If Step 1 generated a loss, you have both a net short-term and net long-term capital loss; apply the capital loss deduction limitations we described above, and ignore Steps 4–9.

Step 4: Separate all long-term capital gains and losses into the three separate rate groups. Any long-term capital loss carried forward from the previous year is placed in the 28 percent group. Also, note that by definition the 25 percent group includes only gains.

Step 5: Net the gains and losses in the 15 percent group. If the result is a net loss, move the net loss into the 28 percent group. Net gains remain in the 15 percent group and move to Step 9.

Step 6: *If the Step 1 result is a short-term capital loss,* move the loss into the 28 percent rate group. Otherwise, ignore this step.

Step 7: Net the gains and losses in the 28 percent rate group to determine if there is a net gain or loss in this group. Net gains in this group are taxed at a maximum rate of 28 percent. Net losses move to the 25 percent group.

Step 8: Net the 25 percent gains with the net loss determined in Step 7. Net gains are taxed at a maximum rate of 25 percent. Net losses move to the 15 percent rate group.

Step 9: Net the 15 percent net gain from Step 5 with the net loss from Step 8. This gain is taxed at a maximum 15 percent rate.

Steps 4 through 9 are designed to maximize the tax benefits of net short-term capital losses, long-term capital losses carryovers, and current year net losses in the 15 percent and 28 percent rate groups.

Example 11-9

What if: Assume that in addition to selling stocks, Jeb sold gold coins and a rental home (with $50,000 of accumulated depreciation) as follows:

Capital Asset	Market Value	Tax Basis	Capital Gain/Loss	Scenario 1 Type
A stock	$ 40,000	$ 5,000	$ 35,000	Long 15%
B stock	20,000	30,000	(10,000)	Long 15%
C stock	20,000	12,000	8,000	Short
D stock	17,000	28,000	(11,000)	Short
Gold coins	4,000	3,000	1,000	Long 28%
Rental home	200,000	80,000	120,000	Long 25% and 15%*
Overall gain			$143,000	

---

*$50,000 of the gain is 25 percent gain (from accumulated depreciation on the property) and the remaining $70,000 is 15 percent gain.

Assume that Jeb did not sell any other capital assets during the year. Jeb recognizes an overall capital gain of $143,000. What is (are) the maximum tax rate(s) applicable to this gain?

Answer: $95,000 of gain subject to a 15 percent maximum rate and $48,000 of gain is subject to a 25 percent rate, computed as follows:

Step 1: $3,000 net short-term capital loss [$8,000 + ($11,000)].

Step 2: $146,000 overall net long-term capital gain, so ignore Step 3 and proceed to Step 4.

Step 4: The $35,000 gain on the A stock, the $10,000 loss on the B stock, and $70,000 of gain from the rental home are placed in the 15 percent group. $50,000 of the gain from the rental property is placed in the 25 percent group and $1,000 gain on the gold coins is placed in the 28 percent group.

Step 5: *$95,000 net 15 percent gain* [$35,000 A stock + (10,000) B stock + $70,000 rental property].

Step 6: Move the $3,000 loss from Step 1 into the 28 percent group.

Step 7: *$2,000 net loss in 28 percent group* [$1,000 gain on gold + ($3,000) short term loss from Step 1]. Move the $2,000 net loss to the 25 percent group.

Step 8: *$48,000 25 percent gain* [$50,000 25 percent gain on rental + ($2,000) loss from Step 7].

Step 9: Not required.

Jeb's netting process is reflected in the following table:

Description	Short-Term	Long-Term Overall	Long-Term 28%	Long-Term 25%	Long-Term 15%
Stock C	$8,000				
Stock D	(11,000)				
Step 1:	(3,000)				
Coins		$ 1,000	1,000		
Unrecaptured §1250 Gain		50,000		50,000	
Remaining Gain from Rental Property		70,000			70,000
Stock A		35,000			35,000
Stock B		(10,000)			(10,000)
Step 2:		$146,000			
Steps 4 and 5:			$1,000	$50,000	$95,000
Step 6:	(3,000) —————→	(3,000)			
Step 7			(2,000) ——→	(2,000)	
Step 8				48,000	
Summary				$48,000	$95,000
Applicable Rate				25%	15%

So, we've learned how to determine the *maximum* tax rates applicable to different types of capital gains. How do we go about actually calculating the effect these gains have on the taxpayer's tax liability? Follow these basic guidelines:

- If the long-term capital gains would have been taxed at a rate of 28 percent or higher if they were ordinary income, the gain is taxed at the maximum rate for their group (15 percent, 25 percent, or 28 percent).
- If the long-term capital gains would have been taxed at a rate of 15 percent or lower if they were ordinary income, the 15 percent gains are taxed at 0 percent, and the 25 percent and 28 percent gains are taxed at the taxpayer's ordinary rate.[31]
- For other situations, use the following steps to determine the tax on the gains:[32]

  Step 1: Fill up the 10 percent and 15 percent tax rate brackets with taxable income, exclusive of long-term capital gains subject to preferential rates.

  Step 2: Next, add any 25 percent rate capital gains to either the 10 percent or 15 percent brackets to the extent room remains in either of these brackets after Step 1. Twenty-five percent rate capital gains included in these brackets are taxed at the ordinary rates applicable to these brackets.

---

[31]Note that the 15 percent gains could be taxed at 0 percent if that is the taxpayer's marginal ordinary rate.

[32]§1(h)

Step 3: Next, add any 28 percent rate capital gains to either the 10 percent or 15 percent brackets to the extent room remains in either of these brackets after Step 2. Twenty-eight percent rate capital gains included in these brackets are taxed at the ordinary rates applicable to these brackets.

Step 4: Next, add any 15 percent rate capital gains to either the 10 percent or 15 percent brackets to the extent room remains in either of these brackets after Step 3. Fifteen percent rate capital gains included in these brackets are taxed at 0 percent.

Step 5: Any capital gains remaining after Steps 1 through 4 are taxed at the maximum rate applicable to the gains (15 percent, 25 percent, or 28 percent).

Example 11-10

What if: Let's return to the facts of the previous example where Jeb recognized a $48,000 25 percent net capital gain and a $95,000 15 percent net capital gain. Also, assume that Jeb's taxable income for 2009 before considering the net capital gains is $10,000. Jeb files as single on his tax return. What is Jeb's gross tax liability for the year?

Answer: $25,175, computed as follows:

Amount and Type of Income	Applicable Rate	Tax	Explanation
$8,350; ordinary	10%	$ 835	$8,350 × 10% The first $8,350 of Jeb's $10,000 of ordinary income is taxed at 10 percent (see single tax rate schedule for this and other computations).
$1,650; ordinary	15%	248	$1,650 × 15%. Jeb's remaining $1,650 of ordinary income ($10,000 − $8,350) is taxed at 15 percent.
$23,950; 25 percent rate capital gains	15%	3,593	23,950 × 15% The end of the 15 percent bracket is $33,950 minus $10,000 ($8,350 + $1,650) already taxed.
$24,050; 25 percent rate capital gains	25%	6,013	$24,050 × 25% $48,000 total 25 percent gain minus $23,950 25 percent gain already taxed at 15 percent.
$95,000; 15 percent rate capital gains	15%	14,250	$95,000 × 15% All of the 15 percent gain would have been taxed at a rate higher than 15 percent, so it is all taxed at 15 percent.
Gross tax liability		**$24,939**	

Limitations on Capital Losses

We've previously discussed the general rule that taxpayers may deduct capital losses against capital gains in the netting process and that individual taxpayers may deduct up to $3,000 ($1,500 if married filing separately) of net capital losses against ordinary income in a given year. This general rule, however, is subject to certain exceptions as described below.

Losses on the Sale of Personal-Use Assets   As previously described, personal-use assets fall within the category of capital assets. When taxpayers sell personal-use assets, what are the tax consequences? Consider an engaged taxpayer who calls off the wedding plans. After getting the ring back from his former fiancée, the taxpayer sells the engagement ring for more than its purchase price. Does he recognize a taxable gain? Absolutely—the gain from the sale of a personal-use asset is taxable even though it was not purchased for its appreciation potential. The tax rate on the gain depends on the amount of time between the date the taxpayer purchased the ring and the date he sold it and on the netting process involving the seller's other capital gains and losses during the year. What if a taxpayer sold her car for less than she paid for it? Does she get to deduct the capital loss? Unfortunately, no—losses on the sale of personal-use assets are *not* deductible, and therefore never become part of the netting process.

Capital Losses on Sales to Related Parties   When taxpayers sell capital assets at a loss to related parties, they are not able to deduct the loss.[33] As we described in detail in Chapter 10, the related party acquiring the asset may eventually be allowed to deduct all, a portion, or none of the disallowed loss on a subsequent sale.

Wash Sales   Consider the case of a taxpayer attempting to do some tax planning near the end of the year: She has invested in the stock of several corporations; some of these investments have appreciated while others have declined in value. The taxpayer wants to capture the tax benefit of the stock losses in the current year to offset ordinary income (up to $3,000) or to offset other capital gains she has already recognized during the year. However, she can't deduct the losses until she sells the stock. Why might this be a problem? If the taxpayer believes that the stocks with unrealized losses are likely to appreciate in the near future, she may prefer *not* to sell those stocks but rather to keep them in her investment portfolio. What might this taxpayer do to deduct the losses while continuing to hold the investment in the stocks? For one, she might be tempted to sell the stocks and then immediately buy them back. Or, she might buy more of the same stock and then sell the stock she originally held to recognize the losses. With this strategy, she hopes to realize (and then recognize or deduct) the losses and, at the end of the day, still hold the stocks in her investment portfolio.

Although this might sound like a great plan, certain **wash sale** tax rules prevent this strategy from accomplishing the taxpayer's objective. A wash sale occurs when an investor sells or trades stock or securities at a loss *and* within 30 days *either before or after* the day of sale buys substantially identical stocks or securities.[34] Because the day of sale is included, the 30 days before and after period creates a 61-day window during which the wash sale provisions may apply.[35] When the wash sale provisions apply to a sale of stock, realized losses are not recognized; instead, the amount of *the unrecognized loss is added to the basis of the newly acquired stock.* Congress created this rule to prevent taxpayers from accelerating losses on securities that have declined in value without actually altering their investment in the securities. The 61-day period ensures that taxpayers cannot deduct losses from stock sales without exposing themselves to the risk that the stock they sold will subsequently increase in value.

---

[33]§267(a). §267(b) defines related parties and limits related-party losses. Because we described this concept in detail in Chapter 10, we merely raise the issue here.

[34]Substantially identical stocks or securities include contracts or options to buy substantially identical securities. However, corporate bonds and preferred stock are not generally considered substantially identical to common stock of the same corporation.

[35]§1091.

THE KEY FACTS

28 Percent and 25 Percent Rate Capital Gains

- Certain capital gains are taxable at maximum rates of 25 percent or 28 percent.
  · Unrecaptured §1250 gains are taxed at a maximum rate of 25 percent.
  · Gains from collectibles and from qualified small business stock (after the 50 percent exclusion) held for longer than five years are taxed at a maximum rate of 28 percent.

- When taxpayers have 25 percent or 28 percent rate capital gains, an expanded netting process applies.
  · The expanded netting process generally requires that losses be applied to higher rate groups before lower rate groups.

- When taxable income without long-term capital gains would be taxed in the 28 percent or higher ordinary income rate bracket, the capital gains in each rate group are simply taxed according to the capital gains rate applicable to each group. Otherwise applicable capital gains rates must be adjusted to reflect their inclusion in lower ordinary income rate brackets.

Nick and Rachel Sutton own 100 shares of Cisco stock that they purchased in June 2008 for $50 a share. On December 21, 2009, Nick and Rachel sell the shares for $40 a share to generate cash for the holidays. This sale generates a capital loss of $1,000 [$4,000 sale proceeds (100 × $40) − $5,000 cost basis ($50 × 100)]. Later, however, Nick and Rachel decide that Cisco might be a good long-term investment. On January 3, 2010 (13 days later), the Suttons purchase 100 shares of Cisco stock for $41 a share ($4,100). Do the Suttons *realize* a short- or long-term capital loss on the December 21 sale?

Answer: Long-term capital loss. They held the stock for more than one year (June 2008 to December 2009) before selling.

How much of the realized $1,000 long-term capital loss can the Suttons recognize or deduct on their 2009 tax return?

Answer: Zero. Because the Suttons sold the stock at a loss and purchased the same stock within the 61-day period centered on the date of sale (30 days before December 21, December 21, and 30 days after December 21), the wash sale rules disallow the loss in 2009. Had the Suttons waited just another 18 days to repurchase the Cisco shares, they could have avoided the wash sale rules. In that case, under the general rules for capital loss deductibility, the Suttons *would* be able to deduct the $1,000 capital loss from the sale against their ordinary income on their 2009 income tax return.

What basis will the Suttons have in the Cisco stock they purchased (or repurchased) on January 3, 2010?

Answer: $5,100. Under the wash sale rules, the Suttons add the $1,000 disallowed loss to the basis of the stock they purchased on January 3. Thus, they now own 100 shares of Cisco stock with a $5,100 basis in the shares, which is $1,000 more than they paid for it.

What if: How much of the $1,000 realized loss would the Suttons have recognized if they had only purchased 40 shares of Cisco stock instead of 100 shares on January 3, 2010?

Answer: $600. The wash sale rules disallow the loss to the extent taxpayers acquire other shares in the 61-day window. In this situation, the Suttons only acquired 40 percent (40 of 100) of the shares they sold at a loss within the window. Consequently, they must disallow 40 percent, or $400, of the loss and they are allowed to deduct the remaining $600 loss.

Balancing Tax Planning Strategies for Capital Assets with Other Goals

When taxpayers invest in capital assets and hold the assets for more than a year, they receive at least two benefits. First, they are able to defer recognizing gains on the assets until they sell them—the longer the deferral period, the lower the present value of the capital gains tax when taxpayers ultimately sell the assets. Second, they pay taxes on the gains at preferential rates. These tax advantages provide taxpayers with a greater after-tax rate of return on these investments than they would obtain from less tax-favored assets that earn equivalent before-tax rates of return. Investors who quickly sell investments pay taxes on gains at higher, ordinary rates and incur significantly greater transaction costs. Nevertheless, taxpayers should balance the tax benefits available for holding assets with the risk that the asset values will have declined by the time they want to sell the assets.

What if: Assume the Suttons decide to purchase Intel stock for $100,000 and hold half of the shares for 5 years to purchase the Park City home and the other half for 18 years to pay for Lea's education. If the Intel stock grows at a constant 8 percent before-tax rate and does not pay any dividends, how much cash will the Suttons accumulate after taxes for the Park City home?

Answer: $69,946, computed as follows:

Description	Amount	Explanation
(1) Proceeds from sale	$73,466	$[\$50,000 \times (1 + .08)^5]$.
(2) Basis in fund shares	50,000	This is the nondeductible investment in the shares.
(3) Gain realized on sale	$23,466	(1) − (2).
(4) Tax rate on gain	× 15%	Low rate for long-term capital gain.*
(5) Tax on gain	$ 3,520	(3) × (4).
After-tax cash for Park City home	**$69,946**	(1) − (5).

*Assumes the Suttons don't have any capital losses.

What after-tax rate of return will the Suttons earn on the money invested for the Park City home?

Answer:[36]   6.94 percent $[(\$69,946/\$50,000)^{1/5} - 1]$.

How much cash will the Suttons accumulate after taxes for Lea's education?

Answer: $177,331, computed as follows:

Description	Amount	Explanation
(1) Proceeds from sale	$199,801	$[\$50,000 \times (1 + .08)^{18}]$.
(2) Basis in fund shares	50,000	This is the nondeductible investment in the shares.
(3) Gain realized on sale	$149,801	(1) − (2).
(4) Tax rate on gain	× 15%	Low rate for long-term capital gain.*
(5) Tax on gain	$ 22,470	(3) × (4).
After-tax cash for education goal	**$177,331**	(1) − (5).

*Assumes the Suttons don't have capital losses.

What after-tax rate of return will the Suttons earn on the money invested for Lea's education?

Answer: 7.29 percent. $[(\$177,331/\$50,000)^{1/18} - 1]$.

Intuitively, why is the after-tax rate of return greater for the 18-year investment than for the 5-year investment?

Answer: Although both the 5-year and the 18-year investments are taxed at preferential capital gains rates, taxes are deferred a longer period of time for the 18-year investment and, as a result, are less on a present value basis.

Taxes in the Real World   *Seeking Long-Term Capital Gains and Diversification*

Investors seeking long-term capital gains and diversification of their investments frequently invest in so-called tax efficient mutual funds. Like other mutual funds, tax efficient mutual funds invest in a portfolio of stock and other securities; but, unlike other mutual funds, they actively employ tax planning strategies to reduce current distributions and to increase the likelihood that recognized investment gains will be taxed at favorable long-term capital gains rates. One basic tax planning strategy they employ is a simple buy and hold strategy rather than frequently trading securities the way other mutual funds do. Exchange traded funds, or ETFs, are also popular among traditional investors in tax efficient mutual

(continued on page 11-22...)

---

[36]In general, the formula for computing the after-tax rate of return on any investment is $(FV/I)^{1/n} - 1$ where FV is the future value after taxes, I is the investment and n is the number of investment periods. Financial calculators designate this calculation as the IRR or internal rate of return.

funds. ETFs are securities that typically derive their value from an investment index such as the S&P 500. Thus, like tax efficient mutual funds, they provide a measure of investment diversification. However, unlike tax efficient mutual funds whose actions determine when and how investment returns are taxed, investors in ETFs have greater control over the timing and character of investment returns from ETF's because they are treated like individual stocks for tax purposes.

Source: Eleanor Laise, "Less-Taxing Fund Choices," *The Wall Street Journal,* October 29, 2006.

When investing in capital assets, taxpayers run the risk that some of their investments may decline in value. Thus, a productive strategy for managing investments in capital assets is to sell investments with built-in losses. This strategy is commonly referred to as "loss harvesting." By selectively selling loss assets, taxpayers can reduce their taxes by deducting up to $3,000 against their ordinary income and by reducing the amount of capital gains that would otherwise be subject to tax during the year. This is particularly beneficial for taxpayers who have short-term capital gains that will be taxed at higher ordinary rates absent offsetting capital losses. Note, however, that taxpayers should not sell investments to gain tax benefits if they believe that the potential economic benefit of holding the investment outweighs the tax benefits of selling the stock. Also, keep in mind that capital losses on stock sales may not be deductible due to the wash sale rules (see above).

LO3 PORTFOLIO INCOME: TAX EXEMPT

So far in this chapter, we have discussed investments that are taxed at different rates and at different times depending on the nature of the investment. Some other investments are, for policy reasons, never explicitly taxed. Among these tax-favored investments are municipal bonds, life insurance, and educational savings plans. Other tax-exempt vehicles meant to stimulate retirement savings are discussed in Chapter 13.

Municipal Bonds

Municipal bonds are debt instruments issued by state and local governments to build roads, schools, and for other governmental needs.[37] Similar to U.S. Treasury securities, municipal bonds are generally considered to be less risky than corporate bonds. In most cases, municipal bond interest is not subject to federal income tax.[38] However, it may be subject to state income taxes if the bondholder holds municipal bonds from a state that is not the state of his primary residence.[39] For example, a taxpayer residing in Arizona would not pay Arizona state income tax on the interest from municipal bonds issued by the state of Arizona, but she would for municipal bonds issued by Utah.

Why does the federal government grant municipal bonds tax-favored status? The answer is, to subsidize the expenditures of state and local governments. Investors are attracted to municipal bonds because they are tax favored relative to similar

---

[37]The District of Columbia as well as U.S. possessions such as Puerto Rico may also issue tax-exempt municipal bonds.

[38]Interest from certain municipal bonds issued to fund activities of a more private nature, such as redevelopment and stadium construction, is included as a preference item in the alternative minimum tax calculation. These bonds are referred to as *private activity bonds.*

[39]States determine residency status by such factors as voter registration, property ownership, and amount of time spent in the state.

taxable bonds. Increased demand drives the price up—and conversely the yield, or interest rate, down— for municipal bonds relative to taxable bonds. The yield on municipal bonds represents the rate that a state, in effect, pays to borrow money. In essence, the federal government is willing to forego tax revenues so that state and local governments may borrow from bond investors at a lower rate.

Viewed from an investor's perspective, the subsidy state and local governments receive when issuing municipal bonds is reflected as lower rates of return relative to alternative rates of return available on taxable bonds. These lower rates of return are economically similar to other taxes on investment income because they subsidize municipal governments while leaving investors in municipal bonds with lower investment returns than they would have received otherwise. As we described in Chapter 1, differences in rates of return on municipal bonds relative to taxable bonds are sometimes referred to as **implicit taxes** as opposed to **explicit taxes,** which are actually levied by and paid to governmental entities. To make correct investment choices, investors must consider implicit taxes when comparing investment alternatives.

Example 11-13

In addition to their other investment options, Nick and Rachel are considering investing in Arizona municipal bonds paying interest of 5 percent annually because they heard they are "tax free." They decide to compare the General Electric corporate bonds with the Arizona municipal bonds. Assume the Arizona bonds are similar to the GE bonds in all respects except for how they are taxed and the rate of return on the Arizona bonds. Recall that when Nick and Rachel previously considered purchasing the taxable GE bonds, they learned that the bonds paid interest annually at a before-tax rate of 8 percent. Given this information, should Nick and Rachel invest in Arizona municipal bonds?

Answer: No. With a 30 percent marginal tax rate, they would earn a 5.6 percent after-tax return on the GE bonds (see Example 11-3), but only a 5 percent after-tax return on the Arizona bonds.

Would their decision change if they expected their marginal tax rate to increase to 40 percent?

Answer: Yes. With a 40 percent marginal tax rate, their after-tax rate of return on the GE bonds decreases to 4.8 percent [8% × (1 − 40%)]. If they expected their rate to increase to 40 percent, the Arizona bonds would be the superior investment!

This example illustrates an important truism: taxpayers with high marginal tax rates prefer tax-favored investments like municipal bonds. Why? Because the explicit tax that taxpayers with high marginal tax rates avoid is greater than the implicit tax they incur when purchasing municipal bonds. The converse also is true—taxpayers with low marginal tax rates prefer explicitly taxed investments like corporate bonds because the explicit taxes they actually pay are less than the implicit taxes they avoid on tax-favored assets like municipal bonds.

Life Insurance

Many people think of life insurance solely as a product designed to financially protect a family in the event of an untimely death of another family member. In addition to insuring one's own life or the life of a family member, however, it is possible to purchase an insurance policy on the life of a nonfamily member such as a business partner. Moreover, companies frequently insure the lives of their key executives and name themselves as beneficiaries.

Although you may not have previously thought of life insurance as an investment, life insurance companies also offer life insurance policies with an investment component in addition to the insurance component. This type of insurance often is referred to as **whole life insurance** whereas insurance without a savings component is called **term insurance.** The premiums paid for whole life policies—minus various insurers' costs—are invested by the insurance company in stocks, bonds, and other securities. In the event the policy is cashed in before the death of the insured individual, the beneficiary receives the **cash surrender value** of the policy, which approximates the value of the invested premiums and the associated investment gains. In reality, the cash surrender value is somewhat less than this amount because of the administrative and other fees insurance companies charge to provide their products.

As we described in Chapter 5, taxpayers receiving life insurance proceeds on the death of the insured exclude the proceeds from gross income. To some extent, the tax-advantaged treatment of life insurance permits individuals to use life insurance policies as tax-favored vehicles to acquire investments that would be taxed if held in normal investment accounts.[40] As long as the investment gains within the life insurance policy remain untapped until the death of the insured, they are tax-exempt. However, if a policy is cashed in early, the cash surrender value is not tax-exempt. The beneficiary of the policy is taxed at *ordinary rates* on the total investment *gains* from the policy—that is, the difference between the cash surrender value of the policy and the premiums invested.

Example 11-14

Nick's father, Dale, recently purchased a policy to insure his life and named Nick and Rachel as beneficiaries. The policy, at a one-time cost of $50,000, promises returns of 8 percent per year if Dale dies after 18 years—his normal life expectancy. How much will Nick and Rachel receive after-tax if Dale dies in 18 years and what would be their after-tax rate of return?

Answer: $199,801. [$50,000 $\times$ (1 + .08)^{18}]. Proceeds paid on the death of the insured are not taxable, so the life insurance policy generates an 8 percent before- and after-tax return.

How much will they receive after-tax if Dale dies prematurely in five years and what would be their after-tax rate of return?[41]

Answer: $73,466. [$50,000 $\times$ (1 + .08)^5]. Proceeds paid on the death of the insured are not taxable, so the life insurance policy generates an 8 percent before- and after-tax return.

How much will *Dale* receive after-tax if he decides to cash in the policy after five years while he is still living (his ordinary rate is 30%) and what would be his after-tax rate of return?

Answer: $66,426 and 5.8 percent, computed as follows:

Description	Amount	Explanation
(1) Cash surrender value received	$73,466	[$50,000 $\times$ (1 + .08)^5].
(2) Initial cost of policy	50,000	Investment in policy.
(3) Gain on cash in	$23,466	(1) − (2).
(4) Ordinary marginal rate	× 30%	
(5) Taxes payable on cash in	7,040	(3) × (4).
(6) After-tax proceeds	$66,426	(1) − (5).
After-tax rate of return	5.8%	[(66,246/50,000)$^{1/5}$ − 1].

---

[40]Tax rules require life insurance policies to provide minimum levels of actual life insurance to prevent life insurance from being used by investors solely as tax-exempt investment vehicles.

[41]For the sake of simplicity, we assume the life insurance purchased in this example functions as a pure investment contract. That is, we assume the life insurance policy will generate a before-tax rate of return of 8 percent regardless of when Dale dies. In reality, if Dale were to die prematurely, the rate of return on the policy would likely be greater than 8 percent because life insurance contracts typically specify a fixed payout regardless of when the insured dies.

Although life insurance, with its tax-favored status, might appear to be an ideal investment, various aspects of life insurance limit its desirability as an investment vehicle. Life insurance products tend to be weighed down with high commissions and fees, which reduce before-tax returns relative to other investment alternatives. Moreover, investors who purchase life insurance and plan to cash in their investments at a predetermined time are constrained because they must wait until the insured individual dies to minimize the tax burden on their investment.

Educational Savings Plans

To encourage families to save for their children's college education, Congress has created tax-favored educational savings accounts that shield investment returns from income taxes.[42] When donors contribute to these plans, they designate how their contributions will be invested within the plans. The investment returns then accumulate tax-free. When distributions are made from these plans, earnings are distributed tax-free provided they are used for qualified education costs. One well-known tax-advantaged account is the Coverdell Educational Savings Account. With a Coverdell account, yearly contributions to the account are limited to $2,000 for each beneficiary, and distributions may be used to pay for qualified educational costs of kindergarten through 12th grade and qualified higher education expenses such as tuition, books, fees, supplies, and reasonable room and board.[43] The $2,000 contribution limit for Coverdell accounts phases out as AGI increases from $190,000 to $220,000 for married filing jointly taxpayers, and from $95,000 to $110,000 for all other taxpayers.

Another tax-advantaged educational savings vehicle gaining in popularity is the **qualified tuition program** or **529 plan.** 529 plans allow parents, grandparents, and other individuals to contribute up to the maximum allowed by state-sponsored 529 plans to fund the qualified educational costs of future *college* students.[44] Earnings in 529 plans are distributed tax-free provided they are used for qualified *higher* education expenses. If, on the other hand, distributions are made to the beneficiary for other purposes, investment returns are taxed to the beneficiary at the beneficiary's tax rate and are subject to an additional 10 percent penalty while distributions to the beneficiary in excess of investment returns are treated as gifts.[45] Distributions to contributors (e.g., parents, grandparents) in excess of their contributions are included in contributors' gross income.

Example 11-15

Assume Nick and Rachel decide to invest $50,000 in the state of Arizona 529 plan to fund Lea's college education. Assuming an 8 percent annual return, how much money, after-taxes, would this investment produce for Lea's college education in 18 years and what after-tax rate of return would the investment earn?

(continued on page 11-26...)

---

[42]As we discussed in Chapter 5, taxpayers may also use U.S. savings bonds as a tax efficient means of saving for higher education. Interest from U.S. savings bonds (series EE and I) is excluded from taxable income to the extent it is used to pay for certain higher education costs.

[43]§530(b). This definition of qualified higher education expenses is consistent with the definition used in §221(d)(2) to determine if interest paid on education-related loans is deductible (see Chapter 6).

[44]Contribution limits vary according to the state administering the 529 plan. The median contribution limit is approximately $235,000. In addition, more than half the states offer a state tax deduction or credit to residents contributing to the 529 plan sponsored by the state in which the contributors reside.

[45]Under §529(c)(3), multiple distributions received under these circumstances are treated as annuities. As a result, a portion of each distribution would be treated as a gift with the remainder treated as income.

Answer: $199,801. [$50,000 \times (1 + .08)^{18}$]. Because the income is tax exempt, the before- and after-tax rate of return is 8 percent. This calculation is exactly the same as the calculation we used to determine what the value of the life insurance policy on Dale's life would be if he dies in 18 years. If used to cover Lea's qualified higher educational expenses, none of the $149,801 in earnings on the $50,000 investment would ever be taxed![46]

What amount would the Suttons have after taxes if they withdrew the balance of their 529 account after five years to use the money to help fund the Park City home and what after-tax (and penalty) rate of return would they earn?

Answer: $64,079 proceeds after-tax and penalty and 5.1 percent after-tax and penalty rate of return.

Description	Amount	Explanation
(1) Total proceeds before taxes and penalties	$73,466	$50,000 \times (1 + .08)^5$.
(2) Total investment in plan	50,000	Amount initially invested in plan.
(3) Gain on distribution	$23,466	(1) − (2).
(4) The Suttons' marginal ordinary tax rate	× 30%	
(5) Taxes payable on distribution of proceeds	($7,040)	(3) × (4) taxed because proceeds not used for education.
(6) After-tax proceeds	$66,426	(1) + (4).
(7) Penalty rate for noneducational use	10%	
(8) Penalty for noneducational use of proceeds	(2,347)	(3) × (7).
(9) Proceeds after taxes and penalties	$64,079	(1) + (5) + (8).
After-tax and penalty rate of return	5.1%	[($64,079/50,000)^{1/5} − 1].

529 plans and other tax-advantaged educational savings vehicles compare favorably with other investment alternatives when it comes to saving for educational costs. While Coverdell plans allow investors some latitude in deciding how to invest contributed funds, the states and organizations that administer 529 plans provide limited investment options. Families looking for greater flexibility when investing for higher education may be willing to trade the tax advantages of these vehicles for the possibility of greater investment returns elsewhere. Investors should consider these plans within the context of their overall investment philosophy.

529 plans and Coverdell savings accounts also offer significant nontax advantages relative to some alternative education savings strategies. In calculating eligibility for financial aid, colleges and universities weight assets held by students more heavily than those held by parents. Because 529 and Coverdell accounts are generally considered parental assets, they are less likely to affect the amount of financial aid a student receives compared to investments held in the student's name.

PORTFOLIO INCOME SUMMARY

As we've discussed the tax consequences of various investments up to this point in the chapter, we have proceeded from the least tax-advantaged (taxed annually at ordinary rates) to the most tax-advantaged (tax-exempt). By moving along this

[46]This analysis reflects the federal income tax impications of investing in a 529 plan. State income taxes as well as state and federal gift taxes may also be an important consideration.

EXHIBIT 11-5   Portfolio Income Summary

Rank	Example of Investment	Income Type	Timing of Taxation	Tax Rate
1	Municipal bonds	Tax-exempt income	Never	Zero
2	Growth stock	Appreciation in capital assets	Deferred	Capital gains
3	Stock in electric utility company	Dividends	Current	Capital gains
4	Certificate of deposit	Taxable interest	Current	Ordinary

continuum from investments taxed annually at ordinary rates (corporate bonds[47]) to investments taxed annually at capital gains rates (dividend-paying stock), investors are in essence employing the conversion planning strategy referred to repeatedly throughout this text. As taxpayers move from dividend-paying stock to growth stock, which provides tax deferral in addition to preferential tax rates, taxpayers combine the conversion strategy with the basic strategy of shifting income from one time period to another. Finally, taxpayers also rely on conversion when they choose to purchase either tax-exempt municipal bonds or when they invest in tax-exempt vehicles like insurance and educational savings plans.

Exhibit 11-5 reviews and ranks investments from best to worst based solely on their tax characteristics.

With the exception of the municipal bond investment, the differences in after-tax returns are driven solely by the tax treatment of each investment.

In this chapter and elsewhere in this text, we emphasize that tax planning must not be done in a vacuum without considering all relevant parties and taxpayers' economic and personal objectives. Because investments typically are not designed to accommodate the specific needs of each individual investor, considering the other party in the deal is not as relevant when investing as it is in other transactions. However, it is vital that investors carefully balance the tax characteristics of their investment options with the other attributes of their investment options such as risk and liquidity. Similarly, investors must be sure to consider implicit taxes when purchasing tax-favored assets like municipal bonds.

Example 11-16

After doing some basic research on investments that might be suitable savings vehicles for the Park City vacation home and Lea's Ivy League education, Nick and Rachel must now decide how to invest $50,000 for 5 years and another $50,000 for 18 years. Given the following summary information from prior examples, how should Nick and Rachel invest their money if they were to base their decision on the tax characteristics alone?

Investment	5 Years After-Tax Rate of Return	18 Years After-Tax Rate of Return	Reference
Corporate bonds (GE)	5.6%	5.6%	Example 11-1.
Dividend-paying stocks (Xerox)	6.80%	6.80%	Example 11-4.
Growth stock (Intel)	**6.94%**	7.29%	Example 11-12.
Municipal bonds (Arizona 5% yield)	5%	5%	Example 11-13.
529 college savings plan (Arizona)	N/A	**8%**	Example 11-15.

Note: Except for the Arizona municipal bonds, all other investments are assumed to yield 8 percent before tax. Because of implicit taxes, the Arizona bond only yields 5 percent.

(continued on page 11-28...)

---

[47]We refer here to corporate bonds issued or acquired at face value.

Answer: To save for the Park City home, the best alternative would be an investment in the Intel stock. This option is superior to the other remaining alternatives from a tax perspective because it combines the power of tax deferral with the conversion of ordinary income into capital gains. Note, however, that the tax deferral benefit in this instance is not significant given the limited deferral period.

To save for Lea's education, the Suttons would do best to use the Arizona 529 plan because it generates the greatest after-tax rate of return among the alternatives. Purchasing the Intel stock would be the next best alternative for the Suttons because the power of conversion and deferral over an 18-year time horizon generates after-tax returns that are close to being tax-exempt. Recall that 529 plans limit the range of investments savers may select relative to a privately managed investment account. If the Suttons feel this is a significant constraint, they may decide to invest in growth stocks and either forgo or limit their contributions to the 529 plan.

PORTFOLIO INVESTMENT EXPENSES

L04

Now that we've discussed how *income* from various forms of investments is taxed and how tax rules affect after-tax returns, let's explore the deductibility of expenses taxpayers incur to acquire or maintain their investments. We first discuss tax consequences associated with **investment expenses** and we conclude by discussing the deductibility of **investment interest expense.** Even though the names of these two deductions sound very similar, investment expenses and investment interest expense are two *different* deductions with different deductibility limitations. So, when you are reading about an investment-related expense, pay careful attention to whether the expense is an *investment expense* or *investment interest expense.* Exhibit 11-6 provides a description of these expenses and the limitations on the deductibility of the expenses.

Investment Expenses

Just as taxpayers can deduct ordinary and necessary business expenditures when conducting business activities, individual taxpayers are allowed to deduct ordinary and necessary expenses they incur in investment activities to produce or collect income and for expenses they pay or incur to manage property held for producing

EXHIBIT 11-6 Summary of Investment-Related Expenses

Item	Investment Expense	Investment *Interest* Expense
Description	Expenses (other than interest) incurred to generate investment income.	Interest expense on loans used to acquire investments.
Deduction type	Miscellaneous itemized deduction (subject to 2 percent of AGI floor).	Interest expense itemized deduction.
Deduction limitations	Deductible only when investment expenses and other miscellaneous itemized deductions exceed 2 percent of AGI floor.	Deduction limited to taxpayer's net investment income for the year. Net investment income is gross investment income reduced by *deductible investment expenses.*
Nondeductible amounts due to limitations	Deduct it in the year incurred or lose it.	Carryover indefinitely.

income—such as safe deposit box rental fees, attorney and accounting fees that are necessary to produce investment income, and expenses for investment advice, among other things.[48]

The arrangement makes sense if you think about it: The government taxes investment income, so it is willing to allow taxpayers to deduct expenses they incur to generate investment income. Conversely, to the extent taxpayers incur expenses to produce tax-exempt income, such as municipal bond interest, they are not allowed to deduct the related expenses.[49] For example, a taxpayer who keeps a fully taxable corporate bond in a safe deposit box would be allowed an investment expense deduction for the cost of renting the box, but one who keeps a tax-exempt municipal bond in a safe deposit box would not.

The bad news here for taxpayers is that investment expenses are treated as miscellaneous itemized deductions subject to the 2 percent of AGI floor.[50] Thus, taxpayers with investment expenses will only realize tax benefits from these expenses if they itemize deductions *and* their total miscellaneous itemized deductions (fees for investment advice, tax return preparation fees, an employee's job-related magazine subscriptions, and other unreimbursed employee business expenses—see Chapter 6)—including investment expenses—exceed 2 percent of their AGI. Consequently, it is likely that taxpayers with taxable investments and investment expenses will receive little tax benefit, if any, from the expenses.

> **THE KEY FACTS**
> Investment-Related Expenses
> ■ Investment expenses deducted as miscellaneous itemized deductions are subject to the 2 percent of AGI floor.
> · Expenses other than interest incurred to generate investment income.
> · No carryover of amounts not currently deductible.

Example 11-17

Nick and Rachel Sutton met several times with a financial planner who advised them regarding some difficult investment decisions. Nick and Rachel paid the advisor $500 for her services. Also, during the year Nick and Rachel paid a CPA $300 to prepare their tax return. The Suttons had no other miscellaneous itemized deductions for the year. Do the Suttons gain any tax benefit from the $500 they paid to the financial planner (their AGI is $170,000)?

Answer: No. The $500 payment is a deductible investment expense for Nick and Rachel. However, to receive any tax benefit from the payment, their total miscellaneous itemized deductions must exceed 2 percent of their AGI. The computation for their deductible investment expense is as follows:

Description	Amount
Investment expenses	$ 500
Tax return preparation fees	300
Total miscellaneous itemized deductions	$ 800
Less: 2 percent of AGI ($170,000 × 2%)	3,400
Miscellaneous itemized deductions over 2 percent of AGI floor.	$ 0

Because their miscellaneous itemized deductions are less than 2 percent of their AGI, the Suttons do not gain any tax benefit from the $500 investment expense (it does not offset taxable income).

In fact, the Suttons could have paid another $2,600 of investment expenses before they would have exceeded the 2 percent of AGI threshold and received *any* tax benefit from the payment ($3,400 − $800).

[48]IRC §212. Rental expenses are also deductible under §212 as we discuss in Chapter 8.
[49]§265.
[50]See Chapter 6 for a discussion of the tax treatment of miscellaneous itemized deductions. Also note that as we discussed in Chapter 6, investment expenses from rental and royalty-related activities are deductible as *for* AGI and not as itemized deductions.

Investment Interest Expense

When taxpayers borrow money to acquire investments, the interest expense they pay on the loan is investment interest expense. For example, if you borrow funds to buy stock, any interest you pay on the loan would be considered investment interest expense. Investment interest expense is deductible as an itemized deduction.[51] Unlike investment expenses, the investment interest expense deduction is *not* a miscellaneous itemized deduction subject to the 2 percent of AGI floor. It is, however, subject to a different limitation. A taxpayer's investment interest expense deduction for the year is limited to the taxpayer's **net investment income** for the year.[52]

Net Investment Income   Net investment income is gross investment income reduced by *deductible* investment expenses. Deductible investment expenses are investment expenses that actually reduce taxable income *after* applying the 2 percent of AGI floor.[53] Gross investment income includes interest, annuity, and royalty income not derived in the ordinary course of a trade or business. It also includes net *short*-term capital gains, net capital losses (short- and long-term), and nonqualifying dividends. However, investment income generally does not include net long-term capital gains and qualifying dividends because this income is taxed at a preferential rate.

Example 11-18

During the year, Nick and Rachel recognized the following income from investments: $3,000 of qualifying dividends and $500 of taxable interest. What is the Suttons' gross investment income?

Answer: $500. The taxable interest is included and the qualifying dividends are excluded because they are taxed at a preferential rate.

What is the Suttons' *net* investment income?

Answer: $500. Recall that net investment income is gross investment income minus deductible (taxable income reducing) investment expenses. We learned in Example 11-17 that the Suttons' deductible investment expenses are $0. Thus, their net investment income is $500 ($500 − $0).

Taxpayers may deduct their investment interest expense up to the amount of their net investment income. Any investment interest expense in excess of net investment income is carried over and treated as though it was incurred in the next year when it is subject to the same limitations.[54] The carryover amount never expires. That is, taxpayers can carry over the excess investment interest expense until they generate sufficient net investment income to deduct it.

---

[51]§163.

[52]The investment interest expense limitation is calculated on Form 4952. Note that taxpayers can avoid the limitations on investment interest expense by acquiring the investment assets with funds from a qualifying home equity loan. As we discuss in Chapter 14, interest on home equity loans is generally fully deductible.

[53]When taxpayers have both investment expenses and other miscellaneous itemized deductions subject to the 2 percent of AGI floor, deductible amounts in excess of the 2 percent of AGI floor are considered to first come from investment expenses up to the total amount of investment expenses and then from other miscellaneous itemized deductions.

[54]In lieu of deducting investment interest expense, taxpayers may elect to capitalize it to the basis of the investment property purchased with the loan generating the investment interest expense. See Reg. §1.266-1(c)(1).

Example 11-19

In July of this year, the Suttons purchased a parcel of undeveloped land as an investment for $120,000. They made a $20,000 down payment and financed the remaining $100,000 with a loan from their local credit union. The interest rate on the loan was 9 percent, payable annually. During the year, the Suttons paid $4,500 in interest expense on the loan. Because the loan was used to purchase an investment, the interest expense is investment interest expense. What amount of this investment interest expense are the Suttons allowed to deduct this year?

Answer: $500. Although they incurred $4,500 of investment interest expense, their deduction for the current year is limited to their $500 net investment income (see Example 11-18). The $4,000 of investment interest expense that is not deductible this year is carried forward until the Suttons generate enough net investment income to deduct it.

Election to Include Long-Term Capital Gains and Qualifying Dividends in Investment Income
When we described the types of income included in investment income, we mentioned that net long-term capital gains and qualifying dividends generally are excluded from investment income because these types of income are taxed at a preferential rate that is lower than the ordinary income tax rate. Congress decided that it wasn't right to allow income that is taxed at a preferential rate to increase the amount of deductions that offset income taxed at an ordinary rate. However, Congress allows taxpayers to *elect to include* preferentially taxed income in investment income if they are willing to subject this income to tax at the ordinary (not preferential) tax rates.

Taxpayers who make this election benefit from increasing their net investment income and thus increasing their current year investment interest expense deduction. But, this additional deduction comes at a price because they must subject their net long-term capital gains and qualifying dividends included in investment income to ordinary tax rates. Note that the election is not an all or nothing proposition. Taxpayers can elect to include all or only a portion of their net long-term capital gains and qualifying dividends in investment income. However, whatever they include in investment income, they must subject to tax at the ordinary tax rates.

Example 11-20

In Examples 11-18 and 11-19, we discovered that the Suttons paid $4,500 of investment interest expense during the year but were only able to deduct $500 of the interest expense because their net investment income was only $500. However, as indicated in Example 11-18, the Suttons also received $3,000 of qualifying dividends that were *excluded* from the net investment income computation. The Suttons may elect to increase their investment income by the amount of the qualifying dividends (and increase their investment interest expense deduction), but by doing so, they must subject the qualifying dividends to their ordinary tax rate (30 percent) instead of the preferential rate (15 percent). Thus, the Suttons are faced with a choice of whether to include the $3,000 dividend in investment income and tax it at ordinary rates (alternative 1) or to exclude it from investment income and tax it at preferential rates (alternative 2).[55] How much more investment interest expense are they allowed to deduct under alternative 1 than alternative 2?

(*continued on page 11-32...*)

THE KEY FACTS

Investment-Related Expenses

■ Investment *interest* expense.
· Itemized deduction not subject to the 2 percent of AGI floor.
· Interest expense on loans used to purchase taxable investments.
· Deductible to the extent of net investment income.
(*continued*)

[55]While this example presents only two options, the Suttons may elect to include any amount of the dividends in investment income.

(concluded)
· Net investment income is gross investment income minus deductible investment expenses.
· Investment income includes interest, annuity, and other investment-type income not taxed at the preferential rate (long-term capital gains and qualifying dividends).
· Taxpayers can elect to include long-term capital gains and dividends in investment income but must tax them at the ordinary not the preferential rate.
· Investment interest expense not deducted carries forward indefinitely.

Answer: $3,000 more under alternative 2, computed as follows:

Alternative 1: *Include the $3,000 dividends in investment income.*

Description	Amount	Explanation
(1) Increase in net investment income	$3,000	Elect to include dividends in net investment income.
(2) **Increase in investment interest expense deduction**	$3,000	Investment interest expense deduction increased from $500 to $3,500.
(3) Tax benefit from additional deduction	$ 900	(2) × 30%.
(4) Tax cost of taxing dividends at ordinary rate	$ 450	(1) × (30% − 15%).
(5) Current savings from election to include dividends in net investment income	$ 450	(3) − (4).
Investment interest expense carryforward	$1,000	$4,500 total − $3,500 deducted.

Alternative 2: *Exclude the $3,000 dividends from investment income.*

Description	Amount	Explanation
Forgone tax benefit available *this year* under alternative 1	$ 450	Under alternative 2, the Suttons don't receive the tax savings available under alternative 1.
(1) Increase in investment interest expense carryforward	$3,000	Investment interest expense not deducted under alternative 2.
Total investment interest expense carryforward	$4,000	(1) + $1,000 investment interest expense carryforward under alternative 1.

Whether or not it makes sense to elect to include net long-term capital gains and qualifying dividends in investment income depends on the taxpayers' circumstances and their personal preferences. As we see in Example 11-20, the Suttons could save $450 this year by electing to include this income in investment income. However, by doing so, they are forgoing $3,000 of investment interest expense carryforward ($4,000 − $1,000) that would be available to offset ordinary income in future years.

LO5

PASSIVE ACTIVITY INCOME AND LOSSES

Taxpayers may invest in business and business-related activities in (1) ways in which the taxpayer is taxed on *portfolio income* from the investment or (2) ways in which the taxpayer is taxed directly on the *actual income* from the business. For example, taxpayers acquiring stock in a **taxable corporation** or acquiring bonds issued by a corporation are taxed on the portfolio income these investments generate in the form of dividends and interest. On the other hand, a taxpayer purchasing rental property and holding title to the property in her own name or a taxpayer forming a business as a sole proprietor is taxed on the actual income these activities generate. Similarly, a taxpayer could acquire a partial interest in a trade or business or rental activity by acquiring an ownership interest in a **flow-through entity** such as a partnership, limited liability company (taxed as a partnership), or an S corporation. With partnerships, limited liability companies, and S corporations, the operating income or loss from their trade or business and rental activities flows through to the taxpayer and is treated as ordinary income or ordinary loss. If trade or business or rental activities (held either directly or indirectly through flow-through entities) generate ordinary income, taxpayers report it on their tax returns and pay taxes on it. However, if the activities generate losses, the losses must clear three hurdles to be currently deductible. The three hurdles are (1) tax basis, (2) at-risk amount, and (3) passive loss limits.

The tax basis hurdle limits a taxpayer's deductible losses to the taxpayer's tax basis in the activity. This limitation is very similar to loss limitations that apply when a taxpayer sells an asset such as corporate stock or other property. Recall that the formula for determining gain or loss on an exchange is the amount realized less the taxpayer's adjusted basis in the property. If a taxpayer were to sell an asset for nothing, the loss would be the amount of her basis in the property, but no more.

Obviously, in order to apply the tax basis loss limitation, we must first compute the taxpayer's tax basis in the activity. Assuming a taxpayer invests only cash in a business activity, the taxpayer's initial basis in the activity is the amount of cash the taxpayer invests (including borrowed funds) and the taxpayer's share of the activity's debt.[56] In general, a taxpayer's share of the activity's debt is included in her tax basis because it is economically equivalent to debt the taxpayer may have incurred outside of the activity to obtain cash to invest in the activity. In addition, a taxpayer's share of the *undistributed* income from the activity increases the taxpayer's basis because it is treated as an additional investment of cash in the activity. In a similar vein, distributions of cash and losses reduce tax basis; but if the taxpayer's losses from an activity exceed her tax basis in the activity, the losses are suspended until the taxpayer generates enough tax basis to absorb the loss.

Example 11-21

What if: Assume that instead of investing solely in assets that generate portfolio income, Nick and Rachel used $10,000 of the inheritance from Nick's grandmother to acquire a 5 percent interest in a limited partnership (a flow-through entity) called Color Comfort Sheets (CCS). CCS uses unique fabric blends to manufacture extremely comfortable bed sheets. As 5 percent owners, 5 percent of the actual income and loss of the business flows through to Nick and Rachel each year and is treated as though they received the income directly. However, as limited partners, Nick and Rachel are not involved in managing CCS's business activities. Assuming CCS has no debt, what is Nick and Rachel's tax basis in their CCS limited partnership interest?

Answer: $10,000, the amount of cash they invested in the business.

What if: Assuming CCS had total debt of $100,000 and Nick and Rachel's share of this debt was deemed to be $5,000, what would be the Suttons' tax basis in their CCS limited partnership interest?

Answer: $15,000, the amount of cash they invested directly plus their share of CCS's debt.

What if: Assuming CCS generated $300,000 of ordinary income in the first year after the Suttons invested, how much of this income would the Suttons recognize on their joint return?

Answer: $15,000. Because CCS is a flow-through entity, the Suttons' share of the business income ($300,000 × 5%) would be taxed to them as if they had received the income directly. Note that this income allocation would increase their tax basis in CCS by $15,000 up to $25,000 if they leave their share of the income in CCS.

(*continued on page 11-34...*)

---

[56]Special rules may apply when a taxpayer invests or contributes other types of property to the activity. In addition, debt from an activity is allocated to investors in varying degrees depending on the type of entity, e.g., S corporation, partnership, sole proprietorship, within which the activity is housed. These rules are beyond the scope of this discussion.

> **What if:** Assuming CCS did not have any debt and generated a ($300,000) ordinary loss in the first year after the Suttons invested, how much of this loss would the Suttons be allowed to deduct based solely on the tax basis limitation?
>
> **Answer:** $10,000, because their 5 percent share of the loss, or $15,000, is limited to their tax basis in their CCS interest. This loss allocation would reduce their tax basis in CCS to $0 and they would have a suspended ($5,000) loss. They must gain additional basis in the future in order to deduct this suspended loss.

When a loss from a business or business-related activity clears the tax basis hurdle, it next must clear an **at-risk** hurdle on its journey toward deductibility.[57] The at-risk rules are meant to limit the ability of investors to deduct "artificial" ordinary losses produced with certain types of debt. These rules limit ordinary losses to a taxpayer's amount at risk in an activity. Generally, a taxpayer is considered to be at risk in an activity to the extent of any cash personally contributed to the activity.[58] Additionally, a taxpayer's amount at risk also includes her share of any amount borrowed for use in the activity *if she is personally liable for repayment.* As with the tax basis calculation, a taxpayer's share of undistributed income increases the taxpayer's amount at risk in the activity and cash distributions reduce the amount at risk. Because the computation of tax basis and at-risk amount are so similar, a taxpayer's tax basis and her at-risk amount in the activity are frequently the same so that when she clears the tax basis hurdle for deducting a loss, she also clears the at-risk hurdle. However, the tax basis may exceed the at-risk amount when the taxpayer's share of the activity's liabilities included in her tax basis includes liabilities that the taxpayer is not personally liable to repay. For example, taxpayers with limited partnership interests in a partnership are usually not at risk for their share of partnership debt because they are usually not economically at risk or responsible for paying the debts of the limited partnership.[59] Taxpayers, including limited partners, are, however, allowed to include their share of debt for "qualified nonrecourse financing" in their at-risk amount even though they are not personally liable to repay the debt.[60] Qualified nonrecourse financing is debt from the activity that (1) represents a legitimate loan and was borrowed to fund real estate used in the activity and (2) was borrowed from a person or entity actively and regularly engaged in the business of lending money. Losses that do not clear the at-risk hurdle are suspended until the taxpayer generates more at-risk amounts to absorb the loss or until the activity is sold. Exhibit 11-7 summarizes the items included in calculating a taxpayer's tax basis and at-risk amount.

Example 11-22

> **What if:** Assume the same facts as in the previous example. The Suttons acquired a limited partnership interest in Color Comfort Sheets (CCS) limited partnership for $10,000. What is their at-risk amount in CCS?
>
> **Answer:** $10,000, the cash they invested in the CCS limited partnership interest.
>
> *(continued on page 11-35...)*

[57]§465.

[58]The amount at risk also includes the tax basis of other property a taxpayer contributes to the activity.

[59]Limited partners are usually only allocated a share of the partnership's "nonrecourse" debt. Because nonrecourse debt is debt for which no partner has economic risk of loss, partners are generally not "at risk" with respect to this type of debt.

[60]§465(b)(6)

EXHIBIT 11-7   Items Affecting Tax Basis and At-Risk Amount

Item	Effect on Tax Basis	Effect on At-Risk Amount
Cash invested	+	+
Share of debt responsible to repay	+	+
Share of debt not responsible to repay: Qualified nonrecourse financing	+	+
Share of debt not responsible to repay: Other	+	No effect
Share of income	+	+
Cash distributions	−	−
Share of loss	−	−

Assuming that CCS incurred $100,000 of debt and that the Suttons' share of the debt is $5,000, what is the Suttons' at-risk amount in CCS?

Answer: $10,000. Even though the Suttons are allowed to include their $5,000 share of CCS's debt in their tax basis for CCS, they are not allowed to include the debt in their at-risk amount because, as limited partners, they are not personally liable for this debt, so they are not economically at risk with respect to this amount.

What if: Assuming the Suttons' share of CCS's debt is $5,000 and that CCS generated a $300,000 ordinary loss in the first year after the Suttons invested, how much of the Suttons' $15,000 share of this loss would they be allowed to deduct after applying the tax basis and at-risk limitations?

Answer: $10,000. The Suttons' tax basis is $15,000, but their at-risk amount is only $10,000; consequently, their entire $15,000 share of loss clears the tax basis hurdle, but only $10,000 of the loss clears the at-risk hurdle. Thus, the Suttons may deduct $10,000 of the loss reducing their amount at risk to zero, but they must wait until they are again at risk in order to deduct the $5,000 loss that is suspended at the at-risk level or until they sell their limited partnership interest.

What if: Assume that the Suttons' share of CCS's debt is $5,000 but that CCS is involved in rental real estate activities and that its debt is considered to be qualified nonrecourse financing. Further assume that the Suttons' share of CCS's loss for the year is $15,000. What amount of this loss are the Suttons allowed to deduct after applying the tax basis and at-risk limitations?

Answer: $15,000. The Suttons' tax basis in their CCS interest is $15,000, and their at-risk amount is also $15,000. Because qualified nonrecourse financing is included in their amount at risk, the Suttons may deduct the entire $15,000 loss (subject to the passive activity loss limits discussed below).

Even when a taxpayer has sufficient tax basis and sufficient amounts at risk to absorb a loss in a business-related activity, the loss may still be limited by the **passive activity loss rules.** Prior to 1986, investors were able to use ordinary losses from certain passive activities to offset portfolio income (interest, dividends, and capital gains), salary income, and self-employment income, including income from other trades or businesses they were actively involved in managing. During this time, a **tax shelter** industry thrived by marketing investments to wealthy investors designed primarily to generate ordinary losses that could be used to shield other income from tax. To combat this practice, Congress introduced the passive activity loss rules.[61] Specifically, these rules limit the ability of investors in certain passive activities involving trade or businesses housed in flow-through entities and in rental property,

[61]§469

EXHIBIT 11-8   Tests for Material Participation

Individuals are considered material participants for the activity if they meet any _one_ of these tests:

1. The individual participates in the activity more than 500 hours during the year.
2. The individual's activity constitutes substantially all of the participation in such activity by all individuals including nonowners.
3. The individual participates more than 100 hours during the year, and the individual's participation is not less than any other individual's participation in the activity.
4. The activity qualifies as a "significant participation activity" (more than 100 hours spent during the year) and the aggregate of all "significant participation activities" is greater than 500 hours for the year.
5. The individual materially participated in the activity for any five of the preceding 10 taxable years.
6. The individual materially participated for any three preceding years in any personal service activity (personal services in health, law, accounting, architecture, etc.)
7. Taking into account all the facts and circumstances, the individual participates on a regular, continuous, and substantial basis during the year.

---

including real estate, to use their ordinary losses from these activities currently to reduce taxable income.[62] The passive activity loss rules are applied to any losses remaining _after_ applying the tax basis and at-risk loss limits described above.

Passive Activity Definition

The **passive activity loss rules** define a passive activity as "any activity which involves the conduct of a trade or business, and in which the taxpayer does not materially participate."[63] According to the tax code, participants in rental activities, including rental real estate, and limited partners in partnerships are generally deemed to be passive participants, and participants in all other trade or business activities are passive unless their involvement in an activity is "regular, continuous, and substantial." Clearly, these terms are quite subjective and difficult to apply. Fortunately, regulations provide more certainty in this area by listing seven separate tests for material participation.[64] An individual can be classified as a material participant in an activity by meeting any one of the seven tests in Exhibit 11-8. As this exhibit indicates, investors who purchase rental property or a trade or business without intending to be involved in the management of the trade or business are classified as passive participants, and these activities are classified as passive activities with respect to them.

Income and Loss Categories

Under the passive activity loss rules, each item of a taxpayer's income or loss for the year is placed in one of three categories. Losses from _the passive category_ cannot offset income from other categories. The three different categories are as follows (see Exhibit 11-9):

1. _Passive activity income or loss_—income or loss from an activity in which the taxpayer is not a material participant.[65]

---

[62]Before passage of the passive activity loss rules, the "at-risk rules" in §465 were adopted in an attempt to limit the ability of investors to deduct "artificial" ordinary losses. Given the similarity of the at risk and tax basis computations, especially for real estate investments, the at-risk rules were not entirely successful at accomplishing this objective. The passive activity loss rules were adopted as a backstop to the at-risk rules and both sets of rules may potentially apply to a given activity.

[63]The term _trade or business_ is also deemed to include property held for the production of income, such as rental property.

[64]§1.469-5T

[65]According to §1.163-8T, interest from debt used to purchase a passive activity is allocated to that activity and either reduces passive income or increases passive loss from the activity.

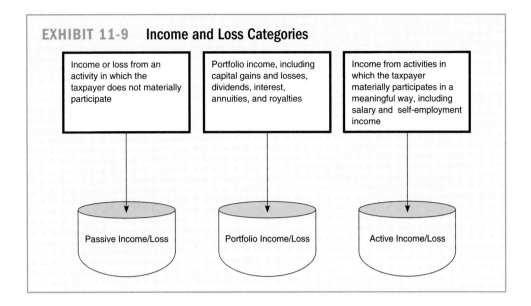

EXHIBIT 11-9   Income and Loss Categories

Income or loss from an activity in which the taxpayer does not materially participate	Portfolio income, including capital gains and losses, dividends, interest, annuities, and royalties	Income from activities in which the taxpayer materially participates in a meaningful way, including salary and self-employment income
Passive Income/Loss	Portfolio Income/Loss	Active Income/Loss

2. *Portfolio income*—income from investments including capital gains and losses, dividends, interest, annuities, and royalties.

3. *Active business income*—income from sources in which the taxpayer is a material participant. For individuals, this includes salary and self-employment income. Thus, an individual with income in this category is no longer an investor with respect to this source of income given that we define investors in this chapter as individuals with portfolio and/or passive income and losses.

The impact of segregating taxpayers' income in these categories is to limit their ability to apply passive activity losses against income in the other two categories. In effect, passive activity losses are suspended and remain in the passive income or loss category until the taxpayer generates current year passive income, either from the passive activity producing the loss or from some other passive activity, or until the taxpayer sells the activity that generated the passive loss.[66] On the sale, in addition to reporting gain or loss from the sale of the property, the taxpayer is allowed to deduct suspended passive losses against sources of income from any of the three categories.

Example 11-23

What if: Let's return to the facts in the previous example where the Suttons' share of CCS loss was ($15,000), their tax basis in their CCS interest is $15,000, and their at-risk amount in the activity is $10,000. Further assume that the Suttons received $170,000 in combined salary, $4,000 of taxable interest income from corporate bonds, $3,000 of dividends, and $5,000 of long-term capital gains. Finally, assume that the Suttons also owned a rental condominium that generated $8,000 of net income. How would each of these income or loss items be allocated among the passive, portfolio, and active income and loss categories?

Answer: The Suttons' ($10,000) loss from CCS remaining after applying the tax basis and at risk loss limits is placed in the passive category because, as limited partners, the Suttons did not materially participate in the activity. Further, their $8,000 of net income from their rental property is included in the passive category because rental activities are generally considered to be passive. The

(continued on page 11-38...)

---

[66]To utilize suspended passive losses on the disposition of a passive activity, the disposition must be a fully taxable transaction.

THE KEY FACTS

Passive Activity Losses

■ Ordinary losses from flow-though entities and other enterprises will be classified as passive if the taxpayer is not a material participant.

■ Losses from limited partnerships and from rental activities, including rental real estate, are generally deemed to be passive losses.

■ Passive loss rules limit losses from passive activities to passive income from other sources.
· Active business income such as salary and self employment income is not passive income.
· Investment-type income such as interest and dividends is portfolio income, not passive income.
· Passive losses in excess of passive income are suspended and deductible against passive income in the future or when the taxpayer sells the passive activity generating the loss.

$4,000 of taxable interest income, $3,000 of dividends, and $5,000 of long-term capital gains are all included in the portfolio income category. Finally, the $170,000 of salary is included in the active income category.

What if: What is the Suttons' AGI for the year assuming, other than the items described above, no other items affect their AGI?

Answer: $182,000, computed as follows:

Description	Amount	Explanation
(1) Active income	$170,000	Salary.
(2) Portfolio income	12,000	Interest of $4,000; dividends of $3,000; $5,000 of long-term capital gains.
(3) Passive income	0	($10,000) passive loss that clears tax basis and at-risk hurdles and $8,000 of passive income. However, the passive loss clearing the basis and at-risk hurdles is deductible only to the extent of passive income. The suspended passive loss is ($2,000).
AGI	$182,000	(1) + (2) + (3).

What if: Assume the facts above and that at the beginning of next year the Suttons sell their limited partnership interest for $12,000 ($7,000 in cash and $5,000 debt relief from the purchaser assuming their share of partnership debt). Given that their tax basis on the date of sale is $0, what effect does the sale have on their AGI?

Answer: $5,000 increase in AGI, computed as follows:

Description	Amount	Explanation
(1) Capital gain	$12,000	Gain realized = $12,000 − $0 tax basis.
(2) Ordinary loss	($5,000)	The loss that was previously suspended at the at-risk level becomes an at-risk amount on the sale (it is no longer suspended). The loss is fully deductible because the loss leaves the passive category and enters the active category on the sale of the interest in the activity.
(3) Ordinary loss	($2,000)	This is the loss that was suspended at the passive loss level last year.
Effect on AGI	$ 5,000	(1) + (2) + (3).

Rental Real Estate Exception to the Passive Activity Loss Rules

Tax laws are renowned for exceptions to rules and, not surprisingly, the general rule that passive activity losses cannot be used to offset nonpassive types of income is subject to a few important exceptions. The one we choose to discuss here applies to lower-to-middle income individuals with rental real estate.[67] A taxpayer

---

[67]§469(b)(7) provides another important exception to the general rule that all real estate activities are passive. To overcome this presumption, taxpayers must spend more than half their time working in real estate trades or businesses and for more than 750 hours during the year. This exception benefits individuals that spend a substantial amount of time in activities like real estate development and construction.

who is an **active participant in a rental activity** may be allowed to deduct up to $25,000 of the rental loss against other types of income. To be considered an active participant, the taxpayer must (1) own at least a 10 percent of the rental property, and (2) participate in the process of making management decisions such as approving new tenants, deciding on rental terms, and approving repairs and capital expenditures.

Consistent with a number of tax benefits, the exception amount for active owners is phased out as income increases: The $25,000 maximum exception amount is phased out by 50 cents for every dollar the taxpayer's adjusted gross income (before considering the rental loss) exceeds $100,000. Consequently, the entire $25,000 is phased-out when the taxpayer's adjusted gross income reaches $150,000.

Example 11-24

What if: Assume that Jeb Landers, Rachel's father, owns and rents a condominium. Jeb is involved in approving new tenants for the rental home and in managing its maintenance. During the year, he reported a net loss of $5,000 from the rental activity, and he had sufficient tax basis and at-risk amounts to absorb the loss. Further, his only sources of income during the year were $126,000 of salary and $22,000 of long-term capital gains. Given Jeb's $5,000 loss from his rental home, how much of the loss could he deduct currently?

Answer: $1,000. Because Jeb meets the definition of an "active participant" and has adjusted gross income of less than $150,000, before considering his rental loss, he may deduct a portion of the loss against his other income. His $1,000 deduction is computed as follows:

Description	Amount	Explanation
(1) Maximum deduction available before phase-out	$25,000	
(2) Phase-out of maximum deduction	$24,000	[($148,000 − 100,000) × .5].
(3) Maximum deduction in current year	$ 1,000	(1) − (2).
(4) Rental loss in current year	$ 5,000	
(5) Rental loss deductible in current year	$ 1,000	Lesser of (3) or (4).
Passive loss carryforward	$ 4,000	(3) − (4).

What if: Assume that Jeb's salary for the year had been $50,000 and he reported $22,000 from the sale of his stock, how much of his rental loss could he deduct currently?

Answer: Because Jeb's adjusted gross income would only be $72,000 under this scenario, he could deduct his entire $5,000 rental loss during the year.

THE KEY FACTS

Rental Real Estate Losses

■ Rental real estate exception to passive loss rules.
· Applies to active participants in rental property.
· Deduct up to $25,000 of rental real estate loss against ordinary income.
· $25,000 maximum deduction phased out by 50 cents for every dollar of AGI over $100,000 (excluding the rental loss deduction).
· Fully phased out at $150,000 of AGI.

CONCLUSION

Investors and their advisors face numerous tax rules that apply to investment income and expenses. Understanding these rules is important, not only to comply with the tax law, but also to make wise investment choices. Investments differ in terms of their potential for implementing the conversion and shifting tax planning strategies. Failing to consider these strategies when investing will lead to less than optimal results. By carefully weighing nontax investment objectives along with the tax characteristics of different investment options, informed investors will be better equipped to select investments appropriate for them.

SUMMARY

L01   Explain how interest income and dividend income are taxed.

- Investors seeking current income invest in interest-bearing securities or dividend-paying stocks.
- Interest income received from certificates of deposit, U.S. Treasury securities, corporate bonds, and other similar investments is typically taxed annually at ordinary rates.
- Accrued market discount on bonds and interest earned on U.S. savings bonds is taxed at sale or maturity, while original issue discount on bonds is taxed annually.
- Bond premiums increase the tax basis of bonds and affect the amount of capital gains or losses investors report.
- Taxpayers may elect to amortize bond premiums to reduce the amount of annual interest reported on bonds purchased at a premium.
- Dividend income, like interest income, is taxed annually when it is received. However, most dividend income currently is taxed at preferential capital gains rates.
- Explicit tax rates favor dividend income over interest income.
- After-tax returns from interest and dividend-paying investments are not affected by an investor's investment horizon because the income they generate is taxed annually.

L02   Compute the tax consequences associated with the disposition of capital assets, including the netting process for calculating gains and losses.

- When taxpayers sell stock, they may determine the basis of the stock using the specific identification method or the FIFO method.
- Capital assets held for more than one year generate long-term capital gains or losses on sale or disposition. Other capital assets generate short-term capital gains or losses on sale or disposition.
- Generally, net long-term capital gains in excess of net short-term losses are taxed at a maximum 15 percent tax rate.
- Unrecaptured §1250 gain is taxed at a maximum 25 percent rate, and gains from collectibles and §1202 stock are taxed at a maximum 28 percent rate.
- Up to $3,000 of net capital losses are deductible against ordinary income for the year.
- A taxpayer's capital gains and losses for the year are reported on Schedule D of Form 1040.
- Wash sale provisions prevent taxpayers from selling stock at a loss, deducting the loss, and replacing the stock sold with the same stock or substantially identical securities.
- Losses on the disposition of property held for personal use are not deductible.
- Because of the deferral of the capital gains tax, after-tax returns from capital assets will increase as an investor's investment horizon increases.

L03   Describe common sources of tax-exempt investment income and explain the rationale for exempting some investments from taxation.

- To promote certain social goals, the income from some investments and investment vehicles is exempt from federal income taxes.
- Interest from municipal bonds issued by state and local governments is exempt from federal income tax. However, states tax municipal bond interest their residents receive from other states.
- Because of their tax-exempt status, municipal bonds yield lower pretax rates of return relative to similar taxable bonds. This lower relative rate of return is referred to as an *implicit tax.*
- Proceeds from life insurance policies are tax-exempt unless the policy has been cashed in early. In that case, the recipient is taxed on the difference between the amount invested in the policy and the proceeds received.
- Investment income earned within a 529 or other education savings plan is tax-exempt provided it is used to pay for certain qualifying educational expenses.

Calculate the deduction for portfolio investment-related expenses, including investment expenses and investment interest expense.

- Investment expenses are miscellaneous itemized deductions subject to the 2 percent of AGI floor.
- Investment interest expense is deductible to the extent of net investment income.
- Net investment income is investment income minus deductible investment expenses.
- Net long-term capital gains and qualifying dividends are not included in investment income unless the taxpayer elects to tax the income as ordinary income.

Understand the distinction between portfolio investments and passive investments and apply tax basis, at-risk, and passive activity loss limits to losses from passive investments.

LO5

- A taxpayer's losses from flow-through entities and other trade or business activities are deductible to the extent they clear the tax basis, at-risk, and passive activity loss hurdles.
- A taxpayer's ordinary losses from flow-through entities and other trade or business activities may be classified as passive if the taxpayer's involvement is not regular, continuous, and substantial.
- A taxpayer's losses from rental activities are, with limited exceptions, deemed to be passive regardless of taxpayer's activity level.
- A taxpayer's passive losses from an activity are limited to passive income from all other sources until disposition of the activity. On disposition, current and prior passive losses from an activity can be used without limitation.
- A rental real estate exception allows taxpayers to deduct up to $25,000 of losses from rental real estate annually provided they are actively involved in managing the rental real estate and have adjusted gross income of less than $150,000.

KEY TERMS

active participant in a rental activity (11-39)
after-tax rate of return (11-1)
amortization (11-4)
at risk (11-34)
basis (11-5)
before-tax rate of return (11-2)
bond (11-2)
bond discount (11-4)
bond premium (11-4)
capital asset (11-9)
cash surrender value (11-24)
certificate of deposit (11-2)
collectibles (11-11)
dividend (11-•2)
ex-dividend date (11-7)
explicit tax (11-23)
first-in first-out (FIFO) method (11-10)
face value (11-2)
flow-through entities (11-32)

implicit tax (11-23)
investment expenses (11-28)
investment income (11-2)
investment interest expense (11-28)
long-term capital gains or losses (11-11)
market discount (11-5)
market premium (11-5)
maturity (11-5)
maturity value (11-2)
mutual fund (11-2)
net capital gain (11-13)
net investment income (11-30)
net long-term capital gain (11-13)
net long-term capital loss (11-13)
net short-term capital gain (11-13)
net short-term capital loss (11-13)
nonbusiness bad debt (11-11)
operating income (11-2)
operating loss (11-2)
original issue discount (11-4)

passive activity loss rules (11-36)
passive investments (11-2)
portfolio investments (11-2)
qualified dividends (11-7)
qualified small business stock (11-11)
qualified tuition plans (529 plans) (11-25)
short-term capital gains or losses (11-11)
specific identification method (11-10)
tax basis (11-9)
tax shelter (11-35)
taxable corporations (11-32)
term insurance (11-24)
Treasury bond (11-4)
Treasury note (11-4)
unrecaptured §1250 gain (11-11)
U.S. savings bonds (11-4)
wash sale (11-19)
whole life insurance (11-23)
zero-coupon bonds (11-4)

DISCUSSION QUESTIONS

1. **(LO1)** Describe how interest income and dividend income are taxed. What are the similarities and differences in their tax treatment?
2. **(LO1)** What is the underlying policy rationale for the current tax rules applicable to interest income and dividend income?
3. **(LO1)** Compare and contrast the tax treatment of interest from a Treasury bond and qualifying dividends from corporate stock.
4. **(LO1)** How are Treasury notes and Treasury bonds treated for federal and state income tax purposes?
5. **(LO1)** Why would taxpayers generally prefer the tax treatment of market discount to the treatment of original issue discount on corporate bonds?
6. **(LO1)** In what ways are U.S. savings bonds treated more favorably for tax purposes than corporate bonds?

research

planning

7. **(LO1)** When should investors consider making an election to amortize market discount on a bond into income annually? [*Hint:* see §1278(b).]
8. **(LO1)** Why might investors purchase interest-paying securities rather than dividend-paying stocks?
9. **(LO1)** Compare and contrast the tax treatment of dividend-paying stocks and growth stocks.
10. **(LO1)** Do after-tax rates of return for investments in either interest- or dividend-paying securities increase with the length of the investment? Why or why not?
11. **(LO2)** What is the definition of a capital asset? Give examples of capital assets.
12. **(LO2)** Why does the tax law allow a taxpayer to defer gains accrued on a capital asset until the taxpayer actually sells the asset?
13. **(LO2)** Why does the tax law provide preferential rates on certain capital gains?
14. **(LO2)** Cameron purchases stock in Corporation X and in Corporation Y. Neither corporation pays dividends. The stocks both earn an identical before-tax rate of return. Cameron sells stock in Corporation X after three years and he sells the stock in Corporation Y after five years. Which investment likely earned a greater after-tax return? Why?
15. **(LO2)** What is the deciding factor in determining whether a capital gain is a short-term or long-term capital gain?
16. **(LO2)** What methods may taxpayers use to determine the adjusted basis of stock they have sold?
17. **(LO2)** What tax rate applies to net short-term capital gains?
18. **(LO2)** What limitations are placed on the deductibility of capital losses for individual taxpayers?
19. **(LO2)** What happens to capital losses that are not deductible in the current year?
20. **(LO2)** Are all long-term capital gains taxable at the same maximum rate? If not, what rates apply to long-term capital gains?

planning

21. **(LO2)** David, a taxpayer currently in the highest tax rate bracket, has the option to purchase either stock in a Fortune 500 company or qualified small business stock in his friend's corporation. All else equal, which of the two will he prefer from a tax perspective if he intends to hold the stock for six years? Which would he prefer if he only plans to hold the stock for two years?
22. **(LO2)** What is a "wash sale"? What is the purpose of the wash sale tax rules?

23. **(LO2)** Nick does not use his car for business purposes. If he sells his car for less than he paid for it, does he get to deduct the loss for tax purposes? Why or why not?

24. **(LO2)** Describe three basic tax planning strategies available to taxpayers investing in capital assets.

25. **(LO2)** Clark owns stock in BCS Corporation that he purchased in January of the current year. The stock has appreciated significantly during the year. It is now December of the current year, and Clark is deciding whether or not he should sell the stock. What tax and nontax factors should Clark consider before making the decision on whether to sell the stock now?

■ **planning**

26. **(LO2)** Under what circumstances would you expect the after-tax return from an investment in a capital asset to approach that of tax-exempt assets assuming equal before-tax rates of return?

27. **(LO3)** Why does the federal government exempt municipal bond interest from federal income tax?

28. **(LO3)** Why do taxpayers have an incentive to purchase municipal bonds from within their own states?

29. **(LO3)** What is an "implicit tax" and how does it affect a taxpayer's decision to purchase municipal bonds?

30. **(LO3)** How do taxpayers' explicit marginal tax rates affect their decision to purchase municipal bonds?

31. **(LO3)** Is there a natural clientele for municipal bonds? If so, why?

32. **(LO3)** In what sense can life insurance be viewed as an investment?

33. **(LO3)** How are life insurance proceeds taxed when paid after the insured individual's death?

34. **(LO3)** How are life insurance proceeds taxed if a policy is cashed out early?

35. **(LO3)** List the important nontax issues to consider when purchasing life insurance as an investment.

36. **(LO3)** How are state-sponsored 529 educational savings plans taxed if investment returns are used for educational purposes? Are the returns taxed differently if they are not ultimately used to pay for education costs?

37. **(LO3)** Why would someone saving for college consider investing in something other than a 529 plan?

■ **planning**

38. **(LO4)** Are dividends and capital gains considered to be investment income for purposes of determining the amount of a taxpayer's deductible investment interest expense for the year?

39. **(LO4)** How is the amount of net investment income determined for a taxpayer with investment expenses and other noninvestment miscellaneous itemized deductions?

40. **(LO4)** What limitations are placed on the deductibility of investment interest expense? What happens to investment interest expense that is not deductible because of the limitations?

41. **(LO4)** When taxpayers borrow money to buy municipal bonds, are they allowed to deduct interest expense on the loan? Why or why not?

42. **(LO5)** What types of losses may potentially be characterized as passive losses?

43. **(LO5)** What are the implications of treating losses as passive?

44. **(LO5)** What tests are applied to determine if losses should be characterized as passive?

45. **(LO5)** All else being equal, would a taxpayer with passive losses rather have wage income or passive income?

■ **planning**

■ **planning**   46. **(LO1, LO2, LO3)** Laurie is thinking about investing in one or several of the following investment options:

Corporate bonds
529 plan
Dividend-paying stock
Life insurance
Savings account
Treasury bonds
Growth stock

a. Assuming all seven options earn similar returns before taxes, rank Laurie's investment options from highest to lowest according to their after-tax returns.

b. Which of the investments employ the deferral and/or conversion tax planning strategies?

c. How does the time period of the investment affect the returns from these alternatives?

d. How do these alternative investments differ in terms of their nontax characteristics?

PROBLEMS

47. **(LO1)** Anne's marginal income tax rate is 30 percent. She purchases a corporate bond for $10,000 and the maturity, or face value, of the bond is $10,000. If the bond pays 5 percent per year before taxes, what is Anne's after-tax rate of return from the bond if the bond matures in one year? What is her after-tax rate of return if the bond matures in 10 years?

48. **(LO1)** Matt recently deposited $20,000 in a savings account paying a guaranteed interest rate of 4 percent for the next 10 years. If Matt expects his marginal tax rate to be 20 percent for the next 10 years, how much interest will he earn after-tax for the first year of his investment? How much interest will he earn after-tax for the second year of his investment? If he withdraws enough cash every year to pay the tax on the interest he earns, how much will he have in the account after four years? How much will he have in the account after seven years?

49. **(LO1)** Dana intends to invest $30,000 in either a Treasury bond or a corporate bond. The Treasury bond yields 5 percent before tax and the corporate bond yields 6 percent before tax. Assuming Dana's federal marginal rate is 25 percent and her marginal state rate is 5 percent, which of the two options should she choose? If she were to move to another state where her marginal state rate would be 10 percent, would her choice be any different? Assume that Dana itemizes deductions.

50. **(LO1)** At the beginning of his current tax year David invests $12,000 in original issue U.S. Treasury bonds with a $10,000 face value that mature in exactly 10 years. David receives $700 in interest ($350 every six months) from the Treasury bonds during the current year, and the yield to maturity on the bonds is 5 percent.

a. How much interest income will he report this year if he elects to amortize the bond premium?

b. How much interest will he report this year if he does not elect to amortize the bond premium?

51. **(LO1)** Seth invested $20,000 in Series EE savings bonds on April 1. By December 31, the published redemption value of the bonds had increased to $20,700. How much interest income will Seth report from the savings bonds in the current year absent any special election?

52. **(LO1)** At the beginning of her current tax year, Angela purchased a zero-coupon corporate bond at original issue for $30,000 with a yield to maturity of 6 percent. Given that she will not actually receive any interest payments until the bond matures in 10 years, how much interest income will she report this year assuming semiannual compounding of interest?

53. **(LO1)** At the beginning of his current tax year, Eric bought a corporate bond with a maturity value of $50,000 from the secondary market for $45,000. The bond has a stated annual interest rate of 5 percent payable on June 30 and December 31, and it matures in five years on December 31. Absent any special tax elections, how much interest income will Eric report from the bond this year and in the year the bond matures?

54. **(LO1)** Hayley recently invested $50,000 in a public utility stock paying a 3 percent annual dividend. If Hayley reinvests the annual dividend she receives net of any taxes owed on the dividend, how much will her investment be worth in four years if the dividends paid are qualifying dividends? (Hayley's marginal income tax rate is 28 percent.) What will her investment be worth in four years if the dividends are nonqualifying?

55. **(LO1)** Five years ago, Kate purchased a dividend-paying stock for $10,000. For all five years, the stock paid an annual dividend of 4 percent before tax and Kate's marginal tax rate was 25 percent. Every year Kate reinvested her after-tax dividends in the same stock. For the first two years of her investment, the dividends qualified for the 15 percent capital gains rate; however, for the last three years the 15 percent dividend rate was repealed and dividends were taxed at ordinary rates.

    ■ **planning**

    a. What is the current value (at the beginning of year 6) of Kate's investment assuming the stock has not appreciated in value?

    b. What will Kate's investment be worth three years from now (at the beginning of year 9) assuming her marginal tax rate increases to 35 percent for the next three years?

56. **(LO2)** John bought 1,000 shares of Intel stock on October 18, 2006, for $30 per share plus a $750 commission he paid to his broker. On December 12, 2009, he sells the shares for $42.50 per share. He also incurs a $1,000 fee for this transaction.

    a. What is John's adjusted basis in the 1,000 shares of Intel stock?

    b. What amount does John realize when he sells the 1,000 shares?

    c. What is the gain/loss for John on the sale of his Intel stock? What is the character of the gain/loss?

57. **(LO2)** Dahlia is in the 28 percent tax rate bracket and has purchased the following shares of Microsoft common stock over the years:

Date Purchased	Shares	Basis
7/10/2001	400	$12,000
4/20/2002	300	$10,750
1/29/2003	500	$12,230
11/02/2005	250	$ 7,300

If Dahlia sells 800 shares of Microsoft for $40,000 on December 20, 2009, what is her capital gain or loss in each of the following assumptions?

    a. She uses the FIFO method.

    b. She uses the specific identification method and she wants to minimize her current year capital gain.

research

58. **(LO2)** Karyn loaned $20,000 to her co-worker to begin a new business several years ago. If her co-worker declares bankruptcy on June 22ⁿᵈ of the current year, is Karyn allowed to deduct the bad debt loss this year? If she can deduct the loss, what is the character of the loss?

59. **(LO2)** Sue has 5,000 shares of Sony stock that has an adjusted basis of $27,500. She sold the 5,000 shares of stock for cash of $10,000 and she also received a piece of land as part of the proceeds. The land was valued at $20,000 and had an adjusted basis to the buyer of $12,000. What is Sue's gain or loss on the sale of 5,000 shares of Sony stock?

60. **(LO2)** Matt and Meg Comer are married. They do not have any children. Matt works as a history professor at a local university and earns a salary of $52,000. Meg works part-time at the same university. She earns $21,000 a year. The couple does not itemize deductions. Other than salary, the Comer's only other source of income is from the disposition of various capital assets (mostly stocks).

a. What is the Comer's tax liability for 2009 if they report the following capital gains and losses for the year?

Short-term capital gains	$ 7,000
Short-term capital losses	($2,000)
Long-term capital gains	$15,000
Long-term capital losses	($6,000)

b. What is the Comer's tax liability for 2009 if they report the following capital gains and losses for the year?

Short-term capital gains	$ 1,500
Short-term capital losses	$ 0
Long-term capital gains	$15,000
Long-term capital losses	($10,000)

61. **(LO2)** Grayson is in the 25 percent tax rate bracket and has the sold the following stocks in 2009:

	Date Purchased	Basis	Date Sold	Amount Realized
Stock A	1/23/1985	$ 7,250	7/22/2009	$ 4,500
Stock B	4/10/2009	$14,000	9/13/2009	$17,500
Stock C	8/23/2007	$10,750	10/12/2009	$15,300
Stock D	5/19/1999	$ 5,230	10/12/2009	$12,400
Stock E	8/20/2009	$ 7,300	11/14/2009	$ 3,500

a. What is Grayson's net short-term capital gain or loss from these transactions?
b. What is Grayson's net long-term gain or loss from these transactions?
c. What is Grayson's overall net gain or loss from these transactions?
d. What amount of the gain, if any, is subject to the preferential rate for certain capital gains?

62. **(LO2)** George bought the following amounts of Stock A over the years:

	Date Purchased	Number of Shares	Adjusted Basis
Stock A	11/21/1985	1,000	$24,000
Stock A	3/18/1991	500	$ 9,000
Stock A	5/22/2000	750	$27,000

On October 12, 2009, he sold 1,200 of his shares of Stock A for $38 per share.

a. How much gain/loss will George have to recognize if he uses the FIFO method of accounting for the shares sold?

b. How much gain/loss will George have to recognize if he specifically identifies the shares to be sold by telling his broker to sell all 750 shares from the 5/22/2000 purchase and 450 shares from the 11/21/1985 purchase?

63. **(LO2)** During the current year, Ron and Anne sold the following assets:

Capital Asset	Market Value	Tax Basis	Holding Period
L stock	$ 50,000	$41,000	> 1 year
M stock	28,000	39,000	> 1 year
N stock	30,000	22,000	< 1 year
O stock	26,000	33,000	< 1 year
Antiques	7,000	4,000	> 1 year
Rental home	300,000*	90,000	> 1 year

*$30,000 of the gain is 25 percent gain (from accumulated depreciation on the property).

a. Given that Ron and Anne have taxable income of only $20,000 (all ordinary) before considering the tax effect of their asset sales, what is their gross tax liability for 2009 assuming they file a joint return?

b. Given that Ron and Anne have taxable income of $150,000 (all ordinary) before considering the tax effect of their asset sales, what is their gross tax liability for 2009 assuming they file a joint return?

64. **(LO2)** During the current year, Ken and Marie sold the following assets:

Capital Asset	Market Value	Tax Basis	Holding Period
R stock	$ 34,000	$48,000	> 1 year
S stock	18,000	27,000	> 1 year
T stock	33,000	31,000	< 1 year
U stock	17,000	18,000	< 1 year
Stamp collection	8,000	11,000	> 1 year
Rental home	350,000*	90,000	> 1 year

*$70,000 of the gain is 25 percent gain (from accumulated depreciation on the property).

a. Given that Ken and Marie have taxable income of only $30,000 (all ordinary) before considering the tax effect of their asset sales, what is their gross tax liability for 2009 assuming they file a joint return?

b. Given that Ken and Marie have taxable income of $120,000 (all ordinary) before considering the tax effect of their asset sales, what is their gross tax liability for 2009 assuming they file a joint return?

65. **(LO2)** In 2009, Tom and Amanda Jackson (married filing jointly) have $200,000 of taxable income before considering the following events:

- On May 12, 2009, they sold a painting (art) for $110,000 that was inherited from Grandma on July 23, 2007. The fair market value on the date of Grandma's death was $90,000 and Grandma's adjusted basis of the painting was $25,000.
- Applied a long-term capital loss carryover from 2008 of $10,000.
- Recognized a $12,000 loss on 11/1/09 sale of bonds (acquired on 5/12/00).
- Recognized a $4,000 gain on 12/12/09 sale of IBM stock (acquired on 2/5/09).
- Recognized a $17,000 gain on the 10/17/09 sale of rental property (the only §1231 transaction) of which $8,000 is reportable as gain subject to the 25 percent maximum rate and the remaining $9,000 is subject to the 15 percent maximum rate (the property was acquired on 8/2/03).

- Recognized a $12,000 loss on 12/20/09 sale of bonds (acquired on 1/18/09).
- Recognized a $7,000 gain on 6/27/09 sale of BH stock (acquired on 7/30/01).
- Recognized an $11,000 loss on 6/13/09 sale of QuikCo stock (acquired on 3/20/02).
- Received $500 of qualifying dividends on 7/15/09.

Complete the required capital gains netting procedures and calculate the Jackson's 2009 tax liability.

66. **(LO2)** For 2009, Sherri has a short-term loss of $2,500 and a long-term loss of $4,750.

a. How much loss can Sherri deduct in 2009?

b. How much loss will Sherri carryover to 2010, and what is the character of the loss carryover?

67. **(LO2)** Jermaine has the following losses during the current year:

Loss	Amount
Short-term capital loss	($10,000)
Long-term capital loss	($25,000)

How much capital loss can Jermaine deduct this year against his ordinary income?

68. **(LO2)** Three years ago, Adrian purchased 100 shares of stock in X Corp. for $10,000. On December 30 of year 4, Adrian sells the 100 shares for $6,000.

a. Assuming Adrian has no other capital gains or losses, how much of the loss is Adrian able to deduct on her year 4 tax return?

b. Assume the same facts as in part (a), except that on January 20 of year 5, Adrian purchases 100 shares of X Corp. stock for $6,000. How much loss from the sale on December 30 of year 4 is deductible on Adrian's year 4 tax return? What basis does Adrian take in the stock purchased on January 20 of year 5?

69. **(LO2)** Christopher sold 100 shares of Cisco stock for $5,500 in the current year. He purchased the shares several years ago for $2,200. Assuming his marginal ordinary income tax rate is 28 percent and he has no other capital gains or losses, how much tax will he pay on this gain?

70. **(LO2)** Christina, who is single, purchased 100 shares of Apple Inc. stock several years ago for $3,500. During her year-end tax planning, she decided to sell 50 shares of Apple for $1,500 on December 30. However, two weeks later, Apple introduced the iPhone and she decided that she should buy the 50 shares (cost of $1,600) of Apple back before prices skyrocket.

a. What is Christina's deductible loss on the sale of 50 shares? What is her basis in the 50 new shares?

b. Assume the same facts, except that Christina repurchased only 25 shares for $800. What is Christina's deductible loss on the sale of 50 shares? What is her basis in the 25 new shares?

research

71. **(LO2)** Arden purchased 300 shares of AMC common stock several years ago for $1,500. On April 30, Arden sold the shares of AMC common for $500 and then purchased 250 shares of AMC preferred stock two days later for $700. The AMC preferred stock is not convertible into AMC common stock. What is Arden's deductible loss from the sale of the 300 shares of AMC common stock?

72. **(LO2)** Shaun bought 300 shares of Dental Equipment, Inc., several years ago for $10,000. Currently the stock is worth $8,000. Shaun's marginal tax rate this year is 25 percent and he has no other capital gains or losses. Shaun expects to have a marginal rate of 30 percent next year, but also expects to have a long-term capital gain of $10,000. To minimize taxes, should Shaun sell the stock on December 31 of this year or January 1 of next year (ignore the time value of money)?   ■ **planning**

73. **(LO2)** Irene is saving for a new car she hopes to purchase either four or six years from now. Irene invests $10,000 in a growth stock that does not pay dividends and expects a 6 percent annual before-tax return (the investment is tax deferred). When she cashes in the investment after either four or six years, she expects the applicable marginal tax rate on long-term capital gains to be 25 percent.   ■ **planning**

    a. What will be the value of this investment four and six years from now?

    b. When Irene sells the investment, how much cash will she have after taxes to purchase the new car (four and six years from now)?

74. **(LO2)** Komiko Tanaka invests $12,000 in LymaBean, Inc. LymaBean does not pay any dividends. Komiko projects that her investment will generate a 10 percent before-tax rate of return. She plans to invest for the long term.   ■ **planning**

    a. How much cash will Komiko retain, after taxes, if she holds the investment for 5 years and then she sells it when the long-term capital gains rate is 15 percent?

    b. What is Komiko's after-tax rate of return on her investment in part (a)?

    c. How much cash will Komiko retain, after taxes, if she holds the investment for 5 years and then sells when the long-term capital gains rate is 25 percent?

    d. What is Komiko's after-tax rate of return on her investment in part (c)?

    e. How much cash will Komiko retain, after taxes, if she holds the investment for 15 years and then she sells when the long-term capital gains rate is 15 percent?

    f. What is Komiko's after-tax rate of return on her investment in part (e)?

75. **(LO2)** Becky recently discovered some high-tech cooking technology that has advantages over microwaves and traditional ovens. She received a patent on the technology that gives her exclusive rights to the technology for 20 years. Becky would prefer to retain the patent, but she doesn't want to deal with the manufacturing and marketing of the technology. She was able to reach a compromise. A little over a year after she secured the patent, Becky signed a contract with DEF Company giving DEF control to manufacture and market the technology. In exchange, Becky is to receive a royalty based on the sales of the technology. For tax purposes, Becky is not sure how to treat her arrangement with DEF. If the exchange with DEF is treated as a sale, she will recognize long-term capital gain because the patent is a capital asset held for more than a year. If the exchange is not treated as a sale, Becky will recognize ordinary income as she receives the royalties. (*Hint:* IRC §1235 and www.aicpa.org/pubs/taxadv/online/aug2000/clinic5a.htm)   ■ **research**

    a. Is it possible for Becky to treat the exchange with DEF as a sale even though she never relinquishes actual title of the patent? If so, what requirements must she meet to treat the contract as a sale for tax purposes?

    b. Does your answer to the question above change if Becky's contract with DEF gave DEF Company control over the income from the patent for the next 10 years of the patent's remaining 19-year life?

76. **(LO3)** The Johnsons recently decided to invest in municipal bonds because their marginal tax rate is 40 percent. The return on municipal bonds is currently   ■ **planning**

3.5 percent and the return on similar taxable bonds is 5 percent. Compare the after-tax returns of the municipal and taxable bonds.

a. Which type of bond should the Johnsons select?

b. What type of bond should the Johnsons select if their marginal tax rate was 20 percent?

c. At what marginal tax rate would the Johnsons be indifferent between investing in either taxable or municipal bonds?

77. **(LO3)** Lynette VanWagoner purchased a life insurance policy to insure her mother Idon. Idon is currently 64. Insurance companies predict that women in her condition will live, on average, to be 81 years old. Lynette makes a one-time payment of $100,000 to purchase a life insurance policy on Idon's life. The policy provides for a $1,000,000 death benefit and promises returns of 7 percent per year.

a. How much will Lynette receive after taxes if Idon dies in 14 years?

b. How much will Lynette receive after taxes if Idon dies prematurely in seven years?

c. How much will Lynette receive after taxes if Lynette decides to cash in the policy after four years when Idon is still living and Lynette's marginal tax rate is 28 percent?

78. **(LO3)** Ben recently made a one-time investment of $20,000 in the Florida 529 educational savings plan for his three-year-old son, Mitch. Assume the plan yields a constant 6 percent return for the next 15 years.

a. How much money will be available for Mitch after taxes when he begins college at age 18?

b. Assume, instead, that when Mitch turns 18, he decides to forego college and spend his time as a traveling artist. If Mitch's parents give him the amount in the 529 plan to pursue his dreams, how much will he keep after taxes if his marginal tax rate is 10 percent?

79. **(LO4)** Rich and Shauna Nielson file a joint tax return and they itemize deductions. Assume their marginal tax rate on ordinary income is 25 percent. The Nielsons incur $2,000 in miscellaneous itemized deductions, excluding investment expenses. They also incur $1,000 in noninterest investment expenses during the year. What tax savings do they receive from the investment expenses under the following assumptions:

a. Their AGI is $90,000.

b. Their AGI is $130,000.

80. **(LO4)** Mickey and Jenny Porter file a joint tax return and they itemize deductions. The Porters incur $2,000 in employment-related miscellaneous itemized deductions. They also incur $3,000 of investment interest expense during the year. The Porters' income for the year consists of $150,000 in salary, and $2,500 of interest income.

a. What is the amount of the Porters' investment interest expense deduction for the year?

b. What would their investment interest expense deduction be if they also had a ($2,000) long-term capital loss?

■ planning   81. **(LO4)** On January 1 of year 1, Nick and Rachel Sutton purchased a parcel of undeveloped land as an investment. The purchase price of the land was $150,000. They paid for the property by making a down payment of $50,000 and borrowing $100,000 from the bank at an interest rate of 6 percent per year. At the end of the first year, the Suttons paid $6,000 of interest to the bank. During year 1, the Suttons only source of income was salary. On December 31 of year 2, the Suttons paid $6,000 of interest to the bank and sold the land for $210,000. They used $100,000 of the sale proceeds to pay off the $100,000 loan. The Suttons itemize deductions and are subject to a marginal ordinary income tax rate of 35 percent.

a. Should the Suttons treat the capital gain from the land sale as investment income in year 2 in order to minimize their year 2 tax bill?

b. How much does this save them in year 2?

82. **(LO4)** George recently received a great stock tip from his friend, Mason. George didn't have any cash on hand to invest, so he decided to take out a $20,000 loan to facilitate the stock acquisition. The loan terms are 8 percent interest with interest-only payments due each year for five years. At the end of the five-year period the entire loan principal is due. When George closed on the loan on April 1, 2009, he decided to invest $16,000 in stock and to use the remaining $4,000 to purchase a four-wheel recreation vehicle. Mason is unsure how he will treat the interest paid on the $20,000 loan. In 2009, Mason paid $1,200 interest expense on the loan. For tax purposes, how should he treat the 2009 interest expense? (*Hint:* visit www.irs.gov and consider IRS Publication 550.)

■research

83. **(LO5)** Larry recently invested $9,000 in purchasing a limited partnership interest. His share of the debt in the partnership is $11,000, but he is not personally responsible for paying the debt in the event the partnership cannot pay it. In addition, Larry's share of the limited partnership loss for the year is $2,000, his share of income from a different limited partnership was $1,000, and he had $3,000 of dividend income from the stock he owns.

a. What is Larry's tax basis in the limited partnership after considering his $2,000 loss for the year?

b. What is Larry's at-risk amount in the limited partnership after considering the $2,000 loss for the year?

c. How much of Larry's $2,000 loss from the limited partnership can he deduct in the current year?

84. **(LO5)** Joe recently invested $11,000 in purchasing a limited partnership interest. His share of the debt in the partnership is $3,000, but he is not personally responsible for paying the debt in the event the partnership cannot pay it. In addition, Joe's share of the limited partnership loss for the year is $12,000, his share of income from a different limited partnership was $3,000, and he had $7,000 of dividend income from the stock he owns.

a. What is Joe's tax basis in the limited partnership after considering his $12,000 loss for the year?

b. What is Joe's at-risk amount in the limited partnership after considering the $12,000 loss for the year?

c. How much of Joe's $12,000 loss from the limited partnership can he deduct in the current year?

85. **(LO5)** Rubio recently invested $15,000 in purchasing a limited partnership interest. His share of the debt in the partnership is $5,000, but he is not personally responsible for paying the debt in the event the partnership cannot pay it. In addition, Rubio's share of the limited partnership loss for the year is $22,000, his share of income from a different limited partnership was

$5,000, and he had $40,000 in wage income and $10,000 in long-term capital gains.

   a. What is Rubio's tax basis in the limited partnership after considering his $22,000 loss for the year?

   b. What is Rubio's at-risk amount in the limited partnership after considering the $22,000 loss for the year?

   c. How much of Rubio's $22,000 loss from the limited partnership can he deduct in the current year?

86. **(LO5)** Anwar owns a rental home and is involved in maintaining it and approving renters. During the year he has a net loss of $8,000 from renting the home. His other sources of income during the year were a salary of $111,000 and $34,000 of long-term capital gains. How much of Anwar's $8,000 rental loss can he deduct currently if he has no sources of passive income?

COMPREHENSIVE PROBLEMS

■ planning

87. As noted in the chapter, Nick inherited $100,000 with the stipulation that he "invest it to financially benefit his family." Nick and Rachel decided they would invest the inheritance to help them accomplish two financial goals: purchasing a Park City vacation home and saving for Lea's education.

	Vacation Home	Lea's Education
Initial investment	$50,000	$50,000
Investment horizon	5 years	18 years

The Suttons have a marginal income tax rate of 30 percent (capital gains rate of 15 percent), and have decided to investigate the following investment opportunities.

	5 Years	After-Tax Rate of Return	18 Years	After-Tax Rate of Return
Corporate bonds	5.75%		4.75%	
Dividend-paying stock (no appreciation)	3.50%		3.50%	
Growth stock	Future Value is $65,000		Future Value is $140,000	
Municipal bonds	3.20%		3.10%	
Qualified tuition program	5.75%		5.50%	

Complete the two after-tax rates of return columns for each investment, and provide investment recommendations for the Suttons.

88. During 2009, your clients, Mr. and Mrs. Howell, owned the following investment assets:

Investment Assets	Date Acquired	Purchase Price	Broker's Commission Paid at Time of Purchase
300 shares of IBM common	11/22/06	$ 10,350	$ 100
200 shares of IBM common	4/3/07	$ 43,250	$ 300
3,000 shares of Apple preferred	12/12/07	$147,000	$1,300
2,100 shares of Cisco common	8/14/08	$ 52,500	$ 550
420 shares of Vanguard mutual fund	3/2/09	$ 14,700	No load fund*

*No commissions are charged when no load mutual funds are bought and sold.

Because of the downturn in the stock market, Mr. and Mrs. Howell decided to sell most of their stocks and mutual fund in 2009 and to reinvest in municipal bonds. The following investment assets were sold in 2009:

Investment Assets	Date Sold	Sale Price	Broker's Commission Paid at Time of Sale
300 shares of IBM common	5/6/09	$ 13,700	$ 100
3,000 shares of Apple preferred	10/5/09	$221,400	$2,000
2,100 shares of Cisco common	8/15/09	$ 63,250	$ 650
451 Shares of Vanguard mutual fund	12/21/09	$ 15,700	No load fund*

*No commissions are charged when no load mutual funds are bought and sold.

The Howells' broker issued them a Form 1099 showing the sales proceeds net of the commissions paid. For example, the IBM sales proceeds were reported as $13,600 on the Form 1099 they received.

In addition to the sales reflected in the table above, the Howells provided you with the following additional information concerning 2009:

- The Howells received a Form 1099 from the Vanguard mutual fund reporting a $900 long-term capital gain distribution. This distribution was reinvested in 31 additional Vanguard mutual fund shares on 6/30/09.
- In 2004, Mrs. Howell loaned $6,000 to a friend who was starting a new multilevel marketing company called LD3. The friend declared bankruptcy in 2009, and Mrs. Howell has been notified she will not be receiving any repayment of the loan.
- The Howells have a $2,300 short-term capital loss carryover and a $4,800 long-term capital loss carryover from prior years.
- The Howells did not instruct their broker to sell any particular lot of IBM stock.
- The Howells earned $3,000 in municipal bond interest, $3,000 in interest from corporate bonds, and $4,000 in qualifying dividends.
- The Howells paid $5,000 in investment interest expense during the year ($1,000 is attributable to their municipal bond investments).
- The Howells paid $2,000 for investment advice during the year but did not have any additional miscellaneous itemized deductions.
- Assume the Howells have $130,000 of wage income during the year.

a. Go to the IRS web site (www.IRS.gov) and download the most current version of Schedule D. Use page 1 of Schedule D to compute net long-term and short-term capital gains. Then, compute the Howells' tax liability for the year (ignoring the alternative minimum tax) assuming they file a joint return, have no dependents, and their itemized deductions total $25,000.

b. Are there any tax planning recommendations related to the stock sales that you should have shared with the Howells before their decision to sell?

c. Assume the Howells' short-term capital loss carryover from prior years is $82,300 rather than $2,300 as indicated above. If this is the case, how much short-term and long-term capital loss carryover remains to be carried beyond 2009 to future tax years?

89. WAR (We Are Rich) has been in business since 1979. WAR is an accrual method sole proprietorship that deals in the manufacturing and wholesaling of various types of golf equipment. Hack & Hack CPAs have filed accurate tax

returns for WAR's owner since WAR opened its doors. The managing partner of Hack & Hack (Jack) has gotten along very well with the owner of WAR—Mr. Someday Woods. However, in early 2009, Jack Hack and Someday Woods played a round of golf and Jack, for the first time ever, actually beat Mr. Woods. Mr. Woods was so upset that he fired Hack & Hack and has hired you to compute his 2009 tax liability. Mr. Woods was able to provide you with the following information from prior tax returns. The taxable income numbers reflect the results from all of Mr. Woods's activities *except for the items separately stated.* You will need to consider how to handle the separately stated items for tax purposes. (*Note that the 2004–2008 numbers do not reflect capital loss carryovers.)

	2004	2005	2006	2007	2008
Ordinary taxable income*	$ 4,000	$ 2,000	$94,000	$170,000	$250,000
Other items not included in ordinary taxable income:					
Net gain (loss) on disposition of §1231 assets	$ 3,000	$10,000		($6,000)	
Net long-term capital gain (loss) on disposition of capital assets	($15,000)	$ 1,000	($7,000)		($5,000)

In 2009, Mr. Woods had taxable income in the amount of $460,000 *before* considering the following events and transactions that transpired in 2009:

a. On January 1, 2009, WAR purchased a plot of land for $100,000 with the intention of creating a driving range where patrons could test their new golf equipment. WAR never got around to building the driving range; instead, WAR sold the land on October 1, 2009, for $40,000.

b. On August 17, 2009, WAR sold its golf testing machine, "Iron Byron" and replaced it with a new machine "Iron Tiger." "Iron Byron" was purchased and installed for a total cost of $22,000 on February 5, 2005. At the time of sale, "Iron Byron" had an adjusted tax basis of $4,000. WAR sold "Iron Byron" for $25,000.

c. In the months October through December 2009, WAR sold various assets to come up with the funds necessary to invest in WAR's latest and greatest invention—the three-dimple golf ball. Data on these assets are provided below:

Asset	Placed in Service (or purchased)	Sold	Initial Basis	Accumulated Depreciation	Selling Price
Someday's black leather sofa (used in office)	4/4/08	10/16/09	$ 3,000	$ 540	$ 2,900
Someday's office chair	3/1/07	11/8/09	$ 8,000	$3,000	$ 4,000
Marketable securities	2/1/06	12/1/09	$12,000	$ 0	$20,000
Land held for investment	7/1/08	11/29/09	$45,000	$ 0	$48,000
Other investment property	11/30/07	10/15/09	$10,000	$ 0	$ 8,000

d. Finally, on May 7, 2009, WAR sold the building where they tested their plutonium shaft, lignite head drivers. WAR purchased the building on January 5, 1997, for $190,000 ($170,000 for the building, $20,000 for the land). At the time of the sale, the accumulated depreciation on the building was $50,000. WAR sold the building (with the land) for $300,000. The fair market value of the land at the time of sale was $45,000.

Compute Mr. Woods's taxable income *after* taking into account the transactions described above. In addition, record the effects of the transactions above in Mr. Woods's Schedule D and Schedule 4797 (use the most current version of these schedules) to be attached to his Form 1040.

KAPLAN SCHWESER CPA SIMULATIONS

KAPLAN SCHWESER

Please visit the Online Learning Center (www.mhhe.com/spilker2010) to access the following Kaplan Schweser CPA Simulation:

The simulation for **Pria Patel** covers capital gains and losses; home office expenses; business income and expense; NOL; charitable contributions; and capital expenditures.

Compensation

Learning Objectives

Upon completing this chapter you should be able to:

LO 1 Discuss and explain the tax implications of compensation in the form of salary and wages from the employer's and employee's perspectives.

■

LO 2 Describe and distinguish the tax implications of various forms of equity-based compensation from the employer's and employee's perspectives.

■

LO 3 Compare and contrast taxable and nontaxable fringe benefits and explain the employee and employer tax consequences associated with fringe benefits.

J ulie and Ethan Clark and their two children have been settled into their life in San Diego, California, for some time. Julie has decided her career is at a crossroads. On the one hand, her employment as a mid-level executive for Premier Computer Corporation (PCC) is going well, but the work is not as challenging as it used to be. She suspects that, given her skills and abilities, she could put her career on the fast track with the right opportunity, engaging in more fulfilling work and gaining a significant increase in compensation.

Julie was sitting at her desk contemplating her career when she received yet another call from a corporate headhunter. While she usually quickly dismisses such

calls, this time she gave her full attention. He asked if she had any interest in a vice president of marketing position with a publicly traded company located nearby. After the headhunter answered a few of her questions, Julie gave him the go-ahead to set up an interview.

A couple of weeks later, Julie had been through two rounds of interviews for the marketing VP position when she received a call informing her that she was the one Technology Products, Inc. (TPI), wanted for the job and that an offer letter with the details was on its way. The letter indicated TPI was offering a $280,000 salary (a nice increase from her current salary). TPI was also offering her a choice of certain types of equity-based compensation, some nice fringe benefits, and the opportunity to participate in

Storyline Summary	
Taxpayers:	Julie and Ethan Clark
Location:	San Diego, California
Employment status:	Julie—mid-level executive for Premier Computer Corporation (PCC); current salary $240,000 Ethan—mechanical engineer; current salary $70,000
Filing status:	Married filing jointly
Deductions:	Contributions to employer-sponsored retirement plan; itemized deductions
Dependents:	Two children
Marginal ordinary tax rate:	40 percent
Current situation:	Julie is considering an offer for the vice president of marketing position with Technology Products, Inc.

the company's qualified retirement plan. While excited by the letter, Julie knew she needed to learn more about the equity-based compensation alternatives and the other forms of compensation TPI was offering before she could adequately evaluate the offer and reach her decision.

to be continued . . .

As TPI's letter to Julie illustrates, employers are able to offer many different forms of compensation to employees. They can also pay some compensation currently and defer some to the future. Each type of compensation has unique tax and nontax consequences.

This chapter addresses the tax and nontax consequences of current compensation from both the employee's and the employer's perspective. The next chapter addresses future compensation.

LO1 SALARY AND WAGES

Current compensation paid to **employees** in the form of **salary** and **wages**, usually paid in cash, has tax consequences to both employees and employers. Below, we address the tax (and nontax) considerations of salary and wages from the employee's perspective followed by the employer's perspective.

Employee Considerations for Salary and Wages

Employees receiving salary generally earn a fixed amount of compensation for the year no matter how many hours they work. In addition, salaried employees may be eligible for bonuses based on satisfying certain criteria. In contrast, employees receiving wages generally get paid by the hour. Salary, bonus, and wages are taxed to employees as ordinary income. Employees generally report income from salary and wages as they receive it.[1]

At the end of each year, employees receive a **Form W-2** (see Exhibit 12-1) from their employers summarizing their salary or wage compensation and the various withholding amounts during the year.[2] Employees simply report their wages on page 1, line 7 of the 1040 federal tax return and report their income taxes withheld on line 62 of page 2.

Withholding Taxes   When they begin employment with a firm, employees complete a **Form W-4** to supply the information the firm needs to withhold the correct amount of tax from each paycheck. Specifically, employees use Form W-4 to indicate (1) whether to withhold at the single rate or at the lower married rate, (2) the number of withholding or "personal" allowances the employee chooses to claim (the more personal allowances claimed, the less the withholding amount), and (3) whether the employee wants an additional amount of tax withheld each period above the amount based on the number of allowances claimed.

---

[1]Treas. Reg. §1.451-1(a).

[2]Compensation received by taxpayers who are not employees is not considered to be salary and wages. Compensation for self-employed taxpayers is discussed in Chapter 8.

EXHIBIT 12-1   2008 Form W-2

22222	a Employee's social security number		
	OMB No. 1545-0008		

b Employer identification number (EIN)	1 Wages, tips, other compensation	2 Federal income tax withheld
c Employer's name, address, and ZIP code	3 Social security wages	4 Social security tax withheld
	5 Medicare wages and tips	6 Medicare tax withheld
	7 Social security tips	8 Allocated tips
d Control number	9 Advance EIC payment	10 Dependent care benefits

e Employee's first name and initial Last name Suff.	11 Nonqualified plans	12a
	13 Statutory employee Retirement plan Third-party sick pay	12b
	14 Other	12c
		12d
f Employee's address and ZIP code		

15 State Employer's state ID number	16 State wages, tips, etc.	17 State income tax	18 Local wages, tips, etc.	19 Local income tax	20 Locality name

Form **W-2** Wage and Tax Statement   **2008**   Department of the Treasury—Internal Revenue Service

Copy 1—For State, City, or Local Tax Department

In general, the withholding tables are designed so that employers will withhold taxes fairly close to the amount of the taxpayer's actual tax liability—if the employee claims the same number of withholding allowances on her W-4 as the number of personal and dependency exemptions she claims on her tax return. However, there are special circumstances in which this general rule does not hold. Taxpayers who itemize deductions, have high income, have deductible losses, file jointly with an employed spouse, or have other special tax circumstances may need to adjust the number of withholding allowances claimed to have the desired amount of taxes withheld.[3] Thus, a married taxpayer with three dependent children would generally elect to have taxes withheld based on the married withholding table and report five withholding allowances on the W-4 (one for herself, her spouse, and each dependent). In this situation, assuming none of the special circumstances described above, the taxpayer's withholding would be very close to her actual tax liability when she files her tax return for the year. However, because the tables assume taxpayers *don't* itemize deductions, they may require employers to withhold more taxes than are necessary from taxpayers who report a significant amount of itemized deductions. Taxpayers in this situation can claim additional withholding allowances on Form W-4 above and beyond the number of their dependents. Each extra withholding allowance claimed by taxpayers reduces the amount of income taxes their employers will withhold. Taxpayers should claim enough extra allowances to ensure that the desired amount of tax is withheld from their paychecks.[4]

Through the W-4, taxpayers can manage the withholding on their salary or wages—whether it is to *decrease* withholding through increasing the number of personal allowances, or to *increase* withholding by either reducing personal

---

[3]See IRS publication 505 "Tax Withholding and Estimated Tax" for other circumstances.

[4]The taxpayer could use actual IRS withholding tables to compute the number of allowances required to have the desired amount of taxes withheld, or the taxpayer could solicit help from his payroll department in determining the right number of allowances.

THE KEY FACTS

Employment-Related Forms

■ Form W-2
· Summarizes an employee's taxable salary and wages.
· Provides annual federal and state withholding information.
· Generated by employer on an annual basis.

■ Form W-4
· Supplies an employee's withholding information to employer.
· Generated by employee.
· Remains constant unless employee makes changes.

allowances or by specifying an additional amount to be withheld. Further, employees can revise the information on the W-4 throughout the year.[5] Taxpayers who, given their income, have underwithheld at any point during the year can increase their withholdings to catch up before the end of the year. For example, a taxpayer who has underwithheld taxes through September can increase her withholdings for October, November, and December to catch up. Because the IRS generally assumes that withholdings are made evenly throughout the year, taxpayers are treated as though most of the withholding increase was made earlier in the year, and the late withholding will likely not cause them to suffer tax underpayment penalties (see Chapter 7).[6]

Taxpayers in any of the special circumstances outlined above should complete their W-4s with care to ensure proper withholding.[7] Julie and Ethan, from our opening storyline, will together earn $310,000 of salary with their current employers. Because they itemize deductions and make deductible contributions to employer-provided retirement accounts, they project their taxable income at $280,000 for the year. Based on this projection, the Clarks will incur a $70,221 tax liability for the year. After consulting with their respective payroll departments, Julie and Ethan learn that if each files a Form W-4 with four personal allowances and has tax withheld at the married rate, Julie will have $54,463 withheld and Ethan will have $4,002 withheld. In total, they will have $58,465 withheld, leaving a withholding shortfall of $11,756.[8] To equalize their withholding and their anticipated liability, the Clarks can reduce the number of withholding allowances they're claiming, have taxes withheld at the higher single rate, and/or have an additional amount withheld from each paycheck. They decide to have an extra $980 withheld from Julie's monthly paycheck ($11,760 for the year) to cover their withholding. Julie's completed Form W-4 without her signature is presented in Exhibit 12-2.

EXHIBIT 12-2   Form W-4

Form **W-4**	**Employee's Withholding Allowance Certificate**	OMB No. 1545-0074
Department of the Treasury Internal Revenue Service	▶ **Whether you are entitled to claim a certain number of allowances or exemption from withholding is subject to review by the IRS. Your employer may be required to send a copy of this form to the IRS.**	20**08**

1 Type or print your first name and middle initial.	Last name		2 Your social security number
Julie	Clark		123 45 6789

Home address (number and street or rural route)	3 ☐ Single ☐ Married ☐ Married, but withhold at higher Single rate.
1250 Beach Street	**Note.** If married, but legally separated, or spouse is a nonresident alien, check the "Single" box.
City or town, state, and ZIP code	4 If your last name differs from that shown on your social security card,
San Diego, CA 92101	check here. You must call 1-800-772-1213 for a replacement card. ▶ ☐

5	Total number of allowances you are claiming (from line **H** above **or** from the applicable worksheet on page 2)	**5**	4
6	Additional amount, if any, you want withheld from each paycheck	**6** $	980
7	I claim exemption from withholding for 2008, and I certify that I meet **both** of the following conditions for exemption.		

• Last year I had a right to a refund of **all** federal income tax withheld because I had **no** tax liability **and**
• This year I expect a refund of **all** federal income tax withheld because I expect to have **no** tax liability.
If you meet both conditions, write "Exempt" here . . . . ▶ | **7** |

Under penalties of perjury, I declare that I have examined this certificate and to the best of my knowledge and belief, it is true, correct, and complete.

Employee's signature
(Form is not valid
unless you sign it.) ▶   Date ▶

8 Employer's name and address (Employer: Complete lines 8 and 10 only if sending to the IRS.)	9 Office code (optional)	10 Employer identification number (EIN)

For Privacy Act and Paperwork Reduction Act Notice, see page 2.   Cat. No. 10220Q   Form **W-4** (2008)

[5]Most employers require an employee to submit a revised Form W-4 at least two weeks before the end of the pay period for which the new withholding amount is to take effect.

[6]See instructions for Form 2210: Underpayment of Estimated Tax by Individuals, Estates, and Trusts.

[7]Note the bottom of Form W-4 indicates that it is signed under penalties of perjury.

[8]While Julie and Ethan are only required to pay 90 percent of their current tax liability to avoid penalty, they prefer to not have a large liability at the end of the year—even if it is suboptimal from a time value perspective.

FICA (Payroll Taxes)   As we discuss in detail in Chapter 7, employees must pay **FICA taxes** on their wages.[9] FICA tax consists of both a Social Security and a Medicare component. Employees pay **Social Security tax** at a rate of 6.2 percent on their wage base, and **Medicare tax** at a rate of 1.45 percent on their wages.[10] As we describe in Chapter 7, the wage base on which employees pay Social Security taxes is limited to an annually determined amount, which is indexed for inflation. The wage base limitation reflects the fact that the benefits an employee may ultimately receive are also capped. The limits apply to each taxpayer's wages regardless of marital or tax filing status. The 2009 limit is $106,800, which is a $4,800 increase over the $102,000 limit in 2008.[11] There is no wage base for the Medicare component of the FICA tax. In other words, employees' first $106,800 of wages are subject to the Social Security tax and employees' entire wages are subject to the Medicare tax. We defer to Chapter 7 for a more detailed discussion on *employee*-related FICA tax considerations.

Example 12-1

Ethan and Julie have salaries of $70,000 and $240,000, respectively. What are Ethan's and Julie's FICA taxes for the current year?

Answer: Ethan's FICA tax is $7,637, computed as follows:

Description	Amount	Reference
(1) Compensation subject to FICA tax	$ 70,000	
(2) Social Security tax base limit for 2009	$106,800	
(3) Compensation subject to Social Security tax	$106,800	Lesser of (1) and (2).
(4) Social Security tax rate	6.2%	
(5) Social Security tax	$ 6,622	(3) × (4).
(6) Medicare tax rate	1.45%	
(7) Medicare tax	$ 1,015	(1) × (6).
FICA taxes	$ 7,637	(5) + (7).

Answer: Julie's FICA tax is $10,102, computed as follows:

Description	Amount	Reference
(1) Compensation subject to FICA tax	$240,000	
(2) Social Security tax base limit for 2007	$106,800	
(3) Compensation subject to Social Security tax	$106,800	Lesser of (1) and (2).
(4) Social Security tax rate	6.2%	
(5) Social Security tax	$ 6,622	(3) × (4).
(6) Medicare tax rate	1.45%	
(7) Medicare tax	$ 3,480	(1) × (6).
FICA taxes	$ 10,102	(5) + (7).

[9]FICA stands for Federal Insurance Contributions Act.

[10]As discussed in the "employer" section, employers must also pay FICA taxes on behalf of the employee.

[11]The 2007 amount was $97,500.

Employer Considerations for Salary and Wages

Storyline Summary	
Taxpayer:	TPI Corporation
Location:	San Diego, California
Ownership:	Publicly traded corporation
Industry:	Manufacturing high-technology products
CEO:	Daniel Hewitt
Marginal tax rate:	35 percent
Current Situation:	Recruiting Julie Clark for marketing vp position

Deductibility of Salary Payments   Employers computing taxable income under the cash method of accounting generally deduct salary and wages when they pay the employee.[12] Employers computing taxable income under the accrual method generally deduct wages payable to employees as the employees earn the wages.[13] This general rule holds even in situations when the employer accrues compensation expense in one year but actually pays the employee in the subsequent year, as long as the company makes the payment within 2½ months after the employer's year-end. If the employer pays the employee more than 2½ months after the employer's year-end, the wages are considered deferred compensation and are not deductible by the employer until the employee recognizes the salary as income (that is, receives payment).[14] Because most employers pay regular salary and wages to employees each month (or more frequently), the 2½ month rule is likely to be more of an issue for accrued compensation, such as one-time year-end bonuses, than it is for normal wages.

In situations when the employer and employee are "related" parties, special rules apply. In this context, the definition of related parties includes an employee/shareholder who owns more than 50 percent of the value of the employer corporation.[15] When the corporation and employee/shareholder are related parties, a corporation is not allowed to deduct the compensation expense until the employee/shareholder (related party) includes the payment in income.[16] Therefore, for an accrual basis company paying compensation, such as wages or a bonus, to a related employee, the 2½ month rule does not apply. Because theoretically related parties are considered to be the same taxpayer to some extent, the tax laws limit their ability to accelerate deductions and enjoy the immediate tax benefits while at the same time deferring income and delaying the payment of taxes.

Because employers are required to match FICA taxes paid by employees (they must pay as much FICA tax on an employee's behalf as the employee is required to pay for herself), their before-tax cost of providing salary (the cost *before*

---

[12]Treas. Reg. §1.461-1(a)(1).

[13]Treas. Reg. §1.461-1(a)(2). See Chapter 8 for a detailed discussion of the cash and accrual accounting methods.

[14]Treas. Reg. §1.404(b)-1T(A-2). We discuss tax issues and consequences relating to deferred compensation in Chapter 13.

[15]See §267(b) for the complete definition of "related" parties.

[16]§267(a)(2).

subtracting the tax benefit of the deduction) is greater than the salary itself.[17] However, the after-tax cost of providing this salary is generally much less than the before-tax cost, because the employer deducts the salary and associated FICA taxes paid. The formula for computing the after-tax cost of the salary (the cost after subtracting the tax savings from the deduction), or any deductible expense, for that matter, is as follows:

$$\text{Deductible Expenditure} \times (1 - \text{Marginal Tax Rate})$$

Example 12-2

What is PCC's before-tax and after-tax costs of paying Julie a $240,000 salary? (Note PCC's marginal tax rate is 35 percent.)

Answer: $249,525 before taxes and $162,566 after taxes, computed as follows:

Description	Amount	Explanation
Before tax cost of salary:		
(1) Compensation subject to FICA tax	$240,000	
(2) Social Security tax base limit for 2009	$106,800	
(3) Compensation subject to Social Security tax	$106,800	Lesser of (1) and (2).
(4) Social Security tax rate	6.2%	
(5) Social Security tax	$ 6,622	(3) × (4).
(6) Medicare tax rate	1.45%	
(7) Medicare tax	$ 3,480	(1) × (6).
(8) FICA taxes	$ 10,102	(5) + (7).
(9) Total before-tax cost	$250,102	(1) + (8).
(10) (1 − marginal tax rate)	× 65%	(1 − 35%).
After-tax cost of salary	**$162,566**	(9) × (10).

Limits on salary deductibility. Employers are generally allowed to deduct reasonable compensation paid to employees.[18] Determining whether compensation is reasonable in amount is a **facts and circumstances test** that involves considering the duties of the employee, the complexities of the business, and the amount of salary compared with the income of the business among other things. The amount of salary in excess of the amount considered reasonable is not deductible. The reasonable compensation limit typically applies to closely held businesses where the employee is also an owner of the company or the employee is a relative of the business owner. For large corporations, another limitation applies that is generally more restrictive than the reasonableness limitation.

Responding to a growing public perception that executives of publicly traded corporations were being overpaid at the expense of shareholders and that the government was subsidizing (paying a part of) the excess by allowing corporations to deduct the high salaries, in 1993 Congress enacted §162(m) of the Internal Revenue Code.[19] This provision limits the deduction for compensation paid to the CEO and

THE KEY FACTS

Limits on Salary Deductibility Publicly Traded Corporations

■ $1,000,000 maximum annual compensation deduction per person.
· Limited—applies to CEO and four other highest compensated officers.
· Does not apply to performance-based compensation.

---

[17]Employers may be required to pay other expenses based on the employee wages such as workers' compensation insurance. While these other expenses are not addressed in this discussion, the concepts are the same as for the FICA taxes.

[18]As we discussed in Chapter 8, all business expenses (not just compensation) must be reasonable in amount to be fully deductible.

[19]Nelson, Daniel, "Section 162(m) Revisited," *Tax Notes Today,* January 10, 2005, pp. 8–22.

the four other most highly compensated officers to $1,000,000 each, per year.[20] However, certain exceptions allow companies to pay and deduct compensation in excess of the $1 million limit. For example, the limit does not apply to compensation based on (1) performance (this is the most significant of the exceptions in terms of dollars and frequency of application), (2) commissions, (3) contributions to qualified retirement plans, or (4) other tax-free benefits.

While most publicly traded corporations are aware of and are sensitive to the limitation, they may take different approaches in dealing with it. For example, as described in the following excerpt from its proxy statement (see Exhibit 12-3 below), Callaway Golf attempts to maximize its compensation deduction, yet it acknowledges that there are situations when, in order to achieve its nontax goals, it may provide compensation to executives that is not deductible.

EXHIBIT 12-3   Excerpt from Callaway Golf Proxy Statement

The tax deductibility of compensation should be maximized where appropriate.

The Compensation Committee reviews its compensation plans in light of applicable tax provisions, including section 162(m), and may revise compensation plans from time to time to maximize deductibility. However, the Compensation Committee may approve compensation in the future, as it has in the past, that does not qualify for deductibility where it is appropriate to do so in light of other competing interests and goals or where, because of the ambiguities and uncertainties as to the application and interpretation of section 162(m) and the regulations issued thereunder, the Company's compensation plans, or a part of them, fail to qualify.

In contrast, PepsiCo, Inc., takes a slightly different approach. As indicated in the following excerpt from its proxy statement (see Exhibit 12-4), PepsiCo caps its salaries at $1 million. Apparently, the firm wants to make sure salaries paid to executives are fully deductible.

EXHIBIT 12-4   Excerpt from PespiCo, Inc., Proxy Statement

Base Salary: The relative levels of base salary for the CEO and the other executive officers are based on the underlying accountabilities of each executive's position and reflect each executive officer's scope of responsibility. The salaries are reviewed on a regular basis and are benchmarked against similar positions among the peer group companies. *Individual salaries are capped at $1 million* (emphasis added).

The difference in philosophy between Callaway and Pepsi may be driven by nontax considerations. To be deductible, compensation to executives in excess of $1 million generally must be performance-based. This means that the executives bear the risk that they won't receive the additional compensation if certain performance benchmarks like stock-price targets aren't met. Some companies may decide they don't want their executives to shoulder this risk, so they pay them salaries in excess of the deductible amount to guarantee a certain level of compensation. Companies may also decide to cap executive salaries at $1 million just to avoid the public perception that they are being fiscally irresponsible by paying more than the deductibility limits.

---

[20]To be deductible, compensation (just like all deductible business expenses) must be "reasonable" irrespective of the $1 million deduction limitation. See Chapter 8 for a discussion of the reasonableness limitation on business expenses.

Example 12-3

Several years ago, TPI was actively searching for a new CEO. The board of directors eventually chose Daniel Hewitt. During negotiations, Daniel indicated he wanted a $2 million salary (Option 1) in addition to the equity-based compensation the board was offering. While this level of salary could be considered reasonable, the board of directors was concerned about the $1 million limitation on deductible salary, so the board offered an alternative proposal. Under this proposal, TPI would pay Daniel a $1 million salary and offer him an additional $1.2 million of bonus, contingent on achieving realistic financial performance goals for TPI (Option 2). Confident he could meet the financial goals, Daniel accepted the offer. Assuming the performance goals are met, what is TPI's after-tax cost of providing the compensation under Option 1 and Option 2?

Answer: $1,672,779 under Option 1 and $1,454,039 under Option 2, computed as follows:

	Option 1 ($2,000,000 salary $0 bonus)	Option 2 ($1,000,000 salary $1,200,000 bonus)	Explanation
Before-tax cost:			
(1) Total compensation	$2,000,000	$2,200,000	Salary + bonus.
(2) Social Security taxes for employee	$ 6,622	$ 6,622	($106,800 × 6.2%).
(3) Medicare taxes for employee	$ 29,000	$ 31,900	(1) × 1.45%.
(4) Total before-tax cost	$2,035,622	$2,238,522	(1) + (2) + (3).
(5) Deductible amount	$1,035,622	$2,238,522	Option 1: $1M salary not deductible.
(6) Marginal tax rate	× 35%	× 35%	
(7) Tax savings from compensation deduction	362,468	783,483	(5) × (6).
After-tax cost	$1,673,154	$1,455,039	(4) − (7).

Assuming the performance goals are met, both parties benefit from the arrangement. Daniel prefers Option 2 because it provides him with $200,000 more of before-tax compensation ($2.2M − $2M). TPI also prefers Option 2 because it costs $218,115 less after taxes than Option 1 ($1,673,154 − $1,455,039). Of course, Daniel is the one who must bear the risk of the contingent compensation in Option 2, so he must consider this risk before accepting the offer.

As this example illustrates, the $1 million dollar deduction limitation can have a considerable impact on the after-tax cost of providing compensation to corporate executives. However, employers frequently utilize the options described above to craft offers that meet the needs of both parties.

EQUITY-BASED COMPENSATION

LO2

continued from page 12-2 . . .
As she read TPI's offer letter more carefully, Julie discovered that on the first day of January following her acceptance of the offer, she would be granted 10,000 shares of restricted stock, 50 incentive stock options (ISOs), and 200 nonqualified options (NQOs). Each of the incentive and nonqualified options gives her the right to purchase 100 shares of stock at a fixed price equal to the market value of TPI stock on

the date of grant. As she read on, Julie noticed that she would not be able to exercise either type of stock option (that is, purchase TPI stock for the exercise price stated in the options) until the options vested (the options become hers when they vest), which will be two years from the grant date. Further, Julie understood that, after the restricted stock vests (one year from the grant date on January 1), she would be free to do what she wanted with it. The last detail Julie noticed when reading this part of the offer letter was that both types of options will expire 10 years from the grant date. She understood this to mean that if she did not exercise her options sometime before their expiration date, she would lose them.

Although it was obvious to Julie that the value of the options and restricted stock would increase as the share price of TPI increased from the current share price of $5 per share, she remained unsure about the terminology used in this section of the letter, and she realized she needed to know more about the economic and tax implications of stock options and restricted stock before making her decision.

to be continued . . .

Equity-based compensation such as stock options and restricted stock provides risks and potential rewards not available with other forms of compensation. If the employer's stock price increases after it grants options and restricted stock, employees can be rewarded handsomely. On the other hand, if employer stock prices don't increase, the value of restricted stock will be limited and stock options will expire worthless.

Employers use equity-based compensation, in part, to motivate their employees to take ownership in their companies. When employees hold employer options and stock, their compensation is more directly tied to the fortunes of their employer and its shareholders—employees' compensation increases in tandem with their employer's stock price. This philosophy is reflected in an excerpt from Intel's proxy statement presented in Exhibit 12-5.

In addition to its motivational effects, equity-based compensation has traditionally brought employers cash flow benefits as well. How? Unless employers purchase their own stock in a market transaction to satisfy option exercises and stock grants, there are no cash outflows associated with this form of compensation. In fact, employers actually *receive* cash from their employees in the amount of the exercise price on the options exercised. There are a couple of downsides to this benefit, however. First, employers experience the opportunity cost of selling shares at a discounted price to employees rather than selling the shares at fair market value on the open market. Second, because employers must issue new shares to satisfy option exercises and stock grants, the total number of shares outstanding increases, and, therefore, earnings per share are diluted, which is a detriment to existing stockholders. The

EXHIBIT 12-5   Excerpt from Intel's 2005 Proxy Statement

The use of stock options has long been a vital component of our overall compensation philosophy, which is premised on the principle that any long-term pay-for-performance incentive compensation should be closely aligned with stockholders' interests. We believe that over the years, we have been very successful in achieving this objective through the use of fixed-price stock options for the majority of our employees. Fixed-price stock options align employees' interests directly with those of our other stockholders, because an increase in stock price after the date of award is necessary for employees to realize any value, thus rewarding employees only upon improved stock price performance.

only way for employers to mitigate this problem without increasing earnings is to use their cash reserves to acquire their own publicly traded shares to satisfy the options exercise.[21] However, from a cash-flow perspective, this is no different from paying cash compensation.

Stock Options

Stock options differ from restricted stock in that (1) employees have to use cash to purchase employer stock once they are allowed to exercise the options and (2) there is a greater likelihood that options, which have expiration dates, will ultimately be worthless. When stock options **vest,** employees are legally entitled to buy or exercise employer stock at a stipulated price, referred to as the exercise or **strike price.** Options may be exercised anytime between the vesting date and the expiration date of the options.[22] If the share price does not go above the exercise price at some point during this interval, employees will not exercise their options and the options will expire without providing them any benefit.

As suggested in Exhibit 12-6, the future value of stock option awards will depend on the exercise price, the company's future share price, the exercise date of the options, and the timing for selling the shares received from the **option exercise.**

Example 12-4

Given the assumptions in the stock option time line shown in Exhibit 12-6, how much will it cost Julie to exercise her options at the end of year 3 (before taxes), and how much will she have if she immediately sells the acquired shares (before taxes)?[23]

Answer: $125,000 cost to exercise; $375,000 remaining after sale, calculated as follows:

Description	Amount	Explanation
(1) Shares acquired	25,000	Given (20,000 NQOs and 5,000 ISOs).
(2) Exercise price	$ 5	Exhibit 12-6.
(3) Cash needed to exercise	$125,000	(1) × (2).
(4) Market price	$ 20	Exhibit 12-6.
(5) Market value of shares	$500,000	(1) × (4).
Net proceeds upon sale	$375,000	(5) − (3).

If, in the prior example, Julie didn't have enough cash on hand to cover the $125,000 cost of exercising the options, she could simultaneously exercise the options and sell the stock, using $125,000 of the proceeds from the stock sale to pay for exercising the options. This so-called cashless exercise is typically facilitated using the services of an employer-provided stockbroker.

---

[21]Because earnings per share is calculated by dividing earnings by the number of shares of stock outstanding, earnings per share could even increase when new shares are issued to satisfy option exercises if earnings increase by an amount that more than offsets the effect of issuing new shares into the market.

[22]Vesting dates are frequently specified as future calendar dates or they may be triggered when certain events occur (i.e., predefined performance objectives are met, or the company has been sold).

[23]According to the facts presented in Exhibit 12-6, Julie could have exercised her options as early as the vesting date for her options at the end of year 2. We assume she waits one year to exercise her options to better illustrate the implications of deferring the option exercise beyond the vesting date. In reality, it is quite common for employees to exercise their stock options on the vesting date.

EXHIBIT 12-6   Sample Timeline for Incentive and Nonqualified Options

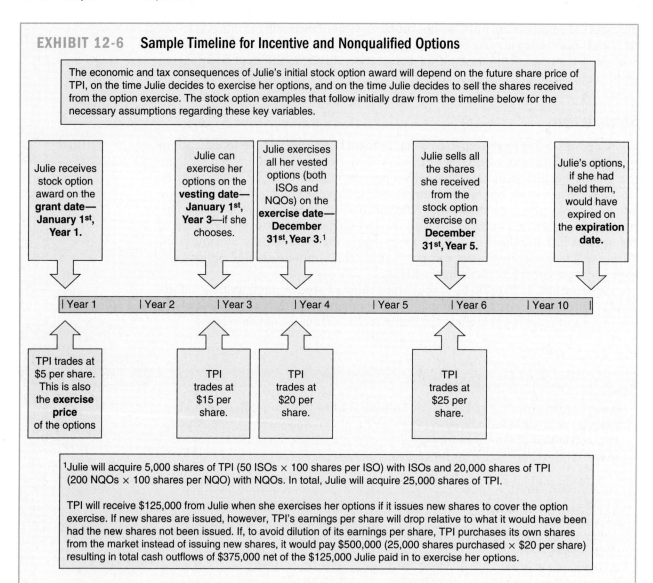

The economic and tax consequences of Julie's initial stock option award will depend on the future share price of TPI, on the time Julie decides to exercise her options, and on the time Julie decides to sell the shares received from the option exercise. The stock option examples that follow initially draw from the timeline below for the necessary assumptions regarding these key variables.

Julie receives stock option award on the **grant date—January 1st, Year 1.**

Julie can exercise her options on the **vesting date—January 1st, Year 3**—if she chooses.

Julie exercises all her vested options (both ISOs and NQOs) on the **exercise date—December 31st, Year 3.**[1]

Julie sells all the shares she received from the stock option exercise on **December 31st, Year 5.**

Julie's options, if she had held them, would have expired on the **expiration date.**

| Year 1 | Year 2 | Year 3 | Year 4 | Year 5 | Year 6 | Year 10 |

TPI trades at $5 per share. This is also the **exercise price** of the options

TPI trades at $15 per share.

TPI trades at $20 per share.

TPI trades at $25 per share.

[1]Julie will acquire 5,000 shares of TPI (50 ISOs × 100 shares per ISO) with ISOs and 20,000 shares of TPI (200 NQOs × 100 shares per NQO) with NQOs. In total, Julie will acquire 25,000 shares of TPI.

TPI will receive $125,000 from Julie when she exercises her options if it issues new shares to cover the option exercise. If new shares are issued, however, TPI's earnings per share will drop relative to what it would have been had the new shares not been issued. If, to avoid dilution of its earnings per share, TPI purchases its own shares from the market instead of issuing new shares, it would pay $500,000 (25,000 shares purchased × $20 per share) resulting in total cash outflows of $375,000 net of the $125,000 Julie paid in to exercise her options.

An employee who uses options to purchase shares experiences an increase in net worth equal to the difference between the exercise price and the market value of the acquired shares on the date of exercise. This difference is called the **bargain element.** In Example 12-4, the bargain element is $15 per share and the total bargain element is $375,000 (25,000 shares × $15 per share).

Example 12-5

What if: What is Julie's economic loss from her stock options if the TPI shares fall to $3 per share and remain there after the options are granted?

Answer: Zero. If TPI's stock price never increases above the $5 per share exercise price before the expiration date of the options, Julie would never exercise her options to purchase TPI shares and those options would expire worthless.

Employee Considerations for Stock Options   Stock options are classified for tax purposes as either **incentive stock options** (ISOs) or **nonqualified stock options** (NQOs). They differ in terms of when and how the bargain element is taxed. To appreciate these differences, it's important to understand what happens on the **grant date,** the vesting date, the **exercise date,** and the date the shares are ultimately sold.

For either type of option, employees experience no tax consequences on the grant date or vesting date. However, when they exercise *nonqualified* stock options, employees report ordinary income equal to the total bargain element on the shares of stock acquired—whether they hold the shares or sell them immediately.[24] A taxpayer's basis in nonqualified stock options acquired is the fair market value on the date of exercise. Thus the basis includes the exercise price plus the ordinary income the taxpayer recognizes on the exercise (the bargain element). In contrast, when they exercise *incentive* stock options, employees don't report any income for regular tax purposes (as long as they don't immediately sell their shares). Their basis in shares acquired with ISOs is the exercise price. The holding period for stock acquired with NQOs and ISOs begins on the exercise date.

When taxpayers exercise incentive stock options, the bargain element is added to their alternative minimum taxable income. This increases the likelihood that taxpayers exercising incentive stock options will be required to pay the alternative minimum tax—this is almost always true if the bargain element is large. We discuss the alternative minimum tax in Chapter 7.

Example 12-6

On the date Julie exercises her options (Example 12-4), she acquires 20,000 shares with NQOs (200 NQOs × 100 shares per NQO) and 5,000 shares of TPI with ISOs (50 ISOs × 100 shares per ISO). Given that the bargain element for each share she purchased is $15, how much income will Julie report on the day she exercises the options?

Answer: $300,000 ordinary income from the NQOs, calculated below, and $0 for the ISOs (she must include the bargain element of $15,000 in her AMT calculation).

Description	Amount	Explanation
(1) Shares acquired with NQOs	20,000	
(2) Market price per share	$ 20	Exhibit 12-6.
(3) Exercise price	$ 5	Exhibit 12-6.
(4) Bargain element per share	$ 15	(2) − (3).
Bargain element (ordinary income)	$300,000	(1) × (4).

What is Julie's basis in the 20,000 shares she acquired with NQOs?

Answer: $400,000. [$100,000 (20,000 shares × $5 per share strike price) + $300,000 (bargain element—ordinary income).]

What is Julie's basis in the 5,000 shares she acquired through ISOs?

Answer: $25,000. (5,000 shares acquired × $5 per share exercise price.)

Once they've exercised their stock options, employees face different choices depending on the type of option. Employees who purchase stock with NQOs and retain the stock are in the same position for tax purposes as any other investor: their basis in the stock is the fair market value on the date they exercised the options

---

[24]The bargain element income is reflected on employees' Form W-2 and the applicable income and payroll taxes are withheld.

(this is the exercise price of the stock plus the bargain element), and any *future* appreciation or depreciation of the stock will be treated for tax purposes as either short-term or long-term capital gain or loss depending on the holding period, which begins on the date of exercise. Moreover, employees using nonqualified options to purchase employer stock are also in the same economic position as any other investor in that the value of the stock is subject to market risk (the risk that the value of the stock will go down). To avoid overweighting their investment portfolios with a single stock, employees exercising nonqualified options often immediately sell all or a significant portion of the shares acquired on the exercise date, a practice referred to as a **same-day sale.**[25]

Example 12-7

Five years after Julie exercised her NQOs and acquired 20,000 TPI shares with a basis of $20 per share, she sold all of the shares for $25 per share. What is the amount and character of the gain she will recognize on the sale?

Answer: $100,000 long-term capital gain, calculated as follows:

Description	Amount	Explanation
(1) Amount realized (sale proceeds)	$500,000	(20,000 × $25).
(2) Adjusted basis	400,000	Example 12-6.
Long-term capital gain recognized	$100,000	(1) − (2).

What if: If Julie sold the shares for $25 per share six months after she exercised them, what is the character of the $100,000 gain she recognizes on the sale?

Answer: Short-term capital gain because she held the shares for one year or less before selling.

Employees who acquire shares through the exercise of ISOs also have an additional tax incentive: if they hold such shares *for at least two years after the grant date and one year after the exercise date,* they will not only be able to defer paying taxes on the bargain element, but they will also be able to have the bargain element taxed at preferential long-term capital gain rates.[26] In essence, employees will treat the difference between the sale proceeds and the adjusted basis (the exercise price) as a long-term capital gain in the year of disposition. Thus, employees prefer ISOs to NQOs.

Example 12-8

Five years after Julie exercised her ISOs and acquired 5,000 TPI shares with a basis of $5 per share, she sold all of the shares for $25 per share. What is the amount and character of the gain she will recognize on the sale?

Answer: Julie will recognize a $100,000 long-term capital gain, calculated as follows:

Description	Amount	Explanation
(1) Amount realized	$125,000	(5,000 × $25).
(2) Adjusted basis	25,000	Example 12-6.
Long-term capital gain recognized	$100,000	(1) − (2).

---

[25]In addition to limiting market risk, employees also engage in same-day sales to cover all or a portion of the exercise price associated with the options exercised, to pay the taxes triggered when nonqualified options are exercised, and to fund planned purchases.

[26]§422(a)(1).

If the two-year and one-year requirements are not met, the premature sale of stock is classified as a **disqualifying disposition,** and the bargain element is taxed at the time of sale *as if* the option had been a nonqualified option. Thus, when holders of ISOs execute same-day sales, they forego the benefit of taxing the bargain element at lower capital gains rates—but they do so in order to eliminate the market risk they would otherwise have to bear if they attempted to satisfy the two-year and one-year holding period requirements.

Example 12-9

What if: Assume that Julie exercised her ISOs and executed a same-day sale on the 5,000 shares on the vesting date (January 1, year 3) when the share price was $15, what is the amount and character of income she will recognize on these transactions?

Answer: $50,000 ordinary income. Because Julie's sale is a disqualifying disposition, the transactions are recast as though she exercised nonqualified options. See computations below.

Description	Amount	Explanation
(1) Shares acquired with ISOs that were disqualified (became NQOs)	5,000	
(2) Market price per share	$ 15	
(3) Exercise price	$ 5	Exhibit 12-6.
(4) Bargain element per share	$ 10	(2) − (3).
Bargain element (ordinary income)	$50,000	(1) × (4).

> **THE KEY FACTS**
>
> **Nonqualified Stock Options (NQOs)**
>
> ■ No tax consequences on grant date.
>
> ■ On exercise date, bargain element is treated as ordinary (compensation) income to employee.
> · Employee holds stock with holding period beginning on date of exercise.
>
> ■ Employers deduct bargain element as compensation expense on exercise date.

Employer Considerations for Stock Options   As is true for employees, an employer's tax treatment of stock options depends on whether the options are incentive stock options (ISOs) or nonqualified options (NQOs).

Nonqualified options.   With nonqualified options, employers deduct the bargain element that employees recognize as income when the employees exercise the nonqualified options. From the employer's perspective, no other date is relevant for tax purposes.

Example 12-10

In year 3, Julie exercises NQOs to acquire 20,000 shares of TPI and she reports $300,000 of ordinary income for the bargain element of the exercise (see Example 12-6). How much compensation expense for Julie's stock option exercise can TPI deduct in year 3?

Answer: $300,000. TPI can deduct the bargain element of Julie's exercise.

Note that this tax deduction is not tied to a cash payment. Thus, unless employers purchase their own publicly traded shares to satisfy their employees' stock option exercises, they'll be entitled to a tax deduction without incurring any cash outflow.[27]

Another important tax benefit associated with nonqualified options derives from the fact that income from NQOs is usually viewed as performance-based compensation. As a result, employers frequently use these options to circumvent the $1,000,000

---

[27]To avoid diluting earnings per share, employers frequently purchase their own stock from the markets rather than issue new shares to satisfy employee stock option exercises.

deduction limitation imposed by §162(m). In fact, the stock option income of key executives at publicly traded companies usually dwarfs their cash salaries.[28]

Incentive stock options. Employers typically don't view incentive stock options as favorably as nonqualified options, because (1) ISOs don't provide them with the same tax benefits (no tax deduction) and (2) the IRS regulatory requirements can be cumbersome. No matter what the circumstances, employers never receive any tax deductions related to ISOs. For this reason, firms with high marginal tax rates may lose significant tax benefits by issuing ISOs rather than NQOs. On the other hand, start-up companies or firms with net operating losses may actually benefit by issuing ISOs instead of NQOs. Due to their low or nonexistent marginal tax rates, companies in this position may not lose tax benefits by granting ISOs; however, because of the potential tax benefits ISOs provide to their employees relative to NQOs, they may be able to persuade their employees to accept relatively fewer ISOs.

Accounting issues. Historically, a major reason that companies used stock options to compensate their employees was the favorable accounting treatment stock options were afforded. Before 2006, companies were not required to reflect stock options as an expense in their financial statements. Thus, before 2006, companies that used stock options in lieu of cash salary typically reported higher earnings than equally situated firms that were not heavy users of stock options. To increase the comparability of financial statements as well as to ensure that the true cost of stock options would be reflected in the financial statements, the FASB mandated the expensing of stock options for financial accounting purposes for years beginning on or after January 1, 2006.[29] Under the new rules, firms must measure the economic value of options on the grant date and then amortize this cost on a straight-line basis over the vesting period of the options.[30]

Example 12-11

What if: Assume that an accounting employee benefits specialist calculated the economic value of Julie's stock option grant (NQOs and ISOs) to be $32,000. Also assume that Julie's options vest 50 percent in year 1 (the year of the grant) and 50 percent in year 2. What compensation expense for year 1 and year 2 would TPI report for Julie's stock options under FAS 123R?

Answer: $16,000 ($32,000 × 50%) in year 1 and $16,000 in year 2.

As you probably realize by now, the tax rules governing the treatment of stock options differ markedly from generally accepted accounting principles in terms of both the amount and the timing of the stock option expense. To compare the tax and **book treatment,** we present TPI's book expense and tax deduction resulting from its stock option grant to Julie (given prior assumptions) in Exhibit 12-7.

The tremendous difference between the book and tax numbers presented in Exhibit 12-7 is driven by the increase in TPI's share price, from $5 on the date of grant to $20 on the date of exercise.

[28]An extreme example of this is Barry Diller, CEO and chairman of the board at InterActiveCorp, who received $726,000 of salary and options with a total market value of approximately $294 million in 2005.

[29]FASB Statement No. 123 (revised 2004), Share-Based Payment (FAS 123R).

[30]Although the exercise price of compensatory stock options typically equals the stock price on the date of grant, compensatory options are, nevertheless, economically valuable on the grant date. They have economic value because the stock price may eventually exceed the exercise price before the options expire. To determine economic value, firms typically use either the Black-Scholes option pricing model or the Binomial pricing model.

EXHIBIT 12-7   **TPI's Tax Deductions and Book Expense from Stock Option Grant to Julie**

	Tax Deduction if Stock Price Increases	Tax Deduction if Stock Price Decreases	Book Expense
Year 1	$ 0	$0	$16,000
Year 2	$ 0	$0	$16,000
Year 3	$300,000	$0*	$ 0

*There would be no exercise because the market price exceeds the exercise price.

Restricted Stock

Like stock options described above, **restricted stock** can't be sold or otherwise treated as owned by employees until they legally have the right to sell the shares on the vesting date. However, unlike the stock acquired through options exercises, employees receive restricted stock on the vesting date *without having to pay for it,* after which they can either sell it immediately or retain it.

As indicated in the timeline in Exhibit 12-8, the initial value of an employee's restricted stock award depends on the share price of the stock on the vesting date.

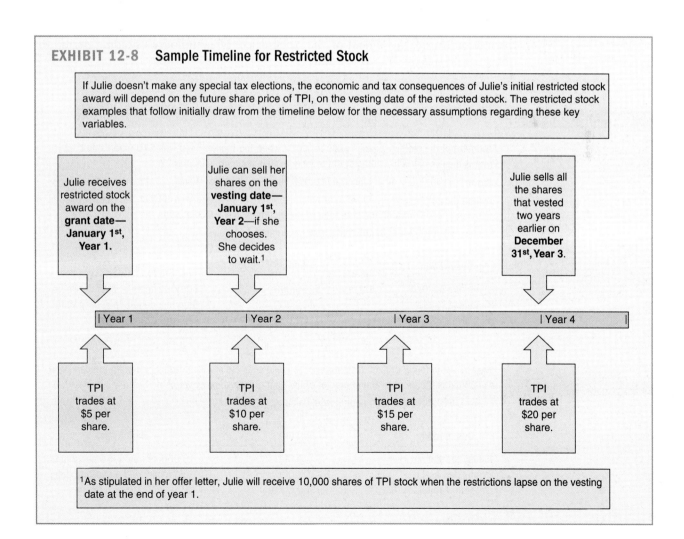

EXHIBIT 12-8   **Sample Timeline for Restricted Stock**

If Julie doesn't make any special tax elections, the economic and tax consequences of Julie's initial restricted stock award will depend on the future share price of TPI, on the vesting date of the restricted stock. The restricted stock examples that follow initially draw from the timeline below for the necessary assumptions regarding these key variables.

Julie receives restricted stock award on the **grant date— January 1st, Year 1.**

Julie can sell her shares on the **vesting date— January 1st, Year 2**—if she chooses. She decides to wait.[1]

Julie sells all the shares that vested two years earlier on **December 31st, Year 3**.

| Year 1 | | Year 2 | | Year 3 | | Year 4 | |

TPI trades at $5 per share.

TPI trades at $10 per share.

TPI trades at $15 per share.

TPI trades at $20 per share.

[1] As stipulated in her offer letter, Julie will receive 10,000 shares of TPI stock when the restrictions lapse on the vesting date at the end of year 1.

Example 12-12

Given the assumptions regarding the restricted stock in Exhibit 12-8, by how much would Julie's wealth increase on the vesting date?

Answer: Julie's wealth would increase by $100,000 (10,000 shares × $10 per share).

What if: Assume that the stock decreased to $3 per share on the vesting date, by how much would Julie's wealth increase or decrease on the vesting date?

Answer: $30,000 increase ($3 × 10,000). Until the vesting date, Julie was not entitled to any economic benefit from the restricted stock. On the vesting date, however, she is entitled to stock valued at $30,000. Thus, the vesting of Julie's restricted stock increases her wealth even if the stock price decreases between the grant date and vesting date (unlike options that would be worthless).

THE KEY FACTS

Restricted Stock *without* §83(b) Election

- No tax consequences on grant date.
- Employee recognizes ordinary income on value of stock on vesting date.
- Holding period for stock begins on vesting date.
- Employer deducts value of stock on vesting date.

Employee Considerations for Restricted Stock   Restricted stock is taxed like non-qualified options with two important distinctions: while employees receiving NQOs are taxed at ordinary rates on the bargain element of the shares when they exercise their options, employees receiving restricted stock are taxed on the *full fair market value* of the shares *on the date the restricted stock vests.* They are taxed on the fair market value of the stock because they are entitled to receive the stock without any payment requirements (contrast with the exercise price for stock options). Any subsequent appreciation in the value of the stock is taxed as either long-term or short-term capital gain or loss when the taxpayer sells the stock, depending on the holding period and future movement of the stock price. The employee's holding period for the stock begins on the vesting date.

Example 12-13

Assume that the restricted stock vests in year 2 when the market price was $10 (see Exhibit 12-8). What is the amount and character of the income Julie recognizes in year 2?

Answer: $100,000 ordinary income (10,000 shares × $10 per share).

Assume the same facts as above and that Julie sells the shares in year 3 when the market price is $20? What is the amount and character of the income she will recognize on the sale?

Answer: $100,000 long-term capital gain, calculated as follows:

Description	Amount	Explanation
(1) Amount realized	$200,000	10,000 shares × $20 per share.
(2) Adjusted basis	100,000	Gain recognized on vesting date.
Long-term capital gain	$100,000	(1) − (2).

What if: Assume the original facts except that Julie sells the shares in year 3 when the market price is $4. What is the amount and character of the gain or loss she recognizes on the sale?

Answer: $60,000 long-term capital loss, calculated as follows:

Description	Amount	Explanation
(1) Amount realized	$ 40,000	10,000 shares × $4 per share.
(2) Adjusted basis	100,000	Gain recognized on vesting date.
Long-term capital loss	($60,000)	(1) − (2).

§83(b) election.   The tax laws allow employees who receive restricted stock to make a tax election that can significantly change the tax consequences by treating the stock nearly the same as vested stock. Up until 30 days after the grant date, employees can make what is known as a **§83(b) election;** once made, however, this election is irrevocable. If the employee makes the §83(b) election, the value of the restricted stock is taxed on the grant date rather than the date on which the stock vests. The effect of the election is to accelerate the tax on the market value of the restricted shares—which, you'll recall from Chapter 3, is usually not desirable. However, if the employee expects the share price to increase after the grant date, making the election converts ordinary income to long-term capital gain (which, assuming the shares are held for more than one year after the grant date, results in a lower preferential tax rate when the taxpayer sells the shares). Without the §83(b) election, the employee reports nothing in income when the shares are granted, but is taxed on their fair market value at ordinary rates when the stock vests. With the §83(b) election, the employee simply pays tax at ordinary rates on the market value of the shares at the grant date.

> **THE KEY FACTS**
>
> Restricted Stock *with*
> Section §83(b)Election
>
> ▌ On grant date, employee recognizes market value of stock as ordinary income.
>
> ▌ Employee takes fair market value basis in stock.
>
> ▌ Holding period for stock begins on grant date.
>
> ▌ If employee never vests, no deduction for basis in stock.
>
> ▌ Employer deducts value of stock on grant date.

Example 12-14

What if: How much tax would Julie pay in year 1 if she does not make a §83(b) election?

Answer: $0. The stock has not vested yet so she has no income.

What if: How much tax would Julie pay in year 1 if she makes a §83(b) election?

Answer: $20,000 [$50,000 ordinary income (10,000 shares × $5 per share) × 40 percent marginal ordinary tax rate].

What if: How much tax would Julie pay in year 2 if she did *not* make a §83(b) election in year 1 (the stock is trading at $10 a share on the vesting date)?

Answer: $40,000 [$100,000 ordinary income (10,000 shares × $10 per share) × 40 percent marginal ordinary tax rate].

What if: How much tax would Julie pay in year 2 if she made the §83(b) election in year 1?

Answer: $0. With the §83(b) election, Julie treated the stock as though it vested in year 1, not year 2, so she does not have a taxable event in year 2 when the stock actually vests.

What if: How much tax would Julie pay in year 3 when she sells the stock for $20 a share (on December 31) if she did *not* make the §83(b) election in year 1?

Answer: $15,000 [$200,000 (10,000 × $20) − $100,000 adjusted basis (fair market value on vesting date in year 2) = $100,000. $100,000 × 15 percent long-term capital gains rate = $15,000].

What if: How much tax would Julie pay in year 3 when she sells the stock for $20 a share (on December 31) if she made the §83(b) election in year 1?

Answer: $22,500 [$200,000 (10,000 × $20) − $50,000 adjusted basis (fair market value in year 1 when made §83(b) election) = $150,000. $150,000 × 15 percent long-term capital gains rate = $22,500].

Given the analyses above what amount of taxes would Julie save by making the §83(b) election?

Answer: $12,500 ($55,000 with election; $42,500 without), computed as follows:

Taxes Payable

Description	With Election	Without Election
Year 1 taxes on ordinary income	$20,000	$ 0
Year 2 taxes on ordinary income	0	40,000
Year 3 taxes on long-term capital gains	22,500	15,000
Total taxes	$42,500	$55,000

(*continued on page 12-20 . . .*)

> Note that Julie saves taxes because the election allowed her to convert $50,000 in income from ordinary income taxed at 40 percent into long-term capital gain taxed at 15 percent.
>
> Also note that this computation overstates to some degree the benefits of making the §83(b) election because it ignores the time value of money. In order to have a greater portion of her gains taxed at capital gains rates, Julie gave up some tax deferral when she accelerated $50,000 of income from year 3 into year 1.

Employees making the §83(b) election essentially trade off some additional current tax now in order to convert ordinary income into long-term capital gains later. Accordingly, the §83(b) election is advisable when the potential for growth in the stock value is high and the amount of additional current tax is manageable. If an employee makes a §83(b) election and then forfeits the stock for any reason, the employee cannot deduct the loss on the forfeiture.[31] Thus, the risk of making the election is that if the stock value declines the employee would have paid taxes on value that the employee never receives.

Employer Considerations for Restricted Stock   Like the tax treatment of non-qualified options, the employer's deduction for restricted stock equals the amount of ordinary income reported by its employees. The timing of the deduction is determined by the employee's decisions regarding the §83(b) election. If the employee makes an 83(b) election, the employer claims the deduction in the year the restricted stock is granted. Otherwise, the employer claims a deduction when the restrictions lapse. Some employers believe that restricted stock is a superior form of compensation to stock options. See Apple Inc.'s 2008 proxy statement in Exhibit 12-9.

The accounting treatment for restricted stock is similar to the accounting treatment for stock options.[32] If restricted stock grants vest over time, the value of restricted stock on the *date of grant* is amortized pro rata over the vesting period.

EXHIBIT 12-9   **Excerpt from Apple Inc.'s 2008 Proxy Statement**

Restricted Stock Units Minimize Dilution and Support Long-Term Focus. Since fiscal year 2004, all equity awards to the named executive officers have been RSUs rather than stock options. A grant of RSUs gives an officer the right to receive a specified number of shares of the Company's common stock, at no cost to the officer, if the officer remains employed at the Company until the RSUs vest. RSUs granted in 2004 also provide for accelerated vesting if the named executive officer is terminated without cause or on a change of control, RSUs granted before 2007 provide for accelerated vesting on a change of control, and all RSUs provide for accelerated vesting upon the death of the officer. The compensation value of an RSU does not depend solely on future stock price increases; at grant, its value is equal to the Company's stock price. Although its value may increase or decrease with changes in the stock price during the period before vesting, an RSU will have value in the long term, encouraging retention. By contrast, the entire compensation value of a stock option depends on future stock price appreciation. Accordingly, RSUs can deliver significantly greater share-for-share compensation value at grant than stock options, and the Company can offer comparable grant date compensation value with fewer shares and less dilution for its shareholders.

[31]Reg. §1.83-2(a).
[32]FAS 123R.

Example 12-15

What if: Given the assumptions in Exhibit 12-8, what amount can TPI deduct for tax purposes in year 1 and in year 2 assuming Julie does *not* make a §83(b)?

Answer: $0 in year 1 and $100,000 in year 2 (10,000 shares of restricted stock vested × $10 per share market price at vesting date).

What if: What amount can TPI deduct in year 1 and in year 2 if Julie *does* make a §83(b) election?

Answer: $50,000 in year 1 (10,000 shares of restricted stock awarded × $5 per share market price on the grant date) and $0 in year 2.

What amount is TPI's compensation expense for financial accounting purposes for Julie's restricted stock in year 1 and in year 2?

Answer: $50,000 book expense in year 1. Because the value of Julie's restricted stock award on the date of grant is $50,000, TPI must amortize that expense on its books over the vesting period, which in this case is just one year (it has a one year vesting period).

Other nontax issues. Since it became clear that accounting rules were changing in 2006 to require employers to record a book expense for stock option grants, as had historically been the case for restricted stock, the popularity of restricted stock has increased relative to stock options. Other factors besides the accounting rule change also help to explain this trend. For example, companies with stagnant or declining stock prices realized that stock options granted when their stock prices were higher, so-called underwater options, were no longer motivating their employees. To address this problem, they replaced some or all of their stock options with restricted stock that, unlike stock options, retains some value even when a company's stock price is falling.[33]

> **THE KEY FACTS**
>
> Restricted Stock Expense: GAAP vs. Tax
>
> ■ For tax purposes, employers deduct the market value of stock when the employee recognizes income. For GAAP purposes, employers deduct the grant date value.

Equity-Based Compensation Summary

To summarize our discussion of the tax treatment of equity-based compensation, Exhibit 12-10 highlights the general tax treatment of nonqualified options, incentive

EXHIBIT 12-10   **Reportable Income and Deductions from Equity Based Compensation (for given time frame and stock prices)**

	Party Affected	NQOs	ISOs	Restricted Stock
Grant Date-Year 1 Stock Price = $1/share	Employee	No Effect	No Effect	No Effect
	Employer	No Effect	No Effect	No Effect
Vesting Date-Year 4 Stock Price = $6/share	Employee	No Effect	No Effect	$6/share Ordinary Income
	Employer	No Effect	No Effect	$6/share Ordinary Deduction
Exercise Date for Options-Year 6 Stock Price = $11/share	Employee	$10/share Ordinary Income	No Effect*	N/A
	Employer	$10/share Ordinary Deduction	No Effect	N/A
Sale Date-Year 8 Stock Price = $16/share	Employee	$5/share LT Capital Gain	$15/share LT Capital Gain	$10/share Capital Gain
	Employer	No Effect	No Effect	No Effect

*$10 per share is included in alternative minimum taxable income.

[33]Microsoft is an extreme example of this trend. In July 2003, it announced it was replacing all of its employee's stock options with restricted stock.

stock options, and restricted stock on a per share basis from both employee and employer perspectives given an arbitrary time series of share prices. In addition to future share prices, the table below assumes options are exercisable for the share price on the grant date.

L03 FRINGE BENEFITS

continued from page 12-10 . . .
The final section of TPI's offer letter indicated Julie would receive fringe benefits in the form of health and dental insurance (value of $18,000), $750,000 of group-term life insurance, a biannual $30,000 automobile allowance, monthly parking, and a flexible spending account for medical expenses. ∎

Employees generally receive most of their compensation in the form of cash salary or wages. However, employers often provide noncash benefits to employees in addition to their cash compensation. These **fringe benefits** range from the common (health insurance) to the exotic (use of a corporate aircraft). As a general rule, because fringe benefits are employee compensation, they are taxable to the employee on receipt. In fact, fringe benefits are specifically mentioned in the definition of gross income. As we indicated in Chapter 5, IRC Section 61(a) indicates that, "gross income means all income from whatever source derived, including . . . (1) Compensation for services, including fees, commissions, *fringe benefits,* and similar items (emphasis added)." This definition of income notwithstanding, the tax laws specifically *exclude* certain fringe benefits from an employee's taxable income. Thus, some fringe benefits are taxable and others are not.

Taxable Fringe Benefits

Taxable fringe benefits are fringe benefits not specifically excluded from income. Congress views many of the taxable fringe benefits as luxuries and chooses not to subsidize them. Taxable fringe benefits could include such things as below-market interest rate loans (see discussion in Chapter 5), gym memberships, season tickets to the local NBA team, an automobile allowance for a personal automobile, or anything else not specifically excluded by the tax laws. Employers generally provide taxable fringe benefits to executives and higher salaried employees rather than to the rank and file employees.

Employee Considerations for Taxable Fringe Benefits From an employee's perspective, taxable fringe benefits are treated just like cash. Employees recognize ordinary compensation income when they receive taxable benefits and, just as they do with salary, pay FICA taxes on the value of the benefit. As a result, taxable fringe benefits cost employees the amount of tax they must pay on the benefits.

> **THE KEY FACTS**
>
> Taxable Fringe Benefits
>
> ∎ Employees recognize compensation income on all benefits received unless specifically excluded by tax laws.
>
> ∎ Employees treat benefits received like taxable cash compensation.
>
> ∎ Employer deducts cost and pays employee's share of FICA taxes on benefit.

Example 12-16

Julie's offer includes a biannual auto allowance of up to $30,000. That is, every other year, TPI will reimburse Julie for an automobile purchase up to $30,000. TPI provides this benefit to executives that interact with the public on a regular basis. Julie purchases a Toyota 4Runner with a retail price of $35,000. What tax is Julie required to pay if she uses the allowance to apply toward the purchase? What is Julie's after-tax cost of the automobile if her marginal tax rate is 40 percent?

Answer: $12,435 in total taxes and $17,435 after-tax cost, computed as follows:

Description	Amount	Explanation
(1) Fair market value of Toyota	$35,000	
(2) Automobile allowance	30,000	Taxable fringe benefit.
(3) Julie's additional cost	5,000	(1) − (2).
(4) Income tax on allowance	12,000	(2) × 40% (given).
(5) FICA taxes on automobile allowance (Medicare)	435	(2) × 1.45% (Julie is over the Social Security wage base).
(6) Total taxes paid	12,435	(4) + (5).
Total after-tax cost	**$17,435**	(3) + (6).

From Julie's perspective, this is a pretty good deal—particularly if she was willing to pay the market price for the car.

Employees may prefer a taxable benefit to an equivalent amount of cash when they benefit from employer-provided quantity or group discounts associated with the benefit. For example, many companies provide (pay premiums for) **group-term life insurance** as a fringe benefit, in part, because they can purchase the insurance at a lower rate than employees can purchase it individually. However, employees must recognize a certain amount of taxable income when employers pay life insurance premiums for the employee for policies with a death benefit in excess of $50,000.[34] Consequently, a portion of the group-term life insurance benefit is taxable and a portion is nontaxable. In these circumstances, the employer determines the employee's taxable amount using a table provided in the Treasury Regulations. An excerpt of this table is provided in Exhibit 12-11.[35] To compute the annual taxable benefit, taxpayers use the following steps:

Step 1: Subtract $50,000 from the death benefit of their employer-provided group-term life insurance policy.

Step 2: Divide the Step 1 result by $1,000.

EXHIBIT 12-11   Uniform Premiums for $1,000 of Group-Term Life Insurance Protection

5-year Age Bracket	Cost per $1,000 of Protection for One Month
Under 25	$0.05
25 to 29	.06
30 to 34	.08
35 to 39	.09
40 to 44	.10
45 to 49	.15
50 to 54	.23
55 to 59	.43
60 to 64	.66
65 to 69	1.27
70 and above	2.06

[34]§79

[35]Treas. Reg. §1.79-3(d)(2) provides an age-based table and instructions to calculate the employee's includable amount.

Step 3: Multiply the result from Step 2 by the cost per $1,000 of protection for one month from the table (Exhibit 12-11) based on the taxpayer's age.

Step 4: Multiply the outcome of Step 3 by 12 (months).

Example 12-17

Julie's offer from TPI includes $750,000 of group-term life insurance. TPI's cost to provide Julie the insurance is $500 per year. If Julie were to purchase the insurance herself she would pay $2,000 per year. Assume that Julie is 37 years old. Based on the Treasury's table (see Exhibit 12-11), the monthly premium per $1,000 of insurance is $.09 cents. What is Julie's taxable compensation from receiving the group-term life benefit? What does this benefit cost Julie?

Answer: $756 of taxable compensation and $313 cost (all taxes). Julie's cost is the income and Medicare taxes she must pay on the compensation, calculated as follows:

Group-Term Life Insurance Description	Amount	Explanation
(1) Insurance coverage	$750,000	Provided by employer.
(2) Excluded coverage	($50,000)	Nontaxable portion.
(3) Taxable benefit	$700,000	(1) − (2).
(4) Monthly cost per $1,000	0.09	Taxable portion per $1,000 from Exhibit 12-11.
(5) Monthly benefit	$ 63	[(3)/$1,000] × (4).
(6) Months	× 12	Annualize monthly taxable amount.
(7) Annual taxable benefit	$ 756	(5) × (6).
(8) Income taxes	$ 302	(7) × 40%.
(9) FICA taxes	$ 11	(7) × 1.45% (Julie is over Social Security wage base limit so she pays only Medicare portion of FICA taxes).
Tax cost of benefit	$ 313	(8) + (9).

Note that Julie's income is not based on TPI's actual cost of providing the policy.

Taxpayers receiving taxable fringe benefits may experience some financial strain because they must pay the tax on the benefits. Frequently, when corporations provide taxable fringe benefits to senior executives, they also provide the executives enough cash to cover the taxes so the benefit costs the executive nothing.[36] This is commonly referred to as a *gross-up.* For example, GE's 2006 proxy statement reveals that it made payments of $14,245 to Jeffrey R. Immelt, its CEO, and indicates that the additional cash is "for the payment of taxes with respect to financial counseling, tax preparation services and personal use of NBCU car service."[37] Employees can choose to forgo a benefit if they prefer not to pay taxes on it.

---

[36]Note that the cash payment to the executive is also taxable, so the company often pays additional cash to the executive to pay the taxes on the payment for taxes. Companies generally choose a formula to determine how much cash they need to pay the employee in addition to the taxable benefit to ensure the benefit costs the employee nothing. That is, the company uses a formula to determine the amount that it will "gross up" the benefit.

[37]While GE's formula reimbursed Mr. Immelt for $14,245 of taxes on taxable benefits of $76,614 (18.6 percent), this is less than some plans that provide such "gross ups" of over 60 percent in an attempt to eliminate the tax on the taxable gross up.

Employer Considerations for Taxable Fringe Benefits   Like employees, employers treat taxable fringe benefits just like cash compensation. That is, the employer has an outlay for the cost of the benefit and must pay the employer's share of FICA taxes on the taxable portion of benefits it provides to employees. The employer deducts its *cost* of the benefit (plus FICA taxes), *not the value* of the benefit to the employee. As we mention above, employers are often able to purchase fringe benefits at a lower cost than can individual employees. For example, employers may receive a group discount for purchasing life insurance, automobiles, financial or tax planning services, or accident insurance.

Example 12-18

In Example 12-17, TPI provided Julie with $750,000 of group-term life insurance. Its cost of providing the entire $750,000 of coverage is $500 per year. If Julie were to purchase the policy herself, it would cost her $2,000 per year. Assuming TPI's marginal tax rate is 35 percent, what is TPI's after-tax cost of the partially taxable group-term life insurance benefit it provided to Julie?

Answer: TPI's after-tax cost of the benefit provided is $330, calculated as follows:

Description	Amount	Explanation
(1) Cost of policy	$500	
(2) Income tax benefit	(175)	(1) × 35%.
(3) FICA taxes paid	7	(1) × 1.45% (over the Social Security tax wage base).
(4) FICA tax benefit	(2)	(3) × 35%.
Total after-tax cost	$330	(1) + (2) + (3) + (4).

Finally, employers may discriminate between employees when providing taxable benefits. That is, they can select which employees receive the taxable benefits and which do not. Not surprisingly, the more highly compensated employees tend to receive these benefits. For example, as described in an excerpt from Wal-Mart's proxy statement in Exhibit 12-12, Wal-Mart's perquisite and supplemental benefits provides certain officers with use of the company aircraft and home security systems. Wal-Mart is unlikely to offer these same benefits to its hourly store clerks.

Taxes in the Real World   *Fringe Benefits*

A Perk Takes Off

The Wall Street Journal
By Christina Cheddar Berk
April 11, 2005

"When Charles K. Gifford stepped down as chairman of Bank of America Corp. in January, he could look forward to a comfortable retirement. Mr. Gifford will receive an annual pension of $3.1 million for life. As the former chief executive of Fleet Financial Group, he also took home $16.4 million stemming from the 1999 merger with BankBoston that formed FleetBoston Financial Corp., which Bank of America bought last year.

And the 62-year-old former executive will receive perks, potentially for life, including choice tickets for as many as 15 Boston Red Sox baseball games a year. If Mr. Gifford isn't in Boston on game day, he needn't worry. He can summon a private jet, provided by Bank of America, to fly him and a handful of friends there in time for the first pitch. Mr. Gifford has access to as many as 120 hours of flight time a year. He doesn't even need to be on board—he can dispatch a plane to ferry his guests.

Bank of America said in filings with the Securities and Exchange Commission that this perk is in part compensation to Mr. Gifford for his continued availability to provide the Charlotte, N.C., company with services including advice and consulting. That's a common justification, along with security concerns, for giving retired executives use of corporate jets."

EXHIBIT 12-12   Excerpt from Walmart's Proxy Statement

Perquisites and supplemental benefits: . . . Executive Officers are entitled to a limited number of perquisites and supplemental benefits. For certain Executive Officers, these include:
- Personal use of Company aircraft,
- A land line telephone in their primary residence,
- An annual senior executive physical, and
- Equipment, maintenance, and monitoring of security systems in their homes.

Nontaxable Fringe Benefits

For policy reasons, Congress specifically excludes certain fringe benefits, such as health insurance, from employees' taxable income to encourage employers to provide the benefits.[38] We refer to excluded benefits as **nontaxable fringe benefits.** Other nontaxable benefits enable taxpayers to become or stay employed, including meals or lodging for the convenience of the employer, educational assistance, dependent-care benefits, moving expense benefits, and transportation-related benefits. Finally, some benefits are excluded for simplicity's sake, such as no-additional-cost services, qualified employee discounts, and *de minimis* (small) fringe benefits. Exhibit 12-13 provides a partial list of nontaxable fringe benefits. Below, we discuss these benefits in more detail.

Group-Term Life Insurance   As we mentioned in the taxable benefits section, employees may exclude from income the employer-provided benefit for the first $50,000 of group-term life insurance.[39] Any remaining group-term life insurance benefit is taxable. An employer may not discriminate between employees in providing nontaxable group-term life insurance benefits.

Health and Accident Insurance and Benefits   When employers pay for **health and accident insurance** for an employee and the employee's spouse and dependents, the employee excludes the benefit from her taxable income.[40] For example, if TPI pays health premiums of $18,000 for Julie and her family, Julie is not required to include this $18,000 fringe benefit in her taxable income.[41] Further, when employees receive cash reimbursements for medical care, they can exclude the reimbursement from taxable income.[42] For example, if TPI reimburses Julie for $450 of medical co-payments she makes during the year, Julie excludes the $450 from her taxable income. Generally, employers may not discriminate between employees when providing health and accident insurance benefits.[43]

Meals and Lodging for the Convenience of the Employer   The value of certain meals and lodging the employer provides to an employee may be excluded from an employee's income if the benefit meets two criteria: (1) the meals and lodging are

---

[38]The nontaxable fringe benefits are listed with "items specifically excluded from gross income" in §§101-140 of the Internal Revenue Code. Employers are generally prohibited from discriminating among employees with respect to nontaxable fringe benefits (they cannot offer them only to executives). This chapter indicates whether or not discrimination for a particular benefit is allowed. However, the discrimination rules are complex and vary from benefit to benefit in ways too numerous to explain in detail.

[39]§79.

[40]§106.

[41]If Julie were to purchase the health insurance with after-tax dollars the equivalent would be $30,743 (after 40 percent of income taxes and 1.45 percent for FICA).

[42]§105(b). Although, reimbursement in excess of costs is included in income.

[43]However, employers may exclude part-time employees from participation.

EXHIBIT 12-13   Common Forms of Nontaxable Fringe Benefits

Benefit	Description
Group-term life insurance (§79)	Employer-paid premiums on up to $50,000 group-term life insurance policy are excluded from employees' income.
Health benefits (§§ 105-106)	Employer-paid premiums covering health, medical, and dental insurance and the benefits provided through the insurance.
Meals or lodging for the convenience of the employer (§119)*	Meals provided on employer's premises and lodging provided by the employer as a condition of employment.
Employee educational assistance (§127)	Up to $5,250 exclusion for tuition, books, and fees. See IRS Publication 970, *Tax Benefits for Education.*
Dependent care benefits (§129)	Up to $5,000 exclusion for cost of providing care for a dependent under 13 years old or disabled.
No-additional-cost services [§132(a)(1)]	Benefits that don't cost the employer a material amount.
Qualified employee discounts [§132(a)(2)]	Reduced prices on employer's product within certain limits.
Working condition fringe [§132(a)(3)]*	A benefit provided by an employer that would be deductible as an ordinary and necessary business expense by the employee if the employee rather than the employer paid the expense.
De minimis fringe [§132(a)(4)]*	Relatively small and infrequently provided benefits.
Qualified transportation fringe benefits [§132(a)(5)]*	Mass transit passes, qualified parking, or use of company owned car pool vehicles (vans).
Qualified moving expense reimbursement [§132(a)(6)]*	Reimbursement for allowable moving expenses such as moving household goods and travel.
Cafeteria plans (§125)	A plan where employees can choose from among various nontaxable fringe benefits or cash. Taxable to the extent employees receive cash.

*Employer may discriminate in providing this benefit.

provided on the employer's business premises to the employee (and the employee's spouse and dependents, if any) and (2) the meals and lodging are provided for the convenience of the employer.[44] For example, employers may provide meals at their place of business so employees can continue working efficiently without taking time off to go out to eat. Accounting firms frequently provide meals to tax professionals working late during tax season. Employers are allowed to deduct the full cost of meals provided to employees for the convenience of the employer. That is, the cost is not subject to the 50 percent deductibility limitation on meals we discussed in Chapter 8.[45] Employers may generally discriminate between employees **for the convenience of the employer benefits.**

Example 12-19

What if: Assume that last year Julie purchased 25 meals, at a cost of $500, on evenings when she worked late. Julie turned in expense reports and receipts for the meals totaling $500, which PCC reimbursed. What is the amount Julie must include in income?

Answer: Julie will not include the value of any of the overtime meals into income because they were provided for PCC's convenience.

[44]§119(a)(1).
[45]§274(n).

EXHIBIT 12-14 **Excerpt from JetBlue Airways' Web Site**

Flight Benefits

• You and your immediate family members are eligible for unlimited stand-by on JetBlue flights and passes on partner airlines.
• Your designated buddy or significant other may also be eligible.

In some situations, employers may provide lodging for employees and require employees to live on the business premises as a condition of their employment. In these cases, employees may exclude the value of the lodging from taxable income.[46] For example, an employer may require an apartment complex manager to live in an apartment in the complex (free of charge) so the employee can respond to tenant needs, provide security, and handle emergencies. The apartment manager can exclude the value of the lodging from taxable income.

Employee Educational Assistance   Employees can exclude from income up to $5,250 of employee **educational assistance benefits** covering tuition, books, and fees.[47] Amounts received in excess of this limit are taxed as compensation to the employee. (See IRS Publication 970 for details related to education benefits.) This includes amounts employers provide for employee undergraduate or graduate level courses or for courses that lead to a professional degree. Amounts excluded from income cannot qualify for educational deductions or credits (such as the hope and lifetime learning credits).

Dependent Care Benefits   Employees can exclude up to $5,000 for benefits paid or reimbursed by employers for caring for children under age 13 or dependents or spouses who are physically or mentally unable to care for themselves.[48] Excluded amounts do not qualify for the dependent care credit (see Chapter 7).

No-Additional-Cost Services   Employees can exclude the value of **no-additional-cost services.** These are any services employers provide to employees in the ordinary course of business that incur no substantial costs (including opportunity costs).[49] For example, airline companies can provide employees with free flight benefits on a space-available basis, hoteliers can allow employees to use vacant hotel rooms, and telephone companies can provide free basic phone service to their employees—all without the employees recognizing taxable income. Exhibit 12-14 (above) provides an excerpt from the JetBlue Airways Web site that describes no-cost benefits it provides to its employees.[50]

Example 12-20

What if: Assume that Julie's current employer, PCC, has a division that provides wireless Internet service and virus protection software. Because PCC has such a large contract with a national provider, its contract has sufficient bandwidth to allow employees to use the service without incurring additional cost. The market value of the services is $1,080 per year. What amount of this benefit must Julie include in her taxable income?

Answer: $0. Julie may exclude the value of the wireless Internet from her income because it qualifies as a no-additional-cost service under §132.

---

[46]§119(a)(2).
[47]§127(a)(2). The discrimination and eligibility rules are provided in §127(b)(2).
[48]§129.
[49]§132(a)(1).
[50]From JetBlue Web site: www.jetblue.com/about/work/benefits.html.

EXHIBIT 12-15   Excerpt from General Electric's Web Site

GE Employee Product Purchase Plan

Employees get substantial discounts on GE products, including refrigerators, washers and dryers, and air conditioners. You can also buy GE products through the GE Appliance Store where you can purchase products directly and save on average 20 percent off typical retail prices.

Qualified Employee Discounts   Employers frequently allow employees to purchase their goods and services at a discount. Employees may exclude **qualified employee discounts** from income as long as they don't acquire *goods* at a price below the employer's cost or *services* at more than a 20 percent discount of the price of the services to customers.[51] This can be a fairly significant nontaxable benefit to employees, particularly for higher priced products. For example, Ford Motor Company could allow employees a substantial discount on its Ford, Land Rover, Jaguar, or Volvo brand cars. Also, Exhibit 12-15 presents an excerpt from the General Electric Web site describing the GE employee product purchase plan that allows employees to acquire home appliances at a significant discount.[52]

From a nontax perspective, employers can use this qualified fringe benefit to entice and retain employees who would otherwise purchase the employer's brand or product.

Example 12-21

What if: Assume that Julie's current employer, PCC, allows all employees to purchase computers (both laptops and desktops) from its retail stores at cost. Julie purchased two computers during the current year: a $1,600 laptop (retails for $2,100, with a cost basis to PCC of $1,500) and a $1,300 desktop (retails for $1,800, with a cost basis of $1,250). Julie saved $500 ($2,100 − $1,600) on the laptop and $500 ($1,800 − $1,300) on the desktop as well. What amount of the savings must Julie include in her taxable income?

Answer: Julie can exclude the entire savings from her income because the savings are a qualified employee discount under §132.

What if: Suppose that that the laptop Julie purchased for $1,600 has a cost basis of $1,700 (instead of $1,500 as stated above). What amount of the tax savings on the laptop must Julie include in her taxable income?

Answer: $100. Because Julie's cost of the computer is $100 less than PCC's cost, Julie must include $100 in her income.

What if: Assume that Julie's current employer, PCC, allows all employees to receive one free computer each year. Julie selected the $1,600 laptop (retails for $2,100, with a cost basis to PCC of $1,500) as her free computer. What amount must PCC include in Julie's taxable income?

Answer: $1,500. Julie's cost of the computer ($0) is $1,500 less than PCC's cost. Therefore, she must include $1,500 in income. Employee discounts only qualify as a qualified employee discount under §132 to the extent it doesn't exceed the employer's cost basis.

Working Condition Fringe Benefits   Employees may exclude from income any benefit or reimbursement of a benefit provided by an employer that would be deductible as an ordinary and necessary expense by the employee if the employee rather than

---

[51]§132(a)(2).

[52]General Electric's Web site: www.gecareers.com/GECAREERS/html/us/whyGE/benefits/other.html.

the employer paid the expense (or the employer did not reimburse the employee). For example, if a company or firm reimburses its employees for professional licensing costs or dues (CPA or bar fees or dues), the reimbursement may be excluded from an employee's income.[53] Additionally, telephones or computers provided to employees for business use may be excluded. Employers may discriminate between employees with respect to **working condition fringe benefits.**

Example 12-22

What if: Assume that Julie's employer reimburses executives for business-related continuing education courses as well as travel related to such education. Julie attended a certificate (nondegree program) course at the University of Chicago this year. Her costs were as follows: $2,500 for the course, $600 for airfare, $800 for hotels, and $200 for books and course materials. PCC reimbursed Julie for the entire $4,100 ($2,500 + $600 + $800 + $200). What amount of the reimbursement must Julie include in her taxable income?

Answer: $0. The reimbursement qualifies as a working condition fringe benefit under §132.

What if: Assume that Ethan's employer allows all its engineers to take home products for consumer testing and evaluation. For example, Ethan is currently designing a new disk brake system for mountain bikes. So Ethan is allowed to check out up to three mountain bikes at a time to see how various different brake systems work. The annual rental value of products Ethan uses is $2,500. What amount of the annual rental value must Ethan include in his taxable income?

Answer: $0. The value of the consumer testing products is an excludible working condition fringe benefit under §132.

De Minimis **Fringe Benefits**   Employees can also exclude from income occasional or incidental *de minimis* **fringe benefits** (very small).[54] These typically include occasional personal use of a copy machine, company-sponsored picnics, noncash traditional holiday gifts (Thanksgiving turkey or Christmas ham), and occasional tickets to sporting or theatrical events. Employers are allowed to discriminate between employees when providing *de minimis* fringe benefits. Who do you think gets to use a company's NBA tickets—the new employee or the boss?

Qualified Transportation Fringe   Employees may exclude from income the value of certain transportation benefits they receive from employers, whether employers pay for these benefits directly or reimburse employees for the transportation costs.[55] These **qualified transportation fringe benefits** eligible for exclusion include the value of company-owned car pool vehicles for commuting to and from work, the cost of mass transit passes, and the cost of qualified parking near the work place. In 2009, the maximum exclusion for the car pool vehicle and mass transit pass is $120 per month and the maximum exclusion for the qualified parking benefit is $230 per month.[56]

Qualified Moving Expense Reimbursement   Employees receiving payments (or reimbursements) from employers for **qualified moving expense reimbursements** may exclude the payments from taxable income to the extent that they do not deduct the moving expenses.[57] As we discussed in Chapter 6, qualified moving expenses include

---

[53]Employees can exclude reimbursements from their income if they properly document their expenses through expense reports, mileage logs, and receipts.

[54]§132(a)(4).

[55]§132(f)(1).

[56]The 2008 amounts are $115 for mass transit passes and $220 for parking.

[57]§132(a)(6).

the cost of moving household items and travel, including lodging, for the employee and dependents as long as the employee's move meets certain distance and length of employment tests. Employees are, however, taxed on payments they receive from employers for house-hunting trips, temporary housing allowances, and reimbursements for expenses related to the sale of their prior residence.

Cafeteria Plans and Flexible Spending Accounts (FSAs)

Employers choose the benefits they make available to employees. Some employers offer a standard package of benefits that employees can either take or leave. Standard benefits typically include health and dental insurance for the employee and her family, **dependent care benefits,** and group-term life insurance for the employee. However, a standard benefit plan is not optimal for all employees because each employee has his or her own needs. So how can employers tailor their benefits to the needs of employees? The answer is cafeteria plans and flexible spending accounts.

Under a **cafeteria plan,** employers determine the total cost of benefits they are willing to provide for each employee. Each employee then either chooses (or buys) benefits up to the determined amount from a menu of nontaxable fringe benefits or may receive a cash equivalent in lieu of forgone benefits.[58] However, cash received from a cafeteria plan is taxable compensation to employees. Cafeteria plans are popular because each employee may desire different types of nontaxable fringe benefits. For example, if an employer provides $3,000 of dependent care benefits to every employee, the benefits would be worthless to employees without dependents. Through a cafeteria plan, employees can select the benefits best suited to their needs. For example, instead of selecting dependent care benefits, an employee with no dependents could choose any combination of nontaxable benefits such as dental insurance, educational benefits, employer §401(k) contributions, or cash if none of the benefits is desirable.

Employers can also offer **flexible spending accounts (FSAs),** which allow employees to set aside a portion of their before-tax salary for payment of either health and/or dependent-care benefits. These plans allow employees to set aside either employee contributions (on a before-tax basis) or employer contributions (a leftover cafeteria plan amount) to pay for medical-related expenses (such as co-payments and prescriptions) or dependent care. Generally, taxpayers must use amounts placed in flexible spending accounts to pay for qualified benefits they expend funds on during the FSA plan year (which is often the calendar year), or they forfeit the remaining balance of the account. However, employers may allow employees to use the remaining balance from one year within two and a half months of the next FSA plan year.[59]

Employee and Employer Considerations for Nontaxable Fringe Benefits

Nontaxable fringe benefits are very attractive to employees because their after-tax cost of these benefits is zero.[60] They do not pay for the benefits and they are not taxed on the value of the benefits they receive. In contrast to taxable fringe benefits, nontaxable fringe benefits cannot, with a few exceptions noted above, be provided on a discriminatory basis (may not be provided to some employees and not others). Employers deduct the cost of providing the benefits, which (thanks to group or quantity discounts) can be considerably lower than the cost to the employee of purchasing the benefit separately. IRS publication 15-B "Employer's Tax Guide to Fringe Benefits" (available at www.IRS.gov) provides tax guidance for employers providing fringe benefits.

THE KEY FACTS

Nontaxable Fringe Benefits

- Specifically identified in the Code.
- Employee excludes benefit from taxable income.
- Employer deducts cost when benefit is paid.

---

[58]§125.

[59]Employers can elect to allow employees to use funds set aside for one year until March 15 of the following year under Notice 2005-42. If employers don't make the election, employees must use their account balance by December 31 of the current year or they lose it after year-end.

[60]Furthermore, there are nontax reasons for employees to value nontaxable benefits, such as the fact that many employer-provided group health insurance plans allow for preexisting health conditions that employees cannot obtain on their own.

Tax Planning with Fringe Benefits

The fact that employees can exclude nontaxable fringe benefits from taxable income, while employers can deduct them, gives rise to compensation-related tax-planning opportunities that may benefit both employee and employer.

Example 12-23

Julie currently spends $200 a month on parking near PCC's place of business. TPI proposed to reimburse Julie for her parking costs. What amount of this reimbursement would be a nontaxable qualified transportation fringe to Julie?

Answer: All $2,400. Julie can exclude up to $230 per month ($2,760 per year) as a qualified transportation fringe.

What if: Assume that TPI would not reimburse Julie's parking costs unless Julie is willing to accept a reduction in salary. Assuming Julie is subject to a 40 percent marginal tax rate, how much salary should Julie be willing to forgo to receive the $2,400 of nontaxable parking benefits?

Answer: $4,099, computed as follows:

Description	Amount	Explanation
(1) Annual fringe benefit	$2,400	
(2) Marginal ordinary tax rate	40%	
(3) Medicare tax rate on salary	1.45%	Julie is over Social Security tax wage base limit.
(4) Total marginal tax rate on income	41.45%	(2) + (3).
Before-tax compensation required to pay for annual fringe benefit	$4,099	(1)/[1 − (4)].

Not surprisingly, employees who desire a particular nontaxable fringe benefit should always prefer that nontaxable benefit over an equivalent amount of taxable benefits. At the same time, however, because employers deduct the cost of taxable and nontaxable compensation or benefits, they should be indifferent between providing a given level of taxable compensation and providing an equivalent level of nontaxable fringe benefits.

Example 12-24

What if: Assume that instead of a parking benefit, TPI would pay Julie $4,099 of salary that she would use to pay for her parking and FICA taxes. What would be TPI's after-tax cost of paying $4,099 of salary to Julie assuming its marginal tax rate is 35 percent?

Answer: $2,699, calculated as follows:

Description	Amount	Explanation
(1) Taxable salary paid	$4,099	
(2) Income tax benefit	(1,435)	(1) × 35%.
(3) FICA taxes paid	59	(1) × 1.45% (over the SS cap).
(4) FICA tax benefit	(21)	(3) × 35%.
Total after-tax cost of salary	$2,702	(1) + (2) + (3) + (4).

What if: Assume that TPI were to provide Julie $2,400 of qualified transportation fringe benefits in the form of parking. What would be its after-tax cost of paying the $2,400 nontaxable fringe benefit to Julie assuming its marginal tax rate is 35 percent?

Answer: $1,560, calculated as follows:

Description	Amount	Explanation
(1) Nontaxable fringe benefit paid	$2,400	Given.
(2) Income tax benefit	(840)	(1) × 35%
Total after-tax cost of nontaxable benefit	$1,560	(1) − (2).

Can an employer and an employee work together to implement the conversion tax planning strategy to make both the employee and employer better off by substituting desired nontaxable fringe benefits for taxable salary in the compensation package? The answer is yes!

Example 12-25

As shown in Example 12-23, Julie is indifferent between receiving (1) $4,099 in salary ($2,400 after-taxes) and (2) $2,400 in nontaxable parking benefits. Consequently, if TPI paid Julie $2,400 in non-taxable benefits and any amount of additional salary she would be better off than she would by receiving no parking and $4,099 in salary. As shown in Example 12-24, TPI would be better off after taxes by providing Julie with (1) $2,400 in nontaxable benefits (cost of $1,560) rather than (2) salary of $4,099 (cost of $2,699). What amount of salary could TPI provide in addition to the $2,400 of nontaxable benefits and remain indifferent between providing the parking and the additional salary and providing salary of $4,099?

Answer: $1,732, calculated as follows:

Description	Amount	Explanation
(1) After-tax cost of salary	$2,702	Example 12-24.
(2) After-tax cost of fringe benefit	$1,560	Example 12-24.
(3) After-tax indifference point	$1,142	(1) − (2).
(4) After-tax cost percentage	65.94%	(1 + .0145) × (1 − .35).*
Before-tax salary	$1,732	(3)/(4).

*Where (1 + .0145) is the before-tax salary plus FICA tax and (1 − .35) is the after-tax conversion factor.

To summarize, if TPI pays Julie's parking costs and provides her with additional salary of any amount below $1,732, it will be better off than it would be by not providing the parking and paying her $4,099 in salary. Julie is better off if TPI pays her parking and gives her any additional salary than she is if they don't pay her parking but pay her $4,099 of salary.

Fringe Benefits Summary

Fringe benefits, both taxable and nontaxable, can make up a significant portion of an employee's compensation. Fringe benefits are taxable unless the tax laws specifically exclude them from gross income. Nontaxable fringe benefits are generally excluded for public policy reasons, while taxable fringe benefits usually represent a

EXHIBIT 12-16   **Excerpt from Disney Company's Proxy Statement Dealing with Fringe Benefits**

The Walt Disney Company Notice of Annual Meeting and Proxy Statement
Benefits and perquisites

The following table identifies the incremental cost to the Company of each item included in Other Annual Compensation in the Summary Compensation Table that exceeds 25 percent of the total for each executive officer for each year in which the total for the officer exceeded $50,000.

		COMPONENTS OF OTHER ANNUAL COMPENSATION				
	Year	**Automobile Benefit**	**Personal Air Travel**	**Security**	**Other**	**Total**
Robert A. Iger	2006	$14,400	$67,879	$578,656		$660,935
	2005	14,400	54,998	438,176	$4,109	511,683

In accordance with the SEC's recent interpretations of its rules, for fiscal 2006 this table includes the incremental cost of some items that are provided to executives for business purposes but which may not be considered integrally related to the executive's duties. In addition, the cost of providing security for Mr. Iger, which previously had been set forth in a separate table, is now included in this table for fiscal 2005 and fiscal 2006. As previously reported, in 2004, the cost of providing security for Mr. Iger was $474,116.

The column labeled Other in the table above includes, for those named executive officers who elected to receive it, reimbursement of up to $450 for health club membership or exercise equipment, reimbursement for up to $1,500 for an annual physical exam and reimbursement of expenses for financial consulting. Executives also receive the following items for which the Company does not incur incremental costs: complimentary access to the Company's theme parks and some resort facilities, discounts of Company merchandise and resort facilities, and access to tickets for sporting and other events for personal use if the tickets are not needed for business use. The table does not include medical benefits coverage, life and disability insurance protection, reimbursement for educational expenses and access to favorably priced group insurance coverage that are offered through programs that are available to substantially all of the Company's salaried employees.

luxury perk. At this point, you should be able to distinguish between taxable and nontaxable fringe benefits. Exhibit 12-16 presents an excerpt from Disney Company's proxy statement. Read through the excerpt and see if you can determine which of the benefits Mr. Iger received are taxable and which are nontaxable?

Mr. Iger's taxable benefits include the automobile, personal air travel, security, health club membership, annual physical exam, reimbursement for financial consulting, and perhaps part of the group-term life insurance. Mr. Iger's nontaxable benefits include theme park access (a no-additional-cost service), merchandise discounts (qualified employee discount), occasional sporting events (*de minimis* fringe benefit), educational expense reimbursements, health insurance, and group-term life insurance (some of this coverage may be taxable).

Recall the fringe benefits included in Julie's offer letter: health insurance (valued at $18,000), $750,000 of group-term life insurance, and a flexible spending account (no amounts given; assume she elects $1,500). She also received an annual parking benefit of $2,400. Which benefits are taxable and which are nontaxable? Exhibit 12-17 summarizes how each of these benefits is classified for tax purposes, Julie's after-tax benefit, and TPI's after-tax cost.

EXHIBIT 12-17   Summary of Julie's Nonsalary Benefits from TPI

Benefit	Nontaxable Fringe	Taxable Fringe	Employee After-Tax Benefit	Employer After-Tax Cost
Auto allowance		X	**$17,565** ($30,000 − 12,435)	**$19,783** [($30,000 + 435) × (1 − .35)]
Health and dental insurance	X		**$18,000** [$18,000 × (1 − .0)]	**$11,700** [$18,000 × (1 − .35)]
Flexible spending account	X		**$1,500** [$1,500 × (1 − .0)]	**$975** [$1,500 × (1 − .35)]
Parking reimbursement	X		**$2,400** [$2,400 × (1 − .0)] (Example 12-23)	**$1,560** ($2,400 − $840) (Example 12-24)
Group-term life insurance	X	X	**$1,687** ($2,000 − $313)* (Examples 12-17, 18)	**$330** (Example 12-18)
Total			**$41,152**	**$34,348**

*This is the fair market value of the benefit less the actual taxes payable by Julie.

CONCLUSION

In our economy, individuals and employers routinely make choices involving compensation issues. As they do so, they must understand how alternative forms of compensation are taxed. In this chapter, we have discussed the tax compliance and planning implications associated with common types of payment including salary and wages, equity-based compensation (such as stock options and restricted stock), and taxable and nontaxable fringe benefits from both employee and employer perspectives. Throughout, we have emphasized that both tax and nontax issues must be considered in the broader context of compensation planning. Armed with the information provided in this chapter, future employees and employers can approach the compensation decisions they will undoubtedly face with more confidence and insight.

SUMMARY

Discuss and explain the tax implications of compensation in the form of salary and wages from the employer's and employee's perspectives.

L01

- Employees are taxed on salary at ordinary income rates.
- Employees use Form W-4 to supply their employer with withholding information. Employees can use the W-4 to manage withholding throughout the year because withholding is treated as though it is withheld evenly throughout the year for estimated tax purposes.
- Employees' wages are subject to FICA tax. The Social Security component is 6.2 percent and the Medicare component is 1.45 percent. The Social Security tax applies to the first $106,800 of income in 2009. The wage base on the Medicare tax is unlimited.
- Cash-basis employers deduct wages when paid. Accrual-basis employers deduct wages when accrued as long as the wages are paid within 2.5 months of year-end. If paid after 2.5 months of year-end, wages are deductible when the employee recognizes the income (when paid). When a corporation accrues wages to a related-party employee (more than 50 percent ownership), the wages are not deductible until the employee recognizes the income (when paid).

- Employers are responsible for matching employees' FICA taxes.
- Employers' after-tax cost of wages is the cost of the wages including FICA taxes minus the tax benefit of the deduction for the wages and the FICA taxes.
- For publicly traded corporations, the tax deduction for nonperformance-based compensation paid to the CEO and four other most highly compensated officers is $1,000,000 per year.

LO2 Describe and distinguish the tax implications of various forms of equity-based compensation from the employer's and employee's perspectives.

- Stock options and restricted stock are common forms of equity-based compensation. Although both reward employees for increases in the stock price of their employers, there are fundamental economic differences between them.
- Stock options are treated as either nonqualified or incentive stock options for tax purposes.
- Employees recognize taxable income equal to the bargain element on nonqualified options when they are exercised. Employers are able to deduct the bargain element when nonqualified options are exercised. Any appreciation in the value of shares subsequent to the exercise of nonqualified options is treated as capital gain by employees when the shares are sold.
- If certain holding period requirements are met, employees exercising incentive stock options don't recognize any income until the shares received from the exercised options are sold. When the shares are sold, the difference between the exercise price and the share price is long-term capital gain. Employers are not permitted a deduction for incentive stock options.
- Generally, employees prefer incentive stock options and employers prefer nonqualified options because of differences in the way the two types of options are taxed.
- Employers treat stock options differently for book and tax purposes.
- Employees recognize taxable income from restricted stock equal to the fair market value of the stock on the vesting date. Employers receive a corresponding tax deduction.
- Employees may elect to recognize taxable income from restricted stock on the date it is received rather than on the vesting date if they make an §83(b) election. Although this election accelerates the recognition of income, it gives the employee the ability to convert ordinary income from further appreciation into capital gain.

LO3 Compare and contrast taxable and nontaxable fringe benefits and explain the employee and employer tax consequences associated with fringe benefits.

- Nontaxable or qualified fringe benefits allow both employees and employers to be better off. This is because the employer is allowed a deduction for the benefits, just as they would with a taxable fringe benefit. However, the qualified fringe benefit is not included in an employee's income.
- Qualified fringe benefits make both employers and employees better off only if the employee wants or desires the benefit offered. Cafeteria plans allow employers to offer employees the choice between qualified benefits (health insurance, for example) or taxable compensation.

KEY TERMS

bargain element (12-12)
book treatment (12-16)
cafeteria plan (12-31)
de minimis fringe benefit (12-30)
dependent care benefit (12-31)
disqualifying disposition (12-15)
educational assistance benefit (12-28)
employee (12-2)
exercise date (12-13)

facts and circumstances test (12-7)
FICA taxes (12-5)
flexible spending account (FSA) (12-31)
for the convenience of the employer benefits (12-27)
Form W-2 (12-2)
Form W-4 (12-2)
fringe benefits (12-22)

grant date (12-13)
group-term life insurance (12-23)
health and accident insurance (12-26)
incentive stock option (12-13)
Medicare tax (12-5)
no-additional-cost services (12-28)
nonqualified stock option (12-13)
nontaxable fringe benefit (12-26)
option exercise (12-11)

qualified employee discount (12-29)

qualified moving expense reimbursement (12-30)

qualified transportation fringe benefit (12-30)

restricted stock (12-17)

salary (12-2)

same-day sale (12-14)

§83(b) election (12-19)

Social Security tax (12-5)

strike price (12-11)

taxable fringe benefit (12-22)

vest (12-11)

wages (12-2)

working condition fringe benefit (12-30)

DISCUSSION QUESTIONS

1. **(LO1)** Shane is an employee who has had a relatively consistent income over the years. His withholding is pretty much right on target with his actual tax liability, so he rarely has much of a tax refund or tax due with his tax return. At the beginning of this year, Shane sold some property at a large gain. What issues relating to withholding should Shane consider? What would you advise him to do?   ■ planning

2. **(LO1)** Juanita recently started employment for Maple Corporation. For tax purposes, Juanita files as a head-of-household filing status with three dependents. Juanita needs to determine the number of "withholding exemptions" to claim on her W-4 form. Should she claim four withholding exemptions or should she claim more? What factors should she consider in making this determination?   ■ planning

3. **(LO1)** Are taxpayers' entire wages subject to the FICA tax? Explain.

4. **(LO1)** Nicole and Braxton are each 50 percent shareholders of NB Corporation. Nicole is also an employee of the corporation. NB is a calendar-year taxpayer and uses the accrual method of accounting. The corporation pays its employees monthly on the first day of the month after the salary is earned by the employees. What issues must NB consider with respect to the deductibility of the wages it pays to Nicole if Nicole is Braxton's sister? What issues arise if Nicole and Braxton are unrelated?

5. **(LO1)** Holding all else equal, does an employer with a higher marginal tax rate or lower marginal tax rate have a lower after-tax cost of paying a particular employee's salary?

6. **(LO1)** What are nontax reasons why a corporation may choose to cap its executives' salaries at $1 million?

7. **(LO1)** What are tax reasons why a corporation may choose to cap its executives' salaries at $1 million?

8. **(LO1)** Lea is a highly paid executive with MCC, Inc., a publicly traded corporation. What are the circumstances under which MCC will be able to deduct more than $1 million of compensation paid to Lea during the year?

9. **(LO2)** From an *employee* perspective, how are incentive stock options treated differently than nonqualified stock options for tax purposes? In general, for a given number of options, which type of stock option should employees prefer?

10. **(LO2)** From an *employer* perspective, how are incentive stock options treated differently than nonqualified stock options for tax purposes? In general, for a given number of options, which type of stock option should employers prefer?

11. **(LO2)** Why do employers use stock options in addition to salary to compensate their employees? For employers, are stock options treated more favorably than salary for tax purposes?

12. **(LO2)** What is a "disqualifying disposition" of incentive stock options and how does it affect employees who have exercised incentive stock options?

13. **(LO2)** Compare and contrast how employers record book and tax expense for stock options.

14. **(LO2)** How is the tax treatment of restricted stock different from that of nonqualified options? How is it similar?

15. **(LO2)** Matt just started work with Boom Zoom, Inc., a manufacturer of credit card size devices for storing and playing back music. Due to the popularity of its devices, analysts expect Boom Zoom's stock price to increase dramatically. In addition to his salary, Matt received Boom Zoom restricted stock. How will Matt's restricted stock be treated for tax purposes? Should Matt consider making the §83(b) election? What are the factors he should consider in making this decision? Would this election help or hurt Boom Zoom?

16. **(LO2)** What risks do employees making a §83(b) election on a restricted stock grant assume?

17. **(LO3)** Explain the differences and similarities between fringe benefits and salary as forms of compensation.

18. **(LO3)** When an employer provides group-term life insurance for an employee, what are the tax consequences to the employee? What are the tax consequences for the employer?

19. **(LO3)** Compare and contrast the employer's tax consequences of providing taxable versus nontaxable fringe benefits.

20. **(LO3)** Mike is working his way through college and trying to make ends meet. Tara, a friend, is graduating soon and tells Mike about a really great job opportunity. She is the onsite manager for an apartment complex catering to students. The job entails working in the office for about 10 hours a week, collecting rent each month, and answering after-hours emergency calls. The pay is $10 per hour, plus a rent-free apartment (worth about $500 per month). Tara then tells him the best part: the rent-free apartment is tax-free as well. Knowing that you are a tax student, Mike asks you if the rent-free apartment is really tax-free or if this is just another scam. Explain to Mike whether the compensation for the apartment is really a nontaxable benefit.

21. **(LO3)** Assume that a friend has accepted a position working as an accountant for a large automaker. As a signing bonus, the employer provides the traditional cash incentive, but also provides the employee with a vehicle not to exceed a retail price of $25,000. Explain whether the value of the vehicle is included, excluded, or partially included in the employee's taxable income.

22. **(LO3)** Explain why an employee might accept a lower salary to receive a nontaxable fringe benefit. Why might an employee not accept a lower salary to receive a nontaxable fringe benefit?

23. **(LO3)** Describe a cafeteria plan and discuss why an employer would provide a cafeteria plan for its employees.

24. **(LO3)** Explain why Congress allows employees to receive certain fringe benefits free of tax but others are taxable?

25. **(LO3)** Explain the policy reason for including the value of country club memberships provided to an executive as a taxable fringe benefit.

26. **(LO3)** Describe the circumstances in which an employee may not value a nontaxable fringe benefit.

PROBLEMS

27. **(LO1)** Anna is single with one four-year-old child. She earns a monthly salary in 2009 of $5,000.

   a. If she claims two withholding allowances, how much will her employer withhold from her monthly paycheck? (*Hint:* Go to www.irs.gov and search for withholding tables.)

   b. If she claims four withholding allowances, how much will her employer withhold from her monthly paycheck?

c. Assuming that she has no other income, claims the standard deduction, and claims one personal and one dependency deduction, what is Anna's tax liability for the year? How many withholding allowances should she claim to equalize (approximately) her withholding and her tax liability?

28. **(LO1)** Baker works for Company ATT for all of 2009. What is his FICA obligation under the following circumstances:

a. Baker is single and earns a salary of $50,000.

b. Baker is single and earns a salary of $110,000.

c. Baker is married and earns a salary of $50,000. His spouse earns $25,000 per year.

d. Baker is married and earns a salary of $50,000. His spouse earns $55,000 per year.

29. **(LO1)** Rasheed works for AD Company and earns $350,000 in salary during 2009. Assuming he has no other sources of income, what amount of Social Security taxes and what amount of Medicare taxes will Rasheed pay for the year?

30. **(LO1)** North Inc. is a calendar-year, accrual-basis taxpayer. At the end of year 1, North accrued and deducted the following bonuses for certain employees for financial accounting purposes.

- $7,500 for Lisa Tanaka, a 30 percent shareholder.
- $10,000 for Jared Zabaski, a 35 percent shareholder.
- $12,500 for Helen Talanian, a 20 percent shareholder.
- $5,000 for Steve Nielson, a 0 percent shareholder.

Unless stated otherwise, assume these shareholders are unrelated.

How much of the accrued bonuses can North Inc. deduct in year 1 under the following alternative scenarios?

a. North paid the bonuses to the employees on March 1 of year 2.

b. North paid the bonuses to the employees on April 1 of year 2.

c. North paid the bonuses to employees on March 1 of year 2 and Lisa and Jared are related to each other, so they are treated as owning each other's stock in North.

d. North paid the bonuses to employees on March 1 of year 2 and Lisa and Helen are related to each other, so they are treated as owning each other's stock in North.

31. **(LO1)** Lynette is the CEO of publicly traded TTT Corporation and earns a salary of $200,000 in 2009. Assume TTT has a 35 percent marginal tax rate.

a. What is TTT Corporation's after-tax cost of paying Lynette's salary excluding FICA taxes?

b. What is TTT Corporation's after-tax cost of paying Lynette's salary including FICA taxes?

32. **(LO1)** Marcus is the CEO of publicly traded ABC Corporation and earns a salary of $1,500,000. Assume ABC has a 35 percent marginal tax rate.

a. What is ABC's after-tax cost of paying Marcus's salary (excluding FICA taxes)?

b. Now assume that Marcus, in addition to the $1.5 million salary, earns a performance-based bonus of $500,000. What is ABC's after-tax cost of paying Marcus's salary (excluding FICA taxes)?

33. **(LO1)** Ramon has finally arrived. He has interviewed for the CEO position with MMM Corporation. They have presented him with two alternative compensation offers. Alternative 1 is for a straight salary of $2,500,000. Option 2 is

■ **planning**

for a salary of $1,000,000 and performance-based compensation of up to $2,000,000. Assume that Ramon has a marginal tax rate of 40 percent, MMM has a marginal tax rate of 35 percent, and ignore FICA taxes for this problem. Answer the questions under each of the following alternative scenarios.

a. If Ramon is 100 percent certain he can meet the qualifications for the full performance-based compensation, which offer should he choose?

b. If Ramon believes there is only a 20 percent chance that he can meet the performance-based requirements, which offer should he choose (assume he is risk neutral)?

c. What is MMM's after-tax cost of providing Ramon with Option 1?

d. What is MMM's expected after-tax cost of providing Ramon with Option 2 if it believes there is a 40 percent chance Ramon will qualify for the performance-based compensation?

34. **(LO2)** Cammie received 100 NQOs (each option provides a right to purchase 10 shares of MNL stock for $10 per share) at the time she started working for MNL Corporation four years ago when MNL's stock price was $8 per share. Now that MNL's stock price is $40 per share, she intends to exercise all of her options. After acquiring the 1,000 MNL shares with her options, she held the shares for over one year and sold them at $60 per share.

a. What are Cammie's tax consequences on the grant date, the exercise date, and the date she sold the shares, assuming her ordinary marginal rate is 30 percent and her capital gains rate is 15 percent?

b. What are MNL Corporation's tax consequences on these dates assuming its marginal tax rate is 35 percent?

■ **planning**

35. **(LO2)** Yost received 300 NQOs (each option gives Yost the right to purchase 10 shares of Cutter Corporation stock for $15 per share) at the time he started working for Cutter Corporation three years ago. Cutter's stock price was $15 per share. Yost exercises all of his options when the share price is $26 per share. Two years after acquiring the shares, he sold them at $47 per share.

a. What are Yost's tax consequences (amount of income/gain recognized and amount of taxes payable) on the grant date, the exercise date, and the date he sells the shares, assuming his ordinary marginal rate is 35 percent and his capital gains rate is 15 percent?

b. What are Cutter Corporation's tax consequences (amount of deduction and tax savings from deduction) on these dates, assuming its marginal tax rate is 25 percent?

c. Assume that Yost is cash poor and needs to perform a same-day sale in order to buy his shares. Due to his belief that the stock price is going to increase significantly, he wants to maintain as many shares as possible. How many shares must he sell in order to cover his purchase price and taxes payable on the exercise?

d. Assume that Yost's options were exercisable at $20 and expired after five years. If the stock only reached $18 dollars during its high point during the five-year period, what are Yost's tax consequences on the grant date, the exercise date, and the date the shares are sold, assuming his ordinary marginal rate is 35 percent and his capital gains rate is 15 percent?

36. **(LO2)** Haven received 200 NQOs (each option gives him the right to purchase 20 shares of Barlow Corporation stock for $7 per share) at the time he started working for Barlow Corporation three years ago when its stock price was $7 per share. Now that Barlow's share price is $50 per share, he intends to exercise all of his options. After acquiring the 4,000 Barlow shares with his options, he

intends to hold the shares for more than one year and then sell the shares when the price reaches $75 per share.

    a. What are the cash flow effects of these transactions to Haven assuming his ordinary marginal rate is 30 percent and his capital gains rate is 15 percent?

    b. What are the cash flow effects for Barlow Corporation resulting from Haven's option exercise if Barlow's marginal tax rate is 35 percent?

37. **(LO2)** Mark received 10 ISOs (each option gives him the right to purchase 10 shares of Hendricks Corporation stock for $5 per share) at the time he started working for Hendricks Corporation five years ago when Hendricks's share price was $5 per share. Now that Hendricks's share price is $35 per share, he intends to exercise all options and hold all of his shares for more than year. Assume that more than a year after exercise, Mark sells the stock for $35 a share.

    a. What are Mark's tax consequences on the grant date, the exercise date, and the date he sells the shares, assuming his ordinary marginal rate is 30 percent and his capital gains rate is 15 percent?

    b. What are Hendricks's tax consequences on these dates, assuming its marginal tax rate is 25 percent?

38. **(LO2)** Antonio received 40 ISOs (each option gives him the right to purchase 20 shares of Zorro stock for $3 per share) at the time he started working for Zorro Corporation six years ago. Zorro's share price was $3 per share at the time. Now that Zorro's share price is $50 per share, he intends to exercise all of his options and immediately sell all the shares he receives from the options exercise.

    a. What are Antonio's tax consequences on the grant date, the exercise date, and the date the shares are sold, assuming his ordinary marginal rate is 30 percent and his capital gains rate is 15 percent?

    b. What are Zorro's tax consequences on these dates, assuming its marginal tax rate is 25 percent?

    c. What are the cash flow effects of these transactions to Antonio, assuming his ordinary marginal rate is 25 percent and his capital gains rate is 15 percent?

    d. What are the cash flow effects to Zorro Corporation resulting from Antonio's option exercise if Zorro's marginal tax rate is 35 percent?

39. **(LO2)** Harmer Inc. is now a successful company. In the early days (before it became profitable), it issued incentive stock options (ISOs) to its employees. Now Harmer is trying to decide whether to issue nonqualified options (NQOs) or ISOs to its employees. Initially, Harmer would like to give each employee 20 options. For purposes of this problem, assume that the options are exercised in three years (*three years from now*) and that the underlying stock is sold in five years (*five years from now*). Also assume the following facts:

■ **planning**

- The after-tax discount rate for both Harmer Inc. and its employees is 10 percent.
- Corporate tax rate is 35 percent.
- Personal (employee) ordinary income rate is 40 percent.
- Personal (employee) capital gains rate is 15 percent.
- Exercise price of the options is $7.
- Market price of Harmer at date of grant is $5.
- Market price of Harmer at date of exercise is $25.
- Market price of Harmer at date of sale is $35.

Answer the following questions:

    a. Considering these facts, which type of option plan, nonqualified (NQO) or incentive (ISO), should Harmer Inc. prefer?

b. Assuming Harmer issues NQOs, what is Harmer's tax benefit from the options for each employee in the year each employee exercise the NQOs?

c. Assuming Harmer issues ISOs, what is the tax benefit to Harmer in the year the ISOs are exercised?

d. Which type of option plan should Harmer's employees prefer?

e. What is the present value of each employee's after-tax cash flows if the employees receive ISOs?

f. What is the present value of each employee's after-tax cash flows if the employees receive NQOs?

g. How many NQOs would Harmer have to grant to keep its employees indifferent between NQOs and 10 ISOs?

40. **(LO2)** Dave recently received 1,000 shares of restricted stock from his employer, RKK Corporation, when the share price was $7 per share. Dave's restricted shares will vest in two years. After that, he intends to hold the shares for two more years when he intends to sell them to help fund the purchase of a new home. Dave predicts the share price of RKK will be $30 per share when his shares vest and will be $40 per share when he sells them.

a. If Dave's stock price predictions are correct, what are the tax consequences to Dave if his ordinary marginal rate is 30 percent and his capital gains rate is 15 percent?

b. If Dave's stock price predictions are correct, what are the tax consequences to RKK if its marginal rate is 35 percent?

41. **(LO2)** Dave recently received 1,000 shares of restricted stock from his employer, RKK Corporation, when the share price was $7 per share. On receiving the restricted stock, Dave made the §83(b) election. Dave's restricted shares will vest in two years. After that, he intends to hold the shares for two more years when he intends to sell them to help fund the purchase of a new home. Dave predicts the share price of RKK will be $30 per share when his shares vest and will be $40 per share when he sells them. Assume that Dave's price predictions are correct and answer the following questions:

a. What are the tax consequences to Dave if his ordinary marginal rate is 30 percent and his capital gains rate is 15 percent?

b. What are the tax consequences to RKK if its marginal rate is 35 percent?

c. Assume that Dave made the §83(b) election upon receiving the shares, what are the tax consequences to Dave if his ordinary marginal rate is 30 percent and his capital gains rate is 15 percent?

d. Assume that Dave made the §83(b) election upon receiving the shares, what are the tax consequences to RKK if its marginal rate is 35 percent?

42. **(LO2)** Jessica recently received 10,000 shares of restricted stock from her employer, Rocket Corporation, when the share price was $10 per share. On receiving the restricted stock, Jessica made the §83(b) election. Jessica's restricted shares will all vest in four years. After the shares vest, she intends to sell them immediately to fund an around-the-world cruise. Unfortunately, Jessica decided that she couldn't wait four years and quit her job to start her cruise two years after receiving the restricted shares.

a. What are the tax consequences to Jessica in the year she receives the restricted shares, assuming her marginal tax rate is 33 percent and her capital gains rate is 15 percent?

b. What are the tax consequences to Jessica in the year she leaves, assuming her marginal tax rate is 33 percent and her capital gains rate is 15 percent?

43. **(LO2)** Anna recently received 5,000 shares of restricted stock from her employer, Jarbal Corporation, when the share price was $5 per share. On receiving the restricted stock, Anna made the §83(b) election. Anna's restricted shares will all vest in two years. After the shares vest, she intends to sell them immediately to purchase a condo. True to her plan, Anna sold the shares immediately after they were vested.

    a. What are the tax consequences to Anna in the year she receives the restricted shares?

    b. What are the tax consequences to Anna in the year the shares vest if the stock is valued at $1 per share on the day the shares vest?

    c. What are the tax consequences to Anna in the year the shares vest if the stock is valued at $9 per share on the day the shares vest?

    d. What are the tax consequences to Anna in the year the shares vest if the stock is valued at $5 per share on the day the shares vest?

44. **(LO2)** Tyra recently started working for Hatch Corporation. New employees must choose immediately between receiving seven NQOs (each NQO provides the right to purchase for $5 per share 10 shares of Hatch stock) or 50 restricted shares. Hatch's stock price is $5 on Tyra's start date. Either form of equity-based compensation will vest in two years. Tyra believes that the stock will be worth $15 per share in two years and $25 in four years when she will sell the stock. Tyra's marginal tax rate is 30 percent and her capital gains rate is 15 percent. Assume that Tyra's price predictions are correct, answer the following questions (ignore present value, use nominal dollars):

    ■ **planning**

    a. What are the cash-flow effects to Tyra in the year she receives the options, the year the options vest and she exercises the options, and in the year she sells the stock if she chooses the NQOs?

    b. What are the cash-flow effects to Tyra in the year she receives the restricted stock, in the year the stock vests, and in the year she sells the stock if Tyra chooses the restricted stock?

    c. What are the cash-flow effects to Tyra in the year she receives the restricted stock, the year the stock vests, and the year she sells the stock if she makes a §83(b) election?

    d. What recommendation would you give Tyra? Explain.

45. **(LO3)** Nicole's employer provides her with an automobile allowance of $20,000 every other year. Her marginal tax rate is 30 percent. Poe Corporation has a marginal tax rate of 35 percent. Answer the following questions relating to this fringe benefit.

    a. What is Nicole's after-tax benefit if she receives the allowance this year (ignore payroll taxes)?

    b. What is Poe's after-tax cost of providing the auto allowance (ignore payroll taxes)?

    c. What is Nicole's after-tax benefit if she receives the allowance this year, and her salary is below the Social Security wage base limit (include FICA taxes in your analysis)?

    d. What is Poe's after-tax cost of providing the auto allowance, and her salary is under the Social Security wage base limit (include FICA taxes in your analysis)?

    e. What is Nicole's after-tax benefit if she receives the allowance this year, and her salary is over the Social Security wage base (include payroll taxes in your analysis)?

    f. What is Poe's after-tax cost of providing the auto allowance if her salary is over the Social Security wage base (include payroll taxes in your analysis)?

research

46. **(LO3)** Bills Corporation runs a defense contracting business that requires security clearance. To prevent unauthorized access to its materials, Bills requires its security personnel to be on duty except for a 15-minute break every two hours. Since the nearest restaurants are a 25-minute round trip, Bills provides free lunches to its security personnel. Bills has never included the value of these meals in its employees' compensation. Bills is currently under audit and the IRS agent wants to deny Bills a deduction for past meals. The agent also wants Bills to begin including the value of the meals in employee compensation starting with the current year. As Bills' tax advisor, give it a recommendation on whether to appeal the agent's decision (*Hint:* see *Boyd Gaming Corp.*, CA-9, 99-1 USTC ¶50,530 (Acq.), 177 F3d 1096).

planning

47. **(LO3)** Lars Osberg, a single taxpayer with a 35 percent marginal tax rate, desires health insurance. The health insurance would cost Lars $8,500 to purchase if he pays for it himself (Lars's AGI is too high to receive any tax deduction for the insurance as a medical expense). Volvo, Lars's employer, has a 40 percent marginal tax rate. Answer the following questions about this benefit (ignore payroll taxes in your analysis).

a. What is the maximum amount of before-tax salary Lars would give up to receive health insurance from Volvo?

b. What would be the after-tax cost to Volvo to provide Lars with health insurance if it could purchase the insurance through its group plan for $5,000?

c. Assume that Volvo could purchase the insurance for $5,000. Lars is interested in getting health insurance and he is willing to receive a lower salary in exchange for the health insurance. What is the least amount by which Volvo would be willing to reduce Lars's salary while agreeing to pay his health insurance?

d. Will Volvo and Lars be able to reach an agreement by which Volvo will provide Lars's health insurance?

planning

48. **(LO3)** Seiko currently has salary of $85,000, a 30 percent marginal tax rate, and fancies European sports cars. She purchases a new auto each year. Seiko is currently a manager for an office equipment company. Her friend, knowing of her interest in sports cars, tells her about a manager position at the local BMW and Porsche dealer. The new position pays only $75,000 per year, but it allows employees to purchase one new car per year at a discount of $15,000. This discount qualifies as a nontaxable fringe benefit. In an effort to keep Seiko as an employee, her current employer offers her a $10,000 raise. Answer the following questions about this analysis (ignore payroll taxes in your analyses).

a. What is the annual after-tax cost to her current employer (office equipment company that has a 35 percent marginal tax rate) to provide Seiko with the $10,000 increase in salary?

b. Financially, which offer is better for Seiko on an after-tax basis and by how much? (Assume that Seiko is going to purchase the new car whether she switches jobs or not.)

c. What salary would Seiko need to receive from her current employer to make her financially indifferent (after taxes) between receiving additional salary from her current employer and accepting a position at the auto dealership?

49. **(LO1, LO3)** JDD Corporation provides the following benefits to its employee, Ahmed (age 47):

Salary	$300,000
Health insurance	$ 10,000
Dental insurance	$ 2,000
Life insurance	$ 3,000
Dependent care	$ 5,000
Professional dues	$ 500
Personal use of company jet	$200,000

Assume the life insurance is a group-term life insurance policy that provides $200,000 of coverage for Ahmed.

   a. Assuming Ahmed is subject to a marginal tax rate of 30 percent, what is his after-tax benefit of receiving each of these benefits (ignoring FICA taxes)?

   b. Assuming Ahmed is subject to a marginal tax rate of 30 percent, what is his after-tax benefit of receiving each of these benefits (including FICA taxes)?

   c. Assuming JDD Corp.'s marginal tax rate is 35 percent, what is its after-tax cost of providing these benefits to Ahmed ignoring FICA taxes (assume the before tax cost of each benefit is equal to the values stated in the problem)?

   d. Assuming JDD Corp.'s marginal tax rate is 35 percent, what is its after-tax cost of providing these benefits to Ahmed including FICA taxes (assume the before tax cost of each benefit is equal to the values stated in the problem)?

50. **(LO3)** Gray's employer is now offering group-term life insurance. The company will provide each employee with $100,000 of group-term life insurance. It costs Gray's employer $300 to provide this amount of insurance to Gray each year. Assuming that Gray is 52 years old, use the table in Treasury Regulation §1.79-3(d)(2) to determine the monthly premium that Gray must include in income as a result of receiving the group-term life benefit?

51. **(LO3)** Brady graduated from SUNY New Paltz with his bachelor's degree recently. He works for Makarov & Company CPAs. The firm pays his tuition ($10,000 per year) for him so that he can receive his Master of Science in Taxation, which will qualify him to sit for the CPA exam. How much of the $10,000 tuition benefit does Brady need to include in income?

52. **(LO3)** Meg works for Freedom Airlines in the accounts payable department. Meg and all other employees receive free flight benefits (for the employee, family, and 10 free buddy passes for friends per year) as part of their employee benefits package. If Meg uses 30 flights with a value of $12,350 this year, how much must she include in her compensation this year?

53. **(LO3)** Sharmilla works for Shasta Lumber, a local lumber supplier. The company annually provides each employee with a Shasta Lumber shirt so that employees look branded and advertise for the business while wearing the shirts. Are Shasta's employees required to include the value of the shirts in income?

54. **(LO3)** LaMont works for a company in downtown Chicago. The firm encourages employees to use public transportation (to save the environment) by providing them with transit passes at a cost of $250 per month.

   a. If LaMont receives one pass (worth $250) each month, how much of this benefit must he include in his taxable income each year?

   b. If the company provides each employee with $250 per month in parking benefits, how much of the parking benefit must LaMont include in his taxable income each year?

55. **(LO3)** Jasmine works in Washington, D.C. She accepts a new position with her current firm in Los Angeles. Her employer provides the following moving benefits:

- Temporary housing for one month—$3,000.
- Transportation for her household goods—$4,500.
- Flight and hotel for a house-hunting trip—$1,750.
- Flights to Los Angeles for her and her family—$2,000.

By how much do these benefits increase her taxable income (ignoring any AGI-related phase-outs)?

56. **(LO3)** Jarvie lives to bike. In fact, he has always turned down better paying jobs to work in bicycle shops where he gets an employee discount. At Jarvie's current shop, Bad Dog Cycles, each employee is allowed to purchase four bicycles a year

at a discount. Because road bikes have higher profit margins, employees receive a 30 percent discount. Employees also normally receive a 20 percent discount on mountain bikes. During the current year, Jarvie bought the following bikes:

Description	Retail Price	Cost	Employee Price
Specialized road bike	$3,200	$2,000	$2,240
Rocky Mountain mountain bike	$3,800	$3,200	$3,040
Trek road bike	$2,700	$2,000	$1,890
Yeti mountain bike	$3,500	$2,500	$2,800

a. What amount is Jarvie required to include in taxable income from these purchases?

b. What amount of deductions is Bad Dog allowed to claim from these transactions?

57. **(LO1, LO3)** Matt works for Fresh Corporation. Fresh offers a cafeteria plan that allows each employee to receive $15,000 worth of benefits each year. The menu of benefits is as follows:

Benefit	Cost
Health insurance–single	$ 5,000
Health insurance–with spouse	$ 8,000
Health insurance–with spouse and dependents	$11,000
Dental and vision	$ 1,500
Dependent care–any specified amount up to $5,000	Variable
Adoption benefits–any specified amount up to $5,000	Variable
Educational benefits–any specified amount (no limit)	Variable
401(k)–any specified amount up to $10,000	Variable
Cash–any specified amount up to $15,000 plan benefit	Variable

For each of the following independent circumstances, determine the amount of income Matt must recognize and the amount of deduction Fresh may claim (ignore payroll taxes):

a. Matt selects the single health insurance and places $10,000 in his 401(k).

b. Matt selects the single health insurance, is reimbursed $5,000 for MBA tuition, and places the remainder in his 401(k).

c. Matt selects the single health insurance and is reimbursed for MBA tuition of $10,000.

d. Matt gets married and selects the health insurance with his spouse and takes the rest in cash to help pay for the wedding.

e. Matt's spouse gets better benefits than he does, so he selects $10,000 of 401(k) and the balance in cash.

f. Matt elects to take all cash.

COMPREHENSIVE PROBLEMS

■ planning

58. Pratt is ready to graduate and leave College Park. His future employer offers the following four compensation packages.

Benefit Description	Option 1	Option 2	Option 3	Option 4
Salary	$60,000	$50,000	$45,000	$45,000
Health insurance	$ 0	$ 5,000	$ 5,000	$ 5,000
401(k)	$ 0	$ 5,000	$ 5,000	$ 5,000
Restricted stock	$ 0	$ 0	$ 5,000	$ 0
NQOs				$ 5,000

Assume that the restricted stock is 1,000 shares that trade at $5 per share on the grant date and are expected to be worth $10 per share on the vesting date at the end of Pratt's first year. Assume that the NQOs (100 options that each allow the employee to purchase 20 shares at $5 strike price). The stock trades at $5 per share on the grant date and is expected to be worth $10 per share on the vesting date at the end of Pratt's first year. Also assume that Pratt spends on average $3,000 on health-related costs that would be covered by insurance if he has coverage. Assume that Pratt's marginal tax rate is 35 percent.

a. What is the after-tax value of each compensation package?

b. If Pratt's sole consideration is maximizing after-tax compensation, which scheme should he select?

59. Santini's new contract for 2009 indicates the following compensation and benefits:

Benefit Description	Amount
Salary	$130,000
Health insurance	$ 9,000
401(k) employer match ISOs	$ 6,000
Restricted stock granted	$ 2,500
Bonus	$ 5,000
Hawaii trip	$ 4,000
Group-term life insurance	$ 1,600
Parking ($265 per month)	$ 3,000

Santini is 54 years old at the end of the current year. He is single and has no dependents. Assume that the employer matches $1 for $1 for the first $6,000 that the employee contributes to his 401(k) during the year. The 100 ISOs each allow the purchase of 10 shares of stock at a strike price of $5 (also the market price on the date of grant). The ISOs vest in two years when the stock price is expected to be $15 and Santini expects to sell the shares in three years when the market price is $20. The restricted stock grant is 500 shares granted when the market price was $5 per share. Assume that the stock vests on December 31, 2009, and that the market price on that date is $7.50 per share. Also assume that Santini is willing to make any elections to reduce equity-based compensation taxes. The Hawaii trip was given to him as the outstanding sales person for 2008. The group-term life policy gives him $150,000 of coverage. Assume that Santini does not itemize deductions for the year. Determine Santini's taxable income, income tax liability, and payroll tax liability for 2009.

60. Sylvana is given a job offer with two alternative compensation packages to choose from. The first package offers her $250,000 annual salary with no qualified fringe benefits. The second package offers $235,000 annual salary plus health and life insurance benefits. If Sylvana were required to purchase the health and life insurance benefits herself, she would need to pay $10,000 annually after taxes. Assume her marginal tax rate is 33 percent (Ignore payroll taxes in your analysis.)

■ planning

a. Which compensation package should she choose and by how much would she benefit in after-tax dollars by choosing this package?

b. Assume the second package offers $240,000 plus the benefits instead of $235,000 plus benefits. Which compensation package should she choose and by how much would she benefit in after-tax dollars by choosing this package?

chapter

13

Retirement Savings and Deferred Compensation

Learning Objectives

Upon completing this chapter, you should be able to:

LO 1 Describe the tax and nontax aspects of employer-provided defined benefit plans from both the employer's and employee's perspective.

LO 2 Explain and determine the tax consequences associated with employer-provided defined contribution plans, including traditional 401(k) and Roth 401(k) plans.

LO 3 Describe the tax implications of deferred compensation from both the employer's and employee's perspective.

LO 4 Determine the tax consequences of traditional and Roth Individual Retirement Accounts and explain the differences between them.

LO 5 Describe the retirement savings options available to self-employed taxpayers and compute the limitations for deductible contributions to retirement accounts for self-employed taxpayers.

LO 6 Compute the saver's credit.

Storyline Summary	
Taxpayer:	Tina Hillman
Location:	Chicago, Illinois
Employment status:	Graduating student about to begin career in tax department of Corporate Business Associates
Starting salary:	$60,000 per year
Filing status:	Single
Dependents:	None
Marginal tax rate:	Current year 15 percent, next year 25 percent
Taxpayer:	Lisa Whitlark
Location:	Chicago, Illinois
Employment status:	Recently promoted to Chief Financial Officer (CFO) for Corporate Business Associates
Salary:	$400,000
Marginal tax rate:	33 percent
Dependents:	Spouse and three children
Taxpayer:	Dave Allan
Location:	Chicago, Illinois
Employment status:	Recently retired as CFO for Corporate Business Associates after 20 years of employment with the company
Salary at retirement:	$450,000
Retirement benefits:	Participant in Corporate Business Associates' defined benefit plan, 401(k) plan, and nonqualified deferred compensation plan
Filing status:	Married filing jointly
Dependents:	Spouse
Marginal tax rate:	35 percent for current year
Taxpayer:	Corporate Business Associates (CBA)
Location:	Chicago, Illinois
Marginal tax rate:	35 percent
Status:	Publicly traded corporation

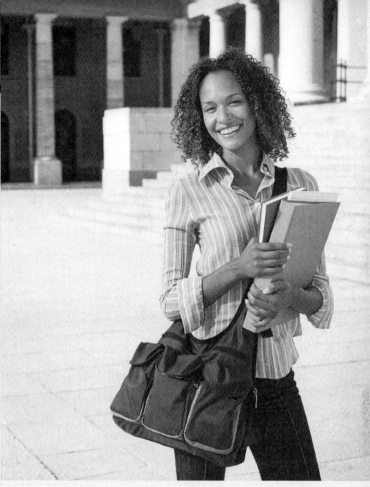

Tina Hillman

Tina Hillman had just completed her last exam, finally fulfilling the requirements for a bachelor's degree in accounting. It was the end of June and she would finally have some time to vacation and see her family before September when she will start her professional career working in the tax department of Corporate Business Associates (CBA). While Tina was looking forward to the time off, she was also anxious to start making money instead of just spending it. She had a great experience during her internship at CBA last year. She had some challenging but enjoyable work assignments and she got along very well with the staff. Overall, she was excited about the work opportunities she would get at CBA.

Tina recently received an information packet on the benefits available to her as a CBA employee. The information indicated that Tina would be

13-1

eligible to participate in CBA's 401(k) plan on January 1 of next year. Tina plans on contributing to the plan as soon as she is eligible because CBA matches employee contributions to the plan dollar for dollar up to 4 percent of each employee's salary. In the meantime, Tina wonders if she has any retirement savings options during the current year while waiting to participate in CBA's plan.

Lisa Whitlark

Lisa Whitlark was finally getting used to her new responsibilities. She was recently promoted to the position of Chief Financial Officer (CFO) for CBA. Lisa threw her name into the ring a few months ago when CBA announced that Dave Allan, the former CFO, would be retiring. Lisa had been working as CBA's tax director for the last 10 years. As a top executive of the company, Lisa was now eligible to participate in CBA's nonqualified deferred compensation program. She didn't have this option as a tax director. Lisa knew she should consider both tax and nontax factors when deciding whether and to what extent she will participate in the plan.

Dave Allan

Dave Allan couldn't believe that he was actually retiring at the end of this year. Looking back, his successful career had passed so quickly. At age 72, he was now ready to move on and spend time seeing the world with his wife. Dave's retirement plans were going to be quite expensive. Fortunately, he had accumulated substantial retirement benefits during his CBA career. Dave would be receiving retirement benefits from CBA's defined benefit plan, 401(k) plan, and nonqualified deferred compensation plan. He knew he had some choices about the timing and amounts of his distributions from these plans. Dave wanted to be sure to evaluate both the tax and nontax considerations before making these decisions. ■

At different stages in their careers, taxpayers are likely to face issues similar to those confronting Tina, Lisa, and Dave. Saving for retirement is not always easy to do because it requires foregoing cash now in order to receive benefits at some point in the future. However, not saving for retirement can be a costly mistake because it's not likely that government-promised Social Security benefits alone will satisfy most taxpayers' retirement needs.[1] Many employers help employees save for retirement by sponsoring retirement plans on behalf of their employees. These plans may be "qualified" retirement plans or "nonqualified" deferred compensation plans. Qualified plans are subject

---

[1] In its 2008 annual report, the board of trustees for the Social Security Trust Fund reported that under our current system, costs will begin to exceed tax income in 2017 and the fund will be exhausted and unable to pay promised benefits beginning in 2041.

to certain restrictions not applicable to nonqualified plans. Both qualified and nonqualified plans are useful tools through which employers can achieve various compensation-related goals. In this chapter, we discuss the tax and nontax consequences of qualified retirement plans and nonqualified plans to both employers and to employees, including issues relating to contributions to and distributions from these plans. We also discuss individually managed retirement savings plans available to certain individual taxpayers and qualified retirement plans available to self-employed taxpayers.

EMPLOYER-PROVIDED QUALIFIED PLANS

Traditional **qualified retirement plans** grew from a Congressional concern that, if unregulated, employers might not adequately fund and protect employee pension benefits and that they might be tempted to provide lavish retirement plans to highly compensated employees such as executives and business owners to the detriment of rank-and-file employees. To address these concerns, Congress mandated that employer-provided plans only receive tax-favored qualified plan status if they meet certain requirements ensuring the plan does not discriminate against rank-and-file employees and if promised benefits are secure. Over the years, the rules addressing these issues have evolved, but the concept of a qualified plan eligible for favorable tax treatment remains the same.

Employer-provided qualified plans can be generally classified as **defined benefit plans** or **defined contribution plans.** As the name suggests, defined benefit plans spell out the specific benefit the employee will receive on retirement. In contrast, defined contribution plans specify the maximum annual contributions that employers and employees may contribute to the plan. While we explore both basic plan types below, we emphasize defined contribution plans because they are much more common than defined benefit plans.

DEFINED BENEFIT PLANS

L01

Defined benefit plans are traditional pension plans used by many older and more established companies and tax-exempt organizations. These plans provide standard retirement benefits to employees based on a fixed formula. The formula to determine the standard retirement benefit is usually a function of years of service and employees' compensation levels as they near retirement. For employees who retire in 2009, the maximum annual benefit an employee can receive is the *lesser* of (1) 100 percent of the average of the employee's three highest years of compensation or (2) $195,000.[2]

THE KEY FACTS

Defined Benefit Plans

∎ Employer specifies benefit employee receives on retirement based on years of service and salary.

(continued)

Example 13-1

CBA provides a defined benefit plan for its employees. The plan uses a fixed formula to determine employee benefits. The formula specifies a benefit of 2 percent for each year of service, up to a maximum of 50 percent (25 years of service), of the average of the employee's three highest years of salary. In 2009, Dave retires from CBA. On the date of retirement, Dave had been a CBA employee for 20 years plus a couple of months. The average of his three highest years of salary was $420,000. What is Dave's annual benefit from the defined benefit plan?

Answer: $168,000 a year. The benefit is calculated by multiplying 40 percent (2 percent for each of his 20 years of service) by $420,000 (the average of his highest three years of salary).

(continued on page 13-4...)

---

[2]IRC §415(b)(1), this maximum benefit is adjusted annually for inflation.

(concluded)

■ Maximum annual benefit for employees who retire in 2009 is the lesser of (1) 100% of the average of the employee's three highest years of compensation or (2) $195,000.

■ Employee must vest to receive benefits using
· 5-year cliff vesting schedule
· 7-year graded vesting schedule

What if: Assume the same facts except that Dave's three highest years of salary was $600,000. What is the annual benefit he will receive from the plan?

Answer: $195,000. The lesser of (1) $240,000 ($600,000 × 40%) or (2) $195,000.

Vesting

We've discussed the idea that an employee's benefit is based on the number of years she works for an employer. When an employee works for an employer for only a short time before leaving, her benefit depends on her salary, the number of full years she worked for the employer, and the employer's vesting schedule. **Vesting** is the process of becoming legally entitled to a certain right or property. Thus, a taxpayer vests (becomes legally entitled to retirement benefits) as she meets certain requirements set forth by the employer. The most restrictive vesting requirements an employer can impose on a qualified defined benefit plan is either a five-year "cliff" or seven-year graded vesting schedule.[3] Under the **cliff vesting** option, after a certain period of time, benefits vest all at once. With a **graded vesting** schedule, the employee's vested benefit increases each year she works for the employer. Exhibit 13-1 features the five-year cliff and seven-year graded vesting schedules for defined benefit plans.

Example 13-2

What if: As we described in Example 13-1, CBA provides a defined benefit plan to its employees. Under the plan, employees earn a benefit equal to 2 percent of their average salary for their three highest years of compensation for every year of service. CBA implements a seven-year graded vesting schedule as part of the plan. If Tina works for CBA for four years, earning annual salaries of $60,000, $65,000, $70,000, and $75,000, and then leaves to work for another employer, what benefit would she be entitled to receive (her vested benefit)?

Answer: $2,240, computed as follows:

Description	Amount	Explanation
(1) Average of three highest years of salary	$70,000	($65,000 + 70,000 + 75,000)/3.
(2) Benefit percentage	× 8%	Four years of service × 2 percent per year.
(3) Full annual benefit	$ 5,600	(1) × (2).
(4) Vesting percentage	× 40%	Four years of service on 7-year graded vesting schedule (See Exhibit 13-1).
Vested benefit	$ 2,240	(3) × (4) Amount that she is allowed to keep.

Tina would forfeit her unvested benefit of $3,360 ($5,600 − $2,240 vested benefit).

What if: Assume the same facts except that CBA uses a five-year cliff schedule. What would be Tina's vested benefit?

Answer: $0. She did not work for CBA for five years so she would not vest in CBA's defined benefit plan.

---

[3]§411(a) specifies maximum vesting periods for employer contributions to qualified plans. Employers are allowed to adopt more generous vesting requirements if they choose (e.g., immediate vesting).

EXHIBIT 13-1   Defined Benefit Plans Minimum Vesting Schedules*

Full Years of Service	5-year Cliff	7-year Graded
1	0%	0%
2	0%	0%
3	0%	20%
4	0%	40%
5	100%	60%
6	N/A	80%
7	N/A	100%

*Percent of employee benefit no longer subject to forfeiture.

Funding, Accounting, and Plan Maintenance

To ensure that employers are able to meet their defined benefit plan obligations, employers are required to annually contribute enough to the plan to fund their expected future liabilities under the plan. The amount of the required annual contribution to a plan is based on certain assumptions about the number of participants in the plan, the life expectancies and expected retirement age of those covered under the plan, and the anticipated tax-exempt rate of return earned by contributions to the plan. The required contribution is determined on an aggregate basis rather than employee-by-employee.

To account for defined benefit plans in their *financial statements,* employers compare anticipated returns from pension assets with expected pension costs, given the attributes of plan participants, to determine the amount of pension expense (if expected costs exceed anticipated returns) or pension income (if anticipated returns exceed expected costs) to record each year. Under this approach, the measurement of anticipated returns and future pension costs is dependent on actuarial and management estimates. In contrast, for tax purposes, employers deduct *actual contributions* to the plan for a given year as long as they make the contributions by the extended tax return due date for that year.[4] Because the process for determining annual required contributions differs markedly from the method used to determine pension expense on the books, tax expense may be greater than or less than book expense from year to year, depending on the circumstances of the particular employer.

From a nontax perspective, a defined benefit plan imposes administrative burdens and risks on the employer sponsoring the plan. A significant amount of work is required to track employee benefits and to compute required contributions to the plan. Because defined benefit plans require employers to provide particular benefits to employees on retirement, the employer bears the investment risk associated with investments within the plan. Beyond the additional administrative costs and risk, defined benefit plans impose significant funding costs on employers relative to alternative retirement plans. Consequently, in recent years, many employers have begun replacing defined benefit plans with defined contribution plans.

Distributions

When their benefits have vested, employees are entitled to receive future distributions according to the provisions of the plan—these distributions are taxable as ordinary income in the year received.[5] Distributions from defined benefit plans (and defined contribution plans) are subject to early distribution requirements and to minimum

THE KEY FACTS

Defined Benefit Plans

- Employer must annually fund expected future liability under plan.
  - Employer, not employee, bears investment risk of plan.
- Early and minimum distribution rules apply, but usually not restrictive.

[4]IRC §404(a)(6).

[5]Distributions of both defined benefit plans and defined contribution plans are reported to taxpayers on Form 1099R.

distribution requirements. Distributions violating these requirements are penalized. However, because defined benefit plans typically don't permit payout arrangements that would trigger the early distribution or minimum distribution penalties, these penalties are of greater concern to participants in defined contribution plans. Consequently, we address these penalties in more detail when we discuss distributions from defined contribution plans.

L02

DEFINED CONTRIBUTION PLANS

THE KEY FACTS

Traditional Defined Contribution Plans: Overview

■ Employer specifies amount it will contribute to employee's retirement account, *not* the amount the employee will receive at retirement.
· Employers typically match employee contributions.

■ Employee chooses how funds are invested and bears market risk.

Defined contribution plans provide an alternative approach for employers to help employees save for retirement. While defined contribution plans and defined benefit plans have similar overall objectives, they are different in important ways. First, employers maintain separate accounts for *each* employee participating in a defined contribution plan. Second, defined contribution plans specify the up-front contributions the employer will make to the employee's separate account rather than specifying the ultimate benefit the employee will receive from the plan. Third, employees are frequently allowed to contribute to their own defined contribution plans, and in many instances they contribute more than their employers. Finally, employees are generally free to choose how amounts in their retirement accounts are invested. If investments in the plan perform well, employees benefit; if the investments perform poorly, employees suffer the financial consequences. Thus, relative to defined benefit plans, defined contribution plans shift the funding responsibility and investment risk from the employer to the employee.

Taxes in the Real World *Retirement Benefits*

More Companies Ending Promises for Retirement

New York Times
By Mary Williams Walsh

January 9, 2006

The death knell for the traditional company pension has been tolling for some time now. Companies in ailing industries like steel, airlines and auto parts have thrown themselves into bankruptcy and turned over their ruined pension plans to the federal government.

Now, with the recent announcements of pension freezes by some of the cream of corporate America—Verizon, Lockheed Martin, Motorola and, just last week, I.B.M.—the bell is tolling even louder. Even strong, stable companies with the means to operate a pension plan are facing longer worker lifespans, looming regulatory and accounting changes and, most important, heightened global competition. Some are deciding they either cannot, or will not, keep making the decades-long promises that a pension plan involves.

I.B.M. was once a standard-bearer for corporate America's compact with its workers, paying for medical expenses, country clubs and lavish Christmas parties for the children. It also rewarded long-serving employees with a guaranteed monthly stipend from retirement until death.

Most of those perks have long since been scaled back at I.B.M. and elsewhere, but the pension freeze is the latest sign that today's workers are, to a much greater extent, on their own. Companies now emphasize 401(k) plans, which leave workers responsible for ensuring that they have adequate funds for retirement and expose them to the vagaries of the financial markets.

"I.B.M. has, over the last couple of generations, defined an employer's responsibility to its employees," said Peter Capelli, a professor of management at the Wharton School of Business at the University of Pennsylvania. "It paved the way for this kind of swap of loyalty for security."

Mr. Capelli called the switch from a pension plan to a 401(k) program "the most visible manifestation of the shifting of risk onto employees." He added: "People just have to deal with a lot more risk in their lives, because all these things that used to be more or less assured—a job, health care, a pension—are now variable."

Employers may provide different types of defined contribution plans such as 401(k) (used by for-profit companies), 403(b) plans (used by nonprofit organizations, including educational institutions), and 457 plans (used by government agencies), profit sharing plans, and money purchase pension plans.[6] Employers may even offer multiple defined contribution plans. Because of their popularity, we use 401(k) plans here to represent the general category of defined contribution plans. However, no matter what defined contribution plan(s) employers provide, employers must ensure that they meet certain requirements relating to annual contribution limits and vesting requirements. Also, to a greater extent than with defined benefit plans, *participants* in defined contribution plans must be careful to avoid the penalties associated with either early distributions or insufficient **minimum distributions** from these plans. Although, minimum distribution requirements have been suspended for 2009 distributions under the Worker, Retiree, and Employer Recovery Act of 2008 passed in December of 2008.

Employer Matching

Employers, but not employees, typically contribute to certain defined contribution plan types such as profit sharing (contributions may be made based on a fixed formula based on profits or may be at the employer's discretion) and money purchase plans (contributions are a fixed percentage of the employee's compensation). In contrast, employees contribute to 401(k) type plans. Many employers also "match" employee contributions to these plans. When deciding whether to contribute to a 401(k) plan, employees should take into account their employer's matching policy. For companies matching employee contributions, the match can range from a small percentage (25 cents on the dollar) to a multiple of the employee's contribution.[7] A dollar-for-dollar match gives employees a 100 percent immediate return on their contributions. Therefore, whenever possible, employees should contribute enough to receive the full match from the employer because, subject to the employer's vesting requirements, the match represents an immediate, no-risk return on the amount contributed.

Example 13-3

Tina's offer from CBA includes participation in its 401(k) plan effective the beginning of next year. The plan's formula provides that CBA will match employee contributions on a two-for-one basis up to employee contributions of 4 percent of the employee's annual salary. Next year when she's eligible, Tina will contribute 4 percent of her salary to the plan. Assuming a $60,000 salary for next year, how much will Tina contribute and how much will CBA contribute to Tina's 401k account?

Answer: Tina will contribute $2,400 ($60,000 × 4%) to her 401(k) plan and CBA will contribute $4,800 ($2,400 × 2).

Contribution Limits

For 2009, the sum of employer *and* employee contributions to an employee's defined contribution account(s) is limited to the *lesser* of (1) $49,000 ($54,500 for employees who are at least 50 years of age by the end of the year) or (2) 100 percent of the employee's compensation for the year.[8] *Employee* contributions to an employee's 401(k) account are limited to $16,500 (or $22,000 for employees that reach age 50 by the end of the year).[9] While this limit applies only to employee contributions, the $49,000 (or $54,500) limit still applies to the sum of employer and employee

THE KEY FACTS

Traditional Defined
Contribution Plans:
Contribution Limits

■ 2009 overall contribution limits for sum of employer and employee contributions.
· Lesser of $49,000 ($54,500 for employees 50 years old by year-end) or 100 percent of employee's annual compensation.

■ 2009 employee contribution limit to 401(k) plan:
· $16,500 or
· $22,000 for employees 50 years old by year-end.

---

[6]401(k), 403(b), and 457 plans reflect the code sections describing the plans.
[7]For example, Chevron contributes $4 to its 401(k) plan for every $1 contributed by its employees.
[8]Section 415(c)(1). However, the amount is indexed for inflation under §415(d)(1)(C).
[9]Section 402(g)(1). However, the amount is indexed for inflation under §402(g)(4).

contributions. For example, if an employee under age 50 contributes the maximum $16,500 to her employer-sponsored 401(k) plan in 2009, the employer's contribution would be limited to $32,500 ($49,000 − $16,500).[10] Because of this limit on employer contributions, highly compensated employees may not be able to receive the full employer match available to other employees.

Example 13-4	

Before Dave retires at the end of 2009 he continues to contribute to his CBA-sponsored 401(k) plan. CBA matches employee contributions on a two-for-one basis up to 4 percent of the employee's salary. Dave is 72 years old at the end of the year and he earned a salary of $450,000 during the year. Dave contributed $22,000 to his 401(k) account. How much would CBA contribute to Dave's 401(k) account?

Answer: $32,500 [$54,500 (Dave is 50+ years old) minus $22,000 (Dave's contribution)]. Without the limitation, CBA would have contributed $36,000 ($450,000 × 4% × 2) to Dave's account.

What if: Assume Dave contributed $20,000 to his 401(k) account. How much would CBA contribute to his account?

Answer: $34,500. Note that this is a better deal for Dave because $54,500 ends up in his account either way, but he only funded $20,000 of the contribution instead of $22,000.

Vesting

When employees contribute to defined contribution plans, they *immediately* vest in their *own* contributions. However, employees vest in employer contributions based on the employer's vesting schedule. The minimum vesting requirements for defined contribution plans are a bit more accelerated than the five-year cliff and seven-year graded vesting schedules applicable to defined benefit plans. For defined contribution plans, employers have the option of providing three-year cliff or six-year graded vesting. These vesting schedules are presented in Exhibit 13-2.

After-Tax Cost of Contributions

Employees effectively deduct their contributions to defined contribution plans, except for Roth 401(k) plans (discussed below), because contributions are removed from their taxable salary.[11] When employees contribute to traditional defined

EXHIBIT 13-2 **Defined Contribution Plans Minimum Vesting Schedules***

Full Years of Service with Employer	3-year Cliff	6-year Graded
1	0%	0%
2	0%	20%
3	100%	40%
4	N/A	60%
5	N/A	80%
6	N/A	100%

*Percent of employer contributions no longer subject to forfeiture.

[10]If an employee participates in more than one defined contribution plan, these limits apply to the total employee and employer contributions to all defined contribution plans. Thus, in a situation where the employee participates in more than one defined contribution plan, the contribution limits for any one defined contribution plan may be less than the overall contribution limits described here.

[11]While employee contributions to defined contribution plans are excluded from the employee's W-2 income for regular tax purposes, contributions to these plans do not reduce the employee's income subject to FICA taxes. That is, the employee will pay the same FICA taxes no matter how much the employee contributes to a defined contribution plan.

contribution plan accounts, they are contributing "before-tax" dollars because the contribution represents the cost of the contribution before considering the tax savings generated by the contribution. The employee's after-tax contribution (or after-tax cost of making the contribution) is the before-tax contribution minus the tax savings generated by the contribution.

Example 13-5

In Example 13-3, Tina contributed $2,400 to her CBA-sponsored traditional 401(k) account in her first full calendar year with CBA. Given Tina's marginal tax rate of 25 percent, what is the after-tax cost of her $2,400 contribution?

Answer: $1,800 computed as follows:

Description	Amount	Explanation
(1) Before-tax contribution	$2,400	Cost of contribution before tax savings.
(2) Tax savings from contribution	(600)	$2,400 deduction × 25 percent marginal tax rate.
After-tax cost of contribution	$1,800	(1) − (2).

Distributions

When employees receive distributions from defined contribution plans (other than Roth 401(k) plans), the distributions are taxed as ordinary income. However, when employees receive distributions (or take withdrawals) from defined contribution plans either too early or too late, they must pay a penalty in addition to the ordinary income taxes they owe on the distributions. Generally, employees who receive distributions before they reach (1) 59½ years of age or (2) 55 years of age *and* have separated from service (retired or let go) are subject to a 10 percent nondeductible penalty on the amount of the early distributions.

Example 13-6

What if: Assume that when she reaches 60 years of age, Lisa Whitlark retires from CBA and receives a $60,000 distribution from her 401(k) account in the year she retires. Assuming her marginal ordinary tax rate is 33 percent, what amount of tax will Lisa pay on the distribution?

Answer: $19,800 ($60,000 × 33%).

What if: Assume that when Lisa is 57 years of age and still employed by CBA, she requests and receives a $60,000 distribution from her 401(k) account. What amount of tax and penalty is Lisa required to pay on the distribution?

Answer: $19,800 taxes ($60,000 × 33%) + $6,000 penalty ($60,000 × 10%).

What if: Assume that Lisa is fired from CBA when she is 57 years old. In that same year, she requests and receives a $60,000 distribution from her 401(k) account. What amount of tax and penalty is Lisa required to pay on the distribution?

Answer: $19,800 taxes ($60,000 × 33%) + $0 penalty (she is over 55 years of age and has separated from service with CBA).

Taxpayers who fail to receive minimum distributions pertaining to years *other than 2009* are also penalized. (Recall that minimum distribution requirements for

EXHIBIT 13-3   **Abbreviated Uniform Lifetime Table**

Age of Participant	Distribution Period	Applicable Percentage*
70	27.4	3.65%
71	26.5	3.77%
72	25.6	3.91%
73	24.7	4.05%
74	23.8	4.20%
75	22.9	4.37%
76	22.0	4.54%
77	21.2	4.72%

*The applicable percentage is calculated by dividing one by the relevant distribution period.

distributions pertaining to 2009 were suspended under the "Worker, Retiree, and Employer Recovery Act of 2008" enacted in December of 2008.) Taxpayers must receive distributions from the plan *for* the year in which the employee reaches 70½ years of age or the year in which the employee retires, if later (2009 excluded). Taxpayers may defer receiving the first required distribution until April 1 of the later of (1) the year after the year in which the employee reaches 70½ years of age or (2) the year after the year in which the employee retires.[12] Minimum distributions pertaining to subsequent years generally must be made by the end of the years to which they pertain.

The amount of the minimum required distribution for a particular year is the taxpayer's account balance at the end of the year prior to the year to which the distribution pertains multiplied by a percentage from an IRS Uniform Lifetime Table. The percentage is based on the taxpayer's age at the end of the year to which the distribution pertains. An abbreviated version of the table is presented in Exhibit 13-3.[13]

Example 13-7

What if: Suppose that Dave retires from CBA in 2008 at age 72. When must Dave receive his minimum distribution for 2008 from his 401(k) account?

Answer: By April 1, 2009.

What if: Assuming Dave's 401(k) account balance on December 31, 2007, was $3,500,000, what is the amount of the minimum distribution Dave must receive by April 1, 2009?

Answer: $136,850 ($3,500,000 × 3.91%). The percentage from the IRS table for determining this minimum distribution is based on Dave's age at the end of 2008, which is 72 years old.

What if: Assuming Dave's 401(k) account balance on December 31, 2008, is $3,700,000, what is the minimum distribution Dave must receive sometime during 2009 (in addition to the $136,850 distribution by April 1)?

Answer: $0. The minimum distribution requirements for 2009 distributions were suspended. If they had not been suspended, Dave would have been required to receive an additional distribution of $149,850 for 2009 ($3,700,000 × 4.05%) in 2009.

---

[12]The amount of the required minimum distribution *for the year* in which a retired employee turns 70½ is the same whether the employee receives the distribution in the year she turns 70½ or whether she defers receiving the distribution until the next year (no later than April 1).

[13]See Reg. §1.401(a)(9)-9 Q&A 2 to reference the full version of the table. This table applies in most circumstances.

The consequences for failing to receive timely minimum distributions from defined contribution plans are even more severe than receiving distributions too early. Taxpayers incur a 50 percent nondeductible penalty on the amount of a minimum distribution the employee should have received but did not. For this reason, it is vital that payouts from defined contribution plans be monitored to avoid not only the 10 percent premature distribution penalty, but also the 50 percent penalty for late withdrawals.

Example 13-8

What if: In the previous example, we determined that Dave must receive a minimum distribution of $136,850 from his 401(k) account by April 1, 2009. If Dave does not receive any distribution before April 1, 2009, what penalty will he be required to pay?

Answer: $68,425 ($136,850 × 50%). This nondeductible penalty is a strong incentive to take the required minimum distributions or at least to take the penalty into consideration when developing a distribution plan.

What if: Assume that Dave received his first distribution from his 401(k) account on March 1, 2009, in the amount of $100,000. But, he did not receive any other distributions before April 1, 2009. What penalty is Dave required to pay?

Answer: $18,425 [($136,850 − $100,000) × 50%]

In contrast to defined benefit plans, defined contribution plans often provide distribution options that could trigger the penalty for premature distributions for the uninformed or unwary. For example, an employee who retires (or is fired) and takes a lump-sum distribution from her defined contribution account in a year before the year in which she turns 55 will be subject to a 10 percent early distribution penalty on the entire amount of the distribution. Employees who receive such lump-sum distributions may avoid the 10 percent penalty by electing to "roll over" (deposit) the distributions into one of the individually managed retirement plans we discuss later in this chapter.

After-Tax Rates of Return

For a given before-tax rate of return, the longer the taxpayer defers distributions from a qualified retirement account, the greater the taxpayer's after-tax rate of return on the account, because deferring the distribution reduces the present value of the tax paid on the distribution. Taxpayer's after-tax rates of return are also sensitive to the taxpayer's marginal tax rates at the time she contributes to the plan and at the time she receives distributions from the plan. All else equal, the higher her marginal tax rate at the time she contributes to the plan, the higher the after-tax rate of return (the higher tax rate makes the deduction more valuable), and the lower her marginal tax rate at the time she receives distributions from the plan the higher the after-tax rate of return (the lower rate reduces the taxes on the income).

Of course, any employer contributions to an employee's account, such as CBA's two-for-one matching contributions to Tina's account, significantly increases the after-tax rate of return (and after-tax accumulation) because the contributions increase the employee's after-tax proceeds, but the employee's cost of these contributions is zero.

EXHIBIT 13-4 **Defined Benefit Plan vs. Defined Contribution Plan Summary**

	Defined Benefit Plan	Defined Contribution Plan
Benefits	• Specifies benefit employee receives on retirement. • Maximum benefit in 2009 lesser of (1) 100 percent of average of highest three years compensation or (2) $195,000.	• Specifies the amounts employer and employee contribute to the account. • Ultimate benefit depends on earnings on contributions.
Payout type	• Life annuity. • Lump sum distribution of the present value of standard benefit.	• Life annuity. • Lump sum. • Fixed number of years.
Funding requirements	• Employers fund increase in expected future liability each year.	• No funding requirement other than to make required contributions to employee accounts.
Employer's contributions tax deductible?	• Yes.	• Yes, but limited to 25 percent of aggregate employee annual compensation.
Employee's contributions tax deductible?	• No employee contributions.	• Yes, subject to limitations on the amount that can be contributed [$16,500 ($22,000 if 50 or older) maximum contribution to 401(k) plan in 2009].
Contribution limits	• Not applicable.	• In 2009, lesser of (1) $49,000 ($54,500 for taxpayers at least 50 years of age at end of year) and (2) 100 percent of the employee's compensation for year.
Other factors	• All employees paid from same account. • Heavy administrative burden. • Employer assumes investment risk.	• Separate accounts for each employee. • Employees make investment choices. • Employees assume investment risk.
Vesting requirements	• 5-year cliff or • 7-year graded	• 3-year cliff or • 6-year graded • Employee contributions vest immediately.
Distributions	• Taxed as ordinary income. • No 10 percent penalty if 55 years of age and retired. • Minimum distributions for years other than 2009 required by April 1 of year after the later of (1) year employee reaches 70½ or (2) year employee retires.	• Taxed as ordinary income (except Roth type accounts). • No 10 percent penalty if 55 years of age and retired or otherwise separated from service. • Minimum distributions requirements same as for defined benefit plan.

Exhibit 13-4 summarizes the tax aspects of defined benefit and defined contribution plans.

Roth 401(k) Plans

Employers that provide **traditional 401(k)** plans to employees may also provide **Roth 401(k)** plans. As we discuss below, employee tax consequences for Roth 401(k) plans differ from tax consequences of other traditional defined contribution plans.

When employers provide a Roth 401(k) plan, *employees* may elect to contribute to the Roth 401(k) *instead of or in addition to* contributing to a traditional 401(k) plan. However, *employer* contributions to an employee's 401(k) account must go to the employee's *traditional* 401(k) account rather than the employee's Roth 401(k) account. Consequently, the balance in an employee's Roth 401(k) account must consist of only the employee's contributions and the earnings on those contributions. Because employers providing Roth 401(k) plans to employees are not allowed to contribute to the Roth plan, these employers are required to maintain traditional 401(k) accounts for each employee participating in the Roth 401(k) plan.

In contrast to contributions to traditional 401(k) plans, employee contributions to Roth 401(k) accounts are *not* deductible and, therefore, do not produce any immediate tax savings for employees. Consequently, employees contributing to Roth 401(k) plans are contributing after-tax dollars. That is, employees wanting to contribute a certain amount to a Roth 401(k) plan must earn more than that specified amount in order to have the desired contribution amount remaining *after* paying taxes on the amount they earn. For example, assume an employee in a 20 percent marginal tax bracket wants to contribute $2,000 to a Roth 401(k) plan. To earn the funds to make this contribution, the employee must earn $2,500 before taxes. The tax on the $2,500 of income is $500 ($2,500 × 20%). This leaves the taxpayer with $2,000 after taxes ($2,500 before taxes minus $500 in taxes) to contribute to the Roth 401(k) plan.

Example 13-9

What if: Let's assume that CBA offers a Roth 401(k) plan in addition to its traditional 401(k) plan. In her first full calendar year of employment with CBA, Tina elects to contribute 4 percent of her $60,000 salary to CBA's Roth 401(k) plan instead of CBA's traditional 401(k) plan. What is Tina's after-tax cost of this $2,400 contribution?

Answer: $2,400. Her after-tax cost is her $2,400 contribution because the contribution does not generate any tax savings.

What is Tina's before-tax cost of the contribution? That is, how much did Tina need to earn before taxes to fund the $2,400 after-tax contribution?

Answer: $3,200. Because her marginal tax rate is 25 percent, she needs to earn $3,200 before taxes [$2,400/(1 − .25)] to have $2,400 to contribute to the Roth 401(k) after taxes [$3,200 × (1 − .25)] When she contributes $2,400 *after taxes* to the Roth 401(k), she is contributing $3,200 *before taxes*.

While contributions to Roth 401(k) accounts are not deductible and, as a result, do not generate any current tax savings, *qualified* distributions from a Roth 401(k) account are excluded from gross income. Because contributions to Roth 401(k) accounts are not deductible and distributions from Roth 401(k) accounts are not taxable, the after-tax rate of return on a Roth 401(k) does not depend on marginal tax rates. The after-tax rate of return on a Roth 401(k) account is the same as the before-tax rate of return.

Example 13-10

What if: In the previous example, Tina contributed $2,400 after taxes to her Roth 401(k) account in her first calendar year on the job with CBA. Let's assume that Tina leaves this contribution in the account until she retires in 40 years at the age of 63, that her contribution earns an annual 8 percent before-tax rate of return, and that her marginal tax rate will be 30 percent when she receives the

(*continued on page 13-14...*)

distribution. How much will Tina have accumulated after taxes if she withdraws the initial contribution and all the earnings on the contribution when she retires?

Answer: $52,139 ($2,400 × 1.08^{40}$).

Tina's after-tax rate of return on her $2,400 after-tax contribution is exactly 8 percent, the same as the before-tax rate of return. With a Roth 401(k) the after-tax rate of return should always equal the before-tax rate return because the after-tax cost of the contribution and the after-tax accumulation on distribution are not affected by the taxpayers' marginal tax rates at the time of contribution or at the time of distribution.

Qualified distributions from Roth 401(k) accounts are those made after the employee's account has been open for five taxable years *and* the employee is at least 59½ years of age. All other distributions are nonqualified distributions. When a taxpayer receives a *non*qualified distribution from a Roth 401(k) account, the tax consequences of the distribution depends on the extent to which the distribution is from the account earnings and the extent to which it is from the employee's contributions to the account. Nonqualified distributions of the account *earnings* are fully taxable and are subject to the 10 percent early distribution penalty. Nonqualified distributions of the taxpayer's account *contributions* are not subject to tax because the taxpayer did not deduct these amounts. If less than the entire balance in the plan is distributed, the amount contributed is determined by multiplying the amount distributed the nontaxable portion of the distribution is determined by multiplying by the ratio of contributions in the plan to the total plan balance.

Example 13-11

What if: In the previous example, Tina contributed $2,400 to CBA's Roth 401(k) plan, her account generated an 8 percent before-tax return, and she withdrew the entire balance 40 years after the contribution. Let's assume that after year 6, Tina needs cash, so she withdraws $1,000 from the account when her marginal tax rate is 28 percent. How much tax and penalty, if any, is Tina required to pay on this nonqualified distribution?

Answer: $104 tax and $37 penalty, computed as follows:

Description	Amount	Explanation
(1) Nondeductible contribution to Roth 401(k)	$2,400	Beginning of year 1.
(2) Account balance end of year 6	3,808	$2,400 × 1.08^6$.
(3) Nonqualified distribution end of year 6	1,000	
(4) Percentage of distribution that is not taxable	63.03%	(1)/(2).
(5) Nontaxable portion of distribution	630	(3) × (4).
(6) Taxable portion of distribution	370	(3) − (5).
(7) Marginal tax rate in year 6	28%	
(8) Regular income tax on distribution	**104**	(6) × (7).
(9) Penalty tax percentage for early distributions	10%	
(10) Penalty tax on early distribution	**37**	(6) × (9).
Total tax and penalty on early distribution	**$ 141**	(8) + (10).

Finally, it is important to note that the minimum distribution requirements applicable to traditional 401(k) accounts also apply to Roth 401(k) accounts.

EXHIBIT 13-5   Traditional 401(k) Plan vs. Roth 401(k) Plan Summary

	Traditional 401(k) Plans	Roth 401(k) Plans
Employer contributions allowed	• Yes.	• No.
Tax consequences to employer	• Contributions deductible when paid.	• Not applicable.
Tax consequences to employee	• Contributions are deductible.	• Contributions not deductible.
Distributions	• Taxed as ordinary income. • No 10 percent penalty if 55 years of age and retired. • If life annuity or joint and survivor annuity no penalty even if not 55 years of age. • Minimum distributions for years other than 2009 required by April 1 of the later of (1) the year after the year in which the employee reaches 70½ or (2) the year after the year in which the employee retires. • Failure to meet minimum distribution timing and amount requirements triggers 50 percent penalty. • Nonqualified distributions (i.e., early distributions) trigger ordinary tax and penalty tax on earnings.	• Qualified distributions not taxed. • Qualified distributions when funds in account for 5 years and employee has reached the age of 59½. • Same as for traditional 401(k) plans. • Same as for traditional 401(k) plans. • Same as for traditional 401(k) plans. • If nonqualified distribution, recover contributions based on ratio of contributions to total value of account.

Comparing Traditional Defined Contribution Plans and Roth 401(k) Plans

We've described and discussed the tax consequences associated with participating in traditional and Roth 401(k) plans. So which is better for employees? If given a choice, which type of 401(k) plan should you contribute to? As we've discussed, current and future marginal tax rates are an important factor to consider. In general terms, the traditional 401(k) plans will generate higher (lower) after-tax rates of return than Roth 401(k) plans when taxpayers' marginal tax rates *decrease* (*increase*) from the time of contribution to the time of distribution. Exhibit 13-5 summarizes and compares traditional 401(k) plans and Roth 401(k) plans.

NONQUALIFIED DEFERRED COMPENSATION   `L03`

So far, our discussion has emphasized the tax and nontax aspects of employer-provided *qualified* defined benefit and defined contribution plans. In addition to or perhaps in lieu of these types of qualified plans, employers may offer **nonqualified deferred compensation** plans to certain employees.

Nonqualified Plans vs. Qualified Defined Contribution Plans

Deferred compensation plans permit employees to defer (or contribute) current salary in exchange for a future payment from the employer. From an employee's perspective, the tax consequences of contributions to and distributions from nonqualified plans receive tax treatment similar to qualified defined contribution plans. For example, just as with defined contribution plans, employee contributions to non-qualified deferred compensation plans (NQDC) reduce an employee's taxable income in the year of contribution.[14] Also, just as with qualified plans, employees are not taxed on the balance in their account until they receive distributions. Finally, like distributions from qualified plans, distributions from nonqualified deferred compensation plans are taxed as ordinary income.

Example 13-12

CBA provides a nonqualified deferred compensation plan under which executives may elect to defer up to 10 percent of their salary. Dave Allan has been participating in the plan by deferring a portion of his salary each year for the last 15 years. The balance in his deferred compensation account is currently $2,000,000. In keeping with the fixed payment schedule Dave elected under the plan, he receives a $50,000 distribution. What amount of tax must Dave pay on the distribution (recall that his marginal tax rate is 35 percent)?

Answer: $17,500 ($50,000 × .35).

THE KEY FACTS

Nonqualified Deferred Compensation Plans

■ Employees defer current income in exchange for future payment.
· Employee taxed when payment received.
· Employee generally selects deemed investment choices up front to determine return on deferral.
· Just like traditional deferred compensation plans, after-tax rate of return depends on before-tax rate of return, marginal tax rate at time of deferral, and marginal tax rate at time of distribution.
· Payment not guaranteed. If employer doesn't pay, employee becomes unsecured creditor.

For employers, NQDC plans are treated differently than qualified plans. For example, because nonqualified plans are not subject to the same restrictive requirements pertaining to qualified plans, employers may discriminate in terms of whom they allow to participate in the plan. In fact, employers generally restrict participation in nonqualified plans to more highly compensated employees. Also, employers are not required to "fund" nonqualified plans. That is, employers are not required to formally set aside and accumulate funds specifically to pay the deferred compensation obligation when it comes due. Rather, employers typically retain funds deferred by employees under the plan, use the funds for business operations, and pay the deferred compensation out of their general funds when it becomes payable. Because employers retain, control, and generate income on funds deferred by employees under nonqualified plans, employers are allowed to *deduct only actual payments* of deferred compensation to employees. That is, employers cannot deduct the amount of deferred compensation they accrue each year. Thus, for tax purposes, an employer may not deduct the deferred compensation when an employee initially earns the compensation even though the employer becomes liable for the deferred compensation payment. In contrast, for financial accounting purposes, companies generally expense deferred compensation in the year employees earn it and record a corresponding deferred compensation liability.[15]

Employee Considerations

Should employees participate in nonqualified plans when given the chance? The decision obviously involves several considerations. First, employees must decide if the benefits they expect to receive from qualified retirement plans (or other sources) will be adequate to provide for their expected costs during retirement. Next, employees should consider whether they can afford to defer current salary. This may not be a significant concern for most eligible participants, however, because nonqualified plans are generally available only to highly compensated employees who likely may not have the liquidity concerns that lower-compensated employees may face. Also, employees should consider the expected rate of return on the deferred salary relative to what they could earn on the salary by receiving it currently and personally investing it.

---

[14]Technically, employees participating in NQDC plans defer the receipt of current salary and employers credit the employee's account for the amount of the deferral. This has the same effect as if the employee had actually made a deductible contribution to her account as an employee participating in a defined contribution plan would do.

[15]Employers record additional expense and liability as earnings on the deferred compensation accumulate.

Generally, larger employers allow employees participating in nonqualified plans to choose how their deferred compensation will be invested from among alternative investments provided under the plan (money market, various bond funds, and stock funds among others). However, because employers *do not actually invest* compensation deferred under the plan on the employee's behalf, the employer credits the employee's account "as if" the employee's contributions had been invested in the employee's *deemed* investment choices. The description of Coca-Cola Company's nonqualified retirement plan, presented in Exhibit 13-6, illustrates this concept:

EXHIBIT 13-6   Description of Nonqualified Retirement Plan

Excerpt from proxy statement

The Coca-Cola Company Deferred Compensation Plan (the "DCP") is a non-qualified and unfunded deferred compensation program offered to a select group of U.S. based management or highly compensated employees. Eligible participants may defer up to 80% of base salary. Gains and losses are credited based on the participant's election of a variety of deemed investment choices. The Company **does not** match any employee deferral or guarantee a return. Participants' accounts may or may not appreciate and may even depreciate depending on the performance of their deemed investment choices. . . . All deferrals are paid out in cash upon distribution. . . . Participants may schedule a distribution during employment, or may opt to receive their balance after termination of employment.

Just as with qualified defined contribution plans, other than Roth 401(k) plans, an employee's after-tax rate of return on deferred compensation depends on the employee's investment choices *and* on the employee's marginal tax rates at the time of the contribution and at the time of the distribution.[16]

Example 13-13

As a new executive with CBA, Lisa Whitlark is eligible to participate in its nonqualified deferred compensation plan. Recall that CBA provides a nonqualified deferred compensation plan under which executives may elect to defer up to 10 percent of their salary. In her first year with CBA, Lisa elects to defer $40,000 of salary ($400,000 × 10%) under the plan. Because her current marginal income tax rate is 33 percent, she saves $13,200 in taxes by deferring the salary ($40,000 × 33%). Consequently, her after-tax cost of deferring the compensation is $26,800. She plans to receive a distribution from the nonqualified plan in 20 years when she expects her marginal tax rate to be 28 percent. Lisa selects a stock index fund as her "deemed" investment choice. She expects the fund to provide an 8 percent before-tax rate of return on her $40,000 deferral. What will Lisa receive after-taxes from her $40,000 deferral?

Answer: $134,235 after-tax accumulation, computed as follows:

Description	Amount	Explanation
Before-tax contribution	$ 40,000	Deferral of 10 percent of her current salary.
Times future value factor	$\times 1.08^{20}$	8 percent annual rate of return for 20 years.
Future value of deferred compensation	186,438	Value of deferral/distribution 20 years after deferral.
Minus: taxes payable on distribution	(52,203)	$186,438 value of account × 28 percent marginal tax rate.
After-tax proceeds from distributions	$134,235	Value of account minus taxes payable on distribution.

[16]As discussed previously, after-tax accumulations in Roth 401(k) accounts are not dependent on current and future marginal tax rates.

Deferring salary to a future period is potentially an effective tax planning technique, particularly when the employee anticipates her marginal tax rate to be lower in the year she will receive the deferred compensation than it is in the year she defers the salary. In fact, if employees had complete flexibility as to when they could receive distributions from deferred compensation plans, they would likely accelerate distributions from deferred compensation plans into years they knew with certainty would have relatively low marginal tax rates. This strategy is limited, however, by rules requiring employees to specify the timing of the future payments at the time they decide to participate in deferred compensation plans.[17]

Employees considering participating in nonqualified deferred compensation plans should also consider potential financial risks of doing so. Recall that employers are not required to fund nonqualified plans. So, there's always the possibility that the employer will not have the funds to pay the employee on the scheduled distribution dates (e.g., the employer becomes bankrupt). If the employer is not able to make the payments, the employee becomes an unsecured creditor of the company and may never receive the full compensation owed to her. Consequently, the employee should evaluate the financial stability of the company when deciding whether to defer compensation under the employer's plan.

THE KEY FACTS

Nonqualified Deferred Compensation Plans

■ Employer promises to pay deferred compensation at some point in future.

· Deduct when paid to employee.

· Not required to fund obligation.

· Use to accomplish compensation objectives like avoid $1M deductibility limit on salary and make whole employees who are over contribution limits on qualified plans.

· Employer's marginal tax rates at time of deferral relative to those at time of payment affect after-tax cost of providing deferred compensation relative to current compensation.

Employer Considerations

It's pretty clear that nonqualified plans can provide significant benefits to employees. How might employers benefit from providing nonqualified plans? First, employers may benefit if they are able to earn a better rate of return on the deferred compensation than the rate of return they are required to pay employees participating in the plan. In addition, employers can use nonqualified plans to achieve certain compensation objectives. For example, nonqualified plans could be a component of a compensation package a company may use to attract prospective executives. Also, because deferred compensation is not deductible until it is paid, deferred compensation plans provide a potentially effective way for employers to circumvent the $1 million salary deduction limitation for executives imposed by §162(m) (see Chapter 12 discussion of the limitation). That is, an employer may pay an executive $1 million of current compensation and defer compensation over $1 million to a future period. By doing this, the employer is able to deduct the full $1 million of salary and the entire amount of the deferred compensation as long as the employee has retired at the time the employer pays the deferred compensation. This is because the $1 million deductibility limitation on compensation does not apply if the executive is no longer employed by the company when the company pays the deferred compensation. However, if the executive is still an employee when the deferred compensation is paid, it is subject to the $1 million deduction limit. Exhibit 13-7 provides an excerpt from an IBM proxy statement that mentions the effectiveness of IBM's deferred compensation plan in avoiding the **§162(m) limitation.**

EXHIBIT 13-7 Deferred Compensation and §162(m) Limitation

Excerpt from proxy statement for IBM

The Executive Deferred Compensation Plan permits an executive officer who is subject to section 162(m) and whose salary is above $1 million to defer payment of a sufficient amount of the salary to bring it below the section 162(m) limit.

---

[17]§409A. These rules do provide, however, that specified payments from deferred compensation plans may commence while employees are still employed.

EXHIBIT 13-8   Qualified Plan vs. Nonqualified Plan Summary

	Qualified Plans	Nonqualified Plans
Types	• Defined benefit (Pension). • Defined contribution (401k).	• Deferred compensation.
Requirements	• May not discriminate against "rank and file" employees of the company. • Funding or contribution requirements. • Vesting requirements.	• May discriminate. • Generally provided to executives and highly compensated. • No formal funding requirements (employee essentially unsecured creditor). • No formal vesting requirements.
Tax consequences to employers	• Immediately deduct contributions to plan (amount funded).	• No deduction until paid to employee.
Tax consequences to employees	• Employee contributions deductible unless to Roth-type account. • Employer contributions not immediately taxed. • Earnings deferred until distributed to employee. • Distributions from non-Roth plans treated as ordinary income.	• Employee contributions (or deferrals) deductible. • Taxed as ordinary income when received. • Earnings deferred until distributed to employee.

In the same vein, deferring compensation may be an important tax planning tool for employers in situations where their current marginal tax rates are low (employers currently experiencing net operating losses) and they expect their future marginal tax rates when deferred compensation is paid to be significantly higher (employers expect to return to profitability). In effect, deferring compensation into a year with a higher marginal tax rate increases the after-tax benefit of the compensation deduction, which reduces the after-tax cost of the compensation to the employer.

Exhibit 13-8 summarizes and compares qualified retirement plans and nonqualified deferred compensation plans.

INDIVIDUALLY MANAGED QUALIFIED RETIREMENT PLANS

We've covered tax and nontax issues relating to both qualified and nonqualified employer-sponsored retirement savings plans. However, not all employers provide retirement savings plans, and when they do, some employees may not be eligible to participate, while others who are eligible may elect to not participate in these plans. The tax laws provide opportunities for these taxpayers to provide for their own retirement security through individually managed retirement plans. The **Individual Retirement Account (IRA)** is the most common of the individually managed retirement plans. Other types of individually managed plans are available to self-employed taxpayers.

INDIVIDUAL RETIREMENT ACCOUNTS

L04

Taxpayers who meet certain eligibility requirements can contribute to **traditional IRAs,** to **Roth IRAs,** or to both. Just like traditional and Roth 401(k) plans, traditional IRAs and Roth IRAs have different tax characteristics. In fact, in most respects, the tax characteristics of traditional 401(k) plans mirror those of traditional IRAs and tax characteristics of Roth 401(k) plans mirror those of Roth IRA accounts. To minimize redundancy in this section, we focus on the tax characteristics that differ between employer-sponsored 401(k) plans and self-managed IRAs.

Traditional IRAs

Because the government provides IRAs primarily to help taxpayers who are not able to participate in employer-sponsored retirement plans and to help taxpayers with relatively low levels of income to save for retirement, tax laws restrict who can make *deductible* contributions to traditional IRAs. To be able to deduct contributions to traditional IRAs, taxpayers must (1) *not* be a participant in an employer-sponsored retirement plan or (2) if they are participating in an employer-sponsored plan, they must have income below the thresholds described below.

For taxpayers who do not participate in an employer-sponsored retirement plan, the limit for deductible IRA contributions is $5,000 in 2009 or the amount of *earned* income if it is less.[18, 19] As we discussed in Chapter 5, earned income generally includes income actually earned through the taxpayer's efforts such as wages, salaries, tips, and other employee compensation plus the amount of the taxpayer's net earnings from self-employment. Alimony income is also considered as earned income for this purpose. Taxpayers who are 50 years of age or older at year end may make an additional $1,000 contribution each year in excess of the standard contribution limit. This extra $1,000 limit is granted to allow taxpayers nearing retirement age to "catch up" on contributions they may have not made in previous years.

> **THE KEY FACTS**
>
> Traditional IRAs
>
> ■ 2009 Contribution limit.
> · Lesser of $5,000 or earned income.
> · Taxpayers over 50, lesser of $6,000 or earned income.
>
> ■ If taxpayers participate in employer provided plan:
> · Deduction limit phased-out for single taxpayers with AGI between $55,000 and $65,000 and for married filing jointly taxpayers with AGI between $89,000 and $109,000.
> · Special rules if one spouse covered by plan and other is not.

Example 13-14

In the year she graduated from college, Tina earned $25,000. She earned $5,000 in salary working part-time while she was in school and she earned $20,000 in salary working for CBA from September through December. To get an early start saving for retirement, she decided to contribute $5,000 to a *traditional* IRA. How much of this contribution may Tina deduct?

Answer: $5,000. Because Tina is not participating in an employer-sponsored retirement plan during the current year, Tina may deduct the full $5,000 contribution as a *for* AGI deduction, reducing her AGI from $25,000 to $20,000.

Taxpayers who do participate in an employer-sponsored retirement plan can still make deductible contributions to traditional IRAs subject to certain AGI restrictions. For 2009, unmarried taxpayers with an AGI of $55,000 and below and married taxpayers filing jointly with AGI of $89,000 and below can make fully deductible contributions to an IRA account, subject to the $5,000 overall deduction limitation (or $6,000 if age 50 or older). The $5,000 deduction limitation is phased-out *proportionally* for single taxpayers with AGI between $55,000 and $65,000 and for married taxpayers filing jointly with AGI between $89,000 and $109,000.

---

[18]Lump-sum distributions from qualified plans other than Roth 401(k)s received prior to retirement are frequently rolled over into traditional IRA accounts to avoid the 10 percent premature distribution penalty and current taxation. Rollover contributions are not subject to normal contribution limits for traditional IRAs.

[19]The IRA contribution limit is indexed for inflation.

Example 13-15

In her first full calendar year working for CBA, Tina earns $60,000. Because she contributes $2,400 of her salary to CBA's 401(k) plan, her AGI is $57,600 ($60,000 − $2,400). Tina also would like to make the maximum deductible contribution to her IRA. How much is she allowed to deduct?

Answer: $3,700. The deductible amount before considering AGI limitations is $5,000. However, because Tina is a participant in CBA's retirement plan, the $5,000 deduction limit is subject to phase-out. Because Tina's AGI is 26 percent of the way through the $55,000 − $65,000 phase-out range for a single taxpayer ($2,600/10,000), the $5,000 deductible contribution limit is reduced by 26 percent to $1,760 [$5,000 × (1 − .26)]. So, $3,700 is the maximum deductible contribution she can make to her traditional IRA.

When the $5,000 deductible limitation is phased-out, taxpayers can still make *nondeductible* contributions to reach the $5,000 contribution limit. While these contributions are not deductible, the earnings on the contributions grow tax-free until the taxpayer receives distributions from the IRA. On distribution, the taxpayer is taxed on the earnings generated by the nondeductible contributions but not on the actual nondeductible contributions. When taxpayers take partial distributions from an IRA to which they have made deductible and nondeductible contributions, each distribution consists of a taxable and nontaxable component. The portion of the distribution that is nontaxable is the ratio of the nondeductible contributions to the entire balance in the account at the time of the distribution (nondeductible contributions divided by the entire balance in account). This is exactly the same procedure we used in Example 13-11 to determine the nontaxable portion of nonqualified distributions from Roth 401(k) accounts. Most taxpayers exceeding the deductibility limits on traditional IRAs would likely do better by contributing to a Roth IRA (discussed below), if eligible, instead of making nondeductible contributions to traditional IRAs.

When an employed taxpayer is not participating in an employer-sponsored retirement plan, that taxpayer's unemployed spouse is allowed to contribute to a deductible IRA. Consequently, the couple may jointly contribute up to $10,000 to IRAs for the year ($5,000 for each spouse). To qualify for the full $10,000 contribution, the income-earning spouse must have at least $10,000 of earned income for the year. If one spouse is covered under a qualified plan but the other spouse is not, the uncovered spouse is allowed to contribute up to $5,000 to a traditional IRA. However, the maximum amount deductible for the uncovered spouse is phased-out proportionally for couples with AGI between $166,000 and $176,000.

Taxpayers who are eligible to contribute to an IRA may contribute to the IRA up to April 15 (the unextended tax return due date). That is, as long as the taxpayer makes a contribution to the IRA by April 15 of year 2, the contribution counts as though it were made during year 1 (the prior calendar year).

> ### THE KEY FACTS
> **Traditional IRAs**
>
> ∎ If taxpayer does not participate in employer provided plan but spouse does
> · Deduction limit phased out for AGI between $166,000 and $176,000.
>
> ∎ Distribution taxed as ordinary income
> · If distribution before taxpayer is 59½, 10 percent penalty generally applies.

Distributions   Just as with traditional 401(k) plans, distributions from traditional IRAs are taxed as ordinary income to the taxpayer. Also, taxpayers withdrawing funds from traditional IRAs before reaching the age of 59½ are subject to a 10 percent early distribution penalty on the amount of the withdrawal. The IRA rules exempt certain distributions from the 10 percent penalty for early withdrawal. Among others, these distributions include proceeds distributed in the form of a life annuity and proceeds used for qualifying medical expenses, health insurance premiums for the owner, qualified higher education expenses, or first-time home purchases.[20] Taxpayers are also subject to the same minimum distribution requirements applicable to traditional 401(k) and other qualified retirement plans. Because the distribution rules for traditional IRAs are so similar to the rules for traditional 401(k) accounts,

---

[20]§72(t).

taxpayers with traditional IRAs face virtually the same issues as participants in traditional 401(k) plans when planning for distributions. Thus, they should be careful to avoid the 10 percent penalty while at the same time taking similar steps to maximize the tax deferral on their traditional IRA account balances.

Roth IRAs

As an alternative to deductible IRAs, taxpayers meeting certain requirements can contribute to Roth IRAs. Contributions to Roth IRAs are *not* deductible and *qualifying* distributions from Roth IRAs are *not* taxable. Roth IRAs are subject to the same annual contribution limits as traditional IRAs ($5,000 in 2009; $6,000 if 50 years of age or older).[21]

Whether or not they participate in an employer-sponsored retirement plan, taxpayers are allowed to contribute to Roth IRAs as long as their AGI does not exceed specified thresholds. For unmarried taxpayers filing for 2009, the $5,000 Roth IRA contribution limitation (or $6,000 if age 50 and older) phases out proportionally for AGI between $105,000 and $120,000. For married taxpayers filing joint returns for 2009, the contribution limit phases out for AGI between $166,000 and $176,000. For married taxpayers filing separately, the limit on Roth IRA contributions phases out between AGI of $0 and $10,000.

Distributions   *Qualifying* distributions from Roth IRAs are not taxable. A qualifying distribution is a distribution from funds or earnings from funds in a Roth IRA *if the distribution is at least five years after the taxpayer has opened the Roth IRA*[22] *and the distribution is* (1) made on or after the date the taxpayer reaches 59½ years of age, (2) made to a beneficiary (or to the estate of the taxpayer) on or after the death of the taxpayer, (3) attributable to the taxpayer being disabled, *or* (4) used to pay qualified acquisition costs for first-time homebuyers (limited to $10,000). All other distributions are considered to be *nonqualified* distributions.

Nonqualified distributions are not necessarily taxable, however. Because taxpayers contributing to a Roth IRA contribute after-tax dollars (they don't deduct the contribution), they are able to withdraw the contributions tax-free at any time. However, *nonqualified* distributions of the *earnings* of a Roth IRA are taxable as ordinary income and subject to a 10 percent penalty. Nonqualified distributions are deemed to come first from the taxpayer's contributions and then from the earnings after the total contributions have been distributed. Thus, taxpayers can treat the Roth IRA as an emergency savings account to the extent of their contributions without incurring any penalties.

Example 13-16

What if: Assume that when Tina started working for CBA, she made a one-time contribution of $4,000 to a Roth IRA. Years later, she retired at the age of 65 when the value of her Roth account was $60,000. If Tina receives a $10,000 distribution from her Roth IRA, what amount of taxes (and penalty, if applicable) must she pay on the distribution (assume her ordinary marginal rate is 30 percent)?

Answer: $0 taxes and $0 penalty. Qualified Roth IRA distributions are not taxable.

What if: Assume the same facts as above, except that Tina received a $10,000 distribution when she was 57 years of age. What amount of taxes (and penalty, if applicable) is she required to pay on the distribution (assume a 30 percent ordinary marginal rate)?

(continued on page 13-23...)

---

[21]Participants in Roth 401(k) accounts receiving distributions subject to the 10% premature distribution penalty and current taxation may avoid this outcome by rolling their distributions into a Roth IRA account. In this event, the normal Roth IRA contribution limit does not apply.

[22]The five-year period starts on January 1 of the year in which the contribution was made and ends on the last day of the fifth taxable year.

Answer: $1,800 in total consistng of $1,200 in taxes ($4,000 earnings distributed × 30 percent marginal tax rate) and $600 penalty ($6,000 earnings × 10 percent penalty rate). Because Tina has not reached age 59½ at the time of the distribution, this is a disqualified distribution. Consequently, she is taxed and penalized on the $6,000 distribution of earnings ($10,000 distribution minus $4,000 contribution).

What if: Assume that when Tina was 62 years old, she opened a Roth IRA, contributing $4,000. Three years later, Tina withdrew the entire account balance of $5,000. What amount of taxes (and penalty, if applicable) must Tina pay on the distribution (assume her marginal tax rate is 30 percent)?

Answer: $400 in total consting of $300 taxes ($1,000 earnings × 30 percent marginal tax rate) and $100 penalty ($1,000 earnings × 10 percent penalty rate). The distribution is a disqualified distribution because Tina did not have the Roth IRA open for five years before receiving the distribution. Consequently, she must pay taxes and penalties on the $1,000 account earnings ($5,000 − $4,000).

> **THE KEY FACTS**
>
> Roth IRAs
>
> ■ Rollovers from traditional IRAs to Roth IRAs.
> · Amount withdrawn from traditional IRA fully taxable but not penalized.
> · Must contribute full amount withdrawn to Roth IRA account within 60 days of withdrawal.
> · Amounts withdrawn but not contributed subject to tax and 10 percent penalty.

In contrast to taxpayers with traditional IRAs, taxpayers are *not ever* required to take minimum distributions from Roth IRAs. Thus, taxpayers can minimize distributions from Roth IRAs to maintain a source of tax-free income for as long as possible.

Rollover from Traditional to Roth IRA

Many taxpayers made contributions to traditional IRAs before Roth IRAs were available. Some taxpayers may have contributed to traditional IRAs and then later decided they should have contributed to a Roth IRA. The tax laws accommodate these taxpayers by allowing them to transfer funds from a traditional IRA to a Roth IRA. This transfer of funds is called a **rollover.** When taxpayers do this, however, the entire amount taken out of the traditional IRA is taxed at ordinary rates but is not subject to the 10 percent penalty tax as long as the taxpayer contributes the *full amount* to a Roth IRA within 60 days of the withdrawal from the traditional IRA.

Example 13-17

What if: Let's assume that in the year she graduated from college and began working for CBA, Tina made a fully deductible $4,000 contribution to a *traditional* IRA account. Three years later, when her marginal tax rate is 25 percent, she decides to roll over the entire $5,000 account balance into a Roth IRA. What amount of taxes is she required to pay on the rollover?

Answer: $1,250 ($5,000 × 25%). The entire $5,000 transferred from the IRA to the Roth IRA is taxed at 25 percent but is not subject to the 10 percent early withdrawal penalty. Even though Tina pays $1,250 in taxes on the transfer, she is required to contribute $5,000 to the Roth IRA within 60 days from the time she withdraws the money from the traditional IRA.

What if: What are the tax consequences if Tina pays the $1,250 tax bill and contributes only $3,750 to the Roth IRA account?

Answer: She must pay a $125 penalty. The penalty is 10 percent of the $1,250 that she withdrew from the IRA and did not contribute to the Roth IRA ($5,000 − $3,750).

Why would anyone be willing to pay taxes currently in order to avoid paying taxes later? Typically, a rollover from a traditional to a Roth IRA makes sense when taxpayers' marginal rates are currently low (when the tax costs of the rollover are low) and expected to be significantly higher in the future (when the expected benefits of the rollover are great). The option to roll over traditional IRAs into Roth IRAs is currently not available to taxpayers with AGI over $100,000. However, beginning in 2010, the AGI restriction disappears, providing higher-income taxpayers with the option to roll over amounts in traditional IRAs into Roth IRAs.

Comparing Traditional and Roth IRAs

So, which type of IRA is better for taxpayers? The tax considerations are very similar to those we already discussed when we compared traditional and Roth 401(k) plans. In general, after-tax returns from traditional IRAs will exceed those from Roth IRAs when marginal tax rates are expected to decline.[23] However, after-tax rates of return from Roth IRAs will exceed those from traditional IRAs when tax rates are expected to increase.

Unrelated to marginal tax rates, Roth IRAs have several advantages relative to traditional IRAs. Taxpayers can contribute to Roth IRAs at any age. In contrast, taxpayers are not allowed to make deductible contributions to traditional IRAs once they have reached 70½ years of age. Also, as noted earlier, the minimum distribution requirements for traditional IRAs do not apply to Roth IRAs. This provision permits owners of Roth IRAs to use their accounts to generate tax-free returns long after retirement. Exhibit 13-9 summarizes tax-related requirements for traditional and Roth IRAs.

EXHIBIT 13-9 **Traditional IRA vs. Roth IRA Summary**

	Traditional IRA	Roth IRA
Contributions requirements	• Taxpayer must not be a participant in an employer-sponsored plan or, if participating in an employer-provided plan, must meet certain income thresholds. Those above the threshold will have deductible portion of contribution phased-out.	• No deduction allowed for contributions. Must meet certain income requirements to be able to contribute to a Roth IRA.
Contributions	• Deductible unless participant in employer plan and high AGI. • Nondeductible contributions allowed.	• Not deductible. • May not contribute if high AGI.
Maximum contribution	• Lesser of $5,000 per taxpayer ($6,000 for taxpayers over 50 years old) or earned income.	• Same as traditional IRA.
Contribution dates	• Can contribute up to unextended tax return due date—generally April 15.	• Same as traditional IRA.
Distributions	• Generally taxed as ordinary income. • If made before 59½, generally subject to 10 percent penalty. • If nondeductible contribution made, allocate distribution between taxable and nontaxable amounts similar to annuity rules. • Minimum distributions for years other than 2009 required by April 1 of the later of (1) the year after the year in which the taxpayer reaches 70½ or (2) the year after the year in which the taxpayer retires. • Failure to meet minimum distribution timing and amount requirements triggers 50 percent penalty.	• Qualified distributions not taxed. • Generally, distributions are qualified after account open for five years and employee has reached the age of 59½. • Nonqualified distributions not taxed to extent of prior contributions. • Nonqualified distributions of earnings subject to tax at ordinary rates and 10 percent penalty. • No minimum distribution requirements.

[23]Under certain conditions, after-tax returns from Roth IRAs may exceed those from traditional IRAs even when tax rates are expected to be constant or to drop. See "Trimming Your Taxes: Why Roth 401(k)s Often Beat Conventional 401(k) Plans," *The Wall Street Journal,* September 6, 2006.

SELF-EMPLOYED RETIREMENT ACCOUNTS

We've discussed retirement savings opportunities available to employees. However, many taxpayers are self-employed small business owners who do not have access to employer-sponsored plans.[24] Moreover, individually managed retirement plans such as traditional and Roth IRAs are not particularly attractive to self-employed taxpayers due to the relatively low contribution limits on these plans. What retirement savings options, then, are available to the self-employed?

To help these self-employed taxpayers save for retirement, Congress created a number of retirement savings plans targeted toward self-employed taxpayers. The more popular plans for the self-employed include SEP IRA, SIMPLE IRA, and Individual (or "solo") 401(k) plans. These are all defined contribution plans that generally work the same as employer-provided plans. That is, amounts set aside in these plans are deducted from income, earnings are free from tax until distributed, and distributions from the plans are fully taxable.[25] However, self-employed retirement plans differ markedly in terms of their annual contribution limits. As we discover below, the contribution limits for the individual 401(k) are generally the highest, followed by the SIMPLE IRA, and then the SEP IRA. For self-employed individuals wanting to maximize their contributions, this is often a critical concern. These plans also differ according to their nontax characteristics including their suitability for businesses with employees other than the owner and their administration costs. As you might expect, all of these factors come into play when self-employed small business owners must choose among these plans.[26] We describe each of these plans below.

Simplified Employee Pension (SEP) IRA

A simplified employee pension (SEP) can be administered through an individual retirement account (IRA) called a **SEP IRA**.[27] The owner of a sole proprietorship can make annual contributions directly to her SEP IRA. For 2009, the annual contribution is limited to the *lesser* of (1) $49,000 *minus* other contributions (employee and employer) to the taxpayer's other qualified defined contribution accounts (if any) or (2) 20 percent of the sole proprietor's **net earnings from self-employment**.[28]

> **THE KEY FACTS**
>
> Self-Employed Retirement Accounts
>
> ■ Popular plans include SEP IRAs, SIMPLE plans, and individual 401(k)s.
>
> ■ Similar to (non-Roth) qualified defined contribution plans.
> · Contributions deductible, distributions taxable.

> **THE KEY FACTS**
>
> Self-Employed Retirement Accounts
>
> ■ SEP IRA 2009 contribution limit.
> · Lesser of (1) $49,000 or (2) 20 percent of net earnings from self-employment (Sch. C income × 92.35%).

Example 13-18

What if: Dave receives director compensation of $30,000 during the current year and is reimbursed for all relevant expenses. Due to the specifics of the work arrangement, Dave is treated as a self-employed sole

(*continued on page 13-26...*)

---

[24]Because sole proprietorships with self-employment income are very common, we assume in our examples and explanations here that any self-employment income originates from a sole proprietorship. In some cases, however, partners and LLC members may also have self-employment income.

[25]"Keogh" self-employed defined benefit plans are also an option. Generally, defined benefit plans are attractive to older, self-employed individuals with profitable businesses because they allow for greater deductible contributions. However, they are usually more costly to maintain than the defined contribution plans we mention here.

[26]Many investment firms provide comparisons to help taxpayers select self-employed retirement plans. One particularly good comparison is provided by Fidelity Investments at http://personal.fidelity.com/products/retirement/getstart/newacc/smallbizintro.shtml.cvsr?refpr=rrc50

[27]§408(k).

[28]This is generally calculated by multiplying the owner's net Schedule C income by 92.35%. Chapter 7 addresses self-employment taxes in more detail. Also note that for SEP IRAs no catch-up contributions are allowed for taxpayers 50 years and older.

proprietor for tax purposes. If Dave sets up a SEP IRA for himself, what is the maximum contribution he may make to the plan (assuming he has no other source of employee or self-employment income)?

Answer: $5,541, computed as follows:

Description	Amount	Explanation
(1) First limit on contribution	$49,000	
(2) Net earnings from self-employment	27,705	$30,000 (Schedule C net income) × .9235.
(3) Percentage for limitation based on net earnings from self-employment	20%	
(4) Second limit on contribution	5,541	(2) × (3).
Contribution limit	**$ 5,541**	Lesser of (1) or (4).

What if: Assume Dave is 48 years old at the end of the year. What is his maximum deductible contribution?

Answer: $5,541. Dave's maximum deductible contribution for a SEP IRA does not depend on his age.

Example 13-19

What if: Similar to the facts provided above, let's assume that Dave receives director compensation of $30,000 as a self-employed independent contractor. Further, let's assume Dave also works as an instructor at a local university and that Dave contributed $7,500 and the university contributed $2,500 to Dave's university-sponsored defined contribution account. What is the maximum amount he may contribute to his SEP IRA account?

Answer: $5,541. This is the lesser of (1) $49,000 − $10,000 ($7,500 + $2,500) or (2) 20% × $27,705 ($30,000 × .9235).

What if: Assume the same facts as the previous example except that Dave earned $250,000 of self-employment income instead of $30,000. What is his maximum deductible contribution to this SEP IRA account?

Answer: $39,000, the lesser of (1) $39,000 ($49,000 − $10,000) or (2) $46,175 [20% × ($250,000 × .9235)]. The concept behind this rule is that Dave should not be able to use a self-employed retirement plan to contribute more than the $49,000 maximum allowed for employer-sponsored plans.

Nontax Considerations   If a sole proprietor has hired employees, the sole proprietor *must* contribute to their respective SEP IRAs based on their compensation. Because owners may view this requirement as being too favorable to employees, this plan is best suited for sole proprietors who do not have employees or for situations where owners are willing to provide generous benefits to their employees. From an administrative perspective, SEP IRAs are easy to set up and have relatively low administrative costs from year to year.

Savings Incentive Match Plans for Employees (SIMPLE) IRAs

Savings incentive match plans for employees plans may be administered through an IRA called a SIMPLE IRA.[29] The owner of a sole proprietorship can make deductible contributions to her SIMPLE IRA account. For 2009, the limit on deductible contributions to a SIMPLE IRA is the lesser of (1) $49,000 *minus* other contributions (employee

---

> **THE KEY FACTS**
>
> **Self-Employed Retirement Accounts**
>
> ■ SIMPLE IRA 2009 contribution limit.
> · Least of (1) $49,000, (2) $11,500, or (3) net earnings from self employment.
> · Additional $2,500 contribution for those at least 50 years old at the end of the year.

[29]SIMPLE plans may also be established as a 401(k) plan.

and employer) to the taxpayer's other qualified defined contribution plans (if any) or (2) $11,500. If the sole proprietor is 50 years old as of the end of the year, she may contribute an additional $2,500 to her account (called a "catch-up" contribution). However, the sole proprietor's contribution may not exceed her net earnings from self-employment.

Example 13-20

What if: Assume the same facts as in Example 13-18, except that Dave set up a SIMPLE IRA. Dave is 64 years old at the end of the year, reports $30,000 of self-employment income, and has no other sources of income. What is the maximum amount he can contribute to his SIMPLE IRA account?

Answer: $14,000, computed as follows.

Description	Amount	Explanation
(1) First limit on contribution	$49,000	
(2) Second limit on contributions	11,500	
(3) Third limit on contributions	27,705	Net earnings from self-employment ($30,000 × 92.35%).
(4) Contribution limit before catch-up contribution	11,500	Least of (1), (2), or (3).
(5) Additional catch-up contribution	2,500	Applies for taxpayers 50 years of age or older at end of year.
Total contribution limit	**$14,000**	(4 + (5).

What if: Assume Dave is 48 years old at the end of the year. What is his maximum deductible contribution to his SIMPLE IRA?

Answer: $11,500. This is the same amount as he is allowed to contribute as a 64-year-old, minus the $2,500 catch-up contribution.

Example 13-21

What if: Assume the same facts as Example 13-19, except that Dave set up a SIMPLE IRA plan. Dave is 64 years old, he received $30,000 of self-employment income, and he works as an employee. Dave contributed $7,500 to his account in an employer-sponsored qualified defined contribution plan and Dave's employer contributed $2,500 to the account. What is the maximum amount Dave may contribute to his SIMPLE IRA account?

Answer: $14,000, computed as follows:

Description	Amount	Explanation
(1) First limit on contribution	$39,000	$49,000 − $10,000 (contributions to other qualified plan).
(2) Second limit on contributions	11,500	
(3) Third limit on contributions	27,705	$30,000 × 92.35%
(4) Contribution limit before catch-up contribution.	11,500	Least of (1), (2), or (3).
(5) Additional catch-up contribution	2,500	Applies for taxpayers 50 years of age or older at end of year.
Total contribution limit	**$14,000**	(4) + (5).

What if: Assume the same facts as above except that Dave earned $10,000 of self-employment income rather than $30,000. What is his maximum deductible contribution to his SIMPLE IRA?

Answer: $9,235. Dave would otherwise be able to deduct $14,000, but his contribution is limited to his net earnings from self-employment ($10,000 × .9235).

Nontax Considerations   Sole proprietors with employees may only adopt SIMPLE IRAs if they have 100 or fewer employees earning at least $5,000 a year. However, sole proprietors adopting SIMPLE IRA plans must contribute to the accounts of employees participating in the plan. Thus, SIMPLE IRAs may not be a viable option for sole proprietors who do not want to incur the cost of providing a plan for their employees. Similar to SEP IRAs, SIMPLE IRAs are relatively easy to set up and have relatively low administrative costs.

Individual 401(k)s

Individual 401(k)s are strictly for sole proprietors (and the spouse of the sole proprietor) who do not have employees. Under this type of plan, the sole proprietor can contribute the lesser of (1) $49,000 *minus* other contributions (employee and employer) to the taxpayer's other qualified defined contribution accounts (if any) or (2) 20 percent × net earnings from self-employment (the "employer's contribution") + $16,500 (the employee's contribution). Further, if the sole proprietor is 50 years of age by the end of the tax year, she may contribute and deduct an *additional* $5,500. However, the sole proprietor's contribution may not exceed her net earnings from self-employment.

> **THE KEY FACTS**
>
> Self-Employed Retirement Accounts
>
> ■ Individual 401(k) 2009 contribution limit.
>   · Lesser of (1) $49,000 or (2) 20 percent of net earnings from self employment plus $16,500.
>   · Additional $5,500 contribution for those at least 50 years old at the end of the year.

Example 13-22

What if: Assume the same facts as in Example 13-18, except that Dave set up an individual 401(k) account. Dave is 64 years old at the end of the year, reports $30,000 of self-employment income, and has no other sources of income. What is the maximum amount he can contribute to his individual 401(k) account?

Answer: $26,041, computed as follows:

Description	Amount	Explanation
(1) First limit on contribution	$49,000	
(2) Net earnings from self-employment	27,705	$30,000 (Schedule C net income) × .9235.
(3) Percentage for limitation based on net earnings from self-employment	20%	
(4) Limit on employer's contribution	5,541	(2) × (3).
(5) Limit on employee's contribution	16,500	
(6) Second limitation	22,041	(4) + (5).
(7) Maximum contribution before catch-up contribution	22,041	Lesser of (1) or (6).
(8) Catch-up contribution	5,500	Applies because Dave is 50 or older at end of year.
Total contribution limit	**$27,541**	(7) + (8).

What if: Assume Dave is 48 years old at the end of the year. What is his maximum deductible contribution to his individual 401(k) account?

Answer: $22,041. This is the same as the amount he could contribute as a 64-year-old, minus the catch-up adjustment.

Example 13-23

What if: Assume the same facts as Example 13-20, except Dave (64 years old) set up an individual 401(k) account, he received $250,000 of self-employment income, and he works as an employee. Dave contributed $7,500 to his account in an employer-sponsored qualified defined contribution plan and Dave's employer contributed $2,500 to the account. What is the maximum amount Dave may contribute to his individual 401(k) account?

Answer: $40,000, computed as follows:

Description	Amount	Explanation
(1) First limit on contribution	$ 39,000	$49,000 − $10,000 (other contributions to his qualified retirement accounts).
(2) Net earnings from self-employment	230,875	$250,000 (Schedule C net income) × .9235.
(3) Percentage for limitation based on net earnings from self-employment	20%	
(4) Limit on employer's contribution	46,175	(2) × (3).
(5) Limit on employee's contribution	16,500	
(6) Second limitation	62,675	(4) + (5)
(7) Maximum contribution before catch-up contribution	39,000	Lesser of (1) or (6).
(8) Catch-up contribution	5,500	Applies because Dave is 50 or older at end of year.
Total contribution limit	**$ 44,500**	(7) + (8).

Nontax Considerations   As we mentioned above, the individual 401(k) is not available for sole proprietors with employees, so providing benefits to employees under the plan is not a concern. However, the administrative burden of establishing, operating, and maintaining a 401(k) plan is much higher for a 401(k) plan than the other self-employed plans we've discussed.

SAVER'S CREDIT

LO6

To encourage middle- and low-income taxpayers to take advantage of the retirement savings opportunities discussed in this chapter, Congress provides an additional **saver's credit** for an individual's elective contribution of up to $2,000 to any of the qualified retirement plans discussed in this chapter including employer-sponsored qualified plans, traditional and Roth IRA plans, and self-employed qualified plans. The credit is provided *in addition to* any deduction the taxpayer is allowed for contributing to a retirement account. It is calculated by multiplying the taxpayer's contribution, up to a maximum of $2,000, by the applicable percentage depending on the taxpayer's filing status and AGI.[30] Exhibit 13-10 provides the applicable percentages for 2009 according to a taxpayer's filing status and AGI.[31]

EXHIBIT 13-10   **Applicable Percentages for Saver's Credit by Filing Status and AGI**

Applicable Percentage	Joint Filers AGI	Heads of Household AGI	All Other Filers AGI
50%	0 to $33,000	0 to $24,750	0 to $16,500
20%	$33,000 to $36,000	$24,750 to $27,000	$16,500 to $18,000
10%	$36,000 to $55,500	$27,000 to $41,625	$18,000 to $27,750
No credit available	Above $55,500	Above $41,625	Above $27,750

[30]According to IRC §25B(g), the saver's credit is applied to the taxpayer's remaining tax liability after the application of certain other tax credits including the child tax credit and the Hope and lifetime learning credits.

[31]For this purpose, AGI is determined without considering the foreign earned income exclusion provided for U.S. residents living abroad under IRC §911.

> **THE KEY FACTS**
>
> Saver's Credit
>
> ■ Credit for taxpayers contributing to qualified plan.
>
> ■ Credit is based on contributions up to $2,000, taxpayer's filing status, and AGI.
> · Phased-out as AGI increases.
> · Maximum credit is $1,000.
> · Unavailable for married filing jointly taxpayers with AGI over $55,500, head of household taxpayers with AGI above $41,625, and all other taxpayers with AGI above $27,750.

In addition to restricting the credit to taxpayers with AGI below a certain amount, the credit is also restricted to individuals who are 18 years of age or older and who are not full-time students or claimed as dependents on another taxpayer's return.[32] Although limited in scope, the saver's credit provides some tax benefits for those taxpayers who qualify.

Example 13-24

What if: Tina earned $24,000 during the year she began working for CBA. She earned $4,000 in salary working part-time while she was in school and $20,000 in salary working for CBA from September through December. To get an early start saving for retirement, assume she contributed $4,000 to a traditional IRA. Because Tina did not participate in an employer-sponsored retirement plan during the current year she may deduct the full $4,000 contribution as a *for* AGI deduction, reducing her AGI from $24,000 to $20,000. What amount of saver's credit, if any, is Tina allowed to claim?

Answer: $200 ($2,000 × 10 percent applicable credit).

What if: What saver's credit may Tina claim if her AGI was $15,000?

Answer: $1,000 ($2,000 × 50 percent applicable credit).

CONCLUSION

The decisions that employees like Tina, Lisa, and Dave must deal with highlight the role that tax issues play in this important area. Employers, like their employees, must also pay careful attention to tax considerations when deciding on retirement savings vehicles to offer their employees. Further, as has been a recurring theme throughout this book, nontax issues play an equal, if not more important, role in the retirement savings decisions of both employees and employers.

SUMMARY

LO1
Describe the tax and nontax aspects of employer-provided defined benefit plans from both the employer's and employee's perspective.

- Benefits are determined based on years of service and salary. The maximum annual benefit is capped and adjusted upward annually for inflation.
- Benefits vest over time using either a five-year cliff or seven-year graded vesting schedule.
- Employers deduct cash contributions to fund the plan and employees treat cash distributions as ordinary income in the year received.
- Employers bear market risk with defined benefit plans.
- Premature distribution and minimum distribution penalties don't typically apply to defined benefit distributions.
- Because of the high cost of funding and maintaining defined benefit plans, they are waning in popularity.

LO2
Explain and determine the tax consequences associated with employer-provided defined contribution plans, including traditional 401(k) and Roth 401(k) plans.

- Employers specify the amount they will contribute to traditional plans instead of the annual benefit. However, employers are not permitted to contribute to a Roth 401(k) plan.

---

[32]Generally speaking, "full-time students" are those who are classified as such by the educational organizations referred to in IRC §152(f)(2).

■ Employees may contribute to either a traditional 401(k) or Roth 401(k) plan, and they determine how employer and employee contributions are invested. Thus, employees bear market risk with defined contribution plans.

■ Annual employer and employee contributions are limited and maximum contribution amounts are adjusted annually for inflation.

■ Employer contributions to traditional plans vest over time using either a three-year cliff or six-year graded vesting schedule.

■ Employers deduct their contributions to traditional defined contribution plans.

■ Employee contributions to traditional defined contribution plans are excluded from their taxable wages on Form W-2. Employee contributions to Roth 401(k) plans are included in taxable wages.

■ Distributions from traditional 401(k) plans are taxable at ordinary rates and qualified distributions from Roth 401(k) plans are not taxable.

■ Distributions from both traditional 401(k) and Roth 401(k) plans are subject to premature and minimum distribution penalties. Minimum distribution penalties have been suspended for 2009 distributions.

■ After-tax returns from Roth 401(k) plans are generally superior to those from traditional 401(k) plans when marginal tax rates are increasing.

Describe the tax implications of deferred compensation from both the employer's and employee's perspective.

LO3

■ Employees elect to defer current salary in exchange for promised future payments from the employer.

■ Because the employer's promise of future payment is unsecured, employees recognize ordinary income when future payments are received. Employers wait to deduct payments until cash is actually paid.

■ The after-tax returns and costs from deferred compensation arrangements to employees and employers depend on the current and future marginal tax rates of both the employee and employer. They also depend on the rate of return employers promise employees on deferred salary.

■ Deferred compensation is often used to overcome the constraints imposed on salary and qualified pension plans.

■ Employees bear more risk with deferred compensation relative to other forms of retirement savings because employees are unsecured creditors of their employers.

Determine the tax consequences of traditional and Roth Individual Retirement Accounts and explain the differences between them.

LO4

■ The same inflation-adjusted annual contribution limits apply to both traditional IRAs and Roth IRAs.

■ The deduction for traditional IRA contributions is phased-out for taxpayers covered by a pension plan at work and with AGI above certain inflation-adjusted amounts. Special rules pertain for spouses not covered by an employer plan.

■ The ability to contribute to a Roth IRA is phased-out for individuals with AGI above certain inflation-adjusted amounts.

■ Distributions from traditional IRAs are taxed at ordinary rates. A 10 percent premature distribution penalty generally applies to distributions from traditional IRAs received before age 59½.

■ Distributions from Roth IRAs received after a Roth IRA account has been open for at least five years and after the recipient reaches age 59½ are not taxable. The earnings component of any distributions not meeting these requirements is generally taxable and subject to the 10 percent premature distribution penalty.

■ Taxpayers generally prefer Roth IRAs to traditional IRAs when they expect their marginal tax rates to increase.

> **L05**   Describe the retirement savings options available to self-employed taxpayers and compute the limitations for deductible contributions to retirement accounts for self-employed taxpayers.
>
> - Self-employed individuals may set up their own qualified pension plans such as SEP IRAs, individual 401(k)s, and SIMPLE IRAs.
> - Contribution limits generally parallel those for employer-sponsored plans, allowing self-employed individuals to have the same access to qualified plans that employees have.
> - Contribution limits are generally highest for individual 401(k)s, then SIMPLE IRAs, then SEP IRAs
> - Self-employed individuals with employees may have to incur the cost of covering their employees when they establish a qualified retirement plan.
>
> **L06**   Compute the saver's credit.
>
> - Individuals may receive up to a $1,000 tax credit for contributions they make to IRAs and employer-sponsored qualified plans.
> - The maximum contribution eligible for the credit is $2,000, and the amount of the credit is a function of the taxpayer's filing status and AGI.

KEY TERMS

cliff vesting (13-4)
defined benefit plan (13-3)
defined contribution plan (13-3)
graded vesting (13-4)
Individual Retirement Account (IRA) (13-19)
minimum distributions (13-7)

net earnings from self-employment (13-25)
nonqualified deferred compensation (13-15)
qualified retirement plans (13-3)
rollover (13-23)
Roth 401(k) (13-12)
Roth IRA (13-19)

saver's credit (13-29)
§162(m) limitation (13-18)
SEP IRA (13-25)
traditional 401(k) (13-12)
traditional IRA (13-19)
vesting (13-4)

DISCUSSION QUESTIONS

1. **(LO1, LO2)** How are defined benefit plans different from defined contribution plans? How are they similar?
2. **(LO1)** Describe how an employee's benefit under a defined benefit plan is computed.
3. **(LO1, LO2)** What does it mean to vest in a defined benefit or defined contribution plan?
4. **(LO1, LO2)** Compare and contrast the minimum vesting requirements for defined benefit plans and defined contribution plans.
5. **(LO1, LO2)** What are the nontax advantages and disadvantages of defined benefit plans relative to defined contribution plans?
6. **(LO1)** Describe the maximum annual benefit that taxpayers may receive under defined benefit plans.
7. **(LO1)** Describe the distribution or payout options available to taxpayers participating in qualified defined benefit plans. How are defined benefit plan distributions to recipients taxed?
8. **(LO1)** Describe the minimum distribution requirements for defined benefit plans. Are these requirements typically an item of concern for taxpayers?
9. **(LO1, LO2)** Compare and contrast the employer's responsibilities for providing a defined benefit plan relative to providing a defined contribution plan.

10. **(LO2)** Describe how an employee's benefit under a defined contribution plan is determined.

11. **(LO2)** Is there a limit to how much an employer and/or employee may contribute to an employee's defined contribution account(s) for the year? If so, describe the limit.

12. **(LO2)** Describe the distribution or payout options available to taxpayers participating in qualified defined contribution plans.

13. **(LO2)** When may employees begin to receive defined contribution plan distributions without penalty?

14. **(LO2)** Describe the circumstances under which distributions from defined contribution plans are penalized. What are the penalties?

15. **(LO2)** Brady Corporation has a profit sharing plan that allocates 10 percent of all after-tax income to employees. The profit sharing is allocated to individual employees based on relative employee compensation. The profit sharing contributions vest to employees under a six-year graded plan. If an employee terminates his or her employment before fully vesting, the plan allocates the forfeited amounts among the remaining participants according to their account balances. Is this forfeiture allocation policy discriminatory, and will it cause the plan to lose its qualified status? Use Rev. Rul. 81-10 to help formulate your answer.

   research

16. **(LO2)** What does it mean if an employer "matches" employee contributions to 401(k) plans?

17. **(LO2)** What nontax factor(s) should an employee consider when deciding whether and to what extent to participate in an employer's 401(k) plan?

   planning

18. **(LO2)** What are the differences between a traditional 401(k) and Roth 401(k) plan?

19. **(LO2)** Can employers match employee contributions to Roth 401(k) plans? Explain.

20. **(LO2)** Describe the annual limitation on employer and employee contributions to traditional 401(k) and Roth 401(k) plans.

21. **(LO2, LO3)** When a company is limited in the amount it can contribute to an employee's 401(k) plan, what will it generally do to make the employee whole? Is this likely an issue for rank-and-file employees? Why or why not?

22. **(LO2)** From a tax perspective, how would taxpayers determine whether they should contribute to a traditional 401(k) or a Roth 401(k)?

   planning

23. **(LO2)** Could a taxpayer contributing to a traditional 401(k) plan earn an after-tax return *greater* than the before-tax return? Explain.

24. **(LO2, LO3)** Explain the *tax* similarities and differences between qualified defined contribution plans and nonqualified deferred compensation plans from an *employer's* perspective.

25. **(LO2, LO3)** Explain the *tax* similarities and differences between qualified defined contribution plans and nonqualified deferred compensation plans from an *employee's* perspective.

26. **(LO2, LO3)** Explain the *nontax* similarities and differences between qualified defined contribution plans and nonqualified deferred compensation plans from an *employer's* perspective.

27. **(LO2, LO3)** Explain the *nontax* similarities and differences between qualified defined contribution plans and nonqualified deferred compensation plans from an *employee's* perspective.

28. **(LO3)** From a *tax* perspective, what issues does an employee need to consider in deciding whether to defer compensation under a nonqualified deferred compensation plan or to receive it immediately?

   planning

29. **(LO3)** From a *nontax* perspective, what issues does an employee need to consider in deciding whether to defer compensation under a nonqualified deferred compensation plan or to receive it immediately?

   planning

30. **(LO3)** What are reasons why companies provide nonqualified deferred compensation plans for certain employees?

■ planning

31. **(LO3)** How can companies use deferred compensation to avoid the §162(m) limitation on salary deductibility?

32. **(LO3)** Are companies allowed to decide who can and who cannot participate in nonqualified deferred compensation plans? Briefly explain.

33. **(LO1, LO2, LO3)** How might the ultimate benefits to an employee who participates in a qualified retirement plan of a company differ from an employee who participates in a nonqualified deferred compensation plan of the company if the company experiences bankruptcy before the employee is scheduled to receive the benefits?

34. **(LO4)** What are the primary tax differences between traditional IRAs and Roth IRAs?

■ planning

35. **(LO4)** Describe the circumstances in which it would be more favorable for a taxpayer to contribute to a traditional IRA rather than a Roth IRA and vice versa.

36. **(LO4)** What are the requirements for a taxpayer to make a deductible contribution to a traditional IRA? Why do the tax laws impose these restrictions?

37. **(LO4)** What is the limitation on a deductible IRA contribution for 2009?

38. **(LO4)** Compare the minimum distribution requirements for traditional IRAs to those of Roth IRAs.

39. **(LO4)** How are qualified distributions from Roth IRAs taxed? How are nonqualified distributions taxed?

40. **(LO4)** Explain when a taxpayer will be subject to the 10 percent penalty tax when receiving distributions from a Roth IRA.

41. **(LO4)** Is a taxpayer who contributed to a traditional IRA able to transfer or "roll over" the money into a Roth IRA? If yes, explain the tax consequences of the transfer.

42. **(LO4)** Assume a taxpayer makes a nondeductible contribution to a traditional IRA. How does the taxpayer determine the taxability of distributions from the IRA on reaching retirement?

43. **(LO4)** When a taxpayer makes a nonqualified distribution from a Roth IRA, is the entire amount of the distribution treated as taxable income?

44. **(LO5)** What types of retirement plans are available to self-employed taxpayers?

45. **(LO5)** Compare and contrast the annual limitations on deductible contributions for self-employed taxpayers to SEP IRAs, SIMPLE IRAs, and individual 401(k) accounts. Are these limits imposed separately from limitations on contributions to the taxpayer's other defined contribution plans?

■ planning

46 **(LO5)** What are the nontax considerations for self-employed taxpayers deciding whether to set up a SEP IRA, a SIMPLE IRA, or an individual 401(k)?

47. **(LO6)** What is the saver's credit and who is eligible to receive it?

48. **(LO6)** What is the maximum saver's credit available to taxpayers? What taxpayer characteristics are relevant to the determination?

49. **(LO6)** How is the saver's credit computed?

PROBLEMS

50. **(LO1)** Javier recently graduated and started his career with DNL, Inc. DNL provides a defined benefit plan to all employees. According to the terms of the plan, for each full year of service working for the employer, employees receive a benefit of 1.5 percent of their average salary over their highest three years of

compensation from the company. Employees may accrue only 30 years of benefit under the plan (45 percent). Determine Javier's annual benefit on retirement,
before taxes, under each of the following scenarios:

a. Javier works for DNL for three years and three months before he leaves for
another job. Javier's annual salary was $55,000, $65,000, $70,000, and
$72,000 for years 1, 2, 3, and 4 respectively. DNL uses a five-year cliff vest-
ing schedule.

b. Javier works for DNL for three years and three months before he leaves for
another job. Javier's annual salary was $55,000, $65,000, $70,000, and
$72,000 for years 1, 2, 3, and 4 respectively. DNL uses a seven-year graded
vesting schedule.

c. Javier works for DNL for six years and three months before he leaves for
another job. Javier's annual salary was $75,000, $85,000, $90,000, and
$95,000 for years 4, 5, 6, and 7 respectively. DNL uses a five-year cliff
vesting schedule.

d. Javier works for DNL for six years and three months before he leaves for another job. Javier's annual salary was $75,000, $85,000, $90,000, and $95,000 for
years 4, 5, 6, and 7 respectively. DNL uses a seven-year graded vesting schedule.

e. Javier works for DNL for 32 years and three months before retiring. Javier's
annual salary was $175,000, $185,000, and $190,000 for his final three years
of employment.

51. **(LO1)** Alicia has been working for JMM Corp. for 32 years. Alicia participates
in JMM's defined benefit plan. Under the plan, she is to receive 2 percent of the
average salary of her three highest years of compensation from JMM. She
retired on January 1, 2009. Before retirement, her annual salary was $570,000,
$600,000, and $630,000 for 2006, 2007, and 2008. What is the maximum benefit
Alicia can receive in 2009?

52. **(LO2)** Kim has worked for one employer her entire career. While she was
working, she participated in the employer's defined contribution plan [tradi-
tional 401(k)]. At the end of 2008, Kim retires and the balance in her defined
contribution plan was $2,000,000 at the end of 2007.

a. What is Kim's minimum required distribution for 2008 in 2009 if she is
68 years old at the end of 2008?

b. What is Kim's minimum required distribution for 2008 if she turns 70½
during 2008 and she has not turned 71 years old by the end of 2008? When
must she receive this distribution?

c. What is Kim's minimum required distribution for 2008 in 2009 if she is
73 years old at the end of 2008?

d. Assuming that Kim is 75 years old at the end of 2008 and that her marginal
tax rate in 2008 is 33 percent, what will she have remaining after taxes if she
receives only a distribution of $50,000 for 2008?

53. **(LO2)** Matthew (48 at year end) develops cutting edge technology for SV, Inc.,
located in Silicon Valley. In 2009, Matthew participates in SV's money purchase
pension plan (a defined contribution plan) and in his company's 401(k) plan. Under the money purchase pension plan, SV contributes 15 percent of an employee's
salary to a retirement account for the employee up to the amount limited by the
tax code. Because it provides the money purchase pension plan, SV does not contribute to the employee's 401(k) plan. Matthew would like to maximize his contribution to his 401(k) account after SV's contribution to the money purchase plan.

a. Assuming Matthew's annual salary is $400,000, what amount will SV con-
tribute to Matthew's money purchase plan? What can Matthew contribute
to his 401(k) account in 2009?

b. Assuming Matthew's annual salary is $240,000, what amount will SV contribute to Matthew's money purchase plan? What can Matthew contribute to his 401(k) account in 2009?

c. Assuming Matthew's annual salary is $60,000, what amount will SV contribute to Matthew's money purchase plan? What amount can Matthew contribute to his 401(k) account in 2009?

d. Assume the same facts as c. except that Matthew is 54 years old at the end of the 2009. What amount can Matthew contribute to his 401(k) account in 2009?

54. **(LO2)** In 2009, Maggy (34 years old) is an employee of YBU Corp. YBU provides a 401(k) plan for all its employees. According to the terms of the plan, YBU contributes 50 cents for every dollar the employee contributes. The maximum employer contribution under the plan is 15 percent of the employee's salary (i.e., if allowed, YBU contributes until the employee has contributed 30 percent of her salary).

a. Maggy has worked for YBU corporation for 3½ years before deciding to leave. Maggy's annual salary during this time was $45,000, $52,000, $55,000, and $60,000 (she only received half of her final year's salary). Assuming Maggy contributed 8 percent of her salary (including her 2009 salary) to her 401(k) account, what is Maggy's vested account balance when she leaves YBU (exclusive of account earnings)? Assume YBU uses three-year cliff vesting.

b. Same question as a. except YBU uses six-year graded vesting.

■ planning   c. Maggy wants to maximize YBU's contribution to her 401(k) account in 2009. How much should Maggy contribute to her 401(k) account assuming her annual salary is $100,000 (she works for YBU for the entire year)?

■ planning   d. Same question as c., except Maggy is 55 years old rather than 34 years old at the end of the year.

55. **(LO2)** In 2009, Nina contributes 10 percent of her $100,000 annual salary to her 401(k) account. She expects to earn a 7 percent before-tax rate of return. Assuming she leaves this (and any employer contributions) in the account until she retires in 25 years, what is Nina's after-tax accumulation from her 2009 contributions to her 401(k) account?

a. Assume Nina's marginal tax rate at retirement is 30 percent.

b. Assume Nina's marginal tax at retirement is 20 percent.

c. Assume Nina's marginal tax rate at retirement is 40 percent.

56. **(LO2)** In 2009, Nitai contributes 10 percent of his $100,000 annual salary to a Roth 401(k) account sponsored by his employer, AY, Inc. AY, Inc., matches employee contributions dollar for dollar up to 10 percent of the employee's salary to the employee's traditional 401(k) account. Nitai expects to earn a 7 percent before-tax rate of return. Assuming he leaves his contributions in the Roth 401(k) and traditional 401(k) accounts until he retires in 25 years, what are Nitai's after-tax proceeds from the Roth 401(k) and traditional 401(k) accounts after he receives the distributions assuming his marginal tax rate at retirement is 30%?

■ planning   57. **(LO3)** Marissa participates in her employer's nonqualified deferred compensation plan. For 2009, she is deferring 10 percent of her $320,000 annual salary. Assuming this is her only source of income and her marginal income tax rate is 30 percent, how much *tax* does Marissa save in 2009 by deferring this income?

a. Ignore FICA taxes.

b. Include FICA taxes in your analysis.

58. **(LO3)** Paris participates in her employer's nonqualified deferred compensation plan. For 2009, she is deferring 10 percent of her $320,000 annual salary. Assuming this is her only source of income and her marginal income tax rate is 30 percent, how much does deferring Paris's income save her employer (after taxes) in 2009? Paris's employer's marginal tax rate is 35 percent.

    a. Ignore FICA taxes.
    b. Include FICA taxes in your analysis.

59. **(LO3)** Leslie participates in IBO's nonqualified deferred compensation plan. For 2009, she is deferring 10 percent of her $300,000 annual salary. Based on her deemed investment choice, Leslie expects to earn a 7 percent before-tax rate of return on her deferred compensation, which she plans to receive in 10 years. Leslie's marginal tax rate in 2009 is 30 percent. IBO's marginal tax rate is 35 percent. Ignore payroll taxes in your analysis.

    a. Assuming Leslie's marginal tax rate in 10 years when she receives the distribution is 33 percent, what is Leslie's after-tax accumulation on the deferred compensation?
    b. Assuming Leslie's marginal tax rate in 10 years when she receives the distribution is 20 percent, what is Leslie's after-tax accumulation on the deferred compensation?
    c. Assuming IBO's cost of capital is 8 percent after taxes, how much deferred compensation should IBO be willing to pay Leslie that would make it indifferent between paying 10 percent of Leslie's current salary or deferring it for 10 years?

    ■ planning

60. **(LO3)** XYZ Corporation has a deferred compensation plan under which it allows certain employees to defer up to 40 percent of their salary for five years. (For purposes of this problem, ignore payroll taxes in your computations).

    ■ planning

    a. Assume XYZ has a marginal tax rate of 35 percent for the foreseeable future and earns a before-tax return of 8 percent on its assets. Joel Johnson, XYZ's VP of finance, is attempting to determine what amount of deferred compensation XYZ should be willing to pay in five years that would make XYZ indifferent between paying current salary of $10,000 and paying the deferred compensation. What would you tell him?
    b. Assume Julie, an XYZ employee, has the option of participating in XYZ's deferred compensation plan. Julie's marginal tax rate is 40 percent and she expects the rate to remain constant over the next five years. Julie is trying to decide how much deferred compensation she will need to receive from XYZ in five years to make her indifferent between receiving current salary of $10,000 and receiving the deferred compensation payment. If Julie takes the salary, she will invest it in a taxable corporate bond paying interest at 5 percent annually. What would you tell Julie?

61. **(LO4)** John (age 51) and single has earned income of $3,000. He has $30,000 of unearned (capital gain) income.

    a. If he does not participate in an employer-sponsored plan, what is the maximum deductible IRA contribution John can make in 2009?
    b. If he does participate in an employer-sponsored plan, what is the maximum deductible IRA contribution John can make in 2009?
    c. If he does not participate in an employer-sponsored plan, what is the maximum deductible IRA contribution John can make in 2009 if he has earned income of $10,000?

62. **(LO4)** William is a single writer (age 35) who recently decided that he needs to save more for retirement. His 2009 AGI is $61,000 (all earned income).

    a. If he does not participate in an employer-sponsored plan, what is the maximum deductible IRA contribution William can make in 2009?

    b. If he does participate in an employer-sponsored plan, what is the maximum deductible IRA contribution William can make in 2009?

    c. Assuming the same facts as in b. except his AGI is $75,000, What is the maximum deductible IRA contribution William can make in 2009?

63. **(LO4)** In 2009, Susan (44 years old) is a highly successful architect and is covered by an employee-sponsored plan. Her husband, Dan (47 years old), however, isn't covered by an employer-sponsored plan at work. Dan's earned income for the year is $15,000.

    a. Assuming the couple's AGI is $180,000, what is the maximum deductible IRA contribution Dan can make to a traditional IRA for the current year?

    b. Assuming the couple's AGI is $120,000, what is the maximum deductible IRA contribution Dan can make to a traditional IRA for the current year?

64. **(LO4)** In 2009, Rashaun (62 years old) retired and planned on immediately receiving distributions (making withdrawals) from his traditional IRA account. The current balance of his IRA account is $160,000. Over the years, Rashaun has contributed $40,000 to the IRA. Of his $40,000 contributions, $30,000 was *nondeductible* and $10,000 was *deductible*.

    a. If Rashaun currently withdraws $20,000 from the IRA, how much tax will he be required to pay on the withdrawal if his marginal tax rate is 20 percent?

    b. If Rashaun currently withdraws $70,000 from the IRA, how much tax will he be required to pay on the withdrawal if his marginal tax rate is 30 percent?

65. **(LO4)** Brooklyn has been contributing to a traditional IRA for seven years (all deductible contributions) and has a total of $30,000 in the account. In 2009, she is 39 years old and has decided that she wants to get a new car. She withdraws $20,000 from the IRA to help pay for the car. She is currently in the 25 percent marginal tax bracket. What amount of the withdrawal, after tax considerations, will Brooklyn have available to purchase the car?

66. **(LO4)** Jackson and Ashley Turner (both 45 years old) are married and want to contribute to a Roth IRA for Ashley. In 2009, their AGI is $167,000. Jackson and Ashley each earned half of the income.

    a. How much can Ashley contribute to her Roth IRA if they file a joint return?

    b. How much can Ashley contribute if she files a separate return?

67. **(LO4)** Harriet and Harry Combs (both 37 years old) are married and both want to contribute to a Roth IRA. In 2009, their AGI is $50,000. Harriet earned $46,000 and Harry earned $5,000.

    a. How much can Harriet contribute to her Roth IRA if they file a joint return?

    b. How much can Harriet contribute if she files a separate return?

    c. How much can Harry contribute to his Roth IRA if they file separately?

68. **(LO4)** George (age 42 at year end) has been contributing to a traditional IRA for years (all deductible contributions) and his IRA is now worth $25,000. He is planning on transferring (or rolling over) the entire balance into a Roth IRA account. George's marginal tax rate is 25 percent.

    a. What are the tax consequences to George if he takes $25,000 out of the traditional IRA and puts the entire amount in a Roth IRA?

b. What are the tax consequences to George if he takes $25,000 out of the traditional IRA, pays the taxes due from the IRA distribution, and contributes the remaining distribution to the Roth IRA?

c. What are the tax consequences to George if he takes $25,000 out of the traditional IRA and keeps $10,000 to pay taxes and to make a down payment on a new car?

69. **(LO4)** John is trying to decide whether to contribute to a Roth IRA or a traditional IRA. He plans on making the maximum $5,000 contribution to whichever plan he decides to fund. He currently pays tax at a 30 percent marginal income tax rate but he believes that his marginal tax rate in the future will be 28 percent. He intends to leave the money in the Roth IRA or traditional IRA accounts for 30 years and he expects to earn a 6 percent before-tax rate of return on the account.

a. How much will John accumulate after taxes if he contributes to a Roth IRA?

b. How much will John accumulate after taxes if he contributes to a traditional IRA?

c. Does the Roth IRA or the traditional IRA provide a greater after-tax rate of return? Explain.

■ planning

70. **(LO4)** Over the past three years, Sherry has contributed a total of $12,000 to a Roth IRA account (i.e., $4,000 a year). The current value of the Roth IRA is $16,300. In the current year, Sherry withdraws $14,000 of the account balance to purchase a car. Assuming Sherry is in a 25 percent marginal tax bracket, how much of the $14,000 withdrawal will she retain after taxes to fund her car purchase?

71. **(LO4)** Seven years ago, Halle (currently age 41) contributed $4,000 to a Roth IRA account. The current value of the Roth IRA is $9,000. In the current year Halle withdraws $8,000 of the account balance to use as a down payment on her first home. Assuming Halle is in a 25 percent marginal tax bracket, how much of the $8,000 withdrawal will she retain after taxes to fund her house down payment?

72. **(LO4)** Sarah was contemplating making a contribution to her traditional individual retirement account for 2009. She determined that she would contribute $5,000 to her IRA and she deducted $5,000 for the contribution when she completed and filed her 2010 tax return on February 15, 2009. Two months later, on April 15, Sarah realized that she had not yet actually contributed the funds to her IRA. On April 15, she went to the post office and mailed a $5,000 check to the bank holding her IRA. The bank received the payment on April 17. In which year is Sarah's $5,000 contribution deductible?

■ research

73. **(LO5)** Elvira is a self-employed taxpayer who turns 42 years old at the end of the year (2009). In 2009, her net Schedule C income was $120,000. This was her only source of income. This year, Elvira is considering setting up a retirement plan. What is the maximum amount Elvira may contribute to the self-employed plan in each of the following situations?

a. She sets up a SEP IRA.

b. She sets up a SIMPLE IRA.

c. She sets up an individual 401(k).

■ planning

74. **(LO5)** Hope is a self-employed taxpayer who turns 54 years old at the end of the year (2009). In 2009, her net Schedule C income was $120,000. This was her only source of income. This year, Hope is considering setting up a retirement

■ planning

plan. What is the maximum amount Hope may contribute to the self-employed plan in each of the following situations?

a. She sets up a SEP IRA.

b. She sets up a SIMPLE IRA.

c. She sets up an individual 401(k).

planning   75. **(LO5)** Rita is a self-employed taxpayer who turns 39 years old at the end of the year (2009). In 2009, her net Schedule C income was $300,000. This was her only source of income. This year, Rita is considering setting up a retirement plan. What is the maximum amount Rita may contribute to the self-employed plan in each of the following situations?

a. She sets up a SEP IRA.

b. She sets up a SIMPLE IRA.

c. She sets up an individual 401(k).

planning   76. **(LO5)** Reggie is a self-employed taxpayer who turns 59 years old at the end of the year (2009). In 2009, his net Schedule C income was $300,000. This was his only source of income. This year, Reggie is considering setting up a retirement plan. What is the maximum amount he may contribute to the self-employed plan in each of the following situations?

a. He sets up a SEP IRA.

b. He sets up a SIMPLE IRA.

c. He sets up an individual 401(k).

planning   77. **(LO5)** Hilton is a self-employed taxpayer who turns 59 years old at the end of the year (2009). He is considering setting up a self-employed retirement account. In 2009, Hilton earned self-employment income of $40,000. He was also employed, and his employer provided a 401(k) account. Hilton contributed $8,000 to his employer-sponsored 401(k) account and his employer also contributed $8,000 to his account. What is the maximum amount he may contribute to the self-employed plan in each of the following situations?

a. He sets up a SEP IRA.

b. He sets up a SIMPLE IRA.

c. He sets up an individual 401(k).

planning   78. **(LO5)** Alicia is a self-employed taxpayer who turns 47 years old at the end of the year (2009). She is considering setting up a self-employed retirement account. In 2009, Alicia earned self-employment income of $400,000. She was also employed, and her employer provided a 401(k) account. Alicia contributed $6,000 to her employer-sponsored 401(k) account and her employer also contributed $3,000 to her account. What is the maximum amount she may contribute to the self-employed plan in each of the following situations?

a. She sets up a SEP IRA.

b. She sets up a SIMPLE IRA.

c. She sets up an individual 401(k).

planning   79. **(LO5)** Jason is a self-employed taxpayer who turns 53 years old at the end of the year (2009). He is considering setting up a self-employed retirement account. In 2009, Jason earned self-employment income of $10,000. Jason was also employed, and his employer provided a 401(k) account. Jason contributed $12,000 to his employer-sponsored 401(k) account and his employer also contributed $3,000 to his account. What is the maximum amount he may contribute to the self-employed plan in each of the following situations?

  a. He sets up a SEP IRA.

  b. He sets up a SIMPLE IRA.

  c. He sets up an individual 401(k).

80. **(LO6)** Desmond is 25 years old and he participates in his employer's 401(k) plan. During the year, he contributed $3,000 to his 401(k) account. What is Desmond's 2009 saver's credit in each of the following alternative scenarios?

  a. Desmond is not married and has no dependents. His AGI after deducting his 401(k) contribution is $30,000.

  b. Desmond is not married and has no dependents. His AGI after deducting his 401(k) contribution is $17,500.

  c. Desmond files as a head of household and has AGI of $39,000.

  d. Desmond and his wife file jointly and report an AGI of $30,000 for the year.

81. **(LO6)** Penny is 57 years old and she participates in her employer's 401(k) plan. During the year, she contributed $2,000 to her 401(k) account. Penny's AGI is $26,000 after deducting her 401(k) contribution. What is Penny's 2009 saver's credit in each of the following alternative scenarios?

  a. Penny is not married and has no dependents.

  b. Penny files as a head of household and she has three dependents.

  c. Penny files as a head of household and she has one dependent.

  d. Penny is married and files a joint return with her husband. They have three dependents.

  e. Penny files a separate tax return from her husband. She claims two dependent children on her return.

COMPREHENSIVE PROBLEMS

82. Alex is 31 years old and has lived in Los Alamos, New Mexico, for the last four years where he works at the Los Alamos National Laboratory (LANL). LANL provides employees with a 401(k) plan and for every $1 an employee contributes (up to 9 percent of the employee's salary) LANL contributes $3 (a 3 to 1 match). The plan provides a six-year graded vesting schedule. Alex is now in his fifth year working for LANL, and his current year salary is $150,000. Alex's marginal tax rate is 28 percent in 2009. Answer the following questions relating to Alex's retirement savings in 2009.

  a. Assume that over the past four years, Alex has contributed $45,000 to his 401(k) and his employer has contributed $115,000 to the plan. The plan has an account balance of $175,000. What is Alex's vested account balance in his 401(k)?

  b. Because Alex considers his employer's matching contribution "free money," he wants to maximize the amount of LANL's contributions. What is the least amount Alex can contribute and still maximize LANL's contribution?

  c. In need of cash to build a home theater, Alex withdrew $30,000 from his traditional 401(k) account. What amount of the withdrawal, after taxes and penalties, will Alex have available to complete his project?

  d. Assume that Alex contributes $10,000 to his traditional 401(k) account this year. Also assume that in 30 years, Alex retires (at age 61) and withdraws the $10,000 contribution made this year *and* all the earnings generated by the contribution. Also assume that his marginal tax rate at the time he retires is 25 percent. Ignore any prior or subsequent contributions to his plan. If Alex earns a 6 percent annual before-tax rate of return, what are his after-tax proceeds from the distribution?

e. Assume that Alex is 74 years old at the end of the year (assume the year is not 2009), retired, and that his marginal tax rate is 25 percent. His account balance in his traditional 401(k) was $1,250,000 at the end of last year. What is the minimum distribution Alex must receive from his 401(k) account for this year (not 2009)? If Alex receives a $43,000 distribution from his 401(k) account (his only distribution during the year) what amount will he be able to keep after taxes and penalties (if any)?

f. Assume that Alex retired in 2007 but, as of the end of 2009, he had not received any distributions from his 401(k) account. Further assume that the balance in his 401(k) account at the end of 2008 was $2,000,000. Alex turned 70 years old on February 15, 2009. Is Alex required to receive a distribution for 2009? If so, what is the amount of the required distribution and when must he receive it to avoid a penalty?

83. Tommy (age 47) and his wife, Michelle (age 49), live in Sandusky, Ohio, where Tommy works for Callahan Auto Parts (CAP) as the vice-president of the brakes division. Tommy's 2009 salary is $360,000. CAP allows Tommy to participate in its nonqualified deferred compensation plan in which participants can defer 15 percent of their salary for five years. Tommy also participates in CAP's qualified 401(k) plan. Tommy's current marginal tax rate is 28 percent and CAP's current marginal tax rate is 34 percent.

a. Assuming Tommy earns a 6 percent *after-tax* rate of return and he expects his marginal tax rate to be 30 percent in five years, what before-tax deferred compensation payment in five years would make him indifferent between receiving the deferred compensation payment or 15 percent of his salary now (ignore payroll taxes)?

b. Assuming CAP has an 8% *after-tax* rate of return and expects its marginal tax rate to be 35% in five years, how much would it be willing to pay in five years to be indifferent between paying the deferred compensation or paying 15 percent of Tommy's salary now (ignore payroll taxes)?

c. Will Tommy and CAP be able to come to an agreement on deferring Tommy's salary?

d. Assuming that Tommy has an AGI of $93,000, that Michelle earns $10,000 working part-time but she does not participate in an employer-sponsored retirement plan, and that they file a joint return, what is the maximum deductible contribution Tommy and Michelle may make to a traditional IRA?

e. Tommy has a balance of $55,000 in his traditional IRA. Due to some recent tax cuts, his marginal tax rate is 20 percent, so he would like to roll his traditional IRA into a Roth IRA. What are the tax consequences to Tommy if he takes $55,000 out of the IRA, pays the taxes due from the traditional IRA distribution, and contributes the remaining distribution to the Roth IRA?

84. Gerry (age 56) and Elaine (age 54) have been married for 12 years and file a joint tax return. The couple lives in an apartment in downtown Manhattan. Gerry's father, Mortey, recently retired from Del Boca Vista Corporation (DBVC) where he worked for many years. Mortey participated in DBVC's defined benefit plan. Elaine is an editor and works for Pendent Publishing earning an annual $150,000 salary. Gerry is a self-employed standup comedian, and had net business income of $46,000 in 2009. At the advice of their

neighbor, Gerry and Elaine have come to you to for help in answering several retirement savings-related questions.

a. The DBVC defined benefit plan specifies a benefit of 1.5 percent for each year of service, up to a maximum of 30 percent (20 years of service), of the average of the employee's three highest years of salary. Mortey worked for the company for 25 years and earned $75,000, $78,000, and $84,000 over his final three years of service. What is Mortey's annual benefit from DBVC's defined benefit plan?

b. Elaine has worked at Pendent Publishing since January 1, 2005. The company offers a defined contribution plan. It matches 100 percent of employee contributions to the plan up to 6 percent of her salary. Prior to 2009, Elaine had contributed $40,000 to the plan and her employer had contributed $28,000 to the plan. In 2009, Elaine contributed $16,500 to her traditional 401(k). What is the amount of her employer's matching contribution for 2009? Assuming the company uses a six-year graded vesting schedule, what is Elaine's vested balance in the plan at the end of 2009 (for simplicity, disregard the plan's earnings)?

c. Elaine tells you that her employer has offered her $30,000 in 10 years to defer 10 percent of her current salary (defer $15,000). Assuming that the couple's marginal tax rate is currently 30 percent, they earn an after-tax rate of return of 8 percent, and they expect their marginal tax rate to be 25 percent in 10 years, should Elaine accept her company's offer? What is the minimum amount she should be willing to accept (ignoring nontax factors)?

d. Gerry has a SEP IRA and would like to contribute as much as possible to this account. What is the maximum contribution Gerry can make to his SEP IRA in 2007?

e. Assuming Gerry had a SIMPLE IRA, what is the maximum amount he could contribute to the plan in 2009?

f. Assuming Gerry had an individual 401(k), what is the maximum amount he could contribute to the plan in 2009?

g. Gerry also has a traditional IRA with an account balance of $42,000. He would like to convert the traditional IRA to a Roth IRA. Gerry would like to pay the least amount of tax possible in rolling the account over. How should he accomplish this and what amount of tax will he owe assuming a 30 percent marginal tax rate? What is the amount of the saver's credit assuming the original income information given in this problem?

h. Assume that Gerry rolled over his traditional IRA into a Roth IRA six years ago (rather than in 2009) and that the account now has a balance of $78,000. The couple is considering buying their first home and would like to pay as much down as possible. They have heard from their friends that they can take the funds from their Roth IRA and use it to buy their first home. Are their friends correct? What would you advise them to do?

i. Assume that Gerry and Elaine made $20,000 of total contributions to their qualified retirement accounts in 2009. Also assume that their AGI is $38,000. What is the amount of their saver's credit for 2009?

chapter

14 Tax Consequences of Home Ownership

Learning Objectives

Upon completing this chapter, you should be able to:

LO 1 Compute the taxable gain on the sale of a residence and explain the requirements for excluding gain on the sale.

■

LO 2 Determine the amount of allowable interest expense deductions on loans secured by a residence.

■

LO 3 Discuss the deductibility of real property taxes and describe the first-time home buyer credit.

■

LO 4 Explain the tax issues and consequences associated with rental use of the home, including determining the deductibility of residential rental real estate losses.

■

LO 5 Describe the requirements necessary to qualify for home office deductions and compute the deduction limitations on home office deductions.

Storyline Summary

Taxpayers:	Tyler and Jasmine Jefferson
Location:	Chicago, Illinois
Employment status:	Tyler—Newly hired V.P. of Sales for GLO Corporation earning an annual salary of $225,000 per year. Jasmine—graphic designer, earning an annual salary of $40,000 per year.
Filing status:	Married filing jointly
Dependents:	Two children
Marginal tax rate:	33 percent

W ith the extra income Tyler Jefferson is earning in his new V.P. of Sales position for GLO Corporation, his family now has greater financial flexibility, but with the money comes new possibilities. For one, Tyler and Jasmine Jefferson would like to sell their current home and purchase a larger one closer to Tyler's work. Fortunately, the value of their home has increased considerably since they purchased it, which should allow them to make a substantial down payment on a new home. Still, they would need to acquire financing to make the purchase. Jasmine likes the idea of buying a vacation home in Scottsdale, Arizona. Besides the great weather (she and Tyler both love golf), Scottsdale has the added benefit of being near Jasmine's family. She is trying to sell the second-home idea to Tyler by suggesting that they could rent the house when they're not there to help defray the costs. Finally, Jasmine is seriously considering a transition to self-employment as a graphic designer. She believes, with her experience and contacts, she can find enough clients to keep busy most of the time—and she very much likes the idea of setting aside a room in their primary home as her workplace. ■

When making these decisions, the Jeffersons should consider the tax consequences of their actions. Will they be required to pay taxes on the gain from the sale of their current home? Will the interest expense on the new home be fully deductible? Should they pay points to obtain a lower interest rate on the home loan? What will be the after-tax cost of the loan payments? If they use a home-equity loan to cover personal expenses, is the interest expense deductible? If they borrow money to buy a vacation home, can they deduct interest on the loan? If they rent out the vacation home for part of the year, how do they account for the related income and expenses for tax purposes? If the rental of the second home generates losses, are these losses deductible? If Jasmine sets up a home office, will the Jeffersons be allowed any tax deductions for expenses relating to their home? This chapter answers these and other relevant questions for the Jeffersons and for others interested in the tax consequences of home ownership.

PERSONAL USE OF THE HOME

To buy or to rent? This is a difficult question with no single answer. The decision to purchase a home is a significant one that involves both nontax and tax considerations. Primary nontax factors favoring home ownership include the appreciation potential for the home as an investment. As the value of the home increases, so does the homeowner's net worth. A home is frequently an individual's most significant investment. Therefore, home ownership also involves significant potential risk. When real estate values decline, the owner's net worth declines as well. Homeowners borrowing funds to purchase their home can potentially achieve large returns on their investment due to the power of leverage, but a home is by no means a liquid asset. Furthermore, homeowners must assume the risk associated with the possible default on the loan. If the owner does not make the mortgage payments required by the terms of the loan, the lender may repossess the home. Homeowners also are responsible for the cost or effort required to repair, maintain, and landscape the home. Finally, because building, buying, or selling a home and moving in or out of a home are expensive and time-consuming tasks, home ownership reduces one's ability to relocate to take advantage of new opportunities.

On the tax side, the government clearly smiles on home ownership given the deductions available to homeowners that are unavailable to renters. In fact, in the government's listing of projected "tax expenditures" (tax breaks provided to taxpayers) for the years 2008–2012, the deductibility of mortgage interest on owner-occupied homes is ranked number two.[1] The projections indicate that in 2008 homeowners were expected to save nearly $90 billion in tax payments due to the mortgage interest deduction. Besides the deduction for interest payments made on home-related loans, other tax benefits of home ownership involve excluding gain on the sale of the home, deducting real estate taxes paid on the home, and deducting expenses relating to business offices in the home. Homeowners also may gain tax benefits associated with owning and renting a vacation home. We address the tax consequences of home ownership throughout the remainder of the chapter.

LO1

Exclusion of Gain on Sale of Personal Residence

Because a personal residence is a capital asset, any gain or loss a taxpayer realizes by selling the residence is a capital gain or loss. When a taxpayer sells a personal residence at a loss, the loss is a nondeductible personal loss.[2] However, when a taxpayer sells a personal residence at a gain, the tax consequences are generally much more

---

[1]Number one on the list is the gross income exclusion for employer-paid medical insurance premiums. See http://www.whitehouse.gov/omb/budget/fy2008/pdf/apers/receipts.pdf.

[2]§165(c).

favorable. In fact, taxpayers meeting certain home ownership *and* use requirements can permanently exclude from taxable income all—or at least a portion—of the realized gain on the sale.[3] Gain in excess of the excludable amount generally qualifies as long-term capital gain subject to tax at preferential rates. The amount of the exclusion and the requirements to qualify for the exclusion are described below.

Requirements   To qualify for the exclusion, the taxpayer must meet both ownership and use tests for the residence:

> *Ownership test:* The taxpayer must have owned the property for a total of two or more years during the five-year period ending on the date of the sale. The ownership test prevents a taxpayer from purchasing a home, fixing it up, and soon thereafter selling it and excluding the gain—a real estate investment practice termed **flipping.** In these circumstances, the gain is primarily due to the taxpayer's efforts in remodeling the home, not to general appreciation in the value of the property.

> *Use test:* The taxpayer must have *used* the property as her **principal residence** for a total of two or more years during the five-year period ending on the date of the sale. Congress intended for the exclusion provision to provide tax benefits to homeowners rather than investors or landlords. The use test helps ensure that taxpayers using the exclusion have realized gains from selling the home they actually live in as opposed to selling an investment or rental property. What qualifies as a principal residence? By definition, a taxpayer can have only one "principal" residence. When a taxpayer lives in more than one residence during the year, the determination of which residence is the principal residence depends on the facts and circumstances such as:

- Amount of time the taxpayer spends at each residence during the year.
- The proximity of each residence to the taxpayer's employment.
- The principal place of abode of the taxpayer's immediate family.
- The taxpayer's mailing address for bills and correspondence.

A taxpayer's principal residence *could* be a houseboat, trailer, or condominium—a residence need not be in a fixed location.

Note that the periods of ownership and use need not be continuous nor do they need to cover the same two-year period. In fact, a taxpayer could rent a home and live in it as her principal residence during 2004 and then again during 2006, purchase the home and rent to someone else during 2007 and 2008, and then sell the home at the beginning of 2009—and *still* meet the ownership and use tests!

How do the ownership and use tests apply to married couples filing joint returns? Married couples filing joint returns are eligible for the exclusion if *either* spouse meets the ownership test and *both* spouses meet the principal-use test.

THE KEY FACTS

Exclusion of Gain on Sale of Personal Residence

■ **Exclusion Amount**
· $500,000 for married couples filing joint returns.
· $250,000 for other taxpayers.
· Hardship provisions *maximum exclusion =* full exclusion × months of qualifying ownership and use/24 months.
· Gain eligible for exclusion may be reduced for time home is not used as principal residence if it is being used as a principal residence at the time of the sale.

Example 14-1

When Tyler and Jasmine were married, Jasmine moved into Tyler's home located in Denver, Colorado. Tyler had purchased the home two years before the marriage. After the marriage, the couple lived in the home together as their principal residence for three years before selling the home to move to Chicago. Tyler was the sole owner of the home for the entire five years he resided in the home. Would gain on the sale of the home qualify for the exclusion available to married couples filing jointly even though Jasmine was never an owner of the home?

(continued on page 14-4...)

[3]§121(a). Also see IRS Publication 523 *"Selling Your Home."*

Answer: Yes. Gain on the sale qualifies for the full exclusion available to married couples filing jointly (up to $500,000, as we discuss below) because Tyler met the ownership test and both Tyler and Jasmine met the use test.

What if: Assume that Tyler and Jasmine lived in the home together for only one year before selling it. Would the couple be allowed to exclude any gain on the sale?

Answer: Yes, but because only Tyler meets the ownership and use tests, they would qualify for the exclusion available to *single taxpayers* (up to $250,000, as we discuss below) even if they file a joint return.

Another issue arises when a taxpayer moves out of a home, rents it to another to occupy for a while, and then sells it. Does the taxpayer lose the exclusion because the property is technically a rental property at the time of sale? As we mention above, the tax laws accommodate the taxpayer in this situation because the taxpayer need only use the home as a principal residence for two of the five years preceding the sale. Thus, a taxpayer can still qualify if she moves out and rents the home before selling it. Interestingly, as illustrated in Exhibit 14-1, a taxpayer could technically simultaneously own two residences meeting the ownership and use tests.

While taxpayers may qualify for the exclusion even when they rent homes before selling them, they must consider three issues:

1. If a taxpayer converts a home from a personal residence to a rental property, the tax basis of the home becomes the *lesser* of (a) the taxpayer's basis at the time of the conversion or (b) the fair market value of the home at the time of the conversion (any loss that accrued while the property was personal-use property disappears at the time of the conversion).[4]

2. If a taxpayer deducts depreciation expense (and reduces the basis of the home by the amount of the depreciation expense) while renting it, either before or after using the home as a principal residence, the *gain caused by the reduction in basis from the depreciation expense* is not eligible for the exclusion.[5]

3. If a taxpayer converts a rental home to a principal residence, the basis of the home as a principal residence is the same basis the home had as a rental at the time the rental home was converted to a principal residence. Thus, if at the time of the conversion to personal use, the value of the home is less than the basis of the home, the built-in loss will never be deductible because the rental use has ceased.[6]

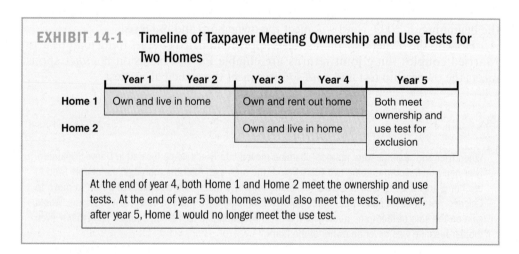

EXHIBIT 14-1   Timeline of Taxpayer Meeting Ownership and Use Tests for Two Homes

At the end of year 4, both Home 1 and Home 2 meet the ownership and use tests. At the end of year 5 both homes would also meet the tests. However, after year 5, Home 1 would no longer meet the use test.

[4]Reg. §1.167(g)-1.
[5]This gain is unrecaptured §1250 gain subject to a maximum tax rate of 25 percent.
[6]To deduct the loss, the taxpayer must sell the home rather than convert it to personal use.

When taxpayers own two homes that meet the requirements and they sell both homes in the same year, can they exclude gain on both homes? Remember the old adage: If it sounds too good to be true, it probably is. Indeed, the tax laws limit each taxpayer to one exclusion every two years. That is, once a taxpayer sells a residence and uses the exclusion on the sale, she will not be allowed to claim another exclusion until at least two years pass from the time of the first sale.

Finally, the exclusion of gain on a sale of a residence provides a great opportunity for contractors in the business of building homes to convert what would otherwise be ordinary income from the taxpayer's trade or business into nontaxable capital gain. Generally when a contractor builds and sells a home for a profit, the gain on the sale is taxable as ordinary business income to the contractor. However, if a contractor builds a home, lives in it for two years, and then sells the home at a profit the gain may qualify for the exclusion. One commentator has pointed out that the gain exclusion provision allows those in the business of building homes to generate the only tax-free business income under the current tax system.[7]

Amount of the Exclusion   Single taxpayers (or married taxpayers when only one spouse meets the requirements) may exclude up to $250,000 of gain on the sale of a principal residence. Married couples filing jointly may exclude up to $500,000 of gain.

Example 14-2

As we described in Example 14-1, the Jeffersons sold their home in Denver, Colorado, and moved to Chicago. Let's assume that Tyler initially purchased the home for $220,000 and the Jeffersons sold the home for $320,000. How much of the $100,000 gain realized on the sale ($320,000 − $220,000) are they allowed to exclude?

Answer: All of it. As we determined in Example 14-1, the Jeffersons qualified for the full exclusion available to married couples filing jointly because Tyler met the ownership test and both Tyler and Jasmine met the use test. Consequently, they are allowed to exclude the entire $100,000 of gain and could have excluded up to $500,000 of gain on the sale.

However, if *either* spouse is ineligible for the exclusion because he or she personally used the $250,000 exclusion on another home sale during the two years before the date of the current sale, the couple's available exclusion is reduced to $250,000. If a widow or widower sells a home that the surviving spouse owned and occupied with the other spouse, the surviving spouse is entitled to the full $500,000 exclusion provided that the surviving spouse sells the home within two years after the date of death of the spouse.

Sometimes taxpayers are unable to meet the ownership and use tests due to unusual or hardship circumstances. For example, a taxpayer may be forced to sell his home before he meets the ownership and use requirements due to a change in employment, significant health issues, or other unforeseen financial difficulties. In such cases, the *maximum* available exclusion is reduced. To qualify for the exclusion due to a change in employment, the taxpayer's new place of employment must be at least 50 miles farther from the residence that is sold than was the previous place of employment.[8] That is, the taxpayer will not qualify unless the taxpayer's commute from the old home to the new job is at least 50 miles longer than the

---

[7]See L. M. Stone, "Obvious Flaws Reduce Confidence in Federal Tax System," *Tax Notes,* February 23, 2004, pp. 1034–35.

[8]If there is no previous place of employment, the distance between the individual's new place of employment and the residence sold must be at least 50 miles.

taxpayer's commute from the old home to the old job.[9] The maximum exclusion available to a taxpayer selling under these circumstances is expressed in the formula presented in Exhibit 14-2.

EXHIBIT 14-2   Formula for Determining Home Sale Exclusion in Hardship Circumstances

Reduced maximum exclusion under hardship circumstances =
Maximum full exclusion × Qualifying months/24 months, where

Maximum full exclusion = $250,000 for single taxpayers or $500,000 for taxpayers filing a joint return.

Qualifying months = the number of months the taxpayer met the ownership and use requirements for the home before *selling* it.

24 months = the number of months taxpayer must own and use home as principal residence to qualify for the full exclusion.[10]

Example 14-3

What if: Let's assume that when the Jeffersons moved from Denver, they purchased a home in Chicago for $275,000 and moved into the home on July 1 of year 0. In January of year 1, Tyler accepted a work opportunity with a different employer located in Miami, Florida. On February 1 of year 1, the Jeffersons sold their home for $295,000 and permanently relocated to Miami. How much of the $20,000 realized gain ($295,000 − $275,000) on their home sale can the Jeffersons *exclude* from taxable income?

Answer: All of it. The Jeffersons lived in the home for only seven months (July 1, year 0 to February 1, year 1), so they do not meet either the ownership or the use test to qualify for the full exclusion. Thus, they must compute their maximum exclusion using the formula presented in Exhibit 14-2 as follows:

$500,000 (max full exclusion) × 7 (qualifying months)/24 = $145,833.

What if: Assume the same facts, except that the Jeffersons realized a $150,000 gain on the sale of their home. How much of the realized gain would they recognize and at what rate would this gain be taxed?

Answer: $150,000 gain realized minus $145,833 exclusion = $4,167 short-term capital gain (the home is a capital asset that the Jeffersons owned for one year or less).

Note, as the previous example illustrates, that under the so-called hardship provision, it is the *maximum exclusion* that is reduced, not necessarily the excludable gain. Consequently, if a taxpayer's gain on the sale of a residence is less than the reduced maximum exclusion, the taxpayer may exclude the full amount of the gain. Finally, the rule limiting taxpayers to claiming one exclusion every two years *does not apply* to taxpayers selling under hardship circumstances.

Limitation on exclusion for nonqualified use.   The amount of gain eligible for exclusion may be limited for taxpayers selling homes after December 31, 2008. The limitation applies if, on or after January 1, 2009, the taxpayer uses the home for something other than a principal residence for a period (termed *nonqualified use*) and then uses the home as a principal residence before selling it. The provision is designed to reduce the excludable gain for taxpayers who use the home as a vacation home or rental property for a period and then convert it to a principal residence before selling

---

[9]You may recall that this is the same test required to determine if a taxpayer qualifies for moving expenses as discussed in Chapter 6.

[10]Taxpayers may choose to use the number of days the taxpayer fully qualified for the exclusion divided by 730 days.

in order to exclude gain (including gain accrued while it was not a principal residence) on the sale. If the limitation applies, the percentage of the gain that is not eligible for exclusion is the ratio of the amount of the nonqualified use divided by the amount of time the taxpayer owned the home (purchase date through date of sale). Note that this provision does not reduce the maximum exclusion. Rather, it reduces the amount of gain eligible for exclusion.

Example 14-4

What if: Suppose that the Jeffersons purchased home 1 on July 1, 2008, for $300,000. They lived in home 1 as their principal residence until July 1, 2011, when they moved to a new principal residence (home 2). They finally sold home 1 on July 1, 2013, for $400,000. What amount of the $100,000 gain on the sale of home 1 ($400,000 amount realized minus $300,000 adjusted basis) may the Jeffersons exclude from gross income?

Answer: All $100,000. The Jeffersons meet the ownership and use tests (they owned and used home 1 as their principal residence for at least two of the five years prior to July 1, 2013) so they qualify for a maximum exclusion of $500,000. Further, the gain eligible for the exclusion is *not* reduced because the Jeffersons stopped using home 1 as a principal residence after July 1, 2011, but they did not use it as a principal residence before they sold it.

What if: Assume the same facts as above, except that on July 1, 2012, the Jeffersons moved back into home 1 and used it as their principal residence until they sold it for $400,000 on July 1, 2013. What amount of the $100,000 gain on the sale of home 1 may the Jeffersons exclude from income?

Answer: $80,000. The Jeffersons meet the ownership and use tests for home 1 and therefore qualify for the maximum $500,000 exclusion. However, because they sold home 1 after January 1, 2009, they stopped using the home as their principal residence for a period (nonqualified use from July 1, 2011–July 1, 2012), and they again used the home as their principal residence before selling (July 1, 2012–July 1, 2013), the gain eligible for exclusion must be reduced. The percentage of the gain that is not eligible for exclusion is 20 percent, which is the amount of nonqualified use (one year; July 1, 2012–July 1, 2013) divided by the total amount of time the Jeffersons owned the home (five years; July 1, 2008–July 1, 2013). Therefore, the Jeffersons must reduce their gain eligible for exclusion by $20,000 ($100,000 gain × 20% reduction percentage), allowing them to exclude $80,000 of the $100,000 gain from gross income.

Exclusion of Gain from Debt Forgiveness on Foreclosure of Home Mortgage   As we discussed in Chapter 5, if, prior to 2007, a lender forecloses (takes possession of) a taxpayer's principal residence, sells the home for less than the taxpayer's outstanding mortgage, and forgives the taxpayer of the remainder of the debt, the taxpayer would be required to include the debt forgiveness in her gross income. However, from January 1, 2007, through December 31, 2012, taxpayers who realize income from this situation are allowed to exclude up to $2 million of debt forgiveness if the debt is secured by the taxpayer's principal residence (the principal residence is collateral for the home) and the debt was incurred to acquire, construct, or substantially improve the home.[11]

Interest Expense on Home-Related Debt   **L02**

A major tax benefit of owning a home is that taxpayers are generally allowed to deduct the interest they pay on their home mortgage loans as an itemized (*from* AGI) deduction. Taxpayers report these itemized deductions on Schedule A of their individual tax Form 1040. For taxpayers that itemize deductions, the mortgage interest expense can generate significant tax savings and reduce the after-tax cost of mortgage payments. Often, this deduction alone exceeds the standard deduction, thus allowing taxpayers to claim other itemized deductions.

[11]§108(h)

Example 14-5

During the current year, Tyler and Jasmine own a home with an average mortgage balance of $300,000. They pay interest at 6 percent annually on the loan. The Jeffersons' marginal income tax rate is 33 percent and, before counting mortgage interest, their itemized deductions exceed the standard deduction. What is the before- and after-tax cost of their mortgage interest expense for the year?

Answer: $18,000 before-tax cost and $12,060 after-tax cost, computed as follows:

Description	Amount	Explanation
(1) Before-tax interest expense	$18,000	$300,000 × 6%. All deductible.
(2) Marginal tax rate	× 33%	
(3) Tax savings from interest expense	5,940	(1) × (2).
After-tax cost of interest expense	**$12,060**	(1) − (3).

Note that the $5,940 tax savings generated by the mortgage interest expense deduction reduces the after-tax cost of their monthly mortgage payment by $495 ($5,940/12).

What if: Assume that instead of buying a home, the Jeffersons rented a home and paid $1,500 a month for rent expense. What would be the before- and after-tax cost of the $18,000 annual rental payments?

Answer: $18,000 before- and after-tax cost of rental payments. Because rental payments are not deductible, they do not generate any tax savings, so the before- and after-tax cost of the rental payments is the same.

Despite the apparent tax savings from buying versus renting a home, it is important to consider that nontax factors could favor renting over purchasing a home.

Taxpayers are allowed to deduct only "qualified" residence interest as an itemized deduction.[12] Qualified residence interest is interest paid on the principal amount of **acquisition indebtedness** and on the principal amount of **home-equity indebtedness.** Both types of indebtedness must be **secured** by a **qualified residence** to qualify. To understand what this means exactly, we need to define a few terms.

Loan secured by residence: The residence is the collateral for the home. If the owner does not make the payments on the loan, the lender may take possession of the home to satisfy the owner's responsibility for the loan.

Qualified residence: The taxpayer's principal residence (as described in the previous section) *and* one other residence. For a taxpayer with *more* than two residences, which property is treated as the second qualified residence is an annual election—that is, the taxpayer can choose to deduct interest related to a particular second home one year and a different second home the next. The second residence is often a vacation home where the taxpayer resides part time. If the taxpayer rents the second residence for part of the year, the residence will qualify if the taxpayer's personal use of the home *exceeds the greater* of (1) 14 days or (2) 10 percent of the number of rental days during the year.[13] Consequently, for a second home to be considered a qualified residence, a taxpayer who rents the home for 100 days must use the home for personal purposes for at least 15 days, and a taxpayer who rents the second home for 200 days must use the home for personal purposes for at least 21 days.

---

[12]See IRS Publication 936, *"Home Mortgage Interest Deduction."*

[13]If the taxpayer does not rent out the property, the taxpayer may choose the property as a qualified residence even if the taxpayer's personal use of the property is 14 days or less.

Acquisition indebtedness: Any debt secured by a qualified residence that is incurred in acquiring, constructing, or substantially improving the residence.

Home-equity indebtedness: Any debt, except for acquisition indebtedness, secured by the taxpayer's qualified residence to *the extent it does not exceed the fair market value of the residence minus the acquisition indebtedness.* That is, for purposes of deducting interest, total qualifying home-related debt cannot exceed the total value of the home. For example, in a rapidly appreciating real estate environment, aggressive lenders sometimes offer "home-equity" loans that result in loan-to-value ratios up to 125 percent. To the extent that the loan exceeds the equity in the home (value minus acquisition indebtedness), the interest is not deductible.[14] This determination is made at the time of the loan, so a subsequent decline in a home's value would not reduce the interest expense deduction.

Borrowers can use the proceeds from a home-equity loan for any purpose, as long as the loan is secured by the residence—hence, the popularity of home-equity loans to consolidate debt and lower monthly payments. However, as we noted in Chapter 7, interest expense on home-equity loans not used to purchase or substantially improve the home is not deductible for AMT purposes. The use of home-equity loans to pay for non-home-related expenditures is an example of the conversion tax planning strategy described in Chapter 3.

Limitations on Home-Related Debt   The tax laws *limit the amount of debt* on which taxpayers can deduct interest expense. Two separate considerations limit the amount of debt that generates qualifying residence (and thus deductible) interest: limitations on the amount of acquisition indebtedness and limitations on the amount of home-equity indebtedness.

Limitation on amount of acquisition indebtedness.   Interest expense of up to $1,000,000 of acquisition indebtedness is deductible as qualified residence interest. Once acquisition indebtedness is established for a qualifying residence (or for the sum of two qualifying residences), only principal payments on the loan(s) can reduce it and only additional indebtedness, secured by the residence(s) *and* incurred to substantially improve the residence(s), can increase it. (Notice the requirements to use funds to *acquire or improve the residence*, a stipulation that markedly differentiates acquisition indebtedness from home-equity indebtedness.)

When a taxpayer **refinances** a mortgage, how does the tax law treat the new loan? Assuming the taxpayer does not use refinance loan proceeds to substantially improve her residence, the refinanced loan is treated as acquisition debt *only to the extent that the principal amount of the refinancing does not exceed the amount of the acquisition debt immediately before the refinancing.* Consequently, any amount borrowed in excess of the remaining principal on the original loan does not qualify as acquisition indebtedness. Interest on the "excess" part of this loan can only be deducted if it qualifies as home-equity indebtedness (described below).

THE KEY FACTS

Home-Related Interest Deduction

■ Deduction allowed for qualified residence interest.
· Principal residence and one other residence.
· If rented out, personal use must exceed greater of (1) 14 days or (2) 10 percent of rental days to be qualified residence.
· Acquisition indebtedness.
· Home-equity indebtedness.

THE KEY FACTS

Home-Related Interest Deduction

■ Acquisition Indebtedness
· Proceeds used to acquire or substantially improve home.
· Limited to $1,000,000.
· Principal payments permanently reduce amount.

Example 14-6

What if: Assume that when they moved to Chicago, the Jeffersons purchased a home costing $330,000 by making a down payment of $300,000 and taking out a $30,000 loan secured by the home. During the next few years, the Jeffersons paid $10,000 of principal on the loan, thereby reducing the loan balance to $20,000. Last year, due to a decrease in interest rates and a need for cash,

(continued on page 14-10...)

---

[14]This is why advertisements for these loans generally suggest borrowers consult with their tax advisors to determine the deductibility of interest on the loans.

the Jeffersons refinanced their mortgage by taking out a loan, secured by their residence, for $150,000. With the $150,000 they paid off the $20,000 balance on the original loan and used the $130,000 of extra cash for purposes unrelated to the home. After the refinance, what is the Jeffersons' acquisition indebtedness?

Answer: $20,000, the same amount as before the refinance. The only way to increase acquisition indebtedness is to borrow money to substantially improve the home. Thus, the Jeffersons' interest deductions on the home will be limited to the interest expense on the $20,000 acquisition indebtedness plus a limited amount of home-equity indebtedness.

What if: Assume the same facts as above except that the Jeffersons used $40,000 of the cash from the loan to build a new garage on their property. After the refinance, what is the Jeffersons' acquisition indebtedness?

Answer: $60,000 ($20,000 original loan principal + $40,000 used to substantially improve home).

Limitation on amount of home-equity indebtedness. As noted earlier, interest on home-equity indebtedness is deductible as qualified residence interest. However, the amount of qualified home-equity indebtedness is limited to the *lesser* of (1) the fair market value of the qualified residence(s) in excess of the acquisition debt related to the residence(s) and (2) $100,000 ($50,000 for married filing separately). Thus, a taxpayer can deduct interest on up to $100,000 of home-related debt above and beyond acquisition debt (limited to $1,000,000) as long as the debt is secured by the equity in the home(s) no matter what the taxpayer does with the proceeds from the home-equity loan. When deciding whether to borrow money through a home-equity loan, the taxpayer must weight the advantage of the interest deductibility against the risk of losing her home if she does not repay the loan.

Example 14-7

What if: Assume that the Jeffersons' home is worth $400,000 and they have a balance of $290,000 on their original home loan. The Jeffersons are interested in purchasing a $50,000 Chevy Suburban. Wanting to finance the full purchase price, they ask you, their financial planner, whether they should borrow the money with a 6 percent automobile loan from their local credit union or use a home-equity loan at 8 percent to fund the purchase. Assuming their marginal tax rate is 33 percent, what is the after-tax interest rate for the automobile loan and what is the after-tax interest rate for the home-equity loan?

Answer: 6 percent for the automobile loan (same as the before-tax rate because the interest is not deductible) and 5.36 percent for the home equity loan [8% × (1 − 33%)]. After taxes, the home-equity loan appears to be a much better deal than the automobile loan. Before taking out the home-equity loan, however, the Jeffersons should consider the economic consequences if they are not able to repay the loan. If they don't make the payments on the automobile loan, they may lose the automobile; if they don't make the payments on the home-equity loan, they may lose their home.

What if: If the Jeffersons wanted to tap their home-equity loan for $110,000 so that they could buy two automobiles, would they be allowed to deduct the interest on the entire loan?

Answer: No. Even though the home has $110,000 of equity ($400,000 fair market value minus $290,000 acquisition indebtedness), the cap on qualifying home-equity debt is $100,000. Consequently, the Jeffersons would be able to deduct interest on only $100,000 of the $110,000 home-equity loan.

Combined limitation on qualifying debt.   What is the maximum amount of debt on which a taxpayer can deduct qualified residence interest? Because the acquisition indebtedness limit of $1,000,000 and the home-equity indebtedness limit of $100,000 are two separate limits, the maximum amount of debt on which a taxpayer may deduct qualified residence interest is $1,100,000—provided, of course, that the value of the taxpayer's qualified residence (or residences) is at least $1,100,000.

When a taxpayer's home-related debt exceeds the limitations, the amount of deductible interest can be determined in one of two ways. First, the deductible interest can be computed as the product of (1) total interest expense on debt secured by the home and (2) the ratio of **qualified debt** to total debt outstanding on the home. This average interest expense option is summarized as follows:

$$\text{Total interest expense} \times \frac{\text{Qualified debt}}{\text{Total debt}} = \text{Deductible interest}$$

The second method is based on the chronological order of when the loans were executed, rather than as a weighted average. A taxpayer can choose to deduct all interest on earlier loans up to the limit on qualifying debt. Once the limit on qualifying debt is reached, interest on debt above the limit is not deductible. Why might taxpayers opt for this ordering method? This method generates a higher deduction when the earlier loans have a higher interest rate than subsequent loans.

Example 14-8

What if: Assume that the Jeffersons moved to Chicago several years ago and purchased a home that was valued at $330,000 by paying $30,000 down and funding the remaining balance with a 30-year mortgage fixed at 6 percent. At the beginning of last year the value of their home had increased to $400,000 and the principal amount of their original loan had been paid down to $290,000. In need of extra cash for anticipated expenditures unrelated to their home, the Jeffersons borrowed $70,000 at a fixed interest rate of 7 percent with a loan secured by their home. As of the beginning of this year, the value of the Jeffersons' home had increased to $420,000. With a need for still more cash, the Jeffersons decided to take out a third loan secured by their home. The Jeffersons borrowed $50,000 on the third mortgage at an annual interest rate of 9 percent. During the year, they made interest-only payments on all three loans. The interest they paid on these loans is summarized as follows:

Loan	Balance	Rate	Interest Paid
Acquisition indebtedness:			
Original home loan	$290,000	6%	$17,400
Home equity indebtedness:			
Home-equity loan 1	70,000	7%	4,900
Home-equity loan 2	50,000	9%	4,500
Totals	$410,000		$26,800

How much of the $26,800 interest expense can the Jeffersons deduct this year using the average interest rate option?

Answer: $25,493. Plugging the numbers into the formula for this option (see above) yields the following:

$$\$26,800 \times \frac{\$390,000}{\$410,000} = \$25,493$$

Where the total interest expense is $26,800, the qualifying debt is $390,000 ($290,000 acquisition indebtedness + $100,000 limit on home-equity indebtedness), and the total debt is $410,000 ($290,000 + $70,000 + $50,000).

(*continued on page 14-12...*)

How much of the $26,800 interest expense can the Jeffersons deduct this year using the chronological order method of determining interest expense?

Answer: $25,000. The first loan is the original home loan. Because the loan is acquisition debt and is under the $1,000,000 acquisition debt limit, the entire $17,400 interest on this loan is deductible. The second mortgage of $70,000 was executed next. Because this loan is a home-equity loan and is under the $100,000 home-equity limit, the entire $4,900 interest on this loan is deductible. Finally, the third mortgage of $50,000 was executed last. However, because only $30,000 of this debt is qualifying home-equity debt ($100,000 limit minus $70,000 second mortgage) only $2,700 of interest on this loan is deductible ($30,000 × 9%). Thus, under the chronological order option, the Jeffersons can deduct $25,000 of the interest expense ($17,400 + $4,900 + $2,700).

Note that the $25,493 interest deduction under the first option is higher than the $25,000 interest expense under the second option because the first home-equity loan has a lower interest rate than the second home-equity loan.

Finally, even though there are separate limits on acquisition indebtedness and home-equity indebtedness, both limits can apply to the same loan.

Example 14-9

Refer back to Example 14-6 where we assumed the Jeffersons refinanced their $20,000 home loan by borrowing $150,000 against their home and paying off the original $20,000 loan. Of course, the Jeffersons can deduct interest on the $20,000 acquisition debt on the loan. How much interest on the remaining $130,000 of the loan are the Jeffersons allowed to deduct?

Answer: The Jeffersons can deduct interest on $100,000 of the remaining $130,000 loan because this is the amount that qualifies as home-equity indebtedness. Interest on the other $30,000 of loan principal is not deductible.

Assuming they paid $9,000 of interest expense on these loans during the year, the Jeffersons could deduct $7,200 of the interest, computed under the average interest rate option as follows:

$$\$9,000 \times \frac{\$120,000}{\$150,000} = \$7,200$$

Note that because in this example the Jeffersons have only one loan (part acquisition debt and part home-equity debt, and part neither), the second (chronological order) method of deducting interest expense does not apply.

Mortgage Insurance   Taxpayers are allowed to deduct as qualified residence interest expense premiums paid or accrued on mortgage insurance (insurance premiums paid by the borrower to protect the lender against the borrower defaulting on the loan).[15] To qualify, the premiums for the mortgage insurance must be paid or accrued in connection with acquisition indebtedness on a qualified residence. The (itemized) deduction is phased out by 10 percent of for every $1,000 (or fraction thereof) that the taxpayer's AGI exceeds $100,000.

Points   A home buyer arranging financing for a home typically incurs several loan-related fees or expenses including charges for "points." A **point** is 1 percent of the principal amount of the loan. Buyers may pay points to compensate lenders for the service of providing the loan; these points are commonly referred to as **loan origination fees**

---

[15]§163(h)(3)(E).

and are not tax deductible. In contrast, taxpayers may pay points to lenders in exchange for reduced interest rates on loans. These points are commonly referred to as **discount points.** Because they effectively represent prepaid interest, points paid for a reduced interest rate are immediately deductible as **qualified residence interest** if the following requirements are met:[16]

1. The amounts paid must conform to an established business general practice of charging points for loans in the area in which the residence is located, and the amount of the points paid must not exceed the amount generally charged in that area.

2. The amounts must be paid in connection with the acquisition of the taxpayer's *principal residence* and the loan *must be secured by that residence* (the deduction for points is not available for points paid in connection with a loan for a second home).

3. The buyer must provide enough funds in the down payment on the home to at least equal the cost of the points (the buyer is not allowed to borrow from the lender to pay the points). However, points paid by the *seller* to the lender in connection with the taxpayer's loan are treated as paid directly by the taxpayer. Consequently, such points are generally deductible by the buyer.

Note that points paid for a reduced interest rate in *refinancing* a home loan are not immediately deductible by the homeowner. These points must be amortized and deducted on a straight-line basis over the life of the loan.[17]

Now that we understand how the tax laws treat points, let's consider the home buyer's decision of whether or not to pay points to obtain a lower interest rate on a home loan. From an economic standpoint, the buyer must choose between (1) paying extra money up front and having lower monthly mortgage payments or (2) paying less initially and having larger monthly payments.

When the taxpayer can afford to pay points, deciding whether or not to do so generally requires a "break-even" analysis. Essentially, the taxpayer determines how long it will take to recoup the after-tax cost of the point(s) through the after-tax interest savings on the loan. Generally speaking, the longer the taxpayer plans on staying in the home and maintaining the loan (not refinancing it), the more likely it is financially beneficial to pay points to obtain a lower interest rate. However, paying points can be costly if, after too short a time, the taxpayer sells the home or refinances the home loan. In these situations, the taxpayer may not reach the break-even point.

Example 14-10

Tyler and Jasmine are seeking financing for their new $800,000 home. They are paying $500,000 down and borrowing the remaining $300,000 to be paid back over 30 years. They have the choice of paying two discount points ($6,000) and getting a fixed interest rate of 5 percent or paying no discount points and getting a fixed interest rate of 6 percent. Assuming the points meet the immediate deductibility requirements, the Jeffersons' marginal tax rate is 33 percent, and they pay interest only for the first three years of the loan, what is the Jeffersons' break-even point for paying the points?

(continued on page 14-14...)

---

[16]Rev. Proc. 94-27 1994-1 C.B. 613.

[17]See Chapter 2 research memo and *J.R. Huntsman v. Comm.* (8 Cir., 1990), 90-2 USTC par. 50,340, rev'g 91 TC 917 (1988) for a limited exception to this rule

Answer: Two years, approximated by considering the first year of the loan as follows:

Loan summary: $300,000; 6 percent rate with no points. 5 percent rate with two points ($6,000). Assume the Jeffersons pay interest only for the first three years.

Description	Amounts	Calculation
(1) Initial cash outflow from paying points	($6,000)	$300,000 × 2%.
(2) Tax benefit from deducting points	+1,980	(1) × 33%.
(3) After-tax cost of points	(4,020)	(1) + (2).
(4) Before-tax *savings per year* from 5% vs. 6% interest rate	3,000	[$300,000 × (6% − 5%)].
(5) *Forgone tax benefit per year* of higher interest rate	(990)	(4) × 33%.
(6) After-tax savings per year of 5% vs. 6% interest rate	$2,010	(4) + (5).
Break-even point in years	2 years	(3)/(6).

The break-even analysis in Example 14-10, while a useful exercise, oversimplifies the calculations a bit. Why? It oversimplifies because it doesn't take into account the present value of the savings, nor does it take into account the increasing principal that would be paid on a traditional principal-and-interest-type loan. In reality, the cost of the points is immediate while the savings comes later—so the break-even point on a present value basis is likely a little longer than two years. Also, the more principal paid on the loan, the less the amount of interest paid each month—so savings from the lower interest rate declines over time, which would also extend the break-even point.

Because points paid on a refinancing are deducted over the life of the loan, the break-even point for paying points on a refinanced mortgage is longer than the break-even point for an original mortgage.

Example 14-11

What if: Assume that due to recent interest rate declines, the Jeffersons have decided to refinance the $300,000 mortgage on their home with a new 30-year loan. The Jeffersons have the option of paying two discount points ($6,000) and obtaining a 5 percent interest rate or obtaining a 6 percent interest rate with no discount points. Assuming the Jeffersons' marginal tax rate is 33 percent and they pay interest only for the first three years of the loan, what is the Jeffersons' approximate break-even point for paying the points on the refinance?

Answer: 2.89 years, calculated as follows:

Loan summary: $300,000; 6 percent rate with no points. 30 years or 5 percent rate with two points ($6,000). Assume the Jeffersons pay interest only for the first three years.

Description	Points	Notes
(1) Initial cash outflow from paying points	($6,000)	$300,000 × 2%.
(2) Tax benefit from deducting points	0	(1) + (2).
(3) After tax cost of points	(6,000)	
(4) Before-tax savings per year from 5% vs. 6% interest rate	3,000	[$300,000 × (6 − 5)%].
(5) Forgone tax benefit per year of higher interest payments	(990)	(4) × 33%.
(6) After-tax savings per year of 5% vs. 6% interest rate	2,010	(4) + (5).
(7) Annual tax savings from amortizing points	66	(1)/30 years × 33%.
(8) Annual after-tax cash flow benefit of paying points	$2,076	(6) + (7).
Break-even point in years	2.89 years	(3)/(8).

The reason for the longer break-even point is that the points effectively cost more because they are not immediately deductible in a refinance.

Real Property Taxes

Owners of personal residences and other types of real estate such as land, rental properties, business buildings, and other types of real property are generally required to pay **real property taxes.** These taxes are assessed by local governments and are based on the fair market value of the property.[18] Real property taxes support general public welfare by providing funding for public needs such as schools and roads.

Local governments set the tax rates applied to the value of the property annually based on financial needs for the year. The applicable rates may depend on the type of real estate. For example, the tax rate for real estate used in a business may be higher than the rates for residential real property. Real property tax payments are deductible by businesses or by taxpayers conducting self-employment activities against business income as *for* AGI deductions, by landlords against rental income as *for* AGI deductions, and by individuals as itemized deductions. As we discussed in Chapter 6, in 2009, taxpayers who do not itemize deductions are allowed to deduct real property taxes by increasing the amount of their basic standard deduction by the lesser of (1) the amount of real property taxes paid during the year or (2) $500 ($1,000 for a married couple filing jointly).

Taxpayers are not allowed to deduct fees paid for setting up water and sewer services, and assessments for local benefits such as streets and sidewalks.[19] Taxpayers generally add these expenditures to the basis of their property.

Frequently, homeowners pay their real estate taxes through an **escrow** (holding) **account** with their mortgage lender. Each monthly payment to the lender includes an amount that represents roughly one-twelfth of the anticipated real property taxes for the year. The actual tax payment (or payments if the taxes are due more than once a year) is made by the mortgage company with funds accumulated in the escrow account. When does the homeowner get to deduct the property taxes? The homeowner gets to deduct the property taxes when the actual taxes are paid to the taxing jurisdiction, not when the homeowner makes payments for taxes to the escrow account.

Because property taxes are generally payable to the government only once or twice a year, who is responsible for paying the taxes when an owner sells a personal residence or another type of real estate during the year? Is the owner at the time the taxes are due responsible for paying the full amount of the taxes? Does the person who makes the tax payment also receive the corresponding tax deduction? In most situations, the buyer and seller divide the responsibility for the tax payments based on the portion of the property tax year that each party held the property. This allocation of taxes between buyer and seller is generally spelled out on the **settlement statement** when the sale becomes final. The settlement statement details the monies paid out and received by the buyer and seller in the transaction (see Appendix A to this chapter for a sample settlement statement). For tax purposes, it doesn't matter who actually pays the tax, although generally the current owner has the responsibility to do so. The tax deduction is based on the relative amount of time each party owned the property during the year (or period over which the property taxes are payable).[20]

---

[18]Local governments tend to understate the fair market value of property when appraising it to minimize the chances that the taxpayer will contest the appraisal.

[19]Reg. §1.164-4(a).

[20]The seller gets a deduction for the taxes allocable for the period of time up to and including the day *before* the date of the sale. The taxes allocable to the day of the sale through the end of the property tax year are deductible by the buyer.

THE KEY FACTS

Real Estate Taxes and First-Time Home Buyer Credit

- Applies to homes, land, business buildings, and other types of real estate.
- Homeowners frequently pay real property tax bill to escrow account.
  · Deduction timing based on payment of taxes to governmental body and not escrow account.
- When homeowners sell home during year.
  · Deduction is based on proportion of year taxpayer lived in home no matter who actually pays tax.
- First-time home buyer refundable credit for first-time home buyers purchasing home on or after April 9, 2008, and before July 1, 2009.
  · Lesser of 10 percent of purchase price or $7,500 ($3,750 if married filing separately).
  · Credit must be paid back over 15 years.

Example 14-12

On February 1 of year 1, Tyler and Jasmine purchased a new home for $800,000. At the time of the purchase, it was estimated that the property tax bill on the home for the year would be $12,000 ($800,000 × 1.5%). Assuming the tax bill is paid and that the property tax bill is based on a calendar year, how much will the Jeffersons *deduct* in property taxes for year 1?

Answer: $11,000. Because the seller lived in the home for one-twelfth of the year (January) and the Jeffersons lived in the home for eleven-twelfths of the year (February through December) the seller will deduct $1,000 of the property taxes (one-twelfth) and the Jeffersons will deduct (as an itemized deduciton) eleven-twelfths ($11,000).

First-Time Home Buyer Tax Credit

Recent changes in the tax laws allow taxpayers to claim a *nonrefundable* tax credit equal to the lesser of (1) 10 percent of the purchase price of a home or (2) $7,500 ($3,750 for married taxpayers filing separately).[21] The credit is available for first-time home buyers purchasing homes on or after April 9, 2008, and before July 1, 2009. A first-time home buyer is a person who did not own a *principal* residence during the three-year period before purchasing the new home. The credit phases out proportionally for married taxpayers filing jointly with modified AGI between $150,000 and $170,000 and for other taxpayers with modified AGI between $75,000 and $95,000. For this purpose, modified AGI is AGI before considering the foreign earned income exclusion and certain other exclusions.[22] Qualifying taxpayers purchasing a home in 2009 may claim the credit on their 2008 or 2009 tax return. If they purchase the residence after filing a 2008 tax return, they have the option of filing an amended 2008 tax return to claim the credit for 2008.

Example 14-13

What if: Suppose the Jeffersons' had rented for several years. On May 1, 2009, they purchased a new home for $300,000. How much first-time home buyer credit may they claim if their AGI is $140,000?

Answer: $7,500, the lesser of (1) $30,000 (10 percent x $300,000 purchase price of the home) and (2) $7,500.

Assume the same facts as above, except their AGI is $160,000. How much first-time home buyer credit may they claim?

Answer: $3,750. They qualified for the $7,500 credit, but they lose one-half of the credit because their $160,000 AGI is one-half of the way through the $20,000 phase-out range between $150,000 to $170,000 of AGI.

Assuming the Jeffersons are allowed to claim the entire credit without phase-out, how do they claim the credit?

Answer: They may (1) claim the credit on their 2009 tax return; (2) claim it when they file their 2008 tax return; or (3) if they had already filed their 2008 return by May 1 when they acquired the home, they can file an amended 2008 tax return to claim the credit.

The first-time home buyer credit is unlike other personal federal tax credits because taxpayers must repay the credit via equal installments over a 15-year period beginning in the second tax year after the year in which they purchased the residence

[21]§36.
[22]§36(b)(2)(B).

that qualified them for the credit. If a taxpayer sells or no longer uses the home as her personal residence before repaying the credit, the balance of the credit is due in the year in which the residence is sold or is no longer used as a principal residence. The amount of the credit due in these circumstances may not exceed the amount of gain from the sale of the residence to an unrelated person.

Example 14-14

What if: Suppose the Jeffersons purchased a home on May 1, 2009, and that they qualified for and claimed a $7,500 first-time home buyer credit. When are they required to start paying back the credit, and what is the amount of their first payback installment payment?

Answer: The Jeffersons are required to begin making $500 annual payments to pay back the credit when they file their 2011 tax return. They will make the $500 payments each year from 2011 through 2025.

What if: Suppose the Jeffersons sell their home in 2012, after they had made one $500 installment payment. How much of the credit are they required to pay back when they file their 2012 tax return?

Answer: $7,000. They paid $500 of the $7,500 credit with their 2011 tax return and they must pay the remainder of the unpaid balance of the credit with their 2012 tax return.

RENTAL USE OF THE HOME

LO4

A taxpayer with the financial wherewithal to do so may purchase a second home as a vacation home, a rental property, or a combination of the two. A taxpayer may own a second home outright or may share ownership with others through a timeshare or fractional ownership arrangement. The nontax benefits of owning a second home include a fixed vacation destination, the ability to trade the use of the home with an owner of a home in a different destination, the opportunity for generating income through rentals, and the potential appreciation of the second home as an investment. The nontax costs of owning a second home include the initial cost of the home, the extra cost of maintaining the home, the hassle of dealing with renters or property managers, and the downside risk associated with holding the second home as an investment.

In contrast to a taxpayer's primary residence, the tax consequences of owning a second home depend on the number of days the taxpayer uses the home for personal purposes and how many days the taxpayer rents the home. The personal vs. rental use can be categorized in one of three ways:

1. Primarily personal use with minimal rental use (a personal residence).
2. Significant personal and rental use (a vacation home).
3. Minimal personal use with significant rental use (a rental property).

To make these determinations, the taxpayer needs to calculate the number of days the rental property was used for personal use during the year and the number of days the property was rented out during the year. So what counts as a day of personal use and what counts as a day of rental use? Exhibit 14-3 summarizes rules for determining the days of personal use.

THE KEY FACTS

Rental Use of the Home

■ Tax treatment depends on amount of personal and rental use. The three categories are:
· Primarily personal with minimum rental (principal residence).
· Significant personal and rental use (vacation home).
· Minimal personal use with significant rental use (rental property).

EXHIBIT 14-3   **Personal Use and Deemed Personal Use of a Home**

(1) Taxpayer stays in home.[23]
(2) Relative of an owner stays in the home, even if the relative pays full fair market value rent.
(3) A nonowner stays in the home under a vacation home exchange or swap arrangement.
(4) Taxpayer rents out the property for less than fair market value.

---

[23]This includes use by a co-owner even when the co-owner pays a usage fee.

Rental use includes (1) days when the property is rented out at fair market value and (2) days spent repairing or maintaining the home for rental use. Days when the home is available for rent, but not actually rented out, *do not count* either as personal days or as rental days.

Property Used Primarily for Personal Purposes with Minimal Rental Use (Residence)

The law is simple for homeowners who rent the home for a minimal amount of time during the year. Taxpayers who live in a home for at least 15 days and rent it out for 14 days or less are not required to include the gross receipts in rental income and are not allowed to deduct any expenses related to the rental. The owner is, however, allowed to deduct qualified residence interest and real property taxes on the second home as itemized deductions or in the case of real property taxes as an additional standard deduction for non-itemizers.

Example 14-15

The Jeffersons purchased a vacation home in a golf community in Scottsdale, Arizona, in January of year 1. They spent 10 days vacationing in the home in early March and another 15 days vacationing in the home in mid-December. In early February, they rented the home for 14 days to a group of golfers who were in town to attend a PGA Tour golf tournament and to play golf. The Jeffersons received $6,000 in rent from the group and the Jeffersons incurred $1,000 of expenses relating to the rental home. The Jeffersons did not rent the property again for the rest of the year. How much will the $5,000 net income from the rental increase their taxable income?

Answer: Zero! Because the Jeffersons lived in the home for at least 15 days (25 days) and rented the home for fewer than 15 days (14 days) during year 1, they do not report the rental income to the IRS and they do not deduct expenses associated with the rental. The Jeffersons saved $1,650 in taxes by excluding the $5,000 of net rental income ($5,000 net income x 33 percent marginal tax rate). Note that the Jeffersons can also deduct the mortgage interest and real property taxes on the property for the *full year* as itemized deductions.

Taxes in the Real World   *Extreme Tax Savings Strategy?*

Newsweek reports that *Extreme Makeover: Home Edition* signs a contract with the contestants to rent the home from the contestant for 10 days. The "makeover" or improvements of the home take the place of rental payments. Because the rental period is less than 15 days, the value of the improvements, which would otherwise be taxable income, is not reported as taxable income by the contestant.[24]

Note that this appears to be a fairly aggressive interpretation of the tax law in this situation. In fact, the IRS has suggested in a nonbinding information letter that "to the extent that the value of the improvements constitutes a prize or an award . . . it cannot also be considered rent, and therefore could not qualify for the exclusion from gross income under §280A(g) of the Code."[25]

A taxpayer with a strategically located second (or even first) home can take advantage of this favorable tax rule by renting the property and excluding potentially large rental payments from those in town to attend high-profile events such as certain college football games (for example, games for Notre Dame University or the University of Texas), the Olympics, the Masters golf tournament, the Super Bowl, and Mardi Gras.

[24]D. McGinn, "Television: Tax Trouble for ABC's 'Extreme' Winners?" *Newsweek,* May 17, 2004, p. 12.
[25]INFO 2006-12, release date March 31, 2006.

Property with Significant Personal and Significant Rental Use (Vacation Home)

To fall into this category, the taxpayer must have (1) rented the home for more than 14 days during the year and (2) used the home for personal purposes for *more than the greater* of (a) 14 days or (b) 10 percent of the number of rental days during the year. Note that this is the same test we discussed earlier in the chapter that the taxpayer must meet in order for the home to qualify for mortgage interest expense deductions. For example, a taxpayer who rents her home for 200 days and uses the home for personal purposes for *more than* 20 days (200 days × 10%) is subject to the rules applicable to property in this category. If the same taxpayer uses the home for personal purposes for 20 days or less, the taxpayer is *not* subject to the rules in this category, but would apply the rules in the next category (minimal personal use and significant rental use).

When the home falls within the significant personal and rental use category, the rental income is included in gross income and the expenses relating to the home are allocated between personal and rental use. The expenses allocated to personal use are not deductible unless they are deductible under other nonrental tax provisions as itemized deductions (mortgage interest and property taxes) or in the case of real property taxes as a limited additional standard deduction for nonitemizers. The expenses allocated to the rental use are deductible but only to the extent of gross income from the property.[26]

When the total amount of deductions allocable to rental use exceeds gross rental income, the deductions must be deducted in a particular sequence. In general terms, the deduction sequence is unfavorable for taxpayers, because it is designed to maximize taxpayer deductions for expenses that would be deductible even without any rental use of the home (mortgage interest and real property taxes) and to minimize the allowable depreciation deductions for the home. Amounts not deducted in the current year as rental deductions are either deducted as itemized deductions (mortgage interest and real property taxes on Schedule A of Form 1040) or carried forward to the next tax year (all other deductions).

Expenses allocable to the rental use are divided into one of three categories or "tiers." Tier 1 expenses are deducted first, followed by tier 2 expenses, and then tier 3 expenses. The tier 1, 2, and 3 expenses for rental property are described in Exhibit 14-4 as follows:

EXHIBIT 14-4   Rental Expenses by Tier and Deduction Sequence

Tier 1
Expenses that are deductible without regard to the rental activity including mortgage interest expense and real property taxes that are deductible in any event as itemized deductions.

↓

Tier 2
All other expenses attributable to the rental activity other than depreciation expense including payments for utilities, maintenance, and other direct expenses

↓

Tier 3
Depreciation expense

---

[26]Interest and property taxes allocated to the rental are deductible for AGI no matter the amount of gross income from the rental property. See §280A(c)(5).

EXHIBIT 14-5   **Tax Court vs. IRS Method of Allocating Expenses**

Rental Allocation	Tax Court Method	IRS Method
Mortgage interest and property taxes (tier 1 expenses)	$\text{Expense} \times \dfrac{\text{Total rental days}}{365}$	$\text{Expense} \times \dfrac{\text{Total rental days}}{\text{Total days used}}$
All other expenses	$\text{Expense} \times \dfrac{\text{Total rental days}}{\text{Total days used}}$	$\text{Expense} \times \dfrac{\text{Total rental days}}{\text{Total days used}}$

Expenses within each tier are *generally* allocated to rental use based on the ratio of the number of days of rental use to the total number of days the property was used for rental and personal purposes (See Exhibit 14-5). All expenses not allocated to rental use are allocated to personal use.

The only potential exception to the general allocation rule involves the allocation of mortgage interest expense and real property taxes (tier 1 expenses). The IRS and the Tax Court disagree on how to allocate these particular expenses. The IRS allocates these expenses the same way as all other expenses. However, the Tax Court allocates *interest* and *taxes* to rental use based on the fraction of days that the property was rented over the *number of days in the year*, rather than the number of days the property was used for any purpose during the year.[27] The IRS and Tax Court allocation methods are described in Exhibit 14-5.

The Tax Court justifies its approach by pointing out that interest expense and property taxes accrue over the entire year regardless of the level of personal or rental use. The Tax Court method generally favors the taxpayer because it tends to allocate less interest expense and real property taxes to the rental use, which reduces the tier 1 expenses and allows more tier 2 and tier 3 expenses to be deducted when the gross income limitation applies. That is, the sum of the taxpayer's deductible personal (*from* AGI) and rental expenses (*for* AGI) associated with the rental home under the Tax Court method generally will exceed the sum of personal (*from* AGI) and rental expenses (*for* AGI) associated with the home under the IRS method when the gross income limitation applies. This is because the taxpayer does not lose deductions for the extra interest and real property taxes allocated to personal use under the Tax Court method because these expenses are allowed as itemized deductions on Schedule A.

Example 14-16

At the beginning of year 1, the Jeffersons purchased a vacation home in Scottsdale, Arizona, for $400,000. They paid $100,000 down and financed the remaining $300,000 with a 6 percent mortgage secured by the home. During the year, the Jeffersons used the home for personal purposes for 30 days and rented the home for 200 days, receiving $37,000 of rental income. Thus, the home falls in the significant personal and rental use category. How are their expenses allocated to the rental use under the IRS and Tax Court methods?

(*continued on page 14-21...*)

[27]The Tax Court method of allocating these expenses is also referred to as the Bolton method after the taxpayer in the court case in which the Tax Court approved this method of allocating deductions. While the court case initially was tried in the Tax Court, the decision in favor of the taxpayer was appealed to the Ninth Circuit Court that also ruled in favor of the taxpayer and sanctioned the use of the Tax Court or Bolton method of allocating interest expense. *Bolton v. Commissioner*, 82-2 USTC ¶9699 (CA 9), Affirming Tax Court, 77 TC 104.

Answer: See the following summary of allocation of expenses associated with the home:

Allocation Method to Rental Use

Expense	Amount	Tier	IRS Method (200/230)	Tax Court Method (200/365 Tier 1 200/230 other)
Interest	$18,000	1	$15,652	$ 9,863
Real estate taxes	5,000	1	4,348	2,740
Total tier 1 expenses	**$23,000**	**1**	**$20,000**	**$12,603**
Utilities	4,500	2	3,913	3,913
Repairs	1,800	2	1,565	1,565
Insurance	3,500	2	3,043	3,043
Maintenance	3,200	2	2,782	2,782
Total tier 2 expenses	**$13,000**	**2**	**$11,303**	**$11,303**
Tier 3: Depreciation	**13,939**	**3**	**$12,121**	**$12,121**
Total expenses on property	$49,939			

Net income from rental	IRS Method	Tax Court Method
Rental receipts	$37,000	$37,000
Less tier 1 expenses	(20,000)	(12,603)
Income after tier 1 expenses	17,000	24,397
Less tier 2 expenses	(11,303)	(11,303)
Income after tier 2 expenses	5,697	13,094
Less: tier 3 expenses	(5,697)	(12,121)
Taxable rental income	**$ 0**	**$ 973**
Deductible personal expenses (interest and property taxes)	$ 3,000	$10,397
Deductible rental expenses (sum of tier 1, 2, and 3 expenses)	37,000	36,027
Total personal and rental expenses	**$40,000**	**$46,424**

Note that under the Tax Court method, the Jeffersons are able to deduct $7,397 more in itemized deductions for interest and real property taxes than they do under the IRS method, and they deduct $973 fewer rental expenses (*for* AGI) under the Tax Court method relative to the IRS method. In total, the Jeffersons are allowed to deduct $6,424 more in total deductions under the Tax Court method than the IRS method in the current year. However, under the IRS method, the Jeffersons are allowed to carry forward to next year the $6,424 in depreciation expense that they were not allowed to deduct in the current year ($12,121– $5,697). Under the Tax Court method, they were able to deduct all of their expenses so they do not carry forward any expenses to future years.

Taxpayers would report their rental activities on Schedule E of Form 1040. The deductible tier 1, tier 2, and tier 3 expenses are *for* AGI deductions. Exhibit 14-6 displays the completed Schedule E for the Jefferson's Scottsdale vacation home using the Tax Court method.

Property Used Primarily for Rental Purposes with Minimal or No Personal Use (Rental)

To fall into this category, the taxpayer must (1) rent the property for 15 days or more and use the property for personal purposes for no more than the *greater of* (a) 14 days or (b) 10 percent of the total days the property is rented. Consequently,

---

THE KEY FACTS

Rental Use of the Home

▎ Significant personal and rental use.

· Use home for personal purposes for greater of (1) 15 days or (2) more than 10 percent of rental days.

· Allocate expenses between rental use and personal use.

· Interest and taxes allocated to personal use deducted as itemized deductions and all other expenses allocated to personal not deductible.

· IRS method allocates interest and taxes to rental use based on rental use to total use for the year while Tax Court method allocates to rental use based on rental use to total days in entire year.

· Rental deductions limited to gross rental income. When limited deduct tier 1 (interest and taxes) first, then tier 2 (all expenses except interest, taxes, and depreciation), and then tier 3 (depreciation).

THE KEY FACTS

Rental Use of the Home

▎ Property used primarily for rental with minimal personal use.

· Must rent for 15 days or more and limit personal use to *greater* of (1) 14 days or (2) 10 percent of rental days.

· Allocate expenses to rental and personal use.

· Rental deductions in excess of rental income are deductible subject to passive loss limitation rules.

· Interest expense allocated to personal use not deductible.

EXHIBIT 14-6   Jeffersons' Schedule E for Vacation Home Rental

SCHEDULE E (Form 1040)	Supplemental Income and Loss	OMB No. 1545-0074
Department of the Treasury Internal Revenue Service (99)	(From rental real estate, royalties, partnerships, S corporations, estates, trusts, REMICs, etc.) ▶ Attach to Form 1040, 1040NR, or Form 1041. ▶ See Instructions for Schedule E (Form 1040).	2008 Attachment Sequence No. **13**

Name(s) shown on return	Your social security number
Tyler and Jasmine Jefferson	321 ┊ 54 ┊ 9876

Part I   Income or Loss From Rental Real Estate and Royalties Note. If you are in the business of renting personal property, use **Schedule C** or **C-EZ** (see page E-3). If you are an individual, report farm rental income or loss from **Form 4835** on page 2, line 40.

1 List the type and address of each **rental real estate property**:

A Residence
   3 hole in one blvd. Scottsdale, AZ 85262

B ....

C ....

2 For each rental real estate property listed on line 1, did you or your family use it during the tax year for personal purposes for more than the greater of:
- 14 days **or**
- 10% of the total days rented at fair rental value?
(See page E-3)

	Yes	No
A	✓	
B		
C		

			Properties				Totals (Add columns A, B, and C.)	
Income:			A	B	C			
3	Rents received	3	$37,000			3		
4	Royalties received	4				4		
Expenses:								
5	Advertising	5						
6	Auto and travel (see page E-4)	6						
7	Cleaning and maintenance	7	2,782					
8	Commissions	8						
9	Insurance	9	3,043					
10	Legal and other professional fees	10						
11	Management fees	11						
12	Mortgage interest paid to banks, etc. (see page E-5)	12	9,863			12		
13	Other interest	13						
14	Repairs	14	1,565					
15	Supplies	15						
16	Taxes	16	2,740					
17	Utilities	17	3,913					
18	Other (list) ▶	18						
19	Add lines 5 through 18	19				19		
20	Depreciation expense or depletion (see page E-5)	20	12,121			20		
21	Total expenses. Add lines 19 and 20	21	36,027					
22	Income or (loss) from rental real estate or royalty properties. Subtract line 21 from line 3 (rents) or line 4 (royalties). If the result is a (loss), see page E-5 to find out if you must file **Form 6198**	22	$973					
23	Deductible rental real estate loss. **Caution.** Your rental real estate loss on line 22 may be limited. See page E-5 to find out if you must file **Form 8582.** Real estate professionals **must** complete line 43 on page 2	23	( )	( )	( )			

24	**Income.** Add positive amounts shown on line 22. **Do not** include any losses	24	$973
25	**Losses.** Add royalty losses from line 22 and rental real estate losses from line 23. Enter total losses here	25	( )
26	**Total rental real estate and royalty income or (loss).** Combine lines 24 and 25. Enter the result here. If Parts II, III, IV, and line 40 on page 2 do not apply to you, also enter this amount on Form 1040, line 17, or Form 1040NR, line 18. Otherwise, include this amount in the total on line 41 on page 2	26	$973

For Paperwork Reduction Act Notice, see page E-8 of the instructions.   Cat. No. 11344L   Schedule E (Form 1040) 2008 a taxpayer who rents the home for 100 days may use it for 14 days of personal use and still qualify for this category. If a taxpayer rents the home for 200 days, she must limit her personal use to 20 days for the property to qualify. For property in this category, the taxpayer includes the rental receipts in gross income and deducts all of the rental expenses *allocated to the rental use* of the property. When the property is used for even a day for personal purposes, the expenses must be allocated between the rental usage and the personal usage. In this situation, however, the law does *not allow* the taxpayer to deduct mortgage interest not allocated to rental use because the taxpayer does not meet the minimum amount of personal use required for the deduction (the home is not a qualified residence—see our earlier discussion on interest expense). However, the taxpayer is still allowed to deduct real property taxes not allocated to the rental. In contrast to the significant personal and rental use category, if the rental expenses exceed the gross income from the rental for property in this category, the loss is deductible subject to the passive activity restrictions discussed below.

Example 14-17

Assume the same facts we used in Example 14-16 except that the Jeffersons *did not use the home at all for personal purposes.* They received $37,000 in gross rental income for the year and incurred $49,939 of expenses relating to the rental property. How much can the Jeffersons deduct?

Answer: The good news is that the deductions are not limited to gross income from the rental so they can deduct all $49,939, generating a ($12,939) loss on the property ($37,000 − $49,939). The bad news is that, as we discuss below, the loss may not be immediately deductible due to the passive activity loss limitations.

Exhibit 14-7 summarizes the tax rules relating to a home used for rental purposes depending on the extent of rental (and personal use).

Losses on Rental Property A rental property can be a great investment that gets the best of all worlds. It could (1) appreciate in value, (2) produce annual positive cash flow (rental receipts exceed expenses other than depreciation), and (3) generate tax losses that reduce the taxes the owner is required to pay on other sources of income. Consider the Jeffersons' second-home property, purchased for $400,000 and used primarily as a rental home (see Example 14-16), which we'll assume has appreciated to $440,000 by the end of year 1. The property has appreciated by $40,000, produced a positive cash flow of $1,000 [$37,000 rental income minus expenses other than depreciation of $36,000 ($49,939 total expenses minus depreciation expense of $13,939)], and generated a net tax loss of $12,939. This tax loss apparently saves the Jeffersons $4,270 in taxes [($12,939) × 33% marginal tax rate].

Thus, the increase in the Jeffersons' wealth from their second-home investment in year 1 appears to be $45,270 ($40,000 appreciation + $1,000 rental cash flow + $4,270 tax savings). But as noted elsewhere in this text, when a tax outcome seems too good to be true, it usually is. Read on.

Passive activity loss rules. In Chapter 11, we introduced the **passive activity loss** rules that indicate taxpayers may only deduct passive losses for a year to the extent of their passive income. We also learned that, by definition, a rental activity (including a second home rental) is considered to be a passive activity. Because they are passive losses, losses from rental property are generally not allowed to offset other ordinary or investment type income. However, as we also discussed in Chapter 11, a

THE KEY FACTS

Rental Losses

- Losses on home rentals are passive losses.

- Passive loss rules generally limit losses from passive activities such as rental to passive income from other sources.
  - Passive losses in excess of passive income are suspended and deductible against passive income in the future or when the taxpayer sells the passive activity generating the loss.

- Rental real estate exception to passive loss rules
  - Applies to active participants in rental property.
  - Deduct up to $25,000 of rental real estate loss against ordinary income.
  - $25,000 maximum deduction phased out by 50 cents for every dollar of AGI over $100,000 (excluding the rental loss deduction). Fully phased out at $150,000 of AGI.

EXHIBIT 14-7   **Summary of Tax Rules Relating to Home Used for Rental Purposes**

	Primarily Personal Use and Minimal Rental Use	Significant Personal and Rental Use	Significant Rental Use and Minimal Personal Use
Classification test	Reside in home for at least 15 days and rent home for fewer than 15 days during the year.	Rent home for 15 days or more and use home for personal purposes for more than the greater of (1) 14 days or (2) 10 percent of the total rental days.	Rent home for 15 days or more, and limit personal use to the greater of (1) 14 days or (2) 10 percent of the rental days.
Rental revenue	Exclude from gross income.	Include in gross income.	Include in gross income.
Treatment of mortgage interest and real estate taxes	Deductible as itemized deductions.	Allocate between personal-use days and rental days; interest and taxes allocated to rental days are deductible as rental expenses; interest and taxes allocated to personal-use days are deductible as itemized deductions.	Allocated between personal-use days and rental days; interest and taxes allocated to rental days are deductible as rental expenses; taxes allocated to personal-use days are deductible as itemized deductions; interest allocated to personal-use days is not deductible.
Treatment of all other expenses	Not deductible.	Allocate between personal-use days and rental days; expenses allocated to personal-use days are not deductible; expenses allocated to rental days are deductible as rental expenses to the extent of gross income from the property; when expenses allocated to rental days exceed the rental income, must use tier system for determining allowed deductions.	Allocated between personal-use days and rental days; expenses allocated to personal-use days are not deductible; expenses allocated to rental days are deductible and can generate loss but loss is subject to passive activity rules.
Excess expenses.	Not applicable.	Rental expenses in excess of rental income are carried forward to the next year.	Not applicable; rental expenses are deductible, even if they create a rental loss.

taxpayer who is an **active participant** in the rental activity may be allowed to deduct up to $25,000 of the rental loss against other types of income.[28] Consistent with a number of tax benefits, the exception amount for active owners is phased out as income increases: the $25,000 maximum exception amount is phased out by 50 cents for every dollar the taxpayer's adjusted gross income (before considering the rental loss) exceeds $100,000. Consequently, the entire $25,000 is phased out when the taxpayer's adjusted gross income reaches $150,000.

---

[28]§469(i).

Example 14-18

The Jeffersons incurred a $12,939 passive loss from their Scottsdale rental home, and they did not receive any passive income during the year. Assuming their current year AGI is $250,000 and that they are considered to be active participants in the rental activity, how much of the rental loss are the Jeffersons allowed to deduct this year under the rental real estate exception to the passive activity loss rules?

Answer: $0. Because their adjusted gross income exceeds $150,000, the $25,000 deduction exception to the passive activity loss rules is completely phased out. Consequently, the Jeffersons are not allowed to deduct any of the $12,939 rental loss from year 1.

What if: How much of the $12,939 loss could the Jeffersons deduct if their adjusted gross income (before considering the rental loss) was $120,000?

Answer: They could deduct the entire $12,939 loss. The $25,000 exception amount would be reduced by a $10,000 phase-out [50 cents × ($120,000 − $100,000)]. The maximum amount of the rental loss that can offset ordinary income would therefore be reduced from $25,000 to $15,000 ($25,000 − $10,000 phased out). However, because their loss is less than $15,000, they may deduct the entire $12,939 rental loss against their other sources of income in year 1.

Are passive losses from rental real estate activities that taxpayers are not allowed to deduct in the current year permanently disallowed? No, these losses are suspended until the taxpayer generates passive income or until the taxpayer sells the property that generated the passive loss. On the sale, in addition to reporting gain or loss from the sale of the property, the taxpayer will be allowed to deduct suspended passive losses against ordinary income.

BUSINESS USE OF THE HOME

L05

Because a personal residence is a personal-use asset, utility payments and depreciation due to wear and tear are not deductible expenses. However, taxpayers who use their home—or at least part of their home—for business purposes may be able to deduct expenses associated with their home use if they meet certain stringent requirements.[29]

To qualify for **home office deductions,** a taxpayer must use her home—or part of her home—*exclusively and regularly* as either (1) the principal place of business for any of the taxpayer's trade or businesses, or (2) as a place to meet with patients, clients, or customers in the normal course of business.

Let's consider these requirements in turn. When a taxpayer has more than one business location, including the home, which is her principal place of business? This is a facts-and-circumstances determination based upon (a) the total time spent doing work at each location, (b) the facilities for doing work at each location, and (c) the relative amount of income derived from each location. By definition, a taxpayer's principal place of business also includes the place of business used by the taxpayer for the administrative or management activities of the taxpayer's trade or business *if there is no other fixed location of the trade or business where the taxpayer conducts substantial administrative or management activities of the trade or business.*

If a taxpayer meets with clients or patients in her home during the normal course of business, she qualifies for the home office deduction even if the home is not her principal place of business. However, the clients or patients must visit the taxpayer's home *in person.* Communication through telephone calls or other types of communication technology does not qualify.

---

[29]§280A. If taxpayers rent the home they occupy and they meet the requirements for business use of the home, they can deduct part of the rent they pay. To determine the amount of the deduction, multiply the rental payment by the percentage of the home used for business purposes.

Example 14-19	

Jasmine recently quit her job as an employee for an advertising firm because, with the move to the new home, the commute was too long. She has decided to go it alone as a self-employed graphic designer. She uses a large room in the basement of the Jeffersons' new home as her office. The room has been wired for all of her office needs. Does this space qualify for a home office deduction?

Answer: A qualified yes. While Jasmine will spend a good deal of time meeting with clients on location, she has no other fixed location for her trade or business. Consequently, as long as the office is used *exclusively* for business purposes, the Jeffersons qualify for home office deductions subject to certain limitations described below.

> **THE KEY FACTS**
>
> **Home Office Deduction**
>
> ■ Deductibility limits on expenses allocated to office.
> · If employee, deducted as unreimbursed employee business expense.
> · If self-employed, deducted for AGI but deduction limited to business income before the deduction.
> · If deduction is limited by income limitation, apply the same tiered system as used for rental property when deductions are limited to rental income.
>
> ■ Depreciation expense
> · Reduces basis in home.
> · Gain on sale due to depreciation is ineligible for exclusion.
> · This gain is taxed at a maximum 25 percent rate as unrecaptured Sec. 1250 gain.

Finally, note that an *employee* (not a self-employed taxpayer) who otherwise meets these requirements qualifies for home office deductions only if the employee's use of the home is considered to be for the convenience of the employer. Generally, with such strict requirements, only self-employed taxpayers and employees such as outside salespersons or full-time telecommuters who have no office space anywhere except at home can qualify for the deductions.

Direct vs. Indirect Expenses

When a taxpayer qualifies for home office deductions the deductions are limited to expenses that are related—either directly or indirectly—to the business. Direct expenses are expenses incurred in maintaining the room or part of the home that is set aside for business use. Direct expenses include painting or costs of other repairs to the area of the home used for business.[30] These expenses are deductible in full as home office expenses. Indirect expenses are expenses incurred in maintaining and using the home. Indirect expenses include insurance, utilities, interest, real property taxes, general repairs, and depreciation on the home as if it were used entirely for business purposes. In contrast to direct expenses, only indirect expenses *allocated* to the home office space are deductible.

How do taxpayers allocate indirect expenses to the home office space? If the rooms in the home are roughly of equal size, the taxpayer may allocate the indirect expenses to the business portion of the home based on the number of rooms. In a 10-room home, a taxpayer using one room for qualifying business use is allowed to deduct 10 percent of the indirect expenses. Alternatively, the taxpayer may allocate indirect expenses based on the amount of the space or square footage of the business-use room relative to the total square footage in the home. If the home is 5,000 square feet and the home office is 250 square feet, the taxpayer may deduct 5 percent of the indirect expenses. Unrelated expenses such painting a room not used for business purposes are not deductible.

Example 14-20	

The Jeffersons moved into their new $800,000, 6,000-square-foot home on February 1 of the current year. Jasmine quit her job and set up a 420-square-foot home office in the basement on that same date. Through the end of the calendar year, the Jeffersons incurred several expenses relating to their

(continued on page 14-27...)

---

[30]The basic local telephone service charge, including taxes, for the first telephone line into a home is a nondeductible personal expense. However, charges for business long-distance phone calls on that line, as well as the cost of a second line into the home used exclusively for business, are deductible business expenses. However, these expenses are not deducted as home office expenses. Rather, these expenses are deducted separately on the appropriate form or schedule. Taxpayers filing Schedule C (Form 1040), would deduct these expenses on line 25 as utilities.

home (see table below). Assuming they qualify for the home office deduction, they would sum the direct expenses and the indirect expenses allocated to the office. They would allocate the indirect expenses based on the square footage of the office compared to the rest of the home. What amount of home-related expenses would qualify as home office expenses?

Answer: $5,413. See allocation below. All direct expenses and 7 percent of the indirect expenses would be allocated to the home office (420 office square footage/6,000 home square footage). The Jeffersons would allocate the expenses as follows:

Total Expense	Type	(A) Amount	(B) Office %	(A) × (B) Home Office Expense
Painting office	Direct	$ 200	100%	$ 200
Electricity	Indirect	2,600	7%	182
Gas and other utilities	Indirect	2,500	7%	175
Real property taxes	Indirect	11,000	7%	770
Home interest expense	Indirect	27,917	7%	1,954
Homeowner's insurance	Indirect	5,000	7%	350
Depreciation	Indirect	25,454	7%	1,782
Total expenses		$74,671		$5,413

The expenses attributable to the home office are deductible subject to the limitations discussed below.

Limitations on Deductibility of Expenses

Deductions of home office expenses are subject to limitation. Home office expenses for employees are treated as unreimbursed employee business expenses that are itemized deductions subject to the 2 percent of AGI floor. Consequently, employees who qualify for the home office deduction are unlikely to receive much if any tax benefit for their home office expenses. A different set of restrictions applies to deductions for home office expenses incurred by self-employed taxpayers. Let's discuss the restrictions applicable to self-employed taxpayers to determine which expenses are deducted and which are carried over to a subsequent year in situations when the current year deductions are limited.

Like vacation home expenses, total home office expenses that are deductible by self-employed taxpayers in any given year are limited to the gross income derived from the business use of the home. In this context, gross income means the taxpayer's net income from the business (Schedule C income) *before* deducting any *home office expenses*.[31] Home office expenses that the taxpayer cannot currently deduct are carried over and deducted in the following year subject to the same business income limitation.

The sequence of deductions for the home office follows the exact same sequence of deductions for homes with significant personal use and significant rental use. Tier 1–type expenses that would be deductible as itemized deductions (interest and taxes) are deducted first. Tier 2–type expenses are deducted second, and Tier 3–type expense (depreciation) is deducted last. Just as with rental homes, the deduction sequence is designed to maximize taxpayer business deductions for expenses that would be deductible without any business use of the home and to minimize the allowable depreciation deductions for the home. Note, however, that if the home-based business is profitable—specifically, if it produces taxable income—the expenses allocated to the home office can be deducted without limitation. In these situations, the order in which the expenses are deducted does not matter.

[31]Interest and property taxes allocated to the home office are deductible for AGI no matter the amount of gross income from the business activity. See §280A(c)(5).

It is important to note that, when a taxpayer deducts depreciation as a home office expense, the depreciation expense reduces the taxpayer's basis in the home. Consequently, when the taxpayer sells the home, the gain on the sale will be greater than it would have been had the taxpayer not deducted depreciation expense. Further, the gain on the sale of the home attributable to the depreciation deductions is *not* eligible to be excluded under the home sale exclusion provisions. Rather, this gain is treated as unrecaptured §1250 gain and is subject to a maximum 25 percent tax rate.

Example 14-21

At the beginning of the year, the Jeffersons' basis in their home was $800,000. Jasmine's first-year home office deductions included $1,782 in depreciation expense. Let's assume that this is the only depreciation expense the Jeffersons ever deduct. What is their adjusted basis in the home?

Answer: The depreciation write-off reduces the basis to $798,218 ($800,000 − $1,782).

What if: Now, assume that after the Jeffersons meet the ownership and use tests for the home sale exclusion, they sell the home for $900,000. The Jeffersons realize a gain of $101,782 on the sale. How much of the gain are they able to exclude?

Answer: They can exclude $100,000 of gain. However, they are not allowed to exclude the $1,782 gain caused by the depreciation expense for the home office. The Jeffersons must pay $446 of tax on the gain ($1,782 × 25% unrecaptured §1250 gain).

Allowing taxpayers to deduct part of their home-related expenses as business expenses creates temptations for taxpayers to deduct home-related expenses that don't meet the requirements. Not surprisingly, the IRS is very concerned about taxpayers inappropriately deducting expenses relating to their home. Consequently, expenses for business use of the home are some of the most highly scrutinized deductions available to taxpayers. Self-employed taxpayers must file a separate Form 8829 "Expenses for Business Use of Your Home" when deducting home office expenses on a tax return. With the high level of scrutiny applied to home office expenses, taxpayers should be sure to have documentation available to support their deductions.

CONCLUSION

When deciding whether to invest in a home as a primary residence, a vacation home, or even a rental home, prospective owners should consider both nontax and tax factors relating to the ownership of the property. The tax code includes several provisions favorable to homeowners. This chapter is intended to provide current and prospective homeowners with enough insight on tax and nontax consequences of home ownership to allow them to make informed investment and compliance decisions when applicable.

SETTLEMENT STATEMENT

A. Settlement Statement

U.S. Department of Housing
and Urban Development

OMB Approval No. 2502-0265
(expires 11/30/2009)

B. Type of Loan

1. ☐ FHA 2. ☐ FmHA 3. ☐ Conv. Unins. 4. ☐ VA 5. ☐ Conv. Ins.	6. File Number:	7. Loan Number:	8. Mortgage Insurance Case Number:

C. Note: This form is furnished to give you a statement of actual settlement costs. Amounts paid to and by the settlement agent are shown. Items marked "(p.o.c.)" were paid outside the closing; they are shown here for informational purposes and are not included in the totals.

D. Name & Address of Borrower:	E. Name & Address of Seller:	F. Name & Address of Lender:

G. Property Location:	H. Settlement Agent:	
	Place of Settlement:	I. Settlement Date:

J. Summary of Borrower's Transaction		**K. Summary of Seller's Transaction**	
100. Gross Amount Due From Borrower		**400. Gross Amount Due To Seller**	
101. Contract sales price		401. Contract sales price	
102. Personal property		402. Personal property	
103. Settlement charges to borrower (line 1400)		403.	
104.		404.	
105.		405.	
Adjustments for items paid by seller in advance		**Adjustments for items paid by seller in advance**	
106. City/town taxes to		406. City/town taxes to	
107. County taxes to		407. County taxes to	
108. Assessments to		408. Assessments to	
109.		409.	
110.		410.	
111.		411.	
112.		412.	
120. Gross Amount Due From Borrower		**420. Gross Amount Due To Seller**	
200. Amounts Paid By Or In Behalf Of Borrower		**500. Reductions In Amount Due To Seller**	
201. Deposit or earnest money		501. Excess deposit (see instructions)	
202. Principal amount of new loan(s)		502. Settlement charges to seller (line 1400)	
203. Existing loan(s) taken subject to		503. Existing loan(s) taken subject to	
204.		504. Payoff of first mortgage loan	
205.		505. Payoff of second mortgage loan	
206.		506.	
207.		507.	
208.		508.	
209.		509.	
Adjustments for items unpaid by seller		**Adjustments for items unpaid by seller**	
210. City/town taxes to		510. City/town taxes to	
211. County taxes to		511. County taxes to	
212. Assessments to		512. Assessments to	
213.		513.	
214.		514.	
215.		515.	
216.		516.	
217.		517.	
218.		518.	
219.		519.	
220. Total Paid By/For Borrower		**520. Total Reduction Amount Due Seller**	
300. Cash At Settlement From/To Borrower		**600. Cash At Settlement To/From Seller**	
301. Gross Amount due from borrower (line 120)		601. Gross amount due to seller (line 420)	
302. Less amounts paid by/for borrower (line 220)	( )	602. Less reductions in amt. due seller (line 520)	( )
303. Cash ☐ From ☐ To Borrower		**603. Cash ☐ To ☐ From Seller**	

L. Settlement Charges

		Paid From Borrowers Funds at Settlement	Paid From Seller's Funds at Settlement
700. Total Sales/Broker's Commission based on price $ @ % =			
Division of Commission (line 700) as follows:			
701. $ to			
702. $ to			
703. Commission paid at Settlement			
704.			
800. Items Payable In Connection With Loan			
801. Loan Origination Fee %			
802. Loan Discount %			
803. Appraisal Fee to			
804. Credit Report to			
805. Lender's Inspection Fee			
806. Mortgage Insurance Application Fee to			
807. Assumption Fee			
808.			
809.			
810.			
811.			
900. Items Required By Lender To Be Paid In Advance			
901. Interest from to @$ /day			
902. Mortgage Insurance Premium for months to			
903. Hazard Insurance Premium for years to			
904. years to			
905.			
1000. Reserves Deposited With Lender			
1001. Hazard insurance months @$ per month			
1002. Mortgage insurance months @$ per month			
1003. City property taxes months @$ per month			
1004. County property taxes months @$ per month			
1005. Annual assessments months @$ per month			
1006. months @$ per month			
1007. months @$ per month			
1008. months @$ per month			
1100. Title Charges			
1101. Settlement or closing fee to			
1102. Abstract or title search to			
1103. Title examination to			
1104. Title insurance binder to			
1105. Document preparation to			
1106. Notary fees to			
1107. Attorney's fees to			
(includes above items numbers:)			
1108. Title insurance to			
(includes above items numbers:)			
1109. Lender's coverage $			
1110. Owner's coverage $			
1111.			
1112.			
1113.			
1200. Government Recording and Transfer Charges			
1201. Recording fees: Deed $; Mortgage $; Releases $			
1202. City/county tax/stamps: Deed $; Mortgage $			
1203. State tax/stamps: Deed $; Mortgage $			
1204.			
1205.			
1300. Additional Settlement Charges			
1301. Survey to			
1302. Pest inspection to			
1303.			
1304.			
1305.			
1400. Total Settlement Charges (enter on lines 103, Section J and 502, Section K)			

SUMMARY

Compute the taxable gain on the sale of a residence and explain the requirements for excluding gain on the sale.   **LO1**

- If they meet ownership and use requirements, married taxpayers may exclude $500,000 of gain on the sale of their principal residence. Single taxpayers may exclude up to $250,000 of gain on the sale of their principal residence.
- To qualify for the exclusion on the sale of real estate, taxpayers must own and use the home as their principal residence for two of the previous five years preceding the sale.
- The amount of gain eligible for exclusion may be reduced if after December 31, 2008, the taxpayer uses the home as a vacation home or rental property and then uses the home as a principal residence before selling it.

Determine the amount of allowable interest expense deductions on loans secured by a residence.   **LO2**

- Taxpayers may deduct interest on up to $1,000,000 of acquisition indebtedness of their principal residence and one other residence.
- Taxpayers may deduct interest on up to $100,000 of home-equity indebtedness on their principal residence and one other residence.
- Taxpayers may immediately deduct points paid to reduce the interest rate on qualifying home mortgages used to acquire the taxpayer's principal residence. Points paid to reduce the interest rate on a loan refinancing are deductible over the life of the loan.

Discuss the deductibility of real property taxes and describe the first-time home buyer credit.   **LO3**

- Taxpayers deduct real property taxes when the taxes are paid to the taxing jurisdiction and not when the taxes are paid to an escrow account.
- When a piece of real property is sold during the year, the tax deduction for the property is allocated to the buyer and seller based on the portion of the year that each held the property no matter who pays the taxes.
- First-time home buyers may claim a refundable credit of up to $7,500 ($3,750 for married taxpayers filing separately) for home purchases on or after April 8, 2008, and before July 1, 2009. The credit phases-out based on taxpayers' modified AGI.
- Taxpayers must pay back the home buyer credit in 15 equal annual installments beginning two years after the year in which they purchase the residence that qualified them for the credit. If a taxpayer sells or no longer uses the home as her personal residence before repaying the credit, she must pay the balance of the credit in the year the residence was no longer used as her personal residence.

Explain the tax issues and consequences associated with rental use of the home, including determining the deductibility of residential rental real estate losses.   **LO4**

- Taxpayers who live in a home for 15 days or more and rent the home out for 14 days or less do not include gross rental receipts in taxable income and do not deduct rental expenses.
- Taxpayers who reside in and rent out a home for a significant portion of the year include rental receipts in income and must allocate home-related expenses between rental and personal use. The rental expenses are deductible in a particular sequence. The amount of deductible expenses for the year cannot exceed the rental income from the property.
- Taxpayers who rent a home with minimal or no personal use include rental receipts in income and deduct all rental expenses. In this situation expenses can exceed the income but the loss is subject to the passive activity rules.
- Taxpayers who own a second home through a timeshare or fractional ownership arrangement determine the use of the home based on the personal and rental use of all of the owners.
- Taxpayers may be able to deduct up to $25,000 of loss on their rental home if they are active participants with respect to the property. This deduction is phased out for taxpayers with adjusted gross income between $100,000 and $150,000.

L05 Describe the requirements necessary to qualify for home office deductions and compute the deduction limitations on home office deductions.

- To deduct expenses relating to a home office, the taxpayer must use the home exclusively and regularly for business purposes.
- Home-related expenses are allocated between business expenses and personal expenses based on the size of the office relative to the size of the home.
- Expenses allocated to the office are deducted in a particular sequence. Expenses allocated to the home office cannot exceed the taxpayer's net business income before considering the home office deduction.

KEY TERMS

acquisition indebtedness (14-8)

active participant (14-24)

discount points (14-13)

escrow account (14-15)

flipping (14-3)

home-equity indebtedness (14-8)

home office deductions (14-25)

loan origination fee (14-12)

passive activity income or loss (14-23)

point (14-12)

principal residence (14-3)

qualified debt (14-11)

qualified residence (14-8)

qualified residence interest (14-13)

real property taxes (14-15)

refinance (14-9)

secured loan (14-8)

settlement statement (14-15)

DISCUSSION QUESTIONS

1. **(LO1)** A taxpayer owns a home in Salt Lake City, Utah, and a second home in St. George, Utah. The taxpayer sells the home in St. George at a gain. How does the taxpayer determine which home is her principal residence for purposes of qualifying for the exclusion of gain on the sale of a personal residence?

2. **(LO1)** What are the ownership and use requirements that a taxpayer must meet to qualify for the exclusion of the gain on the sale of a residence?

3. **(LO1)** Under what circumstances, if any, can a taxpayer fail to meet the ownership and use requirements but still be able to exclude all of the gain on the sale of a principal residence?

4. **(LO1)** Under what circumstances can a taxpayer meet the ownership and use requirements for a residence but still not be allowed to exclude gain on the sale of the residence?

5. **(LO1)** A taxpayer purchases and lives in a home for a year. The home appreciates in value by $50,000. The taxpayer sells the home after her employer transfers her to an office in a nearby city. The taxpayer buys a new home. What information do you need to obtain to determine whether the taxpayer is allowed to exclude the gain on the sale of the first home?

6. **(LO2)** Juanita owns a principal residence in New Jersey, a cabin in Montana, and a houseboat in Hawaii. All of these properties have mortgages on which Juanita pays interest. What limits, if any, apply to Juanita's mortgage interest deductions? And explain whether deductible interest is deductible *for* AGI or *from* AGI.

7. **(LO2)** Barbi really wants to acquire an expensive automobile (perhaps more expensive than she can really afford). She has two options. Option 1: finance the purchase with an automobile loan from her local bank at a 7 percent interest rate, or Option 2: finance the purchase with a home-equity loan at a rate of

7 percent. Compare and contrast the tax and nontax factors Barbi should consider before deciding which loan to use to pay for the automobile. Barbi typically has more itemized deductions than the standard deduction amount.

8. **(LO2)** Lars and Leigha saved up for years before they purchased their dream home. They were considering (1) using all of their savings to make a large down payment on the home (90 percent of the value of the home) and barely scraping by without the backup savings, or (2) making a more modest down payment (50 percent of the value of the loan) and holding some of the savings in reserve as needed if funds get tight. They decided to go with the large down payment because they figured they could always refinance the home to pull some equity out of the home if things got tight. What advice would you give them about the tax consequences of their decision?

9. **(LO2)** How are acquisition indebtedness and home-equity indebtedness similar? How are they dissimilar?

10. **(LO2)** Why might it be good advice from a tax perspective to think hard before deciding to quickly pay down mortgage debt?

11. **(LO2)** Can portions of one loan secured by a residence consist of both acquisition indebtedness and home-equity indebtedness? Explain.

12. **(LO2)** When a taxpayer has loans that in total exceed the limits for deductibility, how does the taxpayer determine the amount of the deductible interest expense?

13. **(LO2)** Compare and contrast the characteristics of a deductible point from a nondeductible point on a first home mortgage.

14. **(LO2)** Is the break-even period generally longer for points paid to reduce the interest rate on initial home loans or points paid for the same purpose on a refinance? Explain.

15. **(LO2)** Under what circumstances is it likely economically beneficial to pay points to reduce the interest rate on a home loan?

■ planning

16. **(LO2)** Harry decides to finance his new home with a 30-year fixed mortgage. Because he figures he will be in this home for a long time he decides to pay a fully deductible discount point on his mortgage to reduce the interest rate. Assuming Harry itemizes deductions and has a constant marginal tax rate over time, will the time required to recover the cost of the discount point be shorter or longer if Harry makes extra principal payments starting in the first year than it would be if he does not make any extra principal payments?

17. **(LO3)** A taxpayer sold a piece of real property in year 1. The amount of year 1 real property taxes was estimated at the closing of the sale and the amounts were allocated between the buyer and the taxpayer. At the end of year 1, the buyer receives a property tax bill that turns out to be higher than the estimate. After paying the tax bill, the buyer contacts the taxpayer at the beginning of year 2 and asks the taxpayer to pay the taxpayer's share of the shortfall. The taxpayer sends a check to the buyer. Should the taxpayer be concerned that she won't get to deduct the extra tax payment because it was paid to the buyer and not to the taxing jurisdiction? Explain.

18. **(LO3)** Is a homeowner allowed a property tax deduction for amounts included in the monthly mortgage payment that are earmarked for property taxes? Explain.

19. **(LO3)** How is the first-time home buyer credit similar to an interest-free loan from the government? How is it different from an interest-free loan?

20. **(LO4)** For taxpayers that own second homes, how does the taxpayer distinguish a day of personal use from a day of rental use?

21. **(LO4)** Is it possible for a taxpayer to receive rental income that is not subject to taxation? Explain.

■ planning

22. **(LO4)** Halle just acquired a vacation home. She plans on spending several months each year vacationing in the home and she plans on renting the property for the rest of the year. She is projecting tax losses on the rental portion of the property for the year. She is not too concerned about the losses because she is confident she will be able to use the losses to offset her income from other sources. Is her confidence misplaced? Explain.

■ planning

23. **(LO4)** A taxpayer stays in a second home for the entire month of September. He would like the home to fall into the significant personal and rental use category for tax purposes. What is the maximum number of days he can rent out the home and have it qualify?

24. **(LO4)** Compare and contrast the IRS method and the Tax Court method for allocating expenses between personal use and rental use for vacation homes. Include the Tax Court's justification for departing from the IRS method in your answer.

25. **(LO4)** In what circumstances is the IRS method for allocating expenses between personal use and rental use for second homes more beneficial to a taxpayer than the Tax Court method?

26. **(LO4)** Under what circumstances would a taxpayer who generates a loss from renting a home that is primarily rental-use property be able to fully deduct the loss? What potential limitations apply?

27. **(LO4)** Describe the circumstances in which a taxpayer acquires a home and rents it out and is not allowed to deduct a portion of the interest expense on the loan the taxpayer used to acquire the home.

28. **(LO4)** Is it possible for a rental property to generate a positive annual cash flow and at the same time produce a loss for tax purposes? Explain.

29. **(LO4, LO5)** How are the tax issues associated with home offices and vacation homes used as rentals similar? How are the tax issues or requirements dissimilar?

30. **(LO5)** Are employees or self-employed taxpayers more likely to qualify for the home office deduction? Explain.

31. **(LO5)** Compare and contrast the manner in which employees and employers report home office deductions on their tax returns.

32. **(LO5)** For taxpayers qualifying for home office deductions, what are considered to be indirect expenses of maintaining the home? How are these expenses allocated to personal and home office use?

33. **(LO5)** What limitations exist for self-employed taxpayers in deducting home office expenses, and how does the taxpayer determine which deductions are deductible and which are not in situations when the overall amount of the home office deduction is limited?

34. **(LO1, LO5)** A self-employed taxpayer deducts home office expenses. The taxpayer then sells the home at a $100,000 gain. Assuming the taxpayer meets the ownership and use tests, does the full gain qualify for exclusion? Explain.

PROBLEMS

35. **(LO1)** Steve and Stephanie Pratt purchased a home in Spokane, Washington, for $400,000. They moved into the home on February 1 of year 1. They lived in the home as their primary residence until June 30 of year 5, when they sold the home for $700,000. The Pratts' marginal tax rate is 34 percent.

   a. How much in taxes will they be required to pay on the gain on the sale of the home?

   b. Assume the original facts, except that Steve and Stephanie live in the home until January 1 of year 3 when they purchased a new home and rented the original home. They finally sell the original home on June 30 of year 5 for $700,000. Ignoring any issues relating to depreciation taken on the home while it was being rented, what amount of taxes will the Pratts be required to pay on the sale of the home?

c. Assume the same facts as in (b), except that the Pratts lived in the home until January of year 4 when they purchased a new home and rented the first home. What amount of taxes will the Pratts need to pay if they sell the first home on June 30 of year 5 for $700,000?

36. **(LO1)** Steve and Stephanie Pratt purchased a home in Spokane, Washington, for $400,000. They moved into the home on February 1 of year 1. They lived in the home as their primary residence until November 1 of year 1, when they sold the home for $500,000. The Pratts' marginal tax rate is 34 percent.

a. Assume that the Pratts sold their home and moved because they don't like their neighbors. How much gain will the Pratts recognize on their home sale? At what rate, if any, will the gain be taxed?

b. Assume the Pratts sell the home because Stephanie's employer transfers her to an office in Utah. How much gain will the Pratts recognize on their home sale?

c. Assume the same facts as in (b), except that the Pratts sell their home for $700,000. How much gain will the Pratts recognize on the home sale?

d. Assume the same facts as (b), except that on December 1 of year 0 the Pratts sold their home in Seattle and excluded the $300,000 gain from income on their year 0 tax return. How much gain will the Pratts recognize on the sale of their Spokane home?

37. **(LO1)** Steve Pratt, who is single, purchased a home in Spokane, Washington, for $400,000. He moved into the home on February 1 of year 1. He lived in the home as his primary residence until June 30 of year 5, when he sold the home for $700,000. Steve's ordinary marginal tax rate is 34 percent.

a. How much in taxes will Steve be required to pay on the gain on the sale of the home?

b. Assume the original facts, except that the home is Steve's vacation home and he vacations there four months each year. Steve does not ever rent the home to others. What gain must Steve recognize on the home sale?

c. Assume the original facts, except that Steve married Stephanie on February 1 of year 3 and the couple lived in the home until they sold it in June of year 5. Under state law, Steve owned the home by himself. How much gain must Steve and Stephanie recognize on the sale (assume they file a joint return in year 5)?

d. Assume the original facts, except that Stephanie moved in with Steve on March 1 of year 3 and the couple was married on March 1 of year 4. Under state law, the couple jointly owned Steve's home beginning on the date they were married. On December 1 of year 3, Stephanie sold her home that she lived in before she moved in with Steve. She excluded the entire $50,000 gain on the sale on her individual year 3 tax return. What amount of gain must the couple recognize on the sale in June of year 5?

38. **(LO1)** Celia has been married to Daryl for 52 years. The couple has lived in their current home for the last 20 years. On October of year 0, Daryl passed away. Celia decided to sell their home and move into a condominium. What is the maximum exclusion Celia is entitled to if she sells the home on December 15 of year 1?

39. **(LO1)** Sarah purchased a home on January 1, 2007, for $600,000. She eventually sold the home for $800,000. What amount of the $200,000 gain on the

sale may Sarah exclude from gross income in each of the following alternative situations?

a. Sarah used the home as her principal residence until July 1, 2012. She used the home as a vacation home from July 1, 2012, until she sold it on July 1, 2014.

b. Sarah used the property as a vacation home until July 1, 2012. She then used the home as her princiapl residence from July 1, 2012, until she sold it on July 1, 2014.

c. Sarah used the home as a vacation home from January 1, 2007, until January 1, 2013. She used the home as her principal residence from January 1, 2013, until she sold it on July 1, 2014.

d. Sarah used the home as a vacation home from January 1, 2007, until July 1, 2008. She used the home as her principal residence from July 1, 2008, until she sold it on July 1, 2011.

40. **(LO2)** Javier and Anita Sanchez purchased a home on January 1, 2009, for $500,000 by paying $200,000 down and borrowing the remaining $300,000 with a 7 percent loan secured by the home. The loan requires interest-only payments for the first five years. The Sanchezes would itemize deductions even if they did not have any deductible interest. The Sanchezes' marginal tax rate is 30 percent.

a. What is the after-tax cost of the interest expense to the Sanchezes in year 1?

b. Assume the original facts, except that the Sanchezes rent a home and pay $21,000 in rent during the year. What is the after-tax cost of their rental payments?

c. Assuming the interest expense is their only itemized deduction for the year and that Javier and Anita file a joint return, have great eyesight, and are under 60 years of age, what is the after-tax cost of their 2009 interest expense?

41. **(LO2)** Javier and Anita Sanchez purchased a home on January 1 of year 1 for $500,000 by paying $50,000 down and borrowing the remaining $450,000 with a 7 percent loan secured by the home. The loan requires interest-only payments for the first five years. The Sanchezes would itemize deductions even if they did not have any deductible interest. The Sanchezes' marginal tax rate is 30 percent.

a. Assume the Sanchezes also took out a second loan secured by the home for $80,000 to fund expenses unrelated to the home. The interest rate on the second loan is 8 percent. The Sanchezes make interest-only payments on the loan in year 1. What is the amount of their deductible interest expense on the second loan in year 1?

b. Assume the original facts and that the Sanchezes take out a second loan secured by the home in the amount of $50,000 to fund expenses unrelated to the home. The interest rate on the second loan is 8 percent. The Sanchezes make interest-only payments during the year. What is the amount of their deductible interest expense on the second loan in year 1?

42. **(LO2)** Javier and Anita Sanchez purchased a home on January 1 of year 1 for $500,000 by paying $200,000 down and borrowing the remaining $300,000 with a 7 percent loan secured by the home. The loan requires interest-only payments for the first five years. The Sanchezes would itemize deductions even if they did not have any deductible interest. The Sanchezes' marginal tax rate is 30 percent. On January 1, the Sanchezes also borrowed money on a second loan secured by the home for $75,000. The interest rate on the loan is 8 percent and the Sanchezes make interest-only payments in year 1 on the second loan.

a. Assuming the Sanchezes use the second loan to landscape the yard to their home, how much of the interest expense on the second loan are they allowed to deduct in year 1?

b. Assume the original facts and that the Sanchezes use the $75,000 loan proceeds for an extended family vacation. How much of the interest expense on the second loan are they allowed to deduct in year 1?

c. Assume the original facts, except that the Sanchezes borrow $120,000 on the second loan and they use the proceeds for an extended family vacation and other personal expenses. How much of the second loan interest expense are the Sanchezes allowed to deduct in year 1?

43. **(LO2)** On January 1, Arthur and Aretha Franklin purchased a home for $1.5 million by paying $200,000 down and borrowing the remaining $1.3 million with a 7 percent loan secured by the home.

 a. What is the amount of the interest expense the Franklins may deduct in year 1?

 b. Assume that in year 2, the Franklins pay off the entire loan but at the beginning of year 3, they borrow $300,000 secured by the home at a 7 percent rate. They make interest-only payments on the loan during the year. What amount of interest expense may the Franklins deduct in year 3 on this loan? Does it matter what they do with the loan proceeds? Explain.

 c. Assume the same facts as in (b), except that the Franklins borrow $80,000 secured by their home. What amount of interest expense may the Franklins deduct in year 3 on this loan? Does it matter what they do with the loan proceeds? Explain.

44. **(LO2)** Last year, Eva took out a $50,000 home-equity loan from her local credit union. At the time she took out the loan, her home was valued $350,000. At time of the loan, Eva's original mortgage on the home was $265,000. At the end of this year, her original mortgage is $260,000. Unfortunately for Eva, during the current year, the value of her home dropped to $280,000. Consequently, as of the end of the current year, Eva's home secured $310,000 of home-related debt but her home is only valued at $280,000. Assuming Eva paid $15,000 of interest on the original mortgage and $3,500 of interest on the home-equity loan during the year, how much qualified residence interest can Eva deduct for the year?

45. **(LO2)** On January 1 of year 1, Jason and Jill Marsh acquired a home for $500,000 by paying $400,000 down and borrowing $100,000 with a 7 percent loan secured by the home. On June 30 of year 1, the Marshes needed cash so they refinanced the original loan by taking out a new $250,000 7 percent loan. With the $250,000 proceeds from the new loan, the Marshes paid off the original $100,000 loan and used the remaining $150,000 to fund their son's college education.

 a. What amount of interest expense on this loan may the Marshes deduct for the year?

 b. Assume the same facts as in (a), except that the Marshes use the $150,000 cash from the refinancing to add two rooms and a garage to their home.

46. **(LO2)** On January 1 of year 1 Brandon and Alisa Roy purchased a home for $1.5 million by paying $500,000 down and borrowing the remaining $1 million with a 7 percent loan secured by the home. On the same day, the Roys took out a second loan, secured by the home, in the amount of $300,000.

■ planning

 a. Assuming the interest rate on the second loan is 8 percent, what is the maximum amount of the interest expense on these two loans deductible by the Roys in year 1?

 b. Assuming the interest rate on the second loan is 6 percent, what is the maximum amount of interest expense on these two loans that the Roys may deduct in year 1?

research

47. **(LO2)** Jennifer has been living in her current principal residence for three years. Six months ago Jennifer decided that she would like to purchase a second home near a beach so she can vacation there for part of the year. Despite her best efforts, Jennifer has been unable to find what she is looking for. Consequently, Jennifer recently decided to change plans. She purchased a parcel of land for $200,000 with the intention of building her second home on the property. To acquire the land, she borrowed $200,000 secured by the land. Jennifer would like to know whether the interest she pays on the loan before construction on the house is completed is deductible as mortgage interest.

   a. How should Jennifer treat the interest if she has begun construction on the home and plans to live in the home in 12 months?

   b. How should Jennifer treat the interest if she hasn't begun construction on the home but plans to live in the home in 15 months?

   c. How should Jennifer treat the interest if she has begun construction on the home but doesn't plan to live in the home for 37 months?

planning

48. **(LO2)** Rajiv and Laurie Amin are recent college graduates looking to purchase a new home. They are purchasing a $200,000 home by paying $20,000 down and borrowing the other $180,000 with a 30-year loan secured by the home. The Amins have the option of (1) paying no discount points on the loan and paying interest at 8 percent or (2) paying one discount point on the loan and paying interest of 7.5 percent. Both loans require the Amins to make interest-only payments for the first five years. Unless otherwise stated, the Amins itemize deductions irrespective of the amount of interest expense. The Amins are in the 25 percent marginal ordinary income tax bracket.

   a. Assuming the Amins *do not itemize deductions,* what is the break-even point for paying the point to get a lower interest rate?

   b. Assuming the Amins do itemize deductions, what is the break-even point for paying the point to get a lower interest rate?

   c. Assume the original facts, except that the amount of the loan is $300,000. What is the break-even point for the Amins for paying the point to get a lower interest rate?

   d. Assume the original facts, except that the $180,000 loan is a refinance instead of an original loan. What is the break-even point for paying the point to get a lower interest rate?

   e. Assume the original facts, except that the amount of the loan is $300,000 and the loan is a refinance and not an original loan. What is the break-even point for paying the point to get a lower interest rate?

49. **(LO3)** In year 1, Peter and Shaline Johnsen moved into a home in a new subdivision. Theirs was one of the first homes in the subdivision. In year 1, they paid $1,500 in property taxes to the state government, $500 to the developer of the subdivision for an assessment to pay for the sidewalks, and $900 for property taxes on land they hold as an investment. What amount of taxes are the Johnsens allowed to deduct assuming their itemized deductions exceed the standard deduction amount before considering any property tax deductions?

50. **(LO3)** Jesse Brimhall is single. In 2009, his itemized deductions were $5,000 before considering any real property taxes he paid during the year. Jesse's adjusted gross income was $70,000 (also before considering any property tax deductions). In 2009, he paid real property taxes of $3,000 on property 1 and $800 of real property taxes on property 2.

   a. If property 1 is Jesse's primary residence and property 2 is his vacation home (he does not rent it out at all) what is his taxable income after taking property taxes into account.

b. If property 1 is Jesse's business building (he owns the property) and property 2 is his primary residence, what is his taxable income after taking property taxes into account?

c. If property 1 is Jesse's primary residence and property 2 is a parcel of land he holds for investment, what is his taxable income after taking property taxes into account.

51. **(LO3)** Kirk and Lorna Newbold purchased a new home on August 1 of year 1 for $300,000. At the time of the purchase, it was estimated that the real property tax rate for the year would be .5 percent of the property's value. Because the taxing jurisdiction collects taxes on a July 1 year-end, it was estimated that the Newbolds would be required to pay $1,375 in property taxes for the property tax year relating to August through June of year 2 (i.e., $300,000 × .05% × 11/12). The seller would be required to pay the $125 for July of year 1. Along with their monthly payment of principal and interest, the Newbolds paid $125 to the mortgage company to cover the property taxes. The mortgage company placed the money in escrow and used the funds in the escrow account to pay the property tax bill in July of year 2. The Newbold's itemized deductions exceed the standard deduction before considering real property taxes.

a. How much in real property taxes can the Newbolds deduct for year 1?

b. How much in real property taxes can the Newbolds deduct for year 2?

c. Assume the original facts, except that the Newbolds were not able to collect $125 from the seller for the property taxes for July of year 1. How much in real property taxes can the Newbolds deduct for year 1 and year 2?

d. Assume the original facts, except that the tax bill for July 1 of year 1 through June 30 of year 2 turned out to be $1,200 instead of $1,500. How much in real property taxes can the Newbolds deduct in year 1 and year 2?

52. **(LO3)** Jenae and Terry Hutchings own a parcel of land as tenants by entirety. That is, they both own the property but when one of them dies the other becomes the sole owner of the property. For nontax reasons, Jenae and Terry decide to file separate tax returns for the current year. Janae paid the entire $3,000 property tax bill for the land. How much of the $3,000 property tax payment is each spouse entitled to deduct in the current year?

53. **(LO4)** After renting an apartment for five years, Todd and Diane purchased a new home for $230,000 on March 1, 2009. Assuming they file a joint tax return, what amount of first-time home buyer credit can they claim in each of the following alternative situations?

a. Todd and Diane's AGI is $110,000.

b. Todd and Diane's AGI is $165,000.

c. Todd and Diane's AGI is $200,000

54. **(LO4)** Harold recently moved out of the apartment he has been renting for the last four years (he owned a small home for two years before he started renting) and into a condominium he purchased on May 1, 2009, for $70,000. Answer the following questions relating to Harold's first-time home buyer credit.

a. What amount of credit may Harold claim on the purchase of the condominium?

b. When and how does Harold claim the credit?

c. When is Harold required to begin repaying the credit and how much must he pay back each year?

d. If Harold sells his home in May 2012, how much credit must he pay back and when must he pay it back?

research

55. **(LO4)** For her 90th birthday, Jamie (a widow) purchased a new home on September 1, 2008, and appropriately claimed a first-time home buyer credit of $7,500 on her 2008 tax return. Jamie followed the appropriate schedule for paying back the credit. However, in December 2014, Jamie passed away of old age. Is Jamie (or her estate) responsible for paying the unpaid balance of the credit? Explain.

56. **(LO4)** Several years ago, Junior acquired a home that he vacationed in part of the time and he rented out part of the time. During the current year Junior:

- Personally stayed in the home for 22 days.
- Rented it to his favorite brother at a discount for 10 days.
- Rented it to his least favorite brother for eight days at the full market rate.
- Rented it to his friend at a discounted rate for four days.
- Rented the home to third parties for 58 days at the market rate.
- Did repair and maintenance work for two days.
- Marketed the property and made it available for rent for 150 days during the year.

How many days of personal use and how many days of rental use did Junior experience on the property during the year?

57. **(LO4)** Dillon rented his personal residence at Lake Tahoe for 14 days while he was vacationing in Ireland. He resided in the home for the remainder of the year. Rental income from the property was $6,500. Expenses associated with use of the home for the entire year were as follows:

Real property taxes	$ 3,100
Mortgage interest	12,000
Repairs	1,500
Insurance	1,500
Utilities	3,900
Depreciation	13,000

a. What effect does the rental have on Dillon's AGI?

b. What effect does the rental have on Dillon's itemized deductions?

Use the following facts to answer problems 58 and 59.

Natalie owns a condominium near Cocoa Beach in Florida. This year, she incurs the following expenses in connection with her condo:

Insurance	$1,000
Mortgage interest	3,500
Property taxes	900
Repairs & maintenance	650
Utilities	950
Depreciation	8,500

During the year, Natalie rented out the condo for 75 days, receiving $10,000 of gross income. She personally used the condo for 35 days during her vacation.

58. **(LO4)** Assume Natalie uses the *IRS* method of allocating expenses to rental use of the property.

a. What is the total amount of *for* AGI (rental) deductions Natalie may deduct in the current year related to the condo?

b. What is the total amount of itemized deductions Natalie may deduct in the current year related to the condo?

c. If Natalie's basis in the condo at the beginning of the year was $150,000, what is her basis in the condo at the end of the year?

59. **(LO4)** Assume Natalie uses the *Tax Court* method of allocating expenses to rental use of the property.

  a. What is the total amount of *for* AGI (rental) deductions Natalie may deduct in the current year related to the condo?

  b. What is the total amount of itemized deductions Natalie may deduct in the current year related to the condo?

  c. If Natalie's basis in the condo at the beginning of the year was $150,000, what is her basis in the condo at the end of the year?

Use the following facts to answer problems 60–62.

Alexa owns a condominium near Cocoa Beach in Florida. This year, she incurs the following expenses in connection with her condo:

Insurance	$2,000
Mortgage interest	6,500
Property taxes	2,000
Repairs & maintenance	1,400
Utilities	2,500
Depreciation	14,500

During the year, Alexa rented out the condo for 100 days. She did not use the condo at all for personal purposes during the year. Alexa's AGI from all sources other than the rental property is $200,000. Unless otherwise specified, Alexa has no sources of passive income.

60. **(LO4)** Assume Alexa receives $30,000 in gross rental receipts.

  a. What effect do the expenses associated with the property have on her AGI?

  b. What effect do the expenses associated with the property have on her itemized deductions?

61. **(LO4)** Assuming Alexa receives $20,000 in gross rental receipts, answer the following questions:

  a. What effect does the rental activity have on her AGI for the year?

  b. Assuming that Alexa's AGI from other sources is $90,000, what effect does the rental activity have on Alexa's AGI? Alexa makes all decisions with respect to the property.

  c. Assuming that Alexa's AGI from other sources is $120,000, what effect does the rental activity have on Alexa's AGI? Alexa makes all decisions with respect to the property.

  d. Assume that Alexa's AGI from other sources is $200,000. This consists of $150,000 salary, $10,000 of dividends, and $25,000 of long-term capital gain and net rental income from another rental property in the amount of $15,000. What effect does the Cocoa Beach Condo rental activity have on Alexa's AGI?

62. **(LO4)** Assume that in addition to renting the condo for 100 days, Alexa uses the condo for eight days of personal use. Also assume that Alexa receives $30,000 of gross rental receipts. Answer the following questions:

  ■ planning

  a. What is the total amount of *for* AGI deductions relating to the condo that Alexa may deduct in the current year? Assume she uses the IRS method of allocating expenses between rental and personal days.

  b. What is the total amount of *from* AGI deductions relating to the condo that Alexa may deduct in the current year? Assume she uses the IRS method of allocating expenses between rental and personal days.

  c. Would Alexa be better or worse off after taxes if she uses the Tax Court method of allocating expenses?

63. **(LO5)** Brooke owns a sole proprietorship in which she works as a management consultant. She maintains an office in her home where she meets with clients, prepares bills, and performs other work-related tasks. The home office is 300 square feet and the entire house is 4,500 square feet. Brooke incurred the following home-related expenses during the year.

Real property taxes	$ 3,600
Interest on home mortgage	14,000
Operating expenses of home	5,000
Depreciation	12,000
Repairs to home theater room	1,000

What amount of each of these expenses is allocated to the home office?

Use the following facts to answer problems 64 and 65.

Rita owns a sole proprietorship in which she works as a management consultant. She maintains an office in her home where she meets with clients, prepares bills, and performs other work-related tasks. Her business expenses, other than home office expenses, total $5,600. The following home-related expenses have been allocated to her home office.

Real property taxes	$1,600
Interest on home mortgage	5,100
Operating expenses of home	800
Depreciation	1,600

Also, assume that not counting the sole proprietorship, Rita's AGI is $60,000.

64. **(LO5)** Assume Rita's consulting business generated $15,000 in gross income.

   a. What is Rita's home office deduction for the current year?
   b. What is Rita's AGI for the year?
   c. What types and amounts of expenses will she carry over to next year?

65. **(LO5)** Assume Rita's consulting business generated $13,000 in gross income for the current year.

   a. What is Rita's home office deduction for the current year?
   b. What is Rita's AGI for the year?
   c. Assume the original facts, except that Rita is an employee and not self-employed. Consequently, she does not receive any gross income from the (sole proprietorship) business and she does not incur any business expenses unrelated to the home office. Finally, her AGI is $60,000 consisiting of salary from her work as an employee. What effect does her home office expenses have on her itemized deductions?
   d. Assuming the original facts, what types and amounts of expenses will she carry over to next year?

66. **(LO1, LO5)** Alisha, who is single, owns a sole proprietorship in which she works as a management consultant. She maintains an office in her home where she meets with clients, prepares bills, and performs other work-related tasks. She purchased the home at the beginning of year 1 for $400,000. Since she purchased the home and moved into it she has been able to deduct $10,000 of depreciation expenses to offset her consulting income. At the end of year 3, Alisha sold the home for $500,000. What is the amount of taxes Alisha will be required to pay on the gain from the sale of the home? Alisha's ordinary marginal tax rate is 30 percent.

COMPREHENSIVE PROBLEMS

67. Derek and Meagan Jacoby recently graduated from State University and Derek accepted a job in business consulting while Meagan accepted a job in computer programming. Meagan inherited $75,000 from her grandfather who recently passed away. The couple is debating whether they should buy or rent a home. They located an apartment that meets their needs. The monthly rent is $2,250. They also found a three-bedroom home that costs $475,000. The Jacobys could use Meagan's inheritance for a down payment on the home. Thus, they would need to borrow $400,000 to acquire the home. They have the option of paying two discount points to receive a fixed interest rate of 4.5 percent on the loan or paying no points and receiving a fixed interest rate of 5.75 percent for a 30-year fixed loan.

■ planning

   Though anything could happen, the couple expects to live in the home for no more than five years before relocating to a different region of the country. Derek and Meagan don't have any school-related debt, so they will save the $75,000 if they don't purchase a home. Also, consider the following information:

   - The couple's marginal tax rate is 25 percent.
   - Regardless of whether they buy or rent, the couple will itemize their deductions.
   - If they buy, the Jacobys would purchase and move into the home on January 1 of year 1.
   - If they buy the home, the property tax year runs from July 1 through June 30. The taxes payable on the home on June 30 of year 1 are $3,600. The taxes payable on the home on June 30 of year 2 are $4,000.
   - Disregard loan-related fees not mentioned above.
   - If the couple does not buy a home, they will put their money into their savings account where they earn 5 percent annual interest.
   - Assume all unstated costs are equal between the buy and rent option.

Required:

Help the Jacobys with their decisions by answering the following questions:

   a. If the Jacobys decide to rent the home, what is their after-tax cost of the rental for the first year?
   b. What is the approximate break-even point in years (or months) for paying the points to receive a reduced interest rate (to simplify this computation, assume the Jacobys will make interest-only payments)?
   c. What is the after-tax cost of living in the home for the first year? Assume that the Jacoby's interest rate is 5.75 percent, they do not pay discount points, they make interest-only payments for the first year, and the value of the home does not change during the year. Also consider the after-tax cost of the property tax they must pay because they live in the home during year 1.
   d. Assume that on March 1 of year 2, the Jacobys sold their home for $525,000, so that Derek and Meagan could accept job opportunities in a different state. The Jacobys used the sale proceeds to (1) pay off the $400,000 principal of the mortgage, (2) pay a $10,000 commission to their real estate broker, and (3) make a down payment on a new home in the different state. However, the new home cost only $300,000. What gain or loss do the Jacobys realize and recognize on the sale of their home and what amount of taxes must they pay on the gain, if any (assume they make interest only payments on the loan)?

e. Assume the same facts as in (d), except that the Jacobys sell their home for $450,000 and they pay a $7,500 commission. What effect does the sale have on their year 2 income tax liability? Recall that the Jacobys are subject to an ordinary marginal tax rate of 25 percent and assume that they do not have any other transactions involving capital assets in year 2.

68. James and Kate Sawyer were married on New Year's Eve of 2008. Before their marriage, Kate lived in New York and worked as a hair stylist for one of the city's top salons. James lives in Atlanta where he works for a public accounting firm earning an annual salary of $100,000. After their marriage, Kate left her job in New York and moved into the couple's newly purchased 3,200-square-foot home in Atlanta. Kate incurred $2,200 of qualified moving expenses. The couple purchased the home on January 3, 2009 by paying $100,000 down and obtaining a $240,000 mortgage for the remainder (assume they paid exactly one-half of a year's worth of interest on this loan by June 30). The interest rate on this loan was 7 percent and the Sawyers made interest-only payments on the loan through June 30, 2009. On July 1, 2009 because the value of their home had increased to $400,000, the Sawyers were in need of cash, and interest rates had dropped, the Sawyers refinanced their home loan. On the refinancing, they borrowed $370,000 at 6 percent interest. They made interest-only payments on the home loan through the end of the year and they spent $20,000 of the loan proceeds improving their home (assume they paid exactly one-half of a year's worth of interest on this loan by year end).

Kate wanted to try her hand at making it on her own in business, and with James's help, she started Kate's Beauty Cuts, LLC. She set up shop in a 384-square-foot corner room of the couple's home and began to get it ready for business. The room conveniently had a door to the outside providing customers direct access to the shop. Before she opened the doors to the business, Kate paid $2,100 to have the carpet replaced with a tile floor. She also paid $1,200 to have the room painted with vibrant colors, and $650 to have the room rewired for appropriate lighting. Kate ran an ad in the local newspaper and officially opened her shop on January 24, 2009. By the end of the year, Kate's Beauty Cuts, LLC. generated $40,000 of *net* income before considering the home office deduction. The Sawyers incurred the following home-related expenditures during 2009:

- $4,200 of real property taxes.
- $2,000 for homeowner's insurance.
- $2,400 for electricity.
- $1,500 for gas and other utilities.

They determined depreciation expense for their entire house was $7,300.

Also, on March 2, Kate was able to finally sell her one-bedroom Manhattan condominium for $478,000. She purchased the condo, which she had lived in for six years prior to her marriage, for $205,000.

Kate owns a vacation home in Myrtle Beach, South Carolina. She purchased the home several years ago, largely as an investment opportunity. To help cover the expenses of maintaining the home, James and Kate decided to rent the home out. They rented the home for a total of 106 days at fair market value (this included eight days that they rented the home to James's brother Jack). In addition to the 106 days, Kate allowed a good friend and customer, Clair, to stay in the home for half-price for two days. James and Kate stayed in the home for six days for a romantic getaway and three days in order to do some home repair and maintenance work. The rental revenues from the home in year 1 were $18,400. The Sawyers incurred the following expenses associated with the home.

- $9,100 of interest expense.
- $3,400 of real property taxes.
- $1,900 for homeowner's insurance.
- $1,200 for electricity.
- $1,600 for gas, other utilities, and landscaping.
- $5,200 for depreciation.

Required:

Determine the Sawyer's taxable income for 2009. Disregard self-employment taxes for Kate and disregard the phase-out of itemized deductions. Assume the couple paid $4,400 in state income taxes and files a joint return. The Sawyers use the method of allocating expenses to the rental that minimizes their *overall taxable income for 2009*.

KAPLAN SCHWESER CPA SIMULATIONS

KAPLAN) SCHWESER

Please visit the Online Learning Center (www.mhhe.com/spilker2010) to access the following Kaplan Schweser CPA simulation:

The simulation for **Michael and Marshall Morgan** covers individual income tax issues, including itemized deductions; rental income and expenses; deductions for AGI; filing requirements; AMT; and dependents with summer job income.

Please visit the Online Learning Center (www.mhhe.com/spilker2010) to access the following Kaplan Schweser CPA simulation:

The simulation for **Colt and Cara West** covers individual income tax issues, including business income/expense; home office deduction; NOL; charitable donations; and capital expenditures.

Tax Forms

All tax forms can be obtained from the IRS Web site: www.irs.gov.

Form **1040**

Department of the Treasury—Internal Revenue Service

U.S. Individual Income Tax Return 2008   (99)   IRS Use Only—Do not write or staple in this space.

For the year Jan. 1–Dec. 31, 2008, or other tax year beginning , 2008, ending , 20	OMB No. 1545-0074

Label

(See instructions on page 14.)

Use the IRS label. Otherwise, please print or type.

L A B E L

H E R E

Your first name and initial	Last name	Your social security number
If a joint return, spouse's first name and initial	Last name	Spouse's social security number
Home address (number and street). If you have a P.O. box, see page 14.	Apt. no.	▲ You **must** enter your SSN(s) above. ▲
City, town or post office, state, and ZIP code. If you have a foreign address, see page 14.		

Checking a box below will not change your tax or refund.

Presidential Election Campaign ▶ Check here if you, or your spouse if filing jointly, want $3 to go to this fund (see page 14) ▶ ☐ **You** ☐ **Spouse**

Filing Status

Check only one box.

1 ☐ Single
2 ☐ Married filing jointly (even if only one had income)
3 ☐ Married filing separately. Enter spouse's SSN above and full name here. ▶
4 ☐ Head of household (with qualifying person). (See page 15.) If the qualifying person is a child but not your dependent, enter this child's name here. ▶ _____
5 ☐ Qualifying widow(er) with dependent child (see page 16)

Exemptions

If more than four dependents, see page 17.

6a ☐ **Yourself.** If someone can claim you as a dependent, **do not** check box 6a
b ☐ **Spouse**
c **Dependents:**

(1) First name Last name	(2) Dependent's social security number	(3) Dependent's relationship to you	(4) ✓ if qualifying child for child tax credit (see page 17)
			☐
			☐
			☐
			☐

d Total number of exemptions claimed

Boxes checked on 6a and 6b _____
No. of children on 6c who:
• lived with you _____
• did not live with you due to divorce or separation (see page 18) _____
Dependents on 6c not entered above _____
Add numbers on lines above ▶ ☐

Income

Attach Form(s) W-2 here. Also attach Forms W-2G and 1099-R if tax was withheld.

If you did not get a W-2, see page 21.

Enclose, but do not attach, any payment. Also, please use **Form 1040-V.**

7	Wages, salaries, tips, etc. Attach Form(s) W-2	7	
8a	**Taxable** interest. Attach Schedule B if required	8a	
b	**Tax-exempt** interest. **Do not** include on line 8a	8b	
9a	Ordinary dividends. Attach Schedule B if required	9a	
b	Qualified dividends (see page 21)	9b	
10	Taxable refunds, credits, or offsets of state and local income taxes (see page 22)	10	
11	Alimony received	11	
12	Business income or (loss). Attach Schedule C or C-EZ	12	
13	Capital gain or (loss). Attach Schedule D if required. If not required, check here ▶ ☐	13	
14	Other gains or (losses). Attach Form 4797	14	
15a	IRA distributions 15a	b Taxable amount (see page 23)	15b	
16a	Pensions and annuities 16a	b Taxable amount (see page 24)	16b	
17	Rental real estate, royalties, partnerships, S corporations, trusts, etc. Attach Schedule E	17	
18	Farm income or (loss). Attach Schedule F	18	
19	Unemployment compensation	19	
20a	Social security benefits 20a	b Taxable amount (see page 26)	20b	
21	Other income. List type and amount (see page 28)	21	
22	Add the amounts in the far right column for lines 7 through 21. This is your **total income** ▶	22	

Adjusted Gross Income

23	Educator expenses (see page 28)	23	
24	Certain business expenses of reservists, performing artists, and fee-basis government officials. Attach Form 2106 or 2106-EZ	24	
25	Health savings account deduction. Attach Form 8889	25	
26	Moving expenses. Attach Form 3903	26	
27	One-half of self-employment tax. Attach Schedule SE	27	
28	Self-employed SEP, SIMPLE, and qualified plans	28	
29	Self-employed health insurance deduction (see page 29)	29	
30	Penalty on early withdrawal of savings	30	
31a	Alimony paid b Recipient's SSN ▶	31a	
32	IRA deduction (see page 30)	32	
33	Student loan interest deduction (see page 33)	33	
34	Tuition and fees deduction. Attach Form 8917	34	
35	Domestic production activities deduction. Attach Form 8903	35	
36	Add lines 23 through 31a and 32 through 35	36	
37	Subtract line 36 from line 22. This is your **adjusted gross income** ▶	37	

For Disclosure, Privacy Act, and Paperwork Reduction Act Notice, see page 88.   Cat. No. 11320B   Form **1040** (2008)

Form 1040 (2008)   Page **2**

Tax **and** **Credits**	38	Amount from line 37 (adjusted gross income)	38	
	39a	Check if: { ☐ **You** were born before January 2, 1944, ☐ Blind. } Total boxes ☐ **Spouse** was born before January 2, 1944, ☐ Blind. } checked ▶ 39a		
	b	If your spouse itemizes on a separate return or you were a dual-status alien, see page 34 and check here ▶ 39b ☐		
Standard Deduction for—	c	Check if standard deduction includes real estate taxes or disaster loss (see page 34) ▶ 39c ☐		
	40	**Itemized deductions** (from Schedule A) **or** your **standard deduction** (see left margin) .	40	
• People who checked any box on line 39a, 39b, or 39c **or** who can be claimed as a dependent, see page 34.	41	Subtract line 40 from line 38	41	
	42	If line 38 is over $119,975, or you provided housing to a Midwestern displaced individual, see page 36. Otherwise, multiply $3,500 by the total number of exemptions claimed on line 6d .	42	
	43	**Taxable income.** Subtract line 42 from line 41. If line 42 is more than line 41, enter -0-	43	
• All others:	44	**Tax** (see page 36). Check if any tax is from: **a** ☐ Form(s) 8814 **b** ☐ Form 4972	44	
Single or Married filing separately, $5,450	45	**Alternative minimum tax** (see page 39). Attach Form 6251 . . .	45	
	46	Add lines 44 and 45 . . . . ▶	46	
Married filing jointly or Qualifying widow(er), $10,900	47	Foreign tax credit. Attach Form 1116 if required	47	
	48	Credit for child and dependent care expenses. Attach Form 2441	48	
	49	Credit for the elderly or the disabled. Attach Schedule R .	49	
	50	Education credits. Attach Form 8863	50	
Head of household, $8,000	51	Retirement savings contributions credit. Attach Form 8880 .	51	
	52	Child tax credit (see page 42). Attach Form 8901 if required .	52	
	53	Credits from Form: **a** ☐ 8396 **b** ☐ 8839 **c** ☐ 5695	53	
	54	Other credits from Form: **a** ☐ 3800 **b** ☐ 8801 **c** ☐ _____	54	
	55	Add lines 47 through 54. These are your **total credits**	55	
	56	Subtract line 55 from line 46. If line 55 is more than line 46, enter -0- . . . . . ▶	56	
Other Taxes	57	Self-employment tax. Attach Schedule SE	57	
	58	Unreported social security and Medicare tax from Form: **a** ☐ 4137 **b** ☐ 8919 . .	58	
	59	Additional tax on IRAs, other qualified retirement plans, etc. Attach Form 5329 if required .	59	
	60	Additional taxes: **a** ☐ AEIC payments **b** ☐ Household employment taxes. Attach Schedule H	60	
	61	Add lines 56 through 60. This is your **total tax** . . . . ▶	61	
Payments	62	Federal income tax withheld from Forms W-2 and 1099 . .	62	
	63	2008 estimated tax payments and amount applied from 2007 return	63	
If you have a qualifying child, attach Schedule EIC.	64a	**Earned income credit (EIC)**	64a	
	b	Nontaxable combat pay election � 64b		
	65	Excess social security and tier 1 RRTA tax withheld (see page 61)	65	
	66	Additional child tax credit. Attach Form 8812	66	
	67	Amount paid with request for extension to file (see page 61)	67	
	68	Credits from Form: **a** ☐ 2439 **b** ☐ 4136 **c** ☐ 8801 **d** ☐ 8885	68	
	69	First-time homebuyer credit. Attach Form 5405	69	
	70	Recovery rebate credit (see worksheet on pages 62 and 63) .	70	
	71	Add lines 62 through 70. These are your **total payments** . . . . ▶	71	
Refund Direct deposit? See page 63 and fill in 73b, 73c, and 73d, or Form 8888.	72	If line 71 is more than line 61, subtract line 61 from line 71. This is the amount you **overpaid**	72	
	73a	Amount of line 72 you want **refunded to you.** If Form 8888 is attached, check here ▶ ☐	73a	
	▶ b	Routing number ☐☐☐☐☐☐☐☐☐ ▶ c Type: ☐ Checking ☐ Savings		
	▶ d	Account number ☐☐☐☐☐☐☐☐☐☐☐☐☐☐☐☐☐		
	74	Amount of line 72 you want **applied to your 2009 estimated tax** ▶ 74		
Amount You Owe	75	**Amount you owe.** Subtract line 71 from line 61. For details on how to pay, see page 65 ▶	75	
	76	Estimated tax penalty (see page 65) 76		
Third Party Designee		Do you want to allow another person to discuss this return with the IRS (see page 66)? ☐ **Yes. Complete the following.** ☐ **No** Designee's name ▶ _____ Phone no. ▶ ( ) _____ Personal identification number (PIN) ▶ ☐☐☐☐☐		
Sign Here Joint return? See page 15. Keep a copy for your records.		Under penalties of perjury, I declare that I have examined this return and accompanying schedules and statements, and to the best of my knowledge and belief, they are true, correct, and complete. Declaration of preparer (other than taxpayer) is based on all information of which preparer has any knowledge.		

Your signature	Date	Your occupation	Daytime phone number
			( )
Spouse's signature. If a joint return, **both** must sign.	Date	Spouse's occupation	

Paid Preparer's Use Only	Preparer's signature ▶	Date	Check if self-employed ☐	Preparer's SSN or PTIN
	Firm's name (or yours if self-employed), address, and ZIP code ▶		EIN	
			Phone no. ( )	

Form **1040** (2008)

✸ *Printed on recycled paper*

SCHEDULES A&B
(Form 1040)

Department of the Treasury
Internal Revenue Service   (99)

Schedule A—Itemized Deductions

(Schedule B is on back)

▶ **Attach to Form 1040.**   ▶ **See Instructions for Schedules A&B (Form 1040).**

OMB No. 1545-0074

20**08**

Attachment
Sequence No. **07**

Name(s) shown on Form 1040

Your social security number

Medical and Dental Expenses		**Caution.** Do not include expenses reimbursed or paid by others.
	1	Medical and dental expenses (see page A-1) **1**
	2	Enter amount from Form 1040, line 38 **2**
	3	Multiply line 2 by 7.5% (.075) **3**
	4	Subtract line 3 from line 1. If line 3 is more than line 1, enter -0- **4**
Taxes You Paid (See page A-2.)	5	State and local **(check only one box):**
		a ☐ Income taxes, **or**
		b ☐ General sales taxes **5**
	6	Real estate taxes (see page A-5) **6**
	7	Personal property taxes **7**
	8	Other taxes. List type and amount ▶ _____
		8
	9	Add lines 5 through 8 . . . . **9**
Interest You Paid (See page A-5.)	10	Home mortgage interest and points reported to you on Form 1098 **10**
	11	Home mortgage interest not reported to you on Form 1098. If paid to the person from whom you bought the home, see page A-6 and show that person's name, identifying no., and address ▶
Note. Personal interest is not deductible.		_____
		_____ **11**
	12	Points not reported to you on Form 1098. See page A-6 for special rules. **12**
	13	Qualified mortgage insurance premiums (see page A-6) **13**
	14	Investment interest. Attach Form 4952 if required. (See page A-6.) **14**
	15	Add lines 10 through 14 . . . . **15**
Gifts to Charity If you made a gift and got a benefit for it, see page A-7.	16	Gifts by cash or check. If you made any gift of $250 or more, see page A-7 . . . . . . **16**
	17	Other than by cash or check. If any gift of $250 or more, see page A-8. You **must** attach Form 8283 if over $500 **17**
	18	Carryover from prior year **18**
	19	Add lines 16 through 18 . . . . **19**
Casualty and Theft Losses	20	Casualty or theft loss(es). Attach Form 4684. (See page A-8.) **20**
Job Expenses and Certain Miscellaneous Deductions (See page A-9.)	21	Unreimbursed employee expenses—job travel, union dues, job education, etc. Attach Form 2106 or 2106-EZ if required. (See page A-9.) ▶ _____ **21**
	22	Tax preparation fees **22**
	23	Other expenses—investment, safe deposit box, etc. List type and amount ▶ _____
		23
	24	Add lines 21 through 23 . . . . **24**
	25	Enter amount from Form 1040, line 38 **25**
	26	Multiply line 25 by 2% (.02) **26**
	27	Subtract line 26 from line 24. If line 26 is more than line 24, enter -0- **27**
Other Miscellaneous Deductions	28	Other—from list on page A-10. List type and amount ▶ _____
		_____ **28**
Total Itemized Deductions	29	Is Form 1040, line 38, over $159,950 (over $79,975 if married filing separately)?
		☐ **No.** Your deduction is not limited. Add the amounts in the far right column for lines 4 through 28. Also, enter this amount on Form 1040, line 40. } ▶ **29**
		☐ **Yes.** Your deduction may be limited. See page A-10 for the amount to enter.
	30	If you elect to itemize deductions even though they are less than your standard deduction, check here . . . . ▶ ☐

For Paperwork Reduction Act Notice, see Form 1040 instructions.   Cat. No. 11330X   **Schedule A (Form 1040) 2008**

Name(s) shown on Form 1040. Do not enter name and social security number if shown on other side. | **Your social security number**

Schedule B—Interest and Ordinary Dividends

Attachment
Sequence No. **08**

			Amount
Part I **Interest** (See page B-1 and the instructions for Form 1040, line 8a.)	**1**	List name of payer. If any interest is from a seller-financed mortgage and the buyer used the property as a personal residence, see page B-1 and list this interest first. Also, show that buyer's social security number and address ▶	**1**
Note. If you received a Form 1099-INT, Form 1099-OID, or substitute statement from a brokerage firm, list the firm's name as the payer and enter the total interest shown on that form.	**2**	Add the amounts on line 1	**2**
	3	Excludable interest on series EE and I U.S. savings bonds issued after 1989. Attach Form 8815	**3**
	4	Subtract line 3 from line 2. Enter the result here and on Form 1040, line 8a ▶	**4**

Note. If line 4 is over $1,500, you must complete Part III.

			Amount
Part II **Ordinary** **Dividends** (See page B-1 and the instructions for Form 1040, line 9a.)	**5**	List name of payer ▶	**5**
Note. If you received a Form 1099-DIV or substitute statement from a brokerage firm, list the firm's name as the payer and enter the ordinary dividends shown on that form.	**6**	Add the amounts on line 5. Enter the total here and on Form 1040, line 9a . ▶	**6**

Note. If line 6 is over $1,500, you must complete Part III.

			Yes	No
Part III **Foreign** **Accounts** **and Trusts** (See page B-2.)		You must complete this part if you **(a)** had over $1,500 of taxable interest or ordinary dividends; or **(b)** had a foreign account; or **(c)** received a distribution from, or were a grantor of, or a transferor to, a foreign trust.		
	7a	At any time during 2008, did you have an interest in or a signature or other authority over a financial account in a foreign country, such as a bank account, securities account, or other financial account? See page B-2 for exceptions and filing requirements for Form TD F 90-22.1		
	b	If "Yes," enter the name of the foreign country ▶		
	8	During 2008, did you receive a distribution from, or were you the grantor of, or transferor to, a foreign trust? If "Yes," you may have to file Form 3520. See page B-2		

For Paperwork Reduction Act Notice, see Form 1040 instructions.   **Schedule B (Form 1040) 2008**

SCHEDULE C
(Form 1040)

Department of the Treasury
Internal Revenue Service   (99)

Profit or Loss From Business

(Sole Proprietorship)

▶ Partnerships, joint ventures, etc., generally must file Form 1065 or 1065-B.

▶ Attach to Form 1040, 1040NR, or 1041.   ▶ See Instructions for Schedule C (Form 1040).

OMB No. 1545-0074

20**08**

Attachment
Sequence No. **09**

Name of proprietor

Social security number (SSN)

A Principal business or profession, including product or service (see page C-3 of the instructions)

B Enter code from pages C-9, 10, & 11
▶

C Business name. If no separate business name, leave blank.

D Employer ID number (EIN), if any

E Business address (including suite or room no.) ▶ ....
City, town or post office, state, and ZIP code

F Accounting method: **(1)** ☐ Cash   **(2)** ☐ Accrual   **(3)** ☐ Other (specify) ▶ ....

G Did you "materially participate" in the operation of this business during 2008? If "No," see page C-4 for limit on losses   ☐ Yes ☐ No

H If you started or acquired this business during 2008, check here   . . . . ▶ ☐

Part I Income

1	Gross receipts or sales. **Caution.** See page C-4 and check the box if: ● This income was reported to you on Form W-2 and the "Statutory employee" box on that form was checked, or ● You are a member of a qualified joint venture reporting only rental real estate income not subject to self-employment tax. Also see page C-4 for limit on losses. . . ▶ ☐	**1**
2	Returns and allowances	**2**
3	Subtract line 2 from line 1	**3**
4	Cost of goods sold (from line 42 on page 2)	**4**
5	**Gross profit.** Subtract line 4 from line 3.	**5**
6	Other income, including federal and state gasoline or fuel tax credit or refund (see page C-4).	**6**
7	**Gross income.** Add lines 5 and 6 . . . . ▶	**7**

Part II Expenses. Enter expenses for business use of your home **only** on line 30.

8	Advertising	**8**	18	Office expense	**18**
9	Car and truck expenses (see page C-5).	**9**	19	Pension and profit-sharing plans	**19**
10	Commissions and fees . .	**10**	20	Rent or lease (see page C-6):	
11	Contract labor (see page C-5)	**11**		a Vehicles, machinery, and equipment .	**20a**
12	Depletion	**12**		b Other business property. . .	**20b**
13	Depreciation and section 179 expense deduction (not included in Part III) (see page C-5)	**13**	21	Repairs and maintenance . .	**21**
			22	Supplies (not included in Part III) .	**22**
			23	Taxes and licenses	**23**
			24	Travel, meals, and entertainment:	
				a Travel	**24a**
14	Employee benefit programs (other than on line 19) .	**14**		b Deductible meals and entertainment (see page C-7)	**24b**
15	Insurance (other than health) .	**15**	25	Utilities	**25**
16	Interest:		26	Wages (less employment credits) .	**26**
	a Mortgage (paid to banks, etc.) .	**16a**	27	Other expenses (from line 48 on page 2)	**27**
	b Other	**16b**			
17	Legal and professional services	**17**			

28	**Total expenses** before expenses for business use of home. Add lines 8 through 27 . . . . . ▶	**28**
29	Tentative profit or (loss). Subtract line 28 from line 7	**29**
30	Expenses for business use of your home. Attach **Form 8829**	**30**
31	**Net profit or (loss).** Subtract line 30 from line 29. ● If a profit, enter on both **Form 1040, line 12,** and **Schedule SE, line 2,** or on **Form 1040NR, line 13** (if you checked the box on line 1 as a statutory employee, see page C-7). Estates and trusts, enter on **Form 1041, line 3.** ● If a loss, you **must** go to line 32.	**31**
32	If you have a loss, check the box that describes your investment in this activity (see page C-8). ● If you checked 32a, enter the loss on both **Form 1040, line 12,** and **Schedule SE, line 2,** or on **Form 1040NR, line 13** (if you checked the box on line 1 as a statutory employee, see the line 31 instructions on page C-7). Estates and trusts, enter on **Form 1041, line 3.** ● If you checked 32b, you **must** attach **Form 6198.** Your loss may be limited.	**32a** ☐ All investment is at risk. **32b** ☐ Some investment is not at risk.

For Paperwork Reduction Act Notice, see page C-9 of the instructions.   Cat. No. 11334P   **Schedule C (Form 1040) 2008**

Schedule C (Form 1040) 2008   Page **2**

Part III   **Cost of Goods Sold** (see page C-8)

33   Method(s) used to value closing inventory: **a** ☐ Cost   **b** ☐ Lower of cost or market   **c** ☐ Other (attach explanation)

34   Was there any change in determining quantities, costs, or valuations between opening and closing inventory?
If "Yes," attach explanation . . . . ☐ **Yes**   ☐ **No**

35 Inventory at beginning of year. If different from last year's closing inventory, attach explanation . .	35	
36 Purchases less cost of items withdrawn for personal use	36	
37 Cost of labor. Do not include any amounts paid to yourself	37	
38 Materials and supplies	38	
39 Other costs	39	
40 Add lines 35 through 39	40	
41 Inventory at end of year	41	
42 **Cost of goods sold.** Subtract line 41 from line 40. Enter the result here and on page 1, line 4 . .	42	

Part IV   **Information on Your Vehicle. Complete this part only** if you are claiming car or truck expenses on line 9 and are not required to file Form 4562 for this business. See the instructions for line 13 on page C-5 to find out if you must file Form 4562.

43   When did you place your vehicle in service for business purposes? (month, day, year) ▶ .... / .... / ....

44   Of the total number of miles you drove your vehicle during 2008, enter the number of miles you used your vehicle for:

   a   Business ....   **b**   Commuting (see instructions) ....   **c**   Other ....

45   Was your vehicle available for personal use during off-duty hours?   . . . . ☐ **Yes**   ☐ **No**

46   Do you (or your spouse) have another vehicle available for personal use?. . . . . ☐ **Yes**   ☐ **No**

47a   Do you have evidence to support your deduction?   . . . . ☐ **Yes**   ☐ **No**

   b   If "Yes," is the evidence written? . . . . ☐ **Yes**   ☐ **No**

Part V   **Other Expenses.** List below business expenses not included on lines 8–26 or line 30.

....		
....		
....		
....		
....		
....		
....		
....		
48 **Total other expenses.** Enter here and on page 1, line 27	48	

SCHEDULE D	Capital Gains and Losses	OMB No. 1545-0074

SCHEDULE D
(Form 1040)
Department of the Treasury
Internal Revenue Service   (99)

Capital Gains and Losses

▶ Attach to Form 1040 or Form 1040NR.   ▶ See Instructions for Schedule D (Form 1040).

▶ Use Schedule D-1 to list additional transactions for lines 1 and 8.

OMB No. 1545-0074

2008

Attachment
Sequence No. **12**

Name(s) shown on return   Your social security number

Part I   Short-Term Capital Gains and Losses—Assets Held One Year or Less

(a) Description of property (Example: 100 sh. XYZ Co.)	(b) Date acquired (Mo., day, yr.)	(c) Date sold (Mo., day, yr.)	(d) Sales price (see page D-7 of the instructions)	(e) Cost or other basis (see page D-7 of the instructions)	(f) Gain or (loss) Subtract (e) from (d)
1					

2   Enter your short-term totals, if any, from Schedule D-1, line 2 . . . .   **2**

3   **Total short-term sales price amounts.** Add lines 1 and 2 in column (d) **3**

4   Short-term gain from Form 6252 and short-term gain or (loss) from Forms 4684, 6781, and 8824   **4**

5   Net short-term gain or (loss) from partnerships, S corporations, estates, and trusts from Schedule(s) K-1 . . . .   **5**

6   Short-term capital loss carryover. Enter the amount, if any, from line 8 of your **Capital Loss Carryover Worksheet** on page D-7 of the instructions . . . .   **6** (   )

7   **Net short-term capital gain or (loss).** Combine lines 1 through 6 in column (f) **7**

Part II   Long-Term Capital Gains and Losses—Assets Held More Than One Year

(a) Description of property (Example: 100 sh. XYZ Co.)	(b) Date acquired (Mo., day, yr.)	(c) Date sold (Mo., day, yr.)	(d) Sales price (see page D-7 of the instructions)	(e) Cost or other basis (see page D-7 of the instructions)	(f) Gain or (loss) Subtract (e) from (d)
8					

9   Enter your long-term totals, if any, from Schedule D-1, line 9 . . . .   **9**

10   **Total long-term sales price amounts.** Add lines 8 and 9 in column (d) **10**

11   Gain from Form 4797, Part I; long-term gain from Forms 2439 and 6252; and long-term gain or (loss) from Forms 4684, 6781, and 8824 . . . .   **11**

12   Net long-term gain or (loss) from partnerships, S corporations, estates, and trusts from Schedule(s) K-1 . . . .   **12**

13   Capital gain distributions. See page D-2 of the instructions **13**

14   Long-term capital loss carryover. Enter the amount, if any, from line 13 of your **Capital Loss Carryover Worksheet** on page D-7 of the instructions . . . .   **14** (   )

15   **Net long-term capital gain or (loss).** Combine lines 8 through 14 in column (f). Then go to Part III on the back **15**

For Paperwork Reduction Act Notice, see Form 1040 or Form 1040NR instructions.   Cat. No. 11338H   **Schedule D (Form 1040) 2008**

Part III	Summary

16   Combine lines 7 and 15 and enter the result. **16**

If line 16 is:

- A **gain**, enter the amount from line 16 on Form 1040, line 13, or Form 1040NR, line 14. Then go to line 17 below.
- A **loss**, skip lines 17 through 20 below. Then go to line 21. Also be sure to complete line 22.
- **Zero**, skip lines 17 through 21 below and enter -0- on Form 1040, line 13, or Form 1040NR, line 14. Then go to line 22.

17   Are lines 15 and 16 **both** gains?
     ☐ **Yes.** Go to line 18.
     ☐ **No.** Skip lines 18 through 21, and go to line 22.

18   Enter the amount, if any, from line 7 of the **28% Rate Gain Worksheet** on page D-8 of the instructions . . . . ▶   **18**

19   Enter the amount, if any, from line 18 of the **Unrecaptured Section 1250 Gain Worksheet** on page D-9 of the instructions . . . . ▶   **19**

20   Are lines 18 and 19 **both** zero or blank?
     ☐ **Yes.** Complete Form 1040 through line 43, or Form 1040NR through line 40. Then complete the **Qualified Dividends and Capital Gain Tax Worksheet** on page 38 of the Instructions for Form 1040 (or in the Instructions for Form 1040NR). **Do not** complete lines 21 and 22 below.

     ☐ **No.** Complete Form 1040 through line 43, or Form 1040NR through line 40. Then complete the **Schedule D Tax Worksheet** on page D-10 of the instructions. **Do not** complete lines 21 and 22 below.

21   If line 16 is a loss, enter here and on Form 1040, line 13, or Form 1040NR, line 14, the **smaller** of:

- The loss on line 16 or   ⎫
- ($3,000), or if married filing separately, ($1,500) ⎬ . . . .   **21** (   )
    ⎭

Note. When figuring which amount is smaller, treat both amounts as positive numbers.

22   Do you have qualified dividends on Form 1040, line 9b, or Form 1040NR, line 10b?
     ☐ **Yes.** Complete Form 1040 through line 43, or Form 1040NR through line 40. Then complete the **Qualified Dividends and Capital Gain Tax Worksheet** on page 38 of the Instructions for Form 1040 (or in the Instructions for Form 1040NR).

     ☐ **No.** Complete the rest of Form 1040 or Form 1040NR.

SCHEDULE E
(Form 1040)

Department of the Treasury
Internal Revenue Service   (99)

Supplemental Income and Loss

(From rental real estate, royalties, partnerships,
S corporations, estates, trusts, REMICs, etc.)

▶ **Attach to Form 1040, 1040NR, or Form 1041.**   ▶ **See Instructions for Schedule E (Form 1040).**

OMB No. 1545-0074

2008

Attachment
Sequence No. **13**

Name(s) shown on return

Your social security number

Part I   **Income or Loss From Rental Real Estate and Royalties** Note. If you are in the business of renting personal property, use **Schedule C or C-EZ** (see page E-3). If you are an individual, report farm rental income or loss from **Form 4835** on page 2, line 40.

1 List the type and address of each **rental real estate property:**

A ....

B ....

C ....

2 For each rental real estate property listed on line 1, did you or your family use it during the tax year for personal purposes for more than the greater of:
- **14 days or**
- **10% of the total days rented at fair rental value?**
(See page E-3)

	Yes	No
A		
B		
C		

Income:

			Properties A	Properties B	Properties C		Totals (Add columns A, B, and C.)
3	Rents received	3				3	
4	Royalties received	4				4	

Expenses:

5	Advertising	5					
6	Auto and travel (see page E-4) .	6					
7	Cleaning and maintenance. . .	7					
8	Commissions	8					
9	Insurance	9					
10	Legal and other professional fees	10					
11	Management fees.	11					
12	Mortgage interest paid to banks, etc. (see page E-5)	12				12	
13	Other interest	13					
14	Repairs	14					
15	Supplies	15					
16	Taxes.	16					
17	Utilities	17					
18	Other (list) ▶	18					
19	Add lines 5 through 18	19				19	
20	Depreciation expense or depletion (see page E-5)	20				20	
21	Total expenses. Add lines 19 and 20	21					
22	Income or (loss) from rental real estate or royalty properties. Subtract line 21 from line 3 (rents) or line 4 (royalties). If the result is a (loss), see page E-5 to find out if you must file **Form 6198** . . .	22					
23	Deductible rental real estate loss. **Caution.** Your rental real estate loss on line 22 may be limited. See page E-5 to find out if you must file **Form 8582.** Real estate professionals **must** complete line 43 on page 2	23	( )	( )	( )	( )	

24 **Income.** Add positive amounts shown on line 22. **Do not** include any losses **24**

25 **Losses.** Add royalty losses from line 22 and rental real estate losses from line 23. Enter total losses here.   **25** ( )

26 **Total rental real estate and royalty income or (loss).** Combine lines 24 and 25. Enter the result here. If Parts II, III, IV, and line 40 on page 2 do not apply to you, also enter this amount on Form 1040, line 17, or Form 1040NR, line 18. Otherwise, include this amount in the total on line 41 on page 2 . .   **26**

For Paperwork Reduction Act Notice, see page E-8 of the instructions.   Cat. No. 11344L   **Schedule E (Form 1040) 2008**

Name(s) shown on return. Do not enter name and social security number if shown on other side.	Your social security number

Caution. The IRS compares amounts reported on your tax return with amounts shown on Schedule(s) K-1.

Part II   **Income or Loss From Partnerships and S Corporations**   **Note.** If you report a loss from an at-risk activity for which **any** amount is **not** at risk, you **must** check the box in column **(e)** on line 28 and attach **Form 6198.** See page E-1.

27 Are you reporting any loss not allowed in a prior year due to the at-risk or basis limitations, a prior year unallowed loss from a passive activity (if that loss was not reported on Form 8582), or unreimbursed partnership expenses? ☐ **Yes** ☐ **No**
If you answered "Yes," see page E-7 before completing this section.

28	(a) Name	(b) Enter P for partnership; S for S corporation	(c) Check if foreign partnership	(d) Employer identification number	(e) Check if any amount is not at risk
A			☐		☐
B			☐		☐
C			☐		☐
D			☐		☐

	Passive Income and Loss		Nonpassive Income and Loss		
	(f) Passive loss allowed (attach **Form 8582** if required)	(g) Passive income from **Schedule K–1**	(h) Nonpassive loss from **Schedule K–1**	(i) Section 179 expense deduction from **Form 4562**	(j) Nonpassive income from **Schedule K–1**
A					
B					
C					
D					
29a Totals					
b Totals					

30 Add columns (g) and (j) of line 29a . . . . **30** |
31 Add columns (f), (h), and (i) of line 29b . . . . **31** ( ) |
32 **Total partnership and S corporation income or (loss).** Combine lines 30 and 31. Enter the result here and include in the total on line 41 below **32**

Part III   **Income or Loss From Estates and Trusts**

33	(a) Name	(b) Employer identification number
A		
B		

	Passive Income and Loss		Nonpassive Income and Loss	
	(c) Passive deduction or loss allowed (attach **Form 8582** if required)	(d) Passive income from **Schedule K–1**	(e) Deduction or loss from **Schedule K–1**	(f) Other income from **Schedule K–1**
A				
B				
34a Totals				
b Totals				

35 Add columns (d) and (f) of line 34a . . . . **35** |
36 Add columns (c) and (e) of line 34b . . . . **36** ( ) |
37 **Total estate and trust income or (loss).** Combine lines 35 and 36. Enter the result here and include in the total on line 41 below **37**

Part IV   **Income or Loss From Real Estate Mortgage Investment Conduits (REMICs)—Residual Holder**

38	(a) Name	(b) Employer identification number	(c) Excess inclusion from **Schedules Q,** line 2c (see page E-7)	(d) Taxable income (net loss) from **Schedules Q,** line 1b	(e) Income from **Schedules Q,** line 3b

39 Combine columns (d) and (e) only. Enter the result here and include in the total on line 41 below **39**

Part V   **Summary**

40 Net farm rental income or (loss) from **Form 4835.** Also, complete line 42 below . . . . . . **40** |
41 **Total income or (loss).** Combine lines 26, 32, 37, 39, and 40. Enter the result here and on Form 1040, line 17, or Form 1040NR, line 18 ▶ **41**

42 **Reconciliation of farming and fishing income.** Enter your **gross** farming and fishing income reported on Form 4835, line 7; Schedule K-1 (Form 1065), box 14, code B; Schedule K-1 (Form 1120S), box 17, code T; and Schedule K-1 (Form 1041), line 14, code F (see page E-8) **42**

43 **Reconciliation for real estate professionals.** If you were a real estate professional (see page E-2), enter the net income or (loss) you reported anywhere on Form 1040 or Form 1040NR from all rental real estate activities in which you materially participated under the passive activity loss rules . **43**

SCHEDULE SE
(Form 1040)

Department of the Treasury
Internal Revenue Service   (99)

Self-Employment Tax

▶ **Attach to Form 1040.**   ▶ **See Instructions for Schedule SE (Form 1040).**

OMB No. 1545-0074

2008

Attachment
Sequence No. **17**

Name of person with **self-employment** income (as shown on Form 1040)	Social security number of person with **self-employment** income ▶		

Who Must File Schedule SE

You must file Schedule SE if:

- You had net earnings from self-employment from **other than** church employee income (line 4 of Short Schedule SE or line 4c of Long Schedule SE) of $400 or more, **or**

- You had church employee income of $108.28 or more. Income from services you performed as a minister or a member of a religious order **is not** church employee income (see page SE-1).

Note. Even if you had a loss or a small amount of income from self-employment, it may be to your benefit to file Schedule SE and use either "optional method" in Part II of Long Schedule SE (see page SE-4).

Exception. If your only self-employment income was from earnings as a minister, member of a religious order, or Christian Science practitioner **and** you filed Form 4361 and received IRS approval not to be taxed on those earnings, **do not** file Schedule SE. Instead, write "Exempt—Form 4361" on Form 1040, line 57.

May I Use Short Schedule SE or Must I Use Long Schedule SE?

Note. Use this flowchart **only if** you must file Schedule SE. If unsure, see *Who Must File Schedule SE,* above.

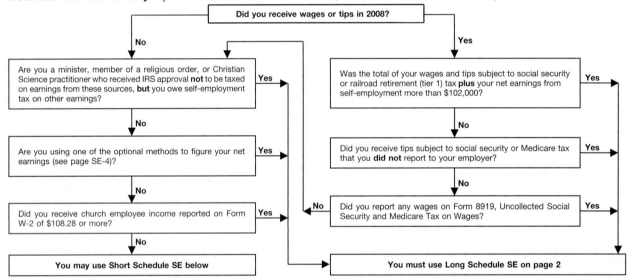

Section A—Short Schedule SE. Caution. Read above to see if you can use Short Schedule SE.

1a	Net farm profit or (loss) from Schedule F, line 36, and farm partnerships, Schedule K-1 (Form 1065), box 14, code A	**1a**	
b	If you received social security retirement or disability benefits, enter the amount of Conservation Reserve Program payments included on Schedule F, line 6b, or listed on Schedule K-1 (Form 1065), box 20, code X	**1b** (	)
2	Net profit or (loss) from Schedule C, line 31; Schedule C-EZ, line 3; Schedule K-1 (Form 1065), box 14, code A (other than farming); and Schedule K-1 (Form 1065-B), box 9, code J1. Ministers and members of religious orders, see page SE-1 for types of income to report on this line. See page SE-3 for other income to report	**2**	
3	Combine lines 1a, 1b, and 2	**3**	
4	**Net earnings from self-employment.** Multiply line 3 by 92.35% (.9235). If less than $400, **do not** file this schedule; you do not owe self-employment tax . . . . ▶	**4**	
5	**Self-employment tax.** If the amount on line 4 is: • $102,000 or less, multiply line 4 by 15.3% (.153). Enter the result here and on **Form 1040, line 57.** • More than $102,000, multiply line 4 by 2.9% (.029). Then, add $12,648 to the result. Enter the total here and on **Form 1040, line 57**	**5**	
6	**Deduction for one-half of self-employment tax.** Multiply line 5 by 50% (.5). Enter the result here and on **Form 1040, line 27** . . .	**6**		

For Paperwork Reduction Act Notice, see Form 1040 instructions.   Cat. No. 11358Z   **Schedule SE (Form 1040) 2008**

Attachment Sequence No. **17**

Name of person with **self-employment** income (as shown on Form 1040)	Social security number of person with **self-employment** income ▶		

Section B—Long Schedule SE

Part I   Self-Employment Tax

Note. If your only income subject to self-employment tax is **church employee income,** skip lines 1 through 4b. Enter -0- on line 4c and go to line 5a. Income from services you performed as a minister or a member of a religious order **is not** church employee income. See page SE-1.

A   If you are a minister, member of a religious order, or Christian Science practitioner **and** you filed Form 4361, but you had $400 or more of **other** net earnings from self-employment, check here and continue with Part I . . . . . ▶ ☐

1a Net farm profit or (loss) from Schedule F, line 36, and farm partnerships, Schedule K-1 (Form 1065), box 14, code A. **Note.** Skip lines 1a and 1b if you use the farm optional method (see page SE-4)	**1a**		
b If you received social security retirement or disability benefits, enter the amount of Conservation Reserve Program payments included on Schedule F, line 6b, or listed on Schedule K-1 (Form 1065), box 20, code X	**1b** (		)
2 Net profit or (loss) from Schedule C, line 31; Schedule C-EZ, line 3; Schedule K-1 (Form 1065), box 14, code A (other than farming); and Schedule K-1 (Form 1065-B), box 9, code J1. Ministers and members of religious orders, see page SE-1 for types of income to report on this line. See page SE-3 for other income to report. **Note.** Skip this line if you use the nonfarm optional method (see page SE-4)	**2**		
3 Combine lines 1a, 1b, and 2	**3**		
4a If line 3 is more than zero, multiply line 3 by 92.35% (.9235). Otherwise, enter amount from line 3	**4a**		
b If you elect one or both of the optional methods, enter the total of lines 15 and 17 here . . .	**4b**		
c Combine lines 4a and 4b. If less than $400, **stop;** you do not owe self-employment tax. **Exception.** If less than $400 and you had **church employee income,** enter -0- and continue. . . . . . ▶	**4c**		
5a Enter your **church employee income** from Form W-2. See page SE-1 for definition of church employee income **5a**			
b Multiply line 5a by 92.35% (.9235). If less than $100, enter -0-	**5b**		
6 **Net earnings from self-employment.** Add lines 4c and 5b	**6**		
7 Maximum amount of combined wages and self-employment earnings subject to social security tax or the 6.2% portion of the 7.65% railroad retirement (tier 1) tax for 2008	**7**	102,000	00
8a Total social security wages and tips (total of boxes 3 and 7 on Form(s) W-2) and railroad retirement (tier 1) compensation. If $102,000 or more, skip lines 8b through 10, and go to line 11 . . . . . . **8a**			
b Unreported tips subject to social security tax (from Form 4137, line 10) **8b**			
c Wages subject to social security tax (from Form 8919, line 10) . . . **8c**			
d Add lines 8a, 8b, and 8c	**8d**		
9 Subtract line 8d from line 7. If zero or less, enter -0- here and on line 10 and go to line 11 . ▶	**9**		
10 Multiply the **smaller** of line 6 or line 9 by 12.4% (.124)	**10**		
11 Multiply line 6 by 2.9% (.029)	**11**		
12 **Self-employment tax.** Add lines 10 and 11. Enter here and on **Form 1040, line 57**	**12**		
13 **Deduction for one-half of self-employment tax.** Multiply line 12 by 50% (.5). Enter the result here and on **Form 1040, line 27** **13**			

Part II   Optional Methods To Figure Net Earnings (see page SE-4)

Farm Optional Method. You may use this method **only** if **(a)** your gross farm income[1] was not more than $6,300, **or (b)** your net farm profits[2] were less than $4,548.

14 Maximum income for optional methods	**14**	4,200	00
15 Enter the **smaller** of: two-thirds (⅔) of gross farm income[1] (not less than zero) or $4,200. Also include this amount on line 4b above	**15**		

Nonfarm Optional Method. You may use this method **only** if **(a)** your net nonfarm profits[3] were less than $4,548 and also less than 72.189% of your gross nonfarm income,[4] **and (b)** you had net earnings from self-employment of at least $400 in 2 of the prior 3 years.

Caution. You may use this method no more than five times.

16 Subtract line 15 from line 14	**16**		
17 Enter the **smaller** of: two-thirds (⅔) of gross nonfarm income[4] (not less than zero) **or** the amount on line 16. Also include this amount on line 4b above	**17**		

[1] From Sch. F, line 11, and Sch. K-1 (Form 1065), box 14, code B.

[2] From Sch. F, line 36, and Sch. K-1 (Form 1065), box 14, code A—minus the amount you would have entered on line 1b had you not used the optional method.

[3] From Sch. C, line 31; Sch. C-EZ, line 3; Sch. K-1 (Form 1065), box 14, code A; and Sch. K-1 (Form 1065-B), box 9, code J1.

[4] From Sch. C, line 7; Sch. C-EZ, line 1; Sch. K-1 (Form 1065), box 14, code C; and Sch. K-1 (Form 1065-B), box 9, code J2.

Tax Terms Glossary

§1231 assets   depreciable or real property used in a taxpayer's trade or business owned for more than one year.

§1231 look-back rule   a tax rule requiring taxpayers to treat current year net §1231 gains as ordinary income when the taxpayer has deducted a §1231 loss as an ordinary loss in the five years preceding the current tax year.

§1245 property   tangible personal property and intangible property subject to cost recovery deductions.

§1250 property   real property subject to cost recovery deductions.

§162(m) limitation   the $1 million deduction limit on nonperformance based salary paid to certain key executives.

§179 election: an incentive for small taxpayers which allows them to immediately expense a certain amount of tangible personal property placed in service during the year.

§197 purchased intangibles   intangible assets which are purchased that must be amortized over 180 months regardless of their actual useful lives.

§291 depreciation recapture   the portion of a corporate taxpayer's gain on real property that is converted to ordinary income rather than §1231 gain. This amount is 20 percent of the lesser of the gain realized or the accumulated depreciation on the asset.

§83(b) election   a special tax election that employees who receive restricted stock or other property with ownership restrictions can make to accelerate income recognition from the normal date when restrictions lapse to the date when the restricted stock or other property is granted. The election also accelerates the employer's compensation deduction related to the restricted stock or other property.

30-day letter   the IRS letter received after an audit that instructs the taxpayer that he or she has 30 days to either (1) request a conference with an appeals officer or (2) agree to the proposed adjustment.

90-day letter   the IRS letter received after an audit and receipt of the 30-day letter that explains that the taxpayer has 90 days to either (1) pay the proposed deficiency or (2) file a petition in the U.S. Tax Court to hear the case. The 90-day letter is also known as the *statutory notice of deficiency*.

A

Abandoned spouse   a married taxpayer whose spouse has left home for the last six months of the year. The taxpayer may qualify for head of household filing status if the taxpayer maintains a household for qualifying child.

Accelerated Cost Recovery System (ACRS) the depreciation system enacted by Congress in 1981 which is based on the concept of set recovery periods and accelerated depreciation methods.

Accountable plan   an employer's reimbursement plan under which employees must submit documentation supporting expenses to receive reimbursement and reimbursements are limited to legitimate business expenses.

Accounting method   an approach for determining the taxable year in which a business recognizes a particular item of income or deduction thereby dictating the timing of when a taxpayer reports income and deductions.

Accounting period   a fixed period in which a business reports income and deductions, generally referred to as a tax year.

Accrual method   method of accounting that generally recognizes income in the period earned and recognizes deductions in the period that liabilities are incurred.

Acquiescence   issued after the IRS loses a trial-level or circuit court case when the IRS has decided to follow the court's adverse ruling in the future. It does not mean that the IRS agrees with the court's ruling. Instead, it simply means that the IRS will no longer litigate this issue.

Acquisition indebtedness   debt secured by a qualified residence that is incurred in acquiring, constructing, or substantially improving the residence.

Action on decision   an IRS pronouncement that explains the background reasoning behind an IRS acquiescence or nonacquiescence.

Active participant in a rental activity   an individual who owns at least 10% of a rental property and participates in the process of making management decisions, such as approving new tenants, deciding on rental terms, and approving repairs and capital expenditures.

Ad valorem tax   a tax based on the value of property.

Adjusted basis   the cost basis of an asset that has yet to be recovered by a business through cost recovery deductions. Adjusted basis can be computed by subtracting the accumulated depreciation, amortization, or depletion from the asset's initial cost basis.

Adjusted gross income (AGI)   gross income less deductions for AGI. AGI is an important reference point that is often used in other calculations.

After-tax rate of return   a taxpayer's before-tax rate of return on an investment minus the taxes paid on the income from the investment. The formula for an after-tax rate of return that is taxed annually is the before tax rate of return $\times$ $(1 -$ marginal tax rate$)$ [i.e., $r = R \times (1 - t)$]. A taxpayer's after-tax rate of return on an investment held for more than one tax period is $r = (FV/I)^{1/n} - 1$, where r is the after-tax rate of return, FV is the after-tax future value of the investment, I is the original investment amount, and n is the number of periods the investment is held.

Alimony   a support payment of cash made to a former spouse. The payment must be made under a written separation agreement or divorce decree that does not designate the payment as something other than alimony, and the payments must cease no later than when the recipient dies.

All-inclusive income concept   definition of income that says that gross income means all income from whatever source derived.

Alternative minimum tax adjustments   adjustments (positive or negative) to regular taxable income to arrive at the alternative minimum tax base.

Alternative minimum tax base (AMT base)   alternative minimum taxable income minus the alternative minimum tax exemption.

Alternative minimum tax exemption   a deduction to determine the alternative minimum tax base that is phased out based on alternative minimum taxable income.

Alternative minimum tax system   a secondary or parallel tax system calculated on an *alternative* tax base that more closely reflects economic income than the regular income tax base. The system was designed to ensure that taxpayers generating income pay some *minimum* amount of income tax each year.

Alternative minimum tax   the additional tax paid when the tentative minimum tax (based on the alternative tax base) exceeds the regular tax (based on the regular tax base).

Amortization   the method of recovering the cost of intangible assets over a specific time period.

Amount realized   the value of everything received by the seller in a transaction (cash, FMV of other property, and relief of liabilities) less selling costs.

Annotated tax service   a tax service arranged by code section. For each code section, an annotated service includes the code section; a listing of the code section history; copies of congressional committee reports that explain changes to the code section; a copy of all the regulations issued for the specific code section; the service's unofficial explanation of the code section; and brief summaries (called annotations) of relevant court cases, revenue rulings, revenue procedures, and letter rulings that address issues specific to the code section.

Annuity   a stream of equal payments over time.

Arm's-length transaction   transactions among unrelated taxpayers, where each transacting party negotiates for his or her own benefit.

Assignment of income doctrine   the judicial doctrine holding that earned income is taxed to the taxpayer providing the service, and that income from property is taxed to the individual who owns the property when the income accrues.

At-risk amount   an investor's risk of loss in a worst case scenario.

Average tax rate   a taxpayer's average level of taxation on each dollar of taxable income. Specifically,

$$\text{Average Tax Rate} = \frac{\textit{Total Tax}}{\textit{Taxable Income}}$$

B

Bargain element (of stock options)   the difference between the fair market value of the employer's stock and the amount employees pay to acquire the employer's stock.

Barter clubs   organizations that facilitate the exchange of rights to goods and services between members.

Basis   a taxpayer's unrecovered investment in an asset that provides a reference point for measuring gain or loss when an asset is sold.

Before-tax rate of return   a taxpayer's rate of return on an investment before paying taxes on the income from the investment.

Bond   a debt instrument issued for a period of more than one year with the purpose of raising capital by borrowing.

Bond discount   the result of issuing bonds for less than their maturity value.

Bond premium   the result of issuing bonds for more than their maturity value.

Boot   property given or received in an otherwise nontaxable transaction such as a like-kind exchange that may trigger gain to a party to the transaction.

Bunching itemized deductions   a common planning strategy in which a taxpayer pays two year's worth of itemized expenses in one year to exceed the standard deduction in that year.

Business activity   a profit-motivated activity that requires a relatively high level of involvement or effort from the taxpayer to generate income.

Business purpose doctrine   the judicial doctrine that allows the IRS to challenge and disallow business expenses for transactions with no underlying business motivation.

Business tax credits   nonrefundable credits designed to provide incentives for taxpayers to hire certain types of individuals or to participate in certain business activities.

C

Cafeteria plan   an employer plan that allows employees to choose benefits from a menu of nontaxable fringe benefits or receive cash compensation in lieu of the benefits.

Capital asset   in general, an asset other than an asset used in a trade or business or an asset such as an account or note receivable acquired in a business from the sale of services or property.

Capital gain property   any asset that would have generated a long-term capital gain if the taxpayer had sold the property for its fair market value instead of contributing the asset to charity.

Capitalization recording an expenditure as an asset on the balance sheet rather than expensing it immediately.

Cash method the method of accounting that recognizes income in the period in which cash, property, or services is received and recognizes deductions in the period paid.

Cash surrender value the amount, if any, the owner of a life insurance policy receives when the policy is cashed in before the death of the insured individual.

Casualty an unexpected, unforseen event driven by forces outside the control of the taxpayer (such as "fire, storm, or shipwreck or other event or theft) that damages or destroys a taxpayer's property.

Ceiling limitations that are maximum amounts for adjustments to taxable income (or credits). The amounts in excess of the ceiling are either lost or carried to another tax year.

Certainty one of the criteria used to evaluate tax systems. Certainty means taxpayers should be able to determine when, where, and how much tax to pay.

Certificate of deposit an interest-bearing debt instrument offered by banks and savings and loans. Money removed from the CD before maturity is subject to a penalty.

Circular 230 regulations issued by the IRS that govern tax practice and apply to all persons practicing before the IRS. There are three parts of Circular 230: Subpart A describes who may practice before the IRS (e.g., CPAs, attorneys, enrolled agents) and what practicing before the IRS means (tax return preparation, representing clients before the IRS, etc.). Subpart B describes the duties and restrictions that apply to individuals governed by Circular 230. Subpart C explains disciplinary proceedings for practitioners violating the Circular 230 provisions.

Citator a research tool that allows one to check the status of several types of tax authorities. A citator can be used to review the history of the case to find out, for example, whether it was subsequently appealed and overturned,

and to identify subsequent cases that cite the case. Citators can also be used to check the status of revenue rulings, revenue procedures, and other IRS pronouncements.

Civil penalties monetary penalties imposed when tax practitioners or taxpayers violate tax statutes without reasonable cause—for example, as the result of negligence, intentional disregard of pertinent rules, willful disobedience, or outright fraud.

Cliff vesting a qualified plan provision allowing for benefits to vest all at once after a period of time has passed.

Collectibles a work of art, a rug or antique, a metal or gem, a stamp or coin, an alcoholic beverage, or other similar items held for investment for more than one year.

Community property systems systems in which state laws dictate how the income and property is legally shared between a husband and a wife.

Commuting traveling from a residence to the place of business.

Constructive receipt doctrine the judicial doctrine that provides that a taxpayer must recognize income when it is actually <u>or</u> constructively received. Constructive receipt is deemed to have occurred if the income has been credited to the taxpayer's account or if the income is unconditionally available to the taxpayer, the taxpayer is aware of the income's availability, and there are no restrictions on the taxpayer's control over the income.

Convenience one of the criteria used to evaluate tax systems. Convenience means a tax system should be designed to facilitate the collection of tax revenues without undue hardship on the taxpayer or the government.

Correspondence examination an IRS audit conducted by mail and generally limited to one or two items on the taxpayer's return. Among the three types of audits, correspondence audits are generally the most common, the most narrow in scope, and least complex. The IRS typically requests supporting documentation for one or more items on the taxpayer's return (e.g., documentation of charitable contributions deducted).

Cost depletion   the method of recovering the cost of a natural resource that allows a taxpayer to estimate or determine the number of units that remain in the resource at the beginning of the year and allocate a pro rata share of the remaining basis to each unit of the resource that is extracted or sold during the year.

Cost recovery   the method by which a company expenses the cost of acquiring capital assets. Cost recovery can take the form of depreciation, amortization, or depletion.

Coupon rate   the interest rate expressed as a percentage of the face value of the bond.

Covenant not to compete   a contractual promise to refrain from conducting business or professional activities similar to those of another party.

Criminal penalties   penalties commonly charged in tax evasion cases (i.e., willful intent to defraud the government). They are imposed only after normal due process, including a trial. Compared to civil cases, the standard of conviction is higher in a criminal trial (beyond a reasonable doubt). However, the penalties are also much higher, such as fines up to $100,000 for individuals plus a prison sentence.

Cutback   a phase-out limit that gradually reduces, but does not completely eliminate, deductions, credits, or other adjustments to taxable income.

D

***De minimis* fringe benefit**   a nontaxable fringe benefit that allows employees to receive occasional or incidental benefits tax free.

Deductions above the line   *for* AGI deductions or deductions subtracted from gross income to determine AGI.

Deductions below the line   *from* AGI deductions or deductions subtracted from AGI to calculate taxable income.

Deductions *for* AGI   deductions subtracted from gross income to determine AGI.

Deductions *from* AGI   deductions that reduce adjusted gross income to determine taxable income. From AGI deductions consist of itemized deductions, standard deductions, and exemptions.

Deductions   amounts that are permitted to reduce gross income in calculating taxable income.

Deferral items, deferred income, or deferrals   realized income that will be taxed as income in a subsequent year.

Deferred like-kind exchange   a like-kind exchange where the taxpayer transfers like-kind property before receiving the like-kind property in exchange. The property to be received must be identified within 45 days and received with 180 days of the transfer of the property given up.

Defined benefit plan   employer-provided qualified plans that spell out the specific benefit employees will receive on retirement.

Defined contribution plan   employer-provided qualified plans which specify the maximum annual contributions employers and/or employees may contribute to the plan.

Dependency exemption   a fixed deduction allowed for each individual who qualifies as a "dependent" of the taxpayer.

Dependent care benefit   a nontaxable fringe benefit that allows employees to receive up to $5,000 of care for children under age 13 or for a spouse or other dependent with physical needs.

Dependent   a person for whom a taxpayer may claim a dependency exemption. To qualify as a dependent a person must be a qualifying child or qualifying relative of the taxpayer.

Depletion   the cost recovery method to allocate the cost of natural resources as they are removed.

Depreciation the cost recovery method to allocate the cost of tangible personal and real property over a specific time period.

Depreciation recapture the conversion of §1231 gain into ordinary income on a sale (or exchange) based on the amount of accumulated depreciation on the property at the time of sale or exchange.

Determination letters rulings requested by the taxpayer, issued by local IRS directors, and generally not controversial. An example of a determination letter is the request by an employer for the IRS to rule that the taxpayer's retirement plan is a "qualified plan."

DIF (Discriminant Function) system the DIF system assigns a score to each tax return that represents the probability that the tax liability on the return has been underreported (a higher score = a higher likelihood of underreporting). The IRS derives the weights assigned to specific tax return attributes from historical IRS audit adjustment data from the National Research Program. The DIF system then uses these (undisclosed) weights to score each tax return based on the tax return's characteristics. Returns with higher DIF scores are then reviewed to determine if an audit is the best course of action.

Direct conversion when a taxpayer receives noncash property as a replacement for property damaged or destroyed in an involuntary conversion rather than a cash payment.

Direct write-off method required method for deducting bad debts for tax purposes. Under this method, businesses deduct bad debt only when the debt becomes wholly or partially worthless.

Disability insurance sometimes called sick pay or wage replacement insurance, pays the insured for wages lost due to injury or disability.

Discharge of indebtedness debt forgiveness.

Discount points points paid to the lender to receive a reduced interest rate on a loan.

Discount rate the taxpayer's rate of return used to determine the present value of future cash inflows (e.g., tax savings) and outflows (taxes paid).

Disqualifying disposition the sale of stock acquired using incentive stock options prior to satisfying certain holding period requirements. Failing to satisfy the holding period requirements converts the options into nonqualified stock options.

Dividends distributions to shareholders of money or property from the corporation's earnings and profits.

Document perfection program a program under which all tax returns are checked for mathematical and tax calculation errors.

Dynamic forecasting the process of forecasting tax revenues that incorporates into the forecast how taxpayers may alter their activities in response to a tax law change.

E

Earmarked tax a tax assessed for a specific purpose (e.g., for education).

Earned income credit a refundable credit designed to help offset the effect of employment taxes on compensation paid to low income taxpayers and to encourage lower income taxpayers to seek employment.

Earned income compensation and other forms of income received for providing goods or services in the ordinary course of business.

Economic performance test the third requirement that must be met for an accrual method taxpayer to deduct an expense currently. The specific event that satisfies the economic performance test varies based on the type of expense.

Economy one of the criteria used to evaluate tax systems. Economy means a tax system should minimize its compliance and administration costs.

Educational assistance benefit a nontaxable fringe benefit that allows an employer to provide a certain amount of education benefits on an annual basis.

Effective tax rate   the taxpayer's average rate of taxation on each dollar of total income (taxable and nontaxable income). Specifically,

$$\text{Effective Tax Rate} = \frac{Total\ Tax}{Total\ Income}$$

Employee   a person who is hired to provide services to a company on a regular basis in exchange for compensation and who does not provide these services as part of an independent business.

Employment taxes   taxes consisting of the Old Age, Survivors, and Disability Insurance (OASDI) tax, commonly called the Social Security tax, and the Medical Health Insurance (MHI) tax known as the Medicare tax.

Equity   one of the criteria used to evaluate a tax system. A tax system is considered fair or equitable if the tax is based on the taxpayer's ability to pay; taxpayers with a greater ability to pay tax, pay more tax.

Escrow account (mortgage-related)   a holding account with a taxpayer's mortgage lender. The taxpayer makes mortgage payments to the lender that includes payment for the interest and principal and payments for property taxes. The lender maintains the payments for property taxes in the escrow account and uses the funds in the account to pay the property taxes when the taxes are due.

Estate tax   a tax based on the fair market values of wealth transfers upon death.

Estimated tax payments   quarterly tax payments that a taxpayer makes to the government if the tax withholding is insufficient to meet the taxpayer's tax liability.

Exchanged basis   the basis of an asset received in a nontaxable exchange. An exchanged basis is generally the basis of the asset given up in a nontaxable exchange.

Excise taxes   taxes levied on the retail sale of particular products. They differ from other taxes in that the tax base for an excise tax typically depends on the *quantity* purchased, rather than a monetary amount.

Excluded income or exclusions   realized income that is exempted from income taxation.

Ex-dividend date   the relevant date for determining who receives a dividend from a stock. Anyone purchasing stock before this date will receive current dividends. Otherwise, the purchaser must wait until subsequent dividends are declared before receiving them.

Exemption   a fixed deduction that eliminates a certain amount of income from the income tax.

Exercise date   the date employees use their stock options to acquire employer stock at a discounted price.

Explicit tax   a tax directly imposed by a government.

F

Face value   a specified final amount paid to the owner of a coupon bond on the date of maturity. The face value is also known as the maturity value.

Facts and circumstances test   a test used to make subjective determination such as whether the amount of salary paid to an employee is reasonable. The test requires the taxpayer and the IRS to consider all the relevant facts and circumstances surrounding the situation in order to make a decision. The relevant facts and circumstance are situation specific.

Federal short-term interest rate   the quarterly interest rate used to determine the interest charged for tax underpayments (federal short-term rate plus 3 percent).

FICA taxes   FICA (Federal Insurance Contribution Act) taxes are a term used to denote both the Social Security and Medicare taxes upon earned income. For self-employed taxpayers, the terms "FICA tax" and "self-employment tax" are synonymous.

Field examination   the least common audit. The IRS conducts these audits at the taxpayer's place of business or the location where the taxpayer's books, records, and source documents are maintained. Field examinations are generally the broadest in scope and most complex of the three audit types. They can last many months to multiple years and generally are limited to business returns and the most complex individual returns.

Filing status filing status places taxpayers into one of five categories (married filing jointly, married filing separately, qualifying widow or widower, head of household, and single) by marital status and family situation as of the end of the year. Filing status determines whether a taxpayer must file a tax return, appropriate tax rate schedules, standard deduction amounts, and several deduction and credit limitation thresholds.

Final regulations regulations that have been issued in final form, and thus, until revoked, they represent the Treasury's interpretation of the Code.

First-in first-out (FIFO) method an accounting method that values the cost of assets sold under the assumption that the assets are sold in the order purchased (i.e., first purchased, first sold).

Fiscal year a year that ends on a day other than December 31.

Flat tax a tax in which a single tax rate is applied throughout the tax base.

Flexible spending account a plan that allows employees to contribute before-tax dollars that may be used for unreimbursed medical expenses or dependent care.

Flipping a term used to describe the real estate investment practice of acquiring a home, repairing or remodeling the home, and then immediately, or soon thereafter, selling it (presumably at a profit).

Floor limitation a minimum amount that an expenditure (or credit or other adjustment to taxable income) must meet before any amount is allowed.

Flow-through entities legal entities like partnerships, limited liability companies, and S corporations that do not pay income tax. Income and losses from flow-through entities are allocated to their owners.

For the convenience of the employer benefits nontaxable benefits employers provide to employees and employee spouses or dependents in the form of meals or lodging if provided on the employer's premises and are provided for a purpose that is helpful or conveniunt for the employer.

Form W-2 used to report wages paid to employees and the taxes withheld from them. The form is also used to report FICA taxes to the Social Security Administration.

Form W-4 a form used by a taxpayer to supply her employer with the information necessary to determine the amount of tax to withhold from each paycheck.

Fringe benefits a noncash benefit provided to an employee as a form of compensation. As a general rule, fringe benefits are taxable. However, certain fringe benefits are excluded from gross income.

Full-inclusion method the method for accounting for advance payments for goods that requires that electing businesses immediately recognize advance payments as taxable income.

Full-month convention convention that allows owners of intangibles to deduct an entire month's amortization in the month of purchase and month of disposition.

G

Gift tax a tax based on the fair market values of wealth transfers by gift.

Gift a transfer of property where no consideration (or inadequate consideration) is paid for the property.

Golsen rule the rule that states that the U.S. Tax Court will abide by the circuit court's rulings that has appellate jurisdiction for a case.

Graded vesting a qualified plan rule that requires an increasing percentage of plan benefits to vest with each additional year of employment.

Graduated taxes taxes in which the tax base is divided into a series of monetary amounts, or brackets, where each successive bracket is taxed at a different (gradually higher or gradually lower) percentage rate.

Grant date (stock options) the date on which employees receive stock options to acquire employer stock at a specified price.

Gross income realized income reduced for any excluded or deferred income.

Group-term life insurance term life insurance provided by an employer to a group of employees.

H

Haircut a phase-out limit that gradually reduces, but does not completely eliminate, deductions, credits, or other adjustments to taxable income.

Half-year convention a depreciation convention that allows owners of tangible personal property to take one-half of a year's worth of depreciation in the year of purchase and in the year of disposition regardless of when the asset was actually placed in service or sold.

Head of household one of five primary filing statuses. A taxpayer may file as head of household if s/he is unmarried as of the end of the year *and* pays more than half of the cost to maintain a household for a qualifying dependent who lives with the taxpayer for more than half of the year; or, s/he pays more than half the costs to maintain a household for a parent who qualifies as the taxpayer's dependent.

Hobby an activity that is motivated by personal motives rather than profit objectives.

Home office deduction deductions relating to the use of an office in the home. When the taxpayer qualifies, expenses are allocated between personal use and business use of the home.

Home-equity indebtedness debt (except for acquisition indebtedness) secured by the taxpayer's qualified residence to the extent it does not exceed the fair market value of the residence over the acquisition indebtedness. Interest paid on up to $100,000 of home-equity indebtedness is allowed as an itemized deduction.

Horizontal equity one of the dimensions of equity. Horizontal equity is achieved if taxpayers in similar situations pay the same tax.

I

Impermissible accounting method an accounting method prohibited by tax laws.

Implicit tax indirect taxes that result from a tax advantage the government grants to certain transactions to satisfy social, economic, or other objectives. They are defined as the reduced before-tax return that a tax-favored asset produces because of its tax advantaged status.

Imputed income income from an economic benefit the taxpayer receives indirectly rather than directly. The amount of the income is based on comparable alternatives.

Incentive stock option a type of stock option that allows employees to defer the bargain element for regular tax purposes until the stock acquired from option exercises is sold. The bargain element is taxed at capital gains rates provided the stock is retained long enough to satisfy certain holding period requirements. Employers cannot deduct the bargain element as compensation expense.

Income effect one of the two basic responses that a taxpayer may have when taxes increase. The income effect predicts that when taxpayers are taxed more (e.g., tax rate increases from 25 to 28 percent), they will work harder to generate the same after-tax dollars.

Income tax a tax in which the tax base is income. Income taxes are imposed by the federal government and by most states.

Independent contractor a person who provides services to another entity, usually under terms specified in a contract. The independent contractor has more control over how and when to do the work than does an employee.

Indirect conversion the receipt of money or other property as a replacement for property that was destroyed or damaged in an involuntary conversion.

Individual retirement account (IRA) a tax-advantaged account in which individuals who have earned income can save for retirement.

Information matching program a program that compares the taxpayer's tax return to information submitted to the IRS from other taxpayers (e.g., banks, employers, mutual funds, brokerage companies, mortgage companies). Information matched includes items such as wages (e.g., Form W-2 submitted by employers), interest income (e.g., Form 1099-INT submitted by banks), dividend income (e.g., Form 1099-DIV submitted by brokerage companies), and so forth.

Inheritance a transfer of property when the owner is deceased (the transfer is made by the decedent's estate).

Installment sale a sale for which the taxpayer receives payment in more than one period.

Intangible assets assets that do not have physical characteristics. Examples include goodwill, covenants not to compete, organizational expenditures, and research and experimentation expenses.

Interest a payment for the use of money.

Internal Revenue Code of 1986 the codified tax laws of the United States. Although the Code is frequently revised, there have only been three different codes since the Code was created in 1939 (i.e., the IRC of 1939, IRC of 1954, and IRC of 1986).

Interpretative regulations the most common regulation; they represent the Treasury's interpretation of the Code, and are issued under the Treasury's general authority to interpret the Code.

Investment activities a profit-seeking activity that is intermittent or occasional in frequency including the production or collection of income or the management, conservation, or maintenance of property held for the production of income.

Investment expenses expenses such as safe deposit rental fees, attorney and accounting fees that are necessary to produce portfolio income. Investment expenses are allowed for individuals as miscellaneous itemized deductions subject to the two percent of AGI floor limitation.

Investment income income received from portfolio type investments. Portfolio income includes capital gains and losses, interest, dividend, annuity, and royalty income not derived in the ordinary course of a trade or business. When computing the deductibility of investment interest expense, however, capital gains and dividends subject to the preferential tax rate are not treated as investment income unless the taxpayer elects to have this income taxed at ordinary tax rates.

Investment interest expense interest paid on borrowings or loans that are used to fund portfolio investments. Individuals are allowed an itemized deduction for qualified investment interest paid during the year.

Involuntary conversion a direct or indirect conversion of property through natural disaster, government condemnation, or accident which allows a taxpayer to defer realized gain if certain requirements are met.

Itemized deductions certain types of expenditures that Congress allows taxpayers to deduct as from AGI deductions.

K

Kiddie tax a tax imposed at the parent's marginal rate on a child's unearned income.

L

Late filing penalty penalty assessed if a taxpayer does not file a tax return by the required date (the original due date plus extension). The penalty equals five percent of the amount of tax owed for each month (or fraction thereof) that the tax return is late with a maximum penalty of 25 percent.

Late payment penalty   penalty assessed if a tax-payer fails to pay the entire balance of tax owed by the original due date of the tax return. The late payment penalty equals .5 percent of the amount of tax owed for each month (or fraction thereof) that the tax is not paid.

Legislative grace   the concept that taxpayers receive certain tax benefits only because Congress writes laws that allow taxpayers to receive the tax benefits.

Legislative regulations   the rarest type of regulation, issued when Congress specifically directs the Treasury Department to create reg-ulations to address an issue in an area of law. In these instances, the Treasury is actually writing the law instead of interpreting the Code. Because legislative regulations actually represent tax law instead of an interpretation of tax law, legislative regulations have more authoritative weight than interpretative and procedural regulations.

LIFO   an accounting method that values the cost of assets sold under the assumption that assets are sold in the reverse order in which they are purchased (i.e., last purchased, first sold).

Like-kind exchange   a nontaxable (or partially taxable) trade or exchange of assets that are similar or related in use.

Listed property   business assets that are often used for personal purposes. Depreciation on list-ed property is limited to the business use portion of the asset.

Loan origination fee   a service fee, usually expressed in terms of points, to the lender for processing the loan. This fee is not tax deductible.

Local tax   taxes imposed by local governments (cities, counties, school districts, etc.)

Long-term capital gains or losses   gains or loss-es from the sale of capital assets held for more than 12 months.

Luxury automobile   an automobile on which the amount of annual depreciation expense is limited because the cost of the automobile exceeds a certain threshold.

M

Marginal tax rate   the tax rate that applies to the *next additional increment* of a taxpayer's taxable income (or to deductions). Specifically,

$$\text{Marginal Tax Rate} = \frac{\Delta Tax}{\Delta Taxable\ Income}$$
$$= \frac{(New\ Total\ Tax - Old\ Total\ Tax)}{(New\ Taxable\ Income - Old\ Taxable\ Income)}$$

"old" refers to the current tax and "new" refers to the tax given the additional income in question.

Market discount   the difference between the amount paid for a bond in a market purchase rather than at original issuance when the amount paid is less than the maturity value of the bond.

Market premium   the difference between the amount paid for a bond in a market purchase rather than at original issuance when the amount paid is greater than the maturity value of the bond.

Marriage benefit   the tax savings married cou-ples receive by filing a joint return relative to the tax they would have paid had they each filed as single taxpayers. This typically occurs when one spouse is either not working or earns significantly less than the other spouse.

Marriage penalty   the extra tax cost a married couple pays by filing a joint return relative to what they would have paid had they each filed as single taxpayers. This typically occurs when both spouses earn approximately the same amount of income.

Married filing jointly   one of five primary filing statuses. A taxpayer may file jointly if s/he is legally married as of the end of the year (or one spouse died during the year and the surviving spouse did not remarry) and both spouses agree to jointly file. Married couples filing joint returns combine their income and deductions and share joint and several liability for the resulting tax.

Married filing separately   one of five primary filing statuses. When married couples file separately, each spouse reports the income he or she received during the year and the deductions he or she paid on a tax return separate from the other spouse.

Maturity value the amount paid to a bondholder when the bond matures and the bondholder redeems the bond for cash.

Maturity the amount of time to the expiration date, or maturity date, of a debt instrument. The maturity of a debt instrument is generally the life of the instrument at which a payment of the face value is due or the instrument terminates.

Medicare tax the Medical Health Insurance (MHI) tax. This tax helps pay medical costs for qualifying individuals. Employees pay the Medicare tax at a rate of 1.45% on all wages. Self-employed taxpayers pay Medicare taxes at a rate of 2.9% of net-earnings from self employment. There is no limit of the amount of wages subject to the Medicare tax.

Mid-month convention a convention which allows owners of real property to take one-half of a month's depreciation during the month when the property was placed in service and in the month it was disposed of.

Mid-quarter convention a depreciation convention for tangible personal property which allows for one-half of a quarter's worth of depreciation in the quarter of purchase and in the quarter of disposition. This convention must be used when more than 40% of tangible personal property is placed into service in the fourth quarter of the tax year.

Minimum tax credit credit available in certain situations for the alternative minimum tax paid. The credit can be used only when the regular tax exceeds the tentative minimum tax.

Miscellaneous itemized deductions deductions representing the sum of certain itemized deductions, such as unreimbursed employee business expenses, investment expenses, and tax preparation fees, that are subject to a special floor limitation.

Mixed-motive expenditures activities that involve a mixture of business and personal objectives.

Modified Cost Recovery System (MACRS) the current tax depreciation system for tangible personal and real property. Depreciation under MACRS is calculated by finding the depreciation method, the recovery period, and the applicable convention.

More likely than not the standard that applies to tax practitioners to determine if they may recommend a tax return position without being subject to IRS penalty under IRC §6694. A tax preparer may recommend a tax return position and avoid penalty if the tax preparer has reasonable belief that the position would *"more likely than not"* (i.e., a greater than 50 percent probability) be sustained on its merits.

Municipal bond the common name for state and local government debt.

Mutual fund a diversified portfolio of securities owned and managed by a regulated investment company.

N

Net capital gain the net gain resulting when taxpayers combine net long-term capital gains with net short-term capital losses.

Net earnings from self-employment the amount of earnings subject to self-employment income taxes. The amount is 92.35% of the net income from a taxpayer's Schedule C (for self-employed taxpayers).

Net investment income gross investment income reduced by deductible investment expenses.

Net long-term capital gain the net gain resulting when taxpayers combine long-term capital gains and losses for the year.

Net long-term capital loss the net loss resulting when taxpayers combine long-term capital gains and losses for the year.

Net short-term capital gain the net gain resulting when taxpayers combine short-term capital gains and losses for the year.

Net short-term capital loss the net loss resulting when taxpayers combine short-term capital gains and losses for the year.

Net unearned income unearned income in excess of a specified threshold amount of a child under the age of 19 or under the age of 24 if a full-time student.

No-additional-cost services a nontaxable fringe benefit that provides employer services to employees with little cost to the employer (e.g., airline tickets or phone service).

Nonacquiescence issued after the IRS loses a trial-level or circuit court case when the IRS has decided to continue to litigate this issue.

Nonbusiness bad debt a loan made for other than business reasons (e.g., as an investment) from a taxpayer to another that is not paid back. A nonbusiness bad debt is considered a short-term capital loss.

Nonqualified deferred compensation a nonqualified plan allowing employees to defer compensation to a future period.

Nonqualified stock option a type of stock option requiring employees to treat the bargain element from options exercised as ordinary income in the tax year options are exercised. Employers may deduct the bargain element as compensation expense in the tax year options are exercised.

Nonrecognition provisions tax laws that allow taxpayers to permanently exclude income from taxation or to defer recognizing realized income until a subsequent period.

Nonrecognition transaction a transaction where at least a portion of the realized gain or loss is not currently recognized.

Nonrefundable personal tax credits personal tax credits that reduce a taxpayer's gross tax liability but are limited to the amount of gross tax liability. Any credit not used in the current year is lost.

Nontaxable fringe benefit an employer provided benefit that may be excluded from an employee's income.

O

Office examination the second most common audit. As the name suggests, the IRS conducts these audits at the local IRS office. These audits are typically broader in scope and more complex than correspondence examinations. Small businesses, taxpayers operating sole proprietorships, and middle- to high-income individual taxpayers are more likely, if audited, to have office examinations.

Operating income the annual income from a trade or business or rental activity.

Operating loss the annual loss from a trade or business or rental activity.

Option exercise the use of a stock option to acquire employer stock at a specified price.

Ordinary and necessary expense interpreted as an expense that is normal or appropriate and that is helpful or conducive to the business activity.

Ordinary asset an asset created or used in a taxpayer's trade or business (e.g. accounts receivable or inventory) that generates ordinary income (or loss) on disposition.

Ordinary income property property contributed to charity that would have generated income taxed at ordinary tax rates if it had been sold instead of contributed.

Organizational expenditures expenses which are (1) connected directly with the creation of a corporation or partnership, (2) chargeable to a capital account, and (3) generally amortized over 180 months (limited immediate expensing may be available).

Original issue discount a type of bond issued for less than the maturity or face value of the bond.

P

Passive activity an activity in which the taxpayer does not materially participate.

Passive activity income or loss income or loss from an activity in which the taxpayer does not materially participate.

Passive activity loss rules   tax rules designed to limit taxpayers' ability to deduct losses from activities in which they don't materially participate against income from other sources.

Passive investments   direct or indirect investments (other than through a taxable corporation) in a trade or business or rental activity in which the taxpayer does not materially participate.

Payment liability   liabilities of accrual method businesses for which economic performance occurs when the business actually *pays* the liability for, among others: worker's compensation; tort; breach of contract or violation of law; rebates and refunds; awards, prizes and jackpots; insurance, warranties, and service contracts provided *to* the business; and taxes.

Percentage depletion   method of recovering cost of natural resource that allows a taxpayer to recover or expense an amount based on a statutorily determined percentage.

Permissible accounting method   accounting method allowed under the tax law. Permissible accounting methods are adopted the first time a taxpayer uses the method on a tax return.

Personal exemption   a fixed deduction allowed for an individual taxpayer and her spouse if filing a joint tax return.

Personal expenses   expenses incurred for personal motives. Personal expenses are not deductible for tax purposes.

Personal property tax   a tax on the fair market value of all types of tangible and intangible property, except real property.

Personal property   all tangible property other than real property.

Phase-outs   limitations that gradually eliminate deductions, credits, or other adjustments to taxable income typically done ratably over a phaseout range (based on AGI or related income measure).

Point   one percent of the principal amount of a loan. A home buyer might pay points to compensate the lender for services or for a lower interest rate. Points paid to compensate

the lender for services are not deductible. Points paid to the lender to reduce the rate of the loan are generally deductible (1) immediately if the loan is an original home loan or (2) over the life of the loan if the loan is a refinance.

Portfolio investments   investments producing dividends, interest, royalties, annuities, or capital gains.

Preferential tax rate   tax rates lower than the tax rate applied to ordinary income.

Preferentially taxed income   income taxed at a preferential rate such as long-term capital gains and qualifying dividends.

Present value   the concept that $1 today is worth more than $1 in the future. For example, assuming an investor can earn a 5% after-tax return, $1 invested today should be worth $1.05 in one year. Hence, $1 today is equivalent to $1.05 in one year.

Primary authority   official sources of the tax law generated by the legislative branch (i.e., statutory authority issued by Congress), judicial branch (i.e., rulings by the U.S. District Court, U.S. Tax Court, U.S. Court of Federal Claims, U.S. Circuit Court of Appeals, or U.S. Supreme Court), or executive/administrative branch (i.e., Treasury or IRS pronouncements).

Principal residence   the main place of residence for a taxpayer during the taxable year.

Private letter rulings   IRS pronouncements issued in response to a taxpayer request for a ruling on specific issues for the taxpayer. They are common for proposed transactions with potentially large tax implications. For the requesting taxpayer, a private letter ruling has very high authority. For all other taxpayers, private letter rulings have little authoritative weight.

Private nonoperating foundations   privately sponsored foundations that disburse funds to other charities.

Private operating foundations   privately sponsored foundations that actually fund and conduct charitable activities.

Procedural regulations   regulations that explain Treasury Department procedures as they relate to administering the Code.

Progressive tax rate structure   a tax rate structure that imposes an increasing marginal tax rate as the tax base increases. As the tax base increases, both the marginal tax rate and the taxes paid increase.

Proportional tax rate structure   also known as a flat tax, this tax rate structure imposes a constant tax rate throughout the tax base. As the tax base increases, the taxes paid increase proportionally.

Proposed regulations   regulations issued in proposed form; they do not carry the same authoritative weight as temporary or final regulations. All regulations are issued in proposed form first to allow public comment on them.

Q

Qualified debt   the amount of debt on which qualified residence interest is paid. This includes debt up to $1,000,000 of acquisition indebtedness and up to $100,000 of home-equity indebtedness.

Qualified dividends   paid by domestic or certain qualified foreign corporations that are eligible for lower capital gains rates.

Qualified educational expenses   consist of tuition and related costs for enrolling the taxpayer, spouse, or a dependent at a post-secondary institution of higher education.

Qualified educational loans   loans whose proceeds are used to pay qualified education expenses.

Qualified employee discount   a nontaxable fringe benefit that provides employer goods at a discount (but not below the employer's cost) and services to employees at up to a 20% discount.

Qualified moving expense reimbursement   a nontaxable fringe benefit which allows employers to pay moving related expenses on behalf of employees.

Qualified production activities income (QPAI)   the *net* income from selling or leasing property that was manufactured in the United States.

Qualified replacement property   property acquired to replace property damaged or destroyed in an involuntary conversion. It must be of a similar or related use to the original property even if the replacement property is real property (rental real estate for rental real estate).

Qualified residence interest   interest paid on acquisition indebtedness and on home-equity indebtedness that is secured by a qualified residence.

Qualified residence   the taxpayer's principal residence and one other residence.

Qualified retirement accounts   plans meeting certain requirements that allow compensation placed in the account to be tax deferred until the taxpayer withdraws money from the account.

Qualified retirement plans   employer-sponsored retirement plans that meet government imposed funding and anti-discrimination requirements.

Qualified small business stock   stock received at original issue from a corporation with a gross tax basis in its assets both before and after the issuance of no more than $50,000,000 and with 80% of the value of its assets used in the active conduct of certain qualified trades or businesses.

Qualified transportation fringe benefit   a nontaxable fringe benefit provided by employers in the form of mass transit passes, parking, or vanpool benefits.

Qualified tuition plans (529 plans)   a state-sponsored program designed to help parents finance education expenses by generating tax free income. 529 plans are administered by certain investment companies and are subject to contribution requirements and investment guidelines.

Qualifying child   an individual who qualifies as as dependent of a taxpayer by meeting a relationship, age, residence, and support test with respect to the taxpayer.

Qualifying relative   an individual who meets a relationship, support, and gross income test may qualify to be a dependent of another taxpayer.

Qualifying widow or widower   one of five primary filing statuses. Applies for up to two years after the year in which the taxpayer's spouse dies (the taxpayer files married filing jointly in the year of the spouse's death) as long as the taxpayer remans unmarried and maintains a household for a dependent child.

Question of fact   a research question that hinges upon the facts and circumstances of the taxpayer's transaction.

Question of law   a research question that hinges upon the interpretation of the law, such as interpreting a particular phrase in a code section.

R

Real property tax   a tax on the fair market value of land and structures permanently attached to land.

Real property   land and structures permanently attached to land.

Realistic possibility   deemed to exist when a tax return position has a one-third (or greater) probability of being sustained administratively (i.e., by the IRS) or judicially (i.e., by the courts) on its merits if challenged.

Realization principle   the proposition that income only exists when there is a transaction with another party resulting in a measurable change in property rights.

Realized gain or loss   the difference between the amount realized and the adjusted basis of an asset sold or otherwise disposed of.

Realized income   income generated in a transaction with a second party in which there is a measurable change in property rights between parties.

Recognized gain or loss   the gain or loss included in gross income on a taxpayer's tax return. This is usually the realized gain or loss unless a nonrecognition provision applies.

Recovery period   a length of time prescribed by statute in which tangible business property is depreciated.

Refinance   when a taxpayer pays off a current loan with the proceeds of a second loan.

Refundable credits   credits that are not limited to the amount of the gross tax liability. If the credit exceeds the gross tax liability, the taxpayer receives a refund for the excess credit.

Regressive tax rate structure   a tax rate structure that imposes a decreasing marginal tax rate as the tax base increases. As the tax base increases, the taxes paid increases, but the marginal tax rate decreases.

Regulations   the Treasury Department's official interpretation of the Internal Revenue Code. Regulations are the highest authority issued by the IRS.

Related-party transaction   financial activities among family members, among owners and their businesses, or among businesses owned by the same owners.

Research and experimentation costs   expenses for research including costs of research laboratories (salaries, materials, and other related expenses). Taxpayers can elect to amortize research and development costs over not less than 60 months from the time benefits are first derived from the research.

Restricted stock   stock employees receive as compensation that may only be sold after the passage of time or after certain performance targets are achieved. Because employees are not entitled to immediately sell the restricted stock they receive, the value of the stock is generally not taxable to employees or deductible by employers until the selling restrictions lapse.

Return of capital   the portion of proceeds from a sale (or distribution) representing a return of the original cost of the underlying property.

Revenue procedures   second in administrative authoritative weight after regulations. Revenue procedures are much more detailed than regulations and explain in greater detail IRS practice and procedures in administering the tax law. Revenue procedures have the same authoritative weight as revenue rulings.

Revenue rulings   second in administrative authoritative weight after regulations. Revenue rulings address the specific application of the Code and regulations to a specific factual situation. Revenue rulings have the same authoritative weight as revenue procedures.

Rollover   a transfer of funds from a qualified retirement plan to another qualified retirement plan, from a qualified retirement plan to a Roth or traditional IRA, or from a traditional IRA to a Roth IRA.

Roth 401(k)   a type of defined contribution plan which allows employees to contribute on an after-tax basis and receive distributions tax free.

Roth IRA   an individually-managed retirement plan permitting individuals to contribute on an after-tax basis and receive distributions tax free.

Roth qualified retirement plans   retirement plans meeting the requirements for qualified plans but not allowing employees a current deduction for contributions. Distributions from Roth qualified retirement plans are tax free.

Royalties   payments taxpayers receive for allowing others to use their tangible or intangible property.

S

Safe-harbor provision   provision of the tax law that reduces or eliminates a taxpayer's liability under the law if the taxpayer meets certain requirements.

Sales tax   a tax imposed on the retail sales of goods (plus certain services). Retailers are responsible for collecting and remitting the tax; typically sales tax is collected at the point of sale.

Same-day sale   phrase used to describe a situation where a taxpayer exercises stock options and then immediately sells the stock received through the option exercise.

Schedule C   the form on which a taxpayer reports the income and deductions for a sole-proprietorship.

Secondary authority   unofficial tax authorities that interpret and explain the primary authorities, such as tax research services, tax articles, newsletters, and textbooks. Secondary authorities may be very helpful in understanding a tax issue, but they hold little weight in a tax dispute (hence, the term *unofficial* tax authorities).

Section 481 adjustment   a change to taxable income associated with a change in accounting methods.

Secured loan   a loan for which property is used as collateral for the loan. If the loan goes into default the lender is only allowed to take possession of the property securing the loan.

Security   a financial instrument including an equity interest in business organizations and creditor interests such as savings accounts, notes, and bonds.

Self-employment taxes   Social Security and Medicare taxes paid by the self employed on a taxpayer's net earnings from self employment. For self-employed taxpayers, the terms "self-employment tax" and "FICA tax" are synonymous.

SEP IRA   a simplified employee pension which can be administered through an individual retirement account.

Settlement statement   a statement that details the monies paid out and received by the buyer and seller in a real estate transaction.

Short-term capital gains or losses   gains or losses from the sale of capital assets held for one year or less.

Sin taxes   taxes imposed on the purchase of goods (e.g., alcohol, tobacco products, etc.) that are considered socially less desirable.

Single   one of five primary statuses available. A taxpayer files as single if s/he is unmarried as of the end of the year and does not qualify for any of the other filing statuses. A taxpayer is considered single if s/he is unmarried or legally separated from his or her spouse under a divorce or separate maintenance decree.

Social Security Tax   the Old Age, Survivors, and Disability Insurance (OASDI) tax. The tax is intended to provide basic pension coverage for the retired and disabled. Employees pay Social Security tax at a rate of 6.2% on the wage base (employers also pay 6.2%). Self-employed taxpayers are subject to a Social Security tax at a rate of 12.4% on their net earnings from self employment. The base on which Social Security taxes are paid is limited to an annually determined amount of wages and/or net earnings from self employment.

Specific identification method   an elective method for determining the cost of an asset sold. Under this method, the taxpayer specifically chooses the assets that are to be sold.

Standard deduction   a fixed deduction offered in lieu of itemized deductions. The amount of the standard deduction depends on the taxpayer's filing status.

Stare decisis   a doctrine meaning that a court will rule consistently with (a) its previous rulings (i.e., unless, due to evolving interpretations of the tax law over time, they decide to overturn an earlier decision) and (b) the rulings of higher courts with appellate jurisdiction (i.e., the courts their cases are appealed to).

Start-up costs   expenses that would be classified as business expenses except that the expenses are incurred before the business begins. These costs are generally capitalized and amortized over 180 months but limited immediate expensing may be available.

State tax   a tax imposed by one of the fifty U.S. states.

Statements on Standards for Tax Services (SSTS)   standards of practice for tax professionals issued by the AICPA. Currently, there are eight SSTS that describe the tax professional standards when recommending a tax return position, answering questions on a tax return, preparing a tax return using data supplied by a client, using estimates on a tax return, taking a tax return position inconsistent with a previous year's tax return, discovering a tax return error, discovering a tax return error during an IRS audit, and giving tax advice to taxpayers.

Static forecasting   the process of forecasting tax revenues based on the existing state of transactions while ignoring how taxpayers may alter their activities in response to a tax law change.

Statute of limitations   defines the period in which the taxpayer can file an amended tax return or the IRS can assess a tax deficiency for a specific tax year. For both amended tax returns filed by a taxpayer and proposed tax assessments by the IRS, the statute of limitations generally ends three years from the *later* of (1) the date the tax return was actually filed or (2) the tax return's original due date.

Step-transaction doctrine   judicial doctrine that allows the IRS to collapse a series of related transactions into one transaction to determine the tax consequences of the transaction.

Student loans   loans where the proceeds are used for qualified educational expenses, but do not include home equity loans.

Substance-over-form doctrine   judicial doctrine that allows the IRS to consider the transaction's substance regardless of its form, and where appropriate, reclassify the transaction according to its substance.

Substantial authority   the taxpayer standard used to determine whether the taxpayer may take a tax return position without being subject to IRS penalty under IRC Sec. 6662. A good CPA evaluates whether supporting authority is substantial or not based upon the supporting and opposing authorities' weight and relevance. Substantial authority suggests that the probability that the taxpayer's position is sustained upon audit or litigation is in the 40 plus percent range or above.

Substitution effect   one of the two basic responses that a taxpayer may have when taxes increase. The substitution effect predicts that when taxpayers are taxed more, rather than work more, they will substitute nontaxable activities (e.g., leisure pursuits) for taxable ones because the marginal value of taxable activities has decreased.

Sufficiency   a standard for evaluating a good tax system. Sufficiency is defined as assessing the aggregate size of the tax revenues that must be generated and ensuring that the tax system provides these revenues.

T

Tax avoidance   the legal act of arranging one's transactions or affairs to reduce taxes paid.

Tax base   the item that is being taxed (e.g., purchase price of a good, taxable income, etc.).

Tax basis   the amount of a taxpayer's unrecovered cost of or investment in an asset.

Tax benefit rule   holds that a refund of an amount deducted in a previous period is only included in income to the extent that the deduction reduced taxable income.

Tax bracket   a range of taxable income taxed at a specified rate.

Tax credits   items that directly reduce a taxpayer's tax liability.

Tax evasion   the willful attempt to defraud the government (i.e., by not paying taxes legally owed). Tax evasion falls outside the confines of legal tax avoidance.

Tax rate schedule   a schedule of progressive tax rates and the income ranges to which the rates apply that a taxpayer may use to compute her gross tax liability.

Tax rate   the level of taxes imposed on the tax base, usually expressed as a percentage.

Tax shelter   an investment or other arrangement designed to produce tax benefits without any expectation of economic profits.

Tax tables   IRS provided tables that specify the federal income tax liability for individuals with taxable income within a specific range. The tables differ by filing status and reflect tax rates that increase with taxable income.

Tax treaties   agreements negotiated between countries that describe the tax treatment of entities subject to tax in both countries (e.g., U.S. citizens earning investment income in Spain). The U.S. president has the authority to enter into a tax treaty with another country after receiving the Senate's advice.

Tax year   a fixed period in which a business reports income and deductions, generally referred to as an accounting period.

Tax   a payment required by a government that is unrelated to any specific benefit or service received from the government.

Taxable corporations   corporations that file a tax return and pay corporate income taxes on their earnings. Taxable corporations are sometimes referred to as "C corporations."

Taxable fringe benefit   a noncash fringe benefit provided by employers to an employee that is included in taxable income (e.g., auto allowance or group-term life over $50,000).

Taxable income   the tax base for the individual income tax.

Technical advice memorandum   ruling issued by the IRS national office, requested by an IRS agent, and generally for a completed transaction.

Temporary regulations   regulations issued with a limited life (three years for regulations issued after November 20, 1988). During their life, temporary regulations carry the same authoritative weight as final regulations.

Tentative minimum tax   the tax on the AMT tax base under the alternative minimum tax system.

Term insurance   a form of life insurance without an investment or savings feature.

Third-party intermediaries   people or organizations that facilitate the transfer of property between taxpayers in a like-kind exchange. Typically, the intermediary receives the cash from selling the property received from the taxpayer and uses it to acquire like-kind property identified by the taxpayer.

Topical tax service   a tax service arranged by subject (i.e., topic). For each topic, topical services identify tax issues that relate to each topic, and then explain and cite authorities relevant to the issue (code sections, regulations, court cases, revenue rulings, etc.).

Trade or business   a profit-motivated activity characterized by a sustained, continuous, high level of individual involvement or effort.

Traditional 401(k)   a popular type of defined contribution plan with before-tax employee and employer contributions and taxable distributions.

Traditional IRA   an individually managed retirement account with deductible contributions and taxable distributions.

Transfer taxes   taxes on the transfer of wealth from one taxpayer to another. The estate and gift taxes are two examples of transfer taxes.

Travel expenses   expenditures incurred while "away from home overnight," including the cost of transportation, meals, lodging, and incidental expenses.

Treasury bond   a debt instrument issued by the U.S. Treasury at face value, at a discount, or at a premium, with a set interest rate and maturity date that pays interest semiannually. Treasury bonds have terms of 30 years.

Treasury note   a debt instrument issued by the U.S. Treasury at face value, at a discount, or at a premium, with a set interest rate and maturity date that pays interest semiannually. Treasury notes have terms of 2, 5, or 10 years.

U

U.S. Circuit Courts of Appeal   the first level of appeals courts after the trial-level courts. There are 13 U.S. Circuit Courts of Appeal; one for the Federal Circuit and 12 assigned to hear cases that originated from a specific circuit (e.g., the 11th Circuit Court of Appeals only hears cases originating within the 11th Circuit).

U.S. Constitution   the founding law of the United States, ratified in 1789.

U.S. Court of Federal Claims   one of the three trial-level courts. It is a national court that only hears monetary claims against the federal government.

U.S. District Court   one of three trial-level courts. It is the only court that allows a jury trial. There is at least one district court in each state.

U.S. savings bonds   debt instruments issued by the U.S. Treasury at face value or at a discount, with a set maturity date. Interest earned from U.S. bonds is paid either at maturity or when the bonds are converted to cash before maturity.

U.S. Supreme Court   the highest court in the United States. The Supreme Court hears only a few tax cases a year with great significance to a broad cross-section of taxpayers or cases litigating issues in which there has been disagreement among the circuit courts. For most tax cases, the Supreme Court refuses to hear the case (i.e., the *writ of certiorari* is denied) and, thus, litigation ends with the circuit court decision.

U.S. Tax Court   a national court that only hears tax cases and where the judges are tax experts. The U.S. Tax Court is the only court that allows tax cases to be heard *before* the taxpayer pays the disputed liability and the only court with a small claims division (hearing claims involving disputed liabilities of $50,000 or less).

Underpayment penalty   the penalty that applies when taxpayers fail to adequately pre-pay their tax liability. The underpayment penalty is determined by multiplying the federal short-term interest rate plus three percentage points by the amount of tax underpayment per quarter.

Unearned income   income from property that accrues as time passes without effort on the part of the owner of the property.

Unemployment tax   the tax that pays for temporary unemployment benefits for individuals terminated from their jobs without cause.

Uniform cost capitalization rules (UNICAP rules)   specify that inventories must be accounted for using full absorption rules to allocate the indirect costs of productive activities to inventory.

Unrecaptured §1231 losses   a net §1231 loss that is deducted as an ordinary loss in one year and has not caused subsequent §1231 gain to be taxed as ordinary income.

Unrecaptured §1250 gain   gain from the sale of real estate held by a noncorporate taxpayer for more than one year in a trade or business or as rental property attributable to tax depreciation deducted at ordinary tax rates. This gain is taxable at a maximum 25% capital gains rate.

Use tax   a tax imposed on the retail price of goods owned, possessed or consumed within a state that were *not* purchased within the state.

V

Value-added tax   a tax imposed on the producer of goods (and services) on the value of goods (services) added at each stage of production. Value-added taxes are common in Europe.

Vertical equity   one of the dimensions of equity. Vertical equity is achieved when taxpayers with greater ability to pay tax, pay more tax relative to taxpayers with a lesser ability to pay tax.

Vest   to become legally entitled to receive a particular benefit without risk of forfeiture.

W

Wash sale   the sale of an investment if that same investment (or substantially identical investment) is purchased within 30 days before or after the sale date. Losses on wash sales are deffered.

Wherewithal to pay   the ability or resources to pay taxes due from a particular transaction.

Whole life insurance   a form of life insurance with an investment or savings component.

Withholdings   taxes collected and remitted to the government by an employer from an employee's wages.

Working condition fringe benefit   a nontaxable fringe benefit provided by employers that would be deductible as an ordinary and necessary business expense if paid by an employee (e.g., reimbursement for professional dues).

Writ of certiorari   a document filed to request the U.S. Supreme Court to hear a case.

Z

Zero coupon bond   a type of bond issued at a discount that pays interest only at maturity.

Comprehensive Tax Return Problems

INDIVIDUAL TAX RETURN PROBLEM 1

Required:

- Use the following information to complete Paul and Judy Vance's 2008 federal income tax return. If information is missing, use reasonable assumptions to fill in the gaps.
- You may need the following forms and schedules to complete the project: Form 1040, Schedule A, Schedule B, Schedule C, Schedule D, Schedule E, Schedule SE, Form 2106-EZ, Form 4562 (for the dental practice), Form 4562 (for the rental property), Form 4797, and Form 8863. The forms, schedules, and instructions can be found at IRS Web site (www.irs.gov). The instructions can be helpful in completing the forms.

Facts:

1. Paul J. and Judy L. Vance are married and file a joint return. Paul is self-employed as a dentist, and Judy is a college professor. Paul and Judy have three children. The oldest is Vince who lives at home. Vince is a law student at the University of Cincinnati and worked part-time during the year, earning $1,500, which he spent for his own support. Paul and Judy provided $6,000 toward Vince's support (including $4,000 for Vince's fall tuition). They also provided over half the support of their daughter, Joan, who is a full-time student at Edgecliff College in Cincinnati. Joan worked part-time as an independent contractor during the year, earning $3,200. Joan lived at home until she was married in December of 2008. She filed a joint return with her husband, Patrick, who earned $20,000 during the year. Jennifer is the youngest and lived in the Vance's home for the entire year. The Vances provide you with the following additional information:

   - Paul and Judy would like to take advantage on their return for any educational expenses paid for their children.
   - Paul and Judy did not receive an economic stimulus payment check last year.
   - The Vances do not want to contribute to the presidential election campaign.
   - The Vances live at 621 Franklin Avenue, Cincinnati, OH 45211.
   - Paul's birthday is 3/5/1954 and his Social Security number is 333-45-6666.
   - Judy's birthday is 4/24/1957 and her Social Security number is 566-77-8888.
   - Vince's birthday is 11/6/1985 and his Social Security number is 576-18-7928.
   - Joan's birthday is 2/1/1989 and her Social Security number is 575-92-4321.
   - Jennifer's birthday is 12/12/1996 and her Social Security number is 613-97-8465.
   - The Vances do not have any foreign bank accounts or trusts.

2. Judy is a lecturer at Xavier University in Cincinnati, where she earned $30,000. The university withheld federal income tax of $3,375, state income tax of $900, Cincinnati city income tax of $375, $1,860 of Social Security tax and $435 of Medicare tax. She also worked part of the year for Delta Airlines. Delta paid her $10,000 in salary; and withheld federal income tax of $1,125, state income tax of $300, Cincinnati city income tax of $125, $620 for Social Security tax, and $145 for Medicare tax.

3. The Vances received $800 of interest from State Savings Bank on a joint account. They received interest of $1,000 on City of Cincinnati bonds they bought in January with the proceeds of a loan from Third National Bank of Cincinnati. They paid interest of $1,100 on the loan. Paul received a dividend of $540 on General Bicycle Corporation stock he owns. Judy received a dividend of $390 on Acme Clothing Corporation stock she owns. Paul and Judy received a dividend of $865 on jointly owned stock in Maple Company. All of the dividends received in 2008 are qualifying dividends.

4. Paul practices under the name "Paul J. Vance, DDS." His business is located at 645 West Avenue, Cincinnati, OH 45211, and his employer identification number is 01-2222222. Paul's gross receipts during the year were $111,000. Paul uses the cash method of accounting for his business. Paul's business expenses are as follows:

Advertising	$ 1,200
Professional dues	490
Professional journals	360
Contributions to employee benefit plans	2,000
Malpractice insurance	3,200
Fine for overbilling State of Ohio for work performed on welfare patient	5,000
Insurance on office contents	720
Interest on money borrowed to refurbish office	600
Accounting services	2,100
Miscellaneous office expense	388
Office rent	12,000
Dental supplies	7,672
Utilities and telephone	3,360
Wages	30,000
Payroll taxes	2,400

In June, Paul decided to refurbish his office. This project was completed and the assets placed in service on July 1. Paul's expenditures included $8,000 for new office furniture, $6,000 for new dental equipment (seven-year recovery period), and $2,000 for a new computer. Paul elected to compute his cost recovery allowance using MACRS. He did not elect to use Section 179 immediate expensing and he chose to not claim any bonus depreciation.

5. Judy's mother, Sarah, died on July 2, 2003, leaving Judy her entire estate. Included in the estate was Sarah's residence (325 Oak Street, Cincinnati, OH 45211). Sarah's basis in the residence was $30,000. The fair market value of the residence on July 2, 2003, was $155,000. The property was distributed to Judy on January 1, 2004. The Vances have held the property as rental property and have managed it themselves. From January 1, 2004, until June 30, 2008, they rented the house to the same tenant. The tenant was transferred to a branch office in California and moved out at the end of June. Since they did not want to bother finding a new tenant, Paul and Judy sold the house on June 30, 2008. They received $140,000 for the house and land ($15,000 for land and $125,000

is allocable to the house), less a 6 percent commission charged by the broker. They had depreciated the house using the MACRS rules and conventions applicable to residential real estate. To compute depreciation on the house, the Vances had allocated $15,000 of the property's basis to the land on which the house is located. The Vances collected rent of $1,000 a month during the six months the house was occupied during the year. They incurred the following related expenses during this period:

Property insurance	$500
Property taxes	800
Maintenance	465
Depreciation (to be computed)	?

6. The Vances sold 200 shares of Capp Corporation stock on September 3, 2008, for $42 a share (minus a $50 commission). The Vances received the stock from Paul's father on June 25, 1979, as a wedding present. Paul's father originally purchased the stock for $10 per share in 1965. The stock was valued at $14.50 per share on the date of the gift. No gift tax was paid on the gift.

7. Judy is required by Xavier University to visit several high schools in the Cincinnati area to evaluate Xavier University students who are doing their practice teaching. However, she is not reimbursed for the expenses she incurs in doing this. During the spring semester (January through April, 2008), she drove her personal automobile 6,800 miles in fulfilling this obligation. Judy drove an additional 6,700 personal miles during 2008. She has been using the car since June 30, 2007.

8. Paul and Judy have given you a file containing the following receipts for expenditures during the year:

Medicine and drugs (net of insurance reimbursement)	$ 376
Doctor and hospital bills (net of insurance reimbursement)	1,148
Medical insurance premiums withheld from Judy's paycheck ($110/month)	1,320
Penalty for underpayment of last year's state income tax	15
Real estate taxes on personal residence	4,762
Interest on home mortgage (paid to Home State Savings & Loan)	8,250
Interest on credit cards (consumer purchases)	595
Cash contribution to St. Matthew's church	3,080
Payroll deductions for Judy's contributions to the United Way	150
Professional dues (Judy)	325
Professional subscriptions (Judy)	245
Fee for preparation of 2007 tax return paid April 12, 2008	500

Assume Cincinnati, Ohio, has a 6.75 percent combined sales tax rate

9. The Vances filed their 2007 federal, state, and local returns on April 12, 2008. They paid the following additional 2007 taxes with their returns: federal income taxes of $630, state income taxes of $250, and city income taxes of $75.

10. The Vances made timely estimated federal income tax payments of $1,500 each quarter during 2008. They made estimated state income tax payments of $300 each quarter and estimated city income tax payments of $160 each quarter. The Vances made all fourth quarter payments on December 31, 2008. They would like to receive a refund for any overpayments.

INDIVIDUAL TAX RETURN PROBLEM 2

Required:

- Use the following information to complete Paige Turner's 2008 federal income tax return. If information is missing, use reasonable assumptions to fill in the gaps.
- You may need the following forms and schedules to complete the project: Form 1040, Schedule A, Schedule B, Schedule C, Schedule D, Schedule E, Schedule SE, Form 2106, Form 4562, Form 4684, and Form 8283. The forms, schedules, and instructions can be found at IRS Web site (www.irs.gov). The instructions can be helpful in completing the forms.

Facts:

1. Paige Turner is single and has two children from her previous marriage. Ali lives with Paige and Paige provides more than half of her support. Leif lives with his father, Will (Lief lived with Will for all of 2008). Will provides more than half of Leif's support. Paige pays "alimony" of $400 per month to Will. The payments are to continue until Leif reaches age 18, when they will be reduced to $150. Paige provides you with the following additional information:
   - She uses the cash method of accounting and a calendar year for reporting.
   - She wishes to contribute to the presidential election campaign.
   - Paige did not receive an economic stimulus payment check last year.
   - Paige lives at 523 Essex Street, Bangor, Maine (04401).
   - Paige's birthday is May 31, 1970.
   - Ali's birthday is October 5, 1999.
   - Leif's birthday is December 1, 1997.
   - Paige's Social Security number is 007-16-4727.
   - Ali's Social Security number is 005-61-7232.
   - Leif's Social Security number is 004-23-3419.
   - Will's Social Security number is 006-45-6333.
   - She does not have any foreign bank accounts or trusts.

2. Paige is employed as a nuclear engineer with Atom Systems Consultants, Inc. (ASCI). Her annual salary is $70,000. ASCI has an extensive fringe benefits program for its employees. Paige's pay stubs indicate that she had $7,230 withheld in federal taxes, $4,987 in state taxes, $4,495 in Social Security taxes, and $1,051 in Medicare taxes. Her taxable compensation includes the following:

Salary	$70,000
− Pension plan payment	(7,000)
− Flexible spending plan contributions	(3,600)
+ Group term life insurance	97
+ Whole life insurance	300
+ Payment of educational costs	See a below
+ Free parking	See b below
+ Health club dues	900
+ Disability pay (see #7 below)	1,200

Paige furnishes you with the following description of the fringe benefits she received from ASCI in 2008.

a. Taking advantage of ASCI's educational assistance program, during the fall Paige enrolled in two graduate engineering classes at a local college. ASCI paid her tuition, fees, and other course-related costs of $2,300.

b. Paige also received free parking in the company's security garage that would normally cost $200 per month.

3. Paige manages the safety program for ASCI. In recognition of her superior handling of three potential crises during the year 2008, Paige was awarded the "Employee Safety Award" on December 15, 2008. The cash award was $500.

4. On January 15, 2008, Paige's father died. From her father's estate, she received stock valued at $30,000 (his basis was $12,000) and her father's house valued at $90,000 (his basis in the house was $55,000).

5. Paige owns several other investments and in February 2009 received a statement from her brokerage firm reporting the interest and dividends earned on the investments for 2008. (See Exhibit A.)

EXHIBIT A   Forms 1099 and 1098

This is important tax information and is being furnished to the Internal Revenue Service.

1099-Div Dividends & Distributions

Entity	Description	Amount
General Dynamics	Gross qualifying dividends	$300

1099-Int Interest

Entity	Description	Amount
New Jersey Economic Development Bonds	Gross interest	$300
IBM bonds		700
State of Nebraska Bonds	Gross interest	200

1098-Mortgage Interest Statement

Entity	Description	Amount
Sunbelt Credit Union	Mortgage interest	$7,100
Northeast Bank	Home equity loan interest	435

Grubstake Mining & Development: preliminary report (preliminary K-1) to Paige for the 2008 tax year

Distribution to shareholder $1,000
Ordinary income (1% of $200,000) $2,000

6. In addition to the investments discussed above, Paige owns 1,000 shares of Grubstake Mining & Development common stock. Grubstake is organized as an S corporation and has 100,000 shares outstanding (S corp. ID number 45-4567890). Grubstake reported taxable income of $200,000 and paid a distribution of $1.00 per share during the current year. Paige tells you that Grubstake typically does not send out its K-1 reports until late April. However, its preliminary report has been consistent with the K-1 for many years. (See Exhibit A.) Paige does not materially participate in Grubstake's activities.

7. Paige slipped on a wet spot in front of a computer store last July. She broke her ankle and was unable to work for two weeks. She incurred $1,300 in medical costs, all of which were paid by the owner of the store. The store also gave her $1,000 for pain and suffering resulting from the injury. ASCI continued to pay her salary during the two weeks she missed because of the accident. ASCI's plan also paid her $1,200 in disability pay for the time she was unable to work. Under this plan ASCI pays the premiums for the disability insurance.

8. Paige received a Form 1099-B from her broker for the sale of the following securities during 2008.

Security	Sale Date	Purchase Date	Sales Price	Commission Paid on Sale	Her Basis
Nebraska Bonds	03/14/08	10/22/04	$2,300	$160	$1,890
Cassill Corp (500 shares)	10/18/08	02/19/08	$8,500	$425	$9,760

9. In addition to the taxes withheld from her salary, she also made timely estimated federal tax payments of $175 per quarter and timely estimated state income tax payments of $150 for the first three quarters. The $150 fourth quarter state payment was made on December 28, 2008. Paige would like to receive a refund for any overpayment.

10. Because of her busy work schedule, Paige was unable to provide her accountant with the tax documents necessary for filing her 2007 state and federal income tax returns by the due date (April 15, 2008). In filing her extension on April 15, 2008, she made a federal tax payment of $750. Her return was eventually filed on June 25, 2008. In August 2008, she received a federal refund of $180 and a state tax refund of $60. Her itemized deductions for 2007 were $12,430.

11. Paige found a renter for her father's house on August 1. The monthly rent is $400, and the lease agreement is for one year. The lease requires the tenant to pay the first and last months' rent and a $400 security deposit. The security deposit is to be returned at the end of the lease if the property is in good condition. On August 1, Paige received $1,200 from the tenant per the terms of the lease agreement. In November, the plumbing froze and several pipes burst. The tenant had the repairs made and paid the $300 bill. In December, he reduced his rental payment to $100 to compensate for the plumbing repairs. Paige provides you with the following additional information for the rental in 2008.

Property taxes	$770
Other maintenance expenses	285
Insurance expense	495
Management fee	350
Depreciation (to be computed)	?

The rental property is located at 35 Harvest Street, Orono, Maine 04473. Local practice is to allocate 12 percent of the fair market value of the property to the land. (See #4.) Paige makes all decisions with respect to the property.

12. Paige paid $2,050 in real estate taxes on her principal residence. The real estate tax is used to pay for town schools and other municipal services.

13. Paige drives a 2008 Acura TL. Her car registration fee (based on the car year) is $50 and covers the period 1/1/08 through 12/31/08. In addition, she paid $280 in property tax to the town based on the book value of the car.

14. In addition to the medical costs presented in #7, Paige incurred the following unreimbursed medical costs:

Dentist	$ 310
Doctor	390
Prescription drugs	215
Over-the-counter drugs	140
Optometrist	125
Emergency room charges	440
LASIK eye surgery	2,000
Chiropractor	265

15. On March 1, Paige took advantage of low interest rates and refinanced her $75,000 home mortgage with her original lender. The new home loan is for 15 years. She paid $215 in closing costs and $1,500 in discount points (prepaid interest) to obtain the loan. The house is worth $155,000 and Paige's basis in the house is $90,000. As part of the refinancing arrangement, she also obtained a $10,000 home equity loan. She used the proceeds from the home equity loan to reduce the balance due on her credit cards. Paige received several Form 1098 statements from her bank for interest paid by her in 2008. Details appear below. (See also Exhibit A on page A-30.)

Primary home mortgage	$7,100
Home equity loan	435
Credit cards	498
Car loan	390

16. On May 14, 2008, Paige contributed clothing to the Salvation Army. The original cost of the clothing was $740. She has substantiation valuing the donation at $360. The Salvation Army is located at 350 Stone Ridge Road, Bangor, Maine 04401. In addition, she made the following cash contributions and received a statement from each of the following organizations acknowledging her contribution:

Larkin College	$850
United Way	125
First Methodist Church	790
Amos House (homeless shelter)	200
Local Chamber of Commerce	100

17. On April 1, 2008, Paige's house was robbed. She apparently interrupted the burglar because all that's missing is an antique brooch she inherited from her grandmother (June 12, 2002) and $300 in cash. Unfortunately, she didn't have a separate rider on her insurance policy covering the jewelry. Therefore, the insurance company reimbursed her only $500 for the brooch. Her basis in the brooch was $6,000 and its fair market value was $7,500. Her insurance policy also limits to $100 the amount of cash that can be claimed in a theft.

18. Paige sells real estate in the evening and on weekends. She runs her business from a rental office she shares with several other realtors (692 River Road Bangor, Maine 04401). The name of her business is Turner Real Estate and the Federal identification number is 05-8799561. Her business code is 531210. Paige has been operating in a business-like way since 1998 and has always shown a profit. She had the following income and expenses from her business:

Commissions earned	$21,250
Expenses:	
Advertising	2,200
Telephone	95
Real estate license	130
Rent	6,000
Utilities	600

She has used her Toyota Camry in her business since June 1, 2007. During 2008, she properly documented 6,000 business miles (500 miles each month). The total mileage on her car (i.e., business and personal-use miles) during the year was 15,000 miles (including 200 miles commuting to and from the real estate office). In 2008, Paige elects to use the standard mileage method to calculate her car expenses. She spent $45 on tolls and $135 on parking related to the real estate business.

19. Paige's company has an accountable expense reimbursement plan for employees from which Paige receives $12,000 for the following expenses:

Airfare	$4,700
Hotel	3,400
Meals	2,000
Car rentals	600
Entertainment	900
Incidentals	400

20. During 2008, Paige also paid $295 for business publications other than those paid for by her employer and $325 for a local CPA to prepare her 2007 tax return.

Code Index

Code Sections Cited

Page numbers followed by n refer to footnotes.

PHOTO CREDITS

Chapter 1: Comstock Images/Jupiter Images
Chapter 2: ©James Hardy/Photo Alto
Chapter 3: Photodisc Collection/Getty Images
Chapter 4: Getty Images/Digital Vision
Chapter 5: Eric Audras/Photoalto/PictureQuest
Chapter 6: Eric Audras/Photoalto/PictureQuest
Chapter 7: Eric Audras/Photoalto/PictureQuest
Chapter 8: Creatas Images
Chapter 9: RF/Corbis
Chapter 10: ©Digital Vison/Punchstock
Chapter 11: PhotoDisc/Getty Images
Chapter 12: Banana Stock/Fotostock
Chapter 13: Banana Stock/Fotostock
Chapter 14: RF/Corbis

Page numbers followed by n refer to footnotes.